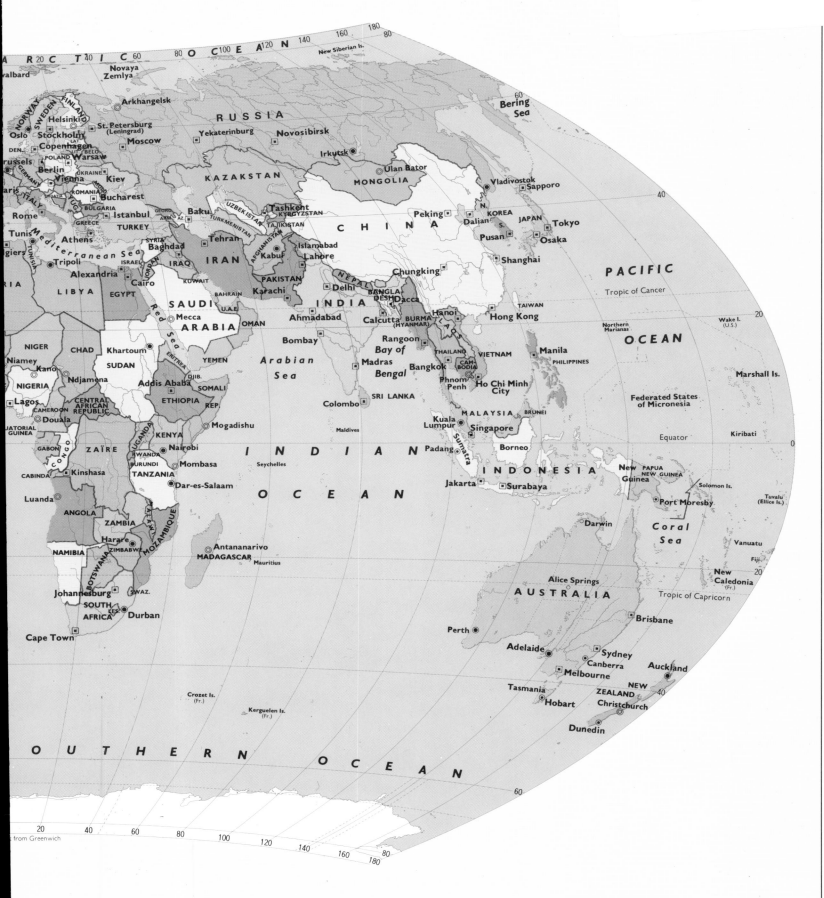

PHILIP'S

ENCYCLOPEDIC WORLD ATLAS

COUNTRY BY COUNTRY

PHILIP'S

ENCYCLOPEDIC WORLD ATLAS

COUNTRY BY COUNTRY

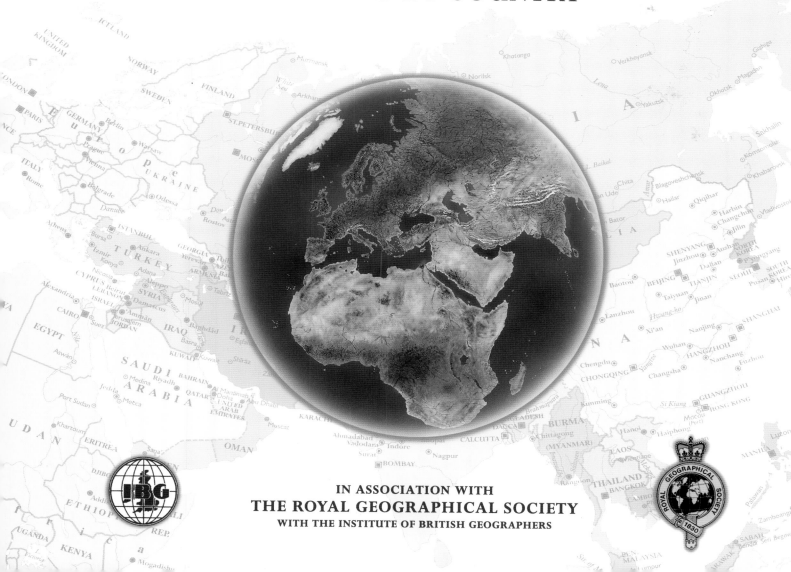

IN ASSOCIATION WITH
THE ROYAL GEOGRAPHICAL SOCIETY
WITH THE INSTITUTE OF BRITISH GEOGRAPHERS

CONTENTS

Compiled by
RICHARD WIDDOWS

Executive Editor
Caroline Rayner

Editor
Kara Turner

Maps prepared by
B.M. Willett, David Gaylard, Ray Smith, Jenny Allen

Information on recent changes to flags provided
and authenticated by the Flag Institute, Chester, UK

PICTURE ACKNOWLEDGEMENTS
Page 14
Science Photo Library /NOAA

INTRODUCTION TO WORLD GEOGRAPHY
Cartography by Philip's

Illustrations
Stefan Chabluk

CONSULTANTS
Philip's are grateful to the following people for acting as specialist
geography consultants on the '*Introduction to World Geography*'
front section:

Professor D. Brunsden, Kings College, University of London, UK
Dr C. Clarke, Oxford University, UK
Dr. I. S. Evans, Durham University, UK
Professor P. Haggett, University of Bristol, UK
Professor K. McLachlan, University of London, UK
Professor M. Monmonier, Syracuse University, New York, USA
Professor M-L. Hsu, University of Minnesota, Minnesota, USA
Professor M. J. Tooley, University of St Andrews, UK
Dr T. Unwin, Royal Holloway, University of London, UK

First published in Great Britain in 1992
by George Philip Limited,
a division of Octopus Publishing Group Limited,
2–4 Heron Quays, London E14 4JB

Second edition 1993
Revised edition 1994
Third edition 1995
Fourth edition 1996
Fifth edition 1997
Revised edition 1998

Cartography by Philip's

Copyright © 1998 George Philip Limited

WORLD STATISTICS

Countries vi
Physical
    Dimensions vii
General Notes viii

INTRODUCTION TO WORLD GEOGRAPHY

Planet Earth 2–3
Restless Earth 4–5
Landforms 6–7
Oceans 8–9
Climate 10–11
Water and
    Vegetation 12–13
Environment 14–15
Population 16–17
The Human Family
    18–19
Wealth 20–21
Quality of Life 22–23
Energy 24–25
Production 26–27
Trade 28–29
Travel and Tourism
    30–31

WORLD MAP SYMBOLS 32

EUROPE 33

Iceland 38
Faroe Islands 38
Norway 39
Sweden 41
Denmark 42
Finland 43
United Kingdom 44
Ireland 49
Netherlands 50
Belgium 51
Luxembourg 52
France 53
Monaco 56
Germany 56
Switzerland 60
Austria 61
Liechtenstein 61
Portugal 62
Andorra 62
Spain 63
Italy 66
San Marino 69
Vatican City 69
Malta 69
Albania 70
Greece 70
Yugoslavia 72
Bosnia-
    Herzegovina 72
Macedonia 72
Slovenia 73
Croatia 73
Bulgaria 73
Hungary 74
Romania 75
Czech Republic 76
Slovak Republic 76
Poland 77
Commonwealth of
    Independent States
    78
Belarus 78
Moldova 78
Ukraine 79
Estonia 80
Latvia 80
Lithuania 80
Georgia 81
Armenia 82
Azerbaijan 82
Russia 88

ASIA 83

Russia 88
Kazakstan 92
Uzbekistan 92
Turkmenistan 92
Kyrgyzstan 93
Tajikistan 93
Turkey 94
Cyprus 95
Lebanon 95
Israel 96
Syria 97
Jordan 98
Saudi Arabia 98
Kuwait 100
Qatar 100
Yemen 100
Bahrain 101
United Arab
    Emirates 101
Oman 101
Iraq 102
Iran 103
Afghanistan 104
Pakistan 105
India 106
Nepal 109
Bhutan 109
Sri Lanka 110
Maldives 110
Bangladesh 111
Mongolia 112
China 113
Macau 116
Taiwan 117
Hong Kong 117
North Korea 118
South Korea 119
Japan 119
Burma
    (Myanmar) 122
Thailand 123
Laos 124
Cambodia 124
Vietnam 124
Malaysia 126
Brunei 127
Singapore 127
Indonesia 128
Philippines 130

AFRICA 131

Morocco 136
Algeria 137
Tunisia 138
Libya 138
Egypt 139
Mauritania 140
Mali 140
Niger 141
Chad 142
Central African
    Republic 142
Sudan 143
Ethiopia 144
Eritrea 144
Djibouti 145
Somalia 145
Senegal 146
The Gambia 146
Guinea-Bissau 146
Guinea 147
Sierra Leone 147
Liberia 148
Ivory Coast
    (Côte d'Ivoire) 148
Burkina Faso 149
Ghana 149
Togo 150
Benin 150
Nigeria 151
São Tomé and
    Príncipe 152
Cameroon 153
Equatorial Guinea 153
Gabon 154
Congo 154
Burundi 154
Zaïre 155
Uganda 156
Rwanda 156
Kenya 157
Malawi 158
Tanzania 158
Mozambique 159
Angola 160
Zambia 160
Zimbabwe 161
Namibia 162
Botswana 162
South Africa 163
Lesotho 164
Swaziland 165
Madagascar 165

INDIAN OCEAN

Seychelles 166
Comoros 166
Mauritius 166
Réunion 166

AUSTRALIA AND OCEANIA 167

Australia 170
Papua New Guinea
    173
Solomon Islands 173
New Caledonia 173
Fiji 174
New Zealand 174
Northern Mariana
    Islands 176
Guam 176
Palau 176
Marshall Islands 177
Federated States of
    Micronesia 177
Nauru 177
Kiribati 177
Tuvalu 177
Vanuatu 178
Tonga 178
Wallis and Futuna
    Islands 178
Western Samoa 178
American Samoa 178
French Polynesia 178
Pitcairn 178

NORTH AND CENTRAL AMERICA 179

Canada 184
United States of
    America 188
Mexico 194
Belize 195
Guatemala 195
Honduras 196
El Salvador 196
Nicaragua 197
Costa Rica 197
Cuba 198
Panama 198
Jamaica 199
Haiti 200
Dominican Republic
    200
Turks and Caicos
    Islands 200
Cayman Islands 200
Bahamas 201
Puerto Rico 201
British Virgin Islands
    201
US Virgin Islands 201
Anguilla 202
St Kitts and
    Nevis 202
Antigua and Barbuda
    202
Montserrat 202
Guadeloupe 202
Dominica 202
Martinique 203
St Lucia 203
St Vincent and the
    Grenadines 203
Grenada 203
Barbados 204
Trinidad and Tobago
    204
Netherlands Antilles
    204
Aruba 204

SOUTH AMERICA 205

Colombia 210
Venezuela 211
Ecuador 212
Peru 212
Guyana 214
Surinam 214
French Guiana 215
Brazil 215
Bolivia 218
Paraguay 218
Uruguay 219
Chile 220
Argentina 221

ATLANTIC OCEAN

Bermuda 222
Cape Verde 222
Azores 223
Madeira 223
Canary Islands 223
Greenland 224
Falkland Islands 224
Ascension 224
St Helena 224
Tristan da Cunha 224

INDEX TO COUNTRY MAPS

225–264

World: Regions in
the News 265

WORLD STATISTICS: COUNTRIES

This alphabetical list includes all the countries and territories of the world. If a territory is not completely independent, then the country it is associated with is named. The area figures give the total area of land, inland water and ice. The population figures are the latest available estimates. The annual income is the Gross National Product per capita in US dollars for 1995.

Country/Territory	Area km² *Thousands*	Area miles² *Thousands*	Population *Thousands*	Capital	Annual Income US$
Adélie Land (Fr.)	432	167	0.03	–	–
Afghanistan	652	252	19,509	Kabul	220
Albania	28.8	11.1	3,458	Tirana	340
Algeria	2,382	920	27,936	Algiers	1,650
American Samoa (US)	0.20	0.08	58	Pago Pago	2,600
Andorra	0.45	0.17	65	Andorra La Vella	14,000
Angola	1,247	481	10,844	Luanda	600
Anguilla (UK)	0.1	0.04	8	The Valley	6,800
Antigua & Barbuda	0.44	0.17	67	St John's	6,390
Argentina	2,767	1,068	34,663	Buenos Aires	7,290
Armenia	29.8	11.5	3,603	Yerevan	660
Aruba (Neths)	0.19	0.07	71	Oranjestad	17,500
Ascension Is. (UK)	0.09	0.03	1.5	Georgetown	–
Australia	7,687	2,968	18,107	Canberra	17,510
Austria	83.9	32.4	8,004	Vienna	23,120
Azerbaijan	86.6	33.4	7,559	Baku	730
Azores (Port.)	2.2	0.87	240	Ponta Delgada	4,500
Bahamas	13.9	5.4	277	Nassau	11,500
Bahrain	0.68	0.26	558	Manama	7,870
Bangladesh	144	56	118,342	Dhaka	220
Barbados	0.43	0.17	263	Bridgetown	6,240
Belarus	207.6	80.1	10,500	Minsk	2,930
Belgium	30.5	11.8	10,140	Brussels	21,210
Belize	23	8.9	216	Belmopan	2,440
Benin	113	43	5,381	Porto-Novo	420
Bermuda (UK)	0.05	0.02	64	Hamilton	27,000
Bhutan	47	18.1	1,639	Thimphu	170
Bolivia	1,099	424	7,900	La Paz/Sucre	770
Bosnia-Herzegovina	51	20	4,400	Sarajevo	2,500
Botswana	582	225	1,481	Gaborone	2,590
Brazil	8,512	3,286	161,416	Brasilia	3,020
British Indian Ocean Terr. (UK)	0.08	0.03	0	–	–
Brunei	5.8	2.2	284	Bandar Seri Begawan	9,000
Bulgaria	111	43	8,771	Sofia	1,160
Burkina Faso	274	106	10,326	Ouagadougou	300
Burma (Myanmar)	677	261	46,580	Rangoon	950
Burundi	27.8	10.7	6,412	Bujumbura	180
Cambodia	181	70	10,452	Phnom Penh	600
Cameroon	475	184	13,232	Yaoundé	770
Canada	9,976	3,852	29,972	Ottawa	20,670
Canary Is. (Spain)	7.3	2.8	1,700	Las Palmas/Santa Cruz	7,900
Cape Verde Is.	4	1.6	386	Praia	870
Cayman Is. (UK)	0.26	0.10	31	George Town	20,000
Central African Republic	623	241	3,294	Bangui	390
Chad	1,284	496	6,314	Ndjaména	200
Chatham Is. (NZ)	0.96	0.37	0.05	Waitangi	–
Chile	757	292	14,271	Santiago	3,070
China	9,597	3,705	1,226,944	Beijing	490
Christmas Is. (Aus.)	0.14	0.05	2	The Settlement	–
Cocos (Keeling) Is. (Aus.)	0.01	0.005	0.6	West Island	–
Colombia	1,139	440	34,948	Bogotá	1,400
Comoros	2.2	0.86	654	Moroni	520
Congo	342	132	2,593	Brazzaville	920
Cook Is. (NZ)	0.24	0.09	19	Avarua	900
Costa Rica	51.1	19.7	3,436	San José	2,160
Croatia	56.5	21.8	4,900	Zagreb	4,500
Cuba	111	43	11,050	Havana	1,250
Cyprus	9.3	3.6	742	Nicosia	10,380
Czech Republic	78.9	30.4	10,500	Prague	2,730
Denmark	43.1	16.6	5,229	Copenhagen	26,510
Djibouti	23.2	9	603	Djibouti	780
Dominica	0.75	0.29	89	Roseau	2,680
Dominican Republic	48.7	18.8	7,818	Santo Domingo	1,080
Ecuador	284	109	11,384	Quito	1,170
Egypt	1,001	387	64,100	Cairo	660
El Salvador	21	8.1	5,743	San Salvador	1,320
Equatorial Guinea	28.1	10.8	400	Malabo	360
Eritrea	94	36	3,850	Asmara	500
Estonia	44.7	17.3	1,531	Tallinn	3,040
Ethiopia	1,128	436	51,600	Addis Ababa	100
Falkland Is. (UK)	12.2	4.7	2	Stanley	–
Faroe Is. (Den.)	1.4	0.54	47	Tórshavn	23,660
Fiji	18.3	7.1	773	Suva	2,140
Finland	338	131	5,125	Helsinki	18,970
France	552	213	58,286	Paris	22,360
French Guiana (Fr.)	90	34.7	154	Cayenne	5,000
French Polynesia (Fr.)	4	1.5	217	Papeete	7,000
Gabon	268	103	1,316	Libreville	4,050
Gambia, The	11.3	4.4	1,144	Banjul	360
Georgia	69.7	26.9	5,448	Tbilisi	560
Germany	357	138	82,000	Berlin/Bonn	23,560
Ghana	239	92	17,462	Accra	430
Gibraltar (UK)	0.007	0.003	28	Gibraltar Town	5,000
Greece	132	51	10,510	Athens	7,390
Greenland (Den.)	2,176	840	59	Godthåb (Nuuk)	9,000
Grenada	0.34	0.13	96	St George's	2,410
Guadeloupe (Fr.)	1.7	0.66	443	Basse-Terre	9,000
Guam (US)	0.55	0.21	155	Agana	6,000
Guatemala	109	42	10,624	Guatemala City	1,110
Guinea	246	95	6,702	Conakry	510
Guinea-Bissau	36.1	13.9	1,073	Bissau	220
Guyana	215	83	832	Georgetown	350
Haiti	27.8	10.7	7,180	Port-au-Prince	800
Honduras	112	43	5,940	Tegucigalpa	580
Hong Kong (China)	1.1	0.40	6,000	–	17,860
Hungary	93	35.9	10,500	Budapest	3,330
Iceland	103	40	269	Reykjavik	23,620
India	3,288	1,269	942,989	New Delhi	290
Indonesia	1,905	735	198,644	Jakarta	730
Iran	1,648	636	68,885	Tehran	4,750
Iraq	438	169	20,184	Baghdad	2,000
Ireland	70.3	27.1	3,589	Dublin	12,580
Israel	27	10.3	5,696	Jerusalem	13,760
Italy	301	116	57,181	Rome	19,620
Ivory Coast	322	125	14,271	Yamoussoukro	630
Jamaica	11	4.2	2,700	Kingston	1,390
Jan Mayen Is. (Nor.)	0.38	0.15	0.06	–	–
Japan	378	146	125,156	Tokyo	31,450
Johnston Is. (US)	0.002	0.0009	1	–	–
Jordan	89.2	34.4	5,547	Amman	1,190
Kazakstan	2,717	1,049	17,099	Alma-Ata	1,540
Kenya	580	224	28,240	Nairobi	270
Kerguelen Is. (Fr.)	7.2	2.8	0.7	–	–
Kermadec Is. (NZ)	0.03	0.01	0.1	–	–
Kiribati	0.72	0.28	80	Tarawa	710
Korea, North	121	47	23,931	Pyŏngyang	1,100
Korea, South	99	38.2	45,088	Seoul	7,670
Kuwait	17.8	6.9	1,668	Kuwait City	23,350
Kyrgyzstan	198.5	76.6	4,738	Bishkek	830
Laos	237	91	4,906	Vientiane	290
Latvia	65	25	2,558	Riga	2,030
Lebanon	10.4	4	2,971	Beirut	1,750
Lesotho	30.4	11.7	2,064	Maseru	660
Liberia	111	43	3,092	Monrovia	800
Libya	1,760	679	5,410	Tripoli	6,500
Liechtenstein	0.16	0.06	31	Vaduz	33,510
Lithuania	65.2	25.2	3,735	Vilnius	1,310
Luxembourg	2.6	1	408	Luxembourg	35,850
Macau (Port.)	0.02	0.006	490	Macau	7,500
Macedonia	25.7	9.9	2,173	Skopje	730
Madagascar	587	227	15,206	Antananarivo	240
Madeira (Port.)	0.81	0.31	300	Funchal	4,500
Malawi	118	46	9,800	Lilongwe	220
Malaysia	330	127	20,174	Kuala Lumpur	3,160
Maldives	0.30	0.12	254	Malé	820
Mali	1,240	479	10,700	Bamako	300
Malta	0.32	0.12	370	Valletta	6,800
Marshall Is.	0.18	0.07	55	Dalap-Uliga-Darrit	1,500
Martinique (Fr.)	1.1	0.42	384	Fort-de-France	3,500
Mauritania	1,030	412	2,268	Nouakchott	510
Mauritius	2.0	0.72	1,112	Port Louis	2,980
Mayotte (Fr.)	0.37	0.14	101	Mamoundzou	1,430
Mexico	1,958	756	93,342	Mexico City	3,750
Micronesia, Fed. States of	0.70	0.27	125	Palikir	1,560
Midway Is. (US)	0.005	0.002	2	–	–
Moldova	33.7	13	4,434	Chişinău	1,180
Monaco	0.002	0.0001	32	Monaco	16,000
Mongolia	1,567	605	2,408	Ulan Bator	400
Montserrat (UK)	0.10	0.04	11	Plymouth	4,500
Morocco	447	172	26,857	Rabat	1,030
Mozambique	802	309	17,800	Maputo	80
Namibia	825	318	1,610	Windhoek	1,660
Nauru	0.02	0.008	12	Yaren District	10,000
Nepal	141	54	21,953	Katmandu	160
Netherlands	41.5	16	15,495	Amsterdam/The Hague	20,710
Neths Antilles (Neths)	0.99	0.38	202	Willemstad	9,700
New Caledonia (Fr.)	19	7.2	181	Nouméa	6,000
New Zealand	269	104	3,567	Wellington	12,900
Nicaragua	130	50	4,544	Managua	360
Niger	1,267	489	9,149	Niamey	270
Nigeria	924	357	88,515	Abuja	310
Niue (NZ)	0.26	0.10	2	Alofi	–
Norfolk Is. (Aus.)	0.03	0.01	2	Kingston	–
Northern Mariana Is. (US)	0.48	0.18	50	Saipan	11,500
Norway	324	125	4,361	Oslo	26,340
Oman	212	82	2,252	Muscat	5,600
Pakistan	796	307	143,595	Islamabad	430
Palau	0.46	0.18	18	Koror	2,260
Panama	77.1	29.8	2,629	Panama City	2,580
Papua New Guinea	463	179	4,292	Port Moresby	1,120
Paraguay	407	157	4,979	Asunción	1,500
Peru	1,285	496	23,588	Lima	1,490
Philippines	300	116	67,167	Manila	830
Pitcairn Is. (UK)	0.03	0.01	0.05	Adamstown	–
Poland	313	121	38,587	Warsaw	2,270
Portugal	92.4	35.7	10,600	Lisbon	7,890
Puerto Rico (US)	9	3.5	3,689	San Juan	7,020
Qatar	11	4.2	594	Doha	15,140
Queen Maud Land (Nor.)	2,800	1,081	0	–	–
Réunion (Fr.)	2.5	0.97	655	Saint-Denis	3,900
Romania	238	92	22,863	Bucharest	1,120
Russia	17,075	6,592	148,385	Moscow	2,350
Rwanda	26.3	10.2	7,899	Kigali	200
St Helena (UK)	0.12	0.05	6	Jamestown	–
St Kitts & Nevis	0.36	0.14	45	Basseterre	4,470
St Lucia	0.62	0.24	147	Castries	3,040
St Pierre & Miquelon (Fr.)	0.24	0.09	6	Saint Pierre	–
St Vincent & Grenadines	0.39	0.15	111	Kingstown	1,730
San Marino	0.06	0.02	26	San Marino	20,000
São Tomé & Príncipe	0.96	0.37	133	São Tomé	330
Saudi Arabia	2,150	830	18,395	Riyadh	8,000
Senegal	197	76	8,308	Dakar	730
Seychelles	0.46	0.18	75	Victoria	6,370
Sierra Leone	71.7	27.7	4,467	Freetown	140
Singapore	0.62	0.24	2,990	Singapore	19,310
Slovak Republic	49	18.9	5,400	Bratislava	1,900
Slovenia	20.3	7.8	2,000	Ljubljana	6,310
Solomon Is.	28.9	11.2	378	Honiara	750
Somalia	638	246	9,180	Mogadishu	500
South Africa	1,220	471	44,000	C. Town/Pretoria/Bloem.	2,900
South Georgia (UK)	3.8	1.4	0.05	–	–
Spain	505	195	39,664	Madrid	13,650
Sri Lanka	65.6	25.3	18,359	Colombo	600
Sudan	2,506	967	29,980	Khartoum	750
Surinam	163	63	421	Paramaribo	1,210
Svalbard (Nor.)	62.9	24.3	4	Longyearbyen	–
Swaziland	17.4	6.7	849	Mbabane	1,050
Sweden	450	174	8,893	Stockholm	24,830
Switzerland	41.3	15.9	7,268	Bern	36,410
Syria	185	71	14,614	Damascus	5,700
Taiwan	36	13.9	21,100	Taipei	11,000
Tajikistan	143.1	55.2	6,102	Dushanbe	470
Tanzania	945	365	29,710	Dodoma	100
Thailand	513	198	58,432	Bangkok	2,040
Togo	56.8	21.9	4,140	Lomé	330
Tokelau (NZ)	0.01	0.005	2	Nukunonu	–
Tonga	0.75	0.29	107	Nuku'alofa	1,610
Trinidad & Tobago	5.1	2	1,295	Port of Spain	3,730
Tristan da Cunha (UK)	0.11	0.04	0.33	Edinburgh	–
Tunisia	164	63	8,906	Tunis	1,780
Turkey	779	301	61,303	Ankara	2,120
Turkmenistan	488.1	188.5	4,100	Ashkhabad	1,400
Turks & Caicos Is. (UK)	0.43	0.17	15	Cockburn Town	5,000
Tuvalu	0.03	0.01	10	Fongafale	600
Uganda	236	91	21,466	Kampala	190
Ukraine	603.7	233.1	52,027	Kiev	1,910
United Arab Emirates	83.6	32.3	2,800	Abu Dhabi	22,470
United Kingdom	243.3	94	58,306	London	17,970
United States of America	9,373	3,619	263,563	Washington, DC	24,750
Uruguay	177	68	3,186	Montevideo	3,910
Uzbekistan	447.4	172.7	22,833	Tashkent	960
Vanuatu	12.2	4.7	167	Port-Vila	1,230
Vatican City	0.0004	0.0002	1	–	–
Venezuela	912	352	21,810	Caracas	2,840
Vietnam	332	127	74,580	Hanoi	170
Virgin Is. (UK)	0.15	0.06	20	Road Town	–
Virgin Is. (US)	0.34	0.13	102	Charlotte Amalie	12,000
Wake Is.	0.008	0.003	0.30	–	–
Wallis & Futuna Is. (Fr.)	0.20	0.08	13	Mata-Utu	–
Western Sahara	266	103	220	El Aaiún	300
Western Samoa	2.8	1.1	169	Apia	980
Yemen	528	204	14,609	Sana	800
Yugoslavia	102.3	39.5	10,881	Belgrade	1,000
Zaïre	2,345	905	44,504	Kinshasa	500
Zambia	753	291	9,500	Lusaka	370
Zimbabwe	391	151	11,453	Harare	540

World Statistics: Physical Dimensions

Each topic list is divided into continents and within a continent the items are listed in order of size. The bottom part of many of the lists is selective in order to give examples from as many different countries as possible. The order of the continents is the same as in the atlas, beginning with Europe and ending with South America. The figures are rounded as appropriate.

World, Continents, Oceans

	km²	miles²	%
The World	509,450,000	196,672,000	–
Land	149,450,000	57,688,000	29.3
Water	360,000,000	138,984,000	70.7
Asia	44,500,000	17,177,000	29.8
Africa	30,302,000	11,697,000	20.3
North America	24,241,000	9,357,000	16.2
South America	17,793,000	6,868,000	11.9
Antarctica	14,100,000	5,443,000	9.4
Europe	9,957,000	3,843,000	6.7
Australia & Oceania	8,557,000	3,303,000	5.7
Pacific Ocean	179,679,000	69,356,000	49.9
Atlantic Ocean	92,373,000	35,657,000	25.7
Indian Ocean	73,917,000	28,532,000	20.5
Arctic Ocean	14,090,000	5,439,000	3.9

Ocean Depths

Atlantic Ocean	m	ft
Puerto Rico (Milwaukee) Deep	9,220	30,249
Cayman Trench	7,680	25,197
Gulf of Mexico	5,203	17,070
Mediterranean Sea	5,121	16,801
Black Sea	2,211	7,254
North Sea	660	2,165

Indian Ocean	m	ft
Java Trench	7,450	24,442
Red Sea	2,635	8,454

Pacific Ocean	m	ft
Mariana Trench	11,022	36,161
Tonga Trench	10,882	35,702
Japan Trench	10,554	34,626
Kuril Trench	10,542	34,587

Arctic Ocean	m	ft
Molloy Deep	5,608	18,399

Mountains

Europe		m	ft
Mont Blanc	*France/Italy*	4,807	15,771
Monte Rosa	*Italy/Switzerland*	4,634	15,203
Dom	*Switzerland*	4,545	14,911
Liskamm	*Switzerland*	4,527	14,852
Weisshorn	*Switzerland*	4,505	14,780
Taschorn	*Switzerland*	4,490	14,730
Matterhorn/Cervino	*Italy/Switzerland*	4,478	14,691
Mont Maudit	*France/Italy*	4,465	14,649
Dent Blanche	*Switzerland*	4,356	14,291
Nadelhorn	*Switzerland*	4,327	14,196
Grandes Jorasses	*France/Italy*	4,208	13,806
Jungfrau	*Switzerland*	4,158	13,642
Grossglockner	*Austria*	3,797	12,457
Mulhacén	*Spain*	3,478	11,411
Zugspitze	*Germany*	2,962	9,718
Olympus	*Greece*	2,917	9,570
Triglav	*Slovenia*	2,863	9,393
Gerlachovka	*Slovak Republic*	2,655	8,711
Galdhöpiggen	*Norway*	2,468	8,100
Kebnekaise	*Sweden*	2,117	6,946
Ben Nevis	*UK*	1,343	4,406

Asia		m	ft
Everest	*China/Nepal*	8,848	29,029
K2 (Godwin Austen)	*China/Kashmir*	8,611	28,251
Kanchenjunga	*India/Nepal*	8,598	28,208
Lhotse	*China/Nepal*	8,516	27,939
Makalu	*China/Nepal*	8,481	27,824
Cho Oyu	*China/Nepal*	8,201	26,906
Dhaulagiri	*Nepal*	8,172	26,811
Manaslu	*Nepal*	8,156	26,758
Nanga Parbat	*Kashmir*	8,126	26,660
Annapurna	*Nepal*	8,078	26,502
Gasherbrum	*China/Kashmir*	8,068	26,469
Broad Peak	*China/Kashmir*	8,051	26,414
Xixabangma	*China*	8,012	26,286
Kangbachen	*India/Nepal*	7,902	25,925
Trivor	*Pakistan*	7,720	25,328
Pik Kommunizma	*Tajikistan*	7,495	24,590
Elbrus	*Russia*	5,642	18,510
Demavend	*Iran*	5,604	18,386
Ararat	*Turkey*	5,165	16,945
Gunong Kinabalu	*Malaysia (Borneo)*	4,101	13,455
Fuji-San	*Japan*	3,776	12,388

Africa		m	ft
Kilimanjaro	*Tanzania*	5,895	19,340
Mt Kenya	*Kenya*	5,199	17,057
Ruwenzori (Margherita)	*Uganda/Zaire*	5,109	16,762
Ras Dashan	*Ethiopia*	4,620	15,157
Meru	*Tanzania*	4,565	14,977
Karisimbi	*Rwanda/Zaire*	4,507	14,787
Mt Elgon	*Kenya/Uganda*	4,321	14,176
Batu	*Ethiopia*	4,307	14,130
Toubkal	*Morocco*	4,165	13,665
Mt Cameroon	*Cameroon*	4,070	13,353

Oceania		m	ft
Puncak Jaya	*Indonesia*	5,029	16,499
Puncak Trikora	*Indonesia*	4,750	15,584
Puncak Mandala	*Indonesia*	4,702	15,427
Mt Wilhelm	*Papua New Guinea*	4,508	14,790
Mauna Kea	*USA (Hawaii)*	4,205	13,796
Mauna Loa	*USA (Hawaii)*	4,170	13,681
Mt Cook	*New Zealand*	3,753	12,313
Mt Kosciusko	*Australia*	2,237	7,339

North America		m	ft
Mt McKinley (Denali)	*USA (Alaska)*	6,194	20,321
Mt Logan	*Canada*	5,959	19,551
Citlaltepetl	*Mexico*	5,700	18,701
Mt St Elias	*USA/Canada*	5,489	18,008
Popocatepetl	*Mexico*	5,452	17,887
Mt Foraker	*USA (Alaska)*	5,304	17,401
Ixtaccihuatl	*Mexico*	5,286	17,342
Lucania	*Canada*	5,227	17,149
Mt Steele	*Canada*	5,073	16,644
Mt Bona	*USA (Alaska)*	5,005	16,420
Mt Whitney	*USA*	4,418	14,495
Tajumulco	*Guatemala*	4,220	13,845
Chirripó Grande	*Costa Rica*	3,837	12,589
Pico Duarte	*Dominican Rep.*	3,175	10,417

South America		m	ft
Aconcagua	*Argentina*	6,960	22,834
Bonete	*Argentina*	6,872	22,546
Ojos del Salado	*Argentina/Chile*	6,863	22,516
Pissis	*Argentina*	6,779	22,241
Mercedario	*Argentina/Chile*	6,770	22,211
Huascaran	*Peru*	6,768	22,204
Llullaillaco	*Argentina/Chile*	6,723	22,057
Nudo de Cachi	*Argentina*	6,720	22,047
Yerupaja	*Peru*	6,632	21,758
Sajama	*Bolivia*	6,542	21,463
Chimborazo	*Ecuador*	6,267	20,561
Pico Colon	*Colombia*	5,800	19,029
Pico Bolivar	*Venezuela*	5,007	16,427

Antarctica		m	ft
Vinson Massif		4,897	16,066
Mt Kirkpatrick		4,528	14,855

Rivers

Europe		km	miles
Volga	*Caspian Sea*	3,700	2,300
Danube	*Black Sea*	2,850	1,770
Ural	*Caspian Sea*	2,535	1,575
Dnepr (Dnipro)	*Black Sea*	2,285	1,420
Kama	*Volga*	2,030	1,260
Don	*Black Sea*	1,990	1,240
Petchora	*Arctic Ocean*	1,790	1,110
Oka	*Volga*	1,480	920
Dnister (Dniester)	*Black Sea*	1,400	870
Vyatka	*Kama*	1,370	850
Rhine	*North Sea*	1,320	820
N. Dvina	*Arctic Ocean*	1,290	800
Elbe	*North Sea*	1,145	710

Asia		km	miles
Yangtze	*Pacific Ocean*	6,380	3,960
Yenisey–Angara	*Arctic Ocean*	5,550	3,445
Huang He	*Pacific Ocean*	5,464	3,395
Ob–Irtysh	*Arctic Ocean*	5,410	3,360
Mekong	*Pacific Ocean*	4,500	2,795
Amur	*Pacific Ocean*	4,400	2,730
Lena	*Arctic Ocean*	4,400	2,730
Irtysh	*Ob*	4,250	2,640
Yenisey	*Arctic Ocean*	4,090	2,540
Ob	*Arctic Ocean*	3,680	2,285
Indus	*Indian Ocean*	3,100	1,925
Brahmaputra	*Indian Ocean*	2,900	1,800
Syrdarya	*Aral Sea*	2,860	1,775
Salween	*Indian Ocean*	2,800	1,740
Euphrates	*Indian Ocean*	2,700	1,675
Amudarya	*Aral Sea*	2,540	1,575

Africa		km	miles
Nile	*Mediterranean*	6,670	4,140
Zaïre/Congo	*Atlantic Ocean*	4,670	2,900
Niger	*Atlantic Ocean*	4,180	2,595
Zambezi	*Indian Ocean*	3,540	2,200
Oubangi/Uele	*Zaïre*	2,250	1,400
Kasai	*Zaïre*	1,950	1,210
Shaballe	*Indian Ocean*	1,930	1,200
Orange	*Atlantic Ocean*	1,860	1,155
Cubango	*Okavango Swamps*	1,800	1,120
Limpopo	*Indian Ocean*	1,600	995
Senegal	*Atlantic Ocean*	1,600	995

Australia		km	miles
Murray–Darling	*Indian Ocean*	3,750	2,330
Darling	*Murray*	3,070	1,905
Murray	*Indian Ocean*	2,575	1,600
Murrumbidgee	*Murray*	1,690	1,050

North America		km	miles
Mississippi–Missouri	*Gulf of Mexico*	6,020	3,740
Mackenzie	*Arctic Ocean*	4,240	2,630
Mississippi	*Gulf of Mexico*	3,780	2,350
Missouri	*Mississippi*	3,780	2,350
Yukon	*Pacific Ocean*	3,185	1,980
Rio Grande	*Gulf of Mexico*	3,030	1,880
Arkansas	*Mississippi*	2,340	1,450
Colorado	*Pacific Ocean*	2,330	1,445
Red	*Mississippi*	2,040	1,270
Columbia	*Pacific Ocean*	1,950	1,210
Saskatchewan	*Lake Winnipeg*	1,940	1,205

South America		km	miles
Amazon	*Atlantic Ocean*	6,450	4,010
Paraná–Plate	*Atlantic Ocean*	4,500	2,800
Purus	*Amazon*	3,350	2,080
Madeira	*Amazon*	3,200	1,990
São Francisco	*Atlantic Ocean*	2,900	1,800
Paraná	*Plate*	2,800	1,740
Tocantins	*Atlantic Ocean*	2,750	1,710
Paraguay	*Paraná*	2,550	1,580
Orinoco	*Atlantic Ocean*	2,500	1,550
Pilcomayo	*Paraná*	2,500	1,550
Araguaia	*Tocantins*	2,250	1,400

Lakes

Europe		km²	miles²
Lake Ladoga	*Russia*	17,700	6,800
Lake Onega	*Russia*	9,700	3,700
Saimaa system	*Finland*	8,000	3,100
Vänern	*Sweden*	5,500	2,100

Asia		km²	miles²
Caspian Sea	*Asia*	371,800	143,550
Aral Sea	*Kazakstan/Uzbekistan*	33,640	13,000
Lake Baykal	*Russia*	30,500	11,780
Tonlé Sap	*Cambodia*	20,000	7,700
Lake Balqash	*Kazakstan*	18,500	7,100

Africa		km²	miles²
Lake Victoria	*East Africa*	68,000	26,000
Lake Tanganyika	*Central Africa*	33,000	13,000
Lake Malawi/Nyasa	*East Africa*	29,600	11,430
Lake Chad	*Central Africa*	25,000	9,700
Lake Turkana	*Ethiopia/Kenya*	8,500	3,300
Lake Volta	*Ghana*	8,500	3,300

Australia		km²	miles²
Lake Eyre	*Australia*	8,900	3,400
Lake Torrens	*Australia*	5,800	2,200
Lake Gairdner	*Australia*	4,800	1,900

North America		km²	miles²
Lake Superior	*Canada/USA*	82,350	31,800
Lake Huron	*Canada/USA*	59,600	23,010
Lake Michigan	*USA*	58,000	22,400
Great Bear Lake	*Canada*	31,800	12,280
Great Slave Lake	*Canada*	28,500	11,000
Lake Erie	*Canada/USA*	25,700	9,900
Lake Winnipeg	*Canada*	24,400	9,400
Lake Ontario	*Canada/USA*	19,500	7,500
Lake Nicaragua	*Nicaragua*	8,200	3,200

South America		km²	miles²
Lake Titicaca	*Bolivia/Peru*	8,300	3,200
Lake Poopo	*Peru*	2,800	1,100

Islands

Europe		km²	miles²
Great Britain	*UK*	229,880	88,700
Iceland	*Atlantic Ocean*	103,000	39,800
Ireland	*Ireland/UK*	84,400	32,600
Novaya Zemlya (N.)	*Russia*	48,200	18,600
Sicily	*Italy*	25,500	9,800
Corsica	*France*	8,700	3,400

Asia		km²	miles²
Borneo	*South-east Asia*	744,360	287,400
Sumatra	*Indonesia*	473,600	182,860
Honshu	*Japan*	230,500	88,980
Celebes	*Indonesia*	189,000	73,000
Java	*Indonesia*	126,700	48,900
Luzon	*Philippines*	104,700	40,400
Hokkaido	*Japan*	78,400	30,300

Africa		km²	miles²
Madagascar	*Indian Ocean*	587,040	226,660
Socotra	*Indian Ocean*	3,600	1,400
Réunion	*Indian Ocean*	2,500	965

Oceania		km²	miles²
New Guinea	*Indonesia/Papua NG*	821,030	317,000
New Zealand (S.)	*Pacific Ocean*	150,500	58,100
New Zealand (N.)	*Pacific Ocean*	114,700	44,300
Tasmania	*Australia*	67,800	26,200
Hawaii	*Pacific Ocean*	10,450	4,000

North America		km²	miles²
Greenland	*Atlantic Ocean*	2,175,600	839,800
Baffin Is.	*Canada*	508,000	196,100
Victoria Is.	*Canada*	212,200	81,900
Ellesmere Is.	*Canada*	212,000	81,800
Cuba	*Caribbean Sea*	110,860	42,800
Hispaniola	*Dominican Rep./Haiti*	76,200	29,400
Jamaica	*Caribbean Sea*	11,400	4,400
Puerto Rico	*Atlantic Ocean*	8,900	3,400

South America		km²	miles²
Tierra del Fuego	*Argentina/Chile*	47,000	18,100
Falkland Is. (E.)	*Atlantic Ocean*	6,800	2,600

GENERAL NOTES

Philip's Encyclopedic World Atlas follows a geographical, rather than an alphabetical sequence, starting with Europe and proceeding through Asia, Africa, Australasia and the Pacific islands, to North and South America and ending with the islands of the Atlantic Ocean. Within each continent the progression is generally west to east and north to south.

Each continent is introduced by maps of the whole region: a physical map and one showing the individual countries, a map showing land use, and some small maps concerned with climate, vegetation and population distribution.

The length of the descriptive entries for each country, as well as the size of its map, tend to reflect the importance and status of the country on a world scale. This is not fixed, however, and a few small countries appear at a map scale which is larger than they would normally merit. Large countries such as the USA, Canada and Russia have maps covering a double page, while for a few densely populated areas – such as the Ruhr in Germany or southern Japan – supplementary maps have been added at a scale larger than the main country map.

The maps are all positioned with north at the top, with the lines of latitude and longitude shown and labelled. Around the edges of the maps are a series of letters and figures, used for locating places from the index.

Place names are spelled in their local forms on the maps, but in the tables and text conventional spellings are generally used. For example, Roma (Rome) will appear with the Italian spelling on the map but in the text it will be referred to as Rome. The maps were corrected up to May 1996 and any changes to place names and boundaries were incorporated up to that time.

For ease of reference, an alphabetical list of the countries described in the main text is given below. Some islands, areas or territories that are part of a country, but separated from it, have been omitted from this list (please refer to the Index on pages 225–264 for the full listing).

Climate graphs
A climate graph has been provided for most countries, usually of the capital or most important town, and some large countries feature two or more. The temperature part shows the average monthly maximum and minimum with a red bar; the monthly average is the black dot centered in this bar. The temperature range mentioned in the climate description means the difference between the highest and the lowest temperature. Because of limited space for the text, the word 'average' has sometimes been omitted, but it should be borne in mind that nearly all climatic statistics are averages and

there can be, and usually are, significant variations from this figure.

Statistical tables
In the country fact-files certain terms have been used which may require some explanation.

AREA The area of the whole country, including inland water areas.

POPULATION The figure given is the latest available estimate from the UN. The population of the cities is taken from the most recent census or survey, and, as far as possible, is for the total geographical urban area and not for the smaller city area within strict administrative boundaries.

ANNUAL INCOME Given in US$ for the latest available year, this is the Gross National Product (GNP) divided by the total population – not average earnings. The GNP is the valuation of production within the country plus the balance of money flowing into and out of the country as a result of financial transactions.

FOREIGN TRADE The latest available imports and exports figures are given, but there may be exceptional factors at work (for example, war or sanctions).

INFANT MORTALITY The number of deaths under one year per 1,000 live births.

LIFE EXPECTANCY The age to which a female or male child born today, applying current rates of mortality, could expect to live.

ALPHABETICAL COUNTRY LIST

Afghanistan 104
Albania 70
Algeria 137
American Samoa 178
Andorra 62
Angola 160
Anguilla 202
Antigua and Barbuda 202
Argentina 221
Armenia 82
Aruba 204
Ascension 224
Australia 170
Austria 61
Azerbaijan 82
Azores 223

Bahamas 201
Bahrain 101
Bangladesh 111
Barbados 204
Belarus 78
Belgium 51
Belize 195
Benin 150
Bermuda 222
Bhutan 109
Bolivia 218
Bosnia-Herzegovina 72
Botswana 162
Brazil 215
Brunei 127
Bulgaria 73
Burkina Faso 149
Burma (Myanmar) 122
Burundi 154

Cambodia 124

Cameroon 153
Canada 184
Canary Islands 223
Cape Verde 222
Cayman Islands 200
Central African Republic 142
Chad 142
Chile 220
China 113
Colombia 210
Commonwealth of
   Independent States 78
Comoros 166
Congo 154
Costa Rica 197
Croatia 73
Cuba 198
Cyprus 95
Czech Republic 76

Denmark 42
Djibouti 145
Dominica 203
Dominican Republic 200

Ecuador 212
Egypt 139
El Salvador 196
Equatorial Guinea 153
Eritrea 144
Estonia 80
Ethiopia 144

Falkland Islands 224
Faroe Islands 38
Fiji 174
Finland 43
France 53
French Guiana 215
French Polynesia 178

Gabon 154
Gambia, The 146
Georgia 81
Germany 56

Ghana 149
Greece 70
Greenland 224
Grenada 203
Guadeloupe 202
Guam 176
Guatemala 195
Guinea 147
Guinea-Bissau 146
Guyana 214

Haiti 200
Honduras 196
Hong Kong 117
Hungary 74

Iceland 38
India 106
Indonesia 128
Iran 103
Iraq 102
Ireland 49
Israel 96
Italy 66
Ivory Coast
   (Côte d'Ivoire) 148

Jamaica 199
Japan 119
Jordan 98

Kazakstan 92
Kenya 157
Kiribati 177
Korea, North 118
Korea, South 119
Kuwait 100
Kyrgyzstan 93

Laos 124
Latvia 80
Lebanon 95
Lesotho 164
Liberia 148

Libya 138
Liechtenstein 61
Lithuania 80
Luxembourg 52

Macau 116
Macedonia 72
Madagascar 165
Madeira 223
Malawi 158
Malaysia 126
Maldives 110
Mali 140
Malta 69
Marshall Islands 177
Martinique 203
Mauritania 140
Mauritius 166
Mexico 194
Micronesia, Federated
   States of 177
Moldova 78
Monaco 56
Mongolia 112
Montserrat 202
Morocco 136
Mozambique 159

Namibia 162
Nauru 177
Nepal 109
Netherlands 50
Netherlands Antilles 204
New Caledonia 173
New Zealand 174
Nicaragua 197
Niger 141
Nigeria 151
Northern Mariana Islands 176
Norway 39

Oman 101

Pakistan 105

Palau 176
Panama 198
Papua New Guinea 173
Paraguay 218
Peru 212
Philippines 130
Pitcairn 178
Poland 77
Portugal 62
Puerto Rico 201

Qatar 100

Réunion 166
Romania 75
Russia 88
Rwanda 156

St Helena 224
St Kitts and Nevis 202
St Lucia 203
St Vincent and the
   Grenadines 203
San Marino 69
São Tomé and
   Principe 152
Saudi Arabia 98
Senegal 146
Seychelles 166
Sierra Leone 147
Singapore 127
Slovak Republic 76
Slovenia 73
Solomon Islands 173
Somalia 145
South Africa 163
Spain 63
Sri Lanka 110
Sudan 143
Surinam 214
Swaziland 165
Sweden 41
Switzerland 60
Syria 97

Taiwan 117
Tajikistan 93
Tanzania 158
Thailand 123
Togo 150
Tonga 178
Trinidad and Tobago 204
Tristan da Cunha 224
Tunisia 138
Turkey 94
Turkmenistan 92
Turks and Caicos Islands 200
Tuvalu 177

Uganda 156
Ukraine 79
United Arab Emirates 101
United Kingdom 44
United States of America 188
Uruguay 219
Uzbekistan 92

Vanuatu 178
Vatican City 69
Venezuela 211
Vietnam 124
Virgin Islands, British 201
Virgin Islands, US 201

Wallis and Futuna
   Islands 178
Western Samoa 178

Yemen 100
Yugoslavia 72

Zaire 155
Zambia 160
Zimbabwe 161

INTRODUCTION TO WORLD GEOGRAPHY

Planet Earth	2	Water & Vegetation	12	Quality of Life	22
Restless Earth	4	Environment	14	Energy	24
Landforms	6	Population	16	Production	26
Oceans	8	The Human Family	18	Trade	28
Climate	10	Wealth	20	Travel & Tourism	30

Planet Earth

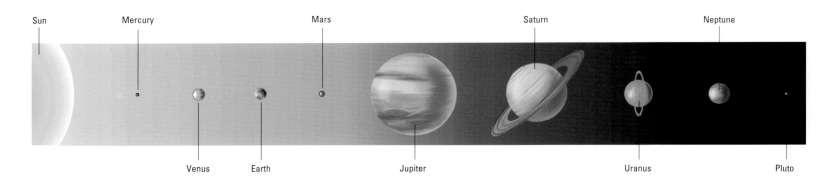

Sun · Mercury · Mars · Saturn · Neptune
Venus · Earth · Jupiter · Uranus · Pluto

The Solar System

A minute part of one of the billions of galaxies (collections of stars) that comprises the Universe, the Solar System lies some 27,000 light-years from the centre of our own galaxy, the 'Milky Way'. Thought to be over 4,700 million years old, it consists of a central sun with nine planets and their moons revolving around it, attracted by its gravitational pull. The planets orbit the Sun in the same direction – anti-clockwise when viewed from the Northern Heavens – and almost in the same plane. Their orbital paths, however, vary enormously.

The Sun's diameter is 109 times that of Earth, and the temperature at its core – caused by continuous thermonuclear fusions of hydrogen into helium – is estimated to be 15 million degrees Celsius. It is the Solar System's only source of light and heat.

Profile of the Planets

	Mean distance from Sun (million km)	Mass (Earth = 1)	Period of orbit (Earth years)	Period of rotation (Earth days)	Equatorial diameter (km)	Number of known satellites
Mercury	57.9	0.055	0.24 years	58.67	4,878	0
Venus	108.2	0.815	0.62 years	243.00	12,104	0
Earth	149.6	1.0	1.00 years	1.00	12,756	1
Mars	227.9	0.107	1.88 years	1.03	6,787	2
Jupiter	778.3	317.8	11.86 years	0.41	142,800	16
Saturn	1,427	95.2	29.46 years	0.43	120,000	20
Uranus	2,871	14.5	84.01 years	0.75	51,118	15
Neptune	4,497	17.1	164.80 years	0.80	49,528	8
Pluto	5,914	0.002	248.50 years	6.39	2,320	1

All planetary orbits are elliptical in form, but only Pluto and Mercury follow paths that deviate noticeably from a circular one. Near perihelion – its closest approach to the Sun – Pluto actually passes inside the orbit of Neptune, an event that last occurred in 1983. Pluto will not regain its station as outermost planet until February 1999.

The Seasons

Seasons occur because the Earth's axis is tilted at a constant angle of 23½°. When the northern hemisphere is tilted to a maximum extent towards the Sun, on 21 June, the Sun is overhead at the Tropic of Cancer (latitude 23½° North). This is midsummer, or the summer solstice, in the northern hemisphere.

On 22 or 23 September, the Sun is overhead at the Equator, and day and night are of equal length throughout the world. This is the autumn equinox in the northern hemisphere. On 21 or 22 December, the Sun is overhead at the Tropic of Capricorn (23½° South), the winter solstice in the northern hemisphere. The overhead Sun then tracks north until, on 21 March, it is overhead at the Equator. This is the spring (vernal) equinox in the northern hemisphere.

In the southern hemisphere, the seasons are the reverse of those in the north.

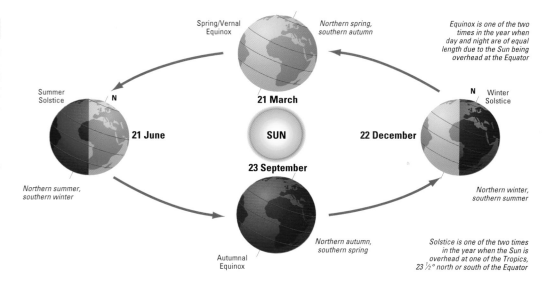

Equinox is one of the two times in the year when day and night are of equal length due to the Sun being overhead at the Equator

Solstice is one of the two times in the year when the Sun is overhead at one of the Tropics, 23½° north or south of the Equator

Day and Night

The Sun appears to rise in the east, reach its highest point at noon, and then set in the west, to be followed by night. In reality, it is not the Sun that is moving but the Earth rotating from west to east. The moment when the Sun's upper limb first appears above the horizon is termed sunrise; the moment when the Sun's upper limb disappears below the horizon is sunset.

At the summer solstice in the northern hemisphere (21 June), the Arctic has total daylight and the Antarctic total darkness. The opposite occurs at the winter solstice (21 or 22 December). At the Equator, the length of day and night are almost equal all year.

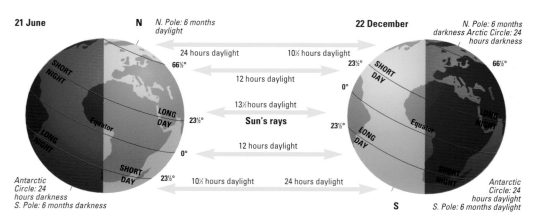

Time

Year: The time taken by the Earth to revolve around the Sun, or 365.24 days.

Leap Year: A calendar year of 366 days, 29 February being the additional day. It offsets the difference between the calendar and the solar year.

Month: The approximate time taken by the Moon to revolve around the Earth. The 12 months of the year in fact vary from 28 (29 in a Leap Year) to 31 days.

Week: An artificial period of 7 days, not based on astronomical time.

Day: The time taken by the Earth to complete one rotation on its axis.

Hour: 24 hours make one day. Usually the day is divided into hours AM (ante meridiem or before noon) and PM (post meridiem or after noon), although most timetables now use the 24-hour system, from midnight to midnight.

Sunrise
Sunset

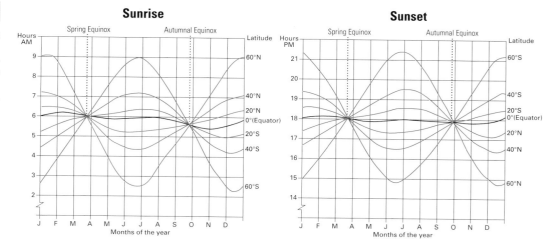

The Moon

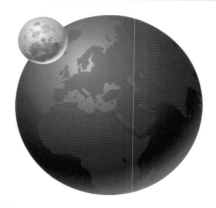

The Moon rotates more slowly than the Earth, making one complete turn on its axis in just over 27 days. Since this corresponds to its period of revolution around the Earth, the Moon always presents the same

Phases of the Moon

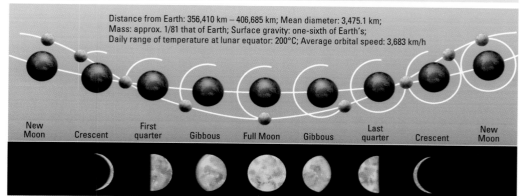

Distance from Earth: 356,410 km – 406,685 km; Mean diameter: 3,475.1 km; Mass: approx. 1/81 that of Earth; Surface gravity: one-sixth of Earth's; Daily range of temperature at lunar equator: 200°C; Average orbital speed: 3,683 km/h

New Moon | Crescent | First quarter | Gibbous | Full Moon | Gibbous | Last quarter | Crescent | New Moon

hemisphere or face to us, and we never see 'the dark side'. The interval between one full Moon and the next (and between new Moons) is about 29½ days – a lunar month. The apparent changes in the

shape of the Moon are caused by its changing position in relation to the Earth; like the planets, it produces no light of its own and shines only by reflecting the rays of the Sun.

Eclipses

When the Moon passes between the Sun and the Earth it causes a partial eclipse of the Sun (1) if the Earth passes through the Moon's outer shadow (P), or a total eclipse (2) if the inner cone shadow crosses the Earth's surface. In a lunar eclipse, the Earth's shadow crosses the Moon and, again, provides either a partial or total eclipse.

Eclipses of the Sun and the Moon do not occur every month because of the 5° difference between the plane of the Moon's orbit and the plane in which the Earth moves. In the 1990s only 14 lunar eclipses are possible, for example, seven partial and seven total; each is visible only from certain, and variable, parts of the world. The same period witnesses 13 solar eclipses – six partial (or annular) and seven total.

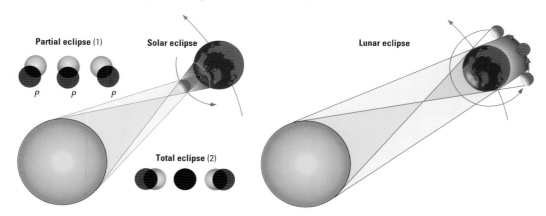

Tides

The daily rise and fall of the ocean's tides are the result of the gravitational pull of the Moon and that of the Sun, though the effect of the latter is only 46.6% as strong as that of the Moon. This effect is greatest on the hemisphere facing the Moon and causes a tidal 'bulge'. When the Sun, Earth and Moon are in line, tide-raising forces are at a maximum and Spring tides occur: high tide reaches the highest values, and low tide falls to low levels. When lunar and solar forces are least coincidental with the Sun and Moon at an angle (near the Moon's first and third quarters), Neap tides occur, which have a small tidal range.

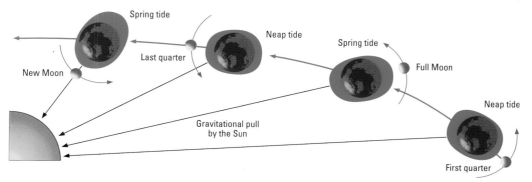

Restless Earth

The Earth's Structure

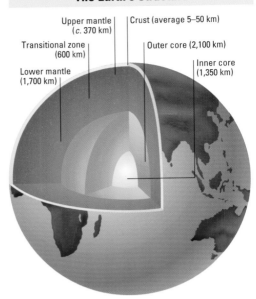

Upper mantle (c. 370 km) | Crust (average 5–50 km)

Transitional zone (600 km) | Outer core (2,100 km)

Lower mantle (1,700 km) | Inner core (1,350 km)

Continental Drift

About 200 million years ago the original Pangaea landmass began to split into two continental groups, which further separated over time to produce the present-day configuration.

180 million years ago

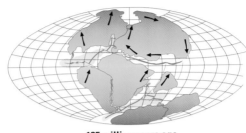

135 million years ago

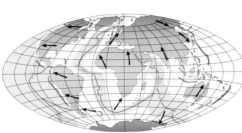

Present day

Trench

Rift

New ocean floor

Zones of slippage

Notable Earthquakes Since 1900

Year	Location	Richter Scale	Deaths
1906	San Francisco, USA	8.3	503
1906	Valparaiso, Chile	8.6	22,000
1908	Messina, Italy	7.5	83,000
1915	Avezzano, Italy	7.5	30,000
1920	Gansu (Kansu), China	8.6	180,000
1923	Yokohama, Japan	8.3	143,000
1927	Nan Shan, China	8.3	200,000
1932	Gansu (Kansu), China	7.6	70,000
1933	Sanriku, Japan	8.9	2,990
1934	Bihar, India/Nepal	8.4	10,700
1935	Quetta, India (now Pakistan)	7.5	60,000
1939	Chillan, Chile	8.3	28,000
1939	Erzincan, Turkey	7.9	30,000
1960	Agadir, Morocco	5.8	12,000
1962	Khorasan, Iran	7.1	12,230
1968	N.E. Iran	7.4	12,000
1970	N. Peru	7.7	66,794
1972	Managua, Nicaragua	6.2	5,000
1974	N. Pakistan	6.3	5,200
1976	Guatemala	7.5	22,778
1976	Tangshan, China	8.2	255,000
1978	Tabas, Iran	7.7	25,000
1980	El Asnam, Algeria	7.3	20,000
1980	S. Italy	7.2	4,800
1985	Mexico City, Mexico	8.1	4,200
1988	N.W. Armenia	6.8	55,000
1990	N. Iran	7.7	36,000
1993	Maharashtra, India	6.4	30,000
1994	Los Angeles, USA	6.6	61
1995	Kobe, Japan	7.2	5,000
1995	Sakhalin Is., Russia	7.5	2,000
1997	N.E. Iran	7.1	2,500
1998	Takhar, Afghanistan	6.1	4,200

The highest magnitude recorded on the Richter scale is 8.9 in Japan on 2 March 1933 which killed 2,990 people. The most devastating earthquake ever was at Shaanxi (Shenshi) province, central China, on 3 January 1556, when an estimated 830,000 people were killed.

Structure and Earthquakes

Mobile land areas

Submarine zones of mobile land areas

Stable land platforms

Submarine extensions of stable land platforms

Mid-oceanic volcanic ridges

Oceanic platforms

1976 ○ Principal earthquakes and dates

Earthquakes are a series of rapid vibrations originating from the slipping or faulting of parts of the Earth's crust when stresses within build up to breaking point. They usually happen at depths varying from 8 km to 30 km. Severe earthquakes cause extensive damage when they take place in populated areas, destroying structures and severing communications. Most initial loss of life occurs due to secondary causes such as falling masonry, fires and flooding.

Earthquakes

Earthquake magnitude is usually rated according to either the Richter or the Modified Mercalli scale, both devised by seismologists in the 1930s. The Richter scale measures absolute earthquake power with mathematical precision: each step upwards represents a tenfold increase in shockwave amplitude. Theoretically, there is no upper limit, but the largest earthquakes measured have been rated at between 8.8 and 8.9. The 12–point Mercalli scale, based on observed effects, is often more meaningful, ranging from I (earthquakes noticed only by seismographs) to XII (total destruction); intermediate points include V (people awakened at night; unstable objects overturned), VII (collapse of ordinary buildings; chimneys and monuments fall) and IX (conspicuous cracks in ground; serious damage to reservoirs).

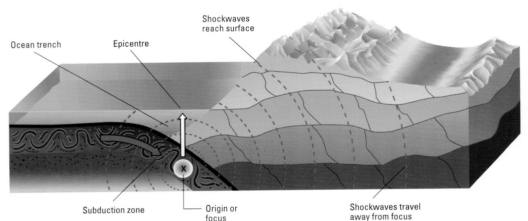

Ocean trench | Epicentre | Shockwaves reach surface

Subduction zone | Origin or focus | Shockwaves travel away from focus

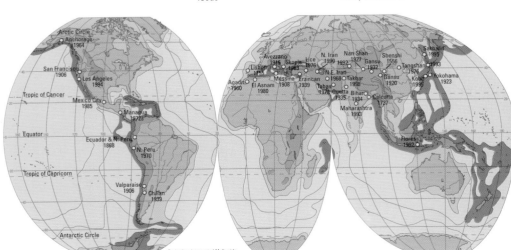

Projection: Interrupted Mollweide

Plate Tectonics

— Plate boundaries   PACIFIC Major plates

➤ Direction of plate movements and rate of movement (cm/year)

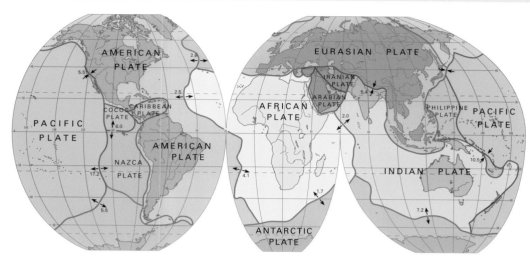

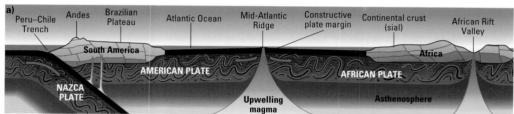

a) Peru–Chile Trench | Andes | Brazilian Plateau | Atlantic Ocean | Mid-Atlantic Ridge | Constructive plate margin | Continental crust (sial) | African Rift Valley

South America
NAZCA PLATE
AMERICAN PLATE
AFRICAN PLATE
Africa
Upwelling magma
Asthenosphere

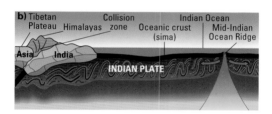

b) Tibetan Plateau | Himalayas | Collision zone | Oceanic crust (sima) | Indian Ocean | Mid-Indian Ocean Ridge

Asia   India
INDIAN PLATE

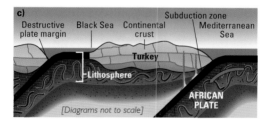

c) Destructive plate margin | Black Sea | Continental crust | Subduction zone | Mediterranean Sea

Turkey
Lithosphere
AFRICAN PLATE

[Diagrams not to scale]

The drifting of the continents is a feature that is unique to Planet Earth. The complementary, almost jigsaw-puzzle fit of the coastlines on each side of the Atlantic Ocean inspired Alfred Wegener's theory of continental drift in 1915. The theory suggested that the ancient super-continent, which Wegener named Pangaea, incorporated all of the Earth's landmasses and gradually split up to form today's continents.

The original debate about continental drift was a prelude to a more radical idea: plate tectonics. The basic theory is that the Earth's crust is made up of a series of rigid plates which float on a soft layer of the mantle and are moved about by continental convection currents within the Earth's interior. These plates diverge and converge along margins marked by seismic activity. Plates diverge from mid-ocean ridges where molten lava pushes upwards and forces the plates apart at rates of up to 40 mm [1.6 in] a year.

The three diagrams, left, give some examples of plate boundaries from around the world. Diagram (a) shows sea-floor spreading at the Mid-Atlantic Ridge as the American and African plates slowly diverge. The same thing is happening in (b) where sea-floor spreading at the Mid-Indian Ocean Ridge is forcing the Indian plate to collide into the Eurasian plate. In (c) oceanic crust (sima) is being subducted beneath lighter continental crust (sial).

Volcanoes

Volcanoes occur when hot liquefied rock beneath the Earth's crust is pushed up by pressure to the surface as molten lava. Some volcanoes erupt in an explosive way, throwing out rocks and ash, whilst others are effusive and lava flows out of the vent. There are volcanoes which are both, such as Mount Fuji. An accumulation of lava and cinders creates cones of variable size and shape. As a result of many eruptions over centuries, Mount Etna in Sicily has a circumference of more than 120 km [75 miles].

Climatologists believe that volcanic ash, if ejected high into the atmosphere, can influence temperature and weather for several years afterwards. The 1991 eruption of Mount Pinatubo in the Philippines ejected more than 20 million tonnes of dust and ash 32 km [20 miles] into the atmosphere and is believed to have accelerated ozone depletion over a large part of the globe.

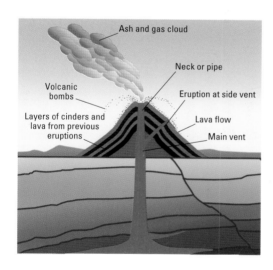

Ash and gas cloud
Neck or pipe
Volcanic bombs
Eruption at side vent
Layers of cinders and lava from previous eruptions
Lava flow
Main vent

Distribution of Volcanoes

Volcanoes today may be the subject of considerable scientific study but they remain both dramatic and unpredictable: in 1991 Mount Pinatubo, 100 km [62 miles] north of the Philippines capital Manila, suddenly burst into life after lying dormant for more than six centuries. Most of the world's active volcanoes occur in a belt around the Pacific Ocean, on the edge of the Pacific plate, called the 'ring of fire'. Indonesia has the greatest concentration with 90 volcanoes, 12 of which are active. The most famous, Krakatoa, erupted in 1883 with such force that the resulting tidal wave killed 36,000 people and tremors were felt as far away as Australia.

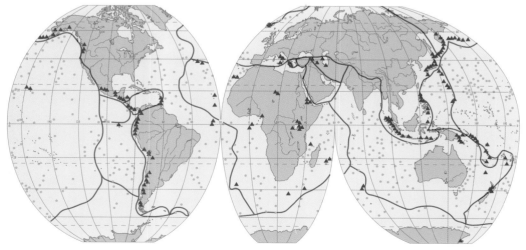

· Submarine volcanoes

▲ Land volcanoes active since 1700

— Boundaries of tectonic plates

Landforms

The Rock Cycle

James Hutton first proposed the rock cycle in the late 1700s after he observed the slow but steady effects of erosion.

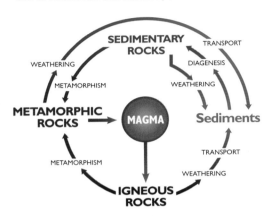

Above and below the surface of the oceans, the features of the Earth's crust are constantly changing. The phenomenal forces generated by convection currents in the molten core of our planet carry the vast segments or 'plates' of the crust across the globe in an endless cycle of creation and destruction. A continent may travel little more than 25 mm [1 in] per year, yet in the vast span of geological time this process throws up giant mountain ranges and creates new land.

Destruction of the landscape, however, begins as soon as it is formed. Wind, water, ice and sea, the main agents of erosion, mount a constant assault that even the most resistant rocks cannot withstand. Mountain peaks may dwindle by as little as a few millimetres each year, but if they are not uplifted by further movements of the crust they will eventually be reduced to rubble and transported away.

Water is the most powerful agent of erosion – it has been estimated that 100 billion tonnes of sediment are washed into the oceans every year. Three Asian rivers account for 20% of this total, the Huang He, in China, and the Brahmaputra and Ganges in Bangladesh.

Rivers and glaciers, like the sea itself, generate much of their effect through abrasion – pounding the land with the debris they carry with them. But as well as destroying they also create new landforms, many of them spectacular: vast deltas like those of the Mississippi and the Nile, or the deep fjords cut by glaciers in British Columbia, Norway and New Zealand.

Geologists once considered that landscapes evolved from 'young', newly uplifted mountainous areas, through a 'mature' hilly stage, to an 'old age' stage when the land was reduced to an almost flat plain, or peneplain. This theory, called the 'cycle of erosion', fell into disuse when it became evident that so many factors, including the effects of plate tectonics and climatic change, constantly interrupt the cycle, which takes no account of the highly complex interactions that shape the surface of our planet.

Mountain Building

Mountains are formed when pressures on the Earth's crust caused by continental drift become so intense that the surface buckles or cracks. This happens where oceanic crust is subducted by continental crust or, more dramatically, where two tectonic plates collide: the Rockies, Andes, Alps, Urals and Himalayas resulted from such impacts. These are all known as fold mountains because they were formed by the compression of the rocks, forcing the surface to bend and fold like a crumpled rug. The Himalayas are formed from the folded former sediments of the Tethys Sea which was trapped in the collision zone between the Indian and Eurasian plates.

The other main mountain-building process occurs when the crust fractures to create faults, allowing rock to be forced upwards in large blocks; or when the pressure of magma within the crust forces the surface to bulge into a dome, or erupts to form a volcano. Large mountain ranges may reveal a combination of those features; the Alps, for example, have been compressed so violently that the folds are fragmented by numerous faults and intrusions of molten igneous rock.

Over millions of years, even the greatest mountain ranges can be reduced by the agents of erosion (most notably rivers) to a low rugged landscape known as a peneplain.

Types of faults: Faults occur where the crust is being stretched or compressed so violently that the rock strata break in a horizontal or vertical movement. They are classified by the direction in which the blocks of rock have moved. A normal fault results when a vertical movement causes the surface to break apart; compression causes a reverse fault. Horizontal movement causes shearing, known as a strike-slip fault. When the rock breaks in two places, the central block may be pushed up in a horst fault, or sink (creating a rift valley) in a graben fault.

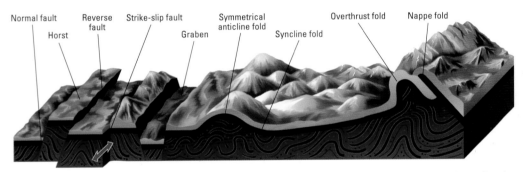

Types of fold: Folds occur when rock strata are squeezed and compressed. They are common therefore at destructive plate margins and where plates have collided, forcing the rocks to buckle into mountain ranges. Geographers give different names to the degrees of fold that result from continuing pressure on the rock. A simple fold may be symmetric, with even slopes on either side, but as the pressure builds up, one slope becomes steeper and the fold becomes asymmetric. Later, the ridge or 'anticline' at the top of the fold may slide over the lower ground or 'syncline' to form a recumbent fold. Eventually, the rock strata may break under the pressure to form an overthrust and finally a nappe fold.

Continental Glaciation

Ice sheets were at their greatest extent about 200,000 years ago. The maximum advance of the last Ice Age was about 18,000 years ago, when ice covered virtually all of Canada and reached as far south as the Bristol Channel in Britain.

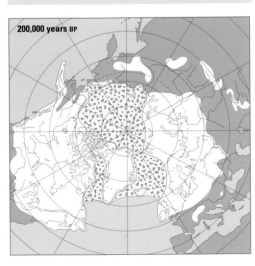

200,000 years BP

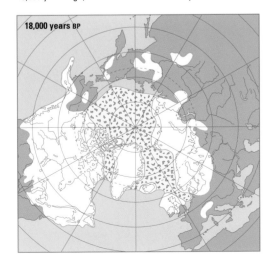

18,000 years BP

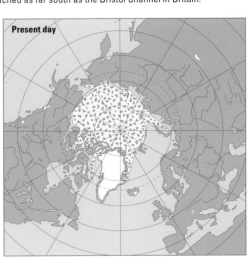

Present day

Natural Landforms

A stylized diagram to show a selection of landforms found in the mid-latitudes.

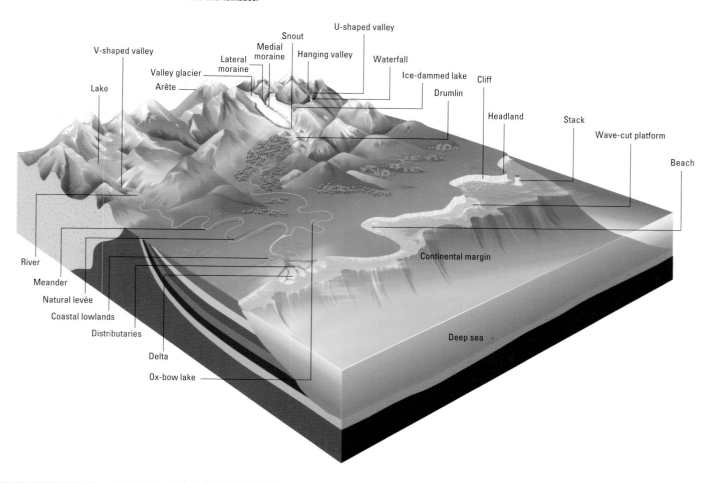

- V-shaped valley
- Valley glacier
- Arête
- Lateral moraine
- Lake
- Medial moraine
- Snout
- Hanging valley
- U-shaped valley
- Waterfall
- Ice-dammed lake
- Drumlin
- Cliff
- Headland
- Stack
- Wave-cut platform
- Beach
- River
- Meander
- Natural levée
- Coastal lowlands
- Distributaries
- Delta
- Ox-bow lake
- Continental margin
- Deep sea

Desert Landscapes

The popular image that deserts are all huge expanses of sand is wrong. Despite harsh conditions, deserts contain some of the most varied and interesting landscapes in the world. They are also one of the most extensive environments – the hot and cold deserts together cover almost 40% of the Earth's surface.

The three types of hot desert are known by their Arabic names: sand desert, called *erg*, covers only about one-fifth of the world's desert; the rest is divided between *hammada* (areas of bare rock) and *reg* (broad plains covered by loose gravel or pebbles).

In areas of *erg*, such as the Namib Desert, the shape of the dunes reflects the character of local winds. Where winds are constant in direction, crescent-shaped *barchan* dunes form. In areas of bare rock, wind-blown sand is a major agent of erosion. The erosion is mainly confined to within 2 m [6.5 ft] of the surface, producing characteristic, mushroom-shaped rocks.

Erg

Hammada

Reg

Surface Processes

Catastrophic changes to natural landforms are periodically caused by such phenomena as avalanches, landslides and volcanic eruptions, but most of the processes that shape the Earth's surface operate extremely slowly in human terms. One estimate, based on a study in the United States, suggested that 1 m [3 ft] of land was removed from the entire surface of the country, on average, every 29,500 years. However, the time-scale varies from 1,300 years to 154,200 years depending on the terrain and climate.

In hot, dry climates, mechanical weathering, a result of rapid temperature changes, causes the outer layers of rock to peel away, while in cold mountainous regions, boulders are prised apart when water freezes in cracks in rocks. Chemical weathering, at its greatest in warm, humid regions, is responsible for hollowing out limestone caves and decomposing granites.

The erosion of soil and rock is greatest on sloping land and the steeper the slope, the greater the tendency for mass wasting – the movement of soil and rock downhill under the influence of gravity. The mechanisms of mass wasting (ranging from very slow to very rapid) vary with the type of material, but the presence of water as a lubricant is usually an important factor.

Running water is the world's leading agent of erosion and transportation. The energy of a river depends on several factors, including its velocity and volume, and its erosive power is at its peak when it is in full flood. Sea waves also exert tremendous erosive power during storms when they hurl pebbles against the shore, undercutting cliffs and hollowing out caves.

Glacier ice forms in mountain hollows and spills out to form valley glaciers, which transport rocks shattered by frost action. As glaciers move, rocks embedded into the ice erode steep-sided, U-shaped valleys. Evidence of glaciation in mountain regions includes cirques, knife-edged ridges, or arêtes, and pyramidal peaks.

Oceans

The Great Oceans

Relative sizes of the world's oceans

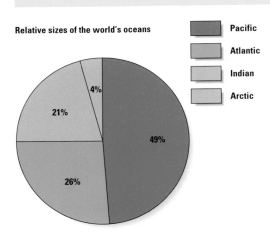

- Pacific
- Atlantic
- Indian
- Arctic

In a strict geographical sense there are only three true oceans – the Atlantic, Indian and Pacific. The legendary 'Seven Seas' would require these to be divided at the Equator and the addition of the Arctic Ocean – which accounts for less than 4% of the total sea area. The International Hydrographic Bureau does not recognize the Antarctic Ocean (even less the 'Southern Ocean') as a separate entity.

The Earth is a watery planet: more than 70% of its surface – over 360,000,000 sq km [140,000,000 sq miles] – is covered by the oceans and seas. The mighty Pacific alone accounts for nearly 36% of the total, and 49% of the sea area. Gravity holds in around 1,400 million cu. km [320 million cu. miles] of water, of which over 97% is saline.

The vast underwater world starts in the shallows of the seaside and plunges to depths of more than 11,000 m [36,000 ft]. The continental shelf, part of the landmass, drops gently to around 200 m [650 ft]; here the seabed falls away suddenly at an angle of 3° to 6° – the continental slope. The third stage, called the continental rise, is more gradual with gradients varying from 1 in 100 to 1 in 700. At an average depth of 5,000 m [16,500 ft] there begins the aptly-named abyssal plain – massive submarine depths where sunlight fails to penetrate and few creatures can survive.

From these plains rise volcanoes which, taken from base to top, rival and even surpass the tallest continental mountains in height. Mount Kea, on Hawaii, reaches a total of 10,203 m [33,400 ft], some 1,355 m [4,500 ft] more than Mount Everest, though scarcely 40% is visible above sea level.

In addition, there are underwater mountain chains up to 1,000 km [600 miles] across, whose peaks sometimes appear above sea level as islands such as Iceland and Tristan da Cunha.

The Ocean Depths

Average and maximum depths of the world's great oceans, in metres

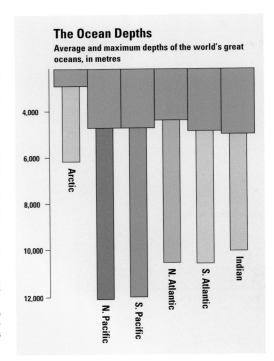

Ocean Currents

January temperatures and ocean currents

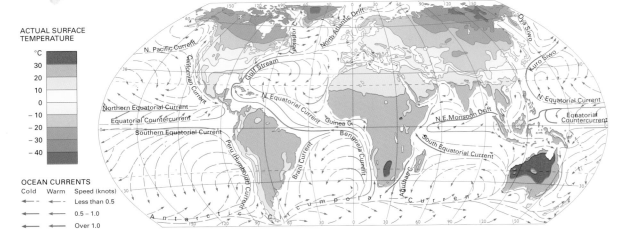

ACTUAL SURFACE TEMPERATURE

°C
30
20
10
0
– 10
– 20
– 30
– 40

OCEAN CURRENTS
Cold   Warm   Speed (knots)
Less than 0.5
0.5 – 1.0
Over 1.0

July temperatures and ocean currents

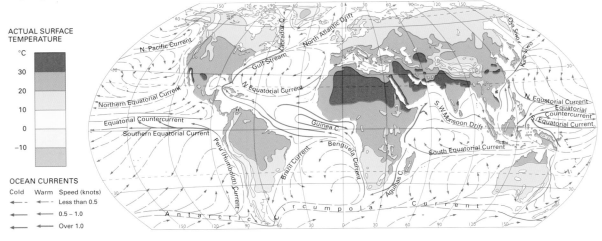

ACTUAL SURFACE TEMPERATURE

°C
30
20
10
0
–10

OCEAN CURRENTS
Cold   Warm   Speed (knots)
Less than 0.5
0.5 – 1.0
Over 1.0

Moving immense quantities of energy as well as billions of tonnes of water every hour, the ocean currents are a vital part of the great heat engine that drives the Earth's climate. They themselves are produced by a twofold mechanism. At the surface, winds push huge masses of water before them; in the deep ocean, below an abrupt temperature gradient that separates the churning surface waters from the still depths, density variations cause slow vertical movements.

The pattern of circulation of the great surface currents is determined by the displacement known as the Coriolis effect. As the Earth turns beneath a moving object – whether it is a tennis ball or a vast mass of water – it appears to be deflected to one side. The deflection is most obvious near the Equator, where the Earth's surface is spinning eastwards at 1,700 km/h [1,050 mph]; currents moving polewards are curved clockwise in the northern hemisphere and anti-clockwise in the southern.

The result is a system of spinning circles known as gyres. The Coriolis effect piles up water on the left of each gyre, creating a narrow, fast-moving stream that is matched by a slower, broader returning current on the right. North and south of the Equator, the fastest currents are located in the west and in the east respectively. In each case, warm water moves from the Equator and cold water returns to it. Cold currents often bring an upwelling of nutrients with them, supporting the world's most economically important fisheries.

Depending on the prevailing winds, some currents on or near the Equator may reverse their direction in the course of the year – a seasonal variation on which Asian monsoon rains depend, and whose occasional failure can bring disaster to millions.

World Fishing Areas

Main commercial fishing areas (numbered FAO regions)

Catch by top marine fishing areas, thousand tonnes (1992)

1. Pacific, NW	[61]	24,199	29.3%
2. Pacific, SE	[87]	13,899	16.8%
3. Atlantic, NE	[27]	11,073	13.4%
4. Pacific, WC	[71]	7,710	9.3%
5. Indian, W	[51]	3,747	4.5%
6. Indian, E	[57]	3,262	4.0%
7. Atlantic, EC	[34]	3,259	3.9%
8. Pacific, NE	[67]	3,149	3.8%

Principal fishing areas

Leading fishing nations

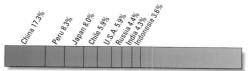

China 17.3% Peru 8.3% Japan 8.0% Chile 5.9% U.S.A. 5.9% Russia 4.4% India 4.3% Indonesia 3.6%

World total (1993): 101,417,500 tonnes
(Marine catch 83.1% Inland catch 16.9%)

Marine Pollution

Sources of marine oil pollution (latest available year)

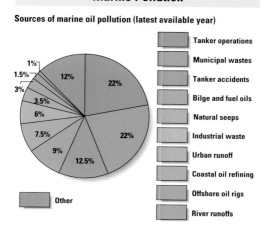

22% — Tanker operations
12% — Municipal wastes
1% — Tanker accidents
1.5% — Bilge and fuel oils
3% — Natural seeps
3.5% — Industrial waste
6% — Urban runoff
7.5% — Coastal oil refining
9% — Offshore oil rigs
12.5% — River runoffs
22% —

Other

Oil Spills

Major oil spills from tankers and combined carriers

Year	Vessel	Location	Spill (barrels)**	Cause
1979	Atlantic Empress	West Indies	1,890,000	collision
1983	Castillo De Bellver	South Africa	1,760,000	fire
1978	Amoco Cadiz	France	1,628,000	grounding
1991	Haven	Italy	1,029,000	explosion
1988	Odyssey	Canada	1,000,000	fire
1967	Torrey Canyon	UK	909,000	grounding
1972	Sea Star	Gulf of Oman	902,250	collision
1977	Hawaiian Patriot	Hawaiian Is.	742,500	fire
1979	Independenta	Turkey	696,350	collision
1993	Braer	UK	625,000	grounding
1996	Sea Empress	UK	515,000	grounding

Other sources of major oil spills

1983	Nowruz oilfield	The Gulf	4,250,000†	war
1979	Ixtoc 1 oilwell	Gulf of Mexico	4,200,000	blow-out
1991	Kuwait	The Gulf	2,500,000†	war

** 1 barrel = 0.136 tonnes/159 lit./35 Imperial gal./42 US gal. † estimated

River Pollution

Sources of river pollution, USA (latest available year)

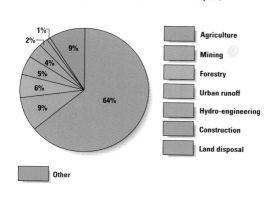

64% —
9% — Agriculture
1% — Mining
2% — Forestry
4% — Urban runoff
5% — Hydro-engineering
6% — Construction
9% — Land disposal

Other

Water Pollution

Severely polluted sea areas and lakes

Polluted sea areas and lakes

Areas of frequent oil pollution by shipping

◤ Major oil tanker spills

▲ Major oil rig blow-outs

▼ Offshore dumpsites for industrial and municipal waste

— Severely polluted rivers and estuaries

The most notorious tanker spillage of the 1980s occurred when the *Exxon Valdez* ran aground in Prince William Sound, Alaska, in 1989, spilling 267,000 barrels of crude oil close to shore in a sensitive ecological area. This rates as the world's 28th worst spill in terms of volume.

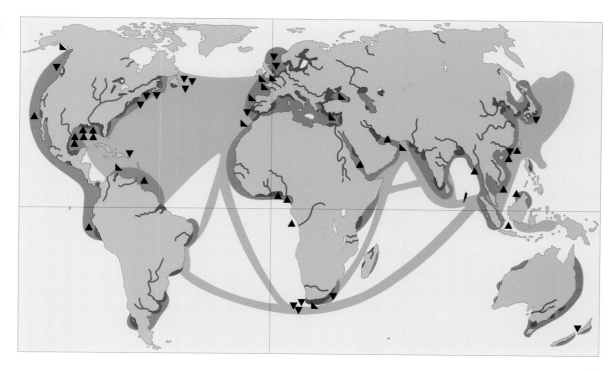

Climate

Climatic Regions

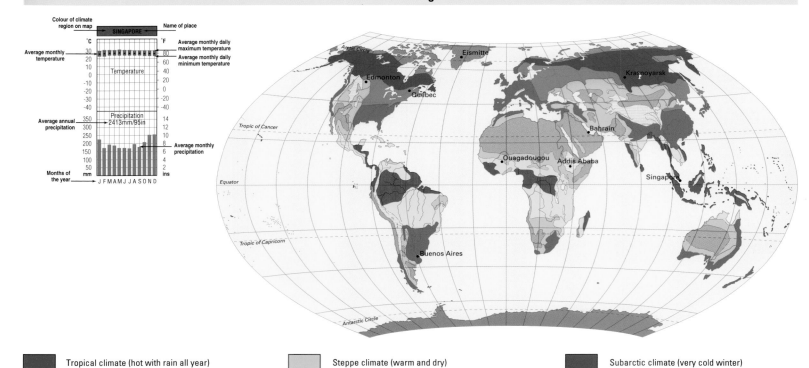

Tropical climate (hot with rain all year)

Desert climate (hot and very dry)

Savanna climate (hot with dry season)

Steppe climate (warm and dry)

Mild climate (warm and wet)

Continental climate (wet with cold winter)

Subarctic climate (very cold winter)

Polar climate (very cold and dry)

Mountainous climate (altitude affects climate)

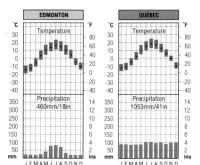
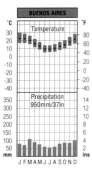
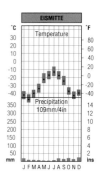
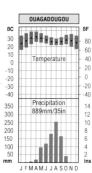
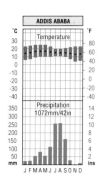
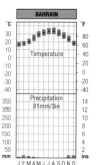
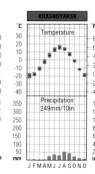

Climate Records

Temperature

Highest recorded shade temperature: Al Aziziyah, Libya, 58°C [136.4°F], 13 September 1922.

Highest mean annual temperature: Dallol, Ethiopia, 34.4°C [94°F], 1960–66.

Longest heatwave: Marble Bar, W. Australia, 162 days over 38°C [100°F], 23 October 1923 to 7 April 1924.

Lowest recorded temperature (outside poles): Verkhoyansk, Siberia, –68°C [–90°F], 6 February 1933.

Lowest mean annual temperature: Plateau Station, Antarctica, –56.6°C [–72.0°F]

Pressure

Longest drought: Calama, N. Chile, no recorded rainfall in 400 years to 1971.

Wettest place (12 months): Cherrapunji, Meghalaya, N. E. India, 26,470 mm [1,040 in], August 1860 to August 1861. Cherrapunji also holds the record for the most rainfall in one month: 2,930 mm [115 in], July 1861.

Wettest place (average): Mawsynram, India, mean annual rainfall 11,873 mm [467.4 in].

Wettest place (24 hours): Cilaos, Réunion, Indian Ocean, 1,870 mm [73.6 in], 15–16 March 1952.

Heaviest hailstones: Gopalganj, Bangladesh, up to 1.02 kg [2.25 lb], 14 April 1986 (killed 92 people).

Heaviest snowfall (continuous): Bessans, Savoie, France, 1,730 mm [68 in] in 19 hours, 5–6 April 1969.

Heaviest snowfall (season/year): Paradise Ranger Station, Mt Rainier, Washington, USA, 31,102 mm [1,224.5 in], 19 February 1971 to 18 February 1972.

Pressure and winds

Highest barometric pressure: Agata, Siberia (at 262 m [862 ft] altitude), 1,083.8 mb, 31 December 1968.

Lowest barometric pressure: Typhoon Tip, Guam, Pacific Ocean, 870 mb, 12 October 1979.

Highest recorded wind speed: Mt Washington, New Hampshire, USA, 371 km/h [231 mph], 12 April 1934. This is three times as strong as hurricane force on the Beaufort Scale.

Windiest place: Commonwealth Bay, Antarctica, where gales frequently reach over 320 km/h [200 mph].

Climate

Climate is weather in the long term: the seasonal pattern of hot and cold, wet and dry, averaged over time (usually 30 years). At the simplest level, it is caused by the uneven heating of the Earth. Surplus heat at the Equator passes towards the poles, levelling out the energy differential. Its passage is marked by a ceaseless churning of the atmosphere and the oceans, further agitated by the Earth's diurnal spin and the motion it imparts to moving air and water. The heat's means of transport – by winds and ocean currents, by the continual evaporation and recondensation of water molecules – is the weather itself. There are four basic types of climate, each of which can be further subdivided: tropical, desert (dry), temperate and polar.

Composition of Dry Air

Nitrogen	78.09%	Sulphur dioxide	trace
Oxygen	20.95%	Nitrogen oxide	trace
Argon	0.93%	Methane	trace
Water vapour	0.2–4.0%	Dust	trace
Carbon dioxide	0.03%	Helium	trace
Ozone	0.00006%	Neon	trace

El Niño

In a normal year, south-easterly trade winds drive surface waters westwards off the coast of South America, drawing cold, nutrient-rich water up from below. In an El Niño year (which occurs every 2–7 years), warm water from the west Pacific suppresses up-welling in the east, depriving the region of nutrients. The water is warmed by as much as 7°C [12°F], disturbing the tropical atmospheric circulation. During an intense El Niño, the south-east trade winds change direction and become equatorial westerlies, re-sulting in climatic extremes in many regions of the world, such as drought in parts of Australia and India, and heavy rainfall in south-eastern USA. An intense El Niño occurred in 1997–8, with resultant freak weather conditions across the entire Pacific region.

Normal year

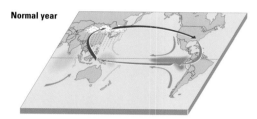

El Niño event

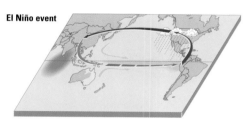

Beaufort Wind Scale

Named after the 19th-century British naval officer who devised it, the Beaufort Scale assesses wind speed according to its effects. It was originally designed as an aid for sailors, but has since been adapted for use on the land.

Scale	Wind speed km/h	mph	Effect
0	0–1	0–1	**Calm** Smoke rises vertically
1	1–5	1–3	**Light air** Wind direction shown only by smoke drift
2	6–11	4–7	**Light breeze** Wind felt on face; leaves rustle; vanes moved by wind
3	12–19	8–12	**Gentle breeze** Leaves and small twigs in constant motion; wind extends small flag
4	20–28	13–18	**Moderate** Raises dust and loose paper; small branches move
5	29–38	19–24	**Fresh** Small trees in leaf sway; wavelets on inland waters
6	39–49	25–31	**Strong** Large branches move; difficult to use umbrellas
7	50–61	32–38	**Near gale** Whole trees in motion; difficult to walk against wind
8	62–74	39–46	**Gale** Twigs break from trees; walking very difficult
9	75–88	47–54	**Strong gale** Slight structural damage
10	89–102	55–63	**Storm** Trees uprooted; serious structural damage
11	103–117	64–72	**Violent storm** Widespread damage
12	118+	73+	**Hurricane**

Conversions

°C = (°F − 32) × 5/9; °F = (°C × 9/5) + 32; 0°C = 32°F
1 in = 25.4 mm; 1 mm = 0.0394 in; 100 mm = 3.94 in

Temperature

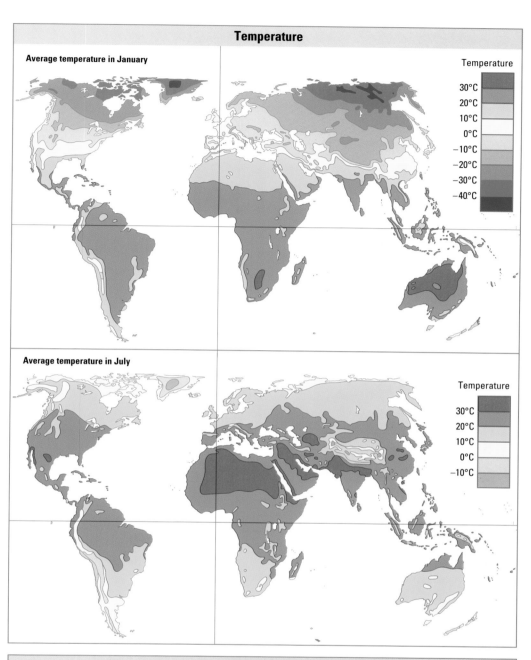

Average temperature in January

Temperature
30°C
20°C
10°C
0°C
−10°C
−20°C
−30°C
−40°C

Average temperature in July

Temperature
30°C
20°C
10°C
0°C
−10°C

Precipitation

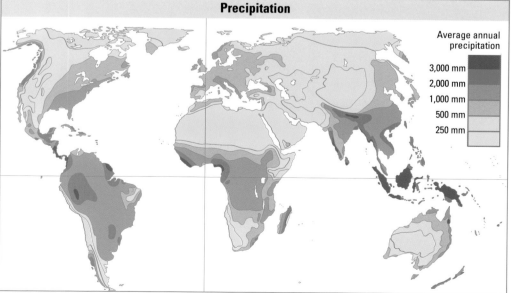

Average annual precipitation
3,000 mm
2,000 mm
1,000 mm
500 mm
250 mm

Water and Vegetation

The Hydrological Cycle

The world's water balance is regulated by the constant recycling of water between the oceans, atmosphere and land. The movement of water between these three reservoirs is known as the hydrological cycle. The oceans play a vital role in the hydrological cycle: 74% of the total precipitation falls over the oceans and 84% of the total evaporation comes from the oceans.

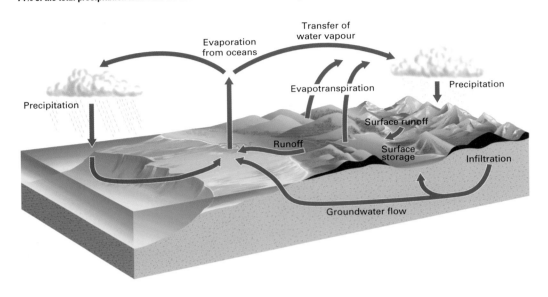

Water Distribution

The distribution of planetary water, by percentage. Oceans and ice-caps together account for more than 99% of the total; the breakdown of the remainder is estimated.

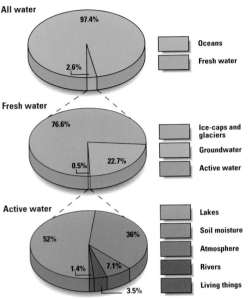

All water — 97.4% 2.6%
- Oceans
- Fresh water

Fresh water — 76.6% 0.5% 22.7%
- Ice-caps and glaciers
- Groundwater
- Active water

Active water — 52% 36% 1.4% 7.1% 3.5%
- Lakes
- Soil moisture
- Atmosphere
- Rivers
- Living things

Water Utilization

Domestic Industrial Agriculture

The percentage breakdown of water usage by sector, selected countries (latest available year)

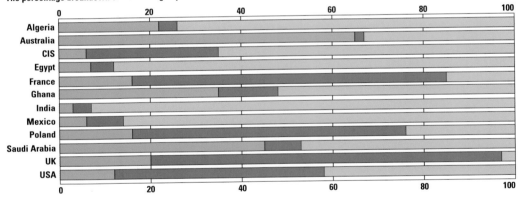

Algeria, Australia, CIS, Egypt, France, Ghana, India, Mexico, Poland, Saudi Arabia, UK, USA

Water Usage

Almost all the world's water is 3,000 million years old, and all of it cycles endlessly through the hydrosphere, though at different rates. Water vapour circulates over days, even hours, deep ocean water circulates over millennia, and ice-cap water remains solid for millions of years.

Fresh water is essential to all terrestrial life. Humans cannot survive more than a few days without it, and even the hardiest desert plants and animals could not exist without some water. Agriculture requires huge quantities of fresh water: without large-scale irrigation most of the world's people would starve. In the USA, agriculture uses 43% and industry 38% of all water withdrawals.

The United States is one of the heaviest users of water in the world. According to the latest figures the average American uses 380 litres a day and the average household uses 415,000 litres a year. This is two to four times more than in Western Europe.

Water Supply

Percentage of total population with access to safe drinking water (average 1990–96)

- Over 90% with safe water
- 75 – 90% with safe water
- 60 – 75% with safe water
- 45 – 60% with safe water
- 30 – 45% with safe water
- Under 30% with safe water

△ Under 80 litres per person per day domestic water consumption

▲ Over 320 litres per person per day domestic water consumption

NB: 80 litres of water a day is considered necessary for a reasonable quality of life.

Least well-provided countries

Afghanistan	23%	Papua New Guinea	28%
Chad	24%	Haiti	28%
Ethiopia	25%	Madagascar	29%

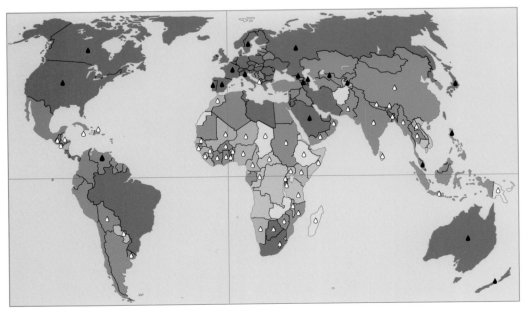

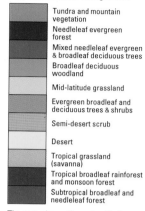

Regional variation in vegetation

Tundra and mountain vegetation

Needleleaf evergreen forest

Mixed needleleaf evergreen & broadleaf deciduous trees

Broadleaf deciduous woodland

Mid-latitude grassland

Evergreen broadleaf and deciduous trees & shrubs

Semi-desert scrub

Desert

Tropical grassland (savanna)

Tropical broadleaf rainforest and monsoon forest

Subtropical broadleaf and needleleaf forest

The map shows the natural 'climax vegetation' of regions, as dictated by climate and topography. In most cases, however, agricultural activity has drastically altered the vegetation pattern. Western Europe, for example, lost most of its broadleaf forest many centuries ago, while irrigation has turned some natural semi-desert into productive land.

Land Use by Continent

- Forest
- Permanent pasture and rough grazing
- Permanent crops and plantations
- Arable
- Non-productive

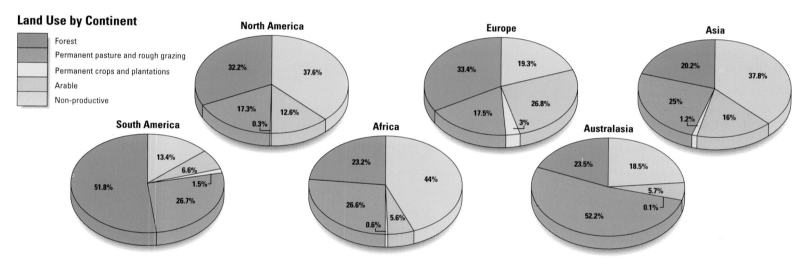

North America: 37.6%, 12.6%, 0.3%, 17.3%, 32.2%

Europe: 19.3%, 26.8%, 3%, 17.5%, 33.4%

Asia: 37.8%, 16%, 1.2%, 25%, 20.2%

South America: 13.4%, 6.6%, 1.5%, 26.7%, 51.8%

Africa: 44%, 5.6%, 0.6%, 26.6%, 23.2%

Australasia: 18.5%, 5.7%, 0.1%, 52.2%, 23.5%

Forestry: Production

Annual production (1993, million cubic metres)

	Forest and woodland (million hectares)	Fuelwood and charcoal	Industrial roundwood*
World	*3,987.9*	*1,875.8*	*1,528.5*
CIS	827.8	51.5	172.9
S. America	829.3	247.8	122.0
N. & C. America	709.8	156.7	586.7
Africa	684.6	493.6	59.5
Asia	490.2	866.4	278.1
Europe	157.3	50.9	272.2
Australasia	157.2	8.7	36.9

Paper and Board

Top producers (1993)**		Top exporters (1993)**	
USA	77,250	Canada	12,896
Japan	27,764	Finland	8,526
China	23,816	USA	7,146
Canada	17,557	Sweden	7,008
Germany	13,034	Germany	4,763

* roundwood is timber as it is felled
** in thousand tonnes

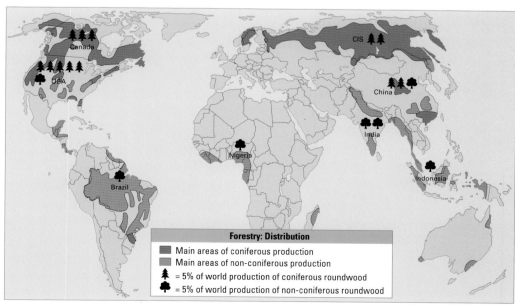

Forestry: Distribution

- Main areas of coniferous production
- Main areas of non-coniferous production
- 🌲 = 5% of world production of coniferous roundwood
- 🌳 = 5% of world production of non-coniferous roundwood

Environment

Humans have always had a dramatic effect on their environment, at least since the development of agriculture almost 10,000 years ago. Generally, the Earth has accepted human interference without obvious ill effects: the complex systems that regulate the global environment have been able to absorb substantial damage while maintaining a stable and comfortable home for the planet's trillions of lifeforms. But advancing human technology and the rapidly-expanding populations it supports are now threatening to overwhelm the Earth's ability to compensate.

Industrial wastes, acid rainfall, desertification and large-scale deforestation all combine to create environmental change at a rate far faster than the great slow cycles of planetary evolution can accommodate. As a result of overcultivation, overgrazing and overcutting of groundcover for firewood, desertification is affecting as much as 60% of the world's croplands. In addition, with fire and chain-saws, humans are destroying more forest in a day than their ancestors could do in a century, upsetting the balance between plant and animal, carbon dioxide and oxygen, on which all life ultimately depends.

The fossil fuels that power industrial civilization have pumped enough carbon dioxide and other so-called greenhouse gases into the atmosphere to make climatic change a near-certainty. As a result of the combination of these factors, the Earth's average temperature has risen by approximately 0.5°C [1°F] since the beginning of the 20th century, and it is still rising.

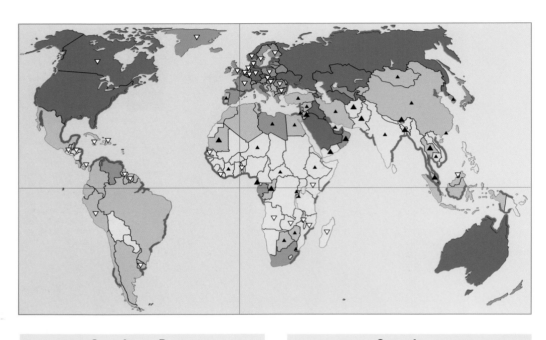

Global Warming

Carbon dioxide emissions in tonnes per person per year (1992)

- Over 10 tonnes of CO_2
- 5 – 10 tonnes of CO_2
- 1 – 5 tonnes of CO_2
- Under 1 tonne of CO_2

Changes in CO_2 emissions 1980–90

- ▲ Over 100% increase in emissions
- ▲ 50–100% increase in emissions
- ▽ Reduction in emissions
- — Coastal areas in danger of flooding from rising sea levels caused by global warming

High atmospheric concentrations of heat-absorbing gases, especially carbon dioxide, appear to be causing a steady rise in average temperatures worldwide – up to 1.5°C [3°F] by the year 2020, according to some estimates. Global warming is likely to bring with it a rise in sea levels that may flood some of the Earth's most densely populated coastal areas.

Greenhouse Power

Relative contributions to the Greenhouse Effect by the major heat-absorbing gases in the atmosphere.

The chart combines greenhouse potency and volume. Carbon dioxide has a greenhouse potential of only 1, but its concentration of 350 parts per million makes it predominate. CFC 12, with 25,000 times the absorption capacity of CO_2, is present only as 0.00044 ppm.

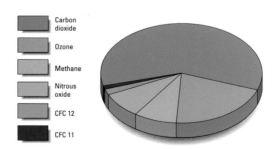

- Carbon dioxide
- Ozone
- Methane
- Nitrous oxide
- CFC 12
- CFC 11

Ozone Layer

The ozone 'hole' over the northern hemisphere on 12 March 1995.

The colours represent Dobson Units (DU). The ozone 'hole' is seen as the dark blue and purple patch in the centre, where ozone values are around 120 DU or lower. Normal levels are around 280 DU. The ozone 'hole' over Antarctica is much larger.

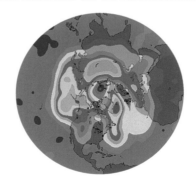

Carbon Dioxide

Carbon dioxide released in millions of tonnes (1992)

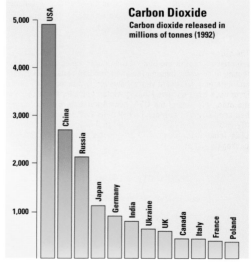

The Greenhouse Effect

Carbon dioxide is increased by burning fossil fuels and cutting forests

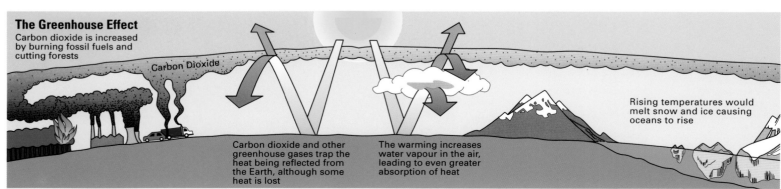

Carbon Dioxide

Rising temperatures would melt snow and ice causing oceans to rise

Carbon dioxide and other greenhouse gases trap the heat being reflected from the Earth, although some heat is lost

The warming increases water vapour in the air, leading to even greater absorption of heat

Desertification

- Existing deserts
- Areas with a high risk of desertification
- Areas with a moderate risk of desertification

- Former areas of rainforest
- Existing rainforest

Forest Clearance

Thousands of hectares of forest cleared annually, tropical countries surveyed 1981–85 and 1987–90. Loss as a percentage of remaining stocks is shown in figures on each column.

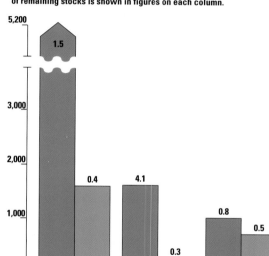

Deforestation

The Earth's remaining forests are under attack from three directions: expanding agriculture, logging, and growing consumption of fuelwood, often in combination. Sometimes deforestation is the direct result of government policy, as in the efforts made to resettle the urban poor in some parts of Brazil; just as often, it comes about despite state attempts at conservation. Loggers, licensed or unlicensed, blaze a trail into virgin forest, often destroying twice as many trees as they harvest. Landless farmers follow, burning away most of what remains to plant their crops, completing the destruction.

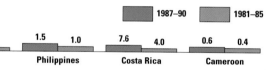

- 1987–90
- 1981–85

Ozone Depletion

The ozone layer, 25–30 km [15–18 miles] above sea level, acts as a barrier to most of the Sun's harmful ultra-violet radiation, protecting us from the ionizing radiation that can cause skin cancer and cataracts. In recent years, however, two holes in the ozone layer have been observed during winter: one over the Arctic and the other, the size of the USA, over Antarctica. By 1996, ozone had been reduced to around a half of its 1970 amount. The ozone (O_3) is broken down by chlorine released into the atmosphere as CFCs (chlorofluorocarbons) – chemicals used in refrigerators, packaging and aerosols.

Air Pollution

Sulphur dioxide is the main pollutant associated with industrial cities. According to the World Health Organization, at least 600 million people live in urban areas where sulphur dioxide concentrations regularly reach damaging levels. One of the world's most dangerously polluted urban areas is Mexico City, due to a combination of its enclosed valley location, three million cars and 60,000 factories. In May 1998, this lethal cocktail was added to by nearby forest fires and the resultant air pollution led to over 20% of the population (three million people) complaining of respiratory problems.

Acid Rain

Killing trees, poisoning lakes and rivers and eating away buildings, acid rain is mostly produced by sulphur dioxide emissions from industry and volcanic eruptions. By the mid 1990s, acid rain had sterilized 4,000 or more of Sweden's lakes and left 45% of Switzerland's alpine conifers dead or dying, while the monuments of Greece were dissolving in Athens' smog. Prevailing wind patterns mean that the acids often fall many hundred kilometres from where the original pollutants were discharged. In parts of Europe acid deposition has slightly decreased, following reductions in emissions, but not by enough.

World Pollution

Acid rain and sources of acidic emissions (latest available year)

Acid rain is caused by high levels of sulphur and nitrogen in the atmosphere. They combine with water vapour and oxygen to form acids (H_2SO_4 and HNO_3) which fall as precipitation.

 Regions where sulphur and nitrogen oxides are released in high concentrations, mainly from fossil fuel combustion

• Major cities with high levels of air pollution (including nitrogen and sulphur emissions)

Areas of heavy acid deposition

pH numbers indicate acidity, decreasing from a neutral 7. Normal rain, slightly acid from dissolved carbon dioxide, never exceeds a pH of 5.6.

- pH less than 4.0 (most acidic)
- pH 4.0 to 4.5
- pH 4.5 to 5.0
- Areas where acid rain is a potential problem

Population

Demographic Profiles

Developed nations such as the UK have populations evenly spread across the age groups and, usually, a growing proportion of elderly people. The great majority of the people in developing nations, however, are in the younger age groups, about to enter their most fertile years. In time, these population profiles should resemble the world profile (even Kenya has made recent progress with reducing its birth rate), but the transition will come about only after a few more generations of rapid population growth.

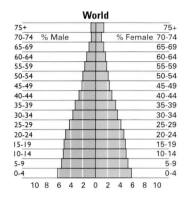

World

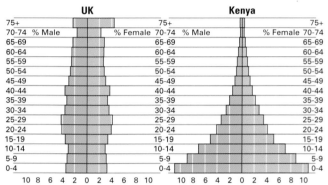

UK

Kenya

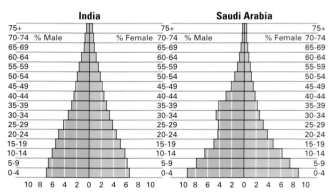

India

Saudi Arabia

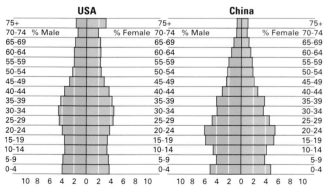

USA

China

Most Populous Nations [in millions (1997)]

1.	China	1,210	9.	Bangladesh	124	17. Egypt	63
2.	India	980	10.	Nigeria	118	18. Thailand	61
3.	USA	268	11.	Mexico	97	19. France	59
4.	Indonesia	204	12.	Germany	82	20. UK	59
5.	Brazil	160	13.	Vietnam	77	21. Ethiopia	59
6.	Russia	148	14.	Philippines	74	22. Italy	58
7.	Pakistan	136	15.	Iran	70	23. Ukraine	52
8.	Japan	126	16.	Turkey	64	24. Burma	48

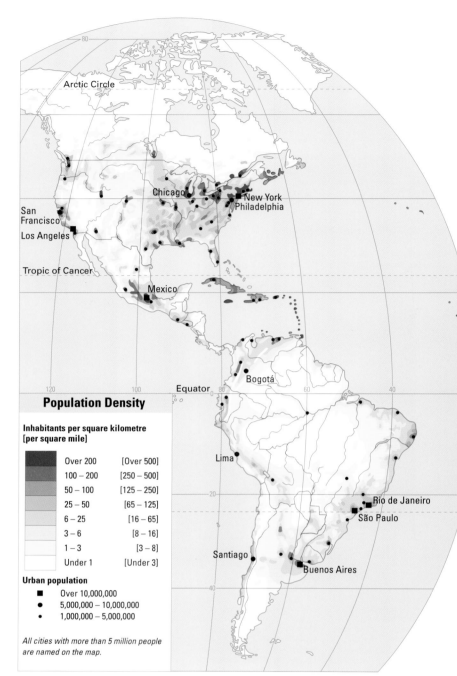

Population Density

**Inhabitants per square kilometre
[per square mile]**

	Over 200	[Over 500]
	100 – 200	[250 – 500]
	50 – 100	[125 – 250]
	25 – 50	[65 – 125]
	6 – 25	[16 – 65]
	3 – 6	[8 – 16]
	1 – 3	[3 – 8]
	Under 1	[Under 3]

Urban population

■ Over 10,000,000

● 5,000,000 – 10,000,000

• 1,000,000 – 5,000,000

All cities with more than 5 million people are named on the map.

Continental Comparisons

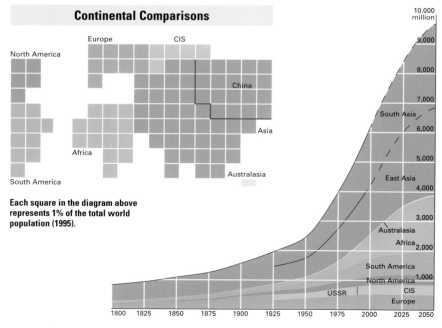

Each square in the diagram above represents 1% of the total world population (1995).

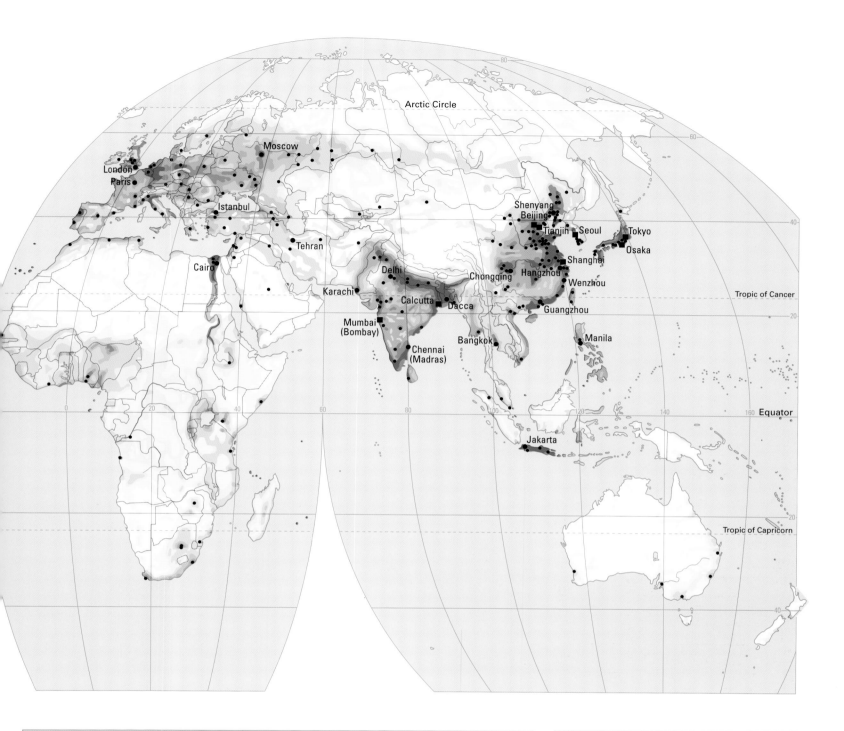

Arctic Circle

Moscow

London
Paris

Istanbul

Tehran

Cairo

Karachi

Delhi

Mumbai
(Bombay)

Calcutta

Dacca

Chennai
(Madras)

Bangkok

Shenyang
Beijing
Tianjin   Seoul   Tokyo
Osaka

Shanghai
Chongqing   Hangzhou
Wenzhou

Guangzhou

Manila

Tropic of Cancer

Equator

Jakarta

Tropic of Capricorn

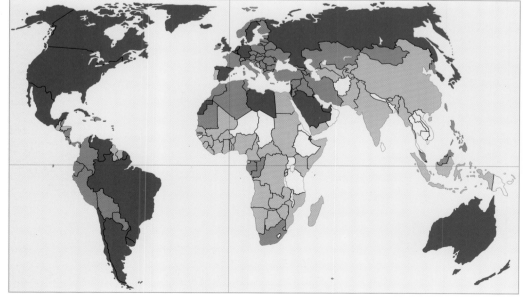

Urban Population

Percentage of total population living in towns and cities (1995)

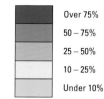

Over 75%

50 – 75%

25 – 50%

10 – 25%

Under 10%

Most urbanized

Singapore	100%
Belgium	97%
Kuwait	95%
Iceland	93%
Venezuela	91%

[UK 89%]

Least urbanized

Rwanda	6%
Bhutan	8%
Burundi	9%
Nepal	12%
Uganda	12%

The Human Family

Predominant Languages

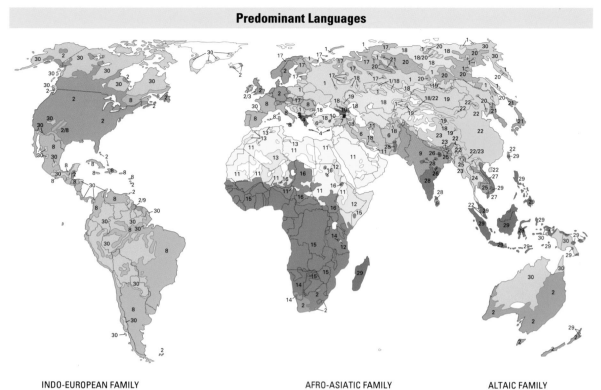

INDO-EUROPEAN FAMILY
1 Balto-Slavic group (incl. Russian, Ukrainian)
2 Germanic group (incl. English, German)
3 Celtic group
4 Greek
5 Albanian
6 Iranian group
7 Armenian
8 Romance group (incl. Spanish, Portuguese, French, Italian)
9 Indo-Aryan group (incl. Hindi, Bengali, Urdu, Punjabi, Marathi)
10 CAUCASIAN FAMILY

AFRO-ASIATIC FAMILY
11 Semitic group (incl. Arabic)
12 Kushitic group
13 Berber group

14 KHOISAN FAMILY

15 NIGER-CONGO FAMILY

16 NILO-SAHARAN FAMILY

17 URALIC FAMILY

ALTAIC FAMILY
18 Turkic group
19 Mongolian group
20 Tungus-Manchu group
21 Japanese and Korean

SINO-TIBETAN FAMILY
22 Sinitic (Chinese) languages
23 Tibetic-Burmic languages

24 TAI FAMILY

AUSTRO-ASIATIC FAMILY
25 Mon-Khmer group
26 Munda group
27 Vietnamese

28 DRAVIDIAN FAMILY (incl. Telugu, Tamil)

29 AUSTRONESIAN FAMILY (incl. Malay-Indonesian)

30 OTHER LANGUAGES

Predominant Religions

Religious Adherents

Religious adherents in millions:

Christian	1,669	Hindu	663
Roman Catholic	*952*	Buddhist	312
Protestant	*337*	Chinese Folk	172
Orthodox	*162*	Tribal	92
Anglican	*70*	Jewish	18
Other Christian	*148*	Sikhs	17
Muslim	966		
Sunni	*841*		
Shia	*125*		

▲ Roman Catholicism

Orthodox and other Eastern Churches

• Protestantism

Sunni Islam

Shia Islam

Buddhism

Hinduism

Confucianism

Judaism

Shintoism

Tribal Religions

United Nations

Created in 1945 to promote peace and co-operation and based in New York, the United Nations is the world's largest international organization, with 185 members and an annual budget of US $2.6 billion (1996–97). Each member of the General Assembly has one vote, while the permanent members of the 15-nation Security Council – USA, Russia, China, UK and France – hold a veto. The Secretariat is the UN's principal administrative arm. The 54 members of the Economic and Social Council are responsible for economic, social, cultural, educational, health and related matters. The UN has 16 specialized agencies – based in Canada, France, Switzerland and Italy, as well as the USA – which help members in fields such as education (UNESCO), agriculture (FAO), medicine (WHO) and finance (IFC). By the end of 1994, all the original 11 trust territories of the Trusteeship Council had become independent.

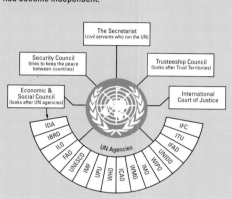

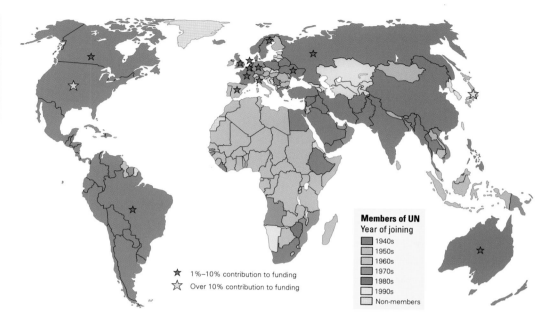

Members of UN
Year of joining
- 1940s
- 1950s
- 1960s
- 1970s
- 1980s
- 1990s
- Non-members

★ 1%–10% contribution to funding
☆ Over 10% contribution to funding

MEMBERSHIP OF THE UN In 1945 there were 51 members; by December 1994 membership had increased to 185 following the admission of Palau. There are 7 independent states which are not members of the UN – Kiribati, Nauru, Switzerland, Taiwan, Tonga, Tuvalu and the Vatican City. All the successor states of the former USSR had joined by the end of 1992. The official languages of the UN are Chinese, English, French, Russian, Spanish and Arabic.

FUNDING The UN budget for 1996–97 was US $2.6 billion. Contributions are assessed by the members' ability to pay, with the maximum 25% of the total, the minimum 0.01%. Contributions for 1996 were: USA 25.0%, Japan 15.4%, Germany 9.0%, France 6.4%, UK 5.3%, Italy 5.2%, Russia 4.5%, Canada 3.1%, Spain 2.4%, Brazil 1.6%, Netherlands 1.6%, Australia 1.5%, Sweden 1.2%, Ukraine 1.1%, Belgium 1.0%.

International Organizations

EU European Union (evolved from the European Community in 1993). The 15 members – Austria, Belgium, Denmark, Finland, France, Germany, Greece, Ireland, Italy, Luxembourg, Netherlands, Portugal, Spain, Sweden and the UK – aim to integrate economies, co-ordinate social developments and bring about political union. These members of what is now the world's biggest market share agricultural and industrial policies and tariffs on trade. The original body, the European Coal and Steel Community (ECSC), was created in 1951 following the signing of the Treaty of Paris.

EFTA European Free Trade Association (formed in 1960). Portugal left the original 'Seven' in 1989 to join what was then the EC, followed by Austria, Finland and Sweden in 1995. Only 4 members remain: Norway, Iceland, Switzerland and Liechtenstein.

ACP African-Caribbean-Pacific (formed in 1963). Members have economic ties with the EU.

NATO North Atlantic Treaty Organization (formed in 1949). It continues after 1991 despite the winding up of the Warsaw Pact. There are 16 member nations.

OAS Organization of American States (formed in 1948). It aims to promote social and economic co-operation between developed countries of North America and developing nations of Latin America.

ASEAN Association of South-east Asian Nations (formed in 1967). Burma and Laos joined in 1997.

OAU Organization of African Unity (formed in 1963). Its 53 members represent over 94% of Africa's population. Arabic, French, Portuguese and English are recognized as working languages.

LAIA Latin American Integration Association (1980). Its aim is to promote freer regional trade.

OECD Organization for Economic Co-operation and Development (formed in 1961). It comprises the 29 major Western free-market economies. Poland, Hungary and South Korea joined in 1996. 'G8' is its 'inner group' comprising Canada, France, Germany, Italy, Japan, Russia, the UK and the USA.

COMMONWEALTH The Commonwealth of Nations evolved from the British Empire; it comprises 16 Queen's realms, 32 republics and 5 indigenous monarchies, giving a total of 53.

OPEC Organization of Petroleum Exporting Countries (formed in 1960). It controls about three-quarters of the world's oil supply. Gabon left the organization in 1996.

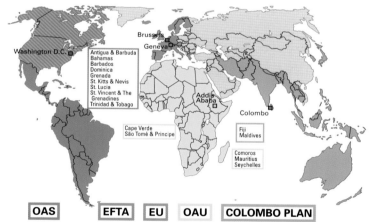

OAS · **EFTA** · **EU** · **OAU** · **COLOMBO PLAN**

ARAB LEAGUE (formed in 1945). The League's aim is to promote economic, social, political and military co-operation. There are 21 member nations.

COLOMBO PLAN (formed in 1951). Its 26 members aim to promote economic and social development in Asia and the Pacific.

★ G8

OECD · **ACP** · **OPEC** · **CIS**

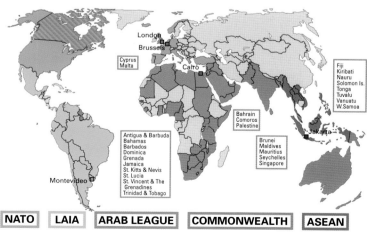

NATO · **LAIA** · **ARAB LEAGUE** · **COMMONWEALTH** · **ASEAN**

Wealth

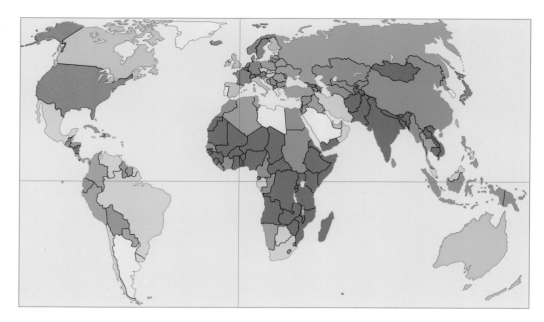

GNP per capita growth rate (%), selected countries, 1985–94

Thailand	8.2	Brazil	−0.4
Chile	6.9	Zimbabwe	−0.6
Japan	3.2	USA	−1.3
Germany	1.9	UK	−1.4
Australia	1.2	Armenia	−12.9

Wealth Creation

The Gross National Product (GNP) of the world's largest economies, US $ million (1995)

1.	USA	7,100,007	23.	Indonesia	190,105
2.	Japan	4,963,587	24.	Turkey	169,452
3.	Germany	2,252,343	25.	Thailand	159,630
4.	France	1,451,051	26.	Denmark	156,027
5.	UK	1,094,734	27.	Hong Kong	142,332
6.	Italy	1,088,085	28.	Norway	136,077
7.	China	744,890	29.	Saudi Arabia	133,540
8.	Brazil	579,787	30.	South Africa	130,918
9.	Canada	573,695	31.	Poland	107,829
10.	Spain	532,347	32.	Finland	105,174
11.	South Korea	435,137	33.	Portugal	96,689
12.	Netherlands	371,039	34.	Israel	87,875
13.	Australia	337,909	35.	Greece	85,885
14.	Russia	331,948	36.	Ukraine	84,084
15.	India	319,660	37.	Singapore	79,831
16.	Mexico	304,596	38.	Malaysia	78,321
17.	Switzerland	286,014	39.	Philippines	71,865
18.	Argentina	278,431	40.	Colombia	70,263
19.	Taiwan	256,300	41.	Venezuela	65,382
20.	Belgium	250,710	42.	Pakistan	59,991
21.	Austria	216,547	43.	Chile	59,151
22.	Sweden	209,720	44.	Peru	55,019

The Wealth Gap

The world's richest and poorest countries, by Gross National Product per capita in US $ (1995)

1.	Luxembourg	41,210	1.	Mozambique	80
2.	Switzerland	40,630	2.	Ethiopia	100
3.	Japan	39,640	3.	Congo (Zaïre)	120
4.	Liechtenstein	38,520	4.	Tanzania	120
5.	Norway	31,250	5.	Burundi	160
6.	Denmark	29,890	6.	Malawi	170
7.	Germany	27,510	7.	Sierra Leone	180
8.	USA	26,980	8.	Rwanda	180
9.	Austria	26,890	9.	Chad	180
10.	Singapore	26,730	10.	Nepal	200
11.	France	24,990	11.	Niger	220
12.	Iceland	24,950	12.	Madagascar	230
13.	Belgium	24,710	13.	Burkina Faso	230
14.	Sweden	23,750	14.	Vietnam	240
15.	Hong Kong	22,990	15.	Uganda	240
16.	Finland	20,580	16.	Bangladesh	240
17.	Canada	19,380	17.	Haiti	250
18.	Italy	19,020	18.	Guinea-Bissau	250
19.	Australia	18,720	19.	Yemen	250
20.	UK	18,700	20.	Nigeria	260

GNP per capita is calculated by dividing a country's Gross National Product by its total population.

Continental Shares

Shares of population and of wealth (GNP) by continent

Population

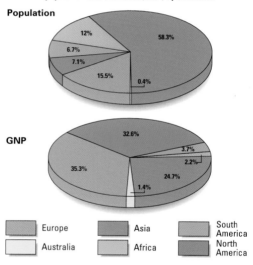

GNP

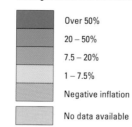

Europe	Asia	South America
Australia	Africa	North America

Inflation

Average annual rate of inflation (1980–93)

Over 50%

20 – 50%

7.5 – 20%

1 – 7.5%

Negative inflation

No data available

Highest average inflation		Lowest average inflation	
Nicaragua	665%	Brunei	−5.1%
Brazil	423%	Oman	−2.3%
Argentina	374%	Saudi Arabia	−2.1%
Peru	316%	Equatorial Guinea	−0.6%
Bolivia	187%	Congo	−0.6%
Israel	70%	Bahrain	−0.3%
Poland	69%	Libya	0.2%

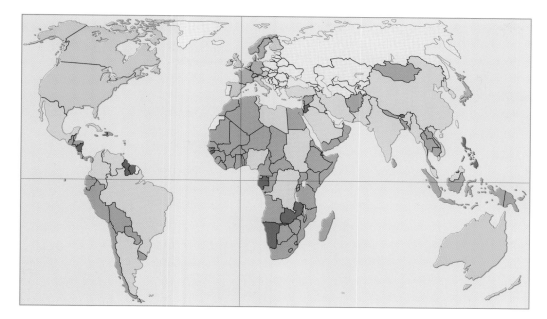

International Aid

Aid provided or received, divided by the total population, in US $ (1995)

Over $100 per person
$10 – $100 per person
$0 – $10 per person
No aid given or received
$0 – $10 per person
$10 – $100 per person
Over $100 per person

Providers

Receivers

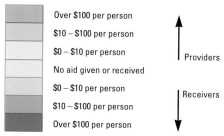

Top 5 providers per capita (1994)		Top 5 receivers per capita (1994)	
France	$279	São Tomé & P.	$378
Denmark	$260	Cape Verde	$314
Norway	$247	Djibouti	$235
Sweden	$201	Surinam	$198
Germany	$166	Mauritania	$153

Debt and Aid

International debtors and the aid they receive (1993)

Although aid grants make a vital contribution to many of the world's poorer countries, they are usually dwarfed by the burden of debt that the developing economies are expected to repay. In 1992, they had to pay US $160,000 million in debt service charges alone – more than two and a half times the amount of Official Development Assistance (ODA) the developing countries were receiving, and US $60,000 million more than total private flows of aid in the same year. In 1990, the debts of Mozambique, one of the world's poorest countries, were estimated to be 75 times its entire earnings from exports.

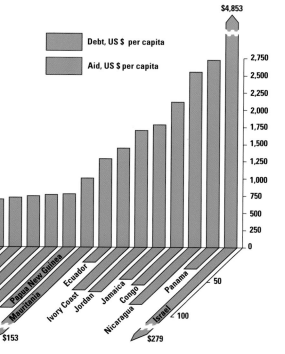

Debt, US $ per capita

Aid, US $ per capita

Distribution of Spending

Percentage share of household spending, selected countries

Food
Medicine & Education
Clothing
Transport
Energy & Housing
Other

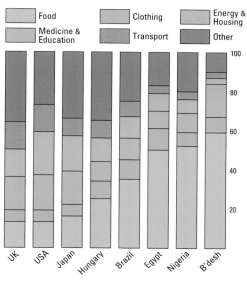

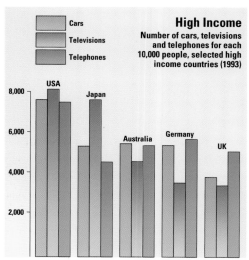

High Income

Cars
Televisions
Telephones

Number of cars, televisions and telephones for each 10,000 people, selected high income countries (1993)

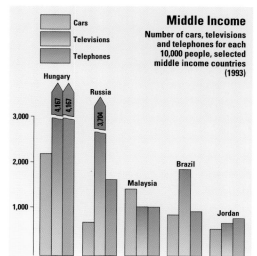

Middle Income

Cars
Televisions
Telephones

Number of cars, televisions and telephones for each 10,000 people, selected middle income countries (1993)

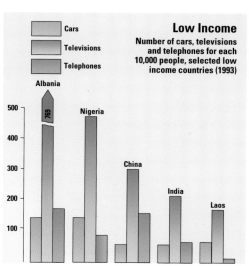

Low Income

Cars
Televisions
Telephones

Number of cars, televisions and telephones for each 10,000 people, selected low income countries (1993)

Quality of Life

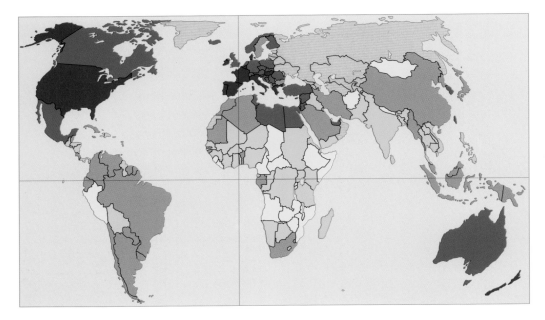

CARTOGRAPHY BY PHILIP'S. COPYRIGHT GEORGE PHILIP LTD

Daily Food Consumption

Average daily food intake in calories per person (latest available year)

Over 3,500 calories per person

3,000 – 3,500 calories per person

2,500 – 3,000 calories per person

2,000 – 2,500 calories per person

Under 2,000 calories per person

No available data

Top 5 countries		**Bottom 5 countries**	
Ireland	3,847 cal.	Mozambique	1,680 cal.
Greece	3,815 cal.	Liberia	1,640 cal.
Cyprus	3,779 cal.	Ethiopia	1,610 cal.
USA	3,732 cal.	Afghanistan	1,523 cal.
Spain	3,708 cal.	Somalia	1,499 cal.

[UK 3,317 calories]

Hospital Capacity

Hospital beds available for each 1,000 people (1993)

Highest capacity		**Lowest capacity**	
Japan	13.6	Bangladesh	0.2
Kazakstan	13.5	Ethiopia	0.2
Ukraine	13.5	Nepal	0.3
Russia	13.5	Burkina Faso	0.4
Latvia	13.5	Afghanistan	0.5
North Korea	13.5	Pakistan	0.6
Moldova	12.8	Niger	0.6
Belarus	12.7	Mali	0.6
Finland	12.3	Indonesia	0.6
France	12.2	Guinea	0.6

[UK 6.4] [USA 4.6]

Although the ratio of people to hospital beds gives a good approximation of a country's health provision, it is not an absolute indicator. Raw numbers may mask inefficiency and other weaknesses: the high availability of beds in Kazakstan, for example, has not prevented infant mortality rates over three times as high as in the United Kingdom and the United States.

Life Expectancy

Years of life expectancy at birth, selected countries (1990–95)

The chart shows combined data for both sexes. On average, women live longer than men worldwide, even in developing countries with high maternal mortality rates. Overall, life expectancy is steadily rising, though the difference between rich and poor nations remains dramatic.

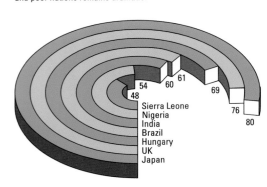

54 Sierra Leone
48 Nigeria
60 India
61 Brazil
69 Hungary
76 UK
80 Japan

Causes of Death

Causes of death for selected countries by % (1992–94)

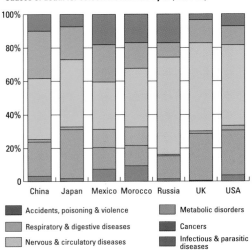

Accidents, poisoning & violence

Respiratory & digestive diseases

Nervous & circulatory diseases

Metabolic disorders

Cancers

Infectious & parasitic diseases

Child Mortality

Number of babies who will die under the age of one, per 1,000 births (average 1990–95)

Over 150 deaths per 1,000 births

100 – 150 deaths per 1,000 births

50 – 100 deaths per 1,000 births

20 – 50 deaths per 1,000 births

10 – 20 deaths per 1,000 births

Under 10 deaths per 1,000 births

Highest child mortality		**Lowest child mortality**	
Afghanistan	162	Hong Kong	6
Mali	159	Denmark	6
Sierra Leone	143	Japan	5
Guinea-Bissau	140	Iceland	5
Malawi	138	Finland	5

[UK 8 deaths]

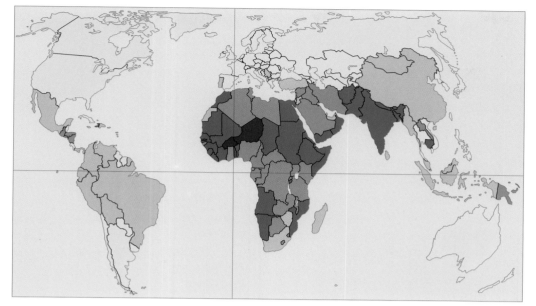

Illiteracy

Percentage of the total population unable to read or write (latest available year)

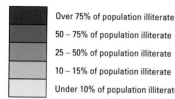

- Over 75% of population illiterate
- 50 – 75% of population illiterate
- 25 – 50% of population illiterate
- 10 – 15% of population illiterate
- Under 10% of population illiterate

Educational expenditure per person (latest available year)

Top 5 countries		Bottom 5 countries	
Sweden	$997	Chad	$2
Qatar	$989	Bangladesh	$3
Canada	$983	Ethiopia	$3
Norway	$971	Nepal	$4
Switzerland	$796	Somalia	$4

Fertility and Education

Fertility rates compared with female education, selected countries (1992–95)

- Percentage of females aged 12–17 in secondary education
- Fertility rate: average number of children borne per woman

Countries (left to right): Denmark, Austria, France, Canada, Belgium, Switzerland, UK, Poland, Australia, Sri Lanka, Malaysia, Turkey, Saudi Arabia, Thailand, Bolivia, Nigeria, Sierra Leone, Niger

Left axis: 0%, 20%, 40%, 60%, 80%, 100%
Right axis: 0, 1, 2, 3, 4, 5, 6, 7

Living Standards

At first sight, most international contrasts in living standards are swamped by differences in wealth. The rich not only have more money, they have more of everything, including years of life. Those with only a little money are obliged to spend most of it on food and clothing, the basic maintenance costs of their existence; air travel and tourism are unlikely to feature on their expenditure lists. However, poverty and wealth are both relative: slum dwellers living on social security payments in an affluent industrial country have far more resources at their disposal than an average African peasant, but feel their own poverty nonetheless. A middle-class Indian lawyer cannot command a fraction of the earnings of a counterpart living in New York, London or Rome; nevertheless, he rightly sees himself as prosperous.

The rich not only live longer, on average, than the poor, they also die from different causes. Infectious and parasitic diseases, all but eliminated in the developed world, remain a scourge in the developing nations. On the other hand, more than two-thirds of the populations of OECD nations eventually succumb to cancer or circulatory disease.

Women in the Workforce

Women in paid employment as a percentage of the total workforce (latest available year)

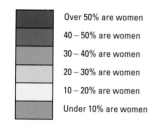

- Over 50% are women
- 40 – 50% are women
- 30 – 40% are women
- 20 – 30% are women
- 10 – 20% are women
- Under 10% are women

Most women in the workforce		Fewest women in the workforce	
Cambodia	56%	Saudi Arabia	4%
Kazakstan	54%	Oman	6%
Burundi	53%	Afghanistan	8%
Mozambique	53%	Algeria	9%
Turkmenistan	52%	Libya	9%

[USA 45] [UK 44]

CARTOGRAPHY BY PHILIP'S. COPYRIGHT GEORGE PHILIP LTD

Energy

Production

[Each square represents 1% of world energy production]

North America

Europe

CIS

Middle East

Africa

Asia

Japan

South America

Australasia

Consumption

[Each square represents 1% of world energy consumption]

North America

Europe

CIS

Middle East

Africa

Asia

Japan

South America

Australasia

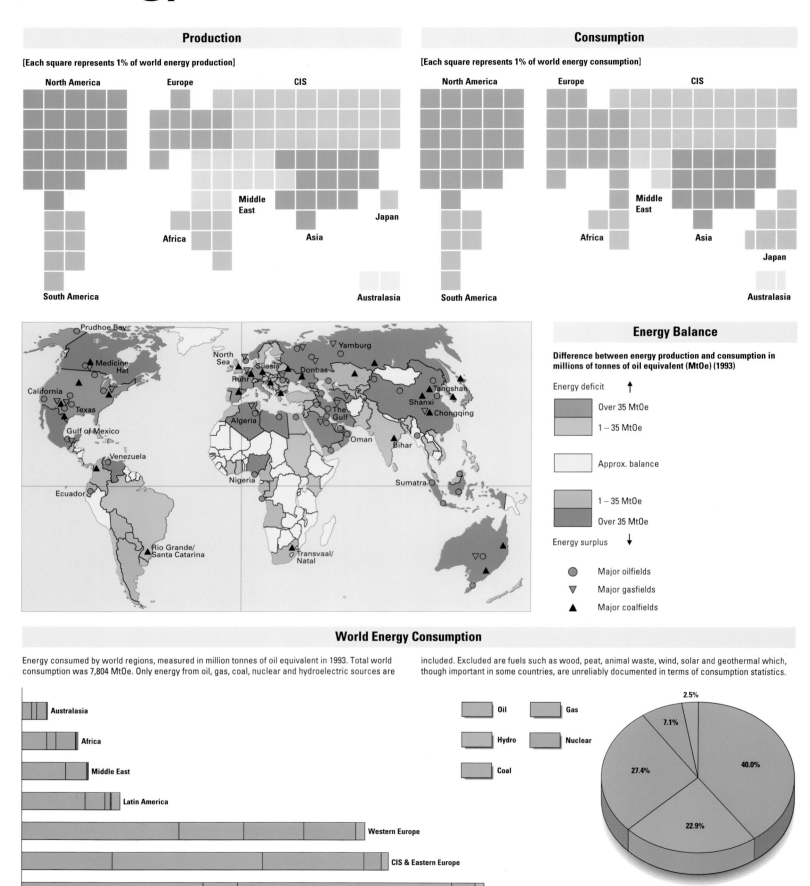

Prudhoe Bay
Medicine Hat
California
Texas
Gulf of Mexico
Venezuela
Ecuador
Rio Grande/Santa Catarina

North Sea
Ruhr
Silesia
Donbas
Algeria
Nigeria
The Gulf
Oman

Yamburg
Tangshan
Shanxi
Chongqing
Bihar
Sumatra

Transvaal/Natal

Energy Balance

Difference between energy production and consumption in millions of tonnes of oil equivalent (MtOe) (1993)

Energy deficit ↑

Over 35 MtOe

1 – 35 MtOe

Approx. balance

1 – 35 MtOe

Over 35 MtOe

Energy surplus ↓

○ Major oilfields

▽ Major gasfields

▲ Major coalfields

World Energy Consumption

Energy consumed by world regions, measured in million tonnes of oil equivalent in 1993. Total world consumption was 7,804 MtOe. Only energy from oil, gas, coal, nuclear and hydroelectric sources are included. Excluded are fuels such as wood, peat, animal waste, wind, solar and geothermal which, though important in some countries, are unreliably documented in terms of consumption statistics.

Australasia

Africa

Middle East

Latin America

Western Europe

CIS & Eastern Europe

Asia

North America

5   10   15   20   25

Oil   Gas   Hydro   Nuclear   Coal

2.5%
7.1%
27.4%
40.0%
22.9%

Energy

Energy is used to keep us warm or cool, fuel our industries and our transport systems, and even feed us; high-intensity agriculture, with its use of fertilizers, pesticides and machinery, is heavily energy-dependent. Although we live in a high-energy society, there are vast discrepancies between rich and poor; for example, a North American consumes 13 times as much energy as a Chinese person. But even developing nations have more power at their disposal than was imaginable a century ago.

The distribution of energy supplies, most importantly fossil fuels (coal, oil and natural gas), is very uneven. In addition, the diagrams and map opposite show that the largest producers of energy are not necessarily the largest consumers. The movement of energy supplies around the world is therefore an important component of international trade. In 1995, total world movements in oil amounted to 1,815 million tonnes.

As the finite reserves of fossil fuels are depleted, renewable energy sources, such as solar, hydro-thermal, wind, tidal and biomass, will become increasingly important around the world.

Nuclear Power

Percentage of electricity generated by nuclear power stations, leading nations (1995)

1. Lithuania	85%	11. Spain	33%
2. France	77%	12. Finland	30%
3. Belgium	56%	13. Germany	29%
4. Slovak Rep.	49%	14. Japan	29%
5. Sweden	48%	15. UK	27%
6. Bulgaria	41%	16. Ukraine	27%
7. Hungary	41%	17. Czech Rep.	22%
8. Switzerland	39%	18. Canada	19%
9. Slovenia	38%	19. USA	18%
10. South Korea	33%	20. Russia	12%

Although the 1980s were a bad time for the nuclear power industry (major projects ran over budget, and fears of long-term environmental damage were heavily reinforced by the 1986 disaster at Chernobyl), the industry picked up in the early 1990s. However, whilst the number of reactors is still increasing, orders for new plants have shrunk. This is partly due to the increasingly difficult task of disposing of nuclear waste.

Hydroelectricity

Percentage of electricity generated by hydroelectric power stations, leading nations (1995)

1. Paraguay	99.9%	11. Rwanda	97.6%
2. Congo (Zaïre)	99.7%	12. Malawi	97.6%
3. Bhutan	99.6%	13. Cameroon	96.9%
4. Zambia	99.5%	14. Nepal	96.7%
5. Norway	99.4%	15. Laos	95.3%
6. Ghana	99.3%	16. Albania	95.2%
7. Congo	99.3%	17. Iceland	94.0%
8. Uganda	99.1%	17. Brazil	92.2%
9. Burundi	98.3%	19. Honduras	87.6%
10. Uruguay	98.0%	20. Tanzania	87.1%

Countries heavily reliant on hydroelectricity are usually small and non-industrial: a high proportion of hydroelectric power more often reflects a modest energy budget than vast hydroelectric resources. The USA, for instance, produces only 9% of power requirements from hydroelectricity; yet that 9% amounts to more than three times the hydropower generated by all of Africa.

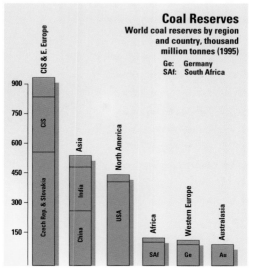

Fuel Exports

Fuels as a percentage of total value of exports (1990–94)

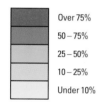

- Over 75%
- 50 – 75%
- 25 – 50%
- 10 – 25%
- Under 10%

Conversion Rates

1 barrel = 0.136 tonnes or 159 litres or 35 Imperial gallons or 42 US gallons

1 tonne = 7.33 barrels or 1,185 litres or 256 Imperial gallons or 261 US gallons

1 tonne oil = 1.5 tonnes hard coal or 3.0 tonnes lignite or 12,000 kWh

1 Imperial gallon = 1.201 US gallons or 4.546 litres or 277.4 cubic inches

Measurements
For historical reasons, oil is traded in 'barrels'. The weight and volume equivalents (shown right) are all based on average-density 'Arabian light' crude oil.

The energy equivalents given for a tonne of oil are also somewhat imprecise: oil and coal of different qualities will have varying energy contents, a fact usually reflected in their price on world markets.

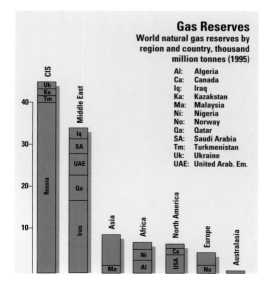

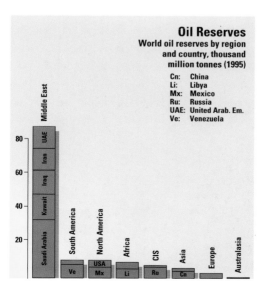

CARTOGRAPHY BY PHILIP'S. COPYRIGHT GEORGE PHILIP LTD

Production

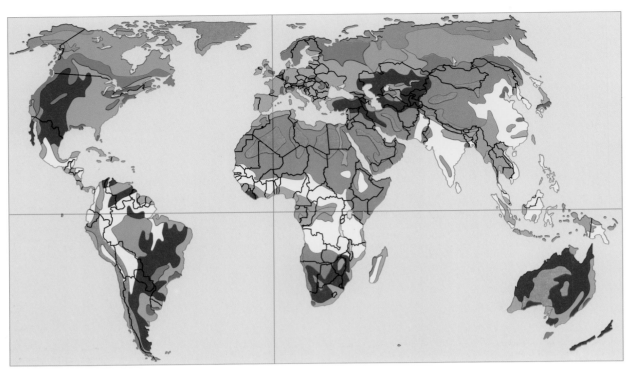

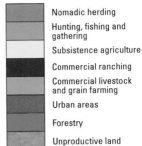

Agriculture

Predominant type of farming or land use.

- Nomadic herding
- Hunting, fishing and gathering
- Subsistence agriculture
- Commercial ranching
- Commercial livestock and grain farming
- Urban areas
- Forestry
- Unproductive land

The development of agriculture transformed human existence more than any other. The whole business of farming is constantly developing: due mainly to new varieties of rice and wheat, world grain production has increased by over 70% since 1965. New machinery and modern agricultural techniques enable relatively few farmers to produce enough food for the world's 5,800 million people.

Staple Crops

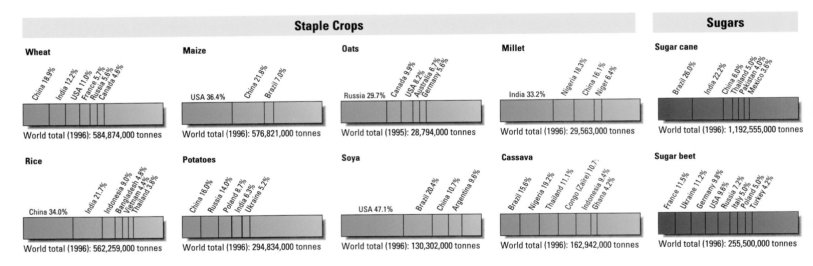

Wheat

China 18.9% | India 12.2% | USA 11.0% | France 5.7% | Russia 5.6% | Canada 4.6%

World total (1996): 584,874,000 tonnes

Maize

USA 36.4% | China 21.6% | Brazil 7.0%

World total (1996): 576,821,000 tonnes

Oats

Russia 29.7% | Canada 9.9% | USA 8.2% | Australia 6.7% | Germany 5.6%

World total (1995): 28,794,000 tonnes

Millet

India 33.2% | Nigeria 18.3% | China 16.1% | Niger 6.4%

World total (1996): 29,563,000 tonnes

Rice

China 34.0% | India 21.7% | Indonesia 9.0% | Bangladesh 4.8% | Vietnam 4.4% | Thailand 3.8%

World total (1996): 562,259,000 tonnes

Potatoes

China 16.0% | Russia 14.0% | Poland 8.7% | India 6.3% | Ukraine 5.2%

World total (1996): 294,834,000 tonnes

Soya

USA 47.1% | Brazil 20.4% | China 10.7% | Argentina 9.6%

World total (1996): 130,302,000 tonnes

Cassava

Brazil 15.6% | Nigeria 19.2% | Thailand 11.1% | Congo (Zaire) 10.7% | Indonesia 9.4% | Ghana 4.2%

World total (1996): 162,942,000 tonnes

Sugars

Sugar cane

Brazil 26.0% | India 22.2% | China 6.0% | Thailand 5.0% | Pakistan 4.0% | Mexico 3.6%

World total (1996): 1,192,555,000 tonnes

Sugar beet

France 11.5% | Ukraine 11.2% | Germany 9.8% | USA 9.6% | Russia 7.2% | Italy 5.0% | Poland 5.0% | Turkey 4.2%

World total (1996): 255,500,000 tonnes

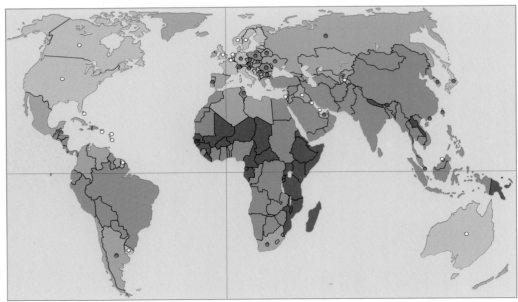

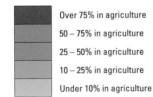

Balance of Employment

Percentage of total workforce employed in agriculture, including forestry and fishing (1990–92)

- Over 75% in agriculture
- 50 – 75% in agriculture
- 25 – 50% in agriculture
- 10 – 25% in agriculture
- Under 10% in agriculture

Employment in industry and services

- Over a third of total workforce employed in manufacturing
- Over two-thirds of total workforce employed in service industries (work in offices, shops, tourism, transport, construction and government)

Mineral Production

*Figures for aluminium are for refined metal; all other figures refer to ore production.

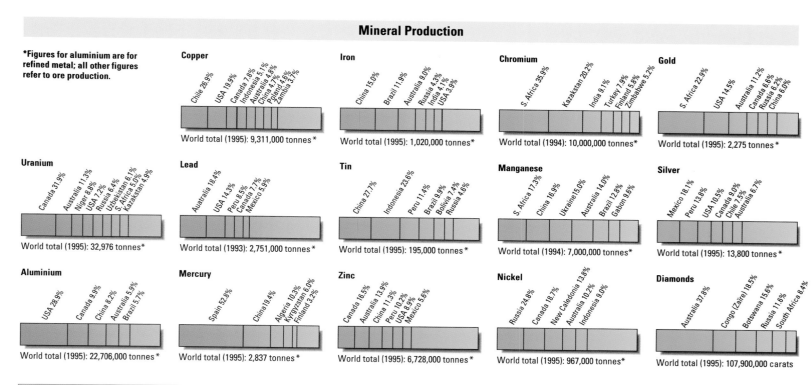

Copper
Chile 26.9% | USA 19.9% | Canada 7.8% | Indonesia 5.1% | Australia 4.8% | China 4.7% | Poland 4.6% | Zambia 3.7%
World total (1995): 9,311,000 tonnes*

Iron
China 15.0% | Brazil 11.9% | Australia 9.0% | Russia 4.3% | India 4.1% | USA 3.9%
World total (1995): 1,020,000 tonnes*

Chromium
S. Africa 35.9% | Kazakstan 20.2% | India 9.1% | Turkey 7.9% | Finland 5.6% | Zimbabwe 5.2%
World total (1994): 10,000,000 tonnes*

Gold
S. Africa 22.9% | USA 14.5% | Australia 11.2% | Canada 6.6% | Russia 6.2% | China 6.0%
World total (1995): 2,275 tonnes*

Uranium
Canada 31.9% | Australia 11.3% | Niger 9.8% | USA 7.2% | Russia 6.4% | Uzbekistan 6.1% | S. Africa 5.0% | Kazakstan 4.9%
World total (1995): 32,976 tonnes*

Lead
Australia 18.4% | USA 14.3% | Peru 8.5% | Canada 7.7% | Mexico 5.9%
World total (1993): 2,751,000 tonnes*

Tin
China 27.7% | Indonesia 23.6% | Peru 11.4% | Brazil 9.9% | Bolivia 7.4% | Russia 4.6%
World total (1995): 195,000 tonnes*

Manganese
S. Africa 17.3% | China 16.9% | Ukraine 15.0% | Australia 14.0% | Brazil 12.8% | Gabon 9.6%
World total (1994): 7,000,000 tonnes*

Silver
Mexico 18.1% | Peru 13.8% | USA 10.5% | Canada 9.0% | Chile 7.5% | Australia 6.7%
World total (1995): 13,800 tonnes*

Aluminium
USA 28.9% | Canada 9.9% | China 8.2% | Australia 5.9% | Brazil 5.7%
World total (1995): 22,706,000 tonnes*

Mercury
Spain 52.8% | China 19.4% | Algeria 10.3% | Kyrgyzstan 6.0% | Finland 3.2%
World total (1995): 2,837 tonnes*

Zinc
Canada 16.5% | Australia 13.9% | China 11.3% | Peru 10.2% | USA 8.9% | Mexico 5.6%
World total (1995): 6,728,000 tonnes*

Nickel
Russia 24.8% | Canada 18.7% | New Caledonia 13.8% | Australia 10.2% | Indonesia 9.0%
World total (1995): 967,000 tonnes*

Diamonds
Australia 37.8% | Congo (Zaire) 18.5% | Botswana 15.6% | Russia 11.6% | South Africa 8.4%
World total (1995): 107,900,000 carats

Mineral Distribution

The map shows the richest sources of the most important minerals. Major mineral locations are named.

Light metals
- ● Bauxite

Base metals
- ■ Copper
- ▲ Lead
- ▽ Mercury
- ▼ Tin
- ◆ Zinc

Iron and ferro-alloys
- ● Iron
- ▽ Chrome
- ▲ Manganese
- ■ Nickel

Precious metals
- ▽ Gold
- ⬨ Silver

Precious stones
- ◆ Diamonds

The map does not show undersea deposits, most of which are considered inaccessible.

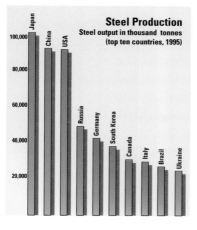

Steel Production
Steel output in thousand tonnes (top ten countries, 1995)

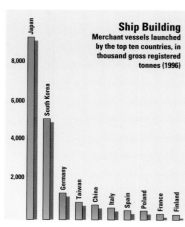

Ship Building
Merchant vessels launched by the top ten countries, in thousand gross registered tonnes (1996)

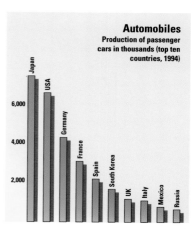

Automobiles
Production of passenger cars in thousands (top ten countries, 1994)

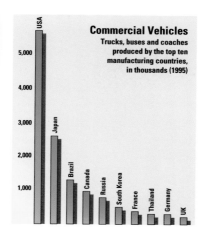

Commercial Vehicles
Trucks, buses and coaches produced by the top ten manufacturing countries, in thousands (1995)

Trade

Share of World Trade

Percentage share of total world exports by value (1995)

- Over 10% of world trade
- 5 – 10% of world trade
- 1 – 5% of world trade
- 0.5 – 1% of world trade
- 0.1 – 0.5% of world trade
- Under 0.1% of world trade

International trade is dominated by a handful of powerful maritime nations. The members of 'G8', the inner circle of OECD (see page 19), and the top seven countries listed in the diagram below, account for more than half the total. The majority of nations – including all but four in Africa – contribute less than one quarter of 1% to the worldwide total of exports; the EU countries account for 40%, the Pacific Rim nations over 35%.

The Main Trading Nations

The imports and exports of the top ten trading nations as a percentage of world trade (1994). Each country's trade in manufactured goods is shown in dark blue.

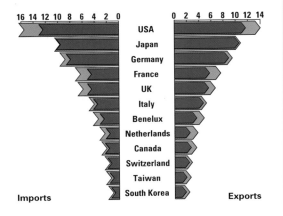

Patterns of Trade

Thriving international trade is the outward sign of a healthy world economy, the obvious indicator that some countries have goods to sell and others the means to buy them. Global exports expanded to an estimated US $3.92 trillion in 1994, an increase due partly to economic recovery in industrial nations but also to export-led growth strategies in many developing nations and lowered regional trade barriers. International trade remains dominated, however, by the rich, industrialized countries of the Organization for Economic Development: between them, OECD members account for almost 75% of world imports and exports in most years. However, continued rapid economic growth in some developing countries is altering global trade patterns. The 'tiger economies' of South-east Asia are particularly vibrant, averaging more than 8% growth between 1992 and 1994. The size of the largest trading economies means that imports and exports usually represent only a small percentage of their total wealth. In export-concious Japan, for example, trade in goods and services amounts to less than 18% of GDP. In poorer countries, trade – often in a single commodity – may amount to 50% of GDP.

Traded Products

Top ten manufactures traded, by value in billions of US $ (latest available year)

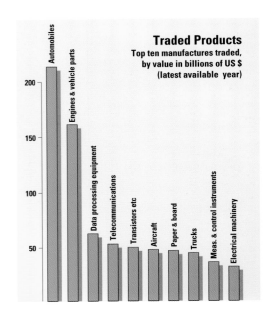

Balance of Trade

Value of exports in proportion to the value of imports (1995)

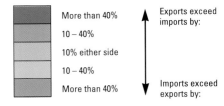

- More than 40% — Exports exceed imports by:
- 10 – 40%
- 10% either side
- 10 – 40%
- More than 40% — Imports exceed exports by:

The total world trade balance should amount to zero, since exports must equal imports on a global scale. In practice, at least $100 billion in exports go unrecorded, leaving the world with an apparent deficit and many countries in a better position than public accounting reveals. However, a favourable trade balance is not necessarily a sign of prosperity: many poorer countries must maintain a high surplus in order to service debts, and do so by restricting imports below the levels needed to sustain successful economies.

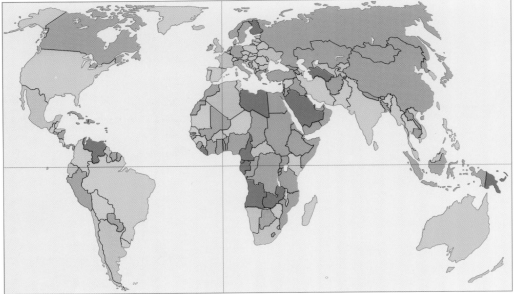

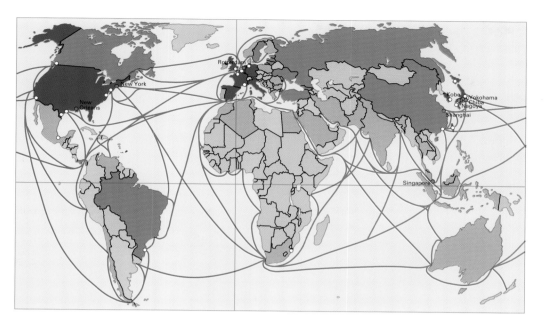

Seaborne Freight

Freight unloaded in millions of tonnes (latest available year)

- Over 100
- 50 – 100
- 10 – 50
- 5 – 10
- Under 5
- Landlocked countries

Major seaports

- ● Over 100 million tonnes per year
- ○ 50–100 million tonnes per year
- — Major shipping routes

Cargoes

Type of seaborne freight

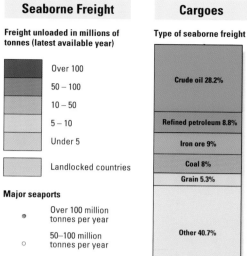

- Crude oil 28.2%
- Refined petroleum 8.8%
- Iron ore 9%
- Coal 8%
- Grain 5.3%
- Other 40.7%

Merchant Fleets

Merchant fleets in thousand gross tonnage (1994). A large number of vessels are registered in Liberia and Panama but they are not part of the national fleet.

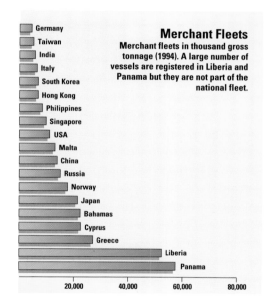

Germany, Taiwan, India, Italy, South Korea, Hong Kong, Philippines, Singapore, USA, Malta, China, Russia, Norway, Japan, Bahamas, Cyprus, Greece, Liberia, Panama

20,000 40,000 60,000 80,000

The Great Ports

Total Cargo Traffic (1995) '000 tonnes

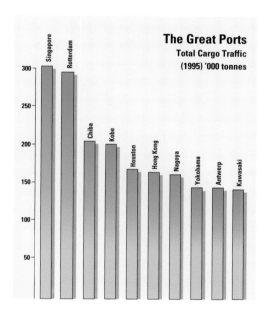

Singapore, Rotterdam, Chiba, Kobe, Houston, Hong Kong, Nagoya, Yokohama, Antwerp, Kawasaki

World Shipping

World merchant fleet by type of vessel and deadweight tonnage (latest available year)

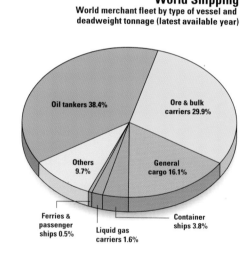

- Oil tankers 38.4%
- Ore & bulk carriers 29.9%
- Others 9.7%
- General cargo 16.1%
- Ferries & passenger ships 0.5%
- Liquid gas carriers 1.6%
- Container ships 3.8%

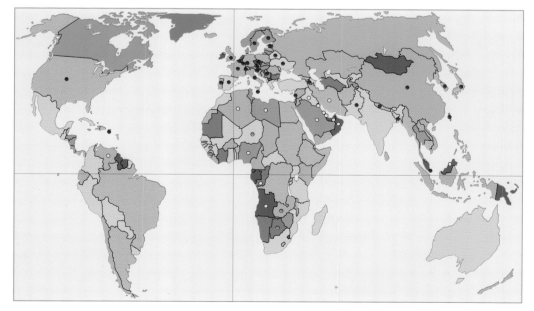

Dependence on Trade

Value of exports as a percentage of Gross National Product (1995)

- Over 50% GNP from exports
- 40 – 50% GNP from exports
- 30 – 40% GNP from exports
- 20 – 30% GNP from exports
- 10 – 20% GNP from exports
- Under 10% GNP from exports

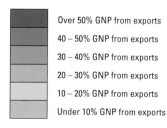

- ● Most dependent on industrial exports (over 75% of total exports)
- ○ Most dependent on fuel exports (over 75% of total exports)
- ◐ Most dependent on mineral and metal exports (over 75% of total exports)

Travel and Tourism

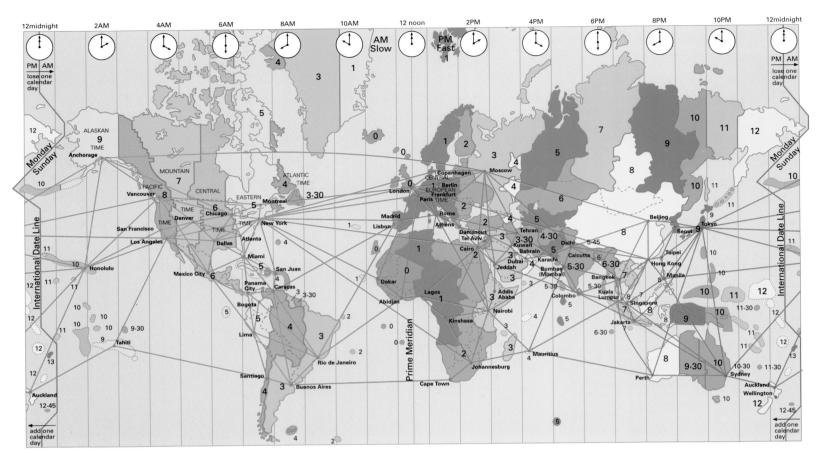

CARTOGRAPHY BY PHILIP'S. COPYRIGHT GEORGE PHILIP LTD

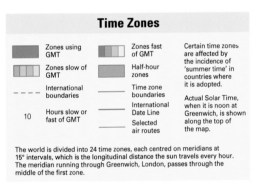

Time Zones

- Zones using GMT
- Zones slow of GMT
- International boundaries
- 10 Hours slow or fast of GMT
- Zones fast of GMT
- Half-hour zones
- Time zone boundaries
- International Date Line
- Selected air routes

Certain time zones are affected by the incidence of 'summer time' in countries where it is adopted.

Actual Solar Time, when it is noon at Greenwich, is shown along the top of the map.

The world is divided into 24 time zones, each centred on meridians at 15° intervals, which is the longitudinal distance the sun travels every hour. The meridian running through Greenwich, London, passes through the middle of the first zone.

Rail and Road: The Leading Nations

Total rail network ('000 km) (1995)	Passenger km per head per year	Total road network ('000 km)	Vehicle km per head per year	Number of vehicles per km of roads
1. USA 235.7	Japan 2,017	USA 6,277.9	USA 12,505	Hong Kong 284
2. Russia 87.4	Belarus 1,880	India 2,962.5	Luxembourg 7,989	Taiwan 211
3. India 62.7	Russia 1,826	Brazil 1,824.4	Kuwait 7,251	Singapore 152
4. China 54.6	Switzerland 1,769	Japan 1,130.9	France 7,142	Kuwait 140
5. Germany 41.7	Ukraine 1,456	China 1,041.1	Sweden 6,991	Brunei..................96
6. Australia 35.8	Austria 1,168	Russia 884.0	Germany 6,806	Italy......................91
7. Argentina 34.2	France 1,011	Canada 849.4	Denmark 6,764	Israel 87
8. France 31.9	Netherlands 994	France 811.6	Austria 6,518	Thailand 73
9. Mexico 26.5	Latvia 918	Australia 810.3	Netherlands 5,984	Ukraine 73
10. South Africa...26.3	Denmark 884	Germany 636.3	UK 5,738	UK 67
11. Poland..........24.9	Slovak Rep. 862	Romania............461.9	Canada 5,493	Netherlands 66
12. Ukraine 22.6	Romania 851	Turkey 388.1	Italy.................4,852	Germany 62

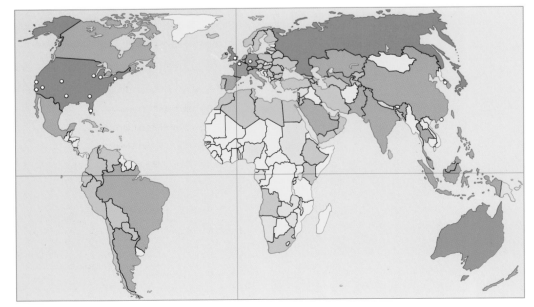

Air Travel

Passenger kilometres (the number of passengers – international and domestic – multiplied by the distance flown by each passenger from the airport of origin) (1994)

- Over 100,000 million
- 50,000 – 100,000 million
- 10,000 – 50,000 million
- 1,000 – 10,000 million
- 500 – 1,000 million
- Under 500 million

○ Major airports (handling over 25 million passengers in 1995)

World's busiest airports (total passengers)	World's busiest airports (international passengers)
1. Chicago (O'Hare)	1. London (Heathrow)
2. Atlanta (Hatsfield)	2. London (Gatwick)
3. Dallas (Dallas/Ft Worth)	3. Frankfurt (International)
4. Los Angeles (Intern'l)	4. New York (Kennedy)
5. London (Heathrow)	5. Paris (De Gaulle)

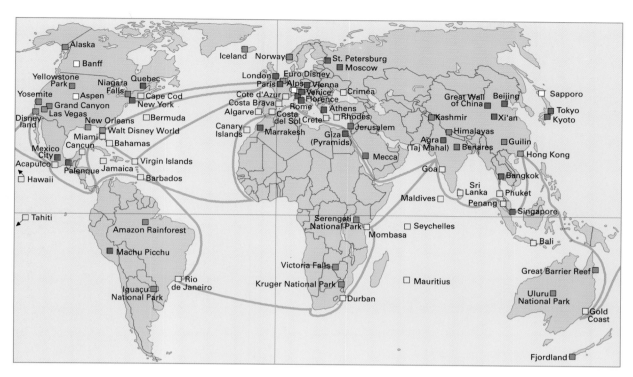

Destinations

- ■ Cultural and historical centres
- □ Coastal resorts
- □ Ski resorts
- ■ Centres of entertainment
- ■ Places of pilgrimage
- ■ Places of great natural beauty
- — Popular holiday cruise routes

Visitors to the USA

Overseas travellers to the USA, thousands (1997 projections)

1. Canada 13,900
2. Mexico 12,370
3. Japan 4,640
4. UK 3,350
5. Germany 1,990
6. France 1,030
7. Taiwan 885
8. Venezuela 860
9. South Korea 800
10. Brazil 785

In 1996, the USA earned the most from tourism, with receipts of more than US $64 billion.

Tourist Spending

Countries spending the most on overseas tourism, US $ million (latest available year)

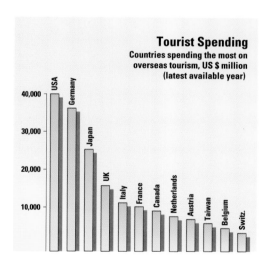

Importance of Tourism

	Arrivals from abroad (1995)	% of world total (1995)
1. France	60,584,000	10.68%
2. Spain	45,125,000	7.96%
3. USA	44,730,000	7.89%
4. Italy	29,184,000	5.15%
5. China	23,368,000	4.12%
6. UK	22,700,000	4.00%
7. Hungary	22,087,000	3.90%
8. Mexico	19,870,000	3.50%
9. Poland	19,225,000	3.39%
10. Austria	17,750,000	3.13%
11. Canada	16,854,000	2.97%
12. Czech Republic	16,600,000	2.93%

The latest figures reveal a 4.6% rise in the total number of people travelling abroad in 1996, to 593 million. Small economies in attractive areas are often completely dominated by tourism: in some West Indian islands, for example, tourist spending provides over 90% of total income.

Tourist Earning

Countries receiving the most from overseas tourism, US $ million (latest available year)

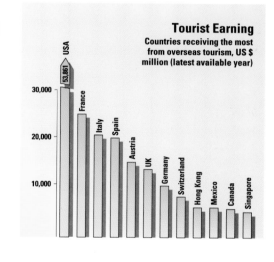

Tourism

Tourism receipts as a percentage of Gross National Product (1994)

- Over 10% of GNP from tourism
- 5 – 10% of GNP from tourism
- 2.5 – 5% of GNP from tourism
- 1 – 2.5% of GNP from tourism
- 0.5 – 1% of GNP from tourism
- Under 0.5% of GNP from tourism

Countries spending the most on promoting tourism, millions of US $ (1996)

Australia 88
Spain 79
UK 79
France 73
Singapore 54

Fastest growing tourist destinations, % change in receipts (1994–5)

South Korea 49%
Czech Republic 27%
India 21%
Russia 19%
Philippines 18%

WORLD MAPS

MAP SYMBOLS

SETTLEMENTS

⌂ PARIS   ■ Berne   ◉ Livorno   ⊙ Brugge   ◎ Algeciras   ○ Fréjus   ○ Oberammergau   ○ Thira

Settlement symbols and type styles vary according to the scale of each map and indicate the importance of towns on the map rather than specific population figures

∴   Ruins or Archæological Sites   ⌣   Wells in Desert

ADMINISTRATION

Boundaries

———   International

— — —   International (Undefined or Disputed)

············   Internal

National Parks

International boundaries show the *de facto* situation where there are rival claims to territory.

Country Names
NICARAGUA

Administrative Areas
KENT
CALABRIA

COMMUNICATIONS

Roads

———   Primary

———   Secondary

-·-·-·   Trails and Seasonal

Railways

———   Primary

———   Secondary

-·-·-·   Under Construction

⌖   Airfields

≍   Passes

ϵ---ϵ   Railway Tunnels

············   Principal Canals

PHYSICAL FEATURES

〜   Perennial Streams

·-·-·   Intermittent Streams

▬   Perennial Lakes

Intermittent Lakes

Swamps and Marshes

Permanent Ice and Glaciers

▲ 2259   Elevations (m)

▼ 2604   Sea Depths (m)

408   Elevation of Lake Surface Above Sea Level (m)

EUROPE

EUROPE

Second smallest of the continents, Europe is topographically subdivided by shallow shelf seas into a mainland block with a sprawl of surrounding peninsulas and off-lying islands. Its western, northern and southern limits are defined by coastlines and conventions. Of the off-lying islands, Iceland, Svalbard, the Faroes, Britain and Ireland are included. So are all the larger islands of the Mediterranean Sea, though more on the grounds of their conquest and habitation by Europeans than by their geographical proximity.

The eastern boundary, between Europe and Asia, is hard to define, and conventions differ. Geographers usually set it along the eastern flank of the Ural Mountains, the Emba River, the north shore of the Caspian Sea, the Kuma and Marich rivers (north of the Caucasus), and the eastern shores of the Azov and Black Seas, and include Turkey west of the Bosphorus. Europe extends from well north of the Arctic Circle almost to latitude 34°N, and includes a wide range of topographies and climates – from polders below sea level to high alpine peaks, from semi-deserts to polar ice caps.

Its geological structure, and some of the forces that have shaped it, show up clearly on a physical map. In the far north lies a shield of ancient granites and gneisses occupying northern Scandinavia, Finland and Karelia. This underlies and gives shape to

the rugged lowlands of this area. The highlands formed later: north and east of the platform lay a marine trough, which was raised, compressed and folded by lateral pressure about 400 million years ago to form the highlands – now well eroded but still impressive – of Norway and north-west Britain.

To the south lay another deep-sea trough, from which a vast accumulation of sediments was raised about 300 million years ago, producing the belt of highlands and well-worn uplands that stretches across Europe from Spain to southern Poland. They include the Cantabrian and central mountains of Iberia, the French Massif Central and uplands of Brittany, the Vosges, Ardennes and Westerwald, the Black Forest, the hills of Cornwall, South Wales and south-west Ireland. A third trough, the Tethys Sea, formed still further south and extended in a wide swathe across Europe and Asia. Strong pressure from a northwards-drifting Africa slowly closed the sea to form the Mediterranean, and raised the 'alpine' mountains that fringe it – the Atlas of North Africa, the Sierra Nevada of Spain, the Pyrenees, the Alps themselves, the Apennines, the Carpathians, the Dinaric Alps and the various ranges of the Balkan Peninsula.

More recently still, however, came the Ice Age. The first ice sheets formed across Eurasia and North America from 2 to 3 million years ago; during

the last million years there have been four major glacial periods in the Alps and three, maybe more, in Scandinavia. The lowland ice melted 8–10,000 years ago, and the Scandinavian and Alpine glaciers retreated, only Iceland and Svalbard keeping ice caps. The accompanying rise in sea level finally isolated Britain.

Physically, Central Europe is divided into three clear structural belts. In the south, the Alpine fold mountains are at their highest and most complex in Switzerland and Austria, but divide eastwards into the Carpathians and the Dinaric Alps of the former Yugoslavia, enclosing the basin in which Hungary lies. A second belt, the central uplands, consisting of block mountains, intervening lowlands and some of Europe's greatest coalfields, stretches from the Ardennes across Germany and the Czech and Slovak Republics to thin out and disappear in Poland. The third belt, the northern lowland, broadens eastwards, and owes its relief largely to glacial deposits.

Two great rivers dominate the drainage pattern: the 1,320 km [820 mls] Rhine rises in the Alps and crosses the central uplands and northern lowland to reach the North Sea. The east-flowing 2,850 km [1,770 mls] Danube cuts right across the fold mountains at Bratislava and again at the Iron Gates (Portile de Fier) on its way to the Black Sea.

The Iberian Peninsula (586,000 sq km [226,000

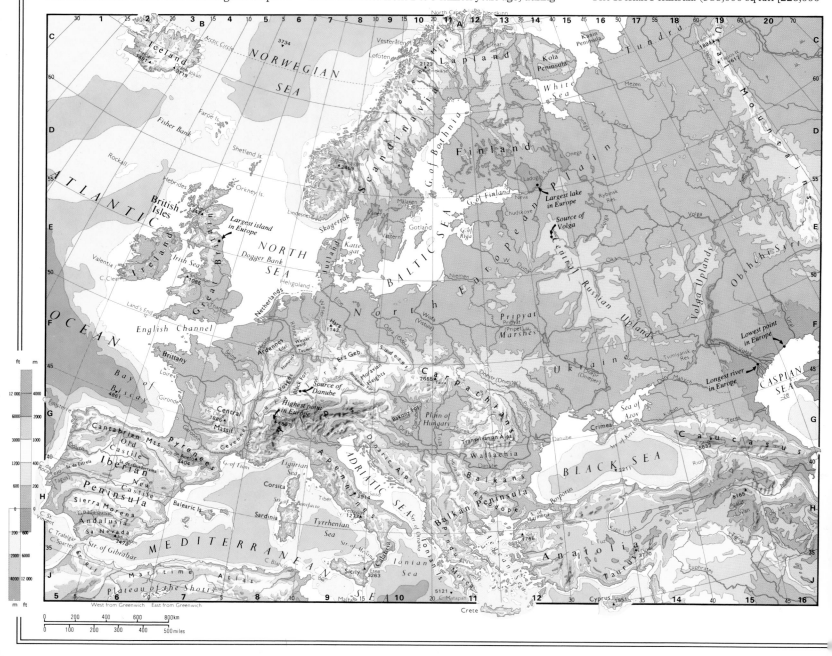

sq mls]) is the largest of the three peninsulas jutting southwards from Europe into the Mediterranean Sea. Stretching through 10° of latitude, it reaches to within 15 km [9.5 mls] of the African coast and extends far enough westwards to merit the title of 'the outpost of Europe'. This position is reflected in the fact that early circumnavigations of Africa and the voyages of Columbus to the New World were launched from Iberian shores.

The core of the peninsula is the Meseta plateau, a remnant of an ancient mountain chain with an average height of 600–1,000 m [1,900–3,280 ft]. Huge faulted mountain ranges, such as the Sierras de Gata, de Gredos and de Guadarrama, traverse the plateau obliquely and terminate westwards in Portugal as rocky headlands jutting into the Atlantic Ocean. Between these upthrust ranges are the wide downwarped basins of Old and New Castile. The plateau is tilted towards the west and its high eastern edge forms a major watershed that overlooks narrow, discontinuous coastal lowlands on the Mediterranean side. The main drainage is through Portugal towards the Atlantic. On its northeastern and southern flanks the Meseta plateau drops abruptly to the Ebro and Guadalquivir (Andalusian) fault troughs; these rise on their outer sides to the lofty mountains of the Pyrenees and the Sierra Nevada, respectively.

The Italian and Balkan peninsulas extend southwards into the Mediterranean Sea. In the north of Italy lies the Plain of Lombardy, drained by the River Po and its tributaries; towering above are the ranges of alpine fold mountains – southern outliers of the European Alps – that mark the boundary between Italy and neighbouring France, Switzerland and Austria. A further range of alpine mountains – the Apennines – runs through peninsular Italy and continues into Sicily.

The western Balkans are made up of alpine fold mountains, running north-west to south-east behind the western coasts – the Dinaric Alps of the former Yugoslavia and the Pindus Mountains (Pindos Oros) of Greece. The Balkan Mountains of Bulgaria represent the southern extension of the great arc of alpine mountains which loop around the lower basin of the Danube. Between them and the Dinaric Alps is the Rhodopi Massif.

Eastern Europe is a relatively huge area, stretching from the Arctic Ocean to the Caspian Sea and the Adriatic to the Urals and including the continent's two largest 'nations' – (European) Russia and the Ukraine. The most common landscape here is undulating plain, comprising coniferous forest as well as massive expanses of arable farmland, but there are impressive mountains too, notably the Carpathians, the Transylvanian Alps and, at the

very eastern corners of Europe, the Caucasus and the Urals.

The tree line in Europe – the boundary marking the northern limit of tree growth – runs north of the Arctic Circle. Only the tundra-covered northern area of Lapland and the Kola Peninsula lie beyond it. Practically all of Europe that lay south of the tree line was originally forested. North of the 60th parallel lay dark, sombre evergreen forests, dominated by spruce and pine. Since the last glacial period the evergreen forests have occupied a swathe 1,200 km [750 mls] wide across central Scandinavia and Finland, broken by marshes, moorlands and lakes, and interspersed with stands of willow and birch. Much of this forest remains today, and is still the haunt of elk, red deer and small populations of wolves, brown bears and lynx.

To the south of the coniferous forest, Europe was covered with deciduous woodland – an ancient forest of oak, ash, birch, beech, and a dozen other familiar species. Favoured by the mild damp climate, this rich forest grew in abundance over the lowlands, foothills and warmer uplands of Europe, limited in the south by dry Mediterranean summers, and in Hungary and the south-west by the aridity of the plains. Virtually the first industrial resource of European man, the forest suffered a thousand years of exploitation and only remnants survive today ■

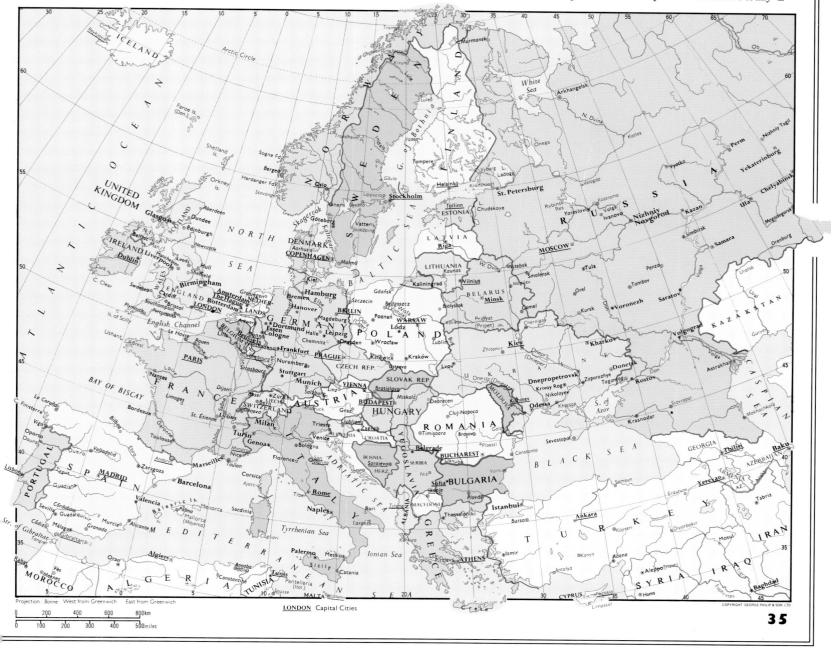

Projection: Bonne   West from Greenwich   East from Greenwich

LONDON Capital Cities

COPYRIGHT GEORGE PHILIP & SON LTD

EUROPE

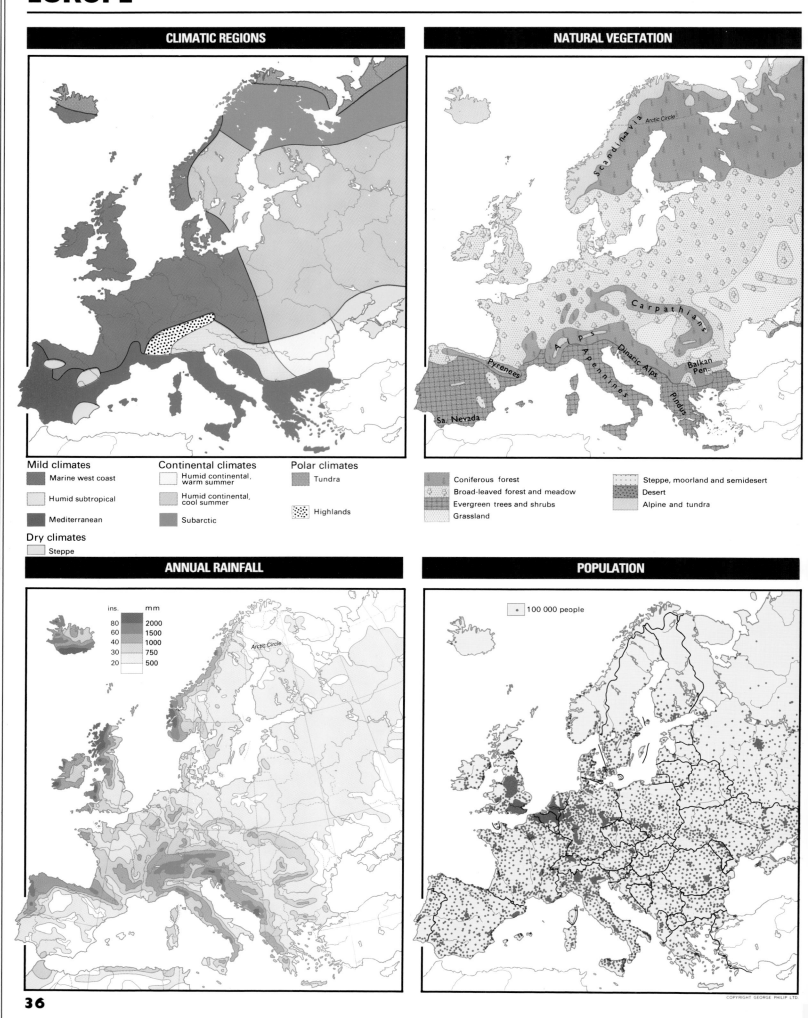

CLIMATIC REGIONS

Mild climates
- Marine west coast
- Humid subtropical
- Mediterranean

Dry climates
- Steppe

Continental climates
- Humid continental, warm summer
- Humid continental, cool summer
- Subarctic

Polar climates
- Tundra
- Highlands

NATURAL VEGETATION

Scandinavia
Arctic Circle
Carpathians
Alps
Apennines
Dinaric Alps
Balkan Pen.
Pyrenees
Pindus
Sa. Nevada

- Coniferous forest
- Broad-leaved forest and meadow
- Evergreen trees and shrubs
- Grassland
- Steppe, moorland and semidesert
- Desert
- Alpine and tundra

ANNUAL RAINFALL

ins.	mm
80	2000
60	1500
40	1000
30	750
20	500

Arctic Circle

POPULATION

- • 100 000 people

LAND USE

Projection: *Bonne*

East from Greenwich

LAND USE

- Arable land
- Arable land with permanent pasture
- Fruit trees, vineyards and market gardens
- Permanent pasture
- Woods and forests
- Rough grazing
- Non-productive land

LIVESTOCK

- Beef cattle
- Dairy cattle
- Sheep

CROPS

- Barley
- Citrus fruits
- Cotton
- Date palms
- Flax
- Maize
- Oats
- Olives
- Potatoes
- Rice
- Rye
- Sugar beet
- Tobacco
- Vines
- Wheat
- Principal fishing areas

MINERALS

- Asbestos
- Bauxite
- Copper
- Gold
- Graphite
- Iron ore
- Lead
- Lead and zinc
- Phosphate
- Salt
- Silver
- Tin
- Uranium
- Zinc
- Sb Antimony
- Cr Chrome
- Mg Magnesium
- Mn Manganese
- Hg Mercury
- Mo Molybdenum
- Ni Nickel
- Ti Titanium

POWER

- Coalfields
- Gasfields
- Oilfields
- Hydroelectric power

LAND USE

Other land 19%

Arable land and permanent crops 30·1%

Woods and forests 32·4%

Permanent pasture 18·5%

Total land area 472.8 million hectares (1 168·3 million acres)

0 100 200 300 400 500 600 km
0 100 200 300 400 miles

EUROPE

ICELAND

Dating from 1915, the flag became official on independence from Denmark in 1944. It uses the traditional Icelandic colours of blue and white and is in fact the same as the Norwegian flag, but with the blue and red colours reversed.

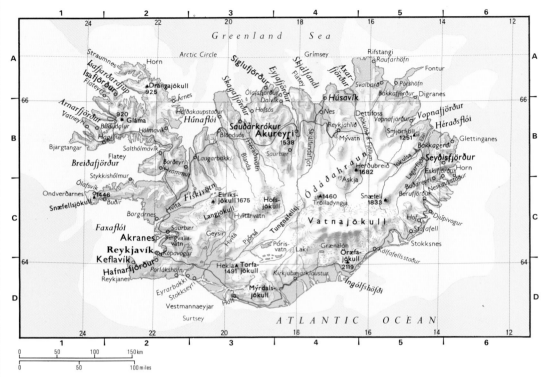

Although the northern tip of Iceland touches the Arctic Circle, thanks to the Gulf Stream the island is relatively warm. The coldest month at Reykjavík, January, is normally 0°C [32°F], the same as Copenhagen; the warmest month is July at 12°C [54°F]. Precipitation falls on 200 days a year, 65 of them as snow. There is very high rainfall on the south coast, exceeding 800 mm [32 in], with half this in the north. Sunshine levels are low, being 5-6 hours from May to August. Gales are frequent most of the year.

COUNTRY Republic of Iceland

AREA 103,000 sq km [39,768 sq mls]

POPULATION 269,000

CAPITAL (POPULATION) Reykjavík (103,000)

GOVERNMENT Multiparty republic with a unicameral parliament

ETHNIC GROUPS Icelandic 94%, Danish 1%

LANGUAGES Icelandic (official)

RELIGIONS Lutheran 95%, Roman Catholic 1%

NATIONAL DAY 17 June

CURRENCY Króna = 100 aurar

ANNUAL INCOME PER PERSON US$23,620

MAIN PRIMARY PRODUCT Fish

MAIN INDUSTRIES Freezing, salting, drying and smoking fish, cement, unwrought aluminium

MAIN EXPORTS Fish products, unwrought aluminium

MAIN IMPORTS Food and live animals, crude materials and petroleum, basic manufactures

DEFENCE Iceland has no defence force

LIFE EXPECTANCY Female 81 yrs, male 75 yrs

Situated far out in the North Atlantic Ocean, Iceland is not only the smallest but also the most isolated of the independent Scandinavian countries. Though politically part of Europe, the island (nearer to Greenland than to Scotland) arises geologically from the boundary between Europe and America – the Mid-Atlantic Ridge.

A central zone of recently active volcanoes and fissures crosses Iceland from Axarfjörður in the north to Vestmannaeyjar in the south, with a side-branch to Reykjanes and an outlying zone of activity around the Snaefellsnes peninsula in the west. During the thousand years that Iceland has been settled, between 150 and 200 eruptions have occurred in the active zones, some building up volcanic cones.

A huge eruption in 1783 destroyed pasture and livestock on a grand scale, causing a famine that reduced the Icelandic population by a quarter. More recent eruptions include the formation of a new island – Surtsey – off the south-west coast in 1963, and the partial devastation of the town of Vestmannaeyjar-Karpstadur, on neighbouring Heimaey, ten years later. Paradoxically, Iceland is also an island of glaciers and ice sheets, with four large ice caps occupying 11% of the surface, and smaller glaciers. A volcanic eruption under the Vatnajökull ice cap in 1996 created a huge subglacial lake, which subsequently burst, causing severe flooding over a wide area.

Colonized by Viking and British farmers in the 9th century, Iceland became a dependency first of Norway, then of Denmark, though mainly self-governing with a parliament (*Althing*) dating from AD 930. This is thought to be the world's first parliament in the modern sense, and is certainly the oldest. Recognized as a sovereign state from 1918, Iceland was united to Denmark through a common sovereign until 1944, when it became a republic.

Since the country was formerly predominantly pastoral, with most of the population scattered in farms and small hamlets, the standard of living depended on the vicissitudes of farming close to the Arctic Circle. Now the economy is based on deep-sea fishing; fish and fish products make up 70% of exports. About a fifth of the land is used for agriculture, but only 1% is actually cultivated for root crops and fodder. The rest is used for grazing livestock.

Geothermal and hydroelectric power provide cheap energy for developing industries, including aluminium smelting and hothouse cultivation; most houses and offices in Reykjavík, the capital, are heated geothermally. About a quarter of the workforce is engaged in the production of energy and manufacturing – processing food and fish, making cement and refining aluminium from imported bauxite. The population is concentrated mainly in settlements close to the coast, over half of them in or near Reykjavík ■

FAROE ISLANDS

In 1948 the Faroe Islands, which are part of Denmark, adopted a flag combining the local arms with the Danish arms. The cross, like that on other Scandinavian flags, is slightly off-centre. Red and blue are ancient Faroese colours; white represents the foam of the sea.

The Faroes are a group of rocky islands situated in the North Atlantic 450 km [280 mls] south-east of Iceland, 675 km [420 mls] from Norway and 300 km [185 mls] from the Shetlands. Like Iceland, they are composed mainly of volcanic material. They were dramatically moulded by glacial action and the landscape forms a forbidding setting for the Faroese farming and fishing settlements. Away from the villages and scattered hamlets, high cliffs are home to millions of seabirds.

Winters are mild for the latitude but the summers are cool. It is usually windy and often overcast or foggy. Sheep farming on the poor soils is the principal occupation, but salted, dried, processed and frozen fish, fishmeal and oil – from cod, whiting, mackerel and herring – comprise the chief exports. Faroese motor vessels are found in all the deep-sea fishing grounds of the North Atlantic and the capital, Tórshavn, has ship-repairing yards. Denmark, Norway and Britain are the main trading partners.

The Faroes have been part of the Danish kingdom since 1386 and from 1851 they sent two representatives to the Danish parliament. Their own elected assembly, dating from 1852, secured a large degree of self-government as a region within the Danish realm in 1948.

The islands left the European Free Trade Association (EFTA) when Denmark switched membership to the European Economic Community (EEC) on 1 January 1973, but did not join the community – though they do have a special associate status allowing for free industrial trade. Since 1940 the currency has been the Faroese króna, which is freely interchangeable with the Danish krone. The people speak Faroese, official (alongside Danish) since 1948. Of the 22 islands, 17 are inhabited ■

COUNTRY Danish self-governing region

AREA 1,400 sq km [541 sq mls]

POPULATION 47,000

CAPITAL (POPULATION) Tórshavn (14,601)

NORWAY

Norway's flag has been used since 1898, though its use as a merchant flag dates back to 1821. The design is based on the Dannebrog flag of Denmark, which ruled Norway from the 14th century until the early 19th century.

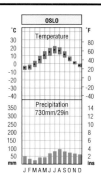

The warm waters and cyclones of the North Atlantic Ocean give the western coastlands of Norway a warm maritime climate of mild winters and cool summers, although wet. The rainfall is heavy on the coast but is less inland and northwards. Inland the winters are more severe and the summers warmer. At Oslo, snow usually begins in November and lies on the ground until late March. Sunshine November to January is only about one hour, but April to August is 6–8 hours per day.

One of the world's most distinctly shaped countries, the kingdom of Norway occupies the western part of the Scandinavian peninsula, from North Cape at latitude 71°N to Lindesnes at 58°N, a north–south distance of over 1,600 km [1,000 mls]. It covers an area far larger than Poland, yet has a population of less than 4.4 million, most of whom live in the southern part of the country, where the capital, Oslo, is situated.

Norway shares a short common frontier in the Arctic with Russia. Unlike its neighbours, Sweden and Finland, which are neutral, Norway is a member of NATO (North Atlantic Treaty Organization), but refused to join the EEC when Britain, Ireland and Denmark decided to enter (on 1 January 1973). As a member of the Nordic Council, Norway co-operates closely with its Scandinavian neighbours on social welfare and education, even though Sweden and Finland left the European Free Trade Association (EFTA) to join the EU in 1995.

The sea has always been a major influence in Norwegian life. A thousand years ago Viking sailors from Norway roamed the northern seas, founding colonies around the coasts of Britain, Iceland and even North America. Today fishing, shipbuilding and the management of merchant shipping lines are of vital importance to the Norwegian economy, and its merchant ships, most of which seldom visit the home ports, earn profits which pay for a third of the country's imports.

Landscape

Norway is a rugged, mountainous country in which communication is difficult. The Norwegian landscape is dominated by rolling plateaus, the *vidda*,

SCANDINAVIA

There are several possible definitions of the term Scandinavia. In the narrow geographical sense it refers to the peninsula shared by Norway and Sweden; in a broader cultural and political sense it includes the five countries of the Nordic Council – Norway, Sweden, Denmark, Finland and Iceland. All except Finland have related languages, and all have a tradition of parliamentary democracy: Finland and Iceland are republics, while the others are constitutional monarchies.

There are also strong historical links between the countries, beginning in the 8th century when their ancestors, the Norsemen, colonized large parts of northern Europe. All have at different times been governed together, Sweden and Finland separating in 1809, Norway and Sweden in 1905, and Denmark and Iceland as recently as 1944.

Because of their northerly position, and their exposure to Atlantic weather systems, the Scandinavian states have a cool, moist climate not favourable to crops. However, because of the long hours of daylight in the northern summer, some surprisingly good crops are grown north of the Arctic Circle.

The Scandinavians were once among the poorest peoples of Europe, but during the last century they have become among the richest, making full use of their limited natural resources, and also seizing the opportunities which their maritime position gave them to become major shipping and fishing nations.

generally 300–900 m [1,000–3,000 ft] high, above which some peaks rise to as much as 1,500–2,500 m [5,000–8,000 ft] in the area between Oslo, Bergen and Trondheim. In the far north the summits are around 1,000 m [3,000 ft] lower.

The highest areas retain permanent ice fields, as in the Jotunheim Mountains above Sognefjord. The Norwegian mountains have been uplifted during three mountain-building episodes over the last 400 million years, and they contain rocks of the earliest geological periods. Intrusions of volcanic material accompanied the uplifting and folding, and there are great masses of granites and gneisses – the source of Norway's mineral wealth.

There are few large areas of flat land in the country, but in the east the *vidda* are broken by deep valleys of rivers flowing to the lowlands of southeast Norway, focused on Oslo. In glacial times the whole country was covered by the great northern ice cap. When it melted about 10,000 years ago it left behind large deposits of glacial moraine, well represented around Oslo in the Raa moraines.

The coast and the islands

The configuration of the coast – the longest in Europe – helps to explain the ease with which the Norwegians took to the sea in their early history and why they have remained a seafaring nation since. The *vidda* are cut by long, narrow, steep-sided fjords on the west coast, shaped by the great northern ice cap. The largest of these, Sognefjord – 203 km [127 mls] long and less than 5 km [3 mls] wide – is the longest inlet in Europe and the best known fjord.

Along the coast there are hundreds of islands, the largest group of which, the Lofoten Islands, lie north of the Arctic Circle. These islands, known as the *skerryguard*, protect the inner coast from the battering of the Atlantic breakers, and provide sheltered leads of water which the coastal ferries and fishing boats can navigate in safety.

Until recently communications along the coast were easier by boat than by land. Oslo is linked by rail to the main towns of the south, and a line reaches north to Bodö at latitude 67.5°N. Roads are difficult to build and costly to maintain, and are often blocked by snow in winter and spring.

There are still several hundred ferries which carry cars across the fjords, but much money has been invested in the building of a north–south trunk road, with bridges across the fjords, to avoid the constant use of ferries. Air transport is of increasing importance and many small airstrips are in use, bringing remote communities into contact with the south.

Agriculture

With two-thirds of the country comprising barren mountains, snowfields or unproductive wastes, and one-fifth forested, less than 3% of the land can be cultivated. The barrenness of the soil, the heavy rainfall, winter snows and the short growing season restrict agriculture, especially in the north, though in the long days of summer good crops of hay, potatoes, quick-growing vegetables and even rye and barley are grown. Near the coast, farming is restricted to the limited areas of level or gently sloping ground beside these sheltered fjords. Cattle and sheep use the slopes above them in the summer but are fed in stalls during the winter. Everywhere fish is caught in the local waters.

COUNTRY Kingdom of Norway

AREA 323,900 sq km [125,050 sq mls]

POPULATION 4,361,000

CAPITAL (POPULATION) Oslo (714,000)

GOVERNMENT Constitutional monarchy with a unicameral legislature

ETHNIC GROUPS Norwegian 97%

LANGUAGES Norwegian (official), Lappish, Finnish

RELIGIONS Christianity (Lutheran 88%)

NATIONAL DAY 17 May; Independence Day (1905)

CURRENCY Krone = 100 ore

ANNUAL INCOME PER PERSON US$26,340

MAIN PRIMARY PRODUCTS Cereals, potatoes, livestock, fruit, timber, fish, crude oil, gas, coal, copper, iron, lead, nickel, titanium, quartz

MAIN INDUSTRIES Mining, oil refining, minerals, shipbuilding, food processing, fishing, forestry

MAIN EXPORTS Crude petroleum 23%, metal products 18%, natural gas 11%, machinery and transport equipment 10%, foodstuffs 8%

MAIN EXPORT PARTNERS UK 27%, Germany 15%, Sweden 11%, Netherlands 7%

MAIN IMPORTS Machinery and transport equipment 28%, metal and metal products 12%, raw materials including fuel 11%, foodstuffs 6%

MAIN IMPORT PARTNERS Sweden 19%, Germany 16%, UK 9%, Denmark 8%

DEFENCE 3.3% of GNP

TOURISM 2,375,000 visitors per year

POPULATION DENSITY 13 per sq km [34 per sq ml]

INFANT MORTALITY 6 per 1,000 live births

LIFE EXPECTANCY Female 81 yrs, male 74 yrs

ADULT LITERACY 99%

PRINCIPAL CITIES (POPULATION) Oslo 714,000 Bergen 195,000 Trondheim 134,000

Resources and industry

Iron and lead ores are found in the north, copper in central Norway and titanium in the south. The extent of Norway's mineral resources is not fully known, and prospecting is still revealing new deposits. Oil and natural gas from the seabed of the North Sea have made a great contribution to the Norwegian economy in recent years, and comprise more than half of the country's export earnings. Statfjord B (899,500 tonnes) is the world's biggest oil platform. Exploitation of all these reserves provides more than enough for the country's needs.

There is no coal in mainland Norway, although some is found in the islands on the Svalbard archipelago in the Arctic Ocean. The lack of coal has been partly compensated for by the development of hydroelectricity, begun in the early 20th century, when the waterfalls of streams and rivers flowing down the steep slopes above the fjords were first harnessed. Later on, inland sites were developed, and the greatest concentration is in the Rjukan Valley, 160 km [100 mls] west of Oslo. Today Norway (which owns five of the world's highest waterfalls) derives 99.6% of its electricity from water power.

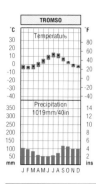

TROMSO

Northern Norway is within the Arctic Circle, but owing to the Gulf Stream the winter temperatures are only just below freezing. Summers are distinctly cool, with July and August temperatures around 10°C [50°F]. Inland, on the same latitude, the temperatures in the winter will be 10°C [18°F] colder, and slightly warmer in the summer. Jan Mayen and Svalbard, well within the Arctic, also benefit from the ameliorating effects of the Gulf Stream.

The availability of cheap electricity made possible the rapid growth of the wood-pulp, paper and chemical industries, and later stimulated the metal-working industries. Many of the industrial sites are on the shores of remote fjords, where cheap electricity and deep-water access for the import of raw materials and for the export of finished products are the determining factors in choosing the location. The aluminium and chemical industries of the south-west coast are typical.

Metalworking has developed in the far north since World War II. After primary treatment iron is exported from Kirkenes to a smelter at Mo-i-Rana, on the coast just south of the Arctic Circle, which uses coal imported from Svalbard. The port of Narvik was connected by rail to the Swedish system in 1903, so that Swedish iron ore could be sent from an ice-free port to supply the iron smelters of Germany and other continental markets. This trade remains important today.

Rapid industrial development since World War II has transformed the Norwegian economy, and has ensured that the Norwegians are among the most prosperous people in Europe. Few people are very wealthy – taxation rates are high – but few are very poor, and an advanced welfare state (common to all the Scandinavian countries) provides good services even to the most isolated or rural communities. The great majority of people own their houses, and many families have second homes on the shores of fjords and lakes. Today's Norwegians are also more generous than their Viking ancestors: the nation is by far Europe's biggest donor of foreign aid per capita, with a figure of 1.1% of GNP – well above the OECD target of 0.7%.

The pre-war economy, dependent on forestry, farming, fishing and seafaring, is still important, but the numbers employed in these industries are dwindling as more and more people move into the new industries and services in the growing towns. There are still few large towns, and all six of those with more than 50,000 population are on the coast. The largest are Oslo, Bergen and Trondheim.

Svalbard is an archipelago (group of islands) of 62,920 sq km [24,295 sq mls] – half as big again as Denmark – sitting halfway between the North Pole and Arctic Circle. Despite this exposed, northerly position, the climate is tempered by the relatively mild prevailing winds from the Atlantic. The largest island is Spitzbergen (or Vestspitzbergen), the former also being used as the name of the whole group.

The rival claims on the islands by the Norwegians, the Dutch and the British lost their importance in the 18th century with the decline of whale hunting, but were raised again in the 20th century with the discovery of coal. A treaty signed in Paris by 40 parties in 1920 finally recognized Norwegian sovereignty in return for mining rights, and in 1925 the islands were incorporated officially into the kingdom of Norway.

Coal remains the principal product, with mines run by Norway and the former Soviet Union, both of which produce similar amounts of coal: Norwegian mines produced 359,000 tonnes in 1992. Soviet citizens outnumbered Norwegians by more than 2 to 1 in 1988; the total population in 1993 was 2,967, of which 1,097 were Norwegian.

Following the success of the North Sea projects, there is now prospecting in Svalbard for oil and natural gas. There are several meteorological stations and a research station, and other residents work on the extensive national parks and nature reserves. An airport opened in 1975 near Longyearbyen, the capital that is named after an American (J.M. Longyear), who in 1905 was the first man to mine coal on Svalbard.

Jan Mayen is a volcanic island of 380 sq km [147 sq mls], north-north-east of Iceland but actually closer to the east coast of Greenland. Desolate, mountainous and partly covered by glaciers, its dominant feature is the volcano of Beerenberg (2,277 m [7,470 ft]), which had been dormant but became active again in 1970.

The island was named in 1614 after the Dutch whaling captain Jan Jacobsz May, but 'discovered' by Henry Hudson in 1608. Though uninhabited, it was used by seal trappers and other hunters, and in 1921 Norway established a meteorological and radio station. In 1929 it was annexed into the kingdom of Norway, and today the only residents are the 30 or so staff at a weather station.

Bjørnøya (Bear Island) lies halfway between Svalbard and the Norwegian mainland, on the cusp of the Norwegian Sea and Barents Sea. Measuring 179 sq km [69 sq mls], it is uninhabited but remains the centre of important cod fisheries; after a long dispute over territorial rights, it was internationally recognized as part of Norway in 1925 ∎

SWEDEN

While Sweden's national flag has been flown since the reign of King Gustavus Vasa in the early 16th century, it was not officially adopted until 1906. The colours were derived from the ancient state coat of arms dating from 1364.

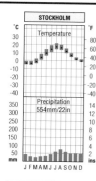

The Gulf Stream warms the southern coastlands, but to the north continental influences take over. The February temperature in the south is just below freezing, but in the north it is –15°C [5°F]. Rainfall is low throughout Sweden, but it lies as snow for over six months in the north. The Baltic is usually frozen for at least five months, but ice is rare on the western coast. In the summer, there is little difference between the north and south, most areas experiencing between 15° and 20°C [59° to 68°F].

The kingdom of Sweden is the largest of the Scandinavian countries in both population and area. It occupies the eastern half of the Scandinavian peninsula, extending southwards to latitude 55°N and having a much smaller Arctic area than either Norway or Finland.

The 1,600 km [1,000 mls] eastern coast, along the shores of the Baltic Sea and the Gulf of Bothnia, extends from the mouth of the Torne River, which forms the border with Finland, to Ystad in the south, opposite the Danish island of Bornholm and the German coast. Sweden also has a coastline facing west along the shores of the Kattegat – the strait that separates Sweden and the Jutland peninsula, which is part of Denmark.

Landscape

Sweden's share of the Scandinavian peninsula is less mountainous than that of Norway. The northern half of the country forms part of the Baltic or Fenno-Scandian Shield, a stable block of ancient granites and gneisses which extends round the head of the Gulf of Bothnia into Finland. This part of Sweden contains most of the country's rich mineral wealth. The shield land is an area of low plateaus which rise gradually westwards.

South of the plateaus area there is a belt of lowlands between the capital city, Stockholm, and the second city, Göteborg (Gothenburg). These lowlands contain several large lakes, the chief of which are Mälar, near Stockholm, and the larger Vänern and Vättern, which are situated in the middle of the lowland belt.

These are all that remains of a strait which, in glacial times, connected the Baltic with the Kattegat. Changes in land and water level during the later stages of the Ice Age led to the breaking of this connection. Now linked by canals, these lakes form an important water route across the country. South of the lakes is a low plateau, rising to 380 m [1,250 ft] above Lake Vättern and sloping gently down to the small lowland area of Skåne (Scania).

Sweden's topography was greatly affected by the Ice Age: the long, narrow lakes which fill the upper valleys of many of the rivers of northern Sweden have been shaped by the action of ice. They are the relics of a much larger lake system which was fed by water from the melting ice sheet and provide excellent natural reservoirs for hydro-electric stations. Some of the most fertile soils in Sweden were formed from material deposited in the beds of such glacial lakes. Elsewhere, glacial moraines and deposits of boulder clay are other reminders of the impact of the Ice Age.

Forestry and agriculture

There are extensive coniferous forests throughout northern Sweden; indeed, half the country's land area is covered with trees. In the south the original cover of mixed deciduous woodland has been cleared for agriculture from the areas of better soil, the typical landscape now being farmland interspersed with forest. This is usually spruce or pine, often with birch – the national tree.

There are better opportunities for agriculture in Sweden than elsewhere in Scandinavia. Cereal crops, potatoes, sugar beet and vegetables are grown for human consumption in Skåne and in central Sweden, but by far the greatest area of cultivated land is given over to the production of fodder crops for cattle and sheep. Dairy farming is highly developed, and Sweden is self-sufficient in milk, cheese and butter production.

Industry and population

Many farmers have left the land since World War II, attracted by the higher wages and more modern life style of the towns. Sweden has been able to create a high standard of living based on industry – despite the fact that, apart from the large iron-ore deposits, many of the essential fuels and raw materials have to be imported. Most of the iron ore obtained from the mines at Kiruna and Gällivare in Arctic Sweden is exported via Narvik and Lulea to Germany.

The development of hydroelectricity has made up for the lack of oil and coal. Sweden is famous for high-quality engineering products such as ball bearings, matchmaking machinery, agricultural machines, motor vehicles (Saab and Volvo), ships, aircraft and armaments (Bofors). In addition to these relatively new industries, the traditional forest-based industries have been modernized. Sweden is among the world's largest exporters of wood pulp and paper and board – as well as being Europe's biggest producer of softwood.

The bulk of the population lives in the lakeland corridor between Stockholm and Göteborg, or around the southern city of Malmö. These citizens, whose forebears worked hard, exploited their resources and avoided war or occupation for nearly two centuries, now enjoy a standard of living that is in many ways the envy of most other Western countries. Sweden has by far the highest percentage figure for public spending in the OECD, with over 70% of the national budget going on one of the widest-ranging welfare programmes in the world.

In turn, the tax burden is the world's highest (some 57% of national income) and some Swedes are beginning to feel that the 'soft' yet paternalistic approach has led to overgovernment, depersonalization and uniformity. The elections of September 1991 saw the end of the Social Democrat government – in power for all but six years since 1932 – with voters swinging towards parties canvassing

ÅLAND

Swedish settlers colonized various coastal tracts of Finland from the 12th century onwards, and the 6.5% of the Finnish population who are Swedish-speaking include all the 25,102 people of Åland, the group of more than 6,500 islands situated between the two countries in the Gulf of Bothnia.

Although the inhabitants voted to secede to Sweden in a 1917 referendum, the result was annulled in 1921 by the League of Nations for strategic reasons and Åland (as Ahvenanmaa) remained a Finnish province. However, the islands were granted considerable autonomy and still enjoy a large degree of 'home rule' with their own flag, postage stamps and representation at the annual assembly of the Nordic Council.

Boasting many important relics of the Stone, Iron and Bronze Ages, the province's income derives mainly from fishing, farming and, increasingly, from tourism.

COUNTRY Kingdom of Sweden

AREA 449,960 sq km [173,730 sq mls]

POPULATION 8,893,000

CAPITAL (POPULATION) Stockholm (1,539,000)

GOVERNMENT Constitutional monarchy and parliamentary state with a unicameral legislature

ETHNIC GROUPS Swedish 91%, Finnish 3%

LANGUAGES Swedish (official), Finnish

RELIGIONS Lutheran 89%, Roman Catholic 2%

NATIONAL DAY 6 June

CURRENCY Swedish krona = 100 öre

ANNUAL INCOME PER PERSON US$24,830

MAIN PRIMARY PRODUCTS Cereals, cattle, sugar beet, potatoes, timber, iron ore, copper, lead, zinc

MAIN INDUSTRIES Engineering, electrical goods, vehicles, mining, timber, paper, wood pulp

MAIN EXPORTS Machinery and transport equipment 43%, paper products 11%, electrical machinery 8%, wood pulp 7%, chemicals 7%

MAIN EXPORT PARTNERS Germany 12%, UK 11%, USA 10%, Norway 9%, Denmark 7%, Finland 7%

MAIN IMPORTS Machinery and transport equipment 36%, chemicals 10%

MAIN IMPORT PARTNERS Germany 21%, UK 9%, USA 8%, Finland 7%, Denmark 7%, Norway 6%

DEFENCE 2.5% of GNP

TOURISM 700,000 visitors per year

POPULATION DENSITY 20 per sq km [51 per sq ml]

INFANT MORTALITY 6 per 1,000 live births

LIFE EXPECTANCY Female 81 yrs, male 75 yrs

ADULT LITERACY 99%

PRINCIPAL CITIES (POPULATION) Stockholm 1,539,000 Göteborg 783,000 Malmö 489,000 Uppsala 181,000

lower taxation. Other attractive policies appeared to include curbs on immigration and diversion of Third World aid (Sweden spends well above the OECD per capita average each year) to the newly independent Baltic states.

Other changes were in the wind, too. A founder member of EFTA – Stockholm played host to the inaugural meetings in 1960 – Sweden nevertheless applied for entry to the EEC in 1991, and finally joined the European Union on 1 January 1995 following a referendum. Sweden is no longer a member of EFTA, but remains a key state in Scandinavia: its long experience of peace and stability, and a wide industrial base built on efficiency and quality, can be grafted on to its strategically central position and relatively large population to form the most important power among the Nordic nations.

While some say that Sweden's biggest problems could be of its own making (though contrary to belief it is Denmark that has the world's highest known suicide rate), it is possible that it will be vulnerable to forces largely beyond its control. Like its neighbours, Sweden suffers from forest-killing acid rain generated mostly by the UK and Germany, and after the shock waves from Chernobyl in 1986 the government was also forced to reconsider its electricity-generating programme, at that time more than 40% dependent on nuclear power ■

DENMARK

The Dannebrog ('the spirit of Denmark') flag is said to represent King Waldemar II's vision of a white cross against a red sky before the Battle of Lyndanisse, which took place in Estonia in 1219. It is possibly the oldest national flag in continuous use.

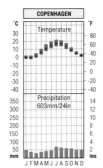

The climate of Denmark reflects that the country is at the meeting of Arctic, continental and maritime influences. The winters, thanks to the warm Atlantic waters, are not too cold, although there may be many nights that are below freezing. The summers are warm. January and February have about 20 frost days, and both of these months have experienced temperatures lower than −20°C [−4°F]. The rainfall is reasonable, falling in all months, with a maximum July to September.

The smallest of the Scandinavian countries (though the second largest in population), Denmark consists of the Jutland (Jylland) peninsula, which is an extension of the North German Plain, and an archipelago of 406 islands, of which 89 are inhabited. The coastline – about 7,300 km [4,500 mls] – is extremely long for the size of the country. The largest and most densely populated of the islands is Zealand (Sjælland), which lies close to the coast of southern Sweden. In October 1994, this was connected to the most important island, Fünen (Fyn), by the Storebaeltstunnel. Copenhagen (København), the capital city, lies on the narrow strait, The Sound, which leads from the Kattegat to the Baltic.

Control of the entrances to the Baltic contributed to the power of Denmark in the Middle Ages, when the kingdom dominated its neighbours and expanded its territories to include Norway, Iceland, Greenland and the Faroe Islands. The link with Norway was broken in 1814, and with Iceland in 1944, but Greenland and the Faroes retain connections with Denmark. The granite island of Bornholm, off the southern tip of Sweden, also remains a Danish possession.

Structurally, Denmark is part of a low-lying belt of sedimentary rocks extending from north Germany to southern Sweden, which are geologically much younger than the rest of Scandinavia. The surface is almost entirely covered by glacial deposits, but the underlying strata are exposed as the 122 m [400 ft] chalk cliffs on the island of Møn. Nowhere in Denmark, however, is higher than 171 m [561 ft] and the country averages just 98 m [30 ft]. Along the west coast of Jutland, facing the North Sea, are lines of sand dunes with shallow lagoons behind them.

Agriculture and industry

Denmark has few mineral resources and no coal, though there is now some oil and natural gas from the North Sea. A century ago this was a poor farming and fishing country, but Denmark has now been transformed into one of Europe's wealthiest industrial nations. The first steps in the process were taken in the late 19th century, with the introduction of co-operative methods of processing and distributing farm produce, and the development of modern methods of dairying and pig and poultry breeding. Denmark became the main supplier of bacon, eggs and butter to the growing industrial nations of Western Europe. Most of the natural fodder for the animals is still grown in Denmark – three-quarters of the land is cultivated and more than 60% is arable – with barley as the principal crop.

From a firm agricultural base Denmark has developed a whole range of industries. Some – brewing, meat canning, fish processing, pottery, textiles and furniture making – use Danish products, while others – shipbuilding, oil refining, engineering and metalworking – depend on imported raw materials. The famous port of Copenhagen is also the chief industrial centre and draw for more than a million tourists each year. At the other end of the scale there is Legoland, the famous miniature town of plastic bricks, built at Billand, north-west of Vejle in eastern Jutland. It was here, in a carpenter's workshop, that Lego was created before it went on to become the world's best-selling construction toy – and a prominent Danish export. The country is also the world's biggest exporter of insulin.

People and culture

Denmark is a generally comfortable mixture of striking social opposites. The Lutheran tradition and the cradle of Hans Christian Andersen's fairy tales co-exist with open attitudes to pornography and one of the highest illegitimacy rates in the West (44%). A reputation for caring and thorough welfare services – necessitating high taxation – is dented somewhat by the world's highest recorded suicide rate.

It is, too, one of the 'greenest' of the advanced nations, with a pioneering Ministry of Pollution that has real power to act: in 1991 it became the first government anywhere to fine industries for emissions of carbon dioxide, the primary 'greenhouse'

COUNTRY Kingdom of Denmark

AREA 43,070 sq km [16,629 sq mls]

POPULATION 5,229,000

CAPITAL (POPULATION) Copenhagen (1,353,000)

GOVERNMENT Constitutional monarchy with a unicameral legislature

ETHNIC GROUPS Danish 97%

LANGUAGES Danish (official)

RELIGIONS Lutheran 91%, Roman Catholic 1%

NATIONAL DAY 16 April; Birthday of HM the Queen

CURRENCY Krone = 100 øre

ANNUAL INCOME PER PERSON US$23,660

MAIN PRIMARY PRODUCTS Livestock, cereals, oil and natural gas

MAIN INDUSTRIES Agriculture and food processing, shipbuilding, chemicals, petroleum refining

EXPORTS US$5,475 per person

MAIN EXPORTS Meat, dairy produce, fish 27%, machinery and electronic equipment 24%, chemicals

MAIN EXPORT PARTNERS Germany 17%, UK 12%, Sweden 11%, USA 8%, Norway 8%

IMPORTS US$5,198 per person

MAIN IMPORTS Machinery and transport equipment 31%, chemicals 10%, foodstuffs 10% mineral fuels and lubricants 9%

MAIN IMPORT PARTNERS Germany 24%, Sweden 12%, UK 7%, Japan 5%, USA 5%, Netherlands 5%, France 5%

DEFENCE 2% of GNP

TOURISM 1,550,000 visitors per year

POPULATION DENSITY 120 per sq km [311 per sq ml]

INFANT MORTALITY 6 per 1,000 live births

LIFE EXPECTANCY Female 79 yrs, male 73 yrs

ADULT LITERACY 99%

PRINCIPAL CITIES (POPULATION) Copenhagen 1,353,000 Århus 271,000 Odense 181,000 Ålborg 157,000

gas. At the same time, Danes register Europe's highest rate of deaths from lung cancer.

Denmark gets on well with its neighbours and partners. On 1 January 1973, along with Britain and Ireland, it joined the EEC – the first Scandinavian country to make the break from EFTA – but it still co-operates closely on social, cultural and economic matters with its five Scandinavian partners in the Nordic Council.

Bornholm is a Danish island well away from the rest of the country and far nearer to the southern tip of Sweden (40 km [25 mls]) than to Copenhagen (168 km [104 mls]). A separate administrative region, it was occupied by Germany in World War II but liberated by the Russians, who returned it to Denmark in 1946.

Measuring 558 sq km [227 sq mls], Bornholm is composed mainly of granite and has poor soils, but deposits of kaolin (china clay) spawned a pottery industry. The principal town and ferry port is Rønne, the fishing port Neksø. Fishing and fish processing, agriculture (mainly cattle rearing) and tourism are the main sources of income – the last-named reliant partly on the island's fine examples of fortified churches ■

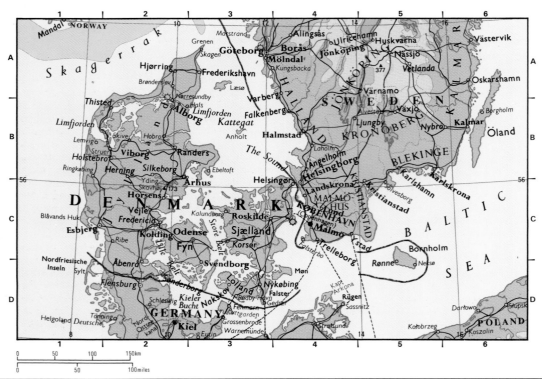

FINLAND

Finland became an independent republic only in 1917 after separation from Russia, then in the throes of the Revolution, and the present flag was adopted soon after. The colours symbolize Finland's blue lakes and white snow.

The dominating feature of Finland's climate is the harshness and length of the winter. A third of Finland is north of the Arctic Circle and here temperatures can reach –30°C [–22°F]. Snow can lie for six months, never clearing from the north-facing slopes. Helsinki has four or five months below 0°C [32°F]. The seas and lakes nearly always freeze in winter. The summers can be hot. Rainfall is low, decreasing northwards and falling mostly from late summer to winter, often as snow.

Located almost entirely between latitudes 60°N and 70°N, Finland is the most northerly state on the mainland of Europe, though Norway's county of Finnmark actually cuts it off from the Arctic Ocean. A third of Finland's total area lies within the Arctic Circle, a far higher proportion than for its two large Scandinavian partners.

The climate of the northern province of Lappi (Lapland) is not as severe as in places which lie in similar latitudes, such as Canada and Siberia, because of the North Atlantic Drift. This influence keeps the Arctic coasts of Europe free from ice all year round.

Finland enjoys a short but warm summer, with average July temperatures at Helsinki of 17°C [63°F] and 13°C [55°F] in Lapland. Because of the high latitudes, summer days are extremely long; indeed, in the Arctic region there is virtually no night throughout the month of June.

Winters are long and cold (Helsinki's January average is 6°C [21°F]) and the days are short. In severe winters the sea freezes for several kilometres offshore and icebreakers have to be used to keep the ports open. Snowfall is not heavy, however, and rail and road transport is seldom badly disrupted.

Landscape

Geologically Finland is made up of a central plateau of ancient crystalline rocks, mainly granites, schists and gneisses, surrounded by lowlands composed of recent glacial deposits. In the 600 million years between the formation of these ancient rocks and the last Ice Age, the surface of the land was worn down to a peneplain, and most of central and southern Finland is below 200 m [650 ft]. However, the roots of an old mountain system running northwest to south-east can still be traced across Lapland and along Finland's eastern border with Russia. Peaks of over 1,000 m [3,000 ft] occur in northern Lapland, near the Swedish and Norwegian borders.

A tenth of the land surface is covered by lakes. Concentrated in the central plateau, they are in most cases long, narrow and shallow, and aligned

COUNTRY Republic of Finland

AREA 338,130 sq km [130,552 sq mls]

POPULATION 5,125,000

CAPITAL (POPULATION) Helsinki (525,000)

GOVERNMENT Multiparty parliamentary republic with a unicameral legislature

ETHNIC GROUPS Finnish 93%, Swedish 6%

LANGUAGES Finnish and Swedish (both official)

RELIGIONS Lutheran 88%, Greek Orthodox 1%

NATIONAL DAY 6 December; Independence Day (1917)

CURRENCY Markka = 100 penniä

ANNUAL INCOME PER PERSON US$18,970

MAIN PRIMARY PRODUCTS Timber, livestock, copper, lead, iron, zinc, fish

MAIN INDUSTRIES Forestry, wood pulp, paper, machinery, shipbuilding, chemicals, fertilizers

EXPORTS US$4,695 per person

MAIN EXPORTS Machinery 27%, paper and paperboard 26%, wood, lumber, cork and wastepaper 10%

MAIN EXPORT PARTNERS Russia and other CIS nations 16%, Sweden 15%, UK 11%, Germany 11%

IMPORTS US$4,964 per person

MAIN IMPORTS Machinery and transport equipment 44%, basic manufactures, textiles and metals 16%, petroleum and petroleum products 10%, chemicals 10%, foodstuffs 5%

MAIN IMPORT PARTNERS Germany 17%, Russia and other CIS nations 14%, Sweden 13%

DEFENCE 2% of GNP

TOURISM 790,000 visitors per year

POPULATION DENSITY 15 per sq km [38 per sq ml]

INFANT MORTALITY 5 per 1,000 live births

LIFE EXPECTANCY Female 80 yrs, male 72 yrs

ADULT LITERACY 99%

PRINCIPAL CITIES (POPULATION) Helsinki 525,000 Espoo 186,000 Tampere 179,000 Turku 162,000

THE LAPPS

Hunters, fishermen and herdsmen living in Arctic Europe, approximately 35,000 Lapps are scattered between Norway (with 20,000), Sweden and Finland, with a small group in Russia. Physically, the short, dark Lapps – or Samer, as they call themselves – are noticeably different from other Scandinavians, though their language, Saarme, is related to Finnish. They probably originated in northern Russia at least 2,000 years ago, and may have been the original inhabitants of Finland. Until the 17th century, when they first learned to domesticate reindeer, they lived entirely by hunting and fishing; thereafter, many followed a semi-nomadic life, driving their herds each summer from their winter settlements at the edge of the forest to the high pastureland.

Industrialization, especially mining and hydroelectric development and the associated roads, has badly affected nomadic herding, and it now occupies only about 10% of Lapps. Most live in fixed settlements in coastal areas, and a steady trickle migrate south, assimilating themselves into modern Scandinavian society.

in a north-west to south-east direction, indicating the line of movement of the ice sheet which scoured out their basins. More than two-thirds of Finland is covered by lakes and forest – a fact that accounts for almost everything from the composition of its exports to the brilliance of its rally-car drivers.

The number of lakes varies from 60,000 to 185,000, depending on the source of the information and the definition used, but whatever the exact figure may be, they dominate the landscape of the southern half of Finland and contribute to its austere beauty. The Saimaa area in the south-east, near the Russian frontier, is Europe's largest inland system.

Although under increasing threat from pollution caused by wood processing and fertilizers as well as acid rain, the lakes are still rich in fish – mainly trout, salmon, pike and perch – and provide a prime source of recreation for huge numbers of Finnish people.

Forests occupy almost 60% of the land surface, the main trees being pine, spruce and birch. Forest-based products – wood pulp, sawn timber, paper and board – still constitute 40% of Finland's exports, but since World War II engineering, ship-building and metallurgical industries have greatly expanded. Formerly a member of EFTA, Finland

saw its economy grow at a faster rate than that of Japan during the 1980s. On 1 January 1995 Finland joined the EU, following a referendum in 1994.

People and culture

Between 1150 and 1809 Finland was under Swedish rule, and one of the legacies of this period is a Swedish-speaking minority of 6% of the total population. In some localities on the south and west coasts, Swedish speakers are in a majority and Åland, an island closer to the Swedish coast than to Finland, is a self-governing province. Many towns in Finland use both Finnish and Swedish names; for example, Helsinki is Helsingfors and Turku is Åbo in Swedish. Finnish bears little relation to Swedish or any Scandinavian language, and is closest to Magyar, the native tongue of Hungary.

While few Finns comply with the clichéd image and run around in the snow before beating their feet with birch twigs, they do try to keep warm in other ways. They consume more vodka per head than the Russians – indeed, it became a serious social problem during the 1980s – and they are the world's most committed consumers of coffee, averaging almost five cups a day ■

EUROPE

UNITED KINGDOM

The first Union flag, combining England's cross of St George and Scotland's cross of St Andrew, dates from 1603 when James VI became James I of England. The Irish emblem, the cross of St Patrick, was added in 1801 to form the present flag.

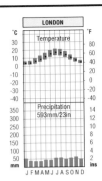

South-eastern England, sheltered from the ocean to the west, is one of the driest parts of the British Isles. Although rainfall varies little throughout the year, greater evaporation creates a deficit between May and August. Like other parts of north-west Europe, London has a small annual temperature range. Its record low is –10°C [14°F] and record high 34°C [93°F]. The metropolis creates its own local climate and nights are generally warmer than in the surrounding countryside.

The British Isles stand on the westernmost edge of the continental shelf – two large and several hundred small islands for the most part cool, rainy and windswept. Despite physical closeness to the rest of Europe (32 km [20 mls] at the nearest point – little more than the distance across London), Britain is curiously isolated, with a long history of political independence and social separation from its neighbours. In the past the narrow seas served the islanders well, protecting them against casual invasion, while Britons in turn sailed to explore and exploit the rest of the world. Now insularity is rapidly breaking down, and Britain is closer to federation with Europe than ever before.

The islands are confusingly named. 'Great Britain', the largest in Europe and eighth largest in the world – so named to distinguish it from 'Little Britain' (Brittany, in France) – includes the kingdoms of England and Scotland and the principality of Wales; Ireland was once a kingdom, but is currently divided into the Province of Northern Ireland, under the British Crown, and the politically separate Republic of Ireland. Great Britain, Northern Ireland, and many off-lying island groups from the Scillies to the Shetlands, together make up the United Kingdom of Great Britain and Northern Ireland, commonly known as the UK. Even isolated Rockall, far out in the Atlantic Ocean, is part of the UK, but the Isle of Man and the Channel Islands are separate if direct dependencies of the Crown, with a degree of political autonomy and their own taxation systems.

Climate

Despite a subarctic position Britain is favoured climatically. Most other maritime lands between 50°N and 60°N – eastern Siberia, Kamchatka, the Aleutian Islands, southern Alaska, Hudson Bay and Labrador in Canada – are colder throughout the year, with longer winters, ice-bound coasts and a shorter growing season. Britain's salvation is the North Atlantic Drift or Gulf Stream, a current of surface water that brings subtropical warmth from the southern Atlantic Ocean, spreading it across the continental shelf of Western Europe and warming the prevailing westerly winds.

Britain's reputation for cloudiness is well merited. Mean duration of sunshine throughout the year is about 5 hours daily in the south, and only 3.5 hours daily in Scotland. At the height of summer only the south-west receives over 7.5 hours of sunshine per day – less than half the hours available. In winter only the south coast, the Severn Estuary, Oxford-

shire and a sliver of south-eastern Essex receive more than 1.5 hours per day, while many northern areas receive less than half an hour daily.

Despite a reputation for rain, Britain is fairly dry. More than half of the country receives less than 750 mm [30 in] annually, and parts of Essex have less than 500 mm [20 in] per year. The wettest areas are Snowdonia with about 5,000 mm [200 in], Ben Nevis and the north-western highlands with 4,300 mm [172 in], and the Lake District with 3,300 mm [132 in].

Population and immigration

Despite insularity the British people are of mixed stock. The earliest immigrants – land-hungry farmers from the Continent – were often refugees from tribal warfare and unrest. The Belgic tribesmen escaping from Imperial Rome, the Romans themselves (whose troops included Spanish, Macedonian and probably North African mercenaries), the Angles, Saxons, Jutes, Danes and Normans, all in turn brought genetic variety; so too did the Huguenots, Sephardic and Ashkenazim Jews, and Dutch, French and German businessmen who followed them. Latterly the waves of immigrants have included Belarussians, Poles, Italians, Ukrainians and Czechs – most, like their predecessors, fugitives from European wars, overcrowding and intolerance.

During the 19th century Britain often took in skilled European immigrants through the front door while steadily losing her own sons and daughters – Scots and Irish peasants in particular – through the back. Most recent arrivals in Britain are immigrants from crowded and impoverished corners of lands once part of the British Empire, notably the West Indies, West Africa, India and Pakistan. These and their descendants now make up about 4% of the population of Britain.

Under Roman rule the population of the British island numbered half to three-quarters of a million. By the time of the Domesday Survey it had doubled, and it doubled again by the end of the 14th century. The Black Death of the late 15th century killed one in every three or four, but numbers climbed slowly; at the Union of 1707, some 6 million English and Welsh joined about 1 million Scots under a single parliament. By 1801 the first national census revealed 8.9 million in England and Wales, and 1.6 million in Scotland; Ireland missed the first two ten-year counts, but probably numbered about 5 million. In 1821 the total British population was 21 million, in 1851 31 million, and in

1921 47 million. The rate of increase has now declined, but some parts of Britain, notably the southeast and the conurbations, are among the most heavily populated areas of the world, with higher densities only in the Netherlands and Taiwan.

England

Landscape: Visitors to England are often amazed at the variety of the landscape. Complex folding, laval outpourings, volcanic upheavals and eruptions, glacial planing, and changes of sea level have all left their marks on the present landscape.

From Northumberland to the Trent, the Pennines extend southwards as an upland with rolling hills, plateaus and fine valleys, many known as 'dales'. The range includes two western outliers – the Forest of Rossendale north of Manchester, and the Forest of Bowland in north Lancashire. To either side lie lowlands – those of Lancashire to the west and of Yorkshire and Nottingham to the east.

The Eden Valley separates the northern Pennines from Cumbria, which includes the Lake District. This is England's most striking mountain mass, a circular area of peaks, deep valleys, splendid lakes and crags. The loftiest peak is Scafell, 978 m [3,210 ft]. In the south-west Exmoor is a fine sandstone upland, and Dartmoor a predominantly granite area with many prominent tors. Elsewhere are isolated hills, small by world standards but dramatic against the small-scale background of Britain, as shown by the Malvern Hills of Worcester and the Wrekin near Shrewsbury.

Much of the English lowland consists of chalk downlands, familiar to continental visitors who enter England through Folkestone or Dover as the famous chalk cliffs. These are the exposed coastal edge of the North Downs, whose scarped northern slope forms a striking feature in the Croydon area of Greater London. The North Downs continue westwards through Surrey to the Hampshire Downs, then south and east as the South Downs, emerging at another coastal landmark – Beachy Head.

There is a northwards extension of downland through the Berkshire and Marlborough Downs to

THE CHANNEL ISLANDS

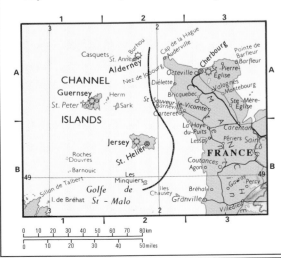

Lying 16 to 48 km [10 to 30 mls] from the coast of France, the Channel Islands are a British dependency covering an area of only 200 sq km [78 sq mls]. The largest are Jersey with 115 sq km [45 sq mls] and 84,400 inhabitants, and Guernsey, with 78 sq km [30 sq mls] and 58,400 people. The other islands – Alderney, Sark and others – are small, with fewer than 3,000 residents.

The only part of the Duchy of Normandy retained by the English Crown after 1204, and the only part of Britain occupied by the Germans in World War II, the islands have their own legal system and government, with lower taxation than that of Britain. This, combined with a favourable

climate and fine coastal scenery, has attracted a considerable number of wealthy residents, notably retired people, and established Jersey and Guernsey as offshore financial centres.

The main produce is agricultural, especially early potatoes, tomatoes and flowers for export to Britain, and the countryside has a vast number of glasshouses. Jersey and Guernsey cattle are famous breeds, introduced to many countries. Holidaymakers visit the islands in large numbers during the summer months, travelling by air or by the various passenger boats, especially from Weymouth. English is the official language but French is widely spoken.

ISLE OF MAN

Covering 590 sq km [227 sq mls], the Isle of Man sits in the Irish Sea almost equidistant from County Down and Cumbria, but actually nearer Galloway in Scotland. The uplands, pierced by the corridor valley from Douglas to Peel, extend from Ramsey to Port Erin. Mainly agricultural, the island is now largely dependent on tourism. Douglas, the capital, has over a third of the population. The IOM is a dependency of the British Crown with its own legislative assembly, legal system and tax controls.

NORTH SEA OIL

The discovery of gas and oil in the North Sea in the 1960s transformed Britain from an oil importer into the world's fifth largest exporter within a decade. Gas from the new fields rapidly replaced coal gas in the British energy system, and by 1981 the country was self-sufficient in oil. In the peak production year of 1986, the British sector of the North Sea produced 141.8 million tonnes of crude oil, accounting for over 20% of UK export earnings; in 1994, the UK was the ninth largest producer of crude oil (4% of the world total) with 124 million tonnes. There were also important new discoveries west of Shetland in 1994: the Foinaven and Schiehallion fields could account for 30% of the UK's known reserves.

In taxes and royalties, North Sea oil gave an immense fillip to British government revenue. There was much discussion as to the best use for this windfall money, which was likely to taper away during the 1990s and vanish altogether in the next century; but it certainly helped finance substantial tax cuts during the controversial years of Mrs Thatcher's government. The sight of North Sea oil wealth flowing south to the Westminster treasury also provoked nationalist resentment in Scotland, off whose coast most of the oil rigs (and much of the gas) are located.

the Chilterns then north again into East Anglia to disappear under the edge of the fens near Cambridge. Formerly forested, the downlands were cleared early for pasture and agriculture, and now provide a rich and varied mixture of woodlands, parklands, fields and mostly small settlements. Chalk appears again in the wolds of Lincolnshire and Yorkshire, emerging at Flamborough Head.

Older rocks, predominantly limestones, form the ridge of the Cotswold Hills, and the rolling, hilly farmlands of Leicestershire, the Lincoln Edge (cut by the River Witham at Lincoln), and finally the North York Moors. In these older rocks are rich iron deposits, mined by Cleveland to supply ores for the steel towns of the Tees Estuary until 1964, and still mined in the Midlands.

England is drained by many fine rivers, of which the greatest are the Thames, the Severn, the fenland Ouse, the Trent, and the great Yorkshire Ouse that receives its tributaries from the many picturesque valleys – the Dales – of the Pennine flank. There are many smaller rivers, and a large number of the old towns that dot England at intervals of 20 km [12 mls] or so were built at their crossing points – generally where dry ground existed above marshes and gave firm sites for building.

Agriculture: England has a rich variety of soils, derived both locally from parent rocks and also from glacial debris or 'drift'. During the 12,000 and more years since the ice retreated, soils have been enriched, firstly by such natural processes as flooding and the growth of forests, latterly by the good husbandry of many generations of farmers. Husbandry improved particularly from the 18th century onwards; the Industrial Revolution was accompanied by an agricultural revolution that resulted in massive increases in crop yields and in the quality of livestock.

Through the 18th and 19th centuries farming became more scientific and more specialized; as the demands from the towns grew, so did the ability of English farmers to meet increasing markets for food. The eastern counties, particularly East Anglia and Holderness (now part of Humberside), became the granaries of England, while the rich, wet grasslands of the west and the Midlands turned pastoral – Cheshire cheese is a famous product of this specialization. There were other local products – the hops of Kent and Hereford, the apples of Worcester, and the fine wools that continued to be the main product of the chalk downlands. In south Lancashire potatoes and vegetables became major crops for sale in the markets of the growing northern industrial towns; market gardening and dairying on a small scale developed near every major settlement, taking advantage of the ready market close at hand.

Scenically England still gives the impression of being an agricultural country. Less than 10% of the area is rough moorland, about 5% is forest, and about another 10% is urban or suburban, leaving roughly three-quarters under cultivation of one kind

or another. Yet only 2% of the working population is currently employed in agriculture, a figure that has declined drastically in recent years. Loss of rural populations has been an inevitable result of agricultural rationalization and improvements in farming methods. Those who deplore this trend might reflect that, though English farming formerly employed many more labourers, it supported them at little more than subsistence level.

Industry and urbanization: England had important reserves of coal, the major fields being on either side of the Pennines (Yorkshire, Lancashire, Northumberland and Durham) and in the Midlands (Derbyshire and Nottinghamshire). These coalfields and extensive reserves of iron ore – now largely defunct – were the basis of the Industrial Revolution of the 18th century, and the industrial growth of the 19th century, which together resulted in major changes in the English landscape.

Areas which previously had only small populations rose to industrial greatness. Perhaps the most striking example was Teesside where, following the exploitation of the Cleveland iron ores, the town of Middlesbrough grew from a small port (7,000 population in 1851) to a large manufacturing centre. Today Middlesbrough and its neighbouring settlements have almost 400,000 inhabitants. Similarly, small mill villages in Lancashire and Yorkshire grew into large towns while the West Midlands pottery towns and villages coalesced into the urban areas of Stoke-on-Trent.

Although the coalfields of the north saw the greatest local expansion of population, London and England's other major ports, such as Liverpool and Bristol, also developed as export markets flourished. These developments were accompanied by significant improvements in communications, including the building of an extensive canal network

(with three canals over the Pennines by 1800) and many new roads.

From the 1840s town growth was rapid, and by the end of the 19th century 80% of the population was urban. While the working-class population was mainly housed in slums, the prosperity of the commercial and professional classes was reflected in the

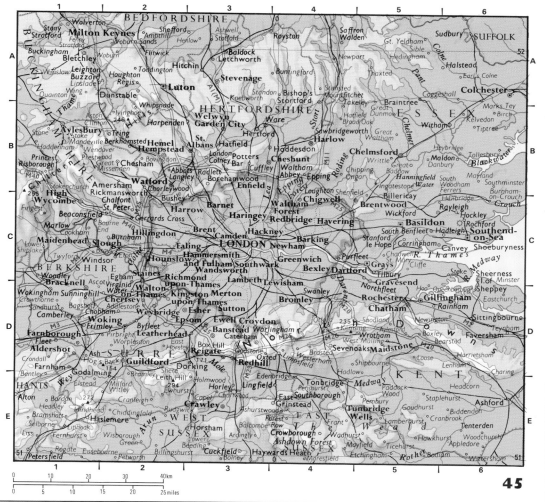

Victorian 'villas' that, in varying degrees of splendour, appeared in select areas of the towns.

This phase of expansion continued until World War I. By the 1930s, however, there were signs that the prosperity of many older and industrial mining areas was threatened and efforts were made to bring new industries to areas of particularly high unemployment, such as the Northumberland and Durham coalfield, West Cumberland, and the South Wales coalfield. In all of these, whole areas had become virtually derelict because their coal was exhausted, or no longer in demand; one such casualty, especially in South Wales, was steam coal for ships, rapidly being replaced by oil.

The main areas of industrial growth since World War I have been around London and also in the West Midlands. A number of towns, for example Coventry, experienced extremely rapid growth. Conscious planning had the aim of controlling industrial expansion and preventing the indiscriminate growth of some towns, for example Oxford and Cambridge.

Today England is a significant steel producer and most of the steel produced is used in other British industries such as shipbuilding and vehicle manufacture – although, as elsewhere in Western Europe, all three industries are currently facing considerable difficulties in the face of strong competition from the Far East and elsewhere. Highly skilled engineering industries are also important and centres include Birmingham, Manchester and Wolverhampton. Textiles are still a major industry, with cotton goods being produced mainly in Lancashire and woollens and worsteds in Yorkshire. Similarly, pottery is still important in the Midlands – though, like most manufacturing in Britain, it is losing out to service industries.

In an age when increased prosperity has spread leisure and the means of travel to millions of people, new emphasis has been placed on recreation. One result is the National Parks scheme, another the many scenic areas under the control of the Countryside Commission and other national bodies. In these areas there are special provisions for conserving the beauty of the English countryside, and creating amenities that help people enjoy them.

Wales

United with England in 1535, Wales still preserves a sense of individuality – a separateness resting on history and sentiment rather than any clear boundary in the countryside. Although only 20% of the population speak Welsh, 75% of the inhabitants do so in the western counties traditionally called Gwynedd and Dyfed. The national sentiment is not only expressed through language, but also through literature, the arts (especially music), sport and political life. Cardiff, the capital, grew rapidly during the 19th century with the iron and steel industry and coal mining, but no Welsh town is centrally

COUNTRY United Kingdom of Great Britain and Northern Ireland
AREA 243,368 sq km [94,202 sq mls]
POPULATION 58,306,000
CAPITAL (POPULATION) London (6,967,000)
GOVERNMENT Constitutional monarchy with a bicameral legislature
ETHNIC GROUPS White 94%, Asian Indian 1%, West Indian 1%, Pakistani 1%
LANGUAGES English (official), Welsh, Scots-Gaelic
RELIGIONS Anglican 57%, Roman Catholic 13%, Presbyterian 7%, Methodist 4%, other Christian 6%, Muslim 2%, Jewish 1%, Hindu 1%, Sikh 1%
CURRENCY Pound sterling = 100 pence
ANNUAL INCOME PER PERSON US$17,970
SOURCE OF INCOME Agriculture 2%, industry 33%, services 65%
MAIN PRIMARY PRODUCTS Oil, natural gas, coal, wheat, fish, sugar
MAIN INDUSTRIES Oil and gas, agriculture, machinery, iron and steel, vehicle manufacture, food processing, textiles, paper, clothing, chemicals, tourism, financial services
MAIN EXPORTS Machinery and transport equipment 35%, rubber, paper and textile manufactures 15%, chemicals and related products 13%, manufactured items 12%, mineral fuels 11%, food, beverages and tobacco 7%
MAIN EXPORT PARTNERS USA 14%, Germany 11%, France 10%, Netherlands 8%, Italy 5%, Belgium–Luxembourg 5%, Ireland 5%

MAIN IMPORTS Machinery and transport equipment 35%, rubber, paper and textile manufactures 18%, manufactured items 14%, chemicals 9%, food and live animals 9%, mineral fuels 6%
MAIN IMPORT PARTNERS Germany 17%, USA 10%, France 9%, New Zealand 7%, South Korea 5%, Japan 5%
EDUCATIONAL EXPENDITURE 5.3% of national budget
DEFENCE 4% of GNP
TOTAL ARMED FORCES 274,800
TOURISM 19,200,000 visitors from abroad (1994), who spent £9,200 million; 23.6 million UK people holidayed abroad.
ROADS 350,407 km [217,733 mls]
RAILWAYS 38,053 km [23,645 mls]
POPULATION DENSITY 240 per sq km [619 per sq ml]
URBAN POPULATION 89%
POPULATION GROWTH 0.1% per year
BIRTHS 14 per 1,000 population
DEATHS 12 per 1,000 population
INFANT MORTALITY 8 per 1,000 live births
LIFE EXPECTANCY Female 79 yrs, male 73 yrs
POPULATION PER DOCTOR 300 people
ADULT LITERACY 99%
PRINCIPAL CITIES (POPULATION) Greater London 6,967,000 Birmingham 1,220,000 Manchester 981,000 Glasgow 720,000 Liverpool 664,000 Leeds 529,000

placed for the whole country; meetings of the boards representing the colleges of the University of Wales – Cardiff, Swansea, Lampeter, Aberystwyth and Bangor – take place at Shrewsbury, an English border town.

Landscape: Wales is predominantly hilly and mountainous, although two-thirds of the rural area is farmland and one-third moorland. The most famous of the highland areas is Snowdonia, now a National Park covering 2,138 sq km [825 sq mls] from Snowdon to Cader Idris. But there are fine upland areas in central Wales, on both sides of the upper Severn Valley which cuts through them to the Dovey Valley and the coastal lowlands facing Cardigan Bay. South of the Severn, in the counties of Powys and Carmarthenshire, the uplands dominate the landscape, and in the Brecon Beacons, south of the Usk Valley on which the old town of Brecon is situated, they provide another National Park, of 1,303 sq km [500 sq mls]. Many of the uplands and high lakes are sources of water for English towns, including Liverpool and Birmingham.

Mining and industry: Some writers on Wales regard the uplands as the country's real heartland, with their sheep pastures and forested valleys, interspersed by farming villages and small towns. But over half the population live in the industrialized area of South Wales, which includes the mining valleys of Glamorgan – all of which ceased to extract coal by the 1990s – and the towns of Newport, Cardiff and Swansea with their traditional heavy metal industries and newer factories for light industry. All are ports, and Cardiff now has many central buildings for the whole of Wales, including the National Museum and the Welsh Office.

No other area of Wales is so heavily dominated by mining and industry as Deeside. Flint and the Wrexham areas are also industrialized, with coalfields now in decline and modern light industries taking their place.

Tourism: Just as the railways stimulated economic growth in South Wales from the 1840s, so on the North Wales coast they stimulated the growth of holiday and residential towns, notably Rhyl, Colwyn Bay and Llandudno. These attracted English residents, many of them retired people from

Lancashire, and the holiday industry boomed. In the motoring age it developed further, so that almost every beach and coastal village had its guest houses, holiday cottages, caravan parks and camping sites. Now tourism has spread to virtually the whole of Wales. In Anglesey, many small places have devoted visitors who favour sailing as well as walking and sea bathing, while this is true also of many ports of the Welsh mainland coast. The south-west has particularly fine scenery, forming the Pembrokeshire National Park, which has a coastal path that is 268 km [167 mls] long.

Wales is rich in scenic attractions. The landscape is dominantly agricultural, with mixed farming, notably for dairying, cattle and sheep. Many upland farmers combine agriculture with the tourist trade, providing guest houses or camping centres. Forestry plantations exist in many upland valleys but the main characteristic is farmland, with country towns placed 20 km [12 mls] or so apart.

Scotland

Scotland is a generally cool, hilly and, in the west, wet country occupying about a third of Great Britain. Physically it can be divided into three parts: the Highlands and Islands, bounded by the edge of the mountains from Stonehaven to the mouth of the Clyde; Central Scotland – sometimes called the central lowland, though it is interspersed by hill ranges; and the Southern Uplands, defined in the north by a fault extending from Dunbar to Girvan, and in the south by the border with England.

The Highlands and Islands: More than half of Scotland's area is in the Highlands and Islands. These are divided by the Great Glen, from Fort William to Inverness, with its three lochs – Lochy, Oich and Ness (where the monster is prone to 'appear' in the tourist season) – linked by the Caledonian Canal. Much of the whisky for which Scotland is famous is produced in the Highlands, notably near the River Spey.

The north-western part of the Highlands has splendid scenery – deep, glaciated valleys dominated by mountains, and only limited areas of farmland, much of it now abandoned.

The financial returns from crofting (small-scale

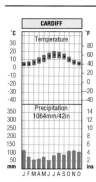

CARDIFF

Winter temperatures are not too cold, the averages for December to February being only 5°C [41°F]; the averages of the lowest in these months is –4 to –2°C [25 to 28°F]. The averages May to October are over 10°C [50°F], and June to August 15°C [59°F] plus. Frost and snow-days are among the lowest in the country. Rainfall at 1,000 mm [39 in] is average for the southern part of the country, falling in all months with a winter peak and on about 180 days per year.

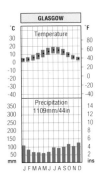

Like most of north-west Europe, Glasgow has a maritime climate with cool summers, mild winters and well-distributed rainfall with an autumn maximum. Variations to the general pattern occur with changes in altitude and proximity to the sea. The Clyde Valley is more sheltered than the estuary where Greenock receives more than 1,500 mm [590 in] of rain annually. At Glasgow rain falls on about 200 days per year. It averages about 3–5 hours of sunshine per day compared to 4–5 hours in the south.

tenant farming) were meagre, and many old croft cottages have become holiday homes. Forests now cover many of the valleys; some of the mountains are deer parks, owned by landlords and let to visitors for seasonal shooting. Railways reach the western coast at Mallaig and Kyle of Lochalsh, from which there are boat services to Skye – now augmented by a controversial new bridge – and the Outer Hebrides. Roads are in part single track with passing places, although they are gradually being improved. At the various villages there are hotels, guest houses and other accommodation for visitors, and the main commercial occupations are fishing and home weaving.

The traditional weaving of Harris tweeds in the Hebrides is now industrially organized, with much of the work done in workshops. Skye has splendid climbing in the Cuillin Hills, and the numerous rivers and lakes are favoured by fishermen. Here, as in the rest of the Highlands, efforts to improve local industries have had some success.

The highland area east of the Great Glen is a richer country, flanked on the east by the lowlands around Aberdeen, which extend into Buchan and then westwards to Moray Firth around Inverness. This is sound farming country, famous for pedigree cattle, and from these lowlands tongues of farmland extend into the valleys of the Dee, Don, Spey and others. Aberdeen and Fraserburgh are major fishing centres. Aberdeen has become increasingly prosperous with the oil extraction from the North Sea, as have many smaller places in the Highlands.

Ben Nevis, at 1,343 m [4,406 ft] dominating the town of Fort William, is the highest summit in the British Isles, and a number of peaks in the Cairngorms, including Ben Macdhui (1,311 m [4,300 ft]), are of almost equal height. Though little known in the past, the Cairngorms have now been developed for winter skiing and summer climbing and fishing. There are still deer forests in the uplands but much of the country is used for sheep farming and tourism. Fort William and a few other centres have industry based on local hydroelectricity – aluminium smelting, for example – but Oban is the main holiday centre in the west.

In the north, the Orkney Islands are connected to Thurso (Scrabster) by boat and also to Aberdeen. Fishing and farming are the main support of the population, with a successful specialization in egg production. The Shetlands have a far harder environment, with craggy hills and limited areas suited to farming, though fishing is prominent, notably at Lerwick. The oil industry has brought great, if temporary, prosperity to some places in these islands.

The Central Lowlands: Scotland's economic heartland includes several ranges of rolling uplands – the Sidlaw Hills north of Dundee, the Ochils south of Perth, and the Pentlands extending in a south-westerly direction from the suburbs of Edinburgh. Most of Scotland's population and industrial activity occurs in this central area, and here too are its two largest cities – Glasgow on innumerable

small glacial hills (drumlins) in the Clyde Valley, and the capital Edinburgh on splendid volcanic ridges, dominated by Arthur's Seat.

Clydeside is still the greatest industrial area of Scotland. Textile industries, engineering and shipbuilding were the basis of the prosperity of Glasgow and its neighbouring towns, which in time grew into one another and held more than a third of Scotland's total population. There is now a wide range of industries in Central Scotland including electronics, printing, brewing and carpet making.

Edinburgh, with its port of Leith, remained much smaller than Glasgow, with only half its population, but is still the administrative centre, and the seat of the main law courts and the National Museum and Library, as well as of many cultural organizations. A favoured centre for retirement in Scotland, it has an increasing tourist trade, particularly during the Edinburgh Festival in the summer. Much of the central area is rich farmland, especially to the east of Edinburgh where the soils have been upgraded by generations of enterprising farmers concentrating on both stock and crops.

The Southern Uplands: Though less spectacular than the Highlands, these include many fine hills, rolling moorlands and rich valleys. From the summit of Merrick (843 m [2,764 ft]) in Galloway can

be seen the Highlands to the north, the plateau of Northern Ireland to the west, and the Lake District, the Pennines and the Isle of Man to the south. The Tweed with its numerous tributaries and – further west – the Esk, Annan, Nith, Ken and Cree provide sheltered valleys for farming, and there is splendid agricultural country in Galloway, where dairying has been particularly successful. Cattle rearing with crop production is more general in the drier east, where many farms specialize in beasts for slaughter. The hills are used for sheep rearing. Some of the towns, notably Hawick and Galashiels, are prominent in the textile industry, especially exports.

Although tourism is relatively less important than in the Highlands, many people come to see the historic centres, such as Melrose and Dryburgh Abbey. To the west, in Galloway, there has been a policy of afforestation on the poorer soils, and several centres have been opened as small museums and educational sites. The coast attracts tourists and Forest Parks, such as that at Glen Trool close to Merrick, have been well laid out for visitors. In the west the towns are small, though there is heavy traffic to Stranraer, the packet station for the shortest sea crossing to Larne in Northern Ireland ■

[For geography of Northern Ireland see page 49.]

1. WEST DUNBARTONSHIRE
2. EAST DUNBARTONSHIRE
3. NORTH LANARKSHIRE
4. CITY OF GLASGOW
5. EAST RENFREWSHIRE
6. RENFREWSHIRE
7. INVERCLYDE
8. CLACKMANNAN
9. FALKIRK
10. WEST LOTHIAN
11. CITY OF ABERDEEN
12. DUNDEE CITY
13. CITY OF EDINBURGH
14. MIDLOTHIAN
15. EAST LOTHIAN
16. NEATH PORT TALBOT
17. RHONDDA CYNON TAFF
18. MERTHYR TYDFIL
19. CAERPHILLY
20. BLAENAU GWENT
21. TORFAEN
22. BRIDGEND
23. VALE OF GLAMORGAN
24. CARDIFF
25. HARTLEPOOL
26. STOCKTON-ON-TEES
27. MIDDLESBROUGH
28. REDCAR AND CLEVELAND
29. KINGSTON UPON HULL
30. CITY & COUNTY OF BRISTOL
31. DARLINGTON
32. STOKE ON TRENT
33. DERBY CITY
34. LEICESTER CITY
35. RUTLAND

36. MILTON KEYNES
37. LUTON
38. THAMESDOWN
39. SOUTHAMPTON
40. PORTSMOUTH
41. BRIGHTON & HOVE
42. BOURNEMOUTH
43. POOLE

The Channel Islands and the Isle of Man are dependencies of the Crown and have their own parliaments. They are not part of the United Kingdom.

The six counties are shown in Northern Ireland. It is divided for local government into 26 districts.

The map shows the 32 unitary authorities in Scotland, the 22 in Wales and the 27 in England as of 1st April 1997.

Capital cities
Administrative Centre
Metropolitan counties (in England)

IRELAND

The Irish flag was first used by nationalists in 1848 in the struggle for freedom from Britain and adopted in 1922 after independence. Green represents the Roman Catholics, orange the Protestants and white stands for peace.

DUBLIC

°C / °F / Temperature / 30 / 20 / 10 / 0 / -10 / -20 / -30 / -40 / 80 / 60 / 40 / 20 / 0 / -20 / -40

Precipitation 762mm/30in / 350 / 300 / 250 / 200 / 150 / 100 / 50 / mm / 14 / 12 / 10 / 8 / 6 / 4 / 2 / ins

J F M A M J J A S O N D

Ireland, open to the Atlantic Ocean, has a mild, damp climate. Humidity is high with frequent fog and low cloud throughout the year. The declining influence of the ocean eastwards is most marked in winter, when temperatures in Dublin are several degrees colder than in the west; rainfall, which is very uniformly distributed throughout the year, is about half that of western coasts that face the prevailing winds off the ocean. Dublin has 762 mm [30 in] rainfall per year, falling on 140 days.

Geographically, Ireland is the whole island west of Britain; the Republic of Ireland (Eire, or the Irish Free State until 1949) comprises the 26 counties governed from Dublin, and Northern Ireland (Ulster) is the six counties that remained part of the United Kingdom from 1921, when the Free State was granted dominion status within the British Commonwealth. Today, the word 'Ireland' is used as political shorthand for the Republic – which occupies some 80% of the island of Ireland.

The original four provinces of Ireland gradually emerged as major divisions from Norman times. Three counties of the present Republic (Donegal, Cavan and Monaghan), together with the six counties which now make up Northern Ireland, formed the old province of Ulster; Connacht, in effect the land beyond the River Shannon, includes the five counties of Leitrim, Sligo, Roscommon, Galway and Mayo; Munster comprises Clare, Limerick, Tipperary, Kilkenny, Waterford, Cork and Kerry; and Leinster consists of the heart of the central lowland and the counties of the south-east (Wicklow, Wexford and Carlow) between Dublin and Waterford harbour.

Landscape

Physically the main outlines of Ireland are simple. In the western peninsulas of Donegal and Connacht ancient rocks were folded to form mountain chains running north-east to south-west; good examples are the fine Derryveagh range of Co. Donegal and the Ox Mountains of Co. Sligo. The highest peaks, for example Errigal, 752 m [2,466 ft], are generally of quartzite, a metamorphosed sandstone. The same trend is seen in the long range, including the Wicklow Mountains, between Dublin Bay and

Waterford harbour in the south-east, and in the Slieve Bloom of the central lowland. The fine east–west ranges of the south, extending from Waterford to the western peninsulas, and the islands of Kerry and West Cork, were formed at a later period. Much of lowland Ireland is floored by rocks contemporary with the coal-bearing measures in England, and these also form some uplands like those around Sligo. Unfortunately these rocks contain little coal; some is mined on a small scale in the Castlecomer area of Co. Kilkenny, and near Lough Allen in the upper Shannon Valley. The basalt lavas that poured out in the north-east of Ireland, forming the desolate Antrim Plateau with its fine scenic cliffs on the famous Coast Road, and the Giant's Causeway, are more recent.

Economy

Agriculture has been the traditional support of the Irish people, though fishing, home crafts and local labouring have been important extra sources of livelihood in the poorer western areas. There is a marked contrast between the richest and the poorest agricultural areas. In the eastern central lowland and the south-east, particularly the lowland areas of Wicklow and Wexford, there are splendid large farms, with pastures supporting fine-quality cattle, sheep, and in some areas racehorses. From Wexford, too, rich farmlands extend through the valleys and lowlands westwards to the counties of Tipperary and Limerick, and from Waterford to Cork and Killarney.

North of the Shannon, in Clare and east Galway, there is intensive sheep and some cattle production; here the glacial deposits are thin and the soils derived from limestones. To the north farming is

COUNTRY Republic of Ireland

AREA 70,280 sq km [27,135 sq mls]

POPULATION 3,589,000

CAPITAL (POPULATION) Dublin (1,024,000)

GOVERNMENT Unitary multiparty republic with a bicameral legislature

ETHNIC GROUPS Irish 94%

LANGUAGES Irish and English (both official)

RELIGIONS Roman Catholic 93%, Protestant 3%

NATIONAL DAY 17 March; St Patrick's Day

CURRENCY Punt = 100 pence

ANNUAL INCOME PER PERSON US$14,128

MAIN PRIMARY PRODUCTS Cereals, potatoes, vegetables, peat, fish, natural gas

MAIN INDUSTRIES Agriculture, food processing, tourism, textiles, clothing, machinery

MAIN EXPORTS Machinery and transport equipment 32%, food and live animals 24%, chemicals 12%

MAIN EXPORT PARTNERS UK 35%, Germany 11%, France 9%, USA 7%, Netherlands 7%

MAIN IMPORTS Machinery and transport equipment 34%, chemicals and related products 12%, foodstuffs 11%, petroleum 5%, clothing 4%

MAIN IMPORT PARTNERS UK 42%, USA 18%, Germany 9%, France 5%, Japan 5%, Netherlands 3%

DEFENCE 1.2% of GNP

TOURISM 3,128,000 visitors per year

POPULATION DENSITY 51 per sq km [132 per sq ml]

LIFE EXPECTANCY Female 78 yrs, male 73 yrs

ADULT LITERACY 99%

PRINCIPAL CITIES (POPULATION) Dublin 1,024,000 Cork 174,000

THE TROUBLES

The Anglo-Irish Treaty of 1921 established southern Ireland – Eire – as an independent state, with the six northern Irish counties, and their Protestant majority, remaining part of the United Kingdom (though Eire's constitution claimed authority over the whole island). Northern Ireland (Ulster) was granted local self-government from the Stormont parliament in Belfast. However, the Protestant majority (roughly two-thirds of the population) systematically excluded the Catholic minority from power and often from employment, despite occasional attacks from the near-moribund IRA – the Irish Republican Army, which had done most of the fighting that led to Eire's independence.

In 1968, inspired by the Civil Rights movement in the southern states of the USA, northern Catholics launched a civil rights movement of their own. But Protestant hostility threatened a bloodbath, and in August 1969 British Prime Minister Harold Wilson deployed army units to protect Catholics from Protestant attack.

Within a short period, the welcome given by Catholics to British troops turned to bitterness; the IRA and many of the Catholic minority came to see them as a hostile occupying force, and there were deaths on both sides. Protestant extremists were quick to form terrorist organizations of their own. In 1971, the British introduced internment without trial for suspected IRA terrorists, removing some of the main security risks from the streets but provoking violent protest demonstrations. In 1972, British troops killed 13 demonstrators in London-

derry, claiming to have been fired upon: the claims were vigorously denied by the demonstrators.

In an attempt to end the alienation of the Catholics, Britain negotiated an agreement with some Protestant politicians to share power in an executive composed of both communities, but the plan collapsed after dissatisfied Protestants staged a general strike. The British government responded by suspending the Stormont parliament and ruling Northern Ireland direct from Westminster. The failure of power-sharing encapsulated the British policy dilemma in Ulster: the Catholics, or most of them, wanted to join the Irish Republic; the Protestants, virtually without exception, did not. Each side bitterly distrusted the other, and long years of sectarian killing only increased the distrust.

The violence continued throughout the 1970s and 1980s, despite a series of political initiatives that included an Anglo-Irish agreement giving the Republic a modest say in Ulster's affairs. Among the conflict's victims were several British politicians, as well as soldiers, policemen, and thousands of ordinary men and women. Armed troops patrolling the streets and almost daily reports of sectarian murders became a way of life. But with the increasing war-weariness of the people, a joint declaration on Northern Ireland was agreed between Britain and Ireland in 1993. Further proposals for a settlement in 1995 led to a resumption of terrorism by the IRA, but talks later resumed to produce a framework for power-sharing which was subsequently approved by referenda in 1998.

mixed, with dairying, meat production, and in some cases specialization on crops such as potatoes and barley. Little wheat is grown; oats are better suited to the damp summer climate.

Farming in much of Ireland is now relatively prosperous, aided by EU grants. The number of people working on the land continues to decline, but that is due to the introduction of machinery, the union of small farms into larger holdings, and the increased opportunities of finding employment in the towns, with overseas emigration still an alternative if not a choice for many Irish workers or families. The tradition of emigration dates back to the great famine of 1846–51, when over a million people fled to Britain and the USA.

Ireland is economically far more prosperous than it was in 1845, when the population of the island numbered 8.5 million. Industrialization only really happened in the north-east, especially Belfast, leaving the Free State an agrarian country from the 1920s. As a result, it has something of a 'Third World' profile: rural (though nearly 29% of the population lives in Dublin and its suburbs), dependent on tourism and, increasingly, high-tech industries such as electronics and pharmaceuticals. Prosperity in the 1960s was followed by a slowdown in growth – when government spending was high – but with a new spirit of economic co-operation the 1980s and 1990s have successfully reversed the trend ∎

NETHERLANDS

The Dutch national flag dates from 1630, during the long war of independence from Spain that began in 1568. The tricolour became a symbol of liberty and inspired many other revolutionary flags around the world.

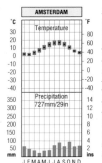

Amsterdam has a climate typical of the coastal margins of north-west Europe. The range of temperature, both daily and annual, is small. Winters are mild with frequent wind and rain from Atlantic depressions. No monthly minimum temperature is below freezing. The prevailing westerly winds which once powered the Dutch wind pumps keep summers cool. Rainfall increases from a spring minimum to a maximum in late summer and autumn, falling on about 130 days per year.

Often, and inaccurately, called Holland – this refers only to the two north-western provinces, where less than 40% of the population lives – the Netherlands is the most crowded country of any size in Europe. Yet the daunting figures for density are only an average: the east and south are relatively sparsely populated, while the figure for the province of Zuid-Holland is 1,080 people per sq km [2,800 per sq ml].

The greatest concentration of population is in the towns and cities of Randstad Holland, a 50 km [31 mls] diameter horseshoe of urban areas, with Dordecht at the centre of the loop. This area, dominant in the Dutch economy, includes most of the major cities, including (clockwise) Hilversum, Utrecht, Dordecht, Rotterdam, The Hague (home of the International Court of Justice), Leiden, Haarlem and Amsterdam, the last still the centre of Dutch cultural life despite being overtaken in size by Rotterdam. Nearly all of this crucial area, rich in history and culture, lies well below sea level.

To anyone travelling westwards from Germany, the Netherlands' density of people is obvious in the landscape, for the fields are smaller, the villages more tightly concentrated with small neat houses, and the land is cultivated more intensively. Over much of the countryside rivers are at a higher level than the surrounding farmland, with villages sited above the flood level.

Seen from the air, most of the Netherlands is made up of richly cultivated fields, mainly rectangular in shape, with water-filled ditches between them along which farmers travel by boat. Control of water is a major problem, for much of the best farmland lies at or below sea level.

Without the protection of dykes and sand dunes along the coast, more than two-fifths of the Netherlands (the 'Low Countries') would be flooded. Constant pumping – formerly by wind pumps (as most picturesque 'windmills' were) and steam pumps, but now by automated motor pumps – lifts surplus water from ditches to canals at a higher level, and from canals to the rivers, particularly the Lek and Waal, which take the waters of the Rhine

to the sea, and the Maas (Meuse in France and Belgium).

The dunes that line much of the coast are carefully guarded against erosion by planting marram grass and, where possible, trees. There are massive dykes to guard the farmland and towns, but in 1953 the exceptionally high tides at the end of January broke through coastal dykes and sand dunes, causing widespread devastation.

For over a thousand years the Dutch have wrested land from the unforgiving North Sea and the process still continues; only in the last 60 years, however, has the balance between reclamation and flooding swung firmly in the people's favour. Since

COUNTRY Kingdom of the Netherlands

AREA 41,526 sq km [16,033 sq mls]

POPULATION 15,495,000

CAPITAL (POPULATION) Amsterdam (1,100,000); Seat of government: The Hague (695,000)

GOVERNMENT Constitutional monarchy with a bicameral legislature

ETHNIC GROUPS Netherlander 95%, Indonesian, Turkish, Moroccan, Surinamese, German

LANGUAGES Dutch (official)

RELIGIONS Roman Catholic 33%, Dutch Reformed Church 15%, Reformed Churches 8%, Muslim 3%

NATIONAL DAY 30 April; Birthday of HM The Queen

CURRENCY Guilder = 100 cents

ANNUAL INCOME PER PERSON US$20,710

SOURCE OF INCOME Agriculture 4%, industry 28%, services 68%

MAIN PRIMARY PRODUCTS Cereals, fruit, vegetables, sugar beet, livestock, fish, oil, gas, salt

MAIN INDUSTRIES Agriculture, food processing, chemicals, iron and steel, clothing and textiles, shipbuilding, printing, diamond cutting, fish

MAIN EXPORTS Machinery and transport equipment 21%, foodstuffs 20%, chemicals and chemical products

MAIN EXPORT PARTNERS Germany 26%, Belgium–Luxembourg 15%, France 11%, UK 11%, Italy 6%

MAIN IMPORTS Machinery and transport equipment 28%, foodstuffs 14%, chemicals 11%, mineral fuels 9%

MAIN IMPORT PARTNERS Germany 26%, Belgium–Luxembourg 15%, UK 8%, France 8%

DEFENCE 2.4% of GNP

TOTAL ARMED FORCES 106,000

TOURISM 6,049,000 visitors per year

ROADS 111,891 km [69,528 mls]

RAILWAYS 2,867 km [1,782 mls]

POPULATION DENSITY 373 per sq km [966 per sq ml]

URBAN POPULATION 89% of population

POPULATION GROWTH 0.37% per year

BIRTHS 13 per 1,000 population

DEATHS 9 per 1,000 population

INFANT MORTALITY 7 per 1,000 live births

LIFE EXPECTANCY Female 81 yrs, male 74 yrs

POPULATION PER DOCTOR 398 people

ADULT LITERACY 99%

PRINCIPAL CITIES (POPULATION) Amsterdam 1,100,000; Rotterdam 1,074,000 The Hague 695,000 Utrecht 546,000 Eindhoven 391,000 Arnhem 308,000

1900 almost 3,000 sq km [1,160 sq mls] have been added to the nation's territory.

The largest and most famous project has been the reclamation of the Zuiderzee, begun in 1920. The major sea barrage of 32 km [21 mls] was completed in 1932, and by 1967 four large 'island' areas were finished, providing some 1,814 sq km [700 sq mls] of former seabed not only for cultivation but also for planned towns and villages. A controversial fifth area, Markerwaard, is under way, leaving the IJsselmeer, a freshwater lake, the only remnant of the original inlet.

The use of land in the Netherlands varies. In the west the concentration on bulb farming is marked near Haarlem in soils of clay mixed with sand. There, too, glasshouse cultivation, combined on many holdings with the growing of flowers and vegetables out-of-doors, is widespread. The Dutch grow and sell more than 3 billion flowers every year.

Much of the produce is exported, some of it by air to London and other north European cities. Some soils are better suited to pastoral farming, with milk, cheese and butter production. In the areas above sea level, farming is varied, with a combination of cattle and crops, including fruit. Gouda has a famous cheese market, and the well-known red-coated round Edam cheeses come from northern areas.

Industry and commerce

Industry and commerce provide support for the greater part of the Dutch population. Mineral resources include china clay, which is abundant, natural gas from the North Sea, and coal, though commercial mining ceased in 1965. The emphasis of modern industry is on oil, steel, chemicals and electrical engineering.

In the area south of Rotterdam a vast port and industrial area, Europoort, has been developed since 1958. Together with Rotterdam's own facilities, the complex is the largest and busiest in the world. The Dutch are skilled at languages, to which a considerable part of the teaching time is given even in primary schools. This is essential to the country's prosperity, for now as in past centuries the Dutch control a main outlet for the commerce of Europe in the port of Rotterdam, with the Rhine Valley and a wider area as its hinterland. The main export markets are the EU partners – Germany, Belgium, the UK and France – while strong trade links with Indonesia recall the Dutch colonial age ■

BELGIUM

The colours of Belgium's flag derive from the arms of the province of Brabant which rebelled against Austrian rule in 1787. It was adopted as the national flag in 1830 when Belgium gained independence from the Netherlands.

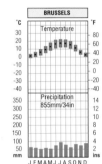

Belgium has a cool temperate maritime climate with the weather systems moving eastwards from the Atlantic. Rainfall is quite heavy in the higher Ardennes plateau with much snow from January to February. At Brussels, no month has a mean temperature below freezing and the summer is pleasantly warm. Temperatures well in excess of 30°C [86°F] have been recorded May to September. The temperatures are lower at all seasons in the higher land to the south of the country.

Throughout a chequered and stormy history as the 'cockpit of Europe', Belgium's fine cities, including Brussels, Ghent and Bruges, have maintained their churches and public buildings, though some have been rebuilt after wars. Following the Napoleonic Wars, from 1815, Belgium and the Netherlands were united as the 'Low Countries', but in 1830, a famous year of ferment in Europe, a National Congress proclaimed independence from the Dutch and in 1831 Prince Leopold of Saxe-Coburg was 'imported from Germany' to become king. At the Treaty of London in 1839 (which the Netherlands also signed), Britain, France and Russia guaranteed the independence of Belgium – and the famous 'scrap of paper' was upheld when Germany invaded Belgium in August 1914. For nearly four weary years the fields of Flanders became the battlefield of Europe.

The division between Belgium and the Netherlands rests on history and sentiment rather than on any physical features. Belgium is predominantly a Roman Catholic country, while the Netherlands is traditionally Protestant (though about 33% of the population are Roman Catholic). Both were neutral in foreign policy, but from 1940 until September 1944 they were occupied by the Nazis.

Since the end of World War II economic progress has been marked, for the geographical advantages Belgium possesses have given it a position of significance in Europe, especially in the EU. The unity of the people, however, is less secure, and by the early 1990s there were growing signs that the fragile alliance which had preserved the nation for so long was beginning to crack.

Of the country's universities, Louvain (Catholic and Belgium's oldest, dating from 1426) provides courses in both Flemish and French; of the universities founded in the 19th century, Ghent (1816) is Flemish and Liège (1817) is French-speaking. At Brussels' Free University (founded in 1834) the courses are mainly in French, but provision is made for Flemish speakers. Gradually the grievances of the Flemish speakers have been removed and in 1974 regional councils were established for Flanders, Wallonia and the Brussels district.

Landscape and agriculture

Physically Belgium may be divided into the uplands of the Ardennes and the lowland plains, which are drained by the Meuse to the Rhine through the Netherlands, and by the Schelde through Antwerp to the North Sea. The Ardennes, rising in Belgium to about 700 m [2,296 ft] at the highest point, is largely moorland, peat bogs and woodland.

Lowland Belgium has varied soils, including some poor-quality sands in the Campine (Kempenland) area near the Dutch frontier, supporting only heaths and woodland. But careful cultivation, sound husbandry and attention to drainage have provided good soils; lowland farming is prosperous, with an emphasis on grain crops, potatoes and vegetables, hops, sugar and fodder beet.

Few hedges exist in the farmed landscape and the holdings are small with intensive cultivation.

THE GREAT DIVIDE

Belgium has always been an uneasy marriage of two peoples: the majority Flemings, speaking a very close relative of Dutch, and the Walloons, who speak French (rather than the old Walloon variation of French). The dividing line between the two communities runs east–west, just south of Brussels, with the capital itself officially bilingual.

Since the inception of the country the Flemings have caught up and overtaken the Walloons in cultural influence as well as in numbers. In 1932 the Belgian government was designated bilingual, and in 1970 the country was effectively splintered into four parts. In the far eastern frontier areas German was the official language; Brussels remained bilingual but its province of Brabant divided; and the other eight provinces were split into four Fleming and four Walloon – with only the dominant language being official.

During the 1980s, as power gradually devolved from the centre to the regions in crucial aspects of education, transport and the economy, the tension between the 'Germanic' Flemings and the 'Latin' Walloons increased in government. The various coalitions of Dutch- and French-speaking Christian Democrats and Socialists – which had held together for more than a decade under the astute stewardship of Prime Minister Wilfried Martens – was seriously undermined by the results of the emergency election of November 1991, with many experts predicting the break-up of the national state into two virtually independent nations by the end of the century. In 1993, Belgium adopted a federal system of government. Each of the regions now has its own parliament, which is responsible for local matters. Elections under this new system were held in 1995.

Traditionally many factory workers of the towns also had a smallholding. There is a small area of polders near the coast, in all less than 500 sq km [200 sq mls], which is rich agricultural land.

Industry and commerce

No minerals other than coal exist in significant quantities and the Belgian emphasis on manufacturing is based on the import of raw materials. The Ardennes includes the country's most productive coalfield (the Campine) in the Sambre-Meuse Valley, centred on the cities of Charleroi and Liège. Charleroi is a coal-mining and metallurgical city while Liège is the centre of the iron industry. The Campine coalfield continues into the Netherlands and Germany, but production has declined in recent years as uneconomic mines have been closed.

Still of major importance, however, is the textile industry, which has existed in the towns of Flanders from medieval times and in its modern form includes a wide range of products. It is associated particularly with Ghent and Bruges, which are equally renowned for their medieval architecture.

It is this part of the country that makes Belgium not only one of Europe's most crowded nations – 332 people per sq km [861 per sq ml] – but the most 'urban' of any reasonably sized independent state, with an official figure of 96.9%.

Belgium's main port is Antwerp, much modernized since 1956. The main industrial centres are served by ship canals, including one of 29 km [18 mls] from Ghent to Terneuzen. Constructed in 1825–7, it can take ships of as much as 67,000 tonnes in capacity. There are canals to Bruges from the North Sea at Zeebrugge, and also to Brussels, both completed in 1922. Barges of 1,510 tonnes capacity can use the 125 km [79 mls] Albert Canal to Liège, opened in 1939, and the Meuse and Sambre are being widened or deepened to take barges of similar capacity. Comparable improvements are being made in the River Schelde between Antwerp and Ghent, and in the Brussels–Charleroi Canal.

COUNTRY Kingdom of Belgium
AREA 30,510 sq km [11,780 sq mls]
POPULATION 10,140,000
CAPITAL (POPULATION) Brussels (952,000)
GOVERNMENT Federal constitutional monarchy
ETHNIC GROUPS Belgian 91% (Fleming 55%, Walloon 32%), Italian 3%, German, French, Dutch, Turkish, Moroccan
LANGUAGES Flemish (Dutch) 57%, Walloon (French) 32%, German 1% – all official languages; 10% of population is officially bilingual
RELIGIONS Roman Catholic 72%, Protestant, Muslim
NATIONAL DAY 21 July; Independent kingdom (1839)
CURRENCY Belgian franc = 100 centimes
ANNUAL INCOME PER PERSON US$21,210
MAIN PRIMARY PRODUCTS Sugar beet, potatoes, livestock, timber, coal
MAIN INDUSTRIES Engineering, iron and steel, petroleum refining, food processing, chemicals, coal, textiles, glassware, diamond cutting
MAIN EXPORTS Vehicles 15%, chemicals 13%, foodstuffs 9%, iron and steel 7%, pearls, precious and semi-precious stones 6%, oil products 3%
MAIN EXPORT PARTNERS France 20%, Germany 20%, Netherlands 15%, UK 8%, USA 5%
MAIN IMPORTS Vehicles and parts 14%, chemicals 10%, foodstuffs 9%, petroleum and petroleum products 7%, non-industrial diamonds 6%
MAIN IMPORT PARTNERS Germany 24%, Netherlands 17%, France 16%, UK 8%, USA 5%, Italy 4%
DEFENCE 1.8% of GNP
TOURISM 3,220,000 visitors per year
POPULATION DENSITY 332 per sq km [861 per sq ml]
INFANT MORTALITY 8 per 1,000 live births
LIFE EXPECTANCY Female 79 yrs, male 72 yrs
ADULT LITERACY 99%

Now, as in past centuries, the lowlands of Belgium, and particularly the city of Brussels (headquarters of the EU, of which Belgium was a founder member), remain a major focus of commercial and political life in Europe ■

LUXEMBOURG

Luxembourg's colours are taken from the Grand Duke's 14th-century coat of arms. The Grand Duchy's flag is almost identical to that of the Netherlands, but the blue stripe is a lighter shade and the flag itself is longer.

Europe's last independent duchy, Luxembourg formed an economic union with Belgium in 1922, extended in 1944 to include the Netherlands under the composite name of Benelux. Luxembourg is a founder member of NATO (1949) and the EEC (1957), and is perhaps best known to Europeans as the host for the Court of the European Communities, the Secretariat of the European Parliament, the European Investment Bank and the European Monetary Co-operation Fund.

Luxembourg consists partly of the picturesque Ardennes, well wooded and famed for its deer and wild boar, but the more prosperous agricultural areas are in the scarplands of Lorraine. Stock rearing, especially of dairy cattle, is important, and crops include grains, potatoes, roots and fruit, and vines in the Moselle Valley. There is also a prosperous iron and steel industry based on rich iron-ore deposits.

Declaring itself a Grand Duchy in 1354, Luxembourg is the only one out of hundreds of independent duchies, which once comprised much of continental Europe, to survive and become a full member of the United Nations. Most Luxembourgers speak both German and French, but the main language is their own Germanic dialect.

With its suburbs, the capital accounts for nearly

COUNTRY Grand Duchy of Luxembourg
AREA 2,590 sq km [1,000 sq mls]
POPULATION 408,000
CAPITAL (POPULATION) Luxembourg (76,500)
GOVERNMENT Constitutional monarchy with a bicameral legislature
ETHNIC GROUPS Luxembourger 71%, Portuguese 10%, Italian 5%, French 3%, Belgian 3%, German 2%
LANGUAGES Letzeburgish (Luxembourgian – official), French, German
RELIGIONS Roman Catholic 95%, Protestant 1%
NATIONAL DAY 23 June; Official birthday of the Grand Duke
CURRENCY Luxembourg franc = 100 centimes
ANNUAL INCOME PER PERSON US$31,780
MAIN INDUSTRIES Iron and steel, banking and financial services, chemicals, agriculture
MAIN EXPORTS Base metals, plastic and rubber manufactures
MAIN IMPORTS Mineral products, base metals and manufactures, machinery, transport equipment
DEFENCE 1.2% of GNP
POPULATION DENSITY 158 per sq km [408 per sq ml]
LIFE EXPECTANCY Female 79 yrs, male 72 yrs
ADULT LITERACY 99%

a third of the country's population. A similar proportion are foreign workers, attracted by opportunities in industry and the many international organizations. Though Luxembourg's population is barely a thousandth of the EU total, it remains a relatively important player in Western European commerce and politics ■

FRANCE

The colours of the French flag originated during the Revolution of 1789. The red and blue are said to represent Paris and the white the monarchy. The present design, adopted in 1794, is meant to symbolize republican principles.

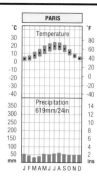

The climate of France is formed from three influences: the Atlantic, the Mediterranean and the continent. With no mountain barriers to affect it, the Atlantic regime extends far inland, giving mild weather with appreciable wind and rain, but little snow. To the east the climate gets warmer, but with colder winters. Towards the mountains and to the south the rainfall increases, snow lying permanently above 3,000 m [12,000 ft]. At Paris, low rainfall is distributed evenly through the year.

A lthough replaced by the Ukraine as Europe's biggest 'country' in 1991, France remains a handsomely proportioned runner-up, well ahead of Spain and more than twice the area of the entire United Kingdom. Yet the nation possesses space as well as size, and while the growth of cities in the years since World War II has been spoken of in terms of crisis (*la crise urbaine*), urban expansion is a problem only in a few special areas, notably Paris and its immediate surroundings. In general, France has stayed predominantly rural.

Many French towns show traces of the country's long history. In the south, for example, at Arles and Carcassonne, there are famous Roman remains. Medieval churches are abundant with splendid cathedrals such as Reims, Amiens and Notre-Dame in Paris. Traces of the period before the 1789 Revolution include the famous châteaux, many of them built or rebuilt in the 18th century, when rich landlords were patrons of the arts.

Frontiers

Frontiers are a natural concern of continental European countries, but of France's 5,500 km [3,440 mls] almost half consists of sea coast and another 1,000 km [620 mls] winds through the mountains of the Pyrenees and the Alps. In general the Pyrenees frontier follows the crest line of the major hills, rather than the watershed between rivers flowing north into France or south into Spain. There are few easy crossings through the Pyrenees into Spain, but good coastal routes exist on the west from Bayonne into the Basque country, and on the east from Perpignan to Gerona.

In the south-east of France, Savoie and the county of Nice were ceded by Italy at the Treaty of Turin in 1860 and in the following year the Prince of Monaco gave Menton and a neighbouring area to France. The cession of Savoie meant that France's territory extended to the summit of Mont Blanc, the highest mountain in Europe outside the Caucasus.

It also gave France part of the shores of Lake

Geneva. Geneva itself is Swiss, but French territory lies within walking distance, and special customs arrangements exist so that people from the French countryside may use the city's trading facilities. North of Geneva the frontier runs through the Jura Mountains to Basle on the Rhine where France, Germany and Switzerland meet. Though Basle itself is in Switzerland, its airport is in France.

North of Basle, for 160 km [100 mls] the border between France and Germany follows the Rhine. Alsace and Lorraine, west of the river, were sought by both countries for centuries, and after the Franco-Prussian War in 1870–1 the whole of Alsace and part of Lorraine were returned to Prussia. This frontier remained until the Treaty of Versailles following World War I, but in World War II it was violated again by the Germans – their third invasion of France in 70 years. The frontiers from the Rhine to the North Sea were defined in their present form during the 18th century.

Local government in France was reorganized during the French Revolution. In 1790 Turgot defined the *départements* as areas in which everyone could reach the central town within one day.

Landscape

Highland France: Most of France lies less than 300 m [1,000 ft] above sea level, but there are several distinctive upland areas. The most impressive are the Alps and the Pyrenees, but they also include the ancient massifs of Brittany and the Central Plateau, the Vosges and that part of the Ardennes which is within France.

The Alps are formed of complex folded rocks of intricate structure, with relief made even more complicated by the successive glaciations of the Ice Age. Areas of permanent snow exist on Mont Blanc and many other high peaks, and visitors to the upper Arve Valley at Chamonix, St-Gervais and other holiday centres have easy access to glaciers. The Alps are visited by tourists throughout the year – in winter for skiing, and in summer for walking on the upland pastures (the original 'alps'). In the French Alps, as in the other alpine areas, hydroelectricity has become universal both for general home use and for industry. The Pyrenees, though comparable to the Alps, lack arterial routes.

The Breton massif includes part of Normandy and extends southwards to the neighbourhood of La Rochelle. In general physical character it is a much dissected hilly area. The Massif Central is more dramatic: it covers one-sixth of France between the Rhône-Saône Valley and the basin of Aquitaine, and its highest summits rise to more than 1,800 m [5,900 ft]; striking examples are Mont du Cantal (1,858 m [6,100 ft]) and Mont Dore (1,866 m [6,200 ft]). Volcanic activity of 10–30 million years ago appears in old volcanic plugs. Earlier rocks include limestones, providing poor soils for agriculture, and coal measures which have been mined for more than a century at St-Étienne and Le Creusot. The Vosges and the Ardennes are areas of poor soil, largely forested.

Lowland France: Although France has striking mountain areas, 60% of the country is less than 250 m [800 ft] above sea level. Fine rivers, including the Rhône, Garonne, Loire and Seine, along with their many tributaries, drain large lowland areas. From the Mediterranean there is a historic route north-

wards through the Rhône-Saône Valley to Lyons and Dijon. North-westwards there is the famous route through the old towns of Carcassonne and Toulouse to Bordeaux on the Gironde estuary, into which the Garonne and the Dordogne flow. This is the basin of Aquitaine, bordered by the Massif Central to the north and the Pyrenees to the south. It is not a uniform lowland – there are several hilly areas and on the coast a belt of sand dunes, the Landes, extending for 200 km [125 mls] from Bayonne to the Gironde estuary.

From Aquitaine there is an easy route to the north, followed by the major railway from Bordeaux to Poitiers, Tours, Orléans and Paris. This lowland is called the Gate of Poitou, though in place of the word 'gate' the French say *seuil* or 'threshold', which is perhaps more appropriate. Crossing the threshold brings the traveller to the Paris basin, in the heart of which is the great city itself.

The ancient centre of Paris lies on the Île de la Cité, where the Seine was easily crossed. The Paris basin is a vast area floored by sedimentary rocks. Those that are resistant to erosion, including some limestones and chalks, form upland areas. The Loire, with its many tributaries in the south-west of the basin, and the Seine, with its numerous affluents (notably the Yonne, Aube, Marne, Aisne and Oise), offer easy routes between the upland areas.

Agriculture

The lowlands of France are warmer than those of England in summer; the cooler winters of the north, with more frost and snow than on the lowlands of England, have little adverse effect on agriculture. Rainfall is moderate, with a summer maximum in the north and a winter maximum in the areas of Mediterranean climate to the south.

Modern improvements in agriculture include the provision of irrigation during the summer months in the south. This has transformed many areas in the Rhône and Durance valleys, and also the coastal lands such as the Crau, south-east of Arles. Without

THE VINEYARDS

While behind Italy in production of both grapes and wine, France remains the drink's spiritual home as well as its greatest per capita consumer. Vines are grown south of a line from Nantes to the Ardennes. In the northern areas they occur on sites with specially favourable climatic qualities, notably good southerly exposure to sunshine; in the southern areas the vine covers a high proportion of the agricultural land.

The threat of disease, the need to preserve the quality of particular named vines, and the necessity of maintaining the export trade all involve government control. Different soils and types of grape, combined with local traditions of treating them, produce a wide range of wines, most of which are consumed locally. In the export market clarets from the Bordeaux area, burgundies from the Rhône Valley south of Dijon, and champagne, an aerated wine from the *pays* of the same name in the Paris basin, are all well known, but there are many other lesser-known wines of which smaller quantities are exported. The quality of the vintage varies each year according to climatic conditions.

irrigation this was a stony, steppelike area; now it supports vast flocks of sheep and has fine hay crops, cut three times a year. Further west in the Camargue, on the Rhône delta, rice is grown with the help of irrigation and there are other areas of rice production close to the Mediterranean. Water comes either from canals, leading into ditches through the fields, or by sprinkler systems from a network of underground pumps; one water point can supply 4 hectares [10 acres].

France's agricultural revolution is far from complete. There are areas where modern technology has made large reclamation schemes possible, but there are still many independent peasant farmers, making a living that is a meagre reward for the labour expended, even with the generous terms of the EU's Common Agricultural Policy (CAP). The younger generation tend to regard emigration to the towns as a more promising way of life.

Alpine areas: In the alpine areas of France, including the Pyrenees, farms are far more numerous on hillslopes having good exposure to sunlight (the *adret*) than on those less favoured (the *ubac*). There are fine upland pastures, apparently retaining their fertility through centuries of use, which provide summer feed for cattle. Although there is still traditional farming in these areas, many people have diversified or emigrated. Some find work in tourist resorts, and many of the old timber-built houses have been bought by people from the cities as holiday homes. The future of peasant farming in mountain areas is a problem that France shares with Switzerland, Austria and Spain.

Mediterranean France: From the French Riviera lowlands extend northwards through the Rhône and Saône valleys and westwards through Languedoc to the neighbourhood of Narbonne. This is the area of Mediterranean climate, having most rain in winter, with wheat, vines and olives as the traditional crops. Wheat is well suited to a Mediterranean climate, for it grows best with a cool, moist period followed by one that is warm and dry. Vines need summer warmth – with temperatures of at least 18°C [64°F] for the greater part of the growing season, and dryness, but not to an excessive degree, during the 70 days from the opening of the buds to maturity. The olive is the traditional tree of the true Mediterranean climate. Originally a native of Egypt, through the

centuries it was planted first in the eastern and later in the western Mediterranean. The ripe, dark purple fruits contain oil, used for cooking; green, unripe olives are commonly used as appetizers.

These three crops are familiar in the south but with them are many more, including maize (the country is the world's fifth largest producer) and a wide range of vegetables. Mediterranean France is not everywhere a land of continuous agriculture, for in places it is interspersed with rocky outcrops unsuited to cultivation but covered with *maquis* or pines. Farmers have made fertile the patches of good soil and adequate moisture, and the general landscape is a mixture of rough hills and limestone pavements surrounding rich areas of cultivation.

Aquitaine: To the west, Aquitaine is not a uniform lowland; the agricultural land is interspersed by hills and plateaus that are generally wooded or left as heathland. It is nevertheless a richly productive area, with arable farming for cereal crops, maize and vegetables, and also pastures for cattle. Aquitaine is also a celebrated wine-producing area, with enormous fields laid out as vineyards. Many of the old farms have disappeared, and even whole villages have been abandoned, for example in the Dordogne, as vines have replaced other, less remunerative crops. Much of the wine is consumed on the home market as the normal *vin ordinaire*, mostly red but including some less favoured whites.

Around Bordeaux the famous claret-producing area includes the Médoc, between the Gironde estuary and the sea: here also are the districts that produce white table wines, such as graves and sauternes. Aquitaine can in fact boast a wide range of red and white wines; several of them, though well known locally, are not exported because the quantity produced is small, and possibly because they do not travel well. Cognac and Armagnac wines are suited to brandy distillation.

Northern France: Northwards from Aquitaine through the lowland Gate (*seuil*) of Poitou, the winters become cooler, with rain in the summer as well as the winter months. Though the summers are cooler in the Paris basin than in Aquitaine, vines flourish on favoured slopes facing south, and many fine French wines come from these northern areas.

As a whole the Paris basin is agriculturally rich, with varied soils. The last Ice Age has left many

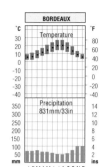

The winters are quite mild and the summers warm; the average temperature for January is 5°C [41°F], and for June to September 18–21°C [64–70°F]. Reasonable rainfall falls fairly evenly throughout the year with a slight maximum in November and December. Rain falls on over 160 days in the year. Snow can fall and there can be 20–35 days with frost each year. The annual amount of sunshine exceeds 2,000 hours, with over seven hours daily April to October.

areas of drifts and windblown soils, here as elsewhere in Europe providing land of great fertility. Between the valleys of the Paris basin lie the *pays*, low plateaus, each with its own characteristics. Some, such as the Beauce, with fertile soils, are suited to crops; others, such as the Sologne, have poor, sandy soils, hard to cultivate and best suited to forest. Local farmers have for centuries adjusted their activity to the qualities of the soil, and now use their specialized production as a basis both for trade with other areas, and for sale in the towns. Despite all the profound changes in French life, the variety of agriculture and land use in the Paris basin remains clear – few areas of the world have so neat a division into units as the *pays* of France.

Finally, to the west of the Paris basin there is the area of ancient rocks covering Brittany and its margins. This area, regarded as archaic but picturesque, has small farms with fields divided by wooded hedges to give a sheltered *bocage* landscape. Rich in medieval churches, old customs and even costumes, it was never of great economic significance. Like Cornwall, in the far south-west of England, it had its own language (still used) and is part of the traditional Celtic west of Europe. There is now increasing pressure for local autonomy in Brittany, expressed particularly in efforts to improve agriculture by upgrading pastures, removing hedges to enlarge fields for animals and cultivation, developing market gardening, and encouraging industrial growth in the towns. Fishing remains a valued resource, while tourism (both from France and neighbouring Europe) brings additional prosperity to Brittany.

Agriculture remains a valued resource in the French economy – France accounts for over 5% of the world's barley and wheat, for example (more of the latter than Canada), and agriculture contributes 17% of export earnings – and politicians make this clear both in Paris and outside France. But there are many changes. In general these appear to reflect the opinion of the American geographer, Isaiah Bowman, that 'man takes the best and lets the rest go'. Poor land is abandoned, perhaps for forest, but promising areas are made rich through investment. Improvements such as drainage, irrigation

COUNTRY French Republic	IMPORTS US$3,427 per person
AREA 551,500 sq km [212,934 sq mls]	**MAIN IMPORTS** Machinery and transport equipment 32%, chemicals 11%, food and live animals 10%, petroleum and petroleum products 8%, textile yarns and fabrics 3%, iron and steel 3%
POPULATION 58,286,000	
CAPITAL (POPULATION) Paris (9,469,000)	
GOVERNMENT Republic with a bicameral legislature	
ETHNIC GROUPS French 93%, Arab 3%, German 2%, Breton 1%, Catalan 1%	**MAIN IMPORT PARTNERS** Germany 20%, Italy 12%, Belgium 9%, UK 7%, USA 7%, Netherlands 6%, Japan 4%
LANGUAGES French (official), Arabic, Breton, Catalan, Basque	**EDUCATIONAL EXPENDITURE** 23% of national budget
	DEFENCE 3.4% of GNP
RELIGIONS Roman Catholic 86%, other Christian 4%, Muslim 3%	**TOTAL ARMED FORCES** 466,300
	TOURISM 60,000,000 visitors per year
NATIONAL DAY 14 July; Fall of the Bastille (1789)	**ROADS** 804,765 km [500,055 mls]
CURRENCY Franc = 100 centimes	**RAILWAYS** 34,647 km [211,528 mls]
ANNUAL INCOME PER PERSON US$22,360	**POPULATION DENSITY** 106 per sq km [274 per sq ml]
SOURCE OF INCOME Agriculture 3%, industry 29%, services 69%	**URBAN POPULATION** 73%
	POPULATION GROWTH 0.4% per year
MAIN PRIMARY PRODUCTS Crude petroleum, natural gas, bauxite, iron ore, agricultural products, lead, zinc, potash	**BIRTHS** 13 per 1,000 population
	DEATHS 10 per 1,000 population
MAIN INDUSTRIES Aluminium, plastics, synthetic fibres and rubber, agriculture, wool, yarn, forestry, fishing, vehicles, steel, cement, paper, petroleum products	**INFANT MORTALITY** 7 per 1,000 live births
	LIFE EXPECTANCY Female 81 yrs, male 73 yrs
	POPULATION PER DOCTOR 333 people
EXPORTS US$3,185 per person	**ADULT LITERACY** 99%
MAIN EXPORTS Machinery and transport equipment 35%, basic manufactures 18%, chemicals and related products 14%, food and live animals 11%	**PRINCIPAL CITIES (POPULATION)** Paris 9,469,000 Lyons 1,262,000 Marseilles 1,087,000 Lille 959,000 Bordeaux 696,000 Toulouse 650,000 Nantes 496,000 Nice 516,000 Toulon 438,000 Grenoble 405,000 Rouen 380,000 Strasbourg 388,000
MAIN EXPORT PARTNERS Germany 17%, Italy 12%, Belgium 9%, UK 9%, USA 7%, Netherlands 5%, Spain 5%	

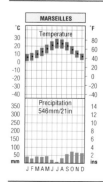

The Mediterranean climate extends over the south-east, pushing northwards into the Rhône Valley and into the mountain foothills, and over Corsica. The winters are very mild, with snow and frost a rarity. The summers are dry and the rain falls mainly September to March but on only around 75 days per year. One feature of the area is its peculiar winds, notably the Mistral, a cold, dry and strong wind which blows southwards during winter and spring, causing crop damage.

and scientific fertilization in some areas counterbalance the decline in agriculture elsewhere, such as in the Alps and the Pyrenees. Loss of people from the land does not indicate a decline in agricultural production but rather an improvement in agricultural efficiency, and the freedom of people, no longer tied to the land, to seek, and generally to find, alternative and more satisfying employment.

Forests

Forests cover one-fifth of France. Most of them are on soils of poor quality, including the sands in parts of the Paris basin, the Vosges and the Landes between Bordeaux and the Spanish frontier, the poor limestones of Lorraine and the clay-with-flints of Normandy. Some of the great forests were planted by landowners as parts of their estates, like those of Fontainebleau and Rambouillet near Paris; others

were planted as barriers between former kingdoms, such as those between Normandy and Picardy.

The greatest single forested area in France is the Landes, covering 10,000 sq km [3,860 sq mls]. This is mainly coniferous forest, interspersed only here and there by farms. Since 1956 attempts have been made to reclaim and replant the extensive areas devastated by fire, and to substitute a more varied rural economy for the exclusive exploitation of the pine forests. In the Alps and the Pyrenees about a quarter of the land is covered with forest.

In France two-thirds of all the woodlands are of deciduous trees, compared with less than a third in Germany, and about 60% of the country's timber, especially for paper pulp-making, has to be imported. Since World War II various laws have been passed to encourage softwood production.

Farms revert to waste when they are no longer

cultivated, and become impenetrable thickets of vegetation. Through most of France this vegetation is known as *maquis*, from the shelter it gives to fugitives: the term *maquis* was given in World War II to the resistance forces in hiding. In dry summers the risk of fire is considerable, especially in the south.

Resources and industry

France is a declining but still significant producer of iron ore (mostly from Lorraine), and several other minerals are also mined, including bauxite, potash, salt and sulphur. There are old coalfields in the north-east, but the output of these does not meet the country's needs. France instead switched to new sources of energy, including experiments with solar power in the Pyrenees and the world's first major tidal power station on the Rance estuary in Brittany, but more significantly utilizing the water of the

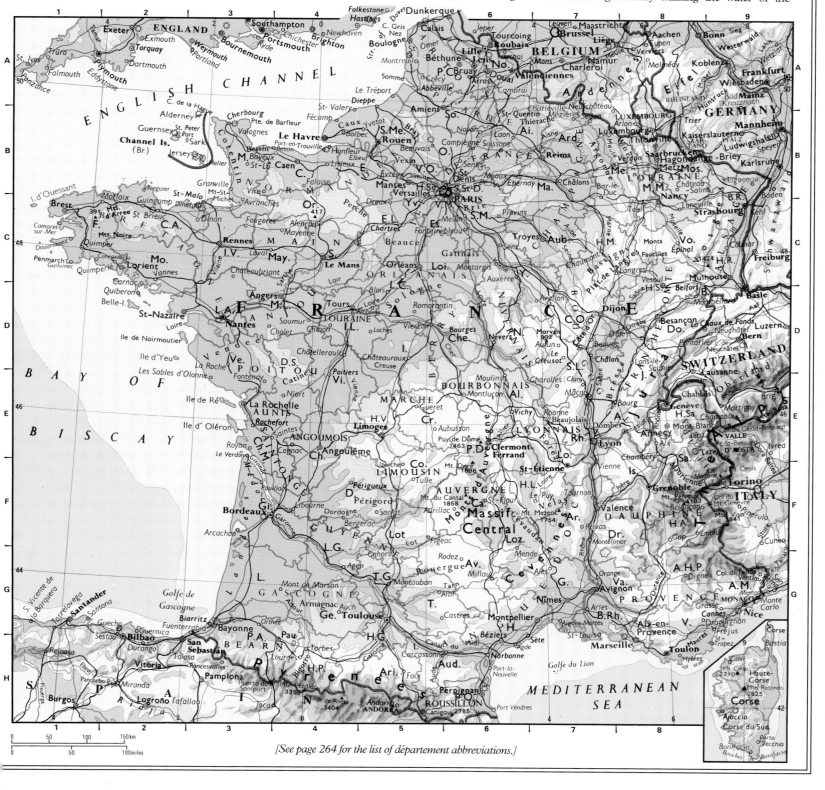

[See page 264 for the list of département abbreviations.]

mountains for hydroelectric power (24% of output) and mined uranium – 5.3% of world production – to make France, after Lithuania, the second highest producer of electricity from nuclear power in the world (75.3% by 1994).

Since World War II the marked industrial expansion in France has been accompanied by a change in the distribution of population. Before the war France was regarded as a country with a fairly even distribution of population between town and country, but from the late 1940s there was a spectacular increase in the urban population. In the first postwar planning period, 1947–53, industrial production rose by 70%, agricultural production by 21% and the standard of living by 30%.

During the following three years there was further expansion, particularly in the chemical and electrical industries. In the period of the third plan, 1958–61, the success of export industries became notable, especially in such products as automobiles, aircraft and electrical goods. In this period, too, natural gas was discovered at Lacq, and such industries as chemicals and aluminium smelting prospered. However, traditional industries, such as textiles and porcelain, are still important, and despite technological innovation and success, France is still weak in 'high-tech' areas compared to Japan, the USA and several European rivals.

Nevertheless, the country's postwar transition to a prosperous, dynamic society has been rapid and pronounced. French life is still focused to a large degree on Paris, where traditional luxury industries, such as perfumes, thrive alongside commerce, light industry, heavy industry and services of all kinds. Virtually all the major French commercial enterprises have their headquarters in Paris – and Paris and district now has almost a fifth of the total population.

The other important industrial centres are on and around the mining areas, and at or near the major ports where imported raw materials are used: Fos, west of Marseilles, for example, and the steel complex at Dunkerque. The aims of modern planning include the development of regional prosperity, based on such centres as Lyons, Marseilles, Toulouse, Nantes, Lille, Nancy and Strasbourg, home to the European parliament. While the industrial attraction of the Paris area remains powerful and population growth continues to exceed that of the second largest urban area, the district around Lyons, the traditional centralization of France is showing signs of weakening and governments of both complexions have sought to reduce state power both in local affairs and the economy.

Modern economic planning in France has been pursued at a time of great difficulty, which included the loss of the colonial territories in North Africa and South-east Asia, as well as the period of unrest in the 1960s, not only in the universities but throughout the country. Consumer industries have prospered, but some critics say that there is still inadequate provision for social services, including housing. Since World War II, there has been agitation about the poor standard of housing throughout France, both rural and urban, much of it obsolete and without basic amenities. Rapid urban growth has resulted in overcrowding and even the growth of poorly built new districts to house immigrants, especially those from Spain and North Africa. The 4 million underprivileged workers from the Maghreb countries have proven to be a difficult political issue in the 1990s.

Achieving expansion and prosperity over the whole country has not been easy. In France, as in most other countries, there remains a disparity

CORSICA

Annexed by France from Genoa in 1768 – just months before the birth of Napoleon Bonaparte, its most famous son – Corsica lies 168 km [105 mls] from France and just 11 km [7 mls] from Sardinia, which is Italian territory. Corsica is divided into two *départements* of France, with its administrative centre at Ajaccio on the west coast. Roughly oval in shape, it is 190 km [118 mls] long and half as wide, with a population of 240,178.

Most of the island is formed of rugged mountains, some reaching to over 2,710 m [8,890 ft]. Only a quarter of Corsica provides rough grazing for sheep and goats; another quarter is in forests with evergreen oak and cork oak to 650 m [2,000 ft], then chestnuts with beech followed by pines to the tree line, between 1,600 and 2,000 m [5,000–6,000 ft]. In winter there is heavy snow on the mountains.

Only 2% of the island is cultivated, mainly in the valleys, on terraced hillsides or on the discontinuous fringe of alluvial lowland along the coasts. Fishing is a primary activity and industries include tunny and lobster canning, chiefly at Ajaccio and Bastia, the two main towns – though tourism is now the principal earner. Separatist terrorist movements are still sporadically active in some areas.

between the richer and poorer areas; for France this is between the east and the west, the richest of all being in closest touch with the great industrial complexes of Germany and the Benelux countries. Though often devastated in European wars, this always emerges in peacetime as one of the most prosperous corners of France ■

MONACO

An independent state since AD 980, Monaco has been ruled by the Grimaldi family since 1297. The colours of the flag, which was officially adopted in 1881, come from the Prince of Monaco's coat of arms.

COUNTRY Principality of Monaco
AREA 1.5 sq km [0.6 sq mls]
POPULATION 32,000
CAPITAL Monaco
LANGUAGES French and Monégasque (official)

The world's smallest nation outside Rome, and by far its most crowded, the tiny principality of Monaco – comprising a rocky peninsula and a narrow stretch of coast – has increased in size by 20% since its land reclamation programme began in 1958. A densely populated modern city-state, it derives its considerable income almost entirely from services: banking, finance, and above all tourism; this is based not just on its Riviera climate but also

on the famous casino. Monégasques are not allowed to gamble there, but there is ample compensation in paying no state taxes.

Monaco has been ruled by the Grimaldi dynasty since 1297, though in 1815 (with the Treaty of Vienna) it came under the protection of the Kingdom of Sardinia; the greater part, including Menton, was annexed by France in 1848 and the remainder came under its protection in 1861 – a situation that

essentially survives today within a customs union. The present monarch, Prince Rainier III (ascended 1949), drew up a new liberalizing constitution in 1962.

Monaco falls into four districts: holiday-oriented Monte Carlo; the old town of Monaco-Ville, with royal palace and cathedral; the shops, banks and smart houses of La Condamine; and the light industries and marinas of Fontvieille ■

GERMANY

The red, black and gold, dating back to the Holy Roman Empire, are associated with the struggle for a united Germany from the 1830s. The horizontal design was officially adopted for the FRG in 1949, and accepted by 'East Germany' on reunification.

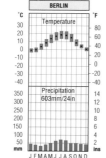

The climate of northern Germany is due mainly to the weather coming in from the Atlantic. January and February are the only months with mean temperatures just below 0°C [32°F], and the summers are warm. Rainfall is moderate, 500–750 mm [20–30 in], falling in all months. Humidity is always high with fog in the autumn and winter can be overcast for long periods. Snow lies for long spells inland and in the hills. When the winds blow from Scandinavia very cold weather follows.

The German Empire that was created under Prussian dominance in 1871, comprising four kingdoms, six grand duchies, five duchies and seven principalities, and centred on the great imperial capital of Berlin, was to last for fewer than 75 years. Even at its greatest extent it left large areas of Europe's German-speaking population outside its boundaries, notably in Austria and large parts of Switzerland. Following the fall of Hitler in 1945, a defeated Germany was obliged to transfer to Poland and the Soviet Union 114,500 sq km [44,200 sq mls] situated east of the Oder and Neisse rivers, nearly a quarter of the country's pre-war area. The German-

speaking inhabitants were expelled – as were most German-speaking minorities in the countries of Eastern Europe – and the remainder of Germany was occupied by the four victorious Allied powers.

The dividing line between the zones occupied by the three Western Allies (USA, UK and France) and that occupied by the USSR rapidly hardened into a political boundary dividing the country. In 1948 West Germany was proclaimed as the independent Federal Republic of Germany (FRG), with a capital at Bonn (deemed 'provisional' pending hoped-for German reunification), and measuring 248,000 sq km [96,000 sq mls]. East Germany be-

came the German Democratic Republic (GDR), a Soviet satellite of 108,000 sq km [41,700 sq mls]. Berlin was similarly divided, the three western sectors of an enclave of occupation becoming 480 sq km [186 sq mls] embedded in the territory

of the GDR, of which the Soviet-occupied East Berlin was deemed to be capital.

On reunification, West and East Germany moved from the ninth and 15th biggest countries in Europe to a combined fourth – still much smaller than France, Spain and Sweden – but with the independence of the Ukraine the following year dropped back to fifth. It is, nevertheless, 12th in the world in terms of population.

Landscape

Germany extends from the North Sea and Baltic coasts in the north to the flanks of the central Alps in the south. The country includes only a narrow fringe of Alpine mountains, with the Zugspitze (2,963 m [9,721 ft]) the country's highest peak. There is, however, a wide section of the associated Alpine foreland bordering Switzerland and Austria, stretching northwards from the foothills of the Alps to the Danube River. The foreland is largely covered by moraines and outwash plains which, with many lakes, including the Bodensee (shared with Switzerland), are relics of the glacial age, and reminders of the many more glaciers that have emerged from the Alpine valleys.

The central uplands of Europe are more amply represented, occupying a broad swathe of Germany. Four types of terrain are found. Block mountains are remnants of pre-Alpine fold mountains shattered and reshaped by the later earth movements. The Harz, Thüringer Wald and Erzgebirge (Ore Mountains) massifs rise above a varied scarpland terrain, notably the Thüringian Basin, which has the fertile Erfurt lowland at its heart.

Uplift was greatest in the south, close to the Alps, producing the Schwarzwald (Black Forest) and Böhmerwald. Between these great blocks of forested mountains are open basins of sedimentary rocks, their resistant bands picked out by erosion as in the magnificent scarp of the Schwäbische Alb, overlooking the Neckar basin.

A third kind of country is provided by down-faulted basins filled with softer deposits of more recent age, notably the Upper Rhine plain between Basle and Mainz. Earth movement and eruptions produced a fourth element, such volcanic mountains as the Vogelsberg and the hot and mineral springs that gave rise to the famous spas. Here is Germany at its most picturesque, with baronial castles on

wooded heights, looking down over vineyards to clustered villages of half-timbered houses, whose occupants still cultivate open-field strips as they have done for centuries.

The northern lowlands, part of the great North European Plain, owe their topography mainly to the retreat of the ice sheets. The most recent moraines, marked by forested ridges that may include good boulder-clay soils, are restricted to Schleswig-Holstein. The rest of the lowland is covered with leached older moraine and sandy outwash, so that in many places soils are poor. The glacial period also left behind loess, windblown dust deposited along the northern edge of the central uplands and in basins within them, providing some of the country's best soils for wheat, malting barley and sugar beet. This belt broadens in the lowland of Saxony around Halle and Leipzig.

The coast is also the product of glaciation and subsequent changes. The low Baltic shore is diversified by long, branching inlets, formed beneath the ice of the glacial period and now beloved by yachtsmen, while inland the most recent moraines have left behind a confused terrain of hills and lakes, but also areas of good soil developed on glacial till. The movement of water around the edge of the ice sheets carved stream trenches (*Urstromtäler*), south-east to north-west; these are now in part occupied by the present rivers, and have also proved convenient for canal construction. The North Sea is fringed by sandy offshore islands, the products of a beach bar now breached by the sea.

Agriculture

Over a quarter of Germany is forested, with particular concentration in the Alps, the massifs of the central uplands, and the poorer areas of the northern lowland. It is amazing that this economically most advanced country has some of Europe's smallest farms, particularly characteristic of southern Germany. Most are used for arable-based mixed farming, with minor livestock enterprises. In the warmer basins tobacco, vegetables and, increasingly, maize are grown. Vineyards and orchards clothe the slopes of the Rhine and its tributaries. Much larger wheat and sugar-beet farms with important livestock enterprises are characteristic of the loess soils on the northern edge of the central uplands. The Bavarian Alpine foreland in the south, and

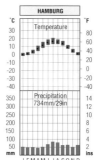

Average temperatures, December to March, are low and frost is usual on over 50 days in this period. The spring is late. The summers are pleasantly warm, the highest recorded temperatures being 34–35°C [93–95°F] in July and August, the averages being 16–17°C [61–62°F]. Moderate rainfall is fairly evenly distributed through the year with a slight peak in July and August. Rain falls on nearly 200 days in the year. Fog is frequent and winter sunshine totals are low.

Schleswig-Holstein in the north, are other areas of above-average farm size. The sandy northern lowland, which used to support a poor agriculture based on rye, potatoes and pigs, increasingly specializes in intensive meat and poultry production. Dairy specialization is typical of the milder north-west and the Alpine fringes.

Because of the generally small size of holdings many farmers seek a supplementary income outside agriculture – often a halfway stage to giving up agriculture altogether. Persons employed in agriculture, who were a quarter of the employed population of the FRG in 1950, accounted for well below 10% on reunification four decades later. With this movement out of agriculture, the average size of holding is steadily but all too slowly rising.

In the GDR, by contrast, all agricultural holdings were brought into 'co-operatives', many of over 500 hectares [1,236 acres] and some up to ten times that size. The East German government's version of the collective farm proved much more efficient than the equivalent in many other Communist states, however, and the economic outlook was quite promising prior to reunification.

As with industry, Germany's world rankings in agricultural production are impressive: third in rye (over 11% of the world total), sugar beet (10%), cheese (9.5%) and pork (5%), and fourth largest producer of barley (7%), butter (7%), milk (6%) and oats (5%). Also important are potatoes, beef and veal.

Minerals and energy

Germany is the most important coal producer of continental Western Europe, though output from the Ruhr, Saar and Aachen fields has dropped since

THE REUNIFICATION OF GERMANY

In 1945, a devastated Germany was divided into four zones, each occupied by one of the victorious powers: Britain, France, the USA and the Soviet Union. The division was originally a temporary expedient (the Allies had formally agreed to maintain German unity), but the Russians published a constitution for the German Democratic Republic in 1946. The split solidified when the Russians rejected a currency reform common to all three Western zones. The German Federal Republic – 'West Germany' – was created in 1949.

Throughout the years of the Cold War, as NATO troops faced Warsaw Pact tanks across the barbed wire and minefields of the new frontier, the partition seemed irrevocable. Although both German constitutions maintained hopes of re-unification, it seemed that nothing short of the total war both sides dreaded could bring it about. The West, with three-quarters of the population, rebuilt war damage and prospered. The East was hailed as the industrial jewel of the Soviet European empire, though some of its people were prepared to risk being shot to escape westwards. By the late 1980s it was clear that the Soviet

empire was crumbling. In the autumn of 1989, thousands of East Germans migrated illegally to the West across the newly open Hungarian border and mass demonstrations in East German cities followed. At first, the government issued a stream of threats, but when it became clear that there would be no Soviet tanks to enforce its rule, it simply packed up. With the frontiers open, it became clear that the 'successful' East German economy was a catastrophic shambles, a scrap-yard poisoned by uncontrolled pollution, with bankruptcy imminent. The choice facing German leaders in 1990 was starkly simple: either unite East and West, or accept virtually the entire Eastern population as penniless refugees.

The West German government, led by Chancellor Helmut Kohl, acted quickly, often bullying the weaker Easterners. The Western Deutschmark became the common currency, and on 3 October 1990 – more than 45 years after Germany had lost the war – the country was formally reunited. However, the costs of restructuring the economy of the East are high, and the German people will be paying them for many years to come.

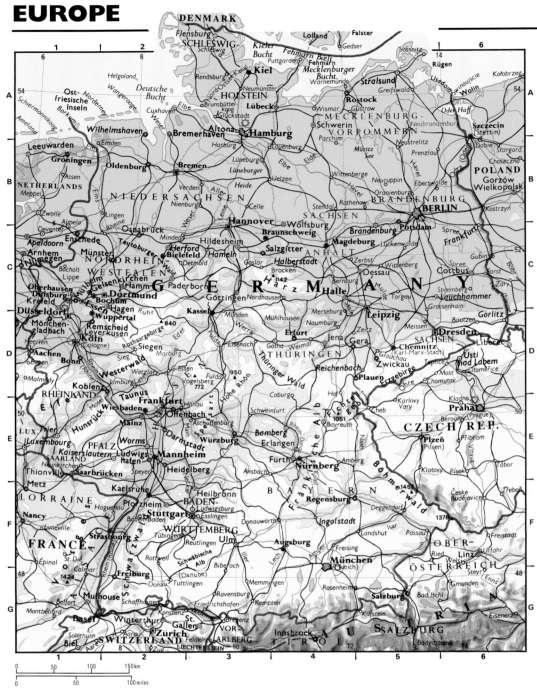

desert' created by Parisian centralization is striking.

When industrial growth came in the 19th century, heavy industry naturally concentrated in the Ruhr and Saar coalfields, but thanks to the railways other production could disperse widely to these existing towns. Since 1945 the Ruhr and Saar coalfields have been undergoing a difficult period of conversion, owing to the problems of the now declining coal, steel and heavy engineering industries. Western Europe's largest industrial region, stretching from Duisburg to Dortmund, the Ruhr ('the forge of Germany') has seen its mines for top-grade coking coal cut from 145 to less than 20 and has been forced to diversify – the western end into petrochemicals based on the Rhine ports and pipelines, the east into lighter and computer-based industry.

By contrast, towns away from the coalfields, especially the great regional capitals of southern Germany, have flourished with the inauguration of modern industries (motor vehicles, electrical equipment, electronics), the growth of administrative and office work, and the division among a number of cities of capital functions formerly in Berlin.

As an advanced industrial country of western type, the role of East Germany within the Soviet-bloc states was to provide technically advanced equipment, receiving in return supplies of raw materials and semi-finished products such as steel. Because of industrial inertia, the location of the important machine-building industry had not greatly changed since capitalist times, being heavily concentrated in and around the southern cities of Leipzig, Chemnitz (then Karl-Marx-Stadt) and Dresden. Other centres were Magdeburg and East Berlin, the leading producer of electrical equipment.

The GDR inherited a traditional strength in precision and optical industries, mostly located in Thüringia (such as the famous Zeiss works at Jena), the base for important developments in industrial instrumentation and electronics. The government tried to steer some major new developments into the rural north and east of the country, including shipbuilding at Rostock – also the site of a new ocean port, to avoid the use of facilities in the FRG – oil refining and chemicals at Schwedt, and iron smelting and steel rolling at Eisenhüttenstadt.

While the inner parts of the greatest cities have tended to lose population, their suburbs and satellites have exploded across the surrounding countrysides, forming vast urban areas of expanding population. In the west and south of the country, an axis of high population growth and high density stretches from the Rhine-Ruhr region (largest of all but checked in expansion by the problems of Ruhr industry) through the Rhine-Main (Frankfurt), Rhine-Neckar (Mannheim-Ludwigshafen) and Stuttgart regions to Munich. In the east and north the densely populated areas are more isolated, centred on Nuremberg, Hanover, Bremen, Hamburg, Dresden, Leipzig and of course Berlin.

the mid-1950s, owing mainly to competition from oil. Some oil and gas is home-produced, mainly extracted from fields beneath the northern lowland, but most of the oil consumed in Germany is delivered by pipeline from Wilhelmshaven, Europoort and the Mediterranean to refineries in the Rhineland and on the Danube.

Brown coal (lignite) is excavated between Cologne and Aachen, but the former GDR (East Germany) was unique in depending for energy supply on this source of low calorific value, economically mined in vast open pits. The older centre of mining was in the lowland of Saxony, between Halle and Leipzig, but the main area of expansion is now in Niederlausitz, south of Cottbus. Brown coal is increasingly reserved for electricity generation, although atomic plants built on the coast and principal rivers are expected to be of increasing importance, with hydroelectric stations concentrated in the Bavarian Alps. Energy needs and feedstock for the important chemical industry around Halle are met by oil brought by pipeline from the former Soviet republics or by tanker through Rostock. The other mineral resource of value is

potash, mined south of the Harz; Germany is the world's third largest producer. The non-ferrous metallic ores of the Harz and other massifs of the central uplands are no longer of great significance, while imported high-grade iron ores have proved more economic than the home ores of the Siegen and Peine-Salzgitter districts.

Settlement and industry

From Neolithic times the core settlement areas of Germany were the fertile lowlands – areas like the northern edge of the central uplands in Lower Saxony and Westphalia, the Upper Rhine plain, the Main and Neckar basins, and the Alpine foreland. From these core areas land-hungry medieval peasants advanced to clear large areas of forest in the uplands, and also streamed eastwards to settle in lands beyond the Elbe and Saale.

The fragmentation of the Holy Roman Empire into a swarm of competing states had a positive side in the founding and fostering by local rulers, large and small, of a dense system of towns, among them future regional capitals like Hanover, Stuttgart or Munich (München). The contrast with the 'French

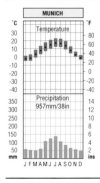

In the south the climate is a little warmer in the summer and slightly colder in winter. It is also wetter, Munich receiving nearly twice as much rain as Berlin. Further south it is even wetter with more snow. The rainfall is much heavier in the summer months. The coming of spring is much earlier in the Rhine Valley and the south. The Föhn wind gets its name from this area. It is a dry warm wind that blows northwards from the Alps, mainly in the summer.

Since 1950 there has been a tendency for the West's population to drift towards the more attractive south. Urban population losses have in part been made up by immigrant workers (nearly 2.5 million at their peak in the early 1970s, with Turkey the principal source), increasingly joined by their families to supplement a German native population – which at the end of the 1960s entered a period of negative growth.

Germany's wary neighbours, fearing that a nation suddenly swollen to nearly 80 million through reunification could swamp Europe, could rest easy. According to a report from the Institute of German Economy, published in 1992, there will be 20 million fewer Germans alive than today by the year 2030, and on current trends the number of young people below the age of 15 will drop from 13.7 million in 1990 to 10 million in 2010. The findings suggested that, as a result, the country would need at least 300,000 new immigrants a year to fill the gap in its labour market.

Communications

Germany has the advantage of the superb Rhine waterway, which from its Alpine sources cuts right across the central uplands to the North Sea. A combination of summer snowmelt from the Alps and autumn–spring rainfall in the central uplands gives it a powerful and remarkably even flow – if increasingly polluted. Although traffic is at its most intensive between Rotterdam and the Rhine-Ruhr region, where Duisburg is the largest inland harbour of Europe, standard 1,350-tonne self-propelled barges can reach Basle. The Rhine–Main–Danube waterway has also opened a through-route to Eastern Europe and the Black Sea, while for north German traffic the Mittelland Canal, following the northern edge of the central uplands, opens up links to the north German ports and Berlin. Unusually for Europe, Germany's rivers and canals carry as much freight as its roads.

Hamburg is Germany's biggest seaport, followed by Bremen with its outport, Bremerhaven. All German ports suffer by being too far from the main centre of European population and economic activity in the Rhinelands; the Belgian and Dutch ports are at a great advantage being closer.

Germany was the first European country to build motorways (Hitler's *Autobahns*, built in the 1930s),

and also enjoys an efficient if highly subsidized railway network. Both are crucial to a country which, on reunification, increased its land borders from nine to ten countries. Air travel, too, both internal and international, is increasingly important.

Administration

The system of powerful federal states (*Länder*) created in the FRG after World War II remained remarkably stable, though huge disparities of size have remained in spite of various reform proposals. Bavaria has by far the largest area, and North Rhine-Westphalia, with the Rhine-Ruhr region at its heart, has the largest population, over a fifth of the German total. At the other extreme are the 'city-states' of Bremen and Hamburg, though Saarland is also small.

In 1990 the ten *Länder* of the FRG (excluding the enclave of West Berlin) were joined by the five rejuvenated old states of the GDR – Brandenburg, Mecklenburg-West Pomerania, Saxony, Saxony-Anhalt and Thüringia – plus the new 'united' Berlin. The East German organization had been very different, the country politically divided into 15 administrative districts (*Bezirke*) under the control of the central government in East Berlin.

The cost of unification

The stability of the federal system may well come under considerable strain in the early years of the reunited Germany. The phenomenal and sustained rise of the FRG from the ashes of World War II to become the world's third biggest economy and its largest exporter – the so-called *Wirtschaftswunder*, or 'economic miracle', accomplished with few natural resources – was already levelling out before the financial costs of reunification (such as the 'two-for-one' Deutschmark for Ostmark deal for GDR citizens) became apparent.

While East Germany had achieved the highest standard of living in the Soviet bloc, it was well short of the levels of advanced EC countries. Massive investment was needed to rebuild the East's industrial base and transport system, and that meant increased taxation. In addition, the new nation found itself funnelling aid into Eastern Europe (Germany led the EC drive for recognition of Slovenia and Croatia) and then into the former Soviet republics. All this took place against a background of continued downturn in world trade: in February 1992

Like defeated Germany itself, Berlin was formally divided between the four victorious powers – despite the fact that it was located in Prussia, 160 km [100 mls] inside Soviet-occupied eastern Germany. In June 1948, in an attempt to bring the whole city under their control, the Soviets closed all road and rail links with the West. The Western Allies supplied the city by a massive airlift; in October 1949 the blockade was abandoned, but Berlin's anomalous situation remained a potential flashpoint, and provoked a series of diplomatic crises – mainly because it offered an easy escape route to the West for discontented East Germans.

In August 1961, alarmed at the steady drain of some of its best-trained people, the East German authorities built a dividing wall across the city. Over the years, the original improvised structure – it was thrown up overnight – became a substantial barrier of concrete and barbed wire, with machine-gun towers and minefields; despite the hazards, many still risked the perilous crossing, and hundreds of would-be refugees – often youngsters – died in the attempt.

The Berlin Wall, with its few, heavily guarded crossing points, became the most indelible symbol of the Cold War, the essential background to every spy thriller. When the East German government collapsed in 1989, the Wall's spontaneous demolition by jubilant Easterners and Westerners alike became the most unambiguous sign of the Cold War's ending.

When East Germany joined the West, it was agreed that Berlin would become the formal capital of the unified state in the year 2000 – until that time, both Berlin and the quiet Rhineland city of Bonn were to be joint capitals.

the German government officially announced the calculation of negative growth – it averaged 8% a year in the 1950s – and the German economy, on paper at least, was 'in recession'.

The costs could be social, too. If Westerners resent added taxes and the burden of the GDR, and if the Easterners resent the overbearing, patronizing attitudes of the old FRG, there could be cultural as well as economic polarization. In 1992 there was the spectacle – not seen in 18 years – of several public sector strikes. More likely, however, are a revived German sense of identity bordering on hegemony, even a swing to the 'right', and a revival of Fascism.

Reunification appeared in the 1990s to be the beginning rather than the end of a chapter in German history. At the very least, it would be a more complicated, expensive and lengthy undertaking than anyone was prepared to envisage as the Berlin Wall came crumbling down ∎

COUNTRY Federal Republic of Germany	**MAIN IMPORTS** Machinery and transport equipment 28%, food and live animals 10%, chemicals 10%, petroleum and petroleum products 7%, clothing 6%, textile yarn
AREA 356,910 sq km [137,803 sq mls]	
POPULATION 82,000,000	**MAIN IMPORT PARTNERS** France 11%, Netherlands 11%, Italy 10%, Belgium 7%, UK 7%, USA 7%, Japan 6%, Switzerland 5%
CAPITAL (POPULATION) Berlin (3,475,000)/ Bonn (297,000)	
GOVERNMENT Federal multiparty republic with a bicameral legislature	**EDUCATIONAL EXPENDITURE** 5.4% of GNP
	DEFENCE 2.4% of GNP
ETHNIC GROUPS German 93%, Turkish 2%, Yugoslav 1%, Italian 1%, Greek, Polish, Spanish	**TOTAL ARMED FORCES** 494,300
	TOURISM 13,209,000 visitors per year
LANGUAGES German (official)	**ROADS** 621,300 km [386,076 mls]
RELIGIONS Protestant 45% (predominantly Lutheran), Roman Catholic 37%, Muslim 2%	**RAILWAYS** 41,000 km [25,477 mls]
	POPULATION DENSITY 230 per sq km [595 per sq ml]
CURRENCY Deutschmark = 100 Pfennig	**URBAN POPULATION** 86%
ANNUAL INCOME PER PERSON US$23,560	**BIRTHS** 11 per 1,000 population
SOURCE OF INCOME Agriculture 1%, industry 38%, services 61%	**DEATHS** 12 per 1,000 population
	INFANT MORTALITY 8 per 1,000 live births
MAIN PRIMARY PRODUCTS Lignite, coal, timber, pigs, cattle, natural gas, salt, silver	**LIFE EXPECTANCY** Female 78 yrs, male 72 yrs
	POPULATION PER DOCTOR 370 people
MAIN INDUSTRIES Motor vehicles, ship construction, iron, cotton yarn, forestry, aluminium, beer, synthetic fibres and rubber, petroleum products	**ADULT LITERACY** 99%
	PRINCIPAL CITIES (POPULATION) Berlin 3,475,000 Hamburg 1,703,000 Munich 1,256,000 Cologne 693,000 Frankfurt-am-Main 660,000 Essen 622,000 Dortmund 602,000 Stuttgart 594,000 Düsseldorf 575,000 Bremen 552,000 Duisburg 537,000 Hanover 525,000 Nürnberg 499,000 Leipzig 491,000 Dresden 479,000
MAIN EXPORTS Machinery and transport equipment 48%, chemicals 13%, manufactured articles 11%, textiles 3%	
MAIN EXPORT PARTNERS France 12%, Italy 9%, Netherlands 9%, UK 9%, USA 9%, Belgium 7%, Switzerland 6%, Austria 5%, Japan 2%	

EUROPE

SWITZERLAND

Switzerland's square flag was officially adopted in 1848, though the white cross on a red shield has been the Swiss emblem since the 14th century. The flag of the International Red Cross, based in Geneva, derives from this Swiss flag.

BERN

The Alpine foreland of northern Switzerland has a central European climate with a marked summer maximum of rainfall. In winter the region is often blanketed in low cloud resulting in a small diurnal range of temperature in contrast with the mountain resorts which lie above the cloud. Precipitation falls mainly as snow between December and March. Summers are warm with a daily average of 8 hours of sunshine in July. December to February, day temperatures at Davos are slightly colder than Bern.

Nearly 60% of Swiss territory is in the Alps, of which two notable peaks are on the Italian border: the Matterhorn (4,478 m [14,700 ft]) and the Monte Rosa (4,634 m [15,200 ft]). The Alps are drained by the upper Rhine tributaries and by the Rhône Valley via Lac Léman (Lake Geneva). Numerous lakes add to the scenic attraction of high mountains with permanent snow, and the Alps have become one of the great tourist attractions of the world. As a result, around 200,000 people work in the hotel and catering industries. Nationally, unemployment is very low by world standards.

Despite its lingering rural, pastoral image, Switzerland is a very advanced country, providing its citizens with the highest per capita income in the world (US$36,410 in 1993), closely followed by Luxembourg and Liechtenstein. The reasons for the high standard of living include neutrality in two World Wars, plentiful hydroelectric power, a central geographical position and rich mineral deposits, including uranium (40% of the country's electricity is now nuclear-derived) and iron ore. It would also be unfair, however – as in the case of Germany and Japan – not to include hard work,

a sense of purpose and organizational ability in the list of attributes.

Agriculture is efficient, with both arable and pastoral farming; a wide range of produce is grown, including maize and other cereals, fruits, vegetables, and grapes for a local wine industry. The mountain pastures are still used for summer grazing, though most of the famous migrations of herds and herders up the mountains in summer no longer take place.

Industry is progressive and prosperous, in particular engineering, metallurgy, chemicals and textiles. Watch- and clockmaking is perhaps the most famed of all Swiss industries, and is still very important to the national economy.

In addition to agricultural and industrial strength Switzerland also has a world trade in banking and insurance, concentrated particularly in Zürich, while its revenues are boosted both by tourism and its position as the headquarters for numerous international bodies. Geneva alone hosts EFTA, GATT and the International Red Cross, as well as ten UN agencies that include WHO, ILO and the High Commission for Refugees (UNHCR), while there are over 140 others: Basle, for example, is home to

the Bank for International Settlements (the central banks' bank). Ironically, Switzerland remains stubbornly outside the UN – a policy whose desirability to the Swiss was confirmed by a referendum held in 1986. However, as Europe moved towards greater economic and political union, Switzerland announced in May 1992 that it would be applying to join the EC, but a December 1992 referendum rejected this proposal.

Switzerland is a multilingual patchwork of 26 cantons, each of which has control over housing and economic policy. Six of the cantons are French-speaking, one Italian-speaking, one with a significant Romansch-speaking community (Graubünden), and the rest speak German. It nevertheless remains a strongly united country, internationally recognized as a permanently neutral power, politically stable with an efficient reservist army, and shrewdly trading with most of the countries of the world ∎

COUNTRY Swiss Confederation (Helvetica)	**MAIN EXPORTS** Non-electrical machinery 20%, electrical machinery 12%, pharmaceuticals 8%, precision instruments 7%, jewellery 7%, watches 6%
AREA 41,290 sq km [15,942 sq mls]	
POPULATION 7,268,000	
CAPITAL (POPULATION) Bern (299,000)	**MAIN EXPORT PARTNERS** Germany 21%, France 9%, USA 9%, Italy 8%, UK 8%, Japan 4%
GOVERNMENT Federal state with a bicameral legislature	**MAIN IMPORTS** Machinery 20%, chemical products 11%, textiles and clothing 10%, precious metals and jewellery 7%
ETHNIC GROUPS Swiss German 64%, Swiss French 19%, Swiss Italian 8%, Yugoslav 3%, Spanish 2%, Romansch	
LANGUAGES French, German, Italian and Romansch (all official)	**MAIN IMPORT PARTNERS** Germany 34%, France 11%, Italy 10%, UK 6%, USA 5%, Japan 5%
RELIGIONS Roman Catholic 46%, Protestant 40%, Muslim 2%	**DEFENCE** 1.6% of GNP
	TOURISM 11,270,000 visitors per year
CURRENCY Swiss franc = 100 centimes	**POPULATION DENSITY** 176 per sq km [456 per sq ml]
ANNUAL INCOME PER PERSON US$33,610	**INFANT MORTALITY** 7 per 1,000 live births
MAIN PRIMARY PRODUCTS Cereals, grapes, potatoes, cattle, timber	**LIFE EXPECTANCY** Female 81 yrs, male 75 yrs
	ADULT LITERACY 99%
MAIN INDUSTRIES Tourism, financial services, machinery, chemicals, clocks and watches	**PRINCIPAL CITIES (POPULATION)** Zürich 915,000 Geneva 393,000 Basle 359,000 Bern 299,000 Lausanne 265,000

THE ALPS

Thrust upwards by continental collision 25 to 30 million years ago, the Alps are Europe's principal mountain range: between north-eastern Italy and eastern Austria, they stretch for over 1,000 km [600 mls] and include Europe's highest mountain, Mont Blanc (4,807 m [15,771 ft]). The Alpine watershed is the source of many great European rivers, including the Rhine and the Po.

Despite the nine major passes that cross them, the mountains were seen by their pastoralist inhabitants and travellers alike as a troublesome obstacle until the 19th century, when interest in mountaineering, originally an English craze, gave puzzled locals new employment as guides. Six tunnels, including one under Mont Blanc, now make access very easy, and tourism (once confined to those eccentric mountaineers) has become a mass industry built around modern winter sports.

Alpine agriculture, once the mainstay of mountain life, is currently in decline, but skiing and summer tourism have brought new prosperity. Throughout the 1980s, the Alps attracted up to 50 million visitors a year, most intent on skiing some of the 40,000 runs that have been created for them. Unfortunately, the impact of mass skiing on the fragile Alpine environment is serious. Thousands of hectares of high forest have been bulldozed to create smooth pistes, denuding the slopes of scarce topsoil as well as creating perfect conditions for massive avalanches: in 1987, more than 60 people were killed by summer mudslides, and almost 50 towns and villages were damaged, some of them severely.

The remaining Alpine forests are also under threat from industrial air pollution. Acid rain, formed from dissolved sulphur dioxide, is destroying trees at an alarming rate: in some districts, two-thirds have been affected, and many of them will never recover.

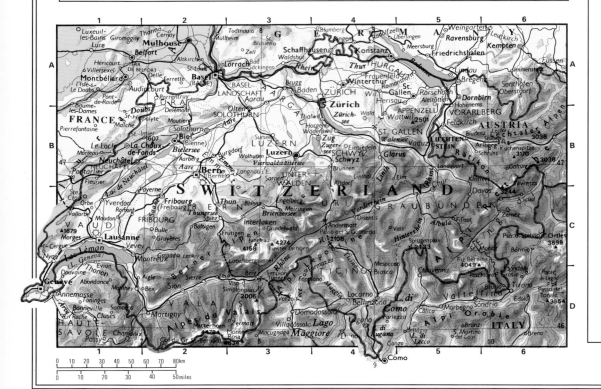

AUSTRIA

According to legend, the colours of the Austrian flag date from the battle of Ptolemais in 1191, when the only part of the Duke of Bebenberg's tunic not bloodstained was under his swordbelt. The design was officially adopted in 1918.

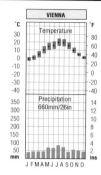

The western Alpine regions have an Atlantic-type climate, while the eastern lowlands are continental. The airflow is mainly from the west, which has twice the rainfall of the east at over 1,000 mm [40 in]. The winters are cold with snow (at Vienna over 60 days), and on the mountains there are glaciers and permanent snow in great depths. In Vienna the January temperature is below freezing and is around 20°C [68°F] in July. The wettest months, June to August, are also the warmest.

A federal republic comprising nine states (*Länder*) – including the capital, Vienna – Austria's present boundaries derive from the Versailles Treaty of 1919, which dissolved the Austro-Hungarian Empire. It was absorbed by the German Reich in 1938, occupied by the Allies in 1945 and recovered its full independence in 1955.

A mountainous country, Austria has two-thirds of its territory and rather less than a third of the population within the eastern Alps, which extend in a series of longitudinal ridges from the Swiss border in the west almost to Vienna in the east. The longitudinal valleys between the ridges accommodate much of the Alpine population.

Austria's lowlands include a section of the northern Alpine foreland, which narrows eastwards towards Vienna and contains the Danube basin. This is Austria's most important east–west route with rail, motorway and river navigation leading through Vienna to Budapest and beyond. Another important lowland is the Burgenland, a rich farming area bordering the eastern Alps and facing southeast towards Hungary.

Unlike Switzerland, Austria has important heavy industries based in large part on indigenous resources. The mountains are a major source of hydroelectric power. Oil and natural gas occur predominantly in the Vienna Basin and are supplemented by imports from the former Soviet republics and from German refineries. Minerals occur in the eastern Alps, notably iron ore in Steiermark (Styria); iron and steel production is located both at Donawitz (near Leoben) in the mountains, and also in the Alpine foreland which has become a major centre of metal, chemical engineering and vehicle manufacturing industries. Various industrial plants are also established around Vienna.

The capital stands at a major European crossroads where the Danube is joined by the Moravian Gate route from the northern lowlands of Europe, and by the Alpine route through the Semmering Pass. A city of political as well as cultural and artistic importance, Vienna is home to OPEC, the International Atomic Energy Agency and the UN Industrial Development Organization, among others, and contains one-fifth of Austria's population.

Like most European countries, Austria experienced low population growth or even a slight reduction in the 1960s and 1970s. Within the country, decline has been greatest in the east, while the west has gained from a higher birth rate, and also from the settlement of refugees and the industrialization of the Tirol since World War II.

Austria's neutrality was enshrined in the constitution in 1955, but unlike Switzerland it has not been frightened to take sides on certain issues. In 1994, two-thirds of the population voted in favour of joining the EU, and on 1 January 1995 Austria, at the same time as Finland and Sweden, became a member. As a result, Austria left the European Free Trade Association (EFTA) in January 1995 ■

COUNTRY Republic of Austria

AREA 83,850 sq km [32,374 sq mls]

POPULATION 8,004,000

CAPITAL (POPULATION) Vienna (1,560,000)

GOVERNMENT Federal multiparty republic

ETHNIC GROUPS Austrian 93%, Slovene 2%, Turkish, German

LANGUAGES German 94% (official), Slovene, Croat, Turkish, Slovak, Magyar

RELIGIONS Roman Catholic 78%, Protestant 6%, Muslim 2%

CURRENCY Schilling = 100 Groschen

ANNUAL INCOME PER PERSON US$23,120

MAIN PRIMARY PRODUCTS Iron ore, lignite, oil and natural gas, graphite, timber, cattle, wheat

MAIN INDUSTRIES Agriculture, tourism, iron and steel, wood products, wine, food processing

MAIN EXPORTS Machinery and transport equipment 34%, iron and steel 7%, paper and board 6%, cork, wood and other crude materials 5%, foodstuffs 3%

MAIN EXPORT PARTNERS Germany 35%, Italy 10%, Switzerland 7%, UK 5%, France 4%

MAIN IMPORTS Machinery and transport equipment 35%, chemicals and pharmaceuticals 10%, mineral fuels and lubricants 7%, foodstuffs 5%

MAIN IMPORT PARTNERS Germany 44%, Italy 9%, Switzerland 5%, Japan 4%, France 4%

DEFENCE 0.9% of GNP

TOURISM 18,257,000 visitors per year

POPULATION DENSITY 95 per sq km [247 per sq ml]

INFANT MORTALITY 9 per 1,000 live births

LIFE EXPECTANCY Female 79 yrs, male 72 yrs

ADULT LITERACY 99%

PRINCIPAL CITIES (POPULATION) Vienna 1,560,000 Graz 238,000 Linz 203,000 Salzburg 144,000 Innsbruck 118,000

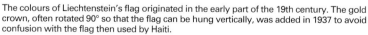

LIECHTENSTEIN

The colours of Liechtenstein's flag originated in the early part of the 19th century. The gold crown, often rotated 90° so that the flag can be hung vertically, was added in 1937 to avoid confusion with the flag then used by Haiti.

COUNTRY Principality of Liechtenstein

AREA 157 sq km [61 sq mls]

POPULATION 31,000

CAPITAL (POPULATION) Vaduz (5,067)

POPULATION DENSITY 197 per sq km [508 per sq ml]

Standing at the end of the eastern Alps between Austria and Switzerland, where the Rhine cuts its way northwards out of the Alpine chains, tiny Liechtenstein became an independent principality within the Holy Roman Empire in 1719 and since then has always managed to escape incorporation into any of Europe's larger states.

Since 1923 Liechtenstein has been in customs and currency union with Switzerland, which also provides overseas representation; and although many Swiss regard it as their 27th canton, it retains full sovereignty in other spheres.

The capital, Vaduz, is situated on the Oberland plateau above the fields and meadows of the Rhine Valley, and rising numbers of tourists (there were as many as 72,000 overnight visitors in 1993) are arriving at its royal castle, intrigued by the notion of this miniature state.

While Liechtenstein is best known abroad for its postage stamps – an important source of income – it is as a haven for international companies, attracted by extremely low taxation and the strictest (most secretive) banking codes in the world, that the state has generated the revenue to produce the highest GDP per capita figure on record.

Since World War II there has also been an impressive growth in specialized manufacturing – the product of a judicious mixture of Swiss engineers, Austrian technicians, Italian workers and international capital investment ■

PORTUGAL

Portugal's colours, adopted in 1910 when it became a republic, represent the soldiers who died in the war (red) and hope (green). The armillary shield – an early navigational instrument – reflects Portugal's leading role in world exploration.

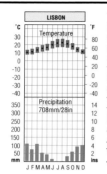

The west coast of the Iberian Peninsula has the oceanic variety of a Mediterranean climate with cooler summers, milder winters and a smaller temperature range than in true Mediterranean lands. Sunshine at Lisbon is abundant, averaging 7.5 hours a day through the year. Frosts are rare, and temperatures over 30°C [86°F] have been recorded March to September, and over 40°C [104°F] in July and August. Most of the rain falls in the winter half of the year, with July and August virtually rainless.

The most westerly of Europe's 'mainland' countries, Portugal occupies an oblong coastland in the south-west of the Iberian peninsula, facing the Atlantic Ocean. Here the Meseta edge has splintered and in part foundered to leave upstanding mountain ranges, particularly in the Serra da Estrêla and its continuation just north of the River Tagus (Tejo), and in the Serra de Monchique.

Agriculture and fishing

The mild, moist airflow from the Atlantic encourages good tree growth. Forests reach a height of at least 1,300 m [4,260 ft] in the north and over a quarter of the country is forested. Pines form the most common species, especially on the sandy 'litorals' near the coast, where large plantations provide timber as well as resin and turpentine. Cork oaks abound in the Tagus Valley and farther south; Portugal is the world's leading producer of the cork that is derived from their bark.

A wide variety of fruits is cultivated, including olives, figs and grapes. Portugal is home to some of the world's greatest vineyards and once ranked fifth in wine production. However, harvests have fallen and in 1993 Portugal ranked eighth in the world, producing 900,000 tonnes of wine.

Most of the grapes are grown north of the Tagus, where the most celebrated speciality is port wine from the Douro Valley near the Portuguese-Spanish frontier. The grape juice is transported by boat down the Douro to Vila Nova, where it is fortified and stored for export. The lower parts of the Douro and Minho basins produce famous sparkling *vinhos verdes*, while the vineyards near the Tagus estuary are noted for white table wines and brandy. In the south the Algarve, with its greater sunshine and aridity, specializes more in liqueurs and muscatels.

The Portuguese economy relies heavily on agriculture and fishing, which together employ over a quarter of the national workforce. These industries are mostly undercapitalized and still rather primitive by European standards, although they provide valuable exports. In the rainy north, the pressure of overpopulation causes fragmented and tiny agricultural holdings (*minifundia*); in the drier south, large holdings (*latifundia*) tend to create monoculture with below-average yields and seasonal unemployment. Recently there has been some investment in irrigation.

The main general crops are food cereals and vegetables, including a wide variety of the beans that form a frequent and favourite item of the Portuguese diet. Maize and rye predominate in the north, and wheat, barley and oats in the south. Of the many farm animals the pig deserves special mention as the forager of the heavy yield of acorns from the cork and evergreen oaks.

Portugal's long coastline provides an important supplementary source of livelihood and of foreign tourist currency. The shallow lagoons yield shellfish, especially oysters; the coastal waters supply sardines, anchovy and tunny; the deep-sea fisheries, long frequented by Portuguese sailors, bring hake, mackerel, halibut and, above all, cod.

Industry

While much of Portuguese industry is concerned with the products of farming, fishing and forestry, the manufacture of textiles and ceramics is also widespread. Modern engineering, associated with a complete iron and steel plant, has been established at Seixal near Lisbon. There is some small-scale mining for copper ores and wolfram (a tungstate of iron and manganese, from which tungsten is obtained), but a relative shortage of power resources is a problem. A small quantity of poor-quality coal is mined annually, and this is supplemented with foreign imports. Great efforts have been made to develop hydroelectric stations in the north, but Portugal remains one of the poorest members of the EU since switching economic allegiance from EFTA on 1 January 1986.

Portugal has two conurbations with over a million inhabitants. Lisbon, the capital, is the chief centre of the country's financial, commercial and industrial concerns and has a fine sheltered harbour in the large Tagus estuary. Porto (Oporto), the main centre for the densely-populated north, has an ocean outport. These two cities still dominate the nation, but during recent decades tourism and rapid residential growth have transformed the subtropical coastline of the Algarve, and have led to a substantial increase in its population ∎

COUNTRY Republic of Portugal	**EXPORTS** US$1,210 per person
AREA 92,390 sq km [35,672 sq mls]	**MAIN EXPORTS** Clothing 26%, machinery and transport equipment 20%, footwear 8%, paper and paper products 8%, agricultural products 7%
POPULATION 10,600,000	
CAPITAL (POPULATION) Lisbon (2,561,000)	**MAIN EXPORT PARTNERS** France 15%, Germany 15%, UK 14%, Spain 11%
GOVERNMENT Multiparty republic with a unicameral legislature	**IMPORTS** US$1,803 per person
ETHNIC GROUPS Portuguese 99%, Cape Verdean, Brazilian, Spanish, British	**MAIN IMPORTS** Machinery 22%, road vehicles 15%, crude petroleum 9%, iron and steel products 4%, chemicals 4%
LANGUAGES Portuguese (official)	**MAIN IMPORT PARTNERS** Germany 14%, Spain 14%, France 12%, Italy 9%, UK 8%
RELIGIONS Roman Catholic 95%	**DEFENCE** 2.9% of GNP
NATIONAL DAY 10 June; Portugal Day	**TOURISM** 20,742,000 visitors per year
CURRENCY Escudo = 100 centavos	**POPULATION DENSITY** 115 per sq km [297 per sq ml]
ANNUAL INCOME PER PERSON US$7,890	**INFANT MORTALITY** 13 per 1,000 live births
MAIN PRIMARY PRODUCTS Cereals, olives, rice, timber, fruit, grapes, vegetables, cork, fish, copper, iron, tungsten, tin, salt	**LIFE EXPECTANCY** Female 78 yrs, male 71 yrs
	ADULT LITERACY 86%
MAIN INDUSTRIES Agriculture, textiles, food processing, wine, chemicals, fishing, mining, machinery, tourism	**PRINCIPAL CITIES (POPULATION)** Lisbon 2,561,000 Oporto 1,174,000

ANDORRA

Andorra is traditionally said to have been granted independence by Charlemagne in the 9th century, after the Moorish Wars. The flag, adopted in 1866, sometimes features the state coat of arms on the obverse in the central yellow band.

COUNTRY Co-principality of Andorra
AREA 453 sq km [175 sq mls]
POPULATION 65,000
CAPITAL (POPULATION) Andorra La Vella (23,000)
POPULATION DENSITY 143 per sq km [371 per sq ml]

Perched near the eastern end of the high central Pyrenees, Andorra consists mainly of six valleys (the Valls) that drain to the River Valira. The population totals about 65,000, a third of whom are native-born.

The rights of the *seigneurie* or co-principality have been shared since 1278 between the Spanish Bishop of Urgel and the French Comte de Foix. The latter's lordship rights passed to the French government, now represented by the prefect of the adjoining *département* of the Eastern Pyrenees. The people of Andorra pay a small annual sum to the bishop and the prefect, and each co-prince is represented in their Council by a *viguier;* but in most other respects the co-principality governs itself, and retains no armed forces.

Physically the country consists of deep glaciated valleys lying at altitudes of 1,000 to 2,900 m [3,280 to 9,500 ft]. On the north a lofty watershed forms the frontier with France and is crossed by a road over the Envalira Pass at 2,400 m [7,870 ft]; to the south the land falls away down the Valira Valley to the Segre Valley in Spain, again followed by the same vital highway. In the colder months the Envalira Pass often becomes snowbound and land communications are then only with Spain.

The climate is severe in winter and pleasantly cool in summer when, because the valleys lie in a rain shadow, slopes above 1,400 m [4,600 ft] often suffer from drought and need irrigation. Some agriculture is possible on the slopes: sheep and cattle are grazed, and crops grow in terraced fields.

Andorra has five main sources of income: stock rearing and agriculture, especially tobacco; the sale of water and hydroelectricity to Catalonia; fees from radio transmission services; tourism, based in winter on skiing; and the sale of duty-free goods and of postage stamps. Of these, tourism and duty-free sales are by far the most important – every year up to 10 million visitors come to Andorra to shop, and to witness this rare surviving example of a medieval principality ∎

SPAIN

The colours of the Spanish flag date back to the old kingdom of Aragon in the 12th century. The present design, in which the central yellow stripe is twice as wide as each of the red stripes, was adopted during the Civil War in 1938.

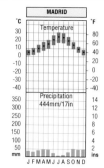

A global position between coastal north-west Europe and Africa, and between the Mediterranean countries of the Old World and the Americas, made Spain a great crossroads. Yet the lofty Pyrenean barrier in the north weakened land contacts with the rest of Europe, while the narrow Strait of Gibraltar in the south encouraged African contacts, lending truth to the cliché that 'Africa begins at the Pyrenees'.

The chief physical feature of Spain is the vast central plateau, the Meseta, which tilts gently towards Portugal. A harsh and often barren area, the plateau is crossed by the Central Sierras, a mountain chain running north-west to south-east. This central divide separates two mountain basins: Old Castile in the north and New Castile in the south.

On the north-eastern and southern edges of the Meseta are large triangular lowlands: the one in the north drains to the Ebro, while the southern lowland drains to the Guadalquivir, the largest river wholly in Spain. Beyond the Ebro trough the land rises to the Pyrenees, which form the Franco-Spanish border and continue westwards in the Cantabrian Mountains. Similarly, the Mediterranean flank of Andalusia rises to a lofty *cordillera* (mountain chain) that culminates in the snowy Sierra Nevada (peaking at

The interior of Spain is a high plateau, isolated from the seas which surround the Iberian Peninsula. Summer days are very hot despite the altitude, above 25°C [77°F] June to September during the day, but at night temperatures fall sharply. Winters are much colder than in coastal districts and frost is not uncommon. Rain is fairly evenly distributed from September to May, but the summer drought is broken only by occasional storms. Madrid has an average of 8 hours sunshine a day over the year.

3,478 m [11,400 ft]). The Mediterranean side of the Meseta has summits of about 2,000 m [6,560 ft] and drops to narrow, discontinuous coastal plains.

Spain has perhaps the widest range of climate of any country in Western Europe. The most striking

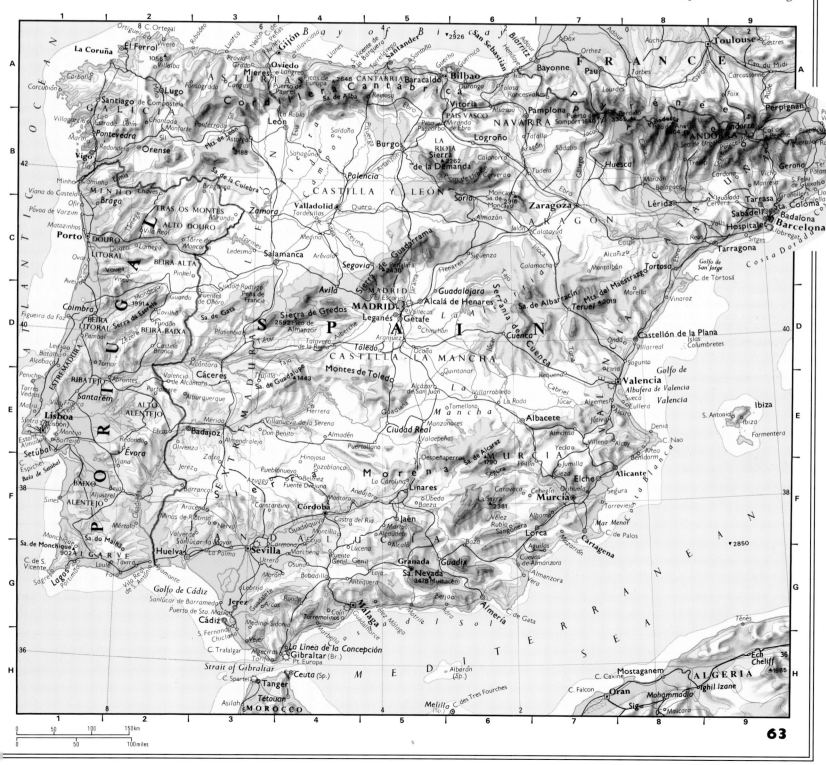

Local rock carvings demonstrate that Gibraltar has been inhabited since Neolithic times. Greeks and Romans also settled here, but the first sure date for colonization is AD 711 when Tariq ibn Zaid, a Berber chieftain, occupied it. Although taken over by Spaniards for a short while in the 14th century, it remained Moorish until 1462. An Anglo-Dutch naval force captured it in 1704 and it was formally recognized as a British possession at the Treaty of Utrecht in 1713. In spite of long sieges and assaults – not to mention pressure from Spain – it has remained British ever since, becoming a strategically vital naval dockyard and air base.

The Rock, as it is popularly known, guards the north-eastern end of the Strait of Gibraltar. It is 6.5 sq km [2.5 sq mls] in area and occupies a narrow peninsula, consisting largely of a ridge thrusting south along the eastern side of Algeciras Bay, terminating in the 30 m [100 ft] cliffs of Europa Point. The topography prohibits cultivation and the Gibraltarians rely on the port, the ship-repairing yards, the military and air bases, and on tourism for their livelihood.

The 28,051 Gibraltarians are of British, Spanish, Maltese, Portuguese and Genoan descent. Though bilingual in Spanish and English, they remain staunchly pro-British. In 1966, following a long-standing claim, the Spanish government called on Britain to give 'substantial sovereignty' of Gibraltar to Spain and closed the border (1.2 km [0.74 mls]) to all but pedestrian traffic. In a 1967 referendum the residents voted to remain under British control, and in 1969 they were granted the status of a self-governing dependency.

Spain closed the frontier completely, preventing thousands of Spaniards from reaching their daily work. The border was reopened fully by Spain in 1985 following British agreement that, for the first time, they would discuss the sovereignty of Gibraltar; but despite being fellow members of NATO (Spain joined in 1982) and the EU (Spain joined on 1 January 1986), no progress was made towards British compliance with the United Nations General Assembly's resolution for an end to Gibraltar's 'colonial status' by 1 October 1996.

contrast is between the humid north and north-west and the mainly arid remainder of the country. Large areas of the country are barren or steppeland, and about a fifth is covered by *matorral*, a Mediterranean scrub like the French *maquis*.

A large part of the farmland is used for pastoral purposes, but there are rich soils in some of the major river valleys, such as the Ebro and the Guadalquivir, and areas of very productive agriculture, especially where there are *huertas* (irrigated market gardens) and *vegas* (irrigated orchards).

Spain's vegetation falls into three broad categories: forest, *matorral* and steppe. Forests (almost 10% of the land surface) are today mainly confined to the rainier north and north-west, with beech and deciduous oak common. Towards the drier south and east, Mediterranean pines and evergreen oaks take over, and forests resemble open parkland. Widespread clearance for fuel and cultivation and grazing by sheep, goats and cattle have turned large areas into *matorral* or shrub.

This low bush growth, often of aromatic evergreen plants, may be dominated over large tracts by one species: thus *romillares* consist predominantly of rosemary, *tomillares* of thyme, *retamales* of broom. Where soils are thin and drought prevalent, *matorral* gives way to steppe, mainly of alfalfa and esparto.

Agriculture

Despite the problems of aridity and poor soils, agriculture occupies nearly a third of the national workforce. Irregular river regimes and deeply incised valleys make irrigation difficult and expensive and, on the higher and drier regions, tracts favourable for cultivation are often isolated by expanses of low fertility where only a meagre livelihood can be wrested from the soil. There are, too, problems connected with the size of farms. In semi-arid Spain large estates (*latifundios*) abound with much seasonal employment or sharecropping, while in the rainy north-west and north excessive fragmentation of small farms (*minifundios*) has proved uneconomic.

It is against this picture of difficulties that the great progress made since 1939 by the *Instituto Nacional de Colonización* (INC) must be viewed. The institute, by means of irrigation, co-operative farming schemes, concentration of landholdings, agricultural credit schemes and technical training, has resettled over a quarter of the land needing reorganization and reclamation. But, generally, crop yields are still comparatively modest and agricultural techniques remain backward.

Stock rearing: Large areas of farmland are used solely or partly for pastoral purposes, which are of great economic importance. Spain has about 20 million sheep, mainly of the native merino type which produces a fine fleece. The Mesta, an old confederation of sheep owners, controls the seasonal migrations on to the summer pastures on the high sierras. Areas too rocky and steep for sheep are given over to goats while cattle, apart from working oxen, are mostly restricted to regions with ample grass and

water – for example the north and north-west. Pigs are bred in the cattle districts of the north, and are also kept to forage the acorns in the large tracts of evergreen oaks in the south. Many working animals are kept, and fighting bulls are bred on the marshes (*marismas*) at the mouth of the Guadalquivir.

Arable crops: The typical arable crops are the classical Mediterranean trio of wheat, olive and vine, with maize important in rainier districts and vegetables and citrus fruits where there is irrigation water. Wheat occupies a third of the cropland and is usually followed in rotation by leguminous pulses or fallow, grazed and so manured by sheep.

In dry areas barley, oats and rye, grown for fodder, replace wheat, and in the wetter north maize dominates both for grain and feed. Rice is harvested in Murcia, Valencia and the Ebro Valley and Spain follows Italy for rice production in Europe.

Fruit growing: Fruits occupy a high and honoured place in Spain's agricultural economy. The olive crop, mainly from large estates in Andalusia, makes Spain the world's chief producer of olive oil. Vines cover about 10% of the cultivated land and only Italy and France exceed the Spanish output of wine. Sherry (from Jérez) is renowned and among Spain's other fine wines are those of Rioja.

For citrus fruit Spain easily outstrips other European producers, the bulk of the crop being Seville oranges destined largely for Britain for making marmalade. Large quantities of other fruits, especially apricots and peaches, are grown with vegetables as a ground crop in market gardens and orchards.

Some of the *huertas* are devoted to industrial crops such as cotton, hemp, flax and sugar beet, while most richer soils in Andalusia are entirely given over to cotton. The poorer steppes yield *esparto* (a strong grass) for papermaking.

Maps of modern Spain clearly indicate the tremendous progress made recently in water reservation and river regulation on all the major rivers. Large new reservoirs have been constructed on the Miño, Duero, Tajo, Guadiana, Guadalquivir and other main rivers as well as numerous dams on the lesser watercourses. The INC, which directs this work, aims at bringing 70,000 hectares [173,000 acres] a year under irrigation as well as undertaking all kinds of land reclamation, drainage, reforestation, settlement schemes and farm co-operative planning.

Mining and industry

Spain is lamentably short of its own supplies of solid and liquid fuels and in an average year produces only small quantities of poor-quality coal (mainly from Asturias at Oviedo), and some lignite from a field south of Barcelona. Small deposits of petroleum found near Burgos and at the mouth of the Ebro have not yet proved economic to develop.

In contrast to fossil fuels, workable mineral ores are widespread. High-quality iron ores, with substantial reserves, occur in Vizcaya, Santander and

COUNTRY Kingdom of Spain

AREA 504,780 sq km [194,896 sq mls]

POPULATION 39,664,000

CAPITAL (POPULATION) Madrid (3,041,000)

GOVERNMENT Constitutional monarchy

ETHNIC GROUPS Castilian Spanish 72%, Catalan 16%, Galician 8%, Basque 2%

LANGUAGES Castilian Spanish (official), Catalan, Galician, Basque

RELIGIONS Roman Catholic 97%

NATIONAL DAY 12 October; Discovery of America (1492)

CURRENCY Peseta = 100 céntimos

ANNUAL INCOME PER PERSON US$13,650

MAIN PRIMARY PRODUCTS Cereals, sugar cane, grapes, fruit, timber, olives, fish, cork, lignite, iron, coal, lead, copper, mercury, tungsten, zinc, tin

MAIN INDUSTRIES Agriculture, wine, food processing, mining, iron and steel, textiles, chemicals, cement

MAIN EXPORTS Transport equipment 17%, machinery and electrical equipment 13%, vegetables and fruit 9%, cast iron, iron and steel 9%, chemicals 7%, mineral fuels 6%

MAIN EXPORT PARTNERS France 15%, USA 10%, Germany 10%, UK 9%, Benelux 8%, Italy 7%

MAIN IMPORTS Machinery and electrical equipment 20%, mineral fuels and petroleum products 19%, chemicals 9%, transport equipment 8%

MAIN IMPORT PARTNERS USA 11%, Germany 11%, France 9%, UK 7%, Mexico 6%, Italy 5%

DEFENCE 1.7% of GNP

TOURISM 57,258,615 visitors per year

POPULATION DENSITY 78 per sq km [203 per sq ml]

LIFE EXPECTANCY Female 80 yrs, male 74 yrs

ADULT LITERACY 98%

PRINCIPAL CITIES (POPULATION) Madrid 3,041,000 Barcelona 1,631,000 Valencia 764,000 Seville 714,000 Zaragoza 607,000 Málaga 531,000 Bilbao 372,000 Las Palmas 372,000 Murcia 342,000 Valladolid 337,000

MALAGA

The narrow coastal plain of southern Spain, sheltered by the Sierra Nevada, is noted for its very hot and sunny summers. Rainfall at Málaga is sparse and, like much of the western Mediterranean region, evenly distributed throughout the winter half of the year – in contrast to the more prominent winter maximum further east. With an average of only 52 rainy days a year, Málaga is one of the most reliable holiday resorts. In winter it records over 5 hours of sunshine a day; 9–11 hours from May to September.

Granada. Bilbao, the chief ore-exporting port, has an important integrated iron and steel plant; so have Oviedo, Gijón and other towns on the north coast.

Many localities yield non-ferrous ores in sufficient quantity to broaden the base of Spain's metallurgical industries. The chief workings are for copper at Río Tinto, lead and silver at Linares and Peñarroya (near Pueblonovo), and mercury at Almadén; in addition, manganese, titanium and sulphur are produced in small quantities and considerable amounts of potassium salts come from Catalonia. Spain is a leading producer of mercury; in 1993 it was second in the world, producing 21.3% of the world total.

But the major Spanish manufacturing industries are based on agriculture rather than minerals. Textiles, including cotton, wool, silk, jute and linen lead the industrial sector. Barcelona, Catalonia's great industrial, financial and commercial centre, is surrounded by textile towns, some specializing in spinning, as at Manresa and Ribas, and others in weaving, as at Sabadell and Granollers.

Cotton fabrics form the chief single product and supply a wide market, especially at home and in Latin America. However, Barcelona has a wide variety of light industries, including engineering, while the heavy metallurgical sectors are located mainly at Bilbao and other north-coast cities. Madrid has become an important centre for consumer goods, particularly electrical appliances.

Food-processing industries are concentrated in the north-east, the chief being flour milling, sugar refining and oil pressing. Fish canning and processing are widespread in the coastal towns and the Galicians and Basques of the Atlantic coastline are skilled fishermen.

Tourism and communications

The relative absence of closely packed industrial plants and industrial pollution, the historical attractions of the relics of a long history dating from the Greeks and Arabs, and the dry warm sunny climate of the Mediterranean south and east have fostered tourism, the greatest of all Spain's non-agricultural industries. In 1993, 57.3 million people visited Spain and the Costa Brava and Costa del Sol are internationally famous as tourist destinations.

Equally significant is the great increase in the number of those who came to live permanently or for most of the year in these picturesque coastlands with warm winters and subtropical vegetation. It was feared that the economic recession that affected Western Europe into the 1990s would substantially reduce Spain's tourist trade, leaving many resorts on the Mediterranean coast with uncertain futures. However, Spain experienced a welcome upturn in tourist numbers in the period 1993–4.

The prime communication routes in Spain focus on Madrid, which has radial links to the peripheral cities. First-class highways radiate to the main ports and good roads connect all the major towns, but minor roads are seldom tarred and for so large a country relatively few vehicles are registered.

Railways likewise converge on Madrid with minor networks around the regional capitals and main ports. The tracks are not of standard European gauge, about 75% being broad gauge and the remainder narrow. The chief land communications with France run at either end of the Pyrenees and are supplemented by several high-level transmontane rail and road routes.

Air travel focuses on the Madrid airport and, particularly for tourism, on 40 other civil airports, many of them with busy international services. The large coastal and ocean-going traffic involves 230 Spanish ports, but the bulk of the overseas trade passes through the modernized harbours – in particular Bilbao, Barcelona, Cartagena, Cádiz and Gijón.

Demography

The population of Spain is most dense on the coastlands and lowlands around the Meseta. Madrid, in the heart of the tableland, forms a grand exception. The capital stands on the small Manzanares River, a tributary of the Tagus, and has a long history dating from early Roman times. The Moors first provided it with clean drinking water and Philip II made it the seat of the national government in 1561. A fine metropolis, it has flourished during the decades since the Civil War (1936–9) and now accommodates about 10% of the total population of continental Spain. The second Spanish city, Barcelona, is a great commercial and industrial centre; in all ways the core of Catalonia, it was given a huge boost by the staging of the summer Olympics in 1992.

The other major cities include Bilbao, the Basque capital and chief urban area of the north coast, long noted for its metallurgy; Cádiz, an important naval centre; Seville, the river port and regional capital of Andalusia; Valencia and Murcia, the largest of the Mediterranean *huerta* cities; Zaragoza, the expanding centre for the Ebro lowland, noted for food processing and engineering; and Málaga, the fast-growing nucleus of the Costa del Sol. Toledo, which was the national capital before Madrid, ranks far below these conurbations in size, but, protected as a national monument, is the finest medieval city that survives almost intact from the golden age of Spain ■

BALEARIC ISLANDS

The Islas Baleares group contains five larger islands (Majorca, Minorca, Ibiza, Formentera, Cabrera) and 11 rocky islets, together covering 5,014 sq km [1,936 sq mls] and spread over 350 km [218 mls].

Majorca (Mallorca), by far the largest island, has limestone ridges on the north-west and south-east with a plain covered with flat-bedded, very fertile marine sediments between them. Minorca (Menorca), the second largest, has limestone plains and small outcrops of crystalline rocks, but nowhere rises above 358 m [1,175 ft].

The typical sunny Mediterranean climate supports an equally typical vegetation. Shrub growth (*matorral* or *garrigue*) still clothes the highest areas and is grazed by sheep and goats. The rainier upper slopes of the hills have been terraced for olives, carobs and vines, while the lower slopes are under market-garden crops. The level lowlands are planted with wheat and barley, usually in rotation with beans. Generally, almonds, apricots and carobs are more important here than vines and citrus fruits. The rural economy is essentially peasant with a high degree of self-sufficiency.

Like most Mediterranean islands the Balearics were settled early. Archaeological remains exist from 1000 BC (Bronze Age) to the Roman period and include boat-shaped burial mounds (*navetas* or *naus*) and conical stone towers (*talayots*) thought to be refuges from piratical raiding parties. Ibiza town and Port Mahon were originally settled from Carthage. During recent times the islands were repeatedly occupied by the British, French and Spanish and remained finally a province of Spain. Each different occupation has left its mark, and Port Mahon has fine buildings representing all these changes of ownership.

Today the population lives mainly either in agricultural villages some way inland or in small ports around the coast. Power resources and raw materials for manufacture are scarce, apart from agricultural products; textile manufacture (wool and cotton) and food processing are the only widespread factory occupations. Handicrafts flourish in response to the tourism that now dominates the whole economy.

Palma, the capital of Majorca and of the Balearic province, continues to grow rapidly. It has a fine harbour with regular sailings to Barcelona, Alicante and Valencia for passengers and the export of Balearic surpluses of almonds, grain, textiles and vegetables. It is also a regular port of call for Mediterranean cruise ships and its airport, one of the busiest in Spain, deals with well over a million visitors annually. Manacor, the only other large centre on Majorca, is an agricultural market town near limestone caves and subterranean lakes that attract numerous tourists. Port Mahon is the capital of Minorca, and Ibiza town is the capital of the small island of the same name.

A Mediterranean-type climate of warm and dry summers with wet and cool winters. The coldest times of the year are the nights of December to March when the average temperature is 6–7°C [43–45°F]. July and August are the warmest months when the average daytime temperature is 29–30°C [84–86°F], with many days getting above 35°C [95°F]. Rainfall is low, being registered on only about 70 days in the year. The months from June to August are almost rainless.

PALMA
Temperature
Precipitation 493mm/19in

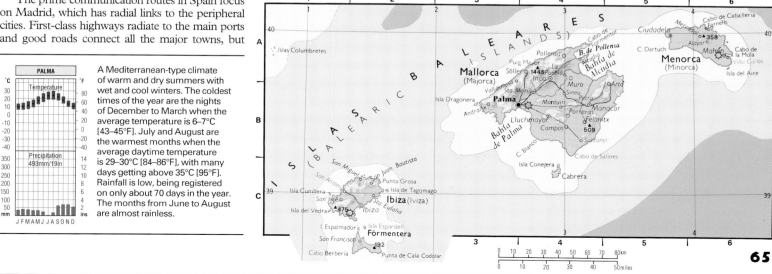

EUROPE

ITALY

When Napoleon invaded Italy in 1796, the French Republican National Guard carried a military standard of vertical green, white and red stripes. After many changes, it was finally adopted as the national flag after the unification of Italy in 1861.

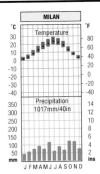

Although the plains of Lombardy lie within the Mediterranean basin they have a climate more like that of central Europe, though with hotter summers and warmer winters. In Milan, January is the only month with average night temperatures just below freezing. Sunshine averages under 5 hours a day, far less than that of southern Italy. Winter is relatively dry and cold with occasional frost and snow. Rainfall is plentiful, with a double maximum in spring and autumn, and falling on 90 days per year.

In 1800 present-day Italy was made up of several political units, including the Papal States, and a substantial part of the north-east was occupied by Austria. The struggle for unification – the *Risorgimento* – began early in the century, but little progress was made until an alliance between France and Piedmont (then part of the kingdom of Sardinia) drove Austria from Lombardy in 1859. Tuscany, Parma and Modena joined Piedmont-Lombardy in 1860, and the Papal States, Sicily, Naples (including most of the southern peninsula) and Romagna were brought into the alliance. King Victor Emmanuel II was proclaimed ruler of a united Italy in Turin the following year, Venetia was acquired from Austria in 1866, and Rome was finally annexed in 1871. Since that time Italy has been a single state, becoming a republic following the abolition of the monarchy by popular referendum in 1946.

North and south

Since unification the population has doubled, and though the rate of increase is notoriously slow today, the rapid growth of population, in a poor country attempting to develop its resources, forced millions of Italians to emigrate during the first quarter of the 20th century. Italy's short-lived African Empire enabled some Italians to settle overseas, but it did not substantially relieve the population pressure. Now there are immigrant Italians to be found on all the inhabited continents. Particularly large numbers settled in the USA, South America and Australia, and more recently large numbers of Italians have moved for similar reasons into northern Europe.

Almost all Italians are brought up as Roman Catholics; since a 1985 agreement between Church and State, Catholic religious teaching is offered, but not compulsory, in schools. The Vatican, though an independent state, is in fact an enclave of Rome.

Despite more than a century of common language, religion and cultural traditions, great differences remain in the ways of life of people in different parts of Italy. These can partly be explained in terms of geography. The long, narrow boot-shaped peninsula, with coastal lowlands on either side of the central Apennines, extends so far south that its toe, and the neighbouring island of Sicily, are in the latitudes of North Africa. Southern Sicily is as far south (36°N) as Tunis and Algiers, while the northern industrial city of Milan (45.5°N) is nearer to London than it is to Reggio in Calabria, the extreme south of peninsular Italy. Given their markedly disparate social and historical backgrounds, the long period of isolation that preceded the unification and widely differing climates, it is hardly surprising that northern and southern Italy retain their independence of character and culture.

The Alps and Apennines

Italy's topographical structure is determined mainly by the events of the Alpine period of mountain building, when the main ranges of the Alps and the Apennines were uplifted together. There are traces of earlier periods in the central Alps, between Mont Blanc (4,807 m [15,771 ft]) on the French border and Monte Rosa (4,634 m [15,203 ft]) on the Swiss border, and in the Carnic Alps in the north-east. Here ancient crystalline rocks predominate, although many of the higher peaks are formed from limestone. The Dolomite Alps, famous for their climbing and skiing resorts, have given their name to a particular form of magnesian limestone.

Generally lower than the Alps, the Apennines reach their highest peaks – almost 3,000 m [9,800 ft] – in the Gran Sasso range overlooking the central Adriatic Sea near Pescara. The most frequently occurring rocks are various types of limestone. The slopes are covered by thin soils and have been subjected to severe erosion, so that in many areas they are suitable only for poor pasture. Between the mountains, however, are long narrow basins, some of which contain lakes. Others have good soils and drainage and provide a basis for arable farming.

Italy is well known for volcanic activity and earthquakes. Three volcanoes are still active – Vesuvius, near Naples, renowned for its burial of Pompeii in AD 79, Etna in Sicily, and Stromboli on an island in the south Tyrrhenian Sea. Traces of earlier volcanism are to be found throughout the country. Ancient lava flows cover large areas, and where they have weathered they produce fertile soils. Mineral deposits, such as the iron ores of Elba and the tin ores of the Mt Annata area, are often associated with earlier volcanic intrusions. Italy is still subject to earthquakes and volcanic eruptions. During the 20th century disasters have occurred at Messina (1908 – the worst in Europe in recent times, with more than 80,000 deaths), Avezzano (1915), Irpinia (1930), Friuli (1976) and Naples (1980).

VENICE

The city of Venice originally grew up on a group of over 100 small islands, lying in a lagoon sheltered from the open Adriatic Sea by a sandbar. It now also includes the mainland suburbs of Mestre and Marghera, where two-thirds of the city's population live. Causeways carry road and rail links to the mainland, but cars are not allowed in the old city. Boats of all types, from the traditional gondolas to the diesel-powered water buses, use the canals which form the 'streets' of Venice.

Venice was once the capital of an imperial republic which, until overthrown by Napoleon in 1797, controlled much of the trade of the Adriatic and the eastern Mediterranean. The heart of the city is around St Mark's Square, where the cathedral and the Palace of the Doges (Dukes) who ruled the republic stand.

The unique site and the rich art treasures attract about 2 million tourists a year, providing a living for tens of thousands of Venetians who cater for them; tourists, too, help to support such craft industries as glassblowing, for which the city is famous. For Expo 2000 the figure is expected to be over 250,000 a day, imposing a massive strain on a city already suffering from erosion, subsidence and pollution.

COUNTRY Italian Republic

AREA 301,270 sq km [116,320 sq mls]

POPULATION 57,181,000

CAPITAL (POPULATION) Rome (2,723,000)

GOVERNMENT Multiparty republic with a bicameral legislature

ETHNIC GROUPS Italian 94%, German, French, Greek, Albanian, Slovene, Ladino

LANGUAGES Italian 94% (official), Sardinian 3%

RELIGIONS Roman Catholic 83%

NATIONAL DAY 2 June; Republic (1946)

CURRENCY Lira = 100 centesimi

ANNUAL INCOME PER PERSON US$19,620

SOURCE OF INCOME Agriculture 3%, industry 32%, services 65%

MAIN PRIMARY PRODUCTS Wheat, barley, vegetables, grapes, fruit, olives, fish oil, natural gas, iron ore, mercury, zinc, lignite, sulphur, marble

MAIN INDUSTRIES Iron and steel, chemicals, food processing, oil refining, vehicles, textiles and clothing, wine, tourism

MAIN EXPORTS Machinery 35%, textiles and clothing 13%, vehicles 9%, chemicals 8%, footwear 5%, petroleum products 3%, iron and steel 3%

MAIN EXPORT PARTNERS Germany 19%, France 17%, USA 9%, UK 7%, Switzerland 5%, Belgium 3%, Spain 3%

MAIN IMPORTS Machinery 29%, textiles and clothing 13%, chemicals 11%, vehicles 9%, petroleum products 8%, footwear 5%, iron and steel 3%

MAIN IMPORT PARTNERS Germany 21%, France 15%, Saudi Arabia 6%, USA 16%, UK 6%, Belgium 5%

EDUCATIONAL EXPENDITURE 4% of GNP

DEFENCE 2% of GNP

TOTAL ARMED FORCES 390,000

TOURISM 51,300,000 visitors per year

ROADS 300,292 [187,683 mls]

RAILWAYS 15,983 km [9,989 mls]

POPULATION DENSITY 193 per sq km [500 per sq ml]

URBAN POPULATION 67%

POPULATION GROWTH 0% per year

BIRTHS 11 per 1,000 population

DEATHS 11 per 1,000 population

INFANT MORTALITY 9 per 1,000 live births

LIFE EXPECTANCY Female 80 yrs, male 73 yrs

POPULATION PER DOCTOR 211 people

ADULT LITERACY 97%

PRINCIPAL CITIES (POPULATION) Rome 2,723,000 Milan 1,359,000 Naples 1,072,000 Turin 953,000 Palermo 697,000 Genoa 668,000 Bologna 401,000 Florence 397,000 Bari 342,000 Catánia 330,000 Venice 306,000 Verona 255,000 Messina 233,000 Táranto 230,000

SARDINIA

Just a little smaller than Sicily, but with less than a third of its population, Sardinia's isolation from the mainstream of Italian life is due partly to its physical position, 480 km [300 mls] from the Italian coast, but the rugged, windswept terrain and lack of resources have also set it apart.

The chief crops on the lowlands are wheat, vines, olives and vegetables, and there are rough pastures for sheep and goats on the scrub-covered hills. Fishing for tuna provides an important source of income for the ports of the west coast. Sardinia is rich in minerals, including lead, zinc, iron ore and lignite, and the island is an increasingly popular tourist destination.

Lombardy

The great triangular plain of Lombardy, lying between the northern Alps and the Apennines, is drained by the River Po, which flows west to east, rising in the Ligurian Alps near the French frontier and flowing across a delta into the Gulf of Venice.

The Lombardy plains are the most productive area of Italy, both agriculturally and industrially. There is no shortage of water, as in the areas further south, although some places are served by irrigation canals. Crops include maize, wheat, potatoes, tomatoes, rice and mulberries – these associated with the development of the silk industry. In the Alpine valleys above the Lombardy plain vines are cultivated.

Industry and urban life in Lombardy is long established. Textiles – silk, cotton, flax and wool – metalworking and food processing all began long before the modern industrial period. Large-scale Italian industry was slower to develop than in Britain and Germany, partly because of the lack of coal, but in Lombardy this has been offset by the availability of hydroelectric power from the Alpine rivers, and by the development of a natural gas field in the area of the Po delta. Oil and gas are also imported by pipeline from Austria. Italy is more dependent on imported energy than any European country, nearly 60% of it oil, though Algeria remains

67

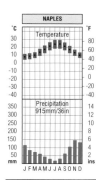

NAPLES

°C Temperature °F

Precipitation
915mm/36in

J F M A M J J A S O N D

Naples lies in the north of the Mezzogiorno, the most typically Mediterranean region in Italy. Summers are hot and very sunny with occasional thunderstorms usually providing the only rain. From May to September sunshine is 8–10 hours per day, with day temperatures of 23–29°C [73–84°F]. Winters are mild and virtually free from frost, with westerly winds bringing abundant rain to the western slopes of the Apennines. November is the wettest month throughout the region.

a major supplier of gas through the Transmed pipeline via Tunisia.

Engineering and metalworking are now the most important industries, centred on Milan and, in Piedmont, on Turin. Lombardy remains dominant, however: the most densely populated region, it accounts for a third of Italy's GDP and some 30% of export earnings, and in the 1992 election the separatist party made huge gains at the expense of established rivals.

Central Italy

Central Italy, between the Po Valley and the River Tiber, is a transitional zone between the industrially developed north and the poor, agrarian south. It contains Rome, which has survived as a capital city for over 2,000 years, Florence and Bologna.

The area has a glorious history of artistic and literary achievement, but with its limited resources, steep slopes and difficult communications it has been left behind in economic development by the more favoured lowlands of the north, and relies heavily on tourism for regional income.

Regions like Tuscany, Umbria and Lazio have considerable autonomy from Rome, with control over health and education, for example, and other devolved powers. Indeed five regions enjoy more autonomy than the rest: French-speaking Valle d'Aosta, in the north-west; Trentino-Alto Adige, the largely German-speaking area in the far north; Friuli-Venézia Giulia in the north-east; and the two island provinces of Sardinia and Sicily.

The Mezzogiorno

The south of Italy, known as the Mezzogiorno, is the least developed part of the country. It displays, in less severe form, many of the characteristics of the developing countries of the Third World. Its people depend for their livelihood on Mediterranean crops produced on small peasant farms too small to lend themselves to modern techniques, although there are some large estates.

Over a third of the people are still in agriculture, with unemployment three or more times that of the north. Though the eight regions of the Mezzogiorno cover some 40% of the land area (including Sicily and Sardinia) and contain more than a third of the country's population, they contribute only about a quarter of the GDP.

The birth rate is much higher than in the north, and there is a serious problem of overpopulation which is partly eased by large-scale, often temporary, migration to the cities of the north and to Italy's more developed partners in the EU, as well as more permanent migration overseas. Migration often exacerbates the problems of the Mezzogiorno, however, as it tends to take away the younger, more active members of society, leaving behind an ageing population.

There are also serious urban problems, caused by the rapid growth of cities such as Naples and Reggio as young people leave the rural areas to live in the slums. As one of Italy's major ports, Naples imports oil, coal, iron ore, chemicals and cotton to provide the raw materials for manufacturing industries. In recent years great efforts have been made by a government-sponsored agency, the Cassa di Mezzogiorno, to found new factories in the Naples area, but they have had little effect on the mass poverty and unemployment of the region.

The problems of the Mezzogiorno, including especially those of the Naples area and Sicily, arise partly from geographical limitations and partly from historical circumstances. They are no longer a problem only for Italy, for the stability and prosperity of Italy is a matter of concern for the rest of Europe, and in particular for the countries of the EU, of which Italy was a founder member. The continuing gulf between north and south has a disturbing effect on the economic and political health of Italy, a country whose people have contributed so much to the civilization of Europe.

Overall, however, Italy has made enormous progress since the devastation of World War II, particularly given its few natural resources and what outsiders have seen as a permanent state of near anarchy presided over by a succession of fragile coalition governments. In fact, Italy's government has always been more stable than it appeared: until the 1990s, coalitions were consistently dominated by the Christian Democrat Party.

Italian individualism continued to fuel the notorious black economy, which boosted official GNP by at least 10% and probably much more while remaining free of government regulation and taxation. When black economy estimates were included in the official GNP in the 1980s, Italy overtook the United Kingdom in the world earning league. By then, the country was an important member of the G8 group. Once poor and agrarian, Italy had earned its place as one of the richest nations in the advanced, industrialized world ■

National capital
Regional capital

0 100 200 300 400 500km
0 100 200 300miles

SICILY

The triangular-shaped island of Sicily lies in a strategic position between the two basins of the Mediterranean, and has had a stormy history as successive powers wishing to dominate the Mediterranean have sought to conquer it. A beautiful island, with both natural and man-made attractions to interest the millions of tourists, it is nevertheless in a low state of economic development and its people are among the poorest in Europe.

There is some industrial development around the ports of Palermo, Catania, Messina and Syracuse, based on imported materials or on oil and natural gas found offshore during the 1960s. The only other local industrial materials are potash, sulphur and salt. However, a large proportion of the inhabitants still live by peasant farming, supplemented by fishing and work in the tourist industry.

There are few permanent streams on Sicily, as the island experiences an almost total drought in summer, and agriculture is restricted by the availability of water. Citrus fruits, vines and olives are among the chief crops. On coastal lowlands such as those around Catania, Marsala and Palermo, wheat and early vegetables are grown. The rapid growth in the population and the strong family ties which exist among Sicilians have, however, led to a situation in which too many people are trying to make a living from tiny parcels of land.

VESUVIUS

Rising steeply from the Plain of Campania, behind the Bay of Naples, the massive cone of Vesuvius forms one of a family of southern Italian volcanoes, clustered in an area of crustal weakness. Others include the nearby island of Ischia, Stromboli and Vulcano of the Lipari Islands, and Etna in eastern Sicily. Ischia's volcanoes last erupted in the 14th century. Stromboli and Vulcano are currently active, emitting lava and gases, and Etna has a long record of eruptions from 475 BC to the present day. In April 1992 an eruption threatened to destroy a village on Etna's slopes.

Vesuvius, which probably arose from the waters of the bay some 200,000 years ago, has been intermittently active ever since; over 30 major eruptions have been recorded since Roman times. However, its slopes are forested or farmed, the fertile volcanic soils producing good crops during the quiescent periods between eruptive spells. There are many settlements on its flanks, and laboratories for volcanic and seismic studies.

The most famous eruption of Vesuvius occurred in AD 79, when the flourishing Roman port of Pompeii and nearby town of Stabiae were engulfed in a rain of ashes. Excavations begun in 1748 have revealed streets, shops, houses, frescoes, statues, and many other artefacts of Roman times – even the bread in the bakery.

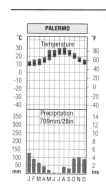

PALERMO

°C Temperature °F

Precipitation
709mm/28in

J F M A M J J A S O N D

This is one of the hottest parts of Italy. The temperature averages are 20–26°C [68–79°F] from May to October, with no month below 10°C [50°F]. Temperatures of just below freezing have been recorded January to March. Sunshine amounts are high with over 10 hours per day June to August. Low rainfall comes mainly in the winter months, falling on about 10 days each month November to February. The *sirocco*, a hot and humid wind from Africa, frequently affects Sicily.

SAN MARINO

The tiny republic of San Marino, enclosed completely within the territory of Italy, has been an independent state since AD 885. The flag's colours – white for the snowy mountains and blue for the sky – derive from the state coat of arms.

COUNTRY Most Serene Republic of San Marino
AREA 61 sq km [24 sq mls]
POPULATION 26,000
CAPITAL (POPULATION) San Marino (4,335)
POPULATION DENSITY 426 per sq km [1,083 per sq ml]

Surrounded by Italy, the tiny independent state of San Marino – the world's smallest republic – lies 20 km [12 mls] south-west of the Adriatic port of Rimini. Most of the territory consists of the limestone mass of Monte Titano (725 m [2,382 ft]), around which are clustered wooded mountains, pastures, fortresses and medieval villages.

The republic is named after St Marinus, the stonemason saint who is said to have first estab-lished a community here in the 4th century AD. Nearly all the inhabitants live in the medieval forti-fied city of San Marino, which is visited by over 3 million tourists a year. The chief occupations are tourism (which accounts for 60% of total revenues), limestone quarrying and the making of wine, textiles and ceramics. San Marino has a friendship and co-operation treaty with Italy dating back to 1862; the ancient republic uses Italian currency, but issues its own stamps, which contribute a further 10% to state revenues. The *de facto* customs union with Italy makes San Marino an easy conduit for the illegal export of lira and certain kinds of tax evasion for Italians.

The state is governed by an elected council and has its own legal system. In 1957 a bloodless takeover replaced the Communist-Socialist regime that had been in power from 1945. It has no armed forces, and police are 'hired' from the Italian constabulary ■

VATICAN CITY

Since the 13th century, the emblem on the flag has represented the Vatican's role as the headquarters of the Roman Catholic Church. Consisting of the triple tiara of the Popes above the keys of heaven given to St Peter, it was adopted in 1929.

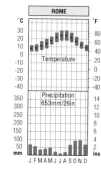

The summers are warm with June to September averages of over 20°C [68°F], but the winters can be cold, with averages in single figures for December to February, and with subzero temperatures having been recorded November to March. There are over 2,500 hours of sunshine per year, ranging from only 3 hours in December, to 8–10 hours from May to September. Reasonable amounts of rain fall mainly in the winter and, in all, on only about 65 days per annum.

The world's smallest nation – a walled enclave on the west bank of the River Tiber in the city of Rome – the Vatican City State exists to provide an independent base for the Holy See, governing body of the Roman Catholic Church and its 952 million adherents round the world. Sustained by invest-ment income and voluntary contribution, it is all that remains of the Papal States which, until 1870, occupied most of central Italy. In 1929 Mussolini recognized the independence of the Vatican City in return for papal recognition of the kingdom of Italy.

The Vatican consists of 44 hectares [109 acres], including St Peter's Square, with a resident popu-lation of about 1,000 – including the country's only armed force of 100 Swiss Guards. The population is made up entirely of unmarried males.

The Commission appointed by the Pope to administer the affairs of the Vatican also has control over a radio station, the Pope's summer palace at Castel Gandolfo and several churches in Rome. The Vatican City has its own newspaper and radio station, police and railway station and issues its own stamps and coins, while the Papacy has since the 1960s played an important role in some areas of international diplomacy.

The popes have been prominent patrons of the arts, and the treasures of the Vatican, including Michelangelo's frescoes in the Sistine Chapel, attract tourists from all over the world. Similarly, the Vatican library contains a priceless collection of manuscripts from both pre-Christian and Christian eras. The popes have lived in the Vatican since the 5th century, apart from a brief period at Avignon in the 14th century ■

COUNTRY Vatican City State
AREA 0.44 sq km [0.17 sq mls]
POPULATION 1,000
CAPITAL Vatican City
GOVERNMENT Papal Commission
LANGUAGES Latin (official), Italian
RELIGIONS Roman Catholic
CURRENCY Vatican lira = 100 centesimi

MALTA

The colours of Malta's flag, adopted on independence in 1964, are those of the Knights of Malta, who ruled the islands from 1530 to 1798. The George Cross was added in 1943 to commemorate the heroism of the Maltese people during World War II.

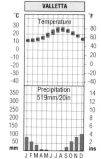

The climate is Mediterranean with hot dry summers and cool wet winters. January to February temperatures average 12°C [54°F], while May to October are over 20°C [68°F], with 26°C [79°F] in July to August. The lowest temperature ever recorded is 5°C [41°F]. June to August have 11–12 hours of sunshine. Rainfall is low with little falling between April and September. It can be a windy island, and the winds bring cool, dry or hot and humid weather depending on its origin.

A former British colony and now an indepen-dent, non-aligned parliamentary republic with-in the Commonwealth, Malta lies in the centre of the Mediterranean, roughly halfway between Gib-raltar and Suez, 93 km [58 mls] south of Sicily and 290 km [180 mls] from North Africa. Its strategic importance arises from its position, and from its possession of magnificent natural harbours – notable among them Grand Harbour and Marsamxett; these lie on either side of the rocky peninsula on which stands the capital, Valletta.

Malta and the neighbouring islands of Comino and Gozo have few natural resources (apart from splendid building stone), and with no rivers and sparse rainfall there are only limited possibilities for agriculture. Yet they constitute one of the world's most densely populated states, with two-thirds of the people living in the 'conurbation' of districts around Valletta. The native islanders are of mixed Arab, Sicilian, Norman, Spanish, English and Italian origin. Arabic, Maltese and English are all spoken.

From the Napoleonic period until after World War II, the Maltese economy depended on agricul-ture (which still involves nearly half the workforce), and the existence of British military bases. Before the last garrison left in 1979 Malta had already obtained independence, and was developing export-oriented industries and 'offshore' business facilities that would replace the income from the military and naval connections. Germany became its chief trad-ing partner ahead of the UK and Italy, though Libya supplies most of its oil.

Year-round tourism, taking advantage of the mild Mediterranean winters and the hot, dry sum-mers, brings 1,185,000 visitors annually to Malta, of whom 49% are from the UK. A major foreign exchange earner, tourism brings in 260 million Maltese lira each year. The country is also develop-ing a new freeport, wharf and storage facilities ■

COUNTRY Republic of Malta
AREA 316 sq km [122 sq mls]
POPULATION 370,000
CAPITAL (POPULATION) Valletta (102,500)
GOVERNMENT Multiparty republic
ETHNIC GROUPS Maltese 96%, British 2%
LANGUAGES Arabic, Maltese, English
RELIGIONS Roman Catholic 96%
NATIONAL DAY 31 March; National Day
CURRENCY Maltese lira = 100 cents
ANNUAL INCOME PER PERSON US$6,800
MAIN PRIMARY PRODUCTS Stone and sand
MAIN INDUSTRIES Tourism, light industry, agriculture
MAIN EXPORTS Manufactured articles, clothing
MAIN IMPORTS Food and live animals, mineral fuels
POPULATION DENSITY 1,171 per sq km [3,033 per sq ml]
LIFE EXPECTANCY Female 76 yrs, male 72 yrs
ADULT LITERACY 87%

EUROPE

ALBANIA

The name of the country means 'land of the eagle'. Following the formation of a non-Communist government in March 1992, the star that had been placed above the eagle's head in 1946 was removed and the flag has reverted to its original form.

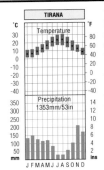

TIRANA

The Mediterranean-type climate in the west, with hot and dry summers and cooler winters, changes in the mountains and valleys of the east and north to become much wetter. November to April there is rain on about every other day. In the coastal lowlands, the temperature rarely drops below freezing. The lowest temperature recorded at Tirana is –8°C [18°F], and over 35°C [95°F] in July to September. In the mountainous interior, cold continental influences bring heavy snowfalls.

By far Europe's poorest country, Albania is also one of the most isolated, separated physically and culturally even from its closest neighbours, Greece and Yugoslavia. The Albanian language has no close affinities with other European languages, and until 1990 the political system, priding itself on being the last fortress of true Marxism-Leninism, emphasized the country's remoteness.

Albania declared independence in 1912, after five centuries under the rule of the Ottoman Turks. A legacy of this period is the fact that, until the government closed all religious establishments in 1967, some 70% of Albanians were Muslims. Today the figure is 65%.

At the end of World War II, an Albanian People's Republic was formed under the Communist leadership that had led the partisans against the Germans. Pursuing a modernization programme on rigid Stalinist lines, the regime of Envar Hoxha at various times associated politically and often

economically with Yugoslavia (up to 1948), the USSR (1948–61), and China (1961–77) before following a fiercely independent policy.

Geographical obstacles have reinforced Albania's linguistic and political isolation. The mountainous interior forms a barrier to penetration from the east. The main ranges, which rise to almost 2,000 m [6,500 ft] are continuations of the Dinaric Alps; these run from north-west to south-east, rising steeply from the coastal lowlands. Limestone is the most common type of rock, although in the central area there are igneous masses rich in mineral ores, including copper, iron, nickel and chromium. Albania relies heavily on exports of chromium for foreign exchange, and is the world's eighth largest producer, contributing 3.2% of the total in 1993.

Although the country has adequate energy resources – including petroleum, brown coal and hydroelectric potential – Albania remains one of the least industrialized countries in Europe, and transport is poorly developed. Horses and mules are widely used in rural areas, and there are no rail links with other countries. Most people still live by farming, with maize, wheat, barley, sugar beet and fruits predominant, though the country has always found it a difficult task feeding a population with a growth rate of 1.3% – one of the highest in Europe.

Hoxha's successor, Ramiz Alia, continued the dictator's austere policies after his death in 1985, but by the end of the decade even Albania was affected by the sweeping changes in Eastern Europe, and in 1990 the more progressive wing of the Communist Party (led by Alia) won the struggle for power. They instituted a wide programme of reform, including the legalization of religion, the encouragement of foreign investment, the introduction of a free market for peasants' produce, and the establishment of pluralist democracy. In the elections of April 1991 the Communists comfortably retained their majority, but two months later the government was brought down by a general strike and an interim coalition 'national salvation' committee took over; this fragile 'government of stability' in turn collapsed after six months. Elections in the spring of 1992 brought to an end the last Communist regime in Europe when the non-Communist Democratic Party won power. In 1996, the Democratic Party took 122 of the 140 seats in the parliament.

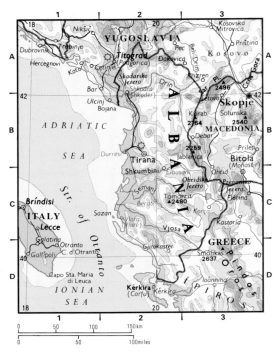

COUNTRY Republic of Albania

AREA 28,750 sq km [11,100 sq mls]

POPULATION 3,458,000

CAPITAL (POPULATION) Tirana (251,000)

GOVERNMENT Multiparty republic with a unicameral legislature

ETHNIC GROUPS Albanian 96%, Greek 2%, Romanian, Macedonian, Montenegrin, Gypsy

LANGUAGES Albanian (official)

RELIGIONS Sunni Muslim 65%, Christian 33%

CURRENCY Lek = 100 qindars

ANNUAL INCOME PER PERSON US$340

MAIN PRIMARY PRODUCTS Copper, chromium, petroleum and natural gas, cereals, fruit, timber, tobacco

MAIN INDUSTRIES Agriculture, petroleum refining, mining, food and tobacco processing, textiles

DEFENCE 2.3% of GNP

POPULATION DENSITY 120 per sq km [312 per sq ml]

LIFE EXPECTANCY Female 75 yrs, male 70 yrs

ADULT LITERACY 85%

PRINCIPAL CITIES (POPULATION) Tirana 251,000 Durrës 86,900 Shkodër 83,700 Elbasan 83,200 Vlorë 76,000 Korçë 67,100

Meanwhile, however, the country experienced periods of chaos and violence, triggered initially by food shortages; in early 1997, severe economic difficulties and the loss of confidence in the government led to extreme civil unrest which quickly spread throughout the country. Large numbers of refugees fled the country to temporary safe havens in Italy and Greece, thereby creating a new set of problems.

After a lifetime of rigid state control, a backward country had been catapulted without real government into modern industrialized Europe, and towards a Western world in recession. By 1995, the annual income per capita figure for Albania had fallen to just US$340, alongside many a struggling nation in what is still called the Third World ■

GREECE

Blue and white became Greece's national colours during the war of independence. Finally adopted in 1970, the flag's design represents the battle cry 'Freedom or Death' used during the struggle against Ottoman (Turkish) domination in the war of 1821–9.

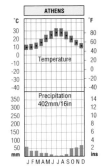

ATHENS

Athens has a climate typical of the eastern Mediterranean basin. A single maximum of rainfall occurs in winter and summers are dry, with no rain falling in July or August on an average of one year in three. At Athens, snow can fall from November to April, but on average on only 2 days January to February. On hot summer days the *calina*, a dusty heat haze, is common. The east coast of Greece is sunny with over 2,700 hours of sunshine a year and has only about half the rainfall of the west.

Mainland Greece consists of a mountainous peninsula which projects 500 km [312 mls] into the Mediterranean from the south-west corner of the Balkans, and an 80 km [50 mls] coastal belt along the northern shore of the Aegean Sea. Nearly a fifth of the total land area of Greece is made up of its 2,000 or so islands, mainly in the Aegean Sea to the east of the main peninsula but also in the Ionian Sea to the west; only 154 are inhabited, but they account for over 11% of the population. Some of the islands of the Dodecanese group in the eastern Aegean lie just 16 km [10 mls] off the coast of Turkey, and northern Corfu in the Ionian Islands

is separated from the Albanian coast by a narrow channel less than 3.2 km [2 mls] across.

The principal structural feature of Greece is the Pindos Mountains, which extend south-eastwards from the Albanian border to cover most of the peninsula. The island of Crete is also structurally related to the main Alpine fold mountain system to which the Pindos range belongs. Its highest peak, Mt Ida, is 2,456 m [8,057 ft] high. In these ranges limestone rocks predominate, though many of the Aegean Islands are of similar formation to the Rhodopi Massif in the north and made up of crystalline rocks.

With so much of Greece covered by rugged

mountains, only about a third of the area is suitable for cultivation, yet 40% of the population depend for their living on agriculture. The average farm size is under 4 hectares [10 acres], though on a few areas of flat land, mostly around the Aegean coasts in

Macedonia and Thrace, large estates are found. Wheat, olives, vines, tobacco and citrus fruits are the chief crops. Most villagers keep a few domestic animals, particularly sheep and goats. The mountain pastures are poor, mainly consisting of scrubland, and many areas have been stripped of what tree cover they once had by goats (notoriously destructive of growing trees), and by the need for wood for ships, house building and charcoal burning.

Greece has been described as a land of mountains and of the sea. Nowhere in Greece is more than 80 km [50 mls] from the sea, and most of the towns are situated on the coast. Greater Athens, which consists of the capital city and its seaport, Piraeus, has a third of the total population and has grown sixfold since 1945. Thessaloníki (Salonica), the second city, is also a seaport, serving not only northern Greece but also southern Yugoslavia. Greece's mountainous terrain makes communications on land difficult, but the country has the world's largest merchant fleet (measured by ownership, not national registry), and in 1996 Greece was the world's largest shipping nation in terms of tonnage. Shipbuilding and repairs are still important industries, while fishing provides a crucial dietary supplement.

In the great days of classical Greece, during the thousand years before Christ, Greek colonies were established all around the shores of the Mediterranean and Black Seas. For a brief period in the 4th century BC, Alexander the Great built an empire which extended from the Danube, through Turkey and the Middle East to the Indus Valley of northern India. Even more important were the great contributions to philosophy, sculpture, architecture and literature made by the early Greeks.

The great epic poems of Greece – the *Iliad* and the *Odyssey* – speak of the exploits of ancient Greek seafarers who travelled around the Mediterranean. Today Greeks are still great seamen and wanderers, and large communities are to be found in the USA, Australia, Canada and Latin America. Since 1960 many Greek migrants have found work in Germany, and the admission of Greece to the EEC (on 1 January 1981) has given further opportunities for Greeks to find work in Western Europe.

COUNTRY Hellenic Republic

AREA 131,990 sq km [50,961 sq mls]

POPULATION 10,510,000

CAPITAL (POPULATION) Athens (3,097,000)

GOVERNMENT Multiparty republic

ETHNIC GROUPS Greek 96%, Macedonian 2%, Turkish 1%, Albanian, Slav

LANGUAGES Greek (official)

RELIGIONS Greek Orthodox 97%, Muslim 2%

CURRENCY Drachma = 100 lepta

ANNUAL INCOME PER PERSON US$7,390

MAIN PRIMARY PRODUCTS Wheat, tobacco, cotton, olives, grapes, bauxite, iron, chrome, crude oil

MAIN INDUSTRIES Agriculture, tourism, chemicals, steel, aluminium, shipping, shipbuilding

MAIN EXPORTS Foodstuffs, olive oil and tobacco 28%, textiles 23%, petroleum products 8%

MAIN EXPORT PARTNERS Germany 25%, Italy 14%, France 9%, UK 9%, USA 6%

MAIN IMPORTS Machinery and transport equipment 23%, foodstuffs and beverages 17%, oil 9%

MAIN IMPORT PARTNERS Germany 20%, Italy 15%, France 8%, Netherlands 7%, Japan 6%, UK 5%

DEFENCE 5.6% of GNP

TOURISM 9,913,267 visitors per year

POPULATION DENSITY 80 per sq km [206 per sq ml]

ADULT LITERACY 94%

PRINCIPAL CITIES (POPULATION) Athens 3,097,000 Thessaloníki 378,000 Piraeus 170,000 Pátrai 155,000

Greece is poorly endowed with industrial raw materials. There are deposits of iron ore, bauxite, nickel and manganese, but no coal and very small amounts of oil. The possibilities for hydroelectric development are severely limited because of the irregularity of the streams, many of which dry up entirely during the long summer drought. Thus Greece must import most of its sources of energy – mainly oil and coal. Industrial activity is largely concerned with the processing of agricultural produce – fruit and vegetables, canning, the production of wine and olive oil, cigarette manufacture, textiles and leather processing. Greece is one of the world's major producers of dried fruits; the word 'currant' is derived from the name of the Greek town of Corinth that lies on the narrow isthmus connecting the southern peninsula of the Pelopónnisos to the mainland. A 4.8 km [3 mls] canal, built in 1893, cuts through the isthmus, linking the Gulf of Corinth with the Aegean.

The tourist industry is vital. Overseas visitors are attracted by the warm climate, the beautiful scenery, especially on the islands, and also by the historical sites which survive from the days of classical Greece. However, a number of factors have combined to limit the importance of tourism in recent years, including the emergence of cheaper rivals like Turkey and Tunisia, the recession in Western countries and the appalling pollution in Athens – by some measures the most polluted city in Europe

outside the former Eastern bloc, with 60% of the nation's manufacturing capacity.

The gap in economic strength and performance between Greece and most of its EU partners remains wide, but the prospect of a single market may help to overcome the traditional obstacles of partisan, often volatile politics, an inflated, slow moving government bureaucracy, and a notorious 'black economy' ∎

CRETE

The island of Crete was the home of the seafaring Minoan civilization, which flourished in the period 3500–1100 BC and left behind a wealth of archaeological sites and artefacts. Most southerly and by far the largest of the Greek islands, Crete has a milder, more maritime climate than the mainland. The rugged south coast, backed by steep limestone mountains, is the more inhospitable side, with winter gales adding to navigation hazards.

Most of the population of 540,000 live in the lowlands of the north, about a quarter of them in the capital Iráklion (the capital) and Khania. Though Greek-speaking, Cretans differ in outlook from the mainlanders; they suffered long occupation by Venetians and then by Turks, remaining under Turkish rule until 1898, 70 years after mainland Greece had been liberated.

EUROPE

YUGOSLAVIA

Only the republics of Serbia and Montenegro now remain in Yugoslavia. The same flag is still used with its colours identifying it as a Slavic state which was once part of the Austro-Hungarian Empire. It used to have a red star in the centre, but this was dropped in 1992.

Yugoslavia by 1993 was an almost figmentary state. Known from 1918 as the State of the Serbs, Croats and Slovenes, and from 1929 as Yugoslavia ('land of the south Slavs'), the unity of the state was under constant threat from nationalist and ethnic tensions. Potential flashpoints existed not only where sections of the Yugoslav patchwork met, but within each patch itself, for centuries of troubled Balkan history had so stirred the region's peoples that there was no area that did not contain at least one aggrieved or distrusted minority.

In the interwar period the country was virtually a 'Greater Serbia', and after Hitler invaded in 1941 Yugoslavs fought both the Germans and each other. The Communist-led Partisans of 'Tito' (Josip Broz, a Croat) emerged victorious in 1945, re-forming Yugoslavia as a republic on the Soviet model. The postwar Tito dictatorship kept antagonisms out of sight, but in 1990, a decade after his death, the first free elections since the war saw nationalist victories in four out of the six federal republics.

The formal secession of Slovenia and Croatia in June 1991 began an irreversible process of disintegration. Slovenia, the most ethnically homogeneous of Yugoslavia's republics, made the transition almost bloodlessly; but the Serbian-dominated federal army launched a brutal campaign against the Croats. The conflict continued until January 1992, when the cease-fire finally held. The fighting then moved to Bosnia-Herzegovina, declared independent in 1992 and at once the theatre of a vicious civil war involving Serbs, Croats and ethnic Bosnian Muslims.

'Yugoslavia' thereafter included only Montenegro and Serbia. However, Serbia had problems of its own: international sanctions had struck at an already war-ravaged economy, causing widespread hardship. In 1998, the fragility of the region was again highlighted when the majority Albanian population in the province of Kosovo fought for self-determination ∎

BOSNIA-HERZEGOVINA

Bosnia-Herzegovina has been fighting for survival since declaring independence in April 1992. With a population made up of 49% Muslims, 31% Serbs and 17% Croats, this volatile combination proved unworkable. At first the Muslim-dominated government allied itself uneasily with the Croat minority, but was at once under attack from the local Serbs, supported by their co-nationals from beyond Bosnia's borders. In their 'ethnic cleansing' campaign, heavily equipped Serbian militias drove poorly armed Muslims from towns they had long inhabited.

By early 1993, the Muslims controlled less than a third of the former federal republic, and even the capital, Sarajevo, became disputed territory under constant shellfire. The Muslim-Croat alliance rapidly disintegrated and refugees approached the million mark. Tougher economic sanctions on Serbia in April 1993 had little effect on the war in Bosnia. A small UN force attempted to deliver relief supplies to civilians and maintain 'safe' Muslim areas, to no avail. Finally, in 1995, the warring parties agreed to a solution – the Dayton Peace Accord. This involved dividing the country into two self-governing provinces, one Bosnian-Serb and the other Muslim-Croat, under a central, unified, multi-ethnic government. Elections were held in 1996 under this new arrangement ∎

MACEDONIA

Macedonia has so far avoided the holocaust of civil war that has marked the passing of Yugoslavia. To begin with, international recognition proved difficult to obtain, since Greece, worried by the consequences for its own Macedonian region, vetoed any acknowledgement of an independent Macedonia on its borders. However, in 1993 the UN accepted the new republic under the name of The Former Yugoslav Republic of Macedonia (FYROM). Diplomatic relations with Greece were assumed in 1995 when Macedonia agreed to remove hints of claims on Greek territory in its constitution ∎

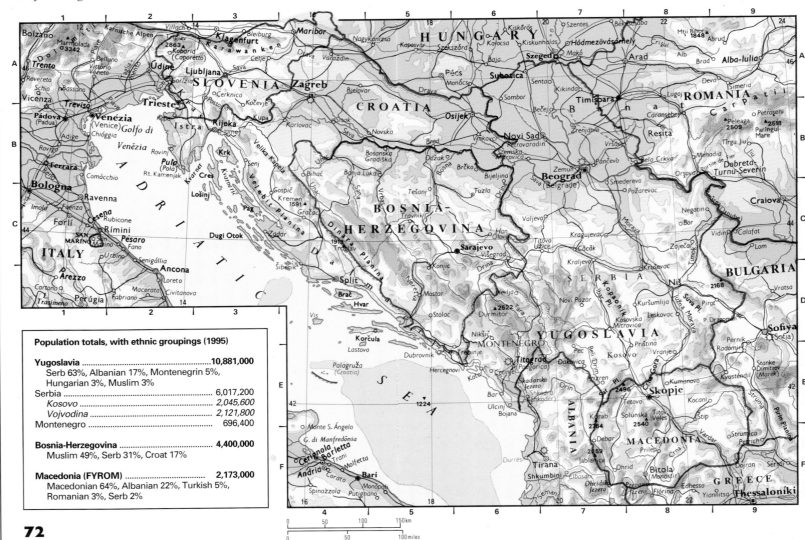

Population totals, with ethnic groupings (1995)	
Yugoslavia	**10,881,000**
Serb 63%, Albanian 17%, Montenegrin 5%, Hungarian 3%, Muslim 3%	
Serbia	6,017,200
Kosovo	*2,045,600*
Vojvodina	*2,121,800*
Montenegro	696,400
Bosnia-Herzegovina	**4,400,000**
Muslim 49%, Serb 31%, Croat 17%	
Macedonia (FYROM)	**2,173,000**
Macedonian 64%, Albanian 22%, Turkish 5%, Romanian 3%, Serb 2%	

SLOVENIA

The Slovene flag, based on the flag of Russia, was originally adopted in 1848. During the Communist period a red star appeared in the centre. This was replaced in June 1991 after independence, with the new emblem showing an outline of Mt Triglav.

COUNTRY Republic of Slovenia (Slovenija)
AREA 20,251 sq km [7,817 sq mls]
POPULATION 2,000,000
CAPITAL (POPULATION) Ljubljana (323,000)
ETHNIC GROUPS Slovene 88%, Croat 3%, Serb 2%, Bosnian 1%
MAIN INDUSTRIES Agriculture, forestry, wine, fishing

Part of the Austro-Hungarian Empire until 1918, Slovenia's Roman Catholic population found ready support from neighbours Italy and Austria (with Slovene populations of about 100,000 and 80,000, respectively) as well as Germany during its fight for recognition in 1991. The most ethnically homogeneous of Yugoslavia's component republics, it stayed relatively free of the violence that plagued Croatia. A mountainous state with access to the Adriatic through the port of Koper, near the Italian border – giving it a flourishing transit trade from landlocked central Europe – it has both strong agricultural sectors (wheat, maize, root crops, livestock) and industry (timber, textiles, steel, vehicles), with mineral resources that include coal, lignite, lead, zinc and mercury. Other important sources of income are winemaking and Alpine tourism. Along with Croatia, Slovenia went furthest in developing a market economy from 1988. After a few days of fighting against the federal army, independence from Belgrade was declared in June 1991 following a peaceful and negotiated withdrawal ■

CROATIA

The red, white and blue flag was originally adopted in 1848. During the Communist period a red star appeared in the centre, but in 1990 this was replaced by the present arms, which symbolize the various parts of the country.

Formerly Yugoslavia's second largest and second most populous republic, Croatia bore the brunt of the Serbian-dominated Yugoslav Army's campaign to resist the break-up of the federation in the autumn war of 1991. Most of the deaths and much of the destruction occurred in this 'U'-shaped state, and the majority of the 650,000 or so refugees were Croats. A massive reconstruction programme is needed to return many towns to anything like normality; the vital tourist industry was also devastated, with the fine medieval city of Dubrovnik on the Dalmatian coast the prime casualty.

COUNTRY Republic of Croatia (Hrvatska)
AREA 56,538 sq km [21,824 sq mls]
POPULATION 4,900,000
CAPITAL (POPULATION) Zagreb (931,000)
ETHNIC GROUPS Croat 78%, Serb 12%, Bosnian 1%

Rivalry between Croats and Serbs goes back centuries – Croatia was politically linked with Hungary, and therefore with Western Europe and the Catholic Church, from 1102 to 1918 – but was fuelled by the Croat position in World War II, when a puppet Fascist regime was set up (including much of Bosnia-Herzegovina) by Germany with the support of the Croatian Catholics.

When war broke out in Bosnia-Herzegovina in 1992, Bosnian Croats occupied parts of the country. But in 1994 Croatia helped to end Croat-Muslim conflict in Bosnia-Herzegovina, and in 1995 it helped to draw up the Dayton Peace Accord. In October 1996, Croatia joined the Council of Europe as its 40th member ■

BULGARIA

The Slav colours of white, green and red were used in the Bulgarian flag from 1878. The national emblem, incorporating a lion (a symbol of Bulgaria since the 14th century), was first added to the flag in 1947, but the crest is now only added for official occasions.

The most subservient of the former Eastern bloc satellites, Bulgaria's links with Russia date back to 1878, when the Tsar's forces liberated the country from five centuries of Ottoman (Turkish) rule. In the period after World War II, and especially under President Zhivkov from 1954, Bulgaria became all too dependent on its overseer; nearly two-thirds of its trade was conducted with the USSR, including most of its energy requirements.

Predictably, Bulgaria was the last and least publicized of the Eastern European countries to fall. In 1990 the Communist Party held on to power under increasing pressure by ousting Zhivkov, renouncing its leading role in the nation's affairs, making many promises of reform and changing its name to the Socialist Party before winning the first free elections since the war – unconvincingly and against confused opposition. With better organization, the Union of Democratic Forces defeated the old guard the following year and began the unenviable task of making the transition to a free market economy.

The new government inherited a host of problems – inflation, food shortages, rising unemployment, strikes, a large foreign debt, a declining traditional manufacturing industry, reduced demand at

The climate of Bulgaria is one of hot summers, cold but not severe winters and moderate rainfall, with a maximum April to August. This is changed by the influence of the nearby seas and the western mountains. The lowlands of the east and south have a much drier and warmer summer. Varna, on the coast, is usually 3–4°C [5–7°F] warmer than Sofia. The Danube lowlands are colder in winter with winds coming in from the continental interior. Temperatures are lower in the mountains.

COUNTRY Republic of Bulgaria
AREA 110,910 sq km [42,822 sq mls]
POPULATION 8,771,000
CAPITAL (POPULATION) Sofia (1,114,000)
GOVERNMENT Multiparty republic
ETHNIC GROUPS Bulgarian 86%, Turkish 10%, Gypsy 3%, Macedonian 3%, Armenian, Romanian, Greek
LANGUAGES Bulgarian (official), Turkish, Romany
RELIGIONS Eastern Orthodox 80%, Sunni Muslim
NATIONAL DAY 3 March; End of Ottoman rule (1878)
CURRENCY Lev = 100 stotinki
ANNUAL INCOME PER PERSON US$1,840
MAIN PRIMARY PRODUCTS Coal, oil and natural gas, lignite, cereals, fruit, cattle, sheep
MAIN INDUSTRIES Agriculture, tobacco, iron and steel, textiles, chemicals, forestry, wine
MAIN EXPORTS Machinery and equipment 57%, foodstuffs, wine and tobacco 14%
MAIN IMPORTS Machinery and equipment 43%, fuels, mineral raw materials and metals 43%, chemicals
POPULATION DENSITY 81 per sq km [211 per sq ml]
LIFE EXPECTANCY Female 76 yrs, male 70 yrs
PRINCIPAL CITIES (POPULATION) Sofia 1,114,000
Plovdiv 379,000 Varna 321,000 Burgas 226,000

home and abroad, increased prices for vital raw materials, and a potential drop in the recently growing revenue from tourism (Bulgaria had 2,335,000 visitors in 1993). In addition there was the nagging worry of a sizeable Turkish minority disaffected with mismanaged attempts at forced assimilation.

With fertile soils but few natural resources, Bulgaria's economy has a distinct agricultural bias, with half the population still earning their living from the land. The most productive agriculture occurs in two lowland areas – the Danubian lowlands of the north, where wheat, barley and maize are the chief crops, and the warmer central valley of the River Maritsa, where grains, cotton, rice, tobacco, fruits and vines are grown.

Separating the two lowland areas are the Balkan Mountains (Stara Planina), which rise to heights of over 2,000 m [6,500 ft]. In the south-facing valleys overlooking the Maritsa plains, plums, vines and tobacco are grown. A particular feature of this area is the rose fields of Kazanluk, from which attar of roses is exported worldwide to the cosmetics industry.

South and west of the Maritsa Valley are the Rhodopi Mountains, containing lead, zinc and copper ores. There are also rich mineral veins of both iron and nonferrous metals in the Stara Planina, north of the capital and chief industrial city, Sofia ■

HUNGARY

The tricolour became popular in the revolution of 1848, though the colours had been in the Hungarian arms since the 15th century. Adopted in 1919, the design was amended in 1957 to remove the state emblem, which had been added in 1949.

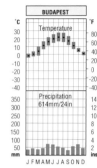

The plains of Hungary have warm, sunny summers and cold winters with snow lying on between 30 and 40 days. At Budapest maximum temperatures exceed 20°C [68°F] from May to September, with the minimum below freezing December to February. There is a double maximum of rainfall, the first in early summer when convectional storms are most active. A second maximum in November becomes a marked feature of the climate towards the south-west.

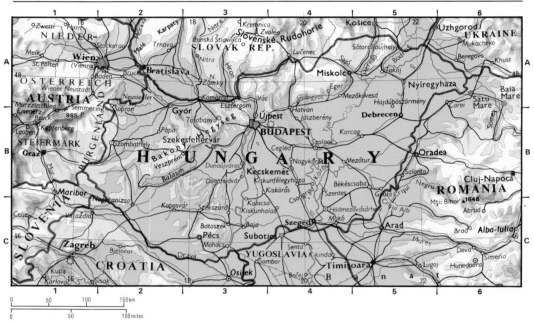

Hungary has reserves of gas, but is poorly endowed with natural resources, bauxite being one of the few plentiful minerals. Industries have been built up on the basis of imported raw materials, mainly from the former USSR. The main industrial centres are in the north of the country, around Miskolc and Budapest, where iron and steel, engineering and chemicals predominate. Aluminium is manufactured north of Lake Balaton.

Unlike its more static neighbours, the new government of Prime Minister Jozsef Antall was able to press on with a rapid transition to a full market economy. The region's first stock market was set up, Budapest was chosen as the European Community's first regional office and Hungary – a founder member of the now defunct Warsaw Pact – applied to join NATO.

Hungary's move away from the classic Eastern European reliance on heavy industry and agriculture would be easier than, say, that of Poland, and many joint ventures with Western capital were inaugurated in the first months of the new democracy. In April 1996, Hungary joined the OECD.

The lack of energy resources, however, remains a concern, and the government has been pursuing an ambitious programme to increase its nuclear capacity from the 1990 figure of 34% of electricity generation. However, Hungary's progress has its cost, with unemployment rising to 632,050 in 1994 – around 10% of the total workforce ■

A s a large part of the Austro-Hungarian Empire, Hungary enjoyed an almost autonomous position within the Dual Monarchy from 1867, but defeat in World War I saw nearly 70% of its territory apportioned by the Treaty of Versailles to Czechoslovakia, Yugoslavia and Romania. Some 2.6 million Hungarians live in these countries today. The government hoped to regain lost land by siding with Hitler's Germany in World War II, but the result was the occupation of the Red Army and, in 1949, the establishment of a Communist state. The heroic Uprising of 1956 was put down by Soviet troops and its leader, Imre Nagy, was executed.

President János Kádár came to power in the wake of the suppression, but his was a relatively progressive leadership, introducing an element of political freedom and a measure of economic liberalism. Before the great upheavals of 1989 Hungary had gone further than any Eastern European Soviet satellite in decentralization and deregulation.

However, failure to tackle the underlying economic problems led in 1988 to some of his own Socialist Workers Party members exerting pressure for change. In 1989 the central committee agreed to a pluralist system and the parliament, previously little more than a rubber-stamp assembly, formally ended the party's 'leading role in society'. In 1990, in the first free elections since the war, Hungarians voted into office a centre-right coalition headed by the Democratic Forum.

Landscape and agriculture

Hungary has two large lowland areas – the aptly named Great Plain (Nagyalföld) which occupies the south-eastern half of the country and is dissected by the country's two main rivers, the Danube and the Tisa, and the Little Plain (Kisalföld) in the north-west. Between them a line of hills runs south-west to north-east from Lake Balaton (72 km [45 mls] long) to the Slovak border.

The Hungarian Plains have some of the most fertile agricultural land in Europe, especially in the areas covered by a mantle of loess (a windblown deposit dating from the Ice Age), but there are also infertile areas of marsh, sand and dry steppeland, where crop growing gives way to grazing.

COUNTRY	Republic of Hungary
AREA	93,030 sq km [35,919 sq mls]
POPULATION	10,500,000
CAPITAL (POPULATION)	Budapest (2,009,000)
GOVERNMENT	Multiparty republic
ETHNIC GROUPS	Magyar 98%, Gypsy, German, Slovak
LANGUAGES	Hungarian (official), German, Slovak
RELIGIONS	Roman Catholic 64%, Protestant 23%
NATIONAL DAY	15 March
CURRENCY	Forint = 100 fillér
ANNUAL INCOME PER PERSON	US$3,330
DEFENCE	3.5% of GNP
TOURISM	22,800,000 visitors per year
POPULATION DENSITY	113 per sq km [292 per sq ml]
LIFE EXPECTANCY	Female 75 yrs, male 68 yrs
ADULT LITERACY	99%
PRINCIPAL CITIES (POPULATION)	Budapest 2,009,000 Debrecen 217,000 Miskolc 191,000 Szeged 179,000

THE DANUBE

With around 300 tributaries and a length of 2,850 km [1,750 mls], the Danube is Europe's second longest river. Rising from a source in the Black Forest in south-west Germany, it flows east and south through Austria, the Slovak Republic, Hungary and Serbia, and forms a large part of the Romanian-Bulgarian frontier before entering the Black Sea through a wide, swampy delta on the border between Romania and the Ukraine.

Navigable as far upstream as Ulm in Bavaria, the Danube passes eight countries in all, and links the three capitals of Vienna, Budapest and Belgrade. It has long been one of Europe's main commercial waterways, and with the ending of the Cold War and the consequent divisions between East and West, it is likely to be of growing importance.

ROMANIA

Romania's colours come from the arms of the provinces that united to form the country in 1861, and the design was adopted in 1948. The central state coat of arms, added in 1965, was deleted in 1990 after the fall of the Communist Ceausescu regime.

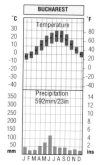

In general, central Europe has a large seasonal range of temperature and a summer rainfall maximum. Winter depressions, which bring so much rain to north-west Europe, are mostly prevented from reaching the east by persistent high pressure. Around Bucharest the heaviest rains fall as thundery showers in spring and early summer, when the air warms rapidly. With over 2,000 hours of sunshine annually, Romania is one of the sunniest parts of Europe.

On three sides, Romania has clearly defined natural boundaries – the Danube in the south, the 200 km [125 mls] Black Sea coast in the east, and the River Prut in the north-east – but in the west the frontier with Hungary crosses the Hungarian Plain, cutting across several tributaries of the River Tisa. This area has a mixed population of Romanians and Hungarians – the western province of Transylvania once belonged to Hungary – and it was here, following the suppression of demonstrations in Timisoara by the secret police (the Securitate), that the army-backed revolt of 1989 began, culminating only days later in the execution of the dictator Nicolae Ceausescu and his wife on Christmas Day, on charges of genocide and corruption.

Landscape

Romania is dominated by a great arc of high fold mountains, the Carpathians, which curve around the plateaus of Transylvania in the heart of the country. South and east of the Carpathians are the plains of the lower Danube. The southern arm of the fold mountains, rising to 2,538 m [8,327 ft], is known as the Transylvanian Alps, the legendary home of Count Dracula. Where these meet the Danube, on the border with Yugoslavia, the river has cut a deep gorge – the Iron Gate (Portile de Fier) – whose rapids over 160 km [100 mls] long have been tamed by the construction of a huge barrage. In the east the Danube delta area has more than 3,000 glaciated lakes and some of Europe's finest wetlands.

There is a great contrast between the fairy-tale landscape of wooded hills in Transylvania and the Carpathians, and the wheat and maize fields of the Danubian lowlands. Despite Ceausescu's manic programmes Romania is still a strong agricultural country, with an export surplus of cereals, timber, fruits and wine, though the agrarian workforce shrank from 75% in 1950 to 18% by 1993. In 1993 the country ranked ninth in maize production and ninth in wine.

Under Ceausescu there was a great drive to develop industries, based on the abundant oil and gas resources of areas on the flanks of the Transylvanian Alps; in 1993 Romania was in the world's top 20 producers of natural gas. The copper, lead, zinc and aluminium industries use domestic supplies, mainly found in the Bihor Massif in Transylvania, but the iron and steel industry, especially the new plant at Galati at the head of the Danubian delta, relies on imported ores.

Bucharest, the capital, lies between the Danube and the Carpathians. An important industrial centre, its manufactures include vehicles, textiles and foodstuffs.

Ceausescu's 24-year rule had been one of the Communist world's most odious. Corrupt and self-seeking, he had nevertheless won plaudits from the West for his independent stance against Soviet control – including a knighthood from Queen Elizabeth II. Coming to power in 1965, he accelerated the party policy of distancing the country from Moscow's foreign aims while pursuing a strict Stalinist approach on the domestic front.

The remorseless industrialization and urbanization programmes of the 1970s caused a severe debt problem, and in the 1980s he switched economic tack, cutting imports and diverting output to exports. But while Romania achieved the enviable status of a net creditor, its people – brainwashed by incessant propaganda – were reduced from sufficiency to subsidence to shortage, with food and energy both savagely rationed. Meanwhile, with many of his relatives in positions of power, Ceausescu built ghettolike 'agro-industrial' housing complexes, desecrating some of the country's finest architecture and demolishing thousands of villages in the process.

After his death, a provisional government of the National Salvation Front (founded only on 22 December 1989) took control; much of the old administrative apparatus was dismantled, the Communist Party was dissolved and religion was relegalized. In May 1990, under Ion Iliescu, the NSF won Romania's first free elections since the war by a huge majority – a result that was judged flawed but not fraudulent by international observers.

The NSF, however, contained many old-guard Communists, and its credibility sank further when Iliescu used miners to curb anti-government demonstrations. Strikes and protests continued, not only against the new authorities but also against the effects of a gradual but nevertheless marked switch to a market economy: food shortages, rampant inflation and rising unemployment. In addition, foreign investment was sluggish, deterred by the political instability. During 1991 the struggle between the two factions of the NSF – conservative President Iliescu (a former Ceausescu Politburo member) and reformist Prime Minister Petre Roman – personified the split that existed right across a country in desperate need of unity.

Another problem appeared with the new independent status of Moldova, which was created from part of Ukraine and Romania in the Hitler-Stalin pact of 1940 (see page 78). Two-thirds of Moldovans speak Romanian, the official language, and people on both sides of the border favour reunification. However, minority groups in Moldova are opposed to this, which has led to fighting.

In November 1991 the parliament in Bucharest voted overwhelmingly for a new constitution enshrining pluralist democracy, human rights and a market economy, with elections set for the spring of 1992. It was not special by the standards of contemporary Eastern European events – but it was a far cry from the despotic reign of Nicolae Ceausescu ∎

COUNTRY Romania

AREA 237,500 sq km [91,699 sq mls]

POPULATION 22,863,000

CAPITAL (POPULATION) Bucharest (2,061,000)

GOVERNMENT Multiparty republic

ETHNIC GROUPS Romanian 89%, Hungarian 7%

LANGUAGES Romanian (official), Hungarian, German

RELIGIONS Romanian Orthodox 87%, Roman Catholic 5%, Greek Orthodox 4%

NATIONAL DAY 23 August; Liberation Day (1945)

CURRENCY Romanian leu = 100 bani

ANNUAL INCOME PER PERSON US$1,120

MAIN PRIMARY PRODUCTS Cereals, sugar, fruit, vegetables, timber, livestock, fish, oil, natural gas

MAIN INDUSTRIES Agriculture, mining, iron and steel, chemicals, forestry, textiles, food processing

LIFE EXPECTANCY Female 74 yrs, male 69 yrs

ADULT LITERACY 97%

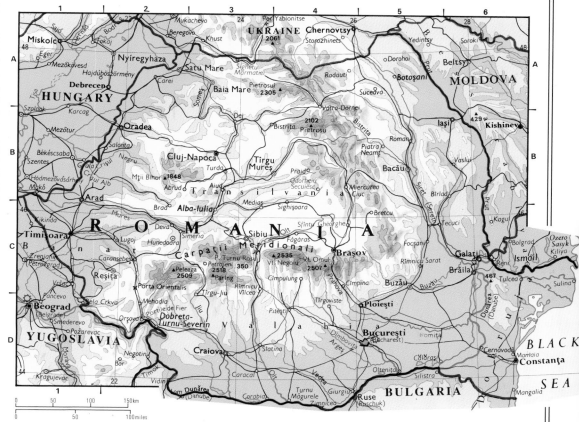

EUROPE

CZECH REPUBLIC

 On independence in January 1993, the Czech Republic adopted the flag of the former Czechoslovakia. It features the red and white of Bohemia with the blue of Moravia and Slovakia, the colours of Pan-Slavic liberation.

COUNTRY Czech Republic
AREA 78,864 sq km [30,449 sq mls]
POPULATION 10,500,000
CAPITAL (POPULATION) Prague (1,217,000)
GOVERNMENT Multiparty republic with a bicameral legislature
ETHNIC GROUPS Czech 81%, Moravian 13%, Slovak 3%
LANGUAGES Czech (official)
RELIGIONS Roman Catholic 39%, Protestant 4%
CURRENCY Czech koruna = 100 haler
ANNUAL INCOME PER PERSON US$2,500
MAIN PRIMARY PRODUCTS Coal, iron ore, uranium, wheat, barley, sugar beet

With 61% of the total land area of the former Czechoslovakia, the Czech Republic is the larger of its two successor states. Created after World War I and reorganized as a federation in 1969, Czechoslovakia was formally broken up on 1 January 1993, when the eastern Slovak Republic became independent in its own right. The Czech Republic is itself composed of two regions, both Czech-speaking, mainly Protestant in religion and with a common history as provinces of the Austrian part of the Austro-Hungarian Empire.

In the west, Bohemia is surrounded by ranges of mountains that enclose a basin drained by the River Elbe and its tributaries. In the centre lies Prague, the historic capital city. The mountains are rich in minerals, while in western Bohemia there are also reserves of hard coal and lignite. Moravia, in the east of the country, is divided from Bohemia by plateau land known as the Moravian Heights.

The Czech Republic is the most highly industrialized of the former Soviet satellites, but agriculture remains well developed, with high yields of most crops suited to the continental climate. Food processing industries are important in the western provinces.

Politics and economy

Czechoslovakia's 'velvet revolution' of 1989 was Eastern Europe's smoothest transition, toppling the old Communist regime by 'people power' and replacing it with a multiparty system headed by President Václav Havel, the country's best-known playwright and noted dissident. It was all different from 1968, when in the 'Prague Spring' Soviet forces suppressed an uprising supporting Alexander Dubcek's attempts to rekindle democracy and break the stranglehold of the party bosses.

As elsewhere in Central and Eastern Europe, the road to a free market economy was not easy, with the resultant inflation, falling production, strikes and unemployment. Politically, too, there were difficulties with pragmatic concerns soon dulling the euphoria of democratization. Principles of the new constitution were still controversial in 1992, when resurgent Slovak nationalism forced the parliamentary vote that ended the old Czechoslovak federation.

But the Czech economy, with a serviceable foreign debt and a skilled and adaptable workforce, was in far better shape than that of, say, Poland, while the break-up was, for the most part, amicable. Border adjustments were negligible and negotiated calmly; after the separation, Czechs and Slovaks maintained a customs union and other economic ties. In 1995, the Czech Republic joined the OECD; the country is also an associate member of the EU ∎

SLOVAK REPUBLIC

 The horizontal tricolour which the Slovak Republic adopted in September 1992 dates from 1848. The red, white and blue colours are typical of Slavonic flags. The three blue mounds in the shield represent the traditional mountains of Slovakia: Tatra, Matra and Fatra.

COUNTRY Slovak Republic
AREA 49,035 sq km [18,932 sq mls]
POPULATION 5,400,000
CAPITAL (POPULATION) Bratislava (448,000)
GOVERNMENT Multiparty republic with a unicameral legislature
ETHNIC GROUPS Slovak, Hungarian, Czech
LANGUAGES Slovak (official), Hungarian, Czech
RELIGIONS Roman Catholic 60%, Protestant 6%, Orthodox 3%
CURRENCY Slovak koruna = 100 halierov
ANNUAL INCOME PER PERSON US$1,900

The other heir to Czechoslovakia, the Slovak Republic consists of a mountainous region in the north, part of the Carpathian system that divides Slovakia from Poland, and a southern lowland area drained by the River Danube. Bratislava, the new nation's chief city, lies in the south, and has become the fourth European capital (Vienna, Budapest and Belgrade are the others) to lie on the river.

Culturally as well as linguistically distinct from their Czech neighbours, the relatively agrarian Slovaks are mainly Roman Catholics. While the Czechs prospered under Austrian rule, Slovakia was subject to Hungarian authority for centuries. Its people suffered from enforced 'Magyarization' and their development was stifled. Divisions were exacerbated from 1939 when Hitler's troops invaded the Czech lands of Bohemia and Moravia. But, even in Communist Czechoslovakia, the Slovaks were in no sense a persecuted minority; their post-1989 independence movement was driven more by the desire to revive their distinct culture than by ethnic grievances.

An OECD member from 1997, Slovakia still maintains close links with its former partner: around 400,000 Slovak workers cross the frontier to work each week, while about 200,000 are still resident in the Czech Republic. Conversely, up to 60,000 Czechs live in Slovakia, but the nation's most substantial minority is Hungarian, with around 600,000 people. Predictably, Slovak independence has raised national aspirations among its Magyar-speaking community, mostly in its southern regions ∎

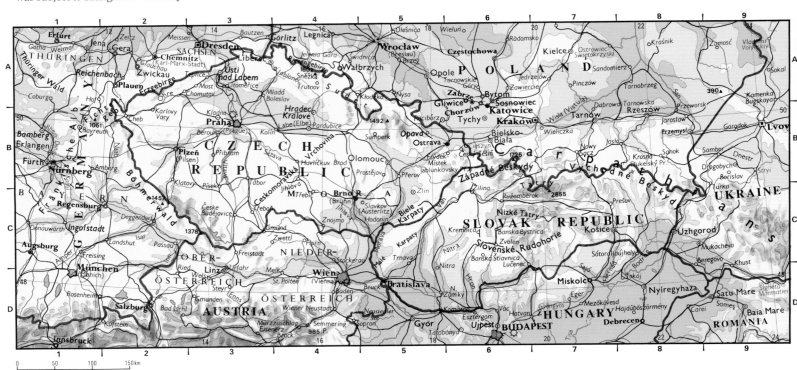

POLAND

The colours of Poland's flag were derived from the 13th-century coat of arms of a white eagle on a red field, which still appears on the Polish merchant flag. The flag's simple design was adopted when Poland became a republic in 1919.

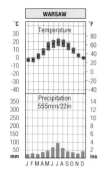

The weather and climate of Poland are transitional between maritime and continental. Warm, humid air masses come in from the west, cold Arctic air from the north and east, and warm air from the south. There is a cold snowy winter – becoming colder southwards and eastwards – and a warm summer with plenty of rain. The southern mountains have a high rainfall. The driest region is the central lowlands. Sunshine amounts exceed 5 hours per day April to September, with over 8 hours in May and June.

The geographical location of Poland has had a strong influence on the country's stormy history. On many occasions powerful neighbours – notably Russia and Germany – have found it all too easy to invade and occupy the land. The most recent frontier changes came at the end of World War II – in which the country lost 6 million people, or a massive 17% of the total population – when Poland gave up territory to the USSR, and in compensation gained parts of Germany as far as the River Oder.

As a result of these changes Poland lost poor agricultural land in the east and gained an important industrial region in the west, including in the south-west Silesia and the former German city of Breslau (now called Wrocław), in the north-west the Baltic port of Stettin (now Szczecin), and in the north the other port of Danzig (now Gdańsk). Acquisition of a length of Baltic coastline gave Poland a chance to develop maritime interests. Now a major fishing nation, Poland's fleets operate worldwide.

Before World War II Poland was primarily an agricultural country, with 65% of the population dependent on farming, but the postwar industrialization drive under Communism reduced this proportion to 19% by 1993, most of them still on privately owned farms. Poland is still, however, a major supplier of agricultural produce: nearly two-thirds of the land surface is farmed, about half of

this area supporting crops of rye and potatoes. Oats, sugar beet, fodder crops, pigs and dairy produce are also important.

Poland's industrial development since World War II has been striking. Coal, lignite, sulphur, lead and zinc are the main mineral products, though Poland is also Europe's top producer of copper ore (seventh in the world) and silver. Underground salt deposits form the basis of important chemical industries. Most of Poland's industrial energy is derived from coal, but oil and natural gas are being developed, and hydroelectric power is being produced in increasing amounts from the Carpathians. Heavy industries include manufacture of steel and cement, and many secondary products. Many of Poland's newer industries are still almost wholly reliant on Russian gas and oil – a difficult position in a changing world.

Poland's reliance on heavy industry, much of it state-controlled and unprofitable, proved to be a major obstacle in the country's 'fast-track' route from Communism to capitalism that followed the pioneering triumph of democratic forces in 1989. The old industries needed drastic measures – re-equipping, restructuring and diversifying – but this could be achieved only with huge assistance from the West; Poland received nearly 70% of all Western credits to Eastern Europe between 1989

COUNTRY Republic of Poland
AREA 312,680 sq km [120,726 sq mls]
POPULATION 38,587,000
CAPITAL (POPULATION) Warsaw (1,643,000)
GOVERNMENT Multiparty republic
ETHNIC GROUPS Polish 98%, Ukrainian 1%
LANGUAGES Polish (official)
RELIGIONS Roman Catholic 94%, Orthodox 2%
NATIONAL DAY 3 May
CURRENCY Zloty = 100 groszy
ANNUAL INCOME PER PERSON US$2,270
MAIN PRIMARY PRODUCTS Cereals, potatoes, sugar beet, fish, timber, copper, iron ore, sulphur, zinc
MAIN INDUSTRIES Machinery, iron and steel, mining, shipbuilding, agriculture, food processing, oil refining
MAIN EXPORTS Machinery and transport equipment 39%, chemicals 11%, fuel and power 10%, metal 10%, textiles and clothing 7%
MAIN EXPORT PARTNERS CIS nations 25%, Germany 14%, Czech and Slovak Republics 6%, UK 7%
MAIN IMPORTS Machinery and transport equipment 36%, chemicals 16%, fuel and power 15%, consumer products 9%, iron and steel products 8%
MAIN IMPORT PARTNERS CIS nations 23%, Germany 21%, Czech and Slovak Republics 6%, Austria 6%, Switzerland 5%
DEFENCE 2.3% of GNP
TOURISM 4,000,000 visitors per year
POPULATION DENSITY 123 per sq km [320 per sq ml]
INFANT MORTALITY 17 per 1,000 live births
LIFE EXPECTANCY Female 76 yrs, male 68 yrs
ADULT LITERACY 99%
PRINCIPAL CITIES (POPULATION) Warsaw 1,643,000 Lódz 834,000 Kraków 745,000 Wroclaw 642,000 Poznan 583,000

and 1991, adding to an already unserviceable foreign debt. Meanwhile, rising inflation and unemployment, coupled with a drastic drop in living standards, led to a resurgence of militant unionism – the very movement that had set Poland on the path to democratization back in 1980.

Under the banner of the independent trade union Solidarity, based originally in the Gdańsk shipyards and led by Lech Walesa, Poland was the first of the Soviet satellites to challenge and bring down its Communist regime. The example set by the Poles (even though they were to be the last Eastern European country to implement full democratic processes, in October 1991), proved an inspiration not only to the other European socialist states but also to the peoples of the Baltic republics.

Elected national president a year earlier, Lech Walesa found it a tough task to form a stable government after the 1991 elections, with the new constitution producing a parliament representing no less than 29 different parties. Solidarity itself had not lived up to its name, dividing in 1990 over personality clashes and the speed of reform. In presidential elections in 1995, Lech Walesa was defeated by ex-Communist Aleksander Kwasniewski. However, Kwasniewski continued to follow westward-looking policies, and in 1996 Poland joined the OECD ■

EUROPE

COMMONWEALTH OF INDEPENDENT STATES

After 74 years, the Union of Soviet Socialist Republics slipped into history a week ahead of schedule on Christmas Day 1991, when Mikhail Gorbachev resigned the leadership of what had become a nation only on paper. His offices in the Kremlin were occupied by Boris Yeltsin, first President of the Russian Federation and driving force behind the 'deconstruction' of the Soviet Union.

Though far from substituted, the USSR was in part replaced by the Commonwealth of Independent States, born in Minsk on 8 December 1991 when Russia, Ukraine and hosts Belarus – between them responsible for 73% of the Soviet population – signed a declaration effectively ending the former superpower's life both as a geopolitical entity and as a force in international relations. Two weeks later, in the Kazakstan capital of Alma Ata, they were joined by Moldova, Armenia, Azerbaijan and the five Asian republics; missing were the three

---

Commonwealth of Independent States

AREA 22,023,900 sq km [8,503,472 sq mls]

POPULATION 274,583,000

HEADQUARTERS (POPULATION) Minsk (1,658,000)

ETHNIC GROUPS Russian 52%, Ukrainian 16%, Uzbek 5%, Belarussian 4%, Kazak 3%, Tartar 2%, Azerbaijani 2%, Armenian 2%, Georgian 1%, Tajik 1%, Moldovan 1%

LANGUAGES Russian (official), Ukrainian and over 100 others

RELIGIONS Orthodox 32%, Muslim 11%, Protestant 3%, Roman Catholic 2%

CURRENCY Various

MAIN PRIMARY PRODUCTS Livestock, timber, fish, cereals, oil and natural gas, iron ore, coal, lignite, bauxite, copper, diamonds, uranium, zinc

MAIN EXPORTS Machinery, iron and steel, crude oil, non-ferrous metals, timber, cotton, vehicles

MAIN IMPORTS Machinery, clothing, ships, minerals, railway rolling stock, footwear

---

Baltic states (already *de facto* independent nations), and Georgia (Georgia eventually joined in 1994). The declaration from the 11 governments covered borders, human rights, ethnic minorities, non-interference and international law; committees were set up to consider foreign affairs, defence, finance, transport and security.

These remarkable events, spread over less than three weeks, were traceable in 1985 to the appointment of Gorbachev as General Secretary of the Communist Party. His unprecedented policies of *glasnost* (openness) and *perestroika* (restructuring) were to have a devastating effect in a very short time. Through increased arms control, the withdrawal of troops from Afghanistan, the retreat from Eastern Europe, the acceptance of German unification and the dissolution of the Warsaw Pact, four decades of Cold War came to an end. The satellites of Eastern Europe and Mongolia abandoned Communist ideology and its Party's monopoly of power, introducing multiparty democracy and the market economy.

The domestic impact was equally dramatic, the republics of the USSR ridding themselves of doctrinaire Communism, adopting pluralism and declaring themselves independent of Moscow. In 1991, the entire system through which the Soviet Union had functioned for seven decades came crumbling down in the course of a calendar year.

The first signs of actual disintegration of the USSR came in January 1991 in Lithuania, and within weeks all three Baltic states had voted for independence, Georgia following in March. Over the next few months Gorbachev tried continually to establish consensus on a new Union treaty and economic reform, but when Yeltsin became directly elected President of Russia in June, his federation took the lead in opposing the Soviet president's increasingly personal and decree-based rule as he attempted to find a middle way between the old guard and the progressives.

While the new laws had produced far-reaching effects on the political and social lives of Soviet citizens, the parallel restructuring of the economy patently failed – not least because the movement to a market economy was constantly hindered by party bureaucrats, factory managers, collective farm chairmen and many others who were unwilling to see the erosion of their positions.

In August hardline Communist leaders ousted Gorbachev – detaining him in his Crimean *dacha* – and a small emergency committee took control of the Soviet Union. Resistance, bravely led by Yeltsin, centred on Moscow, and after three days the coup collapsed. Gorbachev returned to his post in the Kremlin, but his already tenuous position, now undermined by events, was further weakened by the worst harvest for a decade, an energy crisis that included a coal miners' strike, and the collapse of the Soviet Central Bank.

On 21 December Gorbachev was told by the Alma Ata protocol that his services were no longer required; outmanoeuvred by Yeltsin and overtaken by events, he resigned on Christmas Day, and the tricolour flag of Russia replaced the hammer and sickle on the Kremlin. Two days later, the Chamber of Deputies of the Supreme Soviet, the USSR's parliament, formally voted itself out of existence, and the Soviet Union was clinically dead.

The CIS is not a sovereign state. It may well prove more than a useful temporary mechanism to disperse power from the Soviet centre to the republics, which in any case have great power in domestic policy. In the honeymoon period, early in 1992, it sorted out (at least on paper) the prickly issues of strategic nuclear weapons (owned by the three founder members, plus Kazakstan) and the 3.7-million-strong Red Army; governed in the short to medium term by the interdependency created by the Soviet system, it will at least function as a common market. Its real political test, however, will come with disputes between its own members, notably and immediately the ancient problem of Nagorno-Karabakh. But there are others: of all the shared borders, for example, only one (Russia/Belarus) is not contentious ∎

BELARUS

In September 1991, Belarus adopted a red and white flag to replace the one used in the Soviet era. But, in June 1995, after a referendum in which Belarussians voted to improve relations with Russia, this was replaced with a design similar to that of 1958.

COUNTRY Belarus

AREA 207,600 sq km [80,154 sq mls]

POPULATION 10,500,000

CAPITAL (POPULATION) Minsk (1,658,000)

ETHNIC GROUPS Belarussian 80%, Russian, Polish, Ukrainian, Jewish

LANGUAGES Belarussian and Russian (both official)

RELIGIONS Belarussian Orthodox, Roman Catholic, Evangelical

Landlocked and low-lying, a third forested and with 11,000 lakes, Belarus ('White Russia') is not the most endowed of the republics. Though mainly agricultural – 46% of the land being used efficiently for flax, potatoes, cereals, dairying, pigs and peat-digging – it also has the largest petrochemical complex in Europe and the giant Belaz heavy-truck plants; these, however, like its many light industries, are heavily reliant on Russia for

electricity and raw materials, including steel. More integrated into the Soviet economy than any other republic, Belarus was also the most dependent on trade, at nearly 70%.

Most observers were surprised when this most conservative and Communist-dominated of parliaments declared independence on 25 August 1991. The quiet state of the European Soviet Union, it played a big supporting role in its deconstruction

and the creation of the CIS; the latter's first meeting was in Minsk – subsequently chosen as its capital. Like the Ukraine, Belarus has been a separate UN member since 1945, the end of World War II, during which one in four of its population died ∎

MOLDOVA

The flag and eagle are based on those of pre-Communist Romania, and the bull's head is the distinctive emblem of Moldova. The flag was adopted in November 1990. According to the official description, the tricolour represents 'the past, present and future' of Moldova.

COUNTRY Moldova

AREA 33,700 sq km [13,010 sq mls]

POPULATION 4,434,000

CAPITAL (POPULATION) Kishinev (or Chişinău, 700,000)

ETHNIC GROUPS Moldovan 65%, Ukrainian 14%, Russian 13%, Gagauz 4%, Jewish 2%, Bulgarian

LANGUAGES Moldovan (Romanian) – official

RELIGIONS Eastern Orthodox

The most densely populated of the former Soviet republics, Moldova is also ethnically complex. Created by Stalin in his 1940 pact with Hitler by combining the Moldavian part of Ukraine with the larger Bessarabia – the section of Romania between the Prut and Dnestr (Dniester) rivers – its majority 'Moldovan' population is ethnically Romanian, and

people on both sides of the border favour reunification. This is opposed by Russians, Ukrainians and, in the south, the Gagauz, the Christian Orthodox Turks. The last two groups both pronounced their sovereignty before the republic declared independence from Moscow on 27 August 1991.

Though barred from the Black Sea by an arm

of the Ukraine, Moldova is well off. Fertile lands and a tolerant climate provide vines, tobacco and honey as well as more conventional produce, while light industry is expanding ∎

UKRAINE

The colours of the Ukrainian flag were first adopted in 1848 and were heraldic in origin, first used on the coat of arms of one of the medieval Ukrainian kingdoms. The flag was first used in the period 1918–20 and was readopted on 4 September 1991.

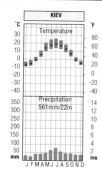

KIEV

Although on the same latitude as many European cities, Kiev is distant from maritime effects. Rainfall is fairly low and evenly distributed throughout the year with a slight summer peak. Snow may lie for over 80 days, and there is precipitation on over 160 days in the year. Winter temperatures are not too severe and only four months are subzero, though frosts can occur on over 180 days. Summers are warm: the months June to August are 20°C [36°F] warmer than January.

The Ukraine became the largest complete nation in Europe with its declaration of independence on 24 August 1991 and the subsequent disintegration of the Soviet Union. It is also a well-populated state: fourth in Europe, discounting Russia, and 22nd in the world.

The western Ukraine comprises the fertile uplands of Volhynia, with the Carpathians cutting across the far western corner of the country. The north is mostly lowlands, with the Dnepr (Dnieper or Dnipro) River at its heart, which include marshes and the state capital of Kiev in addition to arable land. This area, however, suffered most from the Chernobyl nuclear disaster of 1986, with huge tracts of land contaminated by radioactivity.

In the centre of the republic, south of Kiev and west of Kirovograd (Yelizavetgrad), are the rich

lands of *chernozem*, fertile black earth. In the south are dry lowlands bordering the Black Sea and the Sea of Azov, with Odessa the main port. Further south still is the Crimean peninsula, a favourite tourist area for Russians as well as Ukrainians. In the east are the main industrial cities, clustered around the coalfields and iron-ore mines of the vital Donets Basin.

Ukraine's main industries are coal mining, iron and steel, agricultural machinery, petrochemicals and plastics, but there are also numerous food-processing plants based on agricultural output.

Though traditionally 'the granary of the Soviet Union', the Ukraine is neither the largest nor the most efficient producer of grain; Russia accounted for more than 53% of the total in 1988 (Ukraine 24%). In 1993, however, the Ukraine was the world's leading producer of sugar beet and second largest producer of barley, and dominated world manganese production (28.6% of the world total). In 1991 the Ukraine produced nearly a quarter of the total USSR coal output. Not blessed with huge reserves of oil, the Kiev government signed an agreement in February 1992 to secure future supplies from Iran. Even under the Soviet system, Ukraine's intrarepublican trade was less than a third of its total GNP.

The Ukraine's declaration of independence from Moscow was ratified by referendum on 1 December 1991, when Leonid Kravchuk, the former Com-

munist Party ideological secretary, was voted president by direct poll over five rivals. A week later, in Minsk, Kravchuk helped Boris Yeltsin create the basis for the Commonwealth of Independent States, and in the early months of 1992 the Ukraine and Russia reached agreement on a number of potentially explosive issues, not least in the military field, with resolutions on nuclear weapons, the Red Army and the distribution of the Black Sea fleet.

The Ukraine, however, will not be seen as Russia's sidekick. While it suffered many of the economic agonies endured by its massive neighbour – notably chronic food shortages and the hyper-inflation that followed the abolition of price controls – it set out from the beginning to be a fully fledged independent nation. While Russia assumed the diplomatic powers of the Soviet Union, the Ukraine already had a seat at the UN – a reward granted in 1945 for the devastation caused by the German invasion in 1941 and its aftermath. In June 1996, a new constitution was adopted, giving new powers to the president and the right to private ownership ■

COUNTRY Ukraine

AREA 603,700 sq km [233,100 sq mls]

POPULATION 52,027,000

CAPITAL (POPULATION) Kiev (2,643,000)

GOVERNMENT Multiparty republic

ETHNIC GROUPS Ukrainian 73%, Russian 22%, Jewish 1%, Belarussian 1%, Moldovan, Bulgarian, Polish

LANGUAGES Ukrainian (official)

RELIGIONS Ukrainian Orthodox

PRINCIPAL CITIES (POPULATION) Kiev 2,643,000 Kharkov 1,622,000 Dnepropetrovsk 1,190,000 Donetsk 1,121,000 Odesa 1,096,000

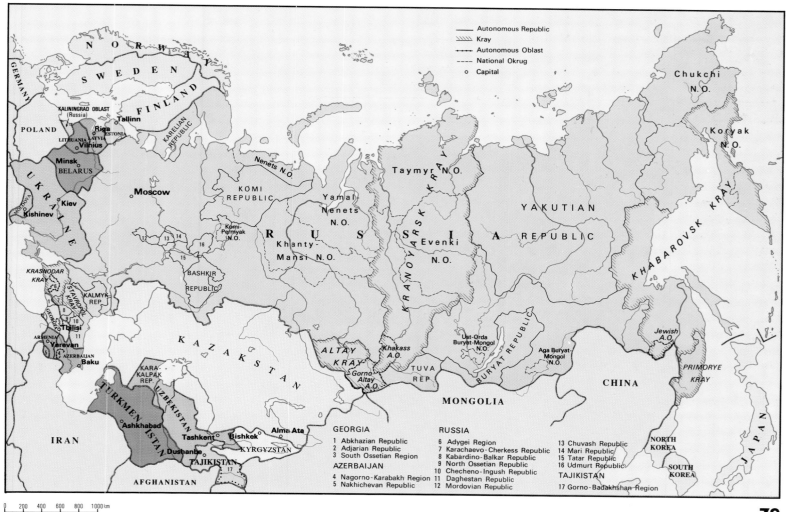

Legend	
——	Autonomous Republic
\\\\\\	Kray
••••	Autonomous Oblast
----	National Okrug
○	Capital

GEORGIA
1 Abkhazian Republic
2 Adjarian Republic
3 South Ossetian Region

AZERBAIJAN
4 Nagorno-Karabakh Region
5 Nakhichevan Republic

RUSSIA
6 Adygei Region
7 Karachaevo-Cherkess Republic
8 Kabardino-Balkar Republic
9 North Ossetian Republic
10 Checheno-Ingush Republic
11 Daghestan Republic
12 Mordovian Republic
13 Chuvash Republic
14 Mari Republic
15 Tatar Republic
16 Udmurt Republic

TAJIKISTAN
17 Gorno-Badakhshan Region

EUROPE

ESTONIA

Used for the independent republic of 1918–40, the Estonian flag was readopted in June 1988. The colours are said to symbolize the country's blue skies, its black earth and the snows of its long winter.

COUNTRY Estonia
AREA 44,700 sq km [17,300 sq mls]
POPULATION 1,531,000
CAPITAL (POPULATION) Tallinn (490,000)
ETHNIC GROUPS Estonian 62%, Russian 30%, Ukrainian 3%, Belarussian 2%, Finnish 1%
LANGUAGES Estonian (official)
RELIGIONS Christian (Lutheran and Orthodox)
POPULATION DENSITY 34 per sq km [88 per sq ml]

Smallest of the three Baltic states, and the least populous of any of the 15 former Soviet republics, Estonia is bounded on the north by the Gulf of Finland and on the west by the Baltic Sea. The country comprises mostly flat, rock-strewn, glaciated lowland, with over 1,500 lakes, and has more than 800 offshore islands, by far the biggest being Saaremaa and Hiiumaa. The largest lake, Chudskoye Ozero, forms much of the border with Russia in the east.

Over a third of the land is forested, and the timber industry is among the country's most important industries, alongside metalworking, shipbuilding, clothing, textiles, chemicals and food processing.

The last is based primarily on extremely efficient dairy farming and pig breeding, but oats, barley and potatoes suit the cool climate and average soils. Fishing is also a major occupation. Like the other two Baltic states, Estonia is not endowed with natural resources, though its shale is an important mineral deposit: enough gas is extracted by processing to supply St Petersburg, Russia's second largest city.

Related ethnically and linguistically to the Finns, the Estonians have managed to retain their cultural identity and now look to increase their links with Europe, and with Scandinavia in particular. But despite having the highest standard of living of any of the 15 former Soviet republics, Estonia has found the free market hard going. In January 1992 the combination of food shortages and an energy crisis forced the resignation of Prime Minister Edgar Savissar, who enjoyed wide popular and parliamentary support. A co-founder of the Popular Front, the country's pro-democracy movement, he was held responsible for a recession which appeared to have hit Estonia far harder than its two neighbours ■

LATVIA

The burgundy and white Latvian flag, revived after independence from the USSR in 1991, dates back to at least 1280. According to one legend, it was first made from a white sheet stained with the blood of a Latvian hero who was wrapped in it.

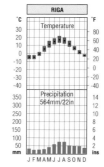

Riga has warm summers and cold winters, with rain or snow in all months. June to August are the warmest months with temperatures over 15°C [59°F], and averages that are subzero from December to March. The temperature extremes are only just over 34°C [93°F] and –29°C [–20°F]. On average, rain will fall on a third of the days in the second half of the year, but the total is relatively light. The weather can be overcast for long periods. Snow cover is light, with many thaws.

Its Baltic coast heavily indented by the Gulf of Riga, Latvia is a small country of flat glaciated lowland, with natural vegetation and agriculture virtually mirroring that of Estonia. So, too, does much of its commerce; like its Baltic neighbours it contains much of the Soviet Union's less traditional, 'clever' industries, while Ventspils is an important conduit for the export of Russian oil and gas. Latvia

COUNTRY Latvia
AREA 64,589 sq km [24,938 sq mls]
POPULATION 2,558,000
CAPITAL (POPULATION) Riga (840,000)
ETHNIC GROUPS Latvian 53%, Russian 34%, Belarussian 4%, Ukrainian 3%, Polish 2%, Lithuanian, Jewish
LANGUAGES Latvian (official)
RELIGIONS Christian (Lutheran, Catholic, Orthodox)
POPULATION DENSITY 40 per sq km [103 per sq ml]

is the most urbanized of the Baltic states, with over 70% of the population living in cities and towns.

Although forming only a slender majority today, the native Latvians (Letts) have a highly developed folklore, their sense of identity honed during the nationalist drive in the late 19th century and re-kindled in the quest for separation from the Soviet Union more than 100 years later. Latvia declared independence in May 1990, two months after Lithuania, and despite a large Russian population the subsequent referendum indicated a substantial majority in favour of a break with Moscow.

Strong ties remain, however. Like its neighbours, Latvia is (in the medium term at least) almost totally reliant on the network of Russian and Ukrainian energy supply, while Russia will not simply surrender the 'Soviet' investments in the country, most obviously in the ports ■

THE BALTIC STATES

The three Baltic republics have always found it hard to establish their nationhood, though their cultures have proved resilient. Estonia and Latvia survived 1,000 years of rule by Danes, Swedes, Lithuanians and Poles before becoming part of the Russian Empire in 1721; Lithuania, once a powerful medieval empire, was united with Poland in 1385 but also came under Russian control in 1795.

Nationalist movements grew in all three countries in the late 19th century, and in 1920, following German occupation, the Soviet Union granted them the status of independent democratic republics. However, all had Fascist coups by the time Hitler assigned them to Stalin in the notorious secret pact of 1939 – operative in 1940, with the establishment of a government acceptable to Moscow.

After three years of occupation by (Nazi) Germany, incorporation into the USSR was confirmed by plebiscite in 1944. On declaring independence in 1990, the Baltic states claimed this was fraudulent and that their countries were never legally part of the Soviet Union. Referenda supported this view, and on 6 September 1991 the transitional State Council of the Soviet Union recognized them as independent sovereign states. All three were United Nations members by the end of the year.

LITHUANIA

The flag was created in 1918, at the birth of the independent republic; it was suppressed after the Soviet annexation in 1940, and restored in November 1988. The colours are reputed to represent Lithuania's rich forests and agricultural wealth.

Largest, most populous and in many ways the most important of the Baltic states, Lithuania is also the most homogeneous, some 80% of its population being staunch Catholics who speak the native language and are proud of their history and culture. From 1988 it was Lithuania which led the 'Balts' in their drive to shed Communism and regain their nationhood; in March 1990 it became the first of the 15 constituent Soviet republics to declare itself an independent, non-Communist country, resulting in the occupation of much of its capital by Soviet troops and a crippling economic blockade not suffered by the other states of the Union.

The successful crusade was led by the emotional president, Vytautus Landsbergis, whose crucial role in the process of 'deconstruction' – and that of his people – was somewhat overshadowed by the figure of Boris Yeltsin and the Russian Federation.

The country consists mostly of a low, glaciated but fairly fertile central lowland used primarily for cattle, pigs and poultry – livestock rearing having been highly intensified under the Soviet collective

system. Crops grown are very similar to those of Estonia, while there are also widespread forests and significant peat reserves, though Lithuania remains pitifully short of natural resources. In the east is an area of forested sandy ridges, dotted with lakes.

A range of industries, among them many of the most advanced programmes in the former Soviet Union, include timber, metalworking, textiles, building materials, fertilizers, fibres and plastics, computers and instruments, and food processing. Craftsmen still make jewellery from amber, a semi-precious fossilized resin found along the Baltic coast.

While Lithuania, in concert with the other Baltic states, seeks to establish closer ties with the rest of Europe – a US$2.5 billion highway is planned, linking the three capitals with Warsaw – it also has simmering ethnic problems of its own. Its significant Polish population, largely self-governing under the Soviets, now fear 'Lithuanization', while the majority who took on Moscow and won resent the pro-Union stance taken by Poles and Russians during their fight for freedom ■

COUNTRY Lithuania
AREA 65,200 sq km [25,200 sq mls]
POPULATION 3,735,000
CAPITAL (POPULATION) Vilnius (576,000)
ETHNIC GROUPS Lithuanian 80%, Russian 9%, Polish 7%, Belarussian 2%
LANGUAGES Lithuanian (official)
RELIGIONS Christian (predominantly Roman Catholic)
POPULATION DENSITY 57 per sq km [148 per sq ml]

GEORGIA

The flag was first adopted in 1917 and lasted until 1921. The colours represent the good times of the past and the future (wine red), the period of Russian rule (black) and the hope for peace (white). It was readopted on independence in 1990.

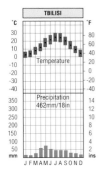

Nestling between the Caucasus and the mountains of Armenia, Tbilisi is sheltered both from the winter cold of central Asia and the heavy rain of the Black Sea coast. The rather sparse rainfall is effective in spring but evaporates quickly in the summer heat when conditions resemble those of the Mediterranean. Rain falls on only about 70 days per year. Winters are less severe than might be expected in a continental location; temperatures rarely fall below freezing in December and January.

Positioned between Russia and Turkey, Georgia comprises four main areas: the Caucasus Mountains in the north, including Mt Elbrus (5,633 m [18,841 ft]) on the Russian border; the Black Sea coastal plain in the west; the eastern end of the mountains of Asia Minor to the south; and a low plateau in the east, protruding into Azerbaijan. Separating the two mountain sections is the crucial Kura Valley, in which the capital Tbilisi stands.

The largest of the three Transcaucasian republics, Georgia is rich in citrus fruits and wine (notably in the Kakhetia region), tea (the main crop), tobacco, wheat, barley and vegetables, while perfumes are made from flowers and herbs and, in Imeretiya, silk is a flourishing industry. Almost 40% forested, it also has a significant stake in timber. Georgia has large deposits of manganese ore (eighth in the world in 1992), but despite reserves of coal and huge hydroelectric potential, most of its electricity is generated in Russia and the Ukraine.

Always a maverick among the Soviet republics, Georgia was the first to declare independence after the Baltic states (April 1991), and deferred joining the CIS until March 1994. When Mikhail Gorbachev resigned, the democratically elected leader of Georgia, Zviad Gamsakhurdia, found himself holed up in Tbilisi's KGB headquarters, under siege from rebel forces representing widespread disapproval of his policies, from the economy to the imprisonment of opponents. In January he fled the country (now ruled by a military council), returning to lead resistance from his home territory in the west, though to little effect. Gamsakhurdia had also been in conflict with the Ossetian minority

in one of the republic's three autonomous regions, who feared being swamped in a new independent nation. In March 1992, Eduard Shevardnadze, the former Soviet foreign minister, agreed to become chairman of the ruling council.

Mostly Orthodox Christians, Georgians have a strong national culture and a long literary tradition based on their own language and alphabet. Land of the legendary Golden Fleece of Greek mythology, the area was conquered by the Romans, Persians and Arabs before establishing autonomy in the 10th century, but Tartars, Persians and Turks invaded before it came under Russian domination around 1800. Renowned for their longevity, the population's most famous product was Josef Stalin, born in Gori, 65 km [40 mls] north-west of Tbilisi ■

COUNTRY Georgia
AREA 69,700 sq km [26,910 sq mls]
POPULATION 5,448,000
CAPITAL (POPULATION) Tbilisi (1,279,000)
ETHNIC GROUPS Georgian 70%, Armenian 8%, Russian 6%, Azerbaijani 6%, Ossetes 3%, Greek 2%, Abkhazian 2%, others 3%
LANGUAGES Georgian (official)

ARMENIA

The flag first used in the period 1918–22 was readopted on 24 August 1990. The colours represent the blood shed in the past (red), the land of Armenia (blue), and the unity and courage of the people (orange).

COUNTRY Armenia
AREA 29,800 sq km [11,506 sq mls]
POPULATION 3,603,000
CAPITAL (POPULATION) Yerevan (1,226,000)
ETHNIC GROUPS Armenian 93%, Azerbaijani 3%, Russian, Kurd
LANGUAGES Armenian (official)

The smallest of the 15 republics of the former Soviet Union, Armenia was also one of the weakest. A rugged, mountainous country landlocked between traditionally hostile neighbours, it has few natural resources (though lead, copper and zinc are mined), limited industry, and registered the poorest agricultural output per head in the Union; the main products are wine, tobacco, olives and rice, the main occupation the raising of livestock. Much of the west is recovering from the earthquake of 1988, in which some 55,000 people died. Its vulnerability is heightened by the lack of support for its conflict with Azerbaijan over Nagorno-Karabakh, and its heavy reliance for energy on other republics.

Originally a much larger independent kingdom centred on Mt Ararat, the legendary resting place of Noah's Ark, Armenia had already been established for more than 1,000 years when it became the first country in the world to make Christianity (Armenian Apostolic) the official state religion in the 4th century. Ever since, its people have been subject to war, occupation and massacre – the most documented example being the genocide by Turks in World War I, when 600,000 Armenians were killed and 1.75 million deported to Syria and Palestine. Today, some 1.5 million live in north-east Turkey, Europe and the USA, with minorities in Azerbaijan (notably Nagorno-Karabakh) and Georgia ■

AZERBAIJAN

This flag was instituted on 5 February 1991. The blue stands for the sky, the red for freedom, and the green for land and the Islamic religion; the crescent and star symbolize Islam, and the points of the star represent the eight races of Azerbaijan.

COUNTRY Azerbaijan
AREA 86,600 sq km [33,436 sq mls]
POPULATION 7,559,000
CAPITAL (POPULATION) Baku (1,081,000)
ETHNIC GROUPS Azerbaijani 83%, Russian 6%, Armenian 6%, Lezgin, Avar, Ukrainian, Tatar
LANGUAGES Azerbaijani (official)

Though now in relative decline, oil is still the mainstay of Azerbaijan's revenue. It was being collected by the Caspian Sea near Baku over 1,000 years ago, and burning natural gas leaking from the ground gave the area its name: 'Land of eternal fire'. Today, along with industries both traditional (iron, timber, carpets) and modern (cement, chemicals, aluminium), it makes the country's economy a viable one. Though much of Azerbaijan is semiarid (there is also a large tract of land below sea level), it nevertheless grows crops such as cotton, grains, rice and grapes, with fishing also important.

As the Azerbaijanis looked to their fellow Shiite Muslims in Iran after independence (declared in August 1991), their biggest problem remained that of their western neighbour, Armenia, and the intractable problem of Nagorno-Karabakh, the predominantly Armenian *oblast* enclave of 192,500 people (77% Armenian, 22% Azerbaijani) in the south-west, scene of bitter fighting and appalling atrocities since 1988. Soviet troops went in early in 1990, and two years later it became a real test for the new CIS to resolve. Ironically, Azerbaijan has itself an enclave, the autonomous republic of Nakhichevan (with a population of 315,000 – 96% Azerbaijani), completely isolated from the main part of the country on the border of Armenia and Turkey. A cease-fire was finally signed on 18 February 1994 in Nagorno-Karabakh under Russian auspices by representatives of Armenia, Azerbaijan and Nagorno-Karabakh ■

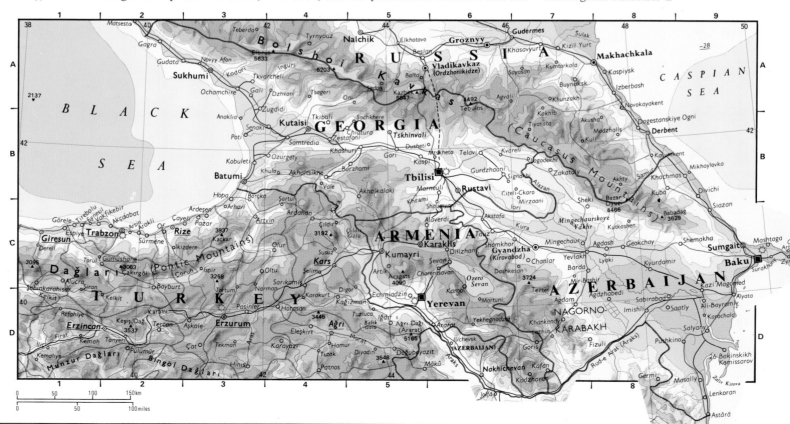

ASIA

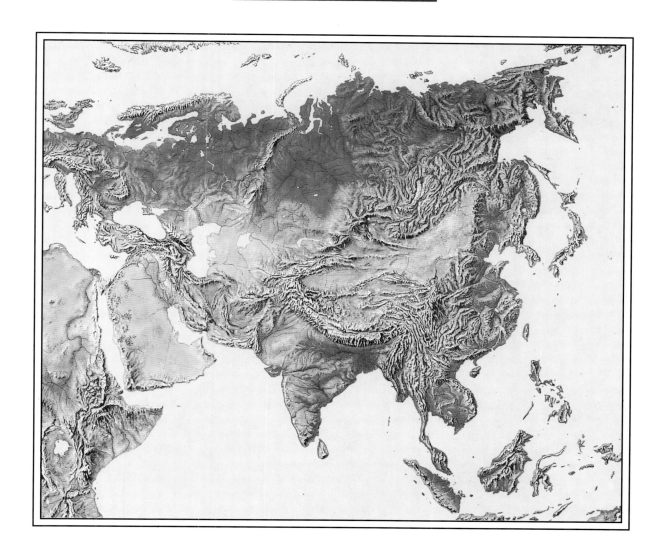

ASIA

The largest continent, accounting for a third of the world's land surface – and well over half its population – Asia extends from the Mediterranean Sea to the Pacific Ocean and from the tropical islands of the East Indies to the frozen shores of the Arctic. Most of its boundary is shoreline, but the boundary with Europe is the subject of some debate.

Geologically, Asia is made up of two vast sets of rock platforms – the Russian and Siberian in the north, and the Arabian, Indian and Chinese platforms in the south, which for eons have converged on each other, squashing between them an enormous extent of sedimentary rocks that were laid down in ancient seas. The platforms provide the great, stable plateaus on the periphery; the sediments have been squeezed and folded into the massive mountain ranges that spread across the continent from Turkey ('Asia Minor') in the west to the Pacific seaboard in the east.

Climatically Asia includes almost every known combination of temperature, precipitation and wind, from the searing heat of Arabia in summer to the biting chill of north-eastern Siberia in winter. Similarly, almost every pattern of vegetation from polar desert and tundra to tropical rainforest can be found within the bounds of this vast continent.

Asia comprises a 'heartland' centred on Siberia, and a series of peripheral areas of widely different character. The heartland includes the tundra wastes of the north, the coniferous forests ('taiga'), and the vast, thinly-populated interior deserts of Mongolia, north-west China and Tibet. Not entirely desert, some of the heartland was traditionally pastoral and is now responding to new agricultural techniques, while the wealth of its minerals is slowly being developed. To the west lie the plains of Russia, homeland of the 16th- and 17th-century invaders who, unlike their many predecessors, finally came to settle in the heartland and organize its massive resources. To the south-west lies the 'fertile crescent' of the Tigris and Euphrates valleys, possibly the world's first centre of agriculture, and beyond it the Mediterranean coastlands of Turkey, Syria, Lebanon and Israel.

From Iran eastwards, right around the shores of the continent and its off-lying islands as far as eastern Siberia, lie the coastlands that contain and support the main masses of Asia's populations. Isolated by the northern mountain barrier, India has traditionally formed a subcontinent in its own right. China, the second great civilization of Asia, centred on the 'Middle Kingdom' of 18 historic provinces, has expanded steadily over the centuries and is a great influence on neighbouring states. Beyond the mainland coasts lie the mountainous but mostly highly fertile islands of the volcanic arcs that skirt the eastern edge of the continental shelf. The populations

of these islands, already high, are among the fastest-growing in the world – though only Japan provides a standard of living comparable to those of the West.

The Indian subcontinent, though a relatively small part of Asia as a whole, is almost continental in its impact on the traveller and in its share (nearly one-fifth) of the world's population. It extends from subequatorial coral beaches in the south to icy mountains overlooking the Vale of Kashmir in the north – approximately in the latitude of Greece.

South Asia is a subcontinent of unity and diversity. Binding it in unity is the annually occurring rhythm of human activities caused by the seasonal reversal of winds in the monsoon. Yet diversity arises from the same cause – the annual vagaries of the monsoon – that bring drought and near-famine to one region, flood and disease to another, in apparently random patterns. There is a cultural unity, too, to which the sensitive traveller reacts, from Kashmir to Cape Comorin (Kanya Kumari). Yet here again is the paradox of extraordinary diversity. Variety of race, language and religion all contribute, often related to invasions, trading connections or a colonial past. At the root of the culture of this subcontinent lies South Asia's millennial role as the cradle of Hinduism and Buddhism.

East Asia comprises the lands to the east of the

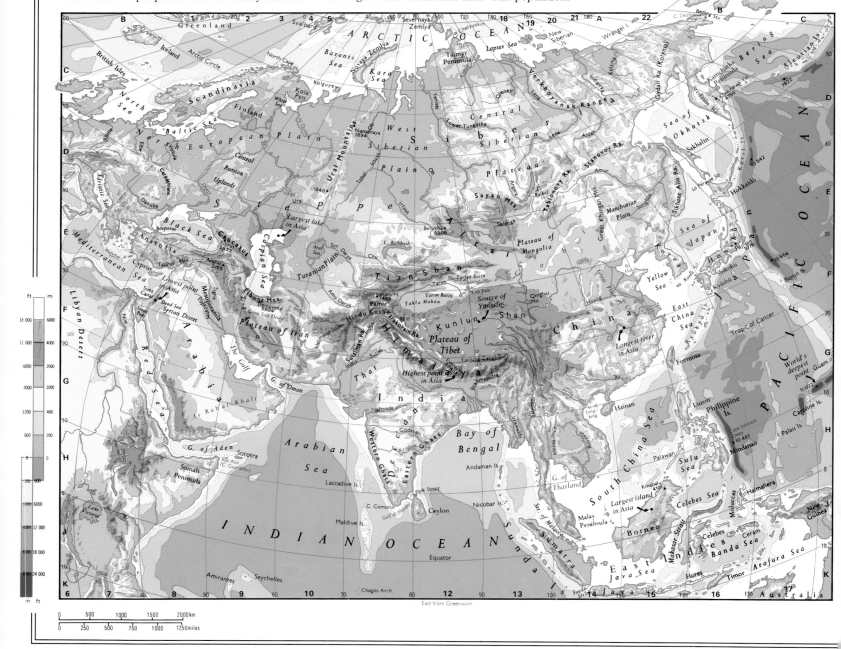

great mountain barrier which runs from south-western China, through the Himalayas, the Kara-koram and the Tian Shan, to the Altai range on the borders of Mongolia, China and Russia. It occupies roughly 9% of the land area of the globe, and exhibits a very great diversity of relief and climate. Altitudes vary from the high Tibetan plateau, where the average elevation is over 4,500 m [14,760 ft], to the floor of the Turfan (Turpan Hami) depression to the north, 154 m [505 ft] below sea level. East Asian climates range from the cold continental of northern Mongolia to the warm humid tropical of southern China and Hainan.

The area contains well over a quarter of mankind. This population is unevenly distributed with the main concentrations in lowland areas open to the influence of the summer monsoon in eastern China, Korea, and Japan. Until recent times the whole area has been strongly dominated by the Chinese civilization.

Only since World War II has the term 'South-east Asia' become widely used to describe the series of peninsulas and islands which lie east of India and south of China. The name was first employed around 1900 to designate a particular trade and shipping area, but the concept of a South-east Asian region goes back a long way. This was recognized by both the Chinese and the Japanese, who respec-

tively called it the Nan Yang and the Nanyo, both meaning the 'southern seas'. Today the region includes Burma, Thailand, Laos, Vietnam, Cambodia, Malaysia, Singapore, Brunei and the islands of Indonesia and the Philippines.

South-east Asia, which lies almost wholly in the humid tropics, is an area of rivers and seas. Each of the mainland states is focused on one major river, with the Irrawaddy in Burma, the Chao Phraya in Thailand, the Mekong in Cambodia and South Vietnam, and the Hongha in North Vietnam. The maritime states, however, revolve around a series of seas and straits, from the highly strategic Strait of Malacca in the west to the Sulu, Celebes and Banda Seas in the east.

The tropical rainforests of South-east Asia are estimated to cover about 250 million hectares [618 million acres]. They are the richest in species of all forest areas in the world. The region is thought to possess some 25,000 species of flowering plants, around 10% of the world's flora.

The evergreen rainforest of the ever-wet, ever-hot tropics is a very complex community. In 20 hectares [49 acres] there can be as many as 350 different species of trees. In the forest, climbing and strangling plants are abundant. Many of the trunks are buttressed, and certain trees bear their flowers and fruits directly on the trunks and branches. The

canopy is the home of a wide range of birds, bats and other mammals, including the orangutan.

Much of the rainforest has now been destroyed by shifting cultivators or felled for timber by extracting companies, and the remaining tracts are also under pressure from mining concerns, rubber companies, hydroelectric developments and tourism.

The peaks and high plateaus of the Himalayas and central Asia are forested up to about 4,000 m [13,000 ft] with an open woodland of pines, cedars, cypresses, bamboos and rhododendrons. Above lies a zone of dwarf shrubs – willows, birches and junipers that spend half their year among snow. This grades into a rough, semi-frozen tundra of coarse sedges and grasses, dotted with cushions of intensely coloured alpine flowers; primulas, edelweiss and gentians become prominent as the snow retreats in early summer. Insects are surprisingly plentiful in the thin, cool air at 4,500–5,500 m [15,000–18,000 ft]. At 6,000 m [19,500 ft] tundra turns to dry desert and both plants and animals become rare.

Larger grazing animals – yaks, hangul deer and blue sheep, for example – emerge from the forest to feed on the high plateaus in summer, and mountain goats and ibex find a living among the high, snow-encrusted crags. Wolves, snow leopards and high-flying eagles are their main predators ∎

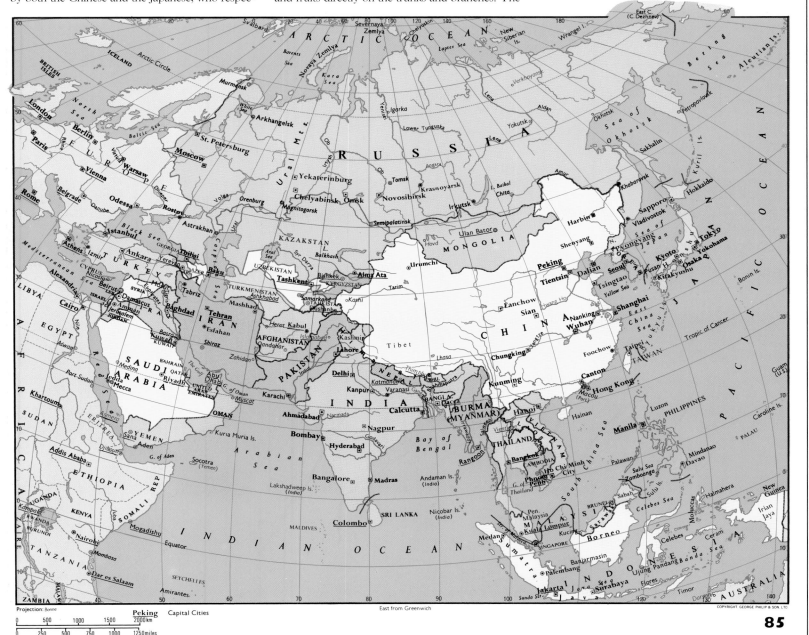

Projection: Bonne

| Peking | Capital Cities |

0   500   1000   1500   2000 km

0   250   500   750   1000   1250 miles

East from Greenwich

COPYRIGHT GEORGE PHILIP & SON, LTD

ASIA

CLIMATIC REGIONS

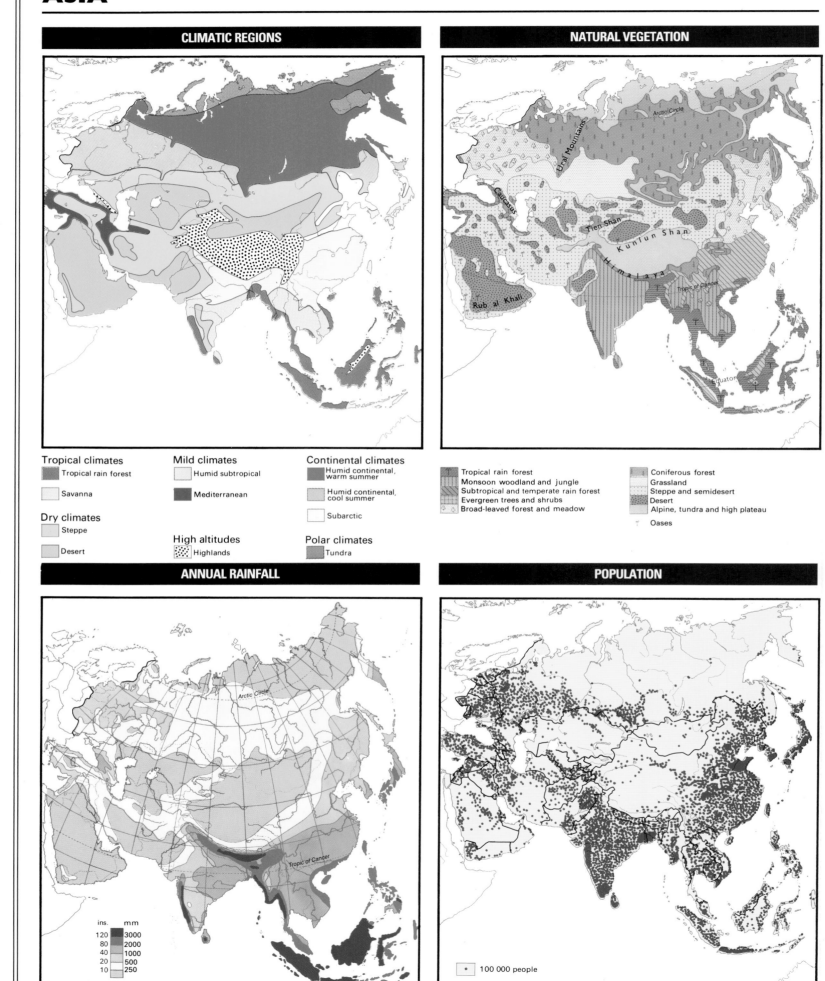

Tropical climates
- Tropical rain forest
- Savanna

Dry climates
- Steppe
- Desert

Mild climates
- Humid subtropical
- Mediterranean

High altitudes
- Highlands

Continental climates
- Humid continental, warm summer
- Humid continental, cool summer
- Subarctic

Polar climates
- Tundra

NATURAL VEGETATION

- Tropical rain forest
- Monsoon woodland and jungle
- Subtropical and temperate rain forest
- Evergreen trees and shrubs
- Broad-leaved forest and meadow
- Coniferous forest
- Grassland
- Steppe and semidesert
- Desert
- Alpine, tundra and high plateau
- Oases

ANNUAL RAINFALL

ins.	mm
120	3000
80	2000
40	1000
20	500
10	250

POPULATION

• 100 000 people

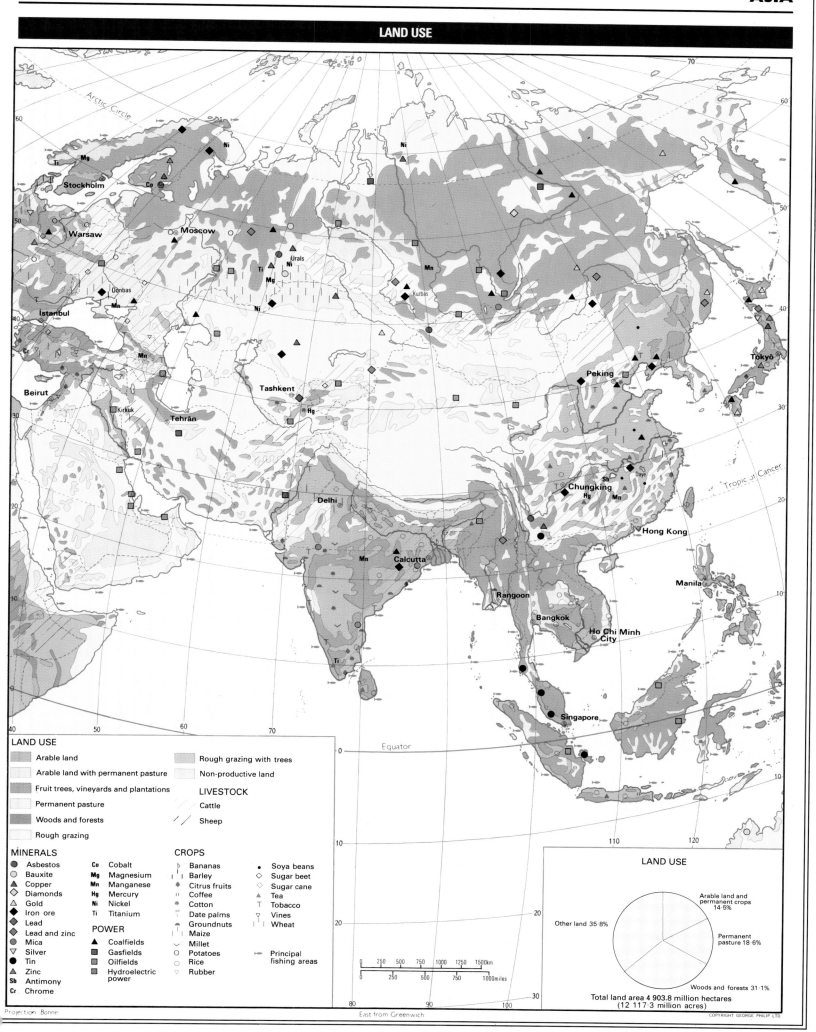

LAND USE

LAND USE

- Arable land
- Arable land with permanent pasture
- Fruit trees, vineyards and plantations
- Permanent pasture
- Woods and forests
- Rough grazing
- Rough grazing with trees
- Non-productive land

LIVESTOCK
- Cattle
- Sheep

MINERALS
- Asbestos
- Bauxite
- Copper
- Diamonds
- Gold
- Iron ore
- Lead
- Lead and zinc
- Mica
- Silver
- Tin
- Sb Antimony
- Cr Chrome

- Co Cobalt
- Mg Magnesium
- Mn Manganese
- Hg Mercury
- Ni Nickel
- Ti Titanium

POWER
- Coalfields
- Gasfields
- Oilfields
- Hydroelectric power

CROPS
- Bananas
- Barley
- Citrus fruits
- Coffee
- Cotton
- Date palms
- Groundnuts
- Maize
- Millet
- Potatoes
- Rice
- Rubber
- Soya beans
- Sugar beet
- Sugar cane
- Tea
- Tobacco
- Vines
- Wheat
- Principal fishing areas

LAND USE

Other land 35·8%
Arable land and permanent crops 14·5%
Permanent pasture 18·6%
Woods and forests 31·1%

Total land area 4 903.8 million hectares
(12 117·3 million acres)

Projection Bonne

East from Greenwich

COPYRIGHT GEORGE PHILIP LTD.

Scale: 250 500 750 1000 1250 1500km / 250 500 750 1000miles

City labels: Stockholm, Warsaw, Moscow, Urals, Donbas, İstanbul, Beirut, Kirkuk, Tehrān, Tashkent, Delhi, Calcutta, Rangoon, Bangkok, Ho Chi Minh City, Singapore, Chungking, Daye, Peking, Hong Kong, Manila, Tōkyō, Kuzbas

RUSSIA

Distinctive Russian flags were first instituted by Peter the Great, based on those of the Netherlands. This flag became the official national flag in 1799 but was suppressed in the Bolshevik Revolution. It was restored on 22 August 1991.

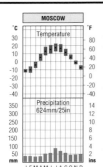

Despite a large temperature range and cold winters (when temperatures rarely rise above freezing, December to February), Moscow has a less extreme continental climate than more easterly parts of Russia. Prevailing westerly winds and the absence of mountains allow the Atlantic Ocean to extend its influence deep into the continent. Rainfall is well distributed, with a slight summer maximum. Winters are cloudy with frequent snow and a very small daily variation in temperature.

It is an indication of the sheer size of the former Soviet Union that, having shed very nearly a quarter of its area with the departure of the 14 republics in 1991, its Russian Federation remains by far the largest country in the world, still getting on for twice the size of Canada, China or the USA.

Diversity certainly characterizes Russia's land-forms, for within the country's borders are to be found rugged peaks and salt flats, glaciers and deserts, marshes and rolling hills as well as broad level plains. In the west the North European Plain occupies the greater part of European Russia as well as much of Ukraine and all of Belarus and the Baltic nations. On the eastern side of the plain are the Ural Mountains; popularly seen as the divide between Europe and Asia, the Urals are low and rounded with few peaks rising above 1,600 m [5,248 ft]. The eastern slopes of the Urals merge into the West Siberian lowland, the largest plain in the world, with extensive low-lying marshes.

The plains of Russia are surrounded on the south and east by mountain ranges of geologically recent origin: the Caucasus, on the borders of Georgia and Azerbaijan; the Altai and Sayan, extending into Mongolia; and, beyond Lake Baykal and the Lena River, the East Siberian ranges at the easternmost tip of the Asian land mass. The Kamchatka peninsula is still geologically unstable – part of the 'Pacific Rim' – and volcanic eruptions and earthquakes occur fairly often.

Much of Russia's landscape bears the imprint of the last Ice Age in the form of chaotic drainage systems, extensive marshlands, lakes and moraines in the lowland areas and cirques and 'U'-shaped valleys in the mountains. More than half the total

LAKE BAYKAL

With a lowest point of 1,620 m [5,315 ft], Lake (*Oz*) Baykal in southern Siberia is the world's deepest lake. Also the largest in Eurasia – at 636 km [395 mls] long by an average width of 48 km [30 mls] it measures some 31,500 sq km [12,160 sq mls], more than the area of Belgium – it is so deep that it is the world's largest body of fresh water and indeed contains no less than a fifth of the fresh water contained in all the world's lakes. Its volume of 23,000 cu km [5,520 cu mls] is as much as the five Great Lakes of North America combined.

Situated in a deep tectonic basin, and fed by 336 rivers and streams, it acts as a reservoir for only one river: the Angara, which flows north to join the Yenisey. Though renowned for its purity and its endemic lifeforms (65% of its 1,500 animal species and 35% of its plant species are unique to Lake Baykal), industrial plants have caused increasing pollution since the 1960s.

The *graben* fault that hosts the arc-shaped lake was caused by gigantic upheavals in the Earth's crust some 80 million years ago; when the climate turned wetter, about 25 million years ago, the lake began to fill – and it is still getting larger. When the *sarma* wind blows from the north-west, it generates waves more than 5 m [16.5 ft] high. Located 80 km [50 mls] from the Mongolian border, Baykal drains an area of 540,000 sq km [208,500 sq mls] – 13% more than the area drained by all five of North America's Great Lakes.

area has permafrost – permanently frozen ground which may extend hundreds of metres in depth.

The rivers that flow across the Russian plains are among the longest and most languid in the world. Drainage in European Russia forms a radial pattern with the hub in the Central Uplands west of Moscow. The Volga flows from this area for 3,700 km [2,300 mls] south to the landlocked Caspian Sea, the world's largest inland body of water. In Siberia the main rivers flow north to the Arctic – among them the Yenisey-Angara, the Ob-Irtysh and the Lena, respectively the fifth, sixth and 11th longest in the world.

Natural regions

Extending latitudinally across Russia, and corresponding to the major climatic belts, are a series of sharply differentiated natural zones – from north to south the tundra, the taiga, the mixed forests and the steppe. The dominant natural zones can also be seen as vertical bands in the mountainous regions.

Tundra: This zone forms a continuous strip north of the Arctic Circle from the Norwegian border to Kamchatka. Climatic conditions here restrict plant growth and soil formation so that the region well deserves its name 'bald mountain top', the meaning of the word 'tundra' in Lapp. Stunted shrubs, mosses, lichens and berry-bearing bushes growing in thin, infertile soils form the vegetation cover, supporting the herds of reindeer which for centuries have formed the basis of the local tribes' economy.

Taiga: Extending south from the boundary with the tundra and occupying about 60% of the country are the coniferous forests that make up the taiga – larger than the Amazonian rainforest. Soils under the forest are acidic and usually unsuitable for cultivation unless fertilized. A major source of wealth in the taiga has always been its large population of fur-bearing animals such as ermine, sable and beaver.

Mixed forest: In the west and east the coniferous forests merge into zones of mixed forest containing both coniferous species and broadleaves such as oak, beech, ash, hornbeam and maple. Today much of the natural vegetation has been cleared for farming, despite the fact that the soils require heavy application of fertilizers to be productive.

Steppe: Sandwiched between the forests to the north and the semi-deserts and deserts of the Central Asian republics to the south is the steppe zone. Hardly any natural vegetation remains in the steppe today as vast expanses have been brought under the plough. The soils of the steppe are *chernozems*, black-earths, and they are among the most fertile in the world. Before conversion into farmland the steppe consisted of extensive grasslands which in the north were interspersed with trees.

Natural resources

Russia's physical environment offers varied opportunities for exploitation. The vast stretches of forest make it the world's largest possessor of softwoods.

The rivers, lakes and seas have yielded marine and freshwater products from early days. In the 11th century fishing villages were already established on the northern coast of European Russia for whaling, sealing and fishing. Today, fish catches are large on the Pacific coast, while in fresh water the sturgeon continues to be valued for its caviar.

Because of the widespread occurrence of poor

soils and harsh climatic conditions, agriculture is confined to a relatively small area. Most of the arable is in the steppe and forest steppe and from the time this was first ploughed it has been used for grains. On the Black Sea coast, subtropical conditions allow the cultivation of wines, tea and citrus fruits.

While agriculture is limited, mineral and energy resources are abundant and formed the basis of the former USSR's powerful industrial economy. Russia's notable mineral deposits are to be found on the Kola peninsula by the Barents Sea, in eastern Siberia and the far east where spectacular discoveries of gold, lead, zinc, copper and diamonds have been made. Iron ore is found in most regions – in 1993, Russia produced 4.3% of the world total (seventh largest producer), amounting to 40 million tonnes; it is also the fourth largest producer of iron and ferro-alloys (42 million tonnes in 1993).

Energy resources are varied. Estimates show Russia to have sufficient coal to last several hundred years, while oil and natural gas deposits are projected to last for several decades, with the main fields in the Volga-Urals region and western Siberia. Large hydropower complexes have also been built on many rivers, though the development of nuclear energy came under review following the 1986 disaster of Chernobyl (in the Ukraine). In 1993, 11.8% of electricity output was nuclear-generated.

History

The present size of Russia is the product of a long period of evolution. In early medieval times the first Slavic state, Kievan Rus, was formed at the junction of the forest and steppe in what is now the Ukraine. As the centuries wore on other states were formed further to the north. All were eventually united under the principality of Muscovy. In the 13th century Mongol hordes from the east penetrated the forests and held sway over the Slavic people there.

It was only in the 16th century that the Mongol yoke was thrown off as the Slavs, under Ivan the Terrible, began to advance across the steppes. This signalled the beginning of a period of expansion from the core area of Slavic settlement to the south, east and west. Expansion across Siberia was rapid and the first Russian settlement on the Pacific, Okhotsk, was established in 1649. Progress across the open steppe was slower but by 1696 Azov, the

COUNTRY Russia

AREA 17,075,000 sq km [6,592,800 sq mls]

POPULATION 148,385,000

CAPITAL (POPULATION) Moscow (9,233,000)

ETHNIC GROUPS Russian 82%, Tatar 4%, Ukrainian 3%, Chuvash 2%

LANGUAGES Russian (official)

RELIGIONS Christian, Muslim, Buddhist

POPULATION DENSITY 9 per sq km [23 per sq ml]

PRINCIPAL CITIES (POPULATION) Moscow 9,233,000
St Petersburg 4,883,000 Nizhniy Novgorod 1,425,000
Novosibirsk 1,418,000 Yekaterinburg 1,347,000

key to the Black Sea, was secured. A series of struggles in the 17th and 18th centuries against the Swedes and Poles resulted in the addition of the Gulf of Finland, the Baltic coast and part of Poland to the growing Russian Empire, and in the 19th century the Caucasus, Central Asia and new territories in the Far East were added.

Russia has been a centralized state throughout its history. A major landmark in the country's history, and indeed in the history of the world, was the 1917 Revolution, when the Tsarist order was overthrown and a Communist government established under Lenin – replacing one form of totalitarianism with another. The years from 1917 witnessed colossal changes, the most dramatic and far-reaching of which took place from the 1930s when Stalin instituted central planning of the economy, collectivized agriculture and began a period of rapid industrialization. After Stalin's death in 1953, Soviet leaders modified some policies but they remained true to the general principles of Communism until the radical approach of Mikhail Gorbachev changed the face of Russia – and the Communist world.

The state that the Communists inherited in 1917 was not merely large; it was also made up of peoples of very diverse ethnic, religious and cultural backgrounds. Among the varied peoples – speaking over 100 languages – the Slavs, consisting of the Russians, Ukrainians and Belarussians, were the most numerous. Other groups include the Turkik and Persian people of Central Asia, the Caucasians, the Baltic peoples, Finno-Ugrians, Mongols and many others. Under Soviet rule the ethnic diversity of the state was recognized in the existence of federal republics (of very disparate size), and in addition autonomous republics and regions were set up to recognize smaller ethnic groups.

Although all parts of Russia are inhabited, even the most remote, the greatest concentration of people has traditionally been in the European part of the country. It was here that in the centuries before the Revolution the first Russian towns with their fortresses (*kremlins*) and onion-domed churches were founded. Outside this settled core there were town and cities which the Russians acquired during their expansion or themselves established on the frontiers. In central Asia the Russians took over what had once been a flourishing urban civilization, gaining towns such as Samarkand, Khiva and Bukhara.

After the Revolution, changes took place in the distribution of population so that the former pattern of a small highly populated core and 'empty' periphery began to break down. Today the settled area extends into Siberia and, in a narrow band, across to the Pacific Ocean. As a result, a far higher proportion of the Russian population is to be found east of the Urals than before the Revolution, even before World War II. This redistribution has been actively encouraged by a regime committed to a policy of developing the east.

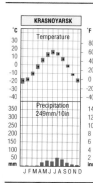

KRASNOYARSK

Though not the most severe climate in Russia, that of Krasnoyarsk is harsh. There are subzero temperature averages for seven months, October to April, with low records exceeding –30°C [–22°F]. Summers are not too warm, though a temperature of over 40°C [104°F] has been measured in July. The annual range of temperature is 36°C [65°F]. Snow lies on the ground for over six months of the year, but the amounts are not great. The rainfall total is low.

THE TRANS-SIBERIAN RAILWAY

The world's longest line, the Trans-Siberian Railway runs for 9,310 km [5,785 mls] from Moscow to Vladivostok and Nakhodka on the Sea of Japan. The Siberian section, beginning at Chelyabinsk in the southern Urals, was built between 1881 and 1905, with an extension around Lake Baykal in 1917, and the line has played a crucial role in opening up Siberia for settlement and industrialization. Today the journey from capital to coast (involving 92 stops in eight time zones) takes over seven days.

Migration to the towns and cities has also been marked since 1917 so that the greater part of the Russian population is now urban. The most famous city is the capital Moscow (Moskva); like the other cities of the North European Plain, it is a mixture of the old and the new, but it is also a mixture of European and Asian styles and cultures.

Economic development

The Soviet government transformed the USSR from an underdeveloped country into the second most powerful industrial nation of the world. At the time of the Revolution (1917) most industrial development was concentrated in a few centres in the European part of the country: Moscow, St Petersburg and, in the Ukraine, the Donbas.

As in many other parts of the world, Soviet industrialization was initially based on the iron and steel industry. In Stalin's drive of the 1930s, heavy national investment went into expanding production in the already existing industrial areas of European Russia and establishing the industry in central and eastern Russia; new large integrated steel mills were built in the southern Urals and on the Kuzbas coalfield in western Siberia. Later the industry was introduced into the Kazak republic on the Karaganda coalfield. Most recently a new plant has been established at Kursk in European Russia.

The shift away from coal as a basis for industrial development to alternative energy sources has taken place later in the Soviet Union than in many other countries. Since the 1960s, however, petroleum and natural gas industries have begun to develop rapidly and the same is true of industries based on hydro-electricity; HEP has been especially important in building up industry in eastern Siberia, where massive installations on the River Angara provide the energy for aluminium production.

Although the introduction of large-scale industry into formerly backward parts of the country has helped to even out levels of development, regional imbalances in production in the territories of the old Soviet Union remain large. The pre-revolutionary foci of development continued to attract a large proportion of available investment and retained their leading position in Soviet industry. This means, effectively, Russia – and of the regions developed since the Revolution only western Siberia can be said today to have a well-developed mature industrial structure. Other parts of the country, and especially the non-Russian republics in the south, still have relatively weak industrial economies.

While overall industrial production forged ahead, agriculture was the 'Achilles' heel' of the Soviet economy, and in several years from the mid-1960s foreign grain had to be imported. Since 1965 there has been an improvement in yields but, even so, output and consumption per capita can only just keep ahead of increases in population.

Soviet farms were of two types, collective (*kolkhozi*) and state (*sovkhozi*). The former were,

according to the official definition, democratically run producers' co-operatives which, in return for a grant of land, delivered some of their produce to the state. In theory free to run their affairs, they were always subject to considerable government interference. The equally large state farms were state-owned and state-managed. Until the 1950s they were relatively uncommon because they were expensive to run, but in the last two decades their number increased. While the greater part of total Soviet agricultural output came from collective and state farms, a large share of market garden produce and some livestock products originated on so-called personal plots.

In the drive for economic development, the Soviet government at first neglected the consumer sector. Growth rates in textiles, food industries and wood processing, for example, lagged behind those for iron and steel production. The paucity of consumer goods, often compounded by gross inefficiencies in the state distribution system, was obvious in the size of the queues that formed whenever scarce products came on sale. Another indication is the existence of a flourishing black market.

During Stalin's rule a conscious policy to restrict foreign trade and maximize self-sufficiency was pursued. With the formation of COMECON, the

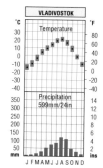

VLADIVOSTOK

The prevailing winds in winter from the bitter north-west give low temperatures to this coastal town at latitude 43°N. Temperatures below –20°C [–4°F] have been recorded in all months from November to March. Snow lies usually from mid-December to mid-February. There are many foggy days in May to July, making the sunshine totals lower in the summer than the winter. Rainfall is quite low, with the monthly total exceeding 100 mm [4 in] in only July to September.

THE KURIL ISLANDS

A chain of 56 windswept volcanically active islands extending 1,200 km [750 mls] between the end of Russia's Kamchatka Peninsula and the tip of Japan's northern island of Hokkaido, the Kurils separate the Sea of Okhotsk from the Pacific Ocean. Totalling 15,600 sq km [6,000 sq mls] but sparsely peopled, they were discovered by the Dutch in 1634, divided between Russia and Japan in the 18th century and ceded to Japan in 1875. At the end of World War II they were seized by Stalin, giving his fleets ice-free northern access to the Pacific. The Japanese, however, still regard the southern section – Etorofu, Kunashir, Shikotan and the Habomai islets – as theirs, referring to them as the 'northern territories' and allotting 7 February as a national day in their honour.

Though there are rich fishing grounds in the territorial waters and the possibility of mineral wealth, it is indeed a matter of honour rather than economics for Tokyo. The Soviets offered to return Shikotan and the Habomai islands in 1956, but the Japanese held out for all four, and the offer was withdrawn. While the advent of Gorbachev and *glasnost* made little difference, the deconstruction of the Soviet Union certainly has: Boris Yeltsin's Russia, desperate for substantial Japanese aid and co-operation, found the islands a stumbling block to assistance. However, more than half of the population who have moved there since 1945 are Russian, and in a 1991 poll the islanders voted 4–1 to remain under Moscow's control.

ASIA

90

Eastern trading bloc, after World War II and the realization that much of Western technology would be useful to its own continued development, the USSR revised trade policy. By the 1980s the Soviet Union was trading with most countries of the world, although the Soviet share of total turnover was small. Again, Russia had the lion's share: while only 15% of its output went to other Soviet republics in 1989, the nearest rivals were Ukraine

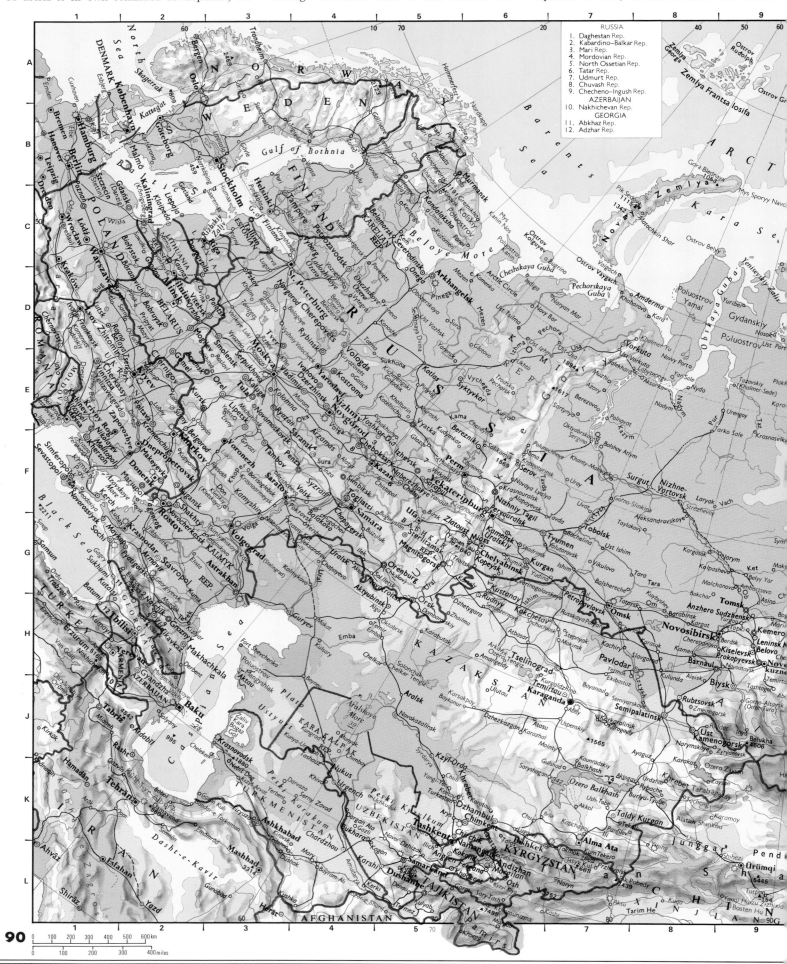

and Kazakstan (32%), while six republics recorded a dependency of more than 60% and another four a figure of more than 50%.

With this apparent status, it may be thought that Russia would not need the Commonwealth of Independent States, its economic strength making it

viable as a major nation and a natural successor internationally to the Soviet Union; indeed, it inherited the USSR's mantle on the UN Security Council and its diplomatic missions worldwide, while applying for membership of CSCE and even NATO.

But Russia, despite its size, fears isolation. With the Eastern European countries and the Baltic states fully independent, the three Caucasus republics unstable, the Asian republics looking increasingly to their Islamic neighbours, and even Mongolia converting to democracy and the free market, Russia has little control of the former 'buffer zones'.

Despite Gorbachev's best and at times brave efforts, the Russian President Boris Yeltsin inherited an economy in crisis, bogged down by lumbering and often obstructive bureaucracy, inept use of resources and an inefficient transport system. After the abolition of price controls sent the cost of basic commodities rocketing, 1992 and 1993 saw food shortages worsen and unemployment rise. However, in spite of these difficulties, the people backed Yeltsin's programme of reforms in a referendum in April 1993, and returned him again as president in July 1996, by a narrow majority over his opponent.

The nation, however, is not homogenous; there are 21 republics, six territories and 49 provinces (*oblasts*). Fighting in the Chechen Republic and its capital Groznyy, from 1994 to 1996, showed that Russia faces continuing problems in maintaining national unity ■

KAZAKSTAN

Although a modest second in size behind Russia among the former Soviet republics, Kazakstan is a colossal country – more than two and a half times the combined area of the other four Central Asian states, over four times the size of Ukraine (Europe's largest 'whole' state), bigger than any nation in Africa and indeed ninth in the world.

This massive new nation, stretching from near the Volga River in the west to the Altai Mountains in the east, comprises mainly vast plains with a mineral-rich central plateau. North to south, the steppe gradually gives way to desert, though irrigation schemes have led to the fertilization of large areas between the Aral Sea and Lake Balkhash, a rich fishing ground. Though its agriculture is tradi-

COUNTRY Kazakstan
AREA 2,717,300 sq km [1,049,150 sq mls]
POPULATION 17,099,000
CAPITAL (POPULATION) Alma Ata (1,198,000)
ETHNIC GROUPS Kazak 40%, Russian 38%, German 6%, Ukrainian 5%, Uzbek, Tatar
RELIGIONS Sunni Muslim, Christian

tionally associated with livestock rearing, Kazakstan accounted for 20% of the cultivated area of the Soviet Union and 12% of its grain output in 1989.

The first extension of the Russian Empire in Central Asia, the area's 'khanates' were gradually subdued or bought off from the 18th century, though rural resistance persisted well into the Soviet era. It was Kazakstan that gave Mikhail Gorbachev his first ethnic problem, when in 1986 nationalist riots erupted after a Russian replaced a Kazak as the republic's Party leader, and in 1991 it led the Central Asian states into the new Commonwealth; indeed, the meeting that finally buried the Soviet Union was held in Alma Ata, testimony to Kazakstan's rank as number three in the hierarchy – an estimate helped by its 1,800 nuclear warheads.

It was not always so. Successive Soviet regimes used the huge republic as a dumping ground and test bed. Stalin exiled Germans and other 'undesirables' there, and Khrushchev experimented with his (largely catastrophic) Virgin Lands Programme; the Soviet missile- and rocket-launching site was located at Baykonur, north-east of the Aral Sea (shrunk by 70% after disastrous Soviet irrigation projects dried up its two feeder rivers), and the USSR's first fast-breeder nuclear reactor was built at Mangyshlak, on the Caspian Sea.

Kazakstan has nevertheless emerged as a powerful entity, wealthier and more diversified than the other Asian republics. Well endowed with oil and

Kazakstan is a large country in the centre of Asia and its climate is markedly continental. The summers are warm and the winters cold, the annual temperature range being 30°C [54°F]. Half the year will experience frost (at Alma Ata) and snow lies for about 100 days. Rainfall is low with only around 250 mm [10 in] in the north and twice this amount in the south, with desert and semi-desert conditions covering large areas.

ALMA ATA
Temperature
Precipitation
597mm/24in

gas, it also has good deposits of chromium ore, uranium, phosphates, tungsten and zinc. Though not industrialized by Western standards, it is growing in oil refining (notably for aviation fuel), metallurgy, engineering, chemicals, footwear, food processing and textiles, the last mostly dependent on homegrown cotton and high-quality native wool.

Kazakstan could provide the 'new order' with a valuable bridge between East and West, between Islam and Christianity; it is the only former Soviet republic whose ethnic population is almost outnumbered by another group (the Russians), and its (Sunni) Muslim revival is relatively muted. Kazakstan's first elected president, Nursultan Nazarbayev, a former Communist party leader, introduced many reforms, including a multiparty system ■

UZBEKISTAN

Only a fraction of Kazakstan's size, but with a larger population, Uzbekistan stretches from the shores of the shrinking Aral Sea, through desert and increasingly fertile semi-arid lands, to the peaks

COUNTRY Uzbekistan
AREA 447,400 sq km [172,740 sq mls]
POPULATION 22,833,000
CAPITAL (POPULATION) Tashkent (2,113,000)
ETHNIC GROUPS Uzbek 71%, Russian 8%, Tajik 5%, Kazak 4%, Tatar 2%, Kara-Kalpak 2%, Crimean Tatar

of the Western Pamirs and the mountainous border with Afghanistan, with a populous eastern spur jutting into Kyrgyzstan.

The fertile sections comprise an intensively irrigated zone that made Uzbekistan the world's fourth largest cotton producer in 1993, contributing 8.2% of the world total; other important agricultural products include rice, astrakhan and hemp. Oil and gas (especially in the desert of Kyzylkum), coal and copper are all important, and in 1993 Uzbekistan was the world's fourth largest producer of uranium.

The Uzbeks were the ruling race in southern Central Asia before the Russians took over in the 19th century. Today, the Russians are a vulnerable minority in the republic noted for ethnic violence, most dangerously between Uzbeks, a Turkic people speaking Jagatai Turkish, and the Tajiks, a Persian people who speak an Iranian dialect. This problem,

Most of the country is extremely dry with less than 200 mm [8 in] of rain a year. This increases in the mountains to over 500 mm [20 in], but is nowhere excessive. There is a winter maximum but near-drought conditions in the summer. The summer is hot and dry; over 40°C [104°F] has been recorded, from May to October, and the winters are not too severe, though the range from January to July is approaching 30°C [54°F].

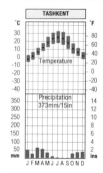

TASHKENT
Temperature
Precipitation
373mm/15in

added to a suspect economy overdependent on one commodity and an enduring reputation for government corruption, could well see Uzbekistan struggle as an independent nation ■

TURKMENISTAN

More than 90% of Turkmenistan is arid, with over half the country covered by the Karakum, Asia's largest sand desert. As much Middle Eastern as Central Asian, its population is found mainly around oases, growing cereals, cotton and fruit, and rearing karakul lambs. Apart from astrakhan rugs and food processing, industry is largely confined to mining sulphur and salt and the production of natural gas, its biggest export.

Dependent on trade with other former Soviet republics for more than 75% of its GDP – and much of that subsidized – Turkmenistan is still a one-party state. Since declaring independence in October 1991 it has looked south to the Muslim countries rather than to the CIS for support – like its Turkic associates, Azerbaijan and Uzbekistan, it has joined the Economic Co-operation Organization formed by Turkey, Iran and Pakistan in 1985 – and its future links with Iran would appear strong ■

COUNTRY Turkmenistan
AREA 488,100 sq km [188,450 sq mls]
POPULATION 4,100,000
CAPITAL (POPULATION) Ashkhabad (411,000)
ETHNIC GROUPS Turkmen 72%, Russian 10%, Uzbek 9%, Kazak 3%, Tatar

KYRGYZSTAN

COUNTRY Kyrgyzstan	
AREA 198,500 sq km [76,640 sq mls]	
POPULATION 4,738,000	
CAPITAL (POPULATION) Bishkek (597,000)	
ETHNIC GROUPS Kyrgyz 52%, Russian 22%, Uzbek 13%, Ukrainian 3%, German 2%, Tatar 2%	
RELIGIONS Sunni Muslim, Christian	

Despite its geographical isolation on the borders of China's Xinjiang province, its mainly mountainous terrain and its conventionally strong links with Moscow, Kyrgyzstan has pursued very aggressive 'European' policies towards Western-style capitalist democracy in the period since independence was declared in August 1991. Its young president, Askar Akayev, introduced rapid privatization, nurtured pluralism, and encouraged trade and investment links with OECD countries. In addition, he established good relations with China, a suspicious neighbour and potential foe.

In 1994, Kyrgyzstan adopted a new constitution, and parliamentary elections were held in 1995.

However, the large Russian minority (in positions of power under the Soviet regime), disenchanted Uzbeks and an influx of Chinese Muslim immigrants have the potential for an ethnic tinderbox.

Though dominated by the western end of the Tian Shan, with peaks rising to the 7,439 m [24,000 ft] of Pik Pobedy on the Chinese border, Kyrgyzstan has a strong agricultural economy. Much of the lower land is pasture for sheep, cattle, goats, horses and yaks (pastoralism is the traditional livelihood of the Mongoloid Kyrgyz, though few nomads remain), while irrigated land produces a wide range of crops from sugar beet and vegetables to rice, cotton, grapes and mulberry trees (for silkworms) ■

TAJIKISTAN

The smallest of the five Central Asian CIS republics, Tajikistan lies on the borders of Afghanistan and China. Only 7% of the country is below 1,000 m [3,280 ft] and the eastern half is almost all above 3,000 m [9,840 ft]. In the north-

west the land is irrigated for wheat, cotton, fruit, vegetables and mulberry trees (for silkworms).

Tajikistan was the poorest of the Soviet republics, and independence (declared in September 1991) brought huge economic problems. The Tajiks are a Persian people, and with a population that is 95% Muslim – albeit Sunnis – the country was the most likely of the Central Asian republics to follow the Islamic fundamentalism of Iran rather than the secular, pro-Western model of Turkey. A new constitution was adopted in 1992 but ethnic

violence broke out, and continued to flare up into 1995. A new parliament was instituted in December 1994 – the 50-member Majlis ■

COUNTRY Tajikistan	
AREA 143,100 sq km [55,250 sq mls]	
POPULATION 6,102,000	
CAPITAL (POPULATION) Dushanbe (602,000)	
ETHNIC GROUPS Tajik 62%, Uzbek 24%, Russian 8%	
RELIGIONS Sunni Muslim, some Christian	

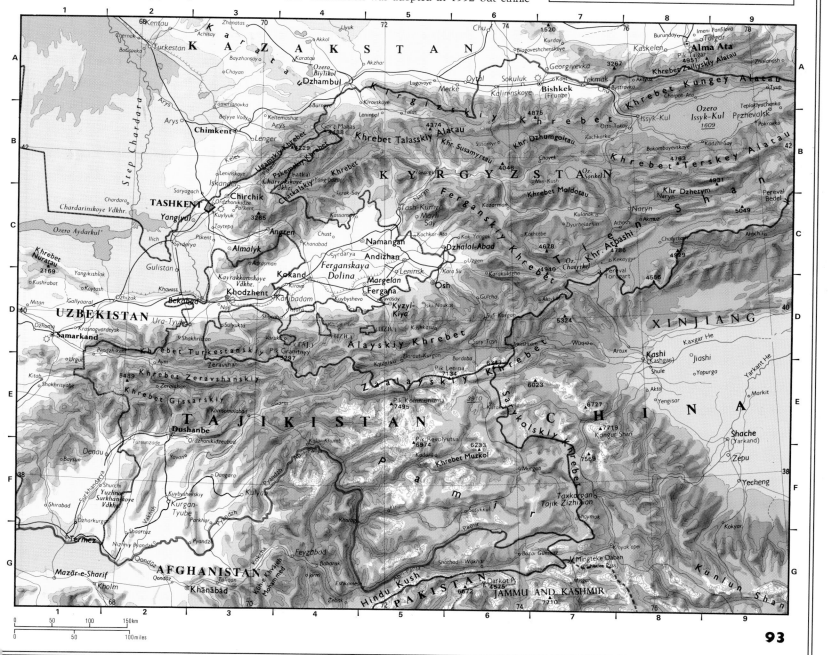

TURKEY

Although the crescent moon and the five-pointed star are symbols of Islam, their presence on Turkey's flag dates from long before the country became a Muslim state. The flag was officially adopted when the republic was founded in 1923.

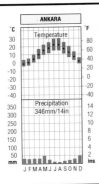

The plateau of Anatolia is a region of continental extremes and slight precipitation. Ankara lies just to the north of the driest part of the plateau which is situated around the large saltwater Lake Tuz. Summer days are hot and sunny, with nights pleasantly cool; over 11 hours of sunshine and temperatures of 15–30°C [59–86°F]. Winters are cold with the mean temperature in January close to freezing. Snow falls on average on 20–30 days a year. Annual rainfall is low, in some years failing from July to October.

The most populous country in south-west Asia, Turkey comprises the broad peninsula of Asia Minor, together with its 'roots' around Lake Van, and in Europe that part of Thrace (Thraki) which lies to the east of the lower Maritsa River. The straits separating the European (5%) and Asiatic parts of Turkey have been of strategic importance for thousands of years. The Dardanelles, joining the Aegean Sea to the Sea of Marmara, are 1.6 km [1 ml] wide at their narrowest point; the Bosphorus, linking the Sea of Marmara to the Black Sea, measures just 640 m [2,100 ft] at one point and is spanned by two suspension bridges at Istanbul.

The heart of the country is the high karst plateau of Anatolia, semi-desert around the central salt lake, but mainly sheep country. The Taurus ranges afford summer grazing for the plateau flocks, and also timber. The northern Pontic ranges are better wooded, with fertile plains. The valleys of the Gediz and Cürüksu, which open westwards from the plateau to the Aegean, export tobacco and figs, while the deltaic plain around Adana grows abundant cotton. The very high and thinly peopled plateaus and ranges to the east of the Euphrates produce chrome, copper and oil.

Istanbul, the former imperial capital of Byzantium and Constantinople, which controls the straits between the Black Sea and the Mediterranean, is the country's chief port and commercial city, but the function of capital has been transferred to the more centrally placed town of Ankara. Turkey, with a rapidly growing population, now has one of the best railway networks in the Middle East, and though lacking in large resources of mineral oil has built up a thriving industrial economy based on imported oil, on coal (from Zonguldak), and above all on hydroelectric power. Though still important, agriculture has been overtaken by manufacturing, particularly textiles and clothing.

Constantinople's huge Ottoman Empire had been in decline for centuries when alliance with Germany in World War I ended in the loss of all non-Turkish areas. Nationalists led by Mustafa Kemal – known later as 'father of the Turks' – rejected peace proposals favouring Greece and after a civil war set up a republic. Turkey's present frontiers were established in 1923, when Atatürk became president, and until 1938 he ruled as a virtual dictator, secularizing and modernizing the traditional Islamic state.

Between 1960 and 1970 the government was overthrown three times by military coups; civilian rule returned in 1983 and since then democracy has been relatively stable, though the country's human rights record remained more Third World than Western European.

The economic progress that partnered political stability in the mid-1980s – growth averaged more than 7% a year – encouraged Turkey to apply for EEC membership in 1987, but the response from Brussels was unenthusiastic. Turkey's disputes with Greece – notably over Ankara's invasion of northern Cyprus in 1974, but also over claims to territory and mineral rights in the Aegean – plus the country's poor human rights record and still-low standard of living were all factors. While Turkey has been a NATO member since 1952, this was likely to remain the EU's position for some time – while the emergence of Islamic fundamentalism raised new doubts about Turkey's 'European' stance.

Situated at one of the world's great geopolitical crossroads, the nation seemed destined to remain sandwiched between Europe and the Middle East. Turkey, nevertheless, has a two-way traffic in people with Western Europe: while tourism is a boom industry (often at the expense of Greece), with 6.5 million visitors a year visiting the country, these are outnumbered by Turkish men working (or seeking work) in EU cities, the majority of them in Germany ∎

COUNTRY Republic of Turkey

AREA 779,450 sq km [300,946 sq mls]

POPULATION 61,303,000

CAPITAL (POPULATION) Ankara (3,028,000)

GOVERNMENT Multiparty republic with a unicameral legislature

ETHNIC GROUPS Turkish 86%, Kurdish 11%, Arab 2%

LANGUAGES Turkish (official), Kurdish

RELIGIONS Sunni Muslim 99%, Eastern Orthodox

NATIONAL DAY 29 October; Republic Day (1923)

CURRENCY Turkish lira = 100 kurus

ANNUAL INCOME PER PERSON US$2,120

MAIN PRIMARY PRODUCTS Cereals, cotton, pulses, sugar beet, cattle, sheep, tobacco, fruit, vegetables, coal, lignite, crude oil, iron, boron, copper, chromium

MAIN INDUSTRIES Agriculture, steel, food processing, textiles, oil, chemicals, fishing, mining

MAIN EXPORTS Textiles 24%, agricultural products 20%, metals 14%, foodstuffs 7%

MAIN EXPORT PARTNERS Germany 18%, Iraq 8%, Italy 7%, USA 7%, UK 5%, France 4%, Saudi Arabia 3%

MAIN IMPORTS Fuels 19%, machinery 17%, chemicals 14%, iron and steel 12%, pharmaceuticals 7%

MAIN IMPORT PARTNERS Germany 14%, USA 11%, Iraq 10%, Italy 7%, UK 6%, France 5%

DEFENCE 4.7% of GNP

TOURISM 6,500,294 visitors per year

POPULATION DENSITY 79 per sq km [204 per sq ml]

INFANT MORTALITY 62 per 1,000 live births

LIFE EXPECTANCY Female 68 yrs, male 65 yrs

ADULT LITERACY 81%

PRINCIPAL CITIES (POPULATION) Istanbul 7,490,000 Ankara 3,028,000 Izmir 2,333,000 Adana 1,472,000 Bursa 1,317,000 Gaziantep 930,000 Antalya 734,000

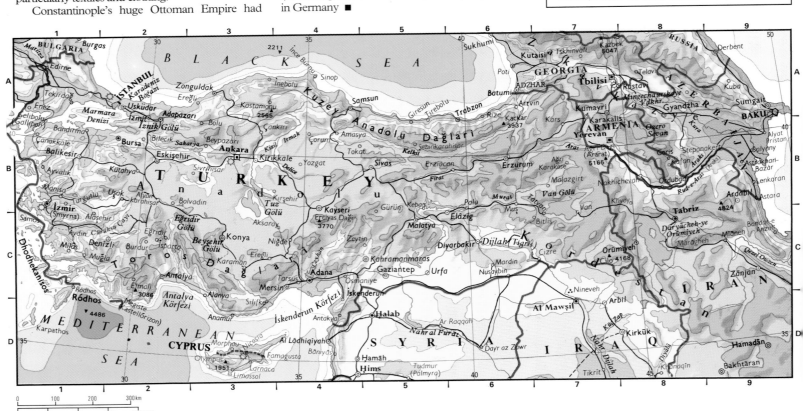

CYPRUS

The design, featuring a map of the island with two olive branches, has been the official state flag since independence from Britain in 1960. However, Cyprus is now divided and the separate communities fly the Greek and Turkish flags.

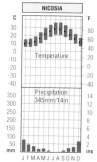

The highest rainfall on the island is in the Troödos Mountains and is under 1,000 mm [40 in]. The rest of the island is very dry with rain on about 60 days per year, and virtually no summer rain. The summers are hot and the winters warm, although the winters are cold in the mountains. The daily temperature in July and August can be very hot – the highest recorded from April to October are all over 40°C [104°F]. The period May to September has over 10 hours of sunshine per day.

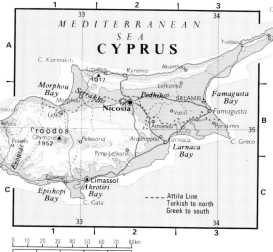

A small but strategically situated island in the Mediterranean, Cyprus is a detached fragment of the mainland mountains to the east. In the south, the broad massif of Troödos, rich in minerals, is a classic example of an ophiolite, or intrusive dome of ancient suboceanic rocks. The northern coast is backed by the long limestone range of Kyrenia. The fertile central plain between Morphou and Famagusta grows fruits, flowers and early vegetables. The former forests were cut mainly in classical times to fuel the copper smelteries; 'kypros' is the Greek for copper. Turks settled in the north of the island during Ottoman rule, from 1571 to 1878, when Cyprus came under British administration. In the 1950s Greek Cypriots, led by Archbishop Makarios (later President), campaigned for union with Greece (Enosis), while the Turks favoured partition. After a guerrilla campaign by EOKA a power-sharing compromise was reached and in 1960 the island became a republic. This fragile arrangement broke down in 1963, and the following year the UN sent in forces to prevent more inter-communal fighting.

In 1968 the Turkish Cypriots set up an 'autonomous administration' in the north, but in 1974, following a coup by Greek-born army officers that deposed Makarios, Turkey invaded the mainland and took control of the northern 40% of the country, displacing 200,000 Greek Cypriots. The UN has since supervised an uneasy partition of the island.

The Greek Cypriot sector has prospered from tourism, British bases, invisible earnings and agriculture, as well as manufacturing. The more agriculturally based north has fared less well: the 'Turkish Republic of Northern Cyprus' is recognized only by Ankara and relies heavily on aid from Turkey ■

COUNTRY Cyprus
AREA 9,250 sq km [3,571 sq mls]
POPULATION 742,000
CAPITAL (POPULATION) Nicosia (178,000)
GOVERNMENT Multiparty republic
ETHNIC GROUPS Greek Cypriot 81%, Turkish Cypriot 19%
LANGUAGES Greek, Turkish
RELIGIONS Greek Orthodox, Muslim
NATIONAL DAY 1 October; Independence Day (1960)
CURRENCY Cyprus pound = 100 cents
ANNUAL INCOME PER PERSON US$8,640
MAIN INDUSTRIES Cement, wine, footwear, cigarettes
MAIN PRIMARY PRODUCTS Asbestos, pyrites, copper
MAIN EXPORTS Wine, vegetables, fruit, clothing, shoes
MAIN IMPORTS Food, petroleum, chemicals
DEFENCE 1.4% of GNP
POPULATION DENSITY 80 per sq km [208 per sq ml]
LIFE EXPECTANCY Female 79 yrs, male 74 yrs
ADULT LITERACY 94%

LEBANON

Adopted on independence in 1943, Lebanon's colours are those of the Lebanese Legion in World War I. The cedar tree, many of which grow in the mountains, has been a Lebanese symbol since biblical times. The colours of the cedar tree were slightly altered in 1996.

The coast of Lebanon has the hot, dry summers and mild, wet winters characteristic of much of the Mediterranean basin. The four months from June to September are almost completely dry. In winter, onshore winds rise against the steep western edge of the Lebanon Mountains bringing heavy rain at sea level with snow at high altitude, raining on every other day between December and February. Close to the sea, there is a small daily range of temperature.

For three decades after its independence from the French mandate in 1944 Lebanon was a relatively peaceful and prosperous country by Middle East standards. An association with France going back a century – before that the country was part of the Ottoman Empire – had bequeathed a distinct Gallic flavour, though with so many racial and religious groups the population was truly cosmopolitan; Beirut, the dominant city, was both a centre of international commerce (the Lebanese are descendants of the Phoenicians, legendary traders and businessmen) and an elegant playground of the wealthy.

All that changed suddenly after March 1975 when this beautiful country saw sporadic conflict spiral into violent civil war between Christians, Muslims and Druses. The complex politics of the next 14 years proved almost unfathomable as Lebanon sank into a seemingly permanent state of ungovernable chaos. Bombing, assassination and kidnapping became routine as numerous factions and private militias – Maronite, Druse, Sunni and Shia groups (including fundamentalists backed by Iran) – fought for control. The situation was complicated by a succession of interventions by Palestinian liberation organizations, Israeli troops, the Syrian Army, Western and then UN forces, as the country became a patchwork of occupied zones and 'no-go' areas.

The core religious confrontation has deep roots: in 1860 thousands of Maronites (aligned to the Catholic Church) were murdered by Druses (so tangential to other Islamic sects that they are now not regarded as Muslims), and Muslim tolerance of

COUNTRY Republic of Lebanon
AREA 10,400 sq km [4,015 sq mls]
POPULATION 2,971,000
CAPITAL (POPULATION) Beirut (1,500,000)
GOVERNMENT Multiparty republic
ETHNIC GROUPS Lebanese 80%, Palestinian 12%, Armenian 5%, Syrian, Kurdish
LANGUAGES Arabic (official), French , English, Armenian
RELIGIONS Muslim 58%, Christian 27%, Druse 3%
CURRENCY Lebanese pound = 100 piastres
ANNUAL INCOME PER PERSON US$1,750
MAIN PRIMARY PRODUCTS Salt, gypsum, tin
DEFENCE 5% of GNP
POPULATION DENSITY 286 per sq km [740 per sq ml]

Christian power after independence lasted only until 1958. Though not directly involved, Lebanon was destabilized by the Arab-Israeli War of 1967, and the exile of PLO leadership to Beirut in 1970. By 1990 the Syrian Army had crushed the two-year revolt of Christian rebels against the Lebanese government, but peace proved fragile and a solution elusive.

At the start of 1996 Israel still occupied the south of the country, while the fundamentalist Hezbollah still controlled much of the Beqaa Valley in the north. In April 1996, in response to missile attacks on settlements in northern Israel, Israeli forces launched a sustained attack on pro-Iranian (Shia) Hezbollah positions in southern Lebanon, resulting in heavy civilian casualties ■

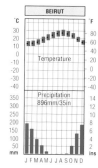

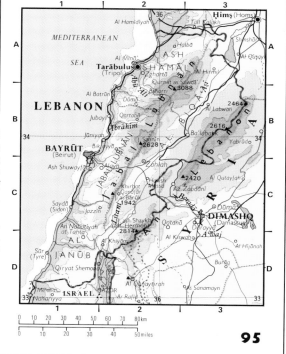

ISRAEL

The blue and white stripes on Israel's flag are based on a Hebrew prayer shawl. In the centre is the ancient six-pointed Star of David. The flag was designed in America in 1891 and officially adopted by the new Jewish state in 1948.

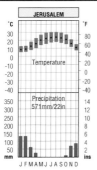

East of the Mediterranean Sea the annual rainfall decreases inland and the length of the summer dry season increases to more than five months. At over 700 m [2,250 ft], Jerusalem has lower temperatures and a greater range than the coastal regions of Israel. To the south, rainfall decreases rapidly to only 70 mm [2.5 in] in the rocky desert around the Dead Sea. There is an average daily sunshine total of over 9 hours, ranging from 6–12 hours.

In 1948 the new Jewish state of Israel comprised the coastal plain, the vale of Esdraelon (Jezreel) behind Haifa, the foothills in the south, most of the hill country of Samaria, and half of Jerusalem with a corridor to the west. It was also the intention of the UN that Israel should acquire either Galilee in the north or the Negev Desert in the south, but in the event both these regions were included.

The rest of Palestine, mainly Judaea and the rift valley west of the river, was added to Jordan, but as a result of the Six Day War in 1967, its administration as the 'West Bank' was taken over by Israel along with East Jerusalem. At the same time the Israelis also occupied the Gaza Strip (Egypt) and the Golan Heights (Syria).

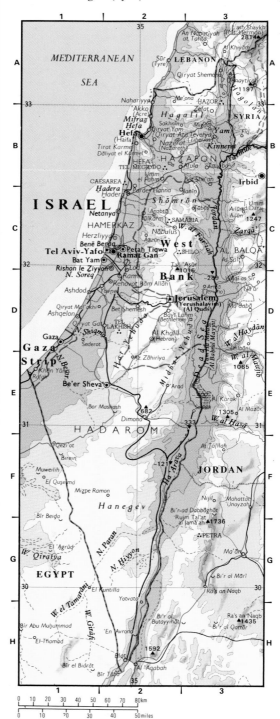

In October 1973, Egypt and Syria launched attacks against Israel in an unsuccessful attempt to regain territories. Egypt and Israel eventually signed a peace treaty in 1979: Israel agreed to withdraw from the Sinai and Egypt recognized Israel. In 1982, Israeli forces invaded Lebanon to destroy PLO strongholds in that country and only left in 1985. From 1987 onwards, Palestinian resistance to Israeli occupation of the Gaza Strip and the West Bank became more and more widespread and violent.

In the 1990s, increased international pressure led to the signing of a treaty in 1993 between Israel and PLO – and a framework document for peace with Jordan was signed in July 1994. But the shocking assassination on 4 November 1995 of Prime Minister Yitzhak Rabin left a great question mark over the peace process, with an upsurge of Jewish nationalism and the onset in early 1996 of terrorist activities by the Arab group Hamas. Rabin's successor, Símon Peres, faced a difficult task to keep the peace process on track; he was subsequently defeated in the June 1996 elections which saw right-wing Binyamin Netanyahu elected prime minister.

Economy and industry

In general, the country is most fertile in the north, and becomes progressively more desertlike towards the south. The object of the Jordan–Western Negev scheme, the most ambitious of Israel's irrigation enterprises, has been to direct through canals and culverts all the water that can be spared from the Upper Jordan and the drainage channels of the coastal plain southwards to the deserts of the Negev. The Upper Jordan Valley is excellent farmland, reclaimed from the swamps of Lake Huleh.

The valley of Jezreel, with a deep alluvial soil washed down from Galilee, is intensively tilled with market gardens. South of the promontory of Carmel, the coastal plain of Sharon is excellent fruit-growing country, but needs irrigation.

Between Sinai and the rift valley, the great wedge of desert plateau known as the Negev accounts for about half the total territory of Israel. Its bedrock is widely covered with blown sand and loess, which will grow tomatoes and grapes in profusion if supplied with fresh water. The Negev south of Be'er Sheva is pioneer territory, with new towns mining oil, copper and phosphates, factories using the potash and salt of the Dead Sea, and farms experimenting with solar power and artificial dew. Carob trees have been planted for fodder, and dairy farms and plantations of bananas and dates have been established with the aid of artesian springs.

Elat on the Gulf of Aqaba is an increasingly successful tourist town and Israel's sea outlet to Africa and most of Asia. From here, a pipeline takes imported oil to the refinery at Haifa. To supplement the facilities of Haifa, Israel built a deep-sea port at Ashdod to replace the old anchorage at Jaffa (Yafo).

Israel has become the most industrialized country in the Near East. Iron is smelted at Haifa and converted to steel at the foundries of Acre. Chemicals are manufactured at Haifa and at plants by the Dead Sea. With the aid of a national electricity grid, factories for textiles, ceramics and other products have been widely established in country towns, including the new foundations of Dimona and Mizpe Ramon in the Negev. Most commercial movement is now along the road network rather than by rail ■

JERUSALEM

Though held sacred by all of the world's three great monotheisms, Jerusalem's religious importance has brought the city little peace. King David's capital in the 11th century BC, with the building of the great Temple of Solomon, it became the cult centre of Judaism. The Temple was destroyed by the Assyrians and rebuilt in the 6th century, reassuming its importance until AD 70, when Jerusalem, Temple and all, was destroyed by Roman legions during the great Jewish Revolt against the Empire. Later, a rebuilt Jerusalem became a great centre of Christian pilgrimage. In the 7th century, the city was captured by the expanding armies of Islam, and for Muslims, too, Jerusalem (al-Quds in Arabic) is also a holy place: it was visited by the Prophet Mohammed during the 'Night Journey' recounted in the Koran, and Muslims also believe that it was from Jerusalem that the Prophet ascended to paradise. The great mosque known as the Dome of the Rock was built on the site of the Jewish Temple.

During the Israeli War of Independence, Arab and Jew fought bitterly for possession of the city: neither could oust the other and until 1967 it was divided by bristling fortifications, with the Wailing Wall, the only surviving part of the old Temple, firmly under Arab control. In the Six Day War, Israeli soldiers at last captured all of the city, to universal Jewish rejoicing and Arab lamentation.

COUNTRY State of Israel

AREA 26,650 sq km [10,290 sq mls]

POPULATION 5,696,000

CAPITAL (POPULATION) Jerusalem (550,000)

GOVERNMENT Multiparty republic

ETHNIC GROUPS Jewish 82%, Arab and others 18%

LANGUAGES Hebrew and Arabic (both official)

RELIGIONS Jewish 82%, Muslim 14%, Christian 2%

NATIONAL DAY 10 May (variable each year); Independence Day (1948)

CURRENCY New Israeli sheqel = 100 agorat

ANNUAL INCOME PER PERSON US$13,760

MAIN PRIMARY PRODUCTS Livestock, natural gas, fruit

MAIN INDUSTRIES Agriculture, mining, food processing, textiles, clothing, fertilizers, cement

MAIN EXPORTS Machinery 29%, diamonds 29%, chemicals 22%, textiles 8%, foodstuffs 5%

MAIN EXPORT PARTNERS USA 31%, UK 8%, Japan 7%, Germany 5%, Hong Kong 5%, Netherlands 5%

MAIN IMPORTS Diamonds 20%, capital goods 15%, consumer goods 11%, fuels and lubricants 8%

MAIN IMPORT PARTNERS USA 16%, Belgium–Luxembourg 15%, Germany 11%, UK 9%, Switzerland 9%, Ireland 6%, France 4%

DEFENCE 11.1% of GNP

TOURISM 1,500,000 visitors per year

POPULATION DENSITY 214 per sq km [554 per sq ml]

LIFE EXPECTANCY Female 78 yrs, male 74 yrs

ADULT LITERACY 95%

SYRIA

The flag of Syria is the one adopted in 1958 by the former United Arab Republic (which included Syria, Egypt and Yemen). At various times in their history Egypt and Syria have shared the same flag, but since 1980 Syria has used this design.

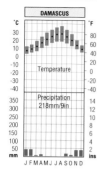

Damascus is isolated from the maritime influence of the Mediterranean by the Lebanon Mountains. Rainfall, confined to winter, is less than on the coast and more variable. The Syrian winter becomes colder further to the east, and frost and snow are not uncommon. Frosts can occur at Damascus between November and March. On the higher mountains, patches of snow persist throughout the year. Summers are very hot and dry with a large diurnal range of temperature of up to 20°C [36°F].

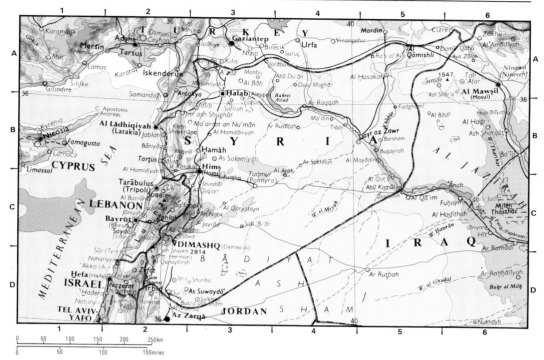

The northern part of the former Ottoman province of the same name, Syria stretches from the Mediterranean to the Tigris, and from the southern edge of the Kurdish plateau in the north to the heart of the Hamad or stony desert in the south. The northern border for most of its length follows the railway from Aleppo to Mosul. Syria has only one large harbour, at Latakia, though the country usually enjoys privileged access to the ports of Lebanon.

The Orontes River flows northwards along the great rift valley, through alternating gorges and wide valleys which have been reclaimed by drainage and irrigation. Near Hamah and Hims the ranges of Lebanon and Anti-Lebanon, which flank the valley to west and east, are relatively low, but further south the Anti-Lebanon rises to the Heights of Hermon, whose snows water the gardens of the capital, Damascus, on the eastern or desert side. In the far south, by the frontier with Jordan, the volcanic mass of Mount Hauran supports a group of oases around the town of Suwayda. The Golan Heights, in the south-west, are occupied by Israel.

Aleppo, the second city of Syria, is set in a well-watered agricultural area. Further east the steppe becomes progressively drier. This was traditionally winter pasture for the nomads who moved in from their summer homes in the mountains of Lebanon, but in recent years, thanks to techniques of dry farming with machinery, it has become a prosperous farming zone, devoted almost exclusively to cotton and cereals. The water from the Euphrates barrage, which produces 70% of the country's electricity, will extend agriculture in this region.

Syria has struck oil in the 'panhandle' by the Tigris in the far north-east, and a pipeline has been laid from there to the Mediterranean. Another pipeline crosses the desert further south from the Kirkuk fields in Iraq to the sea terminal at Baniyas.

President Assad's repressive but stable regime, in power since 1970, was heavily reliant on Arab aid, but Syria's anti-Iraq stance in the 1991 Gulf War will almost certainly result in greater Western assistance to the improving economy. Though small compared to Egypt or Saudi Arabia, Syria's position (both historical and geographical) makes the country a key player in the complicated power game of Middle East politics ∎

THE MIDDLE EAST CONFLICT

Arab-Jewish hostility in the Middle East dates from the so-called Balfour Declaration of 1917, when an embattled British government proposed a 'Jewish national home' in the then Turkish imperial province of Palestine without prejudicing the 'existing rights' of the overwhelmingly Arab population. After World War I, Palestine became a League of Nations mandate under British control; throughout the 1920s, a trickle of Jewish immigrants inspired rioting without noticeably affecting the population balance. But the rise of Nazism in Europe brought floods of Jewish refugees, and Arab-Jewish violence became endemic.

In 1947 the UN proposed a formal partition of the land, accepted by the Jews but rejected by the Palestinians. Even before the British announced they would withdraw in May 1948, 150,000 Arab refugees had fled. On 14 May, the day the British quit, the independence of a new State of Israel was declared. Egypt, Lebanon, Syria, Transjordan and Iraq at once launched an invasion, later joined by Yemen and Saudi Arabia. By the 1949 cease-fire, though, Israel controlled more territory than the partition plan had allocated the Jews. Jerusalem remained a divided city, half controlled by Israel, half by Transjordan (later the Kingdom of Jordan).

An uneasy peace descended, with sporadic border clashes; hundreds of thousands of Palestinians lost their homes. In 1956, full-scale war erupted once more when Israel joined with Britain and France in an attack on Egypt. Egypt's armies were badly mauled, but Israel's borders remained unchanged. In 1967, Israel responded to an Egyptian maritime blockade with a pre-emptive strike that left it in control of the Sinai peninsula, the Gaza Strip, the 'West Bank' of the Jordan and all of Jerusalem. But real peace was no nearer; Israel had acquired an Arab population of several million. Palestinian 'freedom fighters' (or 'terrorists') began a worldwide campaign, including aircraft hijacking, to broadcast their people's plight.

A 1973 Egyptian attack across the Suez Canal, backed by Syria, came close to overrunning Sinai, but Israeli counter-attacks recovered much of the lost territory. Egypt's partial victory eventually led to the 1979 Camp David accord, whereby Israel agreed to return Sinai in exchange for Egyptian recognition of Israel's right to exist. Egypt was excoriated by its former Arab allies, and Palestinian terrorism continued. From 1987 onwards, a Palestinian uprising (the *intifada*) began, which was repressed by Israel. Finally, on 13 September 1993, Israeli prime minister Yitzhak Rabin officially recognized the PLO, and Yasser Arafat, leader of the PLO, renounced world terrorism and recognized the State of Israel, leading to an agreement signed by both sides in Washington in 1993, which provided for limited Palestinian self-rule in the Gaza Strip and Jericho. The subsequent assassination of Rabin led to the election of right-wing Binyamin Netanyahu, which heightened tensions across the region and slowed the peace process.

COUNTRY Syrian Arab Republic

AREA 185,180 sq km [71,498 sq mls]

POPULATION 14,614,000

CAPITAL (POPULATION) Damascus (2,230,000)

GOVERNMENT Unitary multiparty republic with a unicameral legislature

ETHNIC GROUPS Arab 89%, Kurd 6%

LANGUAGES Arabic (official), Kurdish, Armenian

RELIGIONS Muslim 90%, Christian 9%

NATIONAL DAY 17 April

CURRENCY Syrian pound = 100 piastres

ANNUAL INCOME PER PERSON US$1,250

MAIN PRIMARY PRODUCTS Sheep, goats, cattle, cotton, sugar, fruit, cereals, crude oil, natural gas, phosphates, manganese, salt

MAIN INDUSTRIES Agriculture, oil and gas, cotton, wool, metal goods, glass, flour, soap

MAIN EXPORTS Crude petroleum and natural gas 33%, chemicals 29%, textiles and clothing 26%, foodstuffs

MAIN EXPORT PARTNERS Italy 31%, CIS nations 21%, France 10%, Romania 9%, Iran 5%, Germany 5%

MAIN IMPORTS Machinery and equipment 30%, chemicals 21%, foodstuffs 12%, basic metal products 8%, textiles 3%

MAIN IMPORT PARTNERS France 10%, CIS nations 8%, Iran 8%, Germany 8%, Italy 7%, Libya 6%, USA 5%

DEFENCE 16.6% of GNP

POPULATION DENSITY 79 per sq km [204 per sq ml]

LIFE EXPECTANCY Female 69 yrs, male 65 yrs

ADULT LITERACY 68%

PRINCIPAL CITIES (POPULATION) Damascus 2,230,000 Aleppo 1,640,000 Hims 644,000 Latakia 284,000

ASIA

JORDAN

Green, white and black are the colours of the three tribes that led the Arab Revolt against the Turks in 1917, while red is the colour of the Hussein dynasty. The star was added in 1928 with its seven points representing the first seven verses of the Koran.

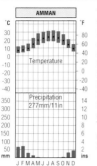

The Jordan Valley marks the eastern limit of the true Mediterranean region, and although Amman lies only a short distance east of Jerusalem, it has a much lower rainfall and a longer dry season. Rain is almost unknown from May to September. Its semi-arid climate is transitional between the Mediterranean type and the true desert to the east. Temperatures are similar on average to those of Jerusalem but summer days are hotter.

After World War I the Arab territories of the Ottoman Empire were divided by the League of Nations and the area east of the River Jordan ('Transjordan') was awarded to Britain as part of Palestine, becoming a separate emirate in 1923. When the mandate ended in 1946 the kingdom became independent, as Jordan, and two years later (in the first Arab-Israeli War) it acquired the West Bank, which was officially incorporated into the state in 1950.

This crucial area, including Arab Jerusalem, was lost to Israel in the 1967 war, and Jordan has since carried the burden of Palestinian refugees on its own limited territory. In the 1970s the guerrillas

THE PALESTINIANS

The sorrowful modern history of the Palestinians began in 1948, when the birth of Israel transformed most of their former territory into a foreign state; some 700,000 fled, most finding no better homes than refugee camps in Jordan, Lebanon and Egypt's Gaza Strip. After the 'Six Day War' in 1967, most Palestinians not already refugees found themselves living under enemy occupation. Since 1964, the Palestine Liberation Organization has existed to free them by 'armed struggle', but the PLO's adoption of international terrorism as a tactic alienated many potential allies. The 1987 *intifada* brought much world support, but by late 1991, when peace talks with Israel at last began, almost half the Palestinian population were still classified as refugees. After long and difficult negotiations, Israel and the PLO finally signed a historic treaty in September 1993: the PLO recognized the state of Israel and Israel granted the Palestinians limited self-rule in the Gaza Strip and Jericho.

using Jordan as a base became a challenge to the authority of King Hussein's government, and after a short civil war the Palestinian leadership fled the country. In 1988 Hussein suddenly renounced all responsibility for the West Bank – a recognition that the PLO and not long-suffering Jordan was the legitimate representative of the Palestinian people.

Palestinians, nevertheless, still formed a majority of the population; Jordan sustains some 900,000 refugees, a figure which puts an intolerable burden on an already weak economy. Jordan is not blessed with the natural resources enjoyed by some Middle East countries – whether oil or water – and a limited agricultural base is supported by mining of phosphates and potash, the main exports.

The country's position was further undermined by the 1991 Gulf War, when despite official neutrality the pro-Iraq, anti-Western stance of the Palestinians did nothing to improve prospects of trade and aid deals with Europe and the USA, Jordan's vital economic links with Iraq having already been severed.

There were, however, signs of political progress: in 1991 the ban on political parties was removed and

COUNTRY	Hashemite Kingdom of Jordan
AREA	89,210 sq km [34,444 sq mls]
POPULATION	5,547,000
CAPITAL (POPULATION)	Amman (1,300,000)
ETHNIC GROUPS	Arab 99% (Palestinian 50%)
GOVERNMENT	Constitutional monarchy
LANGUAGES	Arabic (official)
RELIGIONS	Sunni Muslim 93%, Christian 5%
NATIONAL DAY	25 May; Independence Day (1948)
CURRENCY	Jordan dinar = 1,000 fils
ANNUAL INCOME PER PERSON	US$1,190
POPULATION DENSITY	62 per sq km [161 per sq ml]
LIFE EXPECTANCY	Female 70 yrs, male 66 yrs
ADULT LITERACY	84%

martial law was lifted after a period of 21 years. Multiparty elections were held in 1993, and in October 1994 Jordan and Israel signed a peace treaty ending a state of war which had been going on for over 40 years. The treaty restored some land in the south to Jordan ■

SAUDI ARABIA

The inscription on the Saudi flag above the sword means 'There is no God but Allah, and Muhammad is the Prophet of Allah'. The only national flag with an inscription as its main feature, the design was adopted in 1938.

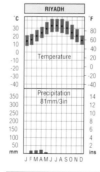

In the interior of Saudi Arabia the diurnal temperature range is much greater than in coastal regions. In the glaring heat of summer, daytime temperatures frequently exceed 40°C [100°F], but fall sharply at night. At over 400 m [1,300 ft] above sea level, Riyadh has unusually cold winters for its latitude, with no rain at all between June and October. Frosts have been recorded in January and February. Most of the rain falls as short but heavy showers in spring, with no rain between June and October.

During and shortly after World War I, the Saudis of Najd (central Arabia) extended their territory at the expense of the Rashidis and Hashemites, and consolidated their control over the greater part of the Arabian peninsula, including the holy cities of Mecca (Makkah) and Medina (Al Madinah). The frontiers with neighbours to the south and east remained ill-defined, but this mattered little until its vast reserves of oil (the world's largest) were tapped after World War II; since then some disputes have been settled, notably the division of the Gulf-shore Neutral Zone with Kuwait.

The heart of the state – the largest in the Middle East but over 95% desert – consists of the province of Najd, within which are three main groups of oases. Najd is enclosed on its east side by a vast arc of sandy desert which broadens out into the two great dune-seas of Arabia, the Nafud in the north, and in the south the Rub' al Khali, or 'Empty Quarter', the largest expanse of sand in the world. Here are found most of the country's Bedouin nomads, still deriving a living as traders and herdsmen.

To the west, Najd is separated from the border hills of the Red Sea by fields of rough basaltic lava. Particularly in its southern section towards the border with Yemen, this coastal strip is quite well supplied with water, and a high storage dam has been built inland from Jizan. The hills of Asir which back the plain here benefit from the summer monsoon, and are extensively terraced to grow grain and orchard trees.

For the most part, however, lack of water is a big problem. Saudi Arabia relies heavily on desalination plants and has the world's biggest on the shores of the Gulf – vulnerable to the oil pollution resulting from the 1991 war against Iraq.

The eastern province, by the shores of the Gulf, is known as the Hasa. Near its chief city of Hufuf in particular, the long underground seepage of water from the Hijaz, the western mountains, breaks out in the artesian springs of the oases. This region contains the country's great oil fields including Ghawar, the world's largest. The oil port of Az Zahran is linked with Riyadh by the only railway;

asphalt roads and, increasingly, air travel are the country's main means of transport.

The world's largest producer and biggest exporter of oil in 1994, Saudi Arabia used the enormous revenues (peaking at more than US$100 billion a year after the 400% price hikes of 1973) to launch a colossal industrial and domestic development programme: a fifth five-year development plan (1990–5) aims to increase manpower by an overall 3.5%, and emphasizes industrial growth, economic development and the expansion of the private industrial base. A strictly Muslim society, Saudi Arabia boasts some of the most advanced facilities in the world, as well as an array of social and educational benefits.

Progress has not always been smooth. In the mid-1980s, world oil prices slumped dramatically, disrupting many of the projects begun in the boom years. Meanwhile, expenditure on defence is high even by the profligate standards of the region. The country's position as the West's staunchest Middle East ally has often conflicted with its role as the guardian of Islam's holy places – hundreds of thousands make the pilgrimage to Mecca every year – and despite large donations to poorer Arab nations (Saudi Arabia is by far the world's biggest donor by percentage of GNP), its commitment to their cherished cause of a Palestinian state has at times appeared relatively weak.

While supporting Iraq against Shiite Iran in the First Gulf War, Saudi Arabia then invited Western forces in to protect it against possible Iraqi aggression following the invasion of Kuwait in 1990, playing a significant role in the quick victory of the Allies over Saddam Hussein in 1991 ■

COUNTRY	Kingdom of Saudi Arabia
AREA	2,149,690 sq km [829,995 sq mls]
POPULATION	18,395,000
CAPITAL (POPULATION)	Riyadh (2,000,000)
GOVERNMENT	Absolute monarchy with a consultative assembly
ETHNIC GROUPS	Arab 92% (Saudi 82%, Yemeni 10%)
LANGUAGES	Arabic (official)
RELIGIONS	Muslim 99%, Christian 1%
NATIONAL DAY	23 September; Unification of the Kingdom (1932)
CURRENCY	Saudi riyal = 100 halalas
ANNUAL INCOME PER PERSON	US$8,000
MAIN EXPORTS	Crude oil 83%, petrochemicals 11%
MAIN EXPORT PARTNERS	Japan 22%, USA 19%
MAIN IMPORTS	Machinery 19%, foodstuffs 17%, transport equipment 14%, textiles 13%, metals 8%
MAIN IMPORT PARTNERS	Japan 17%, USA 15%, UK 8%
DEFENCE	11.8% of GNP
POPULATION DENSITY	9 per sq km [22 per sq ml]
INFANT MORTALITY	58 per 1,000 live births
LIFE EXPECTANCY	Female 68 yrs, male 64 yrs
PRINCIPAL CITIES (POPULATION)	Riyadh 2,000,000 Jedda (Jiddah) 1,400,000 Mecca 618,000 Medina 500,000

MECCA

The holiest city of Islam, Mecca was an important centre of pilgrimage long before the birth of the Prophet Muhammad. Its chief sanctuary, then as now, was the Ka'ba, a square building housing a remarkable and much venerated black stone of probable meteoric origin, said to have been given to the patriarch Abraham by the Archangel Gabriel.

In 632, shortly before his death, the Prophet undertook his own final pilgrimage to the city; the pilgrimage to Mecca – the Hajj – remains the fifth of the Five Pillars of Islam, and every Muslim is expected to make it at least once in a lifetime.

Mecca is also part of the Second Pillar, the duty of prayer, for it is towards the Ka'ba (now enclosed by Mecca's Great Mosque) that the world's Muslims face five times daily when they pray.

At the beginning of the 20th century, Mecca was a provincial town in the Ottoman Empire; now, with a population of over 618,000, it is the administrative capital of the Western Province of Saudi Arabia. Its chief business remains, as ever, the Hajj, with upwards of 1.5 million pilgrims visiting annually. Non-Muslims (infidels) are to this day excluded from the city.

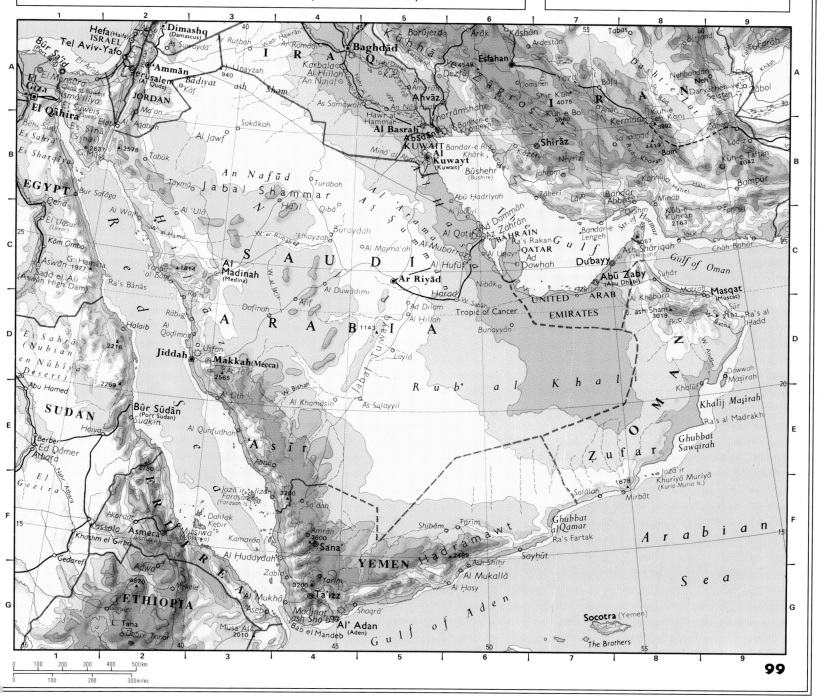

ASIA

KUWAIT

Kuwait's national flag dates from 1961, when the country ceased to be a British protectorate and gained its independence. The flag features the four Pan-Arab colours, the black portion having an unusual trapezium shape.

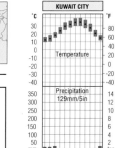

The impressive, if unevenly distributed, prosperity built by the ruling Sabah family in Kuwait since oil was first commercially produced in 1946 was suddenly and brutally undermined by the Iraqi invasion of 1990. Occupying troops were soon expelled by a US-led multinational force, but not before they had set fire to more than 500 oil wells, causing unprecedented pollution, and destroyed almost all industrial and commercial installations.

Kuwait's revenge over the devastation was directed mainly at the huge contingent of Palestinian, Jordanian and Yemeni immigrant workers (seen as pro-Iraq) on whom the economic progress of the country had been founded for more than two decades. Reconstruction was expected to cost hundreds of billions of dollars, but foreign investments made during the good years had produced massive funds to get it under way, using chiefly American rather than European companies ■

COUNTRY State of Kuwait
AREA 17,820 sq km [6,880 sq mls]
POPULATION 1,668,000
CAPITAL (POPULATION) Kuwait City (189,000)
GOVERNMENT Constitutional monarchy
ETHNIC GROUPS Kuwaiti Arab 44%, non-Kuwaiti Arab 36%, various Asian 20%
LANGUAGES Arabic 78%, Kurdish 10%, Farsi 4%
RELIGIONS Muslim 90% (Sunni 63%), Christian 8%, Hindu 2%
CURRENCY Kuwaiti dinar = 1,000 fils
ANNUAL INCOME PER PERSON US$23,350
MAIN EXPORTS Petroleum and petroleum products 87%
MAIN IMPORTS Electrical machinery, transport equipment, chemicals, iron and steel
DEFENCE 62% of GNP
POPULATION DENSITY 94 per sq km [242 per sq ml]
LIFE EXPECTANCY Female 77 yrs, male 72 yrs
ADULT LITERACY 77%

In winter, the northern end of the Gulf comes under the influence of low-pressure systems moving eastwards from the Mediterranean region and rainfall is more reliable than that experienced further down the Gulf. In the wake of low pressure, winds blowing from the north-west bring cooler air to the region. Summers are hot and dry. The frequent *shamal* winds which blow steadily by day give way to calm, sultry nights.

QATAR

The flag was adopted in 1971. The maroon colour is said to result from the natural effect of the sun on the traditional red banner, while the white was added after a British request in 1820 that white should be included in the flags of friendly states in the Arabian Gulf.

Occupying a low, barren peninsula on the Arabian Gulf, the former British protectorate of Qatar derives its high standard of living from oil and gas. Despite diversification into cement, steel and fertilizers, oil and gas still account for over 80% of revenues, and Qatar's gas reserves are enormous.

The economy of the country (and many institutions) is heavily dependent on the immigrant work force, notably from the Indian subcontinent and poorer Middle Eastern states ■

COUNTRY State of Qatar
AREA 11,000 sq km [4,247 sq mls]
POPULATION 594,000
CAPITAL (POPULATION) Doha (243,000)
GOVERNMENT Constitutional absolute monarchy
ETHNIC GROUPS Southern Asian 34%, Qatari 20%
LANGUAGES Arabic (official)
RELIGIONS Sunni Muslim 92%, Christian, Hindu
CURRENCY Qatar riyal = 100 dirhams

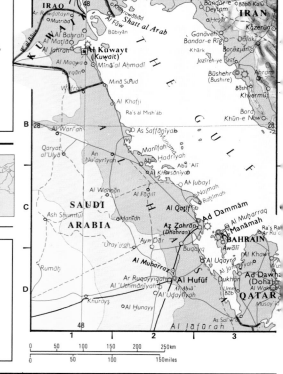

YEMEN

The new straightforward design of Yemen's flag, incorporating the Pan-Arab colours, dates from 1990 when the Yemen Arab Republic (in the north and west) united with the People's Democratic Republic of Yemen (in the south and east).

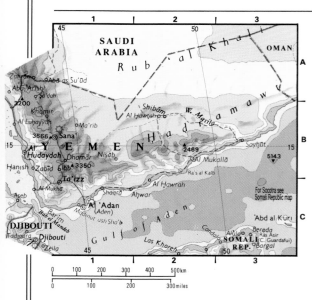

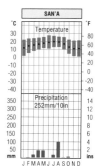

The optimism that greeted unification of the two Yemeni countries in May 1990 proved short-lived; support for Iraq in the Gulf War, publicized by a vote on the UN Security Council, wrought swift revenge from Iraq's Arab enemies on the ending of hostilities, with Kuwait and Saudi Arabia expelling vast numbers of Yemeni workers. This not only removed the main source of earnings for a homeland already struggling with a weak economy, but it also jeopardized hopes of much-needed foreign aid from rich Gulf nations and the West.

The process of marrying the disparate needs of a traditional state (the Yemen Arab Republic – an independent kingdom since 1918 and backed by the Saudis) and the failed regime of the Marxist People's Democratic Republic of Yemen, based in the South Yemen capital of Aden (formerly a vital British staging post on the journey to India) has proved difficult. Though a good deal smaller than the South, the North provided over 65% of the population.

In May 1994 civil war erupted between north and south, with President Saleh (a northerner) attempting to remove the vice-president (a south-

San'a lies at over 2,000 m [6,500 ft], on the eastern side of the Yemen highlands. Temperatures are much lower than at sea level and the diurnal range is very large (over 20°C [36°F] in winter), frost occurring in winter. In August the south-west monsoon brings heavy thunderstorms. As in Ethiopia, across the Red Sea, minor rains occur in spring. The western side of the mountains, famous for coffee plantations, is wetter and cloudier. The yearly average for sunshine hours per day is 9.5.

COUNTRY Republic of Yemen
AREA 527,970 sq km [203,849 sq mls]
POPULATION 14,609,000
CAPITAL (POPULATION) San'a (972,000)
GOVERNMENT Multiparty republic
ETHNIC GROUPS Arab 96%, Somali 1%
LANGUAGES Arabic (official)
RELIGIONS Sunni Muslim 53%, Shiite Muslim 47%
CURRENCY Rial = 100 fils

erner). The war ended in July 1994, following the capture of Aden by government forces. In 1995, Yemen resolved border disputes with Oman and Saudi Arabia, but clashed with Eritrea over uninhabited islands in the Red Sea ■

BAHRAIN

The flag dates from about 1932, with the white section a result of the British request that it be included in the flags of friendly Arab states around the Gulf. Red is the traditional colour of Kharijite Muslims. The serrated edge was added to distinguish between the colours.

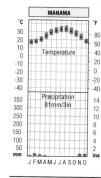

Comprising 35 small islands, by far the largest of them called Bahrain, this relatively liberal state led the region in developing oil production after discovery in 1932. When production waned in the 1970s it diversified into other sectors: its aluminium-smelting plant is the Gulf's largest non-oil industrial complex, and the moves into banking, communications and leisure came when the cosmopolitan centre of Beirut was plunging into chaos. Banking now accounts for some 15% of GDP, while oil takes as much as 20% – though far more of government revenues. Most of the land is barren, but soil imports have created some fertile areas.

Bahrain does have problems, however. Tension between the Sunni and majority Shiite population (the latter favouring an Islamic republic) has been apparent since before independence, and during the First Gulf War Iran responded to Bahrain's support for Iraq by reiterating its claims to the territory. In 1986 a rumbling dispute began with Qatar over claims to a cluster of oil-rich islands, reefs and sandbars; the disagreement was taken by Qatar to the International Court of Justice in 1991 ■

Bahrain island is more humid and has a smaller diurnal range of temperature than other parts of the southern Gulf. The island is noted for extreme heat and humidity in summer, particularly at Muharraq in the north-east. A hot, dry wind, the *shamal*, sometimes blows from the north. Winter nights are relatively chilly and heavy dew may occur. Rainfall occurs mainly as winter thunderstorms. Sunshine levels are high; November to April have 6–9 hours daily, the rest of the year having over 10 hours.

COUNTRY Emirate of Bahrain
AREA 678 sq km [262 sq mls]
POPULATION 558,000
CAPITAL (POPULATION) Manama (143,000)
GOVERNMENT Monarchy (emirate) with a cabinet appointed by the Emir
LANGUAGES Arabic (official), English
ETHNIC GROUPS Bahraini Arab 68%, Persian, Indian and Pakistani 25%, other Arab 4%, European 3%
RELIGIONS Muslim (Shiite majority) 85%, Christian 7%
CURRENCY Bahrain dinar = 1,000 fils
ANNUAL INCOME PER PERSON US$7,870
LIFE EXPECTANCY Female 74 yrs, male 70 yrs
ADULT LITERACY 84%

UNITED ARAB EMIRATES

When seven small states around the Arabian Gulf combined to form the United Arab Emirates in 1971, this flag was agreed for the new nation. It features the Pan-Arab colours, first used in the Arab revolt against the Turks from 1916.

In 1971 six of the seven British-run Trucial States of the Gulf – Abu Dhabi, Ajman, Dubai, Fujairah, Sharjah and Umm al-Qaiwain – opted to form the United Arab Emirates (UAE), with Ras al-Khaimah joining in 1972. It could have been a federation of nine, but Bahrain and Qatar chose independence. Abu Dhabi is more than six times the size of the other countries put together, has the largest population, and is easily the biggest oil producer. Nevertheless, the capitals of Dubai and Sharjah also contain over 250,000 people.

Though mainly low-lying desert, the UAE's oil and gas have provided one of the highest GNP per capita figures in Asia. However, only 20% of the population are citizens – the rest are expatriate workers – and traditional values, sustained by the control of the emirs, remain strong ■

COUNTRY United Arab Emirates
AREA 83,600 sq km [32,278 sq mls]
POPULATION 2,800,000
CAPITAL (POPULATION) Abu Dhabi (243,000)
GOVERNMENT Federation of seven emirates, each with its own government
ETHNIC GROUPS Arab 87%, Indo-Pakistani 9%, Iranian 2%
LANGUAGES Arabic (official), English
RELIGIONS Muslim 95%, Christian 4%
CURRENCY Dirham = 100 fils
ANNUAL INCOME PER PERSON US$22,470
DEFENCE 14.6% of GNP
POPULATION DENSITY 33 per sq km [87 per sq ml]
LIFE EXPECTANCY Female 74 yrs, male 70 yrs
ADULT LITERACY 78%

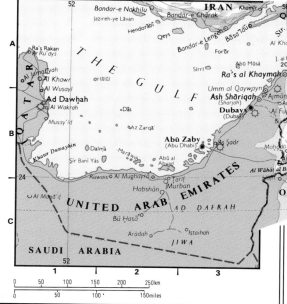

OMAN

Formerly Muscat and Oman, the state's flag was plain red – the traditional colour of the local people. When Oman was established in 1970, the state arms of sword and dagger were added, with stripes of white and green. The proportions of the stripes changed in 1995.

Backward compared to its oil-rich Arabian Gulf neighbours to the west until 1970 – when, with British collusion, Sultan Said was deposed by his son Qaboos – Oman has since made substantial strides, seeing an end to the civil war against Yemen-backed left-wing separatist guerrillas in the southern province of Dhofar (Zufar) and enjoying an expanding economy based on oil reserves far larger than expected when production began modestly in 1967. Petroleum now accounts for more than 90% of government revenues – and because of Oman's detached situation the industry was not hit by the lack of confidence that afflicted the Gulf states in the 1991 war. In addition, huge natural gas reserves were discovered in 1991 that were equal in size to all the finds of the previous 20 years. There are also some copper deposits.

An absolute ruler (as his family heads have been since 1749), Qaboos has tended to forego the usual prestigious projects so favoured by wealthy Arab leaders in favour of social programmes. Even so, by 1995 only one in three adults of this arid, inhospitable country were literate (less than 1% of the land is cultivated), and defence and internal security were taking nearly 18% of the Gross National Product ■

COUNTRY Sultanate of Oman
AREA 212,460 sq km [82,031 sq mls]
POPULATION 2,252,000
CAPITAL (POPULATION) Muscat (350,000)
GOVERNMENT Monarchy with a unicameral consultative council
ETHNIC GROUPS Omani Arab 74% other Asian 21%
LANGUAGES Arabic (official), Baluchi, English
RELIGIONS Muslim 86%, Hindu 13%
CURRENCY Omani rial = 1,000 baizas
ANNUAL INCOME PER PERSON US$5,600
DEFENCE 17.5% of GNP
POPULATION DENSITY 11 per sq km [27 per sq ml]

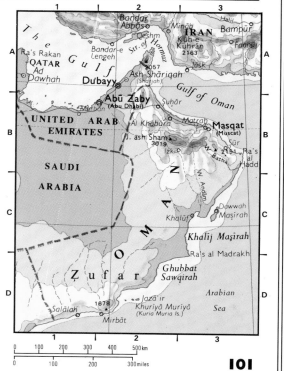

IRAQ

Adopted in 1963 at the time of the proposed federation with Egypt and Syria, Iraq's flag retained the three green stars, symbolizing the three countries, even though the union failed to materialize. The slogan *Allah Akbar* (God is Great) was added in 1991.

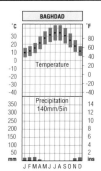

The central plains of Iraq experience the extremes of temperature typical of continental interiors. Winters are cool with occasional frost; temperatures below 10°C [50°F] can be expected at night from November to March. Rain falls between November and April when low-pressure systems invade from the west. In summer it is dry and hot. *Shamal* winds from the north-west raise dust and sand storms by day. Heat and humidity increase southwards towards the Gulf.

Absorbed into the Ottoman (Turkish) Empire in the 16th century, Iraq was captured by British forces in 1916 and after World War I became a virtual colony as a League of Nations-mandated territory run by Britain. The Hashemite dynasty ruled an independent kingdom from 1932 (British occupation 1941–5), but in 1958 the royal family and premier were murdered in a military coup that set up a republic. Ten years later, after struggles between Communists and Pan-Arab Baathists, officers for the latter seized control. From 1969 the vicepresident of this single-party government was Saddam Hussein, who in a peaceful transfer of power became president in 1979. The next year he invaded neighbouring Iran.

The country includes a hilly district in the north-east, and in the west a large slice of the Hamad or Syrian Desert; but essentially it comprises the lower valleys and deltas of the Tigris and Euphrates. Rainfall is meagre, but the alluvium is fertile.

The north-east of Iraq includes part of the Zagros Mountains, where fruits and grains grow without the help of irrigation. The Kirkuk oil field is the country's oldest and largest, and nearby the Lesser Zab River has been impounded behind a high dam. The population here includes many Turks, and Kurdish tribes akin to those in Iran.

In addition to the Kirkuk oil field, which exports by pipeline through Syria and Lebanon, there are reserves of oil near Mosul, Khanaqin and Basra. Basra is connected to the Gulf by the crucial Shatt-al-Arab Waterway, shared with Iran and the ostensible cause of the First Gulf War (Iran–Iraq War).

The Gulf Wars

Supplied with financial help and arms by the West, the Soviets and conservative Arab countries, all of whom shared a fear of the new Islamic fundamentalism in Iran, Saddam amassed the fourth largest army in the world by 1980. His attack on Iran was meant to be a quick, land-grabbing, morale-boosting victory. Instead it led to an eight-year modern version of Flanders which drained Iraqi resolve (over a million men were killed or wounded, many of them fighting fellow Shiites), and nearly crippled a healthy if oil-dependent economy that had, despite colossal defence spending, financed a huge development programme in the 1970s. Even then, Iraq was still the world's sixth biggest oil producer in 1988, and Saddam's regime continued to enjoy support from Western countries.

If Iraq was hit by this long war, it was decimated by the Second Gulf War. In August 1990, having accused Kuwait of wrecking Baghdad's economy by

COUNTRY Republic of Iraq

AREA 438,320 sq km [169,235 sq mls]

POPULATION 20,184,000

CAPITAL (POPULATION) Baghdad (3,841,000)

GOVERNMENT Unitary single-party republic

ETHNIC GROUPS Arab 77%, Kurd 19%, Turkmen 2%, Persian 2%, Assyrian

NATIONAL DAY 17 July; Military revolution (1958)

LANGUAGES Arabic (official), Kurdish, Turkish

RELIGIONS Shiite Muslim 62%, Sunni Muslim 34%

CURRENCY Iraqi dinar = 20 dirhams = 1,000 fils

ANNUAL INCOME PER PERSON US$2,000

MAIN PRIMARY PRODUCTS Crude oil, natural gas, dates, cattle, sheep, cereals, goats, camels

MAIN INDUSTRIES Oil and gas production, food processing, textiles

MAIN EXPORTS Fuels and other energy 98%

MAIN IMPORTS Machinery and transport equipment 40%, manufactured goods 27%, foodstuffs 16%, chemicals 8%

POPULATION DENSITY 46 per sq km [119 per sq ml]

LIFE EXPECTANCY Female 67 yrs, male 65 yrs

ADULT LITERACY 60%

PRINCIPAL CITIES (POPULATION) Baghdad 3,841,000 Basra 617,000 Mosul 571,000

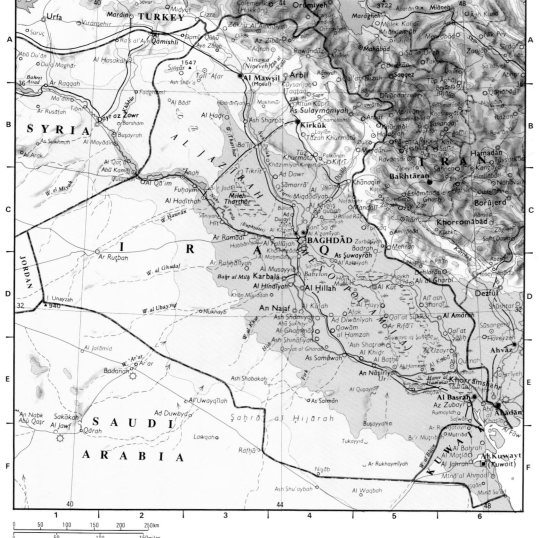

exceeding its oil quota and forcing prices down, Saddam ordered the invasion of Kuwait, then annexed it as an Iraqi province. It gave him more oil and far better access to the Gulf. Unlike a decade before, the international community were almost unanimous in their condemnation of the invasion, and following the imposition of sanctions a multinational force – led by the USA but backed primarily by Britain, France and Saudi Arabia – was dispatched to the Gulf to head off possible Iraqi moves on to Saudi oil fields.

After Saddam failed to accede to repeated UN demands to withdraw his troops, the Second Gulf War began on 16 January 1991 with an Anglo-American air attack on Baghdad, and in late February a land-sea-air campaign freed Kuwait after just 100 hours, Iraq accepting all the terms of the UN cease-fire and coalition troops occupying much of southern Iraq. This, however, did not prevent the brutal suppression of West-inspired revolts by Shiites in the south and Kurds in the north, millions of whom fled their homes. International efforts were made to help these refugees, some of whom had fled to Iran and Turkey, and in September 1996, following Iraqi military manoeuvres in the Kurdish 'safe havens', further US Cruise missile attacks were directed at Iraqi government troops.

Saddam Hussein, though surviving in power, had been left an international leper in charge of a pitiful country. Much of the infrastructure was destroyed in the war, and sanctions, war damage and mismanagement combined to cause economic chaos throughout the country. In December 1998, arguments over UN weapons inspections led to sustained allied US and British military air strikes ■

IRAN

Iran's flag has been in use since July 1980 after the fall of the Shah and the rise of the Islamic republic. Along the edges of the stripes is the legend *Allah Akbar* (God is Great) repeated 22 times; in the centre is the new national emblem.

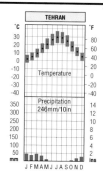

Tehran lies at over 1,200 m [4,000 ft] on the high Iranian plateau, enclosed on all sides by mountains, and experiences the dryness and extreme temperatures of a continental climate. Rain falls on only about 30 days in the year. Summers are hot, sunny and dry with low humidity. Most of the rain falls in winter and spring. Winters are cold with strong north-west winds. Snow and frost occur in most years. The annual range of temperature is over 25°C [45°F].

The most populous and productive parts of Iran lie at the four extremities – the fisheries, rice fields and tea gardens of the Caspian shore in the foothills of the earthquake zone to the north, the sugar plantations and oil fields of Khuzestan to the south (target of the Iraqi invasion in 1980), the wheat fields of Azarbayjan in the west, and the fruit groves of the oases of Khorasan and Seistan in the east. In between are the deserts of Kavir and Lut, and the border ranges which broaden in the west into the high plateaus of the Zagros, the summer retreats of the tribes of Bakhtiars and Kurds.

The cities of the interior depend on ingenious arrangements of tunnels and channels for tapping underground water, and these have been supplemented by high dams, notably at Dezful. The burgeoning capital of Tehran is the crossing point of the country's two great railways, the Trans-Iranian from the Gulf to the Caspian, and the east–west track from Mashhad to Tabriz.

The Islamic Revolution

Called Persia until 1935, the country retained its Shah – thanks first to British and later American support – until 1979, when the emperor's extravagantly corrupt regime (a single-party affair from 1975) was toppled by a combination of students, middle-class professionals and, above, all, clerics offended by the style and pace of Westernization.

The despotism was replaced with another: that of a radical fundamentalist Islamic republic inspired by the return of exiled leader Ayatollah Khomeini. The revolution created a new threat to the conservative Arabs of the Gulf and beyond, who saw it as a dangerous call to challenge the flimsy legitimacy of their own oil-rich governments. The effects would rumble round the Muslim world: 12 years later, in far-off Algeria, the Islamic Salvation Front won the democratic elections.

Many Arab states were less hostile, however, and despite Iranian backing of a series of international terrorist attacks and hostage takings linked to the Palestinian issue, their regime won respect for the steadfast way they fought the Iraqis from 1980–8, when hundreds of thousands of zealous young Shiite men died defending their homeland.

The war left Iran's vital oil production at less than half the level of 1979 (oil production had returned to mid-1970s levels by 1994, at 180 million tonnes per year), and the government began to court the Western powers. Iran's stance during the Second Gulf War (albeit predictable) and a tempering of the militant position to one of peace broker on international issues – led by the liberal President Khatami – encouraged many powers to re-establish closer links with the country. Iran's role has become even more significant since the independence of the neighbouring Muslim republics of the former Soviet Union ■

COUNTRY Islamic Republic of Iran
AREA 1,648,000 sq km [636,293 sq mls]
POPULATION 68,885,000
CAPITAL (POPULATION) Tehran (6,476,000)
GOVERNMENT Unitary Islamic republic, religious leader (elected by Council of Experts) exercises supreme authority
ETHNIC GROUPS Persian 46%, Azerbaijani 17%, Kurdish 9%, Gilaki 5%, Luri, Mazandarani, Baluchi, Arab
LANGUAGES Farsi (or Persian, official), Kurdish, Baluchi, Turkic, Arabic, French
RELIGIONS Shiite Muslim 91%, Sunni Muslim 8%
CURRENCY Rial = 100 dinars
ANNUAL INCOME PER PERSON US$4,750

MAIN PRIMARY PRODUCTS Crude oil, natural gas, lead, chrome, copper, iron, sheep, cattle, cereals, timber
MAIN INDUSTRIES Oil refining, gas, steel, textiles, electrical goods, fishing, sugar, flour milling
MAIN EXPORTS Petroleum products 98%
MAIN IMPORTS Machinery and transport equipment 33%, iron and steel 15%, foodstuffs 13%
DEFENCE 7.1% of GNP
TOURISM 155,000 visitors per year
POPULATION DENSITY 42 per sq km [108 per sq ml]
INFANT MORTALITY 40 per 1,000 live births
LIFE EXPECTANCY Female 68 yrs, male 67 yrs
ADULT LITERACY 65%
PRINCIPAL CITIES (POPULATION) Tehran 6,476,000 Mashhad 1,759,000 Esfahan 1,127,000 Tabriz 1,089,000

THE KURDS

With 15–17 million people dispersed across the territories of five countries – Turkey (8 million), Iran, Iraq, Syria and Armenia – the Kurds form the world's largest stateless nation, and they are likely to remain so. The 1920 Treaty of Sävres, a postwar settlement designed to dismember the old Ottoman Empire, proposed a scheme for Kurdish independence, but it was never implemented.

Neither Arab nor Turk, the Kurds are predominantly Sunni Muslims, and in the past have provided their share of Islam's leaders; indeed, Saladin, the near-legendary nemesis of the Crusaders, was a Kurd. Now, as in the past, the Kurds are an agricultural people; many earn their living by pastoralism, a way of life that pays little attention to borders or the governments that attempt to control them. Since World War II, they have suffered consistent repression by most of their titular overlords. Turkey has regularly used armed force against Kurdish nationalists; an uprising in Iran was put down in 1979–80; and during the Iran–Iraq War of the 1980s, Iraqi forces used chemical weapons – as well as more orthodox brutality – against Kurdish settlements.

The defeat of Iraqi dictator Saddam Hussein by Coalition forces in 1991 inspired another massive uprising, but Saddam's badly weakened army still proved quite capable of murdering Kurdish women and children on a scale that provoked a limited Western intervention. The outcome, though, was upwards of 1.5 million Kurds living in refugee camps, with the dream of Kurdistan no nearer realization.

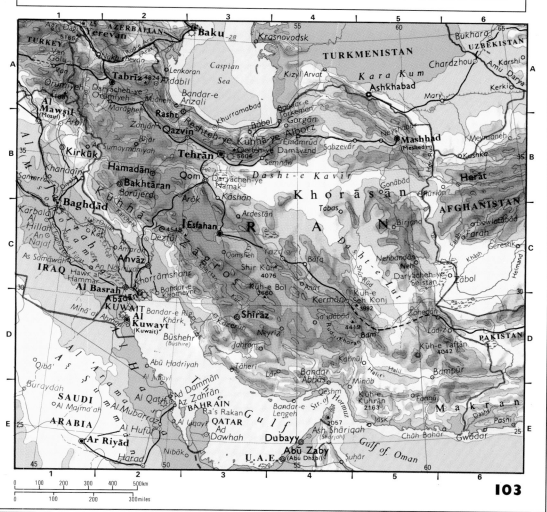

ASIA

AFGHANISTAN

After many changes since the late 1970s, a new national flag was introduced in December 1992 based on the colours used by the Mujaheddin during the civil war. The flag bears the new national arms.

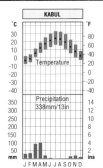

The climate of Afghanistan is governed more by its high altitude and being cut off by mountain ranges than by its latitude. From December to March the air masses come from the cold continental north and bring very cold weather and snow on the mountains. June to September is very hot and dry, with the east getting some rain from a weakened monsoon. Kabul, at 2,000 m [6,000 ft], has a range of temperature from –5°C to 25°C [23–77°F]. There are over 10 hours of sunshine daily, May to August.

Nearly three-quarters of Afghanistan is mountainous, comprising most of the Hindu Kush and its foothills, with several peaks over 6,400 m [21,000 ft], and much of the rest is desert or semi-desert. However, the restoration of the Helmand canals has brought fertility to the far south-west, and the sweet waters of the Hamun support fish and cattle; the plains of the north, near the borders with Turkmenistan, Uzbekistan and Tajikistan, yield most of the country's limited agriculture.

The most profitable crop may well be opium, from poppies grown in the hills of the Pathans adjoining Pakistan's North-West Frontier province. With the Islamic Revolution in Iran and the crackdown in the 'Golden Triangle' of Laos, Burma and Thailand, Pakistan became the world's biggest source of heroin (the derivative drug); but while US pressure saw the Pakistani government start to control production on its side of the border, it could do little to stem the flow from Afghanistan – a prime source of revenue for the Mujaheddin's fight against occupying Soviet forces in the 1980s.

History and politics

Landlocked Afghanistan has always been in a critical position in Asia: the Khyber Pass was both the gateway to India and the back door to Russia. Since earliest times it has been invaded by Persians, Greeks, Arabs, Mongols, Tartars and the British, who finally failed in their attempts to create a buffer state between India and Russia and bowed to Afghan independence after the Third Afghan War in 1921. The latest invaders, entering the country on Christmas Day 1979, were 80,000 men of the Soviet army.

The Soviet forces were sent in support of a Kremlin-inspired coup that removed a revolutionary council set up after the ousting of the pro-Soviet government of Mohammed Daud Khan. Killed in that 1978 coup – the Saur Revolution – Daud Khan had been in power since 1953, first as prime minister and then, after he toppled the monarchy in 1972, as founder, president and prime minister of a fiercely pro-Soviet single-party republic.

The Saur Revolution and subsequent Soviet occupation led to a bitter and protracted civil war, the disparate Muslim tribes uniting behind the banner of the Mujaheddin ('holy warriors') to wage an unrelenting guerrilla war financed by the US and oiled with the co-operation of Pakistan. Despite their vastly superior weaponry and resources, the Soviet forces found it impossible to control the mountain-based rebels in a country the size of Texas, and Afghanistan quickly threatened to turn into an unwinnable war – Moscow's 'Vietnam'.

President Gorbachev began moves to end the conflict soon after coming to power in 1985, and in 1988 a cease-fire was agreed involving both Afghanistan and Pakistan, its main overt ally. In February 1989 the Soviet troops withdrew, leaving the cities in the hands of the pro-Moscow government and the countryside under the control of the Mujaheddin; the civil war intensified, however, fuelled by internecine and traditional feuds.

The war, which cost over a million Afghanis their lives, left what was an already impoverished state almost totally crippled. Before the Soviet invasion Afghanistan had one of the world's poorest records for infant mortality, literacy, women's rights and a host of other measurements, but the occupation reduced the economy to ruins. Before the 1978 Marxist revolution Afghanis abroad sent home remittances worth some US$125 million, and tourism brought in about US$50 million; now all that had gone. Based on natural gas, exports were not helped by the decision of the USSR to cap the wells in 1989.

The greatest problem, however, was one of refugees. Some 2 million people had moved into crowded cities and towns to avoid the Russian shelling, but far more – somewhere between 3 million and 5 million by most accounts, but nearer 6 million according to the UN Commissioner – fled the country altogether, predominantly to Pakistan. This latter estimate, the UN stated in 1990, was around 42% of the entire world total of displaced persons.

In the spring of 1992, after a prolonged onslaught by the Mujaheddin, the government in Kabul finally surrendered. Mujaheddin forces entered Kabul and set up an Islamic government. But, by late 1996, a militant Islamic faction called 'Taliban' (meaning 'students') had occupied Kabul and was in control of most of the country ■

COUNTRY Islamic Republic of Afghanistan

AREA 652,090 sq km [251,772 sq mls]

POPULATION 19,509,000

CAPITAL (POPULATION) Kabul (1,424,000)

GOVERNMENT Islamic republic

ETHNIC GROUPS Pashtun ('Pathan') 52%, Tajik 20%, Uzbek 9%, Hazara 9%, Chahar 3%, Turkmen, Baluchi

LANGUAGES Pashto, Dari (Persian) – both official

RELIGIONS Sunni Muslim 74%, Shiite Muslim 25%

NATIONAL DAY 27 April; Anniversary of Saur Revolution

CURRENCY Afghani = 100 puls

ANNUAL INCOME PER PERSON US$220

MAIN INDUSTRIES Agriculture, carpets, textiles

MAIN EXPORTS Natural gas 42%, dried fruit 26%, fresh fruit 9%, carpets and rugs 7%

MAIN EXPORT PARTNERS CIS nations 55%, Pakistan 16%, India 12%

MAIN IMPORTS Wheat 5%, vegetable oil 4%, sugar 3%

MAIN IMPORT PARTNERS CIS nations 62%, Japan 13%

POPULATION DENSITY 30 per sq km [77 per sq ml]

PAKISTAN

Pakistan's flag was adopted when the country gained independence from Britain in 1947. The green, the crescent moon and five-pointed star are traditionally associated with Islam. The white stripe represents Pakistan's other religions.

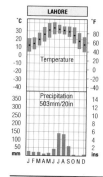

Situated to the south-west of the Himalayas, Lahore has a higher rainfall than Karachi, but still with a marked July and August maxima. Temperatures in the summer are very high, with over 40°C [104°F] having been recorded in every month from March to October, and averages of over 20–30°C [68–86°F]. Night temperatures in winter, though, are very chilly. The annual variation of temperature in Lahore is about 20°C [36°F], while at Karachi it is only 11°C [20°F].

As Egypt is the gift of the Nile, so Pakistan is the gift of the Indus and its tributaries. Despite modern industrialization, irrigated farming is vital both in Punjab, the 'land of the five rivers' (Indus, Jhelum, Beas, Ravi and Sutlej), and on the dry plains flanking the Indus between Khairpur and Hyderabad. The stations at Tarbela (on the Indus) and Mangla (on the Jhelum) are among the world's biggest earth- and rock-filled dams.

West of the Indus delta the arid coastal plain of Makran rises first to the Coast Range, then in successive ridges to the north – stark, arid, deforested and eroded. Between the ridges lie desert basins like that containing the saltmarsh of Hamun-i-Mashkel on the Iranian border. Ridge and basin alternate through Baluchistan and the earthquake zone round Quetta, the *daman-i-koh* ('skirts of the hills') still irrigated by the ancient tunnels called *karez* or *qanats*, for growing cereals and fruit.

North again stretches the famous North-West Frontier province, pushing up between the towering Hindu Kush and Karakoram, with K2, on the border with China, the world's second highest mountain at 8,611 m [28,251 ft]. East of Peshawar lies Kashmir, which Pakistan controls to the west of the 1947 cease-fire line, and India to the east. The cease-fire ended war and appalling internecine slaughter that followed the grant of independence from Britain, when the old Indian Empire was divided between India and Pakistan – Hindu and Muslim states. The Kashmir problem was partly religious – a mainly Muslim population ruled by a Hindu maharaja who acceded to India – but there was also an underlying strategic issue: five rivers rising in or passing through Kashmir or the neighbouring Indian state of Himachal Pradesh are vital to Pakistan's economy, and could not be left in the hands of possible enemies.

Like most developing countries, Pakistan has increased both mineral exploitation and manufacturing industry. To the small oil and coalfield near Rawalpindi has now been added a major resource of natural gas between Sukkur and Multan. Karachi, formerly the capital and developed in the colonial period as a wheat port, is now a considerable manufacturing centre, principally textiles; so is the cultural centre, Lahore, in the north. The well-planned national capital of Islamabad, begun in the 1960s, is still growing to the north-east of Rawalpindi, with the outline of the Murree Hills – refuge for the wealthier citizens on weekends – as a backdrop to the architecture of the new city.

The seventh most populous country in the world, Pakistan is likely to be overtaken by Bangladesh – its former partner separated

by 1,600 km [1,000 mls] of India – by the end of the century. Then East Pakistan, Bangladesh broke away from the western wing of the nation in 1971, following a bitter civil war and Indian military intervention, but neither country state has enjoyed political stability or sound government.

'West' Pakistan's economy has also done better than poor Bangladesh, while reserves of some minerals (notably bauxite, copper, phosphates and manganese) have yet to be exploited. Yet there are huge problems: dependence on textiles, an increasingly competitive area, and on remittances from Pakistani workers abroad, especially in the Middle East (the main source of foreign income); a chronic trade deficit and debt burden; massive spending on defence and security; growing drug traffic through the North-West Frontier; and the added pressure of some 5 million Afghan refugees who fled the

civil war in their homeland. However, the fall of Kabul to Afghan Mujaheddin rebels in the spring of 1992 brought the prospect of an improvement in Pakistan's refugee problem – though it also raised the prospect of renewed Pathan nationalism.

Pakistan has been subject to military rule and martial law for much of its short life, interspersed with periods of fragile democracy resting on army consent. During one such, in 1988, Benazir Bhutto (daughter of the president executed after his government, the country's first elected civilian administration, was overthrown by the army in 1977) was elected prime minister, the first female premier in the Muslim world. Two years later she was dismissed by the president following accusations of nepotism and corruption. She was subsequently re-elected in 1993, but was again dismissed under charges of corruption in November 1996; her party was defeated in the parliamentary elections of early 1997 ■

COUNTRY Islamic Republic of Pakistan

AREA 796,100 sq km [307,374 sq mls]

POPULATION 143,595,000

CAPITAL (POPULATION) Islamabad (204,000)

GOVERNMENT Federal republic

ETHNIC GROUPS Punjabi 60%, Pushtun 13%, Sindhi 12%, Baluchi, Muhajir

LANGUAGES Punjabi 60%, Pashto 13%, Sindhi 12%, Urdu 8%, Baluchi, Brahvi, English

RELIGIONS Muslim 97%, Hindu, Christian, Buddhist

CURRENCY Pakistan rupee = 100 paisa

ANNUAL INCOME PER PERSON US$430

MAIN PRIMARY PRODUCTS Cotton, rice, sugar cane, cereals, dates, tobacco, natural gas, iron ore

MAIN INDUSTRIES Agriculture, cotton, oil refining

MAIN EXPORTS Raw cotton 14%, cotton yarn 12%, cotton fabrics 11%, rice 8%, leather 6%, carpets 6%

MAIN IMPORTS Machinery 18%, mineral oils 16%, chemicals 9%, transport equipment 9%

DEFENCE 7.7% of GNP

POPULATION DENSITY 180 per sq km [467 per sq ml]

LIFE EXPECTANCY Female 59 yrs, male 59 yrs

ADULT LITERACY 36%

The summer monsoon rains decrease rapidly in intensity from the Indian peninsula westwards into Pakistan, leaving much of the Indus lowland arid. Rain falls on only about 20 days in the year, half of these in July and August. Karachi is hot throughout the year but, being on the coast, has a smaller range of temperature than inland. The summer rains are thundery and vary greatly in intensity from year to year. Small amounts of winter rain are brought by low-pressure systems from the west.

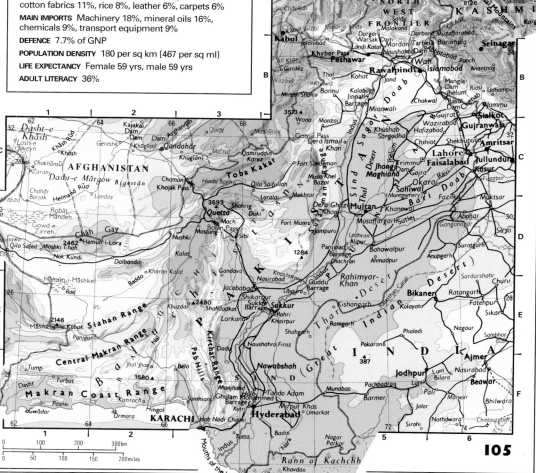

ASIA

INDIA

India's flag evolved during the struggle for freedom from British rule. The orange represents the Hindu majority, green the country's many Muslims and white peace. The Buddhist wheel symbol, the blue *charka*, was added on independence in 1947.

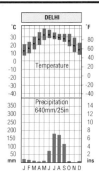

The summer rains, typical of the Indian monsoon, arrive later and are less intense at Delhi than in the lower parts of the Ganges Valley. From November to May, the dry season, there is abundant sunshine and temperatures increase rapidly until the arrival of the rains in June. During the rainy season the temperature is uniformly hot, with little diurnal variation. The latter part of the year is sunny, dry and much cooler. Night temperatures from December to February are usually below 10°C [50°F].

A diamond-shaped country – the world's seventh largest – India extends from high in the Himalayas through the Tropic of Cancer to the warm waters of the Indian Ocean at 8°N. More than 942 million people live here in the world's second most populous state – and its largest democracy.

Landscape and agriculture

The mountainous north: The Himalayan foothills make a stunning backdrop for northern India, rising abruptly from the plains in towering ranks. Harsh dry highlands, sparsely occupied by herdsmen, stretch northwards to the everlasting snows of the Karakoram. Below lie alpine meadows, lakes and woodlands, often grazed in summer by seasonally migrant flocks from lower villages. The fertile Vale of Kashmir has emerald-green rice terraces, walnut and plane trees, and apple and apricot orchards around half-timbered villages.

The wet, forested eastern Himalayas of Assam are ablaze with rhododendrons and magnolias, and terraced for buckwheat, barley and rice growing. The high plateau of Meghalaya ('abode of the clouds') is damp and cool; nearby Cherrapunji has one of the highest rainfalls in the world. Tropical oaks and teaks on the forest ridges of Nagaland, Manipur and Mizoram, bordering Burma, alternate with rice patches and small towns; on the hilltops dry cultivation of rice is practiced.

The plains: The great plains form a continuous strip from the Punjab eastwards. Heavily irrigated by canals engineered in the late 19th century, the rich alluvial soils have provided prosperity for Sikh and Jat farmers of the Punjab and Haryana. Here are grown winter wheat and summer rice, cotton and sugar cane with sorghum in the drier areas, the successful agriculture forming a foundation for linked industrial development.

Somewhat similar landscapes extend east to the plains surrounding Delhi, India's third largest city on the west bank of the Jumna (Yamuna) River. An ancient site, occupied for over 3,000 years, it now includes the Indian capital New Delhi, designed by Sir Edwin Lutyens and built from 1912. Old city and new lie at a focal point of road and rail links, and like many Indian cities rapidly became overcrowded. To the east again are the lowlands of Uttar Pradesh, crisscrossed by the Ganges and Jumna rivers and their many tributaries. Slightly wetter, but less irrigated, these plains are farmed less for wheat and rice than for spiked millet and sorghum.

Among the most densely populated areas of India (the state of Uttar Pradesh has a population larger than Nigeria, Pakistan or Bangladesh), these lowlands support dozens of cities and smaller settlements – notably Agra, with its Red Fort and Taj Mahal, and the sacred cities of Allahabad and Varanasi (Benares). Along the Nepal border the *terai* or hillfoot plains, formerly malaria-infested swamp forest, have now been cleared and made healthy for prosperous farming settlements.

Downstream from Tinpahar ('three hills'), near the Bangladeshi border, the Ganges begins its deltaic splitting into distributary streams, while still receiving tributaries from the north and west. West Bengal consists largely of the rice- and jute-growing lands flanking the distributary streams that flow south to become the Hooghly, on which Calcutta is built. The Ganges-Kobadak barrage now provides irrigation for the north of this tract, while improving both water supply and navigation lower down the Hooghly. The Sundarbans – mangrove and swamp forests at the seaward margin of the Ganges delta – extend eastwards into Bangladesh.

South-west from the Punjab plains lies the Thar or Great Indian Desert, its western fringes in Pakistan but with a broad tract of dunes in the northeastern lowlands in Rajasthan, India's largest state. The desert ranges from perenially dry wastelands of shifting sand to areas capable of cultivation in wet years. As the name Rajasthan implies, this state was once (until 1950) a land of rajahs and princes, palaces and temples. Rajasthan rises in a series of steps to a jagged, bare range of brightly coloured

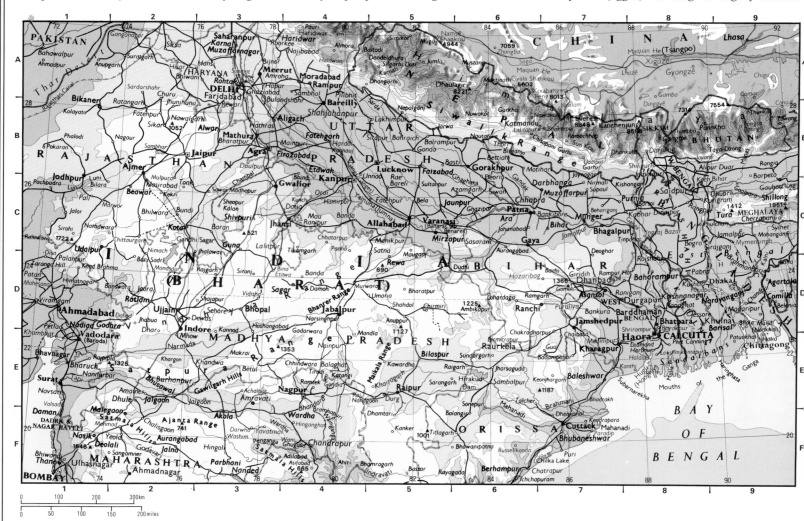

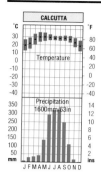

Calcutta has a tropical monsoon climate with windflow in winter the reverse of that in summer. In winter, north-westerlies bring dry, sunny weather with a large daily range of temperature of about 14°C [25°F]. By May, the increasing intensity of the sun gives rise to thunderstorms which precede the northwards sweep of the summer monsoon across the Bay of Bengal, bringing four months of heavy rain and constant high temperature and humidity.

sandstone ridges, the Aravallis, that extend north-eastwards and end at Delhi.

South and west of the Aravallis lie the cotton-growing lands of tropical Gujarat; Ahmadabad is its chief city. Between the Gulfs of Khambhat and Kachchh is the low peninsular plateau of Kathiawar, whose declining deciduous forests still harbour small groups of tribal peoples, and indeed the last of India's native lions. Between this and the Pakistan border stretches the desert salt marsh of the Rann of Kachchh, once an arm of the Arabian Sea and still occasionally flooded by exceptionally heavy rains.

South-east of the Aravallis is an area of transition between the great plains of the north and the uplands and plateaus of peninsular India. First come the Chambal badlands (wastelands south of Agra, now partly reclaimed), then rough hill country extending south-eastwards to Rewa. The River Sone provides a lowland corridor through the hills south of Rewa, and an irrigation barrage provides water for previously arid lands west of Gaya. Eastwards again the hills are forested around Ambikapur and Lohardaga. Industrial development becomes important around the coalfields of the Damodar Valley, centred on Asansol and the developing steel town of Jamshedpur.

Peninsular India: South of the Chambal River and of Indore (a princely capital until 1950) the sandy plateau of the north gives way to forested hills, split by the broad corridors of the Narmada and Tapi rivers. Tribal lands persist in the Satpura Range, and the Ajanta Range to the south is noted for primitive cave paintings near Aurangabad. From here to the south volcanic soils predominate.

Bombay (also called Mumbai), India's second largest city, lies on the coastal lowlands by a broad estuary, among rice fields dotted with low lava ridges. Fishing villages with coconut palms line the shore, while inland rise the stepped, forested slopes and pinnacles of peninsular India's longest mountain chain, the Western Ghats (Sahyadri).

East of the Ghats stretch seemingly endless expanses of cotton and sorghum cultivation. Arid in late winter and spring, and parched by May, they spring to life when the rains break in late May or June. The sleepy market towns follow a similar rhythm, full of activity when the agricultural cycle demands, and then relaxing under the broiling sun.

South from the holiday beaches of Goa (formerly a Portuguese enclave, still Portuguese in flavour), past busy Mangalore, Calicut and Cochin to the state capital of Kerala, Trivandrum, the coast becomes a kaleidoscope of coconut groves and fishing villages, rice fields, scrublands, cashew orchards and tapioca plantations. Here the Ghats are edged with granite, gneiss, sandstone and schist, and clad in heavy rainforest. To the east the peninsula is drier, with rolling plateaus given over to the production of millet, pulses and other dry crops. Sugar, rice and spices are grown where simple engineering provides tanks, stopped with earth or masonry dams, to save

the summer rains; now canals perform the same task. Bangalore and Hyderabad, once sleepy capitals of princely states, are now bustling cities, respectively capitals of Karnataka and Andhra Pradesh.

History

India's earliest settlers were widely scattered across the subcontinent in Stone Age times. The first of its many civilizations developed in the Indus Valley about 2600 BC, and in the Ganges Valley from about 1500 BC. By the 4th and 3rd centuries BC Pataliputra (modern Patna) formed the centre of a loosely held empire that extended across the peninsula and beyond into Afghanistan. This first Indian empire broke up after the death of the Emperor Asoka in 232 BC, to be replaced by many others. The Portuguese who crossed the Indian Ocean in the late 15th century, and the British, Danes, French and Dutch who soon followed, found a subcontinent divided and ripe for plundering.

As a result of battles fought both in Europe and in India itself, Britain gradually gained ascendancy over both European rivals and local factions within the subcontinent; by 1805 the British East India

THE HIMALAYAS

The Earth's highest mountain range, with an average height of 6,100 m [20,000 ft], the Himalayas are structurally part of the high plateau of Central Asia. The range stretches over 2,400 km [1,500 mls] from the Pamirs in the north-west to the Chinese border in the east. There are three main ranges: Outer, Middle and Inner; in Kashmir, the Inner Himalayas divide into five more ranges, including the Ladakh Range and the Karakorams. The world's highest mountain, Mt Everest (8,848 m [29,029 ft]) is on the Tibet-Nepal border; next highest is K2 (8,611 m [28,251 ft]) in the Karakorams, and there are a further six peaks over 8,000 m [26,250 ft].

The name comes from the Nepalese words *him* ('snows') and *alya* ('home of'), and the mountains are much revered in Hindu mythology as the abode of gods. Recently, the hydroelectric potential of the range has inspired more secular reverence: enormous quantities of energy could be tapped, although certainly at some cost to one of the world's most pristine environments.

COUNTRY Republic of India	**MAIN EXPORT PARTNERS** USA 19%, CIS nations 15%, Japan 10%, Germany 6%, UK 6%
AREA 3,287,590 sq km [1,269,338 sq mls]	**IMPORTS** US$24 per person
POPULATION 942,989,000	**MAIN IMPORTS** Non-electrical machinery 18%, mineral fuels 13%, iron and steel 7%, pearls, precious and semi-precious stones 7%, electrical machinery 4%, transport equipment 3%, edible vegetable oil 3%
CAPITAL (POPULATION) New Delhi (301,000)	
GOVERNMENT Multiparty federal republic with a bicameral legislature	
ETHNIC GROUPS Indo-Aryan (Caucasoid) 72%, Dravidian (Aboriginal) 25%, others (mainly Mongoloid) 3%	**MAIN IMPORT PARTNERS** Japan 13%, USA 10%, Germany 9%, UK 8%, CIS nations 5%
LANGUAGES Hindi 30% and English (both official), Telugu 8%, Bengali 8%, Marati 8%, Urdu 5%, and over 200 others	**EDUCATIONAL EXPENDITURE** 3.5% of GNP
RELIGIONS Hindu 83%, Sunni Muslim 11%, Christian 2%, Sikh 2%, Buddhist 1%	**DEFENCE** 2.5% of GNP
	TOTAL ARMED FORCES 1,260,000
NATIONAL DAY 26 January; Republic Day (1950)	**TOURISM** 1,760,000 visitors per year
CURRENCY Rupee = 100 paisa	**ROADS** 1,772,000 km [1,101,000 mls]
ANNUAL INCOME PER PERSON US$290	**RAILWAYS** 61,810 km [38,407 mls]
SOURCE OF INCOME Agriculture 31%, industry 27%, services 41%	**POPULATION DENSITY** 287 per sq km [743 per sq ml]
	URBAN POPULATION 26%
MAIN PRIMARY PRODUCTS Wheat, sugar cane, rice, millet, sorghum, jute, barley, tea, cattle, coal, iron ore, lead, zinc, diamonds, oil and natural gas, bauxite, chromium, copper, manganese	**POPULATION GROWTH** 2.7% per year
	BIRTHS 31 per 1,000 population
	DEATHS 10 per 1,000 population
	INFANT MORTALITY 88 per 1,000 live births
MAIN INDUSTRIES Textiles, chemicals, petroleum products, oil refining, jute, cement, fertilizers, food processing, diesel engines, beverages, iron and steel	**LIFE EXPECTANCY** Female 61 yrs, male 60 yrs
	POPULATION PER DOCTOR 2,439 people
EXPORTS US$19 per person	**ADULT LITERACY** 50%
MAIN EXPORTS Gems and jewellery 17%, clothing 9%, leather and leather manufactures 6%, machinery and transport equipment 6%, cotton fabrics 5%, tea and maté 4%	**PRINCIPAL CITIES (POPULATION)** Bombay (Mumbai) 15,093,000 Calcutta 11,673,000 Delhi 9,882,000 Madras (Chennai) 5,361,000 Hyderabad 4,280,000 Bangalore 4,087,000 Ahmadabad 3,298,000

KASHMIR

Until Indian independence in August 1947, Kashmir's mainly Muslim population was ruled, under British supervision, by a Hindu maharaja. Independence obliged the maharaja to choose between Pakistan or India; hoping to preserve his own independence, he refused to make a decision. In October, a ragtag army of Pathan tribesmen invaded from newly created Pakistan. Looting industriously, the Pathans advanced slowly, and India had time to rush troops to the region. The first Indo-Pakistan war resulted in a partition that satisfied neither side, with Pakistan holding one-third and India the remainder, with a 60% Muslim population. Despite promises, India has refused to allow a plebiscite to decide the province's fate. Two subsequent wars, in 1965 and 1972, failed to alter significantly the 1948 cease-fire lines.

In the late 1980s, Kashmiri nationalists in the Indian-controlled area began a violent campaign in favour of either secession to Pakistan or local independence. India responded by flooding Kashmir with troops and accusing Pakistan of intervention. By the mid 1990s, at least 3,000 Kashmiris had died. India stood accused of torture and repression, and there was little sign of a peaceful end to the conflict.

Company was virtually in control, and the British Indian Empire (which included, however, many autonomous states) was gradually consolidated throughout the 19th and early 20th centuries. Organized opposition to Britain's rule began before World War I and reached a climax after the end of World War II. In August 1947 the Indian subcontinent became independent, but divided into the separate states of India, a mainly Hindu community, and Pakistan, where Muslims formed the vast majority. In the boundary disputes and reshuffling of minority populations that followed perhaps a million lives were lost – and events since then have done little to promote good relations between the two states.

India is a vast country with enormous problems of organization. It has over a dozen major languages, each with a rich literature, and many minor languages. Hindi, the national language, and the Dravidian languages of the south (Tamil, Telugu and Malayalam) are Indo-European; in the north and east occur Sino-Tibetan tongues, and in forested hill refuges are found residual Austric languages. Racial stocks too are mixed, with dark tribal folk in forest remnants, Mongoloids in the north and east, and lighter-coloured skins and eyes in the north-west.

The mosaic of religion also adds variety – and potential conflict. Hinduism is all-pervasive (though the state is officially secular), and Buddhism is slowly reviving in its country of origin (the Buddha was born on the border of India and Nepal about 563 BC). Buddhism's near-contemporary Mahavira

and Jainism are strong in the merchant towns around Mt Abu in the Aravalli hills north of Ahmadabad. Islam contributes many mosques and tombs to the Indian scene, the Taj Mahal being the most famous. The forts of Delhi, Agra and many other northern cities, and the ghost city of Fatehpur Sikri, near Agra, are also Islamic relics of the Mogul period (1556–1707). Despite the formation of Pakistan, India retains a large Muslim minority of about 76 million. Now it is the turn of the Punjab's militant Sikhs, claiming to represent their population of 13 million, who seek separation.

Christian influences range from the elaborate Catholic churches and shrines remaining from Portuguese and French settlement, to the many schools and colleges set up by Christian denominations and still actively teaching; there are also notable church unions in both south and north India. The British period of rule left its own monuments; Bombay and Calcutta both have some notable Victoriana, and New Delhi is a planned Edwardian city.

Communications and development

A more vital memorial is the railway network – a strategic broad-gauge system fed by metre-gauge subsidiaries, with additional light railways, for example to the hill stations of Simla (in Himachal Pradesh), Darjeeling (between Nepal and Bhutan) and Ootacamund (in Tamil Nadu). Among developments since independence are the fast and comfortable intercity diesel-electric trains, but steam engines remain the main workhorses in a country that is the world's third largest coal producer.

The road system also has strategic elements from the Mogul and British past, now part of a national network. Main roads are passable all the year round, and feeder roads are largely all-weather dirt roads taking traffic close to most of India's 650,000 villages. The well-served international airports are linked with good, cheap internal services.

At independence India was already established as a partly industrialized country, and has made great strides during a succession of five-year plans that provided explicitly for both nationalized and private industry. The Damodar coalfield around Asansol has been developed, and several new fields

opened. The Tata family's steel city of Jamshedpur, itself now diversified by other industries, has been complemented by new state plants and planned towns at Durgapur and other places, in collaboration with Britain, Germany and the former Soviet Union. Major engineering factories have been built at Bangalore, Vishakhapatnam and elsewhere (including the ill-fated Bhopal), and oil refineries set up at Barauni in the north-east, and near Bombay for new fields recently developed in the north-west. Several nuclear power stations are in operation, and the massive potential of hydroelectric power is being exploited. Small-scale industry is also being encouraged. Industrial estates have had mixed success, but do well in places like Bangalore where there are enough related industries to utilize interactions.

In the countryside a generation of effort in community and rural development is starting to achieve results, most obviously where the Green Revolution of improved seeds and fertilizers has been successful, for example in the wheatlands of the Punjab and Haryana, or where irrigation has been newly applied and brought success. In such areas it can be argued that the gap between landless labourers and prosperous farmers widens when new methods bring greater yields; but this is one of many social problems that beset a complex, diverse society which appears to be always on the verge of collapse into chaos, but despite its size, burgeoning population and potential for division manages to remain intact.

Sikkim, after Goa the smallest of India's 25 self-governing states, was a Buddhist kingdom before being ruled by Britain from 1866 and protected by India from 1950 to 1975, when following a plebiscite it joined the Union. On the border with Nepal is Mt Kanchenjunga, at 8,598 m [28,028 ft] the world's third highest peak.

Indian islands: The Andaman and Nicobar Islands, in the Bay of Bengal, became an Indian state in 1950 and now form one of the country's seven Union territories (population 280,660); a similar status is held by the Lakshadweep (Laccadive) Islands, off the Malabar Coast, where 27 of the coral atolls are inhabited (population 51,707) ∎

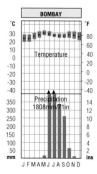

Bombay's climate is hot and humid. January and February are the coldest months, with night temperatures just below 20°C [68°F] – the only time in the year that they go below that figure. The period March to May is hot and then the monsoon rains come, lasting from June to September. Over 2,000 mm [79 in] fall, and from July to August rain falls on 45–50 days; more than 500 mm [20 in] has been recorded in one day. For the rest of the year, the heat returns.

NEPAL

This Himalayan kingdom's uniquely shaped flag was adopted in 1962. It came from the joining together in the 19th century of two triangular pennants – the royal family's crescent moon emblem and the powerful Rana family's sun symbol.

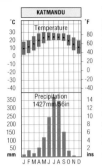

The high altitude of the Himalayan parts of the country give subzero temperatures throughout the year, with the resultant snow, ice and high winds. In the lower regions, however, the temperatures are subtropical and the rainfall quite high, though it tends to be drier in the west. At Katmandu, the day temperatures for most of the year are 25–30°C [77–86°F], but dropping at night to 10–20°C [50–68°F]. The lowest recorded is only just below freezing. Rainfall is quite high, mainly from May to September.

Over three-quarters of Nepal lies in a mountain heartland located between the towering Himalayas, the subject of an inconclusive boundary negotiation with China in 1961, and the far lower Siwalik Range overlooking the Ganges plain. Its innumerable valleys are home to a mosaic of peoples, of Indo-European and Tibetan stock, with a wide range of cultures and religions, and exercising fierce clan loyalties.

This heartland, some 800 km [500 mls] from west to east, is divided between the basins of Nepal's three main rivers – the Ghaghara, Gandak and Kosi. Between the last two, on a smaller river flanked by lake deposits, stands Katmandu, the royal and parliamentary capital, surrounded by emerald rice fields and orchards. The provincial centre of Pokhara is in a similar valley tributary to the Gandak, north of Nuwakot.

South of the Siwalik Range, the formerly swampy and malarious *terai*, or hillfoot plain, is now an economic mainstay, with new farming settlements growing rice, wheat, maize, jute and sugar. Development is encouraged by the *terai* section of the Asian Highway. There are two short railroads from India, Jaynagar–Janakpur and Raxaul–Amlekganj, where the railhead from the south meets the road that takes goods up to Katmandu. As well as general development aid from the West, China has built a road from Tibet to Katmandu, India one from near Nautanwa to Pokhara. Nepal's most

famous assets are the mountains, now an increasing tourist attraction bringing vital revenue to the country. Everest (8,848 m [29,029 ft]) and Kanchenjunga (8,598 m [28,208 ft]) are the tallest peaks of a magnificent range, giving a backdrop that dominates every vista in Nepal.

The authorities now hope for more than increased tourism. Today's plan is for the Himalayas to be tapped for their colossal hydroelectric potential, to supply the factories of India; Nepal's goal is to become the powerhouse of the region. If the scheme envisaged by the government and the World Bank goes ahead, the first stage would be under way by the mid-1990s at Chisapani Gorge.

Financing such schemes – at US$6 billion Chisapani alone is nearly twice the total gross national product – is a huge problem for a country which ranks alongside Laos as the poorest in Asia. With Chinese Tibet to the north and India to the south, the nation is already heavily reliant on Indian trade and co-operation – a fact emphasized when border restrictions operated in the late 1980s. Devoid of coast, independent trade links and mineral resources, Nepal has remained an undeveloped rural country, with more than 90% of the adult population (only one in four of whom can read) working as subsistence farmers. In addition, indiscriminate farming techniques have led to deforestation – in turn resulting in the erosion of precious soils.

While tourism is now encouraged, it was only in

1951 that Nepal was opened up to foreigners. Before that it had been a patchwork of feudal valley kingdoms, and though these were conquered by the Gurkhas in the 18th century – forming the present country – local leaders always displayed more allegiance to their clans than to the state. From the mid-19th century these families (notably the powerful Rana) reduced the power of the central king, but in 1951 the monarchy was re-established. A brief period of democracy ended with the return of autocratic royal rule in 1960 under King Mahendra, but after mass demonstrations and riots his son Birendra, despite attempts at stalling, was forced to concede a new constitution incorporating pluralism and basic human rights in 1990 and the hierarchical system of *panchayats* (rubber-stamping local councils) was over. In May 1991 the first democratic elections for 32 years took place with 10 million voters, and were won by the left-of-centre Nepali Congress Party. Though the birthplace of Buddha (Prince Siddhartha Gautama, c. 563 BC), Nepal remains a predominantly Hindu country ■

COUNTRY Kingdom of Nepal
AREA 140,800 sq km [54,363 sq mls]
POPULATION 21,953,000
CAPITAL (POPULATION) Katmandu (535,000)
GOVERNMENT Constitutional monarchy
ETHNIC GROUPS Nepalese 53%, Bihari 18%, Tharu 5%, Tamang 5%, Newar 3%
LANGUAGES Nepali 58% (official)
RELIGIONS Hindu 86%, Buddhist 8%, Muslim 4%
NATIONAL DAY 28 December; Birthday of the King
CURRENCY Nepalese rupee = 100 paisa
ANNUAL INCOME PER PERSON US$160
MAIN PRIMARY PRODUCTS Rice, cereals, timber, sugar
MAIN EXPORTS Basic manufactures 35%, foodstuffs 23%, machinery and transport equipment 22%
MAIN IMPORTS Basic manufactured goods 30%, machinery and transport equipment 23%, chemicals 13%, mineral fuels 11%, foodstuffs 10%
POPULATION DENSITY 156 per sq km [404 per sq ml]
LIFE EXPECTANCY Female 53 yrs, male 54 yrs

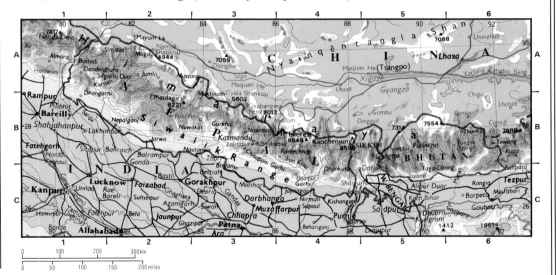

BHUTAN

The striking image on Bhutan's flag is explained by the name of this Himalayan kingdom in the local language, *Druk Yil*, which means 'land of the dragon'. The saffron colour stands for royal power and the orange-red for Buddhist spiritual power.

COUNTRY Kingdom of Bhutan
AREA 47,000 sq km [18,147 sq mls]
POPULATION 1,639,000
CAPITAL (POPULATION) Thimphu (31,000)
POPULATION DENSITY 35 per sq km [90 per sq ml]

Geographically a smaller and even more isolated version of Nepal, the remote mountain kingdom of Bhutan faces many of the same problems and hopes for many of the same solutions – notably the harnessing of hydroelectric power from the Himalayas: India has already built one plant and commissioned two more from King Jigme Singye Wangchuk. The monarch is head of both state and government, though foreign affairs are under Indian guidance following a treaty of 1949.

The world's most 'rural' country (around 6% of the population live in towns and over 90% are dependent on agriculture), Bhutan produces mainly rice and maize as staple crops, and fruit and cardamom as cash crops. Timber is important, too, though outweighed by cement (25% of exports) and talcum (10%) in earning foreign exchange. Despite these activities, plus tourism, the World Bank in 1993 ranked Bhutan the world's sixth poorest country, ahead only of Nepal in Asia, and with a

GNP per capita figure of just US$170. Aircraft and diesel fuels are its main imports.

Like Nepal, Bhutan was subject to a series of prodemocracy demonstrations in 1990, but because the protesters were mainly Hindus there has been little political progress in this predominantly Buddhist country. The Hindu minority, mostly Nepali-speakers, maintain that they are the victims of discrimination, denied basic rights such as religious freedom and the ownership of property ■

ASIA

SRI LANKA

This unusual flag was adopted in 1951, three years after 'Ceylon' gained independence from Britain. The lion banner represents the ancient Buddhist kingdom and the stripes the island's minorities – Muslims (green) and Hindus (orange).

Known as Ceylon until 1972, when it became a Socialist republic, Sri Lanka has been described as 'the pearl of the Indian Ocean'; the island is also its crossroads. First inhabited by forest-dwelling negroid Veddas, it was settled later by brown-skinned Aryans from India. These are now dominant in the population, though diluted by successive waves of incomers. Long-resident Tamils farm in the northern limestone peninsula of Jaffna, and Arab dhow sailors and merchants settled in the ports. After Vasco da Gama's contact with India in the 15th century came new traders and colonists – first Portuguese, then Dutch, then British (in control from 1796 to 1948) – and new immigrant Tamils were brought in from south-east India to farm the plantations.

From mountain core to coral strand stretches the 'wet zone' of south-western Sri Lanka, supporting grassy downs, rainforests and tea gardens near the ancient religious centre of Kandy, and evergreen forests and palm-fringed beaches in the lowlands from Colombo to east of Galle. White Buddhist shrines dot the cultivated land among rice paddies, sugar cane plantations and spice gardens. In contrast are the much drier zones of the north and east.

While light industry has gone some way to diversifying an agricultural base dependent on tea (third in the world after India and China), coconuts and rubber, Sri Lanka's economic progress since independence has been plagued by civil war and communal violence. The main conflict, between the Sinhalese Buddhist majority and the Tamil Hindu minority, led to disorders in 1958, 1971 and 1977; since 1983 the conflict has been virtually continuous as Tamil guerrillas have fought for an independent homeland in the north (Eelam), with Jaffna the capital.

An Indian-brokered cease-fire in 1987 allowed an Indian peacekeeping force in, but it failed to subdue the main terrorist group, the Tamil Tigers, and withdrew in March 1990. Between then and the start of 1992 more than 12,000 people died in renewed clashes between the predominantly Sinhalese government forces and the rebels, despite an agreement on Tamil autonomy. Many civilians, too, have lost their lives, and the conflicts have badly affected the tourist industry. In addition, the authorities were dogged by a rumbling rebellion of the left-wing Sinhalese nationalist movement (JVP) in the south. Banned in 1983, the JVP escalated their campaign after the Indo-Sri Lankan pact of 1987, but their guerrillas were virtually broken by an offensive initiated by the new government – elected democratically after a delay of some six years in 1988. However, in 1993, the country's president was assassinated by a suspected Tamil separatist. Offensives against the Tamil Tigers continued into the late 1990s ■

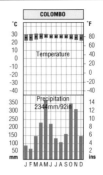

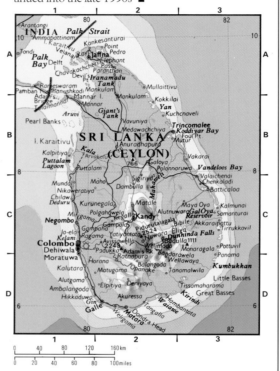

The western side of Sri Lanka has an equatorial climate with a double maximum of rainfall in May and October and very uniform high temperatures throughout the year. The periods of heaviest rain at Colombo mark the advance and retreat of the summer monsoon, which gives a single wet season over the Indian subcontinent to the north. The eastern side of the island, sheltered from the south-west winds, is drier; Trincomalee has an annual rainfall of 1,646 mm [65 in].

COUNTRY Democratic Socialist Republic of Sri Lanka

AREA 65,610 sq km [25,332 sq mls]

POPULATION 18,359,000

CAPITAL (POPULATION) Colombo (1,863,000)

GOVERNMENT Unitary multiparty republic with a unicameral legislature

ETHNIC GROUPS Sinhalese 74%, Tamil 18%, Sri Lankan Moor 7%

LANGUAGES Sinhala and Tamil (both official), English

RELIGIONS Buddhist 69%, Hindu 16%, Muslim 8%, Christian 7%

NATIONAL DAY 4 February; Independence and National Day (1948)

CURRENCY Sri Lankan rupee = 100 cents

ANNUAL INCOME PER PERSON US$600

MAIN PRIMARY PRODUCTS Rice, coconuts, rubber, tea, fish, timber, iron ore, precious and semi-precious stones, graphite

MAIN INDUSTRIES Agriculture, mining, forestry, fishing, textiles, oil refining, cement, food processing

MAIN EXPORTS Tea 27%, rubber 7%, precious and semi-precious stones 6%, coconuts 3%

MAIN EXPORT PARTNERS USA 27%, Germany 8%, UK 6%, Japan 5%, Pakistan 2%

MAIN IMPORTS Petroleum 15%, machinery and transport equipment 13%, sugar 4%, vehicles

MAIN IMPORT PARTNERS Japan 15%, UK 7%, USA 6%, Iran 5%, India 4%, China 3%

DEFENCE 4.9% of GNP

TOURISM 393,700 visitors per year

POPULATION DENSITY 280 per sq km [725 per sq ml]

INFANT MORTALITY 24 per 1,000 live births

LIFE EXPECTANCY Female 74 yrs, male 70 yrs

ADULT LITERACY 89%

PRINCIPAL CITIES (POPULATION) Colombo 1,863,000 Dehiwala 196,000 Moratuwa 170,000

MALDIVES

The Maldives used to fly a plain red flag until the Islamic green panel with white crescent was added early this century. The present design was officially adopted in 1965, after the British left the islands.

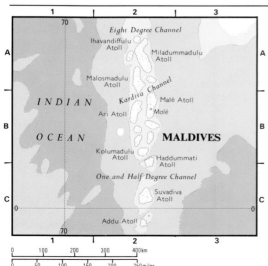

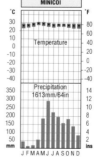

The archipelago of the Maldives comprises over 1,190 small low-lying islands and atolls (202 of them inhabited), scattered along a broad north–south line starting 650 km [400 mls] west-south-west of Cape Comorin.

The islands were settled from Sri Lanka about 500 BC. For a time under Portuguese and later Dutch rule, they became a British protectorate in 1887, administered from Ceylon but retaining local sultanates. They achieved independence in 1965, and the last sultan was deposed three years later.

Adequately watered and covered with tropical vegetation, the islands' crops are coconuts, bananas, mangoes, sweet potatoes and spices, but much food is imported – as are nearly all capital and consumer goods. Fish are plentiful in lagoons and open sea; bonito and tuna are leading exports, together with copra and coir. Tourism, however, has now dis-

Surrounded by the warm waters of the Indian Ocean, the islands are hot throughout the year, with monthly temperature averages of 26–29°C [79–84°F], and even night temperatures going no lower than 23–27°C [73–81°F]. The temperature record is only 37°C [99°F]. Monsoon rainfall is heavy, with an annual total of over 1,500 mm [59 in], most of this falling from June to November, though there is rain in all months; the period from December to March is the driest.

COUNTRY Republic of the Maldives

AREA 298 sq km [115 sq mls]

POPULATION 254,000

CAPITAL (POPULATION) Malé (56,000)

placed fishing as the mainstay of the economy, though its future depends much on political stability; the 1988 coup against the authoritarian nationalist government was put down with Indian troops ■

BANGLADESH

Bangladesh adopted this flag in 1971 following the break from Pakistan. The green is said to represent the fertility of the land, while the red disk, as the sun of independence, commemorates the blood shed in the struggle for freedom.

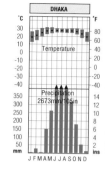

The Ganges delta has a classic monsoon climate. From June to September the winds blow from the south over the Bay of Bengal, bringing very heavy rain, over 240 mm [10 in] per month. On occasions, the winds are so strong they pile the sea water up against the outflowing river, bringing flood devastation. April is the hottest month and temperatures remain high throughout the monsoon season, though with little bright sunshine. January, with winds from the north, is the coldest month.

Battered by a relentless cycle of flood and famine, and plagued by political corruption and a succession of military coups, Bangladesh is perhaps Asia's most pitiful country, once known as Golden Bengal (Sonar Bangla) for its treasures, but gradually plundered and now pushed near to the bottom of the Third World pile. It is – apart from statistically irrelevant city-states and small island countries – the most crowded nation on Earth: the 1995 figure was a density of some 822 people per sq km [2,129 per sq ml], well ahead of the next realistic rival Taiwan (586 per sq km [1,518 per sq ml]) and far greater than Europe's contender Belgium (332 per sq km [861 per sq ml]), which in any case has a much larger urban proportion. The world's ninth biggest population – a figure expected to increase by another 36 million or more between 1988 and 2000 – lives on an area of precarious flat lowlands smaller than the US states of Illinois or Iowa.

Landscape

Apart from a south-eastern fringe of forested ridges east of Chittagong, Bangladesh consists almost entirely of lowlands – mainly the (greater) eastern part of the large delta formed jointly by the Ganges and Brahmaputra. The western part (now West Bengal, in India) is largely the 'dying delta' – its land a little higher and less often flooded, its deltaic channels seldom flushed by floodwaters. In contrast, the heart of Bangladesh, following the main Ganges channel and the wide Brahmaputra, is the 'active delta'. Frequently flooded, with changing channels that are hazardous to life, health and property, the rivers also renew soil fertility with silt washed down from as far away as the mountains of Nepal and Tibet. Indeed, while deforestation in the Himalayan

foothills has caused enough silt to form new 'islands' for the burgeoning Bangladeshi population, it has also led to the blocking of some waterways – 60% of the country's internal trade is carried by boat – and danger to fish stocks, as well as increased risk of flooding.

The alluvial silts of the 'active delta' yield up to three rice crops a year (the world's fourth largest producer), as well as the world's best jute – Bangladesh is the second largest producer in a declining market, and exports high-quality fibre to India; jute and cotton are processed also in post-independence mills, for example at Narayanganj.

There is a large hydroelectric plant at Karnaphuli reservoir, and a modern paper industry using bamboo from the hills. Substantial reserves of coal await exploitation, but a more realistic development may be the planned construction of a 320 km [200 mls] canal to transfer water from the flooding Brahmaputra to the Ganges, in order to increase supplies to India's drought-affected areas. However, in December 1996, the Bangladesh government signed a new treaty with India that provided for sharing the water from the Ganges, heralding an era of improved relations between the two countries.

History and politics

Bangladesh was until 1971 East Pakistan, the oriental wing of the Muslim state set up by the partition of British India in 1947. Separated by 1,600 km [1,000 mls] of India from the politically dominant, Urdu- and Punjabi-speaking western province, the easterners felt the victims of ethnic and economic discrimination. In 1971 resentment turned to war when Bengali irregulars, considerably aided and abetted by Indian troops, convened the indepen-

THE DELTA CYCLONES

Most of Bangladesh is almost unbelievably low and flat, and the people of the coastal fringes are all too familiar with the cyclones from the Bay of Bengal. Even so, 1991 brought the worst in memory: the official death toll was a staggering 132,000 (it may well be higher), and more than 5 million people, almost all of them poor peasants already living around or below the poverty line, were made homeless.

The cyclone caused inestimable damage to the area around Chittagong: crops and fields were inundated with sea water; herds of cattle and goats and flocks of poultry were decimated; dykes were breached and trees ripped up; wells filled up with salt water. The struggling survivors were victims of dysentery and cholera, dehydration and malnutrition. However generous, aid rarely reached the most needy, as it was sifted and filtered down the line despite the efforts of charity administrators. Corrupt practices, like cyclones, are endemic to Bangladesh; funds allocated for concrete cyclone-proof shelters, for example, were appropriated by individuals and government officials. As with most natural disasters – earthquakes, volcanic eruptions, tidal waves, landslips – the cyclones usually affect countries least equipped to deal with them and least able to withstand the losses.

dent state of 'Free Bengal', with Sheikh Mujibur Rahman as head of state.

The Sheikh's assassination in 1975 – during one of four military coups in the first 11 years of independence – led finally to a takeover by General Zia Rahman, who created an Islamic state before being murdered himself in 1981. General Ershad took over in a coup the following year and resigned as army chief in 1986 to take up the civilian presidency, lifting martial law, but by 1990 protests from supporters of his two predecessors toppled him from power and, after the first free parliamentary elections since independence, a coalition government was formed in 1991.

The new authority faced not only the long-term problems of a debt-ridden, aid-reliant country where corruption is a way of life; it also had to deal with the consequences of the worst cyclone in living memory and, from 1992, the increasing prospect of war with Burma, triggered by Rangoon's treatment of the Rohingyas, its Muslim minority. As far back as 1978 Bangladesh took in some 300,000 Rohingyas fleeing persecution, and while most went back, the emigrants of the 1990s are unlikely to follow suit. Meanwhile, both nations amassed troops on a border that snakes its way through misty hills, mahogany forests and rubber plantations.

In June 1996 elections, Shaikh Hasina Wajed, the daughter of the country's first president, was elected prime minister; a few weeks later, in July, the country's new president, Shahabuddin Ahmed, was elected to office unopposed ■

COUNTRY People's Republic of Bangladesh

AREA 144,000 sq km [55,598 sq mls]

POPULATION 118,342,000

CAPITAL (POPULATION) Dhaka (7,832,000)

GOVERNMENT Multiparty republic

ETHNIC GROUPS Bengali 98%, Bihari, tribal groups

LANGUAGES Bengali (official), English, nearly 100 tribal dialects

RELIGIONS Sunni Muslim 87%, Hindu 12%, Buddhist, Christian

NATIONAL DAY 26 March; Independence Day (1971)

CURRENCY Taka = 100 paisas

ANNUAL INCOME PER PERSON US$220

MAIN PRIMARY PRODUCTS Rice, jute, natural gas, sugar cane, cattle, fish, timber, tea, wheat, glass, sand, tobacco

MAIN INDUSTRIES Jute spinning, textiles, sugar, fishing

EXPORTS US$12 per person

MAIN EXPORTS Jute goods and raw jute 33%, fish and fish preparations 12%, hides and skins 12%

MAIN EXPORT PARTNERS USA 30%, Italy 9%, Japan 6%, Singapore 6%, UK 6%

IMPORTS US$33 per person

MAIN IMPORTS Machinery and basic manufactures 24%, foodstuffs 16%, petroleum products 15%

MAIN IMPORT PARTNERS Japan 13%, Canada 10%, Singapore 9%, USA 7%, Germany 6%

DEFENCE 1.8% of GNP

POPULATION DENSITY 822 per sq km [2,129 per sq ml]

LIFE EXPECTANCY Female 53 yrs, male 53 yrs

ADULT LITERACY 36%

PRINCIPAL CITIES (POPULATION) Dhaka (Dacca) 7,832,000 Chittagong 2,041,000 Khulna 877,000 Rajshahi 517,000

ASIA

MONGOLIA

 On Mongolia's flag the blue represents the country's national colour. In the hoist is the Golden Soyonbo, a Buddhist symbol, representing freedom. Within this, the flame is seen as a promise of prosperity and progress.

COUNTRY State of Mongolia
AREA 1,566,500 sq km [604,826 sq mls]
POPULATION 2,408,000
CAPITAL (POPULATION) Ulan Bator (601,000)
GOVERNMENT Multiparty republic
ETHNIC GROUPS Khalkha Mongol 79%, Kazak 6%
LANGUAGES Khalkha Mongolian (official), Chinese, Russian
RELIGIONS Shamanist, Buddhist, Muslim
NATIONAL DAY 11 July; Independence Day (1921)
CURRENCY Tugrik = 100 möngös

Worthy of its harsh, isolated reputation, Mongolia is the world's largest landlocked country and the most sparsely populated. Despite its traditional nomads, more than half the population live in towns, a quarter of them in Ulan Bator, a modern city built in the postwar Soviet mould. Geographically Mongolia divides into two contrasting regions, north and south of a line joining the mountains of the Altai, Hangayn and Hentiyn ranges.

In the north, high mountains alternate with river valleys and lake basins. Pastures are watered enough to support herds of cattle and wheat is grown, especially where black earth soils occur. In the far north-west, where the Altai rise to over 4,000 m [13,120 ft], boreal forests blanket the slopes.

The southern half of the country, still averaging 1,500 m [4,900 ft], has a strong continental climate with meagre, variable rainfall. In these semi-desert steppelands, salt lakes and pans occupy shallow depressions, poor scrub eventually giving way to the arid wastes of the Gobi Desert.

Mongolia is still a land of nomadic pastoralists – less than 1% of the land is cultivated – and huge herds of sheep, goats, yaks, camels and horses form the mainstay of the traditional economy. Herdsmen's families inhabit *ghers* (*yurts*), circular tents covered in felt, and subsist on a diet of milk, cheese and mutton.

Politics and economy

Outer Mongolia broke away from China following the collapse of the Ch'ing dynasty in 1911, but full independence was not gained until 1921 – with Soviet support in what was the world's second Socialist revolution. In 1924 a Communist People's Republic was proclaimed and the country fell increasingly under Soviet influence, the last example being a 20-year friendship and mutual assistance pact signed in 1966.

Textiles and food processing were developed, with aid from the USSR and COMECON also helping to open up mineral deposits such as copper, molybdenum and coking coal; in addition, Mongolia is an important producer of fluorspar . In the late 1980s, minerals overtook the agricultural sector as the country's main source of income.

In recent years Mongolia followed the path of other less remote Soviet satellites, reducing the presence of Soviet troops (1987–9), launching into privatization and developing a free-market economy. The pace of change was frantic after seven decades of authoritarian rule. In 1990, the people demonstrated for more freedom. Free elections in June 1990 resulted in victory for the Mongolian

People's Revolutionary Party (MPRP), which was composed of Communists. Although the MPRP started to move away from Communist policies, it was defeated in elections in 1996 by the opposition Democratic Union coalition ■

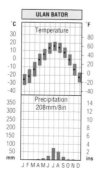 Ulan Bator lies on the northern edge of a vast desert plateau in the heart of Asia. Winters are bitterly cold and dry, and six months have a mean temperature below freezing. In the summer months, the temperatures are moderated by the height of the land above sea level. A large diurnal temperature range of over 15°C [27°F] occurs throughout the year. Rain falls almost entirely in the summer, the amount varying greatly from year to year, and decreasing to the south.

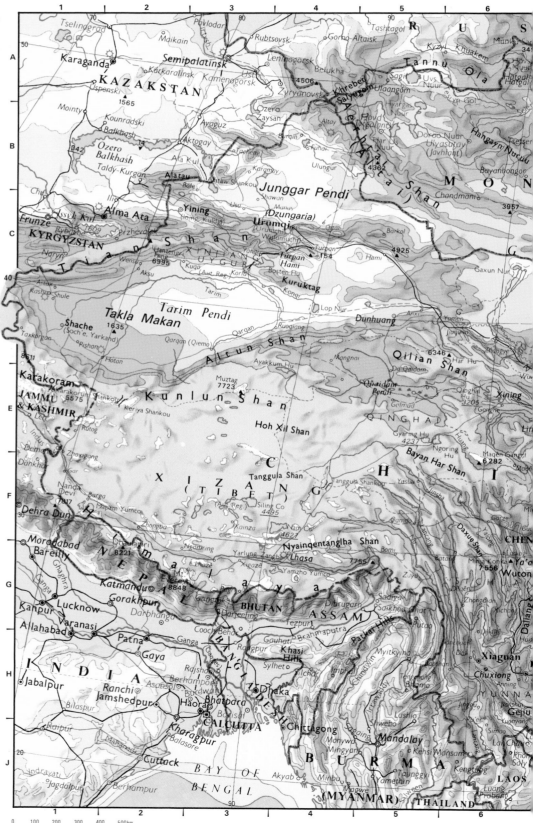

CHINA

Red, the traditional colour of both China and Communism, was chosen for the People's Republic flag in 1949. The large star represents the Communist Party programme, the small stars represent the four principal social classes.

By far the most populous country in the world – one in every five people is Chinese – the People's Republic of China also ranks as the third largest country after Russia and Canada, being marginally bigger than the USA. Before the development of modern forms of transport, the vast size of China often hampered communication between the centre of the country and the peripheries. Distances are huge. By rail, the distance from Beijing (Peking) to Guangzhou (Canton) is 2,324 km [1,450 mls].

One of the main determining influences on the evolution of Chinese civilization had been the geographical isolation of China from the rest of the world. Surrounded to the north, west and south by forests, deserts and formidable mountain ranges, and separated from the Americas by the Pacific Ocean, China until modern times was insulated from frequent contact with other civilizations, and its culture and society developed along highly individual lines. In the 1990s China again finds itself an enigma – the great giant of Communism in an era when the creed is experiencing a global collapse.

Landscape and relief

The Chinese landscape is like a chequerboard in which mountains and plateaus alternate with basins and alluvial plains. There are two intersecting systems of mountain chains, one trending from north-north-east to south-south-west, the other from east to west. Many mountain areas have been devastated by soil erosion through indiscriminate tree felling. The agricultural wealth of China is all in the lowlands of the east – where most of its people live.

Manchuria, in the far north, comprises a wide area of gently undulating country, originally grassland, but now an important agricultural area. The loess lands of the north-west occupy a broad belt from the great loop of the Hwang Ho (Huang He) into the Shanxi and Henan provinces. Here, valley sides, hills and mountains are blanketed in loess – a fine-grained unstratified soil deposited by wind during the last glaciation. Within this region, loess deposits occur widely in the form of plateaus which are deeply incised by spectacular gorges and ravines.

By contrast with the loess lands, the landscape of the densely populated North China Plain is flat and monotonous. Settlement is concentrated in walled villages while large fields are the product of post-1949 land consolidation schemes. Further south the Yangtze delta is a land of large lakes. Water is a predominant element – the low-lying alluvial land with its irrigated rice fields is traversed by intricate networks of canals and other man-made works, many of which date back several centuries.

Far inland in the Yangtze basin, and separated from the middle Yangtze Valley by precipitous river gorges, lies the Red Basin of Sichuan (Szechwan). To the north, west and south, the basin is surrounded by high mountain ranges. The mountains of the Qin Ling ranges, in particular, protect the basin from cold winter winds. With its mild climate and fertile soils, the Red Basin is one of the most productive and densely populated regions of China. Rice fields, often arranged in elaborate terraces, dominate the landscape.

Other distinctive landscapes of southern China include those of north-eastern Guizhou province, where limestone spires and pinnacles rise vertically

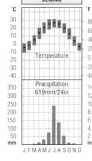

The climate of China is controlled by the air masses of Asia and the Pacific, and the mountains in the west. In the winter the cold, dry Siberian air blows southwards. In the summer the tropical Pacific air dominates, bringing high temperatures and rain. In summer the temperature in eastern China is high with little difference between north and south; in winter there is over 20°C [36°F] difference. Annual rain decreases from over 2,000 mm [80 in] in the south to the desert conditions of the north-west.

TIBET

With an average elevation of 4,500 m [14,750 ft] – almost as high as Europe's Mont Blanc – and an area of 1.2 million sq km [460,000 sq mls], Tibet is the highest and most extensive plateau in the world. It is a harsh and hostile place, and most of its population of just over 2 million people live in the relatively sheltered south of the country.

For much of its history Tibet has been ruled by Buddhist priests – lamas – as a theocracy. The Dalai Lama, a title passed on in successive incarnations from a dying elder to a newborn junior, usually dominated from Lhasa. Between 1720 and 1911 Tibet was under Chinese control, and in 1950 Tibet was reabsorbed by a resurgent Red China; after an unsuccessful uprising in 1959, the Dalai Lama fled to Delhi and a brutal process of forced Chinese acculturation began: in 1961, a report of the International Commission of Jurists accused China of genocide. An 'Autonomous Region of Tibet' was proclaimed in 1965, but during the 1966–76 Cultural Revolution, many Tibetan shrines and monasteries were destroyed.

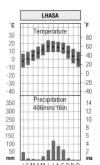

Tibetans call their country 'The Land of Snows', but the Himalayas act as a barrier to rain-bearing winds and the amount of precipitation is low, with Lhasa in the south getting 400 mm [16 in], this decreasing northwards to desert conditions. There is always snow at altitudes higher than about 5,000 m [16,000 ft]. In Lhasa, night temperatures will be below freezing on nearly every night from late October to early April, with the constant wind making this feel much colder.

above small, intensively cultivated plains, and the Guangdong coastal lowlands, with their villages in groves of citrus, bananas, mangoes and palms.

The Hwang Ho and the Yangtze

The two major rivers of China are the Hwang Ho (Huang He) and the Yangtze (Chang Jiang), the world's seventh and third longest. The Hwang Ho, or Yellow River (so called from the large quantities of silt which it transports), is 4,840 km [3,005 mls] long. Also known as 'China's Sorrow', it has throughout history been the source of frequent and disastrous floods. In 1938, dykes along the Hwang Ho were demolished in order to hamper the advance of the Japanese army into northern China, and the river was diverted so as to enter the sea to the south of the Shandong peninsula. In the catastrophic floods which followed, nearly 900,000 lives were lost and 54,000 sq km [21,000 sq mls] of land was inundated. Since 1949, the incidence of flooding has declined sharply, largely as a result of state investment in flood prevention schemes.

The Yangtze, China's largest and most important river, is 6,380 km [3,960 mls] long, and its catchment basin is over twice as extensive as that of the Hwang Ho. Unlike the Hwang Ho, the Yangtze is navigable. During the summer months, ocean-going vessels of 11,000 tonnes may reach Wuhan, and 1,100-tonne barges can go as far upstream as Chongqing. Despite the post-1949 improvement of roads and railways, the Yangtze remains an important transport artery.

Climate and agriculture

Although the Chinese subcontinent includes a wide variety of relief and climate, it can be divided into three broad regions.

Northern China: Throughout northern China, rainfall is light and variable, and is generally insufficient for irrigated agriculture. In winter, temperatures fall to between –1°C and –8°C [30°F and 18°F] and bitterly cold winds blow eastwards across the North China Plain from the steppes of Mongolia. Summer temperatures, by contrast, are little different from those of southern China, and may reach a daily average of 28°C [82°F]. The growing season diminishes northwards and in northern Manchuria only 90 days a year are free of frost. Despite advances in water conservation since World War II, aridity and unreliability of rainfall restrict the range of crops that can be grown. Millet, maize and winter wheat are the staple crops of the North China Plain, while coarse grains and soya beans are cultivated in Manchuria.

Southern China: The area to the south of the Qin Ling ranges receives heavier and more reliable rainfall than the north, and winter temperatures are generally above freezing point. Summer weather, especially in the central Yangtze Valley, is hot and humid. At Nanjing, temperatures as high as 44°C [111°F] have been recorded. Inland, the mild climate and fertile soils of the Red Basin make this an important agricultural region. Rice production is dominant but at lower altitudes the climate is warm enough to allow the cultivation of citrus fruits, cotton, sugar cane and tobacco, of which China is the world's biggest producer.

The far south of China, including Guangdong province and the island of Hainan, lies within the tropics and enjoys a year-round growing season. Irrigated rice cultivation is the economic mainstay of southern China. Double cropping (rice as a main crop followed by winter wheat) is characteristic of the Yangtze Valley; along the coast of Guangdong province two crops of rice can be grown each year, and in parts of Hainan Island the annual cultivation of three crops of rice is possible; the country produces 35% of the world total. Crops such as tea (second in the world), mulberry and sweet potato are also cultivated, and in the far south sugar cane, bananas, and other tropical crops are grown.

The interior: While the Qin Ling ranges are an important boundary between the relatively harsh environments of the north and the more productive lands of the south, a second major line, which follows the Da Hinggan Ling mountains and the eastern edge of the high Tibetan plateau, divides the intensively cultivated lands of eastern China from the mountains and arid steppes of the interior. In the north, this boundary line is marked by the Great Wall of China. Western China includes the Dzungarian basin, the Turfan depression, the arid Takla Makan desert, and the high plateau of Tibet.

Although aridity of climate has hampered the development of agriculture throughout most of western China, oasis crops are grown around the rim of the Takla Makan desert, and farming settlements also exist in the Gansu corridor to the north of the Qilian mountains.

Early history

Early Chinese civilization arose along the inland margins of the North China Plain, in a physical setting markedly harsher (especially in terms of winter temperatures) than the environments of the other great civilizations of the Old World. The Shang dynasty, noted for its fine craftsmanship in bronze, flourished in northern China from 1630 to 1122 BC. Shang civilization was followed by many centuries of political fragmentation, and it was not until the 3rd century BC that China was unified into a centrally administered empire. Under the Ch'in dynasty (221 to 206 BC) the Great Wall of China was completed, while Chinese armies pushed southwards beyond the Yangtze, reaching the southern Chinese coast in the vicinity of Canton.

In succeeding centuries there was a gradual movement of population from the north to the warmer, moister, and more productive lands of the south. This slow migration was greatly accelerated by incursions of barbarian nomads into north China, especially during the Sung dynasty (AD 960 to 1279). By the late 13th century the southern lands, including the Yangtze Valley, probably contained somewhere between 70% and 80% of the Chinese population.

During the Han, T'ang and Sung dynasties, a remarkably stable political and social order evolved within China. The major distinguishing features of Chinese civilization came to include Confucianism, whereby the individual was subordinated to family obligations and to state service, the state bureaucracy, members of which were recruited by public examination, and the benign rule of the emperor – the 'Son of Heaven'. Great advances were made in

COUNTRY People's Republic of China

AREA 9,596,960 sq km [3,705,386 sq mls]

POPULATION 1,226,944,000

CAPITAL (POPULATION) Beijing (12,362,000)

GOVERNMENT Single-party Communist State

ETHNIC GROUPS Han (Chinese) 92%, 55 others

LANGUAGES Mandarin Chinese (official); local dialects spoken in the south and west

RELIGIONS Confucian (officially atheist) 20%, Buddhist 6%, Taoist 2%, Muslim 2%, Christian

NATIONAL DAY 1 October; Proclamation of People's Republic (1949)

CURRENCY Renminbi (yuan) = 10 jiao = 100 fen

ANNUAL INCOME PER PERSON US$370

MAIN PRIMARY PRODUCTS Antimony, coal, fish, gold, iron ore, manganese, natural gas, petroleum, phosphates, pigs, rice, salt, sheep, timber, tobacco, tungsten

MAIN INDUSTRIES Agriculture, cement, forestry, textiles, steel, bicycles, petroleum, newsprint, fertilizers

MAIN EXPORTS Manufactured goods 19%, food and live animals 16%, mineral fuels 13%, chemicals 6%

MAIN EXPORT PARTNERS Hong Kong 32%, Japan 16%, USA 10%, Singapore 1%, UK 1%

MAIN IMPORTS Machinery and transport equipment 40%, chemicals 9%, raw materials 7%, food and live animals 5%

MAIN IMPORT PARTNERS Japan 28%, Hong Kong 14%, USA 12%, Germany 4%

DEFENCE 3.7% of GNP

TOTAL ARMED FORCES 4,860,000

TOURISM 43,700,000 visitors per year

ROADS 942,000 km [588,750 mls]

RAILWAYS 52,487 km [32,804 mls]

POPULATION DENSITY 128 per sq km [331 per sq ml]

BIRTHS 21 per 1,000 population

DEATHS 7 per 1,000 population

INFANT MORTALITY 27 per 1,000 live births

LIFE EXPECTANCY Female 73 yrs, male 69 yrs

POPULATION PER DOCTOR 1,000 people

ADULT LITERACY 70%

PRINCIPAL CITIES (POPULATION) Shanghai 15,082,000 Beijing (Peking) 12,362,000 Tianjin 10,687,000 Shenyang 4,050,000 Chongqing 3,870,000 Wuhan 3,870,000 Guangzhou 3,750,000 Chengdu 2,760,000 Nanjing 2,490,000 Xi'an 2,410,000 Zibo 2,400,000 Harbin 3,120,000 Nanchang 1,440,000

the manufacture of porcelain, silk, metals and lacquerware, while gunpowder, the compass, and printing were among several Chinese inventions which found their way to the West in medieval times. Nevertheless, the economy of pre-modern China was overwhelmingly agricultural, and the peasant class accounted for most of the population.

Despite the geographical diversity and great size of its territory, China during pre-modern times experienced long periods of unity and cohesion rarely disturbed by invasion from outside. Two important dynasties, the Yuan (1279–1368) and the Ch'ing (1644–1912), were established by the Mongols and Manchus respectively, but, almost invariably, alien rulers found it necessary to adopt Chinese methods of government, and the Chinese cultural tradition was preserved intact.

The birth of the Republic

In the 18th century, China experienced a rapid acceleration in the rate of population growth, and living standards began to fall. By the early 19th century, the government was weak and corrupt, and the country suffered frequent famines and political unrest. British victory in the Opium War (1839–42) was followed by the division of China into spheres of influence for the major Western

imperialist powers, and by the establishment of treaty ports, controlled by Western countries, along the Chinese coast and the Yangtze.

Meanwhile, the disintegration of imperial China was hastened by peasant uprisings such as the Taiping rebellion (1850–64), and by the defeat of China in the Sino-Japanese War of 1894–5. Belated attempts were made to arrest the decline of the Chinese empire, but in 1912, and following an uprising in Wuhan, the last of the Chinese emperors abdicated and a republic was proclaimed.

Although the republican administration in Peking was regarded as the legitimate government, real power rested with army generals and provincial governors. Rival generals, or warlords, raised private armies and plunged China into a long and disastrous period of internal disorder. Alternative solutions were offered by two political parties – the Kuomintang (or Chinese Nationalist Party) formed by Sun Yat-sen and later led by Chiang Kai-shek, and the Communist Party. In 1931, Japan seized Manchuria, and in 1937 full-scale war broke out between the two countries. In the bitter fighting which followed, the Communists, under Mao Tsetung, gained the support of the peasantry and proved adept practitioners of guerrilla warfare.

The defeat of Japan in 1945 was followed by a

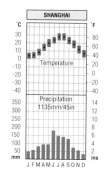

The annual rainfall total decreases from over 2,000 mm [80 in] in the south to the desert conditions of the north-west. Most of this rain falls in the summer months. Summer is also the typhoon season. Northwards the winters get drier and the rain becomes more variable from one year to the next. At Shanghai it rains on average ten days per month. Daily sunshine levels are not high: 4–5 hours from November to March, with only 7.5 hours in August.

civil war which cost 12 million lives: the Communists routed the Xuomintang armies, forcing them to take refuge on the island of Taiwan, and the People's Republic of China was officially proclaimed on 1 October 1949.

Communist China

Under Communist rule the mass starvation, malnutrition and disease which afflicted China before World War II were virtually eliminated, and living standards greatly improved, especially in the countryside.

One of the salient features of the centrally

□ National capital
● Autonomous region capitals
◉ Province capitals

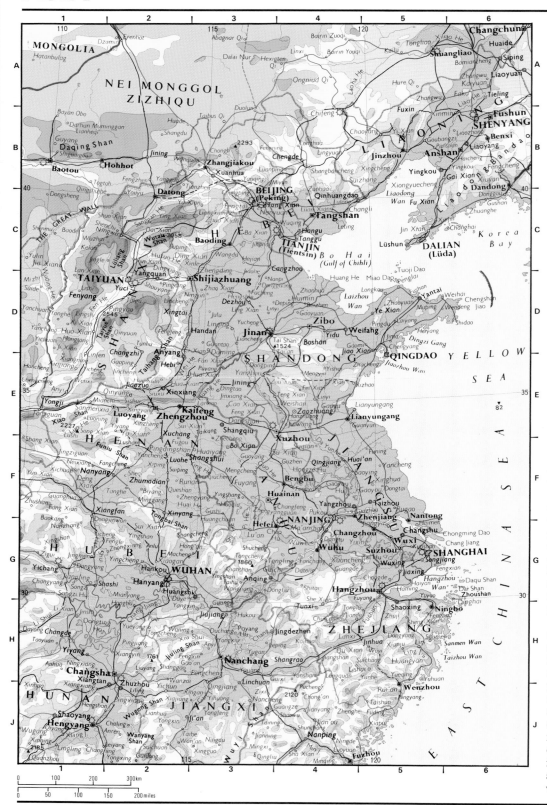

planned economy was the organization of the rural population into 50,000 communes – self-sufficient units of varying size which farm the land collectively. Communes also ran rural industries, and are responsible for the administration of schools and clinics. Labour has been organized on a vast scale to tackle public works such as water conservation, flood control and land reclamation.

Living standards improved markedly, with life expectancy doubling and education improving, though the GNP per capita figure remained that of a poor Third World nation – some 1.5% that of Japan. The agricultural communes were not notably successful, and since peasants have been freed from petty bureaucracy, harvests of the major grain crops went up by over 40% in the decade from 1976.

Although food supply has generally kept abreast of population growth, the size and growth rate of the Chinese population has always given cause for concern. By 1990–5, the population was growing at 1.5% per year, a net annual increase of about 13 million people; penalties and incentives have met with some success; but between 1988 and 2000 it is expected to grow by 187 million – slightly less than the prediction for India, but more than the 1988 totals for Indonesia or Brazil.

Only 10% of the land area of China is cultivable, but environmental constraints are such that there is little prospect of meeting increased food demand by reclaiming land for agriculture. Future growth in food supply must come from continued intensification of land use and gains in yields.

Although China is an agricultural country, government planners, especially since the death of Mao Tse-tung in 1976, have emphasized the need to industrialize. China has sufficient resources in coal, iron ore and oil to support an industrial economy, but it is deficient in capital and industrial technology. While refusing to bow to the wave of political reform sweeping through world socialism in 1990 and 1991 – the country's record on human rights is appalling – the Chinese leadership has loosened the reins on the economy, allowing certain market forces to operate, encouraging further foreign investment and promoting the enormous potential of tourism.

Beijing, the capital city of China, is a governmental and administrative centre of prime importance. Several buildings of outstanding architectural interest, such as the former imperial palace complex (once known as the Forbidden City) and the Temple and Altar of Heaven, have been carefully preserved and are now open to the public. In the 19th and early 20th centuries, with a large community of foreign merchants, Shanghai grew rapidly as a major banking and trading centre. Since 1949, the city has lost its former commercial importance, but it remained China's largest and has emerged as a major centre for iron and steel, ships, textiles and a wide range of engineering products ■

MACAU

Portugal declared Macau independent from China in 1849, and a century later proclaimed it an Overseas Province. This new flag for Macau replaces that of Portugal in the run-up to retrocession to China, on 20 December 1999.

COUNTRY Chinese territory under Portuguese administration
AREA 16 sq km [6 sq mls]
POPULATION 490,000
CURRENCY Pataca = 100 avos

A Portuguese colony from 1557 and for 200 years one of the great trading centres for silk, gold, spices and opium, Macau was overtaken in importance by Hong Kong in the 19th century. When China re-established diplomatic relations with the colonial power in 1979, the coastal enclave was redefined as 'Chinese territory under Portuguese administration', and in 1987 the powers agreed that the territory will return to China in 1999 as a Special Administrative Region of that country – an agreement based on the 'one country, two systems' principle used by China and Britain to settle the future of Hong Kong in 1984.

Macau is a peninsula at the head of the Canton (Pearl) River, 64 km [40 mls] west of Hong Kong and connected to China by a narrow isthmus. The main industries are textiles and tourism, but there is no airport – most visitors arrive via Hong Kong – and the territory, with a population that is 95% Chinese, is heavily reliant on the Chinese mainland for food, water and raw materials ■

TAIWAN

In 1928 the Nationalists adopted this design as China's national flag and used it in the long struggle against Mao Tse-tung's Communist army. When they were forced to retreat to Taiwan (then Formosa) in 1949, the flag went with them.

Taiwan is on the tropic line, but as the central island range reaches over 3,000 m [10,000 ft] at many points, it bears snow in the winter. Taipei has night temperatures below 20°C [68°F] from October to March, but over 30°C [86°F] in the daytime, June to September. There is heavy rainfall, heavier in the east than in the west of the island, falling mainly in the summer. Sunshine levels in the north are quite low – under 3 hours per day from December to March and only over 7 hours in July and August.

Ceded by the Chinese Empire to Japan in 1895, Taiwan was surrendered by the Japanese Army to General Chiang Kai-shek's Nationalist Chinese government in 1945. Beaten by Mao Tse-tung's Communists, some 2 million Nationalists and their leader fled the mainland to the island in the two years before 1949. The influx was met with hostility by the 8 million Taiwanese, and the new regime was imposed with force.

Boosted by help from the US, Chiang's government set about ambitious programmes for land reform and industrial expansion, the latter taking Taiwan into the world's top 20 nations by 1980 and providing high living standards. The island, nevertheless, remained politically isolated, losing its UN seat to Communist China in 1971, and being diplomatically abandoned by the US in 1979, when Washington switched recognition to Beijing. Though few countries take seriously Taipei's claim to be the sole legitimate government of China, the country administers a number of islands (*dao*) off the mainland, notably Quemoy (Jinmen) and Matsu (Mazu).

High mountain ranges, which extend for the entire length of the island, occupy the central and eastern parts of Taiwan, and only a quarter of the island's surface area is cultivated. The central ranges rise to altitudes of over 3,000 m [10,000 ft], and carry dense forests of broadleaved evergreen trees such as camphor and Chinese cork oak. Above 1,500 m [5,000 ft], conifers such as pine, larch and cedar dominate.

With its warm, moist climate, Taiwan provides a highly favourable environment for agriculture, and the well-watered lands of the western coastal plain produce heavy rice crops. Sugar cane, sweet potatoes, tea, bananas and pineapples are also grown. Recently, however, agriculture has declined as industrial output has risen.

COUNTRY Taiwan (Republic of China)
AREA 36,000 sq km [13,900 sq mls]
POPULATION 21,100,000
CAPITAL (POPULATION) Taipei (2,653,000)
GOVERNMENT Unitary multiparty republic with a unicameral legislature
ETHNIC GROUPS Taiwanese (Han Chinese) 84%, mainland Chinese 14%
LANGUAGES Mandarin Chinese (official)
RELIGIONS Buddhist 43%, Taoist and Confucian 49%, Christian 7%
NATIONAL DAY 10 October; Republic proclaimed (1911)
CURRENCY New Taiwan dollar = 100 cents
ANNUAL INCOME PER PERSON US$11,000
MAIN INDUSTRIES Textiles, electrical and electronic goods, chemicals and fertilizers, plastics, agriculture, fishing
MAIN EXPORTS Textiles and clothing 16%, electronic products 12%, information technology 7%, plastic and rubber 6%, footwear 6%, toys and games 5%
MAIN IMPORTS Machinery and electrical equipment 29%, base metals 13%, chemicals 11%, transport equipment 8%, crude oil 5%, foodstuffs 5%
DEFENCE 5.2% of GNP
POPULATION DENSITY 586 per sq km [1,518 per sq ml]
INFANT MORTALITY 6 per 1,000 live births
LIFE EXPECTANCY Female 78 yrs, male 72 yrs
ADULT LITERACY 93%
PRINCIPAL CITIES (POPULATION) Taipei 2,653,000 Kaohsiung 1,405,000 Taichung 817,000 Tainan 700,000 Panchiao 544,000

Taiwan produces a wide range of manufactured goods, including colour television sets, electronic calculators, footwear and ready-made clothing, and is the world's leading shipbreaker. Taipei, the capital, is a modern and affluent city, and an important administrative and cultural centre.

Less than half the size of Ireland or Tasmania, but supporting 21 million people, Taiwan has been a remarkable success story, averaging nearly 9% growth every year from 1953 to the 1990s. The authoritarian regime lifted martial law after nearly 40 years in 1987, a native Taiwanese became president in 1988, and in 1991 came the country's first general election. Technically still at war with Beijing, an intimidating series of naval exercises by China off the coast of Taiwan in 1996 caused grave concern ■

HONG KONG

Hong Kong flew the Blue Ensign from 1841 when it became a British dependent territory until July 1997 when it reverted to Chinese control, becoming a Special Administrative Region of China, and this new flag was adopted.

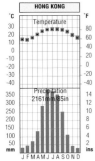

Situated on the south coast of China and within the tropics, Hong Kong experiences the full power of the South-east Asian monsoon. Winter is mild and has enough rain to keep the land green; rain falls on only about 30 days between October and February. The summer is hot and humid with heavy rain, particularly between May and September. Typhoons (cyclones) occur mainly from June to October. Many swing northwards towards Japan but those which cross the coast can do great damage.

COUNTRY Special Administrative Region of China
AREA 1,071 sq km [413 sq mls]
POPULATION 6,000,000
ETHNIC GROUPS Chinese 97%, others 2% (including European)
LANGUAGES English and Chinese (official)
RELIGIONS Buddhist majority, Confucian, Taoist, Christian, Muslim, Hindu, Sikh, Jewish
CURRENCY Hong Kong dollar = 100 cents
ANNUAL INCOME PER PERSON US$17,860
MAIN INDUSTRIES Textiles, electronics, watches, plastic goods, engineering, agriculture and fishing
MAIN EXPORTS Textiles, clothing, plastic and light metal products, electronic goods
MAIN IMPORTS Machinery, manufactures, chemicals
POPULATION DENSITY 5,602 per sq km [14,527 per sq ml]
LIFE EXPECTANCY Female 80 yrs, male 75 yrs
ADULT LITERACY 91%

On 1 July 1997 the British Crown Colony of Hong Kong passed back into the hands of the Chinese government. What Beijing received was Hong Kong Island, 235 smaller islands, the Kowloon peninsula on their province of Guangdong and the 'New Territories' adjoining it.

More important, they inherited the world's biggest container port, its biggest exporter of clothes and its tenth biggest trader. Hong Kong's economy has been so successful since World War II that its huge neighbour will be increasing its export earnings by over 25%; in return, under a 1984 accord, China has agreed to allow the territory to enjoy full economic autonomy and pursue its capitalist path for at least another 50 years. From 1996, increasingly detailed negotiations took place between Britain and China to safeguard the interests of the inhabitants, resulting in a successful handover on 30 June 1997.

Despite some uncertainty over Hong Kong's future role in world affairs, industrial development continued unabated up to the time of changeover: in 1992 Hong Kong embarked on its scheme for a new airport to replace the dangerous Kai Tak – the world's largest civil engineering project is due to be opened in 1998. Nevertheless, the economy has recently shown signs of slowing as some services shifted to rival countries such as Singapore.

The fortunes of this dynamic, densely populated community have been based on manufacturing, banking and commerce, with the sheltered waters between Kowloon and Hong Kong Island providing one of the world's finest natural deep-water harbours. Yet Hong Kong has few natural resources of its own and its prosperity has rested on the ingenuity, acumen and hard work of the people – only time will tell if these attributes will continue to flourish ■

NORTH KOREA

The Korean Democratic People's Republic has flown this flag since the country was split into two separate states in 1948. The colours are those of the traditional Korean standard, but in a new Communist design with a red star.

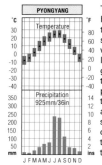

The eastern margins of Eurasia have much more extreme climates than those of the west, as can be seen by comparing Pyongyang with Lisbon at the same latitude. In winter, winds from central Asia give three months of bitterly cold temperatures with some snow, particularly on the mountains to the east; the winter low records are around –28°C [–18°F]. In the summer the wind blows from the ocean, bringing rain and increasing the average temperature by more than 30°C [54°F].

Mountains and rugged hills occupy most of the Korean peninsula, and only 20% of the surface area is suitable for cultivation. The interior of North Korea is a harsh environment, characterized by long and severe winters during which lakes and rivers regularly freeze over. High forested mountains, cut by river gorges, lie along the borders of North Korea and Manchuria. Further south, a chain of bare, eroded mountains runs for almost the entire length of the peninsula, parallel with and close to the eastern coast.

The most productive land in the peninsula occurs along the southern coast, where winters are relatively mild. While South Korea contains the best rice lands in the peninsula, most mineral resources, including coal – which supplies 70% of the country's energy needs – and iron ore, are concentrated in North Korea. Though the North has nearly 55% of the land area, it has only just over a third of the total Korean population.

While the country's collectivist agriculture programme has been reasonably successful – around 90% of cultivated land is under the control of co-operative farms – most of its effort went into the development of heavy industry, a decision which, after initial success, left the economy lagging well behind the 'sunrise' countries of the region, which moved quickly into electronics and computers. Defence, too, continues to be a significant drain on the economy.

The Stalinist regime of North Korea installed by the Soviet Union after World War II – and supported by China during the Korean War of 1950–3 – has been a total dictatorship revolving around the extraordinary and dynastic personality cult of Kim Il Sung and his nominated heir, Kim Jung Il, whom the president also designated his successor as supreme commander of the army. The world's most durable Communist ruler, Kim Il Sung

imposed on North Korea his own unique brand of Marxism-Leninism, resting on the principles of self-reliance and party supremacy, and created a forbidding society virtually closed to foreigners and with few international friends.

As the Cold War ended and the Soviet satellites strived for a new age, North Korea remained isolated from the momentous events taking place outside. In 1991, however, there were quite sudden signs of progress (see South Korea), with various and unexpected breakthroughs appearing to end confrontation on the peninsula.

However, the sudden death of the 'Great Leader' on 8 July 1994, at a time of increasing uncertainty surrounding North Korea's nuclear capabilities, cast a cloud of unease over the region as a whole ∎

COUNTRY Democratic People's Republic of Korea

AREA 120,540 sq km [46,540 sq mls]

POPULATION 23,931,000

CAPITAL (POPULATION) Pyongyang (2,639,000)

GOVERNMENT Single-party socialist republic

ETHNIC GROUPS Korean 99%

LANGUAGES Korean (official), Chinese

RELIGIONS Traditional beliefs 16%, Chondogyo 14%, Buddhist 2%, Christian 1%

NATIONAL DAY 15 August; Independence Day (1945)

CURRENCY North Korean won = 100 chon

ANNUAL INCOME PER PERSON US$1,000

MAIN PRIMARY PRODUCTS Coal, rice, iron ore

MAIN INDUSTRIES Agriculture, iron and steel, chemicals, engineering, cement

MAIN EXPORTS Iron and other metals, agricultural products, textiles

MAIN EXPORT PARTNERS CIS nations 44%, Japan 15%, China 13%

MAIN IMPORTS Crude petroleum, coal, machinery, transport equipment, chemicals, grain

MAIN IMPORT PARTNERS CIS nations 35%, China 19%, Japan 13%

DEFENCE 25.7% of GNP

POPULATION DENSITY 199 per sq km [514 per sq ml]

LIFE EXPECTANCY Female 72 yrs, male 66 yrs

ADULT LITERACY 95%

PRINCIPAL CITIES (POPULATION) Pyongyang 2,639,000 Hamhung 775,000 Chongjin 754,000

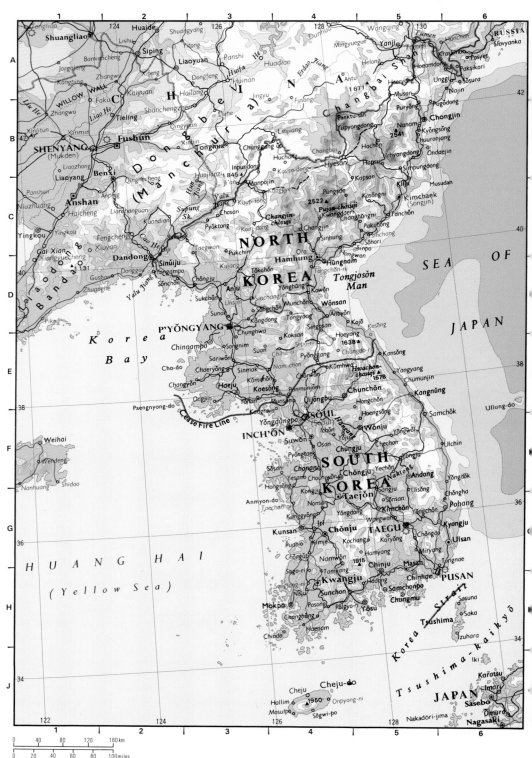

SOUTH KOREA

Adopted in 1950, South Korea's flag is the traditional white of peace. The central emblem signifies nature's opposing forces: the black symbols stand for the four seasons, the points of the compass, and the Sun, Moon, Earth and Heaven.

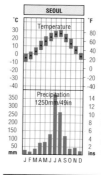

Strong north-westerly winds from central Asia give cold, dry weather in winter. Night temperatures, from December to March, are usually well below freezing. Snow occurs on the western slopes of the mountains to the east of Seoul. Summer is hot and wet, the rapid transition giving rise to sea fog around the coasts in spring as warmer air from the south moves over the cold water surface. In July and August it rains on average every other day; from September to May it usually rains on less than 5 days in a month.

For centuries the Koreans were very much a united people, an independent kingdom – 'Land of the Morning Calm' – knitted together by race, language and culture. Then, in 1910, came annexation by Japan and its harsh colonial rule, followed after World War II with division by the Allied powers into the Soviet (North) and American (South) zones of occupation each side of the 38th parallel. In 1948 the Soviets established a Communist regime in the North, the Americans a republic in the South, and the country – especially after the civil war of 1950–3 – seemed permanently partitioned. With a handful of interruptions, the two

governments retained their hostile positions on the artificial frontier for nearly four decades; then, in 1991, the sides began to talk.

They first came together over a combined table-tennis team, yet only ten months later they had signed a full-blown non-aggression pact. In January 1992, following New Year messages from both presidents talking of unification, they signed a nuclear weapons agreement, setting up a joint control committee. However, deep suspicion remains on both sides. Much depends on events in North Korea following the death in 1994 of Kim Il Sung, but with the re-establishment of heavy border patrols in the North in early 1996, the prospects for an end to all hostilities did not look very promising.

The story of South Korea since the civil war had been a very different one from the North, though it was hardly a Far Eastern oasis of liberalism. While land reform based on smallholdings worked well enough to produce some of the world's highest rice yields (and self-sufficiency in food grains), the real economic miracle came in industrial expansion from the early 1960s. Initiated by a military government – one of several bouts of army rule since the inauguration of the republic – and based on slender natural resources, the schemes utilized cheap, plentiful but well-educated labour to transform the economy and make South Korea one of the strongest countries in Asia. The original manufacturing base of textiles remains important, but South Korea is now a world leader in footwear (first), shipbuilding (second), consumer electronics, toys and vehicles.

Seoul, hiding its pollution and housing shortages as best it could, celebrated the country's growth by hosting the 1988 Olympic Games: from a population of 1.4 million in 1950, it had reached 10.6 million by 1990. The dynamism of the country must now be linked to more liberal policies – and less spending on defence.

The economy was growing, too: at nearly 9% a year from 1960 to 1990. South Korea has now opened up the possibility of trade links with China, which, though Communist, is desperate to broaden its economic possibilities, while approaches

are being made to bodies to recognize the country's achievements and net status. A major breakthrough occurred in 1991 when both North Korea and South Korea were admitted as full members of the United Nations ■

THE KOREAN WAR

Hastily divided in 1945 between a Soviet-occupied North and an American-occupied South, Korea was considered by most Western strategists an irrelevance to the developing Cold War. But when the heavily armed North invaded the South in June 1950, US President Truman decided to make a stand against what he saw (mistakenly) as Moscow-organized aggression. A Soviet boycott of the UN allowed US troops – assisted by contingents from Britain, Canada, France and other allies – to fight under the UN flag, and under General Douglas MacArthur they went on the offensive. American seapower permitted a landing far behind North Korean lines, and soon the Northerners were in retreat.

With some misgivings, Truman ordered his forces north of the 38th parallel, the former partition line. But as US troops neared the Chinese frontier in November 1950, hundreds of thousands of Chinese 'volunteers' surged across the Yalu River and threatened to overwhelm them. They retreated far southwards in disarray, until a 1951 counter-attack slowly pushed back up the country, and the combatants became entrenched along the 38th parallel in a bitter war of attrition that endured until an armistice was negotiated in 1953. Not until 1991, almost 40 years later, were North and South able to agree to a tentative non-aggression pact.

COUNTRY Republic of Korea

AREA 99,020 sq km [38,232 sq mls]

POPULATION 45,088,000

CAPITAL (POPULATION) Seoul (11,641,000)

GOVERNMENT Unitary multiparty republic

ETHNIC GROUPS Korean 99%

LANGUAGES Korean (official)

RELIGIONS Buddhist 28%, Protestant 19%, Roman Catholic 6%, Confucian 1%

NATIONAL DAY 15 August; Independence Day (1945)

CURRENCY South Korean won = 100 chon

ANNUAL INCOME PER PERSON US$7,670

MAIN PRIMARY PRODUCTS Tungsten, rice, fish

MAIN INDUSTRIES Agriculture, chemicals, electronic and electrical goods, shipbuilding, iron and steel

MAIN EXPORTS Transport equipment 11%, electrical machinery 9%, footwear 6%, textile fabrics 5%

MAIN EXPORT PARTNERS USA 39%, Japan 18%, Hong Kong 5%, Germany 4%, UK 3%, Canada 3%

MAIN IMPORTS Petroleum and petroleum products 11%, electronic components 6%, chemicals 5%

MAIN IMPORT PARTNERS Japan 33%, USA 21%, Germany 4%, Australia 3%

DEFENCE 3.8% of GNP

TOURISM 3,600,000 visitors per year

POPULATION DENSITY 455 per sq km [1,179 per sq ml]

LIFE EXPECTANCY Female 73 yrs, male 67 yrs

ADULT LITERACY 97%

PRINCIPAL CITIES (POPULATION) Seoul 11,641,000 Pusan 3,798,000 Taegu 2,229,000 Inchon 1,818,000

JAPAN

The geographical position of Japan in the East is expressed in the name of the country, *Nihon-Koku* (Land of the Rising Sun), and in the flag. Officially adopted in 1870, the simple design had been used by Japanese emperors for many centuries.

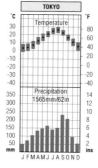

Despite its maritime location, Tokyo experiences a large annual range of temperature (23°C [41°F]) due to the seasonal reversal of wind, blowing from the cold heart of Asia in winter and from the warm Pacific in summer. Winter weather is usually fine and sunny, but cold, dry north-westerly winds often blow, and frost may occur as late as April. Summer in Tokyo is hot and humid with abundant rainfall. The day temperature in August is usually over 30°C [86°F].

The Japanese archipelago lies off the Asian mainland in an arc extending from 45°N to 30°N, occupying a latitudinal range comparable to the Atlantic seaboard of the USA from Maine to Florida. Four large and closely grouped islands (Hokkaido, Honshu, Shikoku and Kyushu) constitute 98% of the nation's territory, the remainder being made up of some 4,000 smaller islands, including the Ryukyus, which lie between Kyushu and Taiwan. Japan is a medium-sized country, smaller than France but slightly larger than Italy.

Japan is a predominantly mountainous country and only 16% of the land is cultivable. Although Japan lacks extensive habitable areas, the population is nevertheless the eighth largest in the world. Limited land must therefore support many people, and Japan is now one of the most densely populated

countries in the world – with an ever-ageing profile.

The Japanese islands occupy a zone of instability in the Earth's crust, and earthquakes and volcanic eruptions are frequent. Throughout Japan, complex folding and faulting has produced an intricate mosaic of landforms, in which mountains and forested hills alternate with small inland basins and coastal plains. The pattern of landforms is further complicated by the presence of several volcanic cones and calderas. The highest mountain in Japan, the majestic cone of Fuji-san (3,776 m [12,388 ft]) is a long-dormant volcano which last erupted in 1707.

In the mountains, fast-flowing torrents, fed by snowmelt in the spring and by heavy rainfall during the summer, have carved out a landscape of deep valleys and sharp ridges. In central Japan, dense mixed forests of oak, beech and maple blanket

mountain slopes to an altitude of 1,800 m [5,900 ft]; further north in Hokkaido, boreal forests of fir and spruce predominate. In central Honshu, the Japan Alps with their snow-capped ridges provide spectacular mountain scenery.

Small but intensively cultivated coastal plains, separated from one another by rugged mountain spurs, make up most of Japan's lowlands. None of the plains is extensive: the Kanto plain, which is the

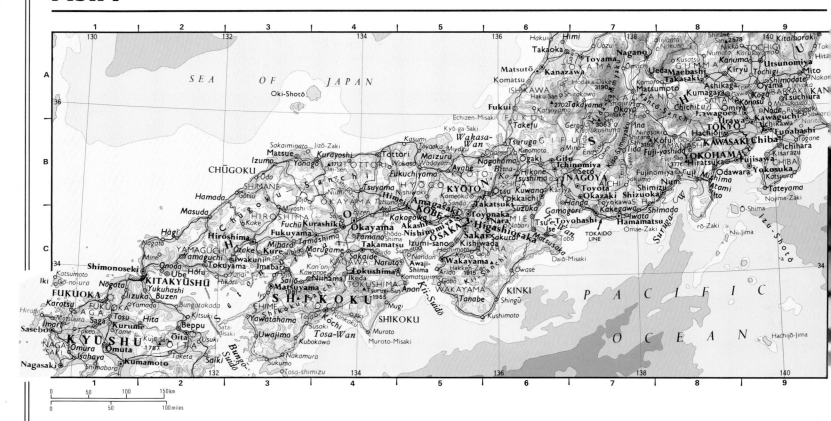

```
0   50   100  150 km
0        50       100 miles
```

largest, covers an area of only 13,000 sq km [5,000 sq mls]. Most of the coastal plains are formed of material deposited by rivers, and their soils have been improved by centuries of careful cultivation.

Early Japan was peopled by immigrants arriving in successive waves from Korea and elsewhere on the Asian mainland. The earliest zone of settlement included northern Kyushu and the coastlands of the Setonaikai (Inland Sea). By the 5th century AD, Japan was divided amongst numerous clans, of which the largest and most powerful was the Yamato. Shinto, a polytheistic religion based on nature worship, had already emerged, as had the Japanese imperial dynasty.

During the next three centuries, Chinese cultural and political influences entered Japan. These included Buddhism, the Chinese script, and Chinese methods of government and administration. At a later stage, Confucianism was also imported. Early cities, modelled on the capital of T'ang-dynasty China, were built at Nara (710) and at Kyoto (794); the latter city remained the seat of the imperial court until 1868.

The adoption of the Chinese system of centralized, bureaucratic government was relatively short-lived. From the early 12th century onwards, political power passed increasingly to military aristocrats, and government was conducted in the name of the emperor by warrior leaders known as *shoguns*. Civil warfare between rival groups of feudal lords was endemic over long periods, but under the rule of the Tokugawa *shoguns* (1603–1867), Japan enjoyed a great period of peace and prosperity; society was feudal and rigidly stratified, with military families (the feudal lords and their retainers, or *samurai*) forming a powerful élite. In the 1630s, Japan embarked on a lengthy phase of enforced isolation from the rest of the world.

This policy of seclusion could not be maintained indefinitely. In 1853, Commodore Perry of the US Navy arrived in Japan and demanded that ports be opened to Western trade. The capitulation of the *shogun* to Perry's demands prepared the way for the overthrow of the Tokugawa government, and the Meiji Restoration (1868) resumed imperial rule.

Under Western-style government, a programme of modernization was set in train. Industrialization proceeded swiftly, and after victories in the Sino-Japanese War (1894–5) and the Russo-Japanese War (1904–5), Japan began to build up an overseas empire which included the colonies of Taiwan and Korea. The growing strength of the Japanese military was demonstrated by the army's seizure of Manchuria in 1931. During the 1930s, and especially after the outbreak of war between Japan and China in 1937, militarist control of the government of Japan grew steadily. In 1941, the launching of a surprise attack on the American naval base of Pearl Harbor, in Hawaii, took Japan – and drew the USA – into World War II.

From its defeat in 1945 to 1952, Japan was administered by US forces. Many liberal and democratic reforms were enacted, and under the new constitution the power of the emperor was much reduced, with sovereignty vested in the people.

The main centres of population and industry are concentrated within a narrow corridor stretching from the Kanto plain, through the coastlands of the Setonaikai, to northern Kyushu. This heavily urbanized zone contains nine cities with populations of over a million and three great industrial regions, centring respectively on Tokyo, Osaka and Nagoya. The capital Tokyo forms the nucleus of a large and congested conurbation, and by most measures remains comfortably the world's most populous metropolis ∎

COUNTRY Japan (Nippon)	**IMPORTS** US$1,713 per person
AREA 377,800 sq km [145,869 sq mls]	**MAIN IMPORTS** Petrol and petroleum products 18%, food and live animals 14%, machinery and transport equipment 11%, metals 10%, chemicals 8%, timber and cork 4%, textile fibres 2%
POPULATION 125,156,000	
CAPITAL (POPULATION) Tokyo (Tokyo–Yokohama, 26,836,000)	
GOVERNMENT Constitutional monarchy	**MAIN IMPORT PARTNERS** USA 21%, Indonesia 5%, South Korea 5%, Australia 5%, China 4%, Saudi Arabia 4%, Taiwan 4%
ETHNIC GROUPS Japanese 99%, Chinese, Korean, Ainu	
LANGUAGES Japanese (official), Chinese, Korean	**EDUCATIONAL EXPENDITURE** 5% of GNP
RELIGIONS Shinto 93%, Buddhism 74%, Christian 1% (most Japanese consider themselves to be both Shinto and Buddhist)	**DEFENCE** 1% of GNP
	TOTAL ARMED FORCES 237,400
	TOURISM 3,747,000 visitors per year
NATIONAL DAY 23 December; the Emperor's birthday	**ROADS** 1,127,500 km [700,600 mls]
CURRENCY Yen = 100 sen	**RAILWAYS** 25,776 km [16,016 mls]
ANNUAL INCOME PER PERSON US$31,450	**POPULATION DENSITY** 331 per sq km [858 per sq ml]
SOURCE OF INCOME Agriculture 2%, industry 41%, services 57%	**URBAN POPULATION** 77%
	POPULATION GROWTH 0.3% per year
MAIN PRIMARY PRODUCTS Rice, vegetables, timber, fish, copper, gold, sulphur, natural gas, coal, lead	**BIRTHS** 12 per 1,000 population
	DEATHS 8 per 1,000 population
MAIN INDUSTRIES Iron and steel, electrical and electronic equipment, cars, ships, textiles, chemicals, food processing, forestry, petroleum refining	**INFANT MORTALITY** 5 per 1,000 live births
	LIFE EXPECTANCY Female 82 yrs, male 76 yrs
	POPULATION PER DOCTOR 600 people
EXPORTS US$2,235 per person	**ADULT LITERACY** 99%
MAIN EXPORTS Machinery, electrical, electronic equipment 36%, vehicles and transport equipment 20%, iron and steel 6%, chemicals 6%, textiles 3%, ships 2%	**PRINCIPAL CITIES (POPULATION)** Tokyo–Yokohama 26,836,000 Osaka 10,601,000 Nagoya 2,159,000 Sapporo 1,732,000 Kobe 1,509,000 Kyoto 1,452,000 Fukuoka 1,269,000 Kawasaki 1,200,000
MAIN EXPORT PARTNERS USA 34%, South Korea 6%, Germany 6%, Taiwan 5%, Hong Kong 4%, UK 3%, China 3%	

THE JAPANESE BOOM

In 1945 Japan lay in ruins, with its major cities in ashes – two of them dangerously radioactive. Its smouldering ports were choked with the sunken remnants of its merchant marine, and its people were demoralized. Less than two generations later, the Japanese economy was second only to that of the USA. Its high-technology products dominated world markets, while Japanese banks and private investors owned huge slices of industry and real estate on every continent.

The far-sighted American Occupation authorities deserve some of the credit. Realizing that industrial recovery could only go hand in hand with political development, they wrote Japan a new constitution. As a link with the past, the Emperor kept his place, but as a constitutional monarch answerable to a democratically elected Diet, with women given full voting rights for the first time. Trade unions, with the right to strike, were established, and land reform eliminated politically subservient tenants: by 1950, 90% of farmland was owner-cultivated. Great industrial conglomerates were broken into smaller units, and education was enormously expanded. Most ordinary Japanese accepted the reforms: they remembered the pain the old ways had brought.

The Korean War in 1950 gave the slowly recovering Japanese economy a tremendous boost. Japanese factories, well paid in American dollars, provided much of the steel, vehicles and other equipment the war demanded. When the Occupation formally ended in 1952, Japan was clearly on the way up. The American military presence, guaranteed by treaty, continued, but caused no resentment; on the contrary, safe beneath the US defence umbrella, Japan could devote its resources to productive industry, not armaments.

The Japanese owed the first stage of their transformation to the Americans; the rest, they did themselves. Carefully planned economic policies, directed by the Ministry of Trade and Industry –

nicknamed 'Japan Inc.'s Corporate Headquarters' – directed investment to key industries. First, the metal, engineering and chemical industries were rationalized and modernized. With the education system producing a steady stream of graduates, already trained in the industrial disciplines their future employers required, results were soon appearing. In the 1950s and 1960s efficient Japanese steelmakers consistently undersold European and American rivals, while producing better-quality steel. 'Made in Japan', once a sneering joke to describe shoddy goods, was taking on an entirely new commercial meaning.

Japan's major weakness was its near-total lack of natural resources; but foresight and planning made up for them. After the 1970s oil crisis, it was clear that the costs of heavy industry were going to rise unprofitably high; besides, the pollution they had brought was reaching dangerous levels. MITI switched resources to automobiles and electronics. Soon, Japan began to capture and dominate these markets, too.

By the 1980s, Japan's trading partners were becoming seriously alarmed. Noting that trade with Japan was largely a one-way traffic – Japan's home market is still notoriously hard to penetrate – they built protective walls of tariffs and duties. Japan responded with its usual flexibility: it bought factories within its rivals' walls, and traded from there. The Tokyo stock market even survived a serious 'crash' in the spring of 1992 – testament to the strength of the national economy. Even so, Japan's colossal trade surpluses in the early 1990s were causing not only resentment but also real danger to the world economic system.

US President Bush secured some trading assurances from the Tokyo government, but these were largely cosmetic – and many economic experts continued to predict that the Japanese GNP figure would indeed be greater than that of the USA by the end of the century.

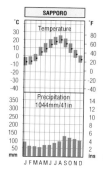

The winters of the north are cold with much snow. At Sapporo temperatures below −20°C [4°F] have been recorded between December and March, and frosts can occur from October to April. The temperature averages from November to May are all below 10°C [50°F]. Rain falls throughout the year, but it is drier February to June. Rainfall is just over 1,000 mm [39 in], but Hokkaido is one of the driest parts of Japan. The summers are warm with temperatures often exceeding 30°C [86°F].

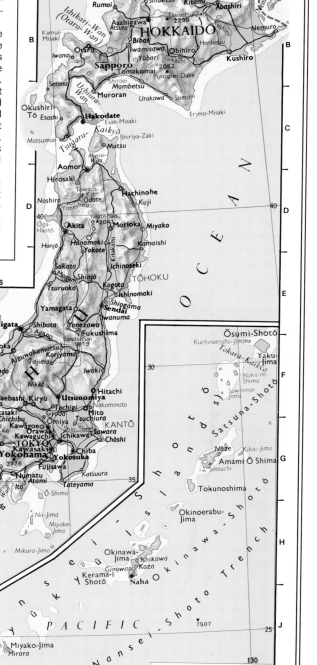

RYŪKYŪ ISLANDS
Continuation southwards in same scale

ASIA

BURMA (MYANMAR)

The colours were adopted following independence from Britain in 1948. The Socialist symbol, added in 1974, includes a ring of 14 stars for the country's states. The gearwheel represents industry and the rice plant symbolizes agriculture.

Once a green and gentle land, rich in agriculture and timber and blessed with many natural resources from precious stones to oil, Burma has become one of the three poorest countries in Asia and run by a regime whose record on human rights is among the world's worst. A change of name – the title Union of Myanmar was officially adopted in 1989 – has not changed the political complexion of a desperate nation.

Geographically, the country has three main regions. The core area is a great structural depression, largely drained by the Chindwin and Irrawaddy rivers. Its coastal zone has a wet climate, but the inner region between Prome and Mandalay constitutes a 'dry zone', sheltered from the south-west monsoon and with an annual rainfall of less than 1,000 mm [40 in]. In this dry zone, which was the original nucleus of the Burmese state, small-scale irrigation has long been practiced in the narrow valleys, and rice, cotton, jute and sugar cane are important crops. Until 1964 Burma was the world's leading exporter of rice (slipping to seventh place by 1993), and the crop still accounts for more than 40% of Burma's meagre export earnings. This central area was also the base of Burmah Oil, hosting the small fields that once made the country the British Empire's second largest producer. Even today it has sufficient oil and gas to meet most of Burma's needs.

To the west lie the fold mountains of the Arakan Yoma, while to the east rises the great Shan Plateau. In the south-east, running down the isthmus that takes Burma on to the Malay Peninsula, are the uplands of the Tenasserim, with hundreds of islands dotted along the coast of the Andaman Sea. More than 60% of the country is forested, rubber plantations augmenting the indigenous teak.

British since 1895, Burma was separate from

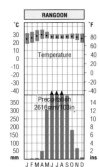

The rain associated with the south-east monsoon affects all the Burmese coastlands (4,000 mm [160 in]), but the rainfall is less in the shadows of the mountain ranges, with a dry zone in the middle Irrawaddy (400 mm [16 in]). The rainy season is May to October, and a very dry period is centred on December to January. Snow falls on the mountains of the north and east, but they also act as a barrier to the colder northern winter winds. Temperatures are high with little annual variation.

India as a crown colony in 1937. A battleground for Japanese and British troops in World War II, it became an independent republic in 1948 and left the Commonwealth. Military dictatorship came in 1962 and a one-party state in 1974, both headed by General Ne Win, leader of the Burma Socialist Programme Party.

'The Burmese Way to Socialism'

The party's rigid combination of state control, Buddhism and isolation, under the banner 'The Burmese Way to Socialism', had disastrous results, the country plunging quickly from prosperity to poverty. Politically, too, Burma was in a perilous state, with over a third of the country in rebel hands.

In the south-east the guerrillas of two Karen liberation movements control large tracts of mountains near the Thai border; in the north and east the Burmese Communist Party holds sway in most of Kachin and a good deal of Shan; here also, at the western end of the 'Golden Triangle', the authorities try to contain the local warlords' trafficking in opium. Another flashpoint is in the west, where Rohinya, the Muslim minority, have been persecuted by the army and repeatedly pushed over the border with Bangladesh in tens of thousands.

Burma spends more than 35% of its budget on 'defence' – much of it on the brutal suppression of political opposition and of human rights. In 1990, the coalition NLD won over 80% of the votes in a multiparty election conceded by the regime following violent demonstrations, but the ruling junta simply refused to accept the result – keeping its leader, Nobel Peace Prize winner Aung San Suu Kyi, under house arrest until July 1995. The powerless opposition were forced to renounce the result and agree to a new and no doubt again ineffective agenda for a return to democracy.

Meanwhile, the country continued to crumble, if with great charm; despite the hideous regime a black market flourishes behind the crumbling colonial façade of Rangoon, once a rival to Bangkok and Singapore. Though some visitors make the trips around the attractions of Rangoon, Mandalay and Pagan, tourism is hardly encouraged by the suspicious government, and much of the country is still closed to foreigners.

Tenth biggest nation in Asia in both area and population, Burma remains an anomaly, holding out almost friendless against the tide of democratic and diplomatic change that swept the world in the late 1980s and early 1990s. It seems that, even with some method of conciliation, it will not long survive in its present form ■

COUNTRY Union of Myanmar (Socialist Republic of the Union of Burma)

AREA 676,577 sq km [261,228 sq mls]

POPULATION 46,580,000

CAPITAL (POPULATION) Rangoon (2,513,000)

GOVERNMENT Transitional government

ETHNIC GROUPS Burman 69%, Shan 9%, Karen 6%, Rakhine 5%, Mon 2%, Chin 2%, Kachin 1%

LANGUAGES Burmese (official), English

RELIGIONS Buddhist 89%, Christian 5%, Muslim 4%

CURRENCY Kyat = 100 pyas

ANNUAL INCOME PER PERSON US$500

MAIN PRIMARY PRODUCTS Zinc, tungsten, nickel, natural gas, oil, rubber, timber, cotton, groundnuts

MAIN INDUSTRIES Forestry, mining, fishing, oil production

MAIN EXPORTS Rice 41%, teak 24%, metals and ores 9%

MAIN EXPORT PARTNERS India 12%, EU countries 12%, African countries 9%, Japan 6%, Middle East 6%

MAIN IMPORTS Machinery 18%, base metals 10%, transport equipment 8%

MAIN IMPORT PARTNERS Japan 33%, EU countries 13%, Eastern Europe 16%

DEFENCE 3.1% of GNP

TOURISM 21,600 visitors per year

POPULATION DENSITY 69 per sq km [178 per sq ml]

INFANT MORTALITY 59 per 1,000 live births

LIFE EXPECTANCY Female 64 yrs, male 61 yrs

ADULT LITERACY 81%

PRINCIPAL CITIES (POPULATION) Rangoon 2,513,000 Mandalay 533,000 Moulmein 220,000 Pegu 150,000

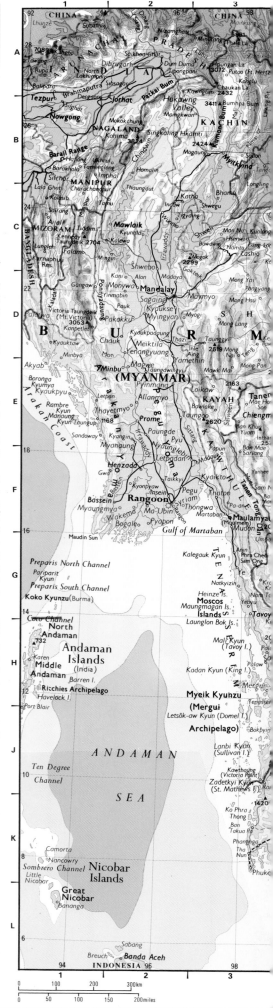

THAILAND

The two red and white stripes are all that remain of Thailand's traditional red-on-white elephant emblem, removed from the flag in 1916. The blue stripe was added in 1917 to show solidarity with the Allies in World War I.

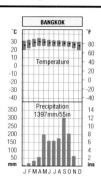

BANGKOK

Precipitation 1397mm/55in

Mountains shelter Bangkok from the rain-bearing south-westerly winds in summer, and although the distribution of rainfall is similar to much of South-east Asia, the total is relatively small, being less than half that of the other side of the mountains, a short distance to the west. Sometimes there can be near-drought conditions in November to April. The warm waters of the Gulf of Thailand to the south sustain high temperatures throughout the year. March to May are the hottest months.

Meaning 'Land of the Free' (*Muang Thai*), and known as Siam until 1939, Thailand is the only South-east Asian country that has not been colonized, or occupied by foreign powers, except in war. Comparable in size to France or Spain, Thailand is centred on the valley of the Chao Phraya River that flows across the central plain extending from the Gulf of Siam to the foothills of the northern mountains. Bounded in the west by the narrow mountain range that borders Burma, and in the east by lower hills separating the plain from the higher Khorat Plateau (Cao Nguyen Khorat), the central plain is Thailand's rice bowl; it presents long vistas, with extensive rice fields, canals and rivers that provide the main routeways, with villages on stilts.

The capital city Bangkok stands at the southern edge of the plain, near the mouth of the Chao Phraya; with a seaport and international airport it is the transport centre of the country. Ornate Buddhist temples stand side by side with modern concrete buildings, and the growing population is already over a tenth of the total. Extraordinarily, the country's next largest city is less than 280,000.

Northern Thailand is a region of fold mountains, with agriculturally rich intermontane basins. The hill forests produce teak and other valuable timbers. Thailand's highest mountain, Doi Inthanon (2,576 m [8,451 ft]), and the high hills surrounding it are the home of many hill tribes who live by shifting cultivation of dry rice and opium poppies; Chiengmai, the beautiful northern capital, lies in this area. The Khorat Plateau to the east is a sandstone region of poor soils supporting savanna woodlands; its main crops are glutinous rice, and cassava (the country is the fourth largest producer in the world, after Brazil, Nigeria and Zaïre). The long southern part of Thailand, linked to the Malay Peninsula by the Isthmus of Kra, is a forested region of rolling hills, producing tin ore and plantation rubber.

Economy and politics

Thailand has long been famous for rice production; though fifth in the world league, it is the biggest exporter and it is still the country's best agricultural earner, despite the increasing importance of several other commodities including rubber, tapioca products and sugar. Wolfram, forest products and fisheries are also being exploited. Industries remain largely underdeveloped, but manufacturing based on cheap labour is expanding rapidly in textiles, clothing, electrical goods and food processing, contributing more to GDP than agriculture since 1984, while local crafts in the villages help to provide overseas income, as does tourism. In 1993 Thailand received nearly 5.5 million visitors (compared with Burma's 21,600).

An absolute monarchy until 1932, when the king graciously surrendered to a bloodless coup that set up a provisional constitution, Thailand has seen a more stable recent history than most of its unfortunate neighbours, though for most of the next 40 years it was dominated by military rulers. Forced into alliance with Japan in World War II, the Thais aligned themselves firmly to the USA after 1945 – a policy that has brought much military, technical and financial aid.

Despite continuing army involvements and interventions – the bloodless coup of 1991, claimed to be protecting King Rama IX and promising a swift return to civilian democracy, was the 17th takeover in half a century – and despite the presence of Cambodian refugees and its use by various camps as a political conduit and military springboard for intentions in South-east Asia, Thailand's subtle and pragmatic approach to life has seen the country prosper. In a system often referred to as 'semi-democracy', constitutional rule propped up by the pillars of military, monarch, bureaucracy and religion, Thailand has managed (not without criticism) to avoid the dreadful events that have afflicted the rest of mainland South-east Asia since the end of World War II – though in May 1992 the un-elected leadership found itself under serious pressure. Hundreds died in protests against the takeover as prime minister by the head of the army, and an uneasy peace was restored only after his removal and an appeal for order from the king. Elections were held and a civilian government under Prime Minister Chuan Leekpai took office.

Situated about 30 km [20 mls] from the Gulf of Thailand, Bangkok is perhaps more dominant in its country's life than any Asian capital. A chaotic city of nearly 6 million people, it is a remarkable mixture of ancient and modern, subtle and gauche. The old city is a place of more than 300 temples and monasteries (*wats*) dotted near canals (*klongs*). Founded as a royal capital in 1782, this 'Venice of the East' is rich in examples of Thai culture, including fantastic statues of Buddha.

The name Bangkok is in fact incorrect: it means 'village of the wild plum' and refers only to the Thon Buri side of the Chao Phraya River; the proper term is Krung Thep ('city of angels' – like Los Angeles). Today, however, it is a sprawling metropolis with high levels of traffic congestion, struggling to absorb the waves of migrants who pour in from the rural areas in search of work ■

COUNTRY Kingdom of Thailand

AREA 513,120 sq km [198,116 sq mls]

POPULATION 58,432,000

CAPITAL (POPULATION) Bangkok (5,876,000)

GOVERNMENT Constitutional monarchy with a multiparty bicameral legislature

ETHNIC GROUPS Thai 80%, Chinese 12%, Malay 4%, Khmer 3%

LANGUAGES Thai (official), Chinese, Malay

RELIGIONS Buddhist 94%, Muslim 4%, Christian 1%

CURRENCY Thai baht = 100 satang

ANNUAL INCOME PER PERSON US$2,040

MAIN PRIMARY PRODUCTS Rice, rubber, maize, sugar cane, cassava, timber, fish, fruit, tin, iron, tungsten

MAIN INDUSTRIES Agriculture, food processing, paper, cement, clothing, mining, forestry

MAIN EXPORTS Textiles and clothing 15%, rice 9%, rubber 7%, tapioca products 5%, canned fish products 4%

MAIN EXPORT PARTNERS USA 19%, Japan 15%, Singapore 9%, Netherlands 7%, Germany 5%, Hong Kong 4%

MAIN IMPORTS Machinery and transport equipment 34%, basic manufactures 20%, chemicals 15%, fuels and lubricants 13%, crude materials 8%, foodstuffs 4%

MAIN IMPORT PARTNERS Japan 26%, USA 12%, Singapore 8%, Germany 6%, Malaysia 4%, China 4%, Taiwan, UK

DEFENCE 2.7% of GNP

TOURISM 5,500,000 visitors per year

POPULATION DENSITY 114 per sq km [295 per sq ml]

INFANT MORTALITY 24 per 1,000 live births

LIFE EXPECTANCY Female 69 yrs, male 65 yrs

ADULT LITERACY 94%

PRINCIPAL CITIES (POPULATION) Bangkok 5,876,000 Nakhon Ratchasima 278,000 Songkhla 243,000

ASIA

LAOS

Since 1975 Laos has flown the flag of the Pathet Lao, the Communist movement which won the long struggle for control of the country. The blue stands for the Mekong River, the white disk for the moon, and the red for the unity and purpose of the people.

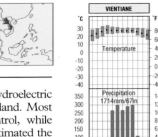

Like much of South-east Asia, Laos experiences the seasonal reversal of winds associated with the monsoon. In winter Vientiane is sheltered from the north-east winds by mountains and the weather is sunny and dry. Rain falls often on only 1–5 days per month, October to April. The temperature increases steadily until April, when south-westerly winds mark the beginning of the wet season. There is great variation in daily sunshine, with 1–3 hours June to September, and 6–7 hours November to March.

Designated Asia's poorest country by the World Bank in 1989, Laos is a narrow, landlocked, largely mountainous country with no railways – the Mekong River is the main artery – where 85% of the sparse population work on collective farms at subsistence level, growing mainly rice. The hilly terrain broadens in the north to a wide plateau, 2,000 m [6,500 ft] above sea level, which includes the Plain of Jars, named after prehistoric stone funerary jars found by early French colonialists.

The Communists took power in 1975 after two decades of chaotic civil war following the departure of the colonial French, their policies bringing isolation and stagnation under the dominance of the Vietnamese government in Hanoi, who had used Laos as a great supply line during their war with the USA.

In 1986 the Politburo embarked on their own version of *perestroika*, opening up trade links with neighbours (notably China and Japan), but most

crucially developing the export of hydroelectric power from the Mekong River to Thailand. Most enterprises are now outside state control, while alternative crops to opium (Laos was estimated the world's third biggest source in the late 1980s) are being tried. Political reform towards a multiparty democracy, however, remains a forlorn hope ■

COUNTRY Lao People's Democratic Republic	**NATIONAL DAY** 2 December
AREA 236,800 sq km [91,428 sq mls]	**CURRENCY** Kip = 100 at
POPULATION 4,906,000	**ANNUAL INCOME PER PERSON** US$290
CAPITAL (POPULATION) Vientiane (449,000)	**MAIN PRIMARY PRODUCTS** Rice, tin, gypsum
GOVERNMENT Single-party socialist republic with a unicameral legislature	**MAIN INDUSTRIES** Subsistence farming
ETHNIC GROUPS Lao 67%, Mon-Khmer 17%, Tai 8%	**MAIN EXPORTS** Electricity 50%, wood 29%, coffee
LANGUAGES Lao (official), French	**MAIN IMPORTS** Machinery and vehicles, petroleum, woven cotton fabrics
RELIGIONS Buddhist 58%, tribal religionist 34%, Christian 2%, Muslim 1%	**POPULATION DENSITY** 21 per sq km [54 per sq ml]
	LIFE EXPECTANCY Female 53 yrs, male 50 yrs
	ADULT LITERACY 54%

CAMBODIA

As well as being associated with Communism and revolution, red is the traditional colour of Cambodia. The silhouette is the historic temple of Angkor Wat. The blue symbolizes the water resources which are so vital to the people of Cambodia.

The heartland of Cambodia is a wide basin drained by the Mekong River, in the centre of which lies the Tonlé Sap ('Great Lake'), a former arm of the sea surrounded by a broad plain. From November to June, when rains are meagre and the Mekong low, the lake drains to the south and away to the sea. During the rainy season and period of high river water in June to October the flow reverses, and the lake more than doubles its area to become the largest freshwater lake in Asia.

The Tonlé Sap lowlands were the cradle of the great Khmer Empire, which lasted from 802 to 1432; its zenith came in the reign of Suryavarman II (1113–50), who built the great funerary temple of Angkor Wat; together with Angkor Thom, the 600 Hindu temples form the world's largest group of religious buildings. The wealth of 'the gentle kingdom' rested on abundant fish from the lake and rice from the flooded lowlands, for which an extensive system of irrigation channels and storage reservoirs was developed.

To the south-west stand low mountain chains, while the northern rim of the country is bounded by the Phanom Dangrek uplands, with a prominent sandstone escarpment. Three-quarters of the country is forested, and 90% of the population live on the fertile plains, mostly in small village settlements;

Phnom Penh, the capital, is the only major city.

Cambodia was under French rule from 1863 as part of French Indo-China, achieving independence in 1954. In a short period of stability during the late 1950s and 1960s the country developed its small-scale agricultural resources and rubber plantations – it has few workable minerals or sources of power – remaining predominantly rural but achieving self-sufficiency in food, with some exports. However, following years of internal political struggles, involvement in the Vietnam War, a destructive civil war and a four-year period of ruthless Khmer Rouge dictatorship – under which Pol Pot ordered the genocide of somewhere between 1 million and 2.5 million people – Cambodia was left devastated.

After the overthrow of Pol Pot in 1979 by Viet-

nam there was civil war between their puppet government of the People's Republic of Kampuchea (Cambodia) and the government of Democratic Kampuchea, a coalition of Prince Sihanouk – deposed by a US-backed coup in 1970 – Son Sann's Khmer People's Liberation Front and the Khmer Rouge, who from 1982 claimed to have abandoned their Communist ideology. It was this strange tripartite government in exile that was recognized by the United Nations.

Denied almost any aid, Cambodia continued to decline, but it was only the withdrawal of Vietnamese troops in 1989, sparking a fear of a Khmer Rouge revival, that forced a settlement. In October 1991, following numerous failures, a UN-brokered peace plan for elections by 1993 was accepted by all parties concerned, and a glimmer of real hope returned to the beleaguered people of Cambodia. A new constitution was adopted in September 1993, restoring the parliamentary monarchy. The Khmer Rouge continued hostilities, but were formally banned in June 1994 ■

COUNTRY State of Cambodia	**RELIGIONS** Buddhist 88%, Muslim 2%
AREA 181,040 sq km [69,900 sq mls]	**CURRENCY** Riel = 100 sen
POPULATION 10,452,000	**ANNUAL INCOME PER PERSON** US$200
CAPITAL (POPULATION) Phnom Penh (920,000)	**MAIN PRIMARY PRODUCTS** Salt, iron ore, phosphates
GOVERNMENT Constitutional monarchy with a unicameral legislature	**MAIN INDUSTRIES** Agriculture
ETHNIC GROUPS Khmer 94%, Chinese 3%, Cham 2%, Thai, Lao, Kola, Vietnamese	**MAIN EXPORTS** Iron and steel, rubber manufactures
LANGUAGES Khmer (official), French	**MAIN IMPORTS** Machinery and transport equipment
	POPULATION DENSITY 58 per sq km [150 per sq ml]
	ADULT LITERACY 35%

VIETNAM

First used by the forces of Ho Chi Minh in the liberation struggle against Japan in World War II, the design was adopted as the national flag of North Vietnam in 1945. It was retained when the two parts of the country were reunited in 1975.

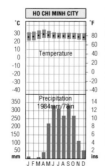

Temperature variation throughout the year is not great. April and May are the hottest months, with the period from November to January the coolest, but never falling below 25°C [77°F]. Night temperatures rarely fall below 20°C [68°F]. There are lower temperatures in the inland mountains. There is heavy rainfall throughout the year, except January to March which are drier, with some years having no rain in these months. Typhoons (cyclones) can hit the coastal areas.

A land of mountains, coastal plains and deltas, Vietnam is perhaps Asia's most strangely shaped country. In the north the coastal lands widen into the valley and delta of the Hongha (Red) River and the valley of the Da. This region has long been the main cultural focus of the country, and it was the original core of the Annamite Empire which came

into being with the revolt against Chinese rule in AD 939. In the south of the country, the coastal plains open out into the great delta of the Mekong, the world's tenth longest river.

For most of their length the coastal lowlands are backed in the west by the mountains of the Annamite Chain, and to the north the country is

dominated by the plateaus of Laos and Tongking, often characterized by an intensely craggy, inhospitable karstic (limestone) landscape. The mountain areas are the home of many different hill peoples.

Vietnam already had a long and turbulent history before the French, following decades of missionary involvement and a military campaign lasting 25 years, made it a French protectorate in 1883, later joined by Laos and Cambodia in the French Indo-Chinese Union. Freedom movements starting early in the 20th century made little headway until the end of World War II, when Communist-led guerrillas under Ho Chi Minh, having fought the Japanese occupation, declared Vietnam once again united and free. There followed a war against the French (1946–54), which produced Communist North Vietnam and non-Communist South Vietnam, and then the cataclysm of over a decade of war against the USA, before reunification as a Communist state.

Vietnam was left exhausted – 2 million of its people died in the American war alone and the countryside was devastated – and the problems facing the new Communist government in 1976 were enormous. Doctrinaire policies and further aggravation of the Western powers in Cambodia did not help its economic and political isolation,

and in 1978 there started the sad saga of the 'Boat People' – peasants fleeing hardship and perhaps persecution in Vietnam to find a new life in Hong Kong and elsewhere; after being put into camps, many were forcibly repatriated years later.

The Hanoi regime softened its position in many ways from the late 1980s, efforts being made to establish diplomatic and trading ties with important international clients and aid donors, Soviet assis-

tance having dwindled with the events in the USSR. In the 1990s, Vietnam began to introduce reforms, and in 1995 relations with the US were normalized when the US opened an embassy in Hanoi.

However, Vietnam remains a poor nation subsisting on agriculture: rice, cassava, maize, sweet potatoes and the world's largest population of ducks. Despite the industries of the north, based on natural resources, the economy needs to diversify ■

COUNTRY Socialist Republic of Vietnam

AREA 331,689 sq km [128,065 sq mls]

POPULATION 74,580,000

CAPITAL (POPULATION) Hanoi (3,056,000)

GOVERNMENT Unitary single-party socialist state

ETHNIC GROUPS Vietnamese 87%, Tho (Tay) 2%, Chinese (Hoa) 2%, Tai 2%, Khmer, Muong, Nung

LANGUAGES Vietnamese (official), Chinese, Tho, Khmer, Muong, Tai, Nung, Miao, Jarai, Rhadé, Hre, Bahnar

RELIGIONS Buddhist 55%, Roman Catholic 7%

NATIONAL DAY 2–3 September

CURRENCY Dong = 10 hao = 100 xu

ANNUAL INCOME PER PERSON US$170

MAIN PRIMARY PRODUCTS Coal, anthracite, lignite, cereals, timber

MAIN INDUSTRIES Mining, food processing, textiles, agriculture

MAIN EXPORTS Raw materials 46%, handicrafts 24%, agricultural products 10%

MAIN EXPORT PARTNERS CIS nations 51%, Hong Kong 14%, Japan 9%, Singapore 9%, Czech and Slovak Republics 5%, EU countries 3%, Poland 2%, Hungary 2%

MAIN IMPORTS Fuel and raw materials 45%, machinery 23%, wheat flour and food products 17%

MAIN IMPORT PARTNERS CIS nations 69%, Japan 8%, Singapore 7%, Hong Kong 3%, EU countries 3%

POPULATION DENSITY 220 per sq km [569 per sq ml]

INFANT MORTALITY 54 per 1,000 live births

LIFE EXPECTANCY Female 66 yrs, male 62 yrs

ADULT LITERACY 92%

PRINCIPAL CITIES (POPULATION) Ho Chi Minh City 3,924,000 Hanoi 3,056,000 Haiphong 1,448,000 Da Nang 370,000

CONFLICT IN INDO-CHINA

Vietnamese conflict dates back at least to 1939, when the Viet Minh coalition of nationalists, including Communists, began agitating for independence from France; by 1945, with experience in anti-Japanese resistance behind them, they would not accept a quiet return to colonial administration after the Japanese collapse. Proclaiming the Democratic Republic of Vietnam, within months they were fighting French troops sent from Europe. Gradually, the Viet Minh, increasingly dominated by a well-organized Communist leadership under Ho Chi Minh, began to overwhelm the French. The USA, alarmed by the Viet Minh's Communism, provided weaponry and logistical support, but Presidents Truman and Eisenhower both refused to allow American military aid. The climax came in May 1954, when a besieged French army surrendered at Dien Bien Phu. At a subsequent peace conference at Geneva, the French abandoned their colony. The country was partitioned between a Communist north, its capital in Hanoi, and a non-Communist south, administered from Saigon. The Geneva accord assumed Vietnamese elections would follow, and included an explicit proviso: the division was 'provisional, and should not in any way be interpreted as constituting a political or territorial boundary'.

Still anxious to avoid military engagement, the USA poured aid into the South, the supposedly Democratic Republic of Vietnam. In fact, as US intelligence reports repeatedly explained to the White House, the republic was far from democratic, and its ruling élite was incapable of running the country, far less inspiring its people's loyalty; most of them would vote Communist if the elections were ever held. The elections were postponed, on the grounds that Communist violence would prevent a fair outcome – probably true, but giving Hanoi justification for a guerrilla campaign in the South, spearheaded by the Viet Cong, heirs to the Viet Minh tradition.

The newly elected US President Kennedy decided to make a stand against Communism in Vietnam, despite the cautious counsel of his most experienced diplomats. American aid was backed up by military advisers, then combat units. The Viet Cong continued to make headway. After Kennedy's assassination in 1963, President Johnson increased the military commitment. US aircraft blasted Vietnam with more explosives than had been used in all of World War II; American casualties began to rise – more than 50,000 would die – and with them the tide of anti-war sentiment back home. By 1968, Johnson was convinced that the war could not be won; he stood down from power. Under his successor, Richard Nixon, the war continued, drawing neighbouring Cambodia into the cauldron. Yet real military progress remained as elusive as ever.

Finally, in 1972, a peace treaty was signed. The Americans withdrew; in 1975 North Vietnamese troops rolled across the 'provisional' border, and the country was reunited. To delay a Communist victory by less than 20 years, the USA had paid a high price in prestige abroad and political discord at home. The Vietnamese had paid vastly higher in lives. And although Vietnam triumphed in a subsequent 1979 war against its former Chinese allies, political repression and economic disaster caused its people to risk their lives by the thousand in seaborne escapes – the refugee 'Boat People' – during the 1980s.

ASIA

MALAYSIA

The red and white bands date back to a revolt in the 13th century. The star and crescent are symbols of Islam; the blue represents Malaysia's role in the Commonwealth. This version of the flag was first flown after federation in 1963.

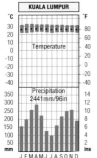

In common with many coastal places close to the Equator, Kuala Lumpur has very uniform temperature throughout the year. The length of daylight and the intensity of the noonday sun varies little from one season to another and the sea is always very warm. The daytime temperature is about 32°C [90°F]. Rainfall is abundant at all seasons, but with a double maximum around the equinoxes, when the tropical rainbelt lies close to the Equator. Rain falls on over 200 days in the year.

The new country of Malaysia was born in 1963 by the joining of the Federation of Malaya (independent from Britain since 1957), the island state of Singapore and the colonies of Sarawak and North Borneo (renamed Sabah). In 1965 Singapore seceded to become an independent nation, and the present federation comprises 11 states and a federal territory (Kuala Lumpur) on the Malay Peninsula, and two states and a federal territory (Labuan) in northern Borneo. The regions are separated by some 650 km [400 mls] of the South China Sea.

The Malay Peninsula is dominated by fold mountains with a north–south axis. There are seven or eight ranges, with frequently exposed granite cores. The most important is the so-called Main Range, which runs from the Thai border to the south-east of Kuala Lumpur, attaining 2,182 m [7,159 ft] at its highest point, Gunong Kerbau. South of the Main Range lies the flat and poorly drained lowland of Johor, which is punctuated by isolated hills, often rising over 1,060 m [3,500 ft]. The small rivers of Malaya have built up a margin of lowland around the coasts.

Northern Borneo has a mangrove-fringed coastal plain, up to 65 km [40 mls] wide, backed by hill country averaging 300 m [1,000 ft] in height. This is dominated by the east–west fold mountains of the interior, which rise from 1,400 m to 2,300 m [4,500 ft to 7,500 ft]; the most striking is the granite peak of Mt Kinabalu (4,101 m [13,455 ft]) in Sabah, Malaysia's highest mountain.

The natural vegetation of most of Malaysia is lowland rainforest and its montane variants. The Malaysian forests, which are dominated by the dipterocarp family of trees, are the richest in species of all the world's forests. Unfortunately, few undisturbed areas remain, mostly in such national parks as the Gunong Mulu in Sarawak and the Kinabalu in Sabah.

An early golden age of Malay political power came in the 15th century with the rise of the kingdom of Malacca, which controlled the important sea routes and trade of the region. In 1414, the ruler

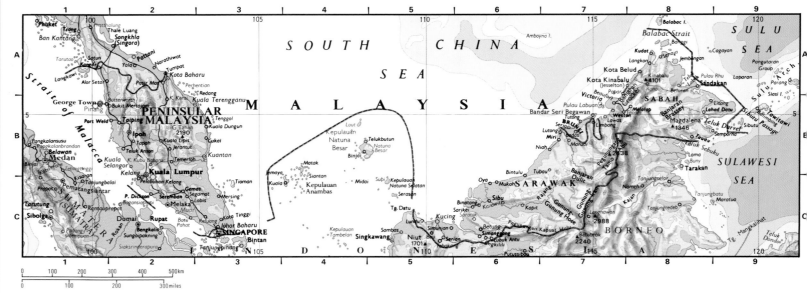

COUNTRY Federation of Malaysia

AREA 329,750 sq km [127,316 sq mls]

POPULATION 20,174,000

CAPITAL (POPULATION) Kuala Lumpur (1,145,000)

GOVERNMENT Federal constitutional monarchy with a bicameral legislature

ETHNIC GROUPS Malay 62%, Chinese 30%, Indian 8%

LANGUAGES Malay (official), Chinese, Tamil, Iban, Dusan, English

RELIGIONS Sunni Muslim 53%, Buddhist 17%, Chinese folk religionist 12%, Hindu 7%, Christian 6%

CURRENCY Ringgit (Malaysian dollar) = 100 cents

ANNUAL INCOME PER PERSON US$3,160

MAIN INDUSTRIES Agriculture, crude oil production, mining, fishing, forestry, food processing, rubber products, chemicals, textiles

MAIN EXPORTS Electronic components 15%, crude petroleum 14%, timber 13%, rubber 9%, palm oil 7%

MAIN EXPORT PARTNERS Japan 20%, Singapore 18%, USA 17%, South Korea 5%, Netherlands 4%

MAIN IMPORTS Electronic components 18%, petroleum products 5%, steel sheets 2%, grain 2%, crude petroleum 2%, sugar 1%

POPULATION DENSITY 61 per sq km [158 per sq ml]

LIFE EXPECTANCY Female 73 yrs, male 69 yrs

ADULT LITERACY 82%

PRINCIPAL CITIES (POPULATION) Kuala Lumpur 1,145,000 Ipoh 383,000 Johor Baharu 329,000 Petaling Jaya 255,000 Tawau 245,000

of Malacca accepted the Islamic faith, which remains the official religion of Malaysia today. The country is, however, characterized by great ethnic, religious and cultural diversity, with Malays of many different origins, Chinese and Indians (mainly brought in by the British to work the tin mines and rubber plantations), Eurasians, Europeans and a number of aboriginal peoples, notably in Sabah and Sarawak.

This patchwork has caused tensions, particularly between the politically dominant Muslim Malays and the economically dominant, mainly Buddhist, Chinese; but while riots did break out in 1969, it has never escalated into serious armed conflict, nor has it prevented remarkable economic growth that has, according to the World Bank ratings, made Malaysia an upper middle-income country.

The traditional mainstays of the economy – rice, plus exports of rubber, palm oil and tin (Malaysia is among the world's biggest producers of all three) – have been supplemented by exploitation of other resources, notably oil and timber, though the pace of the latter is causing concern among environmentalists. Exports are now diverse, from Sarawak's pepper to the new Proton 'national car', and with a growing tourist industry in support Malaysia seems set to join Japan and the four 'little dragons' as a success story of postwar eastern Asia ■

BRUNEI

The yellow background represents the Sultan, with the black and white stripes standing for his two main advisers (*wazirs*). The arms contain the inscription in Arabic 'Brunei, Gate of Peace' and a crescent, the symbol of Islam.

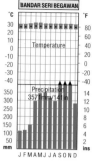

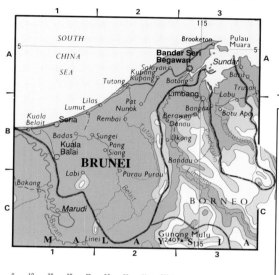

Comprising two small enclaves on the coast of northern Borneo, Brunei rises from humid plains to forested mountains over 1,800 m [6,000 ft] high along the Malaysian border. Formerly a British protectorate, and still a close ally of the UK, the country was already rich from oil (discovered by Shell in 1929) when it became independent in 1983. Today, oil and gas account for 70% of GDP and even more of export earnings – oil 53%, gas 40% – though income from the resultant investments overseas exceeds both. Imports are dominated by machinery, transport equipment, manufactures and foodstuffs. Brunei is, however, currently undergoing a drive towards agricultural self-sufficiency.

The revenues have made Sultan Hassanal Bolkiah (crowned 1968) allegedly the world's richest man, and given his people the second highest income per capita in Asia after Japan. There is no income tax system in Brunei and citizens enjoy free cradle-to-the-grave welfare. All government employees (two-thirds of the workforce) are banned from political activity, and the Sultan and his family retain firm control ■

The climate is hot and humid, the temperatures varying little over the year from a minimum of 24°C [75°F] to a maximum of 30°C [86°F]. Rainfall is heaviest in November and March, when the equatorial monsoon blows onshore. When the monsoon is offshore, from June to August, the weather is a little drier and brighter. Rainfall can exceed 5,000 mm [200 in] high up in the mountainous interior. The amount of sunshine varies between 6.5 and 8.5 hours a day.

COUNTRY The Islamic Sultanate of Brunei
AREA 5,770 sq km [2,228 sq mls]
POPULATION 284,000
CAPITAL (POPULATION) Bandar Seri Begawan (55,000)
GOVERNMENT Constitutional monarchy with an advisory council
ETHNIC GROUPS Malay 69%, Chinese 18%, Indian
LANGUAGES Malay (official), English, Chinese
RELIGIONS Muslim 63%, Buddhist 14%, Christian 10%
CURRENCY Brunei dollar = 100 cents
ANNUAL INCOME PER PERSON US$6,000
POPULATION DENSITY 49 per sq km [127 per sq ml]
LIFE EXPECTANCY Female 77 yrs, male 74 yrs
ADULT LITERACY 86%

SINGAPORE

Adopted in 1959, this flag was retained when Singapore broke away from the Federation of Malaysia in 1963. The crescent stands for the nation's ascent and the stars for its aims of democracy, peace, progress, justice and equality.

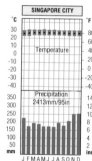

When Sir Stamford Raffles established British influence in 1819, leasing the island and its muddy Malay fishing village for the East India Company, there were only 150 inhabitants. This had not always been so; 'Singapura' (the city of the lion) was an important settlement in the 14th century, but had been destroyed in the rivalry between the great kingdoms of Madjapahit (Java) and Siam. The modern city, originally planned by Raffles, remained under British rule until self-government in 1959. In 1963, Singapore became part of the Federation of Malaysia, but seceded in 1965 to become a fully independent nation.

The republic comprises the main island itself and an additional 54 much smaller islands lying within its territorial waters. The highest point on the main island is Bukit Timah (176 m [577 ft]). The position of Singapore at the southernmost point of the Malay Peninsula, controlling the Strait of Malacca, has throughout history been one of enormous strategic importance.

Singapore is one of the world's most remarkable commercial and industrial experiments. It is, in effect, a city state, its downtown area thick with skyscrapers, the most densely populated country in South-east Asia, and has an economy based on its vast port, manufacturing, commercial and financial services. The port began its modern expansion as a conduit for shipping out tin and rubber from Malaya. Today, one of the world's largest container ports (Rotterdam is the biggest), it handles nearly 75 million tonnes a year, much of it entrepôt (re-export) trade but also involving significant amounts of materials for and from its own thriving industries.

The success of Singapore owes much to the vision and dynamism of Lee Kuan Yew, prime minister from independence in 1959 to 1990, who despite having a predominantly Chinese population in a Malay region made his ambitious policies work. The strategy of industrialization, first labour- and later skill-intensive, gave Singapore an average growth of 7% a year and made it the richest of Asia's four 'little dragons'.

The cost, however, was a lack of genuine democracy, his regime increasingly bordering on a one-party dictatorship; his attitude, essentially, was that Singapore could not afford the luxury – or danger – of political debate. Impressive though the new city may be, most Singaporeans live in massive apartment blocks reminiscent of postwar Eastern Europe, with most aspects of their lives rigidly controlled and much of their former culture buried forever beneath a Western façade.

Lee's groomed successor, Goh Chok Tong, seemed set to continue his policies with equal vigour, turning Singapore into the hub of an expanding region. Despite its political stance, it was in the vanguard of nations opening up links with the reticent Communist countries of Laos, Vietnam and North Korea in the post-*perestroika* era.

The future of his party's wealthy establishment appeared secure, with the island state setting its sights on replacing Hong Kong as eastern Asia's second financial and commercial centre after Tokyo. The feeling nevertheless persisted that Singapore's crucial tertiary activity would give it little to fall back on in the face of a really deep and lasting world recession ■

Uniformly high temperatures, averaging 27°C [80°F], high humidity and heavy rain in all months of the year are typical of a place situated very close to the Equator and surrounded by water. The daytime temperature is usually always above 30°C [86°F]. Rain is frequently intense and thunder occurs on an average of 40 days a year. As in much of the tropics, rainfall varies greatly from year to year, the highest recorded being more than twice the lowest. Rain falls on over 180 days per year.

COUNTRY Republic of Singapore
AREA 618 sq km [239 sq mls]
POPULATION 2,990,000
CAPITAL (POPULATION) Singapore (2,874,000)
GOVERNMENT Unitary multiparty republic with a unicameral legislature
ETHNIC GROUPS Chinese 78%, Malay 14%, Indian 7%
LANGUAGES Chinese, Malay, Tamil, English (all official)
RELIGIONS Buddhist 28%, Muslim 15%, Christian 13%, Taoist 13%, Hindu 5%
NATIONAL DAY 9 August; Independence Day (1965)
CURRENCY Singapore dollar = 100 cents
ANNUAL INCOME PER PERSON US$19,310
MAIN PRIMARY PRODUCTS Rubber, coconuts, vegetables, fruit, fish
MAIN INDUSTRIES Oil refining, oil drilling equipment, chemicals, textiles, shipbuilding, electronic goods

EXPORTS US$16,671 per person
MAIN EXPORTS Machinery and transport equipment 50%, mineral fuels 15%, manufactured goods 8%, chemicals 6%, crude materials 4%, foodstuffs 4%
MAIN EXPORT PARTNERS USA 24%, Malaysia 14%, Japan 9%, Hong Kong 6%, Thailand 6%, Germany 4%
IMPORTS US$18,536 per person
MAIN IMPORTS Machinery and transport equipment 44%, mineral fuels 14%, manufactured goods 9%, chemicals 8%, foodstuffs 5%
MAIN IMPORT PARTNERS Japan 22%, USA 16%, Malaysia 15%, Taiwan 5%, Saudi Arabia 4%
DEFENCE 5.4% of GNP
TOURISM 5,990,000 visitors per year
POPULATION DENSITY 4,838 per sq km [12,510 per sq ml]
INFANT MORTALITY 7 per 1,000 live births
LIFE EXPECTANCY Female 77 yrs, male 72 yrs
ADULT LITERACY 90%

INDONESIA

While the colours date back to the Middle Ages, they were adopted by political groups in the struggle against the Netherlands in the 1920s and became the national flag in 1945, when Indonesia finally proclaimed its independence.

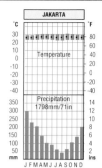

The most remarkable feature of Jakarta's climate is the almost constant high temperature throughout the year. Daytime temperatures reach 29–31°C [84–88°F], only cooling to around 23°C [73°F] at night. This is due to its location on the shores of the hot Java Sea and the uniform intensity of the midday sun and duration of daylight, with an average of over 6 hours of sunshine a day. Rainfall is heaviest in summer, most of it falling in thunderstorms which occur on average 136 days a year.

With the break-up of the Soviet Union in 1991, Indonesia moved up from the fifth to the fourth most populous nation on Earth. It is also the world's largest archipelago, with 13,677 islands (less than 6,000 of which are inhabited) scattered over an enormous area of tropical sea. However, three-quarters of the area is included in the five main centres of Sumatra, Java, Kalimantan (southern Borneo), Sulawesi (Celebes) and Irian Jaya (the western end of New Guinea), which also include over 80% of the people; more than half the population live on Java alone, despite its being only 7% of the land area.

Most of the big islands stand on continental shelves and have extensive coastal lowlands, though Sulawesi and the chain of islands between Java and Irian Jaya rise from deep water. All are mountainous, for this is an area of great crustal activity. Along the arc formed by Sumatra, Java and the Lesser Sunda Islands stand over 200 volcanoes – including Krakatoa (Pulau Rakata).

The natural vegetation of the tropical lowlands is rainforest, which also spreads up into the hills. Much of this has now been cleared by shifting cultivators and replaced by secondary growth, though forest is still the dominant vegetation on most of the less-populated islands. About a tenth of the land

area is under permanent cultivation, mostly rice, maize, cassava and sweet potato, and Indonesia remains essentially an agricultural nation. There are also large plantations of rubber (second in the world), coffee (fifth), tea (fifth), and sugar cane (eighth). Accessible parts of the rainforest are being exploited at an alarming rate for their valuable timber; native forest in Sumatra is now virtually restricted to reserves and national parks, though mountain forests, less vulnerable because they are more isolated, still remain over wide areas. Many of the coasts are lined with mangrove swamps, and several accessible islands are stunningly beautiful; tourism is one of the country's fastest growing sectors.

The population of Indonesia is complex and varied. There is a wide range of indigenous peoples, speaking some 25 different languages and over 250 dialects. Four of the world's major religions – Islam, Hinduism, Christianity and Buddhism – are well represented, though followers of Islam are in the great majority and Indonesia is the world's most populous Muslim nation.

The first important empire in the region was centred at Palembang in south-eastern Sumatra. This was the great maritime power of Sri Vijaya, which held sway from the 8th to 13th centuries over the important trade routes of the Malacca and

Sunda Straits. During the 14th century it was replaced by the kingdom of Madjapahit, centred on the fertile lands of east-central Java. From the 16th century onwards, European influences grew, the area coming progressively under the domination and ruthless exploitation of the Dutch East India Company. Freedom movements starting in the early 20th century found their full expression under Japanese occupation in World War II, and Indonesia declared its independence on the surrender of Japan in 1945. After four years in intermittent but brutal fighting, the Dutch finally recognized the country as a sovereign state in 1949 under Achmed Sukarno, leader of the nationalist party since 1927.

Sukarno's anti-Western stance and repressive policies plunged his sprawling country into chaos and poverty, while costly military adventures drained the treasury. In 1962 he invaded Dutch New Guinea (Irian Jaya) and between 1963 and

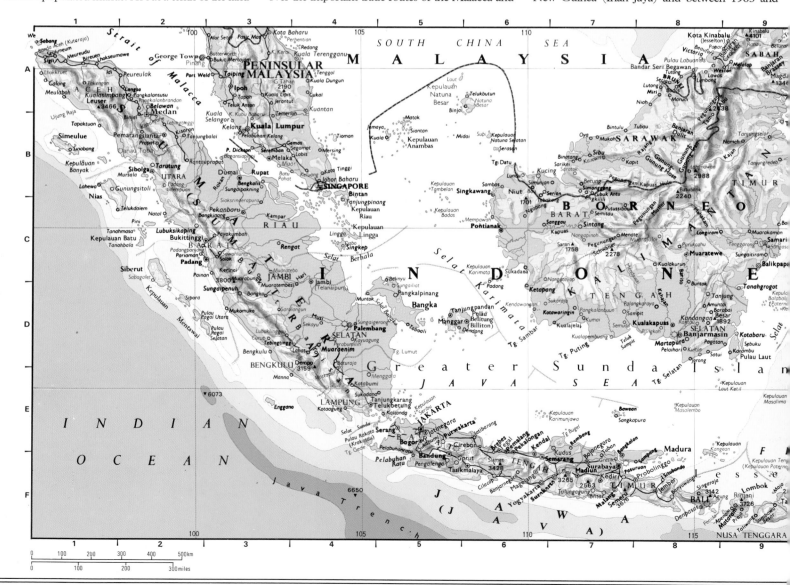

1966 he attempted to destabilize the fledgling Federation of Malaysia by incursions into northern Borneo. Throughout his dictatorship Indonesia seemed to be permanently on the edge of disintegration, government forces fighting separatist movements in various parts of the island chain.

In 1967 Sukarno was toppled by General Suharto, following the latter's suppression of a two-year allegedly Communist-inspired uprising that cost 80,000 lives. However, his military regime, with US technical and financial assistance, brought a period of relatively rapid economic growth, supported by an oil boom that by 1970 accounted for 70% of export earnings – a figure that had shrunk to 33% by 1992. Self-sufficiency in rice and a degree of population control also helped raise living standards, though Java's overcrowding remained a problem, and in 1986 a 'transmigration programme' was initiated to settle large numbers of Javanese on sparsely populated islands, notably on Irian Jaya.

While the Javanese dominate Indonesian affairs, most of the country's wealth – oil, timber, minerals and plantation crops – comes from other islands. Establishing better relations with the West and its ASEAN (Association of South-east Asian Nations) neighbours, the government has now deregulated much of the economy, but corruption and nepotism remain rife and power is firmly in the hands of Golkar, the military-backed coalition which thwarts the aspirations of the two permitted political parties. The army, perhaps correctly, continues to regard itself as the only protector of stability in a country that has proved almost impossible to govern ■

EAST TIMOR

Invaded by Indonesian troops in 1975, East Timor has effectively remained its 21st state despite numerous UN condemnatory resolutions. The end of the Cold War has done little to ease the people's plight; Australia still does not recognize their right to self-determination, while the Western powers leave the problem to the ineffectual UN.

East Timor was a neglected, coffee-growing Portuguese colony for 300 years before Lisbon promised independence in 1974. The 1975 free elections were won by Fretilin, the left-wing nationalists who had fought the empire for years, but the following month Indonesia occupied the territory. Their policies of deportation, resettlement, harassment, torture, bombings, summary executions and massacres – including one filmed by a British film crew in 1991 – have resulted in the deaths of a third of the population (still officially 630,000) and the encampment of 150,000 or more, according to Amnesty International. At the same time, 100,000 Indonesians have been settled in a country rich in sandalwood, marble and coffee, with oil reserves of 5 billion barrels.

Fretilin's fighters, who returned to the hills in 1975, have since kept up a sporadic and dispersed campaign, while the population – mostly Catholic – await international help. In practice, however, East Timor stays closed to the world.

COUNTRY Republic of Indonesia

AREA 1,904,570 sq km [735,354 sq mls]

POPULATION 198,644,000

CAPITAL (POPULATION) Jakarta (11,500,000)

GOVERNMENT Unitary multiparty republic

ETHNIC GROUPS Javanese 39%, Sundanese 16%, Bahasa Indonesian 12%, Madurese 5%, over 300 others

LANGUAGES Bahasa Indonesia (official), Javanese, Sundanese, Dutch, over 200 others

RELIGIONS Sunni Muslim 87%, Christian 10% (Roman Catholic 4%), Hindu 2%, Buddhist 1%

NATIONAL DAY 17 August; Anniversary of the Proclamation of Independence (1945)

CURRENCY Indonesian rupiah = 100 sen

ANNUAL INCOME PER PERSON US$730

MAIN PRIMARY PRODUCTS Rice, cassava, sweet potatoes, sugar cane, soya beans, coffee, tobacco, tea, rubber, fish, timber, oil and natural gas, bauxite

MAIN INDUSTRIES Agriculture, mining, oil refining, fishing, textiles, cement, fertilizers, chemicals

MAIN EXPORTS Crude petroleum 35%, natural gas 14%, wood and cork manufacture 11%, coffee, tea

MAIN IMPORTS Machinery 30%, chemicals 19%, iron and steel 15%, petroleum and petroleum products 9%

TOURISM 1,500,000 visitors per year

POPULATION DENSITY 104 per sq km [270 per sq ml]

LIFE EXPECTANCY Female 65 yrs, male 61 yrs

ADULT LITERACY 83%

PRINCIPAL CITIES (POPULATION) Jakarta 11,500,000 Surabaya 2,421,000 Bandung 2,027,000 Medan 1,686,000 Semarang 1,005,000

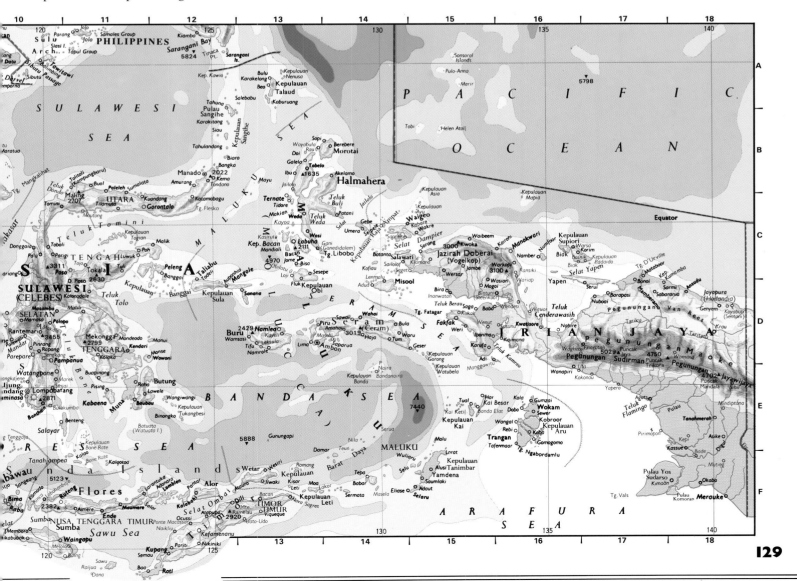

PHILIPPINES

The eight rays of the large sun represent the eight provinces that led the revolt against Spanish rule in 1898, and the three smaller stars stand for the three main island groups. The flag was adopted on independence from the USA in 1946.

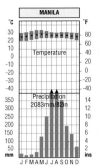

The climate of the Philippines is tropical, the temperature, except in the mountains, rarely dropping below 20°C [68°F]. There is a dry season from December to April, but there is very high rainfall often associated with typhoons in the rest of the year, especially July and August. The latter is particularly true in the eastern Pacific-facing islands and coastlands. The cooler and drier seasons usually coincide. February to May are the sunniest months, with an average of 7–8 hours per day.

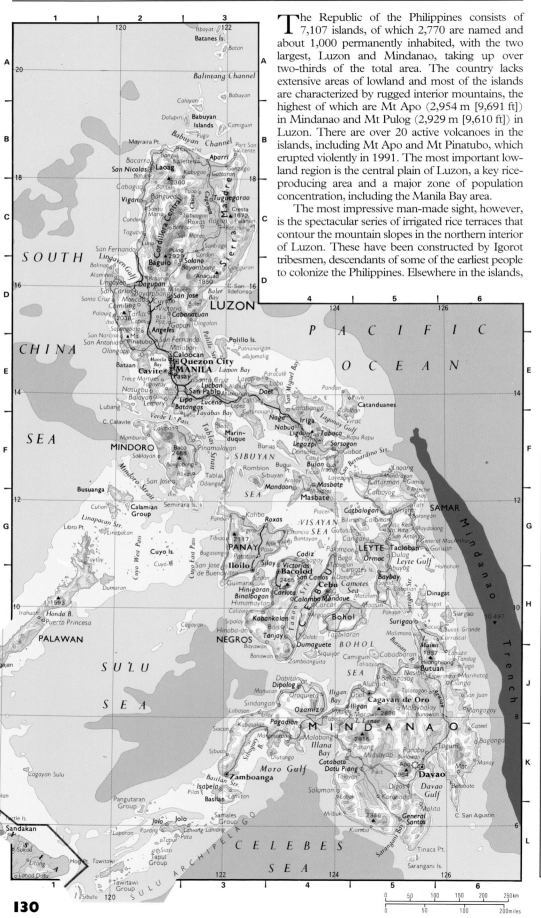

The Republic of the Philippines consists of 7,107 islands, of which 2,770 are named and about 1,000 permanently inhabited, with the two largest, Luzon and Mindanao, taking up over two-thirds of the total area. The country lacks extensive areas of lowland and most of the islands are characterized by rugged interior mountains, the highest of which are Mt Apo (2,954 m [9,691 ft]) in Mindanao and Mt Pulog (2,929 m [9,610 ft]) in Luzon. There are over 20 active volcanoes in the islands, including Mt Apo and Mt Pinatubo, which erupted violently in 1991. The most important lowland region is the central plain of Luzon, a key rice-producing area and a major zone of population concentration, including the Manila Bay area.

The most impressive man-made sight, however, is the spectacular series of irrigated rice terraces that contour the mountain slopes in the northern interior of Luzon. These have been constructed by Igorot tribesmen, descendants of some of the earliest people to colonize the Philippines. Elsewhere in the islands, and especially on Cebu, Leyte and Negros, maize is the staple foodstuff, reflecting the Philippines' former contacts with Spanish America. Another link is Roman Catholicism; over 84% Catholic, and named after King Philip II of Spain, the country is the only predominantly Christian nation of any size in Asia.

Following three centuries of harsh Spanish rule the islands were ceded to the USA in 1898 after the Spanish-American War. Ties with the USA have remained strong, notably during the corrupt regime of President Ferdinand Marcos (1965–86), though in 1991 the Philippines government announced the closure of Subic Bay naval base, the largest in Asia, which took place in 1992.

Marcos was overthrown by the 'people power' revolution that brought to office Corazon Aquino, wife of the opposition leader assassinated in 1983, but the political situation remained volatile, with Communist and Muslim Nationalist rebels undermining stability. Mrs Aquino did not stand in the May 1992 presidential elections. Her successor was former defence secretary General Fidel V. Ramos. The economy, lacking any real natural resources, remains weak, and levels of unemployment and emigration among Filipinos are high ■

COUNTRY Republic of the Philippines

AREA 300,000 sq km [115,300 sq mls]

POPULATION 67,167,000

CAPITAL (POPULATION) Manila (Metro Manila, 9,280,000)

GOVERNMENT Unitary republic with a bicameral legislature

ETHNIC GROUPS Tagalog 30%, Cebuano 24%, Ilocano 10%, Hiligayon Ilongo 9%, Bicol 6%, Samar-Leyte 4%

LANGUAGES Pilipino (Tagalog) and English (both official), Spanish, Cebuano, Ilocano, over 80 others

RELIGIONS Roman Catholic 84%, Aglipayan 6%, Sunni Muslim 4%, Protestant 4%

NATIONAL DAY 12 June; Independence Day (1946)

CURRENCY Philippine peso = 100 centavos

ANNUAL INCOME PER PERSON US$830

MAIN PRIMARY PRODUCTS Copper, coal, iron, nickel, chrome, rice, maize, sugar cane, coconuts, abaca, tobacco, rubber, coffee, pineapples, bananas

MAIN INDUSTRIES Agriculture, food processing, textiles, chemicals, mining, timber, fishing

MAIN EXPORTS Electrical and electronic equipment 20%, clothing 19%, coconut oil and products 8%, minerals 5%, fish 3%, timber 3%

MAIN EXPORT PARTNERS USA 35%, Japan 17%, Netherlands 5%, Germany 5%, Hong Kong 5%

MAIN IMPORTS Mineral fuels 19%, chemicals 13%, parts for electrical equipment 11%, machinery 8%, electrical machinery 7%, base metals 6%

MAIN IMPORT PARTNERS USA 22%, Japan 17%, Taiwan 6%, Kuwait 5%, Hong Kong 5%, Germany 4%

DEFENCE 2.2% of GNP

POPULATION DENSITY 224 per sq km [583 per sq ml]

LIFE EXPECTANCY Female 70 yrs, male 63 yrs

AFRICA

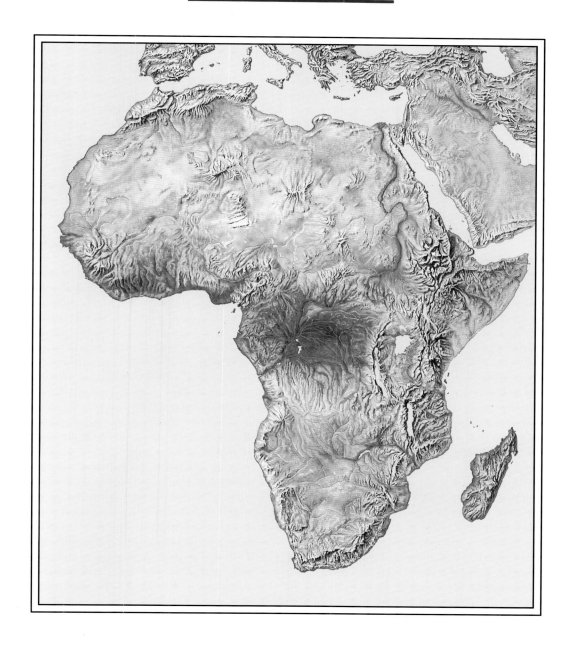

AFRICA

Extending to some 35° north and south of the Equator, the vast continent of Africa covers a wide range of environments. Mediterranean Africa, lying north of the Sahara Desert, includes the sharply folded and eroded Atlas Mountains; the coastal and Nile Valley lands were the home of the ancient civilization of Egypt, with rich evidence of early Phoenician, Greek, Roman and Muslim contacts. The Sahara Desert stretches across northern Africa from west to east, containing the mountain massifs of Hoggar and Tibesti; low-lands to the east are threaded from south to north by the Nile Valley.

South of the Sahara, Africa may be divided by the 1,000 m [3,000 ft] contour line running from south-west (Angola) to north-east (Ethiopia). North of this line the low plateaus of Central and West Africa surround the great basins of the Congo and Niger rivers and the inland basin of Lake Chad. Here are Africa's major areas of tropical rainforest, with savanna dominant on the inner and higher ground. East and south of this contour lie Africa's highest plateaus and mountains, and the complex rift valley systems of north-eastern and East Africa.

The rift valleys of East Africa are part of the most extensive fissure in the Earth's crust, extending south from the Dead Sea, down the Red Sea, across the Ethiopian Highlands, through Kenya to reach the sea again near the mouth of the Zambezi. Both this main rift and its principal branch to the west of Lake Victoria contain deep, long lakes of which Tanganyika, Turkana (formerly Rudolf) and Nyasa are the largest. Here also are the high, open and

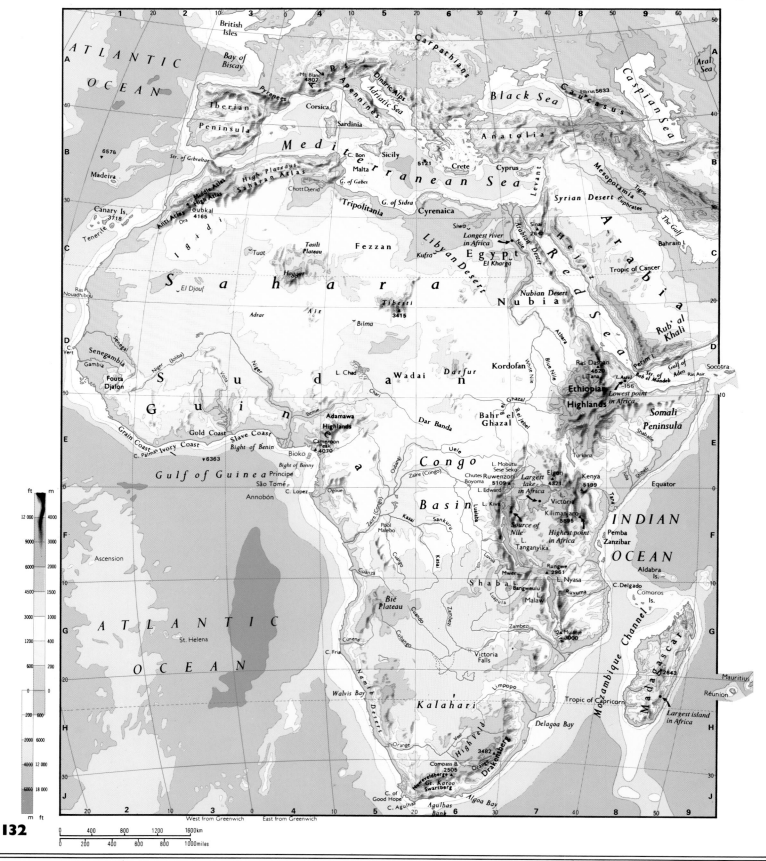

grassy savanna plains with most of Africa's famous wildlife game parks and great snow-capped peaks, notably Kilimanjaro. South and west of the Zambezi River system lie the arid uplands of the Kalahari and Namib deserts, and the dry highlands of Namibia. In the far south a damper climate brings Mediterranean conditions to the plains of South Africa, and to the Drakensberg and Cape Ranges.

The Sahara Desert formed a barrier that was partly responsible for delaying European penetration; Africa south of the Sahara remained the 'Dark

Continent' for Europeans until well into the 19th century. The last 15 years of the century saw the final stages of the European 'scramble for Africa', that resulted in most of the continent being partitioned between and colonized by Britain, France, Germany, Belgium, Portugal and Spain. Today almost all the states of Africa are independent, though traces of their recent colonial history are still evident in their official languages, administrative institutions, legal and educational systems, architecture, transport networks and economics.

The colonial pattern, and the current political pattern succeeding it, were superimposed on a very complex system of indigenous tribal states and cultures. There are many hundreds of ethnic groups, languages and religions; indeed, the peoples of Africa themselves are of many physical types, at many different levels of economic, social and political development, and they have reacted in differing ways to European colonial rule; the continent's peoples are culturally just as heterogeneous as the indigenous peoples of any continent ■

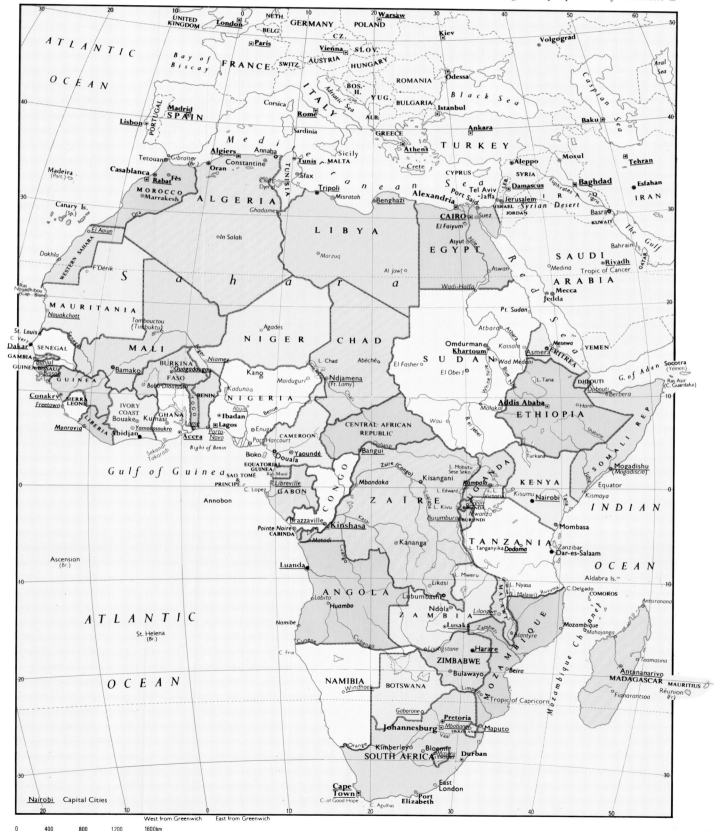

AFRICA

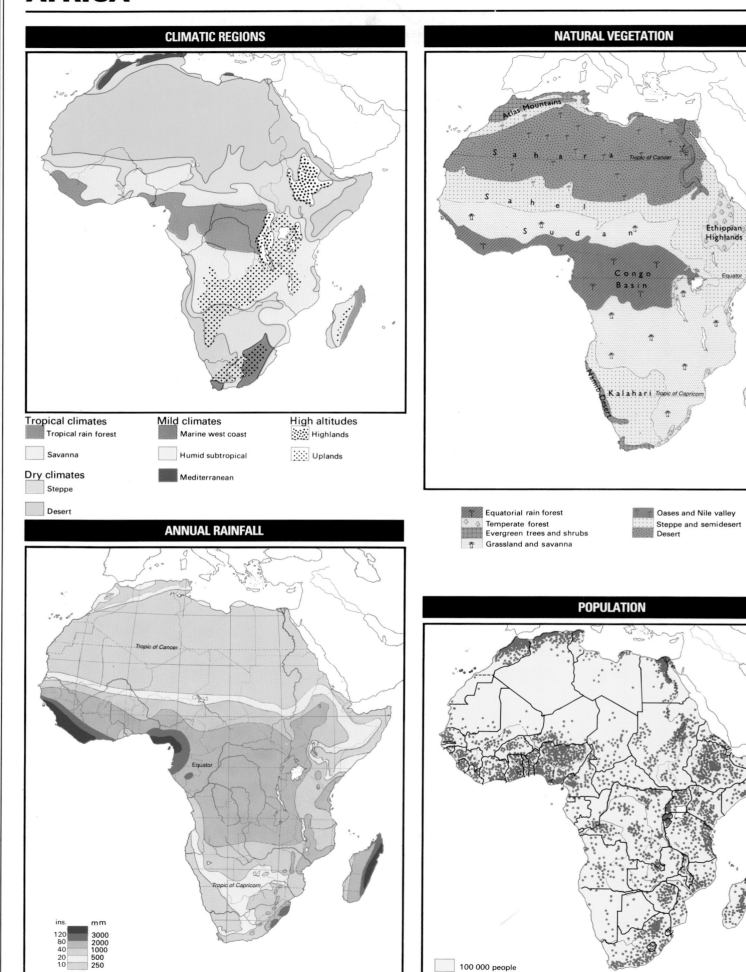

CLIMATIC REGIONS

Tropical climates
- Tropical rain forest
- Savanna

Dry climates
- Steppe
- Desert

Mild climates
- Marine west coast
- Humid subtropical
- Mediterranean

High altitudes
- Highlands
- Uplands

NATURAL VEGETATION

Atlas Mountains
Sahara
Tropic of Cancer
Nile
Sahel
Sudan
Ethiopian Highlands
Congo Basin
Equator
Namib Desert
Kalahari   Tropic of Capricorn

- Equatorial rain forest
- Temperate forest
- Evergreen trees and shrubs
- Grassland and savanna
- Oases and Nile valley
- Steppe and semidesert
- Desert

ANNUAL RAINFALL

Tropic of Cancer
Equator
Tropic of Capricorn

ins.	mm
120	3000
80	2000
40	1000
20	500
10	250

POPULATION

100 000 people

LAND USE

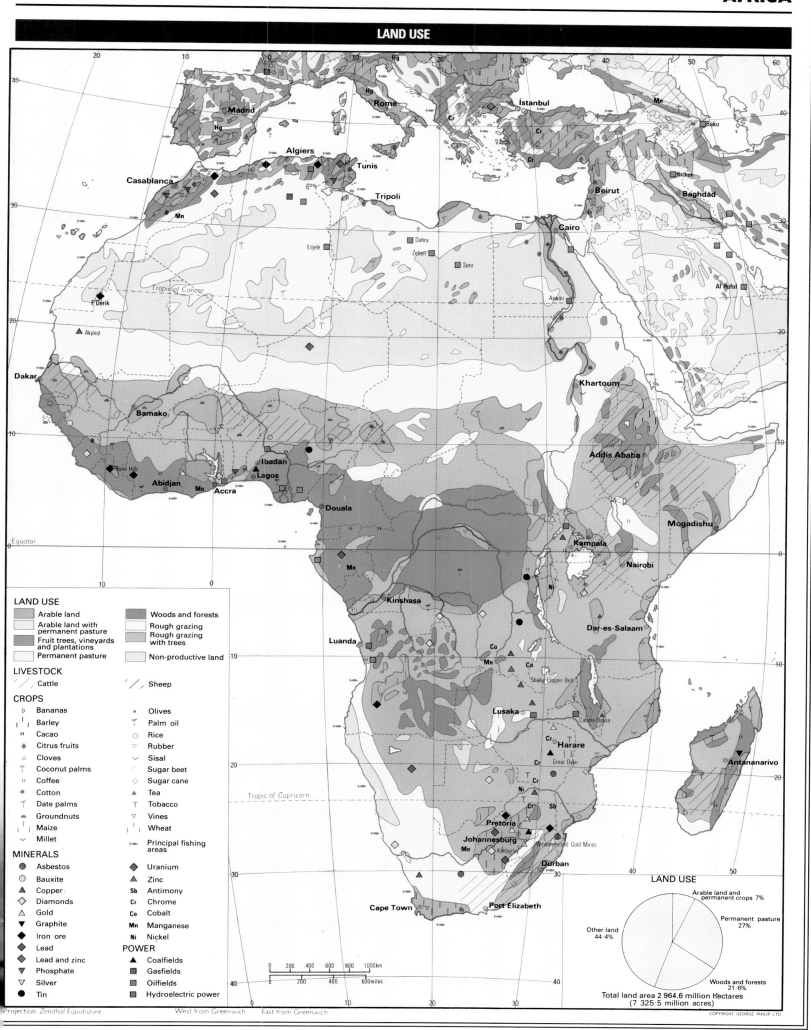

LAND USE

- Arable land
- Arable land with permanent pasture
- Fruit trees, vineyards and plantations
- Permanent pasture
- Woods and forests
- Rough grazing
- Rough grazing with trees
- Non-productive land

LIVESTOCK

- Cattle
- Sheep

CROPS

-) Bananas
- Barley
- Cacao
- Citrus fruits
- Cloves
- Coconut palms
- Coffee
- Cotton
- Date palms
- Groundnuts
- Maize
- Millet
- Olives
- Palm oil
- Rice
- Rubber
- Sisal
- Sugar beet
- Sugar cane
- Tea
- Tobacco
- Vines
- Wheat
- Principal fishing areas

MINERALS

- Asbestos
- Bauxite
- Copper
- Diamonds
- Gold
- Graphite
- Iron ore
- Lead
- Lead and zinc
- Phosphate
- Silver
- Tin
- Uranium
- Zinc
- Sb Antimony
- Cr Chrome
- Co Cobalt
- Mn Manganese
- Ni Nickel

POWER

- Coalfields
- Gasfields
- Oilfields
- Hydroelectric power

LAND USE

Arable land and permanent crops 7%
Permanent pasture 27%
Other land 44·4%
Woods and forests 21·6%

Total land area 2 964.6 million hectares
(7 325·5 million acres)

Projection: Zenithal Equidistant

West from Greenwich   East from Greenwich

COPYRIGHT GEORGE PHILIP LTD.

Madrid, Rome, İstanbul, Baku, Algiers, Tunis, Casablanca, Tripoli, Beirut, Baghdād, Cairo, Kırkuk, Dahra, Zelten, Serīr, Al Hufūf, Aswān, F'Dérik, Akjoujt, Dakar, Khartoum, Bamako, Addis Ababa, Ibadan, Lagos, Accra, Abidjan, Douala, Mogadishu, Kampala, Nairobi, Kinshasa, Dar-es-Salaam, Luanda, Lusaka, Cabora Bassa, Harare, Great Dyke, Antananarivo, Pretoria, Johannesburg, Kimberley, Witwatersrand Gold Mines, Durban, Cape Town, Port Elizabeth, Shaba Copper Belt, Bong Hills

Tropic of Cancer

Equator

Tropic of Capricorn

AFRICA

MOROCCO

A red flag had been flown in Morocco since the 16th century and the star-shaped green pentagram, the Seal of Solomon, was added in 1915. This design was retained when Morocco gained independence from French and Spanish rule in 1956.

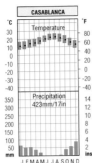

The Atlantic coast of Morocco is washed by the cool Canaries Current which keeps summers notably cool for the latitude, the highest recorded temperatures being only just over 40°C [100°F]. Inland, summers are hot and dry with bright sunshine, but near the coast low cloud and fog are not infrequent. In winter the prevailing winds are westerly, bringing rain from the Atlantic and often heavy snow over the High Atlas Mountains of the interior. Frosts have been recorded at Casablanca.

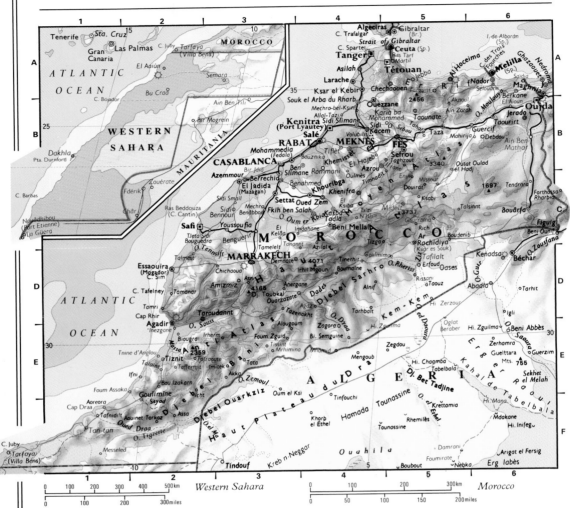

Western Sahara

Morocco

The name Morocco is derived from the Arabic *Maghreb-el-Aksa* (meaning 'the farthest west'). Over the centuries, the country's high mountains have acted as a barrier to penetration, so that Morocco has been much less affected by outside influences than Algeria and Tunisia. Morocco was the last North African territory to succumb to European colonialism; not until 1912 did the Sultan of Morocco accept the French protectorate, in a settlement that also gave Spain control of the Rif Mountains and several enclaves along the coast (of which Ceuta and Melilla remain under Spanish administration).

In 1956 France and Spain gave up their protectorate as Morocco became independent, and in 1958 the international zone of Tangier was incorporated in a unified Morocco, which became an independent kingdom. Ruled since 1961 by the authoritarian and nationalistic regime of King Hassan II, Morocco is today one of only three kingdoms left on the continent of Africa.

Since independence a large proportion of the once-important European and Jewish communities have departed. To the difficulties accompanying reunification were added the burdens of a fast-growing population – nearly half the people are under 15 years old – high unemployment and lack of trained personnel and capital. Yet Morocco has considerable potential for economic development: the country possesses large cultivable areas, abun-

dant water supplies for irrigation and hydroelectric power, and diverse mineral resources including deposits of iron ore, lead and zinc.

Agriculture and industry

More than a third of Morocco is mountainous. The main uplands are the High, Middle and Anti 'arms' of the Atlas Mountains in the west and north, and a plateau in the east. Two principal ways of life exist in the mountains – peasant cultivation and semi-nomadic pastoralism.

In contrast to these, modern economic development is found in the Atlantic plains and plateaus. The major irrigation schemes created during the colonial period are situated here, and the majority of Morocco's agricultural production – citrus fruits, grapes (for wine), vegetables, wheat and barley.

Phosphates, of which Morocco is one of the world's leading exporters and fourth largest producer, are mined around Khouribga as well as in Western Sahara. This is the vital raw material for fertilizers. But the country's modern industry is concentrated in the Atlantic ports, particularly in Casablanca, which is the largest city, chief port and major manufacturing centre.

The biggest growth industry, however, is tourism, based on the Atlantic beaches, the Atlas Mountains and the rich, international history of cities like Casablanca, Tangier, Agadir, Marrakech, Rabat and Fès (Fez), famed not only for its hat but also as

the home of the University of Kairaouin – founded in 859 and the oldest educational institution in the world. Morocco is Africa's biggest tourist destination, the only one attracting more than 3 million visitors a year (1992 figures). Tunisia and Egypt are its nearest rivals.

Western Sahara is a former Spanish possession (and the province of Spanish Sahara from 1960) occupying the desert lands between Mauritania and the Atlantic coast; with an area of 266,000 sq km [102,700 sq mls] it is more than half the size of Morocco. Most of the indigenous population are Sahrawis, a mixture of Berber and Arab, almost all of whom are Muslims. The capital is El Aaiún, which has 97,000 of the country's 220,000 inhabitants. Many of these are desert nomads.

Rich in phosphates – it has the world's largest known deposits of phosphate rock – the country has since the mid-1970s been the subject of considerable conflict, with the Rabat government claiming the northern two-thirds as historically part of 'Greater Morocco'. While Morocco has invested heavily in the two-thirds or so of Western Sahara it controls, the rich earnings from the phosphate exports could finance more economic, social and educational programmes. In the early 1990s, more than 140,000 Sahrawi refugees were living in camps around Tindouf, in western Algeria.

A cease-fire was agreed in 1991 between the Rabat government and the Polisario Front, the Sahrawi liberation movement, which are still in dispute over the territory. In 1992 the peace, overseen by the UN, remained fragile ∎

COUNTRY Kingdom of Morocco

AREA 446,550 sq km [172,413 sq mls]

POPULATION 26,857,000

CAPITAL (POPULATION) Rabat (1,220,000)

GOVERNMENT Constitutional monarchy

ETHNIC GROUPS Arab 70%, Berber 30%

LANGUAGES Arabic (official), Berber

RELIGIONS Muslim 99%, Christian 1%

NATIONAL DAY 3 March; Accession of Hassan II (1961)

CURRENCY Moroccan dirham = 100 centimes

ANNUAL INCOME PER PERSON US$1,030

MAIN INDUSTRIES Agriculture, wine, food processing, textiles, leather goods, fertilizers, mining, forestry

MAIN EXPORTS Food and beverages 27%, phosphoric acid 15%, phosphates 13%, clothing 10%

MAIN IMPORTS Capital goods 21%, crude oil 15%, consumer goods 12%, foodstuffs 11%, sulphur 6%

DEFENCE 4% of GNP

TOURISM 3,250,000 visitors per year

POPULATION DENSITY 60 per sq km [156 per sq ml]

INFANT MORTALITY 68 per 1,000 live births

LIFE EXPECTANCY Female 65 yrs, male 62 yrs

ADULT LITERACY 41%

PRINCIPAL CITIES (POPULATION) Casablanca 2,943,000 Rabat-Salé 1,220,000 Marrakech 602,000 Fès 564,000

ALGERIA

Algeria's flag features traditional Islamic symbols and colours, and the design dates back to the early 19th century. Used by the liberation movement that fought against French rule after 1954, it was adopted on independence in 1962.

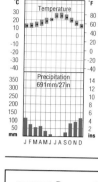

Algiers is exposed to the maritime influences of the Mediterranean Sea but is sheltered from the Sahara to the south by the high Atlas Mountains. The temperature range, both annual and diurnal, is remarkably small: annual 13°C [23°F]; diurnal 6°C [11°F]. Frosts have not been recorded. Rainfall has a winter maximum typical of the Mediterranean region, with amounts varying greatly from year to year. The mountains to the south are often snow-covered in winter.

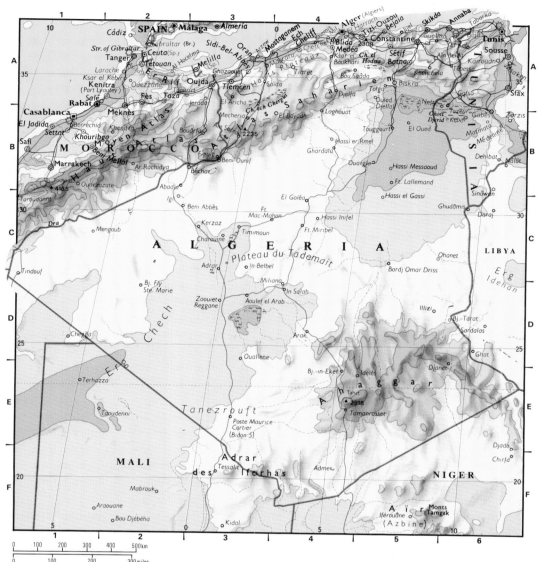

COUNTRY Democratic and Popular Republic of Algeria
AREA 2,381,700 sq km [919,590 sq mls]
POPULATION 27,936,000
CAPITAL (POPULATION) Algiers (1,722,000)
GOVERNMENT Socialist multiparty republic with a unicameral legislature
ETHNIC GROUPS Arab 83%, Berber 16%, French
LANGUAGES Arabic (official), Berber, French
RELIGIONS Sunni Muslim 98%, Christian
NATIONAL DAY 1 November; Anniversary of the Revolution (1954)
CURRENCY Algerian dinar = 100 centimes
ANNUAL INCOME PER PERSON US$1,650
MAIN PRIMARY PRODUCTS Oil, natural gas, phosphates, iron ore, lead, copper, cereals, fruit, timber, livestock
MAIN INDUSTRIES Oil refining, gas, petrochemicals, mining, agriculture, wine, food processing
MAIN EXPORTS Crude oil, petroleum products, natural gas 98%, wine, vegetables and fruit
MAIN IMPORTS Machinery and transport equipment 29%, semi-finished products 29%, foodstuffs 18%
DEFENCE 1.9% of GNP
TOURISM 1,120,000 visitors per year
POPULATION DENSITY 12 per sq km [30 per sq ml]
PRINCIPAL CITIES (POPULATION) Algiers 1,722,000 Oran 664,000 Constantine 449,000 Annaba 348,000

THE ATLAS MOUNTAINS

Extending from Morocco into northern Algeria and Tunisia, the Atlas is a prominent range of fold mountains. Its highest peak and the highest in North Africa, Jebel Toubkal (4,165 m [13,670 ft]), is one of a jagged row – the High Atlas – in central Morocco; the lesser ranges cluster on either side and to the east, generally with a north-east to south-west trend.

In Morocco there are the Anti-Atlas in the south-west, the Middle Atlas in the centre of the country and the Er Rif mountains near the Mediterranean coast. In Algeria the range includes the Saharan Atlas and, further north, the Tell or Maritime Atlas. Heavily glaciated during the Ice Age, the highest Atlas ranges are now capped with alpine tundra and patches of permanent snow. North-facing slopes receive good winter rainfall, and are forested with pines, cedars, and evergreen and cork oaks. Tablelands between the ranges provide high pastures and rich soils for farming. The southern and eastern ranges are drier and covered with semi-desert scrub.

After Sudan, Algeria is the biggest political unit in the Middle East and Africa, and the world's 11th largest nation. However, over 90% of the country's 27.9 million inhabitants live in the Mediterranean coastlands. The vast Saharan territories, covering over 2 million sq km [772,200 sq mls], or about 85% of the total area, are very sparsely populated; most of the inhabitants are concentrated in the oases, which form densely populated 'islands'. The majority of the population speak Arabic, but there is a significant Berber-speaking indigenous minority in the mountainous north-east.

Like its neighbours Morocco and Tunisia, Algeria experienced French colonial rule and settler colonization. Algeria was the first Maghreb country to be conquered by France and the last to receive independence, following years of bitter warfare between nationalist guerrillas and the French armed forces. European settlers acquired over a quarter of the cultivated land, mainly in north-western Algeria, and rural colonization transformed the plains, producing cash crops.

Oil was discovered in the Algerian Sahara in 1956 and Algeria's natural gas reserves are among the largest in the world. The country's crude-oil refining capacity is the biggest in Africa. Since independence in 1962, revenues from oil and gas have provided 65% of all revenues and accounted for over 90% of exports. Industrial developments include iron and steel plants, food processing, chemicals and textiles, while Algeria is one of the few African nations to have its own car-manufacturing facility, producing about a third of its commercial vehicles. While most of the larger industries are nationalized, much of the light industry remains under private control.

Though agriculture has suffered by comparison, about 18% of Algerians are farmers. Arable land accounts for only 3% of Algeria's total land area, but the rich northern coastlands produce wheat, barley, vines and olives, as well as early fruit and vegetables for the European markets, notably France and Italy. Further south, dates are important, but in the mountains the primary occupation of the Berber population is the rearing of sheep, cattle and goats.

At independence in 1962, the socialist FLN (National Liberation Front) formed a one-party government. Opposition parties were permitted in 1989, and in 1991 the Islamic Salvation Front (FIS) won a general election. The FLN, however, cancelled the election results, declared a state of emergency and arrested many FIS leaders. Instability continued into early 1996, with terrorist attacks and car bombs in Blida and elsewhere. A proposal by President Lamine Zerouale to ban political parties based on religion was approved in a referendum in 1996 ■

AFRICA

TUNISIA

The Tunisian flag features the crescent moon and five-pointed star, traditional symbols of Islam. It originated in about 1835 when the country was still officially under Turkish rule and was adopted after independence from France in 1956.

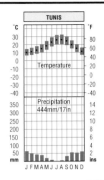

Although most of the rain in Tunisia falls in winter when the region is affected by low pressure, prevailing north-easterly winds from the sea in summer result in a shorter dry season than is found in many parts of the Mediterranean basin. Rain falls on a few days throughout the summer months. The influence of the sea also helps to moderate extremes of temperature, and although they are mostly sunny, summer days are seldom oppressive, humidity being quite low.

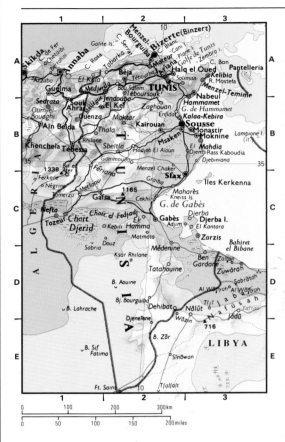

Smallest of the three Maghreb countries that comprise north-west Africa, Tunisia has a long and rich history. It was the first part of the region to be conquered by the Phoenicians, Romans (Carthage is now a suburb of Tunis) and later the Arabs and Turks, and each successive civilization has left a marked impression on the country. Consequently Tunisia has acquired a distinct national identity, with a long tradition of urban life. Close contacts with Europe have always existed – France established a protectorate in 1881 – and the majority of today's 3.2 million tourists a year are European.

Tunisia consists of the eastern end of the Atlas Mountains together with the central steppelands to the south, which are separated from the country's Saharan sector by the vast low-lying salt pans of Chott Djerid. In the north the lower Medjerda Valley and the low-lying plains of Bizerte and Tunis were densely colonized. Major irrigation schemes have been carried out in recent years and these lowlands, which produce cereals, vines, citrus fruits, olives and vegetables, represent the country's most important agricultural area. New industries, coupled with tourism, have transformed a number of coastal towns, including Sfax, Monastir and Sousse. By comparison the interior has been neglected.

After the removal of Habib Bourguiba in 1987, Tunisia remained effectively a one-party (RCD) dictatorship. However, presidential and parliamentary elections were held in March 1994 and were won by President Zine El Abidine Ben Ali – the sole candidate – and the Constitutional Democratic Assembly, which won all seats in government ■

COUNTRY Republic of Tunisia
AREA 163,610 sq km [63,170 sq mls]
POPULATION 8,906,000
CAPITAL (POPULATION) Tunis (1,827,000)
GOVERNMENT Multiparty republic
ETHNIC GROUPS Arab 98%, Berber 1%, French
LANGUAGES Arabic (official), French
RELIGIONS Sunni Muslim 99%
CURRENCY Dinar = 1,000 millimes
ANNUAL INCOME PER PERSON US$1,780
MAIN PRIMARY PRODUCTS Crude oil and natural gas, phosphates, salt, lead, iron, timber, fruit, wheat
MAIN INDUSTRIES Tourism, mining, oil refining, food processing, phosphate processing, textiles
MAIN EXPORTS Petroleum and derivatives 30%, clothing 20%, olive oil 15%, fertilizers 12%
MAIN EXPORT PARTNERS France 22%, Germany 20%, Italy 17%, Belgium 7%
MAIN IMPORTS Machinery 17%, petroleum and derivatives 8%, raw cotton, cotton yarn and fabrics
MAIN IMPORT PARTNERS France 27%, Germany 13%, Italy 11%, USA 6%
TOURISM 3,200,000 visitors per year
POPULATION DENSITY 54 per sq km [141 per sq ml]
LIFE EXPECTANCY Female 69 yrs, male 67 yrs

LIBYA

The simplest of all world flags, Libya's flag represents the nation's quest for a green revolution in agriculture. Libya flew the flag of the Federation of Arab Republics until 1977, when it left the organization.

When the kingdom of Libya gained independence from British and French military administration in 1951, the former Turkish possession and Italian colony was one of the poorest countries in the world, with a predominantly desert environment, few known natural resources and a largely nomadic, poor and backward population. This bleak picture changed dramatically after 1959 with the discovery of vast reserves of oil and gas.

With growing revenues from petroleum and gas exports, important highways were built to link the different regions across the desert, and considerable investment was made in housing, education and health provision. Today, the country's income per head is twice that of its nearest rivals on the African continent – Algeria, Gabon and South Africa. But despite a high population growth rate (3.5%), the process of agricultural development and industrialization still relies heavily on immigrant specialists and workers.

In 1969, a group of 12 army officers overthrew King Idris in a coup and control of all matters has since been in the hands of the Revolutionary Command Council, chaired in dictatorial style by Colonel Muammar Gaddafi. While this includes a violently pro-Palestinian and anti-Western stance, Gaddafi also has long-running disputes with his neighbours, notably Chad and Sudan ■

COUNTRY Socialist People's Libyan Arab Jamahiriya
AREA 1,759,540 sq km [679,358 sq mls]
POPULATION 5,410,000
CAPITAL (POPULATION) Tripoli (960,000)

EGYPT

Egypt has flown a flag of red, white and black (the Pan-Arab colours) since 1958 but with various emblems in the centre. The present design, with the gold eagle emblem symbolizing the Arab hero Saladin, was introduced in 1984.

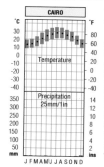

The rainfall of Egypt is very low, falling, if at all, in the months from November to February. The Nile, carrying tropical rainfall northwards to the Mediterranean, is the lifeline of the land. In the south and on the Red Sea coast no rain may fall for many years. The winters are cool, but the summers very hot, getting hotter north to south. Hot dusty winds can blow into the Nile from the surrounding deserts from March to July. Daily sunshine amounts range from 7 hours in December to over 11 hours in June to August.

But for the River Nile, which brings the waters of the East African and Ethiopian Highlands to the Mediterranean, Egypt would scarcely be populated, for 96% of the present population lives in the Nile Valley and its rich delta.

The vast majority of the country, away from the Nile, is desert and semi-desert. Egypt's deserts offer varied landscapes. Beyond the Gulf of Suez and the Suez Canal the Sinai Peninsula in the south is mountainous and rugged; it contains the highest of Egypt's mountains – Gebel Katherina (2,637 m [8,650 ft]) – and is almost entirely uninhabited. The Eastern Desert, between the Nile and the Red Sea, is a much dissected area and parts of the Red Sea Hills are over 2,000 m [6,560 ft].

The Western Desert includes almost three-quarters of Egypt and consists of low vales and scarps, mainly of limestones. Great tank battles were fought over its stony and sandy surfaces in World War II. A number of depressions in the desert surface fall below sea level. There are a number of oases, the most important being Khârga, Dakhla, Farâfra, Baharîya and Siwa. By drawing on deep-seated artesian waters it is hoped to expand the farming area of the first four of these as a contribution to the solution of Egypt's population problem.

The Nile

The Nile Valley was one of the cradles of civilization. The dependable annual flooding of the great river each summer and the discovery of the art of cultivating wheat and barley fostered simple irrigation techniques and favoured co-operation between the farmers. Stability and leisure developed arts and crafts, city life began and the foundations were laid of writing, arithmetic, geometry and astronomy. Great temples and pyramid tombs within the valley remain as memorials to this early civilization – and a magnet for tourists.

Today, even more than in the past, the Egyptian people depend almost entirely on the waters of the

Nile. These are extremely seasonal, and control and storage have become essential during this century. For seasonal storage the Aswan Dam (1902) and the Jebel Awliya Dam in Sudan (1936) were built. The Aswan High Dam (1970), sited 6.4 km [4 mls] above the Aswan Dam, is the greatest of all. Built with massive Soviet aid, it holds back 25 times as much as the older dam and permits year-round storage. Through this dam the Egyptian Nile is now regulated to an even flow throughout the year. The water that has accumulated behind the dam in Lake Nasser (about 5,000 sq km [1,930 sq mls]) is making possible the reclamation of more desert land. The dam is also a source of hydroelectric power and aids the expansion of industry.

Most of Egypt's industrial development has come about since World War II. Textiles, including the spinning, weaving, dyeing and printing of cotton, wool, silk and artificial fibres, form by far the largest industry. Other manufactures derive from local agricultural and mineral raw materials, and include sugar refining, milling, oil-seed pressing, and the manufacture of chemicals, glass and cement. There are also iron-and-steel, oil-refining and car-assembly industries, and many consumer goods such as radios, TV sets and refrigerators are

made. The main cities of Cairo, the capital, and Alexandria are also the major industrial centres.

The Suez Canal, opened in 1869 and 173 km [107 mls] long, is still an important trading route. Though it cannot take the large modern cargo vessels, oil tankers and liners, in 1992 it carried more than 17,400 vessels between the Mediterranean and the Red Sea. The British-built canal was nationalized in 1956 by the Egyptian president, Gamal Abdel Nasser, who from 1954 until his death in 1970 was the leader of Arab nationalism. In 1952 the army had toppled the corrupt regime of King Farouk, the last ruler of a dynasty dating back to 1841. Egypt had previously been part of the Ottoman Empire (from 1517), though British influence was paramount after 1882 and the country was a British protectorate from 1914 to 1922, when it acquired limited independence ■

COUNTRY Arab Republic of Egypt

AREA 1,001,450 sq km [386,660 sq mls]

POPULATION 61,100,000

CAPITAL (POPULATION) Cairo (9,656,000)

GOVERNMENT Multiparty republic with a bicameral legislature

ETHNIC GROUPS Egyptian 99%

LANGUAGES Arabic (official), French, English

RELIGIONS Sunni Muslim 94%, Christian

CURRENCY Egyptian pound = 100 piastres

ANNUAL INCOME PER PERSON US$660

MAIN PRIMARY PRODUCTS Cotton, rice, maize, sugar, sheep, goats, phosphates, oil and natural gas

MAIN INDUSTRIES Oil refining, cement, textiles, fertilizers, iron and steel, tourism

MAIN EXPORTS Mineral products including crude petroleum 65%, textiles 19%

MAIN IMPORTS Foodstuffs 30%, machinery and electrical equipment 20%

DEFENCE 6% of GNP

TOURISM 3,200,000 visitors per year

POPULATION DENSITY 64 per sq km [166 per sq ml]

LIFE EXPECTANCY Female 63 yrs, male 60 yrs

ADULT LITERACY 49%

PRINCIPAL CITIES (POPULATION) Cairo 9,656,000 Alexandria 3,380,000 Giza 2,144,000 Shubra el Kheima 834,000

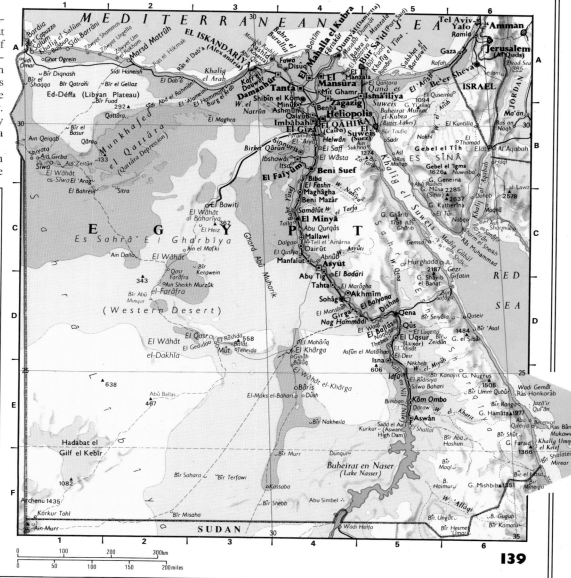

AFRICA

MAURITANIA

The Mauritanian Islamic Republic's flag features the star and the crescent, traditional symbols of the Muslim religion, as is the colour green. It was adopted in 1959, the year before the country gained its independence from France.

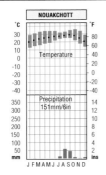

The amount of rain and the length of the wet season increases from north to south. Much of the country receives less than 250 mm [10 in] of rain, due to the dry north-east and easterly winds throughout the year in the north, but the reverse occurs in the south, when south-westerlies bring rain in the summer. Sunshine hours and temperatures are very high, every month having recorded over 40°C [104°F]. The monthly temperature ranges from 30°C [86°F], August to October, to 20°C [68°F] in January.

Over two-thirds of Mauritania – twice the size of France but with just over 2 million people – consists of desert wastes, much of it in the Sahara. Apart from the main north–south highway and routes associated with mineral developments, land communications consist of rough tracks.

Only in the southern third of the country and along the Atlantic coast is precipitation sufficient to support Sahelian thornbush and grassland. Apart from oasis settlements such as Atar and Tidjikdja, the only permanent arable agriculture is in the south, concentrated in a narrow strip along the Senegal River. Crops of millet, sorghum, beans, peanuts and rice are grown, often using the natural late-summer floods for irrigation. When the Senegal River Project is complete, large areas should be developed for irrigated crops of rice, cotton and sugar cane.

Many people are still cattle herders who drive their herds from the Senegal River through the Sahel steppelands in tandem with the seasonal rains. In good years the country's livestock outnumber the human population by about five to one, but the ravages of drought and the development of mining industries in the 1980s – allied to overgrazing – have reduced the nomadic population from three-quarters to less than a third of the national total.

Off the Atlantic coast the cold Canaries Current is associated with some of the richest fishing grounds in the world. The national fishing industry is still evolving and over 110,000 tonnes of fish are landed and processed each year, mainly at the major fishing port of Nouadhibou (Port Etienne).

As the Atlantic coast in the south of the country lacks good harbours, a port and capital city have been constructed at Nouakchott. This now handles a growing proportion of the country's trade, including exports of copper mined near Akjoujt. Exported minerals, particularly high-grade iron ores, worked from the vast reserves around Fdérik, provide most of the country's foreign revenue, though animal products, gum arabic and dates are also exported.

The rulers in Nouakchott surrendered their claims to the southern part of Western Sahara in 1979. The following year slavery was formally abolished, though some estimates put the number of 'Haratines' (descendants of black slaves) still in bondage as high as 100,000. Unlike several of the former colonial territories of West and Central Africa, Mauritania was not affected by the wave of democratization that toppled military and single-party regimes from the late 1980s. However, in 1991, the country adopted a new constitution when the people voted to create a multiparty government. Multiparty and presidential elections, held in 1992, were won by Maaouiya Sidi Ahmed Taya, former president of the military government ■

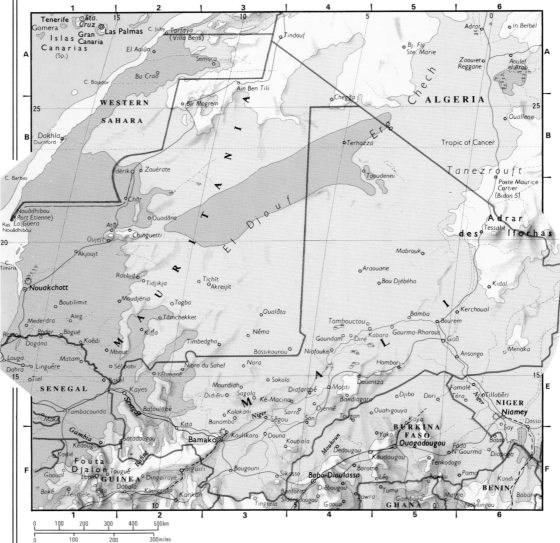

COUNTRY	Islamic Republic of Mauritania
AREA	1,025,220 sq km [395,953 sq mls]
POPULATION	2,268,000
CAPITAL (POPULATION)	Nouakchott (600,000)
GOVERNMENT	Multiparty republic
ETHNIC GROUPS	Moor (Arab-Berber) 70%, Wolof 7%, Tukulor 5%, Soninké 3%, Fulani 1%
LANGUAGES	Arabic (official), Soninké, Wolof, French
RELIGIONS	Sunni Muslim 99%
NATIONAL DAY	28 November; Independence Day
CURRENCY	Ouguiya = 5 khoums
ANNUAL INCOME PER PERSON	US$510
DEFENCE	3.1% of GNP
POPULATION DENSITY	2 per sq km [6 per sq ml]
LIFE EXPECTANCY	Female 50 yrs, male 46 yrs
ADULT LITERACY	36%

MALI

Adopted on independence from France in 1960, Mali's flag uses the Pan-African colours employed by the African Democratic Rally, and symbolizing the desire for African unity. Its design is based on the French tricolour.

In the 14th century the centre of a huge West African Malinka empire based on the legendary city of Timbuktu (Tombouctou), Mali is today a poor, landlocked country consisting mainly of lifeless Saharan desert plains. Water (or the lack of it) dominates the life of the people and most of the country's population is concentrated along the Senegal and Niger rivers, which provide water for stock and irrigation and serve as much-needed communication routes. The Niger and its tributaries support a fishing industry that exports dried fish to neighbouring Ivory Coast, Burkina Faso and Ghana.

With the exception of small areas in the south of the country, irrigation is necessary for all arable crops. The savanna grasslands and highland areas in the Sahelian south-east are free of the tsetse fly (carrier of sleeping sickness), and large numbers of sheep and cattle are traditionally kept in the area, though grazing lands have been decimated by a series of catastrophic droughts. Northern Mali is entirely poor desert, inhabited only by Tuareg and Fulani nomads.

Millet, cotton and groundnuts are important crops on the unirrigated lands of the south, while rice is intensively grown with irrigation. A large irrigation scheme has been developed near Ségou which produces rice, cotton and sugar cane, and there are many other smaller schemes. Industry is confined mainly to one commercial gold mine, salt production and embryonic manufacturing – shoes, textiles, beer and matches.

Mali – a French colony between 1893 and 1960 called French Sudan – was governed by a radical socialist government for the first eight years of independence, before this was overthrown by a bloodless coup under General Moussa Traoré. His repressive military, single-party regime did little for the country – despite successful pressure from aid donor nations to liberalize the planned economy – and in 1987 the World Bank classified Mali as the

world's fourth poorest country; they were still in the bottom 20 in 1996.

In 1985 the government had been involved in a border dispute with neighbouring Burkina Faso; the International Court of Justice finally granted Mali 40% of its claimed land.

Student-led protests finally ended Traoré's 23-year reign in 1991. Following a referendum in 1992, elections were held in which Alphar Oumar Konare became Mali's first democratically elected president. He faced the problem of the Tuareg people demanding a separate homeland ■

COUNTRY Republic of Mali	**RELIGIONS** Muslim 90%, traditional animist beliefs 9%, Christian 1%
AREA 1,240,190 sq km [478,837 sq mls]	**NATIONAL DAY** 22 September; Independence Day (1960)
POPULATION 10,700,000	**CURRENCY** CFA franc = 100 centimes
CAPITAL (POPULATION) Bamako (746,000)	**ANNUAL INCOME PER PERSON** US$300
GOVERNMENT Multiparty republic with a unicameral legislature	**DEFENCE** 2.9% of GNP
ETHNIC GROUPS Bambara 32%, Fulani 14%, Senufo 12%, Soninké 9%, Tuareg 7%, Songhai 7%, Malinké 7%	**POPULATION DENSITY** 9 per sq km [22 per sq ml]
LANGUAGES French (official), languages of the Mande group 60%, including Bambara, Soninké, Malinké	**LIFE EXPECTANCY** Female 48 yrs, male 40 yrs
	ADULT LITERACY 27%

NIGER

Niger's flag was adopted shortly before independence from France in 1960. The circle represents the sun, the orange stripe the Sahara Desert in the north, the green stripe the grasslands of the south, divided by the (white) River Niger.

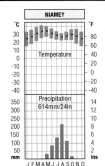

The climate of southern Niger is very similar to other places within the vast tropical grassland belt of northern Africa – the Sahel. From November to April, the hot, dry *harmattan* wind blows from the Sahara Desert, the skies are clear and there is no rain. The period from March to May is the hot season, when the intensity of the sun increases rapidly. But in June, the intertropical rainbelt reaches the region, and the increasing cloud and rain give rise to cooler conditions.

The title Niger, derived from the Tuareg word *n'eghirren* ('flowing water'), is something of a misnomer for the country that bears the river's name. West Africa's great waterway runs through only the extreme south-west of what is, apart from its fertile southern strip, a desolate territory of hot, arid sandy and stony basins.

The monotony of the northern 60% of the country is broken by the jagged peaks of the Aïr Mountains, rising to 1,900 m [6,230 ft] from the desert plains; here rainfall is sometimes sufficient to permit the growth of thorny scrub. However, severe droughts since the 1970s have crippled the traditional life style of the nomads in the area, grazing their camels, horses, cattle and goats, and whole clans have been wiped out as the Sahara slowly makes its way south.

The same period has seen the growth of uranium mining in the mountains by the government in con-

junction with the French Atomic Energy Commission, and this has now overtaken groundnuts as Niger's chief export (in 1993 Niger was the world's second largest producer of uranium, after Canada). The country's reserves of other minerals remain largely untouched. Over 85% of Niger's population still derive their living from agriculture and trading.

The southern part of the country, including the most fertile areas of the Niger basin and around Lake Chad, have also been affected by drought; but here desertification, linked to overgrazing, climbing temperatures as well as water shortage, is a wider problem. The crucial millet and sorghum crops – often grown by slash-and-burn techniques – have repeatedly failed, and migration to the already crowded market towns and neighbouring countries is widespread. The capital of Niamey, a mixture of traditional African, European colonial and modern Third World, is the prime destination for migrants

travelling in search of food and work. South of Niamey is the impressive 'W' national park, shared with Burkina Faso and Benin. The wooded savanna, protecting elephants, buffaloes, crocodiles, cheetahs, lions and antelopes, is intended to attract growing numbers of tourists in the 1990s (Niger received US$17 million from tourism receipts in 1992).

Niger comes close to the bottom of all the world tables measuring aspects of poverty, along with its Sahara/Sahel neighbours, Mali and Chad. French colonial rule came to an end in 1960, and the original post-independence government was over-thrown in 1974, in the wake of a prolonged drought, and military rule followed. Civilian control was reinstated in 1989 (with army backing) and in 1990 a route to democracy was mapped out. In 1992 a multiparty constitution was adopted following a referendum, and elections were held in 1993. However, on 27 January 1996, army officers seized political power in a coup, suspending the constitution and imposing a state of emergency. Total power was assumed by the National Salvation Council (CSN), who claimed they had 'no intention of putting an end to the ongoing democratic process'. Later that year, Colonel Ibrahim Barre Mainassara, the coup leader, was elected president ■

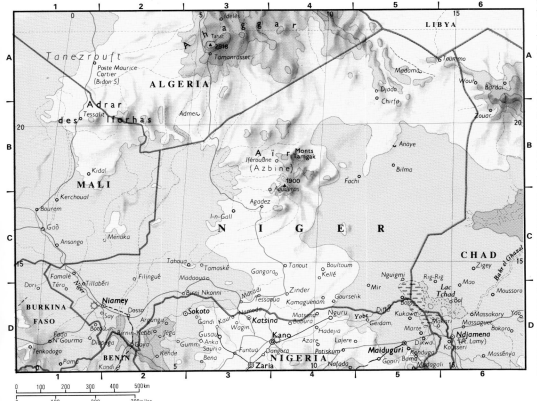

COUNTRY Republic of Niger	
AREA 1,267,000 sq km [489,189 sq mls]	
POPULATION 9,149,000	
CAPITAL (POPULATION) Niamey (398,000)	
GOVERNMENT Multiparty republic	
ETHNIC GROUPS Hausa 53%, Zerma -Songhai 21%, Tuareg 11%, Fulani 10%	
LANGUAGES French (official), Hausa	
RELIGIONS Sunni Muslim 98%	
CURRENCY CFA franc = 100 centimes	
ANNUAL INCOME PER PERSON US$270	
MAIN PRIMARY PRODUCTS Uranium, tin, gypsum, salt	
POPULATION DENSITY 7 per sq km [19 per sq ml]	

AFRICA

CHAD

Adopted in 1959, Chad's colours are a compromise between the French and Pan-African flags. Blue represents the sky, the streams of the south and hope, yellow represents the sun and the Sahara Desert in the north, and red represents national sacrifice.

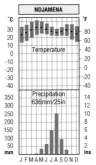

The central regions of Chad lie within the tropical grassland belt traditionally known as the Sudan, which extends across North Africa. The climate is markedly seasonal. A dry season with north-easterly winds extends from November to April. The sky is clear and the daily range of temperature is large. The heat increases until the beginning of the rainy season in June, when cloud and rain bring cooler but more humid conditions.

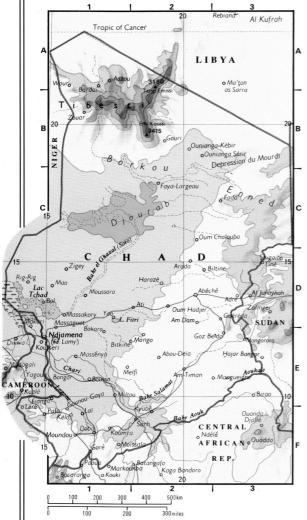

Africa's largest landlocked country, and twice the size of France, its former ruler, Chad is a sprawling, strife-torn, desperately poor state with few industries except for the processing of agricultural products. Over 83% of the population make a living from crop cultivation, notably cotton, or by herding. In the Saharan northern third of the country, a sparse nomadic Arabic population lives in a harsh, hot desert containing extensive tracts of mobile dunes and the volcanic Tibesti Mountains.

The wetter southern portions of the country are covered by wooded savanna and crops of cotton, groundnuts, millet and sorghum are grown – drought permitting – by settled black cultivators. A central bank of thornbush (in the Sahel) provides pasturage for migratory cattle and herds of game, though drought and desertification have combined to wreak havoc here in recent years.

Lake Chad is the focal point of much of the country's drainage, affecting two-thirds of the country. However, most water feeding the lake comes from the rivers Chari and Logone, the only large perennial watercourses in the country and now only streams. Agriculture and population are concentrated along their valleys and in the vicinity of Lake Chad, now shrinking fast – some estimates state that the water area is only 20% of its size in 1970, and the levels much lower; and while fishing is locally important, catches are declining each year.

Since independence Chad has been plagued by almost continuous civil wars, primarily between the Muslim Arab north and the Christian and animist black south, but also with many subsidiary ethnic conflicts. In 1973 Colonel Gaddafi's Libya, supporters of the Arab faction, occupied the mineral-rich Aozou Strip in the far north.

Libya tried incursions further south in 1983 – to back the forces of the previously separate state of Bourkou-Ennedi-Tibesti – and in 1987, to support one of many abortive coups against a succession of

COUNTRY Republic of Chad (Tchad)
AREA 1,284,000 sq km [495,752 sq mls]
POPULATION 6,314,000
CAPITAL (POPULATION) Ndjamena (530,000)
GOVERNMENT Transitional government
ETHNIC GROUPS Bagirmi, Sara and Kreish 31%, Sudanic Arab 26%, Teda 7%, Mbum 6%
LANGUAGES French and Arabic (both official), but more than 100 languages and dialects spoken
RELIGIONS Sunni Muslim 40%, Christian 33%, traditional beliefs 27%
CURRENCY CFA franc = 100 centimes
ANNUAL INCOME PER PERSON US$220
MAIN PRIMARY PRODUCTS Cotton, salt, uranium, fish, sugar, cattle
MAIN INDUSTRIES Cotton ginning, sugar refining
MAIN EXPORTS Cotton, live cattle, animal products
MAIN IMPORTS Cereals, petroleum products, chemicals
DEFENCE 3.8% of GNP
POPULATION DENSITY 5 per sq km [13 per sq ml]
LIFE EXPECTANCY Female 49 yrs, male 46 yrs
ADULT LITERACY 30%

repressive governments in Ndjamena; the former ended in agreement on 'joint withdrawal', the latter in crushing victory for French and Chadian forces.

Diplomatic relations were restored with Libya in 1988, but Chad's massive commitments in maintaining control in the drought-afflicted country as well as on several of its borders – in addition to an impossible foreign debt – make it one of the most troubled nations of Africa ■

CENTRAL AFRICAN REPUBLIC

The national flag of the Central African Republic, adopted in 1958, combines the green, yellow and red of Pan-African unity with the blue, white and red of the flag of the country's former colonial ruler, France.

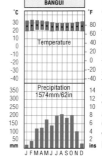

The climate of this landlocked country is tropical. Temperatures rarely fall below 30°C [86°F] during the day, and below 20°C [68°F] at night. The north-east trade winds blow from November to February from the Sahara, causing a dry season with high temperatures. There are no real mountains to affect this airflow. The south-west winds bring a slightly cooler regime and a wet season from July to October. Annual rainfall is high with some rain in all months and little variation in the total figure.

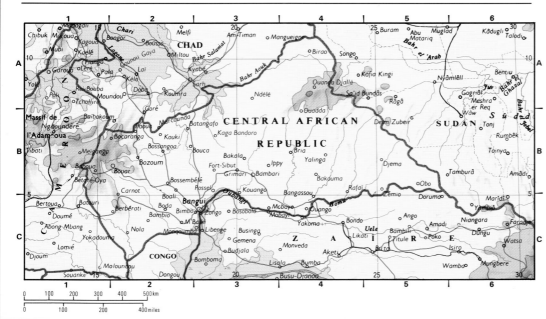

Declared independent in 1960, this former colony of French Equatorial Africa hit the headlines briefly in 1976 when the ex-French Army sergeant Jean-Bedel Bokassa crowned himself head of the 'Central African Empire' in an outrageously lavish ceremony. His extravagance and repressive methods were ended in 1979 with the help of French paratroops, and the self-styled emperor went into exile. He returned in 1986 expecting to regain power, but was sentenced to death – later commuted to life imprisonment. The army continued in power, but moves towards pluralism, approved by voters a decade before, were initiated in 1991. Elections

were held in 1993, but none of the political parties won an overall majority. A new president, Ange-Félix Patasse of the Central African People's Movement, was elected in September 1993. Then, in 1996, an army rebellion was put down with the assistance of French troops.

Lying on an undulating plateau between the Chad and Congo basins, much of the country is savanna. Most farming is for subsistence, but coffee, cotton and groundnuts are exported, as well as timber, uranium and gem diamonds (the main earner) ■

COUNTRY Central African Republic	
AREA 622,980 sq km [240,533 sq mls]	NATIONAL DAY 1 December
POPULATION 3,294,000	CURRENCY CFA franc = 100 centimes
CAPITAL (POPULATION) Bangui (706,000)	ANNUAL INCOME PER PERSON US$390
GOVERNMENT Multiparty republic	MAIN EXPORTS Coffee, cotton, cork, wood and diamonds
ETHNIC GROUPS Banda 29%, Baya 25%, Ngbandi 11%, Azanda 10%, Sara 7%, Mbaka 4%, Mbum 4%	MAIN IMPORTS Cereals, machinery and transport equipment, medicines
LANGUAGES French (official), Sango (most common)	DEFENCE 1.7% of GNP
RELIGIONS Traditional beliefs 57%, Christian 35%, Sunni Muslim 8%	POPULATION DENSITY 5 per sq km [14 per sq ml]
	LIFE EXPECTANCY Female 53 yrs, male 48 yrs
	ADULT LITERACY 38%

SUDAN

The design of Sudan's flag is based on the flag of the Arab revolt used in Syria, Iraq and Jordan after 1918. Adopted in 1969, it features the Pan-Arab colours and an Islamic green triangle symbolizing material prosperity and spiritual wealth.

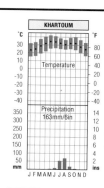

The Sudan, formerly an Anglo-Egyptian Condominium, is the largest state of Africa. It consists essentially of vast clay plains and sandy areas, parts of the Nile basin and the Sahara, but it presents two very different landscapes. The extreme north is virtually uninhabited desert; to the south, nomads move over age-old tribal areas of semi-desert.

The belt across the centre of the country holds most of the population. Here low rainfall, supplemented by wells and small reservoirs for irrigation, allows subsistence farming, but the bulk of the population lives by or near the Blue and White Niles. This is the predominantly Arab part of the Sudan, where 70% of the population live. Cotton and oilseed are grown for export, while sugar cane and sorghum are produced for local consumption.

Southern Sudan presents a very different landscape. Much of it is a great clay plain, fringed by uplands and experiencing a heavy annual rainfall.

The Sudan suffers from an awesome amalgam of ills: ethnic, religious and ideological division; political repression and instability; intermittent civil war, with high spending on 'defence'; economic crisis and massive foreign debt which, to service, would cost three times as much as export earnings; prolonged drought (punctuated by flash floods such as those in 1988, which left 1.5 million home-

less); and an influx of famine-stricken refugees from Ethiopia since the 1980s.

The 17-year-old civil war that ended in 1972 was rekindled in 1983 by the (largely effective) pressure from extremists for the reinstatement of fundamental Sharic law. The renewed rivalries of the Arab north and the non-Muslim south have caused the deaths of hundreds of thousands of people and the decimation of a traditional way of life in an area already prone to drought and severe food shortages.

While power in the land rested in the north with the military council in Khartoum (a city laid out in

Sudan extends from the Sahara Desert almost to the Equator, and the climate changes from desert to equatorial as the influence of the intertropical rainbelt increases southwards. At Khartoum, rain falls during three summer months when the rainbelt is at its most northerly extent. The rain may be squally and accompanied by dust storms called 'haboobs'. There is a large daily range of temperature and summer days are particularly hot.

the pattern of the British flag at the confluence of the White and Blue Niles), there seemed little hope of a return to democracy. But voting in presidential and legislative elections took place in March 1996 ■

COUNTRY Republic of the Sudan
AREA 2,505,810 sq km [967,493 sq mls]
POPULATION 29,980,000
CAPITAL (POPULATION) Khartoum (561,000)
GOVERNMENT Military regime
ETHNIC GROUPS Sudanese Arab 49%, Dinka 12%, Nuba 8%, Beja 6%, Nuer 5%, Azande 3%
LANGUAGES Arabic, Nubian, local languages, English
RELIGIONS Sunni Muslim 73%, traditional beliefs 17%, Roman Catholic 4%, Protestant 2%
NATIONAL DAY 1 January; Independence Day (1956)
CURRENCY Sudanese dinar = 10 Sudanese pounds
ANNUAL INCOME PER PERSON US$750
MAIN PRIMARY PRODUCTS Cotton, dates, livestock, gum arabic, wheat, beans, chromium, crude oil, natural gas
MAIN INDUSTRIES Agriculture, oil, food processing
MAIN EXPORTS Cotton 30%, gum arabic 18%, sesame seeds 9%
MAIN IMPORTS Machinery and transport equipment 33%, manufactured goods 19%, oil products 19%, food and tobacco 16%, chemicals 10%, textiles 3%
DEFENCE 15.8% of GNP
POPULATION DENSITY 12 per sq km [31 per sq ml]
LIFE EXPECTANCY Female 53 yrs, male 51 yrs
ADULT LITERACY 43%
PRINCIPAL CITIES (POPULATION) Khartoum 561,000 Omdurman 526,000

ETHIOPIA

Ethiopia's tricolour was first flown as three separate pennants, one above the other. The colours date from the late 19th century but this sequence was not adopted until 1941. The national emblem, representing the common will of the 68 ethnic groups, was added in 1996.

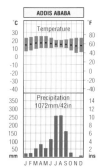

Located at the centre of the Shewan plateau, at an altitude of 2,450 m [8,000 ft], Addis Ababa experiences an average annual temperature of 20°C [68°F], the altitude lowering the expected temperatures for these latitudes. The highest temperatures are in October (22°C [72°F]), with June and July the coolest months at 18°C [64°F]. As much as 1,151 mm [45 in] of rain falls throughout the year, with December to March the driest months. The rainy season tends to lower temperatures.

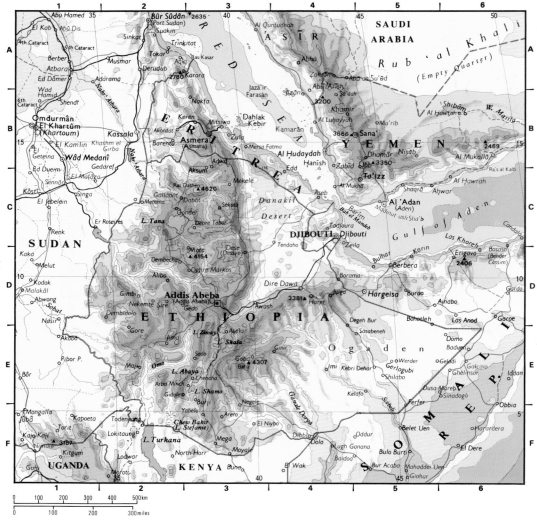

COUNTRY People's Democratic Republic of Ethiopia
AREA 1,128,000 sq km [435,521 sq mls]
POPULATION 51,600,000
CAPITAL (POPULATION) Addis Ababa (2,316,000)
GOVERNMENT Federation of nine provinces
ETHNIC GROUPS Amhara 38%, Galla 35%, Tigre 9%, Gurage 3%, Ometo 3%
LANGUAGES Amharic (*de facto* official), Galla, Tigre

Previously known as Abyssinia, Ethiopia was thrust before the attention of the world late in 1984 by unprecedented television pictures of starving millions – victims not only of famine but also of more than two decades of civil war and a Marxist government determined to enforce hardline economic and social policies.

Ethiopia's main feature is a massive block of volcanic mountains, rising to 4,620 m [15,150 ft] and divided into Eastern and Western Highlands by the Great Rift Valley. The Eastern Highlands fall away gently to the south and east. The Western Highlands, generally higher and far more deeply trenched, are the sources of the Blue Nile and its tributaries. Off their north-eastern flank, close to the Red Sea, lies the Danakil Depression, an extensive desert falling to 116 m [380 ft] below sea level.

Coptic Christianity reached the northern kingdom of Aksum in the 4th century, surviving there and in the mountains to the south when Islam spread through the rest of north-east Africa. These core areas also survived colonial conquest; indeed, Ethiopia (Abyssinia) itself became a colonial power between 1897 and 1908, taking Somali and other peoples into its feudal empire. Invaded by Italy in 1935, Ethiopia became independent again six years later when British troops forced the Italians out.

Emperor Haile Selassie ('the Lion of Judah'), despite promising economic and social reforms following a two-year drought, was deposed after his 44-year rule by a revolutionary military government in 1974. A month later Ethiopia was declared a socialist state: foreign investments and most industries were nationalized and a programme of land collectivization was started, sweeping away the feudal aristocracy. Though the ideology changed, it was still centralized, bureaucratic despotism.

By 1977 President Mengistu had assumed control, and with massive Soviet military and financial aid pursued interlocking policies of eliminating rival left-wing groups, suppressing secessionist movements (in Eritrea, Tigre, Wollo, Gondar and Ogaden) and instituting land reform, including the forced resettlement of millions from their drought-afflicted homelands. His period of 'Red Terror' killed tens of thousands of innocent people.

After a decade of unparalleled disaster driven by drought, Mengistu was finally put to flight in 1991 as Addis Ababa was taken by forces of the EPRDF (Ethiopian People's Revolutionary Democratic Front). The EPRDF announced a caretaker coalition government and plans for multiparty elections, but the administration faced one of the most daunting tasks in the Third World. Relief organizations estimated that of the 25 million people facing starvation in Africa, some 6 million were Ethiopians ■

ERITREA

The new flag was hoisted on 24 May 1993 to celebrate independence from Ethiopia. It is a variation on the flag of the Eritrean People's Liberation Front, and shows an olive wreath which featured on the flag of the region between 1952 and 1959.

COUNTRY Eritrea
AREA 94,000 sq km [36,293 sq mls]
POPULATION 3,850,000
CAPITAL (POPULATION) Asmera (367,500)
GOVERNMENT Transitional government
ETHNIC GROUPS Tigre, Afar, Beja, Saho, Agau
LANGUAGES Arabic and Tigrinya (both official), Tigre, English, Saho, Agail, Afar
POPULATION DENSITY 41 per sq km [106 per sq ml]

Eritrea is a long narrow country bordering the Red Sea. It was conquered by the Italians in 1882 and declared a colony in 1890. Following the Italian defeat in East Africa, Eritrea passed to British military administration. In 1952 it became an autonomous region within the Federation of Ethiopia and Eritrea; ten years later the region was effectively annexed by Haile Selassie and became the far northern province of Ethiopia.

The Eritrean People's Liberation Front (EPLF) then pressed for independence with an unrelenting guerrilla campaign. They held large tracts of the countryside for years while government forces occupied the towns. With the fall of the Mengistu regime in 1991 the EPLF gained agreement on independence for Eritrea; independence was formally declared on 24 May 1993. A new constitution was to be drafted, with multiparty elections scheduled for 1997 at the end of the transition period.

Eritrea was Ethiopia's third largest province but, with 3.8 million people, was only seventh in terms of population. The capital, Asmera, was easily the country's second city (358,000) after Addis Ababa ■

DJIBOUTI

Djibouti's flag was adopted on independence from France in 1977, though its use by the independence movement had begun five years earlier. The colours represent the two principal peoples in the country: the Issas (blue) and the Afars (green).

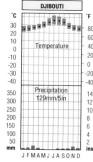

Along the western shores of the Gulf of Aden is a narrow strip of hot, arid lowland between the Gulf and the Ethiopian highlands. The temperature is high throughout the year and summer days are cloudless and exceptionally hot, regularly exceeding 40°C [100°F]. Night temperatures rarely fall below 20°C [68°F]. The sparse and variable rainfall occurs in winter, when northerly winds bring moisture from the Red Sea and the Gulf of Aden. On average, it rains on only 26 days per year.

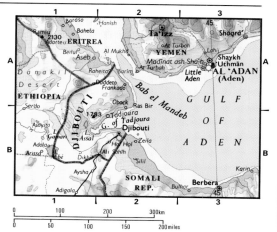

This small state lies in the Afro-Asian rift valley system, forming a hinterland to the Gulf of Tadjoura. Part of Djibouti lies below sea level; much of the low ground is hot, arid and unproductive basalt plain. Mt Goudah, the principal mountain, rises to 1,783 m [5,848 ft], and is covered with juniper and box forest.

Djibouti is important because of the railway link with Addis Ababa, which forms Ethiopia's main artery for overseas trade and was vital to an Ethiopian government whose only other access to the sea was through rebel-held Eritrea. Its town grew from 1862 around a French naval base, which is being redeveloped as a container port, thanks to its important position as a staging post between the Indian Ocean and Red Sea. The French still maintain a garrison there and offer support of various kinds to the authoritarian one-party regime of Hassan Ghouled Aptidon.

Djibouti was previously the French territory of the Afars and Issas. The majority of Afars, most of whom are nomadic, live in Ethiopia and are better known by the Arabic word 'Danakil' while the Issas (or Ishaak) are Somali. This majority dominate the struggling economy, and there is periodic unrest among the underprivileged Afars ■

COUNTRY Republic of Djibouti
AREA 23,200 sq km [8,958 sq mls]
POPULATION 603,000
CAPITAL (POPULATION) Djibouti (383,000)
GOVERNMENT Multiparty republic
ETHNIC GROUPS Issa 47%, Afar 37%, Arab 6%
LANGUAGES Arabic and French (official), Cushitic
RELIGIONS Sunni Muslim 96%, Roman Catholic 4%
CURRENCY Djibouti franc = 100 centimes
ANNUAL INCOME PER PERSON US$1,000
POPULATION DENSITY 26 per sq km [67 per sq ml]
LIFE EXPECTANCY Female 51 yrs, male 47 yrs
ADULT LITERACY 19%

SOMALIA

In 1960 British Somaliland united with Italian Somalia to form present-day Somalia and the flag of the southern region was adopted. It is based on the colours of the UN flag with the points of the star representing the five regions of East Africa where Somalis live.

Nowhere is rainfall heavy, with few places receiving more than 500 mm [20 in] per year. The wettest regions are in the south and in the mountains of the interior. The rains come from March to November, with a slight dry season in the middle. At Mogadishu there is only a monthly temperature variation of a few degrees. The temperatures on the Gulf of Aden coast during June to August can exceed 40°C [104°F]. Frosts can occur in the mountains, which exceed 2,000 m [6,500 ft].

More than twice as large as Italy (which formerly ruled the southern part), the Somali Republic became independent in 1960. The northern section, formerly British Somaliland and the literal 'Horn of Africa', is the highest and most arid, rising to 2,408 m [7,900 ft]; the mountains are an easterly projection of the Ethiopian Highlands, wooded with box and cedar. The east and south have some 500 mm [20 in] rainfall on the coast. Dunes have diverted one of the country's two rivers, the Scebeli, to the south, making it available for irrigation, and bananas are a major export from this area, especially to Italy. Inland is low plain or plateau, an arid landscape with grass and thornbush.

The Somali, though belonging to separate tribes or clans, are conscious of being one people and members of one of Africa's rare nation states. Expatriate Somali living in southern Djibouti, Ogaden (eastern Ethiopia) and north-east Kenya are mostly pastoralists, who move across borders in an increasingly desperate search for pasture and water. The quest for a reunification of all the Somali peoples led to conflict with neighbouring countries, notably Ethiopia and the Ogaden war of 1978, which has continued intermittently since and caused thousands of Somali refugees to flee across the border.

Somalia relied heavily on Soviet aid until Ethiopia went Marxist and sought massive help from Moscow; the revolutionary socialist government of President Siyad Barre, which had seized power and suspended the constitution in 1969, then became increasingly reliant on Italian support and, most important, US aid.

Grievances against the repressive regime, spearheaded by secessionist guerrillas in the north, reached their peak in 1991 with the capture of Mogadishu. Free elections and the independence of the north-east part of the country, as the Somaliland Republic, were promised after the cease-fire and

COUNTRY Somali Democratic Republic
AREA 637,660 sq km [246,201 sq mls]
POPULATION 9,180,000
CAPITAL (POPULATION) Mogadishu (1,000,000)
GOVERNMENT Single-party republic, military dominated
ETHNIC GROUPS Somali 98%, Arab 1%
LANGUAGES Somali, Arabic, English, Italian
RELIGIONS Sunni Muslim 99%
CURRENCY Somali shilling = 100 cents
ANNUAL INCOME PER PERSON US$150
MAIN PRIMARY PRODUCTS Livestock, bananas, maize
MAIN INDUSTRIES Raising livestock, subsistence agriculture, sugar refining
MAIN EXPORTS Livestock, bananas, myrrh, hides
MAIN IMPORTS Petroleum, foodstuffs, construction materials, machinery and parts
POPULATION DENSITY 14 per sq km [37 per sq ml]

Barre's fall from power, but vicious factional fighting continued not only in the capital but also in many parts of the countryside. The Western nations virtually abandoned Somalia to its fate, with thousands dying every week in interclan bloodletting. One of the world's poorest countries – it has one of the highest infant mortality rates at 122 per 1,000, for example – was plunged into anarchy. The situation deteriorated further into 1992, despite UN attempts at mediation and several cease-fires. Much of Mogadishu was reduced to rubble, violence spread to country areas, and tens of thousands of refugees fled to northern Kenya and eastern Ethiopia. In 1993 the UN intervened, sending in a task force of US Marines to protect and oversee the distribution of food aid, but the US troops had to withdraw in 1994. By 1995, Somalia was divided into three distinct regions: the north, the north-east and the south, and had no national government ■

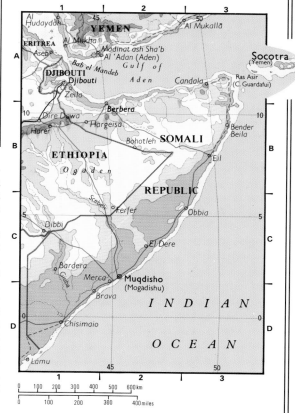

AFRICA

SENEGAL

Apart from the green five-pointed star, which symbolizes the Muslim faith of the majority of the population, Senegal's flag is identical to that of Mali. It was adopted in 1960 when the country gained its independence from France.

On gaining independence in 1960 Senegal had a well-planned capital, a good road network and a top-heavy administration, all legacies from its role as the administrative centre for French West Africa. One-fifth of the country's population lives in Dakar and the area around volcanic Cape Verde (Cap Vert), the most westerly point on mainland Africa. The name derives from the Zenega Berbers, who invaded from Mauritania in the 14th century, bringing Islam with them.

Dakar, once the administrative centre for France's federation of West African colonies, has large modern docks with bunkering and ship-repair facilities and is the nation's major industrial centre. In the north-east of the country, Fulani tribesmen eke out a spartan existence by keeping herds of cattle on the scrub and semi-desert vegetation. In contrast, in the wetter and more fertile south the savanna bushlands are cultivated and cassava, sorghum and rice are grown. About half of the cultivated land produces groundnuts, a crop that still dominates the country's economy and exports. The only other major exports are phosphates.

In an attempt to diversify and stabilize the economy the government is encouraging fishing and tourism, and is involved with Mali and Mauritania in a major scheme to increase irrigated crop production. One of the few African countries to remain stable and democratic through the 1980s, Senegal

COUNTRY Republic of Senegal
AREA 196,720 sq km [75,954 sq mls]
POPULATION 8,308,000
CAPITAL (POPULATION) Dakar (1,729,000)
GOVERNMENT Multiparty republic
ETHNIC GROUPS Wolof 44%, Fulani 24%, Serer 15%, Tukulor 8%, Dyola 8%
LANGUAGES French (official), African languages
RELIGIONS Sunni Muslim 94%, Christian 5%, traditional beliefs and others 1%
CURRENCY CFA franc = 100 centimes
ANNUAL INCOME PER PERSON US$730
MAIN PRIMARY PRODUCTS Groundnuts, phosphates, fish
MAIN INDUSTRIES Agriculture, fishing, seed cotton, cement, textiles
MAIN EXPORTS Groundnuts, phosphates and textiles
MAIN IMPORTS Crude petroleum, cereals, vehicles
DEFENCE 2.1% of GNP
POPULATION DENSITY 42 per sq km [109 per sq ml]
ADULT LITERACY 31%

nevertheless struggles economically, is prone to drought and reliant on aid. Federations with Mali (1959–60) and Gambia (1981–9) were unsuccessful, and since 1989 there have been violent, though sporadic, clashes with Mauritania.

Senegal was the only African colony where French citizenship was granted to the people, and, indeed, the Senegalese were encouraged to become 'black Frenchmen'. As a result many of the Wolof – the largest tribe group and traditionally savanna farmers – are now city dwellers in Dakar, dominating the political, economic and cultural life of the country. Strangely, today's quality of life is for most Senegalese little better than their neighbours' ■

THE GAMBIA

The blue stripe in the Republic of The Gambia's flag represents the Gambia River that flows through the country, while the red stands for the sun overhead and the green for the land. The design was adopted on independence from Britain in 1965.

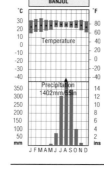

Winds along the West African coast alternate seasonally between dry north-easterlies in winter and moist south-westerlies in summer. The proportion of the year for which the south-westerlies blow – and hence the length of the rainy season – decreases northwards. At Banjul it lasts from June to October, during which period the temperature is very uniform, with warmer nights. In the dry season skies are clear, with over 10 hours of sunshine per day, and the temperature range is much greater.

Britain's first (1765) and last colony in Africa, this small low-lying state forms a narrow strip on either side of the River Gambia, almost an enclave of the French-oriented Senegal. The capital Banjul is also the country's major port, and all the large settlements are on the river, which provides the principal means of communication.

Rice is grown in swamps and on the floodplains of the river (though not enough to feed the country's modest population), with millet, sorghum and cassava on the higher ground. Groundnuts and their derivatives still dominate the economy and provide nine-tenths of export earnings, but a successful tourist industry has now been developed: whether northern Europeans looking for sunshine

or black Americans tracing their ancestry, the number of visitors rose from a few hundred at independence to more than 102,000 in 1991.

The Gambia became a republic in 1970, but in July 1994 a military group, led by Lt. Yayah Jammeh, overthrew the government of Sir Dawda Jawara, who fled into exile ■

COUNTRY Republic of The Gambia
AREA 11,300 sq km [4,363 sq mls]
POPULATION 1,144,000
CAPITAL (POPULATION) Banjul (150,000)
GOVERNMENT Military regime
ETHNIC GROUPS Madinka 40%, Fulani, Wolof, Dyola, Soninké

LANGUAGES English (official), Madinka, Fula, Wolof
RELIGIONS Sunni Muslim 95%, Christian 4%
CURRENCY Dalasi = 100 butut
ANNUAL INCOME PER PERSON US$360
POPULATION DENSITY 101 per sq km [262 per sq ml]
ADULT LITERACY 36%

GUINEA-BISSAU

This flag, using the Pan-African colours, was adopted on independence from Portugal in 1973. It is based on the one used by the PAIGC political party that led the struggle from 1962, who in turn based it on Ghana's flag – the first African colony to gain independence.

Guinea-Bissau is largely composed of swamps and estuaries. On independence in 1974 the country possessed few basic services and agriculture had been severely dislocated by the guerrilla war.

About 82% of the active population are subsistence farmers. Large numbers of livestock are kept on the grasslands in the east, and there is considerable potential for growing irrigated rice and sugar cane. A fishing industry and cash crops such

as tropical fruits, cotton and tobacco are being developed, and there are untapped reserves of bauxite and phosphates as well as offshore oil.

In December 1991 the Supreme Court ended 17 years of socialist one-party rule by legalizing the opposition Democratic Front. However, rivalry between black Guineans (especially predominant Balante) and the mestizo élite remained strong. Multiparty elections were held in 1994 ■

COUNTRY Republic of Guinea-Bissau
AREA 36,120 sq km [13,946 sq mls]
POPULATION 1,073,000
CAPITAL (POPULATION) Bissau (125,000)
GOVERNMENT Multiparty republic
ETHNIC GROUPS Balante 27%, Fulani 23%, Malinké 12%, Mandyako 11%, Pepel 10%
LANGUAGES Portuguese (official), Crioulo
RELIGIONS Traditional beliefs 54%, Muslim 38%
CURRENCY Guinea-Bissau peso = 100 centavos
ANNUAL INCOME PER PERSON US$220
POPULATION DENSITY 30 per sq km [77 per sq ml]
LIFE EXPECTANCY Female 45 yrs, male 42 yrs
ADULT LITERACY 52%

GUINEA

Guinea's Pan-African colours, adopted on independence from France in 1958, represent the three words of the national motto 'Travail, Justice, Solidarité': Work (red), Justice (yellow) and Solidarity (green). The design is based on the French tricolour.

CONAKRY

Temperature

Precipitation
4418mm/174in

Along the coastlands rainfall exceeds 4,000 mm [157 in], declining inland to less than 1,500 mm [59 in]. The wet season lasts from April to October with rain falling almost every day at its height. The sunshine levels are also at their lowest and so this is the coolest period. The highest temperatures coincide with the dry season, when the hot and dry *harmattan* wind blows south-westwards from the Sahara. Temperatures are cooler along the coast and in the highlands.

The first independent state of French-speaking Africa, Guinea is a country of varied landscapes, ranging from the grasslands and scattered woodland of the interior highlands and Upper Niger plains, to the swampy mangrove-fringed plains of the Atlantic coast. Dense forests occupy the western foothills of the Fouta Djalon.

Two-thirds of the population are employed in agriculture and food processing. Bananas, palm oil, pineapples and rice are important crops on the wet Atlantic coastal plain, where swamps and forests have been cleared for agriculture, while in the drier interior cattle are kept by nomadic herdsmen.

France granted the troublesome territory independence after a referendum in 1958, and for more than a quarter of a century Guinea was ruled by the repressive regime of President Ahmed Sékou Touré, who isolated Guinea from the West and leaned towards the Eastern bloc for support. Though reconciled with France in 1978, it was not until after the military coup following Touré's death in 1984 that economic reforms began to work.

Guinea's natural resources are considerable: it has some of the world's largest reserves of high-grade bauxite, and the three large mines account for some 80% of export earnings. The Aredor diamond mine has also been very profitable since opening in 1984, and there is great potential for iron-ore mining and hydroelectric power ■

COUNTRY	Republic of Guinea
AREA	245,860 sq km [94,927 sq mls]
POPULATION	6,702,000
CAPITAL (POPULATION)	Conakry (1,508,000)
GOVERNMENT	Multiparty republic
ETHNIC GROUPS	Fulani 40%, Malinké 26%, Susu 11%
LANGUAGES	French (official), Susu, Malinké
RELIGIONS	Muslim 85%, traditional beliefs 5%
NATIONAL DAY	3 April; Independence Day (1958)
CURRENCY	Guinean franc = 100 cauris
ANNUAL INCOME PER PERSON	US$510
LIFE EXPECTANCY	Female 45 yrs, male 44 yrs
ADULT LITERACY	33%

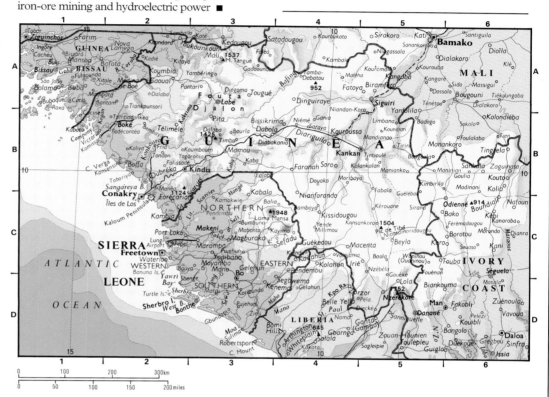

SIERRA LEONE

The colours of Sierra Leone's flag, adopted on independence from Britain in 1961, come from the coat of arms. Green represents the country's agriculture, white stands for peace and blue for the Atlantic Ocean.

FREETOWN

Temperature

Precipitation
4433mm/175in

The coast of Sierra Leone faces directly into the rain-bearing south-west monsoon and is backed by the high Fouta Djalon plateau, which forces the air to ascend and release moisture. For seven months of the year, April to October, rainfall is heavy, reaching a maximum in July of nearly 1,200 mm [47 in]. Temperature and humidity along the coast are uniformly high. In winter the wind is offshore and there is little rain for four months. Day temperatures are around 27–30°C [81–86°F].

Freetown, the capital of Sierra Leone ('lion mountain'), has the best natural harbour in West Africa, and was established as a settlement for freed slaves at the end of the 18th century. At independence in 1961, three-quarters of the population were employed in subsistence agriculture, yet rice had to be imported, and only small surpluses of palm kernel, coffee and ginger were produced.

Revenues from diamond and iron-ore mining, of major importance since the 1930s, plus other minerals, provide the country with funds for education and agricultural developments. Sierra Leone is also one of the few producers of rutile (titanium ore), now its most important export, and is also expanding production of bauxite.

The main centres for the production of coffee, cocoa, and timber products are in the south-east of the country near Kenema. Rice and palm oil are produced throughout Sierra Leone, except in the drier north, where groundnuts and cattle herding are more important. Large-scale mechanized rice cultivation has been established in the bolilands of the north-west, the seasonally-flooded riverine grasslands of the south-east, and the mangrove

COUNTRY	Republic of Sierra Leone
AREA	71,740 sq km [27,699 sq mls]
POPULATION	4,467,000
CAPITAL (POPULATION)	Freetown (505,000)
GOVERNMENT	Transitional government
ETHNIC GROUPS	Mende 35%, Temne 37%, Limba 8%, Kono 5%
LANGUAGES	English (official), Creole, Mende, Limba, Temne
RELIGIONS	Traditional beliefs 51%, Sunni Muslim 39%, Christian 9%
CURRENCY	Leone = 100 cents
ANNUAL INCOME PER PERSON	US$140
MAIN PRIMARY PRODUCTS	Iron ore, bauxite, diamonds, rutile concentrates
MAIN INDUSTRIES	Mining
MAIN EXPORTS	Rutile, diamonds, coffee, bauxite, cocoa beans
MAIN IMPORTS	Food and live animals, mineral fuels, machinery and transport equipment
DEFENCE	2.3% of GNP
POPULATION DENSITY	62 per sq km [161 per sq ml]
LIFE EXPECTANCY	Female 45 yrs, male 41 yrs
ADULT LITERACY	29%

swamps near Port Loko, in an effort to boost rice production. Apart from mills processing palm oil and rice, most factories are in or near Freetown; while, looking to develop Sierra Leone's growing tourist industry, modern hotels were established along the palm-fringed beaches near Freetown.

After independence, Sierra Leone became a monarchy. But after a military government took power in 1968, Sierra Leone became a republic in 1971 and a one-party state in 1978. A majority of the people voted for the restoration of democracy in 1991, but in 1992 a military group seized power. In 1994 and 1995, civil war caused a collapse of law and order in some areas, but multiparty elections were held in 1996, though no voting took place in rural areas, which were considered unsafe ■

AFRICA

LIBERIA

Liberia was founded in the early 19th century as an American colony for freed black slaves. The flag, based on the American flag, was adopted on independence in 1847; its 11 red and white stripes represent the 11 men who signed the Liberian declaration of independence.

West Africa's oldest independent state, Liberia lacks a legacy of colonial administration. A sparsely populated country with large tracts of inaccessible tropical rainforest, Liberia is popularly known for its 'flag of convenience', used by about one-sixth of the world's commercial shipping.

There has been an open-door policy towards foreign entrepreneurs, and the economy began to develop rapidly following the exploitation of large iron-ore deposits by foreign companies, mainly American. Though diamonds and gold have long been worked, iron ore accounts for about half the value of all exports. The economy is a mixture of foreign-owned corporations operating mines and plantations, and of various indigenous peoples who still exist largely as shifting subsistence cultivators.

In 1989, Liberia was plunged into vicious civil war between various ethnic groups when a force led by Charles Taylor invaded from the Ivory Coast. The president, Samuel K. Doe, a former army sergeant who had seized power in a coup in 1980, was assassinated in 1990. But his successor, Amos Sawyer, continued to struggle with rebel groups. Peacekeeping forces from five other West African countries arrived in Liberia in October 1990, but the fighting continued. By mid-1993, an estimated 150,000 people had died and hundreds of thousands were homeless. In 1995, a cease-fire was finally agreed and a council of state, composed of formerly warring leaders, was set up. However, by early 1996 the truce had broken down and violent clashes flared up again between rival factions ∎

COUNTRY Republic of Liberia

AREA 111,370 sq km [43,000 sq mls]

POPULATION 3,092,000

CAPITAL (POPULATION) Monrovia (490,000)

GOVERNMENT Transitional government suspended by military regime

ETHNIC GROUPS Kpelle 19%, Bassa 14%, Grebo 9%, Gio 8%, Kru 7%, Mano 7%

LANGUAGES English (official), Mande, West Atlantic, Kwa

RELIGIONS Christian 68%, traditional beliefs 18%, Muslim 14%

CURRENCY Liberian dollar = 100 cents

ANNUAL INCOME PER PERSON US$800

MAIN PRIMARY PRODUCTS Iron ore, diamonds, gold

MAIN INDUSTRIES Rubber, agriculture, forestry, fishing

MAIN EXPORTS Iron ore and concentrates, natural rubber, coffee, timber, cocoa

MAIN IMPORTS Foodstuffs, machinery and transport equipment, mineral fuels, chemicals

POPULATION DENSITY 28 per sq km [72 per sq ml]

LIFE EXPECTANCY Female 57 yrs, male 54 yrs

IVORY COAST (CÔTE D'IVOIRE)

On independence from France in 1960 this former colony adopted a compromise between the French tricolour and the colours of the Pan-African movement. Orange represents the northern savannas, white is for peace and unity, and green for the forests and agriculture.

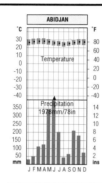

The uniform high temperature and humidity and the double rainfall maxima are a distinctive feature of the climate of the West African coast as far west as Liberia. The total rainfall increases steadily westwards as the south-west monsoon winds of summer have a longer sea track. The heaviest and most prolonged rainfall is in May and June, when the intertropical rainbelt moves northwards ahead of the monsoon. Nearly half the annual rainfall falls in these two months and on about 40 days.

Except for Nigeria, the Ivory Coast is the largest Guinea coastal land – a little larger than Italy. Formally known as Côte d'Ivoire since 1986, it has substantial forests in the south where the basic resources of coffee, cocoa and timber are produced, as well as the lesser crops of bananas and pineapple. The depletion of the rainforest, as in much of West Africa, is rapid.

In terms of such indices as GNP and international trade figures, the relatively stable Ivory Coast is one of Africa's most prosperous countries. This show of prosperity was initiated by the Vridi Canal, opened in 1950, which made Abidjan a spacious and sheltered deep-water port – a rarity in an area

of Africa renowned for barrier reefs. The Ivory Coast's free-market economy has proved attractive to foreign investors, especially French firms, and France has given much aid, particularly for basic services and education. It has also attracted millions of migrant West African workers. On achieving independence, Ivory Coast freed itself economically from support of seven other countries in the French West African Federation. The country is the world's largest exporter of cocoa and Africa's biggest producer of coffee. It has few worked minerals, but its manufacturing industries are developing.

Outward prosperity is visually expressed in Abidjan, whose skyline is a minor Manhattan, and

where most of the 44,000 French live. However, the cost of living for Ivoriens is high; almost everything is centralized in Abidjan – recently replaced as the country's capital by Yamoussoukro (126,000), site of the world's biggest church (consecrated by Pope John Paul II in 1990) – and there are great social and regional inequalities. Nevertheless, a second port has been developed since 1971 at San Pedro, and efforts are being made to develop other towns and the relatively backward north.

In 1990 the country's first multiparty presidential election returned to power Felix Houphouët-Boigny, leader since 1960. On his death in 1993, he was succeeded by Henri Konan Bédié as president ∎

COUNTRY Republic of Côte d'Ivoire

AREA 322,460 sq km [124,502 sq mls]

POPULATION 14,271,000

CAPITAL (POPULATION) Yamoussoukro (126,000)

GOVERNMENT Multiparty republic

ETHNIC GROUPS Akan 41%, Kru 18%, Voltaic 16%, Malinké 15%, Southern Mande 10%

LANGUAGES French (official), African languages

RELIGIONS Muslim 38%, Christian 28%, traditional beliefs 17%

NATIONAL DAY 7 December; Independence Day

CURRENCY CFA franc = 100 centimes

ANNUAL INCOME PER PERSON US$630

MAIN PRIMARY PRODUCTS Petroleum, timber

MAIN INDUSTRIES Agriculture, timber, petroleum

MAIN EXPORTS Cocoa, coffee, timber, canned fish, fruit

MAIN IMPORTS Crude petroleum, machinery and transport equipment, chemicals, vehicles

POPULATION DENSITY 44 per sq km [115 per sq ml]

LIFE EXPECTANCY Female 56 yrs, male 53 yrs

ADULT LITERACY 37%

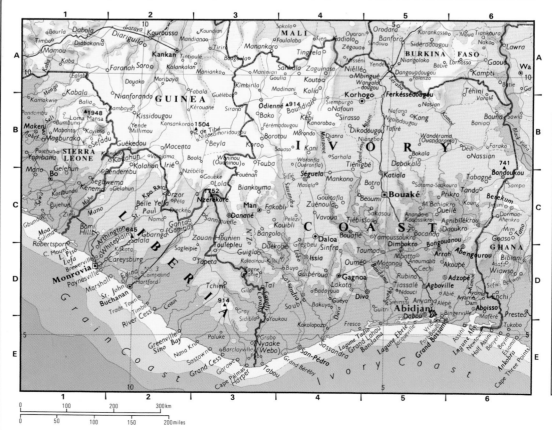

BURKINA FASO

Formerly Upper Volta, this country adopted a new name and flag in 1984, replacing those used since independence from France in 1960. The colours are the Pan-African shades of Burkina Faso's neighbours, representing the desire for unity.

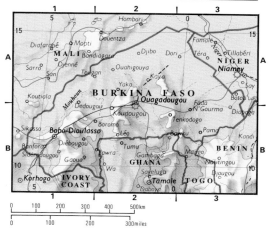

Landlocked Burkina Faso ('land of the upright people') is the successor to Mossi, an early West African state dating from 1100. As large as Italy, and with just over 10 million inhabitants, it is nevertheless overpopulated; the low, seasonal and erratic rainfall, the thin, eroded soils, desertification, and a dearth of other natural resources combine to keep Burkina Faso one of the poorest and most agrarian states in the world, heavily reliant on aid.

The Mossi people, who are the majority tribe, live around Ouagadougou, the capital; another group, the Bobo, dwell around the second city of Bobo Dioulasso. Both grow cotton and millet, guinea corn (sorghum) and groundnuts for food, and collect shea nuts for cooking oil. The nomadic Fulani people keep cattle. Though small surpluses of all these products are sold overseas and to the better-off countries to the south, especially Ivory Coast, remittances sent home by migrants working in those countries probably provide most of Burkina Faso's foreign income. Manganese mining could be developed in the far north-east, though this would necessitate a 340 km [210 mls] extension to the railway from Abidjan already 1,145 km

[715 mls] long. Another hope lies in eliminating the simulium fly, whose bite causes blindness. This would permit settlement and farming of the valleys, which have the most fertile and best-watered lands. Among these is the 'W' national park, shared with Niger and Benin.

COUNTRY Burkina Faso
AREA 274,200 sq km [105,869 sq mls]
POPULATION 10,326,000
CAPITAL (POPULATION) Ouagadougou (634,000)
GOVERNMENT Multiparty republic
ETHNIC GROUPS Mossi 48%, Mandé 9%, Fulani 8%, Bobo 7%
LANGUAGES French (official)
RELIGIONS Traditional beliefs 45%, Sunni Muslim 43%, Christian 12%
CURRENCY CFA franc = 100 centimes
ANNUAL INCOME PER PERSON US$350
MAIN PRIMARY PRODUCTS Sorghum, millet, maize
MAIN INDUSTRIES Agriculture, mining, food processing
MAIN EXPORTS Ginned cotton, livestock
MAIN IMPORTS Transport equipment, non-electrical machinery, petroleum products and cereals
DEFENCE 2.8% of GNP
POPULATION DENSITY 38 per sq km [98 per sq ml]
LIFE EXPECTANCY Female 51 yrs, male 48 yrs
ADULT LITERACY 18%

Plagued by coups and political assassinations, Burkina Faso tasted democracy in 1991, for the first time in more than a decade, when the military regime of Blaise Compaore granted elections. However, 20 opposition parties combined to produce a boycott involving 76% of the electorate, and the government registered a hollow victory. In 1994, a coalition government of ten parties was formed ■

GHANA

Adopted on independence from Britain in 1957, Ghana's flag features the colours first used by Ethiopia, Africa's oldest independent nation. Following Ghana's lead, other ex-colonies adopted them as a symbol of black Pan-African unity.

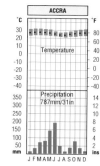

The climate of the coastal regions of Ghana is similar to much of the Guinea coast, with uniformly high temperatures, high humidity and a marked double maximum of rainfall associated with the two passages of the intertropical rainbelt. However, the total rainfall is less than that of coastal regions to the east and west of Ghana, a feature which is attributed to the presence of a local upwell of cooler water offshore. The total rainfall in some years can be as low as 300 mm [12 in].

Formerly known appropriately as the Gold Coast, Ghana's postcolonial name recalls the state which lay north of the upper Niger from the 8th to the 13th centuries, and from whose population some of today's Ghanaians may be descended.

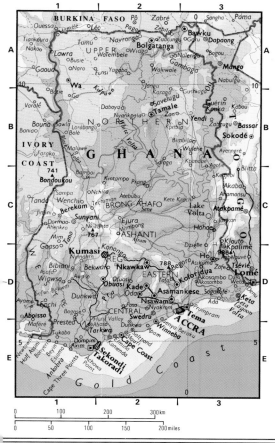

In 1957 Ghana was the first tropical African country to become independent of colonial rule, and until 1966 was led by Dr Kwame Nkrumah, a prominent Third World spokesman and pioneer of Pan-African Socialism. Under him the Akosombo Dam was completed below Lake Volta (one of the world's largest artificial lakes), providing power to smelt imported alumina into aluminium, and for the main towns, mines and industries in the Takoradi-Kumasi-Tema triangle, the most developed part of the country. To build the dam, a second deep-water port was built at Tema, east of Accra, the capital. Tema is now Ghana's main port for imports and for cocoa export.

Cocoa has been the leading export since 1924, and until the late 1970s Ghana was the world's leading producer (it is now fifth). Neighbouring Ivory Coast has now overtaken Ghana both in this and in forestry production. In turn, Ghana has attempted to expand fishing, tourism and agriculture.

Unlike the Ivory Coast, Ghana has long been a producer of minerals – gold has been exploited for a thousand years. However, production of most minerals is currently static or declining. The few remaining gold mines, with the notable exception of Obuasi, are now scarcely economic. Manganese production was recently revived to meet a new demand in battery manufacture, but the country's substantial reserves of bauxite remain undeveloped while imported alumina is used in the Tema aluminium smelter. Industrial diamonds contribute modestly to Ghana's economy.

Nkrumah's overthrow in 1966 was followed by a succession of coups and military governments, with Flight-Lieutenant Jerry Rawlings establishing himself as undoubted leader in 1981. His hardline regime steadied the economy and introduced several

new policies, including the relaxation of government controls. In 1992, the government introduced a new constitution, which allowed for multiparty elections. In late 1992, presidential elections were held and Rawlings defeated his four opponents ■

COUNTRY Republic of Ghana
AREA 238,540 sq km [92,100 sq mls]
POPULATION 17,462,000
CAPITAL (POPULATION) Accra (1,390,000)
GOVERNMENT Multiparty republic with a unicameral legislature
ETHNIC GROUPS Akan, Mossi, Ewe, Ga-Adangme, Gurma
LANGUAGES English (official), Akan 54%, Mossi 16%, Ewe 12%, Ga-Adangme 8%, Gurma 3%, Yoruba 1%
RELIGIONS Protestant 28%, traditional beliefs 21%, Roman Catholic 19%, Muslim 16%
CURRENCY Cedi = 100 pesewas
ANNUAL INCOME PER PERSON US$430
MAIN PRIMARY PRODUCTS Cocoa, maize, cassava, bananas, sorghum, timber, diamonds, gold
MAIN INDUSTRIES Agriculture, mining, bauxite and oil refining, food processing, forestry
MAIN EXPORTS Cocoa 59%, gold 15%, timber 4%, manganese ore 2%, industrial diamonds 1%
MAIN IMPORTS Mineral fuels and lubricants 29%, machinery and transport equipment 26%,
POPULATION DENSITY 71 per sq km [184 per sq ml]
LIFE EXPECTANCY Female 58 yrs, male 54 yrs
ADULT LITERACY 61%

AFRICA

TOGO

Togo's Pan-African colours stand for agriculture and the future (green), mineral wealth and the value of hard work (yellow), and the blood shed in the struggle for independence from France in 1960 (red), with the white star for national purity.

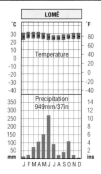

Togo has a tropical climate of high temperatures with little variation throughout the year, and high rainfall, except on the coast and in the north. Temperatures are lower in the central highlands and higher in the north. The wet season is from March to July, but in the south a minor wet season is also experienced from October to November. In the south rain falls on less than 100 days per year, and on average there are over 6 hours of sunshine per day from October to May.

COUNTRY	Republic of Togo
AREA	56,790 sq km [21,927 sq mls]
POPULATION	4,140,000
CAPITAL (POPULATION)	Lomé (590,000)
GOVERNMENT	Multiparty republic
ETHNIC GROUPS	Ewe-Adja 43%, Tem-Kabre 26%, Gurma 16%
LANGUAGES	French (official), Ewe, Kabiye
RELIGIONS	Traditional beliefs 50%, Christian 35%, Sunni Muslim 15%
NATIONAL DAY	27 April; Independence Day (1960)
CURRENCY	CFA franc = 100 centimes
ANNUAL INCOME PER PERSON	US$330
MAIN PRIMARY PRODUCTS	Natural phosphates
MAIN INDUSTRIES	Agriculture, phosphate extraction
MAIN EXPORTS	Phosphates, cotton, coffee, cocoa
MAIN IMPORTS	Foodstuffs, fuels, machinery
DEFENCE	3.1% of GNP
POPULATION DENSITY	73 per sq km [189 per sq ml]
LIFE EXPECTANCY	Female 57 yrs, male 53 yrs
ADULT LITERACY	48%

A small country nowhere more than 120 km [75 mls] wide, Togo stretches inland from the Gulf of Guinea for some 500 km [312 mls] between Ghana to the west and Benin to the east. The Togo-Atacora Mountains cross the country from south-west to north-east, and the major forests and cash crops are in the south-west.

The railway inland from the coast stops at Blitta, in central Togo, and the road is the only means of keeping the poorer, drier northern parts of this awkwardly shaped country in touch with the more developed areas of the south, including the capital and main port of Lomé and the important phosphate mining area, with its port of Kpémé. Phosphates, coffee and cocoa are the important exports, but major food crops are cassava, yams, maize and sorghum millets.

As Togoland, the country was colonized by Germany in 1884 and then occupied by Franco-British troops during World War I. It was partitioned between the two powers under a League of Nations mandate in 1922, with British Togoland later becoming part of Ghana and the larger eastern French section eventually gaining independence as Togo in 1960.

From 1967 Togo was ruled by the military regime of General Gnassingbé Eyadéma, whose government took a pro-Western stance and pioneered privatization in Africa. Following strikes and protests, the principle of multiparty elections was conceded in March 1991, but by the end of the year there were violent clashes between the army and the new civilian government, with old rivalries between Eyadéma's northern Kabye people and the dominant Ewe tribe re-emerging. Multiparty elections for parliament took place in 1994 ■

BENIN

This flag, showing the red, yellow and green Pan-African colours, was first used after independence from France in 1960 and has now been readopted. While Benin was a Communist state after 1975, another flag, showing a red Communist star, was used.

Previously called Dahomey (the name of an old cultured kingdom centred on Abomey), Benin, one of Africa's smallest countries, extends some 620 km [390 mls] north to south, although the coastline is a mere 100 km [62 mls] long.

After the Dutch expelled the Portuguese from

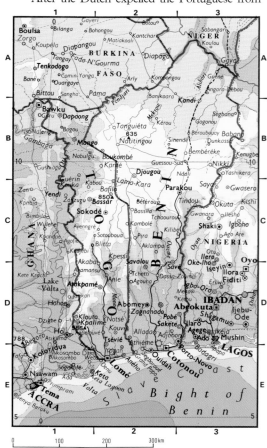

the Gold Coast in 1642, they established their West African headquarters at Ouidah where, until 1961, there was a tiny Portuguese enclave. Several million slaves were shipped from here, mainly to Brazil, where Dahomean customs survive among blacks there. Because of early European contact, and through returned ex-slaves, coastal Benin early acquired an educated élite, as did Senegal, Sierra Leone and Gabon.

Rival tribal kingdoms flourished in this part of Africa for centuries until the French began establishing their presence from around 1850, creating a colony (Dahomey) in 1892 and formally making the country part of French West Africa in 1904.

Before that, from the 13th century, the area had been the western part of the Kingdom (or Empire) of Benin, centred on the Nigerian city of that name and famous for its life-size brass heads and plaques for its ruler, the Oba, from the 15th century. Situated east of Lagos, Benin City is now capital of the Nigerian state of Bendel.

Today's dominant tribe in Benin is the Fon, who (with the Yoruba) occupy the more populous equatorial and fertile south, mostly as subsistence farmers, growing yams, cassava, sweet potatoes and vegetables. In the central parts and some of the north are the Bariba, renowned for their horsemanship, and the Somba, while some Fulani still follow the increasingly precarious nomadic life style in the far north, the least populated of the regions.

In the north, too, are two of West Africa's most beautiful wildlife parks—the Pendjari and the much larger 'W', shared with both Burkina Faso and Niger. Like many neighbouring countries, Benin's government hopes that in the long term these will encourage expansion of tourism, which in 1992 was still just 130,000.

Benin has little to sell, its main exports being palm-oil produce, cotton and groundnuts, with the timber from the central rainforest belt depleting rapidly. Fees from Niger's transit trade through Cotonou are an important additional source of revenue, but illegal trade with Nigeria is also rife. Offshore oil began production in 1982, but output peaked three years later and the industry has since been hampered by low prices.

Following independence from France in 1960, the country experienced a series of coups and power struggles, going through 11 changes of government in 12 years. Then, during the military single-party regime of General Mathieu Kérékou, who in 1974 introduced 'scientific socialism' (and the following year dropped the name Dahomey), Benin found itself sitting awkwardly as a Marxist state between the market-oriented economies of Togo and Nigeria. Kérékou officially abandoned his path in 1989, and in 1990 he was forced to concede multiparty elections in a referendum. He was roundly beaten in March 1991, when the country enjoyed a relatively peaceful return to democracy for the first time in nearly two decades. However, there was an unexpected victory for the former military dictator General Kérékou in the presidential elections of 1996 ■

COUNTRY	People's Republic of Benin
AREA	112,620 sq km [43,483 sq mls]
POPULATION	5,381,000
CAPITAL (POPULATION)	Porto-Novo (179,000)
GOVERNMENT	Multiparty republic
ETHNIC GROUPS	Fon, Adja, Bariba, Yoruba, Fulani, Somba
LANGUAGES	French (official)
RELIGIONS	Traditional beliefs 60%, Christian 23%, Sunni Muslim 15%
NATIONAL DAY	30 November; Independence Day (1960)
CURRENCY	CFA franc = 100 centimes
ANNUAL INCOME PER PERSON	US$380
MAIN PRIMARY PRODUCTS	Palm oil and kernel oil
MAIN INDUSTRIES	Agriculture
MAIN EXPORTS	Fuels, raw cotton, palm products
MAIN IMPORTS	Manufactured goods, textiles
POPULATION DENSITY	48 per sq km [124 per sq ml]

NIGERIA

The design of Nigeria's flag was selected after a competition to find a new national flag in time for independence from Britain in 1960. The green represents the country's forests and the white is for peace.

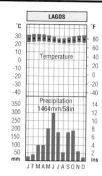

The coastal belt of Nigeria has uniform temperature and humidity through most of the year. The coolest months are July and August when the monsoon brings oceanic air from beyond the Equator, but even then the lowest recorded temperature is 16°C [61°F]. There are two periods of heaviest rain: the long rains with a maximum in June, and the short rains with a maximum in October, with rain on about every other day in the month. Humidity is high and sunshine levels relatively low.

Four times the size of the United Kingdom, whose influence dates from 1861, Nigeria is tropical Africa's most important country. Ranking in the top 15 producers of world oil, there are many other resources (albeit dwarfed in exports by oil), including cocoa in the south-west, timber, rubber and palm oil in the south-centre and east, and cotton and groundnuts in the north.

There are over 88.5 million Nigerians, making it by far the most populous African state; one in every six Africans is Nigerian. It is also the second most populated country of the Commonwealth, and 11th in the world. Natural wealth and substantial armed forces give Nigeria a commanding position in Africa, and its oil and gas reserves are a focus of worldwide interest.

Nigeria's landscape varies from the savanna of the north – much of it under threat of desertification – through mountains and tropical rainforests to the coastal lands on the Gulf of Guinea. The coast has huge expanses of fine sandy beaches, interspersed with mangrove swamps where rivers join the ocean. Much of the country's coast is formed by the Niger delta, behind which lie thousands of creeks and lagoons. Before roads were constructed, these inland waterways provided crucial transport, and boats and canoes still carry people and cargoes between towns and villages in the area. Here the heavy rains produce yams, cassava, maize and vegetables, with rice grown beside rivers and creeks and on large stretches of irrigated land where streams do not flood in the wet seasons.

Further north, in the forest belt, the hills rise towards the Jos Plateau – famous for its holiday resorts – and in the east towards the steep valleys and wooded slopes of the Cameroon Highlands. These areas produce Nigeria's important tree crops – cocoa, rubber, hardwoods and palm oil. North of the Jos Plateau, parkland gives way to grassland, but the savanna becomes increasingly dry and some areas are now little more than semi-arid scrub.

Northern Nigeria is reliant on one precarious wet season, while the south enjoys two. Poor-quality millet and sorghum are the staples, with cotton and groundnuts the main cash crops. Where desertification has not taken hold, livestock are still important – enjoying the absence of the tsetse fly that afflicts the area of moist vegetation in the south.

Nigeria is unique in Africa south of the Sahara for the numerous pre-colonial towns of the south-west (such as Ibadan) and the north (such as Kano). Domestic trade between these and Nigeria's varied regions was developed in pre-colonial days, and is now intense. European contact dates back to the 15th century.

A federation of 30 states and a Federal Capital Territory, Nigeria includes many tribal groups, the largest being the Yoruba of the south-west, the Ibo of the east, and the Hausa, Fulani and Kanuri of the north. The north is predominantly Muslim, and the Islamic influence is increasing in the south, where most people are pagan or Christian. With so many diversities, Nigeria suffers internal stresses and national unity is often strained. Abuja replaced Lagos as the federal capital and seat of government in December 1991.

Though blessed with many natural resources, Nigeria has had an uneasy path since independence in 1960 (becoming a full republic in 1963). Democratically elected governments have found it an

DEMOCRACY IN AFRICA

The great flush of liberty that followed decolonization in the 1950s and 1960s did not bring the rewards of peace, prosperity and self-government that many early African nationalists had envisaged. Instead, within a few years, most of the newly independent African nations had been transformed into corrupt and incompetent dictatorships, at best authoritarian one-party states, usually heavily reliant on Western or Soviet subsidies and often plagued by guerrilla fighting and banditry. Governments were changed, if at all, by means of a coup d'état.

In the late 1980s, however, new hope reached the world's poorest continent. Everywhere, it seemed, dictators were succumbing quite peacefully to popular demands for multiparty elections and many long-running civil wars were coming to an end. By the early 1990s, some form of democracy was in place in 80% of African nations.

But democracy has no easy answer to Africa's chronic problem: its poverty, and the continuing collapse in world prices for most African commodities. In some instances, Western-style democracy may even prove to be impossible, as in Algeria, where in 1992 the military intervened to prevent power passing to elected Islamic fundamentalists, who had sworn to destroy the system that would have given them their victory.

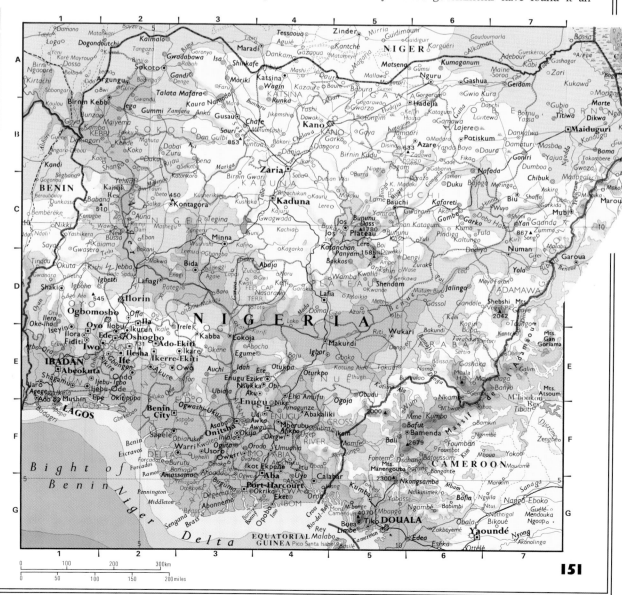

DESERTIFICATION OF THE SAHEL

The Sahel is a wide band of scrub and savanna grassland stretching from Mauritania and northern Senegal in the west through parts of Mali, Burkina Faso, Benin and Niger to southern Chad in the east, and including much of northern Nigeria. To the north is the vast Sahara, the world's largest desert; to the south are the rainforests of tropical West and Central Africa. Though used mainly for pasture, the whole area has irregular and unpredictable rainfall and suffers frequently from drought. Attention was first drawn to the desperate plight of the region by the Sahelian famine of 1973, when hundreds of thousands died, and the problem has since became virtually permanent.

Over the past 30 years, the Sahara has gradually encroached southwards in the world's most blatant example of 'desertification'. The causes are many and interwoven. As well as declining rainfall (possibly as a result of global warming), there are the pressures of a growing population; herdsmen overgrazing the land with their cattle, sheep and goats; overcultivation by farmers;

cutting of ground cover, mainly for fuelwood; and poor or faulty irrigation techniques, where limited water supplies are wasted and the land left too saline or alkaline to support crops.

Ironically, the problem was aggravated in the previous two decades, when above-average rainfall encouraged the expansion of settlement and the cultivation of cash crops into marginal land. Experts estimate that as much as two-thirds of the world's pasture and grazing lands are now in danger from desertification. Africa, and notably the Sahel, is the worst affected: in places the Sahara has advanced more than 350 km [200 mls] in just two decades. The process is containable – even reversible – if the land is allowed to recover and the soil rejuvenated through tree planting, terracing and proper irrigation under careful and consistent management with sufficient funds. But these conditions are rarely found: pressures of population, lack of finance and changing policies all mean that such techniques have not been applied anywhere in the Sahel on a substantial scale.

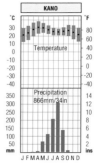

The north of Nigeria extends into the great belt of tropical grassland known as the Sudan which extends across North Africa from the Red Sea to the Atlantic. The climate is markedly seasonal with hot, dry winters and hot, wet summers. In winter the hot, dry *harmattan* blows from the Sahara. With clear skies and no rain, the daily range of temperature is large, in January dropping from 30°C [86°F] in the day to 13°C [55°F] at night. In June, rain approaches from the south, often preceded by tornadoes.

COUNTRY Federal Republic of Nigeria

AREA 923,770 sq km [356,668 sq mls]

POPULATION 88,515,000

CAPITAL (POPULATION) Abuja (306,000)

GOVERNMENT Transitional government

ETHNIC GROUPS Hausa 21%, Yoruba 21%, Ibo 19%, Fulani 11%, Ibibio 6%

LANGUAGES English (official), Hausa, Yoruba, Ibo

RELIGIONS Sunni Muslim 45%, Protestant 26%, Roman Catholic 12%, African indigenous 11%

NATIONAL DAY 1 October; Republic Day (1963)

CURRENCY Naira = 100 kobo

ANNUAL INCOME PER PERSON US$310

SOURCE OF INCOME Agriculture 33%, industry 43%, services 24%

MAIN PRIMARY PRODUCTS Groundnuts, maize, cocoa, cotton, millet, cassava, livestock, rice, timber, iron ore, oil and natural gas, tin, coal

MAIN INDUSTRIES Mining, oil and natural gas, agriculture, fertilizers, vehicles, food processing

MAIN EXPORTS Mineral fuels and lubricants 96%, foodstuffs 2%

MAIN EXPORT PARTNERS USA 18%, Italy 16%, France 16%, Netherlands 12%, Germany 7%, UK 4%

MAIN IMPORTS Machinery and transport equipment 35%, basic manufactures 24%, foodstuffs

MAIN IMPORT PARTNERS UK 20%, USA 13%, Germany 13%, France 9%, Japan 7%

EDUCATIONAL EXPENDITURE 1.7% of GNP

DEFENCE 0.7% of GNP

TOTAL ARMED FORCES 77,500

TOURISM 237,000 visitors per year

ROADS 124,000 km [77,500 mls]

RAILWAYS 3,505 km [2,191 mls]

POPULATION DENSITY 96 per sq km [248 per sq ml]

URBAN POPULATION 37% of population

POPULATION GROWTH 0% per year

LIFE EXPECTANCY Female 54 yrs, male 51 yrs

ADULT LITERACY 53%

PRINCIPAL CITIES (POPULATION) Lagos 10,287,000 Ibadan 1,365,000 Ogbomosho 712,000 Kano 657,000 Oshogbo 442,000 Ilorin 431,000

impossible task to unify and stabilize an unruly jigsaw of more than 250 ethnic and linguistic groups, and civilian administrations have held sway for only ten years since the departure of the British.

An unwieldy tripartite federal structure first introduced in 1954 proved unable to contain rivalries after independence and in 1966 the first Prime Minister, Abubaka Tafawa Balewa, and many other leaders were assassinated in a military coup. A counter-coup brought General Yakubu Gowon to power, but a vicious civil war ensued from 1967 when the Eastern Region, dominated by the Christian Ibo and known as Biafra, attempted to secede from the union after the slaughter of thousands of members of their tribe in the north by Muslim Hausa – and wrangles over increasing oil revenues.

Hundreds of thousands died (most from starvation) before Biafra admitted defeat early in 1971. The federation gradually splintered from three to 21 full states (now 31 including the Federal Capital Territory) to try to prevent one area becoming dominant. Gowon was overthrown in 1975, but another attempt at civilian rule (1979–83) also ended in a military takeover. The latest coup, a bloodless affair in 1985, brought General Ibrahim Babangida to office, and he immediately faced the crucial problems of falling oil prices and mounting foreign debts.

Nigeria's foreign exchange earnings from oil, the country's prime source of income (accounting for over 90% of exports), were halved in a year. Oil production had begun in the 1950s and risen

steadily to a peak of 2.4 million barrels a day in the early 1980s. Foreign exchange earnings peaked in 1980 at US$26 billion, but by the end of the decade this figure had shrunk to US$9 billion.

At the same time the foreign debt, constantly shuffled and rescheduled, had blossomed to US$30 billion in 1993. In seven years the annual income of the average Nigerian has shrunk from US$1,120 (among the top three on the continent) to a meagre US$310. In 1991 the World Bank officially reclassified Nigeria as a low-income rather than middle-income country. In the early 1990s there were, nevertheless, signs of a recovery, with agriculture and some areas of manufacturing growing quickly.

The political scene was changing, too. Presidential elections held in June 1993 were annulled, and Ernest Shoneka was appointed head of state. But on 17 November 1993, General Sani Abacha forced Shoneka to resign and assumed the function of head of state himself. Moshood Abiola, who claimed to have won the annulled 1993 elections, proclaimed himself head of state in June 1994 and was arrested for treason. Then, on 10 November 1995, Ken Saro-Wiwa and eight others, all from Ogoniland, were hanged at Port Harcourt, provoking an international outcry against the military regime of Abacha. As a direct result, Nigeria was suspended from the Commonwealth on 11 November. In 1996, Commonwealth efforts to persuade Nigeria to restore democracy and respect human rights were blocked by Nigerian resistance ■

SÃO TOMÉ AND PRÍNCIPE

Adopted on independence from Portugal in 1975, this variation of the familiar Pan-African colours had previously been the emblem of the national liberation movement. The two black stars represent the two islands that comprise the country.

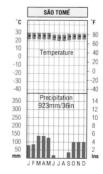

The seasonal change in the wind systems brings to the islands greatly varied monthly rainfall totals. There is a dry season, from June to September, with practically no rain in July and August, and a lesser dry spell in January and February. Rainfall is not high – below 1,000 mm [39 in]. There are also less than half the amounts of possible sunshine. Temperatures are not excessive, 34°C [93°F] being the upper record; the warmest month is March, while the coolest is July.

These mountainous, volcanic and heavily forested Atlantic islands some 145 km [90 mls] apart, comprise little more than twice the area of

COUNTRY The Democratic Republic of São Tomé and Príncipe

AREA 964 sq km [372 sq mls]

POPULATION 133,000

CAPITAL (POPULATION) São Tomé (43,000)

GOVERNMENT Multiparty republic

LANGUAGES Portuguese

Andorra, with São Tomé the larger and more developed of the two. A Portuguese colony since 1522, the islands were suddenly granted independence in 1975, and the cocoa plantations that formed the platform for the economy quickly deteriorated under a one-party hardline socialist state. Reliance on the Soviet Union was lessened from the mid-1980s and the cocoa industry revived – as well as diversification into palm oil, pepper and coffee and the encouragement of tourism. In 1990, Marxism was abandoned altogether and, following the lead from many mainland African nations and

pressure from Portugal (the main trading partner) and France (the major aid donor), São Tomé held multiparty elections in 1991, and again in 1996 when Raul Bragança Neto was elected prime minister ■

CAMEROON

Cameroon's flag employs the Pan-African colours, as used by many former African colonies. The design, with the yellow liberty star, dates from 1975 and is based on the tricolour adopted in 1957 before independence from France in 1960.

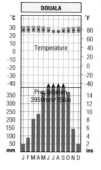

The north-east corner of the Gulf of Guinea is a region of very high rainfall and uniformly high temperatures and humidity. The rain is at its heaviest during the months of July, August and September when the south-west monsoon is at its strongest and steadiest and the temperature hardly varies. Sunshine levels are low, averaging only 3 hours per day. The rainfall on the seaward slopes of Cameroon Peak is even heavier and exceeds 9,000 mm [350 in] in places.

Half the size of neighbouring Nigeria, Cameroon has only a seventh of the population. It is, nevertheless, a remarkably diverse country, stemming from more than 160 ethnic groups (each with their own language) and a colonial past involving several European countries. The mountainous borderlands between Nigeria and Cameroon lie on a line of crustal weakness dating from the break-up of the supercontinent, Gondwanaland. Mostly volcanic, the mountains include Mt Cameroon (4,070 m [13,350 ft]) which is occasionally active. There is desert to the north, dense tropical rainforest in the south and dry savanna in the intermediate area.

The name Cameroon is derived from the Portuguese word *camarões* – meaning the prawns fished by Portuguese explorers' seamen in coastal estuaries – but European contact dates mainly from German rule as a protectorate after 1884. After World War I the country was divided according to League of Nations mandates between France and Britain. The French Cameroons became independent in 1960, while following a 1961 plebiscite the north of the British Cameroons voted to merge with Nigeria, and the south federated with the newly independent state; this became unitary in 1972 and a republic in 1984. Though Cameroon is officially bilingual, the government and public sector are dominated by French-speakers – a fact that continues to upset the rest of the population.

Despite oil production passing its peak in the 1980s and likely to stop before the end of the century, and despite patchy industrial development, Cameroon is one of tropical Africa's better-off nations, with an annual income per person of US$940 and rare self-sufficiency in food. This relative prosperity rests partly on diverse but well-managed agriculture, with extensive plantations of palm, rubber, bananas and other crops in the south-west dating from colonial times. Douala is Cameroon's main port for exports of cocoa, coffee

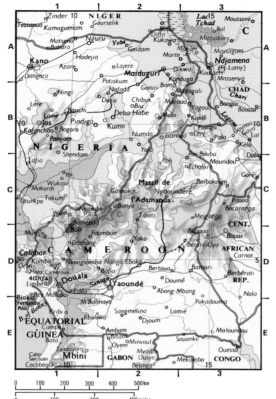

COUNTRY Republic of Cameroon

AREA 475,440 sq km [183,567 sq mls]

POPULATION 13,232,000

CAPITAL (POPULATION) Yaoundé (750,000)

GOVERNMENT Multiparty republic with a bicameral legislature

ETHNIC GROUPS Fang 20%, Bamileke and Mamum 19%, Duala, Luanda and Basa 15%, Fulani 10%

LANGUAGES French and English (both official), Sudanic, Bantu

RELIGIONS Roman Catholic 35%, traditional beliefs 25%, Sunni Muslim 22%, Protestant 18%

NATIONAL DAY 20 May; National Day

CURRENCY CFA franc = 100 centimes

ANNUAL INCOME PER PERSON US$940

MAIN INDUSTRIES Aluminium, cement, rubber, palm oil

MAIN EXPORTS Aluminium products, coffee, cocoa, cotton fibre, logs

MAIN IMPORTS Transport equipment, iron and steel, medicine, textiles

DEFENCE 2.1% of GNP

POPULATION DENSITY 28 per sq km [72 per sq ml]

LIFE EXPECTANCY Female 57 yrs, male 54 yrs

ADULT LITERACY 54%

(the chief cash crops) and aluminium, and for the transit trade of neighbours, while Kribi exports timber. Aluminium is produced at Edéa, using hydroelectric power generated from the Sanaga River, and a railway is being built to the north.

The austerity programme of President Paul Biya, initiated in 1987, appeared to reap rewards by the end of the decade, though there was widespread unrest at the repressive regime (one-party politics was introduced in 1966 by Biya's mentor and predecessor Ahmadou Ahidjo, who had been president since independence). However, elections were held in 1992. Cameroon joined the Commonwealth in November 1995, becoming its 52nd member ■

EQUATORIAL GUINEA

Equatorial Guinea's flag dates from independence from Spain in 1968. Green represents the country's natural resources, blue the sea, red the nation's struggle for independence and the white stands for peace.

At the turn of the 15th century, the Papacy awarded Africa and Asia to Portugal, and the Americas west of 50°W to Spain. The latter sought a source of slaves in Africa, and in 1778 the Portuguese ceded the islands of Fernando Poó (Bioko) and Annobon (Pagalu), together with rights on the mainland, Mbini (Rio Muni), against Spanish agreement to Portuguese advance west of 50°W in Brazil. Plantations of coffee and cocoa were established on these mountainous and volcanic islands, similar to many Caribbean islands.

Mainland Mbini, accounting for over 90% of the country's land area, is very different: less developed, thinly peopled, and with fewer foreign enterprises, except in forestry (especially okoumé and mahogany production) and palm oil. Coffee and cocoa are also grown, though the economy relies heavily on foreign aid. Oil production began in 1992.

Guinea, a name which derives from an ancient African kingdom, was once used to describe the whole coastal region of West Africa. Equatorial

COUNTRY Republic of Equatorial Guinea

AREA 28,050 sq km [10,830 sq mls]

POPULATION 400,000

CAPITAL (POPULATION) Malabo (35,000)

GOVERNMENT Multiparty republic (transitional)

ETHNIC GROUPS Fang 83%, Bubi 10%, Ndowe 4%

LANGUAGES Spanish (official), Fang, Bubi

RELIGIONS Christian (mainly Roman Catholic) 89%

CURRENCY CFA franc = 100 centimes

ANNUAL INCOME PER PERSON US$360

POPULATION DENSITY 14 per sq km [36 per sq ml]

LIFE EXPECTANCY Female 50 yrs, male 46 yrs

ADULT LITERACY 75%

Guinea was granted partial autonomy from Spain in 1963, and gained full independence in 1968. Thanks to its cocoa plantations, Equatorial Guinea once boasted the highest per capita income in West Africa. But after independence, the bloody 11-year dictatorship of President Macías Nguema left the economy in ruins, and the one-party rule of his nephew Teodoro Obiang Nguema Mbasago has since survived several coup attempts. In 1991, the people voted to set up a multiparty democracy, and elections were held in 1993 and 1996, amid many allegations of intimidation and fraud ■

AFRICA

GABON

Gabon's tricolour was adopted on independence from France in 1960. The yellow, now representing the sun, used to be thinner to symbolize the Equator on which the country lies. The green stands for Gabon's forests and the blue for the sea.

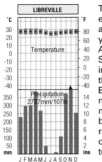

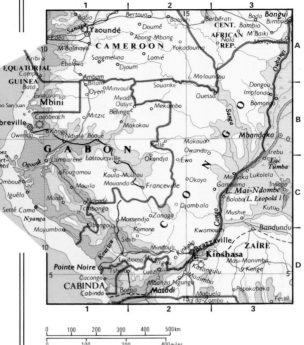

The climate of Gabon is mainly equatorial with uniform heat and humidity throughout the year and very high rainfall. At Libreville the rains last from September to May, with maxima in November and April following the passage of the sun across the Equator at the equinoxes. In these months it rains on over 20 days per month. From June to August winds blow offshore and it is almost rainless. Sunshine levels average only 4–5 hours a day, with monthly totals ranging from 3–6 hours.

The name Gabon derives from that given by a 16th-century Portuguese explorer. In the 19th century the French Navy suppressed the local slave trade, and landed freed slaves at Libreville.

Figures for GNP suggest that Gabon is one of Africa's richest states, but this is misleading: though rich in resources, the country has a low population

COUNTRY Gabonese Republic
AREA 267,670 sq km [103,347 sq mls]
POPULATION 1,316,000
CAPITAL (POPULATION) Libreville (418,000)
GOVERNMENT Multiparty republic
ETHNIC GROUPS Fang 36%, Mpongwe 15%, Mbete 14%
LANGUAGES French (official), Bantu languages
RELIGIONS Christian 96% (Roman Catholic 65%)
CURRENCY CFA franc = 100 centimes
ANNUAL INCOME PER PERSON US$4,050
MAIN INDUSTRIES Agriculture, forestry, petroleum
MAIN EXPORTS Petroleum and petroleum products, manganese, timber, uranium
MAIN IMPORTS Machinery, transport equipment, food products, metal and metal products
DEFENCE 3.7% of GNP
POPULATION DENSITY 5 per sq km [13 per sq ml]
LIFE EXPECTANCY Female 55 yrs, male 52 yrs
ADULT LITERACY 59%

(just over a million in an area larger than the UK), to whom the wealth has not yet spread.

Most of the country is densely forested, and valuable timbers were the main export until 1962. Since then minerals have been developed, as so often in Africa, by foreign companies whose profits leave the country. First came oil and gas from near Port Gentil (oil still provides over 65% of export earnings). Then, the world's largest deposit of manganese was mined at Mouanda, near Franceville, although originally the ore had to be exported through the Congo by a branch of the Congo-Ocean railway. Gabon is the world's fourth biggest producer of manganese and has about a quarter of the world's known reserves. Lastly, there is uranium from nearby Mounana; Gabon, Niger and the Central African Republic are France's main sources of uranium.

Gabon became a one-party state in 1968. Multiparty elections were held in 1990, and presidential elections in 1993 re-elected Omar Bongo ■

CONGO

The People's Republic of the Congo was created in 1970, ten years after it achieved independence from France, becoming Africa's first Communist state. Marxism was officially abandoned in 1990 and this new flag was adopted.

A former French colony and half the area of France, the Congo has over 2.5 million inhabitants. Although astride the Equator, only the near-coastal Mayombe ridges and the east-central and northern parts of the Congo Basin have truly equatorial climate and vegetation, and these are the sources of valuable exports of timber and palm-oil produce.

In 1970, the Congo became Africa's first declared Communist state, but Marxist-Leninist ideology did not prevent the government seeking Western help in exploiting the vast deposits of offshore oil, soon, by far, to be the country's main source of income. The timber industry, in relative decline, has always been hampered by poor transport – despite the spectacular Congo-Ocean railway from Brazzaville (formerly the capital of French Equatorial Africa) to Pointe Noire, the nation's only significant port.

Marxism was officially abandoned in 1990 and the regime announced the planned introduction of a multiparty system. Following a referendum overwhelmingly in favour of a new constitution, elections were held in 1992, with further elections in 1993.

Because of the huge areas of dense forest, 56% of the population live in towns – a high proportion for Africa – though subsistence agriculture, mainly for cassava, occupies a third of the fast-growing workforce ■

COUNTRY People's Republic of the Congo
AREA 342,000 sq km [132,046 sq mls]
POPULATION 2,593,000
CAPITAL (POPULATION) Brazzaville (938,000)
GOVERNMENT Multiparty republic
ETHNIC GROUPS Kongo 52%, Teke 17%, Mboshi 12%, Mbete 5%
LANGUAGES French (official), Kongo, Teke, Ubangi
RELIGIONS Roman Catholic 54%, Protestant 24%
NATIONAL DAY 15 August; Independence Day (1960)
CURRENCY CFA franc = 100 centimes
ANNUAL INCOME PER PERSON US$1,120
MAIN INDUSTRIES Petroleum and forestry
MAIN EXPORTS Petroleum, timber, diamonds
MAIN IMPORTS Machinery, iron, steel, foodstuffs
DEFENCE 3.6% of GNP
POPULATION DENSITY 8 per sq km [20 per sq ml]
LIFE EXPECTANCY Female 57 yrs, male 52 yrs
ADULT LITERACY 63%

BURUNDI

Burundi adopted this unusual design when it became a republic in 1966. The three stars symbolize the nation's motto 'Unity, Work, Progress'. Green represents hope for the future, red the struggle for independence, and white the desire for peace.

From the capital of Bujumbura on Lake Tanganyika a great escarpment rises to the rift highlands – reaching 2,670 m [8,760 ft] – which make up most of Burundi. Cool and healthy, the highlands support a dense but dispersed farming population, the Hutu, and a minority of the unusually tall cattle-owning Tutsi. This is similar to Rwanda, and being also a small country and overpopulated, employment is sought in neighbouring countries. Coffee is widely grown for export throughout the uplands, and cotton is grown on the rift valley floor in the Ruzizi Valley, which forms part of the frontier with Zaïre and links Lake Kivu in the north with Lake Tanganyika in the south.

As in neighbouring Rwanda, the enmity between the Hutu and Tutsi is centuries old. After independence in 1962, the rivalries between the two tribes led to frequent outbreaks of fighting. The Tutsi monarchy was ended in 1966 and Burundi became a republic. But instability continued with coups in 1976, 1987, 1993 and 1996, with massacres of thousands of people as Tutsis and Hutus fought for power ■

COUNTRY Republic of Burundi
AREA 27,830 sq km [10,745 sq mls]
POPULATION 6,412,000
CAPITAL (POPULATION) Bujumbura (235,000)
GOVERNMENT Transitional government
ETHNIC GROUPS Hutu 85%, Tutsi 14%, Twa (pygmy) 1%
LANGUAGES French and Kirundi (both official)
RELIGIONS Roman Catholic 78%, traditional beliefs 13%, Protestant 5%
NATIONAL DAY 1 July; Independence Day (1962)
CURRENCY Burundi franc = 100 centimes
ANNUAL INCOME PER PERSON US$210
POPULATION DENSITY 230 per sq km [597 per sq ml]
LIFE EXPECTANCY Female 51 yrs, male 48 yrs

[For map of Burundi see Rwanda, page 156.]

ZAÏRE

The Pan-African colours of red, yellow and green were adopted for Zaïre's flag in 1971. The central emblem symbolizes the revolutionary spirit of the nation and was used by the Popular Movement of the Revolution, formed in 1967.

The Equator passes through the northern half of Zaïre, and in this zone the rainfall and temperature are high throughout the year. To the north and south is a subtropical zone with slightly lower temperatures and a marked wet and dry season. The climate near the coast, because of a cold ocean current, is cooler and drier. In the east is a mountain climate. At Lubumbashi there is practically no rain from May to September, but from December to February rain falls on 25 days each month.

Formerly made up of several African kingdoms, more recently a Belgian colony, Zaïre and her peoples suffered successively from the slave trade and then the brutal methods and corruption of the Congo Free State (1884–1908), the personal possession of King Leopold II, before Belgium assumed administration until independence was granted in 1960. The country's huge size and small population stretched Belgium's modest resources. Africa's third biggest and the world's 11th biggest country, Zaïre is no less than 77 times the size of its former master.

In colonial days, palm and rubber plantations were developed in the equatorial Congo Basin (the world's second largest river drainage system), with mining on the Congo-Zambezi watershed and coffee growing on the Congo-Nile watershed in the north-east. The Congo (Zaïre) River was developed as a major artery, its rapids and falls bypassed by the railways – including the Boyoma (Stanley), the world's most voluminous, and an important railway built from the river port of Kinshasa to the coastal port of Matadi. Despite its vast size, Zaïre's Atlantic coastline consists of only 27 km [17 mls].

Minerals from the 'Copperbelt' in the far south-eastern province of Shaba (formerly Katanga), refined on the spot, provide much of Zaïre's export income. Most outstanding of many minerals are copper and cobalt (by far the world's leading producer with over 23% of the world total in 1992), with copper accounting for more than half the country's export earnings, but zinc, gold and diamonds (world's second producer) are also important. 'Strategic minerals', including cadmium, also emanate from Shaba. Industry was already substantial at independence, and the massive hydroelectric developments at Inga, below Kinshasa, which supplies power to the mining town of Kolwezi in Shaba, some 1,725 km [1,800 mls] to the south-east, should provide for further expansion under new government policies.

Belgium left the country politically unprepared for its sudden withdrawal, and within days of independence the army mutinied and the richest province, Shaba, tried to secede. Then called the Congo, the country invited the United Nations to intervene, but the appallingly violent civil war lasted three years. In 1965 General Mobutu seized control in a period of sustained confusion and remained in power into the 1990s, declaring a one-party state in 1967, and renaming the nation Zaïre as part of a wide-ranging Africanization policy in 1971.

His long, chaotic dictatorship was a catalogue of repression, inefficiency and corruption in government and unrest, rebellion and poverty among the people, with impenetrably inconsistent policies wreaking havoc in the economy even during the various mineral booms of the 1970s and 1980s.

On the whole, he was supported by the West, notably France, Belgium and the USA, who valued his strategic minerals and his support to the UNITA rebels in Angola and wanted Zaïre outside the Soviet sphere of influence. But with the end of the Cold War that support evaporated; indeed, the US soon pushed hard for reform. This, combined with increasing protests, forced Mobutu in 1990 to concede limited multiparty elections for the summer of 1991, but elections were repeatedly postponed.

Some further rioting occurred in 1993; French and Belgian troops were sent in to restore order while Mobutu tried to cling to power. In 1996, fighting broke out in eastern Zaïre, and in May 1997 rebels led by Laurent Kabila overthrew the government and planned to rename the country 'The Democratic Republic of the Congo' ■

COUNTRY Republic of Zaïre

AREA 2,344,885 sq km [905,365 sq mls]

POPULATION 44,504,000

CAPITAL (POPULATION) Kinshasa (3,804,000)

GOVERNMENT Single-party republic

ETHNIC GROUPS Luba 18%, Kongo 16%, Mongo 14%, Rwanda 10%, Azandi 6%, Bangi and Ngale 6%

LANGUAGES French (official), Lingala (linguafranca), Swahili, Kikongo, Tshiluba

RELIGIONS Roman Catholic 48%, Protestant 29%, indigenous Christian 17%, traditional beliefs 3%

NATIONAL DAY 24 November; Anniversary of the Second Republic (1965)

CURRENCY Zaïre = 100 makuta

ANNUAL INCOME PER PERSON US$250

MAIN PRIMARY PRODUCTS Cassava, plantains and bananas, groundnuts, sugar cane, coffee, rubber, cotton, palm oil, cocoa, tea, timber, oil, gas, copper

MAIN INDUSTRIES Agriculture, food processing, oil refining, textiles and clothing, mining, forestry

MAIN EXPORTS Copper 52%, coffee 16%, diamonds 11%, crude petroleum 8%, cobalt 5%, zinc 1%

MAIN IMPORTS Mining equipment 32%, foodstuffs 15%, energy 14%, transport equipment 8%, consumer goods

DEFENCE 2.9% of GNP

POPULATION DENSITY 19 per sq km [49 per sq ml]

INFANT MORTALITY 75 per 1,000 live births

LIFE EXPECTANCY Female 56 yrs, male 52 yrs

ADULT LITERACY 74%

PRINCIPAL CITIES (POPULATION) Kinshasa 3,804,000 Lubumbashi 739,000 Mbuji-Mayi 613,000

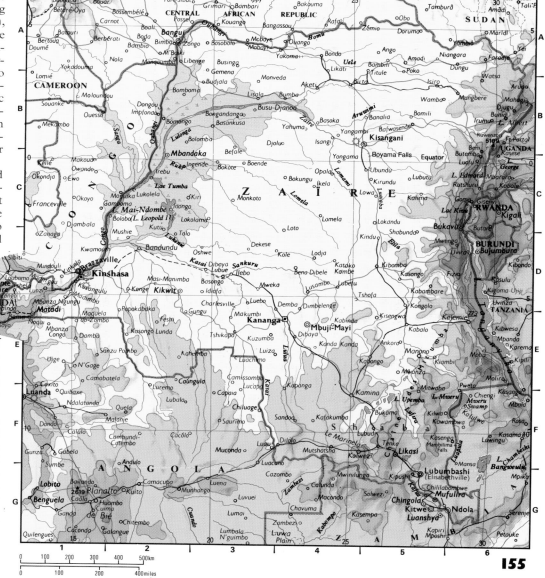

AFRICA

UGANDA

Adopted on independence from Britain in 1962, Uganda's flag is that of the party which won the first national election. The colours represent the people (black), the sun (yellow), and brotherhood (red); the country's emblem is a crested crane.

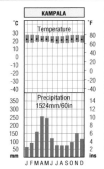

The northern shores of Lake Victoria are the rainiest tract of East Africa due to the moisture provided by the lake. Temperatures show the uniformity associated with the equatorial region but are moderated by altitude. There is a double maximum of rainfall, the heaviest rains occurring after the noonday sun is at its hottest around the equinoxes. Much of the rain falls in thunderstorms which move northwards from the lake by day.

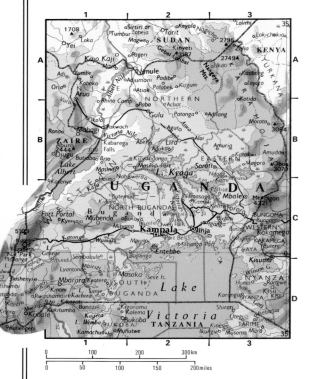

COUNTRY Republic of Uganda

AREA 235,880 sq km [91,073 sq mls]

POPULATION 21,466,000

CAPITAL (POPULATION) Kampala (773,000)

GOVERNMENT Transitional republic

ETHNIC GROUPS Baganda 18%, Banyoro 14%, Teso 9%, Banyan, Basoga, Bagisu, Bachiga, Lango, Acholi

LANGUAGES English and Swahili (both official)

RELIGIONS Roman Catholic 40%, Protestant 29%, traditional beliefs 18%, Sunni Muslim 7%

CURRENCY Uganda shilling = 100 cents

ANNUAL INCOME PER PERSON US$190

DEFENCE 2.9% of GNP

POPULATION DENSITY 91 per sq km [236 per sq ml]

LIFE EXPECTANCY Female 55 yrs, male 51 yrs

bisects the extinct volcano of Mt Elgon (4,321 m [14,176 ft]).

In the south rainfall is abundant in two seasons, and patches of the original rainforest (25% of land area) remain. However, most of the forest has been cleared from the densely settled areas, notably in the historic kingdoms of Buganda and Busoga. Here the banana is a staple of diet, and coffee, tea and sugar are cash crops; Uganda is the world's seventh largest coffee producer. Here, too, are the capital Kampala, and the industrial centre of Jinja, adjacent to the huge Owen Falls hydroelectric plant. The western areas, the former kingdoms of Bunyoro, Toro and Ankole, depend more on cattle rearing.

To the north, one rainy season each year supports a savanna of trees and grassland. Population is generally less dense, and farmers grow finger millet and sorghum, with cotton and tobacco as cash crops. The tsetse fly inhibits cattle keeping in some areas, which have become game parks, but the dry northeast (Karamoja) supports nomadic pastoralists.

Blessed with an equable climate, fertile soils and varied resources, from freshwater fish to copper, Uganda could have lived up to Churchill's colonial description as 'the pearl of Africa'. Instead, independence soon brought two decades of disaster with almost ceaseless internal conflict and a shattered economy.

Between the break from Britain in 1962 and the takeover by Yoweri Museveni in 1986 the country suffered a succession of linked civil wars, violent coups, armed invasions and tribal massacres. The worst of several bad periods was the sordid regime of Idi Amin, who in 1971 ousted the first Prime Minister Milton Obote – then president of a one-party state – and in an eight-year reign of terror killed up to 300,000 people as all political and

human rights were suspended. Amin was finally removed when he tried to annex part of Tanzania and President Nyerere ordered his troops to carry on into Uganda after they had repelled the invaders.

Obote returned to power, but the bloodshed continued and he was ousted again in 1985. The following year brought in Yoweri Museveni, who achieved some success in stabilizing the situation. In 1993 he restored the traditional kingdoms, including Buganda, and national elections were held in 1994, though political parties were not permitted. Museveni was elected president in 1996 ■

RWANDA

Adopted in 1961, Rwanda's tricolour in the Pan-African colours features the letter 'R' to distinguish it from Guinea's flag. Red represents the blood shed in the 1959 revolution, yellow for victory over tyranny, and green for hope.

Uplift on the flank of the western arm of the Great Rift Valley has raised much of Rwanda to well over 2,000 m [6,000 ft]. On the northern border are the perfectly shaped but extinct volcanoes of the Mufumbiro Range, rising to 4,507 m [14,786 ft] and a last reserve of the mountain gorilla.

Rwanda was merged with Burundi by German colonialism in 1899, making Ruanda-Urundi part of German East Africa. Belgium occupied it during World War I, and then administered the territory under a League of Nations mandate, later (1946) a UN trusteeship. In 1959 it was again divided into two, Rwanda finally achieving full independence in 1962, the same year as Burundi.

A small, landlocked and poor rural country, Rwanda is by far Africa's most densely populated state and the steep slopes are intensively cultivated, with contour ploughing to prevent erosion. Exports include coffee (70%), tea, pyrethrum and tungsten, but when conditions permit there is a large movement into neighbouring countries for employment.

As in Burundi, there are deep social and cultural divisions between the farming majority and the traditional, nomadic owners of cattle. Several decades

of ethnic strife climaxed in 1990 when a rebel force of Tutsi 'refugees' invaded from Uganda and occupied much of the north before being repulsed by French, British and Zaïrean troops brought in by the Hutu-dominated Rwanda government. The problems stem from the revolution of 1959, when the Hutu overthrew the aristocratic Tutsi minority rulers in one of the most violent clashes in modern African history.

In February 1991, in return for its neighbours granting Tutsi refugees citizenship, Rwandan leaders agreed to the principle of a return to democracy, but the violence continued into 1992, and erupted again in early 1994 with appalling loss of life following the dual assassination of the presidents of Rwanda and Burundi in an air crash. In 1996 the conflict spread into Zaïre, where Tutsis clashed with Zaïrean troops ■

COUNTRY Republic of Rwanda

AREA 26,340 sq km [10,170 sq mls]

POPULATION 7,899,000

CAPITAL (POPULATION) Kigali (235,000)

GOVERNMENT Transitional government

ETHNIC GROUPS Hutu 90%, Tutsi 9%, Twa 1%

LANGUAGES French, Kinyarwanda, Swahili

RELIGIONS Roman Catholic 65%, Protestant 12%, traditional beliefs 17%, Muslim 9%

CURRENCY Rwanda franc = 100 centimes

KENYA

The Kenyan flag, which dates from independence from Britain in 1963, is based on the flag of the Kenya African National Union, which led the colonial struggle. The Masai warrior's shield and crossed spears represent the defence of freedom.

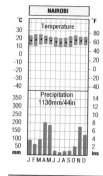

The Equator passes through the centre of Kenya, and while the climate is tropical, it is very much affected by altitude, the western half of the country being over 1,000 m [3,250 ft]. In summer, Nairobi is 10°C [18°F] cooler than Mombasa on the coast. There are two temperature maxima associated with the passage of the sun. Nights can be cool with temperatures around 10°C [50°F], but it never falls below freezing. The rains fall from April to May, with a lesser period from November to December.

Bisected by the Great Rift Valley, the Kenya Highlands were formed by volcanoes and lava flows rising from 1,500 m [4,900 ft] to the snow-capped peak of Mt Kenya at 5,199 m [17,057 ft]. Some 80% of the people crowd into about 15% of the plains in the south-west of the country, where average rainfalls of over 750 mm [30 in] a year support dense farming populations. Corn meal is the staple diet.

The western Highlands descend to the equally populous Lake Victoria basin around Kakamega and Kisii, focusing on Kisumu. Nakuru and Eldoret are farming centres originally settled by Europeans. The modern capital city of Nairobi is within this core area of Kenya, from which derive most of the exports of tea (Kenya is the world's fourth largest producer), coffee, pyrethrum and sisal, with soda ash from the Magadi alkaline lake.

By the standards of tropical Africa, Kenya has a stable and safe economy, even allowing for the traditionally thriving black market and usual reliance on aid. The country could nevertheless be in danger from two explosions, one in AIDS and the other, by contrast, in sheer numbers of people. Though relatively sparse in terms of density, Kenya's high birth rate of 4.2% is expected to produce an increase of 82% in its population between 1988 and

2000 – a figure exceeded only by Haiti. By 1990 it was already registering the world's 'youngest' profile, with more than 52% of the total under 15 years of age.

The 1990s brought signs, too, of increasing political problems as Daniel arap Moi, president since 1978 and successor to the moderate Jomo Kenyatta, found his authoritarian one-party regime under threat. In December 1991, after months of pressure and government defections, he was forced to concede the principle of pluralist democracy – not seen since 1969. The president (a Kalenjin in a country whose affairs have always been dominated by the Kikuyu) was re-elected in multiparty elections in December 1992, though there were many allegations of vote-rigging ■

COUNTRY Republic of Kenya

AREA 580,370 sq km [224,081 sq mls]

POPULATION 28,240,000

CAPITAL (POPULATION) Nairobi (2,000,000)

GOVERNMENT Multiparty republic with a unicameral legislature

ETHNIC GROUPS Kikuyu 18%, Luhya 12%, Luo 11%, Kamba 10%, Kalenjin 10%

LANGUAGES Swahili and English (both official), Kikuyu, over 200 tribal languages

RELIGIONS Christian 73% (Roman Catholic 27%, Protestant 19%, others 27%), traditional beliefs 19%, Muslim 6%

NATIONAL DAY 12 December; Independence Day

CURRENCY Kenya shilling = 100 cents

ANNUAL INCOME PER PERSON US$270

MAIN PRIMARY PRODUCTS Maize, millet, cassava, beans, pyrethrum, tea, coffee, sugar, cattle, sisal

MAIN INDUSTRIES Agriculture, oil refining, food processing, tourism, cement

MAIN EXPORTS Coffee 26%, tea 22%, petroleum products 13%, vegetables and fruit 10%

MAIN IMPORTS Machinery and transport equipment 34%, crude petroleum 20%, chemicals 18%

TOURISM 700,000 visitors per year

POPULATION DENSITY 49 per sq km [126 per sq ml]

LIFE EXPECTANCY Female 63 yrs, male 59 yrs

ADULT LITERACY 75%

AIDS AND POVERTY IN AFRICA

The Acquired Immune Deficiency Syndrome was first identified in 1981, when American doctors found otherwise healthy young men succumbing to rare infections. By 1984, the cause had been traced to the Human Immunodeficiency Virus (HIV), which can remain dormant for many years and perhaps indefinitely; only half of those known to carry the virus in 1981 had developed AIDS ten years later. By the early 1990s, AIDS was still largely restricted to male homosexuals or needle-sharing drug users in the West. However, the disease is spreading fastest among heterosexual men and women in the Third World.

Africa is the most severely hit. In 1991 a World Health Organization (WHO) conference in Dakar, Senegal, was told that AIDS would kill more than 6 million Africans in the coming decade. In the same period, 4 million children would be born with the disease, and millions more would be orphaned by it. In Uganda, an estimated million people are thought to be carrying the virus. The total number of AIDS cases in adults and children reported to the WHO up to the end of 1994 was 1,025,073, but the WHO estimates the real figure is in excess of 4.5 million, of which an estimated 70% are in Africa. Trained people are desperately needed to help the continent's future development. Africans are also more than usually vulnerable to HIV and AIDS infection, partly because of urbanization and sexual freedom. In addition,

most are poor and many are undernourished; many more suffer from various debilitating, non-fatal diseases. Their immune systems are already weak, making them less likely to shrug off exposure to the HIV virus, and more likely to develop full-blown AIDS.

Thus in Africa, a pregnant mother with HIV has a one-in-two chance of passing the virus to her child; in the West, the child of a similarly afflicted mother has only one chance in eight of contracting the infection. African poverty also means that victims have virtually no chance of receiving any of the expensive drugs developed to prolong the lives of AIDS sufferers. Even if researchers succeed in developing an AIDS vaccine, it is likely to be well beyond the reach of countries whose health budget is seldom much more than US$2 a year for each citizen; there are few refrigerators to store such a vaccine, and few needles to administer it safely.

Africa faces millions of individual human tragedies. Yet even so, AIDS-related deaths are unlikely to impinge significantly on continental population growth. At its current rate of increase – 2.97% per annum – Africa by the year 2000 will have acquired more than 243 million extra people – more than 40 times the number of predicted deaths from AIDS. And AIDS is only the newest scourge Africa must suffer. Malaria, measles, a host of waterborne infections and simple malnutrition will kill far more Africans during the same period.

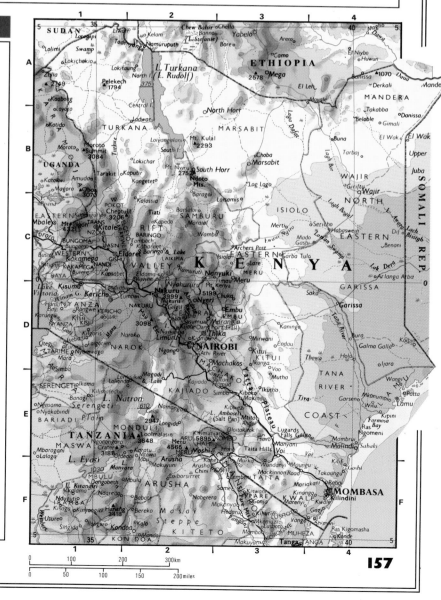

AFRICA

MALAWI

The colours in Malawi's flag come from the flag adopted by the Malawi Congress Party in 1953. The rising sun symbol, representing the beginning of a new era for Malawi and Africa, was added when the country gained independence from Britain in 1964.

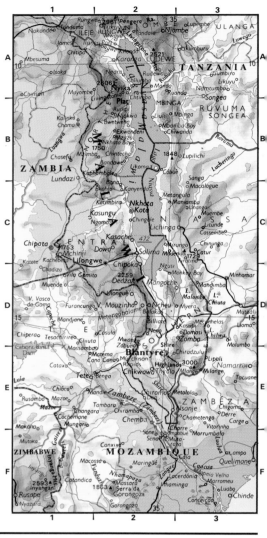

A small, landlocked, hilly if not mountainous country, Malawi's strange shape (nowhere is it more than 160 km [100 mls] wide) derived from a 19th-century missionaries' and traders' route up the Zambezi, Shire and Lake Nyasa (Malawi). The country is relatively poor in natural resources, and compared with its neighbours has a high population density, placing excessive pressure on the land. This problem was inflamed during the 1980s, when Malawi became the main host to nearly a million refugees from neighbouring Mozambique, putting an intolerable burden on an already weak economy, despite massive aid packages.

Industrial and urban development are extremely limited. Most of the commercial activity centres on agriculture, which provides over 90% of Malawi's domestic exports. Tea and tobacco, mostly from large estates, are the principal export crops, while basic foodstuffs such as maize are largely derived from small, quasisubsistence peasant holdings which occupy most of the farmland. Malawi has a long history as an exporter of labour migrants, and large numbers of Malawians still work or seek work abroad, notably in South Africa.

Malawi's recent history has been dominated by one man: Dr Hastings Kumuzu Banda. Already 62 years old, he led the country (formerly Nyasaland) to independence in 1964, and two years later declared a one-party republic with himself as president – for life from 1971. His autocratic regime was different from most of black Africa in being conservative and pragmatic, hostile to socialist neighbours but friendly with South Africa.

At first his austerity programme and agricultural

COUNTRY	Republic of Malawi
AREA	118,480 sq km [45,745 sq mls]
POPULATION	9,800,000
CAPITAL (POPULATION)	Lilongwe (268,000)
GOVERNMENT	Multiparty republic
ETHNIC GROUPS	Maravi (Chewa, Nyanja, Tonga, Tumbuka) 58%, Lomwe 18%, Yao 13%, Ngoni 7%
LANGUAGES	Chichewa and English (both official)
RELIGIONS	Christian (mostly Protestant) 62%, traditional beliefs 21%, Muslim 16%
NATIONAL DAY	6 July; Independence Day (1966)
CURRENCY	Kwacha = 100 tambala
ANNUAL INCOME PER PERSON	US$220
MAIN PRIMARY PRODUCTS	Limestone and timber
MAIN INDUSTRIES	Agriculture, fishing
MAIN EXPORTS	Tobacco, tea and sugar
MAIN IMPORTS	Fuel, vehicles and clothing
DEFENCE	1.4% of GNP
POPULATION DENSITY	83 per sq km [214 per sq ml]
LIFE EXPECTANCY	Female 50 yrs, male 48 yrs
ADULT LITERACY	54%

policies seemed to have wrought an economic miracle, but the 1980s sealed a swift decline and a return to poverty. As well as a million refugees Malawi faced another immediate problem – the world's worst recorded national incidence of AIDS. A multiparty system was restored in 1993, and, in elections in May 1994, Banda and his party were defeated. Bakili Muluzi was elected president ■

TANZANIA

In 1964 Tanganyika united with the island of Zanzibar to form the United Republic of Tanzania and a new flag was adopted. The colours represent agriculture (green), minerals (yellow), the people (black), water and Zanzibar (blue).

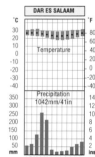

In East Africa the winds blow mainly parallel to the coast throughout the year and rainfall is less than in many equatorial regions. The heaviest rain occurs in April and May, when the intertropical rainbelt moves northwards. It is followed by the south-east winds, which have lost much of their moisture over the mountains of Madagascar before reaching East Africa. The temperature is uniformly high throughout the year.

From the islands of Zanzibar and Pemba, Tanzania extends across the high plateau of eastern Africa, mostly above 1,000 m [3,000 ft], to the rift valleys filled by lakes Tanganyika and Nyasa (Malawi), whose deepest waters reach below sea level. The Northern Highlands flank branches of the eastern rift valley, containing the strongly alkaline Lake Natron and Lakes Eyasi and Manyara, and dominated by the ice-capped extinct volcano of Kilimanjaro which, at 5,895 m [19,340 ft], is the highest mountain in Africa. The Southern Highlands overlook Lake Nyasa at the southern end of the rift system.

Tanzania's population is dispersed into several concentrations mostly on the margins of the country, separated by sparsely inhabited savanna woodland (*miombo*). Attempts to develop the *miombo* woodlands have been hindered by sleeping sickness, drought and poor soils, and traditional settlement is based on shifting cultivation.

Along the coast and on self-governing Zanzibar and other islands are old cities and ruins of the historic Swahili-Arab culture, and the major ports and railway termini of Dar es

Salaam and Tanga. Rail connections enable Dar es Salaam to act as a port for Zambia and, by ferry across Lake Tanganyika, for eastern Zaïre. Local products include sisal and cashew nuts with cloves from Zanzibar and Pemba, and there are some good beach resorts for the tourist industry.

The Northern Highlands centre on Moshi and support intensive agriculture, exporting coffee, tea and tobacco. This contrasts with the nomadic Masai pastoralists of the surrounding plains. Tea also comes from the Southern Highlands. South of Lake Victoria is an important cotton-growing and cattle-rearing area, focusing on Mwanza.

Tanzania was formed in 1964 when mainland Tanganyika – which had become independent from Britain in 1961 – was joined by the small island state of Zanzibar. For 20 years after independence Tanzania was run under the widely admired policies of self-help (*ujamaa*) and egalitarian socialism

pioneered by President Julius Nyerere. While his schemes produced relatively high levels of education and welfare for Africa, economic progress was stifled not only by lack of resources and falling world commodity prices but also by inefficient state corporations and corrupt bureaucracies. As a result the country ranks little better than war-torn states like Ethiopia and the Somali Republic in terms of income, and is almost as dependent on foreign financial aid.

Nyerere stepped down as president in 1985, but retained the (only) party leadership and considerable influence for another five years. In the meantime his successor, Ali Hassan Mwinyi, was attempting to liberalize the economy – if not the political system. Another target was tourism: Tanzania received 202,000 visitors in 1992; this is less than a third of Kenya's total, but there are hopes of a rise.

COUNTRY United Republic of Tanzania	**CURRENCY** Tanzanian shilling = 100 cents
AREA 945,090 sq km [364,899 sq mls]	**ANNUAL INCOME PER PERSON** US$100
POPULATION 29,710,000	**MAIN PRIMARY PRODUCTS** Agricultural and diamonds
CAPITAL (POPULATION) Dodoma (204,000)	**MAIN INDUSTRIES** Agriculture, food processing
GOVERNMENT Multiparty republic	**MAIN EXPORTS** Coffee 26%, cotton 24%, sisal 1%
ETHNIC GROUPS Nyamwezi and Sukama 21%, Swahili 9%, Hehet and Bena 7%, Makonde 6%, Haya 6%	**MAIN IMPORTS** Machinery and industrial goods 73%
LANGUAGES Swahili and English (both official)	**DEFENCE** 3.6% of GNP
RELIGIONS Christian (mostly Roman Catholic) 34%, Sunni Muslim 33% (in Zanzibar 99%), traditional beliefs	**POPULATION DENSITY** 31 per sq km [81 per sq ml]
	INFANT MORTALITY 97 per 1,000 live births
NATIONAL DAY 26 April; Union Day (1964)	**LIFE EXPECTANCY** Female 55 yrs, male 50 yrs
	ADULT LITERACY 64%

Certainly it has many of the prerequisites for a successful tourist industry. There are 17 national parks and reserves – among them the Selous, the largest game reserve in the world; the celebrated Serengeti; and the Ngorongoro crater, renowned for its wildlife. In addition, there are important archaeological sites such as Olduvai Gorge, west of the Serengeti, where in 1964 Louis Leakey, the British archaeologist and anthropologist, discovered the remains of humans some million years old ■

MOZAMBIQUE

The green stripe represents the fertile land, the black stripe Africa and the yellow stripe mineral wealth. The badge on the red triangle contains a rifle, hoe, cogwheel and book, which are all Marxist symbols of the struggle against colonialism.

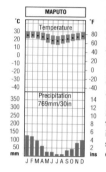

Like other former ex-Portuguese African countries, Mozambique arose from the search for a route around Africa to the riches of Asia; Vasco da Gama and his successors established forts at Beira (Sofala), Quelimane and Moçambique Island. Dutch conquest of Portuguese Asia in the 17th century, and subsequent concentration by the Portuguese on the slave trade from West Africa to the Americas, resulted in decay of Mozambique settlements. However, being so little affected by the slave trade, and acting as a refuge in wars, Mozambique was never depopulated to the extent of Angola, and still maintains a higher population on a smaller area.

Because of the warm Mozambique (Agulhas) Current, all the country is tropical. Coral reefs lie offshore, and the only real natural harbour is Maputo (Lourenço Marques). Here is southern Africa's widest coastal plain, with plantations of coconut, sisal and sugar on the alluvial flats. As in the northern foothills, farmers grow maize, groundnuts, cotton and cashew. Only the inner borderlands are high; because of this and its remoteness from Portugal, Mozambique attracted few European settlers.

At the limit of navigation on the Zambezi is Cabora Bassa, Africa's largest dam, whose power goes largely to South Africa. Large deposits of coal, copper, bauxite and offshore gas have yet to be exploited.

Mozambique forms a transit route for much of the overseas trade of Swaziland, the Transvaal, Zimbabwe and Zambia, involving mainly the ports of Maputo, Beira and Nacala-Velha, just north of Mozambique. Rail, port and handling services provide employment and substantial revenues.

Mozambique has been plagued by civil war since well before Portugal abruptly relinquished control in 1975. Combined with frequent droughts and floods, this has caused tens of thousands of deaths and, by 1989, had reduced the country to the status of the world's poorest.

When the Portuguese rulers and settlers abandoned Mozambique they left behind a country totally unprepared for organizing itself – the literacy rate, for example, was less than 1%. The Marxist-Leninist government of Samora Machel's Frelimo movement, which had been fighting the colonial regime for more than a decade, tried to implement ambitious social policies, but erratic administration, along with a series of natural disasters, reduced the economy to ruins by the mid-1980s.

From the 1970s economic progress was also severely hampered by the widespread activities of the Mozambique National Resistance (MNR, or Renamo), backed first by Rhodesia and later by South Africa. Renamo soon controlled huge areas of the countryside – convoys could only cross the 'Tete Corridor' escorted by Zimbabwean and Malawian forces – forcing more than a million refugees to flee their land, the vast majority of them going to Malawi; by 1988 almost half of all Mozambique's population was reliant on foreign aid.

Well before Machel was mysteriously killed in a plane crash inside South Africa in 1986, his government had been opening up the country to Western investment and influence – a policy continued by his successor, President Joaquim Chissano. In 1989 Frelimo formally abandoned its Marxist ideology, and in 1990 agreed to end one-party rule and hold talks with the rebels. However, the talks dragged on without a permanent cease-fire and hostilities continued to dog the country – relief agencies estimated in 1991 that up to 3 million people had been displaced by the war – and that as many again faced

COUNTRY People's Republic of Mozambique	
AREA 801,590 sq km [309,494 sq mls]	
POPULATION 17,800,000	
CAPITAL (POPULATION) Maputo (2,000,000)	
GOVERNMENT Multiparty republic	
ETHNIC GROUPS Makua/Lomwe 47%, Tsonga 23%, Malawi 12%, Shona 11%, Yao 4%, Swahili 1%, Makonde 1%	
LANGUAGES Portuguese (official), Bantu languages	
RELIGIONS Traditional beliefs 48%, Roman Catholic 31%, Muslim 13%	
NATIONAL DAY 25 June; Independence Day (1975)	
CURRENCY Metical = 100 centavos	
ANNUAL INCOME PER PERSON US$80	
MAIN PRIMARY PRODUCTS Cotton, cereals, cashew nuts, sugar, tea, fruit, sisal, groundnuts, coal	
MAIN INDUSTRIES Agriculture, textiles, chemicals, mining, food processing, fishing	
MAIN EXPORTS Shrimps 39%, cashew nuts 32%, cotton 7%, sugar 3%, copra 3%	
MAIN IMPORTS Foodstuffs 38%, capital equipment 19%, machinery and spare parts 15%, petroleum 10%	
DEFENCE 10.2% of GNP	
POPULATION DENSITY 22 per sq km [56 per sq ml]	
LIFE EXPECTANCY Female 50 yrs, male 47 yrs	

Maputo is located on the coast of Mozambique at the southern end of an extensive lowland. The range of temperature is less than that of the interior plateaus, and summers are hot and humid – partly due to the warm Agulhas Current which flows southwards along the coast. Day temperatures reach 30°C [86°F], rarely dropping below 18°C [64°F] at night. Most of the rain falls in summer, when the intertropical rainbelt is at its furthest south. There is a not entirely rainless dry season in winter.

starvation. The civil war officially ended in 1992, and multiparty elections in 1994 heralded more stable conditions. In 1995, Mozambique became the 53rd member of the Commonwealth ■

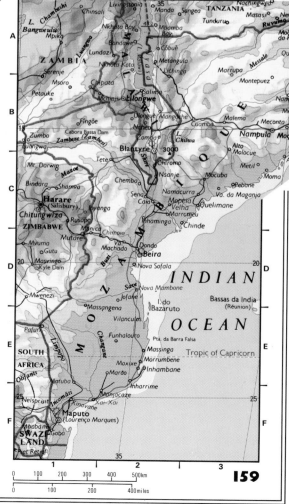

AFRICA

ANGOLA

The flag is based on that of the Popular Movement for the Liberation of Angola during the struggle for independence from Portugal (1975). The emblem, incorporating a half gearwheel and a machete, symbolizes Angola's socialist ideology.

Angola has a tropical climate with temperatures above 20°C [68°F], though slightly lower on the plateau to the east. The rainfall is low on the coast, especially in the south, because the winds are generally blowing over the cold Benguela Current or from the dry, hot interior. At Luanda, rain falls on only about 50 days each year. The wettest parts of the country are in the north and east, and the rainy season is from about November to April.

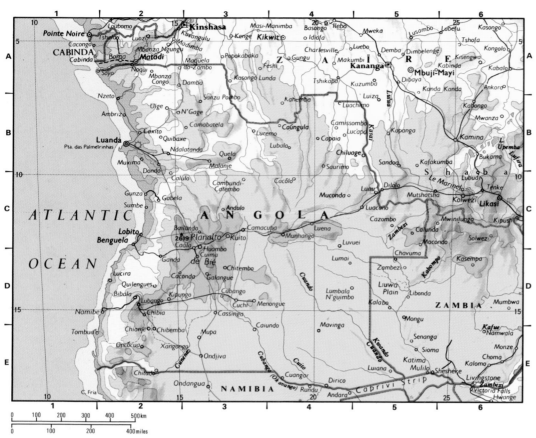

COUNTRY Republic of Angola

AREA 1,246,700 sq km [481,351 sq mls]

POPULATION 10,844,000

CAPITAL (POPULATION) Luanda (2,250,000)

GOVERNMENT Multiparty republic

ETHNIC GROUPS Ovimbundu 37%, Mbundu 22%, Kongo 13%, Luimbe, Humbe, Chokwe

LANGUAGES Portuguese (official), Bantu languages

RELIGIONS Roman Catholic 69%, Protestant 20%, traditional beliefs 10%

NATIONAL DAY 11 November; Independence Day (1975)

CURRENCY Kwanza = 100 lwei

ANNUAL INCOME PER PERSON US$475

MAIN PRIMARY PRODUCTS Coffee, cassava, crude petroleum, diamonds, cotton, sisal

MAIN INDUSTRIES Agriculture, oil-related products

MAIN EXPORTS Mineral products, pearls, gemstones, precious metals

MAIN IMPORTS Base metals, electrical and transport equipment

DEFENCE 35.5% of GNP

POPULATION DENSITY 9 per sq km [23 per sq ml]

LIFE EXPECTANCY Female 48 yrs, male 45 yrs

ADULT LITERACY 43%

More than 13 times the size of its colonial ruler, Portugal, Angola is southern Africa's largest state, extending through 13° of latitude. There is a strong cooling effect from the cold offshore Benguela Current, and climate and vegetation vary from desert on the south coast to equatorial and montane conditions in the centre and north. Thus Angola has exceptionally varied agricultural output, while the coastal waters are rich in fish.

Portugal established Luanda in 1575, and Angola's capital is the oldest European-founded city in Africa south of the Sahara. As a centre of the slave trade, some 3 million captives from Angola passed through it to the Americas; the depopulation dislocated local life for many generations. As a Portuguese colony and then overseas province, Angola's development was hampered by the small population, by Portugal's economic weakness and centralized rule, and more recently by years of persistent guerrilla warfare between rival nationalist groups.

Potentially, Angola is one of Africa's richest countries. Oil reserves are important both on the coast and offshore near Luanda, and in the enclave of Cabinda (separated from Angola by a strip of land belonging to Zaïre), and hydroelectric power and irrigation developments are substantial. Diamonds come from the north-east, and there are unexploited reserves of copper, manganese and phosphates.

Economic progress has been hampered by austere Marxist policies and vast spending on defence and security, but in 1991 the crippling 16-year war between the MPLA government and UNITA rebels ended in a peace accord. Multiparty elections were held in September 1992. The MPLA, which had renounced Marxism-Leninism and was liberalizing the economy, won a majority. However, UNITA's leaders rejected the election result, and the civil war resumed until a new peace accord was signed in 1994 ■

ZAMBIA

The colours of Zambia's distinctive national flag are those of the United Nationalist Independence Party, which led the struggle against Britain. The flying eagle represents freedom. The design was adopted on independence in 1964.

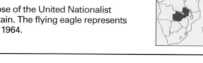

COUNTRY Republic of Zambia

AREA 752,614 sq km [290,586 sq mls]

POPULATION 9,500,000

CAPITAL (POPULATION) Lusaka (982,000)

GOVERNMENT Multiparty republic with a unicameral legislature

ETHNIC GROUPS Bemba 36%, Nyanja 18%, Malawi 14%, Lozi 9%, Tonga 5%

LANGUAGES English (official), Bemba, Tonga, Nyanja Lozi, Lunda, Luvale, Kaonde

RELIGIONS Christian 68%, traditional beliefs 27%

CURRENCY Kwacha = 100 ngwee

ANNUAL INCOME PER PERSON US$370

MAIN PRIMARY PRODUCTS Copper, coal, zinc, lead

MAIN INDUSTRIES Mining, agriculture

MAIN EXPORTS Copper, cobalt, zinc, tobacco

MAIN IMPORTS Machinery, transport equipment

DEFENCE 2.6% of GNP

POPULATION DENSITY 13 per sq km [33 per sq ml]

ADULT LITERACY 75%

A vast expanse of high plateaus in the interior of south-central Africa, most of Zambia (formerly Northern Rhodesia) is drained by the Zambezi and two of its major tributaries, the Kafue and the Luangwa. The latter and the central section of the Zambezi occupy a low-lying rift valley bounded by rugged escarpments. Lake Kariba, formed by damming in 1961 and the second largest artificial lake in Africa, occupies part of the floor of this valley; like the hydroelectric power it generates, the lake is shared with Zimbabwe, though power from the Kafue River now supplements supplies from Kariba. The magnificent Victoria Falls are similarly shared between the two countries. Much of northern Zambia is drained to the Atlantic Ocean by headwaters of the Zaïre (Congo), including the Chambeshi, which loses itself within the vast swamps of the Bangweulu Depression.

Zambia is the world's fifth biggest producer of copper ore, but despite efforts to diversify, the economy remains stubbornly dependent on this one mineral (90% of export earnings in 1990). The Copperbelt, centred on Kitwe, is the dominant urban region, while the capital, Lusaka, provides the other major growth pole. Rural-urban migration has increased markedly since independence in 1964 – Zambia has 'black' southern Africa's highest proportion of town dwellers – but work is scarce.

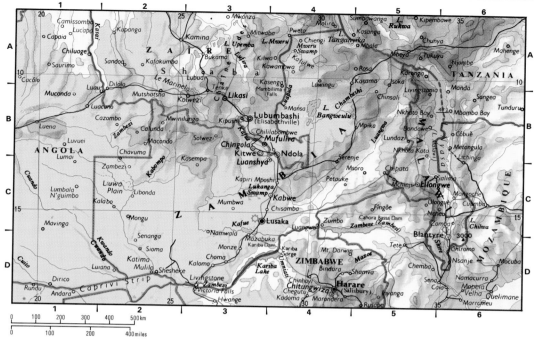

Commercial farming, concentrated in central regions astride the railway, and mostly maize, frequently fails to meet the needs of the growing urban population, but as a landlocked country heavily dependent on international trade, Zambia relies on its neighbours for access to ports via Zimbabwe, Mozambique and South Africa. Alternatives, notably a railway, highway and oil pipeline to Dar es Salaam, have been developed, but Zambia continues to have serious transport problems, compounded by lack of finance.

The leading opponent of British rule, Kenneth Kaunda became president of Zambia in 1964. His government enjoyed reasonable income until the copper crash of the mid-1970s, but his collectivist policies failed to diversify the economy and neglected agriculture. In 1972 he declared the United Nationalist Independence Party (UNIP) the only legal party, and it was nearly 20 years before democracy returned to the country. In the 1991 elections (conceded by Kaunda after intense pressure in 1990), he was trounced by Frederick Chiluba of the Movement for Multiparty Democracy (MMD) – Kaunda's first challenger in 27 years of postcolonial rule. Chiluba inherited a foreign debt of US$4.6 billion – one of the world's biggest per capita figures ■

ZIMBABWE

Adopted when legal independence was secured in 1980, Zimbabwe's flag is based on the colours of the ruling Patriotic Front. Within the white triangle is the soapstone bird national emblem and a red star, symbolizing the party's socialist policy.

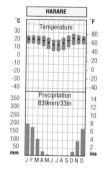

In common with other places on the high interior plateau of southern Africa, Harare has a large diurnal range of temperature, particularly in the dry, sunny winter, and is much cooler than lowlands at the same latitude. Frosts have been recorded from June to August. The main rains of summer are brought by south-easterly winds from the Indian Ocean, usually preceded by isolated thundery outbreaks which extend the rainy season from late October to March, when it usually rains on over 15 days per month.

Formerly Rhodesia (and Southern Rhodesia before 1965), Zimbabwe is a compact country lying astride the high plateaus between the Zambezi and Limpopo rivers. It was nurtured by Britain as a 'white man's country', and when Ian Smith declared UDI in 1965, there were some 280,000 Europeans there. Guerrilla action against the Smith regime soon escalated into a full-scale civil war, eventually forcing a move to black majority rule in 1980. The rift that followed independence, between Robert Mugabe's ruling ZANU and Joshua Nkomo's ZAPU, was healed in 1989 when they finally merged after nearly three decades and Mugabe renounced his shallow Marxist-Leninist ideology. In 1990 the state of emergency that had lasted since 1965 was allowed to lapse – three months after Mugabe had secured a landslide election victory. He was subsequently re-elected president in 1996.

Zimbabwe's relatively strong economy, founded on gold and tobacco but now far more diverse, evolved its virtual self-sufficiency during the days of international sanctions against Smith's white minority regime. After independence in 1980, there was a surge in most sectors, with successful agrarian policies enabling the nation to supply less endowed well-off neighbours with food in good years and the exploitation of the country's rich and varied mineral resources. However, a fast-growing population continues to exert pressure on both land and resources of all kinds ■

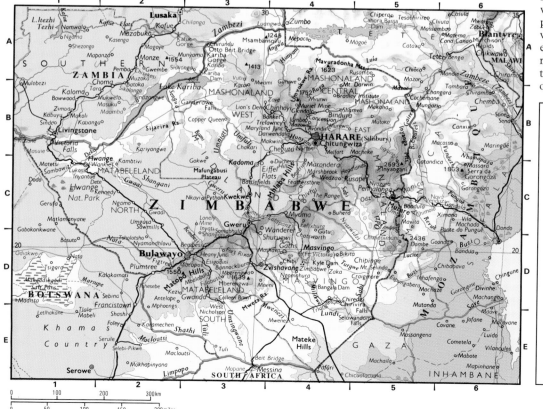

COUNTRY Republic of Zimbabwe

AREA 390,579 sq km [150,873 sq mls]

POPULATION 11,453,000

CAPITAL (POPULATION) Harare (1,189,000)

GOVERNMENT Multiparty republic

ETHNIC GROUPS Shona 71%, Ndebele 16%, other Bantu-speaking Africans 11%, Europeans 2%

LANGUAGES English (official), Shona, Ndebele

RELIGIONS Christian 45%, traditional beliefs 40%

CURRENCY Zimbabwe dollar = 100 cents

NATIONAL DAY 18 April; Independence Day (1980)

ANNUAL INCOME PER PERSON US$540

MAIN PRIMARY PRODUCTS Nickel, copper, coal, cobalt, asbestos, gold, iron ore, silver, tin

MAIN INDUSTRIES Agriculture, mining, manufacturing

MAIN EXPORTS Food, tobacco, cotton lint, asbestos, copper, nickel, iron and steel bars

MAIN IMPORTS Chemicals, mineral fuels, machinery, transport equipment, foodstuffs

DEFENCE 4.3% of GNP

POPULATION DENSITY 29 per sq km [76 per sq ml]

ADULT LITERACY 83%

AFRICA

NAMIBIA

Namibia adopted its flag after independence from South Africa in 1990. The red and white colours symbolize the country's human resources, while the green, blue and the gold sun represent the natural resources, mostly minerals.

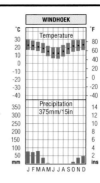

Windhoek lies at 1,700 m [5,500 ft] on the Namibian Plateau and is isolated from the effects of the cold Benguela Current which washes the coast to the west. With little cloud and clear, dry air, the daily range of temperature is much greater than on the coast. Summer days are hot, and frost may occur on winter nights. Thundery rain in summer provides enough water to support vegetation, contrasting with the deserts to the east and west. For most of the year there is about 10 hours of sunshine per day.

Born out of the late 19th-century scramble for Africa, Namibia is a country of enormous diversity, physically and socially. Fringing Namibia's southern Atlantic coastline is the arid Namib Desert (which is virtually uninhabited), separated by a major escarpment from a north–south spine of mountains which culminate in the Khomas Highlands near Windhoek. This rugged spine, built of thick schists and quartzites, rises to 2,483 m [8,150 ft] in the peak of Moltkeblik. To the east the country occupies the fringes of the Kalahari Desert.

Apart from the British enclave of Walvis Bay, Namibia was (as South West Africa) a German protectorate from 1884, before being occupied by the Union of South Africa at the request of the Allied powers in 1915. Granted a League of Nations mandate in 1920, South Africa refused to place the territory under UN trusteeship after World War II, and in 1966 the mandate was cancelled. However, South Africa continued to exploit Namibia, even though in 1971 the International Court of Justice ruled that its occupation of the country was illegal; the main nationalist movement, SWAPO, began a guerrilla campaign supported by Cuba and Angola, but it was not until 1990, following increasing international pressure, that the country eventually won its independence.

In African terms it was well worth fighting over. Although 60% of the population is engaged in agriculture, and offshore the Benguela Current feeds some of the Atlantic's richest fishing grounds, 90% of Namibia's income comes from exports of minerals – notably uranium (5.1% of the world total in 1993) and diamonds. There are also large gas fields and good prospects for oil.

The status of Walvis Bay, the crucial deep-water port and military base, was in doubt at independence, but on 28 February 1994 South Africa renounced all claims and it was returned to Namibia ■

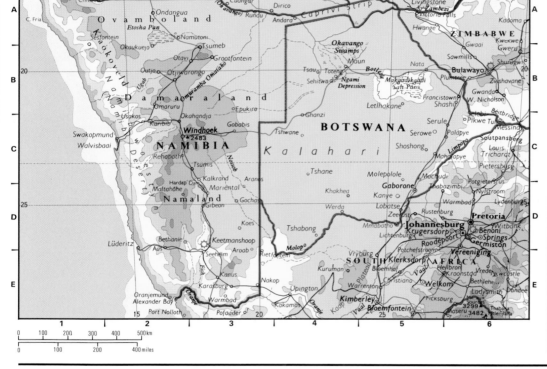

COUNTRY Namibia

AREA 824,290 sq km [318,258 sq mls]

POPULATION 1,610,000

CAPITAL (POPULATION) Windhoek (126,000)

GOVERNMENT Multiparty republic

ETHNIC GROUPS Ovambo 50%, Kavango 9%, Herero 7%, Damara 7%, White 6%, Nama 5%

LANGUAGES English (official)

RELIGIONS Christian 90% (Lutheran 51%), animist

CURRENCY Namibian dollar = 100 cents

ANNUAL INCOME PER PERSON US$1,660

MAIN PRIMARY PRODUCTS Uranium, tin, copper, lead, zinc, silver and diamonds

MAIN INDUSTRIES Mining and agriculture

DEFENCE 2.9% of GNP

POPULATION DENSITY 2 per sq km [5 per sq ml]

LIFE EXPECTANCY Female 60 yrs, male 58 yrs

ADULT LITERACY 40%

BOTSWANA

Botswana's flag dates from independence from Britain in 1966. The white-black-white zebra stripe represents the racial harmony of the people and the coat of the zebra, the national animal. The blue symbolizes the country's most vital need – rainwater.

The British protectorate of Bechuanaland from 1885, Botswana became an independent state after a peaceful six-year transition in 1966. It was then one of the world's poorest countries, with cattle as the only significant export, and its physical environment hardly induced optimism: more than half of the country's land area is occupied by the Kalahari Desert, with much of the rest taken up by salt pans and swamps. Although the Kalahari extends into Namibia and South Africa, Botswana accounts for the greater part of this vast dry upland. It is, however, not a uniform desert: occasional rainfall allows growth of grasses and thorny scrub, enabling the area's sparse human population of about 100,000 – mostly nomadic Bantu herdsmen – to graze their cattle.

Botswana was transformed by the mining of vast diamond resources, starting at Orapa in 1971, and, despite a protracted drought, expanding output in the 1980s made the economy the fastest growing in sub-Saharan Africa, paving the way for wide-ranging social programmes. By 1993, Botswana was producing 14.6% of the world's total, behind Australia and Zaïre.

Politically stable under Seretse Khama, the country's main target became diversification, not only to reduce dependence on diamonds (85% of export earnings) and on South African imports, but also to create jobs for a rapidly expanding – though still relatively sparse – population. Copper has been mined at Selebi-Pikwe since 1974, but the emphasis in the 1980s was put on tourism: 17% of Botswana's huge area (the world's highest figure) is assigned to wildlife conservation and game reserves, and more than half a million visitors a year are drawn to them, mostly from South Africa ■

COUNTRY Botswana

AREA 581,730 sq km [224,606 sq mls]

POPULATION 1,481,000

CAPITAL (POPULATION) Gaborone (135,000)

GOVERNMENT Multiparty republic

ETHNIC GROUPS Tswana 75%, Shona 12%, San (Bushmen) 3%

LANGUAGES English (official), Setswana (Siswana, or Tswana – national language)

RELIGIONS Traditional beliefs 49%, Christian (mainly Anglican) 50%

CURRENCY Pula = 100 thebe

ANNUAL INCOME PER PERSON US$2,590

MAIN PRIMARY PRODUCTS Diamonds, copper, nickel, coal, cobalt, sorghum and pulses

MAIN INDUSTRIES Agricultural and mining

MAIN EXPORTS Diamonds, copper-nickel matte, meat and meat products

MAIN IMPORTS Food, beverages, tobacco, machinery, electrical goods and transport equipment

DEFENCE 8.2% of GNP

POPULATION DENSITY 3 per sq km [6 per sq ml]

LIFE EXPECTANCY Female 64 yrs, male 58 yrs

ADULT LITERACY 74%

SOUTH AFRICA

This new flag was adopted in May 1994, after the country's first multiracial elections were held in April and a new constitution drawn up. The colours are a combination of the ANC colours (black, yellow and green) and the traditional Afrikaner ones (red, white and blue).

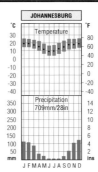

In winter the air is very dry and the sky almost cloudless on the High Veld. The large diurnal range of temperature resembles that of other places situated on the high plateaus of southern Africa; it often exceeds 15°C [27°F]. Summer is the rainy season, when north-easterly winds bring moist air from the Indian Ocean. Rainfall is more abundant and the winter dry season shorter than in western areas at the same latitude. From May to September it usually rains on 1–3 days per month.

Geologically very ancient, South Africa has only scant superficial deposits of sediments less than 600 million years old. Geological history has had a great effect on all aspects of its development.

The country is divisible into two major natural zones – the interior and the coastal fringe – the interior in turn consisting of two major parts. Most of Northern Cape Province and Free State are drained by the Orange River and its important right-bank tributaries which flow with gentle gradients over level plateaus, varying in height from 1,200–2,000 m [4,000–6,000 ft]. The Northern Province is occupied by the Bushveld, an area of granites and igneous intrusions.

The coastal fringe is divided from the interior by the Fringing Escarpment, a feature that makes communication within the country very difficult. In the east the massive basalt-capped rock wall of the Drakensberg, at its most majestic near Mont-aux-Sources and rising to over 3,000 m [over 10,000 ft], overlooks the KwaZulu-Natal and Eastern Cape coastlands. In the west there is a similar divide between the interior plateau and the coastlands, though this is less well developed. The Fringing Escarpment also runs along the south coast, where it is fronted by many independent mountain ranges.

South Africa's economic and political development is closely related to these physical components. The country was first peopled by negroids from the north, who introduced a cattle-keeping, grain-growing culture. Entering by the plateaus of the north-east, they continued southwards into the well-watered zones below the Fringing Escarpment of KwaZulu-Natal and Eastern Cape. Moving into country occupied by Bushmanoid peoples they absorbed some of the latter's cultural features, especially the 'clicks' so characteristic of the modern Zulu and Xhosa languages. By the 18th century these Bantu-speaking groups had penetrated to the south-east.

Simultaneously with this advance, a group of Europeans was establishing a victualling point for the Dutch East India Company on the site of modern Cape Town. These Company employees, augmented by Huguenot refugees, eventually spread out from Cape Town, beginning a movement of European farmers throughout southern Africa and bringing about the development of the Afrikaners. Their advance was channelled in the south by the parallel coastal ranges, so that eventually black and white met near the Kei River. To the north, once the Fringing Escarpment had been overcome, the level surface of the plateaus allowed a rapid spread

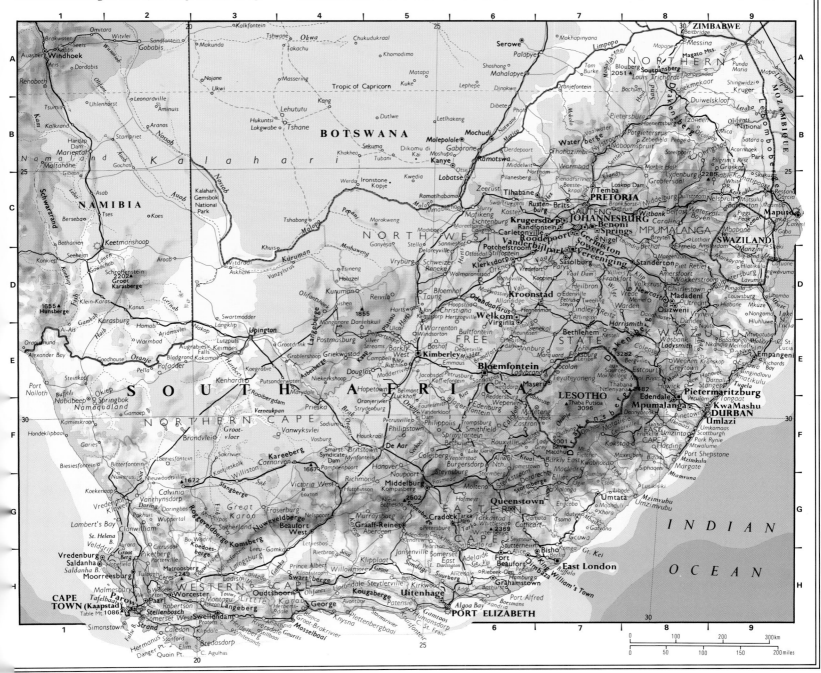

AFRICA

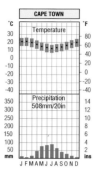

The south-western corner of South Africa has a very different climate from the rest of the country. It lies far enough south to be affected by westerly winds which blow across the Southern Ocean in winter, bringing cloud and rain. The dry, sunny summers and wet winters resemble those of the Mediterranean region, but it is less hot in summer due to the cold Benguela Current flowing northwards along the coast. From October to February, there are over 10 hours of sunshine per day.

COUNTRY Republic of South Africa
AREA 1,219,916 sq km [470,566 sq mls]
POPULATION 44,000,000
CAPITAL (POPULATION) Cape Town (legislative, 1,912,000); Pretoria (administrative, 1,080,000); Bloemfontein (judiciary, 300,000)
GOVERNMENT Multiparty republic
ETHNIC GROUPS Black 76%, White 13%, Coloured 9%, Asian 2%
LANGUAGES Afrikaans, English, Ndebele, North Sotho, South Sotho, Swazi, Tsonga, Tswana, Venda, Xhosa, Zulu (all official)
RELIGIONS Christian 68%, Hindu 1%, Muslim 1%

NATIONAL DAY 31 May; Republic Day (1961)
CURRENCY Rand = 100 cents
ANNUAL INCOME PER PERSON US$2,900
MAIN PRIMARY PRODUCTS Gold, iron ore, copper, uranium, diamonds, coal, zinc, tin, phosphates
MAIN INDUSTRIES Mining, iron and steel, vehicles, food processing, oil refining, agriculture, clothing
MAIN EXPORTS Gold 39%, base metals 14%, mineral products 10%, pearls, chemical products
MAIN IMPORTS Mechanical equipment 31%, transport equipment 14%, chemical products 11%
PRINCIPAL CITIES (POPULATION) Cape Town 1,912,000 East Rand 1,379,000 Johannesburg 1,196,000

northwards. From this colonizing process, aided by an implanting of British people in the south-east and near Durban, the present disposition of black-dominated and white-dominated lands arose.

Stretching from Northern Province's western border with Botswana, running in a horseshoe to the north of Pretoria and then southwards through KwaZulu-Natal and Eastern Cape province, are the so-called homelands – territories occupied almost exclusively by Africans. From the outset the Africans operated a form of mixed agriculture, giving them subsistence but little more. The men were cattle keepers and warriors, the women tilled the plots, in a culture based on extensive holdings of communal land. European farming was also based on extensive holdings but incorporated individual land rights. Not surprisingly, conflict arose from the juxtapositioning of the two groups, and with the discovery of valuable minerals – gold in the Banket deposits of the Witwatersrand, diamonds in the Kimberlite pipes of the Cape, platinum in the Bushveld and coal in the Northern Province and KwaZulu-Natal – both were drastically affected. South Africa still produces 27.2% of the world's gold, and today chromium ore (30.2%), uranium (5.3%), nickel ore (3.7%) and many others may be added to the list.

Exploitation of southern Africa's minerals led to trade with overseas markets and the development of major urban complexes. Johannesburg grew fastest; its growth encouraged the expansion of Durban and to a large extent caused Cape Town and Port Elizabeth to flourish. The appearance of a capitalist, market-oriented economy caused even greater divergence between white and black. The politically

dominant whites reproduced a European-style economy and, after the transfer of political power, developed strong links with Britain.

The African farmers gained little from the mineral boom. With their constant needs for new grazing grounds frustrated by the white farmers, and with taxes to pay, they had little alternative but to seek employment in the cities and mines, and on European-owned farms; the African areas became labour pools. Migrant labour became the normal way of life for many men; agriculture in the Native Reserves (so designated early in the 20th century) stagnated and even regressed.

Small groups of Africans took up urban life in 'locations' which became a typical feature of all towns whatever their size. Separated by a *cordon sanitaire* of industry, a river or the railway line from the white settlement, these townships with their rudimentary housing, often supplemented by shanty dwellings and without any real services, mushroomed during World War II and left South Africa with a major housing problem in the late 1940s. Nowhere was this problem greater than in the Johannesburg area, where it was solved by the building of a vast complex of brick boxes, the South-Western Townships (SOWETO).

The contrast in prosperity between South African whites and blacks, which increased steadily, is nowhere more visibly expressed than in their respective urban areas. The white areas could be Anytown in North America: skyscrapers, multitrack roads and well-tended suburbs. The black towns could only be South African: though rudimentary in what they offer, they are rigidly planned ∎

THE RISE AND FALL OF APARTHEID

From its 1948 institution, apartheid – 'separate development' – meant not only racial segregation but also massive racial discrimination. Over the next generation, a whole body of apartheid law was created. Key measures deprived blacks of political rights except in 'homelands' – modest tracts of poor land. Whites were guaranteed exclusive ownership of most of the country's best land, and most blacks, with no right of residence outside homelands few had ever seen, found themselves foreigners in their own country, obliged to carry passes at all times in a police state.

The African National Congress, the main black political organization, was banned, and black opposition was brutally suppressed. South Africa's racial policies led to increasing isolation from the rest of the world.

Changing demographic patterns (blacks were outnumbering whites more and more) combined with international sanctions made apartheid increasingly unsupportable. The 1989 election of liberal Nationalist President F. W. de Klerk brought dramatic change. Veteran ANC leader Nelson Mandela was released from jail to the negotiating table, and in 1991 de Klerk announced his intention to dismantle the entire structure of apartheid. In 1992, an all-white referendum gave him a mandate to move quickly towards a multiracial democratic system. The first multiracial elections were held in April 1994, after which all internal boundaries were changed and the homelands abolished. A new constitution was adopted in 1996.

LESOTHO

In 1987 this succeeded the flag adopted on independence from Britain in 1966. The white, blue and green represent peace, rain and prosperity – the words of the national motto. The emblem comprises a shield, knobkerrie and ostrich feather sceptre.

COUNTRY Kingdom of Lesotho
AREA 30,350 sq km [11,718 sq mls]
POPULATION 2,064,000
CAPITAL (POPULATION) Maseru (367,000)
GOVERNMENT Constitutional monarchy
ETHNIC GROUPS Sotho 85%, Zulu 15%
LANGUAGES Sesotho and English (both official)
RELIGIONS Christian 93% (Roman Catholic 44%)
CURRENCY Loti = 100 lisente
ANNUAL INCOME PER PERSON US$660
MAIN PRIMARY PRODUCTS Diamonds
MAIN INDUSTRIES Agriculture, mining
MAIN IMPORTS Food, vehicles, clothing, oil products
MAIN EXPORTS Diamonds, mohair, wool
POPULATION DENSITY 68 per sq km [176 per sq ml]
LIFE EXPECTANCY Female 63 yrs, male 54 yrs
ADULT LITERACY 69%

Consisting mainly of a high mountainous plateau deeply fretted by the headwaters of the Orange (Oranje) River, Lesotho declines altitudinally from east to west, with the highest ridges, over 3,000 m [9–10,000 ft], developed on basaltic lavas. This treeless zone with its steep valleys has an excess of water, making it boggy in summer, frozen in winter. It is nevertheless overpopulated. All of this contrasts with the lower narrow western belts of the foothills and lowlands, stretching southwards from Butha-Buthe to Mohale's Hoek. Here the dominant rock is sandstone.

The physical environment and being surrounded on all sides by South Africa provide major economic and political problems for the country. Most of the population are involved in subsistence agriculture, battling for a living against steep slopes and thin soils. The only urban and industrial development lies at Maseru, but the trend is still for people to drift to the small towns or to find employment in the gold and coal mines of South Africa. The country's scenery is conducive to tourism and the altitude allows winter sports; however, massive capital investment, especially in roads, would be necessary to develop this potential ∎

SWAZILAND

The kingdom has flown this distinctive flag, whose background is based on that of the Swazi Pioneer Corps of World War II, since independence in 1968. The emblem has the weapons of a warrior – ox-hide shield, two *assegai* (spears) and a fighting stick.

COUNTRY Kingdom of Swaziland
AREA 17,360 sq km [6,703 sq mls]
POPULATION 849,000
CAPITAL (POPULATION) Mbabane (42,000)
GOVERNMENT Monarchy with a bicameral legislature

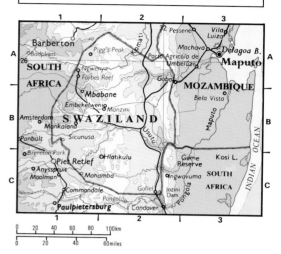

Although the smallest country in sub-Saharan Africa, Swaziland nevertheless reveals strong scenic contrasts. From west to east the country descends in three altitudinal steps: the High Veld, average altitude 1,200 m [4,000 ft], and the Middle Veld, lying between 350 m and 1,000 m [1,000 ft and 3,500 ft], are made of old, hard rocks; the Low Veld, average height 270 m [900 ft], is of softer shales and sandstones in the west, and basalts in the east. Shutting the country in on the east are the Lebombo Mountains (800 m [2,600 ft]). Rivers rising in South Africa completely traverse these belts; their valleys provide communication lines and are sources of perennial water, important for irrigation.

European colonists settled in the late 19th century, and today the main economic features result from basic differences in occupational structures between 'black' and 'white' Swazi. Those derived from European stock are involved in commerce,

industry and, predominantly, production of exports such as sugar, citrus fruits and wood pulp as well as farming cereals and cattle. The majority indigenous Swazi are still mostly engaged in subsistence farming based on maize, with fragmented landholdings and a dispersed settlement pattern. As a result there are few large towns, but the population remains far better off than in Lesotho, with which it is often compared, somewhat unrealistically.

Swaziland, which gained independence from Britain in 1968, is part of a customs union which includes South Africa, but for overseas trade the country relies largely on the port of Maputo, to which it is linked by the only railway. During the 1980s this was frequently inoperative because of the war in Mozambique – while Swaziland was also burdened with a flow of refugees. The kingdom would no doubt rather have tourists: in 1993 there were 349,185 visitors ∎

MADAGASCAR

Madagascar's colours are those of historical flags of South-east Asia, from where the island's first inhabitants came before AD 1000. The present flag was adopted in 1958 when the country first became a republic after French rule.

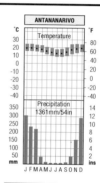

Apart from the east coast, which has rain at all seasons, Madagascar has a summer rainy season and a marked winter dry season. Antananarivo lies in the central highlands and temperatures are considerably moderated by its altitude. The island, especially the north-west, is reputed to be one of the world's most thundery regions. In February tropical cyclones from the Indian Ocean may affect the island. Only on a few occasions have temperatures exceeded 30°C [86°F].

The world's fourth largest island, Madagascar is virtually a semi-continent, bigger than France and immensely varied, physically, ecologically and culturally. Almost all geological eras are represented, and made more vivid by steep faulting, volcanic outpourings and deeply trenched valleys. There are extensive rugged areas, so that soils are often poor and farming unrewarding, and the coasts are hostile, with little natural shelter. The north and east are

hot and wet, and subject to cyclones. The west is drier, and the south and south-west are arid.

Separated from the African mainland for more than 50 million years, Madagascar developed a distinct flora and fauna – over 150,000 plant and animal species are unique to the island. Before the coming of people some 3,000 years ago, nearly all of the island was variously forested, and though much of it was cleared for agriculture a strange collection of animals survived in the remnants – among them 40 species of chameleons, pygmy hippos, elephant birds and the renowned lemurs.

Also unique to the island is its mixture of peoples, derived from several continents. Those on the west side are of Bantu origin, drawn from southern Africa via the Comoros Islands 'bridge'. Those of the centre and east (the Merina or Hova people) came first from Indonesia, as early as 2,000 years ago, with later waves arriving during the 7th to 15th centuries. Other Asians followed, all rice growers, reverent to cattle, and with language and funeral rites similar to those in South-east Asia. They had a monarchy until French occupation in 1895. In the south, the Betsileo are more mixed Bantu-Indonesian, as are other groups, yet all feel 'Malagasy' rather than African or Asian. Many other immigrant groups, including Europeans, Chinese and Indians, have also settled.

Both landscapes and agriculture (predominantly rice with cattle and pigs) in the central highlands are south Asian in character; the east coast and northern highlands are more African, with fallow-farming of food crops and cultivation of coffee, sugar, essential oil plants and spices for export – the country produces two-thirds of the world's vanilla. In the dry west and south nomadic pastoralism is important, and rice is grown by irrigation. Significant minerals are graphite, chromite and mica. Because of the rough terrain, wet season and size of the country, air transport is important, with a network of over 60 airports and airstrips.

The government which took power on indepen-

dence in 1960 continued Madagascar's links with France, but a resurgence of nationalism in the 1970s was followed by the emergence of Didier Ratsiraka, who seized power in 1975 and established a dictatorial one-party socialist state. Under a new constitution approved in 1992, Ratsiraka, whose incompetence had plunged Madagascar into poverty, was defeated in elections in 1993, replaced by the opposition leader, Albert Zafy. However, Ratsiraka was re-elected in presidential elections in 1997.

But with 90% of the forests gone, and the grasslands heavily overgrazed, Madagascar is today one of the most eroded places in the world – and is also one of the poorest countries, with a burgeoning population ∎

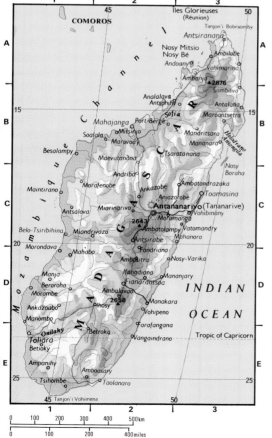

COUNTRY Democratic Republic of Madagascar
AREA 587,040 sq km [226,656 sq mls]
POPULATION 15,206,000
CAPITAL (POPULATION) Antananarivo (1,053,000)
GOVERNMENT Unitary republic with a bicameral legislature
ETHNIC GROUPS Merina 27%, Betsimisaraka 15%, Betsileo 12%, Tsimihety 7%, Sakalava 6%
LANGUAGES Malagasy (official), French, English
RELIGIONS Christian 51% (Roman Catholic 28%) traditional beliefs 47%, Muslim 2%
CURRENCY Malagasy franc = 100 centimes
ANNUAL INCOME PER PERSON US$240
MAIN EXPORTS Coffee, vanilla, sugar and cloves
MAIN IMPORTS Petroleum, chemicals, machinery
POPULATION DENSITY 26 per sq km [67 per sq ml]

INDIAN OCEAN

SEYCHELLES

The Seychelles are a compact group of four large and 36 small granitic islands, plus a wide scattering of coralline islands (14 of them inhabited) lying mainly to the south and west; 82% of the land area is composed of the four main islands which host 98% of the population, the vast majority on lush and mountainous Mahé.

With a tropical oceanic climate, the Seychelles produce copra, cinnamon and tea, though rice is imported. Fishing and luxury tourism are the two main industries. French from 1756 and British from 1814, the islands gained independence in 1976. A year later a political coup set up a one-party socialist state that several attempts have failed to remove. But multiparty democracy was restored when elections were held in 1992.

Formerly part of the British Indian Ocean Territory, Farquhar, Desroches and Aldabra (famous for its unique wildlife) were returned to the Seychelles in 1976. BIOT now includes only the Chagos Archipelago, with Diego Garcia, the largest island, supporting a US naval base ■

COUNTRY	Republic of Seychelles
AREA	455 sq km [176 sq mls]
POPULATION	75,000
CAPITAL (POPULATION)	Victoria (30,000)

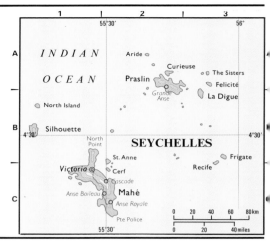

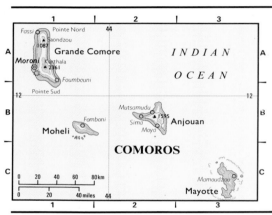

COMOROS

The Comoros are three large mountainous islands and several smaller coral islands, lying at the northern end of the Mozambique Channel. Njazidja (formerly Grande Comoro) rises to an active volcano; Nzwami (Anjouan) is a heavily eroded volcanic massif; Mwali (Mohéli) is a forested plateau. The islands were originally forested; now they are mostly under subsistence agriculture, producing coffee, coconuts, cocoa and spices. Formerly French, the Comoros became independent (without the agreement of France) following a referendum in 1974. One of the world's poorest countries, it is plagued by lack of resources and political turmoil.

Mayotte, the easternmost of the large islands (population 109,600), voted to remain French in the 1974 referendum, and in 1976 became a Territorial Collectivity ■

COUNTRY	French Islamic Republic of the Comoros
AREA	2,230 sq km [861 sq mls]
POPULATION	654,000
CAPITAL (POPULATION)	Moroni (23,000)

MAURITIUS

Mauritius consists of the main island, situated 800 km [500 mls] to the east of Madagascar, Rodruigues (formerly a dependency), 20 nearby islets and the dependencies of the Agalega Islands and the tiny Cargados Carajas shoals (St Brandon). French from 1715 and British from 1810, the colony gained independence within the Commonwealth in 1968.

The main island, fringed with coral reefs, rises to a high lava plateau. Good rainfall (up to 5,000 mm [200 in] a year) and steep slopes have combined to give fast-flowing rivers, now harnessed for limited hydroelectric power. Similar to Réunion in climate and soils, its vast plantations produce sugar cane (now declining but with derivatives like molasses still accounting for over 40% of exports), tea and tobacco, while home consumption centres around livestock and vegetables. To some extent the decline in sugar has been offset by the growth in tourism (374,600 visitors in 1993) and the expansion of textiles and clothing (nearly half of exports), though Mauritius remains heavily in debt – having been a Third World success story in the 1970s.

The islands also suffer from increasing tensions between the Indian majority – descended from contract workers brought in to tend the plantations after the end of slavery in 1834 – and the Creole minority. A republic was created on 12 March 1992 ■

COUNTRY	Mauritius
AREA	1,860 sq km [718 sq mls]
POPULATION	1,112,000
CAPITAL (POPULATION)	Port Louis (144,000)
GOVERNMENT	Multiparty republic
ETHNIC GROUPS	Indian 68%, Creole 27%, Chinese 3%

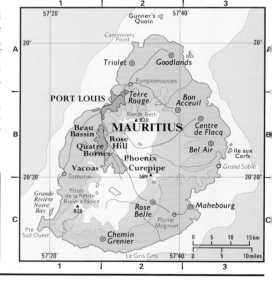

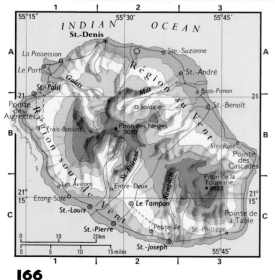

RÉUNION

Réunion is the largest of the Mascarene islands, lying east of Madagascar and south-west of Mauritius and composed of a rugged, mountainous forested centre surrounded by a fertile coastal plain. The volcanic mountains rise in spectacular scenery to the peak of Piton des Neiges (3,070 m [10,076 ft]), which is sporadically active. Réunion receives heavy rainfall from the cool south-east trade winds in winter, while the summers can be oppressively hot and humid. The lowlands are intensely cultivated with huge plantations of sugar cane: providing 75% of exports (plus rum 3%), this remains the island's most significant industry, though vanilla, perfume oils and tea also produce revenue. Local consumption revolves around vegetables, maize and livestock.

Tourism is a big hope for the future, following the success of Mauritius, but unemployment is high and France still subsidizes the islands heavily in return for its use as its main military base in the area. The people of the island – which has a varied and potentially explosive ethnic mix – are divided on its status; as in the other Overseas Departments (Guadeloupe, Martinique and French Guiana), there is increasing pressure on Paris for independence. In 1991 several people were killed in outbreaks of civil unrest ■

COUNTRY	French Overseas Department
AREA	2,510 sq km [969 sq mls]
POPULATION	655,000
CAPITAL (POPULATION)	St-Denis (207,000)
ETHNIC GROUPS	Mixed 64%, East Indian 28%, Chinese 2%, White 1%
RELIGIONS	Roman Catholic 90%, Muslim 1%

AUSTRALIA AND OCEANIA

AUSTRALIA AND OCEANIA

Though a somewhat awkward geographical label, 'Oceania' is a collective term for Australia, New Zealand, most of the Pacific islands and the eastern part of New Guinea. It is characterized by a seemingly bewildering array of islands, of varying origins; some are coral islands, others volcanic and yet others, such as New Guinea, 'continental' islands. Only about 3,000 of the tens of thousands scattered from Palau (Belau) to Easter Island and from Midway to Macquarie are large enough even to merit names. The Pacific is the largest expanse of water in the world, occupying more than a third of the Earth's surface; Magellan's first crossing in 1520–1 took no less than four months. However, its islands are nearly all tiny, and even with Australia 'Oceania' is still far smaller than Europe.

The islands of the south and western Pacific divide into three groups, based as much on ethnic differences as on geography. Melanesia ('black islands') comprises New Guinea and the larger groups close to Australia. The name refers to the dark complexion of the fine-featured people with black, frizzy hair who are today the main indigenous coastal dwellers of the South-west Pacific. Polynesia ('many islands') includes numerous islands in the central Pacific. The basically Caucasoid Polynesians, skilled in navigation, are sometimes termed 'the supreme navigators of history'. Micronesia ('small islands') includes the many minute coral atolls north of Melanesia and a narrow Polynesian 'corridor' linking the Society Islands with South-east Asia. Micronesians today are often markedly Polynesian, but in the west are more Malay or Mongoloid ■

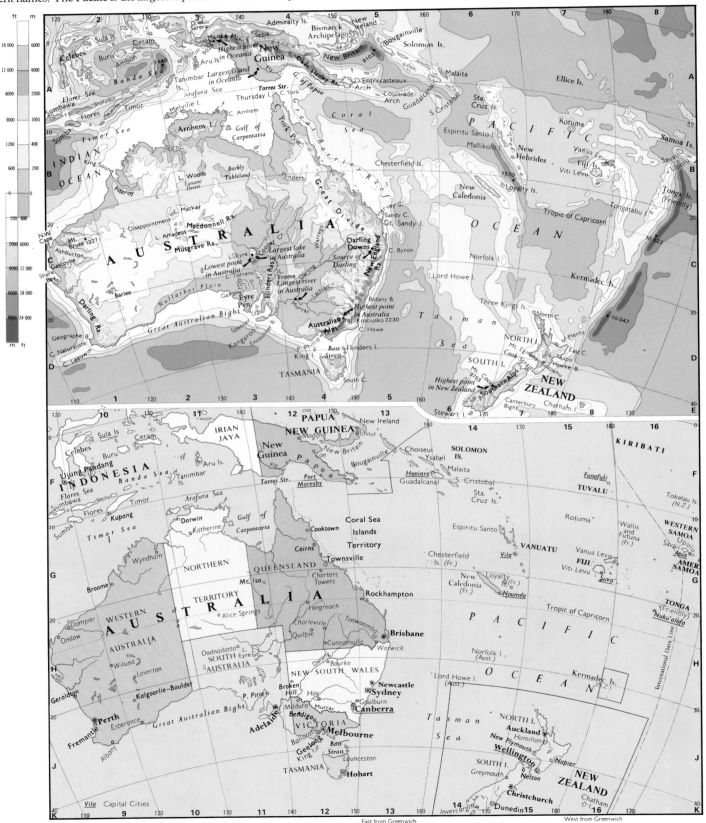

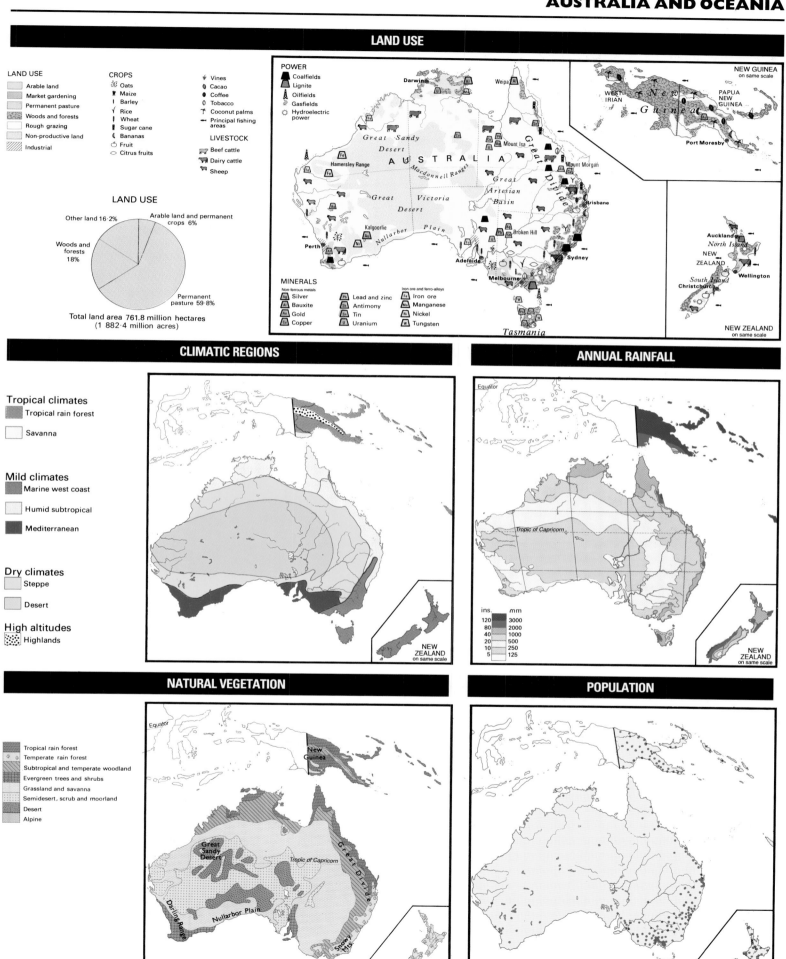

AUSTRALIA AND OCEANIA

LAND USE

LAND USE
- Arable land
- Market gardening
- Permanent pasture
- Woods and forests
- Rough grazing
- Non-productive land
- Industrial

CROPS
- ⚘ Oats
- ⚘ Maize
- I Barley
- Y Rice
- Wheat
- I Sugar cane
- ⚘ Bananas
- ⚘ Fruit
- ⚘ Citrus fruits

- ⚘ Vines
- ⚘ Cacao
- ● Coffee
- ● Tobacco
- ⚘ Coconut palms
- ⚓ Principal fishing areas

LIVESTOCK
- 🐄 Beef cattle
- 🐄 Dairy cattle
- 🐑 Sheep

POWER
- ▲ Coalfields
- ▲ Lignite
- ⚒ Oilfields
- ⚒ Gasfields
- ⚙ Hydroelectric power

MINERALS
Non-ferrous metals
- Ag Silver
- Al Bauxite
- Au Gold
- Cu Copper
- Lead and zinc
- Antimony
- Sn Tin
- U Uranium

Iron ore and ferro-alloys
- Fe Iron ore
- Mn Manganese
- Ni Nickel
- W Tungsten

LAND USE

Other land 16·2%
Arable land and permanent crops 6%
Woods and forests 18%
Permanent pasture 59·8%

Total land area 761.8 million hectares
(1 882·4 million acres)

NEW GUINEA on same scale
WEST IRIAN · New Guinea · PAPUA NEW GUINEA
Port Moresby

Darwin · Weipa
Great Sandy Desert
Hamersley Range
AUSTRALIA
Macdonnell Ranges
Mount Isa
Great Dividing
Mount Morgan
Great Artesian Basin
Brisbane
Great Victoria Desert
Kalgoorlie
Perth
Nullarbor Plain
Broken Hill
Adelaide
Sydney
Melbourne
Tasmania

NEW ZEALAND on same scale
Auckland · North Island · NEW ZEALAND
Christchurch · South Island · Wellington

CLIMATIC REGIONS

Tropical climates
- Tropical rain forest
- Savanna

Mild climates
- Marine west coast
- Humid subtropical
- Mediterranean

Dry climates
- Steppe
- Desert

High altitudes
- Highlands

NEW ZEALAND on same scale

ANNUAL RAINFALL

Equator
Tropic of Capricorn

ins.	mm
120	3000
80	2000
40	1000
20	500
10	250
5	125

NEW ZEALAND on same scale

NATURAL VEGETATION

- Tropical rain forest
- Temperate rain forest
- Subtropical and temperate woodland
- Evergreen trees and shrubs
- Grassland and savanna
- Semidesert, scrub and moorland
- Desert
- Alpine

Equator
New Guinea
Great Sandy Desert
Tropic of Capricorn
Great Dividing
Darling Range
Nullarbor Plain
Snowy Mts.

NEW ZEALAND on same scale

POPULATION

• 100 000 people

NEW ZEALAND on same scale

AUSTRALIA AND OCEANIA

AUSTRALIA

Australia's flag (*far left*), adopted in 1901, features the British Blue Ensign. The five stars represent the Southern Cross and, with the larger star, symbolize the six states. The Aboriginal flag (*left*) has had equal status since 1995.

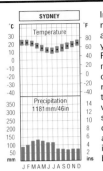

In the south-east, the annual rainfall total is reasonably high and distributed throughout the year, with maxima April to June. Rain falls on 12–13 days each month. The vast valleys inland of the Great Divide, in the lee of the rain-bearing winds, are drier. The temperatures are moderate, with winter night frosts throughout the south and the interior. Snow falls on the uplands of the south-east and Tasmania. Frosts are unknown in Sydney, the lowest temperatures being 2–4°C [36–39°F].

Whether Australia is the world's largest island or its smallest continental land mass – or both, or neither, depending on the school of geography – it is primarily a land of low to medium altitude plateaus that form monotonous landscapes extending for hundreds of kilometres. The edges of the plateaus are more diverse, particularly in the east where deep gorges and waterfalls create rugged relief between the Great Divide and the coast. In the north-west, impressive gorge scenery is found in the Hammersley Range and Kimberley area.

The western half of Australia is formed of ancient rocks. Essentially an arid landscape of worn-down ridges and plateaus, with depressions occupied by sandy deserts and occasional salt lakes, this area has little surface water.

The eastern sixth of the continent, including Tasmania, forms the Eastern Highlands, the zone of greatest relief, greatest rainfall, most abundant vegetation and greatest population. Peaks in this region include Mt Kosciusko, at 2,230 m [7,316 ft] Australia's highest. Much of this area shows signs of volcanic activity in the relatively recent geological past, and these young basalts support nutrient-rich soils in contrast to the generally weathered, nutrient-poor soils of nearly all the remainder of Australia.

Between the western plateaus and Eastern Highlands lie the Carpentaria, central and Murray lowlands. The central lowlands drain to the great internal river systems supplying Lake Eyre, or to

the Bulloo system, or through great inland deltas to the Darling River. The parallel dune ridges of this area form part of a great continent-wide set of dune ridges extending in a huge anti-clockwise arc, eastwards through the Great Victoria Desert, northwards through the Simpson Desert and westwards in the Great Sandy Desert. All these, though inhospitable, are only moderately arid, allowing widespread if sparse vegetation cover.

Vegetation

On the humid margins of the continent are luxuriant forests. These include the great jarrah forests of tall eucalyptus hardwoods in the extreme south-west of Western Australia; the temperate rainforests with Antarctic beech found in Tasmania and on humid upland sites north through New South Wales to the Queensland border; and the tropical and subtropical rainforests found in the wetter areas along the east coast, from the McIllwraith Range in the north to the vicinity of Mallacoota Inlet in the south. Some of the rainforest areas are maintained as managed forests, others are in national parks, but most of the original cover has been cleared for agriculture, particularly for dairying and cattle fattening, and for sugar and banana cultivation north of Port Macquarie.

The most adaptable tree genus in Australia is the *Eucalyptus*, which ranges from the tall flooded gum trees found on the edges of the rainforest to the dry-living mallee species found on sand plains and interdune areas. Acacia species, especially the bright-yellow flowered wattles, are also adapted to a wide range of environments. Associated with this adaptation of plants is the wide variety of animal adaptations, with 277 different mammals, about 400 species of reptiles and some 700 species of birds. Aborigines arriving from Asia over 40,000 years ago brought the dingo, which rapidly replaced the Tasmanian wolf, the largest marsupial predator, and preyed on smaller animals. Fires, lit for hunting and allowed to burn uncontrolled, altered much of the vegetation, probably allowing eucalyptus forests to expand at the expense of the rainforest. However, the Aborigines understood their environment, carefully protecting vital areas of natural food supply,

restricting the use of certain desert waterholes which tradition taught would be reliable in a drought, and developing a resource-use policy which was aimed at living with nature.

European settlement after 1788 upset this ecological balance, through widespread clearing of coastal forests, overgrazing of inland pastures and introduction of exotic species, especially the destructive rabbit. But Europeans also brought the technology which enabled the mineral, water and soil resources of Australia to be developed.

Mineral resources

Much of Australia's growth since the beginning of European settlement has been closely related to the exploitation of mineral resources, which has led directly to the founding, growth and often eventual decline of the majority of inland towns. Broken Hill and Mount Isa are copper-, lead-, zinc- and silver-producing centres, while Kalgoorlie, Bendigo, Ballarat and Charters Towers all grew in the 19th-century gold rushes. Today, less-glamorous minerals support the Australian economy. In Western Australia, the great iron-ore mines of Mount Tom Price, Mount Newman and Mount Goldsworthy are linked by new railways to special ports at Dampier and Port Hedland. Offshore are the oil and gas fields of the north-west shelf.

In the east, the coal mines of central Queensland and eastern New South Wales are linked by rail to bulk-loading facilities at Sarina, Gladstone, Brisbane, Newcastle, Sydney and Port Kembla, which enable this high-grade coking coal to be shipped to worldwide markets and by 1986 had made Australia the biggest exporter (15% of export earnings). Bauxite mining has led to new settlements at Nhulunby and Weipa on the Gulf of

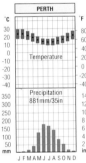

The vast interior of Australia is very dry, and with high temperatures much of the rain that does fall quickly evaporates. There are no great areas of high land that could form a barrier to the rain-bearing winds or a relief to the high temperatures. Along the southern coast the rainfall is slightly higher than in the interior. There is higher rainfall in the extreme south-west of the country around Perth, which experiences a Mediterranean-type climate of hot, dry summers and warm, wet winters.

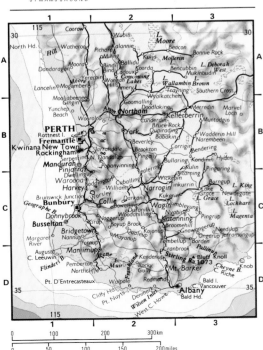

COUNTRY Commonwealth of Australia

AREA 7,686,850 sq km [2,967,893 sq mls]

POPULATION 18,107,000

CAPITAL (POPULATION) Canberra (328,000)

GOVERNMENT Federal constitutional monarchy with a bicameral legislature

ETHNIC GROUPS White 95%, Aboriginal 2%, Asian 1%

LANGUAGES English (official)

RELIGIONS Roman Catholic 26%, Anglican 24%, other Christian 20%, Muslim, Buddhist, Jewish

NATIONAL DAY 26 January; Australia Day

CURRENCY Australian dollar = 100 cents

ANNUAL INCOME PER PERSON US$17,510

SOURCE OF INCOME Agriculture 4%, industry 34%, services 61%

MAIN PRIMARY PRODUCTS Coal, crude petroleum, bauxite, sheep, cattle, timber, zircon, natural gas, gold, silver

MAIN INDUSTRIES Metal fabrication, mining, construction of vehicles and aircraft, agriculture, petrol refining, chemicals, electronics

MAIN EXPORTS Food and live animals 22%, coal, oil and gas 19%, metallic ores 14%, textile fibres 11%, machinery 6%, transport equipment 3%

MAIN EXPORT PARTNERS Japan 25%, USA 12%, New Zealand 5%, South Korea 4%, UK 4%, Germany 3%, Hong Kong 3%, Taiwan 3%

MAIN IMPORTS Machinery and transport equipment 40%, basic manufactures 16%, chemicals 8%, petroleum products 5%, food and live animals 5%

MAIN IMPORT PARTNERS USA 22%, Japan 21%, Germany 8%, UK 7%, New Zealand 4%, Taiwan 4%

EDUCATIONAL EXPENDITURE 5.5% of GNP

DEFENCE 2.4% of GNP

TOTAL ARMED FORCES 62,700

TOURISM 2,783,400 visitors per year

ROADS 840,000 km [525,000 mls]

RAILWAYS 39,251 km [22,657 mls]

POPULATION DENSITY 2 per sq km [6 per sq ml]

URBAN POPULATION 85%

POPULATION GROWTH 1.4% per year

INFANT MORTALITY 7 per 1,000 live births

LIFE EXPECTANCY Female 80 yrs, male 74 yrs

ADULT LITERACY 99%

PRINCIPAL CITIES (POPULATION) Sydney 3,713,000 Melbourne 3,189,000 Brisbane 1,422,000 Perth 1,221,000 Adelaide 1,071,000

Carpentaria, with associated refineries at Kwinana, Gladstone and Bell Bay.

Rum Jungle, south of Darwin, became well known as one of the first uranium mines, but now deposits further east in Arnhem Land are being developed. Meanwhile, new discoveries of ore bodies continue to be made in the ancient rocks of the western half of Australia. Natural gas from the Cooper Basin, just south of Innamincka on Cooper Creek, is piped to Adelaide and Sydney, while oil and gas from the Bass Strait and brown coal from the Yallourn-Morwell area have been vital to the industrial growth of Victoria. Fossil fuels are supplemented by hydroelectric power from major schemes in western Tasmania and the Snowy Mountains and smaller projects near Cairns and Tully in north Queensland.

Australia's mineral wealth is phenomenal. In 1993 it produced over 40% of the world's diamonds, around 13% of gold and iron ore, 8% of silver, 7% of aluminium, nickel, magnesium and uranium, and 5% of zinc and lead. Even this impressive array could not help Australia resist slumps in world demand, however, and by 1991 the country was experiencing its worst recession since the 1920s.

Agriculture

Apart from the empty and largely unusable desert areas in Western Australia and the Simpson Desert, extensive cattle or sheep production dominates all of Australia north and west of a line from Penong in South Australia, through Broken Hill in New South Wales to Bundaberg in Queensland, and east of a line from Geraldton to Esperance in Western Australia. Cattle and sheep populations in this zone are sparse, while individual pastoral holdings are large, some over 400,000 hectares [1 million acres], and towns are both small and far apart.

Some Aborigines retain limited tracts of land in Arnhem Land and on the fringes of the deserts where they live by hunting and gathering, but nearly all Aborigines now live close to government settlements or mission stations. Many are employed as stockmen and seasonal agricultural workers, while thousands of others have migrated to country towns and the major cities.

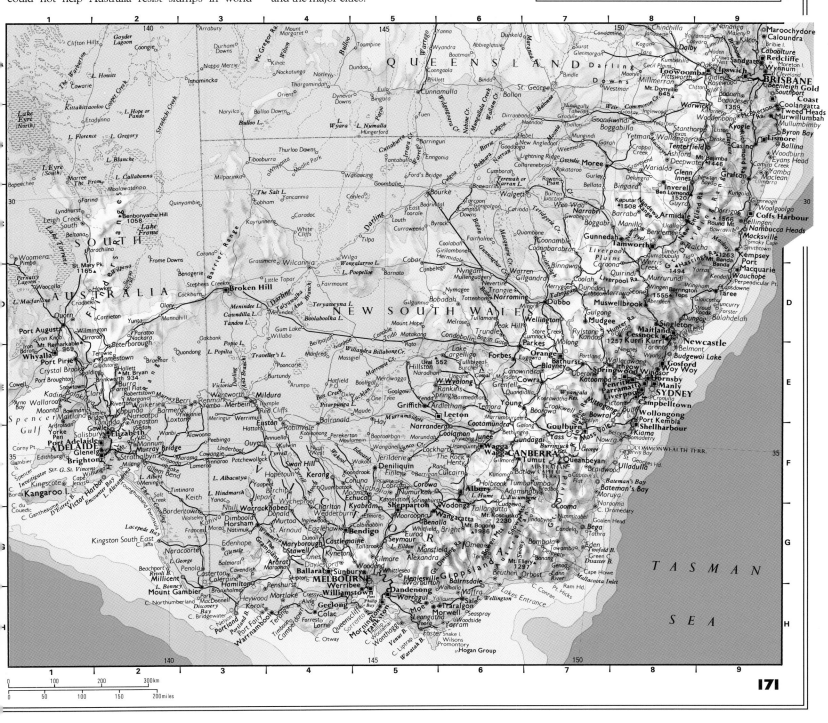

AUSTRALIA AND OCEANIA

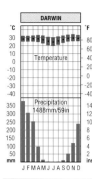

DARWIN

Only 10% of Australia receives more than 1,000 mm [39 in] of rain and these areas are the north, the east coast and the south-west tip of the continent. Much of the centre receives less than 250 mm [10 in], which fails in many years. The northern half of Australia lies within the tropics and the monsoon brings a lot of rain from December to March. Typhoons can hit the northern Queensland coast. Day temperatures in all months are over 30°C [68°F], with night temperatures above 20°C [68°F].

The intensive pastoral and agricultural zones support the bulk of the sheep and cattle of Australia, and wool, mutton and beef production is still the basic industry. The country is the world's largest producer of wool and third in lamb and mutton. Wheat is cultivated in combination with sheep raising over large tracts of the gentle inland slopes of the coastal ranges.

Along the east coast are important cattle, dairy and sugar-cane industries, the latter significant on the east coast from Brisbane to Cairns. Irrigated areas also support cotton, rice, fruit and vegetable crops, largely for consumption within Australia. Wine production around Perth, Adelaide, central Victoria and eastern New South Wales has expanded in recent decades, producing vintages of international renown.

Development

European settlement in Australia began in 1788 as a penal colony in New South Wales, spreading quickly to Queensland and Tasmania. During the 19th century the continent became divided into the states of New South Wales, Queensland (1859), South Australia (1836), Tasmania (1825), Victoria (1851) and Western Australia (1829), with the area now forming the Northern Territory being under the control of South Australia. During this colonial period the state seaport capitals of Sydney, Brisbane, Adelaide, Hobart, Melbourne and Perth became established as the dominant manufacturing, commercial, administrative and legislative centres of their respective states – a position none of them have since relinquished.

In 1901, the states came together to create the Commonwealth of Australia with a federal constitution. Trade between the states became free, and external affairs, defence and immigration policy became federal responsibilities, though health, education, transport, mineral, agricultural and industrial development remained firmly in the hands of each state. Only gradually did powers of taxation give the federal government the opportunity to develop national policies.

The federal capital established at Canberra, in the new Australian Capital Territory, grew from a tiny settlement in 1911 to become a great seat of administration and learning, and the largest inland regional commercial centre. The federal government's territorial responsibilities also include the Northern Territory, self-governing since 1978.

Immigration has changed the ethnic character of Australia since about 1960. Australian society now has Greek, Italian, Yugoslav, Turkish, Lebanese and South-east Asian communities alongside the longer-established Aboriginal, British, Irish, Chinese, Dutch and German communities, though the culture remains strongly British in flavour. Almost 60% of the total Australian population live in Sydney, Melbourne, Adelaide, Brisbane, Perth and Hobart. Migration within the states from inland rural areas to capital cities or coastal towns leaves many rural communities with an ageing population, while the new mining centres have young populations. The most rapid growth outside new mining centres is occurring in coastal towns through migration on retirement and attempts to establish an alternative life style by leaving the big cities.

Soon after 1788, small-scale manufacturing began to supply domestic goods and machinery to the colonial community. Inevitably manufacturing grew in the colonial seaport capitals, especially Sydney and Melbourne, which now have over 60% of all manufacturing industry (though only 40% or so of the total population).

Under the Australian Constitution, the federal government has control over interstate and overseas transport, with the state governments responsible for regulation within their own borders. Seven railway systems thus exist, each state system focusing on its capital city, with the Commonwealth Railways responsible for the Trans-Australian, Central Australian and Northern Territory routes. The notorious differences in gauges between the states have been partially overcome by the construction of the standard-gauge links from Brisbane to Sydney, Sydney to Melbourne, and Sydney to Perth via Broken Hill. The completion of the Tarcoola–Alice Springs route will provide the basic strategic standard-gauge rail network for Australia.

Railways are vital for bulk freight, especially mineral ores, coal and wheat. Among the busiest of the railways are the iron-ore lines in the north-west of Western Australia. Most cattle and sheep, however, are carried by 'road trains' – a powerful unit pulling several trailers.

When coral is alive it sways gently in the sea's currents, but when it dies it forms hard coral 'limestone' rock. The beautiful Great Barrier Reef, off the coast of Queensland in the Coral Sea and the world's biggest, is a maze of some 2,500 reefs exposed only at low tide, ranging in size from a few hundred hectares to 50 sq km [20 sq mls], and extending over an area of 250,000 sq km [100,000 sq mls].

The section extending for about 800 km [500 mls] north of Cairns forms a discontinuous wall of coral, through which narrow openings lead to areas of platform or patch reefs. South of Cairns, the reefs are less continuous, and extend further from the coast. Between the outer reef and the coast are many high islands, remnants of the mainland; coral cays, developed from coral sand on reefs and known locally as low islands, are usually small and uninhabited, exceptions being Green Island and Heron Island.

A major tourist attraction comprising over 400 types of coral and harbouring more than 1,500 species of fish, the modern reefs have evolved in the last 20,000 years, over older foundations exposed to the atmosphere during former low sea levels. Coral is susceptible to severe damage from tropical cyclones and, increasingly, to attack by the crown-of-thorns starfish. Much is now protected as the Great Barrier Reef Marine Park (the world's largest protected sea area), but the existence of oil around and beneath the reef is a great long-term threat to its ecological stability.

A rapidly improving highway system links all major cities and towns, providing easy mobility for a largely car-owning population. Some journeys are still difficult, especially when floods wash away sections of road or sand drifts bury highways. Although 90% of all passenger transport is by road, air services cope with much interstate travel.

Australia is also well served by local broadcasting and television. The radio remains a lifeline for remote settlements dependent on the flying doctor or aerial ambulance, and for many others when floods or bush fires threaten isolated communities.

The worldwide economic depression of the late 1980s was mirrored in Australia by a deterioration of the country's hitherto buoyant export of agricultural products and its worst unemployment for 60 years. It was against this background that the Labour Prime Minister, Bob Hawke, was elected for an unprecedented fourth term, but in 1991 the worsening economic situation forced his replacement by Paul Keating. Under Keating's administration, the key issue of Australia's trade relations, following the extension of the European Union and the success of the Pacific Rim economies, came to the fore, as did the associated question of the country's national identity.

However, elections in 1996 saw Paul Keating voted out of office, and the election of John Howard to the position of prime minister. Unlike Keating, Howard is not a republican, and he is keen to maintain close links with the UK ∎

Marsupials are mammals that give birth to their young at an early stage of development and attach them to their milk glands for a period, often inside a pouch (*marsupium*). Once widespread around the world, they have mostly been ousted by more advanced forms, but marsupials continue to flourish in Australia, New Guinea and South America.

Best known are the big red and grey kangaroos that range over the dry grasslands and forests of Australia. Standing up to 2 m [6.5 ft] tall, they are grazers that now compete for food with cattle and sheep. Bounding at speed they can clear fences of their own height. Wallabies – small species of the same family – live in the forests and mountains.

Australia has many other kinds of marsupials, though several have died out since the coming of Europeans. Tree-living koalas live exclusively on eucalyptus leaves. Heavily built wombats browse in the undergrowth like large rodents, and the fierce-sounding Tasmanian Devils are mild scavengers of the forest floor.

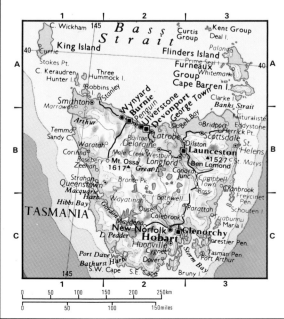

PAPUA NEW GUINEA

When Papua New Guinea became independent from Australia in 1975 it adopted a flag which had been used for the country since 1971. The design includes a local bird of paradise, the *kumul*, in flight and the stars of the Southern Cross constellation.

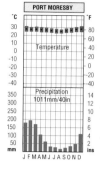

Close to the Equator and surrounded by a warm ocean, Port Moresby has a very small temperature range both diurnally (about 7°C [13°F]) and seasonally (about 3°C [5°F]). Rainfall is far more variable, with a wet season when the humid north-west monsoon blows, and a dry season associated with the south-east trade winds. The total rainfall is small compared with most of New Guinea. Over 3,000 mm [130 in] falls on the north coast, with even higher amounts in the mountains.

Forming part of Melanesia, Papua New Guinea is the eastern section of the island of New Guinea, plus the Bismarck Archipelago and the copper-rich island of Bougainville – geographically, though not politically, part of the Solomons. The backbone of the main island is a high cordillera of rugged fold mountains, averaging between 2,500 m to 4,600 m [8,000 ft to 15,000 ft] in height and covered with tropical montane 'cloud' forest. Isolated valleys and intermontane basins run parallel with the main ranges. Fertile with alluvium and volcanic materials, these are the sites of isolated settlements, even today linked only by light aircraft. The capital city, Port Moresby, is not linked by road to any other major centre, and communication with the highlands depends on the country's 400 airports and airstrips.

The traditional garden crops of the 'highlanders' include kaukau (sweet potato), sugar cane, bananas, maize, cassava and nut-bearing pandans. Pigs are kept mainly for status and ritual purposes. In the lowlands, taro is the staple food, although yams and sago are also important. The main cash crops are coconuts, coffee, cocoa and rubber.

Although the first European contact came as early as 1526, it was only in the late 19th century that permanent German and British settlements were established. After World War II, the UN Trust Territory of New Guinea and the Territory of Papua were administered by Australia. Self-government came in 1973, with full independence in 1975.

While 80% of the population still live by agriculture, minerals (notably copper, gold and silver) have provided an increasingly important share of exports, encouraging 'PNG' to reduce its dependence on Australian aid. Most of the copper, however, comes from the world's biggest mine at Panguna on Bougainville, where demands by the islanders for a greater share of the earnings spiralled into a separatist struggle by 1989 – followed by the closure of the mine, a declaration of independence by the secessionists and a total blockade of the island by the government in Moresby. Despite a peace accord of 1991, the position was still unchanged after three years – with the 'revolution' passing into the hands of criminal gangs ■

COUNTRY	Independent State of Papua New Guinea
AREA	462,840 sq km [178,703 sq mls]
POPULATION	4,292,000
CAPITAL (POPULATION)	Port Moresby (193,000)
GOVERNMENT	Constitutional monarchy
ETHNIC GROUPS	Papuan 84%, Melanesian 15%
LANGUAGES	English (official), Motu
RELIGIONS	Christian 96%, traditional beliefs 3%
NATIONAL DAY	16 September; Independence Day
CURRENCY	Kina = 100 toea
ANNUAL INCOME PER PERSON	US$1,120
MAIN EXPORTS	Gold 39%, copper ore, coffee, timber, cocoa beans, copra
MAIN IMPORTS	Machinery and vehicles 34%, manufactured goods, mineral fuels, foodstuffs
POPULATION DENSITY	9 per sq km [24 per sq ml]
LIFE EXPECTANCY	Female 57 yrs, male 55 yrs
ADULT LITERACY	70%

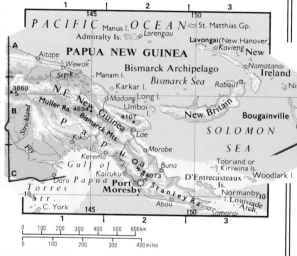

SOLOMON ISLANDS

The double chain of islands forming the Solomons and Vanuatu extends for some 2,250 km [1,400 mls] and represents the drowned outermost crustal fold on the borders of the ancient Australian continent. New Caledonia lies on an inner fold, nearer the mainland. The main islands, all of volcanic origin, are Guadalcanal, Malaita, New Georgia, San Cristóbal, Santa Isabel and Choiseul. The islands are characterized by thickly-forested mountain ranges.

The northern Solomons have a true hot and wet tropical oceanic climate, but further south there tends to be an increasingly long cool season. The coastal plains are used for the subsistence farming that sustains about 90% of the population. While coconuts (giving copra and palm oil) and cocoa are important exports, tuna fish is the biggest earner and lumbering the main industry, with Japan the main market for both. Significant phosphate deposits are also mined on Bellona Island. Plagued by a population growth of 3.5% – half the total is under 20 – the Solomons' progress is faltering, with development hampered by the mountainous and densely forested environment of the six main islands; transport is often impossible between scattered settlements. The economy was also hit by a devastating cyclone in 1986.

Occupied by the Japanese during World War II, the islands were the scene of fierce fighting, notably the battle for Guadalcanal, on which the capital Honiara lies. Known as the British Solomons, the islands won full independence in 1978. Though a stable parliamentary monarchy, political activity is turbulent, and it is likely that a federal republican structure will be introduced during the 1990s ■

COUNTRY	Solomon Islands
AREA	28,900 sq km [11,158 sq mls]
POPULATION	378,000
CAPITAL (POPULATION)	Honiara (37,000)
GOVERNMENT	Constitutional monarchy with a unicameral legislature
ETHNIC GROUPS	Melanesian 94%, Polynesian 4%
LANGUAGES	Many Melanesian languages, English
RELIGIONS	Christian
CURRENCY	Solomon Islands dollar = 100 cents
POPULATION DENSITY	13 per sq km [34 per sq ml]

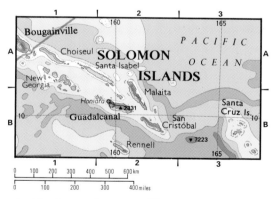

NEW CALEDONIA

Most southerly of the Melanesian countries, New Caledonia comprises the main island of Grande Terre and the dependencies of the Loyalty Islands (Îles Loyauté), Île des Pins and the Bélep archipelago. The remaining islands (many of them coral atolls) are all small and uninhabited.

New Caledonia's economy is dominated by a single commodity, nickel, which accounts for over 56% of export earnings. The world's largest producer in the 1960s, by 1993 it had slipped to fifth place, though still with a healthy 11% of the share and with reserves estimated at more than a third of the world total. Other exports are copra and coffee.

A French possession since 1853 and Overseas Territory from 1958, New Caledonia today has a fundamental split on the question of independence from Paris. The Kanaks, the indigenous Melanesian people (but numbering under half the total), support it; the less numerous French settlers (many of whom fled Algeria after it gained independence) are against it. An agreement for increased autonomy, supposedly leading to independence before the end of the 1990s, helped ease tension but the future looks cloudy. Much may depend on finance: France provides a third of the government budget, but separatists have purchased the islands' largest nickel mine ■

COUNTRY	French Overseas Territory
AREA	18,580 sq km [7,174 sq mls]
POPULATION	181,000
CAPITAL	Nouméa (98,000)

AUSTRALIA AND OCEANIA

FIJI

The Fijian flag, based on the British Blue Ensign, was adopted in 1970 after independence from Britain. The state coat of arms shows a British lion, sugar cane (the most important crop), a coconut palm, bananas and a dove of peace.

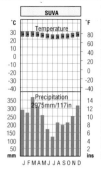

SUVA

The south-east trades blow all year round, producing local contrasts; windward slopes are cloudier and wetter with rainfall exceeding 3,000 mm [120 in]. Rainfall varies greatly from year to year, but usually falls on 200 days per year. Typhoons can cause great damage from December to April. Temperatures are uniformly high throughout the year, rising to 32°C [90°F] in the hot season (from December to April), dropping by only a few degrees at night to 23°C [73°F].

By far the most populous of the Pacific nations, Fiji comprises more than 800 Melanesian islands, the larger ones volcanic, mountainous and surrounded by coral reefs, the rest being low coral atolls. Easily the biggest are Viti (10,430 sq km [4,027 sq mls]), with the capital of Suva on its south coast, and Vanua Levu, just over half the size of the main island, though a very different shape. The islands' economy is basically agricultural, with sugar cane (45% of exports), copra and ginger the main cash crops, and fish and timber also exported. However, nearly 20% of revenues are generated by sales of gold. The main trading partners are the UK and Australia for exports, and the USA, New Zealand and Australia for imports.

Fiji suffers today from its colonial past. The Indian workers brought in by the British for the sugar plantations in the late 19th century out-numbered the native Fijians, but were second-class citizens in terms of electoral representation, economic opportunity and, crucially, land owner-ship. The constitution adopted on independence in 1970 was intended to ease racial tension, but two military coups in 1987 overthrew the recently elected (and first) Indian-majority government, suspended the constitution and set up a Fijian-dominated republic outside the British Commonwealth.

The country finally returned to full civilian rule in 1990, and eventually returned to the Common-wealth in 1997. However, with a new constitution guaranteeing Melanesian political supremacy, many Indians had already emigrated before the elections of 1992, taking their valuable skills with them. The turmoil of the late 1980s also had a disastrous effect on the growing tourist industry – and by the time the situation stabilized many of the Western countries that provide the foreign visitors were already in deep recession ■

COUNTRY	Republic of Fiji
AREA	18,270 sq km [7,054 sq mls]
POPULATION	773,000
CAPITAL (POPULATION)	Suva (75,000)
GOVERNMENT	Republic with a non-elected senate
ETHNIC GROUPS	Fijian 48%, Indian 46%
LANGUAGES	English, Bauan, Hindustani
RELIGIONS	Christian 53%, Hindu 38%, Muslim 8%
NATIONAL DAY	10 October
CURRENCY	Fiji dollar = 100 cents
MAIN PRIMARY PRODUCTS	Sugar cane, copra, ginger
MAIN INDUSTRIES	Agriculture (sugar cane dominating), tourism, mining
MAIN EXPORTS	Sugar, gold, food products
MAIN IMPORTS	Petroleum products, machinery and electrical goods, transport equipment, textile yarn and fibres, iron and steel
POPULATION DENSITY	42 per sq km [110 per sq ml]
LIFE EXPECTANCY	Female 68 yrs, male 64 yrs
ADULT LITERACY	90%

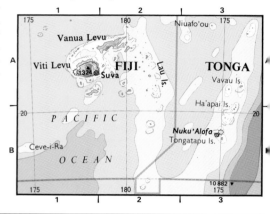

NEW ZEALAND

Like Australia, New Zealand flies a flag based on the design of the British Blue Ensign. Designed in 1869 and adopted in 1907 on acquiring Dominion status, it displays four of the five stars of the Southern Cross constellation.

Geologically part of the Circum-Pacific Mobile Belt of tectonic activity, New Zealand is moun-tainous and partly volcanic. Many of the highest mountains – the Southern Alps and Kaikoura Range of the South Island, for example – were thrust up from the seabed in the past 10 to 15 million years, representing only the latest in a long series of orog-enies. Much of the North Island was formed by volcanic action even more recently, mainly in the past 1 to 4 million years. Minor earthquakes are common, and there are several areas of volcanic and geothermal activity, especially in the North Island.

Its youth makes New Zealand a rugged country with mountains always in sight and about 75% of the total land area above the 200 m [650 ft] contour. The North Island has many spectacular but low ranges, with peaks of 1,200 m to 1,500 m [4,000 ft to 5,000 ft], made up of folded sedimentary rocks that form good soils. Folding and faulting give the eastern half of the island a strong north-east to south-west 'grain', especially in the south-east where the rivers have cut broad, fertile valleys between the ranges. The Coromandel Range and hilly Northland peninsula are softer and more worn, with few peaks over 800 m [12,600 ft].

Overlying these older rocks in the centre and north are massive spreads of lava, pumice and vol-canic tuffs, formed during the past 1 to 3 million years. The great central plateau is dominated by three slumbering volcanoes – Ruapehu (2,797 m [9,176 ft], the North Island's highest peak), Ngauruhoe and Tongariro. Further north extensive fields of lava and ash cones lie across the base of the Northland peninsula, forming a firm, rolling site for the suburbs of Auckland, New Zealand's largest city.

The far larger South Island is also mainly moun-tainous, with an alpine backbone extending obliquely from north-east to south-west. The highest peaks form a central massif, the Southern Alps, clustered around Mt Cook, at 3,753 m [12,313 ft] New Zealand's highest mountain. From this massif, which is permanently ice-capped, glaciers descend on either flank, and on the east the outwash fans of glacier-fed rivers form the Canterbury Plains – South Island's only extensive lowland. The north end of the island has many high, rolling ranges rising to the steeply folded and faulted Kaikoura Ranges of the north-east. In the far south-west (Fjordland), the coast is indented by deep, steeply walled sounds that wind far into the forested mountains.

New Zealand was discovered by Abel Tasman in 1642 and charted thoroughly by James Cook in 1769–70. Both explorers recorded the presence of Maoris – Polynesians who hunted and farmed from well-defended coastal settlements, who were them-selves relatively recent arrivals on the islands. Sealing gangs and whalers were New Zealand's first Euro-pean inhabitants, closely followed by missionaries and farmers from Britain and Australia. By the early 1830s about 2,000 Europeans had settled there.

In 1840 Britain took possession, in a treaty which gave rights and privileges of British subjects to the Maori people. The following decades saw the arrival of thousands of new settlers from Britain, and by mid-century there were over 30,000. Though their relationships with the Maoris (who at this stage out-numbered them two to one) were generally good, difficulties over land ownership led to warfare in the 1860s. Thereafter the Maori population declined while European numbers continued to increase.

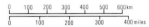

| 0 | 100 | 200 | 300 | 400 | 500 | 600km |
| 0 | 100 | 200 | 300 | 400 miles |

THE MÀORIS

'Strong, raw-boned, well-made, active people, rather above than under the common size . . . of a very dark brown colour, with black hair, thin black beards, and . . . in general very good features.' So Captain James Cook described the Maoris he met in New Zealand in 1770. Of Polynesian stock, the Maoris settled (mainly in North Island) from about AD 800 to 1350. A warlike people, living in small fortified settlements, they cultivated kumaras (sweet potatoes) and other crops, hunted seals and moas (large flightless birds, now extinct) and gathered seafoods.

The Maoris befriended the early European settlers; readily accepting British sovereignty, Christianity and pacification, they rebelled only as more and more of their communal land was bought for the settlers' use. Given parliamen-tary representation from 1876, they eventually integrated fully. Now Maoris form about 9% of New Zealand's population, still living mostly in North Island. Though socially and politically equal in every way to whites, they are still over-represented in the poorer, unskilled sections of the population, separated more by poverty and lack of opportunity than by colour from the mainstream of national life.

COUNTRY New Zealand

AREA 268,680 sq km [103,737 sq mls]

POPULATION 3,567,000

CAPITAL (POPULATION) Wellington (329,000)

GOVERNMENT Constitutional monarchy with a unicameral legislature

ETHNIC GROUPS White 74%, Maori 10%, Polynesian 4%

LANGUAGES English and Maori (both official)

RELIGIONS Anglican 21%, Presbyterian 16%, Roman Catholic 15%, Methodist 4%

NATIONAL DAY 6 February; Treaty of Waitangi (1840)

CURRENCY New Zealand dollar = 100 cents

ANNUAL INCOME PER PERSON US$12,900

MAIN PRIMARY PRODUCTS Sheep, cereals, fruit and vegetables, cattle, fish, coal, natural gas, iron

MAIN EXPORTS Meat and meat preparations 20%, wool 14%, fruit and vegetables 7%, forestry products 7%, hides, skins and pelts 4%, butter 4%, fish 3%

MAIN EXPORT PARTNERS USA 17%, Japan 15%, Australia 15%, UK 9%

MAIN IMPORTS Machinery and electrical goods 26%, transport equipment 15%, chemicals 12%, textiles, clothing and footwear 7%, fuels and oils 5%

MAIN IMPORT PARTNERS Japan 20%, Australia 18%, USA 16%, UK 10%

DEFENCE 1.6% of GNP

TOURISM 1,250,000 visitors per year

POPULATION DENSITY 13 per sq km [34 per sq ml]

LIFE EXPECTANCY Female 79 yrs, male 73 yrs

ADULT LITERACY 99%

PRINCIPAL CITIES (POPULATION) Auckland 896,000 Wellington 326,000 Hamilton 150,000 Waitakere 140,000 Dunedin 110,000 Napier-Hastings 110,000

British settlers found a climate slightly warmer than their own, with longer growing seasons but variable rainfall, sometimes with crippling drought in the dry areas. From 1844, when the first Merinos were introduced from Australia, New Zealand became predominantly a land of sheep, the grassy lowlands (especially in the South Island) providing year-round forage. Huge flocks were built up, mainly for wool and tallow production. From the lowlands they expanded into the hills – the 'high country', which was cleared of native bush and sown with European grasses for pasture. More than half the country is still covered with evergreen forest. The North Island proved more difficult to turn into farmland, later proving its value for dairying.

New Zealand's early prosperity was finally established when the export of frozen mutton and lamb carcasses began in 1882. Soon a steady stream of chilled meat and dairy products – and later of fruit – was crossing the oceans to established markets in Britain, and the country is still the

NEW ZEALAND TERRITORIES

New Zealand comprises not just the two main islands, Stewart Island, Chatham Island and a number of uninhabited outlying islands, but also territories further out in the Pacific, including the Kermadec Islands (with an isolated meteorological station) and Tokelau (population 2,000); formerly part of the Gilbert and Ellice Islands – now called Kiribati – and transferred from Britain to New Zealand in 1926, the group became part of the country in 1949.

The Cook Islands (population 18,500) became an internally self-governing state in 'free association' with New Zealand in 1965; Niue (population 2,300) has had the same status since 1974. These Polynesian islanders have full citizenship, while Wellington controls defence and foreign affairs. The main exports are citrus fruits and juices, copra (coconut), bananas and honey.

world's second biggest producer of lamb. Wheat and other cereals were also grown. High productivity was maintained by applications of fertilizers, mainly based on rock-phosphate mined on Nauru.

New Zealand is a prosperous country, with a high standard of living for a refreshingly harmonious multiracial population. Since 1907 a self-governing Dominion, it long relied on British markets for the export of agricultural produce, and has generally strong ties and affinities with Britain. Though agricultural products are still the main exports, the economy has diversified considerably since World War II, including fish, timber and wood pulp. Iron ores, coal and small amounts of gold are among the few valuable minerals, recently boosted by natural gas and petroleum. Geothermal and hydroelectric

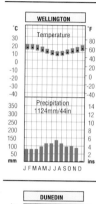

WELLINGTON

The islands are set in a vast ocean which moderates temperatures, and although Wellington is at the same latitude as Rome, in the northern hemisphere (41°), summers are 8°C [14°F] cooler. In the lowlands, no monthly temperature is below freezing. Auckland has briefly registered zero temperatures and subzero temperatures have been recorded in every month in Invercargill. Temperatures above 25°C [77°F] are rare.

Temperature
Precipitation 1124mm/44in

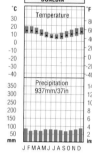

DUNEDIN

New Zealand lies within the influence of westerly winds throughout the year and has a well-distributed rainfall, varying from over 6,000 mm [236 in] on the west coast of the South Island to below 300 mm [12 in] in the lee of the Southern Alps. There is a slight winter maximum and rain usually falls on over half the days in the year. In spite of this, sunshine levels are high, with over 2,000 hours over most of the area.

Temperature
Precipitation 937mm/37in

power are well developed, and timber and forest products are finding valuable overseas markets. Despite the country's isolation, a promising tourist industry is also developing, based on the scenic beauty, abundance of game animals, and relatively peaceful and unhurried way of life.

However, the idyll was showing signs of cracking from the 1970s, beginning when the UK joined the EEC and New Zealand's exports to Britain shrank from 70% to 10%. Along with a re-evaluation of its defence position, the country has had to re-think its previous 'safe' economic strategy – cutting subsidies to farmers, privatization, and seeking new markets in Asia – and, like Australia and most fellow members of the OECD, find a way to survive the recession of the late 1980s and early 1990s ∎

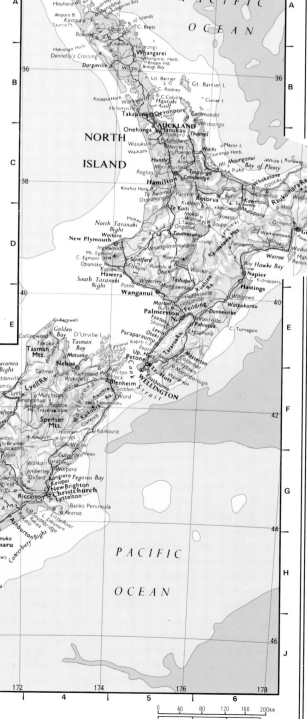

AUSTRALIA AND OCEANIA

NORTHERN MARIANA ISLANDS

The Northern Mariana Islands comprise all 17 Mariana Islands except Guam, the most southerly, with a total land area of 477 sq km [184 sq mls]. Part of the US Trust Territory of the Pacific from 1947, its people voted in a 1975 UN plebiscite for Commonwealth status in union with the USA. Washington approved the change in 1976, granting US citizenship, and internal self-government followed in 1978. The population of 50,000 is concentrated on three of the six inhabited islands, with Saipan accounting for 39,000. Tourism appears to be the key to the future and is growing rapidly: the number of foreign visitors rose from 130,000 in 1984 to over 435,400 in 1990 ■

GUAM

Largest of the Marianas, measuring 541 sq km [209 sq mls], Guam is composed mainly of a coralline limestone plateau, with mountains in the south, hills in the centre and narrow coastal lowlands in the north. Populated for over 3,000 years, charted by Magellan in 1521, colonized by Spain from 1668 but ceded to the USA after the 1896–8 war and occupied by the Japanese 1941–4, it is today – as a 'self-governing unincorporated territory' – of huge strategic importance to Washington, and a third of its usable land is occupied by American naval and air force establishments.

Though parts are highly developed along American lines, there are also traditional villages, beautiful beaches and dense jungles. Textiles, beverages, tobacco and copra are the main exports, but most food is imported. As a Pacific tourist destination, it is second only to Hawaii. All this helps to give Guamanians a relatively high standard of living, with an annual per capita income of over US$7,000.

Almost half the population of 155,000 are Chamorro – of mixed Indonesian, Spanish and Filipino descent – and another quarter Filipino, but 20% of the total is composed of US military personnel and their families. In 1979 a referendum backed a return of much of the military land to civilian use, and a 1982 vote showed support for the Commonwealth status enjoyed by the Northern Marianas ■

PALAU (BELAU)

The last remaining member of the four states that comprised the US Trust Territory of the Pacific, established under UN mandate in 1947 – thanks to sustained American skulduggery – Palau (Belau) voted to break away from the Federated States of Micronesia in 1978, and a new self-governing constitution became effective in 1981. The territory then entered into 'free association with the USA', providing sovereign-state status, but in 1983 a referendum rejected the proposal, since Washington refused to accede to a 92% vote in a 1979 referendum that declared the nation a nuclear-free zone. On 1 October 1994, Palau finally became an independent republic, and in December 1994 Palau joined the UN as the 185th member.

The republic comprises an archipelago of six Caroline groups, totalling 26 islands and over 300 islets varying in terrain from mountain to reef and measuring 458 sq km [177 sq mls]. The country relies heavily on US aid, and the US government is the largest employer.

Eight of the islands are permanently inhabited, including Peleliu (Beleliu) and Angaur. Most of the largely Catholic population speak the official Palauan (Belauan) but English is widely used. The present capital is Koror (population 10,000 – over half the national total of 18,000); a new capital is being built in the east of Babelthuap, the largest island, where coastal plains surround a high jungle interior ■

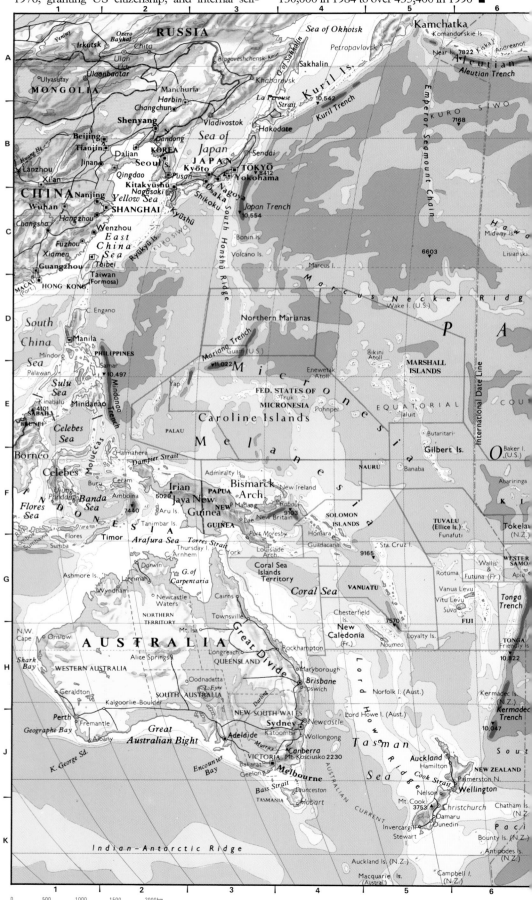

MARSHALL ISLANDS

The Marshall Islands became a republic 'in free association with the USA' in 1986, moving from Trust Territory status to a sovereign state responsible for its own foreign policy but not (until 2001) for its defence and security. Independent since 1991, the country comprises over 1,250 islands and atolls – including the former US nuclear testing sites of Bikini and Enewetak – totalling just 181 sq km [70 sq mls]. The population, mainly Micronesian, Protestant and English-speaking, is 55,000, with nearly half living on Majuro. The economy, based on agriculture and tourism, is heavily supported by aid from the USA, which still retains a missile site on the largest island, Kwajalein ■

FEDERATED STATES OF MICRONESIA

The Federated States of Micronesia became a sovereign state in 1986, when after 17 years of negotiation they entered into 'free association with the USA', which had run them as a US Trust Territory since 1947 and will continue to control defence and security until 2001. They were formally admitted as an independent member of the UN in September 1991.

Comprising the bulk of the Carolines, the Federation – despite a land area of just 705 sq km [272 sq mls] – stretches across more than 3,200 km [2,000 mls] of Pacific, with the Equator as the southern boundary; the 607 islands divide into four groups and range from mountains to low atolls. Over half the area is contributed by the main island, Pohnpei, which also accounts for 33,000 out of a total population of 125,000.

The cultures of the 'FSM', both Micronesian and Polynesian, are diverse, and four main languages are spoken in line with the four states of Yap, Truk, Pohnpei and Kosrae – though English is official. While some areas are highly Americanized, the traditional way of life has survived in others, based on subsistence farming and fishing. Copra is the main crop and phosphate is also exported, while tuna fishing brings in valuable revenue ■

NAURU

A low-lying coral atoll of just 21 sq km [8 sq mls] located halfway between Australia and Hawaii, 40 km [25 mls] south of the Equator, Nauru is the world's smallest republic. The climate is hot and wet, though the rains can fail. Discovered by Britain in 1798, the island was under the control of Germany (1888), Australia (1914), Japan (1942) and Australia again (with a UN trusteeship from 1946) before it gained independence in 1968.

A plateau rising to over 60 m [200 ft], surrounded by a belt of fertile, cultivated land, has provided the island with rich deposits of high-grade phosphate rock, exported to the Pacific Rim countries for fertilizer. The industry, nationalized in 1970, accounts for over 98% of exports, and though Nauru is only the 16th largest world producer this is enough to furnish the population with an average national income of US$10,000 – a similar figure to Spain, Taiwan and Ireland – giving them exemption from taxes and free education and welfare. The native people of mixed Micronesian and Polynesian origin, speak a hybrid Nauruan language and are predominantly Christian (mainly Protestant). They are supplemented by more than 4,000 migrants.

Nauru's future is nevertheless uncertain, since the phosphates are likely to be exhausted by the end of the century. The government is planning to derive new revenues from shipping and air services ■

KIRIBATI

Known as the Gilbert Islands until independence in 1979, the republic of Kiribati comprises three groups of coral atolls – 16 Gilbert Islands, eight Phoenix Islands and 11 of the Line Islands – plus the higher and volcanic Banaba. Though amounting to only 728 sq km [281 sq mls], they are scattered over 5 million sq km [2 million sq mls] of the Pacific, straddling both the Equator and the International Date Line.

Together with the Ellice Islands (which broke away as Tuvalu in 1975), the Gilberts were a British protectorate from 1892 and a colony from 1916; they were occupied by the Japanese in World War II, and recaptured after the battle for Tarawa in 1943. Today the capital has 20,000 residents, out of a total population of 80,000. The people of the islands are almost exclusively Christian, with a slight Roman Catholic majority.

Little of the coral islands rises above 4 m [13 ft], though coconuts, bananas, papayas, and breadfruits are harvested, with taro (babai) laboriously cultivated in deep pits to provide the staple vegetable. Following the exhaustion of Banaba's phosphate deposits in 1980, the main exports are copra (63%), and fish and fish preparations (24%), but Kiribati remains heavily dependent on foreign aid. The future, both medium-term economic and long-term environmental (due to possible rising sea levels from global warming) is bleak, compounded by an overcrowding problem that has forced the resettlement of some 4,700 people in the 1990s ■

TUVALU

Tuvalu became an independent constitutional monarchy within the Commonwealth in 1978, three years after separation from the Gilbert Islands – a decision supported by a large majority in a referendum held in 1974. None of its nine coral atolls – total area 24 sq km [9 sq mls] – rises more than 4.6 m [15 ft] out of the Pacific, and poor soils restrict vegetation to coconut palms, breadfruit trees and bush. The population of 10,000 (a third of whom live on the main island of Funafuti) survive by subsistence farming, raising pigs and poultry, and by fishing. Copra is the only significant export crop, but most foreign exchange comes from the sale of elaborate postage stamps to the world's philatelists. The people are almost all Protestant, speaking both Tuvaluan, a Polynesian-Samoan dialect, and usually English. The population, once far higher, was reduced from about 20,000 to just 3,000 in the three decades after 1850 by Europeans abducting workers for other Pacific plantations ■

VANUATU

An archipelago of 13 large islands and 70 islets, the majority of them mountainous and volcanic in origin, with coral beaches, reefs, forest cover and very limited coastal cultivation, Vanuatu totals 12,190 sq km [4,707 sq mls] in land area. Nearly two-thirds of the population of 167,000 live on four islands, 20,000 of them in the capital of Port-Vila, on the island of Efate.

Formerly the New Hebrides, and governed jointly by France and Britain from 1906, the islands became independent as a parliamentary republic in 1980. The francophone island of Espiritu Santó attempted separation from the anglophone government, and politics have remained unstable. The Melanesian, Bislama-speaking people live largely by subsistence farming and fishing, with copra (45%), beef and veal (14%) the main exports ■

TONGA

Tonga is an absolute monarchy. Since 1965 the ruler has been Taufa'ahau Tupou IV, latest in a line going back a thousand years, who presided over the islands' transition from British protectorate to independent Commonwealth state in 1970. His brother is prime minister on a council that has hereditary chiefs as well as elected representatives; there are no parties.

The archipelago comprises more than 170 islands, 36 of which are inhabited, covering 750 sq km [290 sq mls] in a mixture of low coralline and higher volcanic outcrops. Nearly two-thirds of the Polynesian population – over 107,000 and growing fast – live on the largest island of Tongatapu, 30,000 of them in the capital of Nuku'alofa, site of the royal palace. Vava'u (15,000) in the north is the next most populous. Predominantly Christian, the people speak Tongan, though English is also official.

Most Tongans live off their own produce, including yams, tapioca and fish. While the government owns all land, men are entitled to rent areas to grow food – a policy now under pressure with a burgeoning young population. The main exports are coconut oil products and bananas, with New Zealand the main trading partner. Tourism is starting, with 23,000 visitors to the islands in 1992 ■

WALLIS AND FUTUNA ISLANDS

The smallest, least populous and poorest of France's three Pacific Overseas Territories, the Wallis and Futuna Islands comprise three main islands and numerous islets, totalling 200 sq km [77 sq mls]. Futuna and uninhabited Alofi, main constituents of the Hoorn group, are mountainous; the much larger Uvea, the chief island of the Wallis group, is hilly with coral reefs. Uvea contains 60% of the 13,000 population, 850 of them in the capital of Mata-Utu.

In a 1959 referendum the Polynesian islanders voted overwhelmingly in favour of change from a dependency to an Overseas Territory, and French aid remains crucial to an economy based mainly on tropical subsistence agriculture. The territory shares the currency of the Pacific franc with French Polynesia and New Caledonia ■

WESTERN SAMOA

Western Samoa comprises two large islands, seven small islands and a number of islets, forming a land area of 2,840 sq km [1,097 sq mls]. The main islands of Upolu and Savai'i both have a central mountainous region, surrounded by coastal lowlands and coral reefs. Upolu contains two-thirds of the population of 169,000.

The cradle of Polynesian civilization, Western Samoa first gained independence in 1889, but ten years later became a German protectorate. Administered by New Zealand from 1920 – first under a League of Nations mandate and later a UN trusteeship – the island achieved independence as a parliamentary monarchy in 1962, following a plebiscite. Under a friendship treaty New Zealand handles relations with governments and organizations outside the Pacific islands zone. The first elections using universal suffrage were held in 1991.

The population remains mainly Polynesian, with a Maori majority, and almost exclusively Christian (70% Protestant); Samoan and English are both official languages. The traditional life style still thrives, with 64% of the workforce engaged in agriculture, chiefly tropical fruits and vegetables, and in fishing. The main exports are coconut oil (43%), taro and cocoa, with New Zealand the main partner. Many of the 38,000 tourists a year visit the home of Robert Louis Stevenson – now the official residence of King Malietoa Tanumafili II ■

AMERICAN SAMOA

A self-governing 'unincorporated territory of the USA', American Samoa is a group of five volcanic islands and two atolls covering a land area of 200 sq km [77 sq mls] in the South Pacific, with Tutuila the largest. Swain Island to the north also comes under its administration, taking the total population to about 58,000. More than twice that number of American Samoans live in the USA.

The Samoan Islands were divided in 1899, with British consent, between Germany and the USA along a line 171° west of Greenwich. Although the US naval base at Pago Pago closed in 1951, the American influence in the territory is still vital, giving substantial grants and taking 90% of exports.

While Pago Pago – the recipient of about 5,000 mm [200 in] of rain a year – is the capital, the seat of government is to the east at Fagatogo. There is little prospect of Samoan reunification: the American islands enjoy a standard of living some ten times as high as their neighbours in Western Samoa ■

FRENCH POLYNESIA

French Polynesia consists of 130 islands, totalling only 3,941 sq km [1,520 sq mls] but scattered over 4 million sq km [1.5 million sq mls] of ocean halfway between Australia and South America. Tahiti is the largest island and home to the capital of Papeete.

The tribal chiefs of Tahiti eventually agreed to a French protectorate in 1843, and by the end of the century France controlled all the present islands. They formed an overseas territory from 1958, sending two deputies and a senator to Paris, and in 1984 gained increased autonomy with a territorial assembly. There are calls for independence, but the high standard of living (the annual per capita income is US$7,000) comes largely from the links with France, including a substantial military presence. France began stationing personnel there in 1962, including nuclear testing at Mururoa (the most recent underground tests took place in 1995–6).

The other factor which changed the islands' economy from subsistence agriculture and fishing was tourism. After petroleum re-exports (45%), the main earners are cultured pearls, vanilla and citrus fruits. Almost half the territory's trade is with France, and it shares a currency (the Pacific franc) with New Caledonia and Wallis and Futuna.

The population is 217,000, of which nearly half live on Tahiti – 78,000 in Papeete. Nearly 80% of the people are Polynesian, the rest being French (10%), descendants of Chinese labourers brought in by a British-owned plantation in the 1860s (7%),

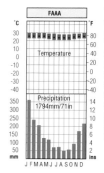

The climate is warm and humid with nearly continuous cloud cover over the mountain peaks. Temperatures remain high throughout the year with a slight maximum in March, during the warm rainy season. Rainfall is abundant and heaviest on the windward slopes (north-facing and east-facing). There are long periods of calm between April and June, when the weather is brighter and drier.

or of mixed descent. Overwhelmingly Christian (Protestant 47%, Roman Catholic 40%), they speak French, the official language, and Tahitian ■

PITCAIRN is a British dependent territory of four islands (48 sq km [19 sq mls]), situated halfway between New Zealand and Panama. Uninhabited until 1790, it was occupied by nine mutineers from HMS *Bounty* and some men and women from Tahiti. The present population of 54, all living in Adamstown on Pitcairn, come under the administration of the British High Commission in Wellington and use the New Zealand dollar ■

NORTH AND CENTRAL AMERICA

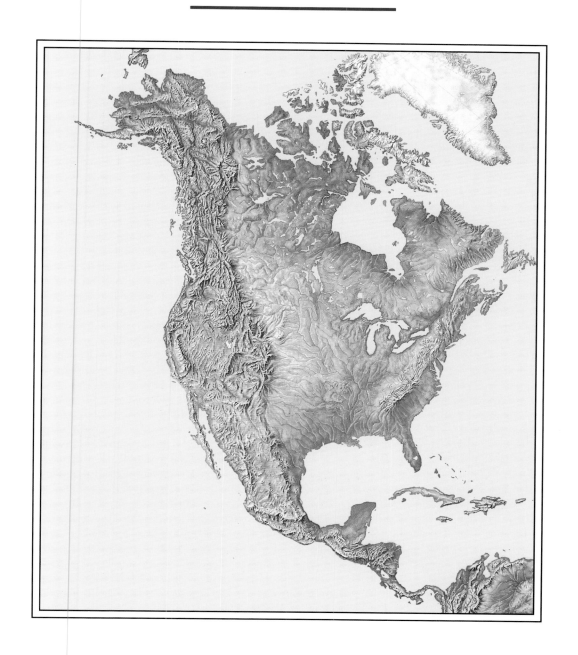

NORTH AND CENTRAL AMERICA

Third largest of the world's continents, North America spans 116° of longitude from Newfoundland to Bering Strait – almost a third of the northern hemisphere; in latitude it extends from the tropical Gulf of Mexico in the south to the Arctic.

With a reputation for containing the biggest and best of everything, North America tends towards superlatives and extremes. Its highest peaks fall short of the highest in Asia and South America, but it includes the world's largest freshwater lake (Lake Superior) and greatest canyon (Grand Canyon, Arizona). Climatic extremes are common, though some of its world records reflect little more than good coverage by an unusually complete network of well-equipped weather stations.

Topography and climate combine to provide an immense range of natural habitats across North America, from mangrove swamps and tropical forests in the south, through hot deserts, prairie, temperate and boreal forests, taiga and tundra to polar deserts in the far north. North America can claim both the largest and oldest known living organisms (giant redwood cedars and bristlecone pines), both found in the western USA.

Standing at the edge of one of the world's six great crustal plates, North America has been subject to pressure and uplift from its neighbouring Pacific plate, with results that show clearly on a physical map. Roughly a third of the continent, including the whole of the western flank, has been thrown into

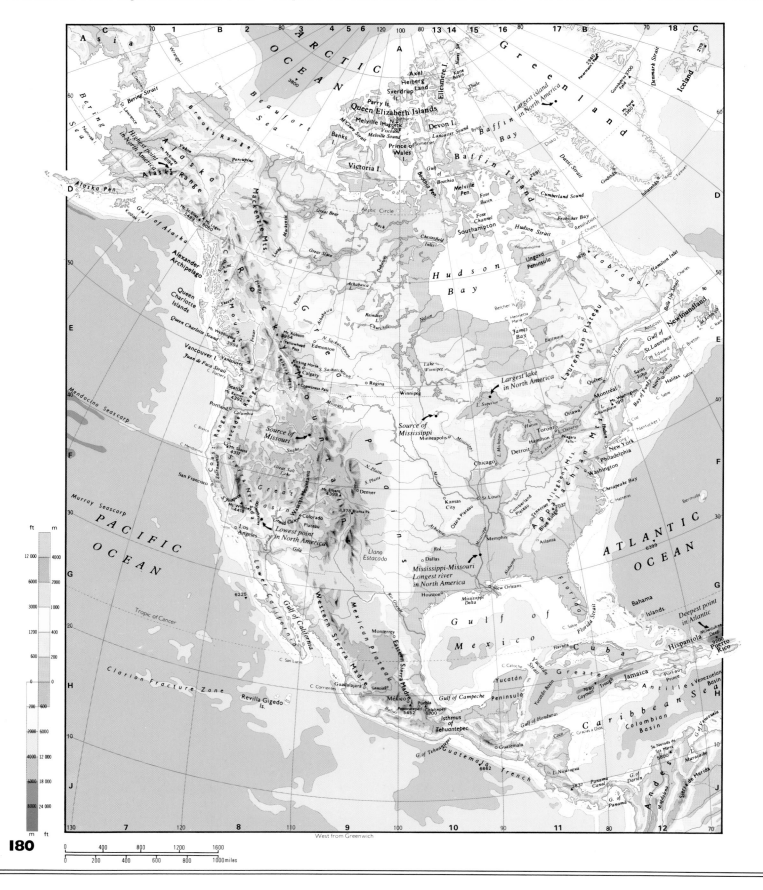

West from Greenwich

a spectacular complex of young mountains, valleys and plateaus – the Western Cordilleras. To the east lie much older mountains, longer-weathered and lower – the Appalachians in the south and the Laurentian Highlands in the north; these are separated from the western ranges by broad interior lowlands drained by the Mississippi–Missouri system.

The bleak northern plains, centred about Hudson Bay, rest on a shield or platform of ancient rocks that underlies most of central and eastern Canada. This Laurentian Shield, though warped and split by crustal movements, was massive enough to resist folding through the successive periods of mountain building that raised the Western Cordilleras. Planed by more than a million years of glaciation throughout the Ice Age, it is now free of permanent ice except on a few of the northern islands. Its surface remains littered with glacial debris that forms thin, waterlogged tundra or forest soils, and the once glaciated region is fringed by a crescent of interlinked lakes and waterways, including the Great Bear Lake and the five Great Lakes.

Central America is the narrow waistline of the Americas, known to the world for the canal that links the two great oceans in Panama. The backbone of the isthmus is mountainous, many of the volcanic vertebrae reaching heights of over 4,000 m [13,000 ft]. It is the most tectonically active zone in the Americas with over 100 large volcanoes and frequent earthquakes ■

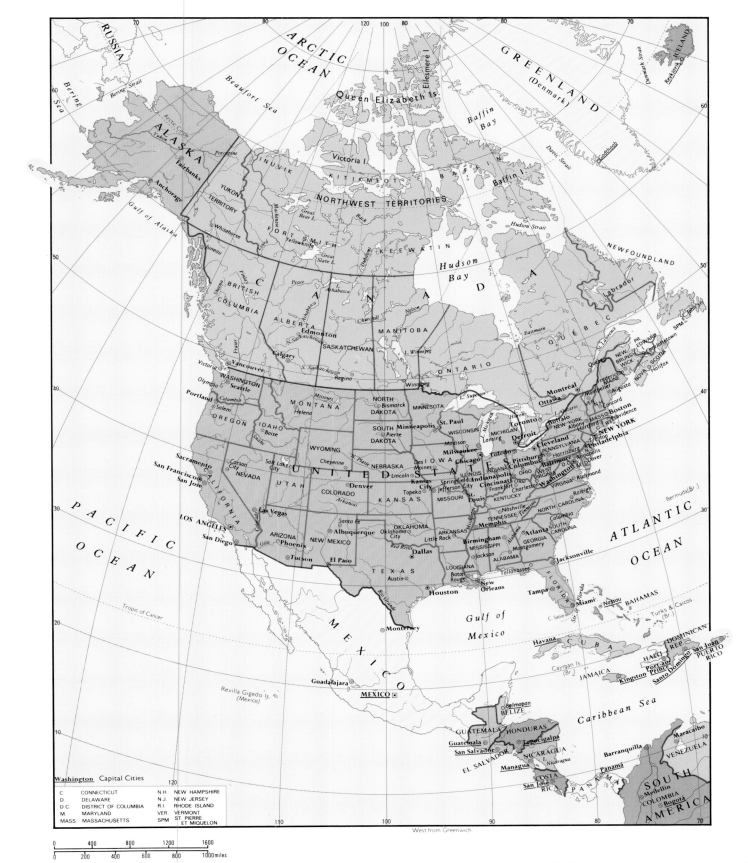

NORTH AND CENTRAL AMERICA

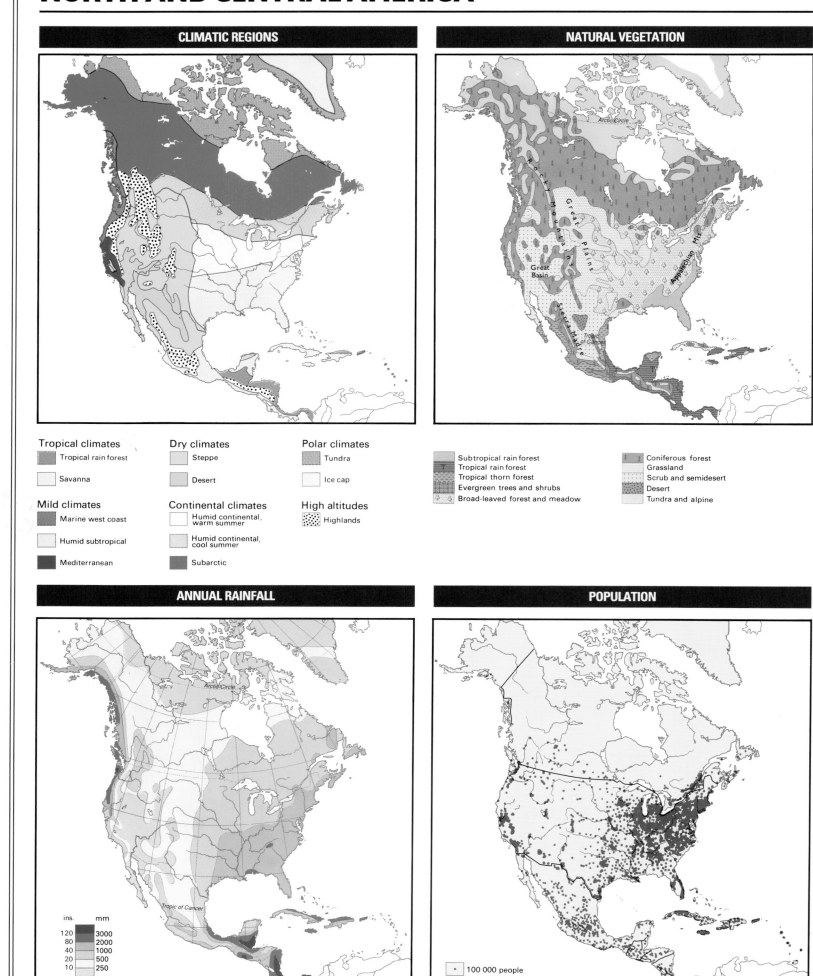

CLIMATIC REGIONS

Tropical climates
- Tropical rain forest
- Savanna

Mild climates
- Marine west coast
- Humid subtropical
- Mediterranean

Dry climates
- Steppe
- Desert

Continental climates
- Humid continental, warm summer
- Humid continental, cool summer
- Subarctic

Polar climates
- Tundra
- Ice cap

High altitudes
- Highlands

NATURAL VEGETATION

- Subtropical rain forest
- Tropical rain forest
- Tropical thorn forest
- Evergreen trees and shrubs
- Broad-leaved forest and meadow
- Coniferous forest
- Grassland
- Scrub and semidesert
- Desert
- Tundra and alpine

ANNUAL RAINFALL

ins.	mm
120	3000
80	2000
40	1000
20	500
10	250

POPULATION

* 100 000 people

LAND USE

LAND USE
- Arable land
- Arable land with grazing
- Market gardening, fruit trees, bushes and orchard land
- Permanent pasture
- Woods and forests
- Woods and forests with grazing land
- Rough grazing
- Non-productive land

LIVESTOCK
- Beef cattle
- Sheep
- Dairy cattle

CROPS
⌇ Bananas	⌄ Sisal
◆ Citrus fruits	• Soya beans
⌒ Coffee	◇ Sugar cane
⬥ Cotton	⊤ Tobacco
• Fruit	▽ Vegetables
⌐ Groundnuts	⊢ Wheat
• Maize	
• Olives	⊢ Principal fishing areas
○ Rice	

MINERALS
● Asbestos	Sb Antimony
○ Bauxite	Co Cobalt
▲ Copper	Mg Magnesium
△ Gold	Hg Mercury
◆ Iron ore	Mo Molybdenum
◆ Lead	Ni Nickel
◆ Lead and zinc	Ti Titanium
● Mica	**POWER**
▼ Phosphate	▲ Coalfields
▽ Silver	■ Gasfields
◆ Uranium	■ Oilfields
▲ Zinc	■ HEP

LAND USE

Arable land and permanent crops 12·7%

Permanent pasture 16·2%

Other land 37·5%

Woods and forests 33·6%

Total land area 2 140.5 million hectares
(5 289·2 million acres)

Projection: Polyconic

West from Greenwich

COPYRIGHT GEORGE PHILIP LTD.

Prudhoe Bay, Mayo, Pine Point, Scheffervillle, Wabush, Flin Flon, Edmonton, Vancouver, Seattle, Timmins, Montréal, Winnipeg, Mesabi, Toronto, Shoshone, Detroit, Niagara, New York, Salt Lake City, Bingham, Chicago, St. Louis, Washington, San Francisco, Los Angeles, Dallas, San Diego, Hurricane Creek, New Orleans, San Antonio, Houston, Monterrey, Havana, Guadalajara, Veracruz, Mexico, Chiapas Tabasco

0 200 400 600 800km
0 100 200 300 400 500miles

NORTH AND CENTRAL AMERICA

CANADA

The British Red Ensign was used from 1892 but became unpopular with Canada's French community. After many attempts to find a more acceptable design, the present flag – featuring the simple maple leaf emblem – was finally adopted in 1965.

A vast confederation of ten provinces and two territories, Canada is the world's second largest country after Russia, and with an even longer coastline (250,000 km [155,000 mls]). Sparsely populated, it has huge areas of virtually unoccupied mountains, forests, tundra and polar desert in the north and west.

To the east lie the Maritime provinces of Newfoundland, Nova Scotia, New Brunswick and Prince Edward Island, and the predominantly French-speaking province of Québec; clustered about the Gulf of St Lawrence, they are based on ancient worn-down mountains – the northern extension of the Appalachians – and the eastern uptilted edge of the even older Canadian Shield. The central province of Ontario borders the Great Lakes, extending north across the Shield to Hudson Bay. Further to the west come the prairie provinces of Manitoba, Saskatchewan and Alberta; like Québec and Ontario, these include fertile farmlands in the south, where most of the population is to be found, and lake-strewn forest on the subarctic wastelands to the north.

South-western Alberta includes a substantial block of the Rocky Mountains, with peaks rising to over 4,000 m [13,120 ft] in Banff, Yoho and Kootenay National Parks. The westernmost province of British Columbia is mountainous, a land of spectacular forests, lakes and fjords, with sheltered valleys harbouring rich farmland. The huge northern area includes the relatively small and mountainous Yukon Territory in the west, bordering Alaska, and the much more extensive Northwest Territories stretching from the 60th parallel to the northern tip of Ellesmere Island.

Exploration and settlement

Norse voyagers and fishermen were probably the first Europeans briefly to visit Canada, but John Cabot's later discovery of North America, in 1497, began the race to annex lands and wealth, with France and Britain the main contenders.

Jacques Cartier's discovery of the St Lawrence River in 1534 gave France a head start; from their settlements near Québec explorers, trappers and missionaries pioneered routes deeply penetrating the northern half of North America. With possible routes to China and the Indies in mind, Frenchmen followed the St Lawrence and Niagara rivers deep into the heartland of the continent, hoping for the riches of another El Dorado.

Discovering the Great Lakes, they then moved north, west and south in their search for trade. From the fertile valley of the upper St Lawrence,

French influence spread north beyond the coniferous forests and over the tundra. To the west and south they reached the prairies – potentially fertile farming country – exploring further to the Rockies and down the Ohio and Mississippi rivers.

By 1763, after the series of wars that gave Britain brief control of the whole of North America, French-speaking communities were already scattered widely across the interior. Many of the southern settlements became American after 1776, when the USA declared independence from Britain, and the northern ones became a British colony.

British settlers had long been established on the Atlantic coast, farming where possible, with supplementary fishing. In the 1780s a new wave of English-speaking settlers – the United Empire Loyalists – moved north from the USA into Nova Scotia, New Brunswick and Lower Canada. With further waves of immigration direct from Britain, English speakers came to dominate the fertile lands between Lakes Huron and Erie. From there they gradually spread westwards.

The birth of Canada

Restricted to the north by intractable coniferous forests and tundra, and to the south by the USA, the settlers spread through Québec into Upper Canada – now Ontario, the only province along the Canadian shores of the Great Lakes. Mostly English-speaking and retaining British traditions, they continued westwards to establish settlements across the narrow wedge of the northern prairie, finally crossing the Rockies to link with embryo settlements along the Pacific coast. So the fertile lowlands of the St Lawrence basin and the pockets of settlement on the Shield alone remained French in language and culture. The bulk of Canada, to east and west, became predominantly British.

Canada's varied topography and immense scale inhibited the development of a single nation; to promote Canadian unity across so wide a continent has been the aim of successive governments for more than two centuries. The union of British Upper Canada and French Lower Canada was sealed by

SAINT-PIERRE ET MIQUELON

The last remaining fragment of once-extensive French possessions in North America, Saint-Pierre et Miquelon comprises eight islands (total area 242 sq km [93 sq mls]) off the south coast of Newfoundland. Settled by Frenchmen in the 17th century and a colony from 1816, it became an overseas department in 1976, thus enjoying – like Martinique, Guadeloupe, Guiana and Réunion – the same status as the departments in Metropolitan France. In 1985, however, it became a 'territorial collectivity' (a status already held by Mayotte), sending one representative to the National Assembly in Paris and one to the Senate. The population of 6,300 (the majority of whom live on Saint-Pierre, the rest on Miquelon) depend mainly on fishing – the cause of disputes with Canada. The French-speaking population of Canada continue to voice separatist claims, most recently in 1995, when, after a hard-fought campaign, Québeckers voted against a move to make Québec a sovereign state. But the majority was less than 1% and this issue seems unlikely to disappear.

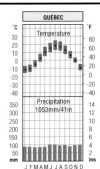

QUÉBEC

The effect of the Great Lakes is felt in the Ontario Peninsula, resulting in slightly warmer winters than in Québec. But the temperatures in northern Canada are extreme: along the Arctic Circle the mean monthly temperatures are below freezing for over seven months of the year. In Québec, rainfall is moderate throughout the year with no marked peak, and with a reasonable amount of snow. Québec has an average of about 1,053 mm [41 in] of rain each year.

the confederation of 1867, when, as the newly named Provinces of Ontario and Québec, they were united with the Maritime core of Nova Scotia and New Brunswick. Three years later the settlement on the Red River entered the confederation as Manitoba, and in the following year the Pacific colonies of Vancouver Island and British Columbia, now united as a single province, completed the link from sea to sea. Prince Edward Island joined in 1873, the prairie provinces of Alberta and Saskatchewan in 1905, and Newfoundland in 1949.

Though self-governing in most respects from the time of the confederation, Canada remained technically subject to the British Imperial parliament until 1931, when the creation of the British Commonwealth made the country a sovereign nation under the crown.

With so much of the population spread out along a southern ribbon of settlement, 4,000 km [2,500 mls] long but rarely more than 480 km [300 mls] wide, Canada has struggled constantly to achieve unity. Transcontinental communications have played a critical role. From the eastern provinces the Canadian Pacific Railway crossed the Rockies to reach Vancouver in 1885. Later, a second rail route, the Canadian National, was pieced together, and the Trans-Canada Highway links the extreme east and west of the country symbolically as well as in fact. Transcontinental air routes link the major centres, and local air traffic is especially important over trackless forests, mountains and tundra. With radio and telephone communications, all parts of the confederation – even the most remote corners of the Arctic territories – are now linked, though the vastness is intimidating and the country spans six time zones: at noon in Vancouver it is already 3:00 P.M. in Toronto, and 4:30 P.M. in St Johns, Newfoundland.

A constant hazard to Canadian nationhood is the proximity of the USA. Though benign, with shared if dwindling British traditions, the prosperous giant to the south has often seemed to threaten the very survival of Canada through economic dominance and cultural annexation. The two countries have the largest bilateral trade flow in the world.

A real and growing threat to unity is the persistence of French culture in Québec province – a last-

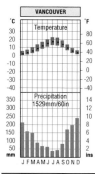

VANCOUVER

West of the Rockies, and to a lesser extent on the eastern coast, the nearby ocean changes the expected climate. At Vancouver, rainfall is high with a maximum from October to March. There is little snow, with only just over 50 frost days. No month has an average minimum below freezing. Summers are cool, with no mean temperatures above 18°C [64°F], the record being 34°C [93°F] in August. Winter temperatures decline a little to the north along this coastal fringe.

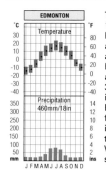

EDMONTON

The July temperature is about 17°C [63°F], but the cold of December is nearly –14°C [6°F], an annual range of over 30°C [54°F], almost as great as in Arctic Canada. But high summer temperatures are recorded in these areas, over 30°C [54°F] having been recorded in all months, April to September. Rainfall is low with a maximum from June to August, and there is little snowfall. On average there are over 210 frost days. Westwards into the Rockies, the snow can reach great depths.

THE TUNDRA

Beyond their habitable southern rim, the northlands of Canada and Alaska are bleak and bare; in the subarctic zone conifers stretch across the continent, but northwards the boreal forest thins and dies out, replaced with tundra. Glaciation has scoured the rocks bare, and soils have had insufficient time to form; the surface thaws in summer, but subsoils remain frozen. Winters are long and bitterly cold, summers brief and cool. Even in the south the season of plant growth is only 70–80 days. Precipitation is light – usually less than 250 mm [10 in] a year, and most of it snow; except where it drifts, the snow seldom lies deep, but it provides cover for vegetation and burrowing animals.

The tundra is covered with low grasses, lichens, mosses and spindly shrubs, providing food for migrating reindeer and resident hares, voles, lemmings and other small browsers and grazers. Their numbers are augmented each summer by hosts of migrant birds – ducks, geese, swans, waders, and many others – that fly in from temperate latitudes to feed on the vegetation and insects.

COUNTRY Canada
AREA 9,976,140 sq km [3,851,788 sq mls]
POPULATION 29,972,000
CAPITAL (POPULATION) Ottawa (921,000)
GOVERNMENT Federal multiparty republic with a bicameral legislature
ETHNIC GROUPS British 34%, French 26%, other European 20%, Asiatic 2%, Native American (Amerindian/Inuit) 2%
LANGUAGES English and French (both official)
RELIGIONS Roman Catholic 47%, Protestant 41%, Eastern Orthodox 2%, Jewish, Muslim, Hindu, Sikh
CURRENCY Canadian dollar = 100 cents
ANNUAL INCOME PER PERSON US$21,260
SOURCE OF INCOME Agriculture 4%, industry 40%, services 56%
MAIN PRIMARY PRODUCTS Coal, cobalt, copper, fish, furs, gold, iron ore, lead, molybdenum, natural gas, nickel, platinum, petroleum, silver, timber, wheat
MAIN INDUSTRIES Transport equipment, food, paper and allied products, primary metal, fabricated metal, electrical and electronics equipment, wood and timber, rubber and plastics
MAIN EXPORTS Passenger vehicles, trucks and parts 26%, food, feed, beverages and tobacco 6%, timber 5%, newspaper print 5%, wood pulp 4%, petroleum 4%, natural gas 3%, industrial machinery 3%

MAIN EXPORT PARTNERS USA 75%, Japan 6%, UK 2%
MAIN IMPORTS Vehicles and parts 26%, machinery 9%, foodstuffs, feed, beverages and tobacco 6%, chemicals 5%, computers 4%, petroleum 3%, iron and steel 2%
MAIN IMPORT PARTNERS USA 68%, Japan 7%, Germany 4%
EDUCATIONAL EXPENDITURE 7.2% of GNP
DEFENCE 2% of GNP
TOTAL ARMED FORCES 89,000
TOURISM 35,731,000 visitors per year [32,427,000 from USA]
ROADS 280,251 km [175,157 mls]
RAILWAYS 93,544 km [58,465 mls]
POPULATION DENSITY 3 per sq km [8 per sq ml]
URBAN POPULATION 77%
POPULATION GROWTH 1.2% per year
BIRTHS 13 per 1,000 population
DEATHS 8 per 1,000 population
INFANT MORTALITY 7 per 1,000 live births
LIFE EXPECTANCY Female 81 yrs, male 74 yrs
POPULATION PER DOCTOR 450 people
ADULT LITERACY 99%
PRINCIPAL CITIES (POPULATION) Toronto 3,893,000 Montréal 3,127,000 Vancouver 1,603,000 Ottawa-Hull 921,000 Edmonton 840,000 Calgary 754,000 Winnipeg 652,000, Québec 646,000 Hamilton 600,000

---

ing political wedge between the western prairie and mountain provinces and the eastern Maritimes. Urbanization and 'Americanization' have fuelled a separatist movement that seeks to turn the province into an independent French-speaking republic. This issue may obscure a wider and more fundamental division in Canadian politics, with the development of a Montréal–Toronto axis in the east, and a Vancouver–Winnipeg axis in the west.

Population and urbanization

Though the population of Canada expanded rapidly from confederation onwards, it remained predominantly rural for many generations; only in recent decades have Canada's cities grown to match those of the USA. At confederation in 1867 about 80% was rural, and only Montréal had passed the 100,000 population mark, with just six towns over 25,000. Not until the end of World War II did the rural and urban elements stand in balance, and today the situation is reversed: 76% of Canada's population is urban.

The metropolitan areas of Toronto and Montréal jointly contain a quarter of the total, and together with Vancouver account for over 30% of the entire population. By contrast the urban centres of Newfoundland and the Maritimes have been relatively stable.

Agriculture and industry

Although farming settlements still dominate the landscape, if not the economy, abandonment of farmland is a serious problem in the eastern provinces, where the agrarian economy – except in such favoured areas as the Annapolis Valley, Nova Scotia – has always been marginal. Through the St Lawrence lowlands and Ontario peninsula farms are more prosperous and rural populations are denser, thinning again along the north shores of the Great Lakes. On the prairies mechanization of grain farming long ago minimized the need for labour, so population densities remain low; the mixed farming communities on the forest margins are often denser. The Pacific coast population is generally concentrated in such rich farming areas as the Okanagan and lower Frazer River basins.

Industry, often dependent on local development of power resources, has transformed many remote and empty areas of Canada. Newfoundland's

Labrador iron-ore workings around Schefferville are powered by the huge hydroelectric plant at Churchill Falls, one of the largest of its kind in the world. Cheap hydroelectric power throughout Québec and Ontario, coupled with improved transmission technology, has encouraged the further development of wood-pulp and paper industries, even in distant parts of the northern forests, and stimulated industry and commerce in the south. Canada is by far the world's leading producer and exporter of paper and board. Mining, too, has helped in the development of these provinces; Sudbury, Ontario, supplies 22.8% of the world's nickel (first in the world), while Canada is also the world's leading producer of zinc ore and uranium.

Tourism is also an important industry; Canada's spectacular open spaces attract visitors from around the world. In the prairie provinces, small marketing, distribution and service centres have been transformed by the enormous expansion of the petrochemical industry; the mineral-rich province of Alberta produces 90% of the country's oil output, and the boom towns of Alberta, Edmonton and Calgary have far outpaced the growth of the eastern cities during recent decades. By contrast – lacking

hydrocarbons, depending mainly on farming, logging and pulping for their prosperity – the settlements of Pacific Canada have on the whole grown slowly, with the notable exception of Vancouver.

The northlands

Canada's northlands, virtually uninhabited apart from small Inuit communities, have an immense, though localized, potential for development. Though the soils are poor and the climate is unyielding, mineral wealth is abundant under the permanently frozen subsoils. Already a major producer of uranium, zinc and nickel, the North also holds vast reserves of copper, molybdenum, iron, cadmium, and other metals of strategic importance; sulphur, potash and asbestos are currently being exploited, and natural gas and petroleum await development beyond the Mackenzie River delta.

Much of this immense mineral wealth will remain in the ground until the high costs of extraction and transportation can be justified. Also, pressure for legislation to protect the boreal forest and tundra against unnecessary or casual damage is rapidly growing – a trend which one day may also curb the massive timber industry ■

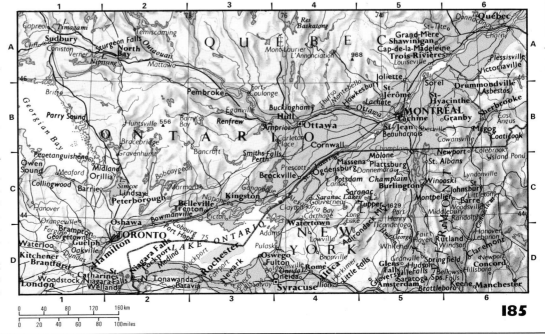

NORTH AND CENTRAL AMERICA

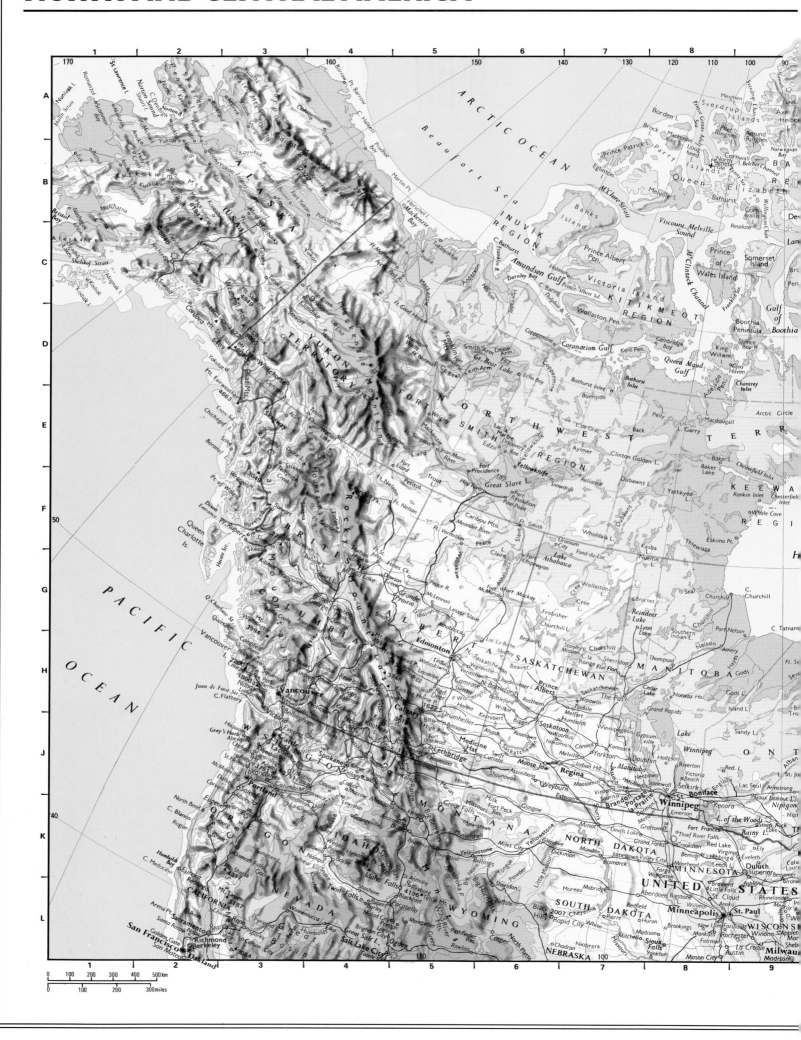

CANADA ADMINISTRATIVE
1 : 40 000 000

⊕ National Capital
◎ Provincial or Territorial Capital
— ∙— ∙— Undemarcated boundary
∙∙∙∙∙∙∙ District boundary

NORTH AND CENTRAL AMERICA

UNITED STATES OF AMERICA

The 'Stars and Stripes' has had the same basic design since 1777, during the War of Independence. The 13 stripes represent the original colonies that rebelled against British rule, and the 50 stars are for the present states of the Union.

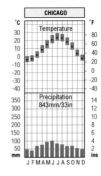

CHICAGO

East of the Rockies, the USA is isolated from the maritime influences of the Pacific and experiences similar extremes to the heart of Eurasia, though the margins of the Great Lakes are warmer in winter and cooler in summer than elsewhere. Temperatures of –20°C [–4°F] have been recorded between December and February. Rainfall is well distributed, with a summer maximum, and the average winter snowfall at Chicago is almost 1,000 mm [40 in].

The world's fourth largest country – and third most populous – the United States of America fills the North American continent between Canada and Mexico and also includes Alaska and the archipelago of Hawaii. Geographically, the main part (of 48 states) falls readily into an eastern section, including the Appalachian Mountains and eastern coastal plain; a central section, including the Mississippi basin and the broad prairie plains from the Dakotas to Texas; and a western section, including the Rocky Mountains and Pacific coastlands.

The East

Eastern North America is crossed by a band of low, folded mountains; though nowhere much above 2,000 m [6,500 ft], they long formed a barrier to settlers. In the north are the Adirondacks, a southern extension of the ancient granite shield of Canada, rising to 1,629 m [5,344 ft]. From Maine to Alabama runs a broad range of sedimentary mountains, the Appalachians. Younger than the Adirondacks (though much older than the Rockies) the Appalachians separate the Atlantic coastlands of the east from the Great Lakes and low plateaus of Ohio, Kentucky and Tennessee.

North-east of New York City lie the six New England states – the fertile wooded country that, at least in summer, made the early settlers feel at home. To the south the coastal plain widens, to be split by the drowned estuaries of the Susquehanna and Potomac rivers, draining into Chesapeake Bay. From Virginia south to Florida smaller rivers drain eastwards, across a much broader plain, many of them entering coastal sounds with offshore sandbars and islands.

In New York state a major spillway cuts through the mountains between the Adirondacks and Appalachians, linking the Great Lakes with the Hudson Valley and the Atlantic Ocean. This is the line of the famous Erie Canal route, the most used of several that gave the early settlers access to the Ohio country beyond the mountains. Other routes led to Pittsburgh and, through the southern Appalachians, into Tennessee. Central Ohio, Indiana and Illinois, which once formed America's Northwest Territory, are rolling uplands and plains, smoothed by glaciation in the north but more rugged in the south, and drained by the Ohio River.

Vegetation: The original vegetation of eastern America, on either flank of the mountains, was broadleaf deciduous forest of oak, ash, beech and maple, merging northwards into yellow birch, hemlock and pine. In the drier Midwest these immense woodlands turned to open country. Patchy grasslands covered northern Indiana and southern Illinois; central Illinois was forested along most watercourses, with prairie bluestem grasses on the drier interfluves. Around the southern Appalachians mixed oak, pine and tulip tree dominated; pines covered the coastal plains to the south and east with bald cypress in northern Florida. Spruce blanketed the highlands from northern Maine to the Adirondacks; spruce, tamarack and balsam fir covered the high Appalachians.

Most of this original forest is now gone, but there is still enough left – and some regenerating on abandoned farmland – to leave the mountains a blaze of colour each autumn. Despite more than 300 years of European settlement, the overall impression of eastern America, seen from the air, is still one of dense semi-continuous forests, except in the extensive farmlands north of the Ohio.

Settlement and development: The eastern USA is the heartland of many of America's rural and urban traditions. In the 19th century European immigrants poured through the ports of Boston, New York, Philadelphia and Baltimore. Many stayed to swell the cities, which grew enormously. Others moved across the mountains to populate the interior and start the farms that fed the city masses. As raw materials of industry – coal and iron ore especially – were discovered and exploited, new cities grew up in the interior. Some were based on old frontier forts: Fort Duquesne became Pittsburgh and Fort Dearborn became Chicago.

Railways spread over the booming farmlands, linking producer and consumer. Huge manufacturing cities, vast markets in their own right, developed along the Great Lakes as people continued to arrive – firstly from abroad, but latterly from the countryside, where mechanization threw people off the land into the cities and factories. In less than a hundred years between the late 18th and 19th centuries the Ohio country passed from Indian-occupied forests and plains to mechanized farmlands of unparalleled efficiency, becoming virtually the granary of the Western world and spawning some of its greatest and wealthiest industrial centres.

While the north boomed, the warmer southern states slipped into rural lethargy; becoming overdependent on cotton cultivation, they remained backward and outside the mainstream of American prosperity. Though fortunes were made on the rich cotton estates of the south-east, Tennessee and the southern Appalachians spelled rural poverty for many generations of settlers.

Today the pattern is much the same, though prosperity has increased throughout the east. The densest concentrations of industry and population lie in the north-east, especially in central New England. New York remains an important financial hub, while Washington, D.C., now part of a vast, sprawling megalopolis, loses none of its significance as the centre of federal government. The southeastern states remain relatively rural and thinly populated, though they are increasingly popular with the retired, notably Florida.

The Central States

Within the 1,400 km [875 mls] from the Mississippi to the foothills of the Rockies, the land rises almost 3,000 m [9,850 ft], though the slope is often imperceptible to the traveller. From the Gulf of Mexico northwards to Minnesota and the Dakotas the rise is even less noticeable, though the flatness is occasionally relieved by the outcrops of uplands – the Ozarks of northern Arkansas, for example. In summer nothing bars the northwards movement of hot moist air from the Gulf of Mexico, nor in winter the southwards movement of dry, cold air from the Arctic. These air masses produce great seasonal contrasts of climate, exacerbated by storms, blizzards and tornadoes. Westwards from the Mississippi the climate grows progressively drier.

The plains are crossed by a series of long, wide rivers, often of irregular flow, that drain off the Rockies: the Missouri, the Platte, the Arkansas, the Canadian and the Red. In contrast to the Ohio,

WASHINGTON • Olympia
OREGON • Salem
MONTANA • Helena
Bismarck • N. DAKOTA
MINNESOTA
IDAHO • Boise
WYOMING
S. DAKOTA • Pierre
St. Paul • WISCONSIN • Madison
MICHIGAN • Lansing
MAINE • Augusta
Montpelier • VT. • N.H. • Concord
Albany • NEW YORK
Hartford • MASS. • Boston
CONN. • R.I.
NEVADA • Carson City
Salt Lake City • UTAH
Cheyenne
NEBRASKA
IOWA • Des Moines
ILLINOIS • INDIANA • OHIO
Springfield • Indianapolis • Columbus
PENNSYLVANIA • Harrisburg • Trenton
Dover • DEL.
Annapolis • MD. • Washington D.C.
CALIFORNIA • Sacramento
COLORADO • Denver
Topeka • Jefferson City
Lincoln
KANSAS
MISSOURI
KENTUCKY • Frankfort
Charleston • WEST VIRGINIA
Richmond • VIRGINIA
Raleigh • NORTH CAROLINA
Nashville • TENNESSEE
ARIZONA • Phoenix
Santa Fe
NEW MEXICO
OKLAHOMA • Oklahoma City
Little Rock • ARKANSAS
Atlanta • GEORGIA
SOUTH CAROLINA
ALABAMA • Montgomery
MISSISSIPPI • Jackson
LOUISIANA • Baton Rouge
Tallahassee
FLORIDA
TEXAS • Austin

C. CONNECTICUT
D. DELAWARE
D.C. DISTRICT OF COLUMBIA
M. MARYLAND
MASS. MASSACHUSETTS
N.H. NEW HAMPSHIRE
N.J. NEW JERSEY
R.I. RHODE ISLAND
VER. VERMONT

CANADA

MEXICO

Alaska and Hawaii are also states

Tropic of Cancer

• National Capital
• State Capital

0 200 400 600 800 1000 km
0 200 400 600 miles

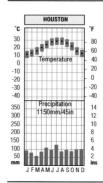

HOUSTON

Southern Texas has a Gulf-type of climate with abundant rain at all seasons to contrast the Great Plains with their winter dry season. In summer the prevailing winds are from the south-east, and in winter from the north-east. In winter, very cold air from Canada may penetrate as far south as the Gulf, causing a sharp fall in temperature, and in autumn the region may be affected by hurricanes. Several degrees of frost can be recorded between November and March.

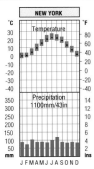

NEW YORK

New York is 40°N, but its average temperature from December to February is only just above freezing. Temperatures lower than –20°C [–4°F] have been recorded from December to February, while the daily high from May to August is above 20°C [68°F], with records of 35–40°C [95–104°F]. Rain and snow are more or less evenly distributed throughout the year, with rain falling on about a third of the days. Sunshine totals are high, averaging 6–9 hours daily from March to October.

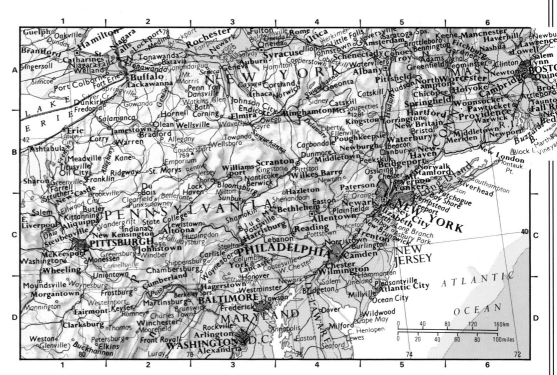

which enabled travellers to pass downstream and so westwards to the Mississippi, these rivers of the plains provided little help to settlers moving westwards, due to their seasonal variations in flow and the effort which was needed to move upstream when floods gave them depth.

Vegetation: West of the margins of the Mississippi, tall bluestem prairie grasses once extended from the Canadian border to southern Texas. Only along the watercourses were there trees – cottonwood and willow in the north, merging into oak and hickory further south. Westwards the prairie grasslands thinned to the bunch grass and needle grass of the Great Plains in a belt from central North Dakota to western Oklahoma; locally favoured areas such as western Nebraska had patches of broadleaf evergreens amidst shrubs and grasses.

West of about meridian 100°W a variety of short grasses stretched from Montana and the Dakotas southwards to north-west Texas: in the far south on the Mexican border low xerophytic shrubs indicated increasing aridity. Higher ground, for example the Black Hills of south-western South Dakota, supported stands of pine.

Settlement and development: Over 30 major tribes of native Indians used these vast and varied plains. Some – the Mandan, the Omaha and the Kansa along the Missouri River, for example – were settled farmers, while on the drier western plains the Blackfoot, Crow, Arapaho, Kiowa and Comanche were nomadic, following the buffalo, the game and the pasture.

European influences revolutionized their lives. By 1800 the horse, introduced from the south by the Spanish, made the Indian population of about 100,000 mobile as never before. Then English- and French-speaking trappers and traders from the east brought firearms; the mounted Indian with a gun became too efficient a hunter, and rapidly depleted his food supply. Behind the traders came white settlers, killing off the buffalo and crowding in other native peoples that they had driven from homelands in the south-east. As railways, cattle trails and the fences of the ranchers crossed the old hunting grounds, Indian farmers and hunters alike lost their traditional lands and livelihoods to the European intruders, and the plains settlement was virtually completed by the late 19th century.

The coming of the railways after the Civil War of the 1860s not only doomed the remnant Indian societies, but also introduced long and often bitter competition between different types of European farming. The dry grasslands that once supported the buffalo could just as well support herds of cattle on the open range, raised to feed the eastern cities. So the range lands often became crop farms. In the dry years that followed soil deterioration and erosion began, becoming a major problem in the early decades of the present century.

With their markets in the cities of the east and in Europe, the plains farmers were caught in a vice

between the desiccation of their farms and the boom and slump of their markets. By the 1930s agricultural depression led to massive foreclosing on mortgaged lands, and when the dust storms of eroded topsoil came the people were driven away – the 'Okies' of Woody Guthrie and John Steinbeck who fled to California. Much farmed land subsequently reverted to ranching.

Farming prospects improved during the later 1930s, when the New Deal brought better price structures. New approaches to farming practice, including dry farming (cropping only one year out of several), contour ploughing, diversification beyond basic grains, and widespread irrigation that was linked to the creation of a vast network of dams and reservoirs, all transformed the plains. Nevertheless these areas are marginal to semi-desert, remaining highly susceptible to periodic changes in precipitation over a wide area; thus a poor snowfall on the Rockies may mean insufficient water for irrigation the following summer. Coupled with worldwide fluctuations in the cereals market (on which Midwest farmers still depend heavily), farming on the plains remains very risky.

The growth of industry: In the Gulf Coast states, petroleum provides a radically different basis for prosperity. Since the exploitation of oil reserves in the early years of the century Oklahoma, Texas and Louisiana have shifted from a dependence on agriculture (notably wheat, cattle, rice and sugar production) to the refining and petrochemical industries. Oil has transformed Dallas–Fort Worth into a major US conurbation, now larger than the twin cities of Minneapolis–St Paul, which were once the chief urban focus of the agricultural economy of the upper Mississippi. At the meeting of the High Plains and the Rocky Mountains, Denver changed from a small elevated railhead town to a wealthy state capital (and further to a smog-ridden metropolis) in response to mineral wealth and the growth of aerospace industries.

Further north the cities of the central USA are great trading centres, dependent on local agriculture for their prosperity. Wholesaling and the transshipping of produce have been crucial since the days of the railheads, but cities like St Louis, Kansas

City and Chicago have been able to diversify far beyond their original role to become major manufacturing centres. Chicago, for example, is the main midwestern focus of the steel industries. Nowadays the interstate freeway system supplements and has partly replaced the railway networks, and air passenger traffic has increased rapidly.

From the air the landscape between the Mississippi and the Rockies is one of quilted farmlands and vast reservoirs, blending into wheatlands with extensive grasslands. Almost all the original vegetation is long gone, and most people now live in the cities, but the landscape still reflects the critical importance of agriculture past and present.

The West

The western USA is a complex mountain and plateau system, rich in scenic beauty and natural history, bordered by a rugged coast that starts in the semi-deserts of the south and ends in the rain-soaked forests of the north. Americans appreciate their far west; for long the final frontier of a youthful, expanding nation, it is still the goal of tens of thousands of immigrants each year and the holiday dream of many more: tourism is the most widespread industry.

Landscape and vegetation: Topographically the west is a land of high mountain ranges divided by high plateaus and deep valleys. The grain of the country runs north-west to south-east, at a right angle to the crustal pressures that produced it, and

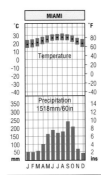

MIAMI

The Florida peninsula enjoys the warmest winters of the US mainland and, with a winter rainfall minimum, the region is an ideal winter holiday resort. The lowest-ever recorded temperature is 1°C [34°F]. The summer is hot and humid with prevailing southerly winds and thundery rain. Hurricanes may affect the region in late summer and partially account for the high rainfall in the months of September and October. Daily sunshine amounts average 7.5–9 hours.

NORTH AND CENTRAL AMERICA

the highest mountains – the Rocky Mountains of a thousand legends – form a spectacular eastern flank. The southern Rockies of Colorado and New Mexico, remnants of an ancient granite plateau, are carved by weathering into ranges of spectacular peaks; Colorado alone has over 1,000 mountains of 3,000 m [10,000 ft] or more. Rising from dry, sandy, cactus-and-sagebrush desert, their lower slopes carry grey piñon pines and juniper scrub, with darker spruce, firs and pines above. At the timberline grow gnarled bristlecone pines, some 3,000 and more years old. Between the ranges,

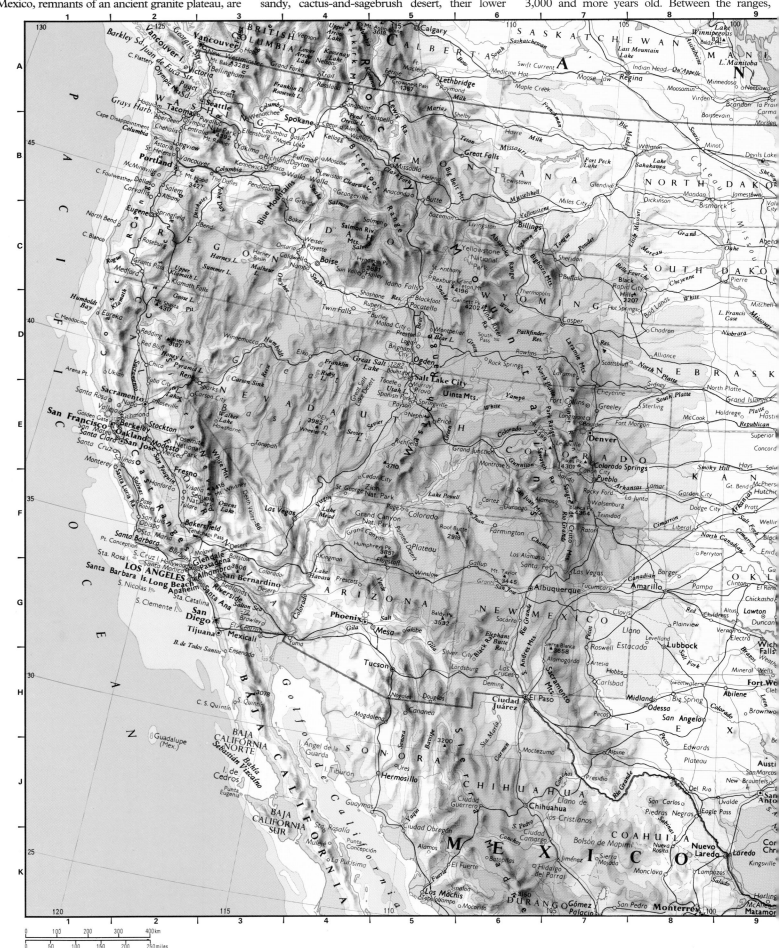

'parks' of mixed forest and grassland support deer and other game in summer grazing. To the south-west are the dry, colourful sandstones of the Colorado Plateau, dotted with cactus and deeply gouged by the Colorado River; to the north lies the Wyoming Basin, a rangeland of rich volcanic soil that once grazed herds of bison, and now supports sheep and cattle. The central Rocky Mountains, towering over western Wyoming, Idaho and Montana, include a number of snow-capped peaks of over 4,000 m [13,000 ft]; their eastern outliers, the Bighorn Mountains, rise 3,000 m [10,000 ft] almost sheer

above the surrounding grasslands. These are the Rockies of the tourists; each year thousands of people visit the many national parks and reserves in the splendid heartland of the Cordilleras. The scenery is matchless, the forests, grasslands, alpine tundras and marshes are ecologically fascinating, and the wild animals are reasonably accessible. There is every chance for tourists to see bison, wapiti, mule deer, moose, black and brown bears, beavers and a host of smaller mammals and birds.

West of the Rockies, beyond the dry plateau scrublands of Arizona, Utah and Nevada, a double chain of mountains runs parallel to the coast from Mexico to Canada. In the arid, sun-baked south they form the desert landscape on either side of the Gulf of California. At Los Angeles they merge, parting again to form the Sierra Nevada and the Coastal Ranges that face each other across the Great Valley of central California. They rejoin in the Klamath Mountains, then continue north on either side of a broad valley – to the west as a lowly coastal chain, to the east as the magnificently forested Cascade Range. By keeping rain away from the interior, these mountains create the arid landscapes of the central Cordilleras.

Climate and agriculture: In the damp winters and dry summers of southern California the coastal mountains support semi-desert scrub; the Sierra Nevada, rising far above them, is relatively well-watered and forested. In the early days of settlement the long, bone-dry summers made farming – even ranching – difficult in the central valley of California. But the peaks of Sierra Nevada, accumulating thick blankets of snow in winter, now provide a reservoir for summer irrigation. Damming and water channelling have made the semi-deserts and dry rangelands bloom all over southern California, which now grows temperate and tropical fruits, vegetables, cotton and other thirsty crops in abundance – despite severe drought from the late 1980s.

Through northern California and Oregon, where annual rainfall is higher and summer heat less intense, the coastal mountains are clothed in forests of tall cedars and firs; notable among them are stands of giant redwood cedars, towering well over 100 m [330 ft]. In coastal Washington Douglas firs, grand firs, Sitka spruce and giant *arborvitae* are the spectacular trees, rivalling the famous giant

redwoods. Forests of giant conifers cover the Cascade Range too, providing the enormous stocks of timber on which the wealth of the American northwest was originally based.

Settlement and development: The Indian cultures of western America included hunting, fishing, seed gathering and primitive irrigation farming. Some were semi-nomadic, others settled, living mostly in small, scattered communities. The first European colonists, spreading northwards from New Spain (Mexico) in the 1760s, made little impact on the Indians. But their forts and missions (which included San Diego, Los Angeles and San Francisco) attracted later settlers who proved more exploitative. From the 1840s pressures increased with the arrival of land-hungry Americans, both by sea and along wagon trails from the east. After a brief struggle, the south-west was sold to the USA; almost immediately the gold rushes brought new waves of adventurers and immigrants.

The Oregon coast, though visited by Spanish, British and Russian mariners in search of furs from the 16th century onwards, was first settled by American fur traders in 1811. Immigration began during the 1830s, the famous Oregon Trail across Wyoming and Idaho from the Mississippi coming into full use during the 1840s. After the establishment of the 49th parallel as the boundary between Canada and the USA, Oregon Territory (including Washington, Idaho and part of Montana) became part of the USA. Here in the north-west the forests and rangelands were equally vital to Indians and to settlers, and many battles were fought before the Indians were subdued and confined in tribal reserves.

Now the wagon trails are major highways, the staging posts, mission stations and isolated forts transformed into cities. Gold mining, once the only kind of mining that mattered, has given way to the delving and processing of a dozen lesser metals, from copper to molybdenum. Fish canning, food processing, electronics and aerospace are major sources of employment. The movie industry is based in Los Angeles, but this urban cluster now has a broad economy based on high-technology industries. The mountain states – once far behind in economic development – have caught up with the rest of the USA. But the enduring beauty of the western mountains remains.

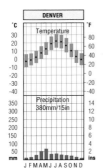

Denver is at an altitude of over 1,500 m [5,000 ft]. The winters are chilly with snow, whereas the summers are pleasantly warm. The daily temperature range is quite high; January's daily daytime average is 6°C [43°F], while the night is –10°C [14°F]. Precipitation is low, with a maximum in April and May, rain falling on ten days in any month. Sunshine levels are high with an average of over 6 hours a day in all months, with over 9 hours in the summer months.

Economy

The years following the Civil War (1861–5) saw the firm establishment of the USA as the world's leading industrial society. Still attracting enormous numbers of emigrants from Europe, its agricultural and industrial output grew at unprecedented rates to the end of the century and beyond.

Agriculture: Stimulated by education, research and new, sophisticated machinery, agriculture developed into a highly mechanized industry for food production and processing. Chicago's agricultural machinery industries transformed the farmers' lives with mass-produced ploughs, tractors, seed drills, reapers and binders. Only a generation after the pioneering days, farmers found themselves tightly integrated into an economic system with such factors as mortgages, availability of spare parts, freight prices and world markets at least as crucial to the success of their efforts as climate and soil.

To the east of the western mountains farming was established in a zonal pattern which remains intact – though much modified – today, a pattern reflecting both the possibilities offered by climate and soils, and the inclinations and national origins of the settlers who first farmed the lands. In the north, from Minnesota to New England, lies a broad belt where dairy farming predominates, providing milk, butter and cheese for the industrial cities. Spring wheat is grown further west, where the climate is drier. The eastern and central states from Nebraska to Ohio form the famous Corn Belt – immensely productive land, formerly prairie and forest, where corn (maize) is the main crop.

Now much extended by the development of new, more tolerant strains, corn production has spread into belts on either side. No longer principally human food, except in the poorer areas of the south, corn is grown mainly for feeding to cattle and pigs, which supply the meat-packing industries. Soya beans, oats and other food and fodder crops grow in the Corn Belt, with wheat and dairy farming prominent along the northern border.

Southwards again, from Oklahoma and Kansas to Virginia, stretches a broad belt of mixed farming where winter wheat and corn alternate as the dominant cereals. In the warmer southern states lies the former Cotton Belt where cotton and tobacco were once the most widespread crops; both are now concentrated into small, highly productive areas where mechanical handling is possible, and the bulk of the land is used for a wide variety of other crops from vegetables to fruit and peanuts.

Throughout American farming there has been a tendency to shift from small-scale operations to large, from labour-intensive to mechanized, and from low-capital to high-capital investment. The main centres of production are now concentrated in the western plains: much of the land originally farmed by the Pilgrim Fathers and other early settlers is now built over, or has reverted to attractive second-growth forest. By concentrating effort in this way,

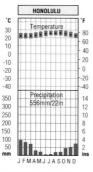

The subtropical islands of Hawaii are cooled by the moisture-laden north-east trades. Temperatures remain high throughout the year, ranging from 26°C [79°F] in the warmest month to 22°C [72°F] in the coolest. Rainfall varies greatly throughout these mountainous islands. Mt Waialeale on Kauai has a rainfall of 12,000 mm [472 in], while Puako on the leeward side of Hawaii receives less than 250 mm [10 in]. The lofty volcanoes Mauna Kea and Mauna Loa are frequently snow-covered.

HAWAII

Most recent and most southerly of the United States, Hawaii is an archipelago of eight large and over 100 smaller volcanic islands in the mid-Pacific, 3,850 km [2,400 mls] south-west of California. Only on the main island are there currently active volcanoes. High rainfall, warmth and rich soils combine to provide a wealth of year-round vegetation; originally forested, the islands are still well covered with trees and shrubs, but now provide commercial crops of sugar cane, cereals, forage for cattle, and a wide range of fruit and vegetables.

Originally settled by Polynesians and visited by James Cook in 1778, Hawaii became a port-of-call for trans-Pacific shipping and a wintering station for New England whalers, but retained its independent status until annexed by the USA in 1898. Only about 2% of its people are full-blooded Polynesians; the rest are of Chinese, Japanese, Korean, Philippine and Caucasian origins. About 80% live on the islands of Oahu, over half of them in the capital city of Honolulu. Agriculture, fishing and food processing are the main industries, though defence and tourism are also important.

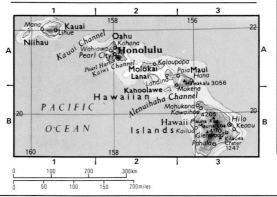

ALASKA

In 1867 the USA bought Alaska from the Tsarist government of Russia for a mere US$7 million. More extensive than the south-western lands acquired from Mexico, Alaska remained a territory for over 90 years, becoming America's largest state in 1959. Geographically, it forms the north-western end of the Western Cordilleras; peaks in the main Alaska Range rise to over 6,000 m [20,000 ft], and the southern 'panhandle' region is a drowned fjordland backed by ice-capped mountains. A gold rush in the 1880s stimulated the later development of other mineral resources – notably copper and, especially, oil. Alaska is the first real test of the USA's resolve to balance economic development and conservation; the six largest US national parks are in Alaska. Some farming is possible on the southern coastal lowlands; the interior tablelands are tundra-covered and rich in migrant birds and mammals.

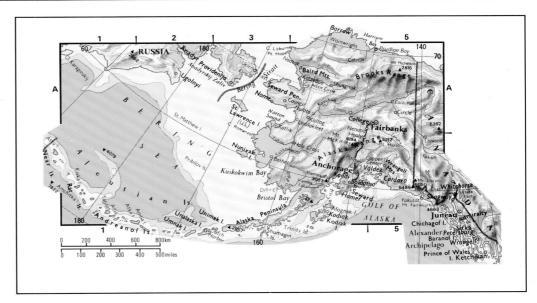

America has become a leading producer of meat, dairy foods, soya beans, corn, oats, wheat, barley, cotton, sugar and many other crops, both for home consumption and export.

Resources and industry: The spread of prosperity throughout a very broad spectrum of the community generated new consumer industries, to satisfy the demands of a large middle class for ever-increasing standards of comfort and material welfare. America became the pioneer of massive-scale industrial production of everything from thumbtacks to automobiles. With almost every material needed for production available within its own boundaries, or readily gained through trading with neighbours, its mining and extractive industries have been heavily exploited from the start.

For several generations coal formed the main source of power and the basis of industrial prosperity. Anthracite from eastern Pennsylvania, good bituminous and coking coals from the Appalachians, Indiana, Illinois, Colorado and Utah are still in demand, and enormous reserves remain. Oil, first drilled in Pennsylvania in 1859, was subsequently found in several major fields underlying the midwest, the eastern and central mountain states, the Gulf of Mexico, California and Alaska. Home consumption of petroleum products has grown steadily: though the USA remains a major producer, it is also by far the world's greatest consumer, and has for long been a net importer of oil. Natural gas, too, is found in abundance, usually in association with oil, and is moved to the main consumer areas through an elaborate, transcontinental network of pipes.

Today the USA is a major producer of iron and steel, mica, molybdenum, uranium and many other primary materials, and a major consumer and exporter of a wide range of manufactured goods. But though the USA remains the world's greatest economic power, its position was being threatened by Japan in the 1990s.

Population: The USA has one of the most diverse populations of any nation in the world. Until about 1860, with the exception of the native Indians and the southern blacks, the population was largely made up by immigrants of British (and Irish) origin, with small numbers of Spanish and French. After the Civil War, however, there was increasing immigration from the countries of central and south-eastern Europe – Italy, the Balkans, Poland, Scandinavia and Russia. This vast influx of Europeans, numbering about 30 million between 1860

and 1920, was markedly different in culture and language from the established population. More recently there have been lesser influxes of Japanese, Chinese, Filipinos, Cubans and Puerto Ricans, with large numbers of Mexicans. Although there are strong influences and pressures towards Americanization, these groups have tended to establish social and cultural enclaves within US society.

The major westwards movement of population through the last century was replaced after 1900 by more subtle but no less important shifts of population away from rural areas and into the cities. Today there is further movement from the old, industrial centres and the tired, outmoded cities that flourished early in the century, away from the ageing buildings and urban dereliction, especially in the north and east, to new centres elsewhere.

The cities that gain population are mostly peripheral, on the Great Lakes and the coasts. The South is especially favoured for its warmth (particularly by retired people) and its closeness to the major source of energy in the USA (and therefore work opportunities) – petroleum. The development of southern petrochemical and electronic industries has helped to relieve rural poverty and given new economic life, though partly at the expense of the North. However, Chicago and the eastern conurba-

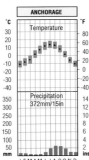

The climate of the southern coastal regions of Alaska is drier and more extreme than might be expected from its maritime position. From November to May, the winds are mainly easterly and winters are cold and dry, though the ports remain ice-free. In summer, south-westerly winds increase in frequency, giving a late summer rainfall maximum. Northwards, beyond the Alaskan Range, the climate becomes drier and bitterly cold in the winter months.

tions – New York, Boston, Philadelphia, Baltimore and Washington – still remain pre-eminent as the centres of US commercial and cultural life.

Since its earliest inception from the 13 colonies, the USA has led the world in industrial, economic and social innovation, creating problems through sheer ebullience and solving them – more or less – through inventiveness and enterprise, and with massive, wealth-bringing resources of energy and materials. The USA today continues to enjoy one of the world's highest material standards of living, and continues to produce a highly skilled, literate and imaginative population ∎

COUNTRY United States of America

AREA 9,372,610 sq km [3,618,765 sq mls]

POPULATION 263,563,000

CAPITAL (POPULATION) Washington, D.C. (4,360,000)

GOVERNMENT Federal republic with a bicameral legislature

ETHNIC GROUPS White 80%, African American 12%, other races 8%

LANGUAGES English (official), Spanish, over 30 others

RELIGIONS Protestant 53%, Roman Catholic 26%, other Christian 8%, Jewish 2%, Muslim 2%

NATIONAL DAY 4 July; Declaration of Independence by Congress (1776)

CURRENCY United States dollar = 100 cents

ANNUAL INCOME PER PERSON US$24,750

SOURCE OF INCOME Agriculture 2%, industry 29%, services 69%

MAIN PRIMARY PRODUCTS Cereals, cotton, tobacco, soya beans, fruit, potatoes, oilseeds, sugar cane, livestock, timber, oil and natural gas, coal, copper, lead, iron ore, zinc, molybdenum, silver, gold

MAIN INDUSTRIES Iron and steel, vehicles, chemicals, telecommunications, aeronautics and space, electronics, computers, textiles, paper, fishing, agriculture, mining

MAIN EXPORTS Machinery and transport equipment 43%, chemicals 10%, foodstuffs, beverages and tobacco 9%, crude materials 8%

MAIN EXPORT PARTNERS Canada 24%, Japan 11%, Mexico 6%, UK 6%, Germany 5%

MAIN IMPORTS Machinery and transport equipment 44%, clothing, footwear and manufactured articles 16%, paper, textiles, diamonds, iron and steel, non-ferrous metals 13%, mineral fuels 11%, foodstuffs 6%

MAIN IMPORT PARTNERS Japan 21%, Canada 18%, Germany 7%, Taiwan 6%, Mexico 5%, UK 4%

EDUCATIONAL EXPENDITURE 7% of GNP

DEFENCE 5.3% of GNP

TOTAL ARMED FORCES 2,124,900

TOURISM 45,793,000 visitors per year

POPULATION DENSITY 28 per sq km [73 per sq ml]

URBAN POPULATION 76%

INFANT MORTALITY 8 per 1,000 live births

LIFE EXPECTANCY Female 80 yrs, male 73 yrs

ADULT LITERACY 99%

PRINCIPAL CITIES (POPULATION) New York 16,329,000 Los Angeles 12,410,000 Chicago 7,561,000 Philadelphia 4,944,000 Washington 4,360,000 Detroit 4,308,000 San Francisco 3,866,000 Houston 3,530,000

NORTH AND CENTRAL AMERICA

MEXICO

The stripes on the Mexican flag were inspired by the French tricolour and date from 1821. The emblem of the eagle, snake and cactus is based on an ancient Aztec legend about the founding of Mexico City. The design was adopted for the Olympic year, 1968.

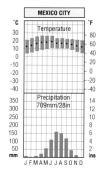

Due to its elevation of over 2,000 m [6,500 ft], temperatures at Mexico City are some 9°C [16°F] lower than on the Gulf coast, though the annual range is about the same. But the daily range of temperature is far greater on the plateau, and frost and snow are not unknown. Rainfall on the plateau is markedly seasonal and decreases northwards to under 250 mm [10 in] where the country widens. From June to September, there is rain on around 21–27 days per month.

The world's largest and most populous Spanish-speaking nation, Mexico has a faster-growing population than any other big country: between 1960 and 1980 it doubled, growing at an unprecedented 3.5% a year. It is thus an astonishingly young society; the average Mexican is a 17-year-old, and 75% of the people are under 30.

The combination of a stable and very high birth rate (now about 17 per thousand) and a declining and now low death rate (about six per thousand) is the main cause of this population explosion. Mexico City (population 1 million in 1930, 8.7 million in 1970, 15 million in 1990) is already the most populous in the Americas and estimated to be the world's largest by 2000, overtaking both Tokyo and São Paulo.

Landscape and vegetation

Mexico is a land of great physical variety. The northern, emptier, half is open basin-and-range country of the Mesa Central. The land rises southwards from the Rio Grande (Rio Bravo del Norte) at the US border, averaging about 2,600 m [8,500 ft] above sea level in the middle, where it is crowned by many snow-capped volcanic cones, Orizaba (5,750 m [18,865 ft]) in the east being the highest.

Though an active earthquake zone, this is the most densely settled part of the country. The Mesa Central ends equally dramatically in the west, where the Sierra Madre Occidental rise to over 4,000 m [13,120 ft], and in the east, where the Sierra Madre Oriental form a backcloth to the modest coastal plain bordering the Gulf of Mexico. In the far northwest is the isolated, 1,220 km [760 mls] mountain-cored peninsula of Baja California.

Mountains dominate southern Mexico, broken only by the low, narrow isthmus of Tehuantepec, which is crossed by railways and roads linking the Gulf ports with Salina Cruz on the Pacific. The flat, low-lying limestone Yucatan peninsula in the southeast is an exception in a country where half the land is over 1,000 m [3,280 ft] above sea level, and a quarter has slopes of over 25 degrees. Deserts characterize the north-west, and tropical rainforest is the natural vegetation of Tehuantepec; over 70% of the country is arid or semi-arid and irrigation is mandatory for agriculture.

Economy

Agriculture occupies half the population but contributes less than a third of the economic product contributed by manufacturing, with metals also important – the country is the world's leading producer of silver. Fresh petroleum discoveries during the 1970s from massive reserves in Tabasco and Campeche have turned Mexico into the world's fifth biggest producer by 1994, much of it exported to the USA, but the economy is now very diverse with food processing, textiles, forestry and tourism all making significant progress. Only an estimated 15–20% of the nation's mineral wealth has been exploited, with precious metals comprising almost half the value of total known mineral reserves.

While the century after independence in 1821 was characterized by political chaos, climaxing in the violent revolution of 1910–21, the post-revolutionary period was steady by Latin American standards, with the PRI in power for more than six decades from 1929 and instituting crucial land reforms in the 1930s. The economy has been dom-

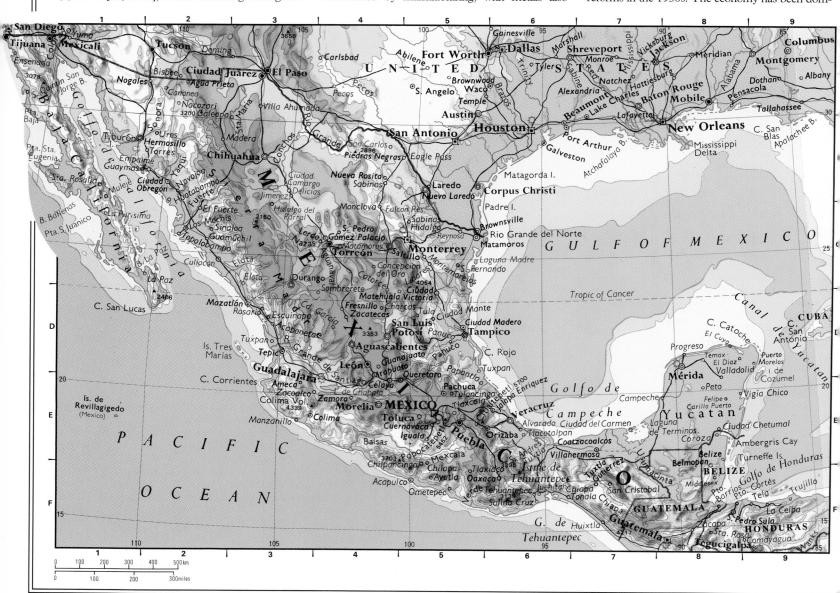

COUNTRY United Mexican States

AREA 1,958,200 sq km [756,061 sq mls]

POPULATION 93,342,000

CAPITAL (POPULATION) Mexico City (15,643,000)

GOVERNMENT Federal multiparty republic

ETHNIC GROUPS Mestizo 60%, Amerindian 30%, European 9%

LANGUAGES Spanish (official), 59 native dialects

RELIGIONS Roman Catholic 90%, Protestant 5%

CURRENCY New peso = 100 centavos

ANNUAL INCOME PER PERSON US$3,750

SOURCE OF INCOME Agriculture 8%, industry 28%, services 63%

MAIN PRIMARY PRODUCTS Wheat, maize, coffee, sorghum, cattle, sugar, cotton, silver, copper, sulphur, coal, lead, iron, gold, oil, natural gas

MAIN INDUSTRIES Oil refining, natural gas, mining, agriculture, aluminium, vehicles, textiles, pottery

MAIN EXPORTS Crude petroleum 38%, engines and vehicle parts 24%, forestry products 15%, energy products 8%, machinery 3%, coffee 2%, shrimps 2%

MAIN EXPORT PARTNERS USA 64%, Japan 6%, Germany 3%

MAIN IMPORTS Machinery and equipment 32%, vehicles and parts 23%, industrial materials 18%, other consumer goods 11%, foodstuffs 6%

MAIN IMPORT PARTNERS USA 62%, Japan 6%, Germany 6%

EDUCATIONAL EXPENDITURE 4.1% of GNP

DEFENCE 0.5% of GNP

TOTAL ARMED FORCES 141,500

TOURISM 16,534,000 visitors per year

ROADS 225,684 km [151,053 mls]

RAILWAYS 19,906 km [12,441 mls]

POPULATION DENSITY 48 per sq km [123 per sq ml]

URBAN POPULATION 74%

POPULATION GROWTH 1.6% per year

INFANT MORTALITY 36 per 1,000 live births

LIFE EXPECTANCY Female 74 yrs, male 67 yrs

POPULATION PER DOCTOR 1,621 people

ADULT LITERACY 87%

PRINCIPAL CITIES POPULATION) Mexico City 15,643,000 Guadalajara 2,847,000 Monterrey 2,522,000 Puebla 1,055,000 León 872,000 Ciudad Juárez 798,000

inated by this regime since oil was nationalized in 1938, enjoying huge growth in the 1970s, when living standards rose considerably, but running into massive debt crises in the 1980s.

Mexico has since pursued the idea of a trading area with Canada and the USA, but rural-urban migration and high unemployment – probably around 40% in many cities – remain the biggest domestic problems. Above all, there is the emigration across the world's busiest border: hundreds of thousands of Mexicans cross into the USA each year, many of them staying as illegal immigrants ■

BELIZE

The badge shows loggers bearing axes and oars, tools employed in the industry responsible for developing Belize. The motto underneath reads '*Sub Umbra Florea*' ('flourish in the shade'), and the tree is a mahogany, the national tree.

COUNTRY Belize

AREA 22,960 sq km [8,865 sq mls]

POPULATION 216,000

CAPITAL (POPULATION) Belmopan (4,000)

GOVERNMENT Constitutional monarchy with a bicameral National Assembly

ETHNIC GROUPS Mestizo (Spanish Maya) 44%, Creole 30%, Mayan Indian 11%, Garifuna (Black Carib Indian) 7%, White 4%, East Indian 3%

LANGUAGES English (official), Creole, Spanish, Indian, Carib

RELIGIONS Roman Catholic 58%, Protestant 29%

NATIONAL DAY 21 September; Independence Day (1981)

CURRENCY Belize dollar = 100 cents

ANNUAL INCOME PER PERSON US$2,440

POPULATION DENSITY 9 per sq km [24 per sq ml]

LIFE EXPECTANCY Female 72 yrs, male 67 yrs

ADULT LITERACY 96%

L arger than El Salvador but with only 3.7% of its population, Belize is a sparsely populated enclave on the Caribbean coast of Central America. The northern half is low-lying swamp, whereas the south is a high corrugated plateau, while offshore lies the world's second biggest coral reef.

Formerly British Honduras, it enjoyed a boom after independence, with processing of citrus fruits and tourism helping to allay the dependency on timber, bananas and sugar, though the latter still accounts for 30% of export earnings. There is also the prospect of an end to the nagging dispute with Guatemala, which initially claimed all of Belizean territory. Over a quarter of the population lives in Belize City, replaced as the capital by Belmopan in 1970 following hurricane damage ■

GUATEMALA

The simple design of Guatemala's flag was adopted in 1871, but its origins date back to the Central American Federation (1823–39) formed with Honduras, El Salvador, Nicaragua and Costa Rica after the break from Spanish rule in 1821.

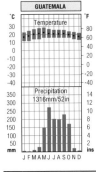

Its position between seas and with a mountainous spine gives a variety of climates. In the lowlands, temperatures are between 25–30°C [77–86°F], but at Guatemala City (1,500 m [5,000 ft]), the extremes are 17°C [63°F] in January and 22°C [72°F] in May. On the Caribbean coast, with the trade winds always blowing onshore, rainfall is high in all months. Rainfall is also high on the Pacific slopes, but inland there is a dry, almost arid, season, in January and February.

COUNTRY Republic of Guatemala

AREA 108,890 sq km [42,042 sq mls]

POPULATION 10,624,000

CAPITAL (POPULATION) Guatemala City (2,000,000)

GOVERNMENT Republic with a unicameral legislature

ETHNIC GROUPS Mayaquiche Indian 45%, Ladino (Mestizo) 42%

LANGUAGES Spanish (official), 20 Indian dialects

RELIGIONS Roman Catholic 75%, Protestant 23%

NATIONAL DAY 15 September; Independence Day

CURRENCY Guatemalan quetzal = 100 centavos

ANNUAL INCOME PER PERSON US$1,110

MAIN PRIMARY PRODUCTS Petroleum, iron, lead, nickel

MAIN EXPORTS Coffee, bananas, sugar, cardamom

MAIN IMPORTS Mineral fuels, chemicals, machinery and transport equipment, manufactured goods

DEFENCE 1.1% of GNP

POPULATION DENSITY 98 per sq km [253 per sq ml]

LIFE EXPECTANCY Female 67 yrs, male 62 yrs

ADULT LITERACY 54%

M ost populous of the Central American countries, Guatemala's Pacific coastline, two and a half times longer than the Caribbean coast, is backed by broad alluvial plains, formed of material washed down from the towering volcanoes that front the ocean. These include extinct Tajumulco (4,217 m [13,830 ft]), the highest peak in Central America.

The plains have been used for commercial-scale agriculture only since the 1950s, when malaria was brought under control and roads were built; cattle and cotton are now more important than the traditional banana crop. The lower mountain slopes yield most of the country's best coffee. Tourism is now becoming an important foreign exchange earner.

While Indians are in the majority, society and government are run on autocratic, often repressive lines by the mestizos of mixed Indian and European stock. The Indians were the principal victims of the army's indiscriminate campaign against left-wing URNG guerrillas in the early 1980s – the acceleration of a policy in place since the 1950s. The 'low-intensity' civil war that followed was still smouldering when a UN-mediated cease-fire became operative in neighbouring El Salvador in 1992. This influence, allied to the government's sudden recognition of Belizean independence in 1991 (Guatemala had claimed the entire territory), would benefit a nation whose human rights record had been appalling. In 1994 a human rights agreement was reached, allowing for the establishment of a UN observer mission. A peace accord was finally signed on 29 December 1996 by the guerilla commanders and President Alvaro Irigoyen, ending a civil war that had lasted 36 years and claimed 140,000 lives ■

HONDURAS

Officially adopted in 1949, the flag of Honduras is based on that of the Central American Federation (*see Guatemala*). Honduras left the organization in 1838, but in 1866 added the five stars to the flag to express a hope for a future federation.

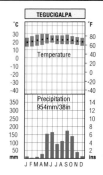

On the northern coast, the average temperatures are between 26–28°C [79–82°F]. At Tegucigalpa (1,000 m [3,250 ft]), these are reduced to 20–24°C [68–75°F], and on the higher land are even lower. The diurnal temperature range can be as much as 15°C [27°F]. The sheltered mountain valleys receive a moderate rainfall of 1,000–1,500 mm [39–59 in], but the coasts and mountains get in excess of 2,000 mm [79 in]. The wet season is from May to October.

Though second largest of the Central American countries, Honduras has a relatively small population. Some 80% of the country is mountainous, with peaks of more than 2,500 m [8,000 ft] in the west. In the south-east, the state has a short 80 km [50 mls] frontage on the Pacific Ocean in the Gulf of Fonseca. Most of Honduras has a seasonal climate that is relatively dry between November and May.

The mountain ranges are metalliferous: lodes of gold drew the first Spanish *conquistadores* to found Tegucigalpa, the capital, in 1524, and silver is still an important export. Mining contributes more to the economy than it does in any other Central American state. The limited lowlands around the Pacific coast form some of the prime cotton lands of the country. Traditional cattle ranching, employing cowboys, is as much in evidence as agriculture. The aromatic pine forests of the east are being consumed by new paper mills on the hot, rain-soaked Caribbean coast. The lower alluvium-filled valleys of the rivers draining into the Caribbean have been reclaimed and the forest replaced by orderly banana plantations.

Honduras was the original 'banana republic' – the world's leading exporter in the interwar years. Today it remains an important crop, accounting for nearly a quarter of exports, with production dominated by two US companies, though coffee is now the largest earner. Dependent on these cash crops, the country is the least industrialized in the region. It is also the most reliant on the USA for trade – quite a claim in Central America: 56% of its imports and 49% of its exports are with the USA.

After a short civil war in the 1920s, a series of military regimes ruled Honduras. However, instability continued to mar the country's progress. In 1969, Honduras fought the short 'Soccer War' with El Salvador that was sparked off by the treatment of fans during a World Cup soccer series. But the underlying reason was that Honduras had forced Salvadoreans in Honduras to give up their land. In 1980, the two countries signed a peace agreement.

Aid from the USA has been crucial, partly in return for services rendered; important strategically to Washington, Honduras allowed US-backed 'Contra' rebels from Nicaragua to operate in Honduras against Nicaragua's left-wing Sandinista government throughout the 1980s. A cease-fire between the Nicaraguan groups was finally signed in 1988, following which the 'Contra' bases were closed down. Since 1980, Honduras has been ruled by civilian governments, though the military retain considerable influence ■

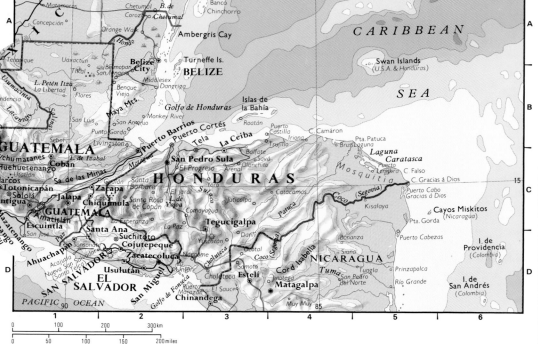

COUNTRY Republic of Honduras

AREA 112,090 sq km [43,278 sq mls]

POPULATION 5,940,000

CAPITAL (POPULATION) Tegucigalpa (739,000)

GOVERNMENT Multiparty republic with a unicameral legislature

ETHNIC GROUPS Mestizo 90%, Amerindian 7%, Black (including Black Carib) 2%, White 1%

LANGUAGES Spanish (official), Black Carib (Garifuna), English Creole, Miskito

RELIGIONS Roman Catholic 85%, Protestant 10%

CURRENCY Honduran lempira = 100 centavos

POPULATION DENSITY 53 per sq km [137 per sq ml]

EL SALVADOR

The original flag, the 'Stars and Stripes', was replaced in 1912 by the current one. The blue and white stripes are a common feature of the flags of Central American countries that gained their independence from Spain at the same time in 1821.

COUNTRY Republic of El Salvador

AREA 21,040 sq km [8,124 sq mls]

POPULATION 5,743,000

CAPITAL (POPULATION) San Salvador (1,522,000)

GOVERNMENT Republic with a unicameral legislature

ETHNIC GROUPS Mestizo 89%, Indian 10%, White 5%

LANGUAGES Spanish (official)

RELIGIONS Roman Catholic 74%

NATIONAL DAY 15 September; Independence Day (1821)

CURRENCY Colón = 100 centavos

ANNUAL INCOME PER PERSON US$1,320

POPULATION DENSITY 273 per sq km [707 per sq ml]

LIFE EXPECTANCY Female 69 yrs, male 64 yrs

ADULT LITERACY 70%

The only Central American country without a Caribbean coast, El Salvador is also the smallest and the most densely populated; pressure on agricultural land, combined with civil war, has led to widespread emigration. The Pacific coastal plain is narrow and backed by a volcanic range averaging about 1,200 m [4,000 ft] in altitude. El Salvador has over 20 volcanoes, some still active, and crater lakes occupying a fertile central plain 400 m to 800 m [1,300 ft to 2,600 ft] above sea level. Urban and rural populations in this belt account for 60% of the total.

This fertile zone also produces 90% of the coffee and tobacco, and most of the maize and sugar – the foundations of the agricultural economy, with coffee usually accounting for over half the total value of exports. The towns are centres of manufacturing for the domestic market. Inland, the frontier with Honduras is marked by mountain ranges that reach heights of 2,000 m [6,560 ft]; previously forested and empty, they are now attracting migrants desperate for agricultural land.

El Salvador was plagued by conflict from the early 1970s and by full-blown civil war from 1980, when the political left joined revolutionary guerrillas against the US-backed extreme right-wing government. During the next 12 years, more than 75,000 people were killed (most of them civilians) and hundreds of thousands were made homeless as the regime received US$4 billion in aid from the USA in abetting the 55,000-strong Salvadorean Army and notorious death squads. After 19 months of UN-mediated talks the two sides agreed to complicated terms at the end of 1991. A cease-fire took effect in February 1992, but the country remained in disarray, with unemployment, for example, standing at more than 50% of the workforce ■

NICARAGUA

Nicaragua's flag, adopted in 1908, is identical to that of the Central American Federation (*see Guatemala*) to which it once belonged. Except for a difference in the shading of the blue and the motif, it is also the same as the flag of El Salvador.

COUNTRY Republic of Nicaragua	
AREA 130,000 sq km [50,193 sq mls]	
POPULATION 4,544,000	
CAPITAL (POPULATION) Managua (974,000)	
GOVERNMENT Multiparty republic	
ETHNIC GROUPS Mestizo 77%, White 10%, Black 9%	
LANGUAGES Spanish (official), Indian, Creole	
RELIGIONS Roman Catholic 91%	
CURRENCY Córdoba oro = 100 centavos	
ANNUAL INCOME PER PERSON US$360	
MAIN PRIMARY PRODUCTS Silver, gold, gypsum, lead	
MAIN EXPORTS Coffee, cotton, sugar and bananas	
MAIN IMPORTS Agricultural goods, oil products	
POPULATION DENSITY 35 per sq km [91 per sq ml]	

Largest and least densely populated of the Central American countries, Nicaragua's eastern half is almost empty. The Caribbean plain is extensive, and the coast is a mixture of lagoons, sandy beaches and river deltas with shallow water and sandbars offshore. With over 7,500 mm [300 in] of rain in some years, it is forested and rich in tropical fauna including crocodiles, turtles, deer, pumas, jaguars and monkeys. Cut off from the populous west of Nicaragua, it was for two centuries the British protectorate of the Miskito Coast, with Bluefields (San Juan del Norte) as the largest settlement.

Inland, the plain gives way gradually to mountain ranges broken by basins and fertile valleys. In the west and south they overlook a great depression which runs from the Gulf of Fonseca south-eastwards and contains Lakes Managua and Nicaragua. Nicaragua (8,264 sq km [3,191 sq mls]) is the largest lake in Central America; though only 20 km [12.5 mls] from the Pacific, it drains to the Caribbean by the navigable San Juan River and formed an important route across the isthmus before the Panama Canal was built. The capital

city, Managua, and other major centres are here, as is much of Nicaragua's industrial development; so, too, are the cotton fields and coffee plantations that provide the country's chief cash crops and exports (23% and 36% respectively).

Forty volcanoes, many active, rise above the lakes; San Cristobál (1,745 m [5,725 ft]) is the highest, still-smoking Momotombo the most spectacular. Earthquakes are common and Managua was virtually destroyed in 1931 and 1972.

Nicaragua has been in a state of civil war almost continuously since the 1960s. In 1979, after a 17-year campaign, the long domination of the corrupt Somoza family (who controlled 40% of the economy) was ended by a popular uprising led by the Sandinista National Liberation Front (FSLN), who went on to win democratic power in 1985. Meanwhile, the USA trained and supplied 'Contra' guerrillas from bases in Honduras and imposed a trade embargo, pushing Nicaragua into increasing dependence on Cuba and the Soviet Union.

A cease-fire agreed in 1989 was followed in 1990 by electoral defeat for Daniel José Ortega Saavedra's Sandinistas at the hands of the US-backed coalition (the National Opposition Union) of Violeta Barrios de Chamorro. The win was due mainly to the state of the economy, which had been reduced to crisis point by a combination of US sanctions and government incompetence; but while the two sides were forced into working uneasily together to try and put the country back on its feet (with the benefit of conditional US aid), fighting frequently broke out between former 'Contra' rebels and ex-Sandinistas. In 1996, the Sandinistas were again defeated and Arnoldo Alemán, leader of the Liberal Alliance Party, became president ■

COSTA RICA

Dating from 1848, Costa Rica's national flag is based on the blue/white/blue sequence of the flag of the Central American Federation (*see Guatemala*), which is itself based on the Argentinian flag, but with an additional red stripe in the centre.

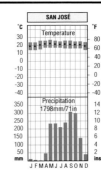

San José is just over 1,000 m [3,250 ft], and its annual average temperature is 20°C [68°F]; on the Pacific or Caribbean coasts this rises to over 27°C [81°F]. December and January are the coolest months, and May is the warmest. The north-east trade winds blow all year along the Caribbean coast, bringing rainfall in excess of 3,000 mm [118 in]. This is lower in the mountains and along the Pacific coast. There is a marked dry season from December to April.

In many ways the exception among the Central American republics, Costa Rica ('rich coast') has become the most European of the republics of the isthmus, with the best educational standards, a long life expectancy, the most democratic and stable system of government, the highest per capita gross domestic product, and the least disparity between the poor and the rich. The abolition of the armed forces in 1948 – it has only 750 civil guards – meant there has been no familiar military regime and its neutral stance has enabled the country to play the role of broker in many regional disputes.

Three mountain ranges form the skeleton of the country. In the south-east the Talamanca ranges rise to 3,837 m [12,585 ft] in Chirripó Grande; further north and west the Central Cordillera includes volcanic Irazú (3,432 m [11,260 ft]) and Poas (2,705 m [8,875 ft]), both active in recent decades; Miravalles (2,020 m [6,627 ft]) is one of four active volcanoes in the Cordillera de Guanacaste.

Coffee grown in the interior has been a cornerstone of the economy since 1850; in this century bananas have become a second major resource, and together they supply nearly half of Costa Rica's overseas earnings. The capital, San José, stands in the fertile Valle Central, in the economic heartland of the country. Drier Guanacaste, in the far north-west, is an important cattle-raising region ■

COUNTRY Republic of Costa Rica	
AREA 51,100 sq km [19,730 sq mls]	
POPULATION 3,436,000	
CAPITAL (POPULATION) San José (1,186,000)	
GOVERNMENT Multiparty republic	
ETHNIC GROUPS White 85%, Mestizo 8%	
LANGUAGES Spanish (official), Creole, Indian	
RELIGIONS Roman Catholic 81%	
CURRENCY Colón = 100 céntimos	
MAIN PRIMARY PRODUCTS Gold, salt, haematite	
ANNUAL INCOME PER PERSON US$1,930	
DEFENCE No armed forces since 1948	
POPULATION DENSITY 67 per sq km [174 per sq ml]	
LIFE EXPECTANCY Female 78 yrs, male 73 yrs	
ADULT LITERACY 93%	

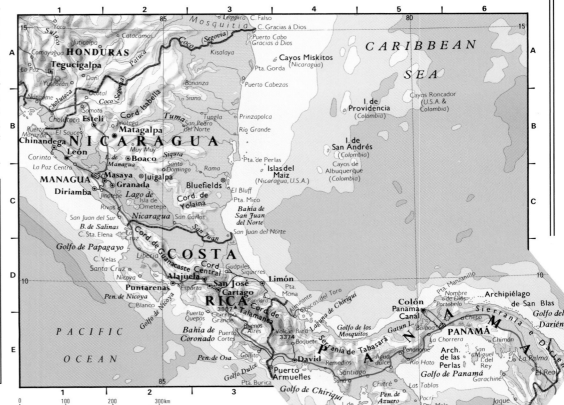

NORTH AND CENTRAL AMERICA

CUBA

First designed in 1849, Cuba's flag, the 'Lone Star' banner, was not officially adopted until the island finally gained its independence from Spain in 1901. The red triangle represents the Cuban people's bloody struggle for independence.

Cuba is encircled by the warm ocean current which is the beginning of what becomes the Gulf Stream. It is just within the tropics and has high temperatures: 22°C [72°F] in January, and 28°C [82°F] in August. The highest temperature ever recorded is 36°C [97°F] and the lowest is 10°C [50°F]. Rainfall is heavier on the northern side of the island and falls in a marked wet season from May to October – this season can also experience hurricanes, often causing widespread devastation.

As large as all the other Caribbean islands put together, Cuba is only 193 km [120 mls] across at its widest, but stretches for over 1,200 km [750 mls] from the Gulf of Mexico to the Windward Passage. Though large, it is the least mountainous of all the Greater Antilles.

Sugar cane remains the outstandingly important cash crop, as it has throughout the century, and Cuba is the world's fourth largest producer behind the giants of Brazil, India and China. It uses over 1 million hectares [2.5 million acres], more than half the island country's cultivated land, and accounts for more than 75% of exports.

Before the 1959 Revolution, the sugar cane was grown on large estates, many of them owned by US companies or individuals, but after these were nationalized the focus of production shifted eastwards to Guayabal, with the USSR and Eastern European countries replacing the USA as the main market. Cattle raising and rice cultivation have also been encouraged to help diversify the economy, while Cuba is also a significant exporter of minerals, principally nickel ore.

A colony until 1898, Cuba took on many Spanish immigrants during the early years of independence. Since the Revolution that deposed the right-wing dictator Fulgencio Batista and brought Fidel Castro to power in 1959 – when 600,000 people fled the island, many of them to Florida – rural development has been fostered in a relatively successful bid to make the quality of life more homogeneous throughout the island. Havana, the chief port and capital, was particularly depopulated.

Cuba's relationship with the USA, which secured its independence from Spain but bolstered the corrupt regimes before the Revolution, has always been crucial. In 1961, US-backed 'exiles' attempted to invade at the Bay of Pigs, and relations worsened still further the following year when the attempted installation of Soviet missiles on Cuban soil almost led to global war. A close ally of the former USSR, Castro has encouraged left-wing revolutionary movements in Latin America and aided Marxist governments in Africa, while emerging as a Third World leader.

The rapid changes in Eastern Europe and the USSR from 1989 to 1991 left Cuba isolated as a hardline Marxist state in the Western Hemisphere, and the disruption of trade severely affected the economy of a country heavily dependent on subsidized Soviet oil and aid, undermining Castro's considerable social achievements. But the country's left-wing policies continued, and elections in February 1993 showed a high level of support from the people for Castro, despite his advancing years ■

COUNTRY Republic of Cuba
AREA 110,860 sq km [42,803 sq mls]
POPULATION 11,050,000
CAPITAL (POPULATION) Havana (2,143,000)
GOVERNMENT Socialist republic
ETHNIC GROUPS White 66%, Mulatto 22%, Black 12%
LANGUAGES Spanish (official)
RELIGIONS Roman Catholic 40%, Protestant 3%
CURRENCY Cuban peso = 100 centavos
ANNUAL INCOME PER PERSON US$1,000
MAIN PRIMARY PRODUCTS Sugar cane, nickel, cobalt, copper, chrome, tobacco, citrus fruits, rice
MAIN INDUSTRIES Agriculture, mining, food processing, tobacco, fishing, textiles, chemicals
DEFENCE 11.3% of GNP
POPULATION DENSITY 97 per sq km [258 per sq ml]
LIFE EXPECTANCY Female 78 yrs, male 74 yrs
ADULT LITERACY 75%
PRINCIPAL CITIES (POPULATION) Havana 2,143,000
Santiago de Cuba 419,000 Camagüey 286,000

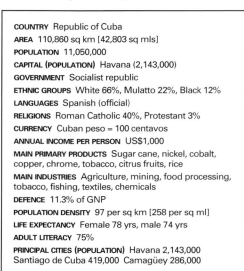
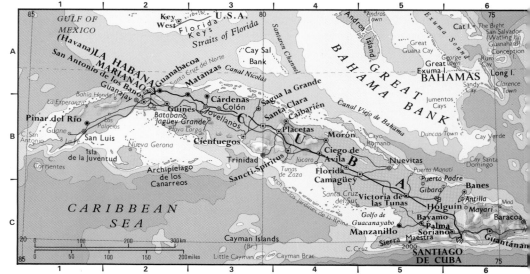

PANAMA

The Panamanian flag dates from the break with Colombia in 1903. Blue stands for the Conservative Party, red for the Liberal Party and white for the hope of peace. The red star represents law and order, and the blue star 'public honesty'.

Less than 60 km [37 mls] wide at its narrowest point, the isthmus of Panama not only links Central and South America but also, via its famous Canal, the Atlantic and Pacific Oceans. Most of the country, including some 750 offshore islands, lies below 700 m [2,300 ft], sweltering daily in tropical heat and high humidity, with heavy downpours marking the May–December rainy season.

Many Panamanians live within about 20 km [12 mls] of the Canal Zone, a quarter of them in the capital city, and 80% of the country's GDP originates here. This includes revenues from free trade, the open-registry merchant fleet (some 12,000 ships), and 'offshore' finance facilities. With exports of bananas, shrimps and mahogany, not to mention substantial US aid, these have given Panama the highest standard of living in Central America – though Western confidence in the economy took a

dive after the crisis of 1989, when the USA invaded to depose General Noriega.

The Panama Canal is 82 km [51 mls] long from deep water at either end (65 km [40 mls] from coast to coast). Three sets of locks at each end lift vessels to the elevated central section 26 m [85 ft] above sea level, which includes Gatun Lake and the 13 km [8 mls] Gaillard Cut through the continental divide.

Though an American-built railway crossed the isthmus in 1855, it was a French company under Ferdinand de Lesseps that began cutting the Canal in 1880, but engineering problems and deaths from disease stopped operations after ten years. In 1903 the province of Panama declared independence from Colombia and granted the USA rights in perpetuity over a Canal Zone 16 km [10 mls] wide. Work on the present Canal began a year later, and it was finally opened for shipping in 1914.

In 1994 there were some 14,029 transits through the Canal – over 38 ships per day – carrying twice the total cargo of 1960. Now running close to capacity, the Canal cannot take fully laden ships of over about 88,000 tonnes, and an alternative Panama Seaway is under discussion. From 1979 sovereignty of the Canal Zone was restored to Panama, and the Canal itself reverts at the end of the century ■

COUNTRY Republic of Panama
AREA 77,080 sq km [29,761 sq mls]
POPULATION 2,629,000
CAPITAL (POPULATION) Panama City (500,000)
GOVERNMENT Multiparty republic
ETHNIC GROUPS Mestizo 60%, Black and Mulatto 20%, White 10%, Amerindian 8%, Asian 2%
LANGUAGES Spanish (official)
RELIGIONS Roman Catholic 84%, Protestant 5%, Muslim 5%
CURRENCY Balboa = 100 centésimos
ANNUAL INCOME PER PERSON US$2,580
LIFE EXPECTANCY Female 75 yrs, male 71 yrs
ADULT LITERACY 90%

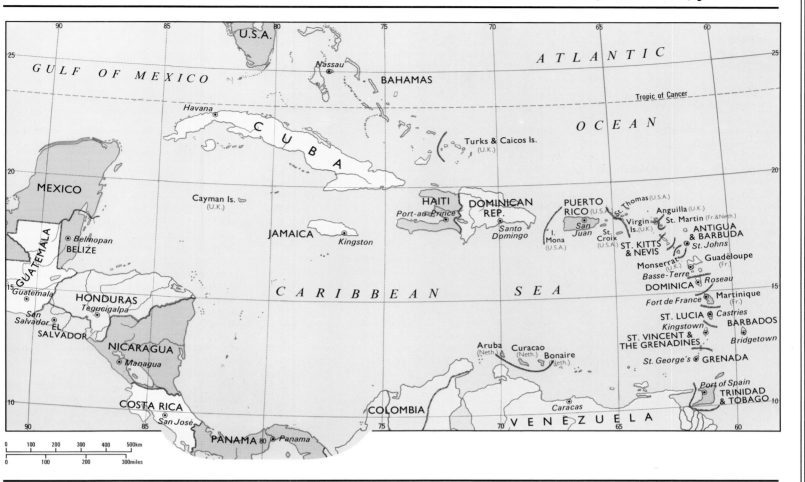

JAMAICA

Jamaica's distinctive flag dates from independence from Britain in 1962. The gold stands for the country's natural resources and sunshine, the green for its agriculture and hope for the future, and black for the nation's hardships.

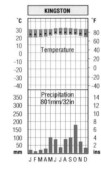

KINGSTON

Temperature

Precipitation
801mm/32in

J F M A M J J A S O N D

The mountains of eastern Jamaica exert a strong influence on rainfall. Kingston, on the south coast and in the lee of the mountains, has 800 mm [31 in] and a dry season from December to April, while Port Antonio, on the windward north-east coast, has 3,500 mm [138 in] and no dry season. The annual total is very variable, mainly due to the irregularity of hurricane rains in August and September. At Kingston, rain falls on about 55 days per year, with sunshine levels at around 8 hours per day.

Third largest of the Caribbean islands and the most populous in the English-speaking 'West Indies', Jamaica has a central range culminating in Blue Mountain Peak (2,256 m [7,402 ft]), from which it declines westwards. Called Xaymaca ('land of wood and water') by the Arawak Indians, half the country lies above 300 m [1,000 ft] and moist south-east trade winds bring rain to the mountains.

The 'cockpit country' in the north-west of the island is an inaccessible limestone area of steep broken ridges and isolated basins. These offered a refuge to escaped slaves prior to emancipation in 1838. Elsewhere the limestone has weathered to

bauxite, an ore of aluminium. Bauxite overlies a quarter of the island; mined since 1952, most is exported as ore, about one-fifth as alumina, making Jamaica the world's third producer and accounting for over 38% of exports. Tourism and bauxite production, Jamaica's two most important industries, comprise almost two-thirds of foreign earnings.

Sugar, a staple product since the island became British in 1655, first made Jamaica a prized imperial possession, and the African slaves imported to work the plantations were the forefathers of much of the present population. But the plantations disappeared and the sugar market collapsed in the 19th century;

today sugar contributes only about 10% of the country's foreign earnings.

Michael Manley's democratic socialist experiment in the 1970s was followed by a modest growth in the 1980s, but unemployment and under-employment are rife, and many Jamaicans leave their country each year to work abroad, mainly in the USA, Canada and the UK ■

COUNTRY Jamaica

AREA 10,990 sq km [4,243 sq mls]

POPULATION 2,700,000

CAPITAL (POPULATION) Kingston (644,000)

GOVERNMENT Constitutional monarchy

ETHNIC GROUPS Black 76%, Afro-European 15%, East Indian and Afro-East Indian 3%, White 3%

LANGUAGES English (official), English Creole, Hindi, Chinese, Spanish

RELIGIONS Protestant 70%, Roman Catholic 8%

CURRENCY Jamaican dollar = 100 cents

ANNUAL INCOME PER PERSON US$1,390

MAIN PRIMARY PRODUCTS Bauxite, sugar, bananas

MAIN INDUSTRIES Mining, agriculture, tourism, sugar

HAITI

Although the colours, first used in 1803, are said to represent the country's two communities (the blacks [blue] and mulattos [red]), the design of Haiti's flag derives from that of France, to which it once belonged. The present version was first used in 1843 and restored in 1986.

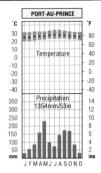

Port-au-Prince is in a relatively sheltered part of the island, but elsewhere altitude and aspect affect the climate. The temperatures along the coast are high with little annual variation from the maxima, July to August. The island is always under the influence of the north-east trade winds which bring rainfall totals of over 2,500 mm [98 in] along the northern coasts. These figures are lower in the south and west. Hurricanes can strike the region between August and November.

Occupying the western third of Hispaniola, the Caribbean's second largest island, Haiti is mainly mountainous with a long, indented coast. Most of the country is centred around the Massif du Nord, with the narrow Massif de la Hotte forming the southern peninsula. In the deep bight between the two lies the chief port and capital, Port-au-Prince. Haiti has few natural resources and most of the workforce is engaged on the land, with coffee the only significant cash crop and accounting for 17% of the country's meagre exports. Two-thirds of the population, however, lives at or below the poverty line, subsisting on agriculture and fishing.

Ceded to France in 1697, a century before the rest of Hispaniola, Haiti developed as a sugar-producing colony. Once the richest part of the Caribbean, it is now the poorest nation in the Western Hemisphere. For nearly two centuries, since a slave revolt made it the world's first independent black state in 1804, it has been bedevilled by military coups, government corruption, ethnic violence and political instability, including a period of US control from 1915 to 1934.

The violent regime of François Duvalier ('Papa Doc'), president from 1957 and declaring himself 'President for Life' in 1964, was especially brutal, but that of his son Jean-Claude ('Baby Doc'), president from 1971, was little better; both used their murderous private militia, the Tontons Macoutes, to conduct a reign of terror. In 1986 popular unrest finally forced Duvalier to flee the country, and the military took over. After another period of political chaos and economic disaster – not helped by the suspension of US aid between 1987 and 1989 – the country's first multiparty elections were held in December 1990, putting in office a radical Catholic priest, Father Jean-Bertrand Aristide, on a platform of sweeping reforms. But with the partisans of the old regime, including the Tontons Macoutes, still powerful, the military took control in September 1991, forcing Aristide to flee (to the USA) after only seven

COUNTRY Republic of Haiti
AREA 27,750 sq km [10,714 sq mls]
POPULATION 7,180,000
CAPITAL (POPULATION) Port-au-Prince (1,402,000)
GOVERNMENT Multiparty republic
ETHNIC GROUPS Black 95%, Mulatto 5%
LANGUAGES Haitian Creole 88%, French 10%
RELIGIONS Christian (Roman Catholic 80%), Voodoo
CURRENCY Gourde = 100 centimes

months of government. Tens of thousands of exiles followed in the ensuing weeks, heading mainly for the US naval base at Guantánamo Bay, in Cuba, in the face of a wave of savage repression, but the US government returned the 'boat people' to Port-au-Prince. Military intervention (as in Panama in 1989) was considered by the Organization of American States, but they imposed a trade embargo instead. Aristide returned as president at the end of 1994 after the military leadership agreed to step down. In 1996 René Préval was elected president ∎

DOMINICAN REPUBLIC

The Dominican Republic's flag dates from 1844, when the country finally gained its independence from both Spain and Haiti. The design developed from Haiti's flag, adding a white cross and rearranging the position of the colours.

COUNTRY Dominican Republic
AREA 48,730 sq km [18,815 sq mls]
POPULATION 7,818,000
CAPITAL (POPULATION) Santo Domingo (2,100,000)
GOVERNMENT Multiparty republic
ETHNIC GROUPS Mulatto 73%, White 16%, Black 11%
LANGUAGES Spanish (official)
RELIGIONS Roman Catholic 93%
CURRENCY Peso = 100 centavos

Second largest of the Caribbean nations in both area and population, the Dominican Republic shares the island of Hispaniola with Haiti, occupying the eastern two-thirds. Of the steep-sided mountains that dominate the island, the country includes the northern Cordillera Septentrional, the huge Cordillera Central (rising to Pico Duarte, at 3,175 m [10,417 ft] the highest peak in the Caribbean), and the southern Sierra de Bahoruco. Between them and to the east lie fertile valleys and lowlands, including the Vega Real and the coastal plains where the main sugar plantations are found. Typical of the area, the Republic is hot and humid close to sea level, while cooler conditions prevail in the mountains; rainfall is heavy, especially in the north-east.

Columbus 'discovered' the island and its Amerindian population (soon to be decimated) on 5 December 1492; the city of Santo Domingo, now the capital and chief port, was founded by his brother Bartholomew four years later and is the oldest in the Americas. For long a Spanish colony, Hispaniola was initially the centrepiece of their empire but later it was to become its poor relation. In 1795 it became French, then Spanish again in 1809, but in 1821 (then called Santo Domingo) it won independence. Haiti held the territory from 1822 to 1844, when on restoring sovereignty it became the Dominican Republic. Growing American influence culminated in occupation from 1916 to 1924, followed by a long period of corrupt dictatorship. Since a

bitter war was ended by US military intervention in 1965, a fledgling democracy has survived violent elections under the watchful eye of Washington.

In the 1990s, growth in industry (exploiting vast hydroelectric potential), mining (nickel, bauxite, gold and silver) and tourism have augmented the traditional agricultural economy based on sugar (still a fifth of exports), coffee, cocoa, tobacco and fruit. This highly Americanized Hispanic society is, however, far from stable ∎

TURKS AND CAICOS ISLANDS

A group of 30 islands (eight of them inhabited), lying at the eastern end of the Grand Bahama Bank, north of Haiti, the Turks and Caicos are composed of low, flat limestone terrain with scrub, marsh and swamp providing little agriculture over their 430 sq km [166 sq mls]. Previously claimed by France and Spain, they have been British since 1766, administered with Jamaica from 1873 to 1959 and a separate Crown Colony since 1973. Nearly a third of the 15,000 population, mainly of mixed Afro-European descent, live in the capital of Cockburn Town on Grand Turk. Tourism has recently overtaken fishing as the main industry. Offshore banking facilities are also expanding ∎

CAYMAN ISLANDS

The Cayman Islands comprise three low-lying islands covering 259 sq km [100 sq mls], south of Cuba, with the capital George Town (population 14,000, in a total of 31,000) on the biggest, Grand Cayman. A dependent territory of Britain (Crown Colony since 1959), they were occupied mainly with farming and fishing until the 1960s, when an economic revolution transformed them into the world's biggest offshore financial centre, offering a secret tax haven to 18,000 companies and 450 banks. The flourishing luxury tourist industry (predominantly from US sources) now accounts for more than 70% of its official GDP and foreign earnings, while a property boom has put beachfront prices on Grand Cayman among the world's highest. An immigrant labour force, chiefly Jamaican, constitutes about a fifth of the population – similar to European and black groups; the rest are of mixed descent ∎

BAHAMAS

The black hoist triangle symbolizes the unity of the Bahamian people and their resolve to develop the island's natural resources. The golden sand and blue sea of the islands are depicted by the yellow and aquamarine stripes.

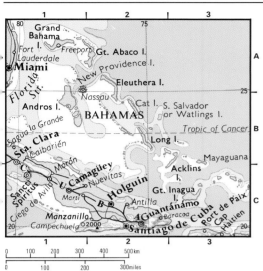

A coral-limestone archipelago of 29 inhabited islands, plus over 3,000 uninhabited cays, reefs and rocks, centred on the Grand Bahama Bank off eastern Florida and Cuba, the Bahamas has developed close ties with the USA since 1973.

Over 90% of its 3.6 million visitors a year are Americans, and tourism now accounts for more than half the nation's revenues, involving some 40% of the workforce. Offshore banking, financial services and a large 'open registry' merchant fleet also offset imports (including most foodstuffs), giving the country a relatively high standard of living. The remainder of the non-administrative population works mainly in traditional fishing and agriculture, notably citrus fruit production.

Though the Bahamas is an independent democracy, it is also élitist. Relations with the USA were strained when it was used as a tax haven for drug traffickers in the 1980s, with government ministers implicated in drug-related corruption ■

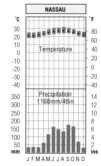

The pleasant subtropical climate is the major tourist attraction of the region. Sea breezes keep the temperatures below 30°C [86°F], but they seldom fall below 15°C [59°F]. In the summer the average temperature is around 27°C [80°F] and in the winter 21°C [70°F]. There is moderate rainfall of about 1,270 mm [50 in], falling with a maximum in the summer months from May to October. Hurricanes, which have in the past been disastrous, occur from July to November.

COUNTRY Commonwealth of the Bahamas
AREA 13,880 sq km [5,359 sq mls]
POPULATION 277,000
CAPITAL (POPULATION) Nassau (190,000)
GOVERNMENT Constitutional monarchy
ETHNIC GROUPS Black 80%, Mixed 10%, White 10%
LANGUAGES English (official), English Creole 80%
RELIGIONS Christian 95%
CURRENCY Bahamian dollar = 100 cents
ANNUAL INCOME PER PERSON US$11,500
LIFE EXPECTANCY Female 76 yrs, male 69 yrs

PUERTO RICO

Puerto Rico fought with Cuba for independence from Spain and their flags are almost identical (the red and blue colours are transposed). The island is a dependent territory of the USA and the flag, adopted in 1952, is flown only with the American 'Stars and Stripes'.

Ceded by Spain to the USA in 1898, Puerto Rico ('rich port') became a self-governing commonwealth in free political association with the USA after a referendum in 1952. Though this gave the island a considerable measure of autonomy, American influence stretches well beyond its constitutional roles in defence and immigration. Full US citizens, Puerto Ricans pay no federal taxes – but nor do they vote in US congressional or presidential elections. Debate over the exact status of the country subsided in the 1970s, the compromise apparently accepted as a sensible middle way between the extremes of being the 51st state of the

USA or completely independent, but resurfaces with the boom years. A referendum in December 1991 narrowly rejected a proposal to guarantee 'the island's distinct cultural identity' – a result interpreted as a move towards statehood. Meanwhile, free access to the USA has relieved the growing pressure created by one of the greatest population densities in the New World, with New York traditionally the most popular destination.

Easternmost of the major Greater Antilles, Puerto Rico is mountainous, with a narrow coastal plain; Cerro de Punta (1,338 m [4,389 ft]) is the highest peak. Flat ground for agriculture is scarce, mainly devoted to cash crops like sugar, coffee, bananas and, since the arrival of Cuban refugees, tobacco, as well as tropical fruits, vegetables and various spices.

However, the island is now the most industrialized and urban nation in the Caribbean – nearly half the population lives in the San Juan area – with chemicals constituting 36% of exports and metal products (based on deposits of copper) a further 17%. Manufacturing, dominated by US companies attracted by tax exemptions, and tourism are now the two

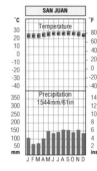

The climate is hot and wet, but there are no great extremes of temperature; the high and low records are 34°C [93°F] and 17°C [63°F]. Of course, altitude lowers the temperatures. The annual temperature range is low. The winds from the north-east or east, blowing over a warm sea, give high rainfall, falling on over 200 days in the year. Every month, except February and March, has in excess of 100 mm [4 in] of rain per month on average.

growth sectors in a country where the standard of living (while low in US terms) is nevertheless the highest in Latin America outside the island tax havens, and rising ■

COUNTRY Commonwealth of Puerto Rico
AREA 8,900 sq km [3,436 sq mls]
POPULATION 3,689,000
CAPITAL (POPULATION) San Juan (1,816,000)
GOVERNMENT Self-governing Commonwealth in association with the USA
ETHNIC GROUPS Spanish 99%, African American, Indian
LANGUAGES Spanish and English (both official)
RELIGIONS Christian (mainly Roman Catholic)
CURRENCY US dollar = 100 cents

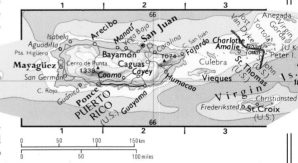

BRITISH VIRGIN ISLANDS

Like their larger American neighbours, the British Virgin Islands were 'discovered' by Columbus in 1493. Most northerly of the Lesser Antilles, they comprise four low-lying islands of note and 36 islets and cays, covering a total of 153 sq km [59 sq mls]. The largest island, Tortola, contains over three-quarters of the total population of 20,000, around a third of which lives in the capital Road Town. Dutch from 1648 but British since 1666, they are now a British dependency enjoying (since 1977) a

strong measure of self-government. Though an increasing rival to the Caymans and the Turks and Caicos in offshore banking from 1985, tourism is the country's main source of income ■

US VIRGIN ISLANDS

The US Virgin Islands were Spanish from 1553, Danish from 1672 and, for a sum of US$25 million, American from 1917 – Washington wishing to protect the approaches to the newly built Panama

Canal. As an 'unincorporated territory', the residents have been US citizens since 1927, and from 1973 have elected a delegate to the House of Representatives. The 68 islands (dominated by the three largest – St Thomas, St Croix and St John) total 340 sq km [130 sq mls] and host a population of 102,000, around 100,000 of them split almost evenly between St Croix and St Thomas, home of the capital Charlotte Amalie. The ethnic breakdown is about 80% black and 15% white. Tourism is now the main industry, notably cruise ships but also airborne day-trippers from the USA to the duty-free shops of St Thomas. The islands have the highest density of hotels and condominiums in the Caribbean ■

NORTH AND CENTRAL AMERICA

ANGUILLA

Deriving its name from its 'discovery' in 1493 by Columbus – *anguil* is Spanish for eel – Anguilla is indeed long and thin, a low coral atoll covered with poor soil and scrub, measuring 96 sq km [37 sq mls]. First colonized by Britain in 1650 and long administered with St Kitts and Nevis, the island was subject to intervention by British troops in 1969 to restore legal government following its secession from the self-governing federation in 1967. Its position as a separate UK dependent territory (colony) was confirmed in 1971 and formalized in 1980.

Of the 8,000 population – largely of African descent and English-speaking – about a quarter lives in the capital of The Valley. The main source of revenue is now tourism ■

ST KITTS AND NEVIS

The first West Indian islands to be colonized by Britain (1623 and 1628), St Kitts and Nevis became independent in 1983. The federation comprises two well-watered volcanic islands, mountains rising on both to around 1,000 m [3,300 ft], and about 20% forested. In past years, St Kitts has been called St Christopher; Nevis derives its name from Columbus (1493), to whom the cloud-covered peaks were reminiscent of Spain's mountains (*nieves* meaning snow). Thanks to fine beaches tourism has replaced sugar, nationalized in 1975, as the main earner ■

ANTIGUA AND BARBUDA

Antigua and Barbuda are strategically situated islands linked by Britain after 1860, gaining internal self-government in 1967 and independence in 1981. They rely heavily on tourism, though some attempts at diversification (notably Sea Island cotton) have been successful. Run by the Antiguan Labour Party almost without break since 1956, its white-owned sugar industry was closed down in 1971. Only 1,400 people live on the game reserve island of Barbuda, where lobster fishing is the main occupation. Antigua is untypical of the Leewards in that despite its height it has no rivers or forests; Barbuda, by contrast, is a well-wooded low coral atoll. The population of the two islands is 67,000 ■

MONTSERRAT

Colonized from 1632 by Britain, which brought in Irish settlers, Montserrat (though still a UK dependent territory) has been self-governing since 1960. The island measures 102 sq km [39 sq mls] and has a population of 11,000, of which 3,500 live in the capital, Plymouth; 96% are of African descent.

Though tourism is the mainstay of the economy it is supported by exports of electronic equipment, Sea Island cotton, fruit and vegetables; unusually for the Caribbean, it is almost self-sufficient in food. Cotton was once the main industry, but new ones have moved in under generous tax concessions ■

GUADELOUPE

Slightly the larger of France's two Caribbean overseas departments, and with a total population of 443,000, Guadeloupe comprises seven islands including Saint-Martin and Saint-Barthélemy to the north-west. Over 90% of the area, however, is taken up by Basse-Terre, which is volcanic – La Soufrière (1,467 m [4,813 ft]) is the highest point in the Lesser Antilles – and the smaller Grande-Terre, made of low limestone; the two are separated by a narrow sea channel called Rivière-Salée (Salt River). The commercial centre of Pointe-à-Pitre (population 25,300) is on Grande-Terre. Food is the biggest import (much of it from France), bananas the biggest export, followed by wheat flour, sugar, rum and aubergines. French aid has helped create a reasonable standard of living, but despite this and thriving tourism – largely from France and the USA – unemployment is high. Though sharing an identical history to Martinique, Guadeloupe has a far stronger separatist movement, which sporadically resorts to acts of terrorism ■

DOMINICA

Dominica has been an independent republic (the Commonwealth of Dominica) since 1978, after 11 years as a self-governing UK colony; Britain and France fought long over the island, ownership decided in 1805 by a ransom of £12,000 (then US$53,000). The population of 89,000 is over 90% African and 6% mixed, with small Asian and white minorities and a settlement of about 500 mainly mixed-blood Carib Indians. Predominantly Christian (75% Catholic), most people speak French patois though English is the official language.

A mountainous ridge forms the island's spine, as it is from this central region that the main rivers flow to the indented coast. Though rich soils support dense vegetation, less than 10% of the land is cultivated; bananas account for 48% of exports, coconut-based soaps for 25%. Much food is imported, and future prospects for a relatively poor Caribbean island depend a good deal on the development of luxury tourism ■

MARTINIQUE

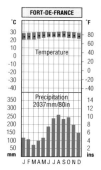

Martinique was 'discovered' by Columbus in 1493, colonized by France from 1635 and, apart from brief British interludes, has been French ever since. It became an overseas department in 1946 – enjoying the same status and representation as *départements* – and, like Guadeloupe, was made an administrative region in 1974. Despite a more homogenous population than its neighbour, the island has a less vociferous independence movement – though in the 1991 elections the separatists made substantial gains, winning 19 of the 41 seats in the provincial assembly.

Martinique comprises three groups of volcanic hills and the intervening lowlands. The highest peak is Mt Pelée, notorious for its eruption of 1902, when in minutes it killed all the inhabitants of St Pierre (estimated at about 28,000) except one – a prisoner saved by the thickness of his cell.

Bananas (40%), rum and pineapples are the main agricultural exports, but tourism (mainly French and American) is the biggest earner. The industrial

The small islands of the Caribbean all have very similar climates with a small annual range of temperature, high humidity, especially in the summer, and a high annual rainfall with a summer maximum. The summer rainfall is mainly in the form of thundery showers, which build up in the afternoon, but in winter the rain tends to be lighter and more prolonged. Hurricanes may occur in August and September, when the sea is at its warmest.

COUNTRY Overseas Department of France
AREA 1,100 sq km [425 sq mls]
POPULATION 384,000
CAPITAL (POPULATION) Fort-de-France (102,000)

sector includes cement, food processing and oil refining, using Venezuelan crude; oil products account for 14% of exports. French government expenditure is higher than on Guadeloupe, at some 70% of GDP, helping provide jobs and retain a better standard of living than its northern compatriot ■

St Martin is divided into the northern two-thirds (Saint-Martin, French and administered as part of Guadeloupe), and the southern third (St Maarten, Dutch and part of the Netherlands Antilles) ■

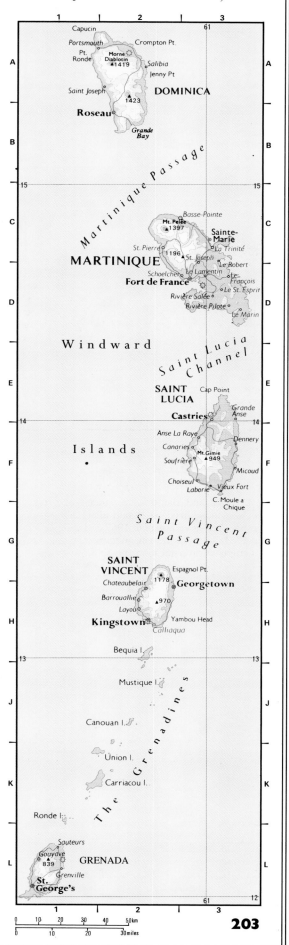

ST LUCIA

First settled by the British in 1605, St Lucia changed hands between Britain and France 14 times before finally being ceded formally in 1814. Internally self-governing as 'Associated State of the UK' from 1967, it gained full independence in 1979. A mountainous, forested island of extinct volcanoes – graphically represented on its flag – St Lucia boasts a huge variety of plant and animal life. To the south of its highest point of Mt Gimie (949 m [3,114 ft]) lies the Qualibou, an area containing 18 lava domes and seven craters. In the west are the

Pitons, rising from the sea to over 750 m [2,460 ft].

Though not poor, St Lucia is still overdependent on bananas (71% of exports), a crop easily hit by hurricane and disease. It is supported by coconuts, coconut products and cocoa, though clothing is the second export, and the free port of Vieux Fort has attracted modern industries. Cruise liners deliver tourists to Castries, and the Grande Cul de Sac Bay to the south is one of the deepest tanker ports in the Americas, used mainly for trans-shipment of oil ■

COUNTRY Saint Lucia
AREA 610 sq km [236 sq mls]
POPULATION 147,000
CAPITAL (POPULATION) Castries (54,000)

ST VINCENT AND THE GRENADINES

St Vincent and the Grenadines comprise the main island (consisting 89% of the area and 95% of the population) and the Northern Grenadines, of which the largest are Bequia, Mustique and Canouan, with Union the furthest south. 'Discovered' in 1498, St Vincent was settled in the 16th century and became a British colony with the Treaty of Versailles in 1783, after a century of conflict with France, often supported by the Caribs – the last of whom were deported to Honduras after the Indian War of 1795–7. The colony became

self-governing in 1969 and independent in 1979.

St Vincent is a mountainous, volcanic island that receives heavy rainfall and boasts luxuriant vegetation. Soufrière (1,178 m [3,866 ft]), which last erupted in the year of independence, is one of two active volcanoes in the eastern Caribbean – Mt Pelée is the other. Less prosperous than its Commonwealth neighbours, there are nevertheless prosperous pockets, notably Mustique and Bequia, where beautiful clean waters have fostered tourism ■

COUNTRY Saint Vincent and the Grenadines
AREA 388 sq km [150 sq mls]
POPULATION 111,000
CAPITAL (POPULATION) Kingstown (27,000)

GRENADA

The most southern of the Windward Islands, the country of Grenada also includes the Southern Grenadines, principally Carriacou. Formally British since 1783, a self-governing colony from 1967 and independent in 1974, it became Communist after a bloodless coup in 1979 when Maurice Bishop established links with Cuba. After Bishop was executed by other Marxists in 1983, the USA (supported by some Caribbean countries) sent in troops to restore democracy, and since the invasion the ailing

economy has been heavily reliant on American aid.

Grenada is known as 'the spice island of the Caribbean' and is the world's leading producer of nutmeg, its main crop. Cocoa, bananas and mace also contribute to exports, but attempts to diversify the economy from an agricultural base have been largely unsuccessful. In the 1990s there were signs that the tourist industry was finally making a recovery after the debilitating events of 1983 ■

COUNTRY Grenada
AREA 344 sq km [133 sq mls]
POPULATION 94,000
CAPITAL (POPULATION) St George's (7,000)

NORTH AND CENTRAL AMERICA

BARBADOS

The flag was adopted on independence from Britain in 1960. The trident had been part of the colonial badge of Barbados and was retained as the centre to its flag. The gold stripe represents the beaches and the two blue stripes are for the sea and the sky.

The most eastern Caribbean country, and first in line for the region's seasonal hurricanes, Barbados is underlain with limestone and capped with coral. Mt Hillaby (340 m [1,115 ft]), the highest point, is fringed by marine terraces marking stages in the island's emergence from the sea. Soils are fertile and deep, easily cultivated except in the eroded Scotland district of the north-east.

Barbados became British in 1627 and sugar production, using African slave labour, began soon afterwards. Cane plantations take up most of the cropped land (over half the total), but at 17% now contributes far less than previously to exports. Manufactures now constitute the largest exports, though tourism is the growth sector and the leading industry (395,979 visitors in 1993), and is the most likely future for this relatively prosperous but extremely overcrowded island; at 612 per sq km [1,584 per sq ml], it is the most densely populated rural society in the world (46% urban). Despite political stability and advanced welfare and education services, emigration (as from many West Indian countries) is high, notably to the USA and the UK ■

COUNTRY Barbados

AREA 430 sq km [166 sq mls]

POPULATION 263,000

CAPITAL (POPULATION) Bridgetown (8,000)

GOVERNMENT Constitutional monarchy with a bicameral legislature

ETHNIC GROUPS Black 80%, Mixed 16%, White 4%

LANGUAGES English (official), Creole 90%

RELIGIONS Protestant 65%, Roman Catholic 4%

CURRENCY Barbados dollar = 100 cents

ANNUAL INCOME PER PERSON US$6,240

POPULATION DENSITY 612 per sq km [1,584 per sq ml]

LIFE EXPECTANCY Female 78 yrs, male 73 yrs

ADULT LITERACY 99%

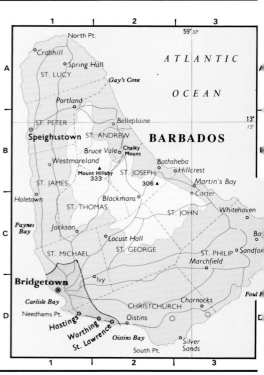

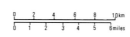

TRINIDAD AND TOBAGO

The islands of Trinidad and Tobago have flown this flag since independence from Britain in 1962. Red stands for the people's warmth and vitality, black for their strength, and white for their hopes and the surf of the sea.

Furthest south of the West Indies, Trinidad is a rectangular island situated just 16 km [10 mls] off Venezuela's Orinoco delta. Tobago is a detached extension of its Northern Range of hills, lying 34 km [21 mls] to the north-east. Trinidad's highest point is Cerro Aripe (940 m [3,085 ft]) in the rugged, forested Northern Range; the capital, Port of Spain, nestles behind the hills on the sheltered west coast.

'Discovered' by Columbus in 1498, Trinidad was later planted for sugar production by Spanish and French settlers before becoming British in 1797. Black slaves worked the plantations until emancipation in 1834, when Indian and some Chinese indentured labourers were brought in. Indian influence is still strong in many villages, with African in others. Tobago was competed for by Spain, Holland and France before coming under British control in 1814, joining Trinidad to form a single colony in 1899. Independence came in 1962 and a republic was established in 1976, though Tobago is pushing for internal self-government.

Oil has been the lifeblood of the nation's economy throughout the 20th century, giving the island a relatively high standard of living, and (with petrochemicals) still accounts for over 70% of exports. Falling prices in the 1980s had a severe effect, however, only partly offset by the growth of tourism and continued revenues from asphalt – the other main resource (occurring naturally) – and gas.

Trinidad experienced a sharp political change in 1986, when after 30 years the People's National Movement was voted out and the National Alliance for Reconstruction coalition took office. After four years of PNM rule, a coalition government took over in 1995, but it faced continuing economic problems and high rates of unemployment ■

PORT OF SPAIN	

The annual temperature range is very small (2°C [4°F]), as would be expected of a coastal location only 10° from the Equator. By day the temperature rises rapidly, setting off heavy showers during the afternoon in the rainy season, but the sky clears in the evenings, which feel pleasantly cool. The wettest months are in summer, when the intertropical rainbelt reaches its most northerly extent and lies close to Trinidad. Sunshine levels are fairly regular at 7–8 hours per day.

COUNTRY Republic of Trinidad and Tobago

AREA 5,130 sq km [1,981 sq mls]

POPULATION 1,295,000

CAPITAL (POPULATION) Port of Spain (60,000)

GOVERNMENT Republic with a bicameral legislature

ETHNIC GROUPS Black 40%, East Indian 40%, Mixed 18%, White 1%, Chinese 1%

LANGUAGES English (official)

RELIGIONS Christian 40%, Hindu 24%, Muslim 6%

CURRENCY Trinidad and Tobago dollar = 100 cents

ANNUAL INCOME PER PERSON US$3,730

POPULATION DENSITY 252 per sq km [654 per sq ml]

LIFE EXPECTANCY Female 75 yrs, male 70 yrs

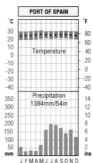

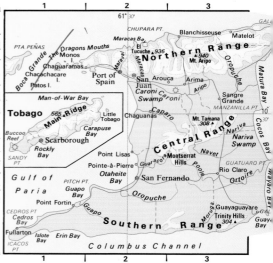

NETHERLANDS ANTILLES

The Netherlands Antilles consists of two very different island groups – Curaçao and Bonaire, off the coast of Venezuela, and Saba, St Eustacius and the southern part of St Maarten, at the northern end of the Leeward Islands, some 800 km [500 mls] away. With Aruba, they formed part of the Dutch East Indies, attaining internal self-government in 1954 as constitutional equals with the Netherlands and Surinam. Curaçao is politically dominant in the federation; it is the largest island, accounting for nearly 45% of the total of 993 sq km [383 sq mls] and 80% of the population of 202,000, over half in the capital Willemstad. The people – mainly mulatto, Creole-speaking and Catholic – are well off by Caribbean standards, enjoying the benefits of an economy buoyed by tourism, offshore banking and oil refining (from Venezuela), mostly for export to the Netherlands, more than the traditional orange liqueur ■

ARUBA

A flat limestone island and the most western of the Lesser Antilles, Aruba measures 193 sq km [75 sq mls]. Incorporated into the Netherlands Antilles in 1845, Aruba held a referendum in 1977, which supported autonomy. With Dutch agreement (in 1981) it separated from the Antilles on 1 January 1986, and full independence is due ■

SOUTH AMERICA

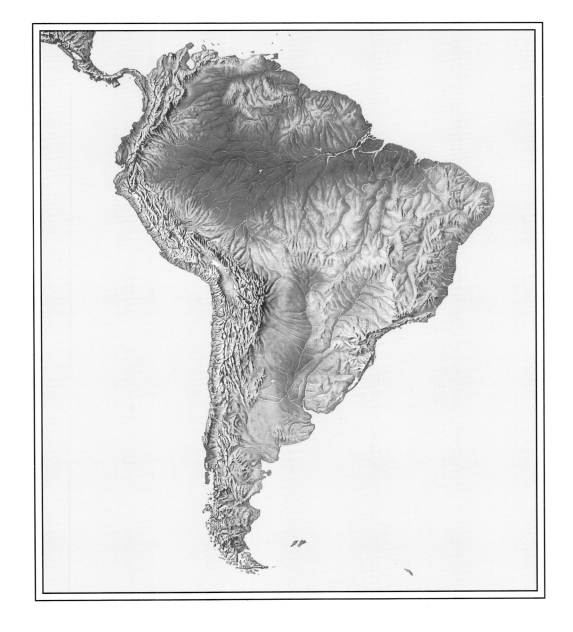

SOUTH AMERICA

Occupying 12% of the Earth's land surface, South America has three structural parts – the Andes Mountains, the river basins and plains, and the ancient eastern highlands. The Andes run almost the entire length of the continent for about 8,000 km [5,000 mls]. Glaciers and snow-fields grace many of the peaks, some of which rise to over 6,500 m [21,000 ft]; Aconcagua (6,960 m [22,834 ft]), in Argentina, is the highest mountain in the world outside Asia. West of the Andes lies a narrow coastal strip, except in the far south and on Tierra del Fuego ('Land of Fire').

Three vast river basins lie to the east of the Andes: the *llanos* of Venezuela, drained by the Orinoco, the Amazon Basin (occupying 40% of the continent), and the great Paraguay–Paraná–Uruguay Basin that empties into the River Plate estuary. The high-lands are the rolling Guiana Highlands of the north, and the more extensive Brazilian plateau that fills and gives shape to South America's eastern bulge. Both are of hard crystalline rock, geologically much older than the Andes, and their presence helps to explain the wanderings and meanderings of the great river systems.

South America has great climatic variety, due partly to the wide latitudinal extent but also to the great range in altitude; 80% falls within the tropics, but height may temper the tropical climate consid-erably – for example in the Altiplano of Bolivia. The natural flora and fauna are equally varied. Long

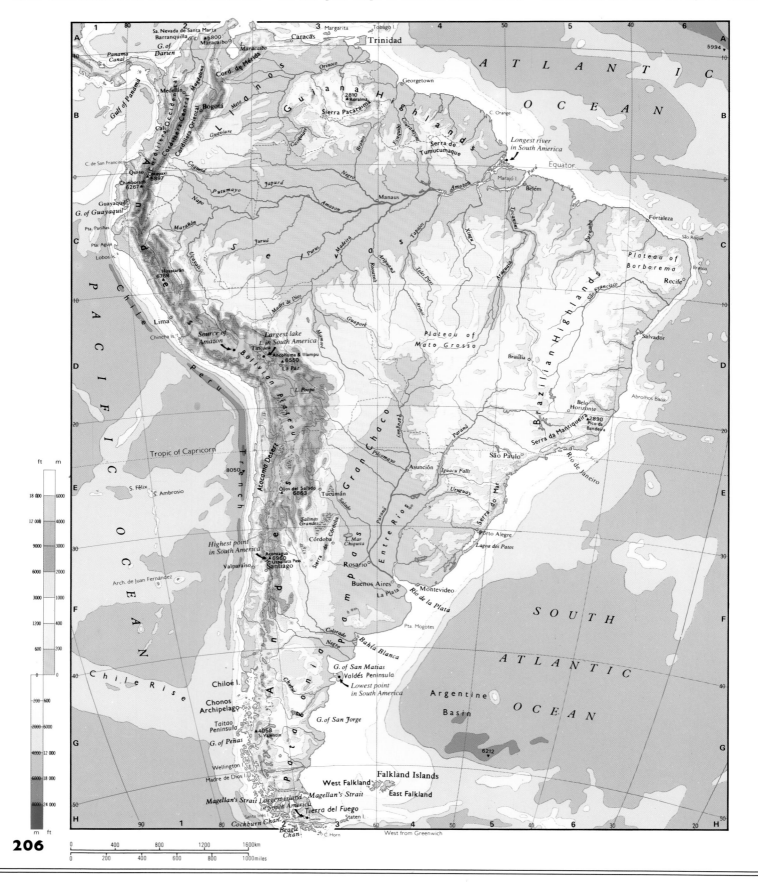

isolation from the rest of the world allowed a great variety of plants and animals to evolve, and this natural variety has not yet been reduced significantly by human pressures. Electric eels, carnivorous piranha fish, manatees, river dolphins, amphibious boa constrictors, sloths, anteaters, armadillos, several kinds of marsupials, camel-like guanacos and llamas, rheas, Andean condors and hummingbirds are some of the many indigenous animals.

Many of the plants found useful to man – potato, cassava, quinoa, squashes, sweet potato, cacao, pineapple and rubber, for example – were originally South American, and the vast forests of the Amazon and Andes may yet contain more. Pressures on the natural fauna and flora are growing, however, in a continent that is, so far, weak on conservation.

South America is prodigal, too, with mineral wealth. Silver and gold were the first attractions but petroleum, iron, copper and tin are also plentiful, and many reserves have yet to be exploited. The people – who may prove to be Latin America's greatest resource – include a rich mix of original Amerindians, Spanish and Portuguese colonial immigrants, African slaves, and a later generation of immigrants and refugees from the turmoils of Europe. Though large and growing fast, the population is still small compared with the vast potential of the continent.

Latin America is generally held to include all the nations of mainland Central America and the Caribbean islands where the Spanish culture is strong ■

BUENOS AIRES   Capital Cities

SOUTH AMERICA

CLIMATIC REGIONS

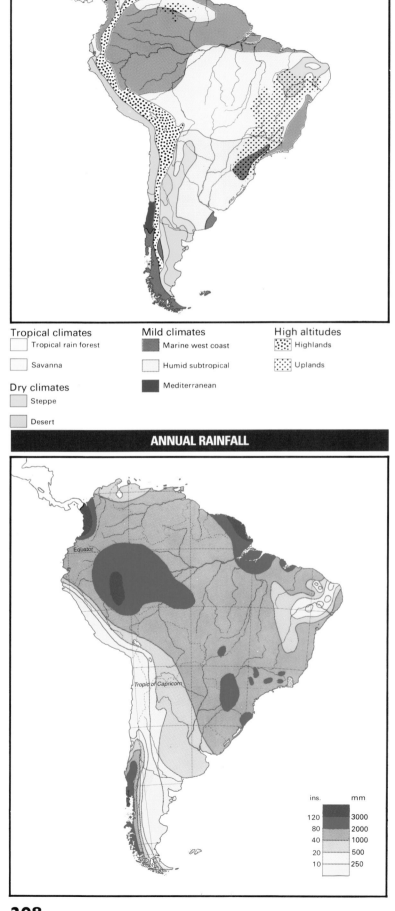

Tropical climates
- Tropical rain forest
- Savanna

Dry climates
- Steppe
- Desert

Mild climates
- Marine west coast
- Humid subtropical
- Mediterranean

High altitudes
- Highlands
- Uplands

NATURAL VEGETATION

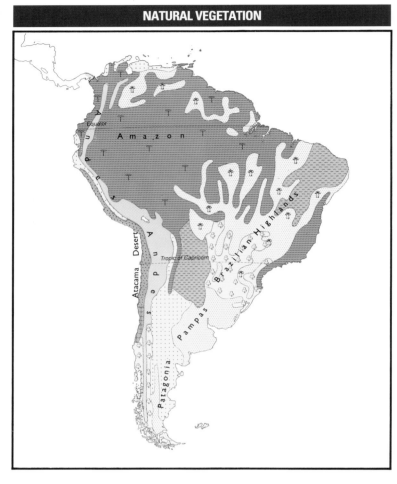

- Tropical rain forest
- Tropical thorn forest
- Temperate rain forest
- Evergreen trees and shrubs
- Grassland and savanna
- Steppe and scrub
- Desert
- Alpine and high plateau

ANNUAL RAINFALL

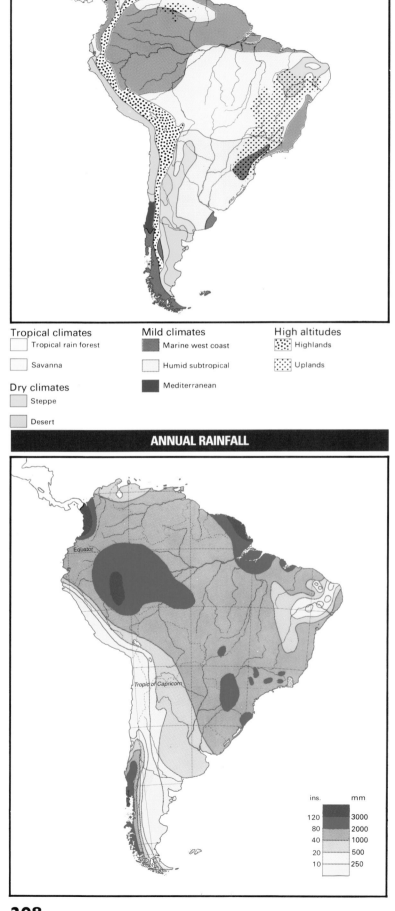

ins.	mm
120	3000
80	2000
40	1000
20	500
10	250

POPULATION

100,000 people

LAND USE

LAND USE

Other land 16·2%

Arable land and permanent crops 5·9%

Permanent pasture 25·2%

Woods and forests 52·7%

Total land area 1 753.7 million hectares
(4 333·4 million acres)

Maracaibo Caracas
Oficina
Cerro Bolivar
Moengo
Bogotá
Mn Serra do Navio
Equator
Quito
Cerro de Pasco
Recife
Cr
Lima
Marcona
La Paz
Colquiri
Ni
Brasília
Sb Potosi
Mn Urucum
Itabira
Morro Velho
Mn
Chuquicamata
Rio de Janeiro
São Paulo
Asunción
El Romeral
Santiago
Mo
El Teniente
Buenos Aires   Montevideo
Concepción
El Chocón
Comodoro Rivadavia

Tropic of Capricorn

0   200 400 600 800 1000 km
0   200 400 600 miles

LAND USE
Arable land
Fruit trees, vineyards and plantations
Permanent pasture
Woods and forests
Rough grazing
Non-productive land

LIVESTOCK
Cattle
Sheep

CROPS
ⅅ Bananas   ◇ Sugar cane
ℓ Cacao   ▲ Tea
◆ Citrus fruits   T Tobacco
ℓ Coffee   ▽ Vines
✿ Cotton   ⅼⅼ Wheat
ⅼⅼ Maize
○ Rice   Principal fishing areas

MINERALS
○ Bauxite   Cr Chrome
▲ Copper   Mn Manganese
◇ Diamonds   Mo Molybdenum
△ Gold   Ni Nickel
◆ Iron ore   **POWER**
◆ Lead and zinc   ▲ Coalfields
◇ Saltpetre   ▣ Oilfields
▽ Silver   ▣ Gasfields
● Tin   ▣ Hydro-
Sb Antimony   electric power

Projection: Lambert's Equivalent Azimuthal

West from Greenwich

COPYRIGHT GEORGE PHILIP LTD.

SOUTH AMERICA

COLOMBIA

Colombia's colours – showing the (yellow) land of the nation separated by the (blue) sea from the tyranny of Spain, whose rule the people fought with their (red) blood – are shared by Ecuador and Venezuela. It was first used in 1806.

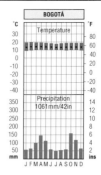

Colombia is split by the northern Andes. The altitude of these mountains fundamentally changes the tropical climate of the country, lowering the temperatures and increasing the amount of rainfall, with permanent snow at the higher levels. Elsewhere, temperatures are high with little annual variation. Rainfall is extremely high on the Pacific coast, but it is drier on the Caribbean coast and in the Magdalena Valley, which experience dry seasons.

Christopher Columbus sighted the country that would bear his name in 1499, and the Spanish conquest of the territory began ten years later. The nation gained independence from Spain after a decade of conflict in 1819, and since the 19th century the two political parties, the proclerical, centralizing Conservatives and the anti-clerical, federal-oriented Liberals, have regularly alternated in power. Their rivalry led to two brutal civil wars (1899–1902 and 1949–57), in which some 400,000 people lost their lives: the 1950s conflict, known as 'La Violencia', claimed 280,000 of them. In 1957 the two parties agreed to form a coalition, and this fragile arrangement – threatened by right-wing death squads, left-wing guerillas and powerful drug cartels – lasted until the Liberal President Virgilio Barco Vargas was elected by a record margin in 1986. But even by the violent standards of South America, Colombia remains politically unstable.

Landscape and agriculture

The Andes cross Colombia from south to north, fanning out into three ranges with two intervening valleys. In the west the low Cordillera Occidental rises from the hot, forested Pacific coastal plain. Almost parallel to it, and separated by the Cauca Valley, is the much higher Cordillera Central; the high peaks of this range, many of them volcanic, rise to over 5,000 m [16,400 ft].

To the east, across the broad valley of the Magdalena River, lies the more complex Cordillera Oriental, which includes high plateaus, plains, lakes and basins; the capital city, Bogotá, is situated on one of the plateaus, at a height of 2,610 m [8,563 ft]. North-west of the mountains lies the broad Atlantic plain, crossed by many rivers. The Andean foothills to the east, falling away into the Orinoco and Amazon basins and densely covered with rainforest (albeit rapidly diminishing), occupy about two-thirds of the total area of the country. Less than 2% of the population, mainly cattle rangers and Indians, live east of the mountains.

Little of the country is under cultivation, but much of the land is very fertile and is coming into use as roads improve. The range of climate for crops is extraordinary and the agricultural colleges have different courses for 'cold-climate farming' and 'warm-climate farming'. The rubber tree grows wild and fibres are being exploited, notably the 'fique', which provides all the country's requirements for sacks and cordage. Colombia is the world's second biggest producer of coffee, which grows mainly in the Andean uplands, while bananas, cotton, sugar and rice are important lowland products. Colombia imports some food, though the country has the capacity to be self-sufficient. Drugs, however, may be the country's biggest industry: it was reported in 1987 that cocaine exports earn Colombia more than its main export, coffee.

Industry

Colombia was the home of El Dorado, the legendary 'gilded one' of the Chibcha Indians, but today the wealth is more likely to be coal or oil. The country has the largest proven reserves of coal in Latin America (20 billion tonnes) and is South America's biggest exporter. Gold, silver, iron ore, lead, zinc, mercury, emeralds (90% of world production) and other minerals are plentiful, and hydroelectric power is increasingly being developed. Petroleum is an important export and source of foreign exchange; large reserves have been found in the north-eastern areas of Arauca and Vichada and in 1991 proven reserves were put at 1.3 billion barrels. Early in 1992 BP stepped up its exploration programme among speculation that its new finds, north-east of Bogotá, were among the world's biggest.

There is compulsory social security funded by employees, employers and the government, but benefits are not evenly spread. Education spending

COUNTRY Republic of Colombia

AREA 1,138,910 sq km [439,733 sq mls]

POPULATION 34,948,000

CAPITAL (POPULATION) Bogotá (5,026,000)

GOVERNMENT Multiparty republic

ETHNIC GROUPS Mestizo 58%, White 20%, Mulatto 14%, Black 4%, mixed Black/Indian 3%, Amerindian 1%

LANGUAGES Spanish (official), over 100 Indian languages and dialects

RELIGIONS Roman Catholic 93%

NATIONAL DAY 20 July; Independence Day (1819)

CURRENCY Peso = 100 centavos

ANNUAL INCOME PER PERSON US$1,280

MAIN PRIMARY PRODUCTS Coal, natural gas, petroleum, silver, gold, iron ore, emeralds

MAIN INDUSTRIES Iron, cement, petroleum industries, vehicles, food processing, paper

MAIN EXPORTS Coffee 43%, crude petroleum 8%, bananas 6%, cotton 3%, coal, emeralds

MAIN EXPORT PARTNERS USA 40%, Germany, Netherlands, Japan

MAIN IMPORTS Machinery 28%, chemicals 18%, vehicles 13%

MAIN IMPORT PARTNERS USA 36%, Japan, Venezuela, Germany, Brazil

POPULATION DENSITY 31 per sq km [79 per sq ml]

INFANT MORTALITY 37 per 1,000 live births

LIFE EXPECTANCY Female 72 yrs, male 66yrs

ADULT LITERACY 87% (Indians 60%)

PRINCIPAL CITIES (POPULATION) Bogotá 5,026,000 Cali 1,719,000 Medellín 1,621,000 Barranquilla 1,064,000 Cartagena 746,000

accounts for nearly 20% of the national budget. Attempts are being made to broaden the industrial base of the economy to counter the decline in domestic demand and the recession being experienced by its neighbours. Foreign investment will be essential, but to achieve this the Liberal government – convincing winners in the 1991 elections – must first defeat the drug barons and the habitual violence that pervades the nation ■

THE DRUGS TRADE

Colombia is notorious for its illegal export of cocaine, and several reliable estimates class the drug as the country's most lucrative source of foreign exchange as kilo after kilo feeds the seemingly insatiable demand from the USA and, to a lesser extent, Western Europe. In addition to the indigenous crop (willingly grown by well-off peasants, though in a neo-feudal setting), far larger amounts of leaf are smuggled in from Bolivia and Peru for refining, processing and 're-export'. US agencies estimated that in 1987 retail sales of South American cocaine totalled US$22 billion – earning about US$2 billion for the producers.

Violence, though focused on the drug capitals of Medellín and Cali, is endemic, with warfare between both rival gangs and between producers and the authorities an almost daily occurrence.

Assassinations of civil servants, judicial officials, police officers or anyone attempting to investigate, control or end the rule of the multimillionaire drug barons are commonplace.

In 1990, as part of US President George Bush's US$10.6 billion 'war on drugs', the governments of these three Andean states – Colombia, Bolivia and Peru – joined forces with the US Drug Enforcement Agency in a concentrated attempt to clamp down on the production and distribution of cocaine. But while early results from Bolivia were encouraging, the situation in Colombia, if anything, hardened, despite the brave attempts of politicians, administrators and police in many areas to break the socio-economic stranglehold of the drug cartels. By 1992 the crackdown was in serious danger of complete failure.

VENEZUELA

The seven stars on the tricolour represent the provinces forming the Venezuelan Federation in 1811 (*see Colombia and Ecuador*). The proportions of the stripes are equal to distinguish it from the flags of Colombia and Ecuador.

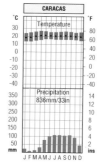

CARACAS

The country has a tropical climate. There is little variation in the temperature from month to month, but there are marked wet and dry seasons, the rain falling from May to November. The north-east trade winds leave little rain in the coastal lowlands, but the total increases when they hit the mountains. The monthly temperature of Caracas on the northern coast is between 19°C and 22°C [66-72°F], but this is much lower on the higher land. Some of the northern Andean peaks have permanent snow.

Sighted by Columbus in 1498, the country was visited by Alonzo de Ojeda and Amerigo Vespucci in 1499, when they named it Venezuela ('Little Venice'). It was part of the Spanish colony of New Granada until 1821 when it became independent, first in federation with Colombia and Ecuador and then, from 1830, as a separate independent republic under the leadership of Simón Bolívar. Between 1830 and 1945, the country was governed mainly by dictators; after frequent changes of president a new constitution came into force in 1961 and since then a fragile civilian-rule democracy has been enjoyed, resting on widespread repression and corruption – almost endemic in South America – with all presidents completing their term of office, despite periodic violence.

Landscape

In the north and north-west of Venezuela, where 90% of the population lives, the Andes split to form two ranges separated from each other by the Maracaibo basin. At 5,007 m [16,427 ft] snow-capped Merida is the highest of several tall peaks in the area. Above 3,000 m [10,000 ft] are the *paramos* – regions of grassland vegetation where Indian villagers live; temperatures are mild and the land is fertile. By contrast, Maracaibo swelters in tropical heat alongside the oil fields that for half a century have produced Venezuela's wealth.

The mountains running west to east behind the coast from Valencia to Trinidad have a separate geological history and gentler topography. Between the ranges are fertile alluvial basins, with many long-established market towns. Caracas, the teeming capital, was one such town before being expanded and modernized on the back of the 1970s oil boom. It now has to take a rapidly swelling population and is fringed with the shanties of hopeful immigrants from poor rural areas.

South of the mountains are the *llanos* of the Orinoco – mostly a vast savanna of trees and grass-lands that floods, especially in the west, during the April–October rains. This is now cattle-raising country. The Orinoco itself rises on the western rim in the Guiana Highlands, a region of high dissected plateaus made famous as the site of Arthur Conan Doyle's *Lost World*, and dense tropical forest makes this still a little-known area.

Not far to the north, however, lies Cerro Bolivar, where iron ore is mined and fed to the steel mills of Ciudad Guayana, a new industrial city built on the Orinoco since 1960. The smelting is powered by hydroelectricity from the nearby Caroni River, and a new deep-water port allows 66,000-tonne carriers to take surplus ore to world markets.

Oil made Venezuela a rich country, but the wealth was always distributed very unevenly and concentrated in the cities – hence the rapid urbanization that made 17 out of every 20 Venezuelans a city dweller and left enormous areas of the country unpopulated. Before the coming of oil, Venezuela was predominantly agricultural, the economy based on coffee, cocoa and cattle.

Commercially viable reserves of oil were found in Venezuela in 1914, and by the 1930s the country had become the world's first major oil exporter – the largest producer after the USA. The industry was nationalized in 1976 but by 1990 there were signs of dangerous dependence on a single commodity controlled by OPEC and in plentiful supply, while the large foreign debt saw austerity measures that triggered a violent reaction from many Venezuelans.

Before the development of the oil industry Venezuela was predominantly an agricultural country, but 85% of export earnings are now from oil and some of the profits from the industry help to fund developments in agriculture and other industries. Gold, nickel, iron ore, copper and manganese are also found and aluminium production has increased following further discoveries of bauxite.

Agriculture can supply only 70% of the country's needs. Only 5% of the arable land is cultivated

COUNTRY Republic of Venezuela

AREA 912,050 sq km [352,143 sq mls]

POPULATION 21,810,000

CAPITAL (POPULATION) Caracas (2,784,000)

GOVERNMENT Federal republic with a bicameral legislature

ETHNIC GROUPS Mestizo 67%, White 21%, Black 10%, Amerindian 2%

LANGUAGES Spanish (official), 30 Amerindian languages and dialects also spoken

RELIGIONS Roman Catholic 94%

CURRENCY Bolívar = 100 céntimos

ANNUAL INCOME PER PERSON US$2,840

MAIN PRIMARY PRODUCTS Foodstuffs, oil, bauxite

MAIN INDUSTRIES Oil refining, steel manufacture, food processing, textiles, vehicles

EXPORTS US$670 per person

MAIN EXPORTS Petroleum 85%, bauxite 9%, iron ore

MAIN EXPORT PARTNERS USA 49%, Germany, Japan, Italy, Brazil, Canada

IMPORTS US$407 per person

MAIN IMPORTS Food, chemicals, manufactured goods

MAIN IMPORT PARTNERS USA 44%, Germany, Japan, Netherlands

DEFENCE 3.6% of GNP

TOURISM 692,400 visitors per year

POPULATION DENSITY 24 per sq km [62 per sq ml]

INFANT MORTALITY 33 per 1,000 live births

LIFE EXPECTANCY Female 74 yrs, male 67 yrs

ADULT LITERACY 90%

PRINCIPAL CITIES (POPULATION) Caracas 2,784,000 Maracaibo 1,364,000 Valencia 1,032,000 Maracay 800,000 Barquisimeto 745,000

and much of that is pasture. The chief crops are sugar cane, coffee, bananas, maize and oranges; there is also substantial dairy and beef production. It is thought that more than 10,000 head of cattle are smuggled into Colombia each month.

Venezuela is still the richest country in South America but now plans to diversify away from the petroleum industry, and foreign investment is being actively encouraged. Demographically stable, with a growing middle class and a proven record in economic planning, it has every chance of increasing its prosperity further in a world economic upturn ■

THE ANGEL FALLS

Called Cherun-Meru by the local Indians, and first known to Europeans in 1910, the world's highest waterfall was 'rediscovered' in 1937 when an American airman called Jimmy Angel flew his small plane into the Guiana Highlands in eastern Venezuela in search of gold – but found instead a natural wonder nearly 20 times the height of Niagara, plunging down from the plateau of Auyán Tepuí, the 'Devil's Mountain'.

Today light aircraft follow his route to take tourists to falls that tumble a total of 979 m [3,212 ft] on the Rio Carrao.

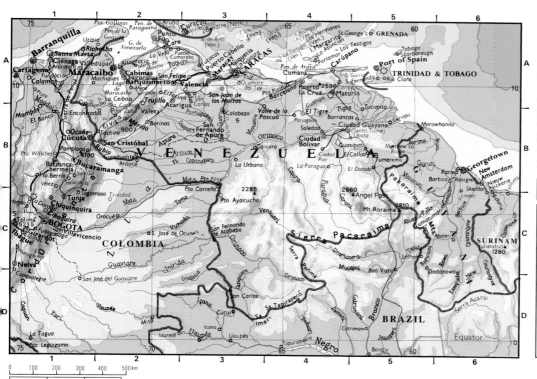

SOUTH AMERICA

ECUADOR

Shared in different proportions by Colombia and Venezuela, Ecuador's colours were used in the flag created by the patriot Francisco de Miranda in 1806 and flown by Simón Bolívar, whose armies also liberated Peru and Bolivia.

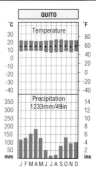

Ecuador lies on the Equator but is bisected by the high Andes, which significantly lower the expected high temperatures. Although offshore there is the cold Peruvian Current, the coastal temperatures are 23–25°C [73-77°F] throughout the year. At Quito, inland at 2,500 m [8,200 ft], this drops to 14–15°C [57–59°F]. There are permanent snowfields and glaciers nearby. Rainfall is low in the extreme south-west, but generally heavy in the east. There is a dry season June to September.

distinct regions – the coastal plain (Costa), the Andes, and the eastern alluvial plains of the Oriente.

The coastal plain, averaging 100 km [60 mls] wide, is a hot, fertile area of variable rainfall. Recently cleared of forests and largely freed of malaria, it is now good farmland where banana farms, coffee and cocoa plantations and fishing are the main sources of income, with the country's commercial centre of Guayaquil a flourishing port.

The Andes form three linked ranges across the country, with several of the central peaks rising above 5,000 m [16,400 ft]. Quito, an old city rich in art and architecture from a colonial past, has a backdrop of snow-capped mountains, among them Cotopaxi – at 5,896 m [19,340 ft] the world's highest active volcano – and Chimborazo (6,267 m [20,556 ft]). The Oriente, a heavily forested upland, is virtually unexploited except for recent developments of oil and natural gas.

Ecuador's economy was based on the export of bananas, for which the country was world leader, and is still the biggest exporter, but this changed from 1972 when oil was first exploited with the opening of the trans-Andean pipeline linking with the tanker-loading port of Esmeraldas. Petroleum and derivatives account for about 40% of export earnings, after peaking at 66% in 1985.

Shortage of power limits much development in the manufacturing industry – even in the mid-1980s only 60% of the population had use of electricity. During the 1970s the manufacture of textiles, cement and pharmaceuticals grew, as did food processing, but there is little heavy industry. Fishing has been affected by the warm water current (El Niño) and there is now an emphasis on greater investment and using much more new technology.

Changes in demand for oil and an earthquake in March 1987, which disrupted much of industry, led the government to suspend payment of interest on its overseas debt, then cancel all debt repayment for the rest of the year. A strict economic recovery programme was put into place and a rescheduling of debt payments agreed in 1989.

COUNTRY Republic of Ecuador
AREA 283,560 sq km [109,483 sq mls]
POPULATION 11,384,000
CAPITAL (POPULATION) Quito (1,101,000)
GOVERNMENT Unitary multiparty republic with a unicameral legislature
ETHNIC GROUPS Mestizo 40%, Amerindian 40%, White 15%, Black 5%
LANGUAGES Spanish (official), Quechua
RELIGIONS Roman Catholic 92%
NATIONAL DAY 10 August; Independence of Quito (1809)
CURRENCY Sucre = 100 centavos
ANNUAL INCOME PER PERSON US$1,170
MAIN PRIMARY PRODUCTS Silver, gold, copper, zinc
MAIN INDUSTRIES Petroleum, agriculture, textiles
MAIN EXPORTS Petroleum and derivatives, seafood, bananas, coffee, cocoa
MAIN IMPORTS Fuels, lubricants, transport equipment, inputs and capital equipment for industry
DEFENCE 2.2% of GNP
POPULATION DENSITY 40 per sq km [104 per sq ml]
LIFE EXPECTANCY Female 69 yrs, male 65 yrs
ADULT LITERACY 88%

The Incas of Peru conquered Ecuador in the 15th century but in 1532 a colony was founded by the Spaniards in the territory, then called Quito. Independence from Spain was achieved in 1822, when it became part of Gran Colombia, and full independence followed in 1830. Today the country's democracy remains intact.

Ecuador's name comes from the Equator, which divides the country unequally; Quito, the capital, lies just within the southern hemisphere. There are three

The Galápagos Islands lie across the Equator 970 km [610 mls] west of Ecuador (of which they form a province), and consist of six main islands and over 50 smaller ones; all are volcanic, some of them active, but only four are inhabited.

Discovered by the Spanish in 1535 but annexed by Ecuador in 1832, the archipelago became famous after the visit of Charles Darwin in 1835, when he collected crucial evidence for his theory of natural selection. The islands contain a large variety of unique endemic species of flora and fauna ∎

PERU

Flown since 1825, the flag's colours are said to have come about when the Argentine patriot General José de San Martin, arriving to liberate Peru from Spain in 1820, saw a flock of red and white flamingos flying over his marching army.

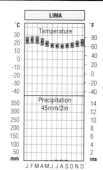

Peru has a great variety of climates; its northern border touches the Equator, over half the country is astride the high Andes, and the prevailing winds from the south-west blow over the cold Peruvian Current of the Pacific Ocean. Desert conditions prevail along the foothills of the Andes. The rainfall increases with altitude, resulting in snow-covered peaks. In the tropical north-eastern lowlands there are high temperatures and high rainfall amounts.

Largest of the Andean states, Peru is spread over coastal plain, mountains and forested Amazon lowlands in the interior. It was formerly the homeland of the Inca and other ancient civilizations, and has a history of human settlement stretching back over 10,500 years. The last Inca empire ended in the 16th century with the arrival of the Spaniards, who made Peru the most important of their viceroyalties in South America.

The coastal plain is narrow and generally arid, cooled by sea breezes from the offshore Humboldt Current. Occasionally it suffers violent rainstorms, associated with shifts in the pattern of surface waters. Rivers that cut through the foothills provide water for irrigated agriculture, mainly of cotton, rice and sugar cane. The middle slopes of the Andes – the Quechua, at heights of 2,000 m to 3,500 m [6,500 ft to 11,500 ft] – are warm-temperate and

fairly well watered. These areas supported the main centres of Indian population in the Inca empire.

Above stand the higher reaches of the Andes, extending westwards in cold inhospitable tablelands at 4,000 m to 4,800 m [13,000 ft to 15,700 ft], cultivated up to 4,200 m [13,700 ft] by peasant farmers and grazed by their sheep, alpacas, llamas and vicuñas. The snowy peaks of the high Andes rise to over 6,000 m [19,500 ft]. Though close to the Pacific, most of the rivers that rise here eventually drain into the Amazon. Their descent to the lowlands is through the *montaña*, a near-impenetrable maze of valleys, ridges and plains, permanently soaked by rain and thickly timbered. Beyond extend the Amazon lowlands – hot, wet and clad mainly in dense tropical rainforest. Occupying half the country, they are thinly inhabited by Indians.

Lima was developed as the Spanish colonial

capital, and through its port of Callao passed much of the trade of Spanish settlers; 19th-century exports included guano (bird droppings, valuable as an agricultural fertilizer) from the offshore islands, and wild rubber. Peru gained independence from Spain in 1824, but difficulties of communication, political strife, earthquakes and other natural disasters, and a chronically unbalanced economy have dogged the country's development.

Today Peru faces many economic, social and

THE ANDES

Created 200 million years ago by the collision of the Nazca plate and the land mass of South America – and still moving at about 12.5 mm [0.5 in] each year – the Andes mountain system extends along the entire west side of the continent from the coast of the Caribbean to Tierra del Fuego for over 6,400 km [4,000 mls], making it the world's longest chain.

It is the highest range outside the Himalayas and Argentina's Cerro Aconcagua, at 6,960 m [22,834 ft], is the highest peak outside Asia. Argentina shares with Chile four of the ten highest summits. In the middle section there are two main chains and elsewhere three, with the breadth exceeding 800 km [500 mls] to the north of latitude 20°S. Altogether the range has 54 peaks over 6,100 m [20,000 ft].

Many of South America's rivers, including the Orinoco, Negro, Amazon and Madeira, rise in the Andes, and the range is home to the continent's largest lake, Titicaca, which lies on the Peru–Bolivia border at 3,812 m [12,506 ft]. The Andes contain numerous volcanoes and are subject almost everywhere to violent earthquakes. Many volcanoes are still active and Cotopaxi in northern central Ecuador is usually regarded as the world's highest (5,896 m [19,457 ft]).

The condor, symbol of the mountains and the world's largest vulture, is now down to a few hundred, despite attempts by several Andean countries – backed by the USA – to increase its dwindling numbers.

In 1910 the Andes were tunnelled, linking the Chilean and Argentine railways by the tunnel, which is 3 km [2 mls] long, at an altitude of 3,200 m [10,500 ft], south-west of Aconcagua.

political problems. Agricultural production has failed to keep up with population, so wheat, rice, meat and other staple foods are imported. Cotton, coffee and sugar are exported. Peru is the leading producer of coca, the shrub used in the illegal production of cocaine, and earnings were thought to be in excess of US$3 billion in the 1980s.

Peru once had the largest fish catch in the world and there are 70 canning factories. Anchoveta was the main target, but fishing was halted from 1976 until 1982 because of depleted stocks. In 1983 a periodic warm current known as 'El Niño' ruined the fishing, but recovery followed from 1986.

Several metals are exported – particularly silver, zinc and lead, though copper is its most important earner – but industrial unrest has reduced production. Exports of oil are growing, however, providing much-needed foreign capital for industrial development, now forthcoming after a lull following Peru's limiting of debt repayment in 1985. Peru's inflation rate – 3,400% in 1989 and a staggering 7,480% in 1990 – settled down to 200% in 1991, the year that many state industries were liberalized.

But, in 1980, when civilian rule was restored, the economic problems facing Peru were coupled with the terrorist activity and involvement in the illegal

drugs trade by the left-wing group called the *Sendero Luminoso* ('Shining Path'), which began guerrilla warfare against the government. In 1990, Alberto Fujimori became president and took strong action. In 1992 he suspended the constitution and dismissed the legislature. The guerrilla leader, Abimael Guzmán, was arrested in 1992, but instability continued. A new constitution was introduced in 1993, giving increased power to the president, who faced many problems in rebuilding the shattered economy. To add to Peru's problems, early in 1991 the country suffered the worst cholera outbreak in the Americas this century, with some 2,500 deaths ∎

COUNTRY	Republic of Peru
AREA	1,285,220 sq km [496,223 sq mls]
POPULATION	23,588,000
CAPITAL (POPULATION)	Lima (6,601,000)
GOVERNMENT	Unitary republic with a bicameral legislature
ETHNIC GROUPS	Quechua 47%, Mestizo 32%, White 12%, Aymara 5%
LANGUAGES	Spanish and Quechua (both official)
RELIGIONS	Roman Catholic 93%, Protestant 6%
NATIONAL DAY	28 July; Independence Day (1821)
CURRENCY	New sol = 100 centavos
ANNUAL INCOME PER PERSON	US$1,490
MAIN PRIMARY PRODUCTS	Iron ore, silver, zinc, tungsten, petroleum, gold, copper, lead, tin, molybdenum
MAIN INDUSTRIES	Food processing, textiles, copper smelting, forestry, fishing
EXPORTS	US$170 per person
MAIN EXPORTS	Copper 19%, petroleum and derivatives 10%, lead 9%, zinc 8%, fishmeal 8%, coffee 5%
MAIN EXPORT PARTNERS	USA 34%, Japan 10%, Belgium 4%, Germany 4%
IMPORTS	US$84 per person
MAIN IMPORTS	Fuels, machinery, chemicals, food, tobacco
MAIN IMPORT PARTNERS	USA 27%, Argentina 9%, Brazil 6%
TOURISM	316,800 visitors per year
POPULATION DENSITY	18 per sq km [48 per sq ml]
INFANT MORTALITY	76 per 1,000 live births
LIFE EXPECTANCY	Female 67 yrs, male 63 yrs
ADULT LITERACY	87%
PRINCIPAL CITIES (POPULATION)	Lima–Callao 6,601,000 Arequipa 620,000 Trujillo 509,000 Chiclayo 410,000

THE INCA CIVILIZATION

The empire of the Incas, centring on Cuzco in the Peruvian highlands, developed from millennia of earlier Andean civilizations that included the Chavin, the Nazca and the Tiahuanaco. The Incas began their conquests about AD 1350, and by the end of the 15th century their empire extended from central Chile to Ecuador. Perhaps some 10 million people owed allegiance to it when it fell to the Spanish *conquistadores* in 1532.

The empire was military and theocratic, with the sun as the focus of worship. Temples and shrines were created for sun worship; the Sun Temple at Cuzco had a circumference of 350 m [1,148 ft], and many other buildings were equally massive. The people were skilled farmers, using elaborate irrigation systems and terraced fields.

Gold and silver were particularly valued by the Incas for ornamentation. They were prized also by the *conquistadores*, who looted them from every corner of the empire and quickly set the Indians to mining more. Fragments of Inca culture and beliefs remain among the Quechua-speaking peoples of Peru and Bolivia.

SOUTH AMERICA

GUYANA

This striking design, adopted by Guyana on independence from Britain in 1966, has colours representing the people's energy building a new nation (red), their perseverance (black), minerals (yellow), rivers (white), and agriculture and forests (green).

Temperatures along the coast are high with an annual variation of only a few degrees; there is a daily range of about 10°C [18°F]. Temperatures are lower on the higher land of the south and west. The north-east trade winds blow constantly, and so the rainfall is high, falling on over 200 days in the year, in a longer and heavier wet season from May to August, and a lesser one, January to December. The rainfall decreases southwards and inland, where the dry season is from September to February.

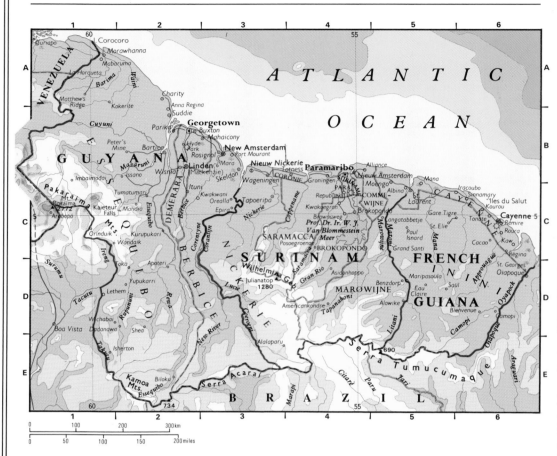

COUNTRY Co-operative Republic of Guyana

AREA 214,970 sq km [83,000 sq mls]

POPULATION 832,000

CAPITAL (POPULATION) Georgetown (200,000)

GOVERNMENT Multiparty republic with a unicameral legislature

ETHNIC GROUPS Asian Indian 49%, Black 36%, Amerindian 7%, Mixed 7%

LANGUAGES English (official), Hindi, Urdu, Amerindian dialects

RELIGIONS Hindu 34%, Protestant 34%, Roman Catholic 18%, Sunni Muslim 9%

CURRENCY Guyanan dollar = 100 cents

ANNUAL INCOME PER PERSON US$350

POPULATION DENSITY 4 per sq km [10 per sq ml]

LIFE EXPECTANCY Female 68 yrs, male 62 yrs

ADULT LITERACY 98%

The 'land of many waters' was settled by the Dutch between 1616 and 1621. The territory was ceded to Britain in 1814, and in 1981 British Guiana was formed. Independent since 1966, Guyana – the only English-speaking country in South America – became a republic in 1970. It is largely uninhabited and 95% of the population live within a few kilometres of the coast, leaving the interior virtually empty.

The vast interior, covering 85% of the land area, includes low forest-covered plateaus, the wooded Rupununi savannas, meandering river valleys, and the spectacular Roraima Massif on the Venezuela–Brazil border. The coastal plain is mainly artificial, reclaimed from the tidal marshes and mangrove swamps by dykes and canals.

Land reclamation for sugar and cotton planting began in the 18th century under Dutch West India Company rule, using slave labour, and continued through the 19th century after the British took over, with indentured Asian labour replacing slaves after emancipation. Today sugar remains the main plan-

tation crop, with production largely mechanized, most of it in the lower Demerara River area.

The Asian community, however, who make up about half the total Guyanan population, are involved in rice growing. Bauxite mining and alumina production are well-established industries, combining with sugar production to provide 80% of the country's overseas earnings. But neither sugar nor rice provide year-round work and unemployment remains a stubborn problem. The economy, which is 80% state-controlled, entered a prolonged economic crisis in the 1970s, and in the early 1980s the situation was exacerbated by the decline in the production and price of bauxite, sugar and rice. Following unrest, the government sought to replace Western aid by turning for help to socialist countries. However, during the late 1980s Western aid and investment were again sought, but these were only forthcoming on condition of restoring free elections in the 1990s ■

SURINAM

Adopted on independence from the Dutch in 1975, Surinam's flag features the colours of the main political parties, the yellow star symbolizing unity and a golden future. The red is twice the width of the green, and four times that of the white.

COUNTRY Republic of Suriname

AREA 163,270 sq km [63,039 sq mls]

POPULATION 421,000

CAPITAL (POPULATION) Paramaribo (201,000)

GOVERNMENT Multiparty republic

ETHNIC GROUPS Asian Indian 37%, Creole 31%, Indonesian 14%, Black, Amerindian, Chinese, Dutch

LANGUAGES Dutch (official), English

RELIGIONS Hindu 27%, Roman Catholic 23%, Sunni Muslim 20%, Protestant 19%

CURRENCY Surinam guilder = 100 cents

ANNUAL INCOME PER PERSON US$1,210

Although Spaniards visited as early as 1499, Surinam was first settled by British colonists in 1651. In 1667 it was ceded to Holland in exchange for Nieuw-Amsterdam, now New York, and was confirmed as a Dutch colony, called Dutch Guiana, in 1816.

Surinam has a coastline of 350 km [218 mls] of Amazonian mud and silt, fringed by extensive mangrove swamps. Behind lies an old coastal plain of sands and clays, bordering a stretch of sandy savanna. The heavily forested interior uplands further to the south are part of the Guiana Highlands, whose weathered soils form the basis of the crucial bauxite industry.

Surinam's hot and humid climate grows an abundance of bananas, citrus fruits and coconuts for export, with rice and many other tropical commodities for home consumption. Plantations were initially worked by African slaves, later by Chinese and East Indian indentured labour. Bauxite and its derivatives, shrimps and bananas are the main exports, but though 92% of the land is covered by forest – the world's highest figure – little is commercially exploited. There is also potential for the expansion of tourism.

In 1980 a military group seized power and abolished the parliament, setting up a ruling National Military Council. Elections were held in 1987 and the country returned to democratic rule in 1988. Another military coup occurred in 1990, but further

elections were held in 1991. In 1992, the government negotiated a peace agreement with the *boschneger*, descendants of African slaves, who in 1986 had launched a rebellion that had disrupted bauxite mining. But instability continued, and in 1993, the Netherlands stopped financial aid after an EU report stated that Surinam had failed to reform the economy and control inflation ■

FRENCH GUIANA

The official flag flown over 'Guyane' is the French tricolour. A French possession since 1676 (apart from 1809–17), the territory is treated as part of mainland France and its citizens send representatives to the Paris parliament.

COUNTRY Department of French Guiana
AREA 90,000 sq km [34,749 sq mls]
POPULATION 154,000
CAPITAL (POPULATION) Cayenne (42,000)
GOVERNMENT Overseas Department of France
ETHNIC GROUPS Creole 42%, Chinese 14%, French 10%, Haitian 7%
LANGUAGES French (official), Creole patois
RELIGIONS Roman Catholic 80%, Protestant 4%
CURRENCY French franc = 100 centimes
POPULATION DENSITY 2 per sq km [4 per sq ml]
ANNUAL INCOME PER PERSON US$5,000

The smallest country in South America, French Guiana has a narrow coastal plain comprising mangrove swamps and marshes, alternating with drier areas that can be cultivated; one such is the site of the capital, Cayenne. Inland, a belt of sandy savanna rises to a forested plateau.

A French settlement was established in 1604 by a group of merchant adventurers, and after brief periods of Dutch, English and Portuguese rule the territory finally became permanently French in 1817. In 1946 – a year after the closure of Devil's Island, the notorious convict settlement –

its status changed to that of an overseas department of France, and in 1974 it also became an administrative region.

The economy is very dependent on France, both for budgetary aid and for food and manufactured goods. The French have also built a rocket-launching station near the coast at Kaurou. Timber is the most important natural resource; bauxite and kaolin have been discovered but are largely unexploited. Only 104 sq km [40 sq mls] of the land is under cultivation where sugar, cassava and rice are grown. Fishing, particularly for shrimps, much

of which are exported, is a leading occupation, and tourism, though in its infancy, has as main attractions the Amerindian villages of the interior and the lush tropical scenery ■

BRAZIL

The sphere bears the motto 'Order and Progress' and its 27 stars, arranged in the pattern of the night sky over Brazil, represent the states and federal district. Green symbolizes the nation's rainforests, and the yellow diamond represents its mineral wealth.

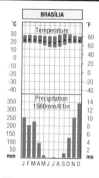

Brazil lies almost entirely within the tropics. The northern half of the country is dominated by the Amazon Basin and, except for the highlands in the south-east, there are no mountains. The monthly temperatures are high – over 25°C [77°F] – and there is little annual variation. Brasília has only a 4°C [7°F] difference between July and October; Rio has twice this range. The hottest part of the country is in the north-east. Frosts occur in the eastern highlands and the extreme south of the country.

By any standard Brazil is a big country. The fifth largest in the world – and the fifth most populous – it covers nearly 48% of South America. Structurally, it has two main regions. In the north lies the vast Amazon Basin, once an inland sea and now drained by a river system that carries one-fifth of the Earth's running water. In the centre and south lies the sprawling bulk of the Brazilian Highlands, a huge extent of hard crystalline rock deeply dissected into rolling uplands. This occupies the heartland (Mato Grosso), and the whole western flank of the country from the bulge to the border with Uruguay.

Landscape

The Amazon River rises in the Peruvian Andes, close to the Pacific Ocean, and many of its tributaries are of similar origin. Several are wide enough to take boats of substantial draught (6 m [20 ft]) from the Andean foothills all the way to the Atlantic – a distance of 5,000 km [3,000 mls] or more.

The largest area of river plain lies in the upper part of the basin, along the frontier with Bolivia and Peru. Downstream the flood plain is relatively narrow, shrinking in width to a few kilometres where the basin drains between the Guiana Highlands in the north and the Brazilian Highlands in the south.

The undulating plateau of the northern highlands carries poor soils; here rainfall is seasonal, and the typical natural vegetation is a thorny scrub forest, used as open grazing for poor cattle herds. Further south scrub turns to wooded savanna – the *campo cerrado* vegetation that covers 2 million sq km [770,000 sq mls] of the interior plateau. It extends into the basin of the Paraná River and its tributaries, most of which start in the coastal highlands and flow west, draining ultimately into the Plate estuary. The Mato Grosso, on the border with Bolivia, is part of this large area and still mostly unexplored.

Conditions are better in the south, with more reliable rainfall. The south-east includes a narrow coastal plain, swampy in places and with abundant rainfall throughout the year; behind rises the Great Escarpment (820 m [2,700 ft]), first in a series of steps to the high eastern edge of the plateau. Over 60% of Brazil's population live in four southern and south-eastern states that account for only 17% of the total area.

History and politics

Brazil was 'discovered' by Pedro Alvarez Cabral on 22 April 1500 and gradually penetrated by Portuguese settlers, missionaries, explorers and prospectors during the 17th and 18th centuries. Many

of the semi-nomadic indigenous Indians were enslaved for plantation work or driven into the interior, and some 4 million African slaves were introduced, notably in the sugar-growing areas of the north-east.

Little more than a group of rival provinces, Brazil began to unite in 1808 when the Portuguese royal court, seeking refuge from Napoleon, transferred from Lisbon to Rio de Janeiro. The eldest surviving son of King Joãs VI of Portugal was chosen as 'Perpetual Defender' of Brazil by a national congress. In 1822 he proclaimed the independence of the country and was chosen as the constitutional emperor with the title Pedro I. He abdicated in 1831 and was succeeded by his son Pedro II, who ruled for nearly 50 years and whose liberal policies included the gradual abolition of slavery (1888).

A federal system was adopted for the United States of Brazil in the 1881 constitution and Brazil

RIO DE JANEIRO AND SÃO PAULO

Much of Brazil's population is concentrated in a relatively small and highly developed 'corner' in the south-east of the country. Rio de Janeiro, discovered by the Portuguese in 1502, lies in a magnificent setting, stretching for 20 km [12 mls] along the coast between mountain and ocean. Though no longer the capital, it remains the focus of Brazil's cultural life, attracting visitors with the world's greatest pre-Lent festival at carnival time.

São Paulo, its early growth fuelled by the coffee boom of the late 19th century, is the most populous city in the southern hemisphere. Estimates state that the 1985 total of 15.5 million will increase to 22.1 million by the year 2000. In both cities the gap between rich and poor is all too evident, the sprawling shanty towns (*favelas*) standing in sharp contrast to sophisticated metropolitan centres.

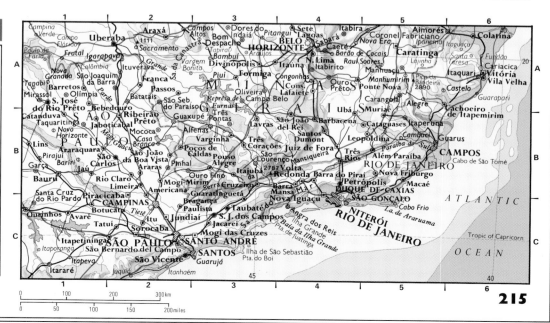

THE AMAZON RAINFOREST

The world's largest and ecologically most important rainforest was still being destroyed at an alarming rate in the late 1980s, with somewhere between 1.5% and 4% disappearing each year in Brazil alone. Opening up the forest for many reasons – logging, mining, ranching, peasant resettlement – the Brazilian authorities did little in real terms when confronted with a catalogue of indictments: decimation of a crucial world habitat; pollution of rivers; destruction of thousands of species of fauna and flora, especially medicinal plants; and the brutal ruination of the lives of the last remaining Amerindian tribes.

Once cut off from the world by impenetrable jungle, hundreds of thousand of Indians have been displaced in the provinces of Rondonia and Acre, principally by loggers and landless migrants, and in Para by mining, dams for HEP and ranching for beef cattle. It is estimated that five centuries ago the Amazon rainforest supported some 2 million Indians in more than 200 tribes; today the number has shrunk to a pitiful 50,000 or so, and many of the tribes have disappeared altogether.

A handful have been relatively lucky – the Yanomani, after huge international support, won their battle in 1991 for a reserve three times the size of Belgium – but for the majority their traditional life style has vanished forever.

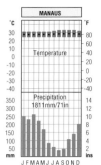

At Manaus, in the centre of the Amazon Basin, there is little difference between the temperature of the warmest month, October (29°C [84°F]), and the coolest, April (27°C [81°F]). The temperatures are not extremely high and the highest recorded was 37°C [99°F]; the lowest was 18°C [64°F]. Rainfall totals are high in this region, especially December to March, with a distinct dry season from June to September, when rain falls on only 5–10 days per month on average.

became a republic in 1889. Until 1930 the country experienced strong economic expansion and prosperity, but social unrest in 1930 resulted in a major revolt and from then until 1945 the country was under the control of President Vargas, who established a strong corporate state similar to that of fascist Italy, although Brazil entered World War II on the side of the Allies. Democracy, often corrupt, prevailed from 1956 to 1964 and from 1985; between were five military presidents of illiberal regimes.

A new constitution came into force in October 1988 – the eighth since independence from the Portuguese in 1822 – which transferred powers from the president to congress and paved the way for a return to democracy in 1990. Today the country comprises 23 states, each with its own directly elected governor and legislature, three territories and the Federal District of Brasília.

Economy and resources

For many decades following the early settlements Brazil was mainly a sugar-producing colony, with most plantations centred on the rich coastal plains of the north-east. Later the same areas produced cotton, cocoa, rice and other crops. In the south, colonists penetrated the interior in search of slaves and minerals, especially gold and diamonds; the city of Ouro Prêto in Minas Gerais was built, and Rio de Janeiro grew as the port for the region.

During the 19th century, São Paulo state became the centre of a huge coffee-growing industry; and while the fortunes made in mining helped to develop Rio de Janeiro, profits from coffee were invested in the city of São Paulo. Immigrants from Italy and Germany settled in the south, introducing farming into the fertile valleys in co-existence with the cattle ranchers and gauchos of the plains.

The second half of the 19th century saw the development of the wild rubber industry in the Amazon Basin, where the city of Manaus, with its world-famous opera house, served as a centre and market; though Manaus lies 1,600 km [1,000 mls]

from the mouth of the Amazon, rubber collected from trees in the hinterland could be shipped out directly to world markets in ocean going steamers. Brazil enjoyed a virtual monopoly of the rubber trade until the early 20th century, when Malaya began to compete, later with massive success.

Vast mineral resources exist, particularly in Minas Gerais and the Amazon area; they include bauxite, tin, iron ore, manganese, chrome, nickel, uranium, platinum and industrial diamonds. Brazil is the world's second-largest producer of iron ore and there are reserves of at least 19,500 million metric tonnes, including the world's biggest at Carajás. Discoveries of new reserves of minerals are frequently being made. The world's largest tin mine is situated in the Amazon region, 50% of the world's platinum is in Brazil, and 65% of the world's supply of precious stones are produced within the country.

The demand for energy has increased rapidly over the years and over a quarter of imports are for crude petroleum. An alternative energy was developed from 1976, made from sugar cane and cassava called ethanol (combustible alcohol), with the aim of reducing demand for petroleum, and in the eight years to 1987 some 3.5 million cars were manufactured to take this fuel; falling oil prices later made this uneconomic. Large investments have been made in hydroelectricity – 93% of the country's electricity is now from water – and the Itaipú HEP station on the Paraná, shared with Paraguay, is the world's largest.

Brazil is one of the world's largest farming countries, and agriculture employs 25% of the population and provides 40% of her exports. The main agricultural exports are coffee, sugar, soya beans, orange juice concentrates (80% of the world total), beef, cocoa, poultry, sisal, tobacco, maize and cotton. Brazil is the world's leading producer of coffee (Colombia is second, with Indonesia third); it is also the top producer of sugar cane, oranges, sisal and cassava.

The Amazon Basin is gradually being opened for the controversial exploitation of forests and mines, with Santarém a new focus of agriculture in a frontier land. There are 35 deep-water ports in Brazil, and the two main oil terminals at São Sebastião and Madre de Jesus are being expanded. Though river transport now plays only a minor part in the movement of goods, for many years rivers gave the only access to the interior, and there are plans to link the Amazon and the Upper Paraná to give a navigable waterway across central Brazil.

A network of arterial roads is being added, replacing the 19th-century railways which have been used to take primary products to markets on the coast. Road transport now accounts for 70% of freight and 97% of passenger traffic.

Population

In 1872 Brazil had a population of about 10 million. By 1972 this had increased almost tenfold, and 1995 saw a figure of 161.4 million Brazilians – with a projected increase to 200 million by the end of the century. Of the economically active population (55 million in 1985), 15 million were engaged in agriculture, 9 million in the service industries, 8 million in manufacturing, 5 million in the wholesale and retail trade, and 3 million in construction.

On 21 April 1960 Rio de Janeiro ceased to be the capital and inland the new city of Brasília, built from 1956 onwards, in many ways encapsulated

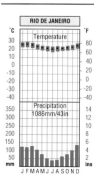

Rio de Janeiro experiences a high rainfall and a marked dry season from May to August – rain falls on only about 20 days from June to August – but not so marked as inland. Most of Brazil has moderate rainfall, but there are very heavy precipitation totals at the mouth and in the headwaters of the Amazon, and on the south-east coast below the highlands. There is an arid zone in the north-east. At Rio de Janeiro, the sun shines for 5–7 hours per day.

COUNTRY	Federative Republic of Brazil
AREA	8,511,970 sq km [3,286,472 sq mls]
POPULATION	161,416,000
CAPITAL (POPULATION)	Brasília (1,596,000)
GOVERNMENT	Federal republic with a bicameral legislature
ETHNIC GROUPS	White 53%, Mulatto 22%, Mestizo 12%, Black 11%, Amerindian
LANGUAGES	Portuguese (official), Spanish, English, French, native dialects
RELIGIONS	Roman Catholic 88%, Protestant 6%
CURRENCY	Real = 100 centavos
ANNUAL INCOME PER PERSON	US$2,920
SOURCE OF INCOME	Agriculture 10%, industry 39%, services 51%
MAIN PRIMARY PRODUCTS	Coal, iron ore, manganese, gold, bauxite, copper, diamonds, petroleum
MAIN INDUSTRIES	Steel, petrochemicals, machinery, consumer goods, cement, offshore oil, shipping, timber
EXPORTS	US$233 per person
MAIN EXPORTS	Transport equipment 12%, soya beans 9%, coffee 8%, iron ore 7%, machinery 6%, footwear 5%
MAIN EXPORT PARTNERS	USA 27%, Japan 6%, Netherlands 6%, Germany 4%, Italy 5%

IMPORTS	US$124 per person
MAIN IMPORTS	Primary products 33%, capital goods 26%, oil and oil products 25%
MAIN IMPORT PARTNERS	USA 20%, Germany 9%, Japan 6%, Saudi Arabia 6%
TOTAL ARMED FORCES	722,000
TOURISM	1,091,000 visitors per year
ROADS	1,675,040 km [1,046,900 mls]
RAILWAYS	29,901 km [18,688 mls]
POPULATION DENSITY	19 per sq km [49 per sq ml]
URBAN POPULATION	76%
POPULATION GROWTH	2.1% per year
BIRTHS	26 per 1,000 population
DEATHS	8 per 1,000 population
INFANT MORTALITY	57 per 1,000 live births
LIFE EXPECTANCY	Female 69 yrs, male 64 yrs
POPULATION PER DOCTOR	1,000 people
ADULT LITERACY	81%

PRINCIPAL CITIES (POPULATION) São Paulo 16,417,000 Rio de Janeiro 9,888,000 Salvador 2,056,000 Belo Horizonte 2,049,000 Fortaleza 1,758,000 Brasília 1,596,000 Curitiba 1,290,000 Recife 1,290,000 Nova Iguaçu 1,286,000 Pôrto Alegre 1,263,000

both the spirit and the problems of contemporary Brazil – a sparkling, dramatic, planned city, deliberately planted in the unpopulated uplands of Goías as a gesture of faith; modern, practical and beautiful, but still surrounded by the shanties of poverty and – beyond them – the challenge of an untamed wilderness. So much of the nation's wealth is still held by the élites of the cities, particularly those of the south-east, and despite grandiose development plans aimed at spreading prosperity throughout the country and despite the international image of fun-loving carnivals, the interior remains poor and underpopulated.

Although possessing great reserves, Brazil has not made the big jump from developing to developed country. The boom of 'the miracle years' from 1968 to 1973, when the economy grew at more than 10% per annum, was not sustained.

Indeed, falls in commodity prices and massive borrowing to finance large and often unproductive projects have combined to make Brazil the world's biggest debtor nation; despite paying back US$69 billion between 1985 and 1991 – a huge drain on any economy – there was still over US$120 billion owed. Inflation during 1990 was nearly 3,000% – down to under 400% in 1991 – and mismanagement and corruption still afflicted administration ∎

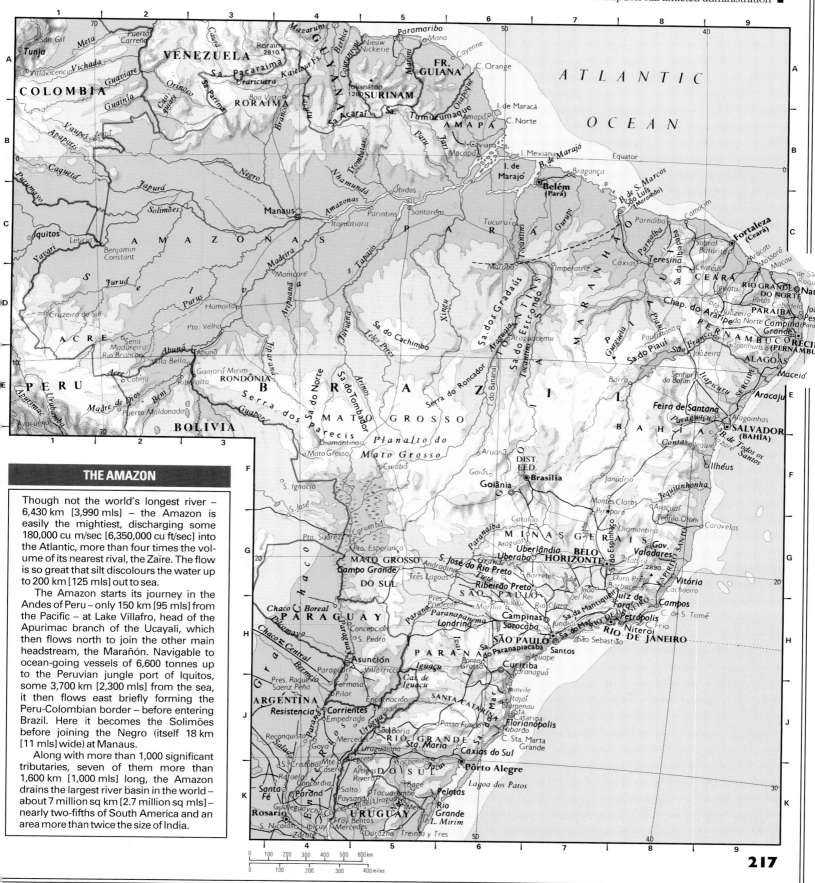

THE AMAZON

Though not the world's longest river – 6,430 km [3,990 mls] – the Amazon is easily the mightiest, discharging some 180,000 cu m/sec [6,350,000 cu ft/sec] into the Atlantic, more than four times the volume of its nearest rival, the Zaïre. The flow is so great that silt discolours the water up to 200 km [125 mls] out to sea.

The Amazon starts its journey in the Andes of Peru – only 150 km [95 mls] from the Pacific – at Lake Villafro, head of the Apurimac branch of the Ucayali, which then flows north to join the other main headstream, the Marañón. Navigable to ocean-going vessels of 6,600 tonnes up to the Peruvian jungle port of Iquitos, some 3,700 km [2,300 mls] from the sea, it then flows east briefly forming the Peru-Colombian border – before entering Brazil. Here it becomes the Solimões before joining the Negro (itself 18 km [11 mls] wide) at Manaus.

Along with more than 1,000 significant tributaries, seven of them more than 1,600 km [1,000 mls] long, the Amazon drains the largest river basin in the world – about 7 million sq km [2.7 million sq mls] – nearly two-fifths of South America and an area more than twice the size of India.

SOUTH AMERICA

BOLIVIA

Dating from liberation in 1825, the tricolour has been used as both national and merchant flag since 1988. The red stands for Bolivia's animals and the army's courage, the yellow for mineral resources, and the green for its agricultural wealth.

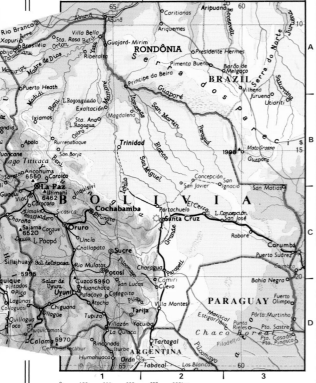

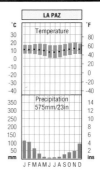

Although within the tropics, La Paz lies at 3,625 m [11,893 ft] on the Bolivian plateau and temperatures are clearly affected by the altitude. The annual range is very small (1°C [2°F]), but temperatures rise rapidly by day and fall sharply at night in the clear air; the diurnal range is very large (10–15°C [18–27°F]), with frequent night frosts in winter. Rainfall, which is often thundery, occurs mainly in the summer months. From April to October, rain falls on less than 10 days per month.

COUNTRY Republic of Bolivia

AREA 1,098,580 sq km [424,162 sq mls]

POPULATION 7,900,000

CAPITAL (POPULATION) La Paz (1,126,000) / Sucre (131,000)

GOVERNMENT Unitary multiparty republic with a bicameral legislature

ETHNIC GROUPS Mestizo 31%, Quechua 25%, Aymara 17%, White 15%

LANGUAGES Spanish, Aymara, Quechua (all official)

RELIGIONS Roman Catholic 94%

CURRENCY Boliviano = 100 centavos

ANNUAL INCOME PER PERSON US$650

MAIN PRIMARY PRODUCTS Tin, sugar cane, rice, cotton

MAIN INDUSTRIES Agriculture, manufacturing, tin mining

POPULATION DENSITY 7 per sq km [17 per sq ml]

LIFE EXPECTANCY Female 58 yrs, male 54 yrs

ADULT LITERACY 78%

THE ALTIPLANO

A high, rolling plateau 3,600 m [12,000 ft] above sea level on the Peruvian border of Bolivia, the Altiplano stretches 400 km [250 mls] north to south between the eastern and western cordilleras of the Andes. Surrounded by high, snow-capped peaks, at its north end lies Lake Titicaca, the highest navigable body of water in the world and according to Indian legend the birthplace of the Inca civilization. To the south are smaller lakes, and extensive salt flats representing old lake beds. Though tropical in latitude the Altiplano is cold, windswept and bleak, by any standards a harsh environment, yet over half the population of Bolivia, including a high proportion of native Indians, make it their home.

The natural vegetation is grassland merging at high levels to *puna* – small bushes and trees forming a harsh scrubland. Summer rains and winter snows bring enough moisture to support grass, and llama and alpaca, from guanacolike ancestors, are herded to provide meat and wool for the peasant farmers.

By far the larger of South America's two land-locked countries, Bolivia is made up of a wide stretch of the Andes and a long, broad Oriente – part of the south-western fringe of the Amazon Basin. The western boundary is the High Cordillera Occidental, crowned by Sajama at 6,520 m [21,400 ft] and many other volcanic peaks. To the east lies the Altiplano, a high plateau which in prehistoric times was a great lake. Eastwards again rises the majestic Cordillera Real, where Illimani, a glacier-covered peak of 6,462 m [21,200 ft], forms a backdrop to La Paz (The Peace), the world's highest capital. In the transmontane region to the north and east lies the huge expanse of the Oriente – foothills and plains extending from the semi-arid Chaco of the south-east through the savannalike *llanos* of the centre to the high, wetter forests of the northern plains.

In pre-Conquest days Bolivia was the homeland of the Tiahuanaco culture (7th–11th centuries AD) and was later absorbed into the Inca empire; Quechua, the Inca language, is still spoken by large Amerindian minorities that constitute the highest proportion of any South American country. Famous for its silver mines, the high Andean area was exploited ruthlessly by the Spanish *conquistadores*; the mine at Potosí, discovered in 1545, proved the richest in the world, and Upper Peru (today's highland Bolivia) was for two centuries one of the most densely populated of Spain's American colonies. In 1824 the local population seized their independence, naming the country after Simón Bolívar, hero of other South American wars of independence. When the era of silver passed, the economy flagged and the country began to lose ground to its neighbours. The Pacific coast was lost to Chile and Peru in 1884 and large tracts of the Oriente were ceded to Brazil (1903) and Paraguay (1935).

Today Bolivia is the poorest of the South American republics, though it has abundant natural resources with large reserves of petroleum, natural gas and many mineral ores. Lack of investment both in these areas and in the agricultural sector do not help the comparatively poor development, but new irrigation schemes in the south-western Oriente may improve local production of staple foods. Over half the working population is engaged in agriculture,

but mining still contributes significantly to the country's wealth. However, Bolivia, once the world's leading tin producer, now ranks sixth with just 8.3% of a rapidly dwindling total. Today's main export may well be coca and refined cocaine, which almost certainly employs 5% of the population; the government, with US help and co-operation with neighbours, is trying to stifle the growing industry.

The collapse of the tin market was linked to the record inflation of 1985 – figures vary between 12,000% and over 20,000%, and the 1980–8 average was the world's worst at 483% – though the rates were more stable by the end of the decade. So, too, in a nation renowned for its political volatility (192 coups in 156 years from independence to 1981), was the government, desperately trying to lift Bolivia to the standards of its neighbours ■

PARAGUAY

Paraguay's tricolour is a national flag with different sides. On the obverse the state emblem, illustrated here, displays the May Star to commemorate liberation from Spain (1811); the reverse shows the treasury seal – a lion and staff, with the words 'Peace and Justice'.

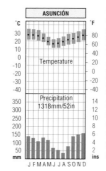

In South America, between 20°S and 30°S, there is a prominent summer wet season. The rain is often heavy and can yield as much as 20 mm [0.8 in] per day in Asunción. Summers throughout the plains of Paraguay are very hot and humid, whereas the winters are mild and relatively dry. Much of the winter rain is associated with surges of cold air from the Southern Ocean, which can give surprisingly low temperatures, especially in the south of the country.

A landlocked nation, Paraguay is bounded mainly by rivers – the Paraná (South America's second longest river) in the south and east, the Pilcomayo in the south-west, and the Paraguay and Apa rivers in the north-west. The middle reach of the Paraguay, navigable for vessels of 1,800 tonnes to Asunción, 1,610 km [1,000 mls] from the sea, divides the country unequally. The eastern third, an extension of the Brazilian plateau at a height of 300 m to 600 m [1,000 ft to 2,000 ft] is densely forested with tropical hardwoods. The western two-thirds is the Northern

Chaco, a flat, alluvial plain rising gently from the damp, marshy Paraguay river valley to semi-desert scrubland along the western border.

Paraguay was settled in 1537 by Spaniards attracted by the labour supply of the native Guarani Indians – and the chance of finding a short cut to the silver of Peru. Forming part of the Rio de la Plata Viceroyalty from 1766, Paraguay broke free in 1811 and achieved independence from Buenos Aires in 1813. For over a century the country struggled for nationhood, torn by destructive internal strife and

conflict with neighbouring states: in 1865–70, war against Brazil, Argentina and Uruguay cost the country more than half its 600,000 people and

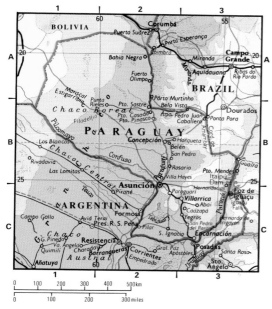

war was followed by political and economic stability.

In 1954 General Stroessner seized power and assumed the presidency. During his dictatorship there was considerable economic growth, particularly in the 1970s, and great emphasis was placed on developing hydroelectricity: by 1976 Paraguay was self-sufficient in electric energy as a result of the completion of the Acaray complex, and a second HEP project (the world's largest) started production in 1984 at Itaipú – a joint US$20 billion venture with Brazil to harness the Paraná. Paraguay was now generating 99.9% of its electricity from waterpower, and another construction on the Paraná – in the south at Yacyretá (near Encarnación) and involving the world's longest dam – was commissioned.

However, demand slackened and income declined, making it difficult for Paraguay to repay foreign debts incurred on the projects, and high inflation and balance of payments problems followed. The economy is being adjusted and as there are no significant mineral sources a return to an agricultural base has been planned for the 1990s.

Hopefully, this will now be happening under the umbrella of democracy. Alfredo Stroessner's regime was a particularly unpleasant variety of despotism, and he ruled with an ever-increasing disregard for human rights during nearly 35 years of fear and fraud before being deposed by his own supporters in 1989. The speeches about reform from his successor, General Andrés Rodríguez,

much of its territory. At a time when most other South American countries were attracting European settlers and foreign capital for development, Paraguay remained isolated and forbidding. Some territory was regained after the Chaco Wars against Bolivia in 1929–35, and in 1947 a period of civil

sounded somewhat hollow, but at the end of 1991 Paraguayans did indeed go to the polls to elect a constituent assembly that would frame a new constitution incorporating a multiparty system. Free multiparty elections held in 1993 resulted in the installation of Juan Carlos Wasmosy, leader of the Colorado Party. Wasmosy was Paraguay's first civilian president since 1954 ■

COUNTRY Republic of Paraguay
AREA 406,750 sq km [157,046 sq mls]
POPULATION 4,979,000
CAPITAL (POPULATION) Asunción (945,000)
GOVERNMENT Multiparty republic
ETHNIC GROUPS Mestizo 90%, Amerindian 3%
LANGUAGES Spanish and Guarani (both official)
RELIGIONS Roman Catholic 96%, Protestant 2%
CURRENCY Guaraní = 100 céntimos
ANNUAL INCOME PER PERSON US$1,550
MAIN PRIMARY PRODUCTS Timber, cattle, limestone, kaolin, gypsum
MAIN INDUSTRIES Agriculture, manufacturing
MAIN EXPORTS Cotton, soya, oilseed, timber
MAIN IMPORTS Petroleum and petroleum products, chemicals, machinery, transport and electrical equipment
POPULATION DENSITY 12 per sq km [32 per sq ml]
LIFE EXPECTANCY Female 70 yrs, male 65 yrs
ADULT LITERACY 91%

URUGUAY

Displayed since 1830, the stripes represent the nine provinces of Uruguay on independence from Spain two years earlier. The blue and white and the May Sun derive from the flag originally employed by Argentina in the colonial struggle.

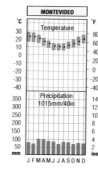

The plains around the estuary of the River Plate have a very even distribution of rainfall throughout the year. Much of the rain is associated with the advance of cold air from the Southern Ocean, which may be accompanied by a Pampero Sucio, a violent squall with rain and thunder followed by cooler, sunny weather. Near to the ocean, the summers are pleasantly warm and the winters less cold than at similar latitudes in the northern hemisphere.

After Surinam, Uruguay is the smallest South American state, a low-lying rolling country of tall prairie grasses and riparian woodlands with the highest land less than 600 m [2,000 ft] above sea level. The Atlantic coast and River Plate estuary are fringed with lagoons and sand dunes; the centre of the country is a low plateau, rising in the north towards the Brazilian border. The Uruguay River forms the western boundary, and is navigable as far as the falls at Salto, 300 km [186 mls] from the Plate.

Originally little more than the hinterland to the Spanish base at Montevideo, Uruguay formed a buffer area between northern Portuguese and western Spanish territories. Though independent in 1828, internal struggles and civil war intervened before the country developed a basis for prosperity. European immigrants settled the coast and the valley of the Uruguay River, farming the lowlands and leaving the highlands for stock rearing.

Meat processing, pioneered at Fray Bentos in the 1860s, was the start of a meat-and-hide export industry that, boosted by railways to Montevideo and later by refrigerated cargo ships, established the nation's fortunes. Today a modern and moderately prosperous country, Uruguay still depends largely on exports of animal products – mostly meat, wool and dairy produce – for its livelihood.

Farming is thus the main industry, though four out of five Uruguayans are urban-living and almost half live in the capital. Moreover, although more than 90% of Uruguay's land could be used for agriculture, only 10% of it is currently under cultivation. The manufacturing industry today is largely centred on food processing and packing, though with a small domestic market the economy has diversified into cement, chemicals, leather, textiles and steel. Uruguay's trading patterns are changing, too, in an

attempt to avoid reliance on Brazil and Argentina, and in 1988 trade agreements with China and USSR were signed. With inadequate supplies of coal, gas and oil, the nation depends on HEP (90%) for its energy, and exports electricity to Argentina.

Since 1828 Uruguay has been dominated by two political parties – Colorados (Liberals) and Blancos (Conservatives) – and from 1904 has been unique in constitutional innovations aimed at avoiding a dictatorship. The early part of the 20th century saw the development of a pioneering welfare state which in turn encouraged extensive immigration. From 1973 until 1985, however, the country was under a strict

military regime accused of appalling human rights abuses, and by 1990 it was still adjusting again to civilian government. Julio Maria Sanguinetti, who led Uruguay back to civilian rule, was re-elected president in 1994 ■

COUNTRY Eastern Republic of Uruguay
AREA 177,410 sq km [68,498 sq mls]
POPULATION 3,186,000
CAPITAL (POPULATION) Montevideo (1,384,000)
GOVERNMENT Unitary multiparty republic with a bicameral legislature
ETHNIC GROUPS White 86%, Mestizo 8%, Black 6%
LANGUAGES Spanish (official)
RELIGIONS Roman Catholic 96%, Protestant 2%, Jewish 1%
CURRENCY Uruguay peso = 100 centésimos
ANNUAL INCOME PER PERSON US$3,910
MAIN PRIMARY PRODUCTS Rice, meat, fruit, fish
MAIN INDUSTRIES Meat processing, food processing, light engineering, cement, chemicals, textiles, steel
MAIN EXPORTS Hides and leather, meat, wool, dairy products, rice, fish
MAIN IMPORTS Fuels, metals, machinery, vehicles
DEFENCE 2.7% of GNP
POPULATION DENSITY 18 per sq km [47 per sq ml]
LIFE EXPECTANCY Female 76 yrs, male 69 yrs
ADULT LITERACY 96%

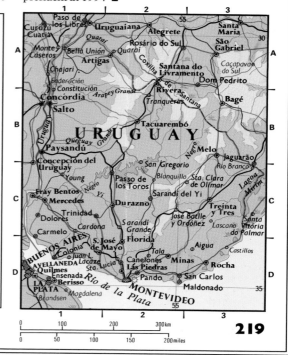

CHILE

Inspired by the US Stars and Stripes, the flag was designed by an American serving with the Chilean Army in 1817 and adopted that year. White represents the snow-capped Andes, blue is for the sky, and red is for the blood of the nation's patriots.

Chile has nearly every type of climate because of its latitudinal extent and the Andes in the east. In northern Chile is the arid Atacama Desert. Rainfall increases southwards and central Chile has a Mediterranean-type climate, with a dry season, November to March, a hot summer and warm winter. Monthly temperatures are never below 5°C [41°F]. In the south, westerly winds all year bring storms and high rainfall. Except in the mountains, Chile does not often experience very low temperatures.

Extending in an extraordinary shape down the west coast of South America from latitude 17°30'S, well inside the tropics, to 55°50'S at Cape Horn, Chile falls into three parallel zones based on the longitudinal folding of the Andes.

From the Bolivian border in the north down as far as 27°S runs an extension of the high plateau of Bolivia. Several volcanic peaks of more than 6,000 m [19,680 ft] mark the edge of the western cordilleras. South of Ojos del Salado the ranges narrow and steepen, then gradually reduce in height as they approach Cape Horn.

The parallel coastal ranges create a rolling, hilly belt, rising to 3,000 m [10,000 ft] or more in the north but generally much lower. Between this belt and the Andes runs the sheltered and fertile central valley, most clearly marked southwards from Santiago; over 60% of the population live in an 800 km [500 mls] stretch of land here.

A Spanish colony from the 16th century, Chile developed as a mining enterprise in the north and a series of vast ranches, or *haciendas*, in the fertile central region. After Chile finally freed itself from Spanish rule in 1818 mining continued to flourish in the north, and in the south Valparaiso developed as a port with the farmlands of the southern valley exporting produce to California and Australia.

The first Christian Democrat president was elected in 1964, but in 1970 he was replaced by President Allende; his administration, the world's first democratically elected Marxist government, was overthrown in a CIA-backed military coup in 1973 and General Pinochet took power as dictator, banning all political activity in a repressive regime. A new constitution took effect from 1981, allowing for an eventual return to democracy, and free elections finally took place in 1989. President Aylwin took office in 1990, but Pinochet secured continued office as commander-in-chief of the armed forces. In 1993, Eduardo Frei was elected president.

Chile's economy continues to depend on agriculture, fishing and, particularly, mining: the country is the world's largest producer of copper ore, and copper accounts for half of all export earnings. Magellanes, the southernmost region that includes Cape Horn and Tierra del Fuego (shared with Argentina), has oil fields that produce about half the country's needs. When the military took over in 1973, inflation was running at about 850%, despite government controls, and Pinochet reintroduced a market economy and abandoned agricultural reform. Economic decline began in 1981, due partly to low world prices for minerals, but by the late 1990s the economy was rapidly recovering ■

COUNTRY Republic of Chile

AREA 756,950 sq km [292,258 sq mls]

POPULATION 14,271,000

CAPITAL (POPULATION) Santiago (4,628,000)

GOVERNMENT Multiparty republic with a bicameral legislature

ETHNIC GROUPS Mestizo 92%, Amerindian 7%

LANGUAGES Spanish (official)

RELIGIONS Roman Catholic 81%, Protestant 6%

CURRENCY Peso = 100 centavos

ANNUAL INCOME PER PERSON US$2,160

MAIN PRIMARY PRODUCTS Copper, coal, petroleum, natural gas, gold, lead, iron ore

MAIN INDUSTRIES Food processing, wine, forestry, iron and steel, copper, cement

DEFENCE 2.7% of GNP

TOURISM 590,000 visitors per year

POPULATION DENSITY 19 per sq km [49 per sq ml]

LIFE EXPECTANCY Female 76 yrs, male 69 yrs

PRINCIPAL CITIES (POPULATION) Santiago 4,628,000 Concepción 312,000 Viña del Mar 312,000

ARGENTINA

The 'celeste' and white stripes, symbol of independence since 1810 around the city of Buenos Aires, became the national flag in 1816 and influenced other Latin American countries. A yellow May Sun, only used on the state flag, was added two years later.

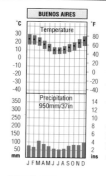

BUENOS AIRES
Temperature
Precipitation
950mm/37in

Argentina, stretching from the tropics almost into Antarctica, with the high Andes to the west and lying in the narrow neck of land between the two oceans, experiences many climates. The north is subtropical, with temperatures around 20°C [68°F] in June and 25°C [77°F] in January. The south is temperate, with May to August above freezing, and 10°C [50°F] in January or February. Rainfall is heaviest in the subtropical north-east and in Patagonia.

Largest of the Spanish-speaking countries of Latin America, but still less than a third of the size of Brazil, Argentina forms a wedge-shaped country from the Tropic of Capricorn to Tierra del Fuego. The western boundary lies high in the Andes, including basins, ridges and peaks of 6,000 m [19,685 ft] in the north. South of the latitude 27°S the ridges merge into a single high cordillera, the highest point being Aconcagua at 6,960 m [22,834 ft], the tallest mountain in the western hemisphere; south of 39°S the Patagonian Andes are lower, but include glaciers and volcanoes. Eastern Argentina is a series of alluvial plains, stretching from the Andean foothills to the sea. The Gran Chaco in the north slopes gradually towards the valley of the Paraná River, from the high desert in the foothills to lowland swamp forest. Further south are the extensive pampas grasslands, damp and fertile near Buenos Aires, drier but still productive elsewhere. Southwards again the pampas give way to the rougher and less hospitable plateaus of Patagonia.

Formerly a dependency of Peru, Argentina ('land of silver') was settled first in the north-west around Salta and San Miguel de Tucumán with strong links to Lima. This area is unusual today in retaining a largely mestizo (mixed Indian and Spanish) population, a remnant of colonial times. In 1776 Argentina, Uruguay, Paraguay and southern Bolivia were disengaged from Peru to form a separate viceroyalty, with its administrative centre in Buenos Aires. After a long war of independence the United Provinces of the Rió de la Plata achieved self-government under Simón Bolívar, but Uruguay, Bolivia and Paraguay separated between 1814 and 1828; it took many years of warfare and turbulence before Argentina emerged as a national entity in 1816, united and centred on Buenos Aires.

Early prosperity, based on stock raising and farming, was boosted from 1870 by a massive influx of European immigrants, particularly Italians and Spaniards for whom the Argentine was a real alternative to the USA. They settled lands recently cleared of Indians and often organized by huge land companies. Britain provided much of the capital and some of the immigrants; families of English and Welsh sheep farmers, still speaking their own languages, are identifiable in Patagonia today. Development of a good railway network to the ports, plus steamship services to Europe and refrigerated vessels, helped to create the strong meat, wool and wheat economy that carried Argentina through its formative years and into the 20th century.

Politics and economy

A military coup in 1930 started a long period of military intervention in the politics of the country. The period from 1976 – the so-called 'dirty war' – saw the torture, wrongful imprisonment and murder ('disappearance') of up to 15,000 people by the military, and up to 2 million people fled the country. In 1982 the government, blamed for the poor state of the economy, launched an ill-fated invasion of the Falkland Islands (Islas Malvinas), a territory they had claimed since 1820. Britain regained possession later that year by sending an expeditionary force, and President Galtieri resigned. Constitutional rule was restored in 1983 under President Raúl Alfonsín, though the military remained influential. The country's economic problems – with their classic Latin American causes of reliance on certain commodities, big borrowing (US$62 billion foreign debt) and maladministration – were inherited by his Peronist successor, Carlos Menem, in 1989. His austerity programme took Argentina through inflation rates of 3,084% and 2,314% down to 85% in 1991 – stable money by previous standards.

His policies of economic liberalization and reduction of state involvement may work. Certainly, Argentina is one of the richest of South America's countries in terms of natural resources, and its population – though remarkably urban, with 85% living in towns and cities – is not growing at anything like the rates seen in most of Africa and Asia. The population, predominantly European and mainly middle-class, nevertheless relies on an economic base that is agricultural: Argentina's farming industry exports wheat, maize, sorghum and soya beans as well as enormous quantities of meat, and produces sugar, oilseed, fruit and vegetables for home consumption. The chief industries, too, are based on food products, and the government aims to switch to manufacturing from agricultural processing. The manufacturing base is around Buenos Aires, where more than a third of the population live, and there is a strong computer industry. Argentina is nearly self-sufficient in petroleum production, and has copper and uranium reserves ∎

COUNTRY Argentine Republic

AREA 2,766,890 sq km [1,068,296 sq mls]

POPULATION 34,663,000

CAPITAL (POPULATION) Buenos Aires (10,990,000)

GOVERNMENT Federal republic

ETHNIC GROUPS European 85%, Mestizo, Amerindian

LANGUAGES Spanish (official), Italian, Guarani

RELIGIONS Roman Catholic 92%, Protestant 2%

CURRENCY Peso = 10,000 australs

ANNUAL INCOME PER PERSON US$7,290

MAIN PRIMARY PRODUCTS Coal, cattle, petroleum, natural gas, zinc, lead, silver

MAIN INDUSTRIES Food processing, wine, cotton yarn, cement, iron and steel, vehicles

EXPORTS US$286 per person

MAIN EXPORTS Vegetable products 43%, textiles and manufactures 4%

MAIN EXPORT PARTNERS Netherlands 10%, Brazil 9%, USA 8%

IMPORTS US$167 per person

MAIN IMPORTS Machinery 23%, chemicals and petrochemicals 21%, mineral products 13%

MAIN IMPORT PARTNERS USA 17%, Brazil 14%, Germany 11%, Bolivia 7%, Japan 7%

DEFENCE 1.7% of GNP

TOURISM 2,870,000 visitors per year

POPULATION DENSITY 13 per sq km [32 per sq ml]

INFANT MORTALITY 29 per 1000 live births

LIFE EXPECTANCY Female 75 yrs, male 68 yrs

ADULT LITERACY 96%

PRINCIPAL CITIES (POPULATION) Buenos Aires 10,990,000 Córdoba 1,198,000 Rosario 1,096,000 Mendoza 775,000 La Plata 640,000

THE PAMPAS

'Pampa' is a South American Indian word describing a flat, featureless expanse: the pampas are the broad, grassy plains that stretch between the eastern flank of the Andes and the Atlantic Ocean. Geologically, they represent outwash fans of rubble, sand, silt and clay, washed down from the Andes by torrents and redistributed by wind and water. Fine soils cover huge expanses of pampas, providing good deep soils in the well-watered areas, but scrub and sandy desert where rainfall and groundwater are lacking.

Early Spanish settlers introduced horses and cattle, and later the best areas of pampas were enclosed for cattle ranching and cultivation. Now the pampas are almost entirely converted to rangelands growing turf grasses (vehicles have mostly replaced the gauchos) or to huge fields producing alfalfa, maize, wheat and flax.

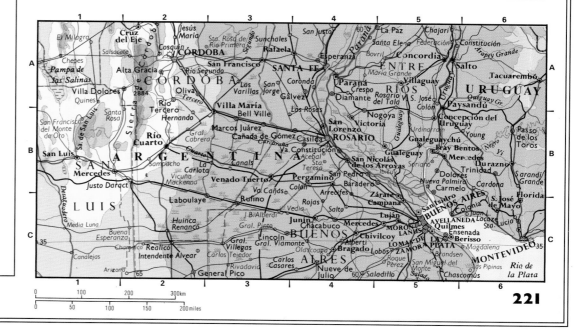

ATLANTIC OCEAN

BERMUDA

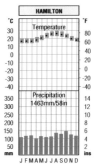

HAMILTON

Temperature

Precipitation 1463mm/58in

J F M A M J J A S O N D

Surrounded by the Atlantic and within the tropics has given Bermuda a mild and equable climate. There is no high land to give appreciable climatic variations. The annual average temperature is mild at about 22°C [72°C], with 10°C [18°F] difference between August (27°C [81°F]) and February (17°C [63°F]). Frosts are unknown, and every month has recorded a temperature higher than 27°C [81°F]. Rainfall is around 1,400 mm [55 in], evenly distributed through the year.

Comprising about 150 small islands, the coral caps of ancient submarine volcanoes rising over 4,000 m [13,000 ft] from the ocean floor, Bermuda is situated 920 km [570 mls] east of Cape Hatteras in North Carolina. Some 20 are inhabited, the vast majority of the population living on the biggest island of Great Bermuda, 21 km [13 mls] long and connected to the other main islands by bridges and causeways. The capital, Hamilton, stands beside a deep harbour on Great Bermuda.

Uninhabited when discovered by the Spaniard Juan Mermúdez in 1503, the islands were taken over by the British more than a century later (following a shipwreck), with slaves brought in from Virginia to work the land. Today, over 60% of the population is of African descent. The pleasant climate, coral sand beaches, historic buildings and pastel-coloured townships attract nearly 506,000 tourists each year, mainly from the USA, but if tourism is the mainstay of the economy, the islands are also a tax haven for overseas companies and individuals.

Food and energy needs dominate imports, while (legal) drugs and medicines account for 57% of exports – though services are the main earners, offsetting a large deficit and giving the islanders an annual per capita income of US$27,0800 (1994), the third highest in the world.

Bermuda remains Britain's oldest colony, but with a long tradition of self-government; the parliament dates from 1603. Ties with the USA are strong, however, and in 1941 part of the islands was leased for 99 years by Washington for naval and air bases. The government is in regular discussions with the USA, UK and Canada over constitutional change, but public opinion continues to oppose moves towards independence ■

COUNTRY British Colony
AREA 53 sq km [20 sq mls]
POPULATION 64,000
CAPITAL (POPULATION) Hamilton (6,000)
ETHNIC GROUPS Black 61%, White 37%
CURRENCY Bermuda dollar = 100 cents

CAPE VERDE

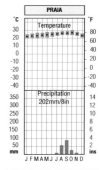

PRAIA

Temperature

Precipitation 202mm/8in

J F M A M J J A S O N D

The oceanic situation of the islands has the effect of tempering a tropical climate. The temperature ranges from 27°C [81°F] in September to 23°C [73°F] in February. Rainfall totals vary throughout the islands. Praia is nearly at the most southerly point in the islands and is one of the wettest regions, but its rainfall total is meagre. Rain falls from August to October, while the rest of the year is generally arid. Nearly all the islands have over 3,000 hours of sunshine in the year.

An archipelago of ten large and five small islands, divided into the Barlavento (windward) and Sotavento (leeward) groups, Cape Verde lies 560 km [350 mls] off Dakar. They are volcanic and mainly mountainous, with steep cliffs and rocky headlands; the highest, Fogo, rises to 2,829 m [9,281 ft] and is active. The islands are tropical, hot for most of the year and mainly dry at sea level. Higher ground is cooler and more fertile, producing maize, groundnuts, coffee, sugar cane, beans and fruit when not subject to the endemic droughts that have killed 75,000 people since 1900. Poor soils and the lack of surface water prohibit development.

Portuguese since the 15th century – and used chiefly as a provisioning station for ships and an assembly point for slaves in the trade from West Africa – the colony became an overseas territory in 1951 and independent in 1975. Linked with Guinea-Bissau in the fight against colonial rule, its socialist single-party government flirted with union in 1980, but in 1991 the ruling PAICV was soundly trounced in the country's first multiparty elections by a newly legalized opposition, the Movement for Democracy.

Cape Verde's meagre exports comprise mainly bananas (36%) and tuna fish (30%), but it has to import much of its food. The only significant minerals are salt and *pozzolana*, a volcanic rock used in making cement. Much of the population's income comes from foreign aid and remittances sent home by the 600,000 Cape Verdeans who work abroad – nearly twice the native population; in the last severe drought (1968–82), some 40,000 emigrated to Portugal alone. Tourism is still in its infancy – only 2,000 visitors a year – lagging well behind the Azores, Madeira and the Canaries. Economic problems have been compounded by tens of thousands of Angolan refugees ■

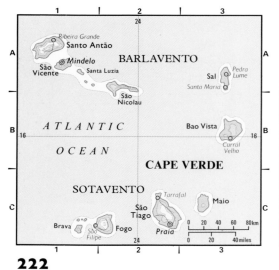

COUNTRY Republic of Cape Verde
AREA 4,030 sq km [1,556 sq mls]
POPULATION 386,000
CAPITAL (POPULATION) Praia (69,000)
ETHNIC GROUPS Mixed 71%, Black 28%, White 1%
LANGUAGES Portuguese (official), Crioulo
RELIGIONS Roman Catholic 97%, Protestant 2%
NATIONAL DAY 5 July; Independence Day (1975)
CURRENCY Cape Verde escudo = 100 centavos
ANNUAL INCOME PER PERSON US$750
MAIN PRIMARY PRODUCTS Maize, coffee, sugar, fruit
POPULATION DENSITY 96 per sq km [248 per sq ml]
LIFE EXPECTANCY Female 69 yrs, male 67 yrs
ADULT LITERACY 53%

COUNTRY Portuguese Autonomous Region
AREA 2,247 sq km [868 sq mls]
POPULATION 240,000
CAPITAL (POPULATION) Ponta Delgada (21,000)
CURRENCY Portuguese escudo = 100 centavos
POPULATION DENSITY 107 per sq km [276 per sq ml]

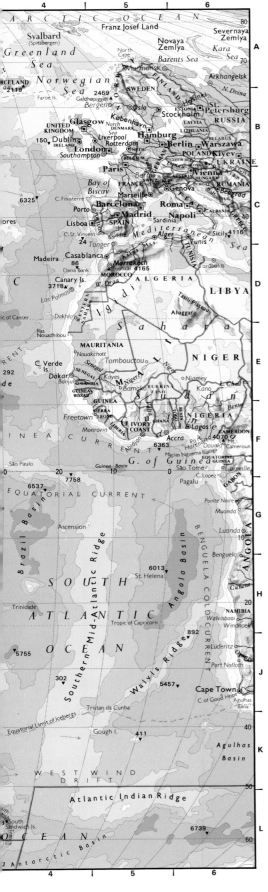

AZORES

Part of the Mid-Atlantic Ridge, the Azores consist of nine large and several small islands situated about 1,200 km [745 mls] west of Lisbon. They divide into three widely separated groups: São Miguel (759 sq km [293 sq mls] out of a total area of 2,247 sq km [868 sq mls]) and Santa Maria are the most easterly; 160 km [100 mls] to the north-west is the central cluster of Terceira, Graciosa, São Jorge, Pico and Faial; another 240 km [150 mls] to the north-west are Flores and the most isolated significant island of Corvo.

Of relatively recent volcanic origin, the islands are mostly mountainous, with high cliffs and narrow beaches of shell gravel or dark volcanic sand. Small-scale farming and fishing are the main occupations, with fruit, wine and canned fish exported (mostly to Portugal), but tourism is an increasingly important sector of the economy.

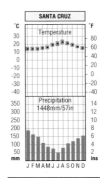

The variation between the hottest and coldest months is usually only about 10°C [18°F], with January to March being 14°C [57°F], and August 23°C [73°F]. Night temperatures rarely fall below 10°C [50°F] and the all-time record is only 29°C [84°F]. There is ample rain all through the year, but the months from December to March have over 150 mm [6 in] per month on average. Santa Cruz is on the most westerly island, and is wetter than the other islands.

The Azores have been Portuguese since the mid-15th century; there were no indigenous people, and its present population of 240,000 is mostly of Portuguese stock. Since 1976 they have been governed as three districts of Portugal, comprising an autonomous region. The capital is Ponta Delgada (population 21,000) on the island of São Miguel, which hosts more than half the total population ∎

MADEIRA

Madeira is the largest of the group of volcanic islands of that name lying 550 km [350 mls] west of the Moroccan coast and 900 km [560 mls] south-west of the national capital, Lisbon. Porto Santo and the uninhabited Ilhas Selvagens and Desertas complete the group, with a total area of 813 sq km [314 sq mls], of which Madeira itself contributes 745 sq km [288 sq mls].

With a warm temperate climate and good soils, Madeira was originally forested, but early settlers cleared the uplands for plantations. The islands form an autonomous region of Portugal ∎

COUNTRY Portuguese Autonomous Region
AREA 813 sq km [314 sq mls]
POPULATION 300,000
CAPITAL (POPULATION) Funchal (45,000)

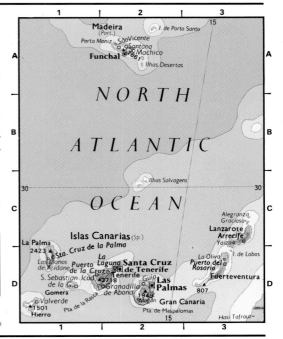

CANARY ISLANDS

The Canary Islands comprise seven large islands and numerous small volcanic islands situated off southern Morocco, the nearest within 100 km [60 mls] of the mainland. The 'inshore' islands of Lanzarote and Fuerteventura are low-lying, while the western group, including Gran Canaria and Tenerife, are more mountainous, the volcanic cone of Pico de Teide rising to 3,718 m [12,198 ft].

The islands, totalling 7,273 sq km [2,807 sq mls] in area, have a subtropical climate, dry at sea level but damp on higher ground. Soils are fertile, supporting farming and fruit growing, mainly by large-scale irrigation. Industries include food and fish processing, boat building and crafts.

Known to ancient European civilizations as the Fortunate Islands, the picturesque Canaries are today a major destination for both winter and summer tourists. Claimed by Portugal in 1341, they were ceded to Spain in 1479, and since 1927 have been divided into two provinces under the names of their respective capitals: Las Palmas de Gran

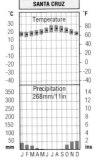

On the coasts of these islands in the Atlantic, the climate is of a Mediterranean type – low rainfall falling on only a few days in the winter months, frosts unknown, and the midday temperatures usually 20–25°C [68–77°F]. But most of the islands rise to central peaks of great height – high enough to carry snow throughout the year. There is thus a climatic variation from coast to peak, giving rise to a vegetation that ranges from arid to fairly dense stands of forest. The daily sunshine amount is 5–9 hours.

COUNTRY Spanish Autonomous Region
AREA 7,273 sq km [2,807 sq mls]
POPULATION 1,700,000
CAPITAL Las Palmas (342,000) / Santa Cruz (223,000)

Canaria (with a population of 342,000, one of Spain's largest cities), and Santa Cruz de Tenerife (population 223,000). The former (56% of the area) includes Gran Canaria, Lanzarote and Fuerteventura; the latter includes Tenerife, La Palma, Gomera and Hierro ∎

ATLANTIC OCEAN

GREENLAND

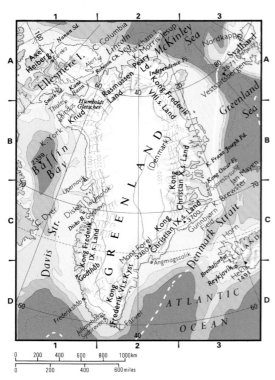

Recognized by geographers as the world's largest island (the Australian mainland being considered a continental land mass), Greenland is almost three times the size of the second largest, New Guinea. However, more than 85% of the land is covered in continuous permafrost, an ice cap with an average depth of about 1,500 m [5,000 ft], and though there are a few sandy and clay plains in the ice-free areas, settlement is confined to the rocky coasts.

The first recorded European to visit this barren desert was Eirike Raudi (Eric the Red), a Norseman from Iceland who settled at Brattahlid in 982. It was he who named the place Greenland – to make it sound attractive to settlers. Within four years, more than 30 ships had ferried pioneers there, founding a colony which would last five centuries.

Greenland became a Danish possession in 1380 and, eventually, an integral part of the Danish kingdom in 1953. After the island was taken into the EEC in 1973 – despite a majority vote against by Greenlanders – a nationalist movement developed and in 1979, after another referendum, a home rule was introduced, with full internal self-government following in 1981. In 1985 Greenland withdrew from the EEC, halving the Community's territory.

The economy still depends substantially on subsidies from Denmark, which remains its chief trading partner. The main rural occupations are sheep rearing and fishing – with shrimps, prawns and mollusks contributing over 60% of exports. The only major manufacturing is fish canning, which has drawn many Inuit to the towns; few now follow the traditional life of nomadic hunters.

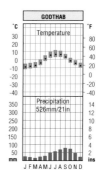

Altitude and latitude affect the climate of Greenland. Godthåb on the warmer south-west coast has over seven months with average temperatures below freezing. Similar temperatures have been recorded in all months. On the inland ice and in the north, the coldest average can be as low as –25 to –40°C [–13 to –40°F]. Precipitation is moderate in the south at around 1,000 mm [39 in], but this declines to less than 250 mm [10 in] in the north.

Most Greenlanders (a mixture of Inuit Eskimo and Danish extraction) live precariously between the primitive and the modern; in the towns, rates of alcoholism, venereal disease and suicide are all high. Yet the nationalist mood prevails, buoyed by abundant fish stocks, lead and zinc from Uummannaq in the north-west, untapped uranium in the south, and possibly oil in the east – and the increase in organized, adventure-oriented tourism. Independence is a daunting task, as the Danes point out: the island is nearly 50 times the size of the mother country with only 1% of the population. However, from 1 January 1997, Inuit name forms became official, emphasizing the resurgence of nationalism ■

COUNTRY Self-governing overseas region of Denmark
AREA 2,175,600 sq km [839,999 sq mls]
POPULATION 59,000

FALKLAND ISLANDS

Comprising two main islands and over 200 small islands, the Falkland Islands lie 480 km [300 mls] from South America. Windswept, virtually treeless, covered with peat moorland and tussock grass, the rolling landscape rises to two points of about 700 m [2,300 ft] – Mt Usborne in East Falkland and Mt Adam in West Falkland. Over half the population lives in (Port) Stanley, the capital situated in a sheltered inlet on East Falkland.

Discovered in 1592 by the English navigator John Davis, the Falklands were first occupied nearly 200 years later – by the French (East) in 1764 and the British (West) in 1765. The French interest, bought by Spain in 1770, was assumed by Argentina when it gained independence in 1806, and the Argentinians retained their settlements there. The British, who had withdrawn on economic grounds back in 1774, had never relinquished their claim, and in 1832 they returned to dispossess the Argentine settlers and start a settlement of their own – one that became a Crown Colony in 1892.

The prospect of rich offshore oil and gas deposits from the 1970s aggravated the long-standing dispute, and in 1982 Argentine forces invaded the islands (*Islas Malvinas* in Spanish) and expelled the Governor. Two months later – after the loss of 725 Argentinians and 225 Britons – the UK regained possession. Anglo-Argentine diplomatic relations were restored in 1990, but the UK refuses to enter discussions on sovereignty.

Life has since been based on the presence of a large British garrison, but in normal times the economy is dominated by sheep farming, almost the only industry, with over 40% of exports comprising high-grade wool, mostly to Britain. The UK gov-

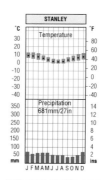

There is a constant westerly wind blowing in from over a cold sea, with gales many times a month. Rainfall is not high and is spread throughout the year, falling on about 150 days, with 50 of them as snow, which rarely settles. The wettest months are December and July. The average summer temperature is not high at 10°C [50°F] – the highest temperature ever recorded was only 24°C [75°F], but the winter minimum is not below freezing. The coldest known temperature was –11°C [12°F].

ernment is also funding a fishing development programme and helping with tourism.

South Georgia and **South Sandwich Island** ceased to be Falklands dependencies in 1985, though they are administered via Stanley. They have had no permanent population since 1966 ■

COUNTRY British Dependent Territory
AREA 12,170 sq km [4,699 sq mls]
POPULATION 2,000

ASCENSION stands in isolation on the Mid-Atlantic Ridge, a triangular volcanic island of 88 sq km [34 sq mls], with a single high peak, Green Mountain (859 m [2,817 ft]), surrounded by hot low-lying ash and lava plains. The mountain climate is cool and damp enough to support a farm, which supplies vegetables for the local community of about 1,500. Ascension has no native population. Administered from St Helena since 1922, its inhabitants are British, St Helenian or American, many of them involved in telecommunications, satellite research and servicing a mid-ocean airstrip ■

ST HELENA is an isolated rectangular, slab-sided island of old volcanic rocks, well off the main line of the Mid-Atlantic Ridge and measuring 122 sq km [47 sq mls]. A tableland deeply dissected by valleys, it has steep cliffs and ridges. The population of about 6,000, mainly of East Indian descent, produce potatoes and other vegetables and raise cattle, sheep and goats on smallholdings. Cultivable land is scarce and many are unemployed. St Helena, a British colony since 1834 and the administrative centre for six of the UK's South Atlantic islands, is heavily dependent on subsidies ■

TRISTAN DA CUNHA is the largest of four scattered islands towards the southern end of the Mid-Atlantic Ridge, a volcanic cone of 2,060 m [6,760 ft], ringed by a lava plain that drops steeply to the sea; a narrow strip of flat ground accommodates the settlement of about 330 inhabitants. The Nightingale and Inaccessible Islands are small, uninhabited islands nearby; Gough Island, 400 km [250 mls] to the south-east, is a craggy, forested island some 13 km [8 mls] long; its only settlement is a weather station. Like Ascension, all are administered as dependencies of St Helena ■

INDEX TO
COUNTRY
MAPS

HOW TO USE THE INDEX

The index contains the names of all the principal places and features shown on the country maps. Each name is followed by an additional entry in italics giving the country or region within which it is located. The alphabetical order of names composed of two or more words is governed primarily by the first word and then by the second. This is an example of the rule:

Ba Don, *Vietnam* **125** **C4**
Ba Ria, *Vietnam* **125** **G4**
Baa, *Indonesia* **129** **F11**
Bab el Mandeb, *Red Sea* . **132** **E8**
Babahoyo, *Ecuador* **212** **C1**

Physical features composed of a proper name (Erie) and a description (Lake) are positioned alphabetically by the proper name. The description is positioned after the proper name and is usually abbreviated:

Erie, L., *N.Amer.* **180** **E11**

Where a description forms part of a settlement or administrative name, however, it is always written in full and put in its true alphabetical position:

Lake City, *U.S.A.* **191** **H15**

Names beginning with M' and Mc are indexed as if they were spelled Mac. Names beginning St. are alphabetized under Saint, but Sankt, Sint, Sant', Santa and San are all spelt in full and are alphabetized accordingly. If the same place name occurs two or more times in the index and all are in the same country, each is followed by the name of the administrative subdivision in which it is located. The names are placed in the alphabetical order of the subdivisions. For example:

Clinton, *Iowa, U.S.A.* **191** **D12**
Clinton, *Mass., U.S.A.* ... **189** **A6**
Clinton, *Okla., U.S.A.* **190** **G9**

The number in bold type which follows each name in the index refers to the number of the page where that feature or place will be found.

The letter and figure which are in bold type immediately after the page number give the imaginary grid square on the map page, within which the feature is situated. This is formed by joining the black ticks outside each map frame. It does not relate to the latitude nor longitude except in the case of the physical maps of the continents.

In some cases the feature itself may fall within the specified square, while the name is outside. Rivers carry the symbol ➔ after their names. A solid square ■ follows the name of a country while, an open square □ refers to a first order administrative area.

Abbreviations used in the index

A.C.T. — Australian Capital Territory
Afghan. — Afghanistan
Ala. — Alabama
Alta. — Alberta
Amer. — America(n)
Arch. — Archipelago
Ariz. — Arizona
Ark. — Arkansas
Atl. Oc. — Atlantic Ocean
B. — Baie, Bahía, Bay, Bucht, Bugt
B.C. — British Columbia
Bangla. — Bangladesh
Barr. — Barrage
Bos. & H. — Bosnia and Herzegovina
C. — Cabo, Cap, Cape, Coast
C.A.R. — Central African Republic
C. Prov. — Cape Province
Calif. — California
Cent. — Central
Chan. — Channel
Colo. — Colorado
Conn. — Connecticut
Cord. — Cordillera
Cr. — Creek
Czech. — Czech Republic
D.C. — District of Columbia
Del. — Delaware
Dep. — Dependency
Des. — Desert
Dist. — District
Dj. — Djebel
Domin. — Dominica
Dom. Rep. — Dominican Republic
E. — East
El Salv. — El Salvador

Eq. Guin. — Equatorial Guinea
Fla. — Florida
Falk. Is. — Falkland Is.
G. — Golfe, Golfo, Gulf, Guba, Gebel
Ga. — Georgia
Gt. — Great, Greater
Guinea-Biss. — Guinea-Bissau
H.K. — Hong Kong
H.P. — Himachal Pradesh
Hants. — Hampshire
Harb. — Harbor, Harbour
Hd. — Head
Hts. — Heights
I.(s). — Île, Ilha, Insel, Isla, Island, Isle
Ill. — Illinois
Ind. — Indiana
Ind. Oc. — Indian Ocean
Ivory C. — Ivory Coast
J. — Jabal, Jebel, Jazira
Junc. — Junction
K. — Kap, Kapp
Kans. — Kansas
Kep. — Kepulauan
Ky. — Kentucky
L. — Lac, Lacul, Lago, Lagoa, Lake, Limni, Loch, Lough
La. — Louisiana
Liech. — Liechtenstein
Lux. — Luxembourg
Mad. P. — Madhya Pradesh
Madag. — Madagascar
Man. — Manitoba
Mass. — Massachusetts
Md. — Maryland
Me. — Maine

Medit. S. — Mediterranean Sea
Mich. — Michigan
Minn. — Minnesota
Miss. — Mississippi
Mo. — Missouri
Mont. — Montana
Mozam. — Mozambique
Mt.(e). — Mont, Monte, Monti, Montaña, Mountain
N. — Nord, Norte, North, Northern, Nouveau
N.B. — New Brunswick
N.C. — North Carolina
N. Cal. — New Caledonia
N. Dak. — North Dakota
N.H. — New Hampshire
N.I. — North Island
N.J. — New Jersey
N. Mex. — New Mexico
N.S. — Nova Scotia
N.S.W. — New South Wales
N.W.T. — North West Territory
N.Y. — New York
N.Z. — New Zealand
Nebr. — Nebraska
Neths. — Netherlands
Nev. — Nevada
Nfld. — Newfoundland
Nic. — Nicaragua
O. — Oued, Ouadi
Occ. — Occidentale
O.F.S. — Orange Free State
Okla. — Oklahoma
Ont. — Ontario
Or. — Orientale
Oreg. — Oregon
Os. — Ostrov

Oz. — Ozero
P. — Pass, Passo, Pasul, Pulau
P.E.I. — Prince Edward Island
Pa. — Pennsylvania
Pac. Oc. — Pacific Ocean
Papua N.G. — Papua New Guinea
Pass. — Passage
Pen. — Peninsula, Péninsule
Phil. — Philippines
Pk. — Park, Peak
Plat. — Plateau
P-ov. — Poluostrov
Prov. — Province, Provincial
Pt. — Point
Pta. — Ponta, Punta
Pte. — Pointe
Qué. — Québec
Queens. — Queensland
R. — Rio, River
R.I. — Rhode Island
Ra.(s). — Range(s)
Raj. — Rajasthan
Reg. — Region
Rep. — Republic
Res. — Reserve, Reservoir
S. — San, South, Sea
Si. Arabia — Saudi Arabia
S.C. — South Carolina
S. Dak. — South Dakota
S.I. — South Island
S. Leone — Sierra Leone
Sa. — Serra, Sierra
Sask. — Saskatchewan
Scot. — Scotland
Sd. — Sound
Sev. — Severnaya
Sib. — Siberia

Slovak — Slovak Republic
Sprs. — Springs
St. — Saint, Sankt, Sint
Sta. — Santa, Station
Ste. — Sainte
Sto. — Santo
Str. — Strait, Stretto
Switz. — Switzerland
Tas. — Tasmania
Tenn. — Tennessee
Tex. — Texas
Tg. — Tanjung
Trin. & Tob. — Trinidad & Tobago
U.A.E. — United Arab Emirates
U.K. — United Kingdom
U.S.A. — United States of America
Ut. P. — Uttar Pradesh
Va. — Virginia
Vdkhr. — Vodokhranilishche
Vf. — Virful
Vic. — Victoria
Vol. — Volcano
Vt. — Vermont
W. — Wadi, West
W. Va. — West Virginia
Wash. — Washington
Wis. — Wisconsin
Wlkp. — Wielkopolski
Wyo. — Wyoming
Yorks. — Yorkshire

A

A Coruña = La Coruña, *Spain* 63 A2
Aachen, *Germany* 58 D1
Aalborg = Ålborg, *Denmark* 42 B2
A'âli en Nîl □, *Sudan* 143 E5
Aalsmeer, *Neths.* 50 D3
Aalst, *Belgium* 51 B3
Aalten, *Neths.* 50 D5
Aarau, *Switz.* 60 A3
Aarberg, *Switz.* 60 B2
Aare →, *Switz.* 60 A3
Aargau □, *Switz.* 60 A3
Aarhus = Århus, *Denmark* 42 B2
Aarschot, *Belgium* 51 B4
Aba, *Nigeria* 151 F4
Âbâdân, *Iran* 103 D2
Abadla, *Algeria* 137 B2
Abagnar Qi, *China* 116 A3
Abak, *Nigeria* 151 G4
Abakaliki, *Nigeria* 151 F4
Abakan, *Russia* 91 H10
Abariringa, *Kiribati* 176 F6
Abashiri, *Japan* 121 B9
Abashiri-Wan, *Japan* 121 A9
Abau, *Papua N. G.* 173 C2
Abay, *Kazakstan* 90 J7
Abaya, L., *Ethiopia* 144 E3
Abaza, *Russia* 90 J9
Abbay = Nîl el Azraq →, *Sudan* 143 D5
Abbeville, *France* 55 A5
Abbieglassie, *Australia* 171 A6
Abbots Langley, *U.K.* 45 B2
Abbottabad, *Pakistan* 105 B5
Abéché, *Chad* 142 D2
Abengourou, *Ivory C.* 148 D6
Åbenrå, *Denmark* 42 D2
Abeokuta, *Nigeria* 151 E1
Aber, *Uganda* 156 B2
Abercorn = Mbala, *Zambia* 161 A5
Aberdare Ra., *Kenya* 157 D2
Aberdeen, *Australia* 171 D8
Aberdeen, *S. Africa* 163 G5
Aberdeen, *U.K.* 46 C7
Aberdeen, *S. Dak., U.S.A.* 190 C9
Aberdeen, *Wash., U.S.A.* 190 B2
Aberystwyth, *U.K.* 46 J5
Abidjan, *Ivory C.* 148 D5
Abilene, *U.S.A.* 190 H9
Abitibi L., *Canada* 187 K11
Abkit, *Russia* 91 C16
Abnûb, *Egypt* 139 C4
Abocho, *Nigeria* 151 E3
Aboisso, *Ivory C.* 148 D6
Abomey, *Benin* 150 D2
Abong Mbang, *Cameroon* 153 D2
Abonnema, *Nigeria* 151 G3
Aboso, *Ghana* 149 E1
Abou-Deïa, *Chad* 142 E2
Abrantes, *Portugal* 63 E2
Abri, *Sudan* 143 A4
Abrolhos Bank, *Brazil* 206 D6
Abrud, *Romania* 75 B2
Abruzzi □, *Italy* 67 E5
Absaroka Range, *U.S.A.* 190 C6
Abû al Khaşib, *Iraq* 102 E6
Abû 'Alî →, *Lebanon* 95 A2
Abu Ballas, *Egypt* 139 E2
Abu Dhabi = Abû Ẓāby, *U.A.E.* 101 B3
Abû Dis, *Sudan* 143 B5
Abû Du'ân, *Syria* 97 A4
Abu Hamed, *Sudan* 143 B4
Abû Kamâl, *Syria* 97 C5
Abu Matariq, *Sudan* 143 D2
Abu Qir, *Egypt* 139 A3
Abu Qireiya, *Egypt* 139 E6
Abu Qurqâs, *Egypt* 139 C4
Abû Simbel, *Egypt* 139 F4
Abu Tig, *Egypt* 139 C4
Abû Zabad, *Sudan* 143 D3
Abû Ẓāby, *U.A.E.* 101 B3
Abuja, *Nigeria* 151 D4
Abunã, *Brazil* 217 E3
Abunã →, *Brazil* 217 E3
Abwong, *Sudan* 143 E4
Aby, Lagune, *Ivory C.* 148 E6
Acajutla, *El Salv.* 196 D1
Acaponeta, *Mexico* 194 D3
Acapulco, *Mexico* 194 F5
Acarigua, *Venezuela* 211 A2
Accra, *Ghana* 149 D3
Acebal, *Argentina* 221 B4
Aceh □, *Indonesia* 128 A1
Achalpur, *India* 106 E3
Achill I., *Ireland* 46 G1
Achinsk, *Russia* 91 H10
Achisay, *Kazakstan* 93 A3
Acklins I., *Bahamas* 201 B3
Aconcagua, *Argentina* 220 E3
Açores, Is. dos = Azores, *Atl. Oc.* 223 C4
Acre = 'Akko, *Israel* 96 B2
Acre □, *Brazil* 217 D1
Acre →, *Brazil* 217 E2
Ad Dammām, *Si. Arabia* 99 C6
Ad Dawhah, *Qatar* 100 D3
Ad Dilam, *Si. Arabia* 99 D5
Ad Dīwānīyah, *Iraq* 102 D4
Ada, *Ghana* 149 D3
Adaja →, *Spain* 63 C4
Adam, Mt., *Falk. Is.* 224 A2
Adamaoua, Massif de l', *Cameroon* 153 C2
Adamawa Highlands = Adamaoua, Massif de l', *Cameroon* 153 C2
Adamello, Mt., *Italy* 67 A3
Adaminaby, *Australia* 171 F7
Adam's Bridge, *Sri Lanka* 110 B1
Adam's Peak, *Sri Lanka* 110 C2
Adana, *Turkey* 94 C4
Adapazarı, *Turkey* 94 A2
Adarama, *Sudan* 143 B5
Adaut, *Indonesia* 129 F15
Adda →, *Italy* 67 B3
Addis Ababa = Addis Abeba, *Ethiopia* 144 D3
Addis Abeba, *Ethiopia* 144 D3
Addlestone, *U.K.* 45 D2
Addo, *S. Africa* 163 H6
Adelaide, *Australia* 171 F2
Adelaide, *S. Africa* 163 H6
Adelaide Pen., *Canada* 186 D8
Aden = Al 'Adan, *Yemen* 100 C1
Aden, G. of, *Asia* 84 G8
Adendorp, *S. Africa* 163 G5
Adh Dhayd, *U.A.E.* 101 B3
Adi, *Indonesia* 129 D15
Adige →, *Italy* 67 B5
Adilabad, *India* 106 F4
Adirondack Mts., *U.S.A.* 191 C16
Adjim, *Tunisia* 138 C3
Adjohon, *Benin* 150 D2
Adjumani, *Uganda* 156 A1
Admer, *Algeria* 137 F4
Admiralty I., *U.S.A.* 193 B5
Admiralty Is., *Papua N. G.* 173 A2
Ado, *Nigeria* 151 E1
Ado Ekiti, *Nigeria* 151 E2
Adonara, *Indonesia* 129 F12
Adoni, *India* 107 E3
Adour →, *France* 55 G3
Adra, *Spain* 63 G6
Adrano, *Italy* 67 J6
Adrar, *Algeria* 137 C3
Adrasman, *Tajikistan* 93 C3
Adré, *Chad* 142 D3
Adrī, *Libya* 138 B2
Adriatic Sea, *Europe* 34 G9
Adua, *Indonesia* 129 D14
Adwa, *Ethiopia* 144 B3
Adzopé, *Ivory C.* 148 D5
Ægean Sea, *Europe* 34 H11
Æolian Is. = Eólie, Is., *Italy* 67 H6
Aerhtai Shan, *Mongolia* 112 B5
Afars & Issas, Terr. of = Djibouti ■, *Africa* 145
Afghanistan ■, *Asia* 104
'Afif, *Si. Arabia* 99 D4
Afikpo, *Nigeria* 151 F4
Afognak I., *U.S.A.* 193 B4
'Afrīn, *Syria* 97 A3
Afula, *Israel* 96 B2
Afyonkarahisar, *Turkey* 94 B2
Agadès = Agadez, *Niger* 141 C3
Agadez, *Niger* 141 C3
Agadir, *Morocco* 136 D2
Agano →, *Japan* 121 E6
Agapa, *Russia* 91 D10
Agats, *Indonesia* 129 E17
Agbélouvé, *Togo* 150 D2
Agboville, *Ivory C.* 148 D5
Agdam, *Azerbaijan* 82 D7
Agdash, *Azerbaijan* 82 C8
Agde, *France* 55 H6
Agdz, *Morocco* 136 D4
Agdzhabedi, *Azerbaijan* 82 D8
Agen, *France* 55 G4
Aginskoye, *Russia* 91 J13
Agnibilékrou, *Ivory C.* 148 C6
Agofie, *Ghana* 149 B3
Agra, *India* 106 B3
Ağri, *Turkey* 82 D4
Agri →, *Italy* 67 G8
Ağrı Dağı, *Turkey* 82 D6
Ağrı Karakose, *Turkey* 94 B7
Agrigento, *Italy* 67 K5
Agrinion, *Greece* 71 D2
Agua Prieta, *Mexico* 194 A2
Aguadas, *Colombia* 210 C1
Aguadilla, *Puerto Rico* 201 A1
Aguadulce, *Panama* 197 E5
Aguarico →, *Ecuador* 212 B3
Aguascalientes, *Mexico* 194 D4
Aguilas, *Spain* 63 G7
Aguja, Pta., *Colombia* 206 C1
Agulhas, C., *S. Africa* 163 H3
Agung, *Indonesia* 128 F8
Agur, *Uganda* 156 B2
Agusan →, *Phil.* 130 J5
Agvali, *Russia* 82 A7
Ahaggar, *Algeria* 137 E5
Ahamansu, *Ghana* 149 C3
Ahiri, *India* 106 F4
Ahlen, *Germany* 59 A3
Ahmadabad, *India* 106 D1
Ahmadnagar, *India* 106 F2
Ahmadpur, *Pakistan* 105 D5
Ahmedabad = Ahmadabad, *India* 106 D1
Ahmednagar = Ahmadnagar, *India* 106 F2
Ahoada, *Nigeria* 151 F3
Ahrax Pt., *Malta* 69 A2
Ahuachapán, *El Salv.* 196 D1
Ahvāz, *Iran* 103 C2
Ahwar, *Yemen* 100 C1
Aichi □, *Japan* 120 B7
Aigle, *Switz.* 60 D1
Aigrettes, Pte. des, *Réunion* 166 B1
Aigua, *Uruguay* 219 D3
Aigues-Mortes, *France* 55 G7
Aihui, *China* 113 A11
Aija, *Peru* 213 D2
Aim, *Russia* 91 F15
Aimere, *Indonesia* 129 F11
Ain □, *France* 55 E8
Aïn Beïda, *Algeria* 137 A5
Aïn Ben Tili, *Mauritania* 140 A3
Aïn Beni Mathar, *Morocco* 136 B6
Ain Dalla, *Egypt* 139 C2
Ain el Mafki, *Egypt* 139 C2
Ain Girba, *Egypt* 139 B1
Ain Qeiqab, *Egypt* 139 B1
Aïn-Sefra, *Algeria* 137 B3
Ain Sheikh Murzûk, *Egypt* 139 D2
Ain Sukhna, *Egypt* 139 B5
Ain Zeitûn, *Egypt* 139 B1
Aïn Zorah, *Morocco* 136 B6
Aïr, *Niger* 141 B4
Air Hitam, *Malaysia* 126 D2
Aire, I. del, *Spain* 65 A6
Aisne □, *France* 55 B6
Aisne →, *France* 55 B6
Aitape, *Papua N. G.* 173 A1
Aiud, *Romania* 75 B3
Aix-en-Provence, *France* 55 G8
Aix-la-Chapelle = Aachen, *Germany* 58 D1
Áíyina, *Greece* 71 E3
Aizuwakamatsu, *Japan* 121 F7
Ajaccio, *France* 55 H9
Ajanta Ra., *India* 106 F2
Ajdâbiyah, *Libya* 138 A4
'Ajmān, *U.A.E.* 101 B3
Ajmer, *India* 106 B2
Ajuy, *Phil.* 130 G4
Akaba, *Togo* 150 D2
Akanthou, *Cyprus* 95 A3
Akaroa, *N.Z.* 175 G4
Akashi, *Japan* 120 C5
Akçaabat, *Turkey* 82 C2
Akelamo, *Indonesia* 129 B14
Aketi, *Zaïre* 155 B4
Akhalkalaki, *Georgia* 82 B5
Akhaltsikhe, *Georgia* 82 B4
Akhelóös →, *Greece* 71 C2
Akhmîm, *Egypt* 139 D4
Akhty, *Russia* 82 B8
Akimiski I., *Canada* 187 J11
Akita, *Japan* 121 D7
Akjoujt, *Mauritania* 140 C1
Akka, *Morocco* 136 C3
'Akko, *Israel* 96 B2
Akkol, *Kazakstan* 90 K7
Akkol, *Kazakstan* 93 A4
Aklampa, *Benin* 150 C2
Aklavik, *Canada* 186 C5
Akmolinsk = Tselinograd, *Kazakstan* 90 H7
Akmuz, *Kyrgyzstan* 93 C8
Aknoul, *Morocco* 136 B5
Ako, *Nigeria* 151 C6
Akola, *India* 106 F3
Akordat, *Eritrea* 144 B2
Akosombo Dam, *Ghana* 149 D3
Akpatok I., *Canada* 187 F12
Akranes, *Iceland* 38 C2
Akreïjit, *Mauritania* 140 D3
Akron, *U.S.A.* 191 D14
Akrotiri Bay, *Cyprus* 95 C1
Aksarka, *Russia* 90 E8
Aksenovo Zilovskoye, *Russia* 91 H13
Akstafa, *Azerbaijan* 82 C6
Aksu, *China* 112 C2
Aksum, *Ethiopia* 144 B3
Aktau, *Russia* 90 H3
Aktogay, *Kazakstan* 90 K8
Aktyubinsk, *Kazakstan* 90 H5
Aktyuz, *Kyrgyzstan* 93 A8
Aku, *Nigeria* 151 E4
Akure, *Nigeria* 151 E2
Akureyri, *Iceland* 38 B4
Akusha, *Russia* 82 B8
Akwa-Ibom □, *Nigeria* 151 G4
Akyab, *Burma* 122 E1
Akzhar, *Kazakstan* 93 A4
Al 'Adan, *Yemen* 100 C1
Al 'Amādīyah, *Iraq* 102 A3
Al Amārah, *Iraq* 102 D6
Al 'Aqabah, *Jordan* 98 C1
Al Arak, *Syria* 97 C4
Al 'Arama, *Si. Arabia* 99 C5
Al Bāb, *Syria* 97 A3
Al Baḥrah, *Kuwait* 100 A1
Al Bārūk, J., *Lebanon* 95 C2
Al Başrah, *Iraq* 102 E6
Al Batrūn, *Lebanon* 95 B2
Al Biqā □, *Lebanon* 95 B2
Al Bu'ayrāt, *Libya* 138 A3
Al Duwādimi, *Si. Arabia* 99 C4
Al Fallūjah, *Iraq* 102 C4
Al Fāw, *Iraq* 102 E6
Al Fujayrah, *U.A.E.* 101 B3
Al Ḥadīthah, *Iraq* 102 C3
Al Hamdānīyah, *Syria* 97 B3
Al Hamīdīyah, *Syria* 97 C2
Al Hasa, *Si. Arabia* 99 C6
Al Ḥasakah, *Syria* 97 A5
Al Ḥawrah, *Yemen* 100 C2
Al Ḥayy, *Iraq* 102 D5
Al Ḥillah, *Iraq* 102 D4
Al Ḥillah, *Si. Arabia* 99 D5
Al Hindīyah, *Iraq* 102 D4
Al Hirmil, *Lebanon* 95 A3
Al Hoceïma, *Morocco* 136 A5
Al Ḥudaydah, *Yemen* 100 B1
Al Hufūf, *Si. Arabia* 99 C6
Al Irq, *Libya* 138 B5
Al Ittihad = Madīnat ash Sha'b, *Yemen* 100 C1
Al Jafr, *Jordan* 98 C2
Al Jaghbūb, *Libya* 138 B5
Al Jahrah, *Kuwait* 100 A1
Al Jamalīyah, *Qatar* 100 D3
Al Janūb □, *Lebanon* 95 D1
Al Jawf, *Libya* 138 C5
Al Jawf, *Si. Arabia* 99 B3
Al Jazirah, *Iraq* 102 C3
Al Jazirah, *Libya* 138 C5
Al Jubayl, *Si. Arabia* 99 C6
Al Junaynah, *Sudan* 143 D1
Al Karak, *Jordan* 98 B2
Al Khābūra, *Oman* 101 B2
Al Khalīl, *Jordan* 98 B1
Al Khawr, *Qatar* 100 D3
Al Khiyām, *Lebanon* 95 D2
Al Kufrah, *Libya* 138 D5
Al Kūt, *Iraq* 102 D5
Al Kuwayt, *Kuwait* 100 A1
Al Labwah, *Lebanon* 95 B3
Al Lādhiqīyah, *Syria* 97 B2
Al Luḥayyah, *Yemen* 100 B1
Al Madīnah, *Si. Arabia* 99 C3
Al-Mafraq, *Jordan* 98 A2
Al Majma'ah, *Si. Arabia* 99 C5
Al Manāmah, *Bahrain* 100 C3
Al Maqwa', *Kuwait* 100 A1
Al Marj, *Libya* 138 A4
Al Maṭlā, *Kuwait* 100 A1
Al Mawşil, *Iraq* 102 A3
Al Mayādin, *Syria* 97 B5
Al Minā', *Lebanon* 95 A2
Al Miqdādīyah, *Iraq* 102 C4
Al Mubarraz, *Si. Arabia* 99 C6
Al Mughayrā', *U.A.E.* 101 B2
Al Muḥarraq, *Bahrain* 100 C3
Al Mukallā, *Yemen* 100 B2
Al Mukhā, *Yemen* 100 C1
Al Musayyib, *Iraq* 102 D4
Al Owuho = Otukpa, *Nigeria* 151 E4
Al Qaḍimah, *Si. Arabia* 99 D3
Al Qaryatayn, *Syria* 97 C3
Al Qaşabát, *Libya* 138 A2
Al Qaṭ'ā, *Syria* 97 C5
Al Qaṭīf, *Si. Arabia* 99 C6
Al Qatrānah, *Jordan* 98 B2
Al Qaṭrūn, *Libya* 138 C3
Al Quds = Jerusalem, *Israel* 96 D2
Al Qunaytirah, *Syria* 97 D2
Al Qurnah, *Iraq* 102 E6
Al Quşayr, *Syria* 97 C3
Al 'Ulā, *Si. Arabia* 99 C2
Al Uqaylah ash Sharqīgah, *Libya* 138 B4
Al Uqayr, *Si. Arabia* 99 C6
Al Wakrah, *Qatar* 100 D3
Al Wusayl, *Qatar* 100 D3
Alabama □, *U.S.A.* 191 H13
Alabama →, *U.S.A.* 191 H13
Alagoas □, *Brazil* 217 E9
Alagoinhas, *Brazil* 217 E9
Alajuela, *Costa Rica* 197 D3
Alalapura, *Surinam* 214 E3
Alaminos, *Phil.* 130 D2
Alamogordo, *U.S.A.* 190 H7
Alamosa, *U.S.A.* 190 F7
Alanya, *Turkey* 94 C3
Alapayevsk, *Russia* 90 F6
Alaşehir, *Turkey* 94 C1
Alaska □, *U.S.A.* 193
Alaska, G. of, *Pac. Oc.* 180 D5
Alaska Peninsula, *U.S.A.* 193 B3
Alaska Range, *U.S.A.* 193 B4
Alataw Shankou, *China* 112 B3
Alatyr, *Russia* 81 C8
Alausi, *Ecuador* 212 C1
Alaverdi, *Armenia* 82 C5
Alawoona, *Australia* 171 F3
'Alayh, *Lebanon* 95 C2
Alaykel, *Kyrgyzstan* 93 D7
Alayor, *Spain* 65 A6
Alayskiy Khrebet, *Kyrgyzstan* 93 D5
Alazan →, *Azerbaijan* 82 B7
Alba, *Italy* 67 B2
Alba Iulia, *Romania* 75 C3
Albacete, *Spain* 63 E6
Albacutya, L., *Australia* 171 F3
Albania ■, *Europe* 70
Albany, *Australia* 170 D3
Albany, *Ga., U.S.A.* 191 H14
Albany, *N.Y., U.S.A.* 189 A5
Albany, *Oreg., U.S.A.* 190 B2
Albany →, *Canada* 187 J11
Albarracín, Sierra de, *Spain* 63 D7
Albemarle Sd., *U.S.A.* 191 F17
Alberche →, *Spain* 63 D4
Albert, L. = Mobutu Sese Seko, L., *Africa* 132 F7
Albert, L., *Australia* 171 F2
Albert Lea, *U.S.A.* 191 D11
Albert Nile →, *Uganda* 156 B1
Alberta □, *Canada* 186 G5
Alberti, *Argentina* 221 C4
Albertinia, *S. Africa* 163 H3
Albertville = Kalemie, *Zaïre* 155 E6
Albi, *France* 55 G5
Albina, *Surinam* 214 C5
Ålborg, *Denmark* 42 B2
Alborz, Reshteh-ye Kūhhā-ye, *Iran* 103 B3
Albula →, *Switz.* 60 C5
Albuquerque, *U.S.A.* 190 G7
Alburquerque, *Spain* 63 E2
Alcalá, *Spain* 63 G5
Alcalá de Henares, *Spain* 63 D5
Alcamo, *Italy* 67 J5
Alcañiz, *Spain* 63 C8
Alcántara, *Spain* 63 D3
Alcaraz, Sierra de, *Spain* 63 E6
Alcaudete, *Spain* 63 F5
Alcázar de San Juan, *Spain* 63 E5
Alchevsk = Kommunarsk, *Ukraine* 81 F5
Alcira, *Spain* 63 E7
Alcobaça, *Portugal* 63 D1
Alcoy, *Spain* 63 E7
Alcudia, *Spain* 65 A4
Alcudia, B. de, *Spain* 65 A4
Aldabra Is., *Seychelles* 132 G8
Aldan, *Russia* 91 G14
Aldan →, *Russia* 91 E14
Alderney, *Chan. Is.* 44 A2
Aldershot, *U.K.* 45 D1
Aleg, *Mauritania* 140 D1
Alegranza, *Canary Is.* 223 C3
Alegre, *Brazil* 215 A5
Alegrete, *Brazil* 217 J5
Aleisk, *Russia* 90 J8
Aleksandrovsk-Sakhalinskiy, *Russia* 91 G17
Aleksandrovskiy Zavod, *Russia* 91 J13
Aleksandrovskoye, *Russia* 90 G8
Além Paraíba, *Brazil* 215 B5
Alençon, *France* 55 C4
Alenuihaha Channel, *U.S.A.* 192 B3
Aleppo = Ḥalab, *Syria* 97 A3
Alès, *France* 55 G7
Alessándria, *Italy* 67 B2
Ålesund, *Norway* 40 E1
Aleutian Is., *Pac. Oc.* 193 B1
Alexander Arch., *U.S.A.* 193 B5
Alexander Bay, *S. Africa* 163 E1
Alexandra, *Australia* 171 G5
Alexandra, *N.Z.* 175 H2
Alexandretta = İskenderun, *Turkey* 94 D4
Alexandria = El Iskandarîya, *Egypt* 139 A3
Alexandria, *Canada* 186 G4
Alexandria, *S. Africa* 163 H6
Alexandria, *U.S.A.* 191 H11
Alexandrina, L., *Australia* 171 F2
Alexandroúpolis, *Greece* 71 B5
Alfenas, *Brazil* 215 B3
Alga, *Kazakstan* 90 H5
Algarve, *Portugal* 63 G1
Algeciras, *Spain* 63 H4
Algemesí, *Spain* 63 E7
Alger, *Algeria* 137 A4
Algeria ■, *Africa* 137
Alghero, *Italy* 67 F2
Algiers = Alger, *Algeria* 137 A4
Algoa B., *S. Africa* 163 H6
Alhama, *Spain* 63 F7
Alhambra, *U.S.A.* 190 G2
Alhucemas = Al Hoceïma, *Morocco* 136 A5
'Alī al Gharbī, *Iraq* 102 D5
Ali-Bayramly, *Azerbaijan* 82 D9
'Alī Khēl, *Afghan.* 104 D5
Aliákmon →, *Greece* 71 B3
Alibo, *Ethiopia* 144 D2
Alicante, *Spain* 63 F7
Alice, *S. Africa* 163 H6
Alice Springs, *Australia* 168 H11
Alicedale, *S. Africa* 163 H6
Aligarh, *India* 106 B3
Alipur, *Pakistan* 105 D5
Alipur Duar, *India* 106 B8
Aliwal North, *S. Africa* 163 F6
Aljustrel, *Portugal* 63 F2
Alkmaar, *Neths.* 50 C3
Allada, *Benin* 150 D2
Allahabad, *India* 106 C5
Allakh-Yun, *Russia* 91 E15
Allal Tazi, *Morocco* 136 B4
Allanmyo, *Burma* 122 E2
Allanridge, *S. Africa* 163 D6
'Allaqi, Wadi →, *Egypt* 139 F5
Allegheny →, *U.S.A.* 189 C1
Allegheny Mts., *U.S.A.* 180 F11
Allentown, *U.S.A.* 189 C4
Alleppey, *India* 107 G2
Alliance, *Surinam* 214 B4
Alliance, *U.S.A.* 190 D8
Allier □, *France* 55 E6
Allier →, *France* 55 D6
Allora, *Australia* 171 A9
Alluitsup Paa = Sydprøven, *Greenland* 224 D2
Alma Ata, *Kazakstan* 93 A8
Almada, *Portugal* 63 E1
Almadén, *Spain* 63 E4
Almalyk, *Uzbekistan* 93 C3
Almansa, *Spain* 63 E7
Almanzor, Pico de, *Spain* 63 D4
Almanzora →, *Spain* 63 G6
Almaty = Alma Ata, *Kazakstan* 93 A8
Almazán, *Spain* 63 C6
Almelo, *Neths.* 50 C6

Almendralejo, *Spain* 63 E3
Almería, *Spain* 63 G6
Almirante, *Panama* 197 E4
Almora, *India* 106 A4
Alnif, *Morocco* 136 D4
Aloi, *Uganda* 156 B2
Alon, *Burma* 122 D2
Alor, *Indonesia* 129 F12
Alor Setar, *Malaysia* 126 A1
Alougoum, *Morocco* 136 E3
Alpes-de-Haute-Provence □, *France* 55 G8
Alpes-Maritimes □, *France* 55 G9
Alphen, *Neths.* 50 D3
Alpine, *U.S.A.* 190 J7
Alps, *Europe* 34 F8
Alsace, *France* 55 C9
Alsask, *Canada* 186 J6
Alsásua, *Spain* 63 A6
Alta Gracia, *Argentina* 221 A2
Altagracia, *Venezuela* 211 A2
Altai = Aerhtai Shan, *Mongolia* 112 B5
Altamaha —►, *U.S.A.* 191 H15
Altanbulag, *Mongolia* 113 A7
Altay, *China* 112 B4
Altdorf, *Switz.* 60 C4
Alto Adige = Trentino-Alto Adige □, *Italy* 67 A4
Alto-Alentejo, *Portugal* 63 E2
Alto Cuchumatanes = Cuchumatanes, Sierra de los, *Guatemala* 196 C1
Alto Molocue, *Mozam.* 159 B3
Alton, *U.K.* 45 E1
Alton, *U.S.A.* 191 E12
Altoona, *U.S.A.* 189 C2
Altstätten, *Switz.* 60 A5
Altun Shan, *China* 112 D3
Altus, *U.S.A.* 190 G9
Alubijid, *Phil.* 130 J5
Alucra, *Turkey* 82 C1
Alusi, *Indonesia* 129 F15
Alvarado, *Mexico* 194 E6
Alvie, *Australia* 171 H4
Alwar, *India* 106 B3
Alxa Zuoqi, *China* 113 D7
Alyaskitovyy, *Russia* 91 D15
Alyata, *Azerbaijan* 82 D9
Am Dam, *Chad* 142 D2
Am-Timan, *Chad* 142 E2
Amadeus, L., *Australia* 168 C3
Amâdi, *Sudan* 143 F4
Amadi, *Zaïre* 155 A5
Amadjuak L., *Canada* 187 E11
Amagasaki, *Japan* 120 C5
Amalner, *India* 106 E2
Amami Ō Shima, *Japan* 121 H9
Amangeldy, *Kazakstan* 90 H6
Amapá, *Brazil* 217 B6
Amapá □, *Brazil* 217 B6
Amarillo, *U.S.A.* 190 G8
Amaro, Mt., *Italy* 67 E6
Amassama, *Nigeria* 151 G3
Amatikulu, *S. Africa* 163 E9
Amatitlán, *Guatemala* 196 C1
Amazon —►, *S. Amer.* 206 C4
Amazonas = Amazon —►, *S. Amer.* 206 C4
Amazonas □, *Brazil* 217 C3
Ambala, *India* 107 B2
Ambalangoda, *Sri Lanka* 110 D1
Ambalavao, *Madag.* 165 D2
Ambam, *Cameroon* 153 E2
Ambanja, *Madag.* 165 A3
Ambarchik, *Russia* 91 B15
Ambartsevo, *Russia* 90 G9
Ambato, *Ecuador* 212 C1
Ambatolampy, *Madag.* 165 C2
Ambatondrazaka, *Madag.* 165 C3
Amberg, *Germany* 58 E4
Ambergris Cay, *Belize* 196 A2
Ambikapur, *India* 106 D6
Ambilobé, *Madag.* 165 A3
Ambo, *Peru* 213 D3
Ambon, *Indonesia* 129 D13
Amboseli L., *Kenya* 157 E2
Ambositra, *Madag.* 165 D2
Ambriz, *Angola* 160 B2
Amderma, *Russia* 90 D7
Ameca, *Mexico* 194 E3
Ameland, *Neths.* 50 A4
Amen, *Russia* 91 A16
American Samoa ■, *Pac. Oc.* 177 G7
Americana, *Brazil* 215 B2
Amersfoort, *Neths.* 50 D4
Amersfoort, *S. Africa* 163 D8
Amersham, *U.K.* 45 B2
Amery, *Australia* 170 A2
Amery, *Canada* 186 H8
Ames, *U.S.A.* 191 D11
Amga, *Russia* 91 F14
Amga —►, *Russia* 91 E14
Amgu, *Russia* 91 J17
Amgun —►, *Russia* 91 G16
Amherst, *Canada* 187 K14
Amiata, Mte., *Italy* 67 D4
Amiens, *France* 55 B5
Amirante Is., *Seychelles* 84 J9
Amizmiz, *Morocco* 136 D3
Amlia I., *U.S.A.* 193 B2
'Ammān, *Jordan* 98 B2
Ammassalik = Angmagssalik, *Greenland* 224 D2
Amorgós, *Greece* 71 E5
Amoy = Xiamen, *China* 113 H10
Ampang, *Malaysia* 126 C1
Ampanihy, *Madag.* 165 E1
Ampenan, *Indonesia* 128 F9
Amper, *Nigeria* 151 D5
Ampthill, *U.K.* 45 A2
Amravati, *India* 106 E3
Amritsar, *India* 107 B2
Amroha, *India* 106 A4
Amsterdam, *Neths.* 50 C3
Amsterdam, *U.S.A.* 189 A5
Amudarya —►, *Uzbekistan* 90 J4
Amund Ringnes I., *Canada* 186 A9
Amundsen Gulf, *Canada* 186 C6
Amuntai, *Indonesia* 128 D8
Amur —►, *Russia* 91 G16
Amurang, *Indonesia* 129 B12
Amursk, *Russia* 91 H16
Amurzet, *Russia* 91 J16
Amyderya = Amudarya —►, *Uzbekistan* 90 J4
An Nabatīyah at Tahta, *Lebanon* 95 D1
An Nabk, *Syria* 97 C3
An Nafūd, *Si. Arabia* 99 B3
An Najaf, *Iraq* 102 D4
An Nāşirīyah, *Iraq* 102 E5
An Nhon, *Vietnam* 125 E5
An Nîl □, *Sudan* 143 B4
An Nîl el Abyad □, *Sudan* 143 D4
An Nîl el Azraq □, *Sudan* 143 D5
An Uaimh, *Ireland* 46 G3
Anabar —►, *Russia* 91 D12
Anaconda, *U.S.A.* 190 B5
Anacuao, Mt., *Phil.* 130 D3
Anadolu, *Turkey* 94 B2
Anadyr, *Russia* 91 A17
Anadyr —►, *Russia* 91 B17
Anadyrskiy Zaliv, *Russia* 91 A17
'Ānah, *Iraq* 102 C2
Anaheim, *U.S.A.* 190 G3
Anaklia, *Georgia* 82 B3
Analalava, *Madag.* 165 B2
Anambas, Kepulauan, *Indonesia* 128 B5
Anambas Is. = Anambas, Kepulauan, *Indonesia* 128 B5
Anamur, *Turkey* 94 D3
Anan, *Japan* 120 C5
Anār, *Iran* 103 C4
Anār Darreh, *Afghan.* 104 E1
Anatolia = Anadolu, *Turkey* 94 B2
Añatuya, *Argentina* 220 D4
Anaye, *Niger* 141 B5
Anbyŏn, *N. Korea* 118 D4
Anchorage, *U.S.A.* 193 B4
Ancohuma, Nevada, *Bolivia* 218 B1
Ancón, *Peru* 213 D2
Ancona, *Italy* 67 C5
Andalgalá, *Argentina* 220 C4
Andalucía □, *Spain* 63 G4
Andalusia, *U.S.A.* 191 H13
Andalusia □ = Andalucía □, *Spain* 63 G4
Andalusia, Reg., *Spain* 34 H6
Andaman Is., *Ind. Oc.* 84 G13
Andara, *Namibia* 162 A4
Anderlues, *Belgium* 51 D3
Andermatt, *Switz.* 60 C4
Anderson, *Ind., U.S.A.* 191 E13
Anderson, *S.C., U.S.A.* 191 G15
Anderson —►, *Canada* 186 C6
Andes, Cord. de los, *S. Amer.* 206 D2
Andhra Pradesh □, *India* 107 E3
Andijon = Andizhan, *Uzbekistan* 93 C5
Andikithira, *Greece* 71 F3
Andizhan, *Uzbekistan* 93 C5
Andkhvoy, *Afghan.* 104 B3
Andoany, *Madag.* 165 A3
Andong, *S. Korea* 118 F5
Andorra ■, *Europe* 63 B9
Andraitx, *Spain* 65 B3
Andreanof Is., *U.S.A.* 193 B1
Ándria, *Italy* 67 F7
Andriba, *Madag.* 165 C2
Andropov = Rybinsk, *Russia* 81 B6
Ándros, *Greece* 71 D4
Andros I., *Bahamas* 201 B1
Andújar, *Spain* 63 F4
Andulo, *Angola* 160 C3
Anécho, *Togo* 150 E2
Anergane, *Morocco* 136 D3
Aneto, Pico de, *Spain* 63 B8
Ang Thong, *Thailand* 123 G4
Ang'angxi, *China* 113 B11
Angara —►, *Russia* 91 G10
Angarsk, *Russia* 91 J11
Angaston, *Australia* 171 E2
Ånge, *Sweden* 40 E3
Angeles, *Phil.* 130 D2
Angerman —►, *Sweden* 40 E4
Angers, *France* 55 D4
Angkor, *Cambodia* 125 E2
Anglesey, *U.K.* 46 H5
Angmagssalik, *Greenland* 224 D2
Ango, *Zaïre* 155 A5
Angola ■, *Africa* 160
Angoulême, *France* 55 E4
Angoumois, *France* 55 E4
Angra dos Reis, *Brazil* 215 C4
Angren, *Uzbekistan* 93 C3
Anguilla ■, *W. Indies* 202 A1
Anholt, *Denmark* 42 B3
Anhua, *China* 116 H1
Anhui □, *China* 116 F4
Anhwei □ = Anhui □, *China* 116 F4
Anie, *Togo* 150 D2
Anin, *Burma* 122 G3
Anjou, *France* 55 D4
Anjouan, *Comoros Is.* 166 B2
Anjozorobe, *Madag.* 165 C2
Anju, *N. Korea* 118 D3
Anka, *Nigeria* 151 B3
Ankang, *China* 113 F8
Ankara, *Turkey* 94 B3
Ankazoabo, *Madag.* 165 D1
Ankazobe, *Madag.* 165 C2
Ankoro, *Zaïre* 155 E5
Anlu, *China* 116 G2
Anmyŏn-do, *S. Korea* 118 G4
Ann, C., *U.S.A.* 189 A6
Ann Arbor, *U.S.A.* 191 D14
Anna Regina, *Guyana* 214 B2
Annaba, *Algeria* 137 A6
Annam = Trung-Phan, *Vietnam* 125 D5
Annapolis, *U.S.A.* 189 D3
Annecy, *France* 55 E8
Anning, *China* 112 H6
Anniston, *U.S.A.* 191 G14
Annobón, *Atl. Oc.* 132 G4
Annotto B., *Jamaica* 199 A5
Annuello, *Australia* 171 F4
Anoka, *U.S.A.* 191 C11
Anqing, *China* 116 G3
Anren, *China* 116 J2
Ansbach, *Germany* 58 E3
Anse Boileau, *Seychelles* 166 C2
Anse Royale, *Seychelles* 166 C2
Anshan, *China* 116 B6
Anshun, *China* 113 H7
Ansirabe, *Madag.* 165 C2
Ansongo, *Mali* 140 E5
Ansudu, *Indonesia* 129 D18
Antabamba, *Peru* 213 E4
Antakya, *Turkey* 94 D4
Antalaha, *Madag.* 165 B3
Antalya, *Turkey* 94 C2
Antalya Körfezi, *Turkey* 94 C2
Antananarivo, *Madag.* 165 C2
Antelope, *Zimbabwe* 161 D2
Antequera, *Spain* 63 G4
Anti Atlas, *Morocco* 136 E3
Anti-Lebanon, *Lebanon* 95 C2
Anticosti, I. d', *Canada* 187 J14
Antigo, *U.S.A.* 191 C12
Antigua, *Guatemala* 196 C1
Antigua, *W. Indies* 202 D5
Antilla, *Cuba* 198 C6
Antioquia, *Colombia* 210 B1
Antipodes Is., *Pac. Oc.* 176 K6
Antofagasta, *Chile* 220 B3
Antongila, Helodrano, *Madag.* 165 B3
Antrim, *U.K.* 46 F3
Antrim, Mts. of, *U.K.* 46 F4
Antsalova, *Madag.* 165 C1
Antsiranana, *Madag.* 165 A3
Antsohihy, *Madag.* 165 B3
Antwerp = Antwerpen, *Belgium* 51 B3
Antwerpen, *Belgium* 51 B3
Antwerpen □, *Belgium* 51 B4
Anupgarh, *India* 106 A1
Anuradhapura, *Sri Lanka* 110 B2
Anvers = Antwerpen, *Belgium* 51 B3
Anxi, *China* 112 D5
Anyama, *Ivory C.* 148 D5
Anyang, *China* 116 E2
Anyi, *Jiangxi, China* 116 H3
Anyi, *Shanxi, China* 116 E1
Anzhero-Sudzhensk, *Russia* 90 H9
Ánzio, *Italy* 67 F5
Aomori, *Japan* 121 D7
Aoreora, *Morocco* 136 F1
Aosta, *Italy* 67 A1
Aoudéras, *Niger* 141 C4
Aouinet Torkoz, *Morocco* 136 F2
Aoulef el Arab, *Algeria* 137 D3
Apalachee B., *U.S.A.* 191 J14
Apapa, *Nigeria* 151 F1
Apaporis —►, *Colombia* 210 E3
Aparri, *Phil.* 130 B3
Apeldoorn, *Neths.* 50 D5
Apennines = Appennini, *Italy* 67 D4
Apia, *W. Samoa* 176 G6
Aplao, *Peru* 213 F4
Apollonia = Marsá Susah, *Libya* 138 A5
Apolo, *Bolivia* 218 B1
Apostle Is., *U.S.A.* 191 B12
Apostolos Andreas, C., *Cyprus* 95 A3
Apoteri, *Guyana* 214 D2
Appalachian Mts., *U.S.A.* 191 F15
Appennini, *Italy* 67 D4
Appingedam, *Neths.* 50 A6
Appledore, *U.K.* 45 E6
Appleton, *U.S.A.* 191 C12
Approuague —►, *Fr. Guiana* 214 C6
Apulia = Púglia □, *Italy* 67 F8
Apure —►, *Venezuela* 211 B3
Apurimac —►, *Peru* 213 D3
Aqabah = Al 'Aqabah, *Jordan* 98 C1
Âqcheh, *Afghan.* 104 B3
Aqîq, *Sudan* 143 B6
Aqmola = Tselinograd, *Kazakstan* 90 H7
'Aqrah, *Iraq* 102 A4
Aqtöbe = Aktyubinsk, *Kazakstan* 90 H5
Aquidauana, *Brazil* 217 G6
Aquin, *Haiti* 200 B1
Ar Rachidiya, *Morocco* 136 C5
Ar Ramādī, *Iraq* 102 C3
Ar Ramthā, *Jordan* 98 A2
Ar Raqqah, *Syria* 97 B4
Ar Riyāḍ, *Si. Arabia* 99 C5
Ar Ru'ays, *Qatar* 100 C3
Ar Ruşāfah, *Syria* 97 B4
Ar Ruṭbah, *Iraq* 102 C1
Ara, *India* 106 C6
'Arab, Bahr el —►, *Sudan* 143 D2
Arab, Khalîg el, *Egypt* 139 A3
Arabia, *Asia* 84 F8
Arabian Desert = Es Sahrâ' Esh Sharqîya, *Egypt* 139 C5
Arabian Gulf = The Gulf, *Asia* 84 F9
Arabian Sea, *Ind. Oc.* 84 G10
Aracaju, *Brazil* 217 E9
Aracataca, *Colombia* 210 A1
Aracati, *Brazil* 217 C9
Aracena, *Spain* 63 F3
Araçuaí, *Brazil* 217 F8
'Arad, *Israel* 96 E2
Arad, *Romania* 75 B1
Arada, *Chad* 142 D2
Aradhippou, *Cyprus* 95 B2
Arafura Sea, *E. Indies* 128 F16
Aragats, *Armenia* 82 C5
Aragón □, *Spain* 63 C7
Aragón —►, *Spain* 63 B6
Araguacema, *Brazil* 217 D6
Araguaia —►, *Brazil* 217 C7
Araguari, *Brazil* 217 G7
Arak, *Algeria* 137 D4
Arāk, *Iran* 103 B2
Arakan Yoma, *Burma* 122 E2
Arakli, *Turkey* 82 C2
Araks —►, *Iran* 34 H16
Aral Sea = Aralskoye More, *Asia* 90 J4
Aralsk, *Kazakstan* 90 J5
Aralskoye More, *Asia* 90 J4
Aran I., *Ireland* 46 E2
Aranjuez, *Spain* 63 D5
Aranos, *Namibia* 162 D3
Aransas Pass, *U.S.A.* 191 K10
Araouane, *Mali* 140 D4
Arapey Grande —►, *Uruguay* 219 A1
Araraquara, *Brazil* 215 B1
Ararat, *Australia* 171 G4
Ararat, Mt. = Ağrı Dağı, *Turkey* 82 D6
Araripe, Chapada do, *Brazil* 217 D8
Araruama, L. de, *Brazil* 215 C5
Arauca, *Colombia* 210 B2
Arauca —►, *Venezuela* 211 B3
Araya, Pen. de, *Venezuela* 211 A4
Arbatax, *Italy* 67 G2
Arbaza, *Russia* 91 J10
Arbīl, *Iraq* 102 A4
Arbroath, *U.K.* 46 C6
Arcachon, *France* 55 F3
Arcadia, *U.S.A.* 191 K15
Archangel = Arkhangelsk, *Russia* 90 D5
Archers Post, *Kenya* 157 C3
Arcila = Asilah, *Morocco* 136 A4
Arctic Bay, *Canada* 186 C9
Arctic Ocean, *Arctic* 84
Arctic Red River, *Canada* 186 C5
Arda —►, *Bulgaria* 73 D4
Ardabīl, *Iran* 103 A2
Ardahan, *Turkey* 82 C4
Ardèche □, *France* 55 F7
Ardenne, *Belgium* 51 E4
Ardennes = Ardenne, *Belgium* 51 E4
Ardennes □, *France* 55 B7
Ardeşen, *Turkey* 82 C3
Ardestān, *Iran* 103 C3
Ardingly, *U.K.* 45 E3
Ardlethan, *Australia* 171 E6
Ardmore, *U.S.A.* 191 G10
Ardrossan, *Australia* 171 E1
Arecibo, *Puerto Rico* 201 A1
Arendal, *Norway* 40 G1
Arendonk, *Belgium* 51 A4
Arenillas, *Ecuador* 212 E1
Arequipa, *Peru* 213 F4
Arero, *Ethiopia* 144 F3
Arévalo, *Spain* 63 C4
Arezzo, *Italy* 67 D4
Argentário, Mte., *Italy* 67 E4
Argentina ■, *S. Amer.* 220
Argentino, L., *Argentina* 220 K3
Argeş —►, *Romania* 75 D5
Arghandab —►, *Afghan.* 104 F2
Argo, *Sudan* 143 B4
Argolikós Kólpos, *Greece* 71 E3
Argonne, *France* 55 B7
Árgos, *Greece* 71 E3
Argostólion, *Greece* 71 D1
Argun —►, *Russia* 91 H14
Argungu, *Nigeria* 151 A2
Arhavi, *Turkey* 82 C3
Århus, *Denmark* 42 B2
Ariana, *Tunisia* 138 A2
Arica, *Chile* 220 A3
Arica, *Colombia* 210 E2
Aride, *Seychelles* 166 A2
Ariège □, *France* 55 H5
Arima, *Trin. & Tob.* 204 A3
Arinos —►, *Brazil* 217 E4
Aripuanã —►, *Brazil* 217 C4
Arîsh, W. el —►, *Egypt* 139 A5
Arizona, *Argentina* 221 C2
Arizona □, *U.S.A.* 190 G4
Arjona, *Colombia* 210 A1
Arka, *Russia* 91 E15
Arkalyk, *Kazakstan* 90 H6
Arkansas □, *U.S.A.* 191 G11
Arkansas —►, *U.S.A.* 191 G12
Arkansas City, *U.S.A.* 191 F10
Arkhangelsk, *Russia* 90 D5
Arklow, *Ireland* 46 H3
Arkticheskiy, Mys, *Russia* 91 B10
Arlanzón —►, *Spain* 63 B5
Arlberg, *Austria* 61 B1
Arles, *France* 55 G7
Arlington, *S. Africa* 163 D7
Arlon, *Belgium* 51 F5
Armagh, *U.K.* 46 F3
Armagnac, *France* 55 G4
Armavir, *Russia* 81 H6
Armenia, *Colombia* 210 C1
Armenia ■, *Asia* 82 C5
Armidale, *Australia* 171 C8
Armstrong, *Canada* 186 J9
Arnaouti, C., *Cyprus* 95 B1
Arnarfjörður, *Iceland* 38 B1
Arnaud —►, *Canada* 187 F12
Árnes, *Iceland* 38 B2
Arnhem, *Neths.* 50 D5
Arnhem, C., *Australia* 168 B3
Arnhem Land, *Australia* 168 B3
Arno —►, *Italy* 67 C3
Arno Bay, *Australia* 171 E1
Arnprior, *Canada* 185 B3
Arnsberg, *Germany* 59 A3
Aroab, *Namibia* 162 D3
Aroroy, *Phil.* 130 F4
Arrabury, *Australia* 171 A3
Arrah = Ara, *India* 106 C6
Arran, *U.K.* 46 E4
Arras, *France* 55 A6
Arrecife, *Canary Is.* 223 C3
Arrecifes, *Argentina* 221 B4
Arrée, Mts. d', *France* 55 C1
Arsin, *Turkey* 82 C2
Árta, *Greece* 71 C1
Artá, *Spain* 65 A5
Arteche, *Phil.* 130 G5
Artem, Ostrov, *Azerbaijan* 82 C9
Artemovsk, *Russia* 91 H10
Artesia, *U.S.A.* 190 H7
Arthington, *Liberia* 148 D1
Arthur —►, *Australia* 172 B1
Arthur's Pass, *N.Z.* 175 G3
Artigas, *Uruguay* 219 A2
Artik, *Armenia* 82 C5
Artois, *France* 55 A6
Artvin, *Turkey* 94 A6
Aru, Kepulauan, *Indonesia* 129 E16
Aru Is. = Aru, Kepulauan, *Indonesia* 129 E16
Arua, *Uganda* 156 A1
Aruanã, *Brazil* 217 F6
Arumpo, *Australia* 171 E4
Arun —►, *U.K.* 45 E2
Arunachal Pradesh □, *India* 107 B6
Arusha, *Tanzania* 158 B2
Aruvi —►, *Sri Lanka* 110 B1
Aruwimi —►, *Zaïre* 155 B4
Arvakalu, *Sri Lanka* 110 B1
Arvayheer, *Mongolia* 113 B7
Arxan, *China* 113 B10
Arys, *Kazakstan* 93 B2
Arys —►, *Kazakstan* 93 A2
Arzamas, *Russia* 81 C7
Arzew, *Algeria* 137 A3
Aş Şadr, *U.A.E.* 101 B3
As Safīrah, *Syria* 97 B3
As Salamīyah, *Syria* 97 B3
As Salt, *Jordan* 98 B2
As Sal'w'a, *Qatar* 100 D3
As Samāwah, *Iraq* 102 E4
As Sukhnah, *Syria* 97 B4
As Sulaymānīyah, *Iraq* 102 B4
Aş Şummān, *Si. Arabia* 99 C5
As Suwaydā', *Syria* 97 D2
As Şuwayrah, *Iraq* 102 D4
Asaba, *Nigeria* 151 F3
Asafo, *Ghana* 149 D1
Asahigawa, *Japan* 121 B8
Asamankese, *Ghana* 149 D2
Asansol, *India* 106 D7
Asbesberge, *S. Africa* 163 E4
Asbestos, *Canada* 185 B6
Asbury Park, *U.S.A.* 189 C5
Ascension I., *Atl. Oc.* 223 G4
Aschaffenburg, *Germany* 58 E3
Áscoli Piceno, *Italy* 67 D5
Ascope, *Peru* 213 C2
Ascot, *U.K.* 45 D1
Aseb, *Eritrea* 144 C4
Asela, *Ethiopia* 144 E3
Asfûn el Matâ'na, *Egypt* 139 D5
Ash, *U.K.* 45 D1
Ash Shamâl □, *Lebanon* 95 A2
Ash Shāmīyah, *Iraq* 102 D4
Ash Shāriqah, *U.A.E.* 101 B3
'Ash Shaṭrah, *Iraq* 102 E5

Ash Shawbak, *Jordan* 98 B1
Ash Shaykh, J., *Lebanon* .. 95 C2
Ash Shuwayfāt, *Lebanon* . 95 C1
Ashanti □, *Ghana* 149 C2
Ashburton, *N.Z.* 175 G3
Ashburton →, *Australia* .. 168 C1
Ashcroft, *Canada* 186 H4
Ashdod, *Israel* 96 D1
Ashdown Forest, *U.K.* 45 E4
Asheville, *U.S.A.* 191 F14
Ashford, *Australia* 171 B8
Ashford, *U.K.* 45 E6
Ashgabat = Ashkhabad, *Turkmenistan* 90 K3
Ashikaga, *Japan* 120 A8
Ashkhabad, *Turkmenistan* . 90 K3
Ashland, *Ky., U.S.A.* 191 E14
Ashland, *Wis., U.S.A.* 191 C11
Ashmûn, *Egypt* 139 B4
Ashqelon, *Israel* 96 D1
Ashton, *S. Africa* 163 H3
Ashuanipi, L., *Canada* 187 H13
Ashurstwood, *U.K.* 45 E4
Asia, Kepulauan, *Indonesia* 129 B15
Asidonhoppo, *Surinam* ... 214 D4
Asifabad, *India* 106 F4
Asike, *Indonesia* 129 E18
Asilah, *Morocco* 136 A4
Asinara, *Italy* 67 F1
Asinara, G. dell', *Italy* 67 F2
Asino, *Russia* 90 H9
'Asīr □, *Si. Arabia* 99 E3
Asir, Ras, *Somali Rep.* 145 A3
Aşkale, *Turkey* 82 D3
Askham, *S. Africa* 163 D3
Askja, *Iceland* 38 C4
Asl, *Egypt* 139 B5
Āsmār, *Afghan.* 104 C6
Asmara = Asmera, *Eritrea* 144 B3
Asmera, *Eritrea* 144 B3
Asni, *Morocco* 136 D3
Aspiring, Mt., *N.Z.* 175 H2
Assa, *Morocco* 136 F2
Assam □, *India* 107 C6
Assen, *Neths.* 50 B5
Assini, *Ivory C.* 148 E6
Assiniboia, *Canada* 186 J6
Assisi, *Italy* 67 D5
Astārā, *Azerbaijan* 82 D9
Asti, *Italy* 67 B2
Astipálaia, *Greece* 71 F6
Aston Clinton, *U.K.* 45 B1
Astorga, *Spain* 63 B3
Astoria, *U.S.A.* 190 B2
Astrakhan, *Russia* 81 G8
Asturias □, *Spain* 63 A3
Asunción, *Paraguay* 219 B2
Aswa →, *Uganda* 156 B3
Aswân, *Egypt* 139 E5
Aswân High Dam = Sadd el Aali, *Egypt* 139 E5
Asyût, *Egypt* 139 C4
Asyûti, Wadi →, *Egypt* .. 139 C4
At Ţafilah, *Jordan* 98 B2
At Tā'if, *Si. Arabia* 99 D3
Atacama, Desierto de, *Chile* 220 C3
Atakpamé, *Togo* 150 D2
Atalaya, *Peru* 213 D3
Atami, *Japan* 120 B8
Atapupu, *Indonesia* 129 F12
Atâr, *Mauritania* 140 C1
Atara, *Russia* 91 E14
Atasu, *Kazakstan* 90 J6
Atauro, *Indonesia* 129 F12
Atbara, *Sudan* 143 B5
'Atbara →, *Sudan* 143 B5
Atbasar, *Kazakstan* 90 H6
Atbashi, *Kyrgyzstan* 93 C8
Atbashi, Khrebet, *Kyrgyzstan* 93 C7
Atchafalaya B., *U.S.A.* 191 J12
Atchison, *U.S.A.* 191 E10
Atebubu, *Ghana* 149 C2
Ath, *Belgium* 51 C2
Athabasca, *Canada* 186 H5
Athabasca →, *Canada* ... 186 G6
Athabasca, L., *Canada* 186 G6
Athenry, *Ireland* 46 H1
Athens = Athínai, *Greece* . 71 D3
Athens, *U.S.A.* 191 G14
Athiéme, *Benin* 150 D2
Athienou, *Cyprus* 95 B2
Athínai, *Greece* 71 D3
Athlone, *Ireland* 46 H2
Áthos, *Greece* 71 B4
Athy, *Ireland* 46 H3
Ati, *Chad* 142 D2
Atiak, *Uganda* 156 A2
Atico, *Peru* 213 F4
Atimonan, *Phil.* 130 E3
Atka, *Russia* 91 D16
Atka, *U.S.A.* 193 B1
Atlanta, *U.S.A.* 191 G14
Atlantic City, *U.S.A.* 189 D5
Atlantic Ocean 222
Atlas Mts. = Haut Atlas, *Morocco* 136 C5
Atlin, *Canada* 186 E3
Atsuta, *Japan* 121 B7
Attawapiskat →, *Canada* . 187 J10
Attendorn, *Germany* 59 B3
Attleboro, *U.S.A.* 189 A6
Attock, *Pakistan* 105 B5
Attopeu, *Laos* 125 D4
Atyrau, *Kazakstan* 90 H3
Aube □, *France* 55 C7
Aube →, *France* 55 C6
Aubel, *Belgium* 51 C5
Auburn, *U.S.A.* 189 A3
Aubusson, *France* 55 E5
Auch, *France* 55 G4
Auchi, *Nigeria* 151 E3
Auckland, *N.Z.* 175 B5
Auckland Is., *Pac. Oc.* 176 K5
Aude □, *France* 55 H6
Aude →, *France* 55 H6
Augrabies Falls, *S. Africa* . 163 E3
Augsburg, *Germany* 58 F4
Augusta, *Italy* 67 K7
Augusta, *Ga., U.S.A.* 191 G15
Augusta, *Maine, U.S.A.* ... 191 B18
Augustów, *Poland* 77 A6
Auna, *Nigeria* 151 C2
Aunis, *France* 55 E3
Auponhia, *Indonesia* 129 D12
Aur, P., *Malaysia* 126 D3
Aurangabad, *Bihar, India* . 106 C6
Aurangabad, *Maharashtra, India* 106 F2
Aurillac, *France* 55 F6
Aurora, *S. Africa* 163 G2
Aurora, *U.S.A.* 191 D12
Aus, *Namibia* 162 D2
Austerlitz = Slavkov, *Czech.* 76 C5
Austin, *Minn., U.S.A.* 191 D11
Austin, *Tex., U.S.A.* 190 J9
Austral Seamount Chain, *Pac. Oc.* 176 H8
Australia ■, *Oceania* 168
Australian Alps, *Australia* . 171 G7
Australian Capital Territory □, *Australia* ... 171 F7
Austria ■, *Europe* 61
Autun, *France* 55 D7
Auvergne, *France* 55 F6
Auxerre, *France* 55 C6
Avallon, *France* 55 D7
Avaré, *Brazil* 215 C1
Aveiro, *Portugal* 63 D1
Avellaneda, *Argentina* 221 C5
Avellino, *Italy* 67 F6
Aversa, *Italy* 67 F6
Aveyron □, *France* 55 G6
Avignon, *France* 55 G7
Ávila, *Spain* 63 D4
Avilés, *Spain* 63 A3
Avoca →, *Australia* 171 F4
Avon →, *Australia* 170 B2
Avondale, *Zimbabwe* 161 B4
Avranches, *France* 55 C3
'Awālī, *Bahrain* 100 C3
Awash, *Ethiopia* 144 D3
Awaso, *Ghana* 149 D1
Awbārī, *Libya* 138 C2
Awgu, *Nigeria* 151 F4
Awjilah, *Libya* 138 B5
Axarfjörður, *Iceland* 38 A4
Axel Heiberg I., *Canada* ... 186 A9
Axim, *Ghana* 149 E1
Axminster, *U.K.* 46 L6
Ayaantang, *Eq. Guin.* 153 B2
Ayabaca, *Peru* 213 B2
Ayabe, *Japan* 120 B5
Ayacucho, *Argentina* 220 F5
Ayacucho, *Peru* 213 E3
Ayaguz, *Kazakstan* 90 K8
Ayamonte, *Spain* 63 G2
Ayan, *Russia* 91 F16
Ayaviri, *Peru* 213 E4
Āybak, *Afghan.* 104 B5
Ayenngré, *Togo* 150 C2
Ayíos Evstrátios, *Greece* .. 71 C4
Aylesbury, *U.K.* 45 B1
Aylesford, *U.K.* 45 D5
Aylmer, L., *Canada* 186 E7
Ayn Zālah, *Iraq* 102 A3
Ayni, *Tajikistan* 93 E2
Ayon, Ostrov, *Russia* 91 B16
Ayr, *U.K.* 46 E5
Aytos, *Bulgaria* 73 B5
Ayu, Kepulauan, *Indonesia* 129 C15
Ayutla, *Guatemala* 196 C1
Ayutla, *Mexico* 194 F5
Ayvalık, *Turkey* 94 B1
Az Zabdānī, *Syria* 97 C2
Az Ẓahrān, *Si. Arabia* 99 C6
Az Zarqā, *Jordan* 98 A2
Az Zubayr, *Iraq* 102 E6
Azamgarh, *India* 106 C6
Azārbayjan = Azerbaijan ■, *Asia* 82 D8
Azare, *Nigeria* 151 B6
A'zāz, *Syria* 97 A3
Azbine = Aïr, *Niger* 141 B4
Azemmour, *Morocco* 136 C3
Azerbaijan ■, *Asia* 82 D8
Azerbaijchan = Azerbaijan ■, *Asia* 82 D8
Azilal, *Morocco* 136 C4
Azogues, *Ecuador* 212 D1
Azores, *Atl. Oc.* 223 C4
Azov, *Russia* 81 G6
Azov, Sea of = Azovskoye More, *Europe* 81 G5
Azovskoye More, *Europe* . 81 G5
Azovy, *Russia* 90 E7
Azrou, *Morocco* 136 B4
Azúa de Compostela, *Dom. Rep.* 200 B3
Azuaga, *Spain* 63 F3
Azuay □, *Ecuador* 212 D1
Azuero, Pen. de, *Panama* . 197 E5
Azul, *Argentina* 220 F5

B

Ba Don, *Vietnam* 125 C4
Ba Ngoi = Cam Lam, *Vietnam* 125 F5
Ba Ria, *Vietnam* 125 G4
Ba Xian, *China* 116 C3
Baa, *Indonesia* 129 F11
Baarle Nassau, *Belgium* .. 51 A4
Baarn, *Neths.* 50 D4
Bab el Mandeb, *Red Sea* .. 132 E8
Babadayhan = Kirovsk, *Turkmenistan* 90 L4
Babahoyo, *Ecuador* 212 C1
Babakin, *Australia* 170 B3
Babana, *Nigeria* 151 C1
Babar, *Indonesia* 129 F14
Babi Besar, P., *Malaysia* .. 126 D3
Babine L., *Canada* 186 G3
Babo, *Indonesia* 129 D15
Bābol, *Iran* 103 B3
Baboua, *C.A.R.* 142 B1
Babruysk = Bobruysk, *Belarus* 81 D3
Babura, *Nigeria* 151 A5
Babuyan Chan., *Phil.* 130 B3
Babuyan I., *Phil.* 130 A3
Babuyan Is., *Phil.* 130 B3
Babylon, *Iraq* 102 D4
Bac Kan, *Vietnam* 125 A3
Bac Ninh, *Vietnam* 125 B3
Bac-Phan, *Vietnam* 125 A3
Bac Quang, *Vietnam* 125 A3
Bacan, *Indonesia* 129 F13
Bacan, Kepulauan, *Indonesia* 129 C13
Bacarra, *Phil.* 130 B2
Bacău, *Romania* 75 B5
Bachelina, *Russia* 90 G7
Back →, *Canada* 186 E8
Baco, Mt., *Phil.* 130 F2
Bacolod, *Phil.* 130 H4
Bacuag, *Phil.* 130 H5
Bacuk, *Malaysia* 126 A2
Bad Ischl, *Austria* 61 B4
Bad Lands, *U.S.A.* 190 D8
Badagara, *India* 107 F0
Badagri, *Nigeria* 151 F1
Badajoz, *Spain* 63 E2
Badakhshān □, *Afghan.* ... 104 B6
Badalona, *Spain* 63 C9
Badampahar, *India* 106 E7
Badas, *Brunei* 127 B1
Badas, Kepulauan, *Indonesia* 128 C5
Baddo →, *Pakistan* 105 E2
Bade, *Indonesia* 129 F18
Baden, *Austria* 61 B5
Baden, *Switz.* 60 A3
Baden-Baden, *Germany* .. 58 F2
Baden-Württemberg □, *Germany* 58 F3
Badgastein, *Austria* 61 B3
Bādghīsāt □, *Afghan.* 104 C2
Badin, *Pakistan* 105 F4
Badulla, *Sri Lanka* 110 C2
Baeza, *Ecuador* 212 B2
Baeza, *Spain* 63 F5
Bafatá, *Guinea-Biss.* 146 D2
Baffin B., *Canada* 187 C10
Baffin I., *Canada* 187 D10
Bafia, *Cameroon* 153 D2
Bafilo, *Togo* 150 C2
Bafing →, *Mali* 140 F2
Bafliyūn, *Syria* 97 A3
Bafoulabé, *Mali* 140 E2
Bāfq, *Iran* 103 C4
Bafwasende, *Zaïre* 155 B5
Bagamoyo, *Tanzania* 158 C3
Bagan Datoh, *Malaysia* ... 126 C1
Bagan Serai, *Malaysia* 126 B1
Baganga, *Phil.* 130 K6
Bagansiapiapi, *Indonesia* . 128 B3
Bagdarin, *Russia* 91 H13
Bagé, *Brazil* 217 K5
Baghdād, *Iraq* 102 C4
Bagherhat, *Bangla.* 111 D1
Baghlān, *Afghan.* 104 C5
Baghlān □, *Afghan.* 104 B5
Bagshot, *U.K.* 45 D1
Baguio, *Phil.* 130 D2
Bahadurabad Ghat, *Bangla.* 111 B1
Bahamas ■, *N. Amer.* 201
Baharampur, *India* 106 D8
Baharîya, El Wâhât al, *Egypt* 139 C3
Bahawalpur, *Pakistan* 105 D5
Bahía = Salvador, *Brazil* .. 217 E9
Bahía □, *Brazil* 217 E8
Bahía, Is. de la, *Honduras* . 196 B3
Bahía Blanca, *Argentina* .. 220 F4
Bahía de Caráquez, *Ecuador* 212 B1
Bahía Honda, *Cuba* 198 B2
Bahía Negra, *Paraguay* ... 219 A2
Bahr el Ahmar □, *Sudan* .. 143 B5
Bahr el Ghazâl □, *Sudan* .. 143 E2
Bahr Salamat →, *Chad* ... 142 E2
Bahr Yûsef →, *Egypt* 139 C4
Bahraich, *India* 106 B5
Bahrain ■, *Asia* 100
Bahret Assad, *Syria* 97 A3
Baia Mare, *Romania* 75 A3
Baie Comeau, *Canada* 187 J13
Baihe, *Taiwan* 117 B2
Ba'ījī, *Iraq* 102 B3
Baikal, L. = Baykal, Oz., *Russia* 91 J12
Baile Atha Cliath = Dublin, *Ireland* 46 H3
Bailundo, *Angola* 160 C3
Bainbridge, *U.S.A.* 191 H14
Baing, *Indonesia* 129 F11
Bā'ir, *Jordan* 98 B2
Baird Mts., *U.S.A.* 193 A4
Bairin Youqi, *China* 116 A4
Bairin Zuoqi, *China* 116 A4
Bairnsdale, *Australia* 171 H6
Bais, *Phil.* 130 H4
Baissa, *Nigeria* 151 E6
Baitadi, *Nepal* 109 A1
Baixo-Alentejo, *Portugal* .. 63 F1
Baiyin, *China* 113 E7
Baja, *Hungary* 74 C3
Baja, Pta., *Mexico* 194 B1
Baja California, *Mexico* ... 194 A1
Bajimba, Mt., *Australia* ... 171 B9
Bajoga, *Nigeria* 151 C6
Bakala, *C.A.R.* 142 B3
Bakchar, *Russia* 90 G8
Bakel, *Senegal* 146 B3
Baker, *U.S.A.* 190 C4
Baker, L., *Canada* 186 E8
Baker I., *Pac. Oc.* 176 F6
Baker Lake, *Canada* 186 E8
Baker Mt., *U.S.A.* 190 A3
Baker's Dozen Is., *Canada* . 187 H11
Bakersfield, *U.S.A.* 190 F2
Bākhtarān, *Iran* 103 B2
Bakkafjörður, *Iceland* 38 B5
Bakkagerði, *Iceland* 38 B6
Bakony Forest = Bakony Hegyseg, *Hungary* 74 B3
Bakony Hegyseg, *Hungary* . 74 B3
Bakori, *Nigeria* 151 B4
Bakouma, *C.A.R.* 142 B4
Baku, *Azerbaijan* 82 C9
Baky = Baku, *Azerbaijan* .. 82 C9
Bālā Morghāb, *Afghan.* ... 104 C2
Balabac I., *Phil.* 130 J1
Ba'labakk, *Lebanon* 95 B3
Balabalangan, Kepulauan, *Indonesia* 128 D9
Balaghat, *India* 106 E4
Balaguer, *Spain* 63 B8
Balaklava, *Australia* 171 E1
Balakovo, *Russia* 81 D8
Balashov, *Russia* 81 E7
Balasore = Baleshwar, *India* 106 E7
Balât, *Egypt* 139 D3
Balaton, *Hungary* 74 B2
Balayan, *Phil.* 130 E2
Balboa, *Panama* 197 E5
Balbriggan, *Ireland* 46 G3
Balcarce, *Argentina* 220 F5
Balchik, *Bulgaria* 73 B5
Balclutha, *N.Z.* 175 J2
Balcombe, *U.K.* 45 E3
Bald Hd., *Australia* 170 D3
Bald I., *Australia* 170 D3
Baldock, *U.K.* 45 A3
Baldwinsville, *U.S.A.* 189 A3
Baldy Peak, *U.S.A.* 190 G5
Baleares, Is., *Spain* 65 B4
Balearic Is. = Baleares, Is., *Spain* 65 B4
Baler, *Phil.* 130 D3
Baler Bay, *Phil.* 130 D3
Baleshwar, *India* 106 E7
Balfate, *Honduras* 196 C3
Bali, *Cameroon* 153 D1
Bali, *Indonesia* 128 F8
Balık Gölü, *Turkey* 82 D5
Balikeşir, *Turkey* 94 B1
Balikpapan, *Indonesia* 128 C9
Baling, *Malaysia* 126 A1
Balintang Channel, *Phil.* .. 130 A3
Balkan Mts. = Stara Planina, *Bulgaria* 73 B2
Balkh □, *Afghan.* 104 B4
Balkhash, *Kazakstan* 90 K7
Balkhash, Ozero, *Kazakstan* 90 K7
Ballarat, *Australia* 171 G4
Ballesteros, *Phil.* 130 B3
Ballidu, *Australia* 170 A2
Ballina, *Australia* 171 B9
Ballina, *Ireland* 46 G1
Ballymena, *U.K.* 46 F3
Balmoral, *Australia* 171 G3
Balmoral, *U.K.* 46 C6
Balonne →, *Australia* 171 B7
Balqash Kol = Balkhash, Ozero, *Kazakstan* 90 K7
Balrampur, *India* 106 B5
Balranald, *Australia* 171 E4
Balsas →, *Mexico* 194 E4
Balta, *Russia* 82 A5
Balta, *Ukraine* 81 F2
Bălţi = Beltsy, *Moldova* ... 81 F2
Baltic Sea, *Europe* 34 D10
Baltîm, *Egypt* 139 A4
Baltimore, *U.S.A.* 189 D3
Baluchistan □, *Pakistan* .. 105 E2
Balygychan, *Russia* 91 D16
Balzar, *Ecuador* 212 C1
Bam, *Iran* 103 D5
Bama, *Nigeria* 151 B7
Bamako, *Mali* 140 F3
Bamba, *Mali* 140 D5
Bambari, *C.A.R.* 142 B3
Bamberg, *Germany* 58 E4
Bambey, *Senegal* 146 B1
Bambili, *Zaïre* 155 A5
Bamenda, *Cameroon* 153 D1
Bāmīān □, *Afghan.* 104 C4
Bamiancheng, *China* 116 A6
Bampūr, *Iran* 103 D5
Ban Aranyaprathet, *Thailand* 123 H5
Ban Ban, *Laos* 125 B2
Ban Bua Chum, *Thailand* . 123 G4
Ban Bua Yai, *Thailand* 123 G5
Ban Don = Surat Thani, *Thailand* 123 K4
Ban Houei Sai, *Laos* 125 B1
Ban Hua Hin, *Thailand* ... 123 H4
Ban Kantang, *Thailand* ... 123 L4
Ban Khe Bo, *Vietnam* 125 C3
Ban Khun Yuam, *Thailand* 122 E3
Ban Mae Sot, *Thailand* ... 122 F3
Ban Me Thuot, *Vietnam* .. 125 F5
Ban Phai, *Thailand* 123 F5
Ban Thateng, *Laos* 125 D4
Banaba, *Kiribati* 176 F5
Banalia, *Zaïre* 155 B5
Banam, *Cambodia* 125 F3
Banamba, *Mali* 140 E3
Bananal, I. do, *Brazil* 217 E6
Banaras = Varanasi, *India* . 106 C5
Bancroft, *Canada* 185 B3
Band-e Torkestān, *Afghan.* 104 C2
Banda, *India* 106 C4
Banda, Kepulauan, *Indonesia* 129 E14
Banda Aceh, *Indonesia* ... 128 A1
Banda Banda, Mt., *Australia* 171 C9
Banda Elat, *Indonesia* 129 E15
Banda Is. = Banda, Kepulauan, *Indonesia* ... 129 E14
Banda Sea, *Indonesia* 129 E14
Bandai-San, *Japan* 121 F7
Bandama →, *Ivory C.* 148 E5
Bandanaira, *Indonesia* 129 E14
Bandar = Machilipatnam, *India* 107 E3
Bandār 'Abbās, *Iran* 103 E4
Bandar-e Anzalī, *Iran* 103 A2
Bandar-e Khomeyni, *Iran* . 103 D2
Bandar-e Lengeh, *Iran* 103 E4
Bandar-e Rīg, *Iran* 103 D3
Bandar-e Torkeman, *Iran* .. 103 B4
Bandar Maharani, *Malaysia* 126 D2
Bandar Penggaram, *Malaysia* 126 D2
Bandar Seri Begawan, *Brunei* 127 A3
Bandawe, *Malawi* 158 B2
Bandeira, Pico da, *Brazil* . 215 A5
Bandiagara, *Mali* 140 E4
Bandırma, *Turkey* 94 A1
Bandon, *Ireland* 46 K1
Bandundu, *Zaïre* 155 D2
Bandung, *Indonesia* 128 F5
Banes, *Cuba* 198 C6
Banff, *Canada* 186 H5
Banff, *U.K.* 46 B6
Banfora, *Burkina Faso* 149 B1
Bang Hieng →, *Laos* 125 D3
Bang Lamung, *Thailand* .. 123 H4
Bang Saphan, *Thailand* ... 123 J4
Bangala Dam, *Zimbabwe* . 161 D4
Bangalore, *India* 107 F3
Banggai, Kepulauan, *Indonesia* 129 D12
Banggi, P., *Malaysia* 126 A8
Banghāzī, *Libya* 138 A4
Bangka, *Sulawesi, Indonesia* 129 B12
Bangka, *Sumatera, Indonesia* 128 D5
Bangka, Selat, *Indonesia* . 128 D5
Bangkalan, *Indonesia* 128 E7
Bangkinang, *Indonesia* ... 128 C3
Bangko, *Indonesia* 128 D3
Bangkok, *Thailand* 123 H4
Bangladesh ■, *Asia* 111
Bangolo, *Ivory C.* 148 C3
Bangor, *U.K.* 46 F4
Bangor, *U.S.A.* 191 B18
Bangued, *Phil.* 130 C2
Bangui, *C.A.R.* 142 C3
Bangui, *Phil.* 130 B2
Bangweulu, L., *Zambia* ... 161 B4
Bani, *Dom. Rep.* 200 B3
Bani, Djebel, *Morocco* 136 C3
Banī Walīd, *Libya* 138 A3
Bania, *Ivory C.* 148 B6
Banīnah, *Libya* 138 A4
Bāniyās, *Syria* 97 B2
Banja Luka, *Bos.-H.* 72 B5
Banjarmasin, *Indonesia* ... 128 D8
Banjarnegara, *Indonesia* .. 128 F6
Banjul, *Gambia* 146 C1
Banket, *Zimbabwe* 161 B4
Bankipore, *India* 106 C6
Banks I., *Canada* 186 B7
Banks Pen., *N.Z.* 175 G4
Banks Str., *Australia* 172 A3
Bankura, *India* 106 D7
Banna, *Phil.* 130 C2
Banningville = Bandundu, *Zaïre* 155 D2
Bannockburn, *Zimbabwe* . 161 D3
Bannu, *Pakistan* 105 B4
Banská Bystrica, *Slovak Rep.* 76 C6
Banská Štiavnica, *Slovak Rep.* 76 C6
Banstead, *U.K.* 45 D3
Banswara, *India* 106 D2

Bantayan, *Phil.* 130 G4
Bantry, *Ireland* 46 K1
Banyak, Kepulauan, *Indonesia* 128 B1
Banyo, *Cameroon* 153 C2
Banyuwangi, *Indonesia* 128 F8
Banzyville = Mobayi, *Zaïre* 155 A3
Bao Vista, *C. Verde Is.* 222 B3
Baode, *China* 116 C1
Baoding, *China* 116 C3
Baoji, *China* 113 E7
Baokang, *China* 116 F1
Baoshan, *China* 112 H6
Baotou, *China* 116 B1
Baoying, *China* 116 F4
Ba'qūbah, *Iraq* 102 C4
Bar, *Montenegro, Yug.* 72 E6
Bar Harbor, *U.S.A.* 191 B18
Bar-le-Duc, *France* 55 C7
Barabai, *Indonesia* 128 D8
Barabinsk, *Russia* 90 H8
Baraboo, *U.S.A.* 191 D12
Baracaldo, *Spain* 63 A5
Baracoa, *Cuba* 198 C6
Baradero, *Argentina* 221 B5
Barahona, *Dom. Rep.* 200 B2
Barakpur, *India* 106 D8
Baran, *India* 106 C3
Baranavichy = Baranovichi, *Belarus* 81 D2
Baranof I., *U.S.A.* 193 B5
Baranovichi, *Belarus* 81 D2
Barapasi, *Indonesia* 129 D17
Barat Daya, Kepulauan, *Indonesia* 129 F13
Barbacena, *Brazil* 215 B4
Barbacoas, *Colombia* 210 D1
Barbados ■, *W. Indies* 204
Barberton, *S. Africa* 163 C9
Barbuda, *W. Indies* 202 C5
Barcelona, *Spain* 63 C9
Barcelona, *Venezuela* 211 A4
Barda, *Azerbaijan* 82 C7
Barddhaman, *India* 106 D8
Bardera, *Somali Rep.* 145 C1
Bardia, *Libya* 138 A6
Bareilly, *India* 106 B4
Barents Sea, *Arctic* 84 A7
Barentu, *Eritrea* 144 B2
Barga, *China* 112 F1
Barguzin, *Russia* 91 H12
Barhi, *India* 106 C7
Bari, *Italy* 67 F8
Bari Doab, *Pakistan* 105 D5
Barīm, *Yemen* 100 C1
Barima →, *Guyana* 214 A1
Barinas, *Venezuela* 211 B2
Baring, C., *Canada* 186 C6
Baringo, *Kenya* 157 C2
Baringo □, *Kenya* 157 C2
Baringo, L., *Kenya* 157 C2
Bârîs, *Egypt* 139 E4
Barisal, *Bangla.* 111 D2
Barito →, *Indonesia* 128 D8
Barking, *U.K.* 45 C4
Barkly East, *S. Africa* 163 F7
Barkly Tableland, *Australia* 168 B3
Barkly West, *S. Africa* 163 E5
Barlee, L., *Australia* 168 C1
Barletta, *Italy* 67 F7
Barmedman, *Australia* 171 E6
Barmer, *India* 107 C1
Barmera, *Australia* 171 E3
Barnato, *Australia* 171 D5
Barnaul, *Russia* 90 H8
Barnet, *U.K.* 45 C3
Barneveld, *Neths.* 50 D4
Barnsley, *U.K.* 46 G7
Barnstaple, *U.K.* 46 L5
Baro, *Nigeria* 151 D3
Baroda = Vadodara, *India* 106 E1
Baroe, *S. Africa* 163 H5
Barpeta, *India* 106 B9
Barquísimeto, *Venezuela* 211 A2
Barra, *Brazil* 217 E8
Barra do Piraí, *Brazil* 215 B4
Barra Falsa, Pta. da, *Mozam.* 159 E2
Barra Mansa, *Brazil* 215 B4
Barraba, *Australia* 171 C8
Barrackpur = Barakpur, *India* 106 D8
Barranca, *Lima, Peru* 213 D2
Barranca, *Loreto, Peru* 213 B2
Barrancabermeja, *Colombia* 210 B1
Barrancas, *Venezuela* 211 B5
Barrancos, *Portugal* 63 F2
Barranquilla, *Colombia* 210 A1
Barre, *U.S.A.* 191 C17
Barreiro, *Portugal* 63 E1
Barrie, *Canada* 185 C1
Barrier Ra., *Australia* 171 C3
Barrington Tops, *Australia* 171 D8
Barringun, *Australia* 171 B5
Barrow, *U.K.* 46 G6
Barrow, *U.S.A.* 193 A4
Barrow, C., *U.S.A.* 180 B4
Barry's Bay, *Canada* 185 B3
Barsham, *Syria* 97 B5
Barsi, *India* 107 E2
Barsoi, *India* 106 C8
Barstow, *U.S.A.* 190 F3
Bartica, *Guyana* 214 B2
Bartlesville, *U.S.A.* 191 F10
Barú, Volcan, *Panama* 197 E3
Barysaw = Borisov, *Belarus* 81 C3
Bas-Rhin □, *France* 55 C9
Basankusa, *Zaïre* 155 B3
Basel, *Switz.* 60 A2
Basellandschaft, *Switz.* 60 A2
Bashkir Republic □, *Russia* 90 G5
Bashkortostan = Bashkir Republic □, *Russia* 90 G5
Basilan, *Phil.* 130 K3
Basilan Str., *Phil.* 130 K3
Basildon, *U.K.* 45 C5
Basilicata □, *Italy* 67 F7
Basim = Washim, *India* 106 F3
Basirhat, *Bangla.* 111 D1
Basle = Basel, *Switz.* 60 A2
Basoka, *Zaïre* 155 B4
Basongo, *Zaïre* 155 D3
Basque Provinces = País Vasco □, *Spain* 63 B6
Basra = Al Başrah, *Iraq* 102 E6
Bass Str., *Australia* 172 A2
Bassano, *Canada* 186 J5
Bassano, *Italy* 67 A4
Bassar, *Togo* 150 C1
Basse Santa-Su, *Gambia* 146 C2
Bassein, *Burma* 122 F2
Basseterre, *St. Kitts & Nevis* 202 C2
Bassigny, *France* 55 C7
Bassikounou, *Mauritania* 140 E4
Bastar, *India* 106 F5
Basti, *India* 106 B5
Bastia, *France* 55 H9
Bastogne, *Belgium* 51 E5
Bat Yam, *Israel* 96 C2
Bata, *Eq. Guin.* 153 B1
Bataan, *Phil.* 130 E2
Batabanó, *Cuba* 198 B2
Batac, *Phil.* 130 B2
Batagoy, *Russia* 91 D14
Batalha, *Portugal* 63 D1
Batamay, *Russia* 91 E14
Batan I., *Phil.* 130 A3
Batanes Is., *Phil.* 130 A3
Batang, *China* 112 G6
Batangafo, *C.A.R.* 142 B2
Batangas, *Phil.* 130 E2
Batanta, *Indonesia* 129 C14
Batatais, *Brazil* 215 A2
Batavia, *U.S.A.* 189 A2
Bateman's B., *Australia* 171 F7
Batemans Bay, *Australia* 171 F7
Bath, *U.K.* 46 K6
Bath, *Maine, U.S.A.* 191 C18
Bath, *N.Y., U.S.A.* 189 A3
Bathurst = Banjul, *Gambia* 146 C1
Bathurst, *Australia* 171 E7
Bathurst, *Canada* 187 J14
Bathurst, *S. Africa* 163 H6
Bathurst, C., *Canada* 186 C6
Bathurst Harb., *Australia* 172 C2
Bathurst I., *Canada* 186 B8
Bathurst Inlet, *Canada* 186 D7
Batlow, *Australia* 171 F6
Batna, *Algeria* 137 A5
Batobato, *Phil.* 130 K6
Baton Rouge, *U.S.A.* 191 J12
Batouri, *Cameroon* 153 D3
Battambang, *Cambodia* 125 E2
Batticaloa, *Sri Lanka* 110 C3
Battle Creek, *U.S.A.* 191 D13
Battle Harbour, *Canada* 187 G15
Battlefields, *Zimbabwe* 161 C3
Battleford, *Canada* 186 H6
Batu, *Ethiopia* 144 E3
Batu, Kepulauan, *Indonesia* 128 C2
Batu Caves, *Malaysia* 126 C1
Batu Gajah, *Malaysia* 126 B1
Batu Is. = Batu, Kepulauan, *Indonesia* 128 C2
Batuata, *Indonesia* 129 E11
Batumi, *Georgia* 82 B3
Baturaja, *Indonesia* 128 D4
Baturité, *Brazil* 217 C9
Baubau, *Indonesia* 129 E11
Bauchi, *Nigeria* 151 C5
Bauchi □, *Nigeria* 151 C6
Bauru, *Brazil* 215 B1
Bautzen, *Germany* 58 D6
Bavaria = Bayern □, *Germany* 58 F4
Bawdwin, *Burma* 122 C3
Bawean, *Indonesia* 128 E7
Bawku, *Ghana* 149 A3
Bawlake, *Burma* 122 E3
Bay City, *U.S.A.* 191 C14
Bayambang, *Phil.* 130 D2
Bayamo, *Cuba* 198 C5
Bayamón, *Puerto Rico* 201 A2
Bayan Har Shan, *China* 112 F5
Bayan Hot = Alxa Zuoqi, *China* 113 D7
Bayan Obo, *China* 116 B1
Bayanaul, *Kazakstan* 90 J7
Bayanhongor, *Mongolia* 112 B6
Bayawan, *Phil.* 130 H3
Baybay, *Phil.* 130 H5
Bayburt, *Turkey* 82 C2
Bayern □, *Germany* 58 F4
Bayeux, *France* 55 B4
Baykal, Oz., *Russia* 91 J12
Baykit, *Russia* 91 G10
Baykonur, *Kazakstan* 90 J6
Bayombong, *Phil.* 130 D2
Bayonne, *France* 55 G3
Bayovar, *Peru* 213 B1
Bayram-Ali, *Turkmenistan* 90 L4
Bayreuth, *Germany* 58 E4
Bayrūt, *Lebanon* 95 B1
Baysun, *Uzbekistan* 93 F1
Bayt Lahm, *Jordan* 98 B1
Bayzhansay, *Kazakstan* 93 A3
Baza, *Spain* 63 G6
Bazar Dyuzi, *Russia* 82 B8
Bazaruto, I. do, *Mozam.* 159 D2
Beachport, *Australia* 171 G2
Beacon, *Australia* 170 A2
Beacon, *U.S.A.* 189 B5
Beaconsfield, *U.K.* 45 C2
Beagle Chan., *S. Amer.* 206 H2
Bear L., *U.S.A.* 190 D5
Béarn, *France* 55 H3
Bearsted, *U.K.* 45 D5
Beata, C., *Dom. Rep.* 200 B2
Beata, I., *Dom. Rep.* 200 B2
Beatrice, *U.S.A.* 191 E10
Beatrice, *Zimbabwe* 161 C4
Beau Bassin, *Mauritius* 166 B1
Beauce, *France* 55 C5
Beauchêne, I., *Falk. Is.* 224 A2
Beaudesert, *Australia* 171 A9
Beaufort, *Malaysia* 126 B7
Beaufort Sea, *Arctic* 180 B5
Beaufort West, *S. Africa* 163 G4
Beauharnois, *Canada* 185 B5
Beaujolais, Mts. du, *France* 55 E7
Beaumont, *U.S.A.* 191 J11
Beaune, *France* 55 D7
Beauvais, *France* 55 B5
Beauval, *Canada* 186 H6
Beaver →, *Canada* 186 H6
Beaver Dam, *U.S.A.* 191 D12
Beawar, *India* 106 C2
Bebedouro, *Brazil* 215 A1
Bečej, *Serbia, Yug.* 72 B7
Béchar, *Algeria* 137 B3
Beckley, *U.S.A.* 191 F15
Beckum, *Germany* 59 A3
Beddouza, Ras, *Morocco* 136 C2
Bedford, *S. Africa* 163 H6
Bedford, *U.K.* 46 J8
Bedford, *U.S.A.* 191 E13
Beenleigh, *Australia* 171 A9
Be'er Sheva', *Israel* 96 E2
Beersheba = Be'er Sheva', *Israel* 96 E2
Befale, *Zaïre* 155 B3
Bega, *Australia* 171 G7
Bei Jiang →, *China* 113 H9
Bei'an, *China* 113 B11
Beibei, *China* 113 G7
Beigang, *Taiwan* 117 B2
Beihai, *China* 113 J8
Beijing, *China* 116 C3
Beijing □, *China* 116 C3
Beilen, *Neths.* 50 B5
Beilpajah, *Australia* 171 D4
Beira, *Mozam.* 159 D2
Beira-Alta, *Portugal* 63 C2
Beira-Baixa, *Portugal* 63 D2
Beira-Litoral, *Portugal* 63 D1
Beirut = Bayrūt, *Lebanon* 95 B1
Beit Bridge, *Zimbabwe* 161 E3
Beizhen, *China* 116 D4
Beja, *Portugal* 63 F2
Béja, *Tunisia* 138 A2
Bejaia, *Algeria* 137 A5
Bekabad, *Uzbekistan* 93 D3
Békéscsaba, *Hungary* 74 B5
Bekok, *Malaysia* 126 D2
Bekwai, *Ghana* 149 D2
Bela, *India* 106 C5
Bela, *Pakistan* 105 F3
Bela Crkva, *Serbia, Yug.* 72 B8
Belarus ■, *Europe* 81 D2
Belau = Palau■, *Pac. Oc.* 176 E2
Belawan, *Indonesia* 128 A2
Belaya Tserkov, *Ukraine* 81 E3
Belcher Chan., *Canada* 186 B9
Belcher Is., *Canada* 187 H11
Belém, *Brazil* 217 B7
Belén, *Paraguay* 219 B2
Belev, *Russia* 81 D5
Belfast, *S. Africa* 163 C8
Belfast, *U.K.* 46 F4
Belfort, *France* 55 D8
Belfort, Territoire de □, *France* 55 D8
Belgaum, *India* 107 E2
Belgium ■, *Europe* 51
Belgorod, *Russia* 81 E5
Belgorod-Dnestrovskiy, *Ukraine* 81 G3
Belgrade = Beograd, *Serbia, Yug.* 72 B7
Belinga, *Gabon* 154 B2
Belinyu, *Indonesia* 128 C5
Beliton Is. = Belitung, Pulau, *Indonesia* 128 D5
Belitung, Pulau, *Indonesia* 128 D5
Belize ■, *Cent. Amer.* 196
Belize City, *Belize* 196 A2
Belkovskiy, Ostrov, *Russia* 91 B13
Bell Bay, *Australia* 172 B2
Bell I., *Canada* 187 H16
Bell Peninsula, *Canada* 187 F10
Bell Ville, *Argentina* 221 B3
Bella Coola, *Canada* 186 G3
Bella Unión, *Uruguay* 219 A1
Bellary, *India* 107 E2
Bellata, *Australia* 171 C7
Belle-Ile, *France* 55 D2
Belle Isle, *Canada* 187 G15
Belle Isle, Str. of, *Canada* 187 H15
Belle Yella, *Liberia* 148 C2
Bellefonte, *U.S.A.* 189 C3
Belleville, *Canada* 185 C3
Belleville, *U.S.A.* 191 F12
Bellingen, *Australia* 171 C9
Bellingham, *U.S.A.* 190 A3
Bellinzona, *Switz.* 60 D4
Belluno, *Italy* 67 A5
Bélmez, *Spain* 63 F4
Belmont, *Australia* 171 E8
Belmont, *S. Africa* 163 E5
Belmopan, *Belize* 196 B2
Belo Horizonte, *Brazil* 215 A4
Belo-Tsiribihina, *Madag.* 165 C1
Belogorsk, *Russia* 91 H15
Beloit, *U.S.A.* 191 D12
Belomorsk, *Russia* 90 C5
Belorussia = Belarus ■, *Europe* 81 D2
Belovo, *Russia* 90 H9
Beloye More, *Russia* 90 C5
Beltana, *Australia* 171 C1
Belton, *U.S.A.* 190 J9
Beltsy, *Moldova* 81 F2
Belukha, *Russia* 90 J9
Beluran, *Malaysia* 126 A8
Belyy, Ostrov, *Russia* 90 C9
Belyy Yar, *Russia* 90 G9
Belyye Vody, *Kazakstan* 93 B3
Bembéréke, *Benin* 150 B3
Bembesi, *Zimbabwe* 161 D3
Bembesi →, *Zimbabwe* 161 D3
Bemidji, *U.S.A.* 191 B10
Ben Gardane, *Tunisia* 138 D3
Ben Lomond, *N.S.W., Australia* 171 C8
Ben Lomond, *Tas., Australia* 172 B3
Ben Nevis, *U.K.* 46 C4
Ben Slimane, *Morocco* 136 B4
Bena, *Nigeria* 151 B3
Bena Dibele, *Zaïre* 155 D4
Benagerie, *Australia* 171 D2
Benahmed, *Morocco* 136 C3
Benalla, *Australia* 171 G5
Benares = Varanasi, *India* 106 C5
Benbonyathe Hill, *Australia* 171 C2
Bencubbin, *Australia* 170 A2
Bend, *U.S.A.* 190 C3
Bender Beila, *Somali Rep.* 145 B3
Bendering, *Australia* 170 B3
Bendery, *Moldova* 81 G2
Bendigo, *Australia* 171 G4
Benē Beraq, *Israel* 96 C2
Benevento, *Italy* 67 F6
Bengal, Bay of, *Ind. Oc.* 84 G12
Bengbu, *China* 116 F4
Benghazi = Banghāzī, *Libya* 138 A4
Bengkalis, *Indonesia* 128 B3
Bengkulu, *Indonesia* 128 D3
Bengkulu □, *Indonesia* 128 D3
Benguela, *Angola* 160 C2
Benguerir, *Morocco* 136 C3
Benha, *Egypt* 139 B4
Beni, *Zaïre* 155 B6
Beni →, *Bolivia* 218 A1
Beni Abbès, *Algeria* 137 C2
Beni Mazâr, *Egypt* 139 C4
Beni Mellal, *Morocco* 136 C4
Beni Ounif, *Algeria* 137 B3
Beni Suef, *Egypt* 139 B4
Benidorm, *Spain* 63 E8
Benin ■, *Africa* 150
Benin, Bight of, *W. Afr.* 132 F4
Benin City, *Nigeria* 151 F2
Benjamin Constant, *Brazil* 217 C2
Bennett, Ostrov, *Russia* 91 B13
Bennington, *U.S.A.* 189 A5
Benoni, *S. Africa* 163 C7
Benque Viejo, *Belize* 196 B2
Benteng, *Indonesia* 129 E10
Bentley, *U.K.* 45 E1
Bentung, *Malaysia* 126 C1
Benue □, *Nigeria* 151 E4
Benue →, *Nigeria* 132 F4
Benxi, *China* 116 B6
Benzdorp, *Surinam* 214 D5
Beo, *Indonesia* 129 A13
Beograd, *Serbia, Yug.* 72 B7
Beppu, *Japan* 120 D2
Beqaa Valley = Al Biqā □, *Lebanon* 95 B2
Berau, Teluk, *Indonesia* 129 D15
Berber, *Sudan* 143 B5
Berbera, *Somali Rep.* 145 B2
Berbérati, *C.A.R.* 142 C2
Berberia, C. del, *Spain* 65 C2
Berbice →, *Guyana* 214 B3
Berdichev, *Ukraine* 81 E2
Berdsk, *Russia* 90 H9
Berdyansk, *Ukraine* 81 G5
Berdychiv = Berdichev, *Ukraine* 81 E2
Berebere, *Indonesia* 129 B14
Berekum, *Ghana* 149 C1
Berenice, *Egypt* 139 E6
Berezina →, *Belarus* 81 D3
Berezniki, *Russia* 90 F6
Berezovo, *Russia* 90 E7
Bérgamo, *Italy* 67 A3
Bergen, *Norway* 40 F1
Bergen-Binnen, *Neths.* 50 C3
Bergen-op-Zoom, *Neths.* 50 E2
Bergerac, *France* 55 F4
Bergheim, *Germany* 59 B1
Bergisch-Gladbach, *Germany* 59 B2
Bergum, *Neths.* 50 A5
Bergville, *S. Africa* 163 E8
Berhala, Selat, *Indonesia* 128 C4
Berhampore = Baharampur, *India* 106 D8
Berhampur, *India* 106 F6
Bering Sea, *Pac. Oc.* 84 C21
Bering Strait, *U.S.A.* 193 A3
Beringovskiy, *Russia* 91 A18
Berisso, *Argentina* 221 C5
Berja, *Spain* 63 G6
Berkane, *Morocco* 136 A6
Berkeley Springs, *U.S.A.* 189 D2
Berkhamsted, *U.K.* 45 B2
Berlaar, *Belgium* 51 B4
Berlin, *Germany* 58 B5
Berlin, *U.S.A.* 191 B17
Bermejo →, *Argentina* 220 C5
Bermuda ■, *Atl. Oc.* 222 D2
Bern, *Switz.* 60 B2
Bern □, *Switz.* 60 C2
Bernburg, *Germany* 58 C4
Berne = Bern, *Switz.* 60 B2
Berne = Bern □, *Switz.* 60 C2
Berner Alpen, *Switz.* 60 C2
Bernina, Piz, *Switz.* 60 C5
Beroroha, *Madag.* 165 D1
Bérouboay, *Benin* 150 B3
Beroun, *Czech.* 76 B3
Berrechid, *Morocco* 136 C3
Berri, *Australia* 171 E3
Berry, *Australia* 171 F8
Berry, *France* 55 D5
Bertoua, *Cameroon* 153 D2
Berufjörður, *Iceland* 38 C5
Berwick, *U.S.A.* 189 B3
Berwick-upon-Tweed, *U.K.* 46 D7
Besalampy, *Madag.* 165 B1
Besançon, *France* 55 D8
Besar, *Indonesia* 128 D8
Beslan, *Russia* 82 A5
Bessemer, *U.S.A.* 191 C12
Bet She'an, *Israel* 96 B3
Bet Shemesh, *Israel* 96 D2
Bétaré Oya, *Cameroon* 153 D3
Bethal, *S. Africa* 163 C8
Bethanie, *Namibia* 162 D2
Bethel, *U.S.A.* 193 B3
Bethlehem = Bayt Lahm, *Jordan* 98 B1
Bethlehem, *S. Africa* 163 E7
Bethlehem, *U.S.A.* 189 C4
Bethulie, *S. Africa* 163 F6
Béthune, *France* 55 A6
Bethungra, *Australia* 171 F6
Betioky, *Madag.* 165 E1
Betong, *Thailand* 123 L4
Betroka, *Madag.* 165 E1
Betsiamites, *Canada* 187 J13
Bettembourg, *Lux.* 52 D2
Bettiah, *India* 106 B6
Betul, *India* 106 E3
Betung, *Malaysia* 126 C6
Betzdorf, *Germany* 59 B3
Beverley, *Australia* 170 B2
Beverley, *U.K.* 46 G8
Beverwijk, *Neths.* 50 C3
Bex, *Switz.* 60 D2
Bexley, *U.K.* 45 C4
Beyin, *Ghana* 149 E1
Beyla, *Guinea* 147 C5
Beyneu, *Kazakstan* 90 J4
Beypazan, *Turkey* 94 B3
Beyşehir Gölü, *Turkey* 94 C2
Bezhitsa, *Russia* 81 D4
Béziers, *France* 55 H6
Bezwada = Vijayawada, *India* 107 E3
Bhadrakh, *India* 106 E7
Bhagalpur, *India* 106 C7
Bhairab →, *Bangla.* 111 D1
Bhairab Bazar, *Bangla.* 111 C2
Bhamo, *Burma* 122 C3
Bhandara, *India* 106 E4
Bhanrer Ra., *India* 106 D4
Bharat = India ■, *Asia* 107
Bharatpur, *India* 106 B3
Bhatiapara Ghat, *Bangla.* 111 C1
Bhatpara, *India* 106 D8
Bhaunagar = Bhavnagar, *India* 106 E1
Bhavnagar, *India* 106 E1
Bhawanipatna, *India* 106 F6
Bhilsa = Vidisha, *India* 106 D3
Bhilwara, *India* 106 C2
Bhima →, *India* 107 E2
Bhind, *India* 106 B4
Bhiwandi, *India* 106 F1
Bhiwani, *India* 106 A3
Bhola, *Bangla.* 111 D2
Bhopal, *India* 106 D3
Bhubaneshwar, *India* 106 F7
Bhuj, *India* 107 C1
Bhusawal, *India* 106 E2
Bhutan ■, *Asia* 109
Biafra, B. of = Bonny, Bight of, *Africa* 132 F4
Biak, *Indonesia* 129 C16
Biała Podlaska, *Poland* 77 C6
Białystok, *Poland* 77 B6
Biaro, *Indonesia* 129 B12
Biarritz, *France* 55 G3
Biasca, *Switz.* 60 D4
Biba, *Egypt* 139 B4
Bibai, *Japan* 121 B8
Bibala, *Angola* 160 D2
Bibane, Bahiret el, *Tunisia* 138 D3
Biberach, *Germany* 58 G3
Bibiani, *Ghana* 149 D1
Bibile, *Sri Lanka* 110 C2

Bida, Nigeria 151 D3
Bidar, India 107 E3
Biddenden, U.K. 45 E6
Bidon 5 = Poste Maurice Cortier, Algeria 137 E3
Bidur, Malaysia 126 C1
Bié, Planalto de, Angola 160 C3
Biel, Switz. 60 B2
Bielé Karpaty, Europe 76 C5
Bielefeld, Germany 58 C2
Bielersee, Switz. 60 B2
Biella, Italy 67 A2
Bielsko-Biała, Poland 77 E3
Bien Hoa, Vietnam 125 F4
Bienne = Biel, Switz. 60 B2
Bienvenue, Fr. Guiana 214 D6
Bienville, L., Canada 187 H12
Biesiesfontein, S. Africa 163 F1
Big Belt Mts., U.S.A. 190 B5
Big Horn Mts. = Bighorn Mts., U.S.A. 190 C7
Big Muddy Cr. —►, U.S.A. 190 B7
Big Sioux —►, U.S.A. 191 D10
Big Spring, U.S.A. 190 H8
Big Trout L., Canada 186 H9
Biggar, Canada 186 J6
Bighorn —►, U.S.A. 190 C7
Bighorn Mts., U.S.A. 190 C7
Bignona, Senegal 146 C1
Bigorre, France 55 H4
Bihać, Bos.-H. 72 B4
Bihar, India 106 C7
Bihar □, India 106 C7
Bijagós, Arquipélago dos, Guinea-Biss. 146 D1
Bijapur, Karnataka, India 107 E2
Bijapur, Mad. P., India 107 E3
Bijār, Iran 103 B2
Bijeljina, Bos.-H. 72 B6
Bijnor, India 106 A3
Bikaner, India 106 B1
Bikfayyā, Lebanon 95 B2
Bikin, Russia 91 J16
Bikini Atoll, Pac. Oc. 176 D5
Bila Tserkva = Belaya Tserkov, Ukraine 81 E3
Bilara, India 106 C1
Bilaspur, India 106 E5
Bilauk Taungdan, Thailand 123 H4
Bilbao, Spain 63 A5
Bilbo = Bilbao, Spain 63 A5
Bildudalur, Iceland 38 B1
Bilecik, Turkey 94 B2
Bilibino, Russia 91 B16
Bilir, Russia 91 E14
Biliran I., Phil. 130 G5
Billericay, U.K. 45 C5
Billings, U.S.A. 190 C6
Billingshurst, U.K. 45 E2
Billiton = Belitung, Pulau, Indonesia 128 D5
Bilma, Niger 141 B5
Biloku, Guyana 214 E2
Biloxi, U.S.A. 191 J13
Biltine, Chad 142 D2
Bima, Indonesia 129 F10
Bimban, Egypt 139 E5
Bimbila, Ghana 149 B3
Bina-Etawah, India 106 D3
Binalbagan, Phil. 130 H4
Binatang, Malaysia 126 C6
Binche, Belgium 51 D3
Binda, Australia 171 A6
Bindle, Australia 171 A7
Bindura, Zimbabwe 161 B4
Bingara, N.S.W., Australia 171 B8
Bingara, Queens., Australia 171 A5
Bingerville, Ivory C. 148 D5
Binghamton, U.S.A. 189 B4
Bingöl Dağlan, Turkey 82 D3
Binh Dinh = An Nhon, Vietnam 125 E5
Binh Son, Vietnam 125 D5
Binjai, Indonesia 128 B2
Binnaway, Australia 171 D7
Binongko, Indonesia 129 E12
Bintan, Indonesia 128 B4
Bintulu, Malaysia 126 B6
Bintuni, Indonesia 129 D16
Binzert = Bizerte, Tunisia 138 A2
Bioko, Eq. Guin. 153 A1
Biougra, Morocco 136 E2
Bîr Abu Hashim, Egypt 139 E6
Bîr Abu Minqar, Egypt 139 D2
Bir Aouine, Tunisia 138 D2
Bîr 'Asal, Egypt 139 D6
Bir Autrun, Sudan 143 B2
Bîr Diqnash, Egypt 139 A1
Bîr el Basur, Egypt 139 B1
Bîr el Gellaz, Egypt 139 A1
Bîr el Shaqqa, Egypt 139 A1
Bîr Fuad, Egypt 139 B1
Bîr Haimur, Egypt 139 F6
Bir Jdid, Morocco 136 B3
Bîr Kanayis, Egypt 139 E5
Bîr Kerawein, Egypt 139 C3
Bîr Maql, Egypt 139 F6
Bîr Misaha, Egypt 139 F2
Bir Mogrein, Mauritania 140 B2
Bîr Murr, Egypt 139 F4
Bîr Nakheila, Egypt 139 E4
Bîr Qatrani, Egypt 139 A1
Bîr Ranga, Egypt 139 E6
Bîr Sahara, Egypt 139 F3
Bîr Seiyâla, Egypt 139 D6
Bir Semguine, Morocco 136 E4
Bîr Shalatein, Egypt 139 F6
Bîr Shût, Egypt 139 E6
Bîr Terfawi, Egypt 139 F3
Bîr Umm Qubûr, Egypt 139 E6
Bîr Ungât, Egypt 139 F6
Bîr Za'farâna, Egypt 139 B5
Bîr Zeidûn, Egypt 139 D6
Bira, Indonesia 129 D15
Biramféro, Guinea 147 A5
Birao, C.A.R. 142 A4
Birch, U.K. 45 B6
Birchip, Australia 171 F4
Birein, Israel 96 F1
Bireuen, Indonesia 128 A1
Birifo, Gambia 146 C2
Birkenhead, U.K. 46 H6
Birket Qârûn, Egypt 139 B4
Bîrlad, Romania 75 B6
Birmingham, U.K. 46 J7
Birmingham, U.S.A. 191 G13
Birmitrapur, India 106 E6
Birni Nkonni, Niger 141 D2
Birnin Gwari, Nigeria 151 B3
Birnin Kebbi, Nigeria 151 A2
Birnin Kudu, Nigeria 151 B5
Birobidzhan, Russia 91 H16
Birr, Ireland 46 H2
Birrie —►, Australia 171 B6
Birsk, Russia 90 F5
Birzebugga, Malta 69 B3
Bisa, Indonesia 129 C13
Biscay, B. of, Atl. Oc. 223 C5
Bishkek, Kyrgyzstan 93 A7
Bisho, S. Africa 163 H7
Bishop's Stortford, U.K. 45 A4
Bisina, L., Uganda 156 B3
Biskra, Algeria 137 A5
Bismarck, U.S.A. 190 C8
Bismarck Arch., Papua N. G. 173 A3
Bismarck Mts., Papua N. G. 173 B1
Bismarck Sea, Papua N. G. 173 A2
Biso, Uganda 156 B1
Bissagos = Bijagós, Arquipélago dos, Guinea-Biss. 146 D1
Bissau, Guinea-Biss. 146 D1
Bissikrima, Guinea 147 B4
Bistriţa, Romania 75 B4
Bistriţa —►, Romania 75 B5
Bitam, Gabon 154 B1
Bitkine, Chad 142 E1
Bitlis, Turkey 94 C7
Bitola, Macedonia 72 F8
Bitolj = Bitola, Macedonia 72 F8
Bitter L. = Buheirat-Murrat-el-Kubra, Egypt 139 B5
Bitterfontein, S. Africa 163 F2
Bitterroot Range, U.S.A. 190 B4
Biu, Nigeria 151 C7
Biwa-Ko, Japan 120 B6
Biyang, China 116 F2
Biylikol, Ozero, Kazakstan 93 A4
Biysk, Russia 90 J9
Bizana, S. Africa 163 F8
Bizerte, Tunisia 138 A2
Bjargtangar, Iceland 38 B1
Bjelovar, Croatia 72 A4
Black = Da —►, Vietnam 125 B3
Black Forest = Schwarzwald, Germany 58 F2
Black Hills, U.S.A. 190 C7
Black Range, U.S.A. 190 H6
Black River, Jamaica 199 B2
Black Sea, Europe 34 G13
Blackburn, U.K. 46 G6
Blackfoot, U.S.A. 190 D5
Blackpool, U.K. 46 G6
Blackwater —►, Ireland 46 K2
Blackwater —►, U.K. 45 B6
Blackwell, U.S.A. 191 F10
Blagodarnoye, Russia 81 H7
Blagoveshchensk, Russia 91 H15
Blagoveshchenskoye, Kazakstan 93 A6
Blairmore, Canada 186 J5
Blanc, C., Tunisia 138 A2
Blanc, Mont, Alps 55 E9
Blanca, B., Argentina 220 G4
Blanca Peak, U.S.A. 190 F7
Blanche, L., Australia 171 B2
Blanchisseuse, Trin. & Tob. 204 A3
Blanco, S. Africa 163 H4
Blanco, C., Costa Rica 197 D2
Blanco, C., Spain 65 B4
Blanco, C., U.S.A. 190 C1
Blanda —►, Iceland 38 B3
Blankenberge, Belgium 51 A1
Blanquillo, Uruguay 219 C2
Blantyre, Malawi 158 E2
Blarney, Ireland 46 K1
Blåvands Huk, Denmark 42 C1
Blayney, Australia 171 E7
Blednaya, Gora, Russia 90 B8
Bleiburg, Austria 61 C4
Blenheim, N.Z. 175 F4
Bletchley, U.K. 45 A1
Blida, Algeria 137 A4
Blitar, Indonesia 128 F7
Blitta, Togo 150 C1
Block I., U.S.A. 189 B6
Bloemfontein, S. Africa 163 E6
Bloemhof, S. Africa 163 D6
Blois, France 55 D5
Blönduós, Iceland 38 B3
Bloomington, Ill., U.S.A. 191 E12
Bloomington, Ind., U.S.A. 191 E13
Bloomsburg, U.S.A. 189 C3
Blouberg, S. Africa 163 A8
Blue Mountains, The, Jamaica 199 B5
Blue Mts., Oreg., U.S.A. 190 C3
Blue Mts., Pa., U.S.A. 189 C3
Blue Nile = An Nîl el Azraq □, Sudan 143 D5
Blue Nile = Nîl el Azraq —►, Sudan 143 D5
Blue Ridge Mts., U.S.A. 191 F15
Bluefield, U.S.A. 191 F15
Bluefields, Nic. 197 C3
Bluff, N.Z. 175 J2
Bluff Knoll, Australia 170 D3
Blumenau, Brazil 217 J6
Bo, S. Leone 147 D3
Bo Hai, China 116 C4
Bo Xian, China 116 F3
Boa Vista, Brazil 217 A4
Boac, Phil. 130 F3
Boaco, Nic. 197 B2
Boatman, Australia 171 A6
Bobadah, Australia 171 D6
Bobbili, India 107 E4
Bobcaygeon, Canada 185 C2
Bobo-Dioulasso, Burkina Faso 149 B1
Bobonaza —►, Ecuador 212 D3
Bóbr —►, Poland 77 C1
Bobraomby, Tanjon' i, Madag. 165 A3
Bobruysk, Belarus 81 D3
Bocanda, Ivory C. 148 C5
Bocaranga, C.A.R. 142 B2
Bocas del Toro, Panama 197 D4
Bocholt, Germany 58 C1
Bochum, Germany 58 C1
Boda, C.A.R. 142 C2
Bodaybo, Russia 91 G13
Boddington, Australia 170 C2
Boden, Sweden 40 C5
Bodiam, U.K. 45 E5
Bodinga, Nigeria 151 A2
Bodø, Norway 40 C3
Bodrog —►, Hungary 74 A5
Boende, Zaïre 155 C3
Boffa, Guinea 147 B2
Bogale, Burma 122 F2
Bogalusa, U.S.A. 191 J12
Bogan Gate, Australia 171 E6
Boggabilla, Australia 171 B8
Boggabri, Australia 171 C8
Bogo, Phil. 130 G4
Bogong, Mt., Australia 171 G6
Bogor, Indonesia 128 E5
Bogorodskoye, Russia 91 G16
Bogoso, Ghana 149 D1
Bogotá, Colombia 210 C1
Bogotol, Russia 90 H9
Boguchany, Russia 91 G11
Bogué, Mauritania 140 D1
Bohemian Forest = Böhmerwald, Germany 58 F5
Böhmerwald, Germany 58 F5
Bohol, Phil. 130 H4
Bohol Sea, Phil. 130 J4
Bohotleh, Somali Rep. 145 B2
Boi, Nigeria 151 C5
Boi, Pta. de, Brazil 215 C3
Boise, U.S.A. 190 C4
Bojador C., W. Sahara 136 B1
Bojana —►, Albania 70 B2
Bojonegoro, Indonesia 128 F7
Boju, Nigeria 151 E4
Bokala, Ivory C. 148 B5
Boké, Guinea 147 B2
Bokhara —►, Australia 171 B6
Bokkos, Nigeria 151 D5
Bokombayevskoye, Kyrgyzstan 93 B8
Bokoro, Chad 142 E1
Bokote, Zaïre 155 C3
Bokpyin, Burma 122 J3
Bokungu, Zaïre 155 C4
Bol, Chad 142 D1
Bolama, Guinea-Biss. 146 D1
Bolan Pass, Pakistan 105 D3
Bolbec, France 55 B4
Bole, China 112 B3
Bolesławiec, Poland 77 D1
Bolgatanga, Ghana 149 A2
Bolinao, Phil. 130 D2
Bolívar, Argentina 220 F5
Bolívar, Colombia 210 D1
Bolívar □, Ecuador 212 C1
Bolivia ■, S. Amer. 218
Bolivian Plateau, S. Amer. 206 D3
Bollon, Australia 171 A6
Bolney, U.K. 45 E3
Bolobo, Zaïre 155 C2
Bologna, Italy 67 C4
Bologoye, Russia 81 B4
Bolomba, Zaïre 155 B2
Boloven, Cao Nguyen, Laos 125 D4
Bolsena, L. di, Italy 67 D4
Bolshereche, Russia 90 G7
Bolshevik, Ostrov, Russia 91 B11
Bolshoi Kavkas, Asia 82 A5
Bolshoy Anyuy —►, Russia 91 B16
Bolshoy Atlym, Russia 90 F7
Bolshoy Begichev, Ostrov, Russia 91 C12
Bolshoy Lyakhovskiy, Ostrov, Russia 91 C13
Bolsward, Neths. 50 B4
Bolton, U.K. 46 G6
Bolu, Turkey 94 B3
Bolvadin, Turkey 94 B2
Bolzano, Italy 67 A4
Boma, Zaïre 155 E1
Bomaderry, Australia 171 F8
Bombala, Australia 171 G7
Bombay, India 106 F1
Bomboma, Zaïre 155 B2
Bomi Hills, Liberia 148 C1
Bomili, Zaïre 155 B5
Bomongo, Zaïre 155 B2
Bon, C., Tunisia 138 A3
Bonang, Australia 171 G7
Bonanza, Nic. 197 B2
Bonavista, Canada 187 H16
Bonawan, Phil. 130 J4
Bondo, Zaïre 155 A4
Bondoukou, Ivory C. 148 C6
Bone, Teluk, Indonesia 129 D11
Bone Rate, Indonesia 129 F11
Bone Rate, Kepulauan, Indonesia 129 E11
Bong Son = Hoai Nhon, Vietnam 125 E5
Bongabong, Phil. 130 F3
Bongandanga, Zaïre 155 B3
Bongor, Chad 142 E1
Bongouanou, Ivory C. 148 D5
Bonifacio, France 55 H9
Bonifacio, Bouches de, Medit. S. 67 F2
Bonifacio, Str. of, Medit. S. 34 G8
Bonin Is. = Ogasawara Gunto, Pac. Oc. 176 C3
Bonn, Germany 58 D1
Bonney, L., Australia 171 G2
Bonnie Rock, Australia 170 A3
Bonny, Nigeria 151 G4
Bonny —►, Nigeria 151 G4
Bonny, Bight of, Africa 132 F4
Bontang, Indonesia 128 C9
Bonthain, Indonesia 129 E10
Bonthe, S. Leone 147 D3
Bontoc, Phil. 130 C2
Bonyeri, Ghana 149 E1
Boolaboolka L., Australia 171 D4
Booligal, Australia 171 E5
Boom, Belgium 51 B3
Boonah, Australia 171 A9
Boorindal, Australia 171 C6
Boorowa, Australia 171 E7
Boothia, Gulf of, Canada 186 D9
Boothia Pen., Canada 186 D9
Booué, Gabon 154 B1
Boquete, Panama 197 E4
Bor, Serbia, Yug. 72 C8
Bôr, Sudan 143 F4
Bor Mashash, Israel 96 E2
Borås, Sweden 40 G2
Borborema, Plat. of, Brazil 206 C6
Borçka, Turkey 82 C3
Borda, C., Australia 171 F1
Bordeaux, France 55 F3
Borden, Australia 170 C3
Borden I., Canada 186 A8
Bordertown, Australia 171 G3
Borðeyri, Iceland 38 B2
Bordj Bourguiba, Tunisia 138 D2
Bordj Fly Ste. Marie, Algeria 137 D2
Bordj-in-Eker, Algeria 137 E4
Bordj Omar Driss, Algeria 137 C5
Bordj-Tarat, Algeria 137 D6
Bordoba, Kyrgyzstan 93 E6
Bordon, U.K. 45 E1
Borehamwood, U.K. 45 B3
Borgarnes, Iceland 38 C2
Borger, Neths. 50 B6
Borger, U.S.A. 190 G8
Borisoglebsk, Russia 81 E6
Borisov, Belarus 81 C3
Borisovka, Kazakstan 93 A2
Borja, Peru 213 B2
Borkou, Chad 142 B2
Borkum, Germany 58 A1
Borneo, E. Indies 84 H15
Bornholm, Denmark 42 C5
Borno □, Nigeria 151 B7
Bornu Yassa, Nigeria 151 B7
Borogontsy, Russia 91 E14
Boromo, Burkina Faso 149 B2
Boronga Kyumba, Burma 122 E1
Borongan, Phil. 130 G5
Borovichi, Russia 81 A4
Borūjerd, Iran 103 B2
Borzhomi, Georgia 82 B5
Borzya, Russia 91 J13
Bosa, Italy 67 G2
Bosanska Gradiška, Bos.-H. 72 B5
Boshan, China 116 D4
Boshof, S. Africa 163 E5
Bosna —►, Bos.-H. 72 B6
Bosna i Hercegovina = Bosnia & Herzegovina ■, Europe 72 C5
Bosnia & Herzegovina ■, Europe 72 C5
Bosnik, Indonesia 129 C17
Bosobolo, Zaïre 155 A3
Bosporus = Karadeniz Boğazı, Turkey 94 A2
Bossangoa, C.A.R. 142 B2
Bossembélé, C.A.R. 142 B2
Bosso, Niger 141 D5
Bosten Hu, China 112 C3
Boston, U.K. 46 H8
Boston, U.S.A. 189 A6
Botany B., Australia 168 D5
Bothaville, S. Africa 163 D6
Bothnia, G. of, Europe 34 C10
Bothwell, Australia 172 C2
Botletle —►, Botswana 162 B5
Botoşani, Romania 75 A5
Botro, Ivory C. 148 C5
Botswana ■, Africa 162
Bottrop, Germany 59 A2
Botucatu, Brazil 215 C1
Bou Djébéha, Mali 140 D5
Bou Izakarn, Morocco 136 E2
Bou Salem, Tunisia 138 A2
Bouaké, Ivory C. 148 C5
Bouar, C.A.R. 142 B2
Bouârfa, Morocco 136 C6
Bouca, C.A.R. 142 B2
Bouches-du-Rhône □, France 55 G7
Boudenib, Morocco 136 C5
Bougainville I., Solomon Is. 173 A1
Bougie = Bejaia, Algeria 137 A5
Bougouni, Mali 140 F3
Boulder, U.S.A. 190 E7
Boulogne, France 55 A5
Boultoum, Niger 141 C4
Boumalne, Morocco 136 D4
Bouna, Ivory C. 148 B6
Boundiali, Ivory C. 148 B4
Bountiful, U.S.A. 190 D5
Bounty Is., Pac. Oc. 176 K6
Bourbonnais, France 55 E6
Bourem, Mali 140 D5
Bourg, France 55 E7
Bourges, France 55 D6
Bourgogne, France 55 D7
Bourke, Australia 171 C5
Bourne End, U.K. 45 C1
Bournemouth, U.K. 46 L7
Bousso, Chad 142 E1
Boutilimit, Mauritania 140 D1
Bouznika, Morocco 136 B4
Bovigny, Belgium 51 D5
Bovingdon, U.K. 45 B2
Bowelling, Australia 170 C2
Bowen Mts., Australia 171 G6
Bowling Green, U.S.A. 191 F13
Bowmans, Australia 171 E1
Bowmanville, Canada 185 D2
Bowral, Australia 171 E8
Bowraville, Australia 171 C9
Box Hill, U.K. 45 D3
Boxley, U.K. 45 D5
Boxtel, Neths. 50 E4
Boyne —►, Ireland 46 G3
Boyni Qara, Afghan. 104 B4
Boyoma, Chutes, Zaïre 132 F6
Boyup Brook, Australia 170 C2
Bozeman, U.S.A. 190 C6
Bozen = Bolzano, Italy 67 A4
Bozoum, C.A.R. 142 B2
Brabant □, Belgium 51 C3
Brač, Croatia 72 D4
Bracciano, L. di, Italy 67 E4
Bracebridge, Canada 185 B2
Brach, Libya 138 B3
Bräcke, Sweden 40 E3
Bracknell, U.K. 45 D1
Brad, Romania 75 C2
Bradenton, U.S.A. 191 J15
Bradford, U.K. 46 G7
Bradford, U.S.A. 189 B2
Bradley Institute, Zimbabwe 161 B4
Braga, Portugal 63 C1
Bragado, Argentina 221 C4
Bragança, Brazil 217 B7
Bragança, Portugal 63 B3
Bragança Paulista, Brazil 215 C2
Brahmanbaria, Bangla. 111 C2
Brahmani —►, India 106 F7
Brahmaputra —►, India 107 C5
Braidwood, Australia 171 F7
Brăila, Romania 75 C6
Brainerd, U.S.A. 191 C11
Braintree, U.K. 45 A5
Brak —►, S. Africa 163 F4
Bramley, U.K. 45 E2
Brampton, Canada 185 D1
Bramshott, U.K. 45 E1
Branco —►, Brazil 217 B3
Branco, C., Brazil 206 C6
Brandenburg = Neubrandenburg, Germany 58 A5
Brandenburg, Germany 58 C5
Brandenburg □, Germany 58 B5
Brandfort, S. Africa 163 E6
Brandon, Canada 186 J7
Brandsen, Argentina 221 C5
Brandvlei, S. Africa 163 F3
Braniewo, Poland 77 A4
Brańsk, Poland 77 C6
Brantford, Canada 187 L11
Branxholme, Australia 171 H3
Brasília, Brazil 217 F7
Braşov, Romania 75 C4
Brass, Nigeria 151 G3
Brass —►, Nigeria 151 G3
Brasschaat, Belgium 51 A3
Brassey, Banjaran, Malaysia 126 B8
Brasted, U.K. 45 D4
Bratislava, Slovak Rep. 76 D5
Bratsk, Russia 91 H11
Brattleboro, U.S.A. 189 A5
Braunschweig, Germany 58 C3
Brava, Somali Rep. 145 D1
Bravo del Norte, R. —► = Grande, Rio —►, U.S.A. 191 K10
Brawley, U.S.A. 190 G3
Bray, Ireland 46 H3

Bray, *U.K.* 45 C1
Brazil ■, *S. Amer.* 217
Brazilian Highlands, *Brazil* 206 D5
Brazos →, *U.S.A.* 191 J10
Brazzaville, *Congo* 154 D2
Brčko, *Bos.-H.* 72 B6
Bream Hd., *N.Z.* 175 B5
Brebes, *Indonesia* 128 E6
Brecon, *U.K.* 46 K6
Breda, *Neths.* 50 E3
Bredasdorp, *S. Africa* 163 H3
Bredbo, *Australia* 171 F7
Bregenz, *Austria* 61 B1
Breiðafjörður, *Iceland* 38 B2
Bremen, *Germany* 58 B2
Bremerhaven, *Germany* 58 A2
Brenner, *Austria* 61 C2
Brent, *U.K.* 45 C3
Brentwood, *U.K.* 45 C4
Bréscia, *Italy* 67 A3
Breslau = Wrocław, *Poland* 77 D2
Bressanone, *Italy* 67 A4
Bresse, *France* 55 E7
Brest, *Belarus* 81 D1
Brest, *France* 55 C1
Brest-Litovsk = Brest, *Belarus* 81 D1
Bretagne, *France* 55 C2
Bretçu, *Romania* 75 C5
Breton Sd., *U.S.A.* 191 J12
Brett, C., *N.Z.* 175 A5
Brewarrina, *Australia* 171 C6
Brewster, Kap, *Greenland* 224 C3
Breyten, *S. Africa* 163 C8
Brezhnev = Naberezhnyye Chelny, *Russia* 82 C9
Bria, *C.A.R.* 142 B4
Briançon, *France* 55 F8
Bribie I., *Australia* 171 A9
Bridgeport, *U.S.A.* 189 B5
Bridgeton, *U.S.A.* 189 D4
Bridgetown, *Australia* 170 C2
Bridgetown, *Barbados* 204 D1
Bridgewater, *Canada* 187 K14
Bridgewater, C., *Australia* 171 H3
Bridport, *Australia* 172 B3
Brie, *France* 55 C6
Brienz, *Switz.* 60 C3
Brienzersee, *Switz.* 60 C3
Brig, *Switz.* 60 D3
Brigham City, *U.S.A.* 190 D5
Bright, *Australia* 171 G6
Brighton, *Australia* 171 F2
Brighton, *U.K.* 46 L8
Brikama, *Gambia* 146 C1
Bríndisi, *Italy* 67 F9
Brinkworth, *Australia* 171 E2
Brisbane, *Australia* 171 A9
Brisbane →, *Australia* 171 A9
Bristol, *U.K.* 46 K6
Bristol, *U.S.A.* 189 B5
Bristol B., *U.S.A.* 193 B4
Bristol Channel, *U.K.* 46 K5
British Columbia □, *Canada* 186 F4
British Guiana = Guyana ■, *S. Amer.* 214
British Honduras = Belize ■, *Cent. Amer.* 196
British Isles, *Europe* 34 E6
Brits, *S. Africa* 163 C7
Britstown, *S. Africa* 163 F4
Brittany = Bretagne, *France* 55 C2
Brno, *Czech.* 76 C4
Brochet, *Canada* 186 G7
Brock I., *Canada* 186 A8
Brocken, *Germany* 58 C4
Brockport, *U.S.A.* 189 A2
Brockville, *Canada* 185 C4
Brodeur Pen., *Canada* 186 C9
Broken Hill = Kabwe, *Zambia* 161 C4
Broken Hill, *Australia* 171 D3
Brokopondo, *Surinam* 214 C4
Brokopondo □, *Surinam* 214 C4
Bromley, *U.K.* 45 D4
Brønderslev, *Denmark* 42 A2
Brong-Ahafo □, *Ghana* 149 C2
Bronkhorstspruit, *S. Africa* 163 C7
Bronte Park, *Australia* 172 B2
Brookhaven, *U.S.A.* 191 H12
Brookings, *U.S.A.* 191 C10
Brooks Ra., *U.S.A.* 193 A5
Broome, *Australia* 168 G10
Broomehill, *Australia* 170 C2
Brownsville, *U.S.A.* 191 K10
Brownsweg, *Surinam* 214 C4
Brownwood, *U.S.A.* 190 H9
Bruas, *Malaysia* 126 B1
Bruay, *France* 55 A6
Bruce, Mt., *Australia* 168 C1
Bruce Rock, *Australia* 170 B3
Bruck, *Austria* 61 A6
Bruges = Brugge, *Belgium* 51 A2
Brugg, *Switz.* 60 A3
Brugge, *Belgium* 51 A2
Brühl, *Germany* 59 B2
Brunei = Bandar Seri Begawan, *Brunei* 127 A3
Brunei ■, *Asia* 127
Brunnen, *Switz.* 60 B4
Brunner, L., *N.Z.* 175 F3
Brunsbüttelkoog, *Germany* 58 A3
Brunswick = Braunschweig, *Germany* 58 C3
Brunswick, *Ga., U.S.A.* 191 H15
Brunswick, *Md., U.S.A.* 189 D3
Brunswick Junction, *Australia* 170 C1
Bruny I., *Australia* 172 C2
Brus Laguna, *Honduras* 196 B4
Brussel, *Belgium* 51 C3
Brussels = Brussel, *Belgium* 51 C3
Bruthen, *Australia* 171 G6
Bruxelles = Brussel, *Belgium* 51 C3
Bryan, *U.S.A.* 191 J10
Bryan, Mt., *Australia* 171 E2
Bryansk, *Russia* 81 D4
Bsharri, *Lebanon* 95 B2
Bū Baqarah, *U.A.E.* 101 B3
Bu Craa, *W. Sahara* 136 A2
Bū Ḥasā, *U.A.E.* 101 C2
Buapinang, *Indonesia* 129 E11
Buba, *Guinea-Biss.* 146 D1
Bubanza, *Burundi* 156 B1
Būbiyān, *Kuwait* 100 A1
Bucaramanga, *Colombia* 210 B2
Bucas Grande I., *Phil.* 130 H6
Buchanan, *Liberia* 148 D2
Bucharest = Bucureşti, *Romania* 75 D5
Buckingham, *Canada* 185 B4
Buckingham, *U.K.* 45 A1
Buckinghamshire □, *U.K.* 45 B1
Bucureşti, *Romania* 75 D5
Budapest, *Hungary* 74 B3
Bude, *U.K.* 46 L5
Budgewoi Lake, *Australia* 171 E8
Búðareyri, *Iceland* 38 C5
Búðir, *Iceland* 38 C2
Budjala, *Zaïre* 155 B3
Buenaventura, *Colombia* 210 C1
Buenos Aires, *Argentina* 221 C5
Buenos Aires, *Costa Rica* 197 E3
Buenos Aires □, *Argentina* 221 C4
Buffalo, *N.Y., U.S.A.* 189 A2
Buffalo, *Wyo., U.S.A.* 190 C7
Buffels →, *S. Africa* 163 F1
Bug →, *Poland* 77 C5
Bug →, *Ukraine* 81 G3
Buga, *Colombia* 210 C1
Buganda, *Uganda* 156 C1
Buganga, *Uganda* 156 C2
Bugasong, *Phil.* 130 G3
Bugel, Tanjung, *Indonesia* 128 E7
Bugibba, *Malta* 69 B2
Bugsuk, *Phil.* 130 J1
Buguma, *Nigeria* 151 G3
Bugun Shara, *Mongolia* 113 B7
Buheirat-Murrat-el-Kubra, *Egypt* 139 B5
Bui, *Russia* 81 A6
Buir Nur, *Mongolia* 113 B9
Buitenpost, *Neths.* 50 A5
Bujumbura, *Burundi* 156 B1
Bukachacha, *Russia* 91 H13
Bukama, *Zaïre* 155 F5
Bukavu, *Zaïre* 155 C6
Bukene, *Tanzania* 158 B1
Bukhara, *Uzbekistan* 90 K4
Bukhoro = Bukhara, *Uzbekistan* 90 K4
Bukit Mertajam, *Malaysia* 126 B1
Bukittinggi, *Indonesia* 128 C3
Bukoba, *Tanzania* 158 A1
Bukuru, *Nigeria* 151 C5
Bukuya, *Uganda* 156 C1
Bula, *Guinea-Biss.* 146 D1
Bula, *Indonesia* 129 D14
Bulahdelah, *Australia* 171 D9
Bulan, *Phil.* 130 F4
Bulandshahr, *India* 106 A3
Būlâq, *Egypt* 139 E4
Bulawayo, *Zimbabwe* 161 D3
Bulgan, *Mongolia* 113 B7
Bulgaria ■, *Europe* 73
Buli, Teluk, *Indonesia* 129 C14
Bullaring, *Australia* 170 B2
Bulle, *Switz.* 60 C2
Bulli, *Australia* 171 E8
Bulloo →, *Australia* 171 A4
Bulloo Downs, *Australia* 171 B4
Bulloo L., *Australia* 171 B3
Bulsar = Valsad, *India* 106 E1
Bultfontein, *S. Africa* 163 E6
Bulu Karakelong, *Indonesia* 129 A13
Bulukumba, *Indonesia* 129 E10
Bulun, *Russia* 91 D13
Bumba, *Zaïre* 155 B4
Bumhpa Bum, *Burma* 122 B3
Bumi →, *Zimbabwe* 161 B3
Buna, *Kenya* 157 C4
Buna, *Papua N. G.* 173 C2
Bunawan, *Agusan del S., Phil.* 130 J6
Bunawan, *Davao del S., Phil.* 130 K5
Bunbah, Khalīj, *Libya* 138 A5
Bunbury, *Australia* 170 C1
Bundi, *India* 106 C2
Bundoran, *Ireland* 46 F2
Bungo-Suidō, *Japan* 120 D3
Bungoma, *Kenya* 157 C1
Bunia, *Zaïre* 155 B6
Bunji, *Pakistan* 105 A6
Buntingford, *U.K.* 45 A4
Buntok, *Indonesia* 128 C8
Bununu Dass, *Nigeria* 151 C5
Bununu Kasa, *Nigeria* 151 C5
Bunyu, *Indonesia* 128 B9
Bunza, *Nigeria* 151 B2
Buol, *Indonesia* 129 B11
Buorkhaya, Mys, *Russia* 91 C13
Buqbua, *Egypt* 139 A1
Bûr Fuad, *Egypt* 139 A5
Bûr Safâga, *Egypt* 139 D6
Bûr Sa'îd, *Egypt* 139 A4
Bûr Sûdân, *Sudan* 143 B6
Bûr Taufiq, *Egypt* 139 B5
Bura, *Kenya* 157 D4
Buraydah, *Si. Arabia* 99 C4
Burbank, *U.S.A.* 190 G2
Burcher, *Australia* 171 E6
Burdur, *Turkey* 94 C2
Burdwan = Barddhaman, *India* 106 D8
Bureya →, *Russia* 91 H15
Burg el Arab, *Egypt* 139 A3
Burgas, *Bulgaria* 73 C5
Burgdorf, *Switz.* 60 B2
Burgenland □, *Austria* 61 B5
Burgersdorp, *S. Africa* 163 F6
Burgos, *Spain* 63 B5
Burgundy = Bourgogne, *France* 55 D7
Burhou, *U.K.* 44 A2
Burias, *Phil.* 130 F4
Burica, Pta., *Costa Rica* 197 E3
Buriram, *Thailand* 123 G5
Burj Sāfitā, *Syria* 97 B2
Burji, *Ethiopia* 144 E3
Burkina Faso ■, *Africa* 149
Burley, *U.S.A.* 190 D5
Burlington, *Iowa, U.S.A.* 191 E12
Burlington, *N.J., U.S.A.* 189 C4
Burlington, *Vt., U.S.A.* 191 C17
Burlyu-Tyube, *Kazakstan* 90 K8
Burma ■, *Asia* 122
Burngup, *Australia* 170 C3
Burnham, *U.K.* 45 C2
Burnham-on-Crouch, *U.K.* 45 B6
Burnie, *Australia* 172 B2
Burnley, *U.K.* 46 G7
Burnoye, *Kazakstan* 93 B4
Burnside →, *Canada* 186 E7
Burqān, *Kuwait* 100 A1
Burqin, *China* 112 B4
Burra, *Australia* 171 E2
Burren Junction, *Australia* 171 C7
Burrinjuck Res., *Australia* 171 F7
Bursa, *Turkey* 94 B2
Burton upon Trent, *U.K.* 46 H7
Burtundy, *Australia* 171 E4
Buru, *Indonesia* 129 D13
Burullus, Bahra el, *Egypt* 139 A4
Burunday, *Kazakstan* 93 A8
Burundi ■, *Africa* 156
Bururi, *Burundi* 156 C1
Burutu, *Nigeria* 151 F2
Bury St. Edmunds, *U.K.* 46 J9
Buryat Republic □, *Russia* 91 H12
Buşayrah, *Syria* 97 B5
Buşayyah, *Iraq* 102 E5
Būshehr, *Iran* 103 D3
Bushenyi, *Uganda* 156 D1
Bushey, *U.K.* 45 C2
Bushire = Būshehr, *Iran* 103 D3
Busie, *Ghana* 149 A1
Businga, *Zaïre* 155 A3
Busoga □, *Uganda* 156 C2
Busra ash Shām, *Syria* 97 D2
Busselton, *Australia* 170 C1
Bussum, *Neths.* 50 C3
Busto Arsizio, *Italy* 67 A2
Busu-Djanoa, *Zaïre* 155 B3
Busuanga, *Phil.* 130 G2
Buta, *Zaïre* 155 B4
Butare, *Rwanda* 156 B2
Butaritari, *Kiribati* 176 E5
Butemba, *Uganda* 156 C1
Butembo, *Zaïre* 155 C6
Butha Qi, *China* 113 B10
Buthabuthe, *Lesotho* 164 A2
Butiaba, *Uganda* 156 B1
Butkhāk, *Afghan.* 104 C5
Butler, *U.S.A.* 189 C1
Butte, *U.S.A.* 190 B5
Butterworth = Gcuwa, *S. Africa* 163 G7
Butterworth, *Malaysia* 126 B1
Butuan, *Phil.* 130 J5
Butuku-Luba, *Eq. Guin.* 153 A1
Butung, *Indonesia* 129 E11
Buturlinovka, *Russia* 81 E6
Buxton, *Guyana* 214 B2
Buyaga, *Russia* 91 F14
Buynaksk, *Russia* 82 A7
Buzău, *Romania* 75 C5
Buzău →, *Romania* 75 C6
Buzen, *Japan* 120 D2
Buzi →, *Mozam.* 159 D2
Buzzards Bay, *U.S.A.* 189 B6
Bydgoszcz, *Poland* 77 B3
Byelarus = Belarus ■, *Europe* 81 D2
Byelorussia = Belarus ■, *Europe* 81 D2
Byfleet, *U.K.* 45 D2
Bylot I., *Canada* 187 C10
Byrock, *Australia* 171 C6
Byron, C., *Australia* 168 C5
Byron Bay, *Australia* 171 B9
Byrranga, Gory, *Russia* 91 C11
Byrranga Mts. = Byrranga, Gory, *Russia* 91 C11
Bystrovka, *Kyrgyzstan* 93 A7
Bysyttakh = Kël, *Russia* 91 D13
Bytom, *Poland* 77 E3
Byumba, *Rwanda* 156 A2

C

Ca Mau = Quan Long, *Vietnam* 125 G3
Ca Mau, Mui, *Vietnam* 125 G3
Caála, *Angola* 160 C3
Cabadbaran, *Phil.* 130 J5
Cabalian, *Phil.* 130 H5
Caballeria, C. de, *Spain* 65 A6
Cabanatuan, *Phil.* 130 D2
Cabedelo, *Brazil* 217 D9
Cabimas, *Venezuela* 211 A2
Cabinda, *Angola* 160 A1
Cabinda □, *Angola* 160 A1
Cabo Frio, *Brazil* 215 C5
Cabo Pantoja, *Peru* 213 A3
Cabonga, Réservoir, *Canada* 187 K12
Caboolture, *Australia* 171 A9
Cabora Bassa Dam = Cahora Bassa Dam, *Mozam.* 159 B1
Cabot Str., *Canada* 187 J15
Cabrera, I., *Spain* 65 C4
Cabriel →, *Spain* 63 E7
Cabugao, *Phil.* 130 C2
Čačak, *Serbia, Yug.* 72 C7
Cacao, *Fr. Guiana* 214 C6
Cáceres, *Spain* 63 E3
Cachéu, *Guinea-Biss.* 146 D1
Cachimbo, Serra do, *Brazil* 217 D5
Cachoeira de Itapemirim, *Brazil* 215 A5
Cachoeira do Sul, *Brazil* 217 J5
Cacólo, *Angola* 160 C4
Caconda, *Angola* 160 D2
Cacongo, *Angola* 160 A1
Cadiz, *Phil.* 130 G4
Cádiz, *Spain* 63 G3
Cádiz, G. de, *Spain* 63 G3
Cadoux, *Australia* 170 A2
Caen, *France* 55 B4
Caernarfon, *U.K.* 46 H5
Caernarvon = Caernarfon, *U.K.* 46 H5
Caesarea, *Israel* 96 B2
Cagayan →, *Phil.* 130 C3
Cagayan de Oro, *Phil.* 130 J5
Cagayan Is., *Phil.* 130 H2
Cagayan Sulu I., *Phil.* 130 K1
Cágliari, *Italy* 67 H2
Cágliari, G. di, *Italy* 67 H2
Caguas, *Puerto Rico* 201 A2
Cahirciveen, *Ireland* 46 J1
Cahora Bassa Dam, *Mozam.* 159 B1
Cahors, *France* 55 G5
Cahuapanas, *Peru* 213 B2
Caia, *Mozam.* 159 C2
Caibarién, *Cuba* 198 B4
Caibiran, *Phil.* 130 G5
Caicara, *Venezuela* 211 B3
Cairns, *Australia* 168 G12
Cairo = El Qâhira, *Egypt* 139 B4
Cairo, *U.S.A.* 191 F12
Caiundo, *Angola* 160 E3
Cajamarca, *Peru* 213 C2
Çakirgol, *Turkey* 82 C2
Calabanga, *Phil.* 130 E4
Calabar, *Nigeria* 151 G4
Calábria □, *Italy* 67 H8
Calahorra, *Spain* 63 B6
Calais, *France* 55 A5
Calamar, *Colombia* 210 A1
Calamba, *Phil.* 130 H4
Calamian Group, *Phil.* 130 G2
Calamocha, *Spain* 63 C7
Calang, *Indonesia* 128 A1
Calapan, *Phil.* 130 F2
Calatayud, *Spain* 63 C6
Calauag, *Phil.* 130 E3
Calavite, C., *Phil.* 130 F2
Calayan, *Phil.* 130 B3
Calbayog, *Phil.* 130 G5
Calca, *Peru* 213 E4
Calcutta, *India* 106 E8
Caldwell, *U.S.A.* 190 C4
Caledon, *S. Africa* 163 H2
Caledon →, *S. Africa* 163 F6
Calella, *Spain* 63 B9
Calgary, *Canada* 186 H5
Cali, *Colombia* 210 D1
Calicut, *India* 107 F2
California □, *U.S.A.* 190 E2
California, G. de, *Mexico* 194 B1
Calitzdorp, *S. Africa* 163 H3
Callabonna, L., *Australia* 171 B2
Callao, *Peru* 213 D2
Calolbon, *Phil.* 130 F4
Caloocan, *Phil.* 130 E2
Caloundra, *Australia* 171 A9
Caltagirone, *Italy* 67 K6
Caltanissetta, *Italy* 67 J6
Calulo, *Angola* 160 C2
Calunda, *Angola* 160 C5
Calvados □, *France* 55 B4
Calvi, *France* 55 H9
Calvinia, *S. Africa* 163 G2
Cam Lam, *Vietnam* 125 F5
Cam Ranh, *Vietnam* 125 F5
Camabatela, *Angola* 160 B3
Camacupa, *Angola* 160 C3
Camagüey, *Cuba* 198 B5
Camaná, *Peru* 213 F4
Camaret, *France* 55 C1
Camarón, C., *Honduras* 196 B4
Cambay = Khambhat, *India* 106 E1
Cambay, G. of = Khambhat, G. of, *India* 107 D1
Camberley, *U.K.* 45 D1
Cambodia ■, *Asia* 125
Cambrai, *France* 55 A6
Cambrian Mts., *U.K.* 46 J5
Cambridge, *N.Z.* 175 C5
Cambridge, *U.K.* 46 J8
Cambridge, *Mass., U.S.A.* 189 A6
Cambridge, *Md., U.S.A.* 191 E16
Cambridge Bay, *Canada* 186 D8
Cambuci, *Brazil* 215 B5
Cambundi-Catembo, *Angola* 160 C3
Camden, *U.K.* 45 C3
Camden, *Ark., U.S.A.* 191 H11
Camden, *N.J., U.S.A.* 189 C4
Cameron Highlands, *Malaysia* 126 B1
Cameroon ■, *Africa* 153
Cameroun, Mt., *Cameroon* 153 D1
Camiguin □, *Phil.* 130 J5
Camiguin I., *Phil.* 130 B3
Camiling, *Phil.* 130 D2
Caminha, *Portugal* 63 B1
Camira Creek, *Australia* 171 B9
Camissombo, *Angola* 160 B4
Camocim, *Brazil* 217 C8
Camopi, *Fr. Guiana* 214 D6
Camopi →, *Fr. Guiana* 214 D6
Camotes Is., *Phil.* 130 H5
Camotes Sea, *Phil.* 130 H4
Campana, *Argentina* 221 C5
Campania □, *Italy* 67 F6
Campbell, *S. Africa* 163 E5
Campbell I., *Pac. Oc.* 176 K5
Campbell Town, *Australia* 172 B3
Campbellton, *Canada* 187 J13
Campbelltown, *Australia* 171 E8
Campbeltown, *U.K.* 46 E4
Campeche, *Mexico* 194 E8
Campeche, G. de, *Mexico* 194 E7
Camperdown, *Australia* 171 H4
Campina Grande, *Brazil* 217 D9
Campinas, *Brazil* 215 C2
Campo, *Cameroon* 153 E1
Campo Grande, *Brazil* 217 G5
Campoalegre, *Colombia* 210 D1
Campobasso, *Italy* 67 E6
Campos, *Brazil* 215 B5
Camrose, *Canada* 186 H5
Can Tho, *Vietnam* 125 G4
Canada ■, *N. Amer.* 186
Cañada de Gómez, *Argentina* 221 B4
Canadian →, *U.S.A.* 191 G10
Çanakkale, *Turkey* 94 B1
Çanakkale Boğazı, *Turkey* 94 B1
Canalejas, *Argentina* 221 C1
Canals, *Argentina* 221 B3
Canandaigua, *U.S.A.* 189 A3
Cananea, *Mexico* 194 A2
Cañar, *Ecuador* 212 D1
Cañar □, *Ecuador* 212 D1
Canarias, Is., *Atl. Oc.* 223
Canarreos, Arch. de los, *Cuba* 198 B2
Canary Is. = Canarias, Is., *Atl. Oc.* 223
Canaveral, C., *U.S.A.* 191 J16
Canbelego, *Australia* 171 C6
Canberra, *Australia* 171 F7
Candala, *Somali Rep.* 145 A3
Candelo, *Australia* 171 G7
Candia = Iráklion, *Greece* 71 F5
Candon, *Phil.* 130 C2
Canea = Khaniá, *Greece* 71 F4
Canelones, *Uruguay* 219 D2
Cañete, *Peru* 213 E3
Cangzhou, *China* 116 C3
Cani, I., *Tunisia* 138 A2
Çankırı, *Turkey* 94 B3
Cann River, *Australia* 171 G7
Cannanore, *India* 107 F2
Cannes, *France* 55 G9
Canon City, *U.S.A.* 190 F7
Canonniers Pt., *Mauritius* 166 A2
Canora, *Canada* 186 J7
Canowindra, *Australia* 171 E7
Cantabria □, *Spain* 63 A5
Cantabrian Mts. = Cantábrica, Cordillera, *Spain* 63 A4
Cantábrica, Cordillera, *Spain* 63 A4
Cantal □, *France* 55 F6
Cantal, Plomb du, *France* 55 F6
Canterbury, *U.K.* 46 K9
Canterbury □, *N.Z.* 175 G3
Canterbury Bight, *N.Z.* 168 E7
Canterbury Plains, *N.Z.* 175 G3
Canton = Guangzhou, *China* 113 H9
Canton, *Miss., U.S.A.* 191 H12
Canton, *Ohio, U.S.A.* 191 D15
Canvey, *U.K.* 45 C5
Cao Xian, *China* 116 F3
Cap-Haïtien, *Haiti* 200 A2
Cap St.-Jacques = Vung Tau, *Vietnam* 125 G4
Capaia, *Angola* 160 B4
Capanaparo →, *Venezuela* 211 B3
Cape Barren I., *Australia* 172 A3
Cape Breton I., *Canada* 187 J15
Cape Coast, *Ghana* 149 E2
Cape Dorset, *Canada* 187 E11
Cape Dyer, *Canada* 187 D12
Cape Fear →, *U.S.A.* 191 G16

Cape Jervis, *Australia* 171 F1
Cape May, *U.S.A.* 189 D4
Cape Town, *S. Africa* 163 H2
Cape Verde Is. ■, *Atl. Oc.* 223 E4
Cape York Peninsula, *Australia* 168 B4
Capel, *U.K.* 45 E3
Capraia, *Italy* 67 D3
Caprera, *Italy* 67 F2
Capri, *Italy* 67 F6
Caprivi Strip, *Namibia* 162 A4
Captain's Flat, *Australia* 171 F7
Caquetá →, *Colombia* 210 E3
Caracal, *Romania* 75 D3
Caracas, *Venezuela* 211 A3
Caradoc, *Australia* 171 C4
Carangola, *Brazil* 215 A5
Caransebeş, *Romania* 75 C2
Caratasca, L., *Honduras* 196 C5
Caratinga, *Brazil* 215 A5
Caravaca, *Spain* 63 F6
Caravelas, *Brazil* 217 G9
Caraveli, *Peru* 213 E4
Carballo, *Spain* 63 A1
Carbonara, C., *Italy* 67 H2
Carbondale, *U.S.A.* 189 B4
Carbonear, *Canada* 187 H16
Carbonia, *Italy* 67 H2
Carcar, *Phil.* 130 H4
Carcasse, C., *Haiti* 200 B1
Carcassonne, *France* 55 H6
Carchi □, *Ecuador* 212 A2
Carcross, *Canada* 186 E3
Cárdenas, *Cuba* 198 B3
Cardiff, *U.K.* 46 K6
Cardigan, *U.K.* 46 J5
Cardigan B., *U.K.* 46 J5
Cardona, *Spain* 63 B9
Cardona, *Uruguay* 219 C1
Carei, *Romania* 75 A2
Careysburg, *Liberia* 148 D1
Cariacica, *Brazil* 215 A6
Caribbean Sea, *W. Indies* 180 H12
Cariboo Mts., *Canada* 186 G4
Caribou, *U.S.A.* 191 A18
Caribou Mts., *Canada* 186 F5
Carigara, *Phil.* 130 G5
Carinda, *Australia* 171 C6
Carinthia □ = Kärnten □, *Austria* 61 C4
Caripito, *Venezuela* 211 A4
Carleton Place, *Canada* 185 B4
Carletonville, *S. Africa* 163 C7
Carlisle, *U.K.* 46 F6
Carlisle, *U.S.A.* 189 C3
Carlisle Bay, *Barbados* 204 D1
Carlos Casares, *Argentina* 221 C4
Carlos Tejedor, *Argentina* 221 C3
Carlow, *Ireland* 46 H3
Carlsbad, *U.S.A.* 190 H7
Carmacks, *Canada* 186 D3
Carman, *Canada* 186 K8
Carmarthen, *U.K.* 46 K5
Carmelo, *Uruguay* 219 D1
Carmona, *Spain* 63 G3
Carnarvon, *S. Africa* 163 F4
Carnot, *C.A.R.* 142 B2
Carnsore Pt., *Ireland* 46 J3
Carolina, *S. Africa* 163 C8
Caroline I., *Kiribati* 176 G8
Caroline Is., *Pac. Oc.* 176 E3
Caroni →, *Venezuela* 211 B4
Caroona, *Australia* 171 C8
Carpathians, *Europe* 34 F11
Carpaţii Meridionali, *Romania* 75 C4
Carpentaria, G. of, *Australia* 168 B3
Carpolac = Morea, *Australia* 171 G3
Carrara, *Italy* 67 C3
Carrascal, *Phil.* 130 H6
Carrick-on-Shannon, *Ireland* 46 G2
Carrick-on-Suir, *Ireland* 46 J2
Carrieton, *Australia* 171 D2
Carson City, *U.S.A.* 190 E2
Carson Sink, *U.S.A.* 190 D3
Cartagena, *Colombia* 210 A1
Cartagena, *Spain* 63 F7
Cartago, *Colombia* 210 C1
Cartago, *Costa Rica* 197 D3
Carterton, *N.Z.* 175 E5
Carthage, *U.S.A.* 191 F11
Cartwright, *Canada* 187 G14
Carúpano, *Venezuela* 211 A4
Casablanca, *Morocco* 136 B3
Casale, *Italy* 67 B2
Casamance →, *Senegal* 146 C1
Cascade, *Seychelles* 166 C2
Cascade Ra., *U.S.A.* 190 C2
Cascades, Pte. des, *Réunion* 166 B3
Caserta, *Italy* 67 F6
Casiguran, *Phil.* 130 D3
Casilda, *Argentina* 221 B4
Casino, *Australia* 171 B9
Casiquiare →, *Venezuela* 211 C3
Casma, *Peru* 213 D2
Caspe, *Spain* 63 C8
Casper, *U.S.A.* 190 D7
Caspian Sea, *Asia* 90 H3
Casquets, *Chan. Is.* 44 A2
Cassiar Mts., *Canada* 186 E4
Cassinga, *Angola* 160 D3
Castellammare del Golfo, *Italy* 67 J5
Castellammare di Stábia, *Italy* 67 F6
Castellón de la Plana, *Spain* 63 D8
Castelo, *Brazil* 215 A5
Castelo Branco, *Portugal* 63 D2
Castelvetrano, *Italy* 67 J5
Casterton, *Australia* 171 G3
Castilla La Mancha □, *Spain* 63 D5
Castilla La Nueva = Castilla La Mancha □, *Spain* 63 D5
Castilla La Vieja = Castilla y Leon □, *Spain* 63 B5
Castilla y Leon □, *Spain* 63 B5
Castillos, *Uruguay* 219 D3
Castlebar, *Ireland* 46 G1
Castlemaine, *Australia* 171 G4
Castlereagh →, *Australia* 171 C7
Castres, *France* 55 G5
Castricum, *Neths.* 50 C3
Castries, *St. Lucia* 203 E3
Castro del Río, *Spain* 63 F4
Çat, *Turkey* 82 D3
Cat I., *Bahamas* 201 B2
Catacamas, *Honduras* 196 C4
Catacáos, *Peru* 213 B1
Cataguases, *Brazil* 215 B5
Catalão, *Brazil* 217 G7
Catalonia = Cataluña □, *Spain* 63 C8
Cataluña □, *Spain* 63 C8
Catamarca, *Argentina* 220 D4
Catanauan, *Phil.* 130 F3
Catanduanes, *Phil.* 130 E4
Catanduva, *Brazil* 215 B1
Catánia, *Italy* 67 J7
Catanzaro, *Italy* 67 H8
Catarman, *Phil.* 130 F5
Catbalogan, *Phil.* 130 G5
Cateel, *Phil.* 130 K6
Caterham, *U.K.* 45 D3
Cathcart, *S. Africa* 163 G6
Catio, *Guinea-Biss.* 146 D1
Catoche, C., *Mexico* 194 D9
Catskill, *U.S.A.* 189 A5
Catskill Mts., *U.S.A.* 189 A4
Cauca →, *Colombia* 210 B1
Caucasus = Bolshoi Kavkas, *Asia* 82 A5
Caúngula, *Angola* 160 B4
Caura →, *Venezuela* 211 B4
Cauvery →, *India* 107 F3
Caux, *France* 55 B4
Cavan, *Ireland* 46 G2
Cavendish, *Australia* 171 G3
Caviana, I., *Brazil* 217 B6
Cavite, *Phil.* 130 E2
Cawndilla L., *Australia* 171 D3
Cawnpore = Kanpur, *India* 106 C4
Caxias, *Brazil* 217 C8
Caxias do Sul, *Brazil* 217 J6
Caxito, *Angola* 160 B2
Cayambe, *Ecuador* 212 B2
Cayambe, *Ecuador* 212 B2
Çayeli, *Turkey* 82 C3
Cayenne, *Fr. Guiana* 214 C6
Cayenne □, *Fr. Guiana* 214 C6
Cayey, *Puerto Rico* 201 A2
Cayman Is. ■, *W. Indies* 198 C3
Cayuga L., *U.S.A.* 189 A3
Cazombo, *Angola* 160 C5
Ceanannus Mor, *Ireland* 46 G3
Ceará = Fortaleza, *Brazil* 217 C9
Ceará □, *Brazil* 217 D9
Cebaco, I. de, *Panama* 197 E4
Cebu, *Phil.* 130 H4
Cechi, *Ivory C.* 148 D5
Cecil Plains, *Australia* 171 A8
Cedar City, *U.S.A.* 190 F4
Cedar Falls, *U.S.A.* 191 D11
Cedar L., *Canada* 186 H7
Cedar Rapids, *U.S.A.* 191 D11
Cedarville, *S. Africa* 163 F7
Cefalù, *Italy* 67 J6
Cegléd, *Hungary* 74 B4
Cehegín, *Spain* 63 F6
Cekhira, *Tunisia* 138 C2
Celaya, *Mexico* 194 E4
Celebes = Sulawesi □, *Indonesia* 129 C10
Celebes Sea = Sulawesi Sea, *Indonesia* 84 H16
Celica, *Ecuador* 212 E1
Celje, *Slovenia* 72 A3
Celle, *Germany* 58 B3
Central □, *Kenya* 157 D2
Central □, *Malawi* 158 C2
Central, Cordillera, *Colombia* 210 C1
Central, Cordillera, *Costa Rica* 197 D3
Central, Cordillera, *Dom. Rep.* 200 A2
Central, Cordillera, *Phil.* 130 C2
Central African Rep. ■, *Africa* 142
Central I., *Kenya* 157 A2
Central Makran Range, *Pakistan* 105 F2
Central Russian Uplands, *Europe* 34 E14
Central Siberian Plateau, *Russia* 84 B14
Centralia, *Ill., U.S.A.* 191 F12
Centralia, *Wash., U.S.A.* 190 B2
Centre de Flacq, *Mauritius* 166 B3
Cephalonia = Kefallinía, *Greece* 71 D1
Ceram = Seram, *Indonesia* 129 D14
Ceram Sea = Seram Sea, *Indonesia* 129 D14
Ceres, *S. Africa* 163 H2
Cerf, *Seychelles* 166 C2
Cerfontain, *Belgium* 51 D3
Cerfs, Is. aux, *Mauritius* 166 B3
Cerignola, *Italy* 67 F7
Cerknica, *Slovenia* 72 A3
Cernavodă, *Romania* 75 D6
Cerro de Punta, Mt., *Puerto Rico* 201 A1
Cervera, *Spain* 63 C9
Cervera del Río Alhama, *Spain* 63 B6
Cesena, *Italy* 67 C5
České Budějovice, *Czech.* 76 C3
Ceskomoravská Vrchovina, *Czech.* 76 B4
Český Těšín, *Czech.* 76 B6
Cessnock, *Australia* 171 D8
Cestos →, *Liberia* 148 D3
Cetinje, *Montenegro, Yug.* 72 E6
Ceuta, *Morocco* 136 A5
Cévennes, *France* 55 G7
Ceyhan →, *Turkey* 94 C4
Ceylon = Sri Lanka ■, *Asia* 110
Cha Pa, *Vietnam* 125 A2
Chablais, *France* 55 E8
Chacabuco, *Argentina* 221 C4
Chachapoyas, *Peru* 213 C2
Chachran, *Pakistan* 105 D4
Chad ■, *Africa* 142
Chad, L. = Tchad, L., *Chad* 142 D1
Chadan, *Russia* 91 J10
Chadron, *U.S.A.* 190 D8
Chadwell St. Mary, *U.K.* 45 C5
Chaeryŏng, *N. Korea* 118 E3
Chagda, *Russia* 91 F14
Chagos Arch., *Ind. Oc.* 84 J11
Chāh Bahār, *Iran* 103 E6
Chāh Gay Hills, *Afghan.* 104 G2
Chahār Borjak, *Afghan.* 104 G1
Chaibasa, *India* 106 E7
Chajari, *Argentina* 221 A5
Chakaria, *Bangla.* 111 D3
Chakhānsūr, *Afghan.* 104 F1
Chakradharpur, *India* 106 D7
Chakwal, *Pakistan* 105 B5
Chala, *Peru* 213 E3
Chalcis = Khalkis, *Greece* 71 D3
Chalfont St. Peter, *U.K.* 45 C2
Chalhuanca, *Peru* 213 E4
Chaling, *China* 116 J2
Chalisgaon, *India* 106 F2
Challapata, *Bolivia* 218 C1
Châlons, *France* 55 B7
Chaman, *Pakistan* 105 C3
Chamba, *India* 107 A2
Chambal →, *India* 106 C3
Chambersburg, *U.S.A.* 189 C3
Chambéry, *France* 55 E8
Chamonix, *France* 55 E9
Champagne, *France* 55 B7
Champaign, *U.S.A.* 191 E12
Champlain, L., *U.S.A.* 191 B17
Chandmani, *Mongolia* 112 C6
Chandpur, *Bangla.* 111 C2
Chandrapur, *India* 106 F4
Ch'ang Chiang = Chang Jiang →, *China* 116 G5
Chang Jiang →, *China* 116 G5
Changane →, *Mozam.* 159 F1
Changchiak'ou = Zhangjiakou, *China* 116 B3
Ch'angchou = Changzhou, *China* 116 G5
Changchun, *China* 116 A6
Changde, *China* 116 H1
Changdo-ri, *N. Korea* 118 E4
Changfeng, *China* 116 F4
Changhai = Shanghai, *China* 116 G5
Changhŭng, *S. Korea* 118 H4
Changhŭngni, *N. Korea* 118 C5
Changjiang, *China* 113 J8
Changjin, *N. Korea* 118 C4
Changjin-chŏsuji, *N. Korea* 118 C4
Changli, *China* 116 C4
Changlun, *Malaysia* 126 A1
Changning, *China* 116 J1
Changping, *China* 116 C3
Changsha, *China* 116 H2
Changshu, *China* 116 G5
Changting, *China* 113 H10
Changyang, *China* 116 G1
Changyŏn, *N. Korea* 118 E3
Changzhi, *China* 116 D2
Changzhou, *China* 116 G5
Chanlar, *Azerbaijan* 82 C7
Channel Is., *U.K.* 44 A2
Channel-Port aux Basques, *Canada* 187 J15
Chantada, *Spain* 63 B2
Chanthaburi, *Thailand* 123 H5
Chantrey Inlet, *Canada* 186 D9
Chao Hu, *China* 116 G4
Chao Phraya →, *Thailand* 123 H4
Chao'an, *China* 113 H10
Chaoyang, *Guangdong, China* 113 H10
Chaoyang, *Liaoning, China* 116 B5
Chapala, L. de, *Mexico* 194 D4
Chapayevo, *Kazakstan* 81 E9
Chapayevsk, *Russia* 81 D9
Chapra = Chhapra, *India* 106 C6
Châr, *Mauritania* 140 C2
Chara, *Russia* 91 G13
Charagua, *Bolivia* 218 C2
Charaña, *Bolivia* 218 C1
Chardara, *Kazakstan* 93 C2
Chardara, Step, *Kazakstan* 93 B2
Chardarinskoye Vdkhr., *Kazakstan* 93 C2
Chardzhou, *Turkmenistan* 90 L4
Charente □, *France* 55 E4
Charente-Maritime □, *France* 55 E3
Charentsavan, *Armenia* 82 C6
Chari →, *Chad* 142 E1
Chārīkār, *Afghan.* 104 C5
Charing, *U.K.* 45 D6
Charity, *Guyana* 214 A2
Chärjew = Chardzhou, *Turkmenistan* 90 L4
Charleroi, *Belgium* 51 D3
Charles, C., *U.S.A.* 191 E17
Charles City, *U.S.A.* 191 D11
Charles Town, *U.S.A.* 189 D3
Charleston, *U.S.A.* 191 G16
Charlestown, *S. Africa* 163 D8
Charlesville, *Zaïre* 155 D3
Charleville = Rath Luirc, *Ireland* 46 J1
Charleville, *Australia* 168 H12
Charleville-Mézières, *France* 55 B7
Charlotte, *U.S.A.* 191 F15
Charlotte Harbor, *U.S.A.* 191 K15
Charlottesville, *U.S.A.* 191 E16
Charlottetown, *Canada* 187 K14
Charlton, *Australia* 171 G4
Charlton I., *Canada* 187 J11
Charlwood, *U.K.* 45 E3
Charolles, *France* 55 E7
Charouine, *Algeria* 137 C3
Charters Towers, *Australia* 168 H12
Chartres, *France* 55 C5
Charvakskoye Vdkhr., *Uzbekistan* 93 B3
Chascomús, *Argentina* 221 C5
Chasovnya-Uchurskaya, *Russia* 91 F15
Château-Salins, *France* 55 B8
Châteaubriant, *France* 55 C3
Châteauroux, *France* 55 D5
Chatelet, *Belgium* 51 D3
Châtellerault, *France* 55 D4
Chatham, *N.B., Canada* 187 K14
Chatham, *Ont., Canada* 187 L11
Chatham, *U.K.* 45 D5
Chatham Is., *Pac. Oc.* 176 K6
Chatkal →, *Uzbekistan* 93 C3
Chatkalskiy Khrebet, *Kyrgyzstan* 93 B4
Chatrapur, *India* 106 F6
Chatsworth, *Zimbabwe* 161 C4
Chattanooga, *U.S.A.* 191 G14
Chatyrkel, Ozero, *Kyrgyzstan* 93 C7
Chatyrtash, *Kyrgyzstan* 93 C8
Chauk, *Burma* 122 D2
Chaukan La, *Burma* 122 A3
Chaumont, *France* 55 C7
Chaves, *Portugal* 63 B2
Chavuma, *Zambia* 161 C2
Chayan, *Kazakstan* 93 A3
Chayek, *Kyrgyzstan* 93 B7
Cheb, *Czech.* 76 B2
Cheboksary, *Russia* 81 B8
Cheboygan, *U.S.A.* 191 C13
Chechaouen, *Morocco* 136 A5
Chechon, *S. Korea* 118 F5
Chegdomyn, *Russia* 91 H16
Chegga, *Mauritania* 140 B4
Chegutu, *Zimbabwe* 161 B4
Chehalis, *U.S.A.* 190 B2
Cheju Do, *S. Korea* 118 J4
Chekiang = Zhejiang □, *China* 116 H5
Cheleken, *Turkmenistan* 90 J3
Chelkar, *Kazakstan* 90 H5
Chelkar Tengiz, Solonchak, *Kazakstan* 90 H5
Chełm, *Poland* 77 D6
Chelmer →, *U.K.* 45 B6
Chełmno, *Poland* 77 B3
Chelmsford, *U.K.* 45 B5
Chełmża, *Poland* 77 B3
Cheltenham, *U.K.* 46 K7
Chelyabinsk, *Russia* 90 G6
Chelyuskin, C., *Russia* 84 A14
Chemin Grenier, *Mauritius* 166 C2
Chemnitz, *Germany* 58 D5
Chen, Gora, *Russia* 91 D15
Chen Xian, *China* 113 H9
Chenab →, *Pakistan* 105 C5
Chencha, *Ethiopia* 144 E3
Chenchiang = Zhenjiang, *China* 116 F4
Chengcheng, *China* 116 E1
Chengchou = Zhengzhou, *China* 116 E2
Chengde, *China* 116 B4
Chengdu, *China* 113 F7
Chengjiang, *China* 112 H6
Ch'engtu = Chengdu, *China* 113 F7
Chengyang, *China* 116 D5
Cheo Reo, *Vietnam* 125 E5
Cheom Ksan, *Cambodia* 125 E3
Chepén, *Peru* 213 C2
Chepes, *Argentina* 221 A1
Chepo, *Panama* 197 E6
Cheptulil, Mt., *Kenya* 157 C2
Cher □, *France* 55 D6
Cher →, *France* 55 D5
Cherbourg, *France* 55 B3
Cherchell, *Algeria* 137 A4
Cherdyn, *Russia* 90 F6
Cheremkhovo, *Russia* 91 J11
Cherepanovo, *Russia* 90 H9
Cherepovets, *Russia* 81 A5
Chergui, Chott ech, *Algeria* 137 A3
Cherkassy, *Ukraine* 81 F3
Cherkasy = Cherkassy, *Ukraine* 81 F3
Cherlak, *Russia* 90 H7
Chernak, *Kazakstan* 93 A2
Chernigov, *Ukraine* 81 E3
Chernihiv = Chernigov, *Ukraine* 81 E3
Chernivtsi = Chernovtsy, *Ukraine* 81 F1
Chernogorsk, *Russia* 91 H10
Chernovtsy, *Ukraine* 81 F1
Chernoye, *Russia* 91 D10
Chernyshovskiy, *Russia* 91 F12
Cherokee, *U.S.A.* 191 D10
Cherrapunji, *India* 106 C9
Cherskiy, *Russia* 91 B15
Cherskogo Khrebet, *Russia* 91 D15
Chertsey, *U.K.* 45 D2
Chesapeake B., *U.S.A.* 191 E16
Chesham, *U.K.* 45 B2
Cheshskaya Guba, *Russia* 90 D6
Cheshunt, *U.K.* 45 B3
Chester, *U.K.* 46 H6
Chester, *U.S.A.* 189 C4
Chesterfield, *U.K.* 46 H7
Chesterfield, Is., *N. Cal.* 168 B5
Chesterfield Inlet, *Canada* 186 F9
Cheviot Hills, *U.K.* 46 E6
Chew Bahir, *Ethiopia* 144 F2
Cheyenne, *U.S.A.* 190 E7
Cheyenne →, *U.S.A.* 190 C8
Cheyne B., *Australia* 170 D3
Chhapra, *India* 106 C6
Chhatak, *Bangla.* 111 B3
Chhatarpur, *India* 106 C4
Chhindwara, *India* 106 E4
Chhlong, *Cambodia* 125 F4
Chi →, *Thailand* 123 F5
Chiamussu = Jiamusi, *China* 113 B12
Chiange, *Angola* 160 E2
Chiapa →, *Mexico* 194 F7
Chiatura, *Georgia* 82 B5
Chiba, *Japan* 120 B9
Chiba □, *Japan* 120 B9
Chibemba, *Angola* 160 E2
Chibia, *Angola* 160 D2
Chibougamau, *Canada* 187 J12
Chicago, *U.S.A.* 191 D13
Chichaoua, *Morocco* 136 D3
Chichester, *U.K.* 46 L8
Chichibu, *Japan* 120 A8
Ch'ich'ihaerh = Qiqihar, *China* 113 B11
Chickasha, *U.S.A.* 190 G9
Chiclana, *Spain* 63 H3
Chiclayo, *Peru* 213 C2
Chico, *U.S.A.* 190 D2
Chico →, *Chubut, Argentina* 220 H4
Chico →, *Santa Cruz, Argentina* 220 J3
Chicopee, *U.S.A.* 189 A6
Chicoutimi, *Canada* 187 K13
Chiddingfold, *U.K.* 45 E2
Chidley, C., *Canada* 187 F13
Chiengi, *Zambia* 161 A4
Chiengmai, *Thailand* 122 E3
Chiese →, *Italy* 67 B3
Chieti, *Italy* 67 E6
Chifeng, *China* 116 B4
Chiguana, *Bolivia* 218 D1
Chiha-ri, *N. Korea* 118 E4
Chihli, G. of = Bo Hai, *China* 116 C4
Chihuahua, *Mexico* 194 B3
Chiili, *Kazakstan* 90 K5
Chikmagalur, *India* 107 F2
Chikwawa, *Malawi* 158 E2
Chilapa, *Mexico* 194 F5
Chilas, *Pakistan* 105 A6
Childress, *U.S.A.* 190 G8
Chile ■, *S. Amer.* 220
Chile Rise, *Pac. Oc.* 206 G1
Chilete, *Peru* 213 C2
Chililabombwe, *Zambia* 161 B3
Chilin = Jilin, *China* 113 C11
Chilka L., *India* 106 F7
Chillán, *Chile* 220 F3
Chillicothe, *U.S.A.* 191 E14
Chiloé, I. de, *Chile* 220 H2
Chilpancingo, *Mexico* 194 F5
Chiltern Hills, *U.K.* 46 K8
Chiluage, *Angola* 160 B5
Chilumba, *Malawi* 158 A2
Chilwa, L., *Malawi* 158 D3
Chimán, *Panama* 197 E6
Chimay, *Belgium* 51 E3
Chimbay, *Uzbekistan* 90 J4
Chimborazo, *Ecuador* 212 C1
Chimborazo □, *Ecuador* 212 C1
Chimbote, *Peru* 213 C2
Chimion, *Uzbekistan* 93 D4
Chimkent, *Kazakstan* 93 B3
Chimoio, *Mozam.* 159 D2
China ■, *Asia* 112
Chinan = Jinan, *China* 116 D3
Chinandega, *Nic.* 197 B1
Chincha Alta, *Peru* 213 E3
Chinchilla, *Australia* 171 A8
Chinchón, *Spain* 63 D5

Chinchou = Jinzhou, *China* 116 B5
Chinde, *Mozam.* 159 C3
Chindo, *S. Korea* 118 H4
Chindwin —►, *Burma* 122 D2
Chingola, *Zambia* 161 B3
Chingole, *Malawi* 158 C2
Ch'ingtao = Qingdao, *China* 116 E5
Chinguetti, *Mauritania* 140 C2
Chinhae, *S. Korea* 118 H5
Chinhoyi, *Zimbabwe* 161 B4
Chiniot, *Pakistan* 105 C5
Chinju, *S. Korea* 118 G5
Chinnampo, *N. Korea* 118 E3
Chinnor, *U.K.* 45 B1
Chinon, *France* 55 D4
Chinsali, *Zambia* 161 B5
Chióggia, *Italy* 67 B5
Chios = Khíos, *Greece* 71 D5
Chipata, *Zambia* 161 C5
Chipinge, *Zimbabwe* 161 D5
Chipoka, *Malawi* 158 D2
Chippewa Falls, *U.S.A.* 191 C11
Chipping Ongar, *U.K.* 45 B4
Chiquián, *Peru* 213 D2
Chiquimula, *Guatemala* 196 C1
Chiquinquira, *Colombia* 210 C1
Chirchik, *Uzbekistan* 93 C3
Chiriquí, G. de, *Panama* 197 E4
Chiriquí, L. de, *Panama* 197 E4
Chirivira Falls, *Zimbabwe* 161 E5
Chirmiri, *India* 106 D5
Chiromo, *Malawi* 158 E2
Chirripó Grande, *Costa Rica* 197 D3
Chisamba, *Zambia* 161 C3
Chisapani Garhi, *Nepal* 109 B3
Chisimaio, *Somali Rep.* 145 D1
Chişinău = Kishinev, *Moldova* 81 G2
Chistopol, *Russia* 81 C9
Chita, *Russia* 91 J13
Chitado, *Angola* 160 E2
Chitembo, *Angola* 160 D3
Chitipa, *Malawi* 158 A1
Chitral, *Pakistan* 105 A5
Chitré, *Panama* 197 E5
Chittagong, *Bangla.* 111 D3
Chittagong □, *Bangla.* 111 C2
Chittaurgarh, *India* 106 C2
Chittoor, *India* 107 F3
Chitungwiza, *Zimbabwe* 161 B4
Chiusi, *Italy* 67 D4
Chivasso, *Italy* 67 B1
Chivhu, *Zimbabwe* 161 C4
Chivilcoy, *Argentina* 221 C4
Chkalov = Orenburg, *Russia* 90 G5
Cho-do, *N. Korea* 118 E2
Choba, *Kenya* 157 B3
Chobham, *U.K.* 45 D2
Chochiwŏn, *S. Korea* 118 F4
Choctawhatchee B., *U.S.A.* 191 J13
Choele Choel, *Argentina* 220 G4
Choiseul, *Solomon Is.* 173 A1
Chojnice, *Poland* 77 B2
Chokurdakh, *Russia* 91 C14
Cholet, *France* 55 D3
Cholpon-Ata, *Kyrgyzstan* 93 A8
Choluteca, *Honduras* 196 D3
Choluteca —►, *Honduras* 196 D3
Choma, *Zambia* 161 D3
Chomutov, *Czech.* 76 A2
Chon Buri, *Thailand* 123 H4
Chonan, *S. Korea* 118 F4
Chone, *Ecuador* 212 B1
Chong'an, *China* 116 J4
Chongde, *China* 116 G5
Chŏngdo, *S. Korea* 118 G5
Chŏngha, *S. Korea* 118 G6
Chongjin, *N. Korea* 118 B5
Chŏngju, *N. Korea* 118 D3
Chŏngju, *S. Korea* 118 F4
Chongli, *China* 116 B3
Chongming Dao, *China* 116 G5
Chongqing, *China* 113 G7
Chŏngŭp, *S. Korea* 118 G4
Chŏnju, *S. Korea* 118 G4
Chonos, Arch. de los, *Chile* 206 G2
Chorleywood, *U.K.* 45 B2
Chŏrwŏn, *S. Korea* 118 E4
Chorzów, *Poland* 77 E3
Chosan, *N. Korea* 118 C3
Chōshi, *Japan* 120 B9
Choszczno, *Poland* 77 B1
Choybalsan, *Mongolia* 113 B9
Christchurch, *N.Z.* 175 G4
Christiana, *S. Africa* 163 D5
Christmas I. = Kiritimati, *Kiribati* 176 E8
Chtimba, *Malawi* 158 A2
Chu, *Kazakstan* 93 A6
Chu —►, *Vietnam* 125 B3
Chuadanga, *Bangla.* 111 C1
Ch'uanchou = Quanzhou, *China* 113 H10
Chubut —►, *Argentina* 220 H4
Chudskoye, Oz., *Estonia* 81 A2
Chūgoku □, *Japan* 120 B3
Chūgoku-Sanchi, *Japan* 120 B3
Chukotskiy Khrebet, *Russia* 91 A16
Chukotskoye More, *Russia* 91 A16
Chulman, *Russia* 91 G14
Chulucanas, *Peru* 213 B1
Chulym —►, *Russia* 90 G9
Chumikan, *Russia* 91 G15
Chumphon, *Thailand* 123 J4
Chumunjin, *S. Korea* 118 E5
Chuna —►, *Russia* 91 G10
Chun'an, *China* 116 H4
Chunchŏn, *S. Korea* 118 E4
Chunggang-ŭp, *N. Korea* 118 B4
Chunghwa, *N. Korea* 118 E3
Chungju, *S. Korea* 118 F5
Chungking = Chongqing, *China* 113 G7
Chungmu, *S. Korea* 118 H5
Chunya, *Tanzania* 158 C1
Chuquibamba, *Peru* 213 E4
Chur, *Switz.* 60 C5
Churchill, *Canada* 186 G8
Churchill —►, *Man., Canada* 186 G8
Churchill —►, *Nfld., Canada* 187 H14
Churchill, C., *Canada* 186 G9
Churchill Falls, *Canada* 187 H13
Churchill L., *Canada* 186 G6
Churchill Pk., *Canada* 186 F4
Churu, *India* 106 B2
Chusovoy, *Russia* 90 F6
Chust, *Uzbekistan* 93 C4
Chuuronjang, *N. Korea* 118 B5
Chuvash Republic □, *Russia* 81 C8
Ci Xian, *China* 116 D2
Ciechanów, *Poland* 77 B4
Ciego de Avila, *Cuba* 198 B4
Ciénaga, *Colombia* 210 A1
Cienfuegos, *Cuba* 198 B3
Cieszyn, *Poland* 77 E3
Cieza, *Spain* 63 F7
Cilacap, *Indonesia* 128 F6
Çıldır, *Turkey* 82 C4
Çıldır Gölü, *Turkey* 82 C4
Cimarron —►, *U.S.A.* 191 G10
Cimone, Mte., *Italy* 67 C3
Cimpina, *Romania* 75 C4
Cimpulung, *Romania* 75 C4
Cinca —►, *Spain* 63 C8
Cincinnati, *U.S.A.* 191 E14
Cinto, Mte., *France* 55 H9
Circle, *U.S.A.* 193 A5
Cirebon, *Indonesia* 128 E6
Citeli-Ckaro, *Georgia* 82 B7
Citlaltépetl, *Mexico* 194 E5
Citrusdal, *S. Africa* 163 G2
Ciudad Bolívar, *Venezuela* 211 B4
Ciudad Chetumal, *Mexico* 194 E8
Ciudad del Carmen, *Mexico* 194 E7
Ciudad Delicias = Delicias, *Mexico* 194 B3
Ciudad Guayana, *Venezuela* 211 B4
Ciudad Juárez, *Mexico* 194 A3
Ciudad Madero, *Mexico* 194 D5
Ciudad Mante, *Mexico* 194 D5
Ciudad Obregón, *Mexico* 194 B2
Ciudad Real, *Spain* 63 E5
Ciudad Rodrigo, *Spain* 63 D3
Ciudad Trujillo = Santo Domingo, *Dom. Rep.* 200 B3
Ciudad Victoria, *Mexico* 194 D5
Ciudadela, *Spain* 65 A5
Civitanova, *Italy* 67 D6
Civitavécchia, *Italy* 67 E4
Cizre, *Turkey* 94 C7
Claire, L., *Canada* 186 G6
Clanwilliam, *S. Africa* 163 G2
Clare, *Australia* 171 E2
Clare I., *Ireland* 46 G1
Clarence —►, *Australia* 171 B9
Clarence —►, *N.Z.* 175 F4
Clark Fork —►, *U.S.A.* 190 B4
Clarke I., *Australia* 172 A3
Clarksdale, *U.S.A.* 191 G12
Clarksville, *U.S.A.* 191 F13
Claveria, *Phil.* 130 B2
Clear, C., *Ireland* 46 K1
Clearfield, *U.S.A.* 189 C2
Clearwater, *U.S.A.* 191 J15
Cleburne, *U.S.A.* 191 H10
Clermont-Ferrand, *France* 55 E6
Clervaux, *Lux.* 52 A2
Cleveland, *Australia* 171 A9
Cleveland, *Miss., U.S.A.* 191 G12
Cleveland, *Ohio, U.S.A.* 191 D14
Cleveland, *Tenn., U.S.A.* 191 G14
Cliffe, *U.K.* 45 C5
Clifton, *Australia* 171 A9
Clifton Hills, *Australia* 171 A2
Clinton, *Canada* 186 H4
Clinton, *Iowa, U.S.A.* 191 D12
Clinton, *Mass., U.S.A.* 189 A6
Clinton, *Okla., U.S.A.* 190 G9
Clinton Colden L., *Canada* 186 E7
Clinton Creek, *Canada* 186 C3
Clocolan, *S. Africa* 163 E7
Clones, *Ireland* 46 G3
Clonmel, *Ireland* 46 J2
Cluj-Napoca, *Romania* 75 B3
Clunes, *Australia* 171 G4
Cluny, *France* 55 E7
Clutha —►, *N.Z.* 175 J2
Clyde —►, *U.K.* 46 D5
Clyde, Firth of, *U.K.* 46 E4
Clyde River, *Canada* 187 C11
Coamo, *Puerto Rico* 201 A2
Coast □, *Kenya* 157 E4
Coast Mts., *Canada* 186 F3
Coast Ranges, *U.S.A.* 190 C2
Coatepeque, *Guatemala* 196 C1
Coatesville, *U.S.A.* 189 C4
Coaticook, *Canada* 185 B6
Coats I., *Canada* 187 F10
Coatzacoalcos, *Mexico* 194 E6
Cobalt, *Canada* 187 K11
Cobán, *Guatemala* 196 C1
Cobar, *Australia* 171 C5
Cóbh, *Ireland* 46 K2
Cobham, *Australia* 171 C3
Cobija, *Bolivia* 218 A1
Cobleskill, *U.S.A.* 189 A4
Cobourg, *Canada* 185 C2
Cobram, *Australia* 171 F5
Cóbué, *Mozam.* 159 A2
Coburg, *Germany* 58 E4
Coca —►, *Ecuador* 212 B2
Cocanada = Kakinada, *India* 107 E4
Cochabamba, *Bolivia* 218 C1
Cochin China = Nam-Phan, *Vietnam* 125 G4
Cochrane, *Canada* 187 K11
Cockburn, *Australia* 171 D3
Cockburn Chan., *Chile* 206 H2
Cockpit Country, The, *Jamaica* 199 A2
Coco —►, *Cent. Amer.* 180 H11
Cocobeach, *Gabon* 154 B1
Cod, C., *U.S.A.* 180 E12
Coeroeni —►, *Surinam* 214 D3
Cœur d'Alene, *U.S.A.* 190 B4
Coffs Harbour, *Australia* 171 C9
Coggeshall, *U.K.* 45 A6
Coghinas —►, *Italy* 67 F2
Cognac, *France* 55 E4
Cohoes, *U.S.A.* 189 A5
Cohuna, *Australia* 171 F4
Coiba, I. de, *Panama* 197 E4
Coimbatore, *India* 107 F2
Coimbra, *Portugal* 63 D1
Coín, *Spain* 63 G4
Cojutepeque, *El Salv.* 196 D2
Colac, *Australia* 171 H4
Colbinabbin, *Australia* 171 G5
Colchester, *U.K.* 45 A6
Colebrook, *Australia* 172 C2
Coleman, *Canada* 186 J5
Colenso, *S. Africa* 163 E8
Coleraine, *Australia* 171 G3
Coleraine, *U.K.* 46 E3
Coleridge, L., *N.Z.* 175 G3
Colesberg, *S. Africa* 163 F5
Coligny, *S. Africa* 163 C6
Colima, *Mexico* 194 E3
Colina do Norte, *Guinea-Biss.* 146 C1
Collarenebri, *Australia* 171 B7
Colleen Bawn, *Zimbabwe* 161 D3
Collie, *Australia* 170 C2
Collingwood, *N.Z.* 175 E4
Colmar, *France* 55 C9
Colne —►, *Essex, U.K.* 45 A6
Colne —►, *Herts., U.K.* 45 C2
Colo —►, *Australia* 171 E8
Cologne = Köln, *Germany* 58 D1
Colomb-Béchar = Béchar, *Algeria* 137 B3
Colombia ■, *S. Amer.* 210
Colombo, *Sri Lanka* 110 C1
Colón, *Argentina* 221 A5
Colón, *Cuba* 198 B3
Colón, *Panama* 197 D5
Colonia, *Uruguay* 219 D1
Colorado □, *U.S.A.* 190 E6
Colorado —►, *Argentina* 220 G4
Colorado —►, *N. Amer.* 190 G4
Colorado —►, *U.S.A.* 191 J10
Colorado Desert, *U.S.A.* 190 G3
Colorado Plateau, *U.S.A.* 190 F5
Colorado Springs, *U.S.A.* 190 E7
Columbia, *Mo., U.S.A.* 191 F11
Columbia, *Pa., U.S.A.* 189 C3
Columbia, *S.C., U.S.A.* 191 G15
Columbia, *Tenn., U.S.A.* 191 G13
Columbia —►, *U.S.A.* 180 E7
Columbia Basin, *U.S.A.* 190 B3
Columbretes, Is., *Spain* 63 D8
Columbus, *Ga., U.S.A.* 191 H14
Columbus, *Miss., U.S.A.* 191 H13
Columbus, *Nebr., U.S.A.* 191 E10
Columbus, *Ohio, U.S.A.* 191 E14
Colville —►, *U.S.A.* 193 A5
Colville, C., *N.Z.* 175 B5
Comácchio, *Italy* 67 B4
Comayagua, *Honduras* 196 C3
Comblain, *Belgium* 51 D5
Comilla, *Bangla.* 111 C3
Comino, *Malta* 69 A2
Commewijne □, *Surinam* 214 C5
Committee B., *Canada* 186 D9
Commoron Cr. —►, *Australia* 171 B8
Communism Pk. = Kommunizma, Pik, *Tajikistan* 93 E5
Como, *Italy* 67 A2
Como, L. di, *Italy* 67 A3
Comodoro Rivadavia, *Argentina* 220 H4
Comorin, C., *India* 107 G3
Comoro Is. = Comoros ■, *Ind. Oc.* 166
Comoros ■, *Ind. Oc.* 166
Comox, *Canada* 186 H3
Compiègne, *France* 55 B6
Compton Downs, *Australia* 171 C6
Côn Dao, *Vietnam* 125 G4
Conakry, *Guinea* 147 C2
Conara Junction, *Australia* 172 B3
Concarneau, *France* 55 C1
Concepción, *Bolivia* 218 B2
Concepción, *Chile* 220 F2
Concepción, *Paraguay* 219 B2
Concepción, L., *Bolivia* 218 C2
Concepción del Oro, *Mexico* 194 C4
Concepción del Uruguay, *Argentina* 221 B5
Concession, *Zimbabwe* 161 B4
Conchos —►, *Mexico* 194 B3
Concord, *N.C., U.S.A.* 191 F15
Concord, *N.H., U.S.A.* 191 C17
Concordia, *Argentina* 221 A5
Concordia, *U.S.A.* 190 E9
Condamine, *Australia* 171 A8
Condobolin, *Australia* 171 D6
Conejera, I., *Spain* 65 C4
Confuso —►, *Paraguay* 219 B2
Congo = Zaïre —►, *Africa* 132 G5
Congo (Kinshasa) = Zaïre ■, *Africa* 155
Congo ■, *Africa* 154
Congo Basin, *Africa* 132 F6
Congonhas, *Brazil* 215 A4
Conjeeveram = Kanchipuram, *India* 107 F3
Conlea, *Australia* 171 C5
Conn, L., *Ireland* 46 G1
Connecticut □, *U.S.A.* 189 B6
Connecticut —►, *U.S.A.* 191 D17
Connellsville, *U.S.A.* 189 C1
Connemara, *Ireland* 46 G1
Conoble, *Australia* 171 D5
Cononaco —►, *Ecuador* 212 C3
Conran, C., *Australia* 171 H7
Conselheiro Lafaiete, *Brazil* 215 A4
Constance = Konstanz, *Germany* 58 G2
Constanţa, *Romania* 75 D6
Constantina, *Spain* 63 F3
Constantine, *Algeria* 137 A5
Constitución, *Uruguay* 219 B1
Contamana, *Peru* 213 C3
Contas —►, *Brazil* 217 F9
Conway, *U.S.A.* 191 G11
Cooch Behar = Koch Bihar, *India* 106 C8
Cook, Mt., *N.Z.* 175 G3
Cook Inlet, *U.S.A.* 193 B4
Cook Is., *Pac. Oc.* 176 G7
Cook Strait, *N.Z.* 175 F5
Cookham, *U.K.* 45 C1
Cookhouse, *S. Africa* 163 H6
Cooktown, *Australia* 168 G12
Coolabah, *Australia* 171 C6
Coolah, *Australia* 171 D7
Coolamon, *Australia* 171 F6
Coolangatta, *Australia* 171 A9
Cooma, *Australia* 171 G7
Coonabarabran, *Australia* 171 C7
Coonamble, *Australia* 171 C7
Coongie, *Australia* 171 A2
Coongoola, *Australia* 171 A5
Cooper Cr. —►, *Australia* 171 A2
Cooperstown, *U.S.A.* 189 A4
Cootamundra, *Australia* 171 E6
Cooyar, *Australia* 171 A9
Copán, *Honduras* 196 C2
Copenhagen = København, *Denmark* 42 C4
Coppename —►, *Surinam* 214 C4
Copper Center, *U.S.A.* 193 B5
Copper Queen, *Zimbabwe* 161 B3
Coppermine, *Canada* 186 D6
Coppermine —►, *Canada* 186 D6
Coquilhatville = Mbandaka, *Zaïre* 155 C2
Corabia, *Romania* 75 D3
Coracora, *Peru* 213 E3
Coral Gables, *U.S.A.* 191 K16
Coral Harbour, *Canada* 187 F10
Coral Sea, *Pac. Oc.* 176 G4
Coral Sea Islands Terr. □, *Australia* 176 G4
Corantijn —►, *Surinam* 214 C3
Corato, *Italy* 67 F8
Corby, *U.K.* 46 J8
Corcubión, *Spain* 63 A1
Cordele, *U.S.A.* 191 H14
Córdoba, *Argentina* 221 A2
Córdoba, *Spain* 63 F4
Córdoba □, *Argentina* 221 A2
Córdoba, Sierra de, *Argentina* 221 A2
Cordon, *Phil.* 130 C3
Cordova, *U.S.A.* 193 B5
Corentyne —►, *Guyana* 214 C3
Corfu = Kérkira, *Greece* 71 C1
Corigliano Cálabro, *Italy* 67 G8
Corinna, *Australia* 172 B1
Corinth = Kórinthos, *Greece* 71 D3
Corinth, *U.S.A.* 191 G13
Corinth, G. of = Korinthiakós Kólpos, *Greece* 71 D3
Corinto, *Nic.* 197 B1
Cork, *Ireland* 46 K1
Cork Harbour, *Ireland* 46 K2
Corn Is. = Maiz, Is. del, *Nic.* 197 C3
Corner Brook, *Canada* 187 H15
Corning, *U.S.A.* 189 B3
Cornwall, *Canada* 185 B4
Cornwall I., *Canada* 186 B9
Cornwallis I., *Canada* 186 B9
Corny Pt., *Australia* 171 F1
Coro, *Venezuela* 211 A2
Corocoro, *Bolivia* 218 C1
Coroico, *Bolivia* 218 B1
Coromandel, *N.Z.* 175 B5
Coromandel Coast, *India* 107 F3
Corona, *Australia* 171 C3
Coronado, B. de, *Costa Rica* 197 E3
Coronation Gulf, *Canada* 186 D7
Coronda, *Argentina* 221 A4
Coronel Pringles, *Argentina* 220 F5
Coronel Suárez, *Argentina* 220 F5
Coronie □, *Surinam* 214 B4
Corowa, *Australia* 171 F5
Corozal, *Belize* 196 A2
Corpus Christi, *U.S.A.* 190 J9
Corque, *Bolivia* 218 C1
Corrèze □, *France* 55 F5
Corrib, L., *Ireland* 46 G1
Corrientes, *Argentina* 220 C5
Corrientes —►, *Peru* 213 B3
Corrientes, C., *Colombia* 210 C1
Corrientes, C., *Cuba* 198 B1
Corrientes, C., *Mexico* 194 E3
Corrigin, *Australia* 170 B2
Corringham, *U.K.* 45 C5
Corry, *U.S.A.* 189 B1
Corse, *France* 55 H9
Corse-du-Sud □, *France* 55 H9
Corsica = Corse, *France* 55 H9
Corsicana, *U.S.A.* 191 H10
Cortez, *U.S.A.* 190 F6
Cortland, *U.S.A.* 189 A3
Cortona, *Italy* 67 D4
Çoruh —►, *Turkey* 82 C3
Çorum, *Turkey* 94 B4
Corumbá, *Brazil* 217 G4
Corunna = La Coruña, *Spain* 63 A2
Corvallis, *U.S.A.* 190 B2
Cosenza, *Italy* 67 H7
Cosquín, *Argentina* 221 A2
Costa Blanca, *Spain* 63 F7
Costa Brava, *Spain* 63 B9
Costa del Sol, *Spain* 63 G5
Costa Dorada, *Spain* 63 C9
Costa Rica ■, *Cent. Amer.* 197
Cotabato, *Phil.* 130 K4
Cotagaita, *Bolivia* 218 D1
Côte-d'Ivoire ■ = Ivory Coast ■, *Africa* 148
Côte-d'Or □, *France* 55 D7
Coteau des Prairies, *U.S.A.* 191 C10
Cotentin, *France* 55 B3
Côtes-d'Armor □, *France* 55 C2
Côtes-du-Nord = Côtes-d'Armor □, *France* 55 C2
Cotonou, *Benin* 150 E2
Cotopaxi, *Ecuador* 212 B1
Cotopaxi □, *Ecuador* 212 C1
Cotswolds, *U.K.* 46 K7
Cottbus, *Germany* 58 C6
Coudersport, *U.S.A.* 189 B2
Couedic, C. du, *Australia* 171 F1
Council, *U.S.A.* 193 A3
Council Bluffs, *U.S.A.* 191 E10
Courantyne —►, *S. Amer.* 206 B4
Courtrai = Kortrijk, *Belgium* 51 C1
Couvin, *Belgium* 51 E3
Coventry, *U.K.* 46 J7
Covilhã, *Portugal* 63 D2
Covington, *U.S.A.* 191 E14
Cowal, L., *Australia* 171 E6
Cowangie, *Australia* 171 F3
Cowarie, *Australia* 171 A1
Cowcowing Lakes, *Australia* 170 A2
Cowell, *Australia* 171 E1
Cowra, *Australia* 171 E7
Cox's Bazar, *Bangla.* 111 E3
Cozumel, I. de, *Mexico* 194 D9
Craboon, *Australia* 171 D7
Cracow = Kraków, *Poland* 77 E4
Cradock, *S. Africa* 163 G6
Craigmore, *Zimbabwe* 161 D5
Craiova, *Romania* 75 D3
Cranbrook, *Tas., Australia* 172 B3
Cranbrook, *W. Austral., Australia* 170 D2
Cranbrook, *Canada* 186 J4
Cranbrook, *U.K.* 45 E5
Cranleigh, *U.K.* 45 E2
Crateús, *Brazil* 217 C8
Crato, *Brazil* 217 D9
Crawley, *U.K.* 45 E3
Crécy, *France* 55 A5
Cree —►, *Canada* 186 G7
Cree L., *Canada* 186 G7
Cremona, *Italy* 67 B3
Cres, *Croatia* 72 B3
Crespo, *Argentina* 221 A4
Cressy, *Australia* 171 H4
Cresta, Mt., *Phil.* 130 C3
Crete = Kriti, *Greece* 71 F4
Creus, C., *Spain* 63 B9
Creuse □, *France* 55 E5
Creuse —►, *France* 55 D4
Crewe, *U.K.* 46 H6
Crimea = Krymskiy Poluostrov, *Ukraine* 81 H4
Crişul Alb —►, *Romania* 75 B1
Crişul Negru —►, *Romania* 75 B1
Crna —►, *Macedonia* 72 F8
Crna Gora = Montenegro □, *Yugoslavia* 72 D6
Crna Gora, *Serbia, Yug.* 72 E8
Croatia ■, *Europe* 72 B4
Crocker, Banjaran, *Malaysia* 126 A8
Cromwell, *N.Z.* 175 H2
Crondall, *U.K.* 45 D1
Cronulla, *Australia* 171 E8
Crookwell, *Australia* 171 E7
Cross —►, *Nigeria* 151 F4
Cross River □, *Nigeria* 151 F5
Crotone, *Italy* 67 H8

Crouch →, *U.K.* 45 C6
Crowborough, *U.K.* 45 E4
Crows Nest, *Australia* 171 A9
Crowsnest Pass, *Canada* 186 J5
Crowthorne, *U.K.* 45 D1
Croydon, *U.K.* 45 D3
Cruz, C., *Cuba* 198 C5
Cruz del Eje, *Argentina* 221 A2
Cruzeiro, *Brazil* 215 B3
Cruzeiro do Sul, *Brazil* 217 D1
Crystal Brook, *Australia* 171 E1
Csongrád, *Hungary* 74 B4
Cu Lao Hon, *Vietnam* 125 F5
Cuamba, *Mozam.* 159 B3
Cuando →, *Angola* 160 E5
Cuango →, *Zaïre* 132 G5
Cuanza →, *Angola* 132 G5
Cuarto →, *Argentina* 221 B3
Cuba ■, *W. Indies* 198
Cuballing, *Australia* 170 C2
Cubango →, *Africa* 132 H6
Cuchi, *Angola* 160 D3
Cuchumatanes, Sierra de los, *Guatemala* 196 C1
Cuckfield, *U.K.* 45 E3
Cúcuta, *Colombia* 210 B2
Cuddalore, *India* 107 F3
Cudgewa, *Australia* 171 F6
Cuenca, *Ecuador* 212 D1
Cuenca, *Spain* 63 D6
Cuenca, Serranía de, *Spain* 63 D6
Cuernavaca, *Mexico* 194 E5
Cuero, *U.S.A.* 191 J10
Cuevas del Almanzora, *Spain* 63 G6
Cuevo, *Bolivia* 218 D2
Cuffley, *U.K.* 45 B3
Cuiabá, *Brazil* 217 F5
Cuilco, *Guatemala* 196 C1
Cuima, *Angola* 160 D3
Cuito →, *Angola* 160 E4
Cukai, *Malaysia* 126 B3
Culcairn, *Australia* 171 F6
Culebra, Isla de, *Puerto Rico* 201 A3
Culebra, Sierra de la, *Spain* 63 B3
Culgoa →, *Australia* 171 B6
Culiacán, *Mexico* 194 C2
Culion, *Phil.* 130 G2
Cullarin Ra., *Australia* 171 E7
Cullera, *Spain* 63 E8
Cumaná, *Venezuela* 211 A4
Cumberland, *U.S.A.* 189 D2
Cumberland →, *U.S.A.* 191 F13
Cumberland Pen., *Canada* 187 D12
Cumberland Plateau, *U.S.A.* 191 G14
Cumberland Sd., *Canada* 187 E12
Cumborah, *Australia* 171 B6
Cumbrian Mts., *U.K.* 46 F6
Cumnock, *Australia* 171 D7
Cunderdin, *Australia* 170 B2
Cunene →, *Angola* 160 E2
Cúneo, *Italy* 67 B1
Cunillera, I., *Spain* 65 C1
Cunnamulla, *Australia* 171 A5
Cupar, *U.K.* 46 D6
Cupica, G. de, *Colombia* 210 C1
Curaray →, *Peru* 213 A3
Curepipe, *Mauritius* 166 B2
Curiapo, *Venezuela* 211 B5
Curieuse, *Seychelles* 166 A2
Curitiba, *Brazil* 217 H6
Currabubula, *Australia* 171 C8
Curral Velho, *C. Verde Is.* 222 B3
Curraweena, *Australia* 171 C5
Currie, *Australia* 172 A1
Curtis Group, *Australia* 172 A2
Çürüksu Çayi →, *Turkey* 94 C1
Curup, *Indonesia* 128 D3
Cuttaburra →, *Australia* 171 A5
Cuttack, *India* 106 F7
Cuxhaven, *Germany* 58 A2
Cuyabeno, *Ecuador* 212 B3
Cuyapo, *Phil.* 130 D2
Cuyo, *Phil.* 130 G2
Cuyo East Pass, *Phil.* 130 G3
Cuyo West Pass, *Phil.* 130 G2
Cuyuni →, *Guyana* 214 B2
Cuzco, *Bolivia* 218 C1
Cuzco, *Peru* 213 E4
Cyangugu, *Rwanda* 156 B1
Cyclades = Kikládhes, *Greece* 71 E4
Cygnet, *Australia* 172 C2
Cyprus ■, *Asia* 95
Cyrenaica, *Libya* 138 B5
Cyrene = Shahhât, *Libya* 138 A5
Czech Rep. ■, *Europe* 76 B3
Czeremcha, *Poland* 77 C6
Częstochowa, *Poland* 77 D3

D

Da →, *Vietnam* 125 B3
Da Lat, *Vietnam* 125 F5
Da Nang, *Vietnam* 125 D5
Da Qaidam, *China* 112 E5
Da Yunhe →, *China* 116 F4
Dab'a, Râs el, *Egypt* 139 A2
Daba Shan, *China* 113 F8
Dabai, *Nigeria* 151 B2
Dabakala, *Ivory C.* 148 B5
Dąbie, *Poland* 77 B1
Dabo, *Indonesia* 128 C4
Dabola, *Guinea* 147 B3
Dabou, *Ivory C.* 148 D5
Daboya, *Ghana* 149 B2
Dabrowa Tarnówska, *Poland* 77 E4
Dabung, *Malaysia* 126 B2
Dacca = Dhaka, *Bangla.* 111 C2
Dacca = Dhaka □, *Bangla.* 111 B2
Dadanawa, *Guyana* 214 D2
Dades, Oued →, *Morocco* 136 D4
Dadiya, *Nigeria* 151 C6
Dadra and Nagar Haveli □, *India* 106 F1
Dadu, *Pakistan* 105 E3
Daet, *Phil.* 130 E4
Dagana, *Senegal* 146 A1
Dagestanskiye Ogni, *Russia* 82 B8
Dagö = Hiiumaa, *Estonia* 81 A1
Dagupan, *Phil.* 130 D2
Dahab, *Egypt* 139 C6
Dahlak Kebir, *Eritrea* 144 B3
Dahod, *India* 106 D2
Dahomey = Benin ■, *Africa* 150
Dahra, *Senegal* 146 B1
Dai Shan, *China* 116 G6
Dai Xian, *China* 116 C2
Daiō-Misaki, *Japan* 120 C6
Dairût, *Egypt* 139 C4
Daisetsu-Zan, *Japan* 121 B8
Dajia, *Taiwan* 117 B2
Dakar, *Senegal* 146 B1
Dakhla, *W. Sahara* 136 B1
Dakhla, El Wâhât el-, *Egypt* 139 D2
Dakingari, *Nigeria* 151 B2
Đakovica, *Serbia, Yug.* 72 E7
Dalaba, *Guinea* 147 B3
Dalai Nur, *China* 116 A3
Dalandzadgad, *Mongolia* 113 C7
Dālbandīn, *Pakistan* 105 D2
Dalby, *Australia* 171 A8
Dalga, *Egypt* 139 C4
Dalhousie, *Canada* 187 J14
Dali, *China* 112 H6
Dalian, *China* 116 C5
Daliang Shan, *China* 112 G6
Dāliyat el Karmel, *Israel* 96 B2
Dallas, *Oreg., U.S.A.* 190 B2
Dallas, *Tex., U.S.A.* 191 H10
Dalmacija = Dalmatia □, *Croatia* 72 D5
Dalmatia □, *Croatia* 72 D5
Dalnegorsk, *Russia* 91 J17
Dalnerechensk, *Russia* 91 J16
Daloa, *Ivory C.* 148 C4
Dalupiri I., *Phil.* 130 B3
Dalvík, *Iceland* 38 B4
Daman, *India* 106 F1
Damanhûr, *Egypt* 139 A4
Damar, *Indonesia* 129 F14
Damaraland, *Namibia* 162 B3
Damascus = Dimashq, *Syria* 97 C2
Damāvand, Qolleh-ye, *Iran* 103 B3
Damba, *Angola* 160 A2
Dame Marie, *Haiti* 200 B1
Damietta = Dumyât, *Egypt* 139 A4
Daming, *China* 116 D3
Damīr Qābū, *Syria* 97 A5
Dammam = Ad Dammām, *Si. Arabia* 99 C6
Damoh, *India* 106 D4
Dampier, *Australia* 168 H9
Dampier, Selat, *Indonesia* 129 C15
Dan Gulbi, *Nigeria* 151 B3
Dana, *Indonesia* 129 F11
Danao, *Phil.* 130 H4
Danbury, *U.K.* 45 B5
Danbury, *U.S.A.* 189 B5
Dandaragan, *Australia* 170 A1
Dandeldhura, *Nepal* 109 A1
Dandenong, *Australia* 171 H5
Dandong, *China* 116 B6
Dangara, *Tajikistan* 93 F3
Danger Is. = Pukapuka, *Cook Is.* 176 G7
Danger Pt., *S. Africa* 163 H2
Dangora, *Nigeria* 151 B4
Dangriga, *Belize* 196 B2
Dangshan, *China* 116 E3
Dangtu, *China* 116 G4
Dangyang, *China* 116 G1
Danielskuil, *S. Africa* 163 E4
Danilov, *Russia* 81 B6
Danissa, *Kenya* 157 B4
Danja, *Nigeria* 151 B4
Dankalwa, *Nigeria* 151 B7
Dankama, *Nigeria* 151 A4
Danlí, *Honduras* 196 D3
Dannemora, *Sweden* 40 F4
Dannevirke, *N.Z.* 175 E6
Dannhauser, *S. Africa* 163 D8
Danshui, *Taiwan* 117 A3
Dansville, *U.S.A.* 189 A2
Danube →, *Europe* 34 F12
Danville, *Ill., U.S.A.* 191 E13
Danville, *Ky., U.S.A.* 191 F14
Danville, *Va., U.S.A.* 191 F15
Danzig = Gdańsk, *Poland* 77 A3
Daoud = Aïn Beïda, *Algeria* 137 A5
Dapitan, *Phil.* 130 J4
Dapong, *Togo* 150 B1
Daqing Shan, *China* 116 B1
Daqu Shan, *China* 116 G6
Dar-es-Salaam, *Tanzania* 158 C3
Dar'ā, *Syria* 97 D2
Daraj, *Libya* 138 B1
Daraut Kurgan, *Kyrgyzstan* 93 E5
Daraw, *Egypt* 139 E5
Darazo, *Nigeria* 151 B6
Darband, *Pakistan* 105 B5
Darbhanga, *India* 106 C7
Dardanelles = Çanakkale Boğazı, *Turkey* 94 B1
Darent →, *U.K.* 45 C4
Dârfûr, *Sudan* 143 D2
Dargai, *Pakistan* 105 A5
Dargan Ata, *Uzbekistan* 90 K4
Dargaville, *N.Z.* 175 B4
Darhan Muminggan Lianheqi, *China* 116 B1
Darién, G. del, *Colombia* 210 B1
Darjeeling = Darjiling, *India* 106 B8
Darjiling, *India* 106 B8
Darkan, *Australia* 170 C2
Darling →, *Australia* 171 E3
Darling Downs, *Australia* 171 A8
Darling Ra., *Australia* 170 B2
Darlington, *U.K.* 46 F7
Darłowo, *Poland* 77 A2
Darmstadt, *Germany* 58 E2
Darnah, *Libya* 138 A5
Darnall, *S. Africa* 163 E9
Darnley B., *Canada* 186 C6
Darsana, *Bangla.* 111 C1
Dartford, *U.K.* 45 C4
Dartmoor, *U.K.* 46 L5
Dartmouth, *Canada* 187 K14
Dartmouth, *U.K.* 46 M5
Dartuch, C., *Spain* 65 A5
Daru, *Papua N. G.* 173 C1
Darvaza, *Turkmenistan* 90 K3
Darvel, Teluk, *Malaysia* 126 B8
Darwha, *India* 106 F3
Darwin, *Australia* 168 G11
Daryoi Amu = Amudarya →, *Uzbekistan* 90 J4
Dās, *U.A.E.* 101 B2
Dashkesan, *Azerbaijan* 82 C7
Dasht →, *Pakistan* 105 F1
Dasht-e Kavīr, *Iran* 103 B4
Dassa-Zoume, *Benin* 150 D2
Datia, *India* 106 C4
Datong, *Anhui, China* 116 G4
Datong, *Shanxi, China* 116 C2
Datu, Tanjung, *Indonesia* 128 B6
Datu Piang, *Phil.* 130 K5
Daudkandi, *Bangla.* 111 C2
Daugava →, *Latvia* 81 B2
Daugavpils, *Latvia* 81 B2
Daule, *Ecuador* 212 C1
Daule →, *Ecuador* 212 C1
Daulpur, *India* 106 B3
Dauphin, *Canada* 186 J7
Dauphiné, *France* 55 F8
Daura, *Borno, Nigeria* 151 B6
Daura, *Kaduna, Nigeria* 151 A4
Davangere, *India* 107 E2
Davao, *Phil.* 130 K5
Davao, G. of, *Phil.* 130 K5
Davenport, *U.S.A.* 191 D12
David, *Panama* 197 E4
Davis Str., *N. Amer.* 180 C14
Davos, *Switz.* 60 C5
Dawaki, *Bauchi, Nigeria* 151 D5
Dawaki, *Kano, Nigeria* 151 B4
Dawson, *Canada* 186 C4
Dawson Creek, *Canada* 186 G4
Daxi, *Taiwan* 117 A3
Daxian, *China* 113 F7
Daxue Shan, *China* 112 F6
Daye, *China* 116 G2
Daylesford, *Australia* 171 G4
Dayong, *China* 116 H1
Dayr az Zawr, *Syria* 97 B5
Dayton, *Ohio, U.S.A.* 191 E14
Dayton, *Wash., U.S.A.* 190 B4
Daytona Beach, *U.S.A.* 191 J15
De Aar, *S. Africa* 163 F5
De Ridder, *U.S.A.* 191 J11
Dead Sea, *Asia* 84 E7
Deal I., *Australia* 172 A3
Dealesville, *S. Africa* 163 E6
Dease →, *Canada* 186 E4
Dease Arm, *Canada* 186 D6
Dease Lake, *Canada* 186 E3
Death Valley, *U.S.A.* 190 F3
Deba Habe, *Nigeria* 151 C6
Debar, *Macedonia* 72 F7
Debdou, *Morocco* 136 B6
Deborah West, L., *Australia* 170 A3
Debre Markos, *Ethiopia* 144 D3
Debre Tabor, *Ethiopia* 144 C3
Debrecen, *Hungary* 74 B5
Decatur, *Ala., U.S.A.* 191 G13
Decatur, *Ga., U.S.A.* 191 G14
Decatur, *Ill., U.S.A.* 191 E12
Deccan, *India* 107 E3
Dedéagach = Alexandroúpolis, *Greece* 71 B5
Dédougou, *Burkina Faso* 149 A1
Deduru →, *Sri Lanka* 110 C1
Dedza, *Malawi* 158 D2
Dee →, *Clwyd, U.K.* 46 H6
Dee →, *Gramp., U.K.* 46 C7
Deepwater, *Australia* 171 B9
Deerdepoort, *S. Africa* 163 B6
Degeh Bur, *Ethiopia* 144 D4
Degema, *Nigeria* 151 G3
Deggendorf, *Germany* 58 F5
Dehibat, *Tunisia* 138 D2
Dehiwala, *Sri Lanka* 110 C1
Dehra Dun, *India* 107 B3
Deinze, *Belgium* 51 B2
Dej, *Romania* 75 B3
Dekese, *Zaïre* 155 D3
Del Rio, *U.S.A.* 190 J8
Delagoa B., *Mozam.* 132 J7
Delareyville, *S. Africa* 163 D6
Delaware □, *U.S.A.* 189 D4
Delaware →, *U.S.A.* 189 D4
Delaware B., *U.S.A.* 191 E17
Delegate, *Australia* 171 G7
Delémont, *Switz.* 60 A2
Delft, *Neths.* 50 D2
Delft I., *Sri Lanka* 110 A1
Delgado, C., *Mozam.* 159 A3
Delgo, *Sudan* 143 B4
Delhi, *India* 106 A3
Delice →, *Turkey* 94 B4
Delicias, *Mexico* 194 B3
Delong, Ostrova, *Russia* 91 B13
Deloraine, *Australia* 172 B2
Delportshoop, *S. Africa* 163 E5
Delungra, *Australia* 171 B8
Demanda, Sierra de la, *Spain* 63 B5
Demba, *Zaïre* 155 E3
Dembecha, *Ethiopia* 144 D2
Dembidolo, *Ethiopia* 144 D2
Demer →, *Belgium* 51 B4
Deming, *U.S.A.* 190 H6
Demnate, *Morocco* 136 D3
Demopolis, *U.S.A.* 191 H13
Dempo, *Indonesia* 128 D4
Den Burg, *Neths.* 50 B3
Den Haag = 's-Gravenhage, *Neths.* 50 D2
Den Helder, *Neths.* 50 B3
Den Oever, *Neths.* 50 B3
Denau, *Uzbekistan* 93 F2
Denbigh, *U.K.* 46 H6
Dendang, *Indonesia* 128 D5
Deng Xian, *China* 116 F1
Denge, *Nigeria* 151 A2
Dengi, *Nigeria* 151 D5
Denia, *Spain* 63 E8
Deniliquin, *Australia* 171 F5
Denizli, *Turkey* 94 C2
Denmark, *Australia* 170 D2
Denmark ■, *Europe* 42
Denmark Str., *Atl. Oc.* 222 A3
Denpasar, *Indonesia* 128 F8
Denton, *U.S.A.* 191 H10
D'Entrecasteaux, Pt., *Australia* 170 D2
D'Entrecasteaux Is., *Papua N. G.* 173 C3
Denu, *Ghana* 149 D3
Denver, *U.S.A.* 190 E7
Deoghar, *India* 106 D7
Deolali, *India* 106 F1
Deoria, *India* 106 C6
Deosai Mts., *Pakistan* 105 A6
Deping, *China* 116 D3
Deputatskiy, *Russia* 91 D14
Dêqên, *China* 112 G6
Dera Ghazi Khan, *Pakistan* 105 D4
Dera Ismail Khan, *Pakistan* 105 C4
Derbent, *Russia* 82 B8
Derby, *U.K.* 46 H7
Dereli, *Turkey* 82 C1
Derg, L., *Ireland* 46 H2
Derryveagh Mts., *Ireland* 46 E2
Derudub, *Sudan* 143 B6
Des Moines, *U.S.A.* 191 D11
Des Moines →, *U.S.A.* 191 E11
Desaguadero →, *Argentina* 221 C1
Desaguadero →, *Bolivia* 218 C1
Deschutes →, *U.S.A.* 190 B3
Dese, *Ethiopia* 144 D3
Desna →, *Ukraine* 81 E3
Despeñaperros, *Spain* 63 F5
Dessau, *Germany* 58 C5
Dessye = Dese, *Ethiopia* 144 D3
D'Estrees B., *Australia* 171 F1
Dete, *Zimbabwe* 161 C2
Detmold, *Germany* 58 C2
Detroit, *U.S.A.* 191 D14
Deurne, *Belgium* 51 B3
Deurne, *Neths.* 50 F4
Deutsche Bucht, *Germany* 58 A2
Deux-Sèvres □, *France* 55 E4
Deva, *Romania* 75 C2
Deventer, *Neths.* 50 D5
Devils Lake, *U.S.A.* 190 B9
Devil's Pt., *Sri Lanka* 110 A1
Devon I., *Canada* 186 B9
Devonport, *Australia* 172 B2
Devonport, *N.Z.* 175 B5
Dewas, *India* 106 D2
Dewetsdorp, *S. Africa* 163 E6
Dezfūl, *Iran* 103 C2
Dezhneva, Mys, *Russia* 91 A17
Dezhou, *China* 116 D3
Dhahran = Az Zahrān, *Si. Arabia* 99 C6
Dhaka, *Bangla.* 111 C2
Dhaka □, *Bangla.* 111 B2
Dhamar, *Yemen* 100 B1
Dhamtari, *India* 106 F5
Dhanbad, *India* 106 D7
Dhangarhi, *Nepal* 109 B1
Dhankuta, *Nepal* 109 C4
Dhar, *India* 106 E2
Dharwad, *India* 107 E2
Dhaulagiri, *Nepal* 109 B2
Dhenkanal, *India* 106 F7
Dhidhimótikhon, *Greece* 71 A6
Dhíkti, *Greece* 71 F5
Dhírfis, *Greece* 71 D4
Dhodhekánisos, *Greece* 71 E6
Dhubri, *India* 106 C9
Dhulasar, *Bangla.* 111 D2
Dhule, *India* 106 E2
Di Linh, Cao Nguyen, *Vietnam* 125 F5
Diafarabé, *Mali* 140 E4
Diamante, *Argentina* 221 A4
Diamantina, *Brazil* 217 G8
Diamantino, *Brazil* 217 F5
Diamond Harbour, *India* 106 E8
Dianra, *Ivory C.* 148 B4
Diapaga, *Burkina Faso* 149 B3
Diariguila, *Guinea* 147 B4
Dibaya, *Zaïre* 155 E4
Dibaya Lubue, *Zaïre* 155 D3
Dibbi, *Ethiopia* 144 F4
Dibrugarh, *India* 107 B6
Dickinson, *U.S.A.* 190 B8
Didiéni, *Mali* 140 E3
Diébougou, *Burkina Faso* 149 B1
Diémbéring, *Senegal* 146 C1
Dien Bien Phu, *Vietnam* 125 B2
Diepenbeek, *Belgium* 51 B5
Dieppe, *France* 55 A5
Dieren, *Neths.* 50 D5
Diest, *Belgium* 51 B4
Differdange, *Lux.* 52 D1
Digby, *Canada* 187 K14
Digges Is., *Canada* 187 F11
Dighinala, *Bangla.* 111 C3
Digne, *France* 55 G8
Digor, *Turkey* 82 C5
Digos, *Phil.* 130 K5
Digranes, *Iceland* 38 A5
Digul →, *Indonesia* 129 F18
Dijon, *France* 55 D7
Dikhil, *Djibouti* 145 B1
Diksmuide, *Belgium* 51 B1
Dikson, *Russia* 90 C9
Dikwa, *Nigeria* 151 B7
Dili, *Indonesia* 129 F12
Dilizhan, *Armenia* 82 C6
Dilling, *Sudan* 143 D3
Dillingham, *U.S.A.* 193 B3
Dilolo, *Zaïre* 155 F4
Dilston, *Australia* 172 B2
Dimashq, *Syria* 97 C2
Dimbaza, *S. Africa* 163 H6
Dimbokro, *Ivory C.* 148 D5
Dimboola, *Australia* 171 G3
Dîmboviţa →, *Romania* 75 D5
Dimitrovgrad, *Bulgaria* 73 C4
Dimitrovgrad, *Russia* 81 C8
Dimona, *Israel* 96 E2
Dinagat, *Phil.* 130 H5
Dinan, *France* 55 C3
Dinant, *Belgium* 51 D4
Dinara Planina, *Croatia* 72 C4
Dinard, *France* 55 C3
Dinaric Alps = Dinara Planina, *Croatia* 72 C4
Ding Xian, *China* 116 C3
Dingalan, *Phil.* 130 D3
Dinghai, *China* 116 G6
Dingtao, *China* 116 E3
Dinguiraye, *Guinea* 147 B4
Dingwall, *U.K.* 46 B5
Dingxiang, *China* 116 D2
Diourbel, *Senegal* 146 B1
Dipolog, *Phil.* 130 J4
Dir, *Pakistan* 105 A5
Diré, *Mali* 140 D4
Dire Dawa, *Ethiopia* 144 D4
Diriamba, *Nic.* 197 C1
Dirico, *Angola* 160 E4
Dirranbandi, *Australia* 171 B7
Disa, *India* 106 D1
Disappointment, C., *U.S.A.* 190 B2
Disappointment, L., *Australia* 168 C2
Disaster B., *Australia* 171 G7
Discovery B., *Australia* 171 H3
Disentis, *Switz.* 60 C4
Dishna, *Egypt* 139 D5
Disina, *Nigeria* 151 B5
Disko, *Greenland* 224 C1
Disko Bugt, *Greenland* 224 C1
Disteghil Sar, *Pakistan* 105 A6
Distrito Federal □, *Brazil* 217 F6
Disûq, *Egypt* 139 A4
Diu I., *India* 107 D1
Divichi, *Azerbaijan* 82 B9
Divnoye, *Russia* 81 G7
Divo, *Ivory C.* 148 D5
Dīwāl Qol, *Afghan.* 104 D4
Dixon, *U.S.A.* 191 D12
Diyadin, *Turkey* 82 D5
Diyarbakır, *Turkey* 94 C6
Djado, *Niger* 141 A5
Djakarta = Jakarta, *Indonesia* 128 E5
Djambala, *Congo* 154 C2
Djanet, *Algeria* 137 D6
Djaul I., *Papua N. G.* 173 A3
Djawa = Jawa, *Indonesia* 128 F6
Djebiniana, *Tunisia* 138 B3
Djelfa, *Algeria* 137 A4
Djeneïene, *Tunisia* 138 E2
Djenné, *Mali* 140 E4
Djerba, *Tunisia* 138 C3
Djerid, Chott, *Tunisia* 138 C1
Djibo, *Burkina Faso* 149 A2
Djibouti, *Djibouti* 145 B2
Djibouti ■, *Africa* 145
Djolu, *Zaïre* 155 B4
Djougou, *Benin* 150 B2
Djoum, *Cameroon* 153 E2

Djourab, Chad 142 C2
Djugu, Zaïre 155 B6
Djúpivogur, Iceland 38 C5
Dmitriya Lapteva, Proliv, Russia 91 C13
Dnepr →, Ukraine 81 G3
Dneprodzerzhinsk, Ukraine 81 F4
Dnepropetrovsk, Ukraine 81 F4
Dnestr →, Europe 81 G3
Dnestrovski = Belgorod, Russia 81 E5
Dnieper = Dnepr →, Ukraine 81 G3
Dniester = Dnestr →, Europe 81 G3
Dnipro = Dnepr →, Ukraine 81 G3
Dniprodzerzhynsk = Dneprodzerzhinsk, Ukraine 81 F4
Dnipropetrovsk = Dnepropetrovsk, Ukraine 81 F4
Dnyapro = Dnepr →, Ukraine 81 G3
Doabi, Afghan. 104 C4
Doba, Chad 142 F1
Doberai, Jazirah, Indonesia 129 C15
Dobo, Indonesia 129 E16
Dobreta-Turnu-Severin, Romania 75 D2
Dobruja, Romania 75 D6
Dodecanese = Dhodhekánisos, Greece 71 E6
Dodge City, U.S.A. 190 F9
Dodoma, Tanzania 158 C2
Doesburg, Neths. 50 D5
Doetinchem, Neths. 50 D5
Dogger Bank, N. Sea 34 D7
Doğubayazıt, Turkey 82 D5
Doha = Ad Dawhah, Qatar 100 D3
Doi, Indonesia 129 B13
Dokkum, Neths. 50 A5
Dolbeau, Canada 187 J12
Dole, France 55 D8
Dolgellau, U.K. 46 J5
Dolgelley = Dolgellau, U.K. 46 J5
Dolomites = Dolomiti, Italy 67 A4
Dolomiti, Italy 67 A4
Dolores, Argentina 220 F5
Dolores, Uruguay 219 C1
Dolphin, C., Falk. Is. 224 A3
Dolphin and Union Str., Canada 186 C6
Doma, Nigeria 151 D4
Domasi, Malawi 158 D3
Dombarovskiy, Russia 90 H5
Dombes, France 55 E7
Domburg, Neths. 50
Domel I. = Letsôk-aw Kyun, Burma 122 J3
Dominica ■, W. Indies 203 A2
Dominican Rep. ■, W. Indies 200
Domo, Ethiopia 144 E6
Domodóssola, Italy 67 A2
Dompim, Ghana 149 E1
Domville, Mt., Australia 171 A8
Don →, Russia 81 G6
Don →, U.K. 46 C7
Don Benito, Spain 63 E3
Don Figuero Mts., Jamaica 199 B3
Donald, Australia 171 G4
Donau →, Austria 61 A6
Donauwörth, Germany 58 F4
Doncaster, U.K. 46 G7
Dondo, Angola 160 B2
Dondo, Mozam. 159 D2
Dondo, Teluk, Indonesia 129 C11
Dondra Head, Sri Lanka 110 D2
Donegal, Ireland 46 F2
Donegal B., Ireland 46 F1
Donets →, Russia 81 G6
Donetsk, Ukraine 81 F5
Donga, Nigeria 151 E5
Dongen, Neths. 50 E3
Donggala, Indonesia 129 C10
Donggou, China 116 C6
Dongguang, China 116 D3
Dongliu, China 116 G3
Dongola, Sudan 143 B4
Dongou, Congo 154 B3
Dongping, China 116 E3
Dongsheng, China 116 C1
Dongshi, Taiwan 117 B3
Dongtai, China 116 F5
Dongting Hu, China 116 H2
Dongxing, China 113 J7
Dongyang, China 116 H5
Donnybrook, Australia 170 C1
Donnybrook, S. Africa 163 F8
Donostia = San Sebastián, Spain 63 A6
Donsol, Phil. 130 F4
Dora Báltea →, Italy 67 B2
Dorchester, U.K. 46 L6
Dorchester, C., Canada 187 E11
Dordogne □, France 55 F4
Dordogne →, France 55 F4
Dordrecht, Neths. 50 E3
Dordrecht, S. Africa 163 G6
Dore, Mt., France 55 F6
Dori, Burkina Faso 149 A3
Doring →, S. Africa 163 G2
Doringbos, S. Africa 163 G2
Dorking, U.K. 45 D3
Dormaa-Ahenkro, Ghana 149 C1
Dorohoi, Romania 75 A5
Döröö Nuur, Mongolia 112 B5
Dorrigo, Australia 171 C9
Dorsten, Germany 59 A2
Dortmund, Germany 58 C2
Doruma, Zaïre 155 A5
Dos Bahias, C., Argentina 220 H4
Dosso, Niger 141 D2
Dothan, U.S.A. 191 H14
Douai, France 55 A6
Douala, Cameroon 153 D1
Douarnenez, France 55 C1
Doubs □, France 55 D8
Doubs →, France 55 D7
Doubtful Sd., N.Z. 175 H1
Doubtless B., N.Z. 175 A4
Douentza, Mali 140 E4
Douglas, S. Africa 163 E5
Douglas, U.K. 46 G5
Douglas, U.S.A. 190 H5
Douirat, Morocco 136 C5
Doumé, Cameroon 153 D2
Dounan, Taiwan 117 B2
Douro →, Europe 34 G5
Douro Litoral, Portugal 63 C2
Douz, Tunisia 138 C2
Dover, Australia 172 C2
Dover, U.K. 46 L9
Dover, U.S.A. 189 D4
Dover, Str. of, Europe 55 A5
Dovrefjell, Norway 40 E2
Dowa, Malawi 158 C2
Dowlat Yār, Afghan. 104 D3
Dowlatābād, Farāh, Afghan. 104 E1
Dowlatābād, Fāryāb, Afghan. 104 B3
Dowshī, Afghan. 104 C5
Draa, C., Morocco 136 F1
Draa, Oued →, Morocco 136 F1
Drachten, Neths. 50 A5
Dragoman, Prokhod, Bulgaria 73 B2
Dragonera, I., Spain 65 B3
Draguignan, France 55 G9
Drake, Australia 171 B9
Drakensberg, S. Africa 163 F7
Dráma, Greece 71 A4
Drammen, Norway 40 F2
Drangajökull, Iceland 38 A2
Drau = Drava →, Croatia 72 B6
Drava →, Croatia 72 B6
Drenthe □, Neths. 50 B5
Dresden, Germany 58 D5
Dreux, France 55 C5
Drina →, Bos.-H. 72 B6
Drogheda, Ireland 46 G3
Drogobych, Ukraine 81 E1
Drohobych = Drogobych, Ukraine 81 E1
Drôme □, France 55 F8
Dromedary, C., Australia 171 G7
Drumheller, Canada 186 H5
Drummondville, Canada 185 B6
Druzhina, Russia 91 C15
Dry Harbour Mts., Jamaica 199 A3
Dschang, Cameroon 153 D1
Du Bois, U.S.A. 189 C2
Dubai = Dubayy, U.A.E. 101 B3
Dubawnt →, Canada 186 F7
Dubawnt, L., Canada 186 F8
Dubayy, U.A.E. 101 B3
Dubbo, Australia 171 D7
Dublin, Ireland 46 H3
Dublin, U.S.A. 191 H15
Dubovka, Russia 81 F7
Dubréka, Guinea 147 B2
Dubrovnik, Croatia 72 E5
Dubrovskoye, Russia 91 G12
Dubuque, U.S.A. 191 D12
Duchang, China 116 H3
Ducie I., Pac. Oc. 176 H9
Dudelange, Lux. 52 D2
Dudhi, India 106 D6
Dudinka, Russia 91 E10
Duero = Douro →, Europe 34 G5
Duffel, Belgium 51 B3
Dugi Otok, Croatia 72 C3
Duisburg, Germany 58 C1
Duiwelskloof, S. Africa 163 B8
Dukhān, Qatar 100 D3
Duki, Pakistan 105 D4
Duku, Bauchi, Nigeria 151 C6
Duku, Sokoto, Nigeria 151 B2
Dulag, Phil. 130 G5
Dulce, G., Costa Rica 197 E3
Dulit, Banjaran, Malaysia 126 B7
Dulq Maghār, Syria 97 A4
Duluth, U.S.A. 191 C11
Dūmā, Lebanon 95 B2
Dūmā, Syria 97 C2
Dumaguete, Phil. 130 J4
Dumai, Indonesia 128 B3
Dumaran, Phil. 130 H2
Dumbarton, U.K. 46 D5
Dumbleyung, Australia 170 C2
Dumfries, U.K. 46 E5
Dumyât, Egypt 139 A4
Dumyât, Masabb, Egypt 139 A4
Dun Laoghaire, Ireland 46 H3
Dunaföldvár, Hungary 74 B3
Dunărea →, Romania 75 C6
Duncan, U.S.A. 190 G9
Dundalk, Ireland 46 G3
Dundas, Canada 185 D1
Dundee, S. Africa 163 E8
Dundee, U.K. 46 D6
Dundoo, Australia 171 A5
Dunedin, N.Z. 175 J3
Dunfermline, U.K. 46 D6
Dungarvan, Ireland 46 J2
Dungog, Australia 171 D8
Dungu, Zaïre 155 A6
Dunhinda Falls, Sri Lanka 110 C2
Dunhuang, China 112 D5
Dunkerque, France 55 A6
Dunkirk = Dunkerque, France 55 A6
Dunkirk, U.S.A. 189 A2
Dunkwa, Central, Ghana 149 E2
Dunkwa, Central, Ghana 149 D2
Dúnleary = Dun Laoghaire, Ireland 46 H3
Dunmore, U.S.A. 189 B4
Dunolly, Australia 171 G4
Dunqul, Egypt 139 F4
Dunstable, U.K. 45 A2
Dunstan Mts., N.Z. 175 H2
Duolun, China 116 B3
Duque de Caxias, Brazil 215 B4
Durance →, France 55 G7
Durango, Mexico 194 C3
Durango, Spain 63 A6
Durango, U.S.A. 190 F6
Duranillin, Australia 170 C2
Durant, U.S.A. 191 G10
Durazno, Uruguay 219 C2
Durazzo = Durrësi, Albania 70 B2
Durban, S. Africa 163 F9
Düren, Germany 59 B1
Durg, India 106 E5
Durgapur, India 106 D7
Durham, U.K. 46 F7
Durham, U.S.A. 191 F16
Durmitor, Montenegro, Yug. 72 D6
Durrësi, Albania 70 B2
D'Urville, Tanjung, Indonesia 129 C17
D'Urville I., N.Z. 175 E4
Dûsh, Egypt 139 E4
Dushak, Turkmenistan 90 L3
Dushanbe, Tajikistan 93 E2
Dusheti, Georgia 82 C6
Düsseldorf, Germany 58 D1
Dutch Harbor, U.S.A. 193 B2
Dutsan Wai, Nigeria 151 C4
Duyun, China 113 H7
Duzdab = Zāhedān, Iran 103 D5
Dvina, Sev. →, Russia 90 D5
Dvinsk = Daugavpils, Latvia 81 B2
Dwellingup, Australia 170 C2
Dyersburg, U.S.A. 191 F12
Dynevor Downs, Australia 171 A5
Dyurbeldzhin, Kyrgyzstan 93 C7
Dzamin Üüd, Mongolia 113 C8
Dzerzhinsk, Belarus 81 C2
Dzerzhinsk, Russia 81 B7
Dzhalal-Abad, Kyrgyzstan 93 C5
Dzhalinda, Russia 91 H14
Dzhambul, Kazakstan 93 A4
Dzhankoi, Ukraine 81 H4
Dzhardzhan, Russia 91 D13
Dzharkurgan, Uzbekistan 93 G1
Dzhelinde, Russia 91 D12
Dzhetygara, Kazakstan 90 H5
Dzhetym, Khrebet, Kyrgyzstan 93 B8
Dzhezkazgan, Kazakstan 90 J6
Dzhikimde, Russia 91 G13
Dzhizak, Uzbekistan 93 D2
Dzhugdzur, Khrebet, Russia 91 F15
Dzhuma, Uzbekistan 93 D1
Dzhumgoltau, Khrebet, Kyrgyzstan 93 B7
Dzhvari, Georgia 82 A4
Dzungaria = Junggar Pendi, China 112 C4
Dzungarian Gate = Alataw Shankou, China 112 B3
Dzuumod, Mongolia 113 B7

E

Eagle Pass, U.S.A. 190 J8
Ealing, U.K. 45 C3
Earl's Colne, U.K. 45 A6
Earnslaw, Mt., N.Z. 175 H2
Easebourne, U.K. 45 E1
East Angus, Canada 185 B6
East Beskids = Vychodné Beskydy, Europe 76 B7
East C., N.Z. 175 C6
East China Sea, Asia 84 E16
East Falkland, Falk. Is. 224 A3
East Grinstead, U.K. 45 E4
East Horsley, U.K. 45 D2
East Indies, Asia 84 J15
East London, S. Africa 163 H7
East Main = Eastmain, Canada 187 J11
East Orange, U.S.A. 189 C5
East Pakistan = Bangladesh ■, Asia 111
East Point, U.S.A. 191 G14
East Schelde → = Oosterschelde, Neths. 50 E2
East Siberian Sea, Russia 91 B15
East Toorale, Australia 171 C5
Eastbourne, N.Z. 175 F5
Eastbourne, U.K. 46 L9
Eastchurch, U.K. 45 D6
Eastern □, Kenya 157 C3
Eastern □, Uganda 156 B3
Eastern Cape, S. Africa 163 G6
Eastern Ghats, India 107 F3
Eastern Group = Lau Is., Fiji 174 A2
Eastern Province □, S. Leone 147 C3
Eastern Transvaal = Mpumalanga □, S. Africa 163 C8
Eastmain, Canada 187 J11
Eastmain →, Canada 187 J11
Easton, U.S.A. 189 C4
Eau Claire, Fr. Guiana 214 D5
Eau Claire, U.S.A. 191 C11
Eban, Nigeria 151 C2
Ebebiyin, Eq. Guin. 153 B2
Ebeltoft, Denmark 42 B3
Eberswalde, Germany 58 B5
Eboli, Italy 67 F7
Ebolowa, Cameroon 153 E1
Ébrié, Lagune, Ivory C. 148 E5
Ebro →, Spain 63 C8
Ech Cheliff, Algeria 137 A4
Echmiadzin, Armenia 82 D5
Echo Bay, Canada 186 D6
Echternach, Lux. 52 C3
Echuca, Australia 171 F5
Ecija, Spain 63 G4
Ecuador ■, S. Amer. 212
Ed Dâmer, Sudan 143 B5
Ed Debba, Sudan 143 B4
Ed-Déffa, Egypt 139 A1
Ed Dueim, Sudan 143 C4
Edam, Neths. 50 C3
Edd, Eritrea 144 C4
Eddystone Pt., Australia 172 B3
Ede, Neths. 50 D4
Ede, Nigeria 151 E2
Édea, Cameroon 153 D1
Eden, Australia 171 G7
Edenbridge, U.K. 45 E4
Edenburg, S. Africa 163 F6
Edendale, S. Africa 163 F8
Edenville, S. Africa 163 D7
Edhessa, Greece 71 B2
Edina, Liberia 148 D2
Edinburgh, U.K. 46 D6
Edirne, Turkey 94 A1
Edithburgh, Australia 171 F1
Edmonton, Canada 186 H5
Edmundston, Canada 187 K13
Edson, Canada 186 H5
Edward →, Australia 171 F4
Edward, L., Africa 132 G6
Edwards Plateau, U.S.A. 190 J8
Eekloo, Belgium 51 B2
Eernegem, Belgium 51 B1
Égadi, Ísole, Italy 67 J4
Eganville, Canada 185 B3
Eger = Cheb, Czech. 76 B2
Eger, Hungary 74 A4
Egersund, Norway 40 G1
Egham, U.K. 45 D2
Eglington I., Canada 186 B7
Egmont, C., N.Z. 175 D4
Egmont, Mt., N.Z. 175 D5
Eğridir, Turkey 94 C2
Eğridir Gölü, Turkey 94 C2
Egume, Nigeria 151 E4
Egvekinot, Russia 91 A17
Egypt ■, Africa 139
Eha Amufu, Nigeria 151 E4
Ehime □, Japan 120 D3
Eifel, Germany 58 E1
Eiffel Flats, Zimbabwe 161 C3
Eil, Somali Rep. 145 B3
Eildon, L., Australia 171 G5
Eindhoven, Neths. 50 F4
Einsiedeln, Switz. 60 B4
Eire ■ = Ireland ■, Europe 46 H2
Eiríksjökull, Iceland 38 C3
Eisenach, Germany 58 D3
Eisenerz, Austria 61 B5
Eiserfeld, Germany 59 B3
Eivissa = Ibiza, Spain 63 E9
Eket, Nigeria 151 G4
Ekibastuz, Kazakstan 90 H7
Ekimchan, Russia 91 G15
El Aaiún, W. Sahara 136 A2
El Aïoun, Morocco 136 B6
El 'Aiyat, Egypt 139 B4
El Alamein, Egypt 139 A3
El 'Arag, Egypt 139 B1
El Aricha, Algeria 137 A3
El 'Arîsh, Egypt 139 A5
El Asnam = Ech Cheliff, Algeria 137 A4
El Badâri, Egypt 139 D4
El Bahrein, Egypt 139 C1
El Ballâs, Egypt 139 D5
El Balyana, Egypt 139 D5
El Bawiti, Egypt 139 C3
El Bayadh, Algeria 137 B4
El Bluff, Nic. 197 C3
El Buheirat □, Sudan 143 E3
El Callao, Venezuela 211 B5
El Carmen, Colombia 210 A1
El Centro, U.S.A. 190 G3
El Cerro, Bolivia 218 C2
El Cuyo, Mexico 194 D8
El Dab'a, Egypt 139 A2
El Deir, Egypt 139 D5
El Dere, Somali Rep. 145 C2
El Diviso, Colombia 210 D1
El Djem, Tunisia 138 B3
El Djouf, Mauritania 140 C3
El Dorado, Ark., U.S.A. 191 H11
El Dorado, Kans., U.S.A. 191 F10
El Dorado, Venezuela 211 B5
El Escorial, Spain 63 D5
El Faiyûm, Egypt 139 B4
El Fâsher, Sudan 143 D2
El Fashn, Egypt 139 B4
El Ferrol, Spain 63 A2
El Fuerte, Mexico 194 C2
El Gedida, Egypt 139 D3
El Geteina, Sudan 143 C4
El Gezira □, Sudan 143 C5
El Gîza, Egypt 139 B4
El Goléa, Algeria 137 C4
El Hajeb, Morocco 136 B4
El Hammam, Egypt 139 A3
El Harrach, Algeria 137 A4
El Heiz, Egypt 139 C3
El 'Idisât, Egypt 139 D5
El Iskandarîya, Egypt 139 A3
El Jadida, Morocco 136 C3
El Jebelein, Sudan 143 D4
El Kab, Sudan 143 B4
El Kala, Algeria 137 A6
El Kalâa, Morocco 136 C3
El Kamlin, Sudan 143 C4
El Kantara, Tunisia 138 C3
El Kef, Tunisia 138 B1
El Khandaq, Sudan 143 B4
El Khârga, Egypt 139 D4
El Khartûm, Sudan 143 C4
El Khartûm Bahrî, Sudan 143 C4
El Ksiba, Morocco 136 C4
El Kuntilla, Egypt 139 B6
El Laqâwa, Sudan 143 D3
El Laqeita, Egypt 139 D5
El Mafâza, Sudan 143 D5
El Mahalla el Kubra, Egypt 139 A4
El Mahârîq, Egypt 139 E4
El-Maks el-Bahari, Egypt 139 E4
El Manshâh, Egypt 139 D4
El Mansûra, Egypt 139 A4
El Manzala, Egypt 139 A4
El Marâgha, Egypt 139 D4
El Matariya, Egypt 139 A4
El Milagro, Argentina 221 A1
El Minyâ, Egypt 139 C4
El Obeid, Sudan 143 D4
El Odaiya, Sudan 143 D3
El Oro □, Ecuador 212 D1
El Oued, Algeria 137 B5
El Paso, U.S.A. 190 H6
El Progreso, Honduras 196 C2
El Qâhira, Egypt 139 B4
El Qantara, Egypt 139 A5
El Qasr, Egypt 139 D3
El Quseima, Egypt 139 A6
El Qusîya, Egypt 139 C4
El Râshda, Egypt 139 D3
El Reno, U.S.A. 190 G9
El Rîdisiya, Egypt 139 E5
El Saff, Egypt 139 B4
El Salvador ■, Cent. Amer. 196
El Sauce, Nic. 197 B1
El Shallal, Egypt 139 E5
El Suweis, Egypt 139 B5
El Thamad, Egypt 139 B6
El Tigre, Venezuela 211 B4
El Tocuyo, Venezuela 211 A2
El Tûr, Egypt 139 C5
El Uqsur, Egypt 139 D5
El Vigía, Venezuela 211 B2
El Wak, Kenya 157 B4
El Waqf, Egypt 139 D5
El Wâsta, Egypt 139 B4
El Wuz, Sudan 143 C4
Elat, Israel 96 H2
Elâzığ, Turkey 94 C6
Elba, Italy 67 D3
Elbasani, Albania 70 C2
Elbe →, Europe 58 A2
Elbert, Mt., U.S.A. 190 E7
Elbeuf, France 55 B5
Elbing = Elbląg, Poland 77 A3
Elbląg, Poland 77 A3
Elbrus, Asia 82 A4
Elburg, Neths. 50 C4
Elburz Mts. = Alborz, Reshteh-ye Kūhhā-ye, Iran 103 B3
Elche, Spain 63 F7
Eldoret, Kenya 157 C1
Electra, U.S.A. 190 G9
Elektrostal, Russia 81 C5
Elele, Nigeria 151 F3
Elephant Butte Reservoir, U.S.A. 190 G6
Elephant Pass, Sri Lanka 110 A2
Eleşkirt, Turkey 82 D4
Eleuthera, Bahamas 201 A2
Elgeyo-Marakwet □, Kenya 157 C1
Elgin, U.K. 46 B6
Elgin, U.S.A. 191 D12
Elgon, Mt., Africa 132 F7
Eliase, Indonesia 129 F14
Elim, S. Africa 163 H2
Elisabethville = Lubumbashi, Zaïre 155 G5
Elista, Russia 81 G7
Elizabeth, Australia 171 F2
Elizabeth, U.S.A. 189 C5
Elizabeth City, U.S.A. 191 F16
Elkhart, U.S.A. 191 D13
Elkhotovo, Russia 82 A5
Elkhovo, Bulgaria 73 C4
Elkins, U.S.A. 191 E15
Elko, U.S.A. 190 D4
Ellef Ringnes I., Canada 186 A8
Ellensburg, U.S.A. 190 B3
Ellenville, U.S.A. 189 B5

Ellery, Mt., *Australia* 171 G7
Ellesmere, L., *N.Z.* 175 G4
Ellesmere I., *Canada* 187 A10
Ellice Is. = Tuvalu ■, *Pac. Oc.* 176 F6
Elliot, *S. Africa* 163 G7
Elliotdale = Xhora, *S. Africa* 163 G7
Ellore = Eluru, *India* 107 E3
Elmalı, *Turkey* 94 C2
Elmina, *Ghana* 149 E2
Elmira, *U.S.A.* 189 B3
Elmore, *Australia* 171 G5
Elsa, *Canada* 186 D4
Elsinore = Helsingør, *Denmark* 42 C4
Elspe, *Germany* 59 B3
Elst, *Neths.* 50 D4
Elstead, *U.K.* 45 E1
Eltham, *N.Z.* 175 D5
Eluanbi, *Taiwan* 117 C3
Eluru, *India* 107 E3
Elvas, *Portugal* 63 E2
Elx = Elche, *Spain* 63 F7
Ely, *U.K.* 46 J9
Ely, *U.S.A.* 190 E4
Elyria, *U.S.A.* 191 D14
Emāmrūd, *Iran* 103 B4
Emba, *Kazakstan* 90 H5
Embarcación, *Argentina* 220 B4
Embetsu, *Japan* 121 A7
Embrun, *France* 55 F8
Embu, *Kenya* 157 D3
Embu □, *Kenya* 157 D3
Emden, *Germany* 58 B1
Emerson, *Canada* 186 K8
Emilia-Romagna □, *Italy* 67 B3
Emme →, *Switz.* 60 B2
Emmeloord, *Neths.* 50 B4
Emmen, *Neths.* 50 B6
Emmental, *Switz.* 60 B2
Empalme, *Mexico* 194 B2
Empangeni, *S. Africa* 163 E9
Empedrado, *Argentina* 220 D5
Emperor Seamount Chain, *Pac. Oc.* 176 B5
Emporia, *U.S.A.* 191 F10
Emporium, *U.S.A.* 189 B2
Empty Quarter = Rub' al Khali, *Si. Arabia* 99 E5
Ems →, *Germany* 58 C2
'En 'Avrona, *Israel* 96 H2
En Nahud, *Sudan* 143 D3
Enaratoli, *Indonesia* 129 D17
Encarnación, *Paraguay* 219 C3
Enchi, *Ghana* 149 D1
Encounter B., *Australia* 171 F2
Ende, *Indonesia* 129 F11
Enderbury I., *Kiribati* 176 F6
Endicott, *U.S.A.* 189 B3
Enewetak Atoll, *Pac. Oc.* 176 E4
Enez, *Turkey* 94 A1
Enfida, *Tunisia* 138 B2
Enfield, *U.K.* 45 B3
Engadin, *Switz.* 60 C6
Engaño, C., *Dom. Rep.* 200 B3
Engelberg, *Switz.* 60 C3
Engels = Pokrovsk, *Russia* 81 E8
Enggano, *Indonesia* 128 E3
Enghien, *Belgium* 51 C3
Engkilili, *Malaysia* 126 C6
England □, *U.K.* 46
English Bazar = Ingraj Bazar, *India* 106 C8
English Channel, *Europe* 34 E6
Enid, *U.S.A.* 190 F9
Enjil, *Morocco* 136 C5
Enkhuizen, *Neths.* 50 B3
Enna, *Italy* 67 J6
Ennedi, *Chad* 142 C3
Enngonia, *Australia* 171 B5
Ennis, *Ireland* 46 H1
Ennis, *U.S.A.* 191 H10
Enniscorthy, *Ireland* 46 J3
Enniskillen, *U.K.* 46 F2
Enns →, *Austria* 61 A4
Enriquillo, L., *Dom. Rep.* 200 B2
Enschede, *Neths.* 50 D6
Ensenada, *Argentina* 221 C5
Ensenada, *Mexico* 194 A1
Entebbe, *Uganda* 156 C2
Entre-Deux, *Réunion* 166 C2
Entre Ríos □, *Argentina* 221 A5
Enugu, *Nigeria* 151 F4
Enugu Ezike, *Nigeria* 151 E4
Éolie, Is., *Italy* 67 H6
Epe, *Neths.* 50 C5
Epe, *Nigeria* 151 E1
Épernay, *France* 55 B7
Épinal, *France* 55 C8
Epira, *Guyana* 214 C3
Episkopi, *Cyprus* 95 C1
Episkopi Bay, *Cyprus* 95 C1
Epping, *U.K.* 45 B4
Epping Forest, *U.K.* 45 B4
Epsom, *U.K.* 45 D3
Epukiro, *Namibia* 162 B3
Equatorial Guinea ■, *Africa* 153
Er Rahad, *Sudan* 143 D4
Er Rif, *Morocco* 136 A5
Er Roseires, *Sudan* 143 D5
Erāwadī Myit = Irrawaddy →, *Burma* 122 F2
Erbil = Arbīl, *Iraq* 102 A4
Ercha, *Russia* 91 C14
Erciyaş Dağı, *Turkey* 94 C4
Ereğli, *Konya, Turkey* 94 C3
Ereğli, *Zonguldak, Turkey* 94 A3
Erenhot, *China* 116 A2
Eresma →, *Spain* 63 C4
Erfenisdam, *S. Africa* 163 E6
Erfoud, *Morocco* 136 D5
Erft →, *Germany* 59 B2
Erfurt, *Germany* 58 D4
Erg Chech, *N. Afr.* 137 D2
Erg Idehan, *Libya* 138 B2
Ergeni Vozvyshennost, *Russia* 81 G7
Érice, *Italy* 67 J5
Erie, L., *N. Amer.* 180 E11
Erímanthos, *Greece* 71 D2
Erimo-misaki, *Japan* 121 C8
Eritrea □, *Africa* 144 B3
Erlangen, *Germany* 58 E4
Erlin, *Taiwan* 117 B2
Ermelo, *S. Africa* 163 D8
Erne, L., *U.K.* 46 F2
Erode, *India* 107 F3
Erris Hd., *Ireland* 46 F1
Ertis = Irtysh →, *Russia* 90 F7
Eruwa, *Nigeria* 151 E1
Erzgebirge, *Germany* 58 D5
Erzin, *Russia* 91 J10
Erzincan, *Turkey* 94 B6
Erzurum, *Turkey* 94 B6
Es Sahrâ' Esh Sharqîya, *Egypt* 139 C5
Es Sînâ', *Egypt* 139 B5
Esan-Misaki, *Japan* 121 C7
Esbjerg, *Denmark* 42 C1
Escanaba, *U.S.A.* 191 C13
Esch, *Neths.* 50
Esch-sur-Alzette, *Lux.* 52 D2
Eschweiler, *Germany* 59 B1
Escuinapa, *Mexico* 194 D3
Escuintla, *Guatemala* 196 C1
Eşfahān, *Iran* 103 C3
Esh Sham = Dimashq, *Syria* 97 C2
Esh Shamâlîya □, *Sudan* 143 B3
Esher, *U.K.* 45 D2
Eshkamesh, *Afghan.* 104 B5
Eshowe, *S. Africa* 163 E9
Esiama, *Ghana* 149 E1
Esil = Ishim →, *Russia* 90 G7
Eskifjörður, *Iceland* 38 C5
Eskimo Pt., *Canada* 186 F9
Eskişehir, *Turkey* 94 B2
Esla →, *Spain* 63 B4
Esmeraldas, *Ecuador* 212 A1
Esmeraldas □, *Ecuador* 212 A1
Esmeraldas →, *Ecuador* 212 A1
Espalmador, I., *Spain* 65 C2
Espardell, I. del, *Spain* 65 C2
Esparta, *Costa Rica* 197 D2
Esperance, *Australia* 168 J10
Esperanza, *Argentina* 221 A4
Esperanza, *Phil.* 130 J5
Espichel, C., *Portugal* 63 F1
Espinal, *Colombia* 210 C1
Espinazo, Sierra del = Espinhaço, Serra do, *Brazil* 217 G8
Espinhaço, Serra do, *Brazil* 217 G8
Espírito Santo □, *Brazil* 217 G8
Espiye, *Turkey* 82 C1
Essaouira, *Morocco* 136 D2
Essen, *Belgium* 51 A3
Essen, *Germany* 58 C1
Essequibo →, *Guyana* 214 B2
Essex □, *U.K.* 45 B5
Esslingen, *Germany* 58 F3
Essonne □, *France* 55 C5
Estados, I. de Los, *Argentina* 220 L4
Estcourt, *S. Africa* 163 E8
Estelí, *Nic.* 197 B1
Estevan, *Canada* 186 K7
Estonia ■, *Europe* 81 A2
Estoril, *Portugal* 63 E1
Estrêla, Serra da, *Portugal* 63 D2
Estremadura, *Portugal* 63 E1
Estrondo, Serra do, *Brazil* 217 D6
Esztergom, *Hungary* 74 A3
Etadunna, *Australia* 171 B1
Etawah, *India* 106 B4
Etchingham, *U.K.* 45 E5
Ete, *Nigeria* 151 E4
Ethiopia ■, *Africa* 144
Ethiopian Highlands, *Ethiopia* 132 E7
Etna, *Italy* 67 J7
Eton, *U.K.* 45 C2
Etosha Pan, *Namibia* 162 A2
Ettelbruck, *Lux.* 52 B2
Euboea = Évvoia, *Greece* 71 D4
Euclid, *U.S.A.* 191 D14
Eucumbene, L., *Australia* 171 F7
Eugene, *U.S.A.* 190 C2
Eugowra, *Australia* 171 E7
Eulo, *Australia* 171 A5
Eupen, *Belgium* 51 C6
Euphrates →, *Asia* 84 F8
Eure □, *France* 55 B5
Eure-et-Loir □, *France* 55 C5
Eureka, *Canada* 186 A9
Eureka, *U.S.A.* 190 D1
Euroa, *Australia* 171 G5
Europa, Picos de, *Spain* 63 A4
Europoort, *Neths.* 50 D2
Evans Head, *Australia* 171 B9
Evanston, *U.S.A.* 191 D13
Evansville, *U.S.A.* 191 F13
Evensk, *Russia* 91 C17
Everest, Mt., *Nepal* 109 B4
Everett, *U.S.A.* 190 A3
Everglades, The, *U.S.A.* 191 K16
Evinayong, *Eq. Guin.* 153 C2
Évora, *Portugal* 63 E2
Évreux, *France* 55 B5
Évvoia, *Greece* 71 D4
Ewell, *U.K.* 45 D3
Ewhurst, *U.K.* 45 E2
Ewo, *Congo* 154 C2
Exaltación, *Bolivia* 218 B1
Exeter, *U.K.* 46 L6
Exmoor, *U.K.* 46 L5
Extremadura □, *Spain* 63 E3
Eyasi, L., *Tanzania* 158 B2
Eyjafjörður, *Iceland* 38 B4
Eynesil, *Turkey* 82 C1
Eyrarbakki, *Iceland* 38 D2
Eyre (North), L., *Australia* 171 B1
Eyre (South), L., *Australia* 171 B1
Eyre Mts., *N.Z.* 175 H2
Eyre Pen., *Australia* 168 D3
Ezousas →, *Cyprus* 95 C1

F

Fabriano, *Italy* 67 D5
Facatativá, *Colombia* 210 C1
Fachi, *Niger* 141 B5
Fada, *Chad* 142 C3
Fada-n-Gourma, *Burkina Faso* 149 B3
Faddeyevskiy, Ostrov, *Russia* 91 B13
Fadghāmī, *Syria* 97 B5
Faenza, *Italy* 67 C4
Fagam, *Nigeria* 151 B5
Făgăras, *Romania* 75 C4
Faggo, *Nigeria* 151 B5
Fair Isle, *U.K.* 46 B9
Fairbanks, *U.S.A.* 193 A5
Fairlie, *N.Z.* 175 G3
Fairmont, *U.S.A.* 191 D10
Fairport, *U.S.A.* 189 A3
Fairweather, Mt., *U.S.A.* 193 B5
Faisalabad, *Pakistan* 105 C5
Faizabad, *India* 106 B5
Fajardo, *Puerto Rico* 201 A2
Fakfak, *Indonesia* 129 D15
Fakobli, *Ivory C.* 148 C3
Faku, *China* 116 A6
Falaise, *France* 55 B4
Falam, *Burma* 122 C1
Falkirk, *U.K.* 46 D5
Falkland Is. ■, *Atl. Oc.* 224
Falkland Sd., *Falk. Is.* 224 A2
Fall River, *U.S.A.* 189 A6
Falmouth, *Jamaica* 199 A2
Falmouth, *U.K.* 46 M4
False B., *S. Africa* 163 H2
Falso, C., *Honduras* 196 C5
Falster, *Denmark* 42 D3
Falun, *Sweden* 40 F3
Famagusta, *Cyprus* 95 B3
Famagusta Bay, *Cyprus* 95 B3
Fan Xian, *China* 116 E3
Fandriana, *Madag.* 165 D2
Fang Xian, *China* 116 F1
Fangchang, *China* 116 G4
Fangcheng, *China* 116 F2
Fangliao, *Taiwan* 117 C3
Fano, *Italy* 67 C5
Fao = Al Fāw, *Iraq* 102 E6
Faradje, *Zaïre* 155 A6
Farafangana, *Madag.* 165 D2
Farâfra, El Wâhât el-, *Egypt* 139 C2
Farāh, *Afghan.* 104 E1
Farāh □, *Afghan.* 104 E1
Faraid, Gebel, *Egypt* 139 E6
Faranah, *Guinea* 147 B4
Farasān, Jazā'ir, *Si. Arabia* 99 F3
Farasan Is. = Farasān, Jazā'ir, *Si. Arabia* 99 F3
Farewell, C., *N.Z.* 175 E4
Farewell C. = Farvel, Kap, *Greenland* 224 D2
Farghona = Fergana, *Uzbekistan* 93 D5
Fargo, *U.S.A.* 191 C10
Faribault, *U.S.A.* 191 C11
Faridpur, *Bangla.* 111 C2
Farim, *Guinea-Biss.* 146 C1
Farina, *Australia* 171 C1
Fâriskûr, *Egypt* 139 A4
Farmington, *U.S.A.* 190 F6
Farnborough, *U.K.* 45 D1
Farnham, *U.K.* 45 D1
Faro, *Portugal* 63 G2
Faroe Is., *Atl. Oc.* 223 B4
Farrell Flat, *Australia* 171 E2
Fársala, *Greece* 71 C2
Fārsī, *Afghan.* 104 D2
Faru, *Nigeria* 151 A3
Farvel, Kap, *Greenland* 224 D2
Fāryāb □, *Afghan.* 104 B3
Fatagar, Tanjung, *Indonesia* 129 D15
Fatehgarh, *India* 106 B4
Fatehpur, *Raj., India* 106 B2
Fatehpur, *Ut. P., India* 106 C5
Fatick, *Senegal* 146 B1
Fatoya, *Guinea* 147 A5
Fauresmith, *S. Africa* 163 F5
Favara, *Italy* 67 K5
Faversham, *U.K.* 45 D6
Favignana, *Italy* 67 J5
Faxaflói, *Iceland* 38 C2
Faya-Largeau, *Chad* 142 C2
Fayetteville, *Ark., U.S.A.* 191 G11
Fayetteville, *N.C., U.S.A.* 191 F16
Fdérik, *Mauritania* 140 B2
Fear, C., *U.S.A.* 191 G16
Featherstone, *Zimbabwe* 161 C4
Fécamp, *France* 55 B4
Fedala = Mohammedia, *Morocco* 136 B3
Federación, *Argentina* 221 A5
Fedjadj, Chott el, *Tunisia* 138 C2
Fehmarn Bælt, *Germany* 58 A4
Fei Xian, *China* 116 E4
Feilding, *N.Z.* 175 E5
Feira de Santana, *Brazil* 217 E9
Felanitx, *Spain* 65 B4
Feldkirch, *Austria* 61 B1
Felicité, *Seychelles* 166 A3
Felipe Carrillo Puerto, *Mexico* 194 E8
Fen He →, *China* 116 E1
Feng Xian, *China* 116 E3
Fengcheng, *Jiangxi, China* 116 H3
Fengcheng, *Liaoning, China* 116 B6
Fengfeng, *China* 116 D2
Fenghua, *China* 116 H5
Fengjie, *China* 113 F8
Fengle, *China* 116 G1
Fengning, *China* 116 B3
Fengtai, *China* 116 C3
Fengxian, *China* 116 G5
Fengxin, *China* 116 H3
Fengyang, *China* 116 F4
Fengzhen, *China* 116 B2
Fenny, *Bangla.* 111 C3
Fenny Stratford, *U.K.* 45 A1
Fens, The, *U.K.* 46 H8
Fenyang, *China* 116 D1
Feodosiya, *Ukraine* 81 H4
Ferfer, *Somali Rep.* 145 C2
Fergana, *Uzbekistan* 93 D5
Ferganskaya Dolina, *Uzbekistan* 93 C4
Ferganskiy Khrebet, *Kyrgyzstan* 93 C6
Fergus Falls, *U.S.A.* 191 C10
Fériana, *Tunisia* 138 B1
Ferkéssédougou, *Ivory C.* 148 B5
Ferlo, Vallée du, *Senegal* 146 B2
Fermoy, *Ireland* 46 J2
Fernando Póo = Bioko, *Eq. Guin.* 153 A1
Fernhurst, *U.K.* 45 E1
Ferozepore = Firozpur, *India* 107 B2
Ferrara, *Italy* 67 B4
Ferreñafe, *Peru* 213 C2
Ferrol = El Ferrol, *Spain* 63 A2
Fès, *Morocco* 136 B5
Feshi, *Zaïre* 155 E2
Feuilles →, *Canada* 187 G12
Feyzābād, *Badākhshān, Afghan.* 104 A6
Feyzābād, *Fāryāb, Afghan.* 104 B3
Fezzan, *Libya* 138 C3
Fianarantsoa, *Madag.* 165 D2
Fianga, *Cameroon* 153 B3
Fichtelgebirge, *Germany* 58 E4
Ficksburg, *S. Africa* 163 E7
Fiditi, *Nigeria* 151 E1
Figeac, *France* 55 F5
Figtree, *Zimbabwe* 161 D2
Figueira da Foz, *Portugal* 63 D1
Figueras, *Spain* 63 B9
Figuig, *Morocco* 136 C6
Fiji ■, *Pac. Oc.* 174
Fika, *Nigeria* 151 B6
Filfla, *Malta* 69 B2
Filiatrá, *Greece* 71 E2
Findlay, *U.S.A.* 191 D14
Fingõe, *Mozam.* 159 B1
Finistère □, *France* 55 C1
Finisterre, C., *Spain* 34 G5
Finland ■, *Europe* 43
Finland, G. of, *Europe* 34 D11
Finlay →, *Canada* 186 F4
Finley, *Australia* 171 F5
Finsteraarhorn, *Switz.* 60 C3
Fiora →, *Italy* 67 E4
Firat = Euphrates →, *Asia* 84 F8
Firenze, *Italy* 67 C4
Firozabad, *India* 106 B4
Firozpur, *India* 107 B2
Fish →, *Namibia* 162 D3
Fish →, *S. Africa* 163 F3
Fishguard, *U.K.* 46 K4
Fitchburg, *U.S.A.* 189 A6
Fitri, L., *Chad* 142 D1
Fitzgerald, *U.S.A.* 191 H14
Fitzroy →, *Australia* 168 B2
Fiume = Rijeka, *Croatia* 72 B3
Fizi, *Zaïre* 155 D6
Fkih ben Salah, *Morocco* 136 C4
Flagstaff, *U.S.A.* 190 G5
Flamborough Hd., *U.K.* 46 G8
Flamingo, Teluk, *Indonesia* 129 E17
Flanders = West-Vlaanderen □, *Belgium* 51 B1
Flandre Occidentale = West-Vlaanderen □, *Belgium* 51 B1
Flandre Orientale = Oost-Vlaanderen □, *Belgium* 51 B2
Flatey, *Barðastrandarsýsla, Iceland* 38 A4
Flatey, *Suður-þingeyjarsýsla, Iceland* 38 B2
Flattery, C., *U.S.A.* 190 A2
Fleet, *U.K.* 45 D1
Flensburg, *Germany* 58 A3
Flesko, Tanjung, *Indonesia* 129 C12
Fleurier, *Switz.* 60 B1
Flevoland □, *Neths.* 50 C4
Flin Flon, *Canada* 186 H7
Flinders →, *Australia* 168 B4
Flinders B., *Australia* 170 D1
Flinders I., *Australia* 172 A3
Flinders Ras., *Australia* 171 D2
Flint, *U.K.* 46 H6
Flint, *U.S.A.* 191 D14
Flint →, *U.S.A.* 191 H14
Flint I., *Kiribati* 176 G8
Flitwick, *U.K.* 45 A2
Florence = Firenze, *Italy* 67 C4
Florence, *Ala., U.S.A.* 191 G13
Florence, *S.C., U.S.A.* 191 G16
Florence, L., *Australia* 171 B1
Flores, *Guatemala* 196 B1
Flores, *Indonesia* 129 F11
Flores Sea, *Indonesia* 129 E10
Florianópolis, *Brazil* 217 J6
Florida, *Cuba* 198 B4
Florida, *Uruguay* 219 D2
Florida □, *U.S.A.* 191 J15
Florida, Straits of, *U.S.A.* 180 G11
Florø, *Norway* 40 E1
Fluk, *Indonesia* 129 C13
Flushing = Vlissingen, *Neths.* 50 F1
Fly →, *Papua N. G.* 173 C1
Fóggia, *Italy* 67 E7
Fogo, *C. Verde Is.* 222 C2
Foix, *France* 55 H5
Folkestone, *U.K.* 46 L9
Fomboni, *Comoros Is.* 166 B1
Fond-du-Lac, *Canada* 186 G7
Fond du Lac, *U.S.A.* 191 D12
Fontainebleau, *France* 55 C6
Fontenay, *France* 55 E3
Fontur, *Iceland* 38 A5
Foochow = Fuzhou, *China* 116 J4
Forbes, *Australia* 171 E6
Forcados, *Nigeria* 151 F2
Forcados →, *Nigeria* 151 F2
Ford's Bridge, *Australia* 171 B5
Forécariah, *Guinea* 147 C2
Forel, Mt., *Greenland* 224 C2
Forest Row, *U.K.* 45 E4
Forez, *France* 55 E7
Forfar, *U.K.* 46 C6
Forlì, *Italy* 67 C4
Formentera, *Spain* 63 E9
Formentor, C. de, *Spain* 65 A4
Formosa = Taiwan ■, *Asia* 117
Formosa, *Argentina* 220 C5
Formosa Bay, *Kenya* 157 E4
Fornells, *Spain* 65 A6
Forrest, *Australia* 171 H4
Forster, *Australia* 171 D9
Fort Albany, *Canada* 187 J11
Fort Beaufort, *S. Africa* 163 H6
Fort Chipewyan, *Canada* 186 G6
Fort Collins, *U.S.A.* 190 E7
Fort-Coulonge, *Canada* 185 B3
Fort-de-France, *Martinique* 203 D3
Fort Dodge, *U.S.A.* 191 D11
Fort Franklin, *Canada* 186 D5
Fort George, *Canada* 187 H11
Fort Good-Hope, *Canada* 186 D5
Fort Hertz = Putao, *Burma* 122 A3
Fort Jameson = Chipata, *Zambia* 161 C5
Fort Lallemand, *Algeria* 137 B5
Fort-Lamy = Ndjamena, *Chad* 142 E1
Fort Lauderdale, *U.S.A.* 191 K16
Fort Liard, *Canada* 186 E5
Fort Liberté, *Haiti* 200 A2
Fort Mackay, *Canada* 186 G6
Fort Macleod, *Canada* 186 J5
Fort MacMahon, *Algeria* 137 C4
Fort McMurray, *Canada* 186 G6
Fort McPherson, *Canada* 186 C5
Fort Miribel, *Algeria* 137 C4
Fort Morgan, *U.S.A.* 190 E7
Fort Myers, *U.S.A.* 191 K15
Fort Nelson, *Canada* 186 F5
Fort Nelson →, *Canada* 186 F4
Fort Norman, *Canada* 186 D5
Fort Peck L., *U.S.A.* 190 B7
Fort Portal, *Uganda* 156 C1
Fort Providence, *Canada* 186 F5
Fort Resolution, *Canada* 186 F6
Fort Rixon, *Zimbabwe* 161 D3
Fort Rosebery = Mansa, *Zambia* 161 B4
Fort Rupert, *Canada* 187 J11
Fort Saint, *Tunisia* 138 E2
Fort Sandeman, *Pakistan* 105 C4
Fort Scott, *U.S.A.* 191 F10
Fort Severn, *Canada* 186 H9
Fort Shevchenko, *Kazakstan* 90 H3
Fort-Sibut, *C.A.R.* 142 B3
Fort Simpson, *Canada* 186 E5
Fort Smith, *Canada* 186 F6
Fort Smith, *U.S.A.* 191 G11
Fort Trinquet = Bir Mogrein, *Mauritania* 140 B2
Fort Vermilion, *Canada* 186 F5
Fort Wayne, *U.S.A.* 191 D13
Fort William, *U.K.* 46 C4

Fort Worth, *U.S.A.* 191 H10
Fort Yukon, *U.S.A.* 193 A5
Fortaleza, *Brazil* 217 C9
Forth, Firth of, *U.K.* 46 D6
Foshan, *China* 113 H9
Fougamou, *Gabon* 154 C1
Fougères, *France* 55 C3
Foul Pt., *Sri Lanka* 110 B3
Foum Assaka, *Morocco* 136 E2
Foum Zguid, *Morocco* 136 E3
Foumban, *Cameroon* 153 D1
Foundiougne, *Senegal* 146 B1
Fouriesburg, *S. Africa* 163 E7
Fournaise, Piton de la, *Réunion* 166 C3
Fouta Djalon, *Guinea* 147 A3
Foux, Cap-à-, *Haiti* 200 A1
Foveaux Str., *N.Z.* 175 J2
Foxe Basin, *Canada* 187 E10
Foxe Chan., *Canada* 187 E10
Foxe Pen., *Canada* 187 E11
Foxton, *N.Z.* 175 E5
Franca, *Brazil* 215 A2
France ■, *Europe* 55
Frances, *Australia* 171 G3
Francés Viejo, C., *Dom. Rep.* 200 A3
Franceville, *Gabon* 154 C2
Franche-Comté, *France* 55 D8
Francisco de Orellana, *Ecuador* 212 B2
Francistown, *Botswana* 162 B6
François L., *Canada* 186 G3
Franeker, *Neths.* 50 A4
Frankado, *Djibouti* 145 A2
Frankfort, *S. Africa* 163 D7
Frankfort, *Ind., U.S.A.* 191 E13
Frankfort, *Ky., U.S.A.* 191 F14
Frankfurt am Main, *Germany* 58 E2
Frankfurt an der Oder, *Germany* 58 C6
Fränkische Alb, *Germany* 58 E4
Frankland →, *Australia* 170 D2
Franklin, *U.S.A.* 189 B1
Franklin B., *Canada* 186 C6
Franklin D. Roosevelt L., *U.S.A.* 190 A4
Franklin L., *U.S.A.* 190 D4
Franklin Mts., *Canada* 186 D5
Franklin Str., *Canada* 186 C8
Frankston, *Australia* 171 H5
Frant, *U.K.* 45 E4
Frantsa Iosifa, Zemlya, *Russia* 90 A9
Franz, *Canada* 187 K10
Franz Josef Land = Frantsa Iosifa, Zemlya, *Russia* 90 A9
Fraser →, *Canada* 186 H3
Fraserburg, *S. Africa* 163 G3
Fraserburgh, *U.K.* 46 B7
Fray Bentos, *Uruguay* 219 C1
Fredericia, *Denmark* 42 C2
Frederick, *U.S.A.* 189 D3
Fredericksburg, *U.S.A.* 191 E16
Fredericton, *Canada* 187 K14
Frederikshåb, *Greenland* 224 D1
Frederikshavn, *Denmark* 42 A3
Fredonia, *U.S.A.* 189 A1
Fredrikstad, *Norway* 40 F2
Free State □, *S. Africa* 163 E6
Freeport, *Bahamas* 201 A1
Freeport, *N.Y., U.S.A.* 189 C5
Freeport, *Tex., U.S.A.* 191 J10
Freetown, *S. Leone* 147 C2
Freibourg = Fribourg, *Switz.* 60 C2
Freiburg, *Germany* 58 G2
Freising, *Germany* 58 F4
Freistadt, *Austria* 61 A4
Fréjus, *France* 55 G9
Fremantle, *Australia* 170 B1
Fremont, *U.S.A.* 191 E10
French Creek →, *U.S.A.* 189 B1
French Guiana ■, *S. Amer.* 214
French Terr. of Afars & Issas = Djibouti ■, *Africa* 145
Fresnillo, *Mexico* 194 D4
Fresno, *U.S.A.* 190 F2
Freycinet Pen., *Australia* 172 C3
Fria, *Guinea* 147 B2
Fria, C., *Namibia* 162 A1
Fribourg, *Switz.* 60 C2
Fribourg □, *Switz.* 60 C2
Friedrichshafen, *Germany* 58 G3
Friendly Is. = Tonga ■, *Pac. Oc.* 174
Friesland □, *Neths.* 50 B4
Frigate, *Seychelles* 166 B3
Frimley, *U.K.* 45 D1
Frio, C., *Brazil* 206 E5
Friuli-Venezia Giulia □, *Italy* 67 A5
Frobisher B., *Canada* 187 E12
Frobisher Bay = Iqaluit, *Canada* 187 E12
Frobisher L., *Canada* 186 G6
Frome, L., *Australia* 171 C2
Frome Downs, *Australia* 171 C2
Front Range, *U.S.A.* 190 E7
Frosinone, *Italy* 67 E5
Frostburg, *U.S.A.* 189 D2
Frunze = Bishkek, *Kyrgyzstan* 93 A7
Frutigen, *Switz.* 60 C2
Frýdek-Místek, *Czech.* 76 B6
Fu Xian, *China* 116 C5
Fucheng, *China* 116 D3
Fuchou = Fuzhou, *China* 116 J4
Fuchū, *Japan* 120 C3
Fuchun Jiang →, *China* 116 G5
Fuding, *China* 116 J5
Fuente Ovejuna, *Spain* 63 F4
Fuentes de Oñoro, *Spain* 63 D3
Fuerte →, *Mexico* 194 C2
Fuerte Olimpo, *Paraguay* 219 A2
Fuerteventura, *Canary Is.* 223 C3
Fuga I., *Phil.* 130 B3
Fugou, *China* 116 F2
Fuhai, *China* 112 B4
Fuji, *Japan* 120 B8
Fuji-San, *Japan* 120 B8
Fujian □, *China* 113 H10
Fujinomiya, *Japan* 120 B8
Fujisawa, *Japan* 120 B8
Fukien = Fujian □, *China* 113 H10
Fukuchiyama, *Japan* 120 B5
Fukui, *Japan* 120 A6
Fukui □, *Japan* 120 A6
Fukuoka, *Japan* 120 D1
Fukuoka □, *Japan* 120 D1
Fukushima, *Japan* 121 F7
Fukuyama, *Japan* 120 C4
Fulda, *Germany* 58 D3
Fulda →, *Germany* 58 D3
Fulton, *U.S.A.* 189 A3
Funabashi, *Japan* 120 B9
Funafuti, *Pac. Oc.* 176 F6
Funchal, *Madeira* 223 A2
Fundación, *Colombia* 210 A1
Fundão, *Portugal* 63 D2
Fundy, B. of, *Canada* 187 K14
Funing, *China* 116 F5
Funiu Shan, *China* 116 F2
Funsi, *Ghana* 149 A1
Funtua, *Nigeria* 151 B4
Fuping, *China* 116 C2
Furnas, Reprêsa de, *Brazil* 215 A3
Furneaux Group, *Australia* 172 A3
Furqlus, *Syria* 97 C3
Fürth, *Germany* 58 E4
Fury and Hecla Str., *Canada* 187 D10
Fusagasuga, *Colombia* 210 C1
Fushan, *China* 116 D5
Fushun, *China* 116 B6
Fuwa, *Egypt* 139 A4
Fuxin, *China* 116 B5
Fuyang, *Anhui, China* 116 F3
Fuyang, *Zhejiang, China* 116 G5
Fuyuan, *China* 113 A12
Fuzhou, *China* 116 J4
Fyn, *Denmark* 42 C2

G

Gaanda, *Nigeria* 151 C7
Gabarin, *Nigeria* 151 B6
Gabela, *Angola* 160 C2
Gabès, *Tunisia* 138 C2
Gabès, G. de, *Tunisia* 138 C2
Gabon ■, *Africa* 154
Gaborone, *Botswana* 162 D5
Gabrovo, *Bulgaria* 73 B3
Gadag, *India* 107 E2
Gadarwara, *India* 106 D4
Gadsden, *U.S.A.* 191 G13
Gafsa, *Tunisia* 138 C1
Gagnoa, *Ivory C.* 148 D4
Gagnon, *Canada* 187 H13
Gagra, *Georgia* 82 A2
Gahini, *Rwanda* 156 A2
Gai Xian, *China* 116 B5
Gainesville, *Fla., U.S.A.* 191 J15
Gainesville, *Ga., U.S.A.* 191 G14
Gairdner, L., *Australia* 168 D3
Gal Oya Res., *Sri Lanka* 110 C3
Galachipa, *Bangla.* 111 D2
Galana →, *Kenya* 157 E3
Galangue, *Angola* 160 D3
Galashiels, *U.K.* 46 E6
Galați, *Romania* 75 C6
Galdhøpiggen, *Norway* 40 E1
Galela, *Indonesia* 129 B13
Galera Point, *Trin. & Tob.* 204 A3
Galesburg, *U.S.A.* 191 E12
Galets →, *Réunion* 166 A1
Gali, *Georgia* 82 A3
Galich, *Russia* 81 A6
Galicia □, *Spain* 63 B2
Galilee = Hagalil, *Israel* 96 B2
Galilee, Sea of = Yam Kinneret, *Israel* 96 B3
Gallabat, *Sudan* 143 D5
Galle, *Sri Lanka* 110 D2
Gállego →, *Spain* 63 C7
Gallinas, Pta., *Colombia* 210 A2
Gallipoli, *Italy* 67 G9
Gällivare, *Sweden* 40 C4
Gallup, *U.S.A.* 190 G6
Gallyaaral, *Uzbekistan* 93 D1
Galong, *Australia* 171 E7
Galveston, *U.S.A.* 191 J11
Gálvez, *Argentina* 221 A4
Galway, *Ireland* 46 H1
Galway B., *Ireland* 46 H1
Gamawa, *Nigeria* 151 B6
Gamay, *Phil.* 130 F5
Gambaga, *Ghana* 149 A2
Gambia ■, *W. Afr.* 146
Gambia →, *W. Afr.* 132 E2
Gambier Is., *Australia* 171 F1
Gamboma, *Congo* 154 C3
Gammouda, *Tunisia* 138 B2
Gananoque, *Canada* 185 C4
Gäncä = Gyandzha, *Azerbaijan* 82 C7
Gand = Ghent, *Belgium* 51 B2
Ganda, *Angola* 160 D2
Gandak →, *India* 106 C7
Gandava, *Pakistan* 105 E3
Gander, *Canada* 187 H15
Ganderowe Falls, *Zimbabwe* 161 B3
Gandhi Sagar, *India* 106 C2
Gandi, *Nigeria* 151 A3
Gandole, *Nigeria* 151 D6
Ganedidalem = Gani, *Indonesia* 129 C13
Ganga →, *India* 106 E9
Ganganagar, *India* 106 A2
Gangara, *Niger* 141 C4
Gangaw, *Burma* 122 D1
Ganges = Ganga →, *India* 106 E9
Gangtok, *India* 106 B8
Gani, *Indonesia* 129 C13
Gannett Peak, *U.S.A.* 190 D6
Gansu □, *China* 112 D6
Ganta, *Liberia* 148 C2
Gantheaume, C., *Australia* 171 F1
Ganyu, *China* 116 E4
Ganzhou, *China* 113 H9
Gao Bang, *Vietnam* 125 A4
Gao'an, *China* 116 H3
Gaomi, *China* 116 D5
Gaoping, *China* 116 E2
Gaoua, *Burkina Faso* 149 B1
Gaoual, *Guinea* 147 A2
Gaoxiong, *Taiwan* 117 C2
Gaoyou, *China* 116 F4
Gaoyou Hu, *China* 116 F4
Gaoyuan, *China* 116 D4
Gap, *France* 55 F8
Gapan, *Phil.* 130 D2
Gar, *China* 112 F1
Garabogazkol Aylagy = Kara Bogaz Gol, Zaliv, *Turkmenistan* 90 J3
Garachiné, *Panama* 197 E6
Garanhuns, *Brazil* 217 D9
Garawe, *Liberia* 148 E3
Garba Tula, *Kenya* 157 C3
Gard □, *France* 55 G7
Garda, L. di, *Italy* 67 A3
Garden City, *U.S.A.* 190 F8
Gardēz, *Afghan.* 104 D5
Gardner, *U.S.A.* 189 A6
Gare Tigre, *Fr. Guiana* 214 C6
Gargano, Mte., *Italy* 67 E7
Garies, *S. Africa* 163 F1
Garigliano →, *Italy* 67 F6
Garissa, *Kenya* 157 D4
Garissa □, *Kenya* 157 D4
Garkida, *Nigeria* 151 C7
Garko, *Nigeria* 151 B5
Garm, *Tajikistan* 93 E3
Garonne →, *France* 55 F4
Garoua, *Cameroon* 153 B2
Garrison Res. = Sakakawea, L., *U.S.A.* 190 B8
Garry, L., *Canada* 186 E8
Garsen, *Kenya* 157 E4
Garu, *Ghana* 149 A3
Garut, *Indonesia* 128 F5
Garvie Mts., *N.Z.* 175 H2
Garwa = Garoua, *Cameroon* 153 B2
Gary, *U.S.A.* 191 D13
Garzê, *China* 112 F6
Garzón, *Colombia* 210 D1
Gasan Kuli, *Turkmenistan* 90 K2
Gascogne, *France* 55 G4
Gascony = Gascogne, *France* 55 G4
Gascoyne →, *Australia* 168 C1
Gashaka, *Nigeria* 151 E6
Gashua, *Nigeria* 151 A6
Gaspé, *Canada* 187 J14
Gaspé, C. de, *Canada* 187 J14
Gaspé, Pén. de, *Canada* 187 J14
Gassol, *Nigeria* 151 D6
Gasteiz = Vitoria, *Spain* 63 A6
Gata, C., *Cyprus* 95 C1
Gata, C. de, *Spain* 63 G6
Gata, Sierra de, *Spain* 63 D3
Gateshead, *U.K.* 46 F7
Gaths, *Zimbabwe* 161 D4
Gâtinais, *France* 55 C6
Gattaran, *Phil.* 130 B3
Gatun, L., *Panama* 197 E5
Gatyana, *S. Africa* 163 G7
Gauhati, *India* 106 C9
Gauteng □, *S. Africa* 163 C7
Gawilgarh Hills, *India* 106 E3
Gawler, *Australia* 171 F2
Gaxun Nur, *China* 112 C6
Gaya, *India* 106 C6
Gaya, *Niger* 141 D2
Gaya, *Nigeria* 151 B5
Gaziantep, *Turkey* 94 C5
Gazli, *Uzbekistan* 90 K4
Gbarnga, *Liberia* 148 C2
Gbekebo, *Nigeria* 151 F2
Gboko, *Nigeria* 151 E5
Gbongan, *Nigeria* 151 E2
Gcuwa, *S. Africa* 163 G7
Gdańsk, *Poland* 77 A3
Gdańska, Zatoka, *Poland* 77 A3
Gdov, *Russia* 81 A3
Gdynia, *Poland* 77 A3
Gebe, *Indonesia* 129 C14
Gebeit Mine, *Sudan* 143 A5
Gebel Musa, *Egypt* 139 C6
Gedaref, *Sudan* 143 C5
Gede, Tanjung, *Indonesia* 128 E4
Gedser, *Denmark* 42 D3
Geel, *Belgium* 51 B4
Geelong, *Australia* 171 H4
Geili, *Sudan* 143 C4
Geita, *Tanzania* 158 B1
Gejiu, *China* 112 H6
Gela, *Italy* 67 K6
Geladi, *Ethiopia* 144 E5
Gelderland □, *Neths.* 50 D5
Geldermalsen, *Neths.* 50 E4
Geldern, *Germany* 59 A1
Geldrop, *Neths.* 50 F4
Geleen, *Neths.* 50 G4
Gelehun, *S. Leone* 147 C3
Gelsenkirchen, *Germany* 58 C1
Gemas, *Malaysia* 126 D2
Gembloux, *Belgium* 51 C4
Gemena, *Zaïre* 155 A3
Gemert, *Neths.* 50 E4
Gemsa, *Egypt* 139 C5
Geneina, Gebel, *Egypt* 139 B5
General Acha, *Argentina* 220 F4
General Alvear, *Argentina* 220 E3
General Cabrera, *Argentina* 221 B2
General MacArthur, *Phil.* 130 G5
General Pico, *Argentina* 221 C2
General Pinto, *Argentina* 221 C3
General Santos, *Phil.* 130 L5
General Viamonte, *Argentina* 221 C4
General Villegas, *Argentina* 221 C3
Genesee →, *U.S.A.* 189 A2
Geneva = Genève, *Switz.* 60 D1
Geneva, *U.S.A.* 189 A3
Geneva, L. = Léman, Lac, *Switz.* 60 C1
Genève, *Switz.* 60 D1
Geng, *Afghan.* 104 F1
Genil →, *Spain* 63 F4
Genk, *Belgium* 51 B5
Gennargentu, Mti. del, *Italy* 67 G2
Genoa = Génova, *Italy* 67 C2
Genoa, *Australia* 171 G7
Génova, *Italy* 67 C2
Génova, G. di, *Italy* 67 C2
Genyem, *Indonesia* 129 D18
Geographe B., *Australia* 170 C1
Geokchay, *Azerbaijan* 82 C8
Georga, Zemlya, *Russia* 90 A8
George, *S. Africa* 163 H4
George →, *Canada* 187 G13
George, L., *N.S.W., Australia* 171 F7
George, L., *S. Austral., Australia* 171 G2
George, L., *Uganda* 156 C1
George, L., *U.S.A.* 191 J15
George Town, *Malaysia* 126 B1
Georgetown, *Canada* 185 D1
Georgetown, *Gambia* 146 C2
Georgetown, *Guyana* 214 B2
Georgetown, *U.S.A.* 191 G16
Georgia □, *U.S.A.* 191 H15
Georgia ■, *Asia* 82 B4
Georgiu-Dezh = Liski, *Russia* 81 E6
Georgiyevka, *Kazakstan* 93 A7
Gera, *Germany* 58 D4
Geraardsbergen, *Belgium* 51 C2
Geraldton, *Australia* 168 H9
Gereshk, *Afghan.* 104 F2
Gerik, *Malaysia* 126 B1
Gerlogubi, *Ethiopia* 144 E5
Germany ■, *Europe* 58
Germiston, *S. Africa* 163 C7
Gerona, *Spain* 63 B9
Gerrards Cross, *U.K.* 45 C2
Gers □, *France* 55 G4
Geser, *Indonesia* 129 D15
Gettysburg, *U.S.A.* 189 C3
Gévaudan, *France* 55 F6
Geysir, *Iceland* 38 C3
Ghaghara →, *India* 106 C6
Ghana ■, *W. Afr.* 149
Ghanzi, *Botswana* 162 C4
Gharb el Istiwa'iya □, *Sudan* 143 F3
Gharbîya, Es Sahrâ' el, *Egypt* 139 C2
Ghard Abû Muharik, *Egypt* 139 C3
Ghardaïa, *Algeria* 137 B4
Ghârib, G., *Egypt* 139 C5
Ghârib, Râs, *Egypt* 139 C5
Gharyān, *Libya* 138 A2
Ghat, *Libya* 138 C1
Ghawdex = Gozo, *Malta* 69 A1
Ghazal, Bahr el →, *Chad* 142 D1
Ghazâl, Bahr el →, *Sudan* 143 E3
Ghazaouet, *Algeria* 137 A3
Ghaziabad, *India* 106 A3
Ghazipur, *India* 106 C6
Ghaznī, *Afghan.* 104 D5
Ghaznī □, *Afghan.* 104 D5
Ghent, *Belgium* 51 B2
Ghot Ogrein, *Egypt* 139 A1
Ghowr □, *Afghan.* 104 D3
Ghugus, *India* 106 F4
Ghūrīān, *Afghan.* 104 D1
Gia Lai = Pleiku, *Vietnam* 125 E5
Gia Nghia, *Vietnam* 125 F4
Giarabub = Al Jaghbūb, *Libya* 138 B5
Giarre, *Italy* 67 J7
Gibara, *Cuba* 198 C6
Gibraltar ■, *Europe* 63 H4
Gibraltar, Str. of, *Medit. S.* 34 H5
Gidole, *Ethiopia* 144 E2
Giessen, *Germany* 58 D2
Gifatin, Geziret, *Egypt* 139 C6
Gifu, *Japan* 120 B6
Gifu □, *Japan* 120 B6
Gijón, *Spain* 63 A4
Gila →, *U.S.A.* 190 G4
Gilbert Is., *Kiribati* 176 F5
Gilf el Kebîr, Hadabat el, *Egypt* 139 E1
Gilgandra, *Australia* 171 D7
Gilgil, *Kenya* 157 D2
Gilgit, *India* 107 A2
Gillingham, *U.K.* 45 D5
Gilmore, *Australia* 171 F6
Gimbi, *Ethiopia* 144 D2
Gin →, *Sri Lanka* 110 D2
Ginâh, *Egypt* 139 D4
Gingin, *Australia* 170 B1
Ginir, *Ethiopia* 144 E4
Ginowan, *Japan* 121 J8
Girardot, *Colombia* 210 C1
Giresun, *Turkey* 94 B5
Girga, *Egypt* 139 D4
Giridih, *India* 106 D7
Girilambone, *Australia* 171 C6
Giro, *Nigeria* 151 B2
Girona = Gerona, *Spain* 63 B9
Gironde □, *France* 55 F3
Gironde →, *France* 55 E3
Gisborne, *N.Z.* 175 D6
Gisenyi, *Rwanda* 156 A1
Gissarskiy, Khrebet, *Tajikistan* 93 E2
Gitega, *Burundi* 156 B2
Giurgiu, *Romania* 75 D4
Giza = El Gîza, *Egypt* 139 B4
Gizhiga, *Russia* 91 C17
Gizhiginskaya Guba, *Russia* 91 D17
Giżycko, *Poland* 77 A5
Gjirokastër, *Albania* 70 D2
Gjoa Haven, *Canada* 186 D8
Glace Bay, *Canada* 187 J15
Gladstone, *Australia* 171 E1
Gláma, *Iceland* 38 B2
Glåma →, *Norway* 40 F2
Glarus, *Switz.* 60 B4
Glasgow, *U.K.* 46 D5
Glauchau, *Germany* 58 D5
Gleiwitz = Gliwice, *Poland* 77 E3
Glen Innes, *Australia* 171 B8
Glencoe, *S. Africa* 163 E8
Glendale, *U.S.A.* 190 G2
Glendale, *Zimbabwe* 161 B4
Glendive, *U.S.A.* 190 B7
Glenelg, *Australia* 171 F2
Glenelg →, *Australia* 171 H3
Glenmorgan, *Australia* 171 A7
Glenorchy, *Australia* 172 C2
Glenreagh, *Australia* 171 C9
Glens Falls, *U.S.A.* 191 C17
Glenwood, *U.S.A.* 192 B3
Gliwice, *Poland* 77 E3
Globe, *U.S.A.* 190 G5
Głogów, *Poland* 77 D1
Gloucester, *Australia* 171 D8
Gloucester, *U.K.* 46 K7
Gloversville, *U.S.A.* 189 A4
Glückstadt, *Germany* 58 A3
Gmünd, *Austria* 61 A5
Gmunden, *Austria* 61 B4
Gniezno, *Poland* 77 C2
Gnowangerup, *Australia* 170 C3
Go Cong, *Vietnam* 125 G4
Goa □, *India* 107 E2
Goalen Hd., *Australia* 171 G7
Goalpara, *India* 106 C9
Goaso, *Ghana* 149 D1
Goba, *Ethiopia* 144 E3
Goba, *Mozam.* 159 F1
Gobabis, *Namibia* 162 C3
Gobi, *Asia* 84 D14
Goch, *Germany* 59 A1
Gochas, *Namibia* 162 D3
Godalming, *U.K.* 45 E2
Godavari →, *India* 107 E4
Godhavn, *Greenland* 224 C1
Godhra, *India* 106 D1
Gods →, *Canada* 186 H9
Gods L., *Canada* 186 H8
Godstone, *U.K.* 45 D3
Godthåb, *Greenland* 224 D1
Godwin Austen = K2, Mt., *Pakistan* 105 A6
Goeie Hoop, Kaap die = Good Hope, C. of, *S. Africa* 163 H2
Goeree, *Neths.* 50 E2
Goes, *Neths.* 50 E1
Gogra = Ghaghara →, *India* 106 C6
Goiânia, *Brazil* 217 F6
Goiás, *Brazil* 217 F6
Goiás □, *Brazil* 217 E6
Goirle, *Neths.* 50 E3
Gojra, *Pakistan* 105 C5
Gold Coast, *Australia* 171 A9
Gold Coast, *W. Afr.* 132 F3
Golden B., *N.Z.* 175 E4
Golden Gate, *U.S.A.* 190 E2
Goldsboro, *U.S.A.* 191 F16
Goleniów, *Poland* 77 B1
Golfito, *Costa Rica* 197 E3

Goma, *Rwanda* 156 A1
Gombe, *Nigeria* 151 C6
Gomel, *Belarus* 81 D3
Gomera, *Canary Is.* 223 D1
Gómez Palacio, *Mexico* 194 C4
Gomogomo, *Indonesia* 129 E16
Gomoh, *India* 106 D7
Gompa = Ganta, *Liberia* 148 C2
Gonābād, *Iran* 103 B5
Gonaïves, *Haiti* 200 A2
Gonâve, G. de la, *Haiti* 200 A1
Gonâve, I. de la, *Haiti* 200 B1
Gonda, *India* 106 B5
Gonder, *Ethiopia* 144 C2
Gondia, *India* 106 E4
Gonghe, *China* 112 E6
Gongola —►, *Nigeria* 151 B6
Gongolgon, *Australia* 171 C6
Goniri, *Nigeria* 151 B7
Gonzaga, *Phil.* 130 B3
Good Hope, C. of, *S. Africa* 163 H2
Goodlands, *Mauritius* 166 A2
Goodooga, *Australia* 171 B6
Goolgowi, *Australia* 171 E5
Goomalling, *Australia* 170 B2
Goombalie, *Australia* 171 C5
Goondiwindi, *Australia* 171 B8
Gooray, *Australia* 171 B8
Goose L., *U.S.A.* 190 D3
Gopalganj, *Bangla.* 111 C2
Gorakhpur, *India* 106 B6
Gorda, Pta., *Nic.* 197 A3
Gordon —►, *Australia* 172 C1
Goré, *Chad* 142 F1
Gore, *Ethiopia* 144 E2
Gore, *N.Z.* 175 J2
Görele, *Turkey* 82 C1
Gorgān, *Iran* 103 B4
Gorgona, I., *Colombia* 210 D1
Gori, *Georgia* 82 B5
Gorinchem, *Neths.* 50 E3
Goris, *Armenia* 82 D7
Gorízia, *Italy* 67 A5
Gorki = Nizhniy Novgorod, *Russia* 81 B7
Gorkiy = Nizhniy Novgorod, *Russia* 81 B7
Gorkovskoye Vdkhr., *Russia* 81 B7
Görlitz, *Germany* 58 D6
Gorlovka, *Ukraine* 81 F5
Gorna Oryakhovitsa, *Bulgaria* 73 B4
Gorno-Altaysk, *Russia* 90 J9
Gorno Slinkino, *Russia* 90 F7
Gorontalo, *Indonesia* 129 B11
Goronyo, *Nigeria* 151 A3
Gorzów Wielkopolski, *Poland* 77 C1
Gosford, *Australia* 171 E8
Goslar, *Germany* 58 C3
Gospič, *Croatia* 72 C3
Göta kanal, *Sweden* 40 G3
Göteborg, *Sweden* 40 G2
Gotha, *Germany* 58 D4
Gotland, *Sweden* 40 G4
Göttingen, *Germany* 58 C3
Gottwaldov = Zlin, *Czech.* 76 C5
Goubangzi, *China* 116 B5
Gouda, *Neths.* 50 D3
Goudhurst, *U.K.* 45 E5
Goudiry, *Senegal* 146 B3
Gough I., *Atl. Oc.* 223 K5
Gouin, Rés., *Canada* 187 K12
Gouitafla, *Ivory C.* 148 C4
Goulburn, *Australia* 171 F7
Goulia, *Ivory C.* 148 A4
Goulimine, *Morocco* 136 F2
Gounou-Gaya, *Chad* 142 F1
Gouri, *Chad* 142 B2
Gourits —►, *S. Africa* 163 H4
Gourma Rharous, *Mali* 140 D5
Governador Valadares, *Brazil* 217 G8
Gowanda, *U.S.A.* 189 A2
Goya, *Argentina* 220 D5
Goyder Lagoon, *Australia* 171 A2
Goyllarisquisga, *Peru* 213 D3
Goz Beïda, *Chad* 142 E3
Gozo, *Malta* 69 A1
Graaff-Reinet, *S. Africa* 163 G5
Gračac, *Croatia* 72 C4
Gracias à Dios, C., *Honduras* 196 C5
Graciosa, I., *Canary Is.* 223 C3
Grado, *Spain* 63 A3
Gradule, *Australia* 171 B7
Graénalon, L., *Iceland* 38 C4
Grafton, *Australia* 171 B9
Grafton, *U.S.A.* 191 B10
Graham Bell, Os., *Russia* 90 A9
Grahamstown, *S. Africa* 163 H6
Graïba, *Tunisia* 138 C2
Grain Coast, *W. Afr.* 148 E2
Grampian Highlands = Grampian Mts., *U.K.* 46 C5
Grampian Mts., *U.K.* 46 C5
Gran —►, *Surinam* 214 C4
Gran Canaria, *Canary Is.* 223 D2
Gran Chaco, *S. Amer.* 206 E3
Gran Paradiso, *Italy* 67 A1
Gran Sasso, *Italy* 67 E5
Granada, *Nic.* 197 C2
Granada, *Spain* 63 G5
Granadilla de Abona, *Canary Is.* 223 D2
Granby, *Canada* 185 B6
Grand Bahama I., *Bahamas* 201 A1
Grand Bassam, *Ivory C.* 148 E5
Grand Béréby, *Ivory C.* 148 E4
Grand-Bourg, *Guadeloupe* 202 G6
Grand Canyon, *U.S.A.* 190 F5
Grand Cess, *Liberia* 148 E3
Grand Falls, *Canada* 187 H15
Grand Forks, *U.S.A.* 191 B10
Grand Island, *U.S.A.* 190 E9
Grand Junction, *U.S.A.* 190 E6
Grand Lahou, *Ivory C.* 148 E5
Grand Popo, *Benin* 150 E2
Grand Rapids, *Canada* 186 H8
Grand Rapids, *U.S.A.* 191 D13
Grand St-Bernard, Col du, *Switz.* 60 D2
Grand Santi, *Fr. Guiana* 214 C5
Grand Teton, *U.S.A.* 190 C6
Grande —►, *Bolivia* 218 B1
Grande —►, *Brazil* 217 G6
Grande, B., *Argentina* 220 K3
Grande, Rio —►, *U.S.A.* 191 K10
Grande Baleine, R. de la —►, *Canada* 187 H11
Grande Comore, *Comoros Is.* 166 A1
Grande de Santiago —►, *Mexico* 194 D3
Grande Prairie, *Canada* 186 G5
Grangeville, *U.S.A.* 190 B4
Granite City, *U.S.A.* 191 F12
Granitnyy, Pik, *Kyrgyzstan* 93 E4
Granollers, *Spain* 63 B9
Grantham, *U.K.* 46 H8
Grants, *U.S.A.* 190 G6
Grants Pass, *U.S.A.* 190 C2
Granville, *France* 55 B3
Gras, L. de, *Canada* 186 E7
Graskop, *S. Africa* 163 B9
Grasse, *France* 55 G9
Grassmere, *Australia* 171 C4
Graubünden □, *Switz.* 60 C5
's-Gravenhage, *Neths.* 50 D2
Gravesend, *Australia* 171 B8
Gravesend, *U.K.* 45 C5
Gravois, Pointe-à-, *Haiti* 200 B1
Grays, *U.K.* 45 C5
Grays Harbor, *U.S.A.* 190 A2
Graz, *Austria* 61 C5
Great Abaco I., *Bahamas* 201 A2
Great Australian Bight, *Australia* 168 D2
Great Baddow, *U.K.* 45 B5
Great Barrier I., *N.Z.* 175 B5
Great Barrier Reef, *Australia* 168 B4
Great Basin, *U.S.A.* 180 F8
Great Bear —►, *Canada* 186 D5
Great Bear L., *Canada* 186 D6
Great Belt = Store Bælt, *Denmark* 42 C3
Great Bend, *U.S.A.* 190 F9
Great Britain, *Europe* 34 E6
Great Dividing Ra., *Australia* 168 C4
Great Dunmow, *U.K.* 45 A5
Great Falls, *U.S.A.* 190 B6
Great Fish = Groot Vis —►, *S. Africa* 163 H6
Great Inagua I., *Bahamas* 201 C3
Great Indian Desert = Thar Desert, *India* 106 B1
Great Karoo, *S. Africa* 163 G3
Great Khingan Mts., *China* 84 D15
Great Lake, *Australia* 172 B2
Great Missenden, *U.K.* 45 B1
Great Plains, *N. Amer.* 180 E9
Great Ruaha —►, *Tanzania* 158 C2
Great Saint Bernard P. = Grand St-Bernard, Col du, *Switz.* 60 D2
Great Salt Desert, *Iran* 103 C5
Great Salt L., *U.S.A.* 190 D5
Great Salt Lake Desert, *U.S.A.* 190 E4
Great Sangi = Sangihe, P., *Indonesia* 129 B12
Great Scarcies —►, *S. Leone* 147 C2
Great Slave L., *Canada* 186 F6
Great Wall, *China* 113 E8
Great Waltham, *U.K.* 45 B5
Great Yarmouth, *U.K.* 46 J9
Great Yeldham, *U.K.* 45 A5
Greater Antilles, *W. Indies* 180 H12
Greater Sunda Is., *Indonesia* 128 E7
Greco, C., *Cyprus* 95 B3
Gredos, Sierra de, *Spain* 63 D4
Greece ■, *Europe* 71
Greeley, *U.S.A.* 190 E7
Greely Fd., *Canada* 186 A9
Green —►, *Ky., U.S.A.* 191 F13
Green —►, *Utah, U.S.A.* 190 E6
Green Bay, *U.S.A.* 191 C12
Green C., *Australia* 171 G7
Greenfield, *U.S.A.* 189 A6
Greenland ■, *N. Amer.* 224
Greenock, *U.K.* 46 D5
Greenore, *Ireland* 46 G3
Greensboro, *U.S.A.* 191 F15
Greensburg, *U.S.A.* 189 C1
Greenville, *Liberia* 148 E2
Greenville, *Ala., U.S.A.* 191 H13
Greenville, *Miss., U.S.A.* 191 H12
Greenville, *S.C., U.S.A.* 191 G15
Greenville, *Tex., U.S.A.* 191 H10
Greenwich, *U.K.* 45 C4
Greenwood, *U.S.A.* 191 H12
Gregory, L., *Australia* 171 B2
Greifswald, *Germany* 58 A5
Gremikha, *Russia* 90 C6
Grenada ■, *W. Indies* 203 L1
Grenadines, *W. Indies* 203 J2
Grenen, *Denmark* 42 A3
Grenfell, *Australia* 171 E6
Grenoble, *France* 55 F8
Grevenbroich, *Germany* 59 B1
Grevenmacher, *Lux.* 52 C3
Grey —►, *N.Z.* 175 F3
Greymouth, *N.Z.* 175 F3
Greytown, *S. Africa* 163 E8
Griekwastad, *S. Africa* 163 E4
Griffin, *U.S.A.* 191 G14
Griffith, *Australia* 171 E5
Grimari, *C.A.R.* 142 B3
Grimsby, *U.K.* 46 G8
Grimsey, *Iceland* 38 A4
Grindelwald, *Switz.* 60 C3
Gris-Nez, C., *France* 55 A5
Grisons = Graubünden □, *Switz.* 60 C5
Groblersdal, *S. Africa* 163 C8
Grodno, *Belarus* 81 C1
Grodzisk, *Poland* 77 C2
Grójec, *Poland* 77 C4
Groningen, *Neths.* 50 A5
Groningen, *Surinam* 214 B4
Groningen □, *Neths.* 50 A6
Groot —►, *S. Africa* 163 H5
Groot Berg —►, *S. Africa* 163 G2
Groot-Brakrivier, *S. Africa* 163 H4
Groot-Kei —►, *S. Africa* 163 G7
Groot Vis —►, *S. Africa* 163 H6
Grootfontein, *Namibia* 162 B3
Grootvloer, *S. Africa* 163 F3
Gross Glockner, *Austria* 61 C3
Grossenhain, *Germany* 58 D5
Grosseto, *Italy* 67 D4
Grouard Mission, *Canada* 186 G5
Groznyy, *Russia* 82 A6
Grudziądz, *Poland* 77 B3
Gruyères, *Switz.* 60 C2
Gryazi, *Russia* 81 D6
Gstaad, *Switz.* 60 C2
Gua, *India* 106 E7
Gua Musang, *Malaysia* 126 B2
Guacanayabo, G. de, *Cuba* 198 C5
Guadalajara, *Mexico* 194 D4
Guadalajara, *Spain* 63 D5
Guadalcanal, *Solomon Is.* 173 B2
Guadalete —►, *Spain* 63 G3
Guadalhorce —►, *Spain* 63 G4
Guadalquivir —►, *Spain* 63 G3
Guadalupe = Guadeloupe ■, *W. Indies* 202 F5
Guadalupe, Sierra de, *Spain* 63 E4
Guadarrama, Sierra de, *Spain* 63 C5
Guadeloupe ■, *W. Indies* 202 F5
Guadiana —►, *Portugal* 63 G2
Guadix, *Spain* 63 G5
Guajará-Mirim, *Brazil* 217 E3
Guajira, Pen. de la, *Colombia* 210 A2
Gualaceo, *Ecuador* 212 D1
Gualán, *Guatemala* 196 C2
Gualeguay, *Argentina* 221 B5
Gualeguaychú, *Argentina* 221 B5
Guam ■, *Pac. Oc.* 176 D3
Guamote, *Ecuador* 212 C1
Guamúchil, *Mexico* 194 C2
Guan Xian, *China* 113 F7
Guanabacoa, *Cuba* 198 A2
Guanacaste, Cordillera del, *Costa Rica* 197 D2
Guanahani = San Salvador, *Bahamas* 201 B2
Guanajay, *Cuba* 198 B2
Guanajuato, *Mexico* 194 D4
Guane, *Cuba* 198 B1
Guangde, *China* 116 G4
Guangdong □, *China* 113 H9
Guanghua, *China* 116 F1
Guangxi Zhuangzu Zizhiqu □, *China* 113 H8
Guangze, *China* 116 J3
Guangzhou, *China* 113 H9
Guánica, *Puerto Rico* 201 A1
Guanipa —►, *Venezuela* 211 A5
Guantánamo, *Cuba* 198 C6
Guantao, *China* 116 D3
Guanyun, *China* 116 E4
Guápiles, *Costa Rica* 197 D3
Guaporé —►, *Brazil* 217 E3
Guaqui, *Bolivia* 218 C1
Guaranda, *Ecuador* 212 C1
Guarapari, *Brazil* 215 A6
Guaratinguetá, *Brazil* 215 C3
Guarda, *Portugal* 63 D2
Guardafui, C. = Asir, Ras, *Somali Rep.* 145 A3
Guarujá, *Brazil* 215 C3
Guarus, *Brazil* 215 B5
Guasdualito, *Venezuela* 211 B2
Guasipati, *Venezuela* 211 B5
Guatemala, *Guatemala* 196 C1
Guatemala ■, *Cent. Amer.* 196
Guaviare —►, *Colombia* 210 C3
Guaxupé, *Brazil* 215 B2
Guayama, *Puerto Rico* 201 A2
Guayaquil, *Ecuador* 212 D1
Guayaquil, G. de, *Ecuador* 212 D1
Guayas —►, *Ecuador* 212 D1
Guaymas, *Mexico* 194 B1
Guazhou, *China* 116 F4
Gûbâl, Madîq, *Egypt* 139 C6
Gubat, *Phil.* 130 F4
Gubio, *Nigeria* 151 B7
Gudata, *Georgia* 82 A2
Guddu Barrage, *Pakistan* 105 E4
Gudermes, *Russia* 82 A7
Guecho, *Spain* 63 A5
Guékédou, *Guinea* 147 C4
Guelma, *Algeria* 137 A5
Guelph, *Canada* 187 L11
Guéné, *Benin* 150 A3
Guercif, *Morocco* 136 B6
Guéréda, *Chad* 142 D3
Guéret, *France* 55 E5
Guernica, *Spain* 63 A6
Guernsey, *U.K.* 44 A1
Guia, *Canary Is.* 223 D2
Guiana Highlands, *S. Amer.* 206 B3
Guichi, *China* 116 G4
Guidong, *China* 116 J2
Guiglo, *Ivory C.* 148 D3
Guildford, *U.K.* 45 D2
Guilin, *China* 113 H8
Guilvinec, *France* 55 C1
Guimaras, *Phil.* 130 H3
Guinea ■, *W. Afr.* 147
Guinea, Gulf of, *Atl. Oc.* 132 F3
Guinea-Bissau ■, *Africa* 146
Güines, *Cuba* 198 B2
Guingamp, *France* 55 C2
Guiping, *China* 113 H8
Güiria, *Venezuela* 211 A5
Guiuan, *Phil.* 130 G5
Guixi, *China* 116 H3
Guiyang, *China* 113 H7
Guizhou □, *China* 113 G7
Gujarat □, *India* 107 C1
Gujranwala, *Pakistan* 105 C6
Gujrat, *Pakistan* 105 C6
Gulbarga, *India* 107 E2
Gulcha, *Kyrgyzstan* 93 D6
Gulfport, *U.S.A.* 191 J13
Gulgong, *Australia* 171 D7
Gulistan, *Uzbekistan* 93 D2
Gulma, *Nigeria* 151 A2
Gulshad, *Kazakstan* 90 K7
Gulu, *Uganda* 156 B2
Gum Lake, *Australia* 171 D4
Gumel, *Nigeria* 151 A5
Gumma □, *Japan* 120 A8
Gummersbach, *Germany* 59 B3
Gummi, *Nigeria* 151 B2
Gümüşhane, *Turkey* 82 C1
Gumzai, *Indonesia* 129 E16
Guna, *India* 106 C3
Gundagai, *Australia* 171 F6
Gungu, *Zaïre* 155 E2
Gunnbjørn Fjeld, *Greenland* 224 C3
Gunnedah, *Australia* 171 C8
Gunners Quoin, *Mauritius* 166 A2
Gunningbar Cr. —►, *Australia* 171 C6
Gunnison —►, *U.S.A.* 190 E6
Guntakal, *India* 107 E3
Guntong, *Malaysia* 126 B1
Guntur, *India* 107 E3
Gunungapi, *Indonesia* 129 E13
Gunungsitoli, *Indonesia* 128 B1
Gunza, *Angola* 160 C2
Guo He —►, *China* 116 F4
Guoyang, *China* 116 F3
Gupis, *Pakistan* 105 A5
Gurdzhaani, *Georgia* 82 B6
Gurkha, *Nepal* 109 B3
Gurley, *Australia* 171 B7
Gurun, *Malaysia* 126 A1
Gurupi —►, *Brazil* 217 B7
Guryev = Atyrau, *Kazakstan* 90 H3
Gusau, *Nigeria* 151 B3
Gushan, *China* 116 C6
Gushi, *China* 116 F3
Gushiago, *Ghana* 149 B3
Gusinoozersk, *Russia* 91 J12
Güstrow, *Germany* 58 A4
Guthrie, *U.S.A.* 191 G10
Guyana ■, *S. Amer.* 214
Guyane française ■ = French Guiana ■, *S. Amer.* 214
Guyang, *China* 116 B1
Guyenne, *France* 55 F4
Guyra, *Australia* 171 C8
Guzhen, *China* 116 F4
Gwa, *Burma* 122 F2
Gwaai, *Zimbabwe* 161 C2
Gwabegar, *Australia* 171 C7
Gwadabawa, *Nigeria* 151 A2
Gwādar, *Pakistan* 105 F1
Gwagwada, *Nigeria* 151 C4
Gwalior, *India* 106 C3
Gwanda, *Zimbabwe* 161 D2
Gwandu, *Nigeria* 151 A2
Gwaram, *Nigeria* 151 C6
Gwarzo, *Nigeria* 151 B5
Gweru, *Zimbabwe* 161 C3
Gwi, *Nigeria* 151 D4
Gwio Kura, *Nigeria* 151 A6
Gwoza, *Nigeria* 151 B7
Gwydir —►, *Australia* 171 B7
Gyandzha, *Azerbaijan* 82 C7
Gyaring Hu, *China* 112 E5
Gydanskiy P-ov., *Russia* 90 D9
Gyöngyös, *Hungary* 74 A4
Györ, *Hungary* 74 A2
Gypsumville, *Canada* 186 J8
Gyumri = Kumayri, *Armenia* 82 C5

H

Ha 'Arava —►, *Israel* 96 F2
Ha Nam = Phu Ly, *Vietnam* 125 B3
Ha'apai Is., *Tonga* 174 B3
Haarlem, *Neths.* 50 C3
Hab Nadi Chauki, *Pakistan* 105 F3
Habaswein, *Kenya* 157 C4
Habiganj, *Bangla.* 111 B3
Hachijō-Jima, *Japan* 120 D9
Hachinohe, *Japan* 121 D8
Hachŏn, *N. Korea* 118 B5
Hackney, *U.K.* 45 C3
Hadarba, Ras, *Sudan* 143 A5
Hadarom □, *Israel* 96 E2
Ḥadd, Ra's al, *Oman* 101 B3
Haddenham, *U.K.* 45 B1
Hadejia, *Nigeria* 151 B5
Hadejia —►, *Nigeria* 151 A6
Haden, *Australia* 171 A9
Ḥadera, *Israel* 96 C2
Ḥadera, N. —►, *Israel* 96 C2
Hadhramaut = Haḍramawt, *Yemen* 100 B2
Hadjeb El Aïoun, *Tunisia* 138 B2
Hadleigh, *U.K.* 45 C6
Hadlow, *U.K.* 45 D5
Hadong, *S. Korea* 118 H5
Haḍramawt, *Yemen* 100 B2
Haeju, *N. Korea* 118 E3
Haenam, *S. Korea* 118 H4
Haerhpin = Harbin, *China* 113 B11
Hafizabad, *Pakistan* 105 C6
Hafnarfjörður, *Iceland* 38 D2
Hagalil, *Israel* 96 B2
Hagen, *Germany* 58 C2
Hagerstown, *U.S.A.* 189 D3
Hagi, *Iceland* 38 B2
Hagi, *Japan* 120 C2
Hagondange-Briey, *France* 55 B8
Hague, C. de la, *France* 55 B3
Hague, The = 's-Gravenhage, *Neths.* 50 D2
Haguenau, *France* 55 B9
Haicheng, *China* 116 C6
Haifa = Ḥefa, *Israel* 96 B2
Haikou, *China* 113 J8
Ḥā'il, *Si. Arabia* 99 B4
Hailar, *China* 113 A10
Hailey, *U.S.A.* 190 C4
Haileybury, *Canada* 187 K11
Hailun, *China* 113 B11
Haimen, *China* 116 G5
Hainan, *China* 84 G14
Hainan □, *China* 113 J8
Hainaut □, *Belgium* 51 C3
Haining, *China* 116 G5
Haiphong, *Vietnam* 125 B4
Haiti ■, *W. Indies* 200
Haiya Junction, *Sudan* 143 B6
Haiyan, *China* 116 G5
Haiyang, *China* 116 D5
Haja, *Indonesia* 129 D14
Ḥajar Bangar, *Sudan* 143 D1
Hajdúböszörmény, *Hungary* 74 A5
Hajiganj, *Bangla.* 111 C2
Hajnówka, *Poland* 77 C6
Hakken-Zan, *Japan* 120 C6
Hakodate, *Japan* 121 C7
Hala, *Pakistan* 105 F3
Ḥalab, *Syria* 97 A3
Ḥalabjah, *Iraq* 102 B5
Halaib, *Sudan* 143 A5
Halbā, *Lebanon* 95 A2
Halberstadt, *Germany* 58 C4
Halden, *Norway* 40 F2
Haldia, *India* 106 E8
Haldwani, *India* 106 A4
Haleakala, *U.S.A.* 192 A3
Half Assini, *Ghana* 149 E1
Halifax, *Canada* 187 K14
Halifax, *U.K.* 46 G7
Halīl —►, *Iran* 103 D6
Hall Beach, *Canada* 187 D10
Halle, *Germany* 58 C4
Hallett, *Australia* 171 E2
Hallim, *S. Korea* 118 J4
Halmahera, *Indonesia* 129 C13
Halmstad, *Sweden* 40 H2
Halq el Oued, *Tunisia* 138 A2
Hals, *Denmark* 42 B2
Hälsingborg = Helsingborg, *Sweden* 40 H2
Halstead, *U.K.* 45 A6
Haltern, *Germany* 59 A2
Hamada, *Japan* 120 B3
Hamadān, *Iran* 103 B2
Hamāh, *Syria* 97 B3
Hamamatsu, *Japan* 120 C7
Hamâta, Gebel, *Egypt* 139 E6
Hamburg, *Germany* 58 A3
Hämeenlinna, *Finland* 43 F2
Hamélé, *Ghana* 149 A1
Hameln, *Germany* 58 C3
Hamerkaz □, *Israel* 96 C2
Hamhung, *N. Korea* 118 D4
Hami, *China* 112 C5
Hamilton, *Australia* 171 G3
Hamilton, *Canada* 185 D1
Hamilton, *N.Z.* 175 C5
Hamilton, *U.K.* 46 D5
Hamilton, *N.Y., U.S.A.* 189 A4
Hamilton, *Ohio, U.S.A.* 191 E14
Hamilton Inlet, *Canada* 180 D14

Hamley Bridge, *Australia* 171 E2
Hamlin = Hameln, *Germany* 58 C3
Hamm, *Germany* 58 C2
Hammamet, *Tunisia* 138 B3
Hammamet, G. de, *Tunisia* 138 B3
Hammerfest, *Norway* 40 A5
Hammersmith and Fulham, *U.K.* 45 C3
Hammond, *U.S.A.* 191 D13
Hammonton, *U.S.A.* 189 C4
Hamrat esh Sheykh, *Sudan* 143 C3
Hamur, *Turkey* 82 D4
Hamyang, *S. Korea* 118 G5
Han Olovo, *Bos.-H.* 72 C6
Han Shui →, *China* 116 G2
Hana, *U.S.A.* 192 A3
Hanamaki, *Japan* 121 D7
Hanau, *Germany* 58 E2
Hancheng, *China* 116 E1
Handa, *Japan* 120 B6
Handan, *China* 116 D2
Handeni, *Tanzania* 158 B3
Hanegev, *Israel* 96 F2
Hanford, *U.S.A.* 190 F2
Hangang →, *S. Korea* 118 F4
Hangayn Nuruu, *Mongolia* 112 B6
Hangchou = Hangzhou, *China* 116 G5
Hangö, *Finland* 43 F2
Hangu, *China* 116 C4
Hangzhou, *China* 116 G5
Hangzhou Wan, *China* 116 G5
Ḥanīsh, *Yemen* 100 B1
Hanko = Hangö, *Finland* 43 F2
Hankou, *China* 116 G2
Hanna, *Canada* 186 H5
Hannibal, *U.S.A.* 191 E11
Hanningfield Water, *U.K.* 45 B5
Hannover, *Germany* 58 C3
Hanoi, *Vietnam* 125 B3
Hanover = Hannover, *Germany* 58 C3
Hanover, *S. Africa* 163 F5
Hanover, *U.S.A.* 189 D3
Hansi, *India* 106 A2
Hanyang, *China* 116 G2
Hanzhong, *China* 113 F7
Hanzhuang, *China* 116 E4
Haora, *India* 106 E8
Haparanda, *Sweden* 40 C5
Hapsu, *N. Korea* 118 B5
Hapur, *India* 106 A3
Har, *Indonesia* 129 E15
Har Hu, *China* 112 D6
Har Us Nuur, *Mongolia* 112 B5
Har Yehuda, *Israel* 96 D2
Ḥaraḍ, *Si. Arabia* 99 D6
Harare, *Zimbabwe* 161 B4
Harazé, *Chad* 142 D2
Harbin, *China* 113 B11
Harbour Grace, *Canada* 187 H16
Harburg, *Germany* 58 B3
Hardangerfjorden, *Norway* 40 F1
Hardap Dam, *Namibia* 162 D3
Hardenberg, *Neths.* 50 C6
Harderwijk, *Neths.* 50 C4
Harding, *S. Africa* 163 F8
Hardinxveld, *Neths.* 50 E3
Hardoi, *India* 106 B4
Hardwar = Haridwar, *India* 106 A3
Harelbeke, *Belgium* 51 C2
Harer, *Ethiopia* 144 D4
Hargeisa, *Somali Rep.* 145 B1
Hari →, *Indonesia* 128 C4
Haridwar, *India* 106 A3
Haringey, *U.K.* 45 C3
Haringhata →, *Bangla.* 111 D2
Harīrūd →, *Asia* 84 E10
Harlingen, *Neths.* 50 A4
Harlingen, *U.S.A.* 190 J9
Harlow, *U.K.* 45 B4
Harney Basin, *U.S.A.* 190 C3
Harney L., *U.S.A.* 190 C3
Härnösand, *Sweden* 40 E4
Harpenden, *U.K.* 45 B3
Harper, *Liberia* 148 E3
Harrietsham, *U.K.* 45 D6
Harris, *U.K.* 46 B3
Harrisburg, *U.S.A.* 189 C3
Harrismith, *S. Africa* 163 E8
Harrison, C., *Canada* 187 G14
Harrisonburg, *U.S.A.* 191 E15
Harrow, *U.K.* 45 C3
Hartbees →, *S. Africa* 163 E3
Hartford, *U.S.A.* 189 B6
Hartlepool, *U.K.* 46 F7
Harts →, *S. Africa* 163 E5
Harvey, *Australia* 170 C1
Harwich, *U.K.* 46 J9
Haryana □, *India* 106 A3
Harz, *Germany* 58 C4
Haslemere, *U.K.* 45 E1
Hasselt, *Belgium* 51 B5
Hasselt, *Neths.* 50 C5
Hassi Inifel, *Algeria* 137 C4
Hassi Messaoud, *Algeria* 137 B5
Hastings, *Barbados* 204 D1
Hastings, *N.Z.* 175 D6
Hastings, *U.K.* 46 L9
Hastings, *U.S.A.* 190 E9
Hastings Ra., *Australia* 171 C9
Hat Nhao, *Laos* 125 E4
Hatay = Antalya, *Turkey* 94 C2
Hatfield, *U.K.* 45 B3
Hatfield Broad Oak, *U.K.* 45 B4
Hatfield P.O., *Australia* 171 E4
Hatgal, *Mongolia* 112 A6
Hathras, *India* 106 B3
Hato Mayor, *Dom. Rep.* 200 B3
Hattah, *Australia* 171 F3
Hattem, *Neths.* 50 C5
Hatteras, C., *U.S.A.* 191 F17
Hattiesburg, *U.S.A.* 191 H12
Hatvan, *Hungary* 74 B4
Hau Bon = Cheo Reo, *Vietnam* 125 E5
Haugesund, *Norway* 40 F1
Hauraki G., *N.Z.* 175 B5
Haut Atlas, *Morocco* 136 C5
Haut-Rhin □, *France* 55 C9
Haute-Corse □, *France* 55 H9
Haute-Garonne □, *France* 55 H5
Haute-Loire □, *France* 55 F7
Haute-Marne □, *France* 55 C7
Haute-Saône □, *France* 55 C8
Haute-Savoie □, *France* 55 E8
Haute-Vienne □, *France* 55 E5
Hautes-Alpes □, *France* 55 F8
Hautes-Pyrénées □, *France* 55 H4
Hauts-de-Seine □, *France* 55 B5
Hauts Plateaux, *Algeria* 137 A4
Havana = La Habana, *Cuba* 198 A2
Havasu, L., *U.S.A.* 190 G4
Havel →, *Germany* 58 B5
Havelange, *Belgium* 51 D4
Haverfordwest, *U.K.* 46 K4
Haverhill, *U.S.A.* 189 A6
Havering, *U.K.* 45 C4
Havlíčkův Brod, *Czech.* 76 B4
Havre, *U.S.A.* 190 B6
Hawaiian Islands, *U.S.A.* 192 B2
Hawaiian Ridge, *Pac. Oc.* 176 C6
Hawea, L., *N.Z.* 175 H2
Hawera, *N.Z.* 175 D5
Hawick, *U.K.* 46 E6
Hawke B., *N.Z.* 175 D6
Hawker, *Australia* 171 D1
Hawkesbury, *Canada* 185 B4
Hawkhurst, *U.K.* 45 E5
Hawsh Mūssá, *Lebanon* 95 C2
Hawthorne, *U.S.A.* 190 E3
Hay, *Australia* 171 E5
Hay River, *Canada* 186 F6
Hayes →, *Canada* 186 H9
Hays, *U.S.A.* 190 E9
Haywards Heath, *U.K.* 45 E3
Hazafon □, *Israel* 96 B2
Hazaribag, *India* 106 D7
Hazelton, *Canada* 186 F3
Hazleton, *U.S.A.* 189 B4
Hazor, *Israel* 96 A3
Headcorn, *U.K.* 45 E6
Headlands, *Zimbabwe* 161 C5
Headley, *U.K.* 45 E1
Healesville, *Australia* 171 G5
Hearst, *Canada* 187 K10
Hebei □, *China* 116 C3
Hebel, *Australia* 171 B6
Hebi, *China* 116 E2
Hebrides, *U.K.* 34 D5
Hebron = Al Khalīl, *Jordan* 98 B1
Hebron, *Canada* 187 F13
Hecate Str., *Canada* 186 F3
Hechi, *China* 113 H7
Hechuan, *China* 113 G7
Heemstede, *Neths.* 50 C3
Heerenveen, *Neths.* 50 B5
Heerlen, *Neths.* 50 G5
Hefa, *Israel* 96 B2
Hefa □, *Israel* 96 B2
Hefei, *China* 116 G4
Hegang, *China* 113 B12
Heidelberg, *Germany* 58 E2
Heidelberg, *S. Africa* 163 H3
Heilbron, *S. Africa* 163 D7
Heilbronn, *Germany* 58 F3
Heilongjiang □, *China* 113 B11
Heilunkiang = Heilongjiang □, *China* 113 B11
Heinze Is., *Burma* 122 G3
Hejian, *China* 116 C3
Hekla, *Iceland* 38 D3
Hekou, *China* 113 J7
Helena, *U.S.A.* 190 B5
Helensburgh, *U.K.* 46 D5
Helensville, *N.Z.* 175 B5
Helgoland, *Germany* 58 A2
Heligoland = Helgoland, *Germany* 58 A2
Heligoland B. = Deutsche Bucht, *Germany* 58 A2
Heliopolis, *Egypt* 139 B4
Hellín, *Spain* 63 F7
Hellshire Hills, *Jamaica* 199 C4
Helmand □, *Afghan.* 104 F2
Helmand →, *Afghan.* 104 F1
Helmond, *Neths.* 50 E4
Helsingborg, *Sweden* 40 H2
Helsingør, *Denmark* 42 C4
Helsinki, *Finland* 43 F2
Helwân, *Egypt* 139 B4
Hemel Hempstead, *U.K.* 45 B2
Henan □, *China* 116 F2
Henares →, *Spain* 63 D5
Henderson, *U.S.A.* 191 F13
Hengelo, *Neths.* 50 D6
Hengshan, *China* 116 J2
Hengshui, *China* 116 D3
Hengyang, *China* 116 J1
Henlow, *U.K.* 45 A3
Hennenman, *S. Africa* 163 D6
Henrietta, Ostrov, *Russia* 91 A13
Henrietta Maria C., *Canada* 187 H10
Hentiyn Nuruu, *Mongolia* 113 B8
Henty, *Australia* 171 F6
Henzada, *Burma* 122 F2
Héraðsflói, *Iceland* 38 B5
Héraðsvötn →, *Iceland* 38 B3
Herāt, *Afghan.* 104 D1
Herāt □, *Afghan.* 104 C1
Hérault □, *France* 55 G6
Hercegnovi, *Montenegro, Yug.* 72 E6
Herðubreið, *Iceland* 38 B4
Hereford, *U.K.* 46 J6
Herentals, *Belgium* 51 B4
Herford, *Germany* 58 C2
Herisau, *Switz.* 60 A5
Herkimer, *U.S.A.* 189 A4
Herm, *Chan. Is.* 44 A2
Hermanus, *S. Africa* 163 H2
Hermidale, *Australia* 171 D6
Hermon, Mt. = Ash Shaykh, J., *Lebanon* 95 C2
Hermosillo, *Mexico* 194 B1
Hernád →, *Hungary* 74 A5
Hernandarias, *Paraguay* 219 C3
Hernando, *Argentina* 221 B2
Herne, *Germany* 59 A2
Herning, *Denmark* 42 B2
Heroica Nogales = Nogales, *Mexico* 194 A2
Herrera, *Spain* 63 E4
Herrick, *Australia* 172 B3
Herschel, I., *Canada* 186 B5
Herstal, *Belgium* 51 C5
Hertford, *U.K.* 45 B3
Hertfordshire □, *U.K.* 45 B3
's-Hertogenbosch, *Neths.* 50 E4
Hertzogville, *S. Africa* 163 E6
Hervey B., *Australia* 168 C5
Herzliyya, *Israel* 96 C2
Hesperange, *Lux.* 52 D2
Hesse = Hessen □, *Germany* 58 D2
Hessen □, *Germany* 58 D2
Hexigten Qi, *China* 116 A4
Heybridge, *U.K.* 45 B6
Heywood, *Australia* 171 H3
Hi Zerzour, *Morocco* 136 D5
Hibbing, *U.S.A.* 191 B11
Hibbs B., *Australia* 172 C1
Hicks, Pt., *Australia* 171 H7
Hida-Sammyaku, *Japan* 120 A7
Hidalgo del Parral, *Mexico* 194 C3
Hierro, *Canary Is.* 223 D1
Higashiōsaka, *Japan* 120 C5
High Atlas = Haut Atlas, *Morocco* 136 C5
High River, *Canada* 186 J5
High Tatra = Tatry, *Slovak Rep.* 76 C7
High Wycombe, *U.K.* 45 C1
Higüay, *Dom. Rep.* 200 B3
Hiiumaa, *Estonia* 81 A1
Ḥijārah, Ṣaḥrā' al, *Iraq* 102 E4
Ḥijāz □, *Si. Arabia* 99 C3
Hijo = Tagum, *Phil.* 130 K5
Hikone, *Japan* 120 B6
Hikurangi, *N.Z.* 175 B5
Hikurangi, Mt., *N.Z.* 175 C6
Hildesheim, *Germany* 58 C3
Hill →, *Australia* 170 A1
Hillaby, Mt., *Barbados* 204 B2
Hillegom, *Neths.* 50 C2
Hillingdon, *U.K.* 45 C2
Hillsboro, *U.S.A.* 191 H10
Hillston, *Australia* 171 E5
Hilo, *U.S.A.* 192 B3
Hilversum, *Neths.* 50 D3
Himachal Pradesh □, *India* 107 B2
Himalaya, *Asia* 84 F12
Himamaylan, *Phil.* 130 H4
Himatnagar, *India* 106 D1
Himeji, *Japan* 120 C5
Himi, *Japan* 120 A6
Ḥimṣ, *Syria* 97 C3
Hinche, *Haiti* 200 A2
Hindhead, *U.K.* 45 E1
Hindmarsh, L., *Australia* 171 F3
Hindu Bagh, *Pakistan* 105 C3
Hindu Kush, *Asia* 84 E11
Hines Creek, *Canada* 186 G5
Hinganghat, *India* 106 F4
Hingoli, *India* 106 F3
Hinigaran, *Phil.* 130 H4
Hinis, *Turkey* 82 D3
Hinna = Imi, *Ethiopia* 144 E4
Hinna, *Nigeria* 151 C6
Hinterrhein →, *Switz.* 60 C5
Hirakud Dam, *India* 106 E6
Hirara, *Japan* 121 K6
Hiratsuka, *Japan* 120 B8
Hirosaki, *Japan* 121 D7
Hiroshima, *Japan* 120 C3
Hiroshima □, *Japan* 120 C3
Hisar, *India* 106 A2
Hispaniola, *W. Indies* 180 H12
Hita, *Japan* 120 D2
Hitachi, *Japan* 120 A9
Hitchin, *U.K.* 45 A3
Hiyyon, N. →, *Israel* 96 G2
Hjälmaren, *Sweden* 40 F3
Hjørring, *Denmark* 42 A2
Hluhluwe, *S. Africa* 163 E9
Ho, *Ghana* 149 D3
Ho Chi Minh City = Phanh Bho Ho Chi Minh, *Vietnam* 125 F4
Hoa Binh, *Vietnam* 125 B3
Hoai Nhon, *Vietnam* 125 E5
Hoare B., *Canada* 187 E12
Hobart, *Australia* 172 C2
Hobbs, *U.S.A.* 190 H7
Hoboken, *Belgium* 51 A3
Hobro, *Denmark* 42 B2
Hobscheid, *Lux.* 52 C1
Hockley, *U.K.* 45 C6
Hoddesdon, *U.K.* 45 B3
Hodgson, *Canada* 186 J8
Hódmezővásárhely, *Hungary* 74 C4
Hodna, Chott el, *Algeria* 137 A5
Hodonín, *Czech.* 76 C5
Hoeamdong, *N. Korea* 118 A6
Hoek van Holland, *Neths.* 50 D2
Hoengsŏng, *S. Korea* 118 F5
Hoeryong, *N. Korea* 118 A5
Hoeyang, *N. Korea* 118 E4
Hof, *Germany* 58 D4
Hof, *Iceland* 38 C5
Höfðakaupstaður, *Iceland* 38 B3
Hofmeyr, *S. Africa* 163 G6
Hofsjökull, *Iceland* 38 C3
Hofsós, *Iceland* 38 B3
Hōfu, *Japan* 120 C2
Hoggar = Ahaggar, *Algeria* 137 E5
Hog's Back, *U.K.* 45 D2
Hoh Xil Shan, *China* 112 E4
Hohe Rhön, *Germany* 58 D3
Hohhot, *China* 116 B1
Hohoe, *Ghana* 149 C3
Hoi An, *Vietnam* 125 D5
Hoi Xuan, *Vietnam* 125 B3
Hokitika, *N.Z.* 175 G3
Hokkaidō □, *Japan* 121 B8
Holbrook, *Australia* 171 F6
Holguín, *Cuba* 198 C5
Hollandia = Jayapura, *Indonesia* 129 D18
Hollidaysburg, *U.S.A.* 189 C2
Hollywood, *U.S.A.* 190 G2
Holman, *Canada* 186 C7
Hólmavík, *Iceland* 38 B2
Holmwood, *U.K.* 45 E3
Holstebro, *Denmark* 42 B1
Holt, *Iceland* 38 D3
Holy Cross, *U.S.A.* 193 B4
Holyhead, *U.K.* 46 H5
Holyoke, *U.S.A.* 189 A6
Homa Bay, *Kenya* 157 D1
Homalin, *Burma* 122 B2
Hombori, *Mali* 140 E5
Home B., *Canada* 187 D11
Homer, *U.S.A.* 193 B4
Homs = Ḥimṣ, *Syria* 97 C3
Homyel = Gomel, *Belarus* 81 D3
Hon Chong, *Vietnam* 125 G3
Honan = Henan □, *China* 116 F2
Honbetsu, *Japan* 121 B8
Honda, *Colombia* 210 C1
Honda Bay, *Phil.* 130 H1
Hondeklipbaai, *S. Africa* 163 F1
Hondo →, *Belize* 196 A2
Honduras ■, *Cent. Amer.* 196
Honduras, G. de, *Caribbean* 180 H11
Honey L., *U.S.A.* 190 D2
Honfleur, *France* 55 B4
Hong Kong ■, *Asia* 113 J9
Hong'an, *China* 116 G2
Hongchŏn, *S. Korea* 118 E5
Hongha →, *Vietnam* 125 B4
Honghu, *China* 116 H2
Hongjiang, *China* 113 G8
Hongshui He →, *China* 113 H8
Hongsŏng, *S. Korea* 118 F4
Hongtong, *China* 116 D1
Hongwon, *N. Korea* 118 C4
Hongze Hu, *China* 116 F4
Honiara, *Solomon Is.* 173 B2
Honjō, *Japan* 121 E7
Honkorâb, Ras, *Egypt* 139 E6
Honolulu, *U.S.A.* 192 A2
Honshū, *Japan* 121 G6
Hoo, *U.K.* 45 D5
Hood, Mt., *U.S.A.* 190 B3
Hoogeveen, *Neths.* 50 B5
Hoogezand, *Neths.* 50 A6
Hooghly = Hugli →, *India* 106 E8
Hooghly → = Hugli →, *India* 106 E8
Hooglede, *Belgium* 51 B1
Hook of Holland = Hoek van Holland, *Neths.* 50 D2
Hoopstad, *S. Africa* 163 D6
Hoorn, *Neths.* 50 C3
Hopa, *Turkey* 82 B3
Hope, *U.S.A.* 191 H11
Hope, L., *Australia* 171 B2
Hopedale, *Canada* 187 G14
Hopefield, *S. Africa* 163 H2
Hopei = Hebei □, *China* 116 C3
Hopetoun, *Australia* 171 F4
Hopetown, *S. Africa* 163 E5
Hopkinsville, *U.S.A.* 191 F13
Hoquiam, *U.S.A.* 190 A2
Horasan, *Turkey* 82 D4
Horgen, *Switz.* 60 B4
Horley, *U.K.* 45 E3
Horlivka = Gorlovka, *Ukraine* 81 F5
Horn, *Austria* 61 A5
Horn, *Ísafjarðarsýsla, Iceland* 38 A2
Horn, *Suður-Múlasýsla, Iceland* 38 B6
Horn, C. = Hornos, C. do, *Chile* 220 L4
Horn, Cape = Hornos, C. do, *Chile* 220 L4
Hornaday →, *Canada* 186 C6
Hornavan, *Sweden* 40 C4
Hornell, *U.S.A.* 189 A2
Hornos, C. do, *Chile* 220 L4
Hornsby, *Australia* 171 E8
Hornu, *Belgium* 51 D2
Horqin Youyi Qianqi, *China* 113 B10
Horqueta, *Paraguay* 219 B2
Horsens, *Denmark* 42 C2
Horsham, *Australia* 171 G3
Horsham, *U.K.* 45 E3
Horton →, *Canada* 186 C6
Hose, Gunung-Gunung, *Malaysia* 126 C7
Hoshangabad, *India* 106 E3
Hosingen, *Lux.* 52 A2
Hospitalet, *Spain* 63 C9
Hot Springs, *Ark., U.S.A.* 191 G11
Hot Springs, *S. Dak., U.S.A.* 190 D8
Hotan, *China* 112 D2
Hotazel, *S. Africa* 163 D4
Hotte, Massif de la, *Haiti* 200 B1
Hou →, *Laos* 125 B2
Houffalize, *Belgium* 51 D5
Houghton Regis, *U.K.* 45 A2
Houhora Heads, *N.Z.* 175 A4
Houma, *U.S.A.* 191 J12
Hounslow, *U.K.* 45 C2
Houston, *U.S.A.* 191 J10
Hovd, *Mongolia* 112 B5
Hövsgöl Nuur, *Mongolia* 112 A6
Howe, C., *Australia* 171 G7
Howick, *S. Africa* 163 E8
Howitt, L., *Australia* 171 A1
Howrah = Haora, *India* 106 E8
Høyanger, *Norway* 40 E1
Hradec Králové, *Czech.* 76 B4
Hrodna = Grodno, *Belarus* 81 C1
Hron →, *Slovak Rep.* 76 D6
Hrvatska = Croatia ■, *Europe* 72 B4
Hsenwi, *Burma* 122 C3
Hsiamen = Xiamen, *China* 113 H10
Hsian = Xi'an, *China* 113 F8
Hsinhailien = Lianyungang, *China* 116 E4
Hsüchou = Xuzhou, *China* 116 E4
Hua Xian, *China* 116 E2
Huacho, *Peru* 213 D2
Huachón, *Peru* 213 D3
Huade, *China* 116 B2
Huai He →, *China* 116 F3
Huai'an, *China* 116 F4
Huaide, *China* 116 A6
Huainan, *China* 116 F3
Huaiyang, *China* 116 F3
Hualian, *Taiwan* 117 B3
Huallaga →, *Peru* 213 B3
Huambo, *Angola* 160 C3
Huancabamba, *Peru* 213 B2
Huancane, *Peru* 213 E5
Huancapi, *Peru* 213 E3
Huancavelica, *Peru* 213 E3
Huancayo, *Peru* 213 D3
Huang Hai = Yellow Sea, *China* 113 E11
Huang He →, *China* 116 D4
Huangchuan, *China* 116 F3
Huangliu, *China* 113 J8
Huangshi, *China* 116 G3
Huangyan, *China* 116 H5
Huánuco, *Peru* 213 D3
Huaraz, *Peru* 213 D2
Huarmey, *Peru* 213 D2
Huascarán, *Peru* 213 C2
Huatabampo, *Mexico* 194 C2
Huayllay, *Peru* 213 D3
Hubei □, *China* 116 G1
Hubli-Dharwad = Dharwad, *India* 107 E2
Huchang, *N. Korea* 118 B4
Hückelhoven, *Germany* 59 B1
Huddersfield, *U.K.* 46 G7
Hudiksvall, *Sweden* 40 E4
Hudson, *U.S.A.* 189 A5
Hudson →, *U.S.A.* 189 C5
Hudson Bay, *Canada* 187 G10
Hudson Str., *Canada* 187 F11
Hudson's Hope, *Canada* 186 G4
Hue, *Vietnam* 125 D4
Huehuetenango, *Guatemala* 196 C1
Huelva, *Spain* 63 G2
Huesca, *Spain* 63 B7
Hugli →, *India* 106 E8
Hui Xian, *China* 116 E2
Huimin, *China* 116 D4
Huinca Renancó, *Argentina* 221 C2
Huizen, *Neths.* 50 C3
Hukou, *China* 116 H3
Hulan, *China* 113 B11
Huld, *Mongolia* 113 C7
Hull, *Canada* 185 B4
Hull, *U.K.* 46 G8
Hullbridge, *U.K.* 45 B5
Hulst, *Neths.* 50 F2
Hulun Nur, *China* 113 B9
Humacao, *Puerto Rico* 201 A2
Humaitá, *Brazil* 217 D3
Humansdorp, *S. Africa* 163 H5

Humber —►, *U.K.* 46 G8
Humboldt, *Canada* 186 J6
Humboldt —►, *U.S.A.* 190 D3
Humboldt Gletscher, *Greenland* 224 B1
Hume, L., *Australia* 171 F6
Humphreys Peak, *U.S.A.* 190 F5
Hūn, *Libya* 138 B3
Húnaflói, *Iceland* 38 B3
Hunan □, *China* 113 G8
Hunedoara, *Romania* 75 C2
Hungary ■, *Europe* 74
Hungary, Plain of, *Europe* 34 F10
Hungerford, *Australia* 171 B5
Hŭngnam, *N. Korea* 118 D4
Huni Valley, *Ghana* 149 D1
Hunsrück, *Germany* 58 E1
Hunter I., *Australia* 172 A1
Hunter Ra., *Australia* 171 D8
Hunters Road, *Zimbabwe* 161 C3
Huntingdon, *U.S.A.* 46 J8
Huntington, *Ind., U.S.A.* 191 E13
Huntington, *W. Va., U.S.A.* 191 E14
Huntly, *N.Z.* 175 C5
Huntsville, *Ala., U.S.A.* 191 G13
Huntsville, *Tex., U.S.A.* 191 J10
Hunyani —►, *Zimbabwe* 161 A4
Huo Xian, *China* 116 D1
Huonville, *Australia* 172 C2
Huoqiu, *China* 116 F3
Huoshao Dao, *Taiwan* 117 C3
Hupeh = Hubei □, *China* 116 G1
Hure Qi, *China* 116 B5
Hurghada, *Egypt* 139 C5
Huron, *U.S.A.* 190 C9
Huron, L., *U.S.A.* 180 E11
Hurunui —►, *N.Z.* 175 G4
Húsavík, *Iceland* 38 B4
Hutchinson, *U.S.A.* 190 E9
Huy, *Belgium* 51 C4
Hvammur, *Iceland* 38 B2
Hvar, *Croatia* 72 D4
Hvítá —►, *Iceland* 38 C2
Hvítárvatn, *Iceland* 38 C3
Hwachon-chosuji, *S. Korea* 118 E4
Hwang Ho = Huang He —►, *China* 116 D4
Hwange, *Zimbabwe* 161 C1
Hyargas Nuur, *Mongolia* 112 B5
Hyde Park, *Guyana* 214 B2
Hyden, *Australia* 170 B3
Hyderabad, *India* 107 E3
Hyderabad, *Pakistan* 105 F3
Hyères, *France* 55 H8
Hyesan, *N. Korea* 118 B4
Hyndman Peak, *U.S.A.* 190 C5
Hyōgo □, *Japan* 120 B5

I

I-n-Gall, *Niger* 141 C3
Ialomiţa —►, *Romania* 75 D6
Iaşi, *Romania* 75 B6
Iba, *Phil.* 130 D2
Ibadan, *Nigeria* 151 E1
Ibagué, *Colombia* 210 C1
Ibar —►, *Serbia, Yug.* 72 C7
Ibaraki □, *Japan* 120 A9
Ibarra, *Ecuador* 212 B2
Iberian Peninsula, *Europe* 34 G6
Iberville, *Canada* 185 B5
Ibi, *Nigeria* 151 D5
Ibicuy, *Argentina* 221 B5
Ibioapaba, Sa. da, *Brazil* 217 C8
Ibiza, *Spain* 63 E9
Ibonma, *Indonesia* 129 D15
Ibrāhīm —►, *Lebanon* 95 B2
Ibshawâi, *Egypt* 139 B4
Ibu, *Indonesia* 129 B13
Içá, *Peru* 213 E3
Içel = Mersin, *Turkey* 94 C4
Iceland ■, *Europe* 38
Icha, *Russia* 91 E18
Ich'ang = Yichang, *China* 116 G1
Ichchapuram, *India* 106 F6
Ichihara, *Japan* 120 B9
Ichikawa, *Japan* 120 B9
Ichilo —►, *Bolivia* 218 B1
Ichinomiya, *Japan* 120 B6
Ichinoseki, *Japan* 121 E7
Ichŏn, *S. Korea* 118 F4
Icht, *Morocco* 136 E2
Icod, *Canary Is.* 223 D1
Idah, *Nigeria* 151 E3
Idaho □, *U.S.A.* 190 C4
Idaho Falls, *U.S.A.* 190 C5
Idd el Ghanam, *Sudan* 143 D2
Idehan Marzūq, *Libya* 138 C2
Idelès, *Algeria* 137 E5
Idfû, *Egypt* 139 E5
Ídhi Óros, *Greece* 71 F4
Ídhra, *Greece* 71 E3
Idi, *Indonesia* 128 A1
Idiofa, *Zaïre* 155 D3
Idlib, *Syria* 97 B3
Idutywa, *S. Africa* 163 G7
Ieper, *Belgium* 51 C1
Ierápetra, *Greece* 71 F5
Ierzu, *Italy* 67 G2
Ifanadiana, *Madag.* 165 D2
Ife, *Nigeria* 151 E2
Iférouâne, *Niger* 141 B4
Ifni, *Morocco* 136 E2
Ifon, *Nigeria* 151 E3
Iforas, Adrar des, *Mali* 140 C6
Ifrane, *Morocco* 136 B5
Iganga, *Uganda* 156 C2
Igarka, *Russia* 90 E9
Igbetti, *Nigeria* 151 D2
Igbo-Ora, *Nigeria* 151 E1
Igboho, *Nigeria* 151 D1
Iğdır, *Turkey* 82 D5
Iglésias, *Italy* 67 H2
Igli, *Algeria* 137 C2
Igloolik, *Canada* 187 D10
'Igma, Gebel el, *Egypt* 139 B5
Iguaçu —►, *Brazil* 217 H5
Iguaçu, Cat. del, *Brazil* 217 J5
Iguaçu Falls = Iguaçu, Cat. del, *Brazil* 217 J5
Iguala, *Mexico* 194 E5
Igualada, *Spain* 63 C9
Iguassu = Iguaçu —►, *Brazil* 217 H5
Iguatu, *Brazil* 217 D9
Iguéla, *Gabon* 154 C1
Ihiala, *Nigeria* 151 F3
Ihosy, *Madag.* 165 D2
Iida, *Japan* 120 B7
Iisalmi, *Finland* 43 D3
Iizuka, *Japan* 120 D1
Ijebu-Igbo, *Nigeria* 151 E1
Ijebu-Ode, *Nigeria* 151 E1
IJmuiden, *Neths.* 50 C3
IJsselmeer, *Neths.* 50 B4
IJsselstein, *Neths.* 50 D3
Ikale, *Nigeria* 151 E2
Ikare, *Nigeria* 151 E3
Ikaría, *Greece* 71 E5
Ikeja, *Nigeria* 151 E1
Ikela, *Zaïre* 155 C4
Ikerre-Ekiti, *Nigeria* 151 E2
Iki, *Japan* 120 C1
Ikire, *Nigeria* 151 E2
İkizdere, *Turkey* 82 C2
Ikom, *Nigeria* 151 F5
Ikot Ekpene, *Nigeria* 151 F4
Ikurun, *Nigeria* 151 E2
Ila, *Nigeria* 151 D2
Ilagan, *Phil.* 130 C3
Ilanskiy, *Russia* 91 H10
Ilaro, *Nigeria* 151 E1
Île-de-France, *France* 55 B6
Ilebo, *Zaïre* 155 D3
Ilek, *Russia* 90 G4
Ilero, *Nigeria* 151 D1
Ilesha, *Kwara, Nigeria* 151 D1
Ilesha, *Oyo, Nigeria* 151 E2
Ilfracombe, *U.K.* 46 L5
Ilhéus, *Brazil* 217 F9
Ili —►, *Kazakstan* 90 K7
Iliamna L., *U.S.A.* 193 B4
Iliç, *Turkey* 82 D1
Ilich, *Kazakstan* 93 C2
Ilichevsk, *Azerbaijan* 82 D6
Iligan, *Phil.* 130 J4
Iligan Bay, *Phil.* 130 J4
Ilin I., *Phil.* 130 G2
Iliodhrómia, *Greece* 71 C3
Ilion, *U.S.A.* 189 A4
Illampu = Ancohuma, Nevada, *Bolivia* 218 B1
Illana B., *Phil.* 130 K4
Ille-et-Vilaine □, *France* 55 C3
Iller —►, *Germany* 58 F3
Illimani, *Bolivia* 218 C1
Illinois □, *U.S.A.* 191 E12
Illinois —►, *U.S.A.* 191 E12
Ilmen, Oz., *Russia* 81 A4
Ilo, *Peru* 213 F4
Ilobu, *Nigeria* 151 E2
Iloilo, *Phil.* 130 H3
Ilora, *Nigeria* 151 E1
Ilorin, *Nigeria* 151 D2
Ilwaki, *Indonesia* 129 F13
Imabari, *Japan* 120 C3
Imandra, Oz., *Russia* 90 C5
Imari, *Japan* 120 D1
Imbâbah, *Egypt* 139 B4
Imbabura □, *Ecuador* 212 B1
Imbaimadai, *Guyana* 214 B1
Imdahane, *Morocco* 136 C3
imeni 26 Bakinskikh Komissarov, *Azerbaijan* 82 D9
Imeni Panfilova, *Kazakstan* 93 A8
Imeni Poliny Osipenko, *Russia* 91 G16
Imi, *Ethiopia* 144 E4
Imishli, *Azerbaijan* 82 D8
Imitek, *Morocco* 136 C3
Imo □, *Nigeria* 151 F4
Imola, *Italy* 67 C4
Imperatriz, *Brazil* 217 C7
Impéria, *Italy* 67 C1
Impfondo, *Congo* 154 B3
Imphal, *India* 107 C6
In Belbel, *Algeria* 137 C3
In Salah, *Algeria* 137 D4
Ina, *Japan* 120 B7
Inanwatan, *Indonesia* 129 D15
Iñapari, *Peru* 213 D5
Inari, *Finland* 43 B2
Inca, *Spain* 65 A4
İnce-Burnu, *Turkey* 94 A4
Inch'ŏn, *S. Korea* 118 F4
Incomáti —►, *Mozam.* 159 F1
Indals —►, *Sweden* 40 E4
Indaw, *Burma* 122 C2
Independence Fjord, *Greenland* 224 A2
India ■, *Asia* 107
Indian Harbour, *Canada* 187 G14
Indian Head, *Canada* 186 J7
Indiana, *U.S.A.* 189 C2
Indiana □, *U.S.A.* 191 E13
Indianapolis, *U.S.A.* 191 E13
Indiga, *Russia* 90 D6
Indigirka —►, *Russia* 91 C14
Indonesia ■, *Asia* 128
Indore, *India* 106 D2
Indravati —►, *India* 106 F4
Indre □, *France* 55 D5
Indre-et-Loire □, *France* 55 D4
Indus —►, *Pakistan* 105 F3
İnebolu, *Turkey* 94 A3
Inezgane, *Morocco* 136 E2
Ingapirca, *Ecuador* 212 D1
Ingatestone, *U.K.* 45 B5
Ingelmunster, *Belgium* 51 B1
Ingende, *Zaïre* 155 C2
Inglewood, *Queens., Australia* 171 B8
Inglewood, *Vic., Australia* 171 G4
Inglewood, *N.Z.* 175 D5
Ingólfshöfði, *Iceland* 38 D4
Ingolstadt, *Germany* 58 F4
Ingore, *Guinea-Biss.* 146 C1
Ingraj Bazar, *India* 106 C8
Ingulec, *Ukraine* 81 G4
Inguri —►, *Georgia* 82 A4
Ingwavuma, *S. Africa* 163 D9
Inhambane, *Mozam.* 159 E2
Inhaminga, *Mozam.* 159 C2
Inharrime, *Mozam.* 159 E2
Ining = Yining, *China* 112 C2
Inini □, *Fr. Guiana* 214 C5
Inírida —►, *Colombia* 210 C3
Inle Aing, *Burma* 122 D3
Inn —►, *Austria* 61 A4
Innamincka, *Australia* 171 A3
Inner Hebrides, *U.K.* 46 C3
Inner Mongolia = Nei Monggol Zizhiqu □, *China* 116 A2
Innisfail, *Canada* 186 H5
Innsbruck, *Austria* 61 B2
Inongo, *Zaïre* 155 C2
Inoucdjouac, *Canada* 187 G11
Inowrocław, *Poland* 77 C3
Inpundong, *N. Korea* 118 B3
Inquisivi, *Bolivia* 218 C1
Insein, *Burma* 122 F2
Intendente Alvear, *Argentina* 221 C2
Interlaken, *Switz.* 60 C3
Inthanon, *Thailand* 122 E3
Inuvik, *Canada* 186 C5
Invercargill, *N.Z.* 175 J2
Inverell, *Australia* 171 B8
Invergordon, *U.K.* 46 B5
Inverness, *U.K.* 46 B5
Investigator Str., *Australia* 171 F1
Inya, *Russia* 90 J9
Inyanga, *Zimbabwe* 161 C5
Inyangani, *Zimbabwe* 161 C5
Inyantue, *Zimbabwe* 161 C1
Inza, *Russia* 81 D8
Iona, *U.K.* 46 D3
Ionian Is. = Iónioi Nísoi, *Greece* 71 D1
Iónioi Nísoi, *Greece* 71 D1
Iori —►, *Azerbaijan* 82 C7
Íos, *Greece* 71 E5
Iowa □, *U.S.A.* 191 D11
Iowa City, *U.S.A.* 191 D11
Ipiales, *Colombia* 210 D1
Ipin = Yibin, *China* 113 G7
Ípiros □, *Greece* 71 C1
Ipoh, *Malaysia* 126 B1
Ippy, *C.A.R.* 142 B3
Ipswich, *Australia* 171 A9
Ipswich, *U.K.* 46 J9
Iqaluit, *Canada* 187 E12
Iquique, *Chile* 220 A3
Iquitos, *Peru* 213 B3
Iracoubo, *Fr. Guiana* 214 C6
Irahuan, *Phil.* 130 H1
Iráklion, *Greece* 71 F5
Iran ■, *Asia* 103
Iran, Gunung-Gunung, *Malaysia* 126 C7
Iran Ra. = Iran, Gunung-Gunung, *Malaysia* 126 C7
Iranamadu Tank, *Sri Lanka* 110 A2
Irapuato, *Mexico* 194 E4
Iraq ■, *Asia* 102
Irbid, *Jordan* 98 A1
Irebu, *Zaïre* 155 C2
Ireland ■, *Europe* 46 H2
Irele, *Nigeria* 151 E2
Iret, *Russia* 91 D17
Irherm, *Morocco* 136 E3
Irhil Mgoun, *Morocco* 136 D4
Irhyangdong, *N. Korea* 118 B5
Iri, *S. Korea* 118 G4
Irian Jaya □, *Indonesia* 129 D17
Irié, *Guinea* 147 C5
Iriga, *Phil.* 130 F4
Iringa, *Tanzania* 158 C2
Iriomote-Jima, *Japan* 121 K5
Iriona, *Honduras* 196 B4
Irish Sea, *Europe* 46 G4
Irkeshtam, *Kyrgyzstan* 93 D6
Irkineyeva, *Russia* 91 G10
Irkutsk, *Russia* 91 J12
Iron Baron, *Australia* 171 E1
Iron Knob, *Australia* 171 D1
Iron Mountain, *U.S.A.* 191 C12
Ironwood, *U.S.A.* 191 C12
Irosin, *Phil.* 130 F4
Irrara Cr. —►, *Australia* 171 B5
Irrawaddy —►, *Burma* 122 F2
Irtysh —►, *Russia* 90 F7
Irumu, *Zaïre* 155 B6
Irún, *Spain* 63 A6
Irunea = Pamplona, *Spain* 63 B6
Irvine, *U.K.* 46 E5
Irymple, *Australia* 171 E3
Isa, *Nigeria* 151 A3
Isabela, *Phil.* 130 K3
Isabela, *Puerto Rico* 201 A1
Isabella, Cord., *Nic.* 197 B2
Ísafjarðardjúp, *Iceland* 38 A2
Ísafjörður, *Iceland* 38 A2
Isangi, *Zaïre* 155 B4
Isar —►, *Germany* 58 F5
Ischia, *Italy* 67 F6
Ise, *Japan* 120 C6
Ise-Wan, *Japan* 120 C6
Isère □, *France* 55 F8
Isère —►, *France* 55 F7
Iserlohn, *Germany* 59 A3
Iseyin, *Nigeria* 151 E1
Isfara, *Tajikistan* 93 D4
Isherton, *Guyana* 214 D1
Ishigaki-Jima, *Japan* 121 K5
Ishikari-Wan, *Japan* 121 B7
Ishikawa, *Japan* 121 J8
Ishikawa □, *Japan* 120 A6
Ishim, *Russia* 90 G7
Ishim —►, *Russia* 90 G7
Ishinomaki, *Japan* 121 E7
Ishkuman, *Pakistan* 105 A6
Ishpeming, *U.S.A.* 191 C12
Isil Kul, *Russia* 90 H7
Isiolo, *Kenya* 157 C3
Isiolo □, *Kenya* 157 C3
Isiro, *Zaïre* 155 B5
Iskander, *Uzbekistan* 93 C3
İskenderun, *Turkey* 94 D4
İskenderun Körfezi, *Turkey* 94 C4
Iski-Naukat, *Kyrgyzstan* 93 D5
Islamabad, *Pakistan* 105 B5
Island L., *Canada* 186 H8
Islay, *U.K.* 46 D3
Isle of Wight □, *U.K.* 46 L7
Isle Royale, *U.S.A.* 191 B12
Ismail, *Ukraine* 81 G2
Ismâ'ilîya, *Egypt* 139 A4
Isna, *Egypt* 139 D5
Isparta, *Turkey* 94 C2
Ispica, *Italy* 67 K7
Ispir, *Turkey* 82 C3
Israel ■, *Asia* 96
Issano, *Guyana* 214 B2
Issia, *Ivory C.* 148 D4
Issyk-Kul, Ozero, *Kyrgyzstan* 93 B8
Istaihah, *U.A.E.* 101 C3
İstanbul, *Turkey* 94 A2
Istra, *Croatia* 72 B2
Istria = Istra, *Croatia* 72 B2
Itabirito, *Brazil* 215 A4
Itajaí, *Brazil* 217 J6
Itajubá, *Brazil* 215 B3
Italy ■, *Europe* 67
Itaperuna, *Brazil* 215 B5
Itapetininga, *Brazil* 215 C2
Itapeva, *Brazil* 215 C1
Itapicuru —►, *Brazil* 217 E9
Itaquari, *Brazil* 215 A6
Itaquatiara, *Brazil* 217 C4
Itararé, *Brazil* 215 C1
Itbayat, *Phil.* 130 A3
Ithaca = Itháki, *Greece* 71 D1
Ithaca, *U.S.A.* 189 A3
Itháki, *Greece* 71 D1
Ito, *Japan* 120 B8
Itonamas —►, *Bolivia* 218 A1
Itsa, *Egypt* 139 B4
Ittoqqortoormiit = Scoresbysund, *Greenland* 224 C3
Itu, *Brazil* 215 C2
Itu, *Nigeria* 151 F4
Ituni, *Guyana* 214 C2
Iturup, Ostrov, *Russia* 91 G18
Ivanhoe, *Australia* 171 D5
Ivano-Frankivsk = Ivano-Frankovsk, *Ukraine* 81 F1
Ivano-Frankovsk, *Ukraine* 81 F1
Ivanovo, *Russia* 81 B6
Ivinghoe, *U.K.* 45 B2
Iviza = Ibiza, *Spain* 63 E9
Ivory Coast ■, *Africa* 148
Ivrea, *Italy* 67 A1
Ivugivik, *Canada* 187 F11
Iwaki, *Japan* 121 F7
Iwakuni, *Japan* 120 C3
Iwamizawa, *Japan* 121 B8
Iwanai, *Japan* 121 B7
Iwanuma, *Japan* 121 E7
Iwata, *Japan* 120 C7
Iwate-San, *Japan* 121 D7
Iwo, *Nigeria* 151 E2
Ixiamas, *Bolivia* 218 B1
Ixopo, *S. Africa* 163 F8
Izabal, L. de, *Guatemala* 196 C2
Izberbash, *Russia* 82 A8
Izegem, *Belgium* 51 B1
Izhevsk, *Russia* 82 B9
Izmayil = Ismail, *Ukraine* 81 G2
İzmir, *Turkey* 94 B1
İzmit, *Turkey* 94 A2
Izra, *Syria* 97 D2
Izumi-sano, *Japan* 120 C5
Izumo, *Japan* 120 B3

J

Jabal Lubnān, *Lebanon* 95 B2
Jabalpur, *India* 106 D4
Jabbūl, *Syria* 97 B3
Jablah, *Syria* 97 B2
Jablonec, *Czech.* 76 A4
Jaboticabal, *Brazil* 215 B1
Jaca, *Spain* 63 B7
Jacarei, *Brazil* 215 C3
Jackson, *Mich., U.S.A.* 191 D14
Jackson, *Miss., U.S.A.* 191 H12
Jackson, *Tenn., U.S.A.* 191 G12
Jacksonville, *Fla., U.S.A.* 191 H15
Jacksonville, *Ill., U.S.A.* 191 E12
Jacksonville, *Tex., U.S.A.* 191 H10
Jacmel, *Haiti* 200 B2
Jacobabad, *Pakistan* 105 E3
Jacqueville, *Ivory C.* 148 E5
Jadotville = Likasi, *Zaïre* 155 F5
Jādū, *Libya* 138 A2
Jaén, *Peru* 213 B2
Jaén, *Spain* 63 F5
Jaffa = Tel Aviv-Yafo, *Israel* 96 C2
Jaffa, C., *Australia* 171 G2
Jaffna, *Sri Lanka* 110 A1
Jagersfontein, *S. Africa* 163 F6
Jagüey Grande, *Cuba* 198 B3
Jahrom, *Iran* 103 D3
Jailolo, *Indonesia* 129 B13
Jailolo, Selat, *Indonesia* 129 C14
Jaintiapur, *Bangla.* 111 B3
Jaipur, *India* 106 B2
Jakarta, *Indonesia* 128 E5
Jalal-Abad = Dzhalal-Abad, *Kyrgyzstan* 93 C5
Jalālābād, *Afghan.* 104 D6
Jalapa, *Guatemala* 196 C1
Jalapa Enríquez, *Mexico* 194 E6
Jaldak, *Afghan.* 104 E4
Jalgaon, *Maharashtra, India* 106 E3
Jalgaon, *Maharashtra, India* 106 E2
Jalingo, *Nigeria* 151 D6
Jalna, *India* 106 F2
Jalón —►, *Spain* 63 C6
Jalpaiguri, *India* 106 B8
Jaluit I., *Pac. Oc.* 176 E5
Jamaari, *Nigeria* 151 B5
Jamaica ■, *W. Indies* 199
Jamalpur, *Bangla.* 111 B2
Jamalpur, *India* 106 C7
Jambe, *Indonesia* 129 C15
Jambi, *Indonesia* 128 C4
Jambi □, *Indonesia* 128 C3
James —►, *U.S.A.* 191 D10
James B., *Canada* 187 H11
Jamestown, *Australia* 171 E2
Jamestown, *S. Africa* 163 F6
Jamestown, *N. Dak., U.S.A.* 190 B9
Jamestown, *N.Y., U.S.A.* 189 B2
Jammu, *India* 107 A2
Jammu & Kashmir □, *India* 107 A2
Jamnagar, *India* 107 D1
Jamshedpur, *India* 106 D7
Jamuna —►, *Bangla.* 111 C1
Jamurki, *Bangla.* 111 C2
Jan Kempdorp, *S. Africa* 163 D5
Jand, *Pakistan* 105 B5
Janesville, *U.S.A.* 191 D12
Janga, *Ghana* 149 A2
Jānī Kheyl, *Afghan.* 104 E5
Januária, *Brazil* 217 F7
Janub Dârfûr □, *Sudan* 143 D2
Janub Kordofân □, *Sudan* 143 D3
Jaora, *India* 106 D2
Japan ■, *Asia* 121
Japan, Sea of, *Asia* 84 E17
Japan Trench, *Pac. Oc.* 176 C3
Japen = Yapen, *Indonesia* 129 C17
Japurá —►, *Brazil* 217 C3
Jarābulus, *Syria* 97 A3
Jarama —►, *Spain* 63 D5
Jardines de la Reina, Arch. de los, *Cuba* 198 C4
Jargalant = Hovd, *Mongolia* 112 B5
Jarosław, *Poland* 77 E6
Jarrahdale, *Australia* 170 B2
Jarvis I., *Pac. Oc.* 176 F8
Jarwa, *India* 106 B5
Jasin, *Malaysia* 126 D2
Jāsk, *Iran* 103 F5
Jasło, *Poland* 77 F5
Jason, Is., *Falk. Is.* 224 A2
Jassy = Iaşi, *Romania* 75 B6
Jászberény, *Hungary* 74 B4
Jatibarang, *Indonesia* 128 E6
Jatinegara, *Indonesia* 128 E5
Játiva, *Spain* 63 E7
Jaú, *Brazil* 215 B1
Jauja, *Peru* 213 D3
Jaunpur, *India* 106 C5
Java = Jawa, *Indonesia* 128 F6
Java Sea, *Indonesia* 128 E5
Java Trench, *Ind. Oc.* 128 F4
Javhlant = Ulyasutay, *Mongolia* 112 B6
Jawa, *Indonesia* 128 F6
Jaya, Puncak, *Indonesia* 129 D17
Jayanti, *India* 106 B8
Jayapura, *Indonesia* 129 D18
Jayawijaya, Pegunungan, *Indonesia* 129 E18
Jaynagar, *India* 106 B7
Jayrūd, *Syria* 97 C3

Jazzīn, Lebanon 95 C1
Jean Marie River, Canada 186 E5
Jean Rabel, Haiti 200 A1
Jeanette, Ostrov, Russia 91 A14
Jebba, Morocco 136 A5
Jebba, Nigeria 151 D2
Jebel, Bahr el →, Sudan 143 F4
Jedburgh, U.K. 46 E6
Jedda = Jiddah, Si. Arabia 99 D3
Jędrzejów, Poland 77 E4
Jeffersonville, U.S.A. 191 F13
Jega, Nigeria 151 B2
Jelenia Góra, Poland 77 D1
Jelgava, Latvia 81 B2
Jemaluang, Malaysia 126 D3
Jemappes, Belgium 51 D2
Jemaya, Indonesia 128 B5
Jember, Indonesia 128 F8
Jembongan, Malaysia 126 A8
Jemeppe, Belgium 51 C5
Jena, Germany 58 D4
Jendouba, Tunisia 138 A2
Jennings, U.S.A. 191 J11
Jeparit, Australia 171 F3
Jequié, Brazil 217 F8
Jequitinhonha →, Brazil 217 F9
Jerada, Morocco 136 B6
Jerantut, Malaysia 126 C2
Jérémie, Haiti 200 B1
Jerez de la Frontera, Spain 63 G3
Jerez de los Caballeros, Spain 63 F3
Jerilderie, Australia 171 F5
Jersey, Chan. Is. 44 B2
Jersey City, U.S.A. 189 C5
Jersey Shore, U.S.A. 189 B3
Jerusalem, Israel 96 D2
Jervis B., Australia 171 F8
Jesselton = Kota Kinabalu, Malaysia 126 A8
Jessore, Bangla. 111 C1
Jesús María, Argentina 221 A2
Jhal Jhao, Pakistan 105 F2
Jhalakati, Bangla. 111 D2
Jhalawar, India 106 D3
Jhang Maghiana, Pakistan 105 C5
Jhansi, India 106 C4
Jharsaguda, India 106 E6
Jhelum, Pakistan 105 B6
Jhelum →, Pakistan 105 D5
Jhunjhunu, India 106 B2
Ji Xian, China 116 D1
Jia Xian, China 116 C1
Jiali, Taiwan 117 C2
Jiamusi, China 113 B12
Ji'an, China 116 J2
Jianchuan, China 112 H6
Jiande, China 116 H4
Jiangling, China 116 G1
Jiangmen, China 113 J9
Jiangshan, China 116 H4
Jiangsu □, China 116 F4
Jiangxi □, China 116 J3
Jiangyin, China 116 G5
Jianning, China 116 J3
Jian'ou, China 116 J4
Jianshui, China 112 H6
Jianyang, China 116 J4
Jiao Xian, China 116 D5
Jiaohe, China 116 D3
Jiaozhou Wan, China 116 E5
Jiaozuo, China 116 E2
Jiawang, China 116 E4
Jiaxing, China 116 G5
Jiayi, Taiwan 117 B2
Jibiya, Nigeria 151 A4
Jibuti = Djibouti ■, Africa 145
Jicarón, I., Panama 197 E4
Jiddah, Si. Arabia 99 D3
Jihlava, Czech. 76 B4
Jihlava →, Czech. 76 C4
Jijel, Algeria 137 A5
Jijiga, Ethiopia 144 D4
Jikamshi, Nigeria 151 B4
Jilin, China 113 C11
Jiloca →, Spain 63 C6
Jilong, Taiwan 117 A3
Jima, Ethiopia 144 E2
Jiménez, Mexico 194 B3
Jimo, China 116 D5
Jin Xian, China 116 C5
Jinan, China 116 D3
Jincheng, China 116 E2
Jindabyne, Australia 171 G7
Jingdezhen, China 116 H3
Jinggu, China 112 H6
Jinghai, China 116 C3
Jingle, China 116 C2
Jingmen, China 116 G1
Jingxi, China 113 H7
Jingziguan, China 116 F1
Jinhua, China 116 H5
Jining, Nei Mongol Zizhiqu, China 116 B2
Jining, Shandong, China 116 E3
Jinja, Uganda 156 C2
Jinjang, Malaysia 126 C1
Jinjini, Ghana 149 C1
Jinnah Barrage, Pakistan 105 B5
Jinotega, Nic. 197 B2
Jinotepe, Nic. 197 C1
Jinshi, China 116 H1
Jinxiang, China 116 E3
Jinzhou, China 116 B5
Jiparaná →, Brazil 217 D3
Jipijapa, Ecuador 212 C1
Jisr ash Shughūr, Syria 97 B2
Jitarning, Australia 170 C3
Jitra, Malaysia 126 A1
Jiu →, Romania 75 D3
Jiujiang, China 116 H3
Jiuling Shan, China 116 H2
Jiuquan, China 112 D6
Jixi, China 113 B12
Jīzān, Si. Arabia 99 F3
João Pessoa, Brazil 217 D9
Jodhpur, India 106 C1
Jofane, Mozam. 159 D2
Jogjakarta = Yogyakarta, Indonesia 128 F6
Johannesburg, S. Africa 163 C7
John Crow Mts., Jamaica 199 B6
Johnson City, N.Y., U.S.A. 189 B3
Johnson City, Tenn., U.S.A. 191 F15
Johnston Falls = Mambilima Falls, Zambia 161 B4
Johnston I., Pac. Oc. 176 D7
Johnstown, N.Y., U.S.A. 189 A4
Johnstown, Pa., U.S.A. 189 C2
Johor Baharu, Malaysia 126 D3
Joinvile, Brazil 217 J6
Jökulsá á Bru →, Iceland 38 B5
Jökulsá á Fjöllum →, Iceland 38 A4
Joliet, U.S.A. 191 D12
Joliette, Canada 187 K12
Jolo, Phil. 130 L2
Jomalig, Phil. 130 E3
Jome, Indonesia 129 C13
Jones Sound, Canada 186 B9
Jonesboro, U.S.A. 191 G12
Jonglei □, Sudan 143 E4
Jönköping, Sweden 40 G3
Jonquière, Canada 187 K13
Joplin, U.S.A. 191 F11
Jordan ■, Asia 98
Jorm, Afghan. 104 B6
Jorong, Indonesia 128 D8
Jos, Nigeria 151 C5
José Batlle y Ordóñez, Uruguay 219 C2
Jotunheimen, Norway 40 E1
Jovellanos, Cuba 198 B3
Jowzjān □, Afghan. 104 B4
Ju Xian, China 116 E4
Juan Bautista Alberdi, Argentina 221 C3
Juan de Fuca Str., Canada 180 E7
Juan Fernández, Arch. de, Pac. Oc. 206 F2
Juan L. Lacaze, Uruguay 219 D1
Juàzeiro, Brazil 217 D8
Juàzeiro do Norte, Brazil 217 D9
Juba →, Somali Rep. 145 D1
Jubayl, Lebanon 95 B2
Jubbulpore = Jabalpur, India 106 D4
Júcar →, Spain 63 E7
Júcaro, Cuba 198 B4
Juchitán, Mexico 194 F6
Judaea = Har Yehuda, Israel 96 D2
Jugoslavia = Yugoslavia ■, Europe 72
Juigalpa, Nic. 197 C2
Juiz de Fora, Brazil 215 B4
Juli, Peru 213 F5
Juliaca, Peru 213 E5
Julianatop, Surinam 214 D3
Julianehåb, Greenland 224 D2
Jülich, Germany 59 B1
Jullundur, India 107 B2
Julu, China 116 D3
Jumbo, Zimbabwe 161 B4
Jumet, Belgium 51 D3
Jumilla, Spain 63 F7
Jumla, Nepal 109 A2
Jumna = Yamuna →, India 106 C5
Junagadh, India 107 D1
Junction City, U.S.A. 191 E10
Jundiaí, Brazil 215 C2
Juneau, U.S.A. 193 B5
Junee, Australia 171 F6
Jungfrau, Switz. 60 C3
Junggar Pendi, China 112 C4
Junglinster, Lux. 52 C2
Junin, Argentina 221 C4
Jūniyah, Lebanon 95 B2
Jur →, Sudan 143 E3
Jura = Schwäbische Alb, Germany 58 F3
Jura, U.K. 46 D4
Jura □, France 55 D8
Jurado, Colombia 210 B1
Juruá →, Brazil 217 C2
Juruena →, Brazil 217 D4
Justo Daract, Argentina 221 B2
Juticalpa, Honduras 196 C3
Jutland = Jylland, Denmark 42 B2
Juventud, I. de la, Cuba 198 B2
Jylland, Denmark 42 B2
Jyväskylä, Finland 43 E2

K

K2, Mt., Pakistan 105 A6
Kaap Plateau, S. Africa 163 E5
Kaapstad = Cape Town, S. Africa 163 H2
Kabaena, Indonesia 129 E11
Kabala, S. Leone 147 C3
Kabale, Uganda 156 D1
Kabalo, Zaïre 155 E5
Kabambare, Zaïre 155 D5
Kabanjahe, Indonesia 128 B2
Kabankalan, Phil. 130 H3
Kabara, Mali 140 D4
Kabare, Indonesia 129 C14
Kabarega Falls, Uganda 156 B1
Kabasalan, Phil. 130 K3
Kabba, Nigeria 151 E3
Kabīr, Zab al →, Iraq 102 B3
Kabkabīyah, Sudan 143 D2
Kabompo →, Zambia 161 C2
Kabongo, Zaïre 155 E5
Kabou, Togo 150 C1
Kaboudia, Rass, Tunisia 138 B3
Kabugao, Phil. 130 B3
Kābul, Afghan. 104 D5
Kābul □, Afghan. 104 C5
Kaburuang, Indonesia 129 A13
Kabwe, Zambia 161 C4
Kachchh, Gulf of, India 107 D1
Kachchh, Rann of, India 107 C1
Kachin □, Burma 122 B3
Kachira, L., Uganda 156 D1
Kachiry, Kazakstan 90 H7
Kackar, Turkey 94 B6
Kadan Kyun, Burma 122 H3
Kade, Ghana 149 D2
Kadina, Australia 171 E1
Kadiyevka, Ukraine 81 F5
Kadoma, Zimbabwe 161 C3
Kâdugli, Sudan 143 D3
Kaduna, Nigeria 151 C4
Kaduna □, Nigeria 151 C4
Kadzharan, Armenia 82 D7
Kadzhi-Say, Kyrgyzstan 93 B8
Kaédi, Mauritania 140 D1
Kaélé, Cameroon 153 B3
Kaesŏng, N. Korea 118 E4
Kāf, Si. Arabia 99 A2
Kafakumba, Zaïre 155 F4
Kafan, Armenia 82 D7
Kafanchan, Nigeria 151 C4
Kafareti, Nigeria 151 C6
Kaffrine, Senegal 146 B1
Kafia Kingi, Sudan 143 E2
Kafirévs, Ákra, Greece 71 D4
Kafr el Dauwâr, Egypt 139 A3
Kafue →, Zambia 161 C3
Kafulwe, Zambia 161 A4
Kaga Bandoro, C.A.R. 142 B3
Kagan, Uzbekistan 90 L4
Kagawa □, Japan 120 C4
Kağizman, Turkey 82 D4
Kahama, Tanzania 158 B1
Kahang, Malaysia 126 D3
Kahemba, Zaïre 155 E2
Kahnūj, Iran 103 D5
Kahoolawe, U.S.A. 192 B2
Kahramanmaraş, Turkey 94 C5
Kai, Kepulauan, Indonesia 129 E15
Kai Besar, Indonesia 129 E15
Kai Is. = Kai, Kepulauan, Indonesia 129 E15
Kai-Ketil, Indonesia 129 E15
Kaiama, Nigeria 151 C1
Kaieteur Falls, Guyana 214 C2
Kaifeng, China 116 E2
Kaihua, China 116 H4
Kaikohe, N.Z. 175 A4
Kaikoura, N.Z. 175 F4
Kaikoura Ra., N.Z. 175 F4
Kailahun, S. Leone 147 C4
Kailu, China 116 B5
Kailua Kona, U.S.A. 192 B3
Kaimana, Indonesia 129 D16
Kaimanawa Mts., N.Z. 175 D6
Kainji Res., Nigeria 151 C2
Kaipara Harbour, N.Z. 175 B5
Kaironi, Indonesia 129 C16
Kairouan, Tunisia 138 B2
Kairuku, Papua N. G. 173 C2
Kaiserslautern, Germany 58 E2
Kaitaia, N.Z. 175 A4
Kaiwi Channel, U.S.A. 192 A2
Kaiyuan, China 116 A6
Kajaani, Finland 43 D3
Kajan →, Indonesia 128 B9
Kajana = Kajaani, Finland 43 D3
Kajang, Malaysia 126 C1
Kajiado, Kenya 157 E2
Kajiado □, Kenya 157 E2
Kajo Kaji, Sudan 143 F4
Kaka, Sudan 143 D4
Kakamas, S. Africa 163 E3
Kakamega, Kenya 157 C1
Kakamega □, Kenya 157 C1
Kakanui Mts., N.Z. 175 H3
Kakegawa, Japan 120 C7
Kakhib, Russia 82 A7
Kakhovka, Ukraine 81 G4
Kakhovskoye Vdkhr., Ukraine 81 G4
Kakinada, India 107 E4
Kakogawa, Japan 120 C5
Kala, Nigeria 151 B7
Kala →, Sri Lanka 110 B1
Kalaa-Kebira, Tunisia 138 B2
Kalabagh, Pakistan 105 B5
Kalabahi, Indonesia 129 F12
Kalabáka, Greece 71 C2
Kalabo, Zambia 161 C2
Kalach, Russia 81 E6
Kalahari, Africa 162 C4
Kalahari Gemsbok Nat. Park, S. Africa 163 C3
Kalai-Khumb, Tajikistan 93 F4
Kalakan, Russia 91 H13
Kalakh, Syria 97 C2
Kalamata, Greece 71 E2
Kalamazoo, U.S.A. 191 D13
Kalannie, Australia 170 A2
Kalao, Indonesia 129 F11
Kalaotoa, Indonesia 129 F11
Kalasin, Thailand 123 F5
Kalat, Pakistan 105 D3
Kalaupapa, U.S.A. 192 A2
Kalemie, Zaïre 155 E6
Kalewa, Burma 122 C2
Kálfafellsstaður, Iceland 38 C5
Kalgan = Zhangjiakou, China 116 B3
Kalgoorlie-Boulder, Australia 168 J10
Kaliakra, Nos, Bulgaria 73 B6
Kalianda, Indonesia 128 E5
Kalibo, Phil. 130 G3
Kalima, Zaïre 155 C5
Kalimantan, Indonesia 128 C8
Kalimantan Barat □, Indonesia 128 C6
Kalimantan Selatan □, Indonesia 128 D8
Kalimantan Tengah □, Indonesia 128 C8
Kalimantan Timur □, Indonesia 128 B9
Kálimnos, Greece 71 E6
Kalinin = Tver, Russia 81 B5
Kaliningrad, Russia 81 C5
Kaliningrad, Russia 81 C1
Kalininskoye, Kyrgyzstan 93 A6
Kaliro, Uganda 156 C2
Kalispell, U.S.A. 190 B5
Kalisz, Poland 77 D3
Kaliua, Tanzania 158 B1
Kalkrand, Namibia 162 C3
Kalmalo, Nigeria 151 A2
Kalmar, Sweden 40 H3
Kalmthout, Belgium 51 A3
Kalmyk Republic □, Russia 81 G8
Kalocsa, Hungary 74 C3
Kalomo, Zambia 161 D3
Kaltungo, Nigeria 151 C6
Kaluga, Russia 81 C5
Kalundborg, Denmark 42 C3
Kalutara, Sri Lanka 110 D1
Kama →, Russia 81 C9
Kamaishi, Japan 121 D8
Kamativi, Zimbabwe 161 C2
Kamba, Nigeria 151 B1
Kambia, S. Leone 147 C2
Kamchatka, P-ov., Russia 91 D18
Kamchatka Pen. = Kamchatka, P-ov., Russia 91 D18
Kamen, Russia 90 H8
Kamenets-Podolskiy, Ukraine 81 F2
Kamenjak, Rt., Croatia 72 B2
Kamensk Uralskiy, Russia 90 G6
Kamenskoye, Russia 91 C17
Kamieskroon, S. Africa 163 F1
Kamina, Zaïre 155 F4
Kamloops, Canada 186 H4
Kamo, Armenia 82 C6
Kamoa Mts., Guyana 214 E2
Kampala, Uganda 156 C2
Kampar, Malaysia 126 B1
Kampar →, Indonesia 128 C3
Kampen, Neths. 50 C5
Kampot, Cambodia 125 G3
Kampuchea = Cambodia ■, Asia 125
Kampung Air Putih, Malaysia 126 B2
Kampung Jerangau, Malaysia 126 B2
Kampung Raja, Malaysia 126 A2
Kampungbaru = Tolitoli, Indonesia 129 B11
Kamrau, Teluk, Indonesia 129 D16
Kamsack, Canada 186 J7
Kamui-Misaki, Japan 121 B7
Kamyanets-Podilskyy = Kamenets-Podolskiy, Ukraine 81 F2
Kamyshin, Russia 81 E7
Kananga, Zaïre 155 E4
Kanash, Russia 81 C8
Kanawha →, U.S.A. 191 E14
Kanazawa, Japan 120 A6
Kanchanaburi, Thailand 123 G4
Kanchenjunga, Nepal 109 B4
Kanchipuram, India 107 F3
Kanda Kanda, Zaïre 155 E4
Kandahar = Qandahār, Afghan. 104 F3
Kandalaksha, Russia 90 C5
Kandangan, Indonesia 128 D8
Kandi, Benin 150 B3
Kandos, Australia 171 D7
Kandy, Sri Lanka 110 C2
Kane, U.S.A. 189 B2
Kane Basin, Greenland 224 A1
Kangar, Malaysia 126 A1
Kangaroo I., Australia 171 F1
Kăngdong, N. Korea 118 D3
Kangean, Kepulauan, Indonesia 128 E8
Kangean Is. = Kangean, Kepulauan, Indonesia 128 E8
Kanggye, N. Korea 118 C3
Kanggyŏng, S. Korea 118 G4
Kanghwa, S. Korea 118 E4
Kangnŭng, S. Korea 118 E5
Kango, Gabon 154 B1
Kani, Ivory C. 148 B4
Kaniapiskau →, Canada 187 G12
Kaniapiskau L., Canada 187 H12
Kanibadam, Tajikistan 93 D3
Kanin, P-ov., Russia 90 C6
Kanin Nos, Mys, Russia 90 C6
Kanin Pen. = Kanin, P-ov., Russia 90 C6
Kaniva, Australia 171 G3
Kankakee, U.S.A. 191 E13
Kankan, Guinea 147 B5
Kanker, India 106 F5
Kankunskiy, Russia 91 G14
Kannauj, India 106 B4
Kannod, India 106 E3
Kano, Nigeria 151 B4
Kano □, Nigeria 151 B5
Kanoroba, Ivory C. 148 B4
Kanowit, Malaysia 126 C6
Kanpetlet, Burma 122 D1
Kanpur, India 106 C4
Kansas □, U.S.A. 190 F9
Kansas →, U.S.A. 191 E10
Kansas City, Kans., U.S.A. 191 E10
Kansas City, Mo., U.S.A. 191 F11
Kansk, Russia 91 H10
Kansŏng, S. Korea 118 E5
Kansu = Gansu □, China 112 D6
Kant, Kyrgyzstan 93 A7
Kanté, Togo 150 B2
Kanthi, India 106 E8
Kanuma, Japan 120 A9
Kanye, Botswana 162 D5
Kaohsiung = Gaoxiong, Taiwan 117 C2
Kaokoveld, Namibia 162 B2
Kaolack, Senegal 146 B1
Kapanga, Zaïre 155 F4
Kapellen, Belgium 51 A3
Kapfenberg, Austria 61 B5
Kapiri Mposhi, Zambia 161 C4
Kāpīsā □, Afghan. 104 C5
Kapit, Malaysia 126 C6
Kapoeta, Sudan 143 F5
Kaposvár, Hungary 74 C2
Kapsan, N. Korea 118 C4
Kapuas →, Indonesia 128 C6
Kapuas Hulu, Pegunungan, Malaysia 126 C7
Kapuas Hulu Ra. = Kapuas Hulu, Pegunungan, Malaysia 126 C7
Kapunda, Australia 171 E2
Kaputar, Australia 171 C8
Kaputir, Kenya 157 B1
Kara, Russia 90 D8
Kara Bogaz Gol, Zaliv, Turkmenistan 90 J3
Kara Kalpak Republic □, Uzbekistan 90 J4
Kara Kum = Karakum, Peski, Turkmenistan 90 K5
Kara Sea, Russia 90 C9
Kara Su, Kyrgyzstan 93 C5
Karabutak, Kazakstan 90 H5
Karachala, Azerbaijan 82 D9
Karachi, Pakistan 105 F3
Karadeniz Boğazı, Turkey 94 A2
Karaga, Ghana 149 A2
Karaganda, Kazakstan 90 J7
Karagayly, Kazakstan 90 J7
Karaginskiy, Ostrov, Russia 91 C18
Karaitivu I., Sri Lanka 110 B1
Karak, Malaysia 126 C2
Karakas, Kazakstan 90 K8
Karakitang, Indonesia 129 B12
Karaklis, Armenia 82 C5
Karakoram Ra., Pakistan 105 A6
Karakul, Tajikistan 93 E6
Karakuldzha, Kyrgyzstan 93 D6
Karakum, Peski, Turkmenistan 90 K5
Karakurt, Turkey 82 D4
Karalon, Russia 91 G13
Karaman, Turkey 94 C3
Karamay, China 112 B3
Karambu, Indonesia 128 D9
Karamea Bight, N.Z. 175 E3
Karamoja □, Uganda 156 B2
Karasburg, Namibia 162 E3
Karasino, Russia 90 E9
Karasu →, Turkey 82 D2
Karasuk, Russia 90 H8
Karatau, Kazakstan 93 A4
Karatau, Kazakstan 93 A3
Karayazı, Turkey 82 D4
Karazhal, Kazakstan 90 J6
Karbalā, Iraq 102 D4
Karcag, Hungary 74 B5
Karda, Russia 91 H11
Kardhítsa, Greece 71 C2
Kareeberge, S. Africa 163 F3
Karelian Republic □, Russia 90 C5
Kargasok, Russia 90 G8
Kargat, Russia 90 H8
Karia ba Mohammed, Morocco 136 B5
Kariba, Zimbabwe 161 A3
Kariba, L., Zimbabwe 161 B2
Kariba Dam, Zimbabwe 161 A3
Kariba Gorge, Zambia 161 D4
Karibib, Namibia 162 C2
Karimata, Kepulauan, Indonesia 128 C6

Karimata, Selat, *Indonesia* 128 C6
Karimata Is. = Karimata, Kepulauan, *Indonesia* 128 C6
Karimunjawa, Kepulauan, *Indonesia* 128 E6
Kariya, *Japan* 120 B6
Karkar I., *Papua N. G.* 173 B2
Karkaralinsk, *Kazakstan* 90 J7
Karkinitskiy Zaliv, *Ukraine* 81 G3
Karkur Tohl, *Egypt* 139 F1
Karl-Marx-Stadt = Chemnitz, *Germany* 58 D5
Karlovac, *Croatia* 72 B4
Karlovy Vary, *Czech.* 76 B2
Karlsbad = Karlovy Vary, *Czech.* 76 B2
Karlskrona, *Sweden* 40 H3
Karlsruhe, *Germany* 58 F2
Karlstad, *Sweden* 40 F3
Karnal, *India* 106 A3
Karnali →, *Nepal* 109 B1
Karnataka □, *India* 107 F2
Kärnten □, *Austria* 61 C4
Karoi, *Zimbabwe* 161 B3
Karonga, *Malawi* 158 A2
Karoonda, *Australia* 171 F2
Karora, *Sudan* 143 B6
Kárpathos, *Greece* 71 F6
Kars, *Turkey* 94 B7
Karsakpay, *Kazakstan* 90 J6
Karshi, *Uzbekistan* 90 L5
Karsun, *Russia* 81 C8
Kartaly, *Russia* 90 G5
Karufa, *Indonesia* 129 D15
Karungu, *Kenya* 157 D1
Karwar, *India* 107 E2
Kas Kong, *Cambodia* 125 F2
Kasache, *Malawi* 158 C2
Kasai →, *Zaïre* 155 D2
Kasama, *Zambia* 161 B4
Kasan-dong, *N. Korea* 118 B4
Kasanga, *Tanzania* 158 C1
Kasangulu, *Zaïre* 155 D1
Kasba, *Bangla.* 111 C3
Kasba L., *Canada* 186 F7
Kasba Tadla, *Morocco* 136 C4
Kasempa, *Zambia* 161 C3
Kasenga, *Zaïre* 155 F6
Kasese, *Uganda* 156 C1
Kāshān, *Iran* 103 B3
Kashi, *China* 112 D1
Kashiwazaki, *Japan* 121 F6
Kashk-e Kohneh, *Afghan.* 104 C1
Kashkasu, *Kyrgyzstan* 93 D5
Kashun Noerh = Gaxun Nur, *China* 112 C6
Kasimov, *Russia* 81 C6
Kasiruta, *Indonesia* 129 C13
Kaskelen, *Kazakstan* 93 A8
Kasongo, *Zaïre* 155 D5
Kasongo Lunda, *Zaïre* 155 E2
Kásos, *Greece* 71 F6
Kaspi, *Georgia* 82 B5
Kaspiysk, *Russia* 82 A8
Kassaba, *Egypt* 139 F3
Kassala, *Sudan* 143 C5
Kassalâ □, *Sudan* 143 C5
Kassansay, *Uzbekistan* 93 C4
Kassel, *Germany* 58 D3
Kassue, *Indonesia* 129 E18
Kastamonu, *Turkey* 94 A3
Kastoría, *Greece* 71 B2
Kasulu, *Tanzania* 158 B1
Kasumkent, *Azerbaijan* 82 B8
Kasungu, *Malawi* 158 C1
Kasur, *Pakistan* 105 C6
Kata, *Russia* 91 G11
Katako Kombe, *Zaïre* 155 D4
Katamatite, *Australia* 171 F5
Katangi, *India* 106 E4
Katangli, *Russia* 91 G17
Katherîna, Gebel, *Egypt* 139 C5
Katihar, *India* 106 C8
Katima Mulilo, *Zambia* 161 D2
Katimbira, *Malawi* 158 C2
Katingan = Mendawai →, *Indonesia* 128 D8
Katiola, *Ivory C.* 148 C5
Katmandu, *Nepal* 109 B3
Katonga →, *Uganda* 156 C1
Katoomba, *Australia* 171 E8
Katowice, *Poland* 77 E3
Katsina, *Nigeria* 151 A4
Katsina □, *Nigeria* 151 A4
Katsina Ala →, *Nigeria* 151 E5
Katsuura, *Japan* 120 B9
Kattegatt, *Denmark* 42 B3
Katwijk-aan-Zee, *Neths.* 50 D2
Kauai, *U.S.A.* 192 A1
Kauai Channel, *U.S.A.* 192 A1
Kaunas, *Lithuania* 81 C1
Kaura Namoda, *Nigeria* 151 A3
Kavacha, *Russia* 91 C18
Kavála, *Greece* 71 B4
Kaw, *Fr. Guiana* 214 C6
Kawagoe, *Japan* 120 A8
Kawaguchi, *Japan* 120 B9
Kawaihae, *U.S.A.* 192 B3
Kawambwa, *Zambia* 161 A4
Kawardha, *India* 106 E5
Kawasaki, *Japan* 120 B9
Kawerau, *N.Z.* 175 C6
Kawio, Kepulauan, *Indonesia* 129 A12
Kawthoolei = Kawthule □, *Burma* 122 F3
Kawthule □, *Burma* 122 F3
Kaya, *Burkina Faso* 149 A2
Kayah □, *Burma* 122 E3
Kayeli, *Indonesia* 129 D13
Kayes, *Mali* 140 E2
Kayima, *S. Leone* 147 C3
Kayoa, *Indonesia* 129 C13
Kayrakkumskoye Vdkhr., *Tajikistan* 93 D3
Kayrunnera, *Australia* 171 C4
Kayseri, *Turkey* 94 B4
Kayuagung, *Indonesia* 128 D4
Kazachinskoye, *Russia* 91 H12
Kazachye, *Russia* 91 C14
Kazakstan ■, *Asia* 90 J6
Kazan, *Russia* 81 C8
Kazan-Rettō, *Pac. Oc.* 176 C3
Kazanlŭk, *Bulgaria* 73 C4
Kazarman, *Kyrgyzstan* 93 C6
Kazbek, *Georgia* 82 A5
Kāzerūn, *Iran* 103 D3
Kazi Magomed, *Azerbaijan* 82 C9
Kazumba, *Zaïre* 155 E3
Kazym →, *Russia* 90 E7
Ké-Macina, *Mali* 140 E4
Kéa, *Greece* 71 E4
Keaau, *U.S.A.* 192 B3
Keban, *Turkey* 94 B5
Kébi, *Ivory C.* 148 B4
Kebili, *Tunisia* 138 C2
Kebnekaise, *Sweden* 40 B4
Kebri Dehar, *Ethiopia* 144 E5
Kecskemét, *Hungary* 74 B4
Kédougou, *Senegal* 146 C3
Keene, *U.S.A.* 189 A6
Keetmanshoop, *Namibia* 162 D3
Keewatin □, *Canada* 186 F9
Kefallinía, *Greece* 71 D1
Kefamenanu, *Indonesia* 129 F12
Keffi, *Nigeria* 151 D4
Keflavík, *Iceland* 38 D2
Kegalla, *Sri Lanka* 110 C2
Keighley, *U.K.* 46 G7
Keimoes, *S. Africa* 163 E3
Keith, *Australia* 171 F3
Keith Arm, *Canada* 186 D5
Kejser Franz Joseph Fjord = Kong Franz Joseph Fd., *Greenland* 224 B3
Kekaygyr, *Kyrgyzstan* 93 C7
Kekri, *India* 106 C2
Kël, *Russia* 91 D13
Kelan, *China* 116 C1
Kelang, *Malaysia* 126 C1
Kelani →, *Sri Lanka* 110 C1
Kelantan →, *Malaysia* 126 A2
Keles →, *Kazakstan* 93 C2
Kelibia, *Tunisia* 138 A3
Kelkit, *Turkey* 82 D2
Kellé, *Congo* 154 B2
Kellerberrin, *Australia* 170 B2
Kellogg, *U.S.A.* 190 B4
Kells = Ceanannus Mor, *Ireland* 46 G3
Kélo, *Chad* 142 F1
Kelowna, *Canada* 186 H4
Kelso, *N.Z.* 175 J2
Keltemashat, *Kazakstan* 93 B3
Keluang, *Malaysia* 126 D3
Kelvedon, *U.K.* 45 B6
Kem, *Russia* 90 C5
Kem-Kem, *Morocco* 136 D5
Kema, *Indonesia* 129 B12
Kemah, *Turkey* 82 D1
Kemaliye, *Turkey* 82 D1
Kemasik, *Malaysia* 126 B3
Kemerovo, *Russia* 90 H9
Kemi, *Finland* 43 C2
Kemi →, *Finland* 43 C2
Kemi älv = Kemi →, *Finland* 43 C2
Kemmuna = Comino, *Malta* 69 A2
Kempsey, *Australia* 171 C9
Kempten, *Germany* 58 G3
Kemsing, *U.K.* 45 D4
Kendal, *Indonesia* 128 E6
Kendal, *U.K.* 46 F6
Kendall, *Australia* 171 D9
Kendari, *Indonesia* 129 D11
Kendawangan, *Indonesia* 128 D6
Kende, *Nigeria* 151 B2
Kendenup, *Australia* 170 D2
Kendrapara, *India* 106 F7
Kendrew, *S. Africa* 163 G5
Kenema, *S. Leone* 147 D3
Keng Tawng, *Burma* 122 D3
Kenge, *Zaïre* 155 D2
Kenhardt, *S. Africa* 163 E3
Kenitra, *Morocco* 136 B4
Kennedy, *Zimbabwe* 161 C2
Kennewick, *U.S.A.* 190 B3
Kenogami →, *Canada* 187 J10
Kenosha, *U.S.A.* 191 D12
Kent □, *U.K.* 45 E5
Kent Group, *Australia* 172 A3
Kent Pen., *Canada* 186 D7
Kentau, *Kazakstan* 93 A2
Kentucky □, *U.S.A.* 191 F13
Kentucky →, *U.S.A.* 191 E13
Kentville, *Canada* 187 K14
Kenya ■, *Africa* 157
Kenya, Mt., *Kenya* 157 D2
Keokuk, *U.S.A.* 191 E11
Kepi, *Indonesia* 129 E18
Kerala □, *India* 107 F2
Kerama-Shotō, *Japan* 121 J8
Kerang, *Australia* 171 F4
Kerch, *Ukraine* 81 H5
Kerchoual, *Mali* 140 D6
Kerema, *Papua N. G.* 173 C2
Keren, *Eritrea* 144 B3
Kerewan, *Gambia* 146 C1
Kericho, *Kenya* 157 D1
Kericho □, *Kenya* 157 D1
Kerinci, *Indonesia* 128 C3
Kerkenna, Is., *Tunisia* 138 C3
Kérkira, *Greece* 71 C1
Kermadec Is., *Pac. Oc.* 176 H6
Kermadec Trench, *Pac. Oc.* 176 J6
Kermān, *Iran* 103 D4
Kermānshāh = Bākhtarān, *Iran* 103 B2
Keroh, *Malaysia* 126 A1
Kerrobert, *Canada* 186 J6
Kerzaz, *Algeria* 137 C3
Keşiş Dağ, *Turkey* 82 D2
Kessel-Lo, *Belgium* 51 B4
Kestell, *S. Africa* 163 E7
Kestenga, *Russia* 90 C5
Ket →, *Russia* 90 G9
Keta, *Ghana* 149 D3
Ketapang, *Indonesia* 128 D6
Ketchikan, *U.S.A.* 193 B5
Kete Krachi, *Ghana* 149 C3
Ketef, Khalîg Umm el, *Egypt* 139 E6
Kewanee, *U.S.A.* 191 E12
Keweenaw B., *U.S.A.* 191 B12
Key West, *U.S.A.* 191 K16
Keyser, *U.S.A.* 189 D2
Kezhma, *Russia* 91 G11
Khabarovo, *Russia* 90 D7
Khabarovsk, *Russia* 91 H16
Khābūr →, *Syria* 97 B5
Khachmas, *Azerbaijan* 82 B9
Khairpur, *Pakistan* 105 E4
Khāk Dow, *Afghan.* 104 C4
Khakhea, *Botswana* 162 D4
Khalkis, *Greece* 71 D3
Khalmer-Sede = Tazovskiy, *Russia* 90 E9
Khalmer Yu, *Russia* 90 D8
Khalturin, *Russia* 81 A8
Khalūf, *Oman* 101 C3
Kham Keut, *Laos* 125 C3
Khambhat, *India* 106 E1
Khambhat, G. of, *India* 107 D1
Khamir, *Yemen* 100 B1
Khān Shaykhūn, *Syria* 97 B3
Khānābād, *Afghan.* 104 B5
Khanabad, *Uzbekistan* 93 C4
Khānaqīn, *Iraq* 102 C4
Khandwa, *India* 106 E3
Khandyga, *Russia* 91 E14
Khanewal, *Pakistan* 105 D5
Khaniá, *Greece* 71 F4
Khanion, Kólpos, *Greece* 71 F4
Khanty-Mansiysk, *Russia* 90 F7
Khapcheranga, *Russia* 91 J13
Kharagpur, *India* 106 E7
Kharan Kalat, *Pakistan* 105 E2
Khârga, El Wâhât el, *Egypt* 139 E4
Khargon, *India* 106 E2
Kharit, Wadi el →, *Egypt* 139 E5
Khārk, Jazireh, *Iran* 103 D3
Kharkiv = Kharkov, *Ukraine* 81 E5
Kharkov, *Ukraine* 81 E5
Kharovsk, *Russia* 81 A6
Khartoum = El Khartûm, *Sudan* 143 C4
Khasavyurt, *Russia* 82 A7
Khashm el Girba, *Sudan* 143 C5
Khashuri, *Georgia* 82 B5
Khaskovo, *Bulgaria* 73 C4
Khatanga, *Russia* 91 D11
Khatanga →, *Russia* 91 D11
Khatyrka, *Russia* 91 B18
Khavast, *Uzbekistan* 93 D2
Khaydarken, *Kyrgyzstan* 93 D4
Khed Brahma, *India* 106 D1
Khemissèt, *Morocco* 136 B4
Khemmarat, *Thailand* 123 F6
Khenchela, *Algeria* 137 A5
Khenifra, *Morocco* 136 C4
Kherson, *Ukraine* 81 G3
Kheta →, *Russia* 91 D11
Khilok, *Russia* 91 J12
Khíos, *Greece* 71 D5
Khirbat Qanāfār, *Lebanon* 95 C2
Khiuma = Hiiumaa, *Estonia* 81 A1
Khiva, *Uzbekistan* 90 K4
Khlong →, *Thailand* 123 H4
Khmelnitskiy, *Ukraine* 81 E2
Khmelnytskyy = Khmelnitskiy, *Ukraine* 81 E2
Khmer Rep. = Cambodia ■, *Asia* 125
Khojak P., *Afghan.* 104 F4
Kholm, *Afghan.* 104 B4
Kholm, *Russia* 81 B3
Kholmsk, *Russia* 91 H17
Khon Kaen, *Thailand* 123 F5
Khonh Hung, *Vietnam* 125 G4
Khonu, *Russia* 91 D15
Khorāsān □, *Iran* 103 B5
Khorat = Nakhon Ratchasima, *Thailand* 123 G5
Khorat, Cao Nguyen, *Thailand* 123 G5
Khorog, *Tajikistan* 93 F4
Khorrāmshahr, *Iran* 103 C2
Khouribga, *Morocco* 136 C4
Khowai, *Bangla.* 111 C3
Khrami →, *Azerbaijan* 82 B6
Khudzhand, *Tajikistan* 93 D3
Khūgīānī, *Qandahar, Afghan.* 104 F4
Khūgīānī, *Qandahar, Afghan.* 104 F3
Khulna, *Bangla.* 111 D1
Khulna □, *Bangla.* 111 D1
Khulo, *Georgia* 82 B4
Khunzakh, *Russia* 82 A7
Khūrīyā Mūrīyā, Jazā 'ir, *Oman* 101 D2
Khushab, *Pakistan* 105 C5
Khuzdar, *Pakistan* 105 E3
Khvājeh Moḩammad, Kūh-e, *Afghan.* 104 B6
Khyber Pass, *Afghan.* 104 D6
Kiama, *Australia* 171 F8
Kiamba, *Phil.* 130 L5
Kiambu, *Kenya* 157 D2
Kiangsi = Jiangxi □, *China* 116 J3
Kiangsu = Jiangsu □, *China* 116 F4
Kibanga Port, *Uganda* 156 C2
Kibangou, *Congo* 154 C1
Kibombo, *Zaïre* 155 D5
Kibondo, *Tanzania* 158 B1
Kibumbu, *Burundi* 156 C2
Kibungu, *Rwanda* 156 A2
Kibuye, *Burundi* 156 C2
Kibuye, *Rwanda* 156 A1
Kibwesa, *Tanzania* 158 C1
Kibwezi, *Kenya* 157 E3
Kichiga, *Russia* 91 C17
Kicking Horse Pass, *Canada* 186 H5
Kidal, *Mali* 140 D6
Kidderminster, *U.K.* 46 J7
Kidira, *Senegal* 146 B3
Kidnappers, C., *N.Z.* 175 D6
Kiel, *Germany* 58 A3
Kiel Kanal = Nord-Ostsee Kanal, *Germany* 58 A3
Kielce, *Poland* 77 D4
Kieler Bucht, *Germany* 58 A3
Kieta, *Papua N. G.* 173 B3
Kiev = Kiyev, *Ukraine* 81 E3
Kiffa, *Mauritania* 140 D2
Kifrī, *Iraq* 102 B4
Kigali, *Rwanda* 156 A2
Kigoma-Ujiji, *Tanzania* 158 B1
Kihee, *Australia* 171 A4
Kii-Suidō, *Japan* 120 C5
Kikai-Jima, *Japan* 121 H9
Kikinda, *Serbia, Yug.* 72 A7
Kikládhes, *Greece* 71 E4
Kikori, *Papua N. G.* 173 B1
Kikwit, *Zaïre* 155 D2
Kilauea Crater, *U.S.A.* 192 B3
Kilcoy, *Australia* 171 A9
Kildare, *Ireland* 46 H3
Kilifi, *Kenya* 157 F4
Kilifi □, *Kenya* 157 E4
Kilimanjaro, *Tanzania* 158 B3
Kilindini, *Kenya* 157 F4
Kilju, *N. Korea* 118 C5
Kilkenny, *Ireland* 46 J2
Killala B., *Ireland* 46 F1
Killarney, *Australia* 171 B9
Killarney, *Ireland* 46 J1
Killíni, *Greece* 71 D2
Kilmarnock, *U.K.* 46 E5
Kilmore, *Australia* 171 G5
Kilosa, *Tanzania* 158 C3
Kilrush, *Ireland* 46 J1
Kilwa Kivinje, *Tanzania* 158 C3
Kimaän, *Indonesia* 129 F18
Kimberley, *S. Africa* 163 E5
Kimchaek, *N. Korea* 118 C5
Kimchŏn, *S. Korea* 118 G5
Kimje, *S. Korea* 118 G4
Kimry, *Russia* 81 B5
Kinabalu, Gunong, *Malaysia* 126 A8
Kindia, *Guinea* 147 B2
Kindu, *Zaïre* 155 D5
Kineshma, *Russia* 81 B6
King, L., *Australia* 170 C3
King Frederick VI Land = Kong Frederik VI.s Kyst, *Greenland* 224 D2
King George B., *Falk. Is.* 224 A2
King George Is., *Canada* 187 G11
King I. = Kadan Kyun, *Burma* 122 H3
King I., *Australia* 172 A1
King Sd., *Australia* 168 B2
King William I., *Canada* 186 D8
King William's Town, *S. Africa* 163 H7
Kingman, *U.S.A.* 190 F4
King's Lynn, *U.K.* 46 H9
Kingscote, *Australia* 171 F1
Kingston, *Canada* 185 C3
Kingston, *Jamaica* 199 B5
Kingston, *N.Z.* 175 H2
Kingston, *N.Y., U.S.A.* 189 B5
Kingston, *Pa., U.S.A.* 189 B4
Kingston South East, *Australia* 171 G2
Kingston-upon-Thames, *U.K.* 45 D2
Kingstown, *St. Vincent* 203 H2
Kingsville, *U.S.A.* 190 J9
Kinkala, *Congo* 154 D2
Kinnarodden, *Norway* 34
Kinoni, *Uganda* 156 D1
Kinross, *U.K.* 46 D6
Kinsale, *Ireland* 46 K1
Kinsha = Chang Jiang →, *China* 116 G5
Kinshasa, *Zaïre* 155 D1
Kinston, *U.S.A.* 191 F16
Kintampo, *Ghana* 149 C2
Kintap, *Indonesia* 128 D8
Kintyre, *U.K.* 46 E4
Kiparissía, *Greece* 71 E2
Kiparissiakós Kólpos, *Greece* 71 E2
Kipembawe, *Tanzania* 158 C1
Kipili, *Tanzania* 158 C1
Kipini, *Kenya* 157 E4
Kipungo, *Angola* 160 D2
Kipushi, *Zaïre* 155 G5
Kirensk, *Russia* 91 G12
Kirghizia = Kyrgyzstan ■, *Asia* 93 B7
Kirghizstan = Kyrgyzstan ■, *Asia* 93 B7
Kirgizia = Kyrgyzstan ■, *Asia* 93 B7
Kiri, *Zaïre* 155 C2
Kiribati ■, *Pac. Oc.* 176 F6
Kırıkkale, *Turkey* 94 B3
Kirillov, *Russia* 81 A5
Kirin = Jilin, *China* 113 C11
Kirindi →, *Sri Lanka* 110 D3
Kiritimati, *Kiribati* 176 E8
Kiriwina Is. = Trobriand Is., *Papua N. G.* 173 C3
Kirkcudbright, *U.K.* 46 F5
Kirkjubæjarklaustur, *Iceland* 38 D4
Kirkland Lake, *Canada* 187 K11
Kirksville, *U.S.A.* 191 E11
Kirkūk, *Iraq* 102 B4
Kirkwall, *U.K.* 46 A3
Kirkwood, *S. Africa* 163 H5
Kirov = Vyatka, *Russia* 81 A8
Kirovabad = Gyandzha, *Azerbaijan* 82 C7
Kirovakan = Karaklis, *Armenia* 82 C5
Kirovo, *Uzbekistan* 93 D4
Kirovograd, *Ukraine* 81 F3
Kirovohrad = Kirovograd, *Ukraine* 81 F3
Kirovsk, *Russia* 90 C5
Kirovsk, *Turkmenistan* 90 L4
Kirovskiy, *Russia* 91 E18
Kirovskoye, *Kyrgyzstan* 93 A4
Kirsanov, *Russia* 81 D7
Kırşehir, *Turkey* 94 B4
Kirteh, *Afghan.* 104 E2
Kirthar Range, *Pakistan* 105 E3
Kiruna, *Sweden* 40 B4
Kirundu, *Zaïre* 155 C5
Kirup, *Australia* 170 C1
Kiryū, *Japan* 120 A8
Kisalaya, *Nic.* 197 A3
Kisangani, *Zaïre* 155 B4
Kisar, *Indonesia* 129 F13
Kisaran, *Indonesia* 128 B2
Kisarazu, *Japan* 120 B9
Kiselevsk, *Russia* 90 H9
Kishanganj, *India* 106 C8
Kishi, *Nigeria* 151 D1
Kishinev, *Moldova* 81 G2
Kishiwada, *Japan* 120 C5
Kishorganj, *Bangla.* 111 B2
Kisii, *Kenya* 157 D1
Kisii □, *Kenya* 157 D1
Kisiju, *Tanzania* 158 C3
Kisizi, *Uganda* 156 D1
Kiskőrös, *Hungary* 74 B3
Kiskunfélegyháza, *Hungary* 74 B4
Kiskunhalas, *Hungary* 74 C4
Kismayu = Chisimaio, *Somali Rep.* 145 D1
Kiso-Sammyaku, *Japan* 120 B7
Kisoro, *Uganda* 156 D1
Kissidougou, *Guinea* 147 C4
Kisumu, *Kenya* 157 D1
Kita, *Mali* 140 F2
Kitab, *Uzbekistan* 93 E1
Kitaibaraki, *Japan* 120 A9
Kitakyūshū, *Japan* 120 C2
Kitale, *Kenya* 157 C1
Kitami, *Japan* 121 B9
Kitchener, *Canada* 187 L11
Kitega = Gitega, *Burundi* 156 B2
Kitgum, *Uganda* 156 A2
Kíthnos, *Greece* 71 E4
Kitikmeot □, *Canada* 186 C7
Kitimat, *Canada* 186 G3
Kittakittaooloo, L., *Australia* 171 A1
Kittanning, *U.S.A.* 189 C1
Kitui, *Kenya* 157 D3
Kitui □, *Kenya* 157 D3
Kitwe, *Zambia* 161 B3
Kivu, L., *Zaïre* 155 C6
Kiyev, *Ukraine* 81 E3
Kiyevskoye Vdkhr., *Ukraine* 81 E3
Kiziguru, *Rwanda* 156 A2
Kızıl Irmak →, *Turkey* 94 A4
Kizil Yurt, *Russia* 82 A7
Kizyl-Arvat, *Turkmenistan* 90 K3
Kladno, *Czech.* 76 B3
Klagenfurt, *Austria* 61 C4
Klaipéda, *Lithuania* 81 B1
Klamath →, *U.S.A.* 190 C1
Klamath Falls, *U.S.A.* 190 C2
Klatovy, *Czech.* 76 B2
Klawer, *S. Africa* 163 G2
Klerksdorp, *S. Africa* 163 D6
Kleve, *Germany* 59 A1
Klipdale, *S. Africa* 163 H3
Klipplaat, *S. Africa* 163 H5
Kłodzko, *Poland* 77 E2

Klondike, *Canada* 186 C3
Klosters, *Switz.* 60 B5
Klouto, *Togo* 150 D1
Kluane L., *Canada* 186 D3
Klyuchevsk Vol., *Russia* 84 C20
Knebworth, *U.K.* 45 B3
Kneïss, Is., *Tunisia* 138 C2
Knob, C., *Australia* 170 D3
Knokke, *Belgium* 51 A1
Knossós, *Greece* 71 F5
Knoxville, *U.S.A.* 191 F14
Knysna, *S. Africa* 163 H4
Ko Chang, *Thailand* 123 H5
Ko Kut, *Thailand* 123 J5
Ko Phra Thong, *Thailand* 122 K3
Ko Tao, *Thailand* 123 J4
Koartac, *Canada* 187 F12
Koba, *Indonesia* 129 E16
Kobarid, *Slovenia* 72 A2
Kobdo = Hovd, *Mongolia* 112 B5
Kōbe, *Japan* 120 C5
København, *Denmark* 42 C4
Koblenz, *Germany* 58 D2
Kobroor, *Indonesia* 129 E16
Kobuleti, *Georgia* 82 B3
Kocaeli = İzmit, *Turkey* 94 A2
Kočani, *Macedonia* 72 E8
Kočevje, *Slovenia* 72 B3
Koch Bihar, *India* 106 C8
Kochang, *S. Korea* 118 G5
Kocheya, *Russia* 91 H14
Kōchi, *Japan* 120 D4
Kōchi □, *Japan* 120 D4
Kochiu = Gejiu, *China* 112 H6
Kochkor-Ata, *Kyrgyzstan* 93 C5
Kochkorka, *Kyrgyzstan* 93 B7
Koddiyar B., *Sri Lanka* 110 B2
Kodiak, *U.S.A.* 193 B4
Kodiak I., *U.S.A.* 193 B4
Kodori →, *Georgia* 82 A3
Koes, *Namibia* 162 D3
Koffiefontein, *S. Africa* 163 E5
Kofiau, *Indonesia* 129 C14
Koforidua, *Ghana* 149 D2
Kōfu, *Japan* 120 B8
Kogan, *Australia* 171 A8
Kogin Baba, *Nigeria* 151 E6
Kogota, *Japan* 121 E7
Koh-i-Bābā, *Afghan.* 104 D4
Kohat, *Pakistan* 105 B5
Kohima, *India* 107 C6
Koin-dong, *N. Korea* 118 C3
Kojŏ, *N. Korea* 118 D4
Kojonup, *Australia* 170 C2
Kok-Yangak, *Kyrgyzstan* 93 C6
Kokand, *Uzbekistan* 93 D4
Kokas, *Indonesia* 129 D15
Kokchetav, *Kazakstan* 90 H7
Kokerite, *Guyana* 214 A1
Koko, *Nigeria* 151 B2
Koko Kyunzu, *Burma* 122 G1
Kokolopozo, *Ivory C.* 148 D4
Kokomo, *U.S.A.* 191 E13
Kokonau, *Indonesia* 129 E17
Koksan, *N. Korea* 118 E4
Koksoak →, *Canada* 187 G12
Kokstad, *S. Africa* 163 F8
Kokuora, *Russia* 91 C14
Kola, *Indonesia* 129 E16
Kola, *Russia* 90 B5
Kola Pen. = Kolskiy Poluostrov, *Russia* 90 C5
Kolahun, *Liberia* 148 B2
Kolaka, *Indonesia* 129 D11
Kolar, *India* 107 F3
Kolayat, *India* 106 B1
Kolchugino = Leninsk-Kuznetskiy, *Russia* 90 H9
Kolda, *Senegal* 146 C1
Kolding, *Denmark* 42 C2
Kole, *Zaïre* 155 D3
Kolepom = Yos Sudarso, Pulau, *Indonesia* 129 F17
Kolguyev, Ostrov, *Russia* 90 C6
Kolhapur, *India* 107 E2
Kolia, *Ivory C.* 148 A4
Kolín, *Czech.* 76 B4
Köln, *Germany* 58 D1
Koło, *Poland* 77 C3
Kołobrzeg, *Poland* 77 A1
Kolokani, *Mali* 140 E3
Kolomna, *Russia* 81 C5
Kolomyya, *Ukraine* 81 F1
Kolonodale, *Indonesia* 129 D11
Kolpashevo, *Russia* 90 G9
Kolpino, *Russia* 81 A4
Kolskiy Poluostrov, *Russia* 90 C5
Kolwezi, *Zaïre* 155 F4
Kolyma →, *Russia* 91 B15
Kôm Ombo, *Egypt* 139 E5
Komandorskiye Is. = Komandorskiye Ostrova, *Russia* 91 D18
Komandorskiye Ostrova, *Russia* 91 D18
Komárno, *Slovak Rep.* 76 D5
Komatipoort, *S. Africa* 163 C9
Komatsu, *Japan* 120 A6
Komenda, *Ghana* 149 E2
Komi Republic □, *Russia* 90 E6
Kommunarsk, *Ukraine* 81 F5
Kommunizma, Pik, *Tajikistan* 93 E5
Komodo, *Indonesia* 129 F10
Komoé, *Ivory C.* 148 E6
Komono, *Congo* 154 C2
Komoran, Pulau, *Indonesia* 129 F18
Komotini, *Greece* 71 A5
Kompasberg, *S. Africa* 163 G5
Kompong Cham, *Cambodia* 125 F3
Kompong Chhnang, *Cambodia* 125 F3
Kompong Som, *Cambodia* 125 G2
Kompong Speu, *Cambodia* 125 F3
Komsberg, *S. Africa* 163 G3
Komsomolabad, *Tajikistan* 93 E3
Komsomolets, Ostrov, *Russia* 91 B10
Komsomolsk, *Russia* 91 H16
Konarhá □, *Afghan.* 104 C6
Kondakovo, *Russia* 91 C15
Kondinin, *Australia* 170 B3
Kondoa, *Tanzania* 158 B2
Kondratyevo, *Russia* 91 H11
Konduga, *Nigeria* 151 B7
Kong, *Ivory C.* 148 B5
Kong, Koh, *Cambodia* 125 F2
Kong Christian IX.s Land, *Greenland* 224 C2
Kong Christian X.s Land, *Greenland* 224 B3
Kong Franz Joseph Fd., *Greenland* 224 B3
Kong Frederik IX.s Land, *Greenland* 224 C1
Kong Frederik VI.s Kyst, *Greenland* 224 D2
Kong Frederik VIII.s Land, *Greenland* 224 B2
Kong Oscar Fjord, *Greenland* 224 B3
Kongju, *S. Korea* 118 G4
Konglu, *Burma* 122 A3
Kongolo, *Zaïre* 155 D5
Kongor, *Sudan* 143 E4
Königsberg = Kaliningrad, *Russia* 81 C1
Konin, *Poland* 77 C3
Konjic, *Bos.-H.* 72 D5
Konkouré →, *Guinea* 147 B2
Kono, *S. Leone* 147 C4
Konongo, *Ghana* 149 D2
Konosha, *Russia* 90 D4
Konotop, *Ukraine* 81 E4
Konqi He →, *China* 112 C3
Końskie, *Poland* 77 D4
Konstanz, *Germany* 58 G2
Kontagora, *Nigeria* 151 C2
Kontum, *Vietnam* 125 E5
Konya, *Turkey* 94 C3
Konza, *Kenya* 157 D2
Kooloonong, *Australia* 171 F4
Koondrook, *Australia* 171 F4
Koorawatha, *Australia* 171 E7
Koorda, *Australia* 170 A2
Kootenay L., *Canada* 186 J4
Kootjieskolk, *S. Africa* 163 G3
Kopaonik, *Serbia, Yug.* 72 D7
Kópavogur, *Iceland* 38 C2
Koper, *Slovenia* 72 B2
Kopeysk, *Russia* 90 G6
Koppies, *S. Africa* 163 D7
Korab, *Macedonia* 72 E7
Korbu, G., *Malaysia* 126 B1
Korça, *Albania* 70 C3
Korce = Korça, *Albania* 70 C3
Korčula, *Croatia* 72 D5
Korea, North ■, *Asia* 118
Korea, South ■, *Asia* 118
Korea Bay, *Korea* 118 E2
Korea Strait, *Asia* 118 H5
Korhogo, *Ivory C.* 148 B4
Koribundu, *S. Leone* 147 D3
Korim, *Indonesia* 129 C16
Korinthiakós Kólpos, *Greece* 71 D3
Kórinthos, *Greece* 71 D3
Kōriyama, *Japan* 121 F7
Kormakiti, C., *Cyprus* 95 A1
Koro, *Ivory C.* 148 B3
Korogwe, *Tanzania* 158 B3
Koroit, *Australia* 171 H3
Koronadal, *Phil.* 130 K5
Körös →, *Hungary* 74 B4
Korsakov, *Russia* 91 H18
Korshunovo, *Russia* 91 G12
Korsør, *Denmark* 42 C3
Korti, *Sudan* 143 B4
Kortrijk, *Belgium* 51 C1
Koryakskiy Khrebet, *Russia* 91 B17
Koryŏng, *S. Korea* 118 G5
Kos, *Greece* 71 E6
Kościan, *Poland* 77 C2
Kosciusko, Mt., *Australia* 171 G6
Kosha, *Sudan* 143 A4
Köshetau = Kokchetav, *Kazakstan* 90 H7
K'oshih = Kashi, *China* 112 D1
Koshtëbë, *Kyrgyzstan* 93 C6
Košice, *Slovak Rep.* 76 C7
Kosŏng, *N. Korea* 118 E5
Kosovska-Mitrovica, *Serbia, Yug.* 72 D7
Koster, *S. Africa* 163 C6
Kôstî, *Sudan* 143 D4
Kostroma, *Russia* 81 B6
Koszalin, *Poland* 77 A2
Kota, *India* 106 C2
Kota Baharu, *Malaysia* 126 A2
Kota Belud, *Malaysia* 126 A8
Kota Kinabalu, *Malaysia* 126 A8
Kota Tinggi, *Malaysia* 126 D3
Kotaagung, *Indonesia* 128 E4
Kotabaru, *Indonesia* 128 D9
Kotabumi, *Indonesia* 128 E4
Kotamobagu, *Indonesia* 129 C12
Kotawaringin, *Indonesia* 128 D7
Kotchandpur, *Bangla.* 111 C1
Kotelnich, *Russia* 81 A8
Kotelnyy, Ostrov, *Russia* 91 B13
Kotka, *Finland* 43 F3
Kotlas, *Russia* 90 E5
Kotonkoro, *Nigeria* 151 B3
Kotor, *Montenegro, Yug.* 72 E6
Kotri, *Pakistan* 105 F3
Kotuy →, *Russia* 91 D11
Kotzebue, *U.S.A.* 193 A4
Koudougou, *Burkina Faso* 149 B2
Kougaberge, *S. Africa* 163 H5
Kouibli, *Ivory C.* 148 C3
Kouilou →, *Congo* 154 D1
Koula-Moutou, *Gabon* 154 C1
Koulen, *Cambodia* 125 E3
Koulikoro, *Mali* 140 F3
Koumbia, *Guinea* 147 A2
Koumboum, *Guinea* 147 B2
Koumpenntoum, *Senegal* 146 B2
Koumra, *Chad* 142 F1
Koundara, *Guinea* 147 A2
Kounradskiy, *Kazakstan* 90 K7
Kourou, *Fr. Guiana* 214 C6
Kouroussa, *Guinea* 147 B4
Kousseri, *Cameroon* 153 A3
Koutiala, *Mali* 140 F3
Kouto, *Ivory C.* 148 A4
Kouvé, *Togo* 150 D2
Kovel, *Ukraine* 81 D1
Kovrov, *Russia* 81 B6
Kowghān, *Afghan.* 104 D2
Kowŏn, *N. Korea* 118 D4
Koyabuti, *Indonesia* 129 D18
Koytash, *Uzbekistan* 93 D1
Koyukuk →, *U.S.A.* 193 A4
Koza, *Japan* 121 J8
Kozáni, *Greece* 71 B2
Kozhikode = Calicut, *India* 107 F2
Kpabia, *Ghana* 149 B3
Kpalimé, *Togo* 150 D1
Kpandae, *Ghana* 149 B3
Kpessi, *Togo* 150 C2
Kra, Isthmus of = Kra, Kho Khot, *Thailand* 123 J4
Kra, Kho Khot, *Thailand* 123 J4
Kra Buri, *Thailand* 122 J3
Kragujevac, *Serbia, Yug.* 72 C7
Krakatau = Rakata, Pulau, *Indonesia* 128 E4
Kraków, *Poland* 77 E4
Kraljevo, *Serbia, Yug.* 72 C7
Kramatorsk, *Ukraine* 81 F5
Krankskop, *S. Africa* 163 E8
Kraskino, *Russia* 91 K16
Kraśnik, *Poland* 77 D5
Krasnodar, *Russia* 81 H5
Krasnogvardeysk, *Uzbekistan* 93 D1
Krasnoperekopsk, *Ukraine* 81 G4
Krasnoselkupsk, *Russia* 90 E9
Krasnoturinsk, *Russia* 90 F6
Krasnoufimsk, *Russia* 90 F6
Krasnouralsk, *Russia* 90 F6
Krasnovodsk, *Turkmenistan* 90 J3
Krasnoyarsk, *Russia* 91 H10
Krasnyy Luch, *Ukraine* 81 F5
Krasnyy Yar, *Russia* 81 G9
Kratie, *Cambodia* 125 F4
Krau, *Indonesia* 129 D18
Kravanh, Phnum, *Cambodia* 125 F2
Krefeld, *Germany* 58 C1
Kremenchug, *Ukraine* 81 F4
Kremenchugskoye Vdkhr., *Ukraine* 81 F4
Kremenchuk = Kremenchug, *Ukraine* 81 F4
Kremnica, *Slovak Rep.* 76 C6
Kribi, *Cameroon* 153 E1
Krishna →, *India* 107 E3
Krishnanagar, *India* 106 D8
Kristiansand, *Norway* 40 G1
Kristiansund, *Norway* 40 D1
Kríti, *Greece* 71 F4
Krivoy Rog, *Ukraine* 81 F4
Krk, *Croatia* 72 B3
Kronshtadt, *Russia* 90 C3
Kroonstad, *S. Africa* 163 D7
Kropotkin, *Russia* 81 H6
Kropotkin, *Russia* 91 G13
Krosno, *Poland* 77 F5
Krotoszyn, *Poland* 77 D2
Kruger Nat. Park, *S. Africa* 163 A9
Krugersdorp, *S. Africa* 163 C7
Kruisfontein, *S. Africa* 163 H5
Krung Thep = Bangkok, *Thailand* 123 H4
Kruševac, *Serbia, Yug.* 72 D8
Krymskiy Poluostrov, *Ukraine* 81 H4
Kryvyy Rih = Krivoy Rog, *Ukraine* 81 F4
Ksabi, *Morocco* 136 C5
Ksar el Boukhari, *Algeria* 137 A4
Ksar el Kebir, *Morocco* 136 A4
Ksar es Souk = Ar Rachidiya, *Morocco* 136 C5
Ksar Rhilane, *Tunisia* 138 D2
Kuala, *Indonesia* 128 B5
Kuala Belait, *Malaysia* 127 B1
Kuala Berang, *Malaysia* 126 B2
Kuala Dungun, *Malaysia* 126 B3
Kuala Kangsar, *Malaysia* 126 B1
Kuala Kelawang, *Malaysia* 126 C2
Kuala Kerai, *Malaysia* 126 B2
Kuala Kubu Baharu, *Malaysia* 126 C1
Kuala Lipis, *Malaysia* 126 B2
Kuala Lumpur, *Malaysia* 126 C1
Kuala Nerang, *Malaysia* 126 A1
Kuala Pilah, *Malaysia* 126 C2
Kuala Rompin, *Malaysia* 126 C3
Kuala Selangor, *Malaysia* 126 C1
Kuala Terengganu, *Malaysia* 126 B2
Kualajelai, *Indonesia* 128 D7
Kualakapuas, *Indonesia* 128 D8
Kualakurun, *Indonesia* 128 C8
Kualapembuang, *Indonesia* 128 D7
Kualasimpang, *Indonesia* 128 A2
Kuandang, *Indonesia* 129 C11
Kuangchou = Guangzhou, *China* 113 H9
Kuantan, *Malaysia* 126 C3
Kuba, *Azerbaijan* 82 B8
Kuban →, *Russia* 81 H5
Kuchinoerabu-Jima, *Japan* 121 F9
Kucing, *Malaysia* 126 C5
Kudara, *Tajikistan* 93 F5
Kudat, *Malaysia* 126 A8
Kudus, *Indonesia* 128 E7
Kudymkar, *Russia* 90 F5
Kueiyang = Guiyang, *China* 113 H7
Kufstein, *Austria* 61 B3
Kūh-e Taftān, *Iran* 103 D6
Kūhestān, *Afghan.* 104 C1
Kuinre, *Neths.* 50 B4
Kuito, *Angola* 160 C3
Kujang, *N. Korea* 118 D3
Kuji, *Japan* 121 D8
Kukawa, *Nigeria* 151 A7
Kukerin, *Australia* 170 C3
Kukup, *Malaysia* 126 D3
Kulai, *Malaysia* 126 D3
Kulal, Mt., *Kenya* 157 B2
Kulanak, *Kyrgyzstan* 93 C7
Kuldja = Yining, *China* 112 C2
Kuli, *Russia* 82 B7
Kulim, *Malaysia* 126 B1
Kulin, *Australia* 170 B3
Kulja, *Australia* 170 A2
Kulunda, *Russia* 90 H8
Kulwin, *Australia* 171 F4
Kulyab, *Tajikistan* 93 F3
Kum Tekei, *Kazakstan* 90 L7
Kumaganum, *Nigeria* 151 A6
Kumagaya, *Japan* 120 A8
Kumai, *Indonesia* 128 D7
Kumamba, Kepulauan, *Indonesia* 129 D17
Kumamoto, *Japan* 120 D1
Kumanovo, *Macedonia* 72 E8
Kumarkhali, *Bangla.* 111 C1
Kumasi, *Ghana* 149 D2
Kumayri, *Armenia* 82 C5
Kumba, *Cameroon* 153 D1
Kumbakonam, *India* 107 F3
Kumbarilla, *Australia* 171 A8
Kumbukkan →, *Sri Lanka* 110 D3
Kŭmchŏn, *N. Korea* 118 E4
Kŭmhwa, *S. Korea* 118 E4
Kumi, *Uganda* 156 C3
Kumo, *Nigeria* 151 C6
Kumon Bum, *Burma* 122 B3
Kumtorkala, *Russia* 82 A7
Kunama, *Australia* 171 F6
Kunashir, Ostrov, *Russia* 91 H18
Kunch, *India* 106 C4
Kungala, *Australia* 171 C9
Kungey Alatau, Khrebet, *Kyrgyzstan* 93 A8
Kungrad, *Uzbekistan* 90 J4
Kungur, *Russia* 90 F6
Kunlong, *Burma* 122 C3
Kunlun Shan, *Asia* 84 E12
Kunming, *China* 112 H6
Kunsan, *S. Korea* 118 G4
Kunshan, *China* 116 G5
Kunya-Urgench, *Turkmenistan* 90 J4
Kuopio, *Finland* 43 E3
Kupa →, *Croatia* 72 B4
Kupang, *Indonesia* 129 F12
Kuqa, *China* 112 C2
Kura →, *Azerbaijan* 82 D9
Kurashiki, *Japan* 120 C4
Kurayoshi, *Japan* 120 B4
Kurday, *Kazakstan* 93 A7
Kure, *Japan* 120 C3
Kurgaldzhino, *Kazakstan* 90 H6
Kurgan, *Russia* 90 G6
Kurgan-Tyube, *Tajikistan* 93 F2
Kuria Maria Is. = Khūrīyā Mūrīyā, Jazā 'ir, *Oman* 101 D2
Kuril Is. = Kurilskiye Ostrova, *Russia* 91 G18
Kuril Trench, *Pac. Oc.* 176 B4
Kurilsk, *Russia* 91 G18
Kurilskiye Ostrova, *Russia* 91 G18
Kurkur, *Egypt* 139 E5
Kurmuk, *Sudan* 143 D5
Kurnool, *India* 107 E3
Kurow, *N.Z.* 175 H3
Kurri Kurri, *Australia* 171 D8
Kursk, *Russia* 81 E5
Kuršumlija, *Serbia, Yug.* 72 D8
Kuruktag, *China* 112 D4
Kuruman, *S. Africa* 163 D4
Kuruman →, *S. Africa* 163 D3
Kurume, *Japan* 120 D1
Kurunegala, *Sri Lanka* 110 C2
Kurupukari, *Guyana* 214 C2
Kurya, *Russia* 91 G12
Kushiro, *Japan* 121 B9
Kushiro →, *Japan* 121 B9
Kushka, *Turkmenistan* 90 L4
Kushrabat, *Uzbekistan* 93 D1
Kushtia, *Bangla.* 111 C1
Kuskokwim →, *U.S.A.* 193 B3
Kuskokwim B., *U.S.A.* 193 B3
Kustanay, *Kazakstan* 90 G6
Kütahya, *Turkey* 94 B2
Kutaisi, *Georgia* 82 B4
Kutaraja = Banda Aceh, *Indonesia* 128 A1
Kutch, Gulf of = Kachchh, Gulf of, *India* 107 D1
Kutch, Rann of = Kachchh, Rann of, *India* 107 C1
Kutkashen, *Azerbaijan* 82 C8
Kutno, *Poland* 77 C3
Kutu, *Zaïre* 155 D2
Kutum, *Sudan* 143 C2
Kuujjuaq, *Canada* 187 G12
Kuŭp-tong, *N. Korea* 118 C3
Kuvasay, *Uzbekistan* 93 D5
Kuwait = Al Kuwayt, *Kuwait* 100 A1
Kuwait ■, *Asia* 100
Kuwana, *Japan* 120 B6
Kuybyshev = Samara, *Russia* 81 D9
Kuybyshev, *Russia* 90 H8
Kuybyshevo, *Uzbekistan* 93 D4
Kuybyshevskiy, *Tajikistan* 93 F2
Kuybyshevskoye Vdkhr., *Russia* 81 C8
Kuylyuk, *Uzbekistan* 93 C3
Küysanjaq, *Iraq* 102 B4
Kuyumba, *Russia* 91 G10
Kuzey Anadolu Dağları, *Turkey* 94 A4
Kuznetsk, *Russia* 81 D8
Kvareli, *Georgia* 82 B6
Kvarner, *Croatia* 72 B3
Kvarnerič, *Croatia* 72 C3
Kwabhaca, *S. Africa* 163 F7
Kwakoegron, *Surinam* 214 C4
Kwale, *Kenya* 157 F4
Kwale, *Nigeria* 151 F3
Kwale □, *Kenya* 157 F4
KwaMashu, *S. Africa* 163 F8
Kwamouth, *Zaïre* 155 D2
Kwangdaeri, *N. Korea* 118 C4
Kwangju, *S. Korea* 118 H4
Kwangsi-Chuang = Guangxi Zhuangzu Zizhiqu □, *China* 113 H8
Kwangtung = Guangdong □, *China* 113 H9
Kwara □, *Nigeria* 151 D2
Kwatisore, *Indonesia* 129 D16
KwaZulu Natal □, *S. Africa* 163 E8
Kweichow = Guizhou □, *China* 113 G7
Kwekwe, *Zimbabwe* 161 C3
Kwinana New Town, *Australia* 170 B1
Kwoka, *Indonesia* 129 C15
Kyabé, *Chad* 142 F2
Kyabram, *Australia* 171 G5
Kyaikto, *Burma* 122 F3
Kyakhta, *Russia* 91 J12
Kyangin, *Burma* 122 E2
Kyaukse, *Burma* 122 D2
Kyauktaw, *Burma* 122 D1
Kycen, *Russia* 91 J11
Kyenjojo, *Uganda* 156 C1
Kyle Dam, *Zimbabwe* 161 D4
Kyneton, *Australia* 171 G4
Kyō-ga-Saki, *Japan* 120 B5
Kyoga, L., *Uganda* 156 B2
Kyogle, *Australia* 171 B9
Kyongju, *S. Korea* 118 G6
Kyŏngsŏng, *N. Korea* 118 B5
Kyōto, *Japan* 120 B5
Kyōto □, *Japan* 120 B5
Kyrenia, *Cyprus* 95 A2
Kyrgyzstan ■, *Asia* 93 B7
Kystatyam, *Russia* 91 E13
Kytal ktakh, *Russia* 91 E13
Kyulyunken, *Russia* 91 E14
Kyunhla, *Burma* 122 C2
Kyurdamir, *Azerbaijan* 82 C8
Kyūshū, *Japan* 120 D1
Kyustendil, *Bulgaria* 73 C1
Kyusyur, *Russia* 91 D13
Kywong, *Australia* 171 F6
Kyyiv = Kiyev, *Ukraine* 81 E3
Kyzyl, *Russia* 91 J10
Kyzyl-Kiya, *Kyrgyzstan* 93 D5
Kyzylkum, Peski, *Uzbekistan* 90 K5
Kyzylsu →, *Kyrgyzstan* 93 E4
Kzyl-Orda, *Kazakstan* 90 K5

L

La Asunción, *Venezuela* 211 A4
La Carlota, *Argentina* 221 B3
La Carlota, *Phil.* 130 H4
La Carolina, *Spain* 63 F5
La Ceiba, *Honduras* 196 C3
La Chaux de Fonds, *Switz.* 60 B1

La Concepción = Ri-Aba, *Eq. Guin.* 153 A1
La Coruña, *Spain* 63 A2
La Crosse, *U.S.A.* 191 D11
La Cruz, *Costa Rica* 197 C2
La Digue, *Seychelles* 166 B3
La Dorada, *Colombia* 210 C1
La Esperanza, *Cuba* 198 B1
La Esperanza, *Honduras* 196 C2
La Estrada, *Spain* 63 B2
La Fé, *Cuba* 198 B1
La Grande, *U.S.A.* 190 B4
La Grange, *U.S.A.* 191 H14
La Guaira, *Venezuela* 211 A3
La Güera, *Mauritania* 140 C1
La Habana, *Cuba* 198 A2
La Isabela, *Dom. Rep.* 200 A3
La Junta, *U.S.A.* 190 F7
La Laguna, *Canary Is.* 223 D2
La Libertad, *Guatemala* 196 B1
La Línea de la Concepción, *Spain* 63 H4
La Louvière, *Belgium* 51 D3
La Mancha, *Spain* 63 E6
La Martre, L., *Canada* 186 E6
La Oliva, *Canary Is.* 223 D3
La Orotava, *Canary Is.* 223 D2
La Palma, *Canary Is.* 223 C1
La Palma, *Panama* 197 E6
La Palma, *Spain* 63 G3
La Paragua, *Venezuela* 211 B4
La Paz, *Argentina* 221 A5
La Paz, *Bolivia* 218 B1
La Paz, *Honduras* 196 C3
La Paz, *Mexico* 194 C2
La Paz, *Phil.* 130 D2
La Paz Centro, *Nic.* 197 C1
La Pedrera, *Colombia* 210 E3
La Perouse Str., *Asia* 84 D18
La Plata, *Argentina* 221 C5
La Possession, *Réunion* 166 A1
La Quiaca, *Argentina* 220 B4
La Rioja, *Argentina* 220 D4
La Rioja □, *Spain* 63 B5
La Robla, *Spain* 63 B5
La Rochelle, *France* 55 E3
La Roda, *Spain* 63 E6
La Romana, *Dom. Rep.* 200 B3
La Sagra, *Spain* 63 F6
La Spézia, *Italy* 67 C3
La Tuque, *Canada* 187 K12
La Unión, *El Salv.* 196 D2
La Urbana, *Venezuela* 211 B3
La Vega, *Dom. Rep.* 200 A3
Labason, *Phil.* 130 J3
Labe = Elbe →, *Europe* 58 A2
Labé, *Guinea* 147 A3
Labi, *Brunei* 127 C1
Labis, *Malaysia* 126 D2
Labo, *Phil.* 130 E3
Laboulaye, *Argentina* 221 C3
Labrador, *Canada* 180 D13
Labrador City, *Canada* 187 H13
Labuan, Pulau, *Malaysia* 126 B7
Labuha, *Indonesia* 129 C13
Labuhanbajo, *Indonesia* 129 F10
Labuk, Teluk, *Malaysia* 126 A8
Labytnangi, *Russia* 90 E8
Lac La Biche, *Canada* 186 H6
Laccadive Is., *Ind. Oc.* 84 G11
Lacepede B., *Australia* 171 G2
Lachine, *Canada* 185 B5
Lachlan →, *Australia* 171 E4
Lachute, *Canada* 185 B5
Lackawanna, *U.S.A.* 189 A2
Lacombe, *Canada* 186 H5
Ladismith, *S. Africa* 163 H3
Lādīz, *Iran* 103 D6
Ladoga, L. = Ladozhskoye Ozero, *Russia* 90 C4
Ladozhskoye Ozero, *Russia* 90 C4
Lady Grey, *S. Africa* 163 F6
Ladybrand, *S. Africa* 163 E7
Ladysmith, *Canada* 186 H3
Ladysmith, *S. Africa* 163 E8
Lae, *Papua N. G.* 173 B2
Læsø, *Denmark* 42 A3
Lafayette, *Ind., U.S.A.* 191 E13
Lafayette, *La., U.S.A.* 191 J11
Lafia, *Nigeria* 151 D4
Lagarfljót →, *Iceland* 38 B5
Laghmān □, *Afghan.* 104 C6
Laghouat, *Algeria* 137 B4
Lagodekhi, *Georgia* 82 B7
Lagonoy Gulf, *Phil.* 130 F4
Lagos, *Nigeria* 151 F1
Lagos, *Portugal* 63 G1
Lagunas, *Peru* 213 B3
Lahad Datu, *Malaysia* 126 B8
Lahaina, *U.S.A.* 192 A2
Lahat, *Indonesia* 128 D4
Lahewa, *Indonesia* 128 B1
Lahiang Lahiang, *Phil.* 130 L3
Lahn →, *Germany* 58 D2
Lahore, *Pakistan* 105 C6
Lahti, *Finland* 43 F2
Lahtis = Lahti, *Finland* 43 F2
Laï, *Chad* 142 F1
Lai Chau, *Vietnam* 125 A2
Laibin, *China* 113 H8
Laidley, *Australia* 171 A9
Laikipia □, *Kenya* 157 C2
Laila = Laylá, *Si. Arabia* 99 D5
Laingsburg, *S. Africa* 163 H3
Laiyang, *China* 116 D5
Laizhou Wan, *China* 116 D4
Lajere, *Nigeria* 151 B6
Lake Cargelligo, *Australia* 171 E6
Lake Charles, *U.S.A.* 191 J11
Lake City, *U.S.A.* 191 H15
Lake Grace, *Australia* 170 C3
Lake Harbour, *Canada* 187 F12
Lake King, *Australia* 170 C3
Lakeland, *U.S.A.* 191 J15
Lakes Entrance, *Australia* 171 H6
Lakewood, *U.S.A.* 191 D14
Laki, *Iceland* 38 C4
Lakonikós Kólpos, *Greece* 71 F3
Lakor, *Indonesia* 129 F13
Lakota, *Ivory C.* 148 D4
Laksham, *Bangla.* 111 C3
Lakshmipur, *Bangla.* 111 D2
Lalapanzi, *Zimbabwe* 161 C4
Lalín, *Spain* 63 B2
Lama Kara, *Togo* 150 C2
Lamar, *U.S.A.* 190 F8
Lamas, *Peru* 213 C2
Lambaréné, *Gabon* 154 C1
Lamberhurst, *U.K.* 45 E5
Lamberts Bay, *S. Africa* 163 G2
Lambeth, *U.K.* 45 C3
Lambi Kyun, *Burma* 122 J3
Lame, *Nigeria* 151 C5
Lamego, *Portugal* 63 C2
Lameroo, *Australia* 171 F3
Lamía, *Greece* 71 C2
Lamitan, *Phil.* 130 K3
Lamon Bay, *Phil.* 130 E3
Lampa, *Peru* 213 E4
Lampang, *Thailand* 123 F4
Lampung □, *Indonesia* 128 E4
Lamu, *Kenya* 157 E4
Lamu □, *Kenya* 157 E4
Lan Xian, *China* 116 D1
Lan Yu, *Taiwan* 117 C3
Lanai I., *U.S.A.* 192 A2
Lanao, L., *Phil.* 130 K4
Lancaster, *U.K.* 46 G6
Lancaster, *U.S.A.* 189 C3
Lancaster Sd., *Canada* 186 C9
Lanchow = Lanzhou, *China* 113 E7
Lanciano, *Italy* 67 E6
Landay, *Afghan.* 104 G2
Landeck, *Austria* 61 B2
Landen, *Belgium* 51 C4
Landes, *France* 55 G3
Landes □, *France* 55 G3
Landi Kotal, *Pakistan* 105 B5
Landquart, *Switz.* 60 B5
Land's End, *U.K.* 46 M4
Landshut, *Germany* 58 F5
Langatabbetje, *Surinam* 214 C5
Langeberg, *S. Africa* 163 H3
Langeberge, *S. Africa* 163 E4
Langjökull, *Iceland* 38 C3
Langklip, *S. Africa* 163 E3
Langkon, *Malaysia* 126 A8
Langnau, *Switz.* 60 B3
Langreo, *Spain* 63 A3
Langres, *France* 55 C7
Langres, Plateau de, *France* 55 C7
Langsa, *Indonesia* 128 A2
Langson, *Vietnam* 125 A4
Languedoc, *France* 55 G7
Langxiangzhen, *China* 116 C3
Langzhong, *China* 113 F7
Lankao, *China* 116 E3
Lansdowne, *Australia* 171 D9
Lansing, *U.S.A.* 191 D13
Lanus, *Argentina* 221 C5
Lanuza, *Phil.* 130 J6
Lanxi, *China* 116 H4
Lanzarote, *Canary Is.* 223 C3
Lanzhou, *China* 113 E7
Lao Cai, *Vietnam* 125 A2
Laoag, *Phil.* 130 B2
Laoang, *Phil.* 130 F5
Laoha He →, *China* 116 A5
Laon, *France* 55 B6
Laos ■, *Asia* 125
Lapithos, *Cyprus* 95 A2
Lapland = Lappland, *Europe* 43 B2
Lappland, *Europe* 43 B2
Laptev Sea, *Russia* 91 C12
L'Áquila, *Italy* 67 E5
Lār, *Iran* 103 D4
Larabanga, *Ghana* 149 B2
Larache, *Morocco* 136 A4
Laramie, *U.S.A.* 190 D7
Laramie Mts., *U.S.A.* 190 D7
Larantuka, *Indonesia* 129 F11
Larap, *Phil.* 130 E3
Larat, *Indonesia* 129 F15
Laredo, *U.S.A.* 190 K9
Laren, *Neths.* 50 D3
Lariang, *Indonesia* 129 C10
Lárisa, *Greece* 71 C2
Larnaca, *Cyprus* 95 B2
Larnaca Bay, *Cyprus* 95 B2
Larne, *U.K.* 46 F4
Larvik, *Norway* 40 F2
Laryak, *Russia* 90 F8
Las Cruces, *U.S.A.* 190 H6
Las Palmas, *Canary Is.* 223 D2
Las Piedras, *Uruguay* 219 D2
Las Pipinas, *Argentina* 221 C6
Las Rosas, *Argentina* 221 B3
Las Tablas, *Panama* 197 E5
Las Varillas, *Argentina* 221 A3
Las Vegas, *N. Mex., U.S.A.* 190 G7
Las Vegas, *Nev., U.S.A.* 190 F4
Lascano, *Uruguay* 219 C3
Lashio, *Burma* 122 C3
Lashkar Gāh, *Afghan.* 104 F2
Lassen Pk., *U.S.A.* 190 D2
Lastoursville, *Gabon* 154 C1
Lastovo, *Croatia* 72 D4
Latacunga, *Ecuador* 212 C1
Latakia = Al Lādhiqīyah, *Syria* 97 B2
Latina, *Italy* 67 F5
Latium = Lazio □, *Italy* 67 E5
Latrobe, *Australia* 172 B2
Latvia ■, *Europe* 81 B2
Lau Is., *Fiji* 174 A2
Lauchhammer, *Germany* 58 C5
Lauenburg, *Germany* 58 B3
Laugarbakki, *Iceland* 38 B3
Launceston, *Australia* 172 B2
Laurel, *U.S.A.* 191 H12
Laurentian Plateau, *Canada* 180 D12
Laurium, *U.S.A.* 191 B12
Lausanne, *Switz.* 60 C1
Laut, *Indonesia* 128 A5
Laut Ketil, Kepulauan, *Indonesia* 128 E9
Laval, *France* 55 C3
Lavongai, *Papua N. G.* 173 A3
Lavras, *Brazil* 215 B3
Lavrentiya, *Russia* 91 A17
Lávrion, *Greece* 71 E4
Lawas, *Malaysia* 126 B7
Lawele, *Indonesia* 129 E11
Lawra, *Ghana* 149 A1
Lawrence, *Kans., U.S.A.* 191 F10
Lawrence, *Mass., U.S.A.* 189 A6
Lawton, *U.S.A.* 190 G9
Lawu, *Indonesia* 128 F7
Laylá, *Si. Arabia* 99 D5
Laysan I., *Pac. Oc.* 176 C7
Lazio □, *Italy* 67 E5
Le Creusot, *France* 55 D7
Le Havre, *France* 55 B4
Le Locle, *Switz.* 60 B1
Le Mans, *France* 55 C4
Le Marinel, *Zaïre* 155 F4
Le Port, *Réunion* 166 A1
Le Puy, *France* 55 F7
Le Tampon, *Réunion* 166 C2
Le Tréport, *France* 55 A5
Le Verdon, *France* 55 E3
Lea →, *U.K.* 45 C4
Leadville, *U.S.A.* 190 E7
Leamington, *U.K.* 46 J7
Leamington Spa = Leamington, *U.K.* 46 J7
Leatherhead, *U.K.* 45 D3
Leavenworth, *U.S.A.* 191 E10
Lebak, *Phil.* 130 K4
Lebanon, *Mo., U.S.A.* 191 F11
Lebanon, *Pa., U.S.A.* 189 C3
Lebanon, *Tenn., U.S.A.* 191 F13
Lebanon ■, *Asia* 95
Lebbeke, *Belgium* 51 B3
Lebomboberge, *S. Africa* 163 B9
Lebrija, *Spain* 63 G3
Lecce, *Italy* 67 F9
Lecco, *Italy* 67 A3
Łęczyca, *Poland* 77 C3
Leduc, *Canada* 186 H5
Lee →, *Ireland* 46 K1
Leech L., *U.S.A.* 191 B10
Leeds, *U.K.* 46 G7
Leeton, *Australia* 171 E6
Leeu Gamka, *S. Africa* 163 H4
Leeuwarden, *Neths.* 50 A4
Leeuwin, C., *Australia* 170 D1
Leeward Is., *Atl. Oc.* 202
Lefka, *Cyprus* 95 B1
Lefkoniko, *Cyprus* 95 B3
Leganés, *Spain* 63 D5
Legazpi, *Phil.* 130 F4
Leghorn = Livorno, *Italy* 67 C3
Legnica, *Poland* 77 D1
Leh, *India* 107 A3
Leicester, *U.K.* 46 J7
Leiden, *Neths.* 50 D2
Leie →, *Belgium* 51 B2
Leighton Buzzard, *U.K.* 45 A2
Leine →, *Germany* 58 B3
Leipzig, *Germany* 58 C5
Leiria, *Portugal* 63 D1
Leith, *U.K.* 46 D6
Leith Hill, *U.K.* 45 E2
Leitrim, *Ireland* 46 G2
Leiyang, *China* 116 J2
Leizhou Bandao, *China* 113 J8
Lek →, *Neths.* 50 D2
Leksula, *Indonesia* 129 D13
Lelystad, *Neths.* 50 C4
Lema, *Nigeria* 151 A2
Léman, Lac, *Switz.* 60 C1
Lemery, *Phil.* 130 E2
Lemmer, *Neths.* 50 B4
Lemvig, *Denmark* 42 B1
Lena →, *Russia* 91 D13
Lenger, *Kazakstan* 93 B3
Lenggong, *Malaysia* 126 B1
Lenham, *U.K.* 45 D6
Lenina, Pik, *Kyrgyzstan* 93 E6
Leninabad = Khudzhand, *Tajikistan* 93 D3
Leninakan = Kumayri, *Armenia* 82 C5
Leningrad = Sankt-Peterburg, *Russia* 81 A3
Leninogorsk = Ridder, *Kazakstan* 90 J8
Leninpol, *Kyrgyzstan* 93 B5
Leninsk, *Russia* 81 F7
Leninsk, *Uzbekistan* 93 D5
Leninsk-Kuznetskiy, *Russia* 90 H9
Leninskoye, *Kazakstan* 93 B3
Leninskoye, *Russia* 91 H16
Lenk, *Switz.* 60 C2
Lenkoran, *Azerbaijan* 82 D9
Lenmalu, *Indonesia* 129 C14
Lenne →, *Germany* 59 A3
Lens, *France* 55 A6
Lensk, *Russia* 91 G13
Lentini, *Italy* 67 K7
Leoben, *Austria* 61 B5
Leominster, *U.S.A.* 189 A6
León, *Mexico* 194 D4
León, *Nic.* 197 B1
León, *Spain* 63 B4
León □, *Spain* 63 B3
León, Montañas de, *Spain* 63 B3
Leongatha, *Australia* 171 H5
Léopold II, Lac = Mai-Ndombe, L., *Zaïre* 155 C2
Leopoldina, *Brazil* 215 B5
Leopoldsburg, *Belgium* 51 B4
Léopoldville = Kinshasa, *Zaïre* 155 D1
Lepel, *Belarus* 81 C3
Lepikha, *Russia* 91 E13
Leping, *China* 116 H3
Léré, *Chad* 142 F1
Lere, *Nigeria* 151 C5
Leribe, *Lesotho* 164 A2
Lérida, *Spain* 63 C8
Lerwick, *U.K.* 46 B9
Les Cayes, *Haiti* 200 B1
Les Minquiers, *Chan. Is.* 44 B2
Les Sables-d'Olonne, *France* 55 E3
Lesbos = Lésvos, *Greece* 71 C5
Leskovac, *Serbia, Yug.* 72 D8
Lesotho ■, *Africa* 164
Lesozavodsk, *Russia* 91 J16
Lesse →, *Belgium* 51 D4
Lesser Slave L., *Canada* 186 G5
Lesser Sunda Is., *Indonesia* 129 F10
Lessines, *Belgium* 51 C2
Lésvos, *Greece* 71 C5
Leszno, *Poland* 77 C2
Letchworth, *U.K.* 45 A3
Lethbridge, *Canada* 186 J5
Lethem, *Guyana* 214 D1
Leti, Kepulauan, *Indonesia* 129 F13
Leti Is. = Leti, Kepulauan, *Indonesia* 129 F13
Leticia, *Colombia* 210 F3
Leting, *China* 116 C4
Letjiesbos, *S. Africa* 163 G4
Letpadan, *Burma* 122 F2
Letpan, *Burma* 122 E1
Letsôk-aw Kyun, *Burma* 122 J3
Letterkenny, *Ireland* 46 F2
Leuk, *Switz.* 60 D2
Leuser, *Indonesia* 128 A1
Leuven, *Belgium* 51 C4
Leuze, *Belgium* 51 C2
Levanger, *Norway* 40 D2
Levelland, *U.S.A.* 190 G8
Leverkusen, *Germany* 58 D1
Levin, *N.Z.* 175 E5
Lévis, *Canada* 187 K13
Levkás, *Greece* 71 D1
Levkôsia = Nicosia, *Cyprus* 95 B2
Lewes, *U.K.* 46 L8
Lewis, *U.K.* 46 A3
Lewis Range, *U.S.A.* 190 A5
Lewisham, *U.K.* 45 C3
Lewisporte, *Canada* 187 H15
Lewistown, *Mont., U.S.A.* 190 B6
Lewistown, *Pa., U.S.A.* 189 C3
Lexington, *U.S.A.* 191 F14
Leyte, *Phil.* 130 G5
Leyte Gulf, *Phil.* 130 G5
Lhasa, *China* 112 G4
Lhazê, *China* 112 G3
Lhokkruet, *Indonesia* 128 A1
Lhokseumawe, *Indonesia* 128 A1
Li Shui →, *China* 116 H1
Li Xian, *China* 116 H1
Lianga, *Phil.* 130 J6
Lianhua, *China* 116 J2
Lianyungang, *China* 116 E4
Liao He →, *China* 116 B5
Liaocheng, *China* 116 D3
Liaodong Bandao, *China* 116 B6
Liaodong Wan, *China* 116 C5
Liaoning □, *China* 116 B5
Liaoyang, *China* 116 B6
Liaoyuan, *China* 116 A6
Liaozhong, *China* 116 B6
Liard →, *Canada* 186 E5
Libau = Liepāja, *Latvia* 81 B1
Libenge, *Zaïre* 155 A2
Liberal, *U.S.A.* 190 F8
Liberec, *Czech.* 76 A3
Liberia, *Costa Rica* 197 D2
Liberia ■, *W. Afr.* 148
Lībīya, Sahrâ', *Africa* 138 C5
Libobo, Tanjung, *Indonesia* 129 C14
Libode, *S. Africa* 163 G7
Libonda, *Zambia* 161 C2
Libourne, *France* 55 F4
Libreville, *Gabon* 154 B1
Libya ■, *N. Afr.* 138
Libyan Desert = Lîbîya, Sahrâ', *Africa* 138 C5
Libyan Plateau = Ed-Déffa, *Egypt* 139 A1
Licata, *Italy* 67 K6
Lichtenburg, *S. Africa* 163 C6
Liechtenstein ■, *Europe* 60 B5
Liège, *Belgium* 51 C5
Liège □, *Belgium* 51 C5
Liegnitz = Legnica, *Poland* 77 D1
Lienyünchiangshih = Lianyungang, *China* 116 E4
Lienz, *Austria* 61 C3
Liepāja, *Latvia* 81 B1
Lier, *Belgium* 51 B3
Liffey →, *Ireland* 46 H3
Ligao, *Phil.* 130 F4
Lightning Ridge, *Australia* 171 B6
Liguria □, *Italy* 67 B2
Ligurian Sea, *Italy* 67 D2
Lihue, *U.S.A.* 192 A1
Lijiang, *China* 112 G6
Likasi, *Zaïre* 155 F5
Likati, *Zaïre* 155 A4
Likoma I., *Malawi* 158 B2
Liling, *China* 116 J2
Lille, *France* 55 A6
Lille Bælt, *Denmark* 42 C2
Lillehammer, *Norway* 40 F2
Lilongwe, *Malawi* 158 D2
Lima, *Indonesia* 129 D13
Lima, *Peru* 213 D2
Lima, *U.S.A.* 191 E14
Limassol, *Cyprus* 95 C1
Limay →, *Argentina* 220 G3
Limbe, *Cameroon* 153 D1
Limbri, *Australia* 171 C8
Limburg □, *Belgium* 51 B5
Limburg □, *Neths.* 50 F5
Limeira, *Brazil* 215 B2
Limerick, *Ireland* 46 J1
Limfjorden, *Denmark* 42 B2
Límnos, *Greece* 71 B5
Limoges, *France* 55 E5
Limón, *Costa Rica* 197 D3
Limousin, *France* 55 F5
Limpopo →, *Africa* 132 J7
Limpsfield, *U.K.* 45 D4
Limuru, *Kenya* 157 D2
Linapacan I., *Phil.* 130 G2
Linapacan Str., *Phil.* 130 G2
Linares, *Mexico* 194 C5
Linares, *Spain* 63 F5
Lincheng, *China* 116 D2
Linchuan, *China* 116 J3
Lincoln, *Argentina* 221 C3
Lincoln, *U.K.* 46 H8
Lincoln, *U.S.A.* 191 E10
Linden, *Guyana* 214 B2
Lindesnes, *Norway* 34 D8
Lindi, *Tanzania* 158 D3
Lindsay, *Canada* 185 C2
Linfen, *China* 116 D1
Ling Xian, *China* 116 D3
Lingayen, *Phil.* 130 B2
Lingayen G., *Phil.* 130 D2
Lingen, *Germany* 58 B2
Lingfield, *U.K.* 45 E4
Lingga, *Indonesia* 128 C4
Lingga, Kepulauan, *Indonesia* 128 C4
Lingga Arch. = Lingga, Kepulauan, *Indonesia* 128 C4
Lingling, *China* 116 J1
Lingshi, *China* 116 D1
Linguére, *Senegal* 146 B1
Lingyuan, *China* 116 B4
Linh Cam, *Vietnam* 125 C3
Linköping, *Sweden* 40 G3
Linqing, *China* 116 D3
Lins, *Brazil* 215 B1
Linslade, *U.K.* 45 A1
Linville, *Australia* 171 A9
Linxi, *China* 116 A4
Linxia, *China* 113 E7
Linyi, *China* 116 E4
Linz, *Austria* 61 A4
Lion, G. du, *France* 55 H7
Lions, G. of = Lion, G. du, *France* 55 H7
Lion's Den, *Zimbabwe* 161 B4
Lipa, *Phil.* 130 E2
Lipari, Is. = Eólie, Is., *Italy* 67 H6
Lipari, Is., *Italy* 67 H7
Lipetsk, *Russia* 81 D6
Lippe →, *Germany* 58 C1
Liptrap C., *Australia* 171 H5
Lira, *Uganda* 156 B2
Liria, *Spain* 63 E7
Lisala, *Zaïre* 155 B3
Lisboa, *Portugal* 63 E1
Lisbon = Lisboa, *Portugal* 63 E1
Lisburn, *U.K.* 46 F4
Lisburne, C., *U.S.A.* 193 A4
Lishi, *China* 116 D1
Lishui, *China* 116 H5
Lisianski I., *Pac. Oc.* 176 C6
Lisichansk, *Ukraine* 81 F5
Lisieux, *France* 55 B4
Liski, *Russia* 81 E6
Lismore, *Australia* 171 B9
Liss, *U.K.* 45 E1
Lisse, *Neths.* 50 D2
Liston, *Australia* 171 B9
Listowel, *Ireland* 46 J1
Litang, *Malaysia* 126 B8
Lithgow, *Australia* 171 E7
Líthinon, Ákra, *Greece* 71 F4

Lithuania ■, Europe 81 B1
Litoměřice, Czech. 76 A3
Little Falls, U.S.A. 189 A4
Little Karoo, S. Africa 163 H3
Little Laut Is. = Laut Ketil, Kepulauan, Indonesia 128 E9
Little Missouri →, U.S.A. 190 B8
Little Rock, U.S.A. 191 G11
Liukang Tenggaja, Indonesia 129 E10
Liuwa Plain, Zambia 161 C2
Liuyang, China 116 H2
Liuzhou, China 113 H8
Liverpool, Australia 171 E8
Liverpool, Canada 187 K14
Liverpool, U.K. 46 H6
Liverpool Plains, Australia 171 C8
Liverpool Ra., Australia 171 D8
Livingston, Guatemala 196 B2
Livingston, U.S.A. 190 C6
Livingstone, Zambia 161 D3
Livingstonia, Malawi 158 A2
Livny, Russia 81 D5
Livorno, Italy 67 C3
Liwale, Tanzania 158 D3
Lizard Pt., U.K. 46 M4
Ljubljana, Slovenia 72 A3
Ljusnan →, Sweden 40 E2
Llandrindod Wells, U.K. 46 J6
Llandudno, U.K. 46 H5
Llanelli, U.K. 46 K5
Llanes, Spain 63 A4
Llano Estacado, U.S.A. 180 F9
Llanos, S. Amer. 206 B2
Lleida = Lérida, Spain 63 C8
Llobregat →, Spain 63 C9
Lloret, Spain 63 B9
Lluchmayor, Spain 65 B4
Lobatse, Botswana 162 D5
Lobito, Angola 160 C2
Lobos, Argentina 221 C5
Lobos, I. de, Canary Is. 223 D3
Lobos Is., Peru 206 C1
Loc Binh, Vietnam 125 A4
Loc Ninh, Vietnam 125 F4
Locarno, Switz. 60 D4
Lochem, Neths. 50 D5
Loches, France 55 D5
Lock Haven, U.S.A. 189 B3
Lockhart, L., Australia 170 C3
Lockport, U.S.A. 189 A2
Lod, Israel 96 D2
Lodhran, Pakistan 105 D5
Lodja, Zaïre 155 D4
Lodwar, Kenya 157 B2
Łódź, Poland 77 D3
Loeriesfontein, S. Africa 163 F2
Lofoten, Norway 40 B3
Logan, U.S.A. 190 D5
Logan, Mt., Canada 186 D3
Logone →, Chad 142 E1
Logroño, Spain 63 B6
Lohardaga, India 106 D6
Loi kaw, Burma 122 E3
Loir →, France 55 D4
Loir-et-Cher □, France 55 D5
Loire □, France 55 E7
Loire →, France 55 D2
Loire-Atlantique □, France 55 D3
Loiret □, France 55 C5
Loja, Ecuador 212 E1
Loja, Spain 63 G5
Loja □, Ecuador 212 E1
Loji, Indonesia 129 C13
Lokandu, Zaïre 155 C5
Lokeren, Belgium 51 B2
Lokichokio, Kenya 157 A1
Lokitaung, Kenya 157 A2
Lokka, Finland 43 B3
Lokoja, Nigeria 151 E3
Lokolama, Zaïre 155 C3
Lola, Guinea 147 D5
Loliondo, Tanzania 158 A2
Lolland, Denmark 42 D3
Lom, Bulgaria 73 A2
Lomami →, Zaïre 155 B4
Lomas de Zamóra, Argentina 221 C5
Lombardia □, Italy 67 A2
Lombardy = Lombardia □, Italy 67 A2
Lomblen, Indonesia 129 F12
Lombok, Indonesia 128 F9
Lomé, Togo 150 E2
Lomela, Zaïre 155 C4
Lomela →, Zaïre 155 C2
Lomié, Cameroon 153 E2
Lommel, Belgium 51 B5
Lomond, L., U.K. 46 D5
Lompobatang, Indonesia 129 E10
Łomza, Poland 77 B5
Londiani, Kenya 157 D2
London, U.K. 45 C3
London Colney, U.K. 45 B3
Londonderry, U.K. 46 E3
Londrina, Brazil 217 H6
Long Beach, U.S.A. 190 G2
Long Branch, U.S.A. 189 C5
Long I., Bahamas 201 B2
Long I., Papua N. G. 173 B2
Long I., U.S.A. 189 B5
Long Xuyen, Vietnam 125 G3
Longford, Australia 172 B2
Longford, Ireland 46 G2
Longhua, China 116 B4
Longiram, Indonesia 128 C8
Longkou, China 116 D5
Longlac, Canada 187 K10
Longmont, U.S.A. 190 E7
Longnawan, Indonesia 128 B8
Longquan, China 116 H4
Longreach, Australia 168 H12
Longview, Tex., U.S.A. 191 H11
Longview, Wash., U.S.A. 190 B2
Lons-le-Saunier, France 55 D8
Loop Hd., Ireland 46 J1
Loose, U.K. 45 D5
Lop Nor = Lop Nur, China 112 D4
Lop Nur, China 112 D4
Lopatina, G., Russia 91 G17
Lopez, Phil. 130 E3
Lopez, C., Gabon 154 C1
Lora, Hamun-i-, Pakistan 105 D1
Lorain, U.S.A. 191 D14
Loralai, Pakistan 105 D4
Lorca, Spain 63 F7
Lord Howe I., Pac. Oc. 176 J4
Lord Howe Ridge, Pac. Oc. 176 J5
Lordsburg, U.S.A. 190 H6
Lorengau, Papua N. G. 173 A2
Loreto, Italy 67 D5
Lorient, France 55 C2
Lorn, Firth of, U.K. 46 D4
Lorne, Australia 171 H4
Lorraine, France 55 B8
Los, Îles de, Guinea 147 C2
Los Alamos, U.S.A. 190 F7
Los Angeles, U.S.A. 190 G2
Los Hermanos, Venezuela 211 A4
Los Llanos de Aridane, Canary Is. 223 D1
Los Mochis, Mexico 194 C2
Los Palacios, Cuba 198 B2
Los Rios □, Ecuador 212 C1
Los Roques, I., Venezuela 211 A3
Los Testigos, Venezuela 211 A4
Loshkalakh, Russia 91 D16
Lošinj, Croatia 72 C3
Lot □, France 55 F5
Lot →, France 55 G4
Lot-et-Garonne □, France 55 G4
Lothair, S. Africa 163 C8
Lötschbergtunnel, Switz. 60 C2
Loubomo, Congo 154 D1
Louga, Senegal 146 A1
Lougheed I., Canada 186 B8
Loughton, U.K. 45 B4
Louis Trichardt, S. Africa 163 A8
Louisiade Arch., Papua N. G. 173 C3
Louisiana □, U.S.A. 191 J11
Louisville, U.S.A. 191 F13
Loulé, Portugal 63 G2
Lourdes, France 55 H4
Lourenço-Marques = Maputo, Mozam. 159 F1
Louth, Australia 171 C5
Louvain = Leuven, Belgium 51 C4
Louwsburg, S. Africa 163 D9
Low Tatra = Nizké Tatry, Slovak Rep. 76 C6
Lowell, U.S.A. 189 A6
Lower Austria = Niederösterreich □, Austria 61 A5
Lower Beeding, U.K. 45 E3
Lower California = Baja California, Mexico 194 A1
Lower Hutt, N.Z. 175 F5
Lower Saxony = Niedersachsen □, Germany 58 B2
Lower Shiplake, U.K. 45 C1
Lower Tunguska = Tunguska, Nizhnyaya →, Russia 91 F10
Lowestoft, U.K. 46 J9
Łowicz, Poland 77 C4
Lowrah →, Afghan. 104 G3
Loxton, Australia 171 E3
Loxton, S. Africa 163 G4
Loyang = Luoyang, China 116 E2
Loyoro, Uganda 156 A3
Lozère □, France 55 F6
Luachimo, Angola 160 B4
Luacono, Angola 160 C5
Lualaba →, Zaïre 155 B4
Lu'an, China 116 G3
Luan Chau, Vietnam 125 A2
Luan Xian, China 116 C4
Luanda, Angola 160 B2
Luang Prabang, Laos 125 B2
Luangwa, Zambia 161 C4
Luangwa →, Zambia 161 C4
Luanping, China 116 B4
Luanshya, Zambia 161 C4
Luapula →, Africa 132 G6
Luarca, Spain 63 A3
Luau, Angola 160 C5
Lubalo, Angola 160 B4
Lubang, Phil. 130 E2
Lubbock, U.S.A. 190 H8
Lübeck, Germany 58 A4
Lubefu, Zaïre 155 D4
Lubero = Luofu, Zaïre 155 C6
Lublin, Poland 77 D5
Lubuagan, Phil. 130 C2
Lubuk Antu, Malaysia 126 C6
Lubuklinggau, Indonesia 128 D3
Lubuksikaping, Indonesia 128 C2
Lubumbashi, Zaïre 155 G5
Lubutu, Zaïre 155 C5
Lucban, Phil. 130 E3
Lucca, Italy 67 C3
Lucena, Phil. 130 E3
Lucena, Spain 63 G4
Lučenec, Slovak Rep. 76 C6
Lucerne = Luzern, Switz. 60 B3
Lucie →, Surinam 214 D3
Lucira, Angola 160 D2
Luckenwalde, Germany 58 C5
Lucknow, India 106 B5
Lüda = Dalian, China 116 C5
Lüdenscheid, Germany 59 B3
Lüderitz, Namibia 162 D2
Ludhiana, India 107 B2
Lüdinghausen, Germany 59 A2
Ludington, U.S.A. 191 C13
Ludwigsburg, Germany 58 F3
Ludwigshafen, Germany 58 E2
Luebo, Zaïre 155 D3
Lufira →, Zaïre 155 F5
Lufkin, U.S.A. 191 H11
Luga, Russia 81 A3
Lugang, Taiwan 117 B2
Lugano, Switz. 60 D4
Lugano, L. di, Switz. 60 D4
Lugansk, Ukraine 81 F6
Lugard's Falls, Kenya 157 E3
Lugo, Spain 63 A2
Lugoj, Romania 75 C2
Lugovoye, Kazakstan 93 A5
Luhansk = Lugansk, Ukraine 81 F6
Luiana, Angola 160 E5
Luiza, Zaïre 155 E3
Luján, Argentina 221 C5
Lukanga Swamp, Zambia 161 C3
Lukenie →, Zaïre 155 D2
Lukolela, Zaïre 155 C2
Lukosi, Zimbabwe 161 C1
Łuków, Poland 77 C5
Lule →, Sweden 40 C4
Luleå, Sweden 40 C5
Lulong, China 116 C4
Lulonga →, Zaïre 155 B2
Lulua →, Zaïre 155 E3
Luluabourg = Kananga, Zaïre 155 E4
Lumai, Angola 160 D4
Lumbala N'guimbo, Angola 160 D4
Lumbwa, Kenya 157 D1
Lumut, Malaysia 126 B1
Lumut, Tg., Indonesia 128 D5
Luna, Phil. 130 C2
Lundazi, Zambia 161 B5
Lundi →, Zimbabwe 161 E4
Lundu, Malaysia 126 C5
Lundy, U.K. 46 L4
Lüneburg, Germany 58 B3
Lüneburg Heath = Lüneburger Heide, Germany 58 B3
Lüneburger Heide, Germany 58 B3
Lünen, Germany 59 A3
Lunéville, France 55 C8
Lungi Airport, S. Leone 147 C2
Luni, India 106 C1
Luni →, India 106 C1
Luo He →, China 116 E2
Luodong, Taiwan 117 A3
Luofu, Zaïre 155 C6
Luoning, China 116 E1
Luoyang, China 116 E2
Luoyuan, China 116 J4
Luozi, Zaïre 155 D1
Luremo, Angola 160 B3
Lusaka, Zambia 161 C3
Lusambo, Zaïre 155 D4
Lushan, China 116 F2
Lushi, China 116 E1
Lushoto, Tanzania 158 B3
Lüshun, China 116 C5
Luta = Dalian, China 116 C5
Luton, U.K. 45 A2
Lutong, Malaysia 126 B7
Lutsk, Ukraine 81 E1
Lutzputs, S. Africa 163 E3
Luvua →, Zaïre 132 G6
Luwuk, Indonesia 129 C11
Luxembourg, Lux. 52 D2
Luxembourg □, Belgium 51 E5
Luxembourg ■, Europe 52
Luxor = El Uqsur, Egypt 139 D5
Luzern, Switz. 60 B3
Luzern □, Switz. 60 B3
Luzhou, China 113 G7
Luzon, Phil. 130 D2
Lviv = Lvov, Ukraine 81 E1
Lvov, Ukraine 81 E1
Lyakhovskiye, Ostrova, Russia 91 C13
Lyaki, Azerbaijan 82 C8
Lyallpur = Faisalabad, Pakistan 105 C5
Lydda = Lod, Israel 96 D2
Lydenburg, S. Africa 163 C8
Łyńa →, Poland 77 A4
Lynchburg, U.S.A. 191 F15
Lyndhurst, Australia 171 C1
Lynn, U.S.A. 189 A6
Lynn Lake, Canada 186 G7
Lyon, France 55 E7
Lyonnais, France 55 E7
Lyons = Lyon, France 55 E7
Lyons, U.S.A. 189 A3
Lys = Leie →, Belgium 51 B2
Lyttelton, N.Z. 175 G4
Lyubertsy, Russia 81 C5

M

Ma'ān, Jordan 98 C2
Ma'anshan, China 116 G4
Ma'arrat an Nu'mān, Syria 97 B3
Maaseik, Belgium 51 B5
Maassluis, Neths. 50 D2
Maastricht, Neths. 50 G4
Mabaruma, Guyana 214 A1
Mabrouk, Mali 140 C5
Macaé, Brazil 215 B5
McAlester, U.S.A. 191 G10
Macao = Macau ■, China 113 J9
Macapá, Brazil 217 B6
Macará, Ecuador 212 E1
Macas, Ecuador 212 D2
Macau, Brazil 217 C9
Macau ■, China 113 J9
Macca Sucker, Jamaica 199 B6
Macclesfield, U.K. 46 H7
M'Clintock Chan., Canada 186 C8
M'Clure Str., Canada 186 B7
McComb, U.S.A. 191 H12
McCook, U.S.A. 190 E8
Macdonnell Ra., Australia 168 C3
Macdougall L., Canada 186 E8
Macedonia = Makedhonía □, Greece 71 B2
Macedonia ■, Europe 72 E8
Macenta, Guinea 147 C4
Macerata, Italy 67 D5
Macfarlane, L., Australia 171 D1
Macgillycuddy's Reeks, Ireland 46 J1
McGregor Ra., Australia 171 A4
Mach, Pakistan 105 D3
Machado = Jiparaná →, Brazil 217 D3
Machakos, Kenya 157 D2
Machakos □, Kenya 157 E3
Machala, Ecuador 212 D1
Macheng, China 116 G3
Machevna, Russia 91 B18
Machico, Madeira 223 A2
Machilipatnam, India 107 E3
Machiques, Venezuela 211 A1
Machupicchu, Peru 213 E4
Macintyre →, Australia 171 B8
Mackay, L., Australia 168 C2
McKeesport, U.S.A. 189 C1
Mackenzie = Linden, Guyana 214 B2
Mackenzie →, Canada 186 B5
Mackenzie Bay, Canada 186 B5
Mackenzie King I., Canada 186 A8
Mackenzie Mts., Canada 186 D4
McKinley, Mt., U.S.A. 193 B4
Mackinnon Road, Kenya 157 F3
Macksville, Australia 171 C9
Maclean, Australia 171 B9
Maclear, S. Africa 163 F7
Macleay →, Australia 171 C9
McLennan, Canada 186 G5
MacLeod Lake, Canada 186 G4
McMinnville, U.S.A. 190 B2
McMurray = Fort McMurray, Canada 186 G6
Mâcon, France 55 E7
Macon, U.S.A. 191 H14
Macondo, Angola 160 C5
McPherson, U.S.A. 190 F9
McPherson Ra., Australia 171 B9
Macquarie Harbour, Australia 172 C1
Macquarie Is., Pac. Oc. 176 K5
Madadeni, S. Africa 163 D8
Madagali, Nigeria 151 C7
Madagascar ■, Africa 165
Madama, Niger 141 A5
Madang, Papua N. G. 173 B2
Madaoua, Niger 141 C3
Madara, Nigeria 151 B6
Madaripur, Bangla. 111 C2
Madauk, Burma 122 F3
Madaya, Burma 122 D2
Made, Neths. 50 E3
Madeira, Atl. Oc. 223
Madeira →, Brazil 217 C4
Madeleine, Is. de la, Canada 187 J14
Madhumati →, Bangla. 111 C1
Madhya Pradesh □, India 106 E3
Madikeri, India 107 F2
Madimba, Zaïre 155 D1
Ma'din, Syria 97 B4
Madīnat ash Sha'b, Yemen 100 C1
Madingou, Congo 154 D2
Madison, S. Dak., U.S.A. 191 D10
Madison, Wis., U.S.A. 191 D12
Madiun, Indonesia 128 F7
Madras = Tamil Nadu □, India 107 F2
Madras, India 107 F3
Madre, L., Mexico 194 C3
Madre, Sierra, Phil. 130 C3
Madre de Dios →, Bolivia 218 A1
Madre de Dios, I., Chile 206 H2
Madrid, Spain 63 D5
Madurai, India 107 G3
Madzhalis, Russia 82 B8
Maebashi, Japan 120 A8
Maestra, Sierra, Cuba 198 C5
Maestrazgo, Mts. del, Spain 63 D7
Maevatanana, Madag. 165 B2
Mafeking = Mafikeng, S. Africa 163 C6
Maféré, Ivory C. 148 D6
Mafeteng, Lesotho 164 B1
Maffra, Australia 171 H6
Mafia I., Tanzania 158 C3
Mafikeng, S. Africa 163 C6
Mafra, Portugal 63 E1
Mafungabusi Plateau, Zimbabwe 161 C3
Magadan, Russia 91 E16
Magadi, Kenya 157 E2
Magadi, L., Kenya 157 E2
Magallanes, Estrecho de, Chile 220 K3
Magangué, Colombia 210 B1
Magburaka, S. Leone 147 C3
Magdalen Is. = Madeleine, Is. de la, Canada 187 J14
Magdalena, Argentina 221 C6
Magdalena, Bolivia 218 B1
Magdalena, Malaysia 126 B8
Magdalena →, Colombia 210 A1
Magdeburg, Germany 58 C4
Magelang, Indonesia 128 F6
Magellan's Str. = Magallanes, Estrecho de, Chile 220 K3
Magenta, L., Australia 170 C3
Maggia →, Switz. 60 D4
Maggiore, L., Italy 67 A2
Magnetic Pole (North) = North Magnetic Pole, Canada 186 B8
Magnitogorsk, Russia 90 G5
Magog, Canada 185 B6
Magoro, Uganda 156 B3
Magosa = Famagusta, Cyprus 95 B3
Magwe, Burma 122 E2
Mahabo, Madag. 165 D1
Mahagi, Zaïre 155 B6
Mahaicony, Guyana 214 B3
Mahajanga, Madag. 165 B2
Mahakam →, Indonesia 128 C9
Mahalapye, Botswana 162 C5
Mahanadi →, India 106 F7
Mahanoro, Madag. 165 C3
Maharashtra □, India 106 F2
Maharès, Tunisia 138 C2
Mahattat 'Unayzah, Jordan 98 C2
Mahaweli →, Sri Lanka 110 B2
Mahdia, Guyana 214 C2
Mahdia, Tunisia 138 B3
Mahé, Seychelles 166 C2
Mahebourg, Mauritius 166 C3
Mahenge, Tanzania 158 C2
Mahesana, India 106 D1
Mahia Pen., N.Z. 175 D6
Mahilyow = Mogilev, Belarus 81 C3
Mahirija, Morocco 136 B6
Mahón, Spain 65 A6
Mahukona, U.S.A. 192 B3
Mahuta, Nigeria 151 B2
Mai-Ndombe, L., Zaïre 155 C2
Maidenhead, U.K. 45 C1
Maidstone, U.K. 45 D5
Maiduguri, Nigeria 151 B7
Maigo, Phil. 130 J4
Maijdi, Bangla. 111 D2
Maikala Ra., India 106 E5
Main →, Germany 58 E2
Maine, France 55 C4
Maine □, U.S.A. 191 B18
Maine-et-Loire □, France 55 D4
Maingkwan, Burma 122 B3
Mainit, L., Phil. 130 H5
Maintirano, Madag. 165 C1
Mainz, Germany 58 E2
Maio, C. Verde Is. 222 C3
Maiquetía, Venezuela 211 A3
Maisi, Cuba 198 C6
Maitland, N.S.W., Australia 171 D8
Maitland, S. Austral., Australia 171 E1
Maiyema, Nigeria 151 B2
Maiz, Is. del, Nic. 197 C3
Maizuru, Japan 120 B5
Majene, Indonesia 129 D10
Maji, Ethiopia 144 E2
Majorca = Mallorca, Spain 65 B4
Maka, Senegal 146 C2
Makale, Indonesia 129 D12
Makamba, Burundi 156 C2
Makari, Cameroon 153 A3
Makarikari = Makgadikgadi Salt Pans, Botswana 162 B5
Makarovo, Russia 91 G12
Makasar = Ujung Pandang, Indonesia 129 E10
Makasar, Selat, Indonesia 128 C9
Makasar, Str. of = Makasar, Selat, Indonesia 128 C9
Makedhonía □, Greece 71 B2
Makedonija = Macedonia ■, Europe 72 E8
Makena, U.S.A. 192 A2
Makeni, S. Leone 147 C3
Makeyevka, Ukraine 81 F5
Makgadikgadi Salt Pans, Botswana 162 B5
Makhachkala, Russia 82 A8
Makian, Indonesia 129 C13
Makindu, Kenya 157 E3
Makinsk, Kazakstan 90 H7
Makiyivka = Makeyevka, Ukraine 81 F5
Makkah, Si. Arabia 99 D3

Makó, *Hungary* 74 C4
Makokou, *Gabon* 154 B1
Makoua, *Congo* 154 B2
Makrai, *India* 106 E3
Makran Coast Range, *Pakistan* 105 F2
Maksimkin Yar, *Russia* 90 G9
Maktar, *Tunisia* 138 B2
Makumbi, *Zaïre* 155 E3
Makurdi, *Nigeria* 151 E4
Makwassie, *S. Africa* 163 D6
Mala, Pta., *Panama* 197 E5
Malabang, *Phil.* 130 K4
Malabar Coast, *India* 107 F2
Malabo = Rey Malabo, *Eq. Guin.* 153 A1
Malabon, *Phil.* 130 E2
Malacca, Str. of, *Indonesia* 128 B3
Malad City, *U.S.A.* 190 D5
Málaga, *Spain* 63 G4
Malaita, *Pac. Oc.* 168 A6
Malakâl, *Sudan* 143 E4
Malakand, *Pakistan* 105 A5
Malamyzh, *Russia* 91 H16
Malang, *Indonesia* 128 F7
Malanje, *Angola* 160 B3
Mälaren, *Sweden* 40 F4
Malatya, *Turkey* 94 C5
Malawi ■, *Africa* 158 C2
Malawi, L., *Africa* 132 H7
Malay Pen., *Asia* 84 H14
Malaybalay, *Phil.* 130 J5
Malaysia ■, *Asia* 126
Malazgirt, *Turkey* 94 B7
Malbork, *Poland* 77 A3
Maldegem, *Belgium* 51 B2
Malden I., *Kiribati* 176 F8
Maldives ■, *Ind. Oc.* 110
Maldon, *U.K.* 45 B6
Maldonado, *Uruguay* 219 D2
Malé, *Maldives* 110 B2
Malé Atoll, *Maldives* 110 B2
Malé Karpaty, *Slovak Rep.* 76 C5
Maléa, Ákra, *Greece* 71 F3
Malebo, Pool, *Africa* 132 G5
Malegaon, *India* 106 F2
Malema, *Mozam.* 159 B3
Malha, *Sudan* 143 C2
Malhão, Sa. do, *Portugal* 63 G2
Malheur L., *U.S.A.* 190 C3
Mali, *Guinea* 147 A3
Mali ■, *Africa* 140
Mali →, *Burma* 122 B3
Mali Kyun, *Burma* 122 H3
Malik, *Indonesia* 129 C12
Malili, *Indonesia* 129 D11
Malin Hd., *Ireland* 46 E3
Malindi, *Kenya* 157 E4
Malines = Mechelen, *Belgium* 51 B3
Maling, *Indonesia* 129 B11
Mallacoota Inlet, *Australia* 171 G7
Mallawi, *Egypt* 139 C4
Mallorca, *Spain* 65 B4
Mallow, *Ireland* 46 J1
Malmesbury, *S. Africa* 163 H2
Malmö, *Sweden* 40 H2
Malombe L., *Malawi* 158 D3
Maloti Mts., *Lesotho* 164 A2
Malta ■, *Europe* 69
Maltahöhe, *Namibia* 162 D2
Maluku, *Indonesia* 129 C13
Maluku □, *Indonesia* 129 D13
Maluku Sea, *Indonesia* 129 C12
Malumfashi, *Nigeria* 151 B4
Malvan, *India* 107 E2
Malvinas, Is. = Falkland Is. ■, *Atl. Oc.* 224
Malyy Lyakhovskiy, Ostrov, *Russia* 91 C13
Mama, *Russia* 91 G12
Mamaia, *Romania* 75 D6
Mamasa, *Indonesia* 129 D10
Mambilima Falls, *Zambia* 161 B4
Mambrui, *Kenya* 157 E4
Mamburao, *Phil.* 130 F2
Mamfe, *Cameroon* 153 D1
Mamoré →, *Bolivia* 218 A1
Mamou, *Guinea* 147 B3
Mamoudzou, *Mayotte* 166 C3
Mampatá, *Guinea-Biss.* 146 D2
Mampong, *Ghana* 149 C2
Mamuju, *Indonesia* 129 D10
Man, *Ivory C.* 148 C3
Man, I. of, *U.K.* 46 G5
Man Na, *Burma* 122 C3
Mana, *Fr. Guiana* 214 C5
Mana, *U.S.A.* 192 A1
Mana →, *Fr. Guiana* 214 B5
Manaar, G. of, *Asia* 84 H11
Manabí □, *Ecuador* 212 B1
Manacor, *Spain* 65 B4
Manado, *Indonesia* 129 B12
Managua, *Nic.* 197 C1
Managua, L., *Nic.* 197 B1
Manakara, *Madag.* 165 D2
Manam I., *Papua N. G.* 173 A1
Manama = Al Manāmah, *Bahrain* 100 C3
Mananara, *Madag.* 165 B3
Mananjary, *Madag.* 165 D2
Manaos = Manaus, *Brazil* 217 C4
Manapouri, L., *N.Z.* 175 J1
Manas, *China* 112 C4
Manas, Gora, *Kyrgyzstan* 93 B4
Manatí, *Puerto Rico* 201 A2
Manaung, *Burma* 122 E1
Manaus, *Brazil* 217 C4
Manay, *Phil.* 130 K6
Manbij, *Syria* 97 A3
Manche □, *France* 55 B3
Manchester, *U.K.* 46 H7
Manchester, *U.S.A.* 189 A6
Manda, *Tanzania* 158 D2
Mandal, *Norway* 40 G1
Mandalay, *Burma* 122 D2
Mandale = Mandalay, *Burma* 122 D2
Mandalī, *Iraq* 102 C4
Mandan, *U.S.A.* 190 B8
Mandaon, *Phil.* 130 G4
Mandar, Teluk, *Indonesia* 129 D10
Mandasor = Mandsaur, *India* 106 D2
Mandaue, *Phil.* 130 H4
Mandera, *Kenya* 157 A4
Mandera □, *Kenya* 157 A4
Mandeville, *Jamaica* 199 B3
Mandioli, *Indonesia* 129 C13
Mandla, *India* 106 E4
Mandritsara, *Madag.* 165 B3
Mandsaur, *India* 106 D2
Mandurah, *Australia* 170 B1
Mandvi, *India* 107 D1
Manfalût, *Egypt* 139 C4
Manfred, *Australia* 171 E4
Mangalia, *Romania* 75 D6
Mangalore, *India* 107 F2
Manggar, *Indonesia* 128 D6
Manggawitu, *Indonesia* 129 D15
Mangkalihat, Tanjung, *Indonesia* 129 B10
Mangla Dam, *Pakistan* 105 B6
Mangnai, *China* 112 D4
Mango, *Togo* 150 B1
Mangoche, *Malawi* 158 D2
Mangole, *Indonesia* 129 D12
Mangonui, *N.Z.* 175 A4
Mangueigne, *Chad* 142 E3
Mangyshlak Poluostrov, *Kazakstan* 90 H3
Manhattan, *U.S.A.* 191 E10
Manica, *Mozam.* 159 D1
Manicaland □, *Zimbabwe* 161 C5
Manicoré, *Brazil* 217 D4
Manicouagan →, *Canada* 187 J13
Manihiki, *Cook Is.* 176 G7
Manikganj, *Bangla.* 111 C2
Manila, *Phil.* 130 E2
Manila B., *Phil.* 130 E2
Manilla, *Australia* 171 C8
Manipur □, *India* 107 C6
Manipur →, *Burma* 122 C1
Manisa, *Turkey* 94 B1
Manistee, *U.S.A.* 191 C13
Manistique, *U.S.A.* 191 C13
Manitoba □, *Canada* 186 H8
Manitoba, L., *Canada* 186 J8
Manitowoc, *U.S.A.* 191 C12
Manizales, *Colombia* 210 C1
Manja, *Madag.* 165 D1
Manjacaze, *Mozam.* 159 F2
Manjhand, *Pakistan* 105 F3
Manjimup, *Australia* 170 D2
Mankato, *U.S.A.* 191 D11
Mankono, *Ivory C.* 148 C4
Manly, *Australia* 171 E8
Manmad, *India* 106 F2
Manna, *Indonesia* 128 E4
Mannahill, *Australia* 171 D2
Mannar, *Sri Lanka* 110 B1
Mannar I., *Sri Lanka* 110 B1
Mannheim, *Germany* 58 E2
Mannum, *Australia* 171 F2
Mano, *S. Leone* 147 C3
Manokwari, *Indonesia* 129 C16
Manombo, *Madag.* 165 D1
Manono, *Zaïre* 155 E5
Manpojin, *N. Korea* 118 C3
Manresa, *Spain* 63 B9
Mansa, *Zambia* 161 B4
Mansel I., *Canada* 187 F10
Mansfield, *Australia* 171 G5
Mansfield, *U.K.* 46 H7
Mansfield, *U.S.A.* 191 D14
Mansoa, *Guinea-Biss.* 146 D1
Manta, *Ecuador* 212 C1
Manta, B. de, *Ecuador* 212 C1
Mantalingajan, Mt., *Phil.* 130 J1
Mantes, *France* 55 B5
Mantiqueira, Serra da, *Brazil* 215 B3
Mántova, *Italy* 67 B3
Mantua = Mántova, *Italy* 67 B3
Manu, *Peru* 213 D4
Manuae, *Cook Is.* 176 G7
Manui, *Indonesia* 129 D12
Manus I., *Papua N. G.* 173 A2
Manyara, L., *Tanzania* 158 B2
Manych →, *Russia* 34 F15
Manych-Gudilo, Oz., *Russia* 81 G7
Manyoni, *Tanzania* 158 B2
Manzai, *Pakistan* 105 C4
Manzala, Bahra el, *Egypt* 139 A4
Manzanares, *Spain* 63 E5
Manzanillo, *Cuba* 198 C5
Manzanillo, *Mexico* 194 E3
Manzanillo, Pta., *Panama* 197 D5
Manzhouli, *China* 113 B9
Manzini, *Swaziland* 165 B2
Mao, *Chad* 142 D1
Maoke Mts., *Indonesia* 168 A3
Maoming, *China* 113 J8
Mapam Yumco, *China* 112 F1
Mapia, Kepulauan, *Indonesia* 129 C16
Maputo, *Mozam.* 159 F1
Maquela do Zombo, *Angola* 160 A2
Maquinchao, *Argentina* 220 G3
Mar, Serra do, *Brazil* 217 J6
Mar Chiquita, L., *Argentina* 220 D4
Mar del Plata, *Argentina* 220 F5
Mara, *Guyana* 214 B3
Marabá, *Brazil* 217 C6
Maracá, I. de, *Brazil* 217 B6
Maracaibo, *Venezuela* 211 A2
Maracaibo, L. de, *Venezuela* 211 A2
Maracay, *Venezuela* 211 A3
Marādah, *Libya* 138 B4
Maradi, *Niger* 141 D3
Marāgheh, *Iran* 103 A2
Marajó, I. de, *Brazil* 217 B6
Maralal, *Kenya* 157 C2
Marama, *Australia* 171 F2
Marampa, *S. Leone* 147 C3
Maran, *Malaysia* 126 C2
Marang, *Malaysia* 126 B2
Maranhão = São Luís, *Brazil* 217 C8
Maranhão □, *Brazil* 217 D7
Maranoa →, *Australia* 171 A7
Marañón →, *Peru* 213 B3
Marão, *Mozam.* 159 E2
Maraş = Kahramanmaraş, *Turkey* 94 C5
Marathón, *Greece* 71 D4
Maratua, *Indonesia* 129 B10
Marawi, *Phil.* 130 J4
Marāwih, *U.A.E.* 101 B2
Marbella, *Spain* 63 G4
Marburg, *Germany* 58 D2
Marchand = Rommani, *Morocco* 136 B4
Marche, *France* 55 E5
Marche □, *Italy* 67 C5
Marche-en-Famenne, *Belgium* 51 D5
Marches = Marche □, *Italy* 67 C5
Marcos Juárez, *Argentina* 221 B3
Marcus I. = Minami-Tori-Shima, *Pac. Oc.* 176 C4
Marcus Necker Ridge, *Pac. Oc.* 176 D5
Mardan, *Pakistan* 105 B5
Mardin, *Turkey* 94 C6
Marek = Stanke Dimitrov, *Bulgaria* 73 C2
Marek, *Indonesia* 129 E10
Maremma, *Italy* 67 D4
Marenyi, *Kenya* 157 F4
Maresfield, *U.K.* 45 E4
Marfa Pt., *Malta* 69 A2
Margarita, I., *Venezuela* 211 A4
Margate, *S. Africa* 163 F8
Margate, *U.K.* 46 K9
Margelan, *Uzbekistan* 93 D5
Margosatubig, *Phil.* 130 K4
Mari Republic □, *Russia* 81 B8
María Grande, *Argentina* 221 A4
Maria I., *Australia* 172 C3
Maria van Diemen, C., *N.Z.* 175 A4
Mariakani, *Kenya* 157 F4
Mariana Trench, *Pac. Oc.* 176 D3
Marianao, *Cuba* 198 A2
Marias →, *U.S.A.* 190 B6
Mariato, Punta, *Panama* 197 E5
Ma'rib, *Yemen* 100 B1
Maribor, *Slovenia* 72 A4
Marīdī, *Sudan* 143 F3
Marie-Galante, *Guadeloupe* 202 G6
Mariecourt, *Canada* 187 F11
Marienberg, *Neths.* 50 C6
Marienbourg, *Belgium* 51 E3
Mariental, *Namibia* 162 D3
Marietta, *U.S.A.* 191 G14
Marihatag, *Phil.* 130 J6
Mariinsk, *Russia* 90 H9
Marília, *Brazil* 217 H6
Marín, *Spain* 63 B1
Marinduque, *Phil.* 130 F3
Marion, *Ill., U.S.A.* 191 F12
Marion, *Ind., U.S.A.* 191 E13
Marion, *Ohio, U.S.A.* 191 E14
Maripasoula, *Fr. Guiana* 214 D5
Mariscal Estigarribia, *Paraguay* 219 B1
Maritsa →, *Bulgaria* 73 C3
Mariupol, *Ukraine* 81 G5
Markovo, *Russia* 91 B17
Marks, *Russia* 81 E8
Marks Tey, *U.K.* 45 A6
Marlow, *U.K.* 45 C1
Marmara, Sea of = Marmara Denizi, *Turkey* 94 A1
Marmara Denizi, *Turkey* 94 A1
Marmolada, Mte., *Italy* 67 A4
Marmora, *Canada* 185 C3
Marne □, *France* 55 B7
Marne →, *France* 55 C7
Marneuli, *Georgia* 82 B6
Maroantsetra, *Madag.* 165 B3
Marondera, *Zimbabwe* 161 C4
Maroni →, *Fr. Guiana* 214 C5
Maroochydore, *Australia* 171 A9
Maroona, *Australia* 171 G4
Maroua, *Cameroon* 153 B3
Marovoay, *Madag.* 165 B2
Marowijne □, *Surinam* 214 D4
Marowijne →, *Surinam* 214 C5
Marquard, *S. Africa* 163 E7
Marquette, *U.S.A.* 191 C12
Marrakech, *Morocco* 136 D3
Marrawah, *Australia* 172 A1
Marree, *Australia* 171 B1
Marromeu, *Mozam.* 159 C2
Marrowie Cr. →, *Australia* 171 E5
Marrupa, *Mozam.* 159 A3
Marsá Matrûh, *Egypt* 139 A2
Marsá Susah, *Libya* 138 A5
Marsabit, *Kenya* 157 B3
Marsabit □, *Kenya* 157 B3
Marsala, *Italy* 67 J5
Marsalforn, *Malta* 69 A1
Marsden, *Australia* 171 E6
Marseille, *France* 55 H8
Marseilles = Marseille, *France* 55 H8
Marsh I., *U.S.A.* 191 J12
Marshall, *Liberia* 148 D2
Marshall, *Mo., U.S.A.* 191 E11
Marshall, *Tex., U.S.A.* 191 H11
Marshall Is. ■, *Pac. Oc.* 176 E5
Marshalltown, *U.S.A.* 191 D11
Martaban, *Burma* 122 F3
Martaban, G. of, *Burma* 122 F3
Martapura, *Kalimantan, Indonesia* 128 D8
Martapura, *Sumatera, Indonesia* 128 E4
Marte, *Nigeria* 151 B7
Martelange, *Belgium* 51 E5
Martha's Vineyard, *U.S.A.* 189 B6
Martigny, *Switz.* 60 D2
Martil, *Morocco* 136 A5
Martinborough, *N.Z.* 175 F5
Martinique ■, *W. Indies* 203 C3
Martinique Passage, *W. Indies* 203 B3
Martinsburg, *U.S.A.* 189 D2
Marton, *N.Z.* 175 E5
Martos, *Spain* 63 F5
Martuni, *Armenia* 82 D6
Maru, *Nigeria* 151 B3
Marudi, *Malaysia* 126 B7
Ma'ruf, *Afghan.* 104 F4
Marugame, *Japan* 120 C4
Marwar, *India* 106 C1
Mary, *Turkmenistan* 90 L4
Maryborough = Port Laoise, *Ireland* 46 H2
Maryborough, *Australia* 171 G4
Maryland □, *U.S.A.* 189 D3
Maryland Junction, *Zimbabwe* 161 B4
Marzūq, *Libya* 138 C2
Masai, *Malaysia* 126 D3
Masaka, *Uganda* 156 D1
Masalembo, Kepulauan, *Indonesia* 128 E8
Masalima, Kepulauan, *Indonesia* 128 F9
Masamba, *Indonesia* 129 D10
Masan, *S. Korea* 118 G5
Masasi, *Tanzania* 158 D3
Masaya, *Nic.* 197 C2
Masbate, *Phil.* 130 F4
Mascara, *Algeria* 137 A3
Masela, *Indonesia* 129 F14
Maseru, *Lesotho* 164 B1
Mashaba, *Zimbabwe* 161 D4
Mashhad, *Iran* 103 B5
Mashi, *Nigeria* 151 A4
Māshkel, Hāmūn-i-, *Pakistan* 105 E1
Mashki Chāh, *Pakistan* 105 D1
Mashonaland Central □, *Zimbabwe* 161 A4
Mashonaland East □, *Zimbabwe* 161 B5
Mashonaland West □, *Zimbabwe* 161 B3
Mashtaga, *Azerbaijan* 82 C9
Masi Manimba, *Zaïre* 155 D2
Masindi, *Uganda* 156 B1
Masindi Port, *Uganda* 156 B2
Masisea, *Peru* 213 C3
Mask, L., *Ireland* 46 G1
Masohi, *Indonesia* 129 D14
Mason City, *U.S.A.* 191 D11
Maspalomas, Pta., *Canary Is.* 223 D2
Masqat, *Oman* 101 B3
Massa, *Italy* 67 C3
Massa, O. →, *Morocco* 136 E2
Massachusetts □, *U.S.A.* 189 A6
Massaguet, *Chad* 142 E1
Massakory, *Chad* 142 D1
Massangena, *Mozam.* 159 D1
Massawa = Mitsiwa, *Eritrea* 144 B3
Massénya, *Chad* 142 E1
Massif Central, *France* 55 F6
Massillon, *U.S.A.* 191 D14
Massinga, *Mozam.* 159 E2
Masterton, *N.Z.* 175 E5
Mastuj, *Pakistan* 105 A5
Mastung, *Pakistan* 105 D3
Masuda, *Japan* 120 C2
Masvingo, *Zimbabwe* 161 D4
Masvingo □, *Zimbabwe* 161 D4
Maşyāf, *Syria* 97 B2
Mât →, *Réunion* 166 A3
Matabeleland North □, *Zimbabwe* 161 C2
Matabeleland South □, *Zimbabwe* 161 D3
Mataboor, *Indonesia* 129 C17
Matad, *Mongolia* 113 B9
Matadi, *Zaïre* 155 E1
Matagalpa, *Nic.* 197 B2
Matagami, L., *Canada* 187 J11
Matagorda I., *U.S.A.* 191 K10
Matak, P., *Indonesia* 128 B5
Matakana, *Australia* 171 D5
Matale, *Sri Lanka* 110 C2
Matam, *Senegal* 146 A3
Matamoros, *Coahuila, Mexico* 194 C4
Matamoros, *Tamaulipas, Mexico* 194 C5
Ma'ṭan as Sarra, *Libya* 138 D5
Matane, *Canada* 187 J13
Matanzas, *Cuba* 198 B2
Matapan, C. = Taínaron, Ákra, *Greece* 71 F2
Matara, *Sri Lanka* 110 D2
Mataram, *Indonesia* 128 F9
Matarani, *Peru* 213 F4
Matatiele, *S. Africa* 163 F7
Mataura, *N.Z.* 175 J2
Matehuala, *Mexico* 194 D4
Mateke Hills, *Zimbabwe* 161 E4
Matelot, *Trin. & Tob.* 204 A3
Matera, *Italy* 67 F8
Matetsi, *Zimbabwe* 161 C1
Mateur, *Tunisia* 138 A2
Mathura, *India* 106 B3
Mati, *Phil.* 130 K6
Matiri Ra., *N.Z.* 175 F4
Matmata, *Tunisia* 138 C2
Mato Grosso □, *Brazil* 217 E5
Mato Grosso, Planalto do, *Brazil* 217 F5
Mato Grosso do Sul □, *Brazil* 217 G5
Matochkin Shar, *Russia* 90 C8
Matopo Hills, *Zimbabwe* 161 D3
Matopos, *Zimbabwe* 161 D2
Matosinhos, *Portugal* 63 C1
Maṭraḥ, *Oman* 101 B3
Matsena, *Nigeria* 151 A5
Matsesta, *Russia* 82 A2
Matsue, *Japan* 120 B3
Matsumae, *Japan* 121 C7
Matsumoto, *Japan* 120 A7
Matsusaka, *Japan* 120 C6
Matsutō, *Japan* 120 A6
Matsuyama, *Japan* 120 C3
Mattagami →, *Canada* 187 K11
Matterhorn, *Switz.* 60 D2
Matthew's Ridge, *Guyana* 214 A1
Matucana, *Peru* 213 D3
Maturín, *Venezuela* 211 A4
Mau Escarpment, *Kenya* 157 D2
Mau Ranipur, *India* 106 C4
Maude, *Australia* 171 E5
Maudin Sun, *Burma* 122 G1
Mauganj, *India* 106 C5
Maui, *U.S.A.* 192 A3
Maulamyaing, *Burma* 122 F3
Maulvibazar, *Bangla.* 111 B3
Maumere, *Indonesia* 129 F11
Maun, *Botswana* 162 B4
Mauna Kea, *U.S.A.* 192 B3
Mauna Loa, *U.S.A.* 192 B3
Maungmagan Is., *Burma* 122 G3
Maures, *France* 55 H8
Mauritania ■, *Africa* 140
Mauritius ■, *Ind. Oc.* 166
Mavinga, *Angola* 160 E4
Mavuradonha Mts., *Zimbabwe* 161 A4
Mawk Mai, *Burma* 122 E3
Mawlaik, *Burma* 122 C2
Maxesibeni, *S. Africa* 163 F8
Maxixe, *Mozam.* 159 E2
May Pen, *Jamaica* 199 C3
Maya →, *Russia* 91 F15
Maya Mts., *Belize* 196 B2
Mayaguana, *Bahamas* 201 B3
Mayagüez, *Puerto Rico* 201 A1
Mayarí, *Cuba* 198 C6
Maydena, *Australia* 172 C2
Mayenne, *France* 55 C4
Mayenne □, *France* 55 C4
Mayfield, *U.K.* 45 E4
Mayfield, *U.S.A.* 191 F12
Mayland, *U.K.* 45 B6
Mayli-Say, *Kyrgyzstan* 93 C5
Maymyo, *Burma* 122 D2
Mayo, *Canada* 186 D4
Mayon Volcano, *Phil.* 130 F4
Mayotte, I., *Mayotte* 166 C3
Mayraira Pt., *Phil.* 130 B2
Mayu, *Indonesia* 129 B13
Mayya, *Russia* 91 F14
Mazabuka, *Zambia* 161 D3
Mazagán = El Jadida, *Morocco* 136 C3
Mazán, *Peru* 213 B4
Mazar-e Sharīf, *Afghan.* 104 B4
Mazarrón, *Spain* 63 F7
Mazaruni →, *Guyana* 214 B2
Mazatenango, *Guatemala* 196 C1
Mazatlán, *Mexico* 194 D3
Mazoe →, *Mozam.* 159 C1
Mazowe, *Zimbabwe* 161 B4
Mazurian Lakes = Mazurskie, Pojezierze, *Poland* 77 B4
Mazurskie, Pojezierze, *Poland* 77 B4
Mbaba, *Senegal* 146 B1
Mbabane, *Swaziland* 165 B1
M'Bahiakro, *Ivory C.* 148 C5
Mbala, *Zambia* 161 A5
Mbale, *Uganda* 156 C3

M'Balmayo, *Cameroon* 153 D2
Mbamba Bay, *Tanzania* 158 D2
Mbandaka, *Zaïre* 155 C2
Mbanza Congo, *Angola* 160 A2
Mbanza Ngungu, *Zaïre* 155 D1
Mbarara, *Uganda* 156 D1
Mbashe →, *S. Africa* 163 G7
Mbatto, *Ivory C.* 148 D5
Mberengwa, *Zimbabwe* 161 D3
Mberengwa, Mt., *Zimbabwe* 161 D3
Mberubu, *Nigeria* 151 F4
Mbeya, *Tanzania* 158 D1
Mbini □, *Eq. Guin.* 153 C2
Mboro, *Senegal* 146 B1
Mboune, *Senegal* 146 B2
Mbour, *Senegal* 146 B1
Mbout, *Mauritania* 140 E1
Mbuji-Mayi, *Zaïre* 155 E4
Mbulu, *Tanzania* 158 B2
Mchinji, *Malawi* 158 C1
Mead, L., *U.S.A.* 190 F4
Meander River, *Canada* 186 F5
Meaux, *France* 55 B6
Mecca = Makkah, *Si. Arabia* 99 D3
Mechelen, *Belgium* 51 B3
Mecheria, *Algeria* 137 B3
Mechra Benâbbou, *Morocco* 136 C3
Mecklenburg-Vorpommern □, *Germany* 58 A5
Mecklenburger Bucht, *Germany* 58 A4
Meconta, *Mozam.* 159 B3
Medan, *Indonesia* 128 B2
Medawachchiya, *Sri Lanka* 110 B2
Medéa, *Algeria* 137 A4
Medellín, *Colombia* 210 C1
Médenine, *Tunisia* 138 C2
Mederdra, *Mauritania* 140 D1
Medford, *U.S.A.* 190 C2
Media Luna, *Argentina* 221 C1
Mediaş, *Romania* 75 C3
Medicine Hat, *Canada* 186 J5
Medina = Al Madīnah, *Si. Arabia* 99 C3
Medina, *Spain* 63 C4
Medina, *U.S.A.* 189 A2
Medina-Sidonia, *Spain* 63 G3
Medinipur, *India* 106 E7
Mediterranean Sea, *Europe* 34 H8
Medjerda, O. →, *Tunisia* 138 A2
Médoc, *France* 55 F3
Medveditsa →, *Russia* 81 F7
Medvezhi, Ostrava, *Russia* 91 B15
Medvezhyegorsk, *Russia* 90 C4
Medway →, *U.K.* 45 D5
Meerut, *India* 106 A3
Mega, *Ethiopia* 144 F3
Mégara, *Greece* 71 D3
Meghalaya □, *India* 106 C9
Meghna →, *Bangla.* 111 D2
Mehadia, *Romania* 75 D2
Mei Xian, *China* 113 H10
Meiganga, *Cameroon* 153 C2
Meighen I., *Canada* 186 A9
Meiktila, *Burma* 122 D2
Meiringen, *Switz.* 60 C3
Meissen, *Germany* 58 D5
Mékambo, *Gabon* 154 B2
Mekhtar, *Pakistan* 105 D4
Meknès, *Morocco* 136 B4
Mekong →, *Asia* 84 H14
Mekongga, *Indonesia* 129 D11
Melaka, *Malaysia* 126 D2
Melalap, *Malaysia* 126 B8
Melanesia, *Pac. Oc.* 176 F4
Melbourne, *Australia* 171 H5
Mélèzes →, *Canada* 187 G12
Melfi, *Chad* 142 E1
Melfort, *Canada* 186 H7
Melfort, *Zimbabwe* 161 B4
Melilla, *Morocco* 136 A6
Melitopol, *Ukraine* 81 G4
Melk, *Austria* 61 A5
Mellégue, O. →, *Tunisia* 138 A2
Mellieha, *Malta* 69 A2
Melo, *Uruguay* 219 B3
Melolo, *Indonesia* 129 F11
Melrose, *Australia* 171 D6
Melun, *France* 55 C6
Melut, *Sudan* 143 D4
Melville, *Canada* 186 J7
Melville, L., *Canada* 187 G14
Melville I., *Australia* 168 B3
Melville I., *Canada* 186 B8
Melville Pen., *Canada* 187 D10
Memba, *Mozam.* 159 B3
Memboro, *Indonesia* 129 F10
Memel = Klaipéda, *Lithuania* 81 B1
Memel, *S. Africa* 163 D8
Memmingen, *Germany* 58 G3
Mempawah, *Indonesia* 128 C6
Memphis, *U.S.A.* 191 G12
Ménaka, *Mali* 140 E6
Menan = Chao Phraya →, *Thailand* 123 H4
Menate, *Indonesia* 128 C7
Mendawai →, *Indonesia* 128 D8
Mende, *France* 55 G6
Mendocino, C., *U.S.A.* 190 D1
Mendocino Seascarp, *Pac. Oc.* 176 B8
Mendoza, *Argentina* 220 E3
Mene Grande, *Venezuela* 211 A2
Menen, *Belgium* 51 C1
Menfi, *Italy* 67 J5
Mengcheng, *China* 116 F3
Menggala, *Indonesia* 128 E4
Mengyin, *China* 116 E4
Mengzi, *China* 112 H6
Menin = Menen, *Belgium* 51 C1
Menindee, *Australia* 171 D4
Menindee L., *Australia* 171 D3
Meningie, *Australia* 171 F2
Menominee, *U.S.A.* 191 C12
Menongue, *Angola* 160 D3
Menorca, *Spain* 65 A6
Mentakab, *Malaysia* 126 C2
Mentawai, Kepulauan, *Indonesia* 128 D2
Menton, *France* 55 G9
Mentz Dam, *S. Africa* 163 H5
Menzel-Bourguiba, *Tunisia* 138 A2
Menzel Chaker, *Tunisia* 138 B2
Menzel-Temime, *Tunisia* 138 A3
Me'ona, *Israel* 96 A2
Meppel, *Neths.* 50 C5
Merabéllou, Kólpos, *Greece* 71 F5
Meran = Merano, *Italy* 67 A4
Merano, *Italy* 67 A4
Merauke, *Indonesia* 129 F18
Merbein, *Australia* 171 E3
Merca, *Somali Rep.* 145 C2
Mercadal, *Spain* 65 A6
Merced, *U.S.A.* 190 E2
Mercedes, *Buenos Aires, Argentina* 221 C5
Mercedes, *Corrientes, Argentina* 220 D5
Mercedes, *San Luis, Argentina* 221 B1
Mercedes, *Uruguay* 219 C1
Mercy C., *Canada* 187 E12
Meredith, C., *Falk. Is.* 224 A2
Merga = Nukheila, *Sudan* 143 B2
Mergui Arch. = Myeik Kyunzu, *Burma* 122 H3
Mérida, *Mexico* 194 D8
Mérida, *Spain* 63 E3
Mérida, *Venezuela* 211 B2
Mérida, Cord. de, *Venezuela* 206 B2
Meriden, *U.S.A.* 189 B6
Meridian, *U.S.A.* 191 H13
Merke, *Kazakstan* 93 A6
Merksem, *Belgium* 51 B3
Merowe, *Sudan* 143 B4
Merredin, *Australia* 170 B3
Merrill, *U.S.A.* 191 C12
Merriwa, *Australia* 171 D8
Merriwagga, *Australia* 171 E5
Merrygoen, *Australia* 171 D7
Mersa Fatma, *Eritrea* 144 B3
Mersch, *Lux.* 52 C2
Merseburg, *Germany* 58 D4
Mersey →, *Canada* 46 H6
Mersin, *Turkey* 94 C4
Mersing, *Malaysia* 126 D3
Merthyr Tydfil, *U.K.* 46 K6
Merton, *U.K.* 45 D3
Meru, *Kenya* 157 C3
Meru □, *Kenya* 157 C3
Mesa, *U.S.A.* 190 G5
Meshed = Mashhad, *Iran* 103 B5
Meshra er Req, *Sudan* 143 E3
Mesolóngion, *Greece* 71 D2
Mesopotamia = Al Jazirah, *Iraq* 102 C3
Messina, *Italy* 67 J7
Messina, *S. Africa* 163 A8
Messina, Str. di, *Italy* 67 J7
Messíni, *Greece* 71 E2
Messiniakós Kólpos, *Greece* 71 E2
Mesta →, *Bulgaria* 73 D2
Meta →, *S. Amer.* 206 B3
Metangula, *Mozam.* 159 A2
Metema, *Ethiopia* 144 C2
Methven, *N.Z.* 175 G3
Metil, *Mozam.* 159 C3
Metlaoui, *Tunisia* 138 C1
Metz, *France* 55 B8
Meulaboh, *Indonesia* 128 A1
Meureudu, *Indonesia* 128 A1
Meurthe-et-Moselle □, *France* 55 B8
Meuse □, *France* 55 B7
Meuse →, *Europe* 55 B7
Mexiana, I., *Brazil* 217 B6
Mexicali, *Mexico* 194 A1
México, *Mexico* 194 E5
Mexico, *U.S.A.* 191 E11
Mexico ■, *Cent. Amer.* 194
Mexico, G. of, *Cent. Amer.* 180 G10
Meymaneh, *Afghan.* 104 B3
Mezen, *Russia* 90 D6
Mezen →, *Russia* 90 D6
Mezökövesd, *Hungary* 74 A4
Mezötúr, *Hungary* 74 B4
Mhlaba Hills, *Zimbabwe* 161 C4
Mhow, *India* 106 E2
Miami, *U.S.A.* 191 K16
Mianchi, *China* 116 E1
Miandrivazo, *Madag.* 165 C2
Mianeh, *Iran* 103 A2
Mianwali, *Pakistan* 105 B5
Mianyang, *China* 116 G2
Miaoli, *Taiwan* 117 B3
Miarinarivo, *Madag.* 165 C2
Miass, *Russia* 90 G6
Michelson, Mt., *U.S.A.* 193 A5
Michigan □, *U.S.A.* 191 C13
Michigan, L., *U.S.A.* 191 D13
Michikamau L., *Canada* 187 H13
Michipicoten, *Canada* 187 K10
Michurinsk, *Russia* 81 D6
Mico, Pta., *Nic.* 197 C3
Micronesia, *Pac. Oc.* 176 E4
Micronesia, Federated States of ■, *Pac. Oc.* 176 E4
Midai, P., *Indonesia* 128 B5
Middelburg, *Neths.* 50 E1
Middelburg, *Eastern Cape, S. Africa* 163 G5
Middelburg, *Eastern Trans., S. Africa* 163 C8
Middelwit, *S. Africa* 163 B6
Middlesboro, *U.S.A.* 191 F14
Middlesbrough, *U.K.* 46 F7
Middletown, *Conn., U.S.A.* 189 B6
Middletown, *N.Y., U.S.A.* 189 B5
Midelt, *Morocco* 136 C5
Midi, Canal du →, *France* 55 G5
Midland, *Canada* 185 C1
Midland, *Mich., U.S.A.* 191 D13
Midland, *Tex., U.S.A.* 190 H8
Midlands □, *Zimbabwe* 161 C3
Midsayap, *Phil.* 130 K5
Midway Is., *Pac. Oc.* 176 C6
Mie □, *Japan* 120 C6
Międzychód, *Poland* 77 C1
Międzyrzec Podlaski, *Poland* 77 C6
Miercurea Ciuc, *Romania* 75 B4
Mieres, *Spain* 63 A3
Mifraz Hefa, *Israel* 96 B2
Migdāl, *Israel* 96 B3
Mihara, *Japan* 120 C3
Mikhaylovka, *Azerbaijan* 82 B9
Míkínai, *Greece* 71 D3
Míkonos, *Greece* 71 E5
Milagro, *Ecuador* 212 C1
Milan = Milano, *Italy* 67 A2
Milang, *Australia* 171 F2
Milano, *Italy* 67 A2
Milâs, *Turkey* 94 C1
Milazzo, *Italy* 67 J7
Mildura, *Australia* 171 E3
Miles City, *U.S.A.* 190 C7
Milford, *U.K.* 45 E2
Milford Haven, *U.K.* 46 K4
Milford Sd., *N.Z.* 175 H1
Milh, Bahr al, *Iraq* 102 D3
Miliana, *Algeria* 137 D4
Miling, *Australia* 170 A2
Milledgeville, *U.S.A.* 191 G14
Millicent, *Australia* 171 G3
Millmerran, *Australia* 171 A8
Millville, *U.S.A.* 189 D4
Milogros, *Phil.* 130 G4
Milos, *Greece* 71 E4
Milparinka, *Australia* 171 B3
Milton, *N.Z.* 175 J2
Milton, *U.S.A.* 189 B3
Milton Keynes, *U.K.* 45 A1
Miltou, *Chad* 142 E1
Milwaukee, *U.S.A.* 191 D12
Milwaukee Deep, *Atl. Oc.* 222 E1
Mim, *Ghana* 149 C1
Min Chiang →, *China* 116 J4
Min Jiang →, *China* 113 G7
Min-Kush, *Kyrgyzstan* 93 B6
Mīnā'al Aḥmadī, *Kuwait* 100 A1
Mīnāb, *Iran* 103 E4
Minami-Tori-Shima, *Pac. Oc.* 176 C4
Minas, *Uruguay* 219 D2
Minas, Sierra de las, *Guatemala* 196 C1
Minas de Riótinto, *Spain* 63 F3
Minas Gerais □, *Brazil* 217 G7
Minbu, *Burma* 122 E2
Minbya, *Burma* 122 D1
Mindanao, *Phil.* 130 J5
Mindanao Sea = Bohol Sea, *Phil.* 130 J4
Mindelo, *C. Verde Is.* 222 A1
Minden, *Germany* 58 C2
Minden, *U.S.A.* 191 H11
Mindiptana, *Indonesia* 129 E18
Mindoro, *Phil.* 130 F2
Mindoro Str., *Phil.* 130 F2
Mindouli, *Congo* 154 D2
Mineral Wells, *U.S.A.* 190 H9
Mingan, *Canada* 187 J14
Mingechaur, *Azerbaijan* 82 C7
Mingechaurskoye Vdkhr., *Azerbaijan* 82 C7
Minggang, *China* 116 F2
Mingin, *Burma* 122 C2
Mingt'iehkaitafan = Mintaka Pass, *Pakistan* 105 A6
Mingxi, *China* 116 J3
Minho, *Portugal* 63 B1
Minna, *Nigeria* 151 C3
Minneapolis, *U.S.A.* 191 C11
Minnedosa, *Canada* 186 J7
Minnesota □, *U.S.A.* 191 C10
Miño →, *Spain* 63 B1
Minorca = Menorca, *Spain* 65 A6
Minore, *Australia* 171 D7
Minot, *U.S.A.* 190 B8
Minqing, *China* 116 J4
Minsk, *Belarus* 81 C2
Mińsk Mazowiecki, *Poland* 77 C5
Minster, *U.K.* 45 D6
Mintaka Pass, *Pakistan* 105 A6
Minûf, *Egypt* 139 B4
Minusinsk, *Russia* 91 H10
Minvoul, *Gabon* 154 B1
Mir, *Niger* 141 D5
Mīrābād, *Afghan.* 104 G1
Miraj, *India* 107 E2
Miram Shah, *Pakistan* 105 B4
Miranda de Ebro, *Spain* 63 B5
Mirango, *Malawi* 158 C2
Mirassol, *Brazil* 215 A1
Mirbāt, *Oman* 101 D2
Mirear, *Egypt* 139 F6
Miri, *Malaysia* 126 B7
Mirnyy, *Russia* 91 F13
Mirpur Khas, *Pakistan* 105 F4
Miryang, *S. Korea* 118 G5
Mirzaani, *Georgia* 82 B7
Mirzapur, *India* 106 C5
Mirzapur-cum-Vindhyachal = Mirzapur, *India* 106 C5
Mishan, *China* 113 B12
Mishbih, Gebel, *Egypt* 139 F6
Mishima, *Japan* 120 B8
Miskitos, Cayos, *Nic.* 197 A4
Miskolc, *Hungary* 74 A4
Misool, *Indonesia* 129 D14
Misrātah, *Libya* 138 A3
Missinaibi →, *Canada* 187 J11
Mississippi □, *U.S.A.* 191 H12
Mississippi →, *U.S.A.* 191 J12
Mississippi River Delta, *U.S.A.* 191 J13
Missoula, *U.S.A.* 190 B5
Missouri □, *U.S.A.* 191 F11
Missouri →, *U.S.A.* 191 F12
Mistassini L., *Canada* 187 J12
Mistretta, *Italy* 67 J6
Misurata = Misrātah, *Libya* 138 A3
Mît Ghamr, *Egypt* 139 A4
Mitan, *Uzbekistan* 93 D1
Mitchell, *U.S.A.* 190 D9
Mito, *Japan* 120 A9
Mitsinjo, *Madag.* 165 B2
Mitsiwa, *Eritrea* 144 B3
Mittagong, *Australia* 171 E8
Mitú, *Colombia* 210 D3
Mitumba, Chaîne des, *Zaïre* 155 F5
Mitumba Mts. = Mitumba, Chaîne des, *Zaïre* 155 F5
Mitwaba, *Zaïre* 155 F5
Mityana, *Uganda* 156 C2
Mitzic, *Gabon* 154 B1
Miyâh, W. el →, *Egypt* 139 E5
Miyah, W. el →, *Syria* 97 C4
Miyake-Jima, *Japan* 120 C9
Miyako, *Japan* 121 D8
Miyako-Jima, *Japan* 121 K6
Miyazu, *Japan* 120 B5
Miyet, Bahr el = Dead Sea, *Asia* 84 E7
Miyun, *China* 116 B3
Mizamis = Ozamiz, *Phil.* 130 J4
Mizdah, *Libya* 138 A2
Mizhi, *China* 116 D1
Mizoram □, *India* 107 C6
Mizpe Ramon, *Israel* 96 F2
Mjøsa, *Norway* 40 F2
Mkomazi →, *S. Africa* 163 F8
Mkuze, *S. Africa* 163 D9
Mkuze →, *S. Africa* 163 D9
Mladá Boleslav, *Czech.* 76 A3
Mlange, *Malawi* 158 E3
Mława, *Poland* 77 B4
Mmabatho, *S. Africa* 163 C6
Moa, *Indonesia* 129 F13
Moa →, *S. Leone* 147 D3
Moabi, *Gabon* 154 C1
Moalie Park, *Australia* 171 B4
Moba, *Zaïre* 155 E6
Mobaye, *C.A.R.* 142 C3
Mobayi, *Zaïre* 155 A3
Moberly, *U.S.A.* 191 E11
Mobile, *U.S.A.* 191 H13
Mobutu Sese Seko, L., *Africa* 132 F7
Moçambique, *Mozam.* 159 B3
Moçâmedes = Namibe, *Angola* 160 D2
Mocho Mts., *Jamaica* 199 B3
Mochudi, *Botswana* 162 C5
Mocimboa da Praia, *Mozam.* 159 A3
Mocoa, *Colombia* 210 D1
Mococa, *Brazil* 215 B2
Mocuba, *Mozam.* 159 C3
Modane, *France* 55 F9
Modder →, *S. Africa* 163 E5
Modderrivier, *S. Africa* 163 E5
Módena, *Italy* 67 B4
Modesto, *U.S.A.* 190 E2
Módica, *Italy* 67 K6
Moe, *Australia* 171 H5
Moengo, *Surinam* 214 B5
Mogadishu = Muqdisho, *Somali Rep.* 145 C2
Mogador = Essaouira, *Morocco* 136 D2
Mogalakwena →, *S. Africa* 163 A7
Mogami →, *Japan* 121 E7
Mogán, *Canary Is.* 223 D2
Mogaung, *Burma* 122 B3
Mogi das Cruzes, *Brazil* 215 C3
Mogi-Guaçu →, *Brazil* 215 A1
Mogi-Mirim, *Brazil* 215 B2
Mogilev, *Belarus* 81 C3
Mogilev-Podolskiy, *Moldova* 81 F2
Mogocha, *Russia* 91 H14
Mogoi, *Indonesia* 129 D15
Mogok, *Burma* 122 C2
Mogumber, *Australia* 170 A1
Mohács, *Hungary* 74 C3
Mohales Hoek, *Lesotho* 164 C1
Mohammedia, *Morocco* 136 B3
Moheli, *Comoros Is.* 166 B1
Mohoro, *Tanzania* 158 C3
Mointy, *Kazakstan* 90 J7
Moisie, *Canada* 187 J13
Moisie →, *Canada* 187 J13
Moïssala, *Chad* 142 F1
Mojave Desert, *U.S.A.* 190 F3
Mojo, *Indonesia* 128 F9
Mokhotlong, *Lesotho* 164 B3
Moknine, *Tunisia* 138 B3
Mol, *Belgium* 51 B4
Molchanovo, *Russia* 90 G9
Moldavia ■ = Moldova ■, *Europe* 81 G2
Molde, *Norway* 40 E1
Moldotau, Khrebet, *Kyrgyzstan* 93 C7
Moldova ■, *Europe* 81 G2
Mole →, *U.K.* 45 D2
Molepolole, *Botswana* 162 C5
Molfetta, *Italy* 67 F8
Moline, *U.S.A.* 191 D12
Moliro, *Zaïre* 155 E6
Molise □, *Italy* 67 E6
Mollendo, *Peru* 213 F4
Mollerin, L., *Australia* 170 A2
Molokai, *U.S.A.* 192 A2
Molong, *Australia* 171 E7
Molotov = Perm, *Russia* 90 F6
Moloundou, *Cameroon* 153 E3
Molteno, *S. Africa* 163 G6
Molu, *Indonesia* 129 E15
Molucca = Maluku, *Indonesia* 129 C13
Molucca Sea = Maluku Sea, *Indonesia* 129 C12
Moluccas = Maluku, *Indonesia* 129 C13
Moma, *Mozam.* 159 C3
Mombasa, *Kenya* 157 F4
Mombetsu, *Japan* 121 B8
Mompós, *Colombia* 210 B1
Møn, *Denmark* 42 D4
Mona, Pta., *Costa Rica* 197 D4
Monaco ■, *Europe* 55 G9
Monaghan, *Ireland* 46 G3
Monastir = Bitola, *Macedonia* 72 F8
Monastir, *Tunisia* 138 B3
Monbetsu, *Japan* 121 A8
Moncada, *Phil.* 130 D2
Moncayo, Sierra del, *Spain* 63 C6
Mönchengladbach, *Germany* 58 D1
Monchique, *Portugal* 63 G1
Monchique, Sa. de, *Portugal* 63 G1
Monclova, *Mexico* 194 C4
Moncton, *Canada* 187 K14
Mondego →, *Portugal* 63 D1
Mondeodo, *Indonesia* 129 D11
Mondovi, *Italy* 67 B1
Mondragon, *Phil.* 130 F5
Monessen, *U.S.A.* 189 C1
Mong Cai, *Vietnam* 125 A4
Mong Lang, *Burma* 122 D3
Mong Nai, *Burma* 122 D3
Mong Ton, *Burma* 122 E3
Mong Yai, *Burma* 122 D3
Mongalla, *Sudan* 143 F4
Monghyr = Munger, *India* 106 C7
Mongla, *Bangla.* 111 D1
Mongo, *Chad* 142 E2
Mongó, *Eq. Guin.* 153 B2
Mongolia ■, *Asia* 112
Mongomo, *Eq. Guin.* 153 C2
Mongonu, *Nigeria* 151 A7
Mongororo, *Chad* 142 E3
Mongu, *Zambia* 161 C2
Monkey Bay, *Malawi* 158 D2
Monkey River, *Belize* 196 B2
Monkoto, *Zaïre* 155 C3
Monmouth, *U.K.* 46 K6
Monópoli, *Italy* 67 F8
Monroe, *La., U.S.A.* 191 H11
Monroe, *Mich., U.S.A.* 191 D14
Monrovia, *Liberia* 148 D1
Mons, *Belgium* 51 D2
Monse, *Indonesia* 129 D11
Mont de Marsan, *France* 55 G4
Mont-St-Michel, *France* 55 C3
Mont-St-Michel, Le = Mont-St-Michel, *France* 55 C3
Montagu, *S. Africa* 163 H3
Montalbán, *Spain* 63 C7
Montana □, *U.S.A.* 190 B5
Montargis, *France* 55 C6
Montauban, *France* 55 G5
Montbéliard, *France* 55 D8
Monte Caseros, *Argentina* 220 D5
Monte Cristi, *Dom. Rep.* 200 A2
Monte Sant' Ángelo, *Italy* 67 E7
Monte Santo, C., *Italy* 67 G3
Montebello, *Canada* 185 B4
Montecristi, *Ecuador* 212 C1
Montego Bay, *Jamaica* 199 A2
Montélimar, *France* 55 F7
Montemorelos, *Mexico* 194 C5
Montenegro □, *Yugoslavia* 72 D6
Montepuez, *Mozam.* 159 B3
Monterey, *U.S.A.* 190 E2
Montería, *Colombia* 210 B1
Monterrey, *Mexico* 194 C5
Montes Claros, *Brazil* 217 F7
Montevideo, *Uruguay* 219 D2
Montgomery = Sahiwal, *Pakistan* 105 C5
Montgomery, *U.K.* 46 J6

Montgomery, U.S.A. 191 H13
Monthey, Switz. 60 D1
Montilla, Spain 63 F4
Montluçon, France 55 E6
Montoro, Spain 63 F4
Montpelier, Idaho, U.S.A. 190 D5
Montpelier, Vt., U.S.A. 191 C17
Montpellier, France 55 G7
Montréal, Canada 185 B5
Montreuil, France 55 A5
Montreux, Switz. 60 C1
Montrose, U.S.A. 190 E6
Montserrat ■, W. Indies 202 E3
Montuiri, Spain 65 B4
Monveda, Zaïre 155 B3
Monywa, Burma 122 D2
Monza, Italy 67 A2
Monze, Zambia 161 D3
Monzón, Spain 63 B8
Mooi River, S. Africa 163 E8
Moolawatana, Australia 171 C2
Mooliabeenee, Australia 170 B1
Moonie, Australia 171 A8
Moonie →, Australia 171 B7
Moonta, Australia 171 E1
Moora, Australia 170 A1
Moore →, Australia 170 B1
Moorefield, U.S.A. 189 D2
Moorhead, U.S.A. 191 C10
Mooroopna, Australia 171 G5
Moorreesburg, S. Africa 163 H2
Moose Jaw, Canada 186 J6
Moosehead L., U.S.A. 191 B17
Moosomin, Canada 186 J7
Moosonee, Canada 187 J11
Mopeia Velha, Mozam. 159 C2
Mopti, Mali 140 E4
Moquegua, Peru 213 F4
Mora, Sweden 40 F3
Moradabad, India 106 A4
Morafenobe, Madag. 165 C1
Moramanga, Madag. 165 C2
Morant Bay, Jamaica 199 C6
Morant Pt., Jamaica 199 C6
Moratuwa, Sri Lanka 110 D1
Morava →, Europe 76 D5
Moravian Hts. = Ceskomoravská Vrchovina, Czech. 76 B4
Morawhanna, Guyana 214 A1
Moray Firth, U.K. 46 B5
Morbihan □, France 55 C2
Morden, Canada 186 K8
Mordovian Republic □, Russia 81 C7
Mordvinia = Mordovian Republic □, Russia 81 C7
Morea, Australia 171 G3
Morea, Greece 34 H11
Moreau →, U.S.A. 190 C8
Morecambe B., U.K. 46 G6
Moree, Australia 171 B7
Morelia, Mexico 194 E4
Morella, Spain 63 D8
Morena, Sierra, Spain 63 F4
Moreton I., Australia 171 A9
Morgan, Australia 171 E2
Morgan City, U.S.A. 191 J12
Morgantown, U.S.A. 189 D1
Morgenzon, S. Africa 163 D8
Morges, Switz. 60 C1
Moriki, Nigeria 151 A3
Morioka, Japan 121 D7
Morlaix, France 55 C2
Mormugao, India 107 E2
Mornington, Australia 171 H5
Moro G., Phil. 130 K4
Morobe, Papua N. G. 173 C2
Morocco ■, N. Afr. 136
Morococha, Peru 213 D3
Morogoro, Tanzania 158 C3
Morombe, Madag. 165 D1
Morón, Argentina 221 C5
Morón, Cuba 198 B4
Morón, Spain 63 G4
Mörön →, Mongolia 113 A7
Morona-Santiago □, Ecuador 212 D2
Morondava, Madag. 165 D1
Morondo, Ivory C. 148 B4
Moroni, Comoros Is. 166 A1
Moronou, Ivory C. 148 D5
Morotai, Indonesia 129 B14
Moroto, Uganda 156 B3
Moroto Summit, Kenya 157 B1
Morphou, Cyprus 95 B1
Morphou Bay, Cyprus 95 B1
Morrelganj, Bangla. 111 D2
Morristown, U.S.A. 191 F14
Morrumbene, Mozam. 159 E2
Morshansk, Russia 81 D6
Mortlake, Australia 171 H4
Morundah, Australia 171 F5
Moruya, Australia 171 F7
Morvan, France 55 D7
Morwell, Australia 171 H5
Moscos Is., Burma 122 G3
Moscow = Moskva, Russia 81 C5
Moscow, U.S.A. 190 B4
Mosel →, Europe 55 C8
Moselle = Mosel →, Europe 55 C8
Moselle □, France 55 B8
Moses Lake, U.S.A. 190 B3
Mosgiel, N.Z. 175 J3
Moshi, Tanzania 158 B3
Mosjøen, Norway 40 C3
Moskva, Russia 81 C5
Moskva →, Russia 81 C5
Mosquera, Colombia 210 D1
Mosquitia, Honduras 196 C5
Mosquitos, G. de los, Panama 197 E4
Moss Vale, Australia 171 F8
Mossaka, Congo 154 C3
Mossburn, N.Z. 175 J2
Mosselbaai, S. Africa 163 H4
Mossendjo, Congo 154 C1
Mossgiel, Australia 171 E5
Mossoró, Brazil 217 C9
Mossuril, Mozam. 159 B3
Most, Czech. 76 A3
Mosta, Malta 69 B2
Mostaganem, Algeria 137 A3
Mostar, Bos.-H. 72 D5
Mostefa, Rass, Tunisia 138 A3
Mosul = Al Mawşil, Iraq 102 A3
Mosulpo, S. Korea 118 J4
Motagua →, Guatemala 196 C2
Motherwell, U.K. 46 D5
Motihari, India 106 B6
Motueka, N.Z. 175 E4
Mouanda, Gabon 154 C2
Moúdhros, Greece 71 C5
Moudjeria, Mauritania 140 D2
Moudon, Switz. 60 C1
Mouila, Gabon 154 C1
Moulamein, Australia 171 F4
Moulins, France 55 E6
Moulmein = Maulamyaing, Burma 122 F3
Moulouya, O. →, Morocco 136 A6
Moultrie, U.S.A. 191 H14
Moundou, Chad 142 F1
Mount Barker, S. Austral., Australia 171 F2
Mount Barker, W. Austral., Australia 170 D2
Mount Darwin, Zimbabwe 161 B4
Mount Fletcher, S. Africa 163 F7
Mount Gambier, Australia 171 H3
Mount Hope, Australia 171 D5
Mount Isa, Australia 168 H11
Mount Lofty Ra., Australia 171 E2
Mount Margaret, Australia 171 A4
Mount Maunganui, N.Z. 175 C6
Mount Morris, U.S.A. 189 A2
Mount Vernon, Ind., U.S.A. 191 F12
Mount Vernon, N.Y., U.S.A. 189 B5
Mourdi, Dépression du, Chad 142 B3
Mourdiah, Mali 140 E3
Mouri, Ghana 149 E2
Mourne Mts., U.K. 46 G4
Mouscron, Belgium 51 C1
Moussoro, Chad 142 D1
Moutier, Switz. 60 B2
Moutong, Indonesia 129 C11
Moyale, Kenya 157 A4
Moyamba, S. Leone 147 C3
Moyen Atlas, Morocco 136 C5
Moyobamba, Peru 213 C2
Moyyero →, Russia 91 E11
Mozambique = Moçambique, Mozam. 159 B3
Mozambique ■, Africa 159
Mozambique Chan., Africa 132 J8
Mozyr, Belarus 81 D3
Mpanda, Tanzania 158 C1
Mpika, Zambia 161 B5
Mpumalanga, S. Africa 163 F8
Mpumalanga □, S. Africa 163 C8
Mpwapwa, Tanzania 158 C2
Mrimina, Morocco 136 E3
Msaken, Tunisia 138 B2
Msambansovu, Zimbabwe 161 A3
Msoro, Zambia 161 C5
Mtilikwe →, Zimbabwe 161 D4
Mtskheta, Georgia 82 B6
Mtubatuba, S. Africa 163 E9
Muang Chiang Rai, Thailand 123 E4
Muang Lamphun, Thailand 122 E3
Muarabungo, Indonesia 128 C3
Muaraenim, Indonesia 128 D4
Muarajuloi, Indonesia 128 C8
Muarakaman, Indonesia 128 C9
Muaratebo, Indonesia 128 C3
Muaratembesi, Indonesia 128 D4
Muaratewe, Indonesia 128 C8
Mubarraz = Al Mubarraz, Si. Arabia 99 C6
Mubende, Uganda 156 C1
Mubi, Nigeria 151 C7
Muconda, Angola 160 C4
Mudanjiang, China 113 B12
Mudgee, Australia 171 D7
Mudon, Burma 122 F3
Mufulira, Zambia 161 B3
Muğla, Turkey 94 C1
Mugu, Nepal 109 A2
Muhammad, Râs, Egypt 139 C6
Muhammad Qol, Sudan 143 A6
Mühlhausen, Germany 58 D3
Muir, L., Australia 170 D2
Mukah, Malaysia 126 C6
Mukawwa, Egypt 139 E6
Mukden = Shenyang, China 116 B6
Mukhtuya = Lensk, Russia 91 G13
Mukinbudin, Australia 170 A3
Mukomuko, Indonesia 128 D3
Muktsar Bhatinda, India 107 B2
Mulde →, Germany 58 C5
Mulgrave, Canada 187 K15
Mulhacén, Spain 63 G5
Mülheim, Germany 58 C1
Mulhouse, France 55 C9
Mull, U.K. 46 D4
Mullaittvu, Sri Lanka 110 A2
Mullengudgery, Australia 171 D6
Muller, Pegunungan, Indonesia 128 C8
Mullingar, Ireland 46 G2
Mullumbimby, Australia 171 B9
Multan, Pakistan 105 D5
Mumbwa, Zambia 161 C3
Mun →, Thailand 123 G5
Muna, Indonesia 129 E11
München, Germany 58 F4
Munchen-Gladbach = Mönchengladbach, Germany 58 D1
Munchŏn, N. Korea 118 D4
Muncie, U.S.A. 191 E13
Münden, Germany 58 D3
Mungallala Cr. →, Australia 171 A6
Mungbere, Zaïre 155 B6
Munger, India 106 C7
Mungindi, Australia 171 B7
Munhango, Angola 160 C4
Munich = München, Germany 58 F4
Munku-Sardyk, Russia 91 J11
Munsan, S. Korea 118 E4
Munshiganj, Bangla. 111 C2
Münster, Germany 58 C2
Muntadgin, Australia 170 B3
Muntok, Indonesia 128 D4
Munyak, Uzbekistan 90 J4
Munzer Dağlari, Turkey 82 D1
Muon Pak Beng, Laos 125 B1
Mupa, Angola 160 E3
Muping, China 116 D5
Muqdisho, Somali Rep. 145 C2
Mur →, Austria 61 C6
Muranda, Rwanda 156 A1
Murang'a, Kenya 157 D2
Murashi, Russia 81 A8
Murban, U.A.E. 101 C2
Murchison Falls = Kabarega Falls, Uganda 156 B1
Murchison Rapids, Malawi 158 E2
Murcia, Spain 63 F7
Murcia □, Spain 63 F6
Mureş →, Romania 75 B1
Mureşul = Mureş →, Romania 75 B1
Murgab, Tajikistan 93 F6
Muriaé, Brazil 215 B5
Muriel Mine, Zimbabwe 161 B4
Müritz See, Germany 58 B5
Murka, Kenya 157 E3
Murmansk, Russia 90 B5
Muro, Spain 65 A4
Murom, Russia 81 C6
Muroran, Japan 121 C7
Muroto-Misaki, Japan 120 D4
Murray, U.S.A. 190 E5
Murray →, Australia 171 F2
Murray Bridge, Australia 171 F2
Murraysburg, S. Africa 163 G5
Murrumbidgee →, Australia 171 E4
Murrumburrah, Australia 171 E7
Murrurundi, Australia 171 D8
Mursala, Indonesia 128 B2
Murtoa, Australia 171 G4
Murwara, India 106 D4
Murwillumbah, Australia 171 B9
Mürzzuschlag, Austria 61 B5
Muş, Turkey 94 B6
Musa Khel Bazar, Pakistan 105 C4
Músá Qal'eh, Afghan. 104 E3
Musaffargarh, Pakistan 105 D5
Musala, Bulgaria 73 C2
Musan, N. Korea 118 A5
Musay'īd, Qatar 100 D3
Muscat = Masqat, Oman 101 B3
Muscat & Oman = Oman ■, Asia 101
Musgrave Ra., Australia 168 C3
Mushie, Zaïre 155 D2
Mushin, Nigeria 151 F1
Musi →, Indonesia 128 D4
Muskegon, U.S.A. 191 D13
Muskegon →, U.S.A. 191 D13
Muskogee, U.S.A. 191 G10
Muslīmiyah, Syria 97 A3
Musmar, Sudan 143 B5
Musoma, Tanzania 158 A1
Musselshell →, U.S.A. 190 B6
Mustang, Nepal 109 A3
Musudan, N. Korea 118 C5
Muswellbrook, Australia 171 D8
Mût, Egypt 139 D3
Mutaray, Russia 91 G11
Mutare, Zimbabwe 161 C5
Muting, Indonesia 129 F18
Mutriba, Kuwait 100 A1
Mutsamudu, Comoros Is. 166 B2
Mutsu-Wan, Japan 121 C7
Muxima, Angola 160 B2
Muy Muy, Nic. 197 B2
Muya, Russia 91 H13
Muzaffarabad, Pakistan 105 A6
Muzaffarnagar, India 106 A3
Muzaffarpur, India 106 C7
Muzhi, Russia 90 E7
Muzkol, Khrebet, Tajikistan 93 F6
Muztag, China 112 E3
Mvuma, Zimbabwe 161 C4
Mvurwi, Zimbabwe 161 B4
Mwanza, Tanzania 158 B1
Mwanza, Zaïre 155 E5
Mweka, Zaïre 155 D3
Mwenezi, Zimbabwe 161 E4
Mwenga, Zaïre 155 D6
Mweru, L., Zambia 161 A4
Mweza Range, Zimbabwe 161 D3
Mwinilunga, Zambia 161 B2
My Tho, Vietnam 125 G4
Myanaung, Burma 122 E2
Myanmar = Burma ■, Asia 122
Myaungmya, Burma 122 F2
Mycenae = Mikínai, Greece 71 D3
Myeik Kyunzu, Burma 122 H3
Myingyan, Burma 122 D2
Myitkyina, Burma 122 B3
Mykolayiv = Nikolayev, Ukraine 81 G3
Mymensingh, Bangla. 111 B2
Mýrdalsjökull, Iceland 38 D3
Mysore = Karnataka □, India 107 F2
Mysore, India 107 F2
Mývatn, Iceland 38 B4
Mzimba, Malawi 158 B2
Mzimkulu →, S. Africa 163 F8
Mzimvubu →, S. Africa 163 G8
Mzuzu, Malawi 158 B2

N

N' Dioum, Senegal 146 A2
Naab →, Germany 58 F4
Naaldwijk, Neths. 50 D2
Naas, Ireland 46 H3
Nababiep, S. Africa 163 F1
Naberezhnyye Chelny, Russia 82 C9
Nabeul, Tunisia 138 A3
Nabire, Indonesia 129 D16
Nabiswera, Uganda 156 B2
Nablus = Nābulus, Jordan 98 A1
Naboomspruit, S. Africa 163 B7
Nabua, Phil. 130 F4
Nābulus, Jordan 98 A1
Nacaome, Honduras 196 D3
Nachingwea, Tanzania 158 D3
Nackara, Australia 171 D2
Nacogdoches, U.S.A. 191 H11
Nacozari, Mexico 194 A2
Nadiad, India 106 D1
Nador, Morocco 136 A6
Nadur, Malta 69 A2
Nadym, Russia 90 E8
Nadym →, Russia 90 E8
Nafada, Nigeria 151 B6
Nafud Desert = An Nafūd, Si. Arabia 99 B3
Nag Hammâdi, Egypt 139 D5
Naga, Phil. 130 F4
Nagaland □, India 107 C6
Nagano, Japan 120 A7
Nagano □, Japan 120 A7
Nagaoka, Japan 121 F6
Nagappattinam, India 107 F3
Nagar Parkar, Pakistan 105 F4
Nagasaki, Japan 120 D1
Nagasaki □, Japan 120 D1
Nagaur, India 106 B2
Nagercoil, India 107 G3
Nagorno-Karabakh, Azerbaijan 82 D7
Nagornyy, Russia 91 G14
Nagoya, Japan 120 B6
Nagpur, India 106 E4
Nagua, Dom. Rep. 200 A3
Nagykanizsa, Hungary 74 C2
Nagykörös, Hungary 74 B4
Naha, Japan 121 J8
Nahanni Butte, Canada 186 E5
Nahīya, Wadi →, Egypt 139 B4
Nain, Canada 187 G13
Nainpur, India 106 E4
Naira, Indonesia 129 E14
Nairn, U.K. 46 B5
Nairobi, Kenya 157 D2
Naivasha, Kenya 157 D2
Naivasha, L., Kenya 157 D2
Najd, Si. Arabia 99 C4
Najibabad, India 106 A4
Najin, N. Korea 118 A6
Naju, S. Korea 118 H4
Naka-no-Shima, Japan 121 G9
Nakamura, Japan 120 D3
Nakfa, Eritrea 144 B3
Nakhichevan, Azerbaijan 82 D6
Nakhl, Egypt 139 B5
Nakhodka, Russia 91 J17
Nakhon Phanom, Thailand 123 F6
Nakhon Ratchasima, Thailand 123 G5
Nakhon Sawan, Thailand 123 G4
Nakhon Si Thammarat, Thailand 123 K4
Nakina, Canada 187 K10
Nakskov, Denmark 42 D3
Naktong →, S. Korea 118 G5
Nakuru, Kenya 157 D2
Nakuru □, Kenya 157 D2
Nakuru, L., Kenya 157 D2
Nal →, Pakistan 105 F2
Nalchik, Russia 82 A5
Nalerigu, Ghana 149 A3
Nalón →, Spain 63 A3
Nālūt, Libya 138 A2
Nam-chon, N. Korea 118 E3
Nam Co, China 112 F4
Nam Dinh, Vietnam 125 B4
Nam-Phan, Vietnam 125 G4
Nam Phong, Thailand 123 F5
Nam Tha, Laos 125 B1
Namacurra, Mozam. 159 C3
Namak, Daryācheh-ye, Iran 103 B3
Namaland, Namibia 162 D2
Namangan, Uzbekistan 93 C5
Namapa, Mozam. 159 B3
Namaqualand, S. Africa 163 F1
Namasagali, Uganda 156 C2
Namatanai, Papua N. G. 173 A3
Namber, Indonesia 129 C16
Nambucca Heads, Australia 171 C9
Nameh, Indonesia 128 B9
Namib Desert = Namibwoestyn, Namibia 162 C2
Namibe, Angola 160 D2
Namibia ■, Africa 162
Namibwoestyn, Namibia 162 C2
Namlea, Indonesia 129 D13
Nampa, U.S.A. 190 C4
Nampula, Mozam. 159 B3
Namrole, Indonesia 129 D13
Namtay, Russia 91 E14
Namtu, Burma 122 C3
Namur, Belgium 51 D4
Namur □, Belgium 51 D4
Namutoni, Namibia 162 A2
Namwala, Zambia 161 C3
Namwŏn, S. Korea 118 G4
Nan, Thailand 123 E4
Nanaimo, Canada 186 H3
Nanam, N. Korea 118 B5
Nanango, Australia 171 A9
Nanao, Japan 121 F5
Nanchang, China 116 H3
Nancheng, China 116 J3
Nanching = Nanjing, China 116 F4
Nanchong, China 113 F7
Nancy, France 55 C8
Nanded, India 106 F3
Nandewar Ra., Australia 171 C8
Nandi □, Kenya 157 C1
Nandurbar, India 106 E2
Nanga Parbat, Pakistan 105 A6
Nangapinoh, Indonesia 128 C7
Nangarhár □, Afghan. 104 D6
Nangatayap, Indonesia 128 C6
Nangeya Mts., Uganda 156 A3
Nanjing, China 116 F4
Nanking = Nanjing, China 116 F4
Nanning, China 113 J7
Nannup, Australia 170 C1
Nanpi, China 116 D3
Nanping, China 116 J4
Nansei-Shotō, Japan 121 J7
Nansen Sd., Canada 186 A9
Nantes, France 55 D3
Nanticoke, U.S.A. 189 B4
Nantong, China 116 F5
Nantucket I., U.S.A. 180 E12
Nanyang, China 116 F2
Nanyuan, China 116 C3
Nanyuki, Kenya 157 C2
Nanzhang, China 116 G1
Náo, C. de la, Spain 63 E8
Naoetsu, Japan 121 F6
Napa, U.S.A. 190 E2
Napanee, Canada 185 C3
Napier, N.Z. 175 D6
Naples = Nápoli, Italy 67 F6
Napo □, Ecuador 212 B2
Napo →, Peru 213 B4
Nápoli, Italy 67 F6
Nappa Merrie, Australia 171 A3
Naqâda, Egypt 139 D5
Nara, Mali 140 E3
Nara □, Japan 120 C6
Naracoorte, Australia 171 G3
Naradhan, Australia 171 E6
Narathiwat, Thailand 123 L5
Narayanganj, Bangla. 111 C2
Narbonne, France 55 H6
Narembeen, Australia 170 B3
Nares Str., N. Amer. 180 A13
Narmada →, India 106 E1
Narman, Turkey 82 C3
Naro, Ghana 149 A1
Narodnaya, Russia 34 B18
Narok, Kenya 157 D2
Narok □, Kenya 157 D2
Narooma, Australia 171 G7
Narrabri, Australia 171 C7
Narran →, Australia 171 B7
Narran, L., Australia 171 B6
Narrandera, Australia 171 F6
Narrogin, Australia 170 C2
Narromine, Australia 171 D7
Narsinghpur, India 106 D4
Narva, Estonia 81 A3
Narvik, Norway 40 B4
Naryan-Mar, Russia 90 D7
Naryilco, Australia 171 B3
Narym, Russia 90 G9
Narymskoye, Kazakstan 90 J8
Naryn, Kyrgyzstan 93 C8
Naryn →, Uzbekistan 93 C5
Nasarawa, Nigeria 151 D4
Naser, Buheirat en, Egypt 139 F5
Nashua, U.S.A. 189 A6
Nashville, U.S.A. 191 F13

Nasik, *India* 106 F1
Nasipit, *Phil.* 130 J5
Nasirabad, *India* 106 C2
Nassau, *Bahamas* 201 A1
Nasser, L. = Naser, Buheirat en, *Egypt* 139 F5
Nasser City = Kôm Ombo, *Egypt* 139 E5
Nassian, *Ivory C.* 148 B6
Nasugbu, *Phil.* 130 E2
Nata, *Botswana* 162 B5
Natagaima, *Colombia* 210 C1
Natal, *Brazil* 217 D9
Natal, *Indonesia* 128 C2
Natashquan, *Canada* 187 H14
Natashquan →, *Canada* 187 H14
Natchez, *U.S.A.* 191 H12
Natchitoches, *U.S.A.* 191 H11
Nathalia, *Australia* 171 F5
Nathdwara, *India* 106 C2
Natimuk, *Australia* 171 G3
Natitingou, *Benin* 150 B2
Natkyizin, *Burma* 122 G3
Natron, L., *Tanzania* 158 A2
Natrûn, W. el →, *Egypt* 139 B3
Natuna Besar, Kepulauan, *Indonesia* 128 A5
Natuna Is. = Natuna Besar, Kepulauan, *Indonesia* 128 A5
Natuna Selatan, Kepulauan, *Indonesia* 128 B6
Naturaliste, C., *Tas., Australia* 172 B3
Naturaliste, C., *W. Austral., Australia* 168 D1
Nau, *Tajikistan* 93 D3
Naumburg, *Germany* 58 D4
Nauru ■, *Pac. Oc.* 176 F5
Naushahra, *Pakistan* 105 B5
Nauta, *Peru* 213 B3
Nautanwa, *India* 106 B6
Navan = An Uaimh, *Ireland* 46 G3
Navarra □, *Spain* 63 B6
Navojoa, *Mexico* 194 B2
Návpaktos, *Greece* 71 D2
Návplion, *Greece* 71 E3
Navrongo, *Ghana* 149 A2
Navsari, *India* 106 E1
Nawabshah, *Pakistan* 105 F3
Nâwah, *Afghan.* 104 E4
Nawakot, *Nepal* 109 B3
Nawalgarh, *India* 106 B2
Náxos, *Greece* 71 E5
Nayakhan, *Russia* 91 C17
Nayé, *Senegal* 146 B3
Nazareth = Nazerat, *Israel* 96 B2
Nazas →, *Mexico* 194 C4
Naze, *Japan* 121 H9
Nazerat, *Israel* 96 B2
Nazir Hat, *Bangla.* 111 D3
Ncheu, *Malawi* 158 D2
Ndalatando, *Angola* 160 B2
Ndali, *Benin* 150 B3
Ndélé, *C.A.R.* 142 A3
Ndendé, *Gabon* 154 C1
Ndjamena, *Chad* 142 E1
Ndjolé, *Gabon* 154 B1
Ndola, *Zambia* 161 B4
Ndoto Mts., *Kenya* 157 B2
Neagh, Lough, *U.K.* 46 F3
Nebine Cr. →, *Australia* 171 B6
Nebit Dag, *Turkmenistan* 90 K3
Nebraska □, *U.S.A.* 190 D8
Nebraska City, *U.S.A.* 191 E10
Nébrodi, Monti, *Italy* 67 J6
Neches →, *U.S.A.* 191 J11
Neckar →, *Germany* 58 E2
Necochea, *Argentina* 220 F5
Neemuch = Nimach, *India* 106 D2
Neepawa, *Canada* 186 J7
Neft-chala = imeni 26 Bakinskikh Komissarov, *Azerbaijan* 82 D9
Nefta, *Tunisia* 138 C1
Negapatam = Nagappattinam, *India* 107 F3
Negele, *Ethiopia* 144 F3
Negev Desert = Hanegev, *Israel* 96 F2
Negoiul, Vf., *Romania* 75 C4
Negombo, *Sri Lanka* 110 C1
Negotin, *Serbia, Yug.* 72 C8
Negril, *Jamaica* 199 A1
Negro →, *Argentina* 206 G3
Negro →, *Brazil* 217 C4
Negro →, *Uruguay* 219 C1
Negros, *Phil.* 130 H4
Nehbandān, *Iran* 103 C5
Neheim, *Germany* 59 A3
Nei Monggol Zizhiqu □, *China* 116 A2
Neiges, Piton des, *Réunion* 166 B2
Neijiang, *China* 113 G7
Neiva, *Colombia* 210 D1
Neixiang, *China* 116 F1
Nejd = Najd, *Si. Arabia* 99 C4
Nekemte, *Ethiopia* 144 D2
Nêkheb, *Egypt* 139 E5
Neksø, *Denmark* 42 D5
Nelkan, *Russia* 91 F15
Nellore, *India* 107 F3
Nelma, *Russia* 91 H17
Nelson, *Canada* 186 J4
Nelson, *N.Z.* 175 F4
Nelson →, *Canada* 186 H9
Nelson, C., *Australia* 171 H3
Nelspoort, *S. Africa* 163 G4
Nelspruit, *S. Africa* 163 C9
Néma, *Mauritania* 140 D3
Neman →, *Lithuania* 81 B1
Nemunas = Neman →, *Lithuania* 81 B1
Nemuro, *Japan* 121 B9
Nemuro-Kaikyō, *Japan* 121 A9
Nemuy, *Russia* 91 G15
Nenagh, *Ireland* 46 H2
Nenana, *U.S.A.* 193 A4
Nenasi, *Malaysia* 126 C3
Nenjiang, *China* 113 A11
Neno, *Malawi* 158 D2
Nenusa, Kepulauan, *Indonesia* 129 A13
Neosho →, *U.S.A.* 191 G10
Nepal ■, *Asia* 109
Nepalganj, *Nepal* 109 B2
Nerchinsk, *Russia* 91 J13
Nerchinskiy Zavod, *Russia* 91 J14
Neretva →, *Croatia* 72 D5
Nerva, *Spain* 63 F3
Nes, *Iceland* 38 B4
Neskaupstaður, *Iceland* 38 B6
Ness, L., *U.K.* 46 B5
Netanya, *Israel* 96 C2
Nete = Nethe →, *Belgium* 51 B3
Nethe →, *Belgium* 51 B3
Netherlands ■, *Europe* 50
Netrakona, *Bangla.* 111 B2
Nettilling L., *Canada* 187 E11
Neubrandenburg, *Germany* 58 A5
Neuchâtel, *Switz.* 60 B1
Neuchâtel □, *Switz.* 60 B1
Neuchâtel, Lac de, *Switz.* 60 B1
Neufchâteau, *Belgium* 51 E5
Neumünster, *Germany* 58 A3
Neunkirchen, *Germany* 58 E1
Neuquén, *Argentina* 220 G3
Neuruppin, *Germany* 58 B5
Neuse →, *U.S.A.* 191 F16
Neusiedler See, *Austria* 61 B6
Neuss, *Germany* 59 B1
Neustrelitz, *Germany* 58 B5
Neva →, *Russia* 81 A3
Nevada □, *U.S.A.* 190 E3
Nevada, Sierra, *Spain* 63 G5
Nevada, Sierra, *U.S.A.* 190 E2
Nevanka, *Russia* 91 H11
Nevers, *France* 55 D6
Nevertire, *Australia* 171 D6
Nevis, *W. Indies* 202 D2
New →, *Guyana* 214 D3
New Albany, *U.S.A.* 191 F13
New Amsterdam, *Guyana* 214 B3
New Angledool, *Australia* 171 B6
New Bedford, *U.S.A.* 189 B6
New Bern, *U.S.A.* 191 F16
New Braunfels, *U.S.A.* 190 J9
New Brighton, *N.Z.* 175 G4
New Britain, *Papua N. G.* 173 B3
New Britain, *U.S.A.* 189 B5
New Brunswick, *U.S.A.* 189 C5
New Brunswick □, *Canada* 187 K14
New Bussa, *Nigeria* 151 C2
New Caledonia, *Pac. Oc.* 168 C6
New Castile = Castilla La Mancha □, *Spain* 63 D5
New Delhi, *India* 106 A3
New England Ra., *Australia* 171 C8
New Georgia Is., *Solomon Is.* 173 A1
New Glasgow, *Canada* 187 K14
New Guinea, *Oceania* 84 J17
New Hampshire □, *U.S.A.* 191 C17
New Hanover = Lavongai, *Papua N. G.* 173 A3
New Hanover, *S. Africa* 163 E8
New Haven, *U.S.A.* 189 B5
New Hebrides = Vanuatu ■, *Pac. Oc.* 176 G5
New Iberia, *U.S.A.* 191 J12
New Ireland, *Papua N. G.* 173 A3
New Jersey □, *U.S.A.* 189 C5
New Kensington, *U.S.A.* 189 C1
New London, *U.S.A.* 189 B6
New Mexico □, *U.S.A.* 190 G6
New Norfolk, *Australia* 172 C2
New Orleans, *U.S.A.* 191 J12
New Providence, *Bahamas* 201 A1
New Ross, *Ireland* 46 J3
New Siberian Is. = Novaya Sibir, Ostrov, *Russia* 91 B14
New Siberian Is. = Novosibirskiye Ostrova, *Russia* 91 B13
New South Wales □, *Australia* 171 D5
New Ulm, *U.S.A.* 191 C10
New Westminster, *Canada* 186 H3
New York □, *U.S.A.* 189 A3
New York City, *U.S.A.* 189 C5
New Zealand ■, *Oceania* 175
Newala, *Tanzania* 158 D3
Newark, *Del., U.S.A.* 189 D4
Newark, *N.J., U.S.A.* 189 C5
Newark, *N.Y., U.S.A.* 189 A3
Newark, *Ohio, U.S.A.* 191 E14
Newburgh, *U.S.A.* 189 B5
Newburyport, *U.S.A.* 189 A6
Newcastle, *Australia* 171 D8
Newcastle, *Canada* 187 K14
Newcastle, *S. Africa* 163 D8
Newcastle, *U.K.* 46 F7
Newdegate, *Australia* 170 C3
Newfoundland □, *Canada* 187 G14
Newham, *U.K.* 45 C4
Newhaven, *U.K.* 46 L9
Newington, *U.K.* 45 D6
Newnan, *U.S.A.* 191 G14
Newport, *Essex, U.K.* 45 A4
Newport, *Gwent, U.K.* 46 K6
Newport, *I. of W., U.K.* 46 L7
Newport, *Ark., U.S.A.* 191 G12
Newport, *Ky., U.S.A.* 191 E14
Newport, *R.I., U.S.A.* 189 B6
Newport News, *U.S.A.* 191 F16
Newry, *U.K.* 46 G3
Newton, *Iowa, U.S.A.* 191 D11
Newton, *Mass., U.S.A.* 189 A6
Newton, *N.J., U.S.A.* 189 B4
Newton Boyd, *Australia* 171 B9
Neya, *Russia* 81 B7
Neyrīz, *Iran* 103 D4
Neyshābūr, *Iran* 103 B5
Nezhin, *Ukraine* 81 E3
Ngabang, *Indonesia* 128 C6
Ngabordamlu, Tanjung, *Indonesia* 129 E16
Ngami Depression, *Botswana* 162 B4
Ngamo, *Zimbabwe* 161 C2
Nganga Eboko, *Cameroon* 153 D2
Ngaoundéré, *Cameroon* 153 C2
Nghai Lo, *Vietnam* 125 A3
Ngoma, *Malawi* 158 C1
Ngomahura, *Zimbabwe* 161 D4
Ngoring Hu, *China* 112 E5
Ngozi, *Burundi* 156 B2
Ngudu, *Tanzania* 158 B1
Nguigmi, *Niger* 141 C5
Nguru, *Nigeria* 151 A6
Nha Trang, *Vietnam* 125 F5
Nhill, *Australia* 171 G3
Niafounké, *Mali* 140 E4
Niagara Falls, *Canada* 185 D2
Niagara Falls, *U.S.A.* 189 A2
Niah, *Malaysia* 126 B7
Niamey, *Niger* 141 D2
Nianforando, *Guinea* 147 B4
Niangara, *Zaïre* 155 A5
Nias, *Indonesia* 128 B1
Nicaragua ■, *Cent. Amer.* 197
Nicaragua, L. de, *Nic.* 197 C2
Nicastro, *Italy* 67 H8
Nice, *France* 55 G9
Nickerie □, *Surinam* 214 D3
Nickerie →, *Surinam* 214 B3
Nicobar Is., *Ind. Oc.* 84 H13
Nicosia, *Cyprus* 95 B2
Nicoya, *Costa Rica* 197 D2
Nicoya, G. de, *Costa Rica* 197 D2
Nicoya, Pen. de, *Costa Rica* 197 D2
Niederösterreich □, *Austria* 61 A5
Niedersachsen □, *Germany* 58 B2
Niefang, *Eq. Guin.* 153 B2
Niekerkshoop, *S. Africa* 163 E4
Niellé, *Ivory C.* 148 A5
Niemen = Neman →, *Lithuania* 81 B1
Nienburg, *Germany* 58 B3
Niers →, *Germany* 59 A1
Nieu Bethesda, *S. Africa* 163 G5
Nieuw Amsterdam, *Surinam* 214 B4
Nieuw Nickerie, *Surinam* 214 B3
Nieuwoudtville, *S. Africa* 163 G2
Nieuwpoort, *Belgium* 51 B1
Nièvre □, *France* 55 D6
Niğde, *Turkey* 94 C4
Nigel, *S. Africa* 163 C7
Niger □, *Nigeria* 151 C2
Niger ■, *W. Afr.* 141
Niger →, *W. Afr.* 132 F4
Nigeria ■, *W. Afr.* 151
Nii-Jima, *Japan* 120 C8
Niigata, *Japan* 121 E6
Niihama, *Japan* 120 C3
Niihau, *U.S.A.* 192 A1
Nijkerk, *Neths.* 50 D4
Nijmegen, *Neths.* 50 E4
Nike, *Nigeria* 151 F4
Nikiniki, *Indonesia* 129 F12
Nikki, *Benin* 150 B3
Nikkō, *Japan* 120 A8
Nikolayev, *Ukraine* 81 G3
Nikolayevsk, *Russia* 81 E8
Nikolayevsk-na-Amur, *Russia* 91 G16
Nikolskoye, *Russia* 91 D18
Nikopol, *Ukraine* 81 G4
Nîl, Nahr en →, *Africa* 132 C7
Nîl el Abyad →, *Sudan* 143 E4
Nîl el Azraq →, *Sudan* 143 D5
Nile = Nîl, Nahr en →, *Africa* 132 C7
Nile □, *Uganda* 156 A1
Nile Delta, *Egypt* 156 A1
Nimach, *India* 106 D2
Nîmes, *France* 55 G7
Nimmitabel, *Australia* 171 G7
Nimneryskiy, *Russia* 91 G14
Nīnawá, *Iraq* 102 A3
Nindigully, *Australia* 171 B7
Nineveh = Nīnawá, *Iraq* 102 A3
Ningbo, *China* 116 H5
Ningde, *China* 116 J4
Ningdu, *China* 116 J3
Ningjin, *China* 116 D3
Ningpo = Ningbo, *China* 116 H5
Ningsia Hui A.R. = Ningxia Huizu Zizhiqu □, *China* 113 E7
Ningwu, *China* 116 C2
Ningxia Huizu Zizhiqu □, *China* 113 E7
Ningxiang, *China* 116 H1
Ninh Binh, *Vietnam* 125 B3
Ninove, *Belgium* 51 C3
Niobrara →, *U.S.A.* 190 D9
Nioro du Rip, *Senegal* 146 C1
Nioro du Sahel, *Mali* 140 E2
Niort, *France* 55 E4
Nipawin, *Canada* 186 H7
Nipigon, L., *Canada* 186 K9
Nirmali, *India* 106 C7
Niš, *Serbia, Yug.* 72 D8
Nişāb, *Yemen* 100 B1
Nishinomiya, *Japan* 120 C5
Nishin'omote, *Japan* 121 K2
Niterói, *Brazil* 215 C4
Nitra, *Slovak Rep.* 76 D5
Nitra →, *Slovak Rep.* 76 D5
Niuafo'ou, *Tonga* 174 A3
Niue, *Cook Is.* 176 G7
Niut, *Indonesia* 128 C6
Nivelles, *Belgium* 51 C3
Nivernais, *France* 55 D6
Nizamabad, *India* 107 E3
Nizhne Kolymsk, *Russia* 91 B15
Nizhne-Vartovsk, *Russia* 90 F8
Nizhneangarsk, *Russia* 91 H12
Nizhnekamsk, *Russia* 81 C9
Nizhneudinsk, *Russia* 91 H11
Nizhneyansk, *Russia* 91 C13
Nizhniy Novgorod, *Russia* 81 B7
Nizhniy Pyandzh, *Tajikistan* 93 G2
Nizhniy Tagil, *Russia* 90 F6
Nizké Tatry, *Slovak Rep.* 76 C6
Njakwa, *Malawi* 158 B2
Njombe, *Tanzania* 158 D2
Nkambe, *Cameroon* 153 C1
Nkawkaw, *Ghana* 149 D2
Nkayi, *Zimbabwe* 161 C3
Nkhota Kota, *Malawi* 158 C2
Nkongsamba, *Cameroon* 153 D1
Nkwanta, *Ghana* 149 C1
Noakhali = Maijdi, *Bangla.* 111 D2
Noatak, *U.S.A.* 193 A4
Nocera, *Italy* 67 F6
Nockatunga, *Australia* 171 A4
Nogales, *Mexico* 194 A2
Nogales, *U.S.A.* 190 H5
Nōgata, *Japan* 120 C1
Noggerup, *Australia* 170 C2
Noginsk, *Russia* 91 F10
Nogoyá, *Argentina* 221 B4
Noi →, *Thailand* 123 G4
Noirmoutier, I. de, *France* 55 D2
Nok Kundi, *Pakistan* 105 D1
Nokhtuysk, *Russia* 91 G13
Nokomis, *Canada* 186 J6
Nola, *C.A.R.* 142 C2
Nombre de Dios, *Panama* 197 D5
Nome, *U.S.A.* 193 A3
Nong Khae, *Thailand* 123 G4
Nong Khai, *Thailand* 123 F5
Nongoma, *S. Africa* 163 D9
Noondoo, *Australia* 171 B7
Noord Brabant □, *Neths.* 50 E3
Noord Holland □, *Neths.* 50 C3
Nóqui, *Angola* 160 A2
Noranda, *Canada* 187 K11
Nord □, *France* 55 A6
Nord-Ostsee Kanal, *Germany* 58 A3
Nordegg, *Canada* 186 H5
Nordhausen, *Germany* 58 C4
Nordkapp, *Norway* 40 A5
Nordkinn = Kinnarodden, *Norway* 34
Nordrhein-Westfalen □, *Germany* 58 C2
Nordvik, *Russia* 91 C11
Norfolk, *Nebr., U.S.A.* 191 D10
Norfolk, *Va., U.S.A.* 191 F16
Norfolk I., *Pac. Oc.* 176 H5
Norg, *Neths.* 50 B5
Norilsk, *Russia* 91 E10
Norley, *Australia* 171 A4
Norman Wells, *Canada* 186 D5
Normandie, *France* 55 B4
Normandy = Normandie, *France* 55 B4
Nørresundby, *Denmark* 42 B2
Norristown, *U.S.A.* 189 C4
Norrköping, *Sweden* 40 G3
Norrland, *Sweden* 40 D4
Norsk, *Russia* 91 H15
North Adams, *U.S.A.* 189 A5
North Atlantic Ocean, *Atl. Oc.* 222 D3
North Battleford, *Canada* 186 H6
North Bay, *Canada* 187 K11
North Bend, *U.S.A.* 190 C2
North Buganda □, *Uganda* 156 C2
North C., *Canada* 187 J15
North C., *N.Z.* 175 A4
North Cape = Nordkapp, *Norway* 40 A5
North Carolina □, *U.S.A.* 191 F15
North Channel, *Canada* 187 L10
North Channel, *U.K.* 46 E4
North Dakota □, *U.S.A.* 190 B8
North Dandalup, *Australia* 170 B1
North Downs, *U.K.* 45 D5
North East Frontier Agency = Arunachal Pradesh □, *India* 107 B6
North Eastern □, *Kenya* 157 C4
North European Plain, *Europe* 34 D12
North Horr, *Kenya* 157 B2
North I., *Kenya* 157 A2
North I., *N.Z.* 175 C5
North Magnetic Pole, *Canada* 186 B8
North Pagai, I. = Pagai Utara, Pulau, *Indonesia* 128 D2
North Platte, *U.S.A.* 190 E8
North Platte →, *U.S.A.* 190 E8
North Rhine Westphalia □ = Nordrhein-Westfalen □, *Germany* 58 C2
North Sea, *Europe* 34 D7
North Sporades = Voriai Sporádhes, *Greece* 71 C4
North Taranaki Bight, *N.Z.* 175 D5
North Thompson →, *Canada* 186 H4
North Tonawanda, *U.S.A.* 189 A2
North-West □, *S. Africa* 163 C5
North West C., *Australia* 168 C1
North West Christmas I. Ridge, *Pac. Oc.* 176 E7
North West Frontier □, *Pakistan* 105 A5
North West Highlands, *U.K.* 46 B4
North West River, *Canada* 187 G14
North West Territories □, *Canada* 186 E7
North York Moors, *U.K.* 46 F7
Northam, *S. Africa* 163 B7
Northampton, *U.K.* 46 J8
Northampton, *U.S.A.* 189 A6
Northcliffe, *Australia* 170 D2
Northern □, *Malawi* 158 B2
Northern □, *S. Africa* 163 A8
Northern □, *Uganda* 156 A2
Northern Cape □, *S. Africa* 163 F2
Northern Ireland □, *U.K.* 46 F3
Northern Marianas ■, *Pac. Oc.* 176 D3
Northern Province □, *S. Leone* 147 C3
Northern Territory □, *Australia* 168 G11
Northfleet, *U.K.* 45 C5
Northumberland, C., *Australia* 171 H3
Northumberland Str., *Canada* 187 K14
Norton, *Zimbabwe* 161 B4
Norton Sd., *U.S.A.* 193 A3
Norwalk, *U.S.A.* 189 B5
Norway ■, *Europe* 40
Norway House, *Canada* 186 H8
Norwegian B., *Canada* 186 B9
Norwegian Sea, *Atl. Oc.* 223 A4
Norwich, *U.K.* 46 J9
Norwich, *U.S.A.* 189 A4
Noshiro, *Japan* 121 D7
Nosok, *Russia* 90 D9
Nossob →, *S. Africa* 163 D3
Nosy Bé, *Madag.* 165 A3
Nosy Boraha, *Madag.* 165 B3
Nosy Mitsio, *Madag.* 165 A3
Nosy Varika, *Madag.* 165 D2
Noto, *Italy* 67 K7
Notre Dame B., *Canada* 187 H15
Notre Dame de Koartac = Koartac, *Canada* 187 F12
Notre Dame d'Ivugivic = Ivugivik, *Canada* 187 F11
Notsé, *Togo* 150 D2
Nottaway →, *Canada* 187 J11
Nottingham, *U.K.* 46 H7
Nouâdhibou, *Mauritania* 140 C1
Nouâdhibou, Ras, *Mauritania* 140 C1
Nouakchott, *Mauritania* 140 D1
Nouméa, *N. Cal.* 168 H14
Noupoort, *S. Africa* 163 G5
Nouveau Comptoir, *Canada* 187 J11
Nouvelle-Calédonie = New Caledonia, *Pac. Oc.* 168 C6
Nova Friburgo, *Brazil* 215 B5
Nova Gaia = Cambundi-Catembo, *Angola* 160 C3
Nova Iguaçu, *Brazil* 215 B4
Nova Lamego, *Guinea-Biss.* 146 D2
Nova Lima, *Brazil* 215 A4
Nova Lisboa = Huambo, *Angola* 160 C3
Nova Mambone, *Mozam.* 159 D2
Nova Scotia □, *Canada* 187 K14
Nova Sofala, *Mozam.* 159 D2
Novara, *Italy* 67 B2
Novaya Lyalya, *Russia* 90 F6
Novaya Sibir, Ostrov, *Russia* 91 B14
Novaya Zemlya, *Russia* 90 C8
Nové Zámky, *Slovak Rep.* 76 D5
Novgorod, *Russia* 81 A4
Novgorod-Severskiy, *Ukraine* 81 D4
Novi Sad, *Serbia, Yug.* 72 B7
Novoataysk, *Russia* 90 H9
Novocherkassk, *Russia* 81 G6
Novokayakent, *Russia* 82 A8
Novokazalinsk, *Kazakstan* 90 J5
Novokuybyshevsk, *Russia* 81 D9
Novokuznetsk, *Russia* 90 H9
Novomoskovsk, *Russia* 81 D5
Novorossiy, *Russia* 81 H5
Novorybnoye, *Russia* 91 D11
Novoshakhtinsk, *Russia* 81 G6

Novosibirsk, Russia 90 H9
Novosibirskiye Ostrova, Russia 91 B13
Novotroitsk, Russia 90 H5
Novouzensk, Russia 81 E8
Novska, Croatia 72 B5
Novvy Port, Russia 90 E8
Novyy Afon, Georgia 82 A3
Nowra, Australia 171 F8
Nowy Sącz, Poland 77 F4
Nowy Tomyśl, Poland 77 C1
Nsanje, Malawi 158 E2
Nsawam, Ghana 149 D2
Nsukka, Nigeria 151 E4
Nubian Desert = Nûbîya, Es Sahrâ En, Sudan 143 A4
Nûbîya, Es Sahrâ En, Sudan 143 A4
Nuboai, Indonesia 129 D17
Nueces →, U.S.A. 190 K9
Nueltin L., Canada 186 G7
Nueva Gerona, Cuba 198 B2
Nueva Rosita, Mexico 194 B4
Nueva San Salvador, El Salv. 196 D1
Nuéve de Julio, Argentina 221 C4
Nuevitas, Cuba 198 B5
Nuevo Laredo, Mexico 194 B5
Nuevo Rocafuerte, Ecuador 212 B3
Nugget Pt., N.Z. 175 J2
Nugrus, Gebel, Egypt 139 E6
Nukheila, Sudan 143 B2
Nuku'Alofa, Tonga 174 B3
Nukus, Uzbekistan 90 K4
Nulato, U.S.A. 193 A4
Nullarbor Plain, Australia 168 D2
Numalla, L., Australia 171 B5
Numan, Nigeria 151 D7
Numata, Japan 120 A8
Numazu, Japan 120 B8
Numfoor, Indonesia 129 C16
Numurkah, Australia 171 F5
Nunivak I., U.S.A. 193 B3
Nunspeet, Neths. 50 C4
Nuratau, Khrebet, Uzbekistan 93 C1
Nuremburg = Nürnberg, Germany 58 E4
Nürestān, Afghan. 104 C6
Nuriootpa, Australia 171 E2
Nürnberg, Germany 58 E4
Nurran, L. = Narran, L., Australia 171 B6
Nusa Tenggara Barat □, Indonesia 128 F9
Nusa Tenggara Timur □, Indonesia 129 F11
Nusaybin, Turkey 94 C6
Nushki, Pakistan 105 D2
Nutak, Canada 187 G13
Nuuk = Godthåb, Greenland 224 D1
Nuwakot, Nepal 109 B3
Nuwara Eliya, Sri Lanka 110 C2
Nuweiba', Egypt 139 B6
Nuweveldberge, S. Africa 163 G3
Nyaake, Liberia 148 E3
Nyah West, Australia 171 F4
Nyahanga, Tanzania 158 A1
Nyahururu, Kenya 157 C2
Nyainqentanglha Shan, China 112 G4
Nyakrom, Ghana 149 D2
Nyâlâ, Sudan 143 D2
Nyamandhlovu, Zimbabwe 161 D2
Nyankpala, Ghana 149 B2
Nyanza, Burundi 156 C1
Nyanza, Rwanda 156 B2
Nyanza □, Kenya 157 D1
Nyasa, L. = Malawi, L., Africa 132 H7
Nyaunglebin, Burma 122 F3
Nyazura, Zimbabwe 161 C5
Nyazwidzi →, Zimbabwe 161 D5
Nyda, Russia 90 E8
Nyeri, Kenya 157 D2
Nyinahin, Ghana 149 D1
Nyíregyháza, Hungary 74 A5
Nykøbing, Denmark 42 D3
Nylstroom, S. Africa 163 B7
Nymagee, Australia 171 D6
Nyngan, Australia 171 D6
Nyon, Switz. 60 C1
Nysa, Poland 77 E2
Nyurba, Russia 91 F13
Nzega, Tanzania 158 B1
N'Zérékoré, Guinea 147 D5
Nzeto, Angola 160 B2

O

Ō-Shima, Japan 120 C8
Oahe, L., U.S.A. 190 C9
Oahu, U.S.A. 192 A2
Oak Ridge, U.S.A. 191 F14
Oakbank, Australia 171 D3
Oakey, Australia 171 A9
Oakland, U.S.A. 190 E2
Oamaru, N.Z. 175 H3
Oaxaca, Mexico 194 F6
Ob →, Russia 90 E8
Oba, Canada 187 K10
Oban, U.K. 46 D4
Obbia, Somali Rep. 145 C3
Oberhausen, Germany 58 C1
Oberon, Australia 171 E7
Oberösterreich □, Austria 61 A4
Obi, Kepulauan, Indonesia 129 C13
Obi Is. = Obi, Kepulauan, Indonesia 129 C13
Obiaruku, Nigeria 151 F3
Óbidos, Brazil 217 C5
Obihiro, Japan 121 B8
Obilatu, Indonesia 129 C13
Obluchye, Russia 91 H16
Obo, C.A.R. 142 B5
Oboa, Mt., Uganda 156 B3
Obock, Djibouti 145 B2
Obozerskaya, Russia 90 D5
Obshchi Syrt, Kazakstan 34 E17
Obskaya Guba, Russia 90 D8
Obuasi, Ghana 149 D2
Obubra, Nigeria 151 F4
Ocala, U.S.A. 191 J15
Ocaña, Spain 63 D5
Occidental, Cordillera, Colombia 210 C1
Ocean City, U.S.A. 189 D5
Ocean I. = Banaba, Kiribati 176 F5
Ochamchire, Georgia 82 A3
Ocho Rios, Jamaica 199 A4
Oconee →, U.S.A. 191 H15
Ocotal, Nic. 197 B1
Ocumare del Tuy, Venezuela 211 A3
Oda, Ghana 149 D2
Ódáðahraun, Iceland 38 B4
Odate, Japan 121 D7
Odawara, Japan 120 B8
Odendaalsrus, S. Africa 163 D6
Odense, Denmark 42 C3
Oder = Odra →, Poland 77 C1
Odesa = Odessa, Ukraine 81 G3
Odessa, Ukraine 81 G3
Odessa, U.S.A. 190 H8
Odienné, Ivory C. 148 B3
Odintsovo, Russia 81 C5
Odiongan, Phil. 130 F3
Odorheiu Secuiesc, Romania 75 B4
Odra →, Poland 77 C1
Odžak, Bos.-H. 72 B5
Of, Turkey 82 C2
Ofanto →, Italy 67 F7
Offa, Nigeria 151 D2
Offenbach, Germany 58 E2
Oga-Hantō, Japan 121 D7
Ogaden, Ethiopia 144 E4
Ōgaki, Japan 120 B6
Ogasawara Gunto, Pac. Oc. 176 C3
Ogbomosho, Nigeria 151 D2
Ogden, U.S.A. 190 D5
Ogdensburg, U.S.A. 191 C16
Oglio →, Italy 67 A3
Ogoja, Nigeria 151 E5
Ogooué →, Gabon 154 B1
Ogowe = Ogooué →, Gabon 154 B1
Ogun □, Nigeria 151 E1
Oguta, Nigeria 151 F3
Ogwashi-Uku, Nigeria 151 F3
Ogwe, Nigeria 151 G4
Ohakune, N.Z. 175 D5
Ohanet, Algeria 137 C5
Ohau, L., N.Z. 175 H2
Ohey, Belgium 51 D4
Ohio □, U.S.A. 191 E14
Ohio →, U.S.A. 191 F12
Ohre →, Czech. 76 A3
Ohridsko, Jezero, Macedonia 70 C3
Ohrigstad, S. Africa 163 B8
Oil City, U.S.A. 189 B1
Oirot-Tura = Gorno-Altaysk, Russia 90 J9
Oise □, France 55 B6
Oisterwijk, Neths. 50 E3
Ōita, Japan 120 D2
Ōita □, Japan 120 D2
Ojos del Salado, Cerro, Argentina 220 C3
Oka →, Russia 34 D15
Okaba, Indonesia 129 F18
Okahandja, Namibia 162 C2
Okandja, Gabon 154 B2
Okara, Pakistan 105 C6
Okaukuejo, Namibia 162 B2
Okavango Swamps, Botswana 162 B4
Okaya, Japan 120 A7
Okayama, Japan 120 C4
Okayama □, Japan 120 B4
Okazaki, Japan 120 B7
Oke-Iho, Nigeria 151 E1
Okeechobee, L., U.S.A. 191 K16
Okene, Nigeria 151 E3
Okha, Russia 91 F17
Okhotsk, Russia 91 E16
Okhotsk, Sea of, Asia 84 C18
Okhotskiy Perevoz, Russia 91 E15
Okhotsko Kolymskoye, Russia 91 D16
Oki-Shotō, Japan 120 A3
Okiep, S. Africa 163 F1
Okigwi, Nigeria 151 F4
Okija, Nigeria 151 F3
Okinawa-Jima, Japan 121 J8
Okinawa-Shotō, Japan 121 H8
Okinerabu-Jima, Japan 121 H8
Okitipupa, Nigeria 151 F2
Oklahoma □, U.S.A. 191 G10
Oklahoma City, U.S.A. 190 G9
Okolo, Uganda 156 B1
Okrika, Nigeria 151 G3
Oktabrsk, Kazakstan 90 H5
Oktyabrskoy Revolyutsii, Os., Russia 91 B10
Oktyabrskoye, Russia 90 F7
Okushiri-Tō, Japan 121 C6
Okuta, Nigeria 151 D1
Ólafsfjörður, Iceland 38 A4
Ólafsvík, Iceland 38 C1
Olanchito, Honduras 196 C3
Öland, Sweden 40 H3
Olary, Australia 171 D2
Olascoaga, Argentina 221 C4
Olavarría, Argentina 220 F5
Ólbia, Italy 67 F2
Old Castile = Castilla y Leon □, Spain 63 B5
Old Harbour, Jamaica 199 C4
Oldenburg, Germany 58 B2
Oldham, U.K. 46 H7
Olean, U.S.A. 189 B2
Olekma →, Russia 91 F13
Olekminsk, Russia 91 F13
Olenek, Russia 91 E12
Olenek →, Russia 91 C12
Oléron, I. d', France 55 E3
Oleśnica, Poland 77 D2
Olga, Russia 91 J17
Olifantshoek, S. Africa 163 D4
Ólimbos, Óros, Greece 71 B2
Olímpia, Brazil 215 A1
Oliva, Argentina 221 A2
Olivenza, Spain 63 E2
Olomouc, Czech. 76 B5
Olongapo, Phil. 130 E2
Olovyannaya, Russia 91 J13
Oloy →, Russia 91 C16
Olpe, Germany 59 B3
Olsztyn, Poland 77 B4
Olt →, Romania 75 D4
Olten, Switz. 60 B3
Olteniţa, Romania 75 D5
Oltu, Turkey 82 C3
Olur, Turkey 82 C4
Olutanga, Phil. 130 K4
Olympia, Greece 71 E2
Olympic Mts., U.S.A. 190 A2
Olympic Nat. Park, U.S.A. 190 B3
Olympus, Mt. = Ólimbos, Óros, Greece 71 B2
Om →, Russia 90 H7
Ōmachi, Japan 120 A7
Omaha, U.S.A. 191 E10
Oman ■, Asia 101
Oman, G. of, Asia 84 F9
Omaruru, Namibia 162 D2
Omate, Peru 213 F4
Ombai, Selat, Indonesia 129 F12
Omboué, Gabon 154 C1
Ombrone →, Italy 67 D4
Omdurmân, Sudan 143 C4
Ometepe, I. de, Nic. 197 C2
Ometepec, Mexico 194 F5
Ōmiya, Japan 120 A9
Ommen, Neths. 50 C5
Omo →, Ethiopia 144 F2
Omolon →, Russia 91 C16
Omsk, Russia 90 H7
Omsukchan, Russia 91 D16
Omul, Vf., Romania 75 C4
Ōmura, Japan 120 D1
Omuramba Omatako →, Namibia 162 A3
Ōmuta, Japan 120 D1
Onang, Indonesia 129 D10
Oncócua, Angola 160 E2
Onda, Spain 63 D8
Ondaejin, N. Korea 118 B5
Ondangua, Namibia 162 A2
Ondo, Nigeria 151 E2
Ondo □, Nigeria 151 E2
Öndörhaan, Mongolia 113 B8
Öndverðarnes, Iceland 38 C1
Onega, Russia 90 C5
Onega →, Russia 34 C14
Onega, L. = Onezhskoye Ozero, Russia 90 D4
Onehunga, N.Z. 175 C5
Oneida, U.S.A. 189 A4
Oneida L., U.S.A. 189 A3
Onekotan, Ostrov, Russia 91 F18
Oneonta, U.S.A. 189 A4
Onezhskoye Ozero, Russia 90 D4
Ongerup, Australia 170 C3
Ongjin, N. Korea 118 E3
Ongniud Qi, China 116 A4
Onguren, Russia 91 H12
Oni, Georgia 82 A5
Onilahy →, Madag. 165 E1
Onitsha, Nigeria 151 F3
Onoda, Japan 120 C2
Onpyŏng-ni, S. Korea 118 J4
Onslow B., U.S.A. 191 G16
Onstwedde, Neths. 50 B6
Ontake-San, Japan 120 B7
Ontario, U.S.A. 190 C4
Ontario □, Canada 186 J9
Ontario, L., U.S.A. 180 E12
Oost-Vlaanderen □, Belgium 51 B2
Oostende, Belgium 51 B1
Oosterhout, Neths. 50 E3
Oosterschelde, Neths. 50 E2
Ootacamund, India 107 F2
Ootmarsum, Neths. 50 C6
Opala, Russia 91 E18
Opala, Zaïre 155 C4
Opanake, Sri Lanka 110 D2
Opava, Czech. 76 B5
Opi, Nigeria 151 E4
Opobo, Nigeria 151 G4
Opol, Phil. 130 J5
Opole, Poland 77 E2
Oporto = Porto, Portugal 63 C1
Opotiki, N.Z. 175 C6
Opua, N.Z. 175 A5
Opunake, N.Z. 175 D4
Oradea, Romania 75 B2
Öræfajökull, Iceland 38 D4
Orai, India 106 C4
Oral = Ural →, Kazakstan 34 F17
Oral = Uralsk, Kazakstan 81 E9
Oran, Algeria 137 A3
Oran, Argentina 220 B4
Orange = Oranje →, S. Africa 163 E1
Orange, Australia 171 E7
Orange, France 55 G7
Orange, U.S.A. 191 J11
Orange, C., Brazil 206 B4
Orange Free State = Free State □, S. Africa 163 E6
Orange Walk, Belize 196 A2
Orangeburg, U.S.A. 191 G15
Orani, Phil. 130 F2
Oranienburg, Germany 58 B5
Oranje →, S. Africa 163 E1
Oranje Vrystaat = Free State □, S. Africa 163 E6
Oranjemund, Namibia 162 E2
Oranjerivier, S. Africa 163 F5
Oras, Phil. 130 G5
Oraşul Stalin = Braşov, Romania 75 C4
Orbe, Switz. 60 C1
Orbetello, Italy 67 E4
Orbost, Australia 171 G6
Orchila, I., Venezuela 211 A3
Ordzhonikidze = Vladikavkaz, Russia 82 A5
Ordzhonikidze, Uzbekistan 93 C3
Ordzhonikidzeabad, Tajikistan 93 E2
Ore Mts. = Erzgebirge, Germany 58 D5
Orealla, Guyana 214 C3
Örebro, Sweden 40 F3
Oregon □, U.S.A. 190 C2
Orekhovo-Zuyevo, Russia 81 C6
Orel, Russia 81 D5
Orenburg, Russia 90 G5
Orense, Spain 63 B2
Orgūn, Afghan. 104 E5
Orhon Gol →, Mongolia 113 A7
Orient, Australia 171 A4
Oriental, Cordillera, Colombia 210 C2
Orihuela, Spain 63 F7
Orinduik, Guyana 214 C1
Orinoco →, Venezuela 211 B5
Orissa □, India 106 F6
Oristano, Italy 67 G2
Oristano, G. di, Italy 67 G2
Orizaba, Mexico 194 E6
Orkney, S. Africa 163 D6
Orkney Is., U.K. 46 A8
Orlando, U.S.A. 191 J15
Orléanais, France 55 C5
Orléans, France 55 C5
Ormara, Pakistan 105 F2
Ormoc, Phil. 130 G5
Orne □, France 55 C4
Örnsköldsvik, Sweden 40 D4
Oro, N. Korea 118 C4
Orocué, Colombia 210 C2
Orodo, Nigeria 151 F3
Oron, Nigeria 151 G4
Oroquieta, Phil. 130 J4
Orotukan, Russia 91 D16
Orroroo, Australia 171 D2
Orsha, Belarus 81 C3
Orsk, Russia 90 H5
Orşova, Romania 75 D2
Ortegal, C., Spain 63 A2
Orthez, France 55 G3
Ortigueira, Spain 63 A2
Ortles, Italy 67 A3
Orto-Tokoy, Kyrgyzstan 93 B8
Ortón →, Bolivia 218 A1
Ortona, Italy 67 E6
Orūmīyeh, Iran 103 A1
Orūmīyeh, Daryācheh-ye, Iran 103 A2
Oruro, Bolivia 218 C1
Orūzgān □, Afghan. 104 D3
Orvieto, Italy 67 D4
Oryakhovo, Bulgaria 73 A2
Osa, Pen. de, Costa Rica 197 E3
Osage →, U.S.A. 191 F11
Ōsaka, Japan 120 C5
Osan, S. Korea 118 F4
Ösel = Saaremaa, Estonia 81 A1
Osh, Kyrgyzstan 93 D5
Oshawa, Canada 185 D2
Oshogbo, Nigeria 151 E2
Oshwe, Zaïre 155 D3
Osijek, Croatia 72 B6
Osipenko = Berdyansk, Ukraine 81 G5
Osizweni, S. Africa 163 D8
Oskaloosa, U.S.A. 191 E11
Oskarshamn, Sweden 40 G3
Öskemen = Ust-Kamenogorsk, Kazakstan 90 J8
Oslo, Norway 40 F2
Oslob, Phil. 130 H4
Oslofjorden, Norway 40 F2
Osmaniye, Turkey 94 C4
Osnabrück, Germany 58 C2
Oss, Neths. 50 E4
Ossa, Mt., Australia 172 B2
Óssa, Oros, Greece 71 C3
Ossining, U.S.A. 189 B5
Ossora, Russia 91 D17
Ostend = Oostende, Belgium 51 B1
Östersund, Sweden 40 D3
Ostfriesische Inseln, Germany 58 A1
Ostrava, Czech. 76 B6
Ostróda, Poland 77 B4
Ostrołęka, Poland 77 B5
Ostrów Mazowiecka, Poland 77 C5
Ostrów Wielkopolski, Poland 77 D2
Ostrowiec-Świętokrzyski, Poland 77 D5
Ōsumi-Kaikyō, Japan 121 K2
Ōsumi-Shotō, Japan 121 F9
Osuna, Spain 63 G4
Oswego, U.S.A. 191 C16
Ōtake, Japan 120 C3
Otaki, N.Z. 175 E5
Otaru, Japan 121 B7
Otaru-Wan = Ishikari-Wan, Japan 121 B7
Otavalo, Ecuador 212 B1
Otavi, Namibia 162 B3
Otford, U.K. 45 D4
Otjiwarongo, Namibia 162 B2
Otoineppu, Japan 121 A8
Otranto, Italy 67 G9
Otranto, Str. of, Italy 34 G10
Otse, S. Africa 163 B6
Ōtsu, Japan 120 B6
Ottawa = Outaouais →, Canada 185 B5
Ottawa, Canada 185 B4
Ottawa, Ill., U.S.A. 191 D12
Ottawa, Kans., U.S.A. 191 F10
Ottawa Is., Canada 187 G10
Otto Beit Bridge, Zimbabwe 161 A3
Ottosdal, S. Africa 163 D6
Ottumwa, U.S.A. 191 E11
Otu, Nigeria 151 D1
Otukpa, Nigeria 151 E4
Otur-kyuyel = Uyandi, Russia 91 C14
Oturkpo, Nigeria 151 E4
Otway, C., Australia 171 H4
Otwock, Poland 77 C5
Ouachita →, U.S.A. 191 H12
Ouachita Mts., U.S.A. 191 G11
Ouadâne, Mauritania 140 C2
Ouadda, C.A.R. 142 B4
Ouagadougou, Burkina Faso 149 A2
Ouahran = Oran, Algeria 137 A3
Ouallene, Algeria 137 D3
Ouanda Djallé, C.A.R. 142 A4
Ouargla, Algeria 137 B5
Ouarzazate, Morocco 136 D3
Oubangi →, Zaïre 155 C2
Oude Rijn →, Neths. 50 D2
Oudenaarde, Belgium 51 C2
Oudenbosch, Neths. 50 E2
Oudtshoorn, S. Africa 163 H4
Oued Zem, Morocco 136 C4
Ouellé, Ivory C. 148 C5
Ouesso, Congo 154 B3
Ouezzane, Morocco 136 B4
Ouidah, Benin 150 E2
Oujda, Morocco 136 B6
Oujeft, Mauritania 140 C1
Ouled Djellal, Algeria 137 A5
Oulmès, Morocco 136 B4
Oulu, Finland 43 D2
Oulu →, Finland 43 D2
Oulujärvi, Finland 43 D3
Oum Chalouba, Chad 142 E2
Oum-er-Rbia, O. →, Morocco 136 C3
Oum Hadjer, Chad 142 D2
Oumé, Ivory C. 148 D5
Ounianga-Kébir, Chad 142 B2
Ounianga Sérir, Chad 142 B2
Our →, Lux. 52 B3
Ourense = Orense, Spain 63 B2
Ourinhos, Brazil 215 C1
Ouro Fino, Brazil 215 B2
Ouro Prêto, Brazil 215 A4
Ouro Sogui, Senegal 146 A3
Ourthe →, Belgium 51 D5
Ouse, Australia 172 C2
Outaouais →, Canada 185 B5
Outat Oulad el Hadj, Morocco 136 B5
Outer Hebrides, U.K. 46 B3
Outjo, Namibia 162 B2
Ouyen, Australia 171 F3
Ovar, Portugal 63 C1
Overflakkee, Neths. 50 E2
Overijssel □, Neths. 50 C5
Oviedo, Spain 63 A3
Ovoro, Nigeria 151 F4
Owase, Japan 120 C6
Owatonna, U.S.A. 191 D11
Owbeh, Afghan. 104 D2
Owego, U.S.A. 189 B3

Owen Falls, *Uganda* 156 C2
Owen Stanley Ra., *Papua N. G.* 173 C2
Owendo, *Gabon* 154 B1
Owens L., *U.S.A.* 190 F3
Owensboro, *U.S.A.* 191 F13
Owerri, *Nigeria* 151 F3
Owo, *Nigeria* 151 E2
Owosso, *U.S.A.* 191 D14
Owyhee →, *U.S.A.* 190 C4
Oxford, *N.Z.* 175 G4
Oxford, *U.K.* 46 K7
Oxley, *Australia* 171 E4
Oxted, *U.K.* 45 D4
Oxus = Amudarya →, *Uzbekistan* 90 J4
Oya, *Malaysia* 126 C6
Oyama, *Japan* 120 A9
Oyapock →, *Fr. Guiana* 214 D6
Oyem, *Gabon* 154 B1
Oymyakon, *Russia* 91 E15
Oyo, *Nigeria* 151 E1
Oyo □, *Nigeria* 151 D1
Oytal, *Kazakstan* 93 A6
Ozamiz, *Phil.* 130 J4
Ozark Plateau, *U.S.A.* 191 F11
Ozarks, L. of the, *U.S.A.* 191 F11

P

P.K. le Roux Dam, *S. Africa* 163 F5
P.W.V. = Gauteng □, *S. Africa* 163 C7
Pa-an, *Burma* 122 F3
Pa Sak →, *Thailand* 123 G4
Paamiut = Frederikshåb, *Greenland* 224 D1
Paarl, *S. Africa* 163 H2
Pab Hills, *Pakistan* 105 F3
Pabo, *Uganda* 156 B2
Pacaraima, Sierra, *Venezuela* 211 C5
Pacasmayo, *Peru* 213 C2
Pachpadra, *India* 106 C1
Pacific Ocean, *Pac. Oc.* 176 E9
Padaido, Kepulauan, *Indonesia* 129 C17
Padang, *Indonesia* 128 C3
Padangpanjang, *Indonesia* 128 C2
Padangsidempuan, *Indonesia* 128 B2
Paddock Wood, *U.K.* 45 E5
Paderborn, *Germany* 58 C2
Padloping Island, *Canada* 187 D12
Padma →, *Bangla.* 111 C2
Pádova, *Italy* 67 B4
Padre I., *U.S.A.* 191 K10
Padua = Pádova, *Italy* 67 B4
Paducah, *U.S.A.* 191 F12
Paengnyong-do, *S. Korea* 118 E2
Paeroa, *N.Z.* 175 C5
Pafúri, *Mozam.* 159 E1
Pag, *Croatia* 72 C3
Paga, *Ghana* 149 A2
Pagadian, *Phil.* 130 K4
Pagai Selatan, P., *Indonesia* 128 D2
Pagai Utara, Pulau, *Indonesia* 128 D2
Pagalu = Annobón, *Atl. Oc.* 132 G4
Pagastikós Kólpos, *Greece* 71 C3
Pagatan, *Indonesia* 128 D9
Pago Pago, *Amer. Samoa* 177 G7
Pahala, *U.S.A.* 192 B3
Pahang →, *Malaysia* 126 C3
Pahiatua, *N.Z.* 175 E5
Paia, *U.S.A.* 192 A3
Pailin, *Cambodia* 125 F2
Painan, *Indonesia* 128 C3
Paint Hills = Nouveau Comptoir, *Canada* 187 J11
Painted Desert, *U.S.A.* 190 F5
País Vasco □, *Spain* 63 B6
Paita, *Peru* 213 B1
Pak Lay, *Laos* 125 C1
Pakaraima Mts., *Guyana* 214 C1
Pakistan ■, *Asia* 105
Pakistan, East = Bangladesh ■, *Asia* 111
Paknam = Samut Prakan, *Thailand* 123 H4
Pakokku, *Burma* 122 D2
Pakse, *Laos* 125 D3
Paktīā □, *Afghan.* 104 D5
Paktīkā □, *Afghan.* 104 E5
Pakwach, *Uganda* 156 B1
Pala, *Chad* 142 F1
Palabek, *Uganda* 156 A2
Palagruža, *Croatia* 72 E4
Palamós, *Spain* 63 B9
Palana, *Australia* 172 A3
Palana, *Russia* 91 D17
Palanan, *Phil.* 130 C3
Palanan Pt., *Phil.* 130 C3
Palangkaraya, *Indonesia* 128 D8
Palanpur, *India* 106 D1
Palapye, *Botswana* 162 C6
Palatka, *Russia* 91 D16
Palatka, *U.S.A.* 191 J15
Palau ■, *Pac. Oc.* 176 E2
Palauk, *Burma* 122 H3
Palawan, *Phil.* 130 H1
Paleleh, *Indonesia* 129 B11
Palembang, *Indonesia* 128 D4
Palencia, *Spain* 63 B4
Palermo, *Italy* 67 J5
Palestine, *U.S.A.* 191 H10
Paletwa, *Burma* 122 D1
Palghat, *India* 107 F2
Pali, *India* 106 C1
Palk Strait, *Asia* 84 H11
Pallisa, *Uganda* 156 C3
Palma, *Mozam.* 159 A3
Palma, *Spain* 65 B3
Palma, B. de, *Spain* 65 B3
Palma Soriano, *Cuba* 198 C6
Palmas, C., *Liberia* 148 E3
Pálmas, G. di, *Italy* 67 H2
Palmeirinhas, Pta. das, *Angola* 160 B2
Palmer, *U.S.A.* 193 B4
Palmerston, *N.Z.* 175 H3
Palmerston North, *N.Z.* 175 E5
Palmi, *Italy* 67 J7
Palmira, *Colombia* 210 C1
Palmyra = Tudmur, *Syria* 97 C3
Palmyra Is., *Pac. Oc.* 176 E7
Palompon, *Phil.* 130 G5
Palopo, *Indonesia* 129 D10
Palos, C. de, *Spain* 63 F7
Palu, *Indonesia* 129 C10
Palu, *Turkey* 94 B6
Pama, *Burkina Faso* 149 B3
Pamir, *Tajikistan* 84 E11
Pamir →, *Tajikistan* 93 F6
Pamlico Sd., *U.S.A.* 191 F17
Pampa, *U.S.A.* 190 G8
Pampa de las Salinas, *Argentina* 221 A1
Pampanua, *Indonesia* 129 D10
Pampas, *Argentina* 220 F4
Pampas, *Peru* 213 D3
Pamplona, *Colombia* 210 B2
Pamplona, *Spain* 63 B6
Pampoenpoort, *S. Africa* 163 F4
Panabo, *Phil.* 130 K5
Panaji, *India* 107 E2
Panamá, *Panama* 197 E5
Panamá ■, *Cent. Amer.* 197
Panamá, G. de, *Panama* 197 E6
Panama Canal, *Panama* 197 E5
Panama City, *U.S.A.* 191 J14
Panão, *Peru* 213 D3
Panaon I., *Phil.* 130 H5
Panay, *Phil.* 130 G3
Pančevo, *Serbia, Yug.* 72 B7
Pancorbo, Paso, *Spain* 63 B5
Pandan, *Antique, Phil.* 130 G3
Pandan, *Catanduanes, Phil.* 130 E4
Pandharpur, *India* 107 E2
Pando, *Uruguay* 219 D2
Pando, L. = Hope, L., *Australia* 171 B2
Pandora, *Costa Rica* 197 D3
Panevėžys, *Lithuania* 81 B1
Panfilov, *Kazakstan* 90 K7
Pangani, *Tanzania* 158 B3
Pangfou = Bengbu, *China* 116 F4
Pangkajene, *Indonesia* 129 E10
Pangkalanbrandan, *Indonesia* 128 A2
Pangkalanbuun, *Indonesia* 128 D7
Pangkalansusu, *Indonesia* 128 A2
Pangkalpinang, *Indonesia* 128 D5
Pangkoh, *Indonesia* 128 D8
Pangnirtung, *Canada* 187 E12
Pangutaran Group, *Phil.* 130 L2
Panjgur, *Pakistan* 105 E2
Panjim = Panaji, *India* 107 E2
Panjinad Barrage, *Pakistan* 105 D5
Pankshin, *Nigeria* 151 D5
Panmunjŏm, *N. Korea* 118 E4
Panna, *India* 106 C4
Pano Lefkara, *Cyprus* 95 B2
Panshan, *China* 116 B5
Pant →, *U.K.* 45 B6
Pantar, *Indonesia* 129 F12
Pante Macassar, *Indonesia* 129 F12
Pantelleria, *Italy* 67 K4
Pánuco, *Mexico* 194 D5
Panyam, *Nigeria* 151 D5
Paola, *Malta* 69 B3
Paoting = Baoding, *China* 116 C3
Paot'ou = Baotou, *China* 116 B1
Paoua, *C.A.R.* 142 B2
Pápa, *Hungary* 74 B2
Papagayo, G. de, *Costa Rica* 197 D2
Papantla, *Mexico* 194 E5
Papar, *Malaysia* 126 A7
Paphos, *Cyprus* 95 C1
Papien Chiang = Da →, *Vietnam* 125 B3
Papua, G. of, *Papua N. G.* 173 C1
Papua New Guinea ■, *Oceania* 173
Papun, *Burma* 122 F3
Pará = Belém, *Brazil* 217 B7
Pará □, *Brazil* 217 C6
Pará □, *Surinam* 214 C4
Paracale, *Phil.* 130 E3
Parachilna, *Australia* 171 C1
Paradip, *India* 106 F7
Parado, *Indonesia* 129 F10
Paragould, *U.S.A.* 191 F12
Paragua →, *Venezuela* 211 B4
Paraguaçu →, *Brazil* 217 E9
Paraguaná, Pen. de, *Venezuela* 211 A2
Paraguarí, *Paraguay* 219 C2
Paraguay ■, *S. Amer.* 219
Paraguay →, *Paraguay* 219 C2
Paraiba = João Pessoa, *Brazil* 217 D9
Paraíba □, *Brazil* 217 D9
Paraíba do Sul →, *Brazil* 215 B5
Parakou, *Benin* 150 C3
Paralimni, *Cyprus* 95 B3
Paramaribo, *Surinam* 214 B4
Paramushir, Ostrov, *Russia* 91 F18
Paran, N. →, *Israel* 96 G2
Paraná, *Argentina* 221 A4
Paraná □, *Brazil* 217 H6
Paraná →, *Argentina* 221 B5
Paranaguá, *Brazil* 217 H6
Paranaíba →, *Brazil* 217 G6
Paranapanema →, *Brazil* 217 H5
Paranapiacaba, Serra do, *Brazil* 217 H6
Parang, *Jolo, Phil.* 130 L2
Parang, *Mindanao, Phil.* 130 K4
Paratoo, *Australia* 171 D2
Parattah, *Australia* 172 C3
Parbhani, *India* 106 F3
Parchim, *Germany* 58 B4
Pardes Hanna, *Israel* 96 B2
Pardubice, *Czech.* 76 B4
Parecis, Serra dos, *Brazil* 217 E4
Paren, *Russia* 91 C17
Parepare, *Indonesia* 129 D10
Pariaguán, *Venezuela* 211 B4
Pariaman, *Indonesia* 128 C2
Parigi, *Indonesia* 129 C10
Parika, *Guyana* 214 B2
Parima, Serra, *Brazil* 217 A3
Parinari, *Peru* 213 B3
Parîng, *Romania* 75 C3
Parintins, *Brazil* 217 C5
Paris, *France* 55 B5
Paris, *U.S.A.* 191 H10
Pariti, *Indonesia* 129 F12
Park Range, *U.S.A.* 190 E7
Park Rynie, *S. Africa* 163 F8
Parkent, *Uzbekistan* 93 C3
Parkersburg, *U.S.A.* 191 E15
Parkes, *Australia* 171 E6
Parkhar, *Tajikistan* 93 F3
Parma, *Italy* 67 B3
Parnaíba, *Brazil* 217 C8
Parnaíba →, *Brazil* 217 C8
Parnassós, *Greece* 71 D3
Pärnu, *Estonia* 81 A2
Páros, *Greece* 71 E5
Parramatta, *Australia* 171 E8
Parry Is., *Canada* 186 B8
Parry Sound, *Canada* 185 B1
Parsons, *U.S.A.* 191 F10
Paru →, *Brazil* 217 B6
Paruro, *Peru* 213 E4
Parvān □, *Afghan.* 104 C5
Parys, *S. Africa* 163 D7
Pas-de-Calais □, *France* 55 A5
Pasadena, *Calif., U.S.A.* 190 G3
Pasadena, *Tex., U.S.A.* 191 J10
Pasaje, *Ecuador* 212 D1
Pasay, *Phil.* 130 E2
Pascagoula, *U.S.A.* 191 J13
Pasco, *U.S.A.* 190 B3
Pasco, Cerro de, *Peru* 213 D3
Pashmakli = Smolyan, *Bulgaria* 73 D3
Pasinler, *Turkey* 82 D3
Pasni, *Pakistan* 105 F1
Paso de los Toros, *Uruguay* 219 C2
Paso Robles, *U.S.A.* 190 F2
Passau, *Germany* 58 F5
Passero, C., *Italy* 67 K7
Passo Fundo, *Brazil* 217 J6
Pastaza □, *Ecuador* 212 C3
Pastaza →, *Peru* 213 B3
Pasto, *Colombia* 210 D1
Pasuruan, *Indonesia* 128 F7
Patagonia, *Argentina* 220 H3
Patan, *India* 106 D1
Patani, *Indonesia* 129 C14
Patchewollock, *Australia* 171 F3
Patchogue, *U.S.A.* 189 B5
Patea, *N.Z.* 175 D5
Pategi, *Nigeria* 151 D3
Patensie, *S. Africa* 163 H5
Paternò, *Italy* 67 J6
Paterson, *U.S.A.* 189 B5
Patharghata, *Bangla.* 111 D2
Pathfinder Reservoir, *U.S.A.* 190 D7
Patiala, *India* 107 B2
Patine Kouka, *Senegal* 146 C2
Pátmos, *Greece* 71 E6
Patna, *India* 106 C6
Patnos, *Turkey* 82 D4
Patonga, *Uganda* 156 B2
Patos, L. dos, *Brazil* 217 K6
Pátrai, *Greece* 71 D2
Pátraikós Kólpos, *Greece* 71 D2
Patta, *Kenya* 157 E4
Pattani, *Thailand* 123 L4
Patti, *Italy* 67 J7
Patuakhali, *Bangla.* 111 D2
Patuca →, *Honduras* 196 B5
Patuca, Punta, *Honduras* 196 B5
Pau, *France* 55 H4
Pauillac, *France* 55 F3
Pauk, *Burma* 122 D2
Paul Isnard, *Fr. Guiana* 214 C5
Paulis = Isiro, *Zaïre* 155 B5
Paulistana, *Brazil* 217 D8
Paulpietersburg, *S. Africa* 163 D9
Paungde, *Burma* 122 E2
Pavia, *Italy* 67 B2
Pavlodar, *Kazakstan* 90 H8
Pavlograd, *Ukraine* 81 F4
Pavlovo, *Russia* 81 C7
Pavlovo, *Russia* 91 F12
Pavlovsk, *Russia* 81 E6
Pawtucket, *U.S.A.* 189 A6
Payakumbuh, *Indonesia* 128 C3
Payerne, *Switz.* 60 C1
Payette, *U.S.A.* 190 C4
Paynesville, *Liberia* 148 D1
Paysandú, *Uruguay* 219 B1
Payson, *U.S.A.* 190 E5
Paz →, *Guatemala* 196 D1
Paz, B. la, *Mexico* 194 C1
Pazar, *Turkey* 82 C3
Pazardzhik, *Bulgaria* 73 C3
Peace →, *Canada* 186 F6
Peace River, *Canada* 186 G5
Peak Hill, *Australia* 171 D7
Peake, *Australia* 171 F2
Pearl Banks, *Sri Lanka* 110 B1
Pearl City, *U.S.A.* 192 A2
Pearl Harbor, *U.S.A.* 192 A2
Peary Land, *Greenland* 224 A2
Pebane, *Mozam.* 159 C3
Pebble, I., *Falk. Is.* 224 A2
Peć, *Serbia, Yug.* 72 E7
Pechenga, *Russia* 90 B6
Pechora →, *Russia* 90 D7
Pechorskaya Guba, *Russia* 90 D7
Pecos, *U.S.A.* 190 H7
Pecos →, *U.S.A.* 190 J8
Pécs, *Hungary* 74 C3
Pedder, L., *Australia* 172 C2
Peddie, *S. Africa* 163 H6
Pédernales, *Dom. Rep.* 200 B2
Pedhikos →, *Cyprus* 95 B3
Pedra Lume, *C. Verde Is.* 222 A3
Pedro Juan Caballero, *Paraguay* 219 B3
Peebinga, *Australia* 171 F3
Peekskill, *U.S.A.* 189 B5
Peel →, *Australia* 171 C8
Peel →, *Canada* 186 C5
Pegasus Bay, *N.Z.* 175 G4
Pegu, *Burma* 122 F2
Pei'ing = Beijing, *China* 116 C3
Pekalongan, *Indonesia* 128 E6
Pekan, *Malaysia* 126 C3
Pekanbaru, *Indonesia* 128 C3
Pekin, *U.S.A.* 191 E12
Peking = Beijing, *China* 116 C3
Pelabuhan Kelang, *Malaysia* 126 C1
Pelabuhan Ratu, Teluk, *Indonesia* 128 F5
Pelabuhanratu, *Indonesia* 128 F5
Pelaihari, *Indonesia* 128 D8
Peleaga, *Romania* 75 C2
Pelée, Mt., *Martinique* 203 C2
Pelekech, *Kenya* 157 A1
Pelendria, *Cyprus* 95 B1
Peleng, *Indonesia* 129 C12
Pella, *S. Africa* 163 E2
Pelly →, *Canada* 186 D4
Pelly L., *Canada* 186 E8
Peloponnese = Pelopónnisos □, *Greece* 71 E2
Pelopónnisos □, *Greece* 71 E2
Peloro, C., *Italy* 67 J7
Pelotas, *Brazil* 217 K5
Pelvoux, Massif de, *France* 55 F8
Pemalang, *Indonesia* 128 E6
Pematangsiantar, *Indonesia* 128 B2
Pemba I., *Tanzania* 158 B3
Pemberton, *Australia* 170 D2
Pembroke, *Canada* 185 B3
Pembroke, *U.K.* 46 K4
Peña de Francia, *Spain* 63 D3
Peñalara, *Spain* 63 C5
Penang = Pinang, *Malaysia* 126 B1
Peñas, C. de, *Spain* 63 A3
Pench'i = Benxi, *China* 116 B6
Pend Oreille L., *U.S.A.* 190 B4
Pendembu, *S. Leone* 147 C3
Pendleton, *U.S.A.* 190 B3
Pendzhikent, *Tajikistan* 93 E1
Penetanguishene, *Canada* 185 C1
Pengalengan, *Indonesia* 128 F5
Penglai, *China* 116 D5
Penguin, *Australia* 172 B2
Penhalonga, *Zimbabwe* 161 C5
Peniche, *Portugal* 63 E1
Penida, *Indonesia* 128 F8
Peninsular Malaysia □, *Malaysia* 126 C2
Penmarch, *France* 55 C1
Penn Yan, *U.S.A.* 189 A3
Pennine Range, *U.K.* 46 F6
Pennsylvania □, *U.S.A.* 189 C2
Penny Str., *Canada* 186 B9
Penola, *Australia* 171 G3
Penonomé, *Panama* 197 E5
Penrhyn Is., *Cook Is.* 176 F7
Penrith, *Australia* 171 E8
Pensacola, *U.S.A.* 191 J13
Penshurst, *Australia* 171 H3
Penshurst, *U.K.* 45 E4
Penticton, *Canada* 186 J4
Pentland Firth, *U.K.* 46 B7
Penza, *Russia* 81 D7
Penzance, *U.K.* 46 M4
Penzhino, *Russia* 91 B17
Penzhinskaya Guba, *Russia* 91 C17
Peoria, *U.S.A.* 191 E12
Perabumilih, *Indonesia* 128 D4
Perche, *France* 55 C4
Perdido, Mte., *Spain* 63 B8
Perdu, Mt. = Perdido, Mte., *Spain* 63 B8
Pereira, *Colombia* 210 C1
Perekerton, *Australia* 171 F4
Pereyaslav Khmelnitskiy, *Ukraine* 81 E3
Pergamino, *Argentina* 221 B4
Péribonca →, *Canada* 187 J12
Périgord, *France* 55 F5
Périgueux, *France* 55 F4
Perijá, Sierra de, *Colombia* 210 A2
Perim I. = Barīm, *Yemen* 100 C1
Perlas, Arch. de las, *Panama* 197 E6
Perlas, Punta de, *Nic.* 197 B3
Perm, *Russia* 90 F6
Pernambuco = Recife, *Brazil* 217 D9
Pernambuco □, *Brazil* 217 D9
Pernatty Lagoon, *Australia* 171 D1
Perpendicular Pt., *Australia* 171 D9
Perpignan, *France* 55 H6
Perryton, *U.S.A.* 190 F8
Persia = Iran ■, *Asia* 103
Persian Gulf = The Gulf, *Asia* 84 F9
Perth, *Australia* 170 B1
Perth, *Canada* 185 C3
Perth, *U.K.* 46 D6
Perth Amboy, *U.S.A.* 189 C5
Peru ■, *S. Amer.* 213
Perúgia, *Italy* 67 D5
Péruwelz, *Belgium* 51 C2
Pervomaysk, *Ukraine* 81 F3
Pervouralsk, *Russia* 90 F6
Pésaro, *Italy* 67 C5
Pescara, *Italy* 67 E6
Peshawar, *Pakistan* 105 B5
Petah Tiqwa, *Israel* 96 C2
Petaling Jaya, *Malaysia* 126 C1
Petange, *Lux.* 52 D1
Petauke, *Zambia* 161 C4
Petén Itzá, L., *Guatemala* 196 B1
Peterborough, *Australia* 171 E2
Peterborough, *U.K.* 46 J8
Peterhead, *U.K.* 46 B7
Peter's Mine, *Guyana* 214 B2
Petersburg, *Alaska, U.S.A.* 193 B5
Petersburg, *Va., U.S.A.* 191 F16
Petersfield, *U.K.* 45 E1
Petit Goâve, *Haiti* 200 B1
Petite-Ile, *Réunion* 166 C2
Petitsikapau, L., *Canada* 187 H13
Petlad, *India* 106 E1
Peto, *Mexico* 194 D8
Petra, *Spain* 65 B4
Petrich, *Bulgaria* 73 D2
Petrograd = Sankt-Peterburg, *Russia* 81 A3
Petropavlovsk, *Kazakstan* 90 G7
Petropavlovsk-Kamchatskiy, *Russia* 91 E18
Petrópolis, *Brazil* 215 B4
Petroşeni, *Romania* 75 C3
Petrovaradin, *Serbia, Yug.* 72 B7
Petrovsk, *Russia* 81 D7
Petrovsk-Zabaykalskiy, *Russia* 91 J12
Petrozavodsk, *Russia* 90 C4
Petrus Steyn, *S. Africa* 163 D7
Petrusburg, *S. Africa* 163 E5
Petworth, *U.K.* 45 E2
Peureulak, *Indonesia* 128 A2
Pevek, *Russia* 91 A16
Pforzheim, *Germany* 58 F2
Phalodi, *India* 106 B1
Phan Rang, *Vietnam* 125 F5
Phan Thiet, *Vietnam* 125 F5
Phangan, Ko, *Thailand* 123 J4
Phangnga, *Thailand* 122 K3
Phanh Bho Ho Chi Minh, *Vietnam* 125 F4
Phatthalung, *Thailand* 123 K4
Phenix City, *U.S.A.* 191 H14
Phetchabun, *Thailand* 123 F4
Phetchabun, Thiu Khao, *Thailand* 123 G5
Phetchaburi, *Thailand* 123 H4
Phichai, *Thailand* 123 F4
Phichit, *Thailand* 123 F4
Philadelphia, *U.S.A.* 189 C4
Philippeville, *Belgium* 51 D3
Philippines ■, *Asia* 130
Philippolis, *S. Africa* 163 F5
Philippopolis = Plovdiv, *Bulgaria* 73 C3
Philipstown, *S. Africa* 163 F5
Phillip I., *Australia* 171 H5
Phillott, *Australia* 171 A5
Phitsanulok, *Thailand* 123 F4
Phnom Dangrek, *Thailand* 123 G6
Phnom Penh, *Cambodia* 125 F3
Phnom Thbeng Meanchey, *Cambodia* 125 E3
Phoenix, *Mauritius* 166 B2
Phoenix, *U.S.A.* 190 G4
Phoenix Is., *Kiribati* 176 F7
Phong Saly, *Laos* 125 A2
Phra Nakhon Si Ayutthaya, *Thailand* 123 G4
Phrae, *Thailand* 123 F4
Phrao, *Thailand* 123 E4
Phu Doan, *Vietnam* 125 A3
Phu Loi, *Laos* 125 B2
Phu Ly, *Vietnam* 125 B3
Phuket, *Thailand* 122 K3
Piacenza, *Italy* 67 B3

Pian Cr. →, Australia 171 C7
Piatra Neamţ, Romania 75 B5
Piauí □, Brazil 217 D8
Piave →, Italy 67 A5
Piazza, Italy 67 K6
Pibor Post, Sudan 143 F5
Picardie, France 55 B6
Picardy = Picardie, France 55 B6
Picayune, U.S.A. 191 J12
Pichincha, □, Ecuador 212 B1
Picton, Australia 171 E8
Picton, Canada 185 C3
Picton, N.Z. 175 F5
Pictou, Canada 187 K14
Pidurutalagala, Sri Lanka 110 C2
Piedmont = Piemonte □, Italy 67 B1
Piedmont Plateau, U.S.A. 191 G15
Piedras, R. de las →, Peru 213 D5
Piedras Negras, Mexico 194 B5
Piemonte □, Italy 67 B1
Pierre, U.S.A. 190 C9
Piet Retief, S. Africa 163 D9
Pietermaritzburg, S. Africa 163 F8
Pietersburg, S. Africa 163 B8
Pietrosul, Romania 75 A4
Piggs Peak, Swaziland 165 A1
Pikes Peak, U.S.A. 190 E7
Piketberg, S. Africa 163 H2
Pilar, Paraguay 219 C2
Pilcomayo →, Paraguay 219 C2
Pilibhit, India 106 A4
Pilica →, Poland 77 D5
Pillaro, Ecuador 212 C1
Pilos, Greece 71 E2
Pilsen = Plzeň, Czech. 76 B2
Pimba, Australia 171 D1
Pimentel, Peru 213 C1
Pinamalayan, Phil. 130 F3
Pinang, Malaysia 126 B1
Pinar del Río, Cuba 198 B1
Pińczów, Poland 77 E4
Pindiga, Nigeria 151 C6
Pindos Óros, Greece 71 C2
Pindus Mts. = Pindos Óros, Greece 71 C2
Pine Bluff, U.S.A. 191 G11
Pine Point, Canada 186 F6
Pinega →, Russia 90 D5
Pinerolo, Italy 67 B1
Pinetown, S. Africa 163 F8
Pingaring, Australia 170 C3
Pingding, China 116 D2
Pingdingshan, China 116 F2
Pingdong, Taiwan 117 C2
Pingdu, China 116 D5
Pingelly, Australia 170 B2
Pingjiang, China 116 H2
Pingliang, China 113 E7
Pingrup, Australia 170 C3
Pingwu, China 113 F7
Pingxiang, Guangxi Zhuangzu, China 113 J7
Pingxiang, Jiangxi, China 116 J2
Pingyao, China 116 D2
Pinhal, Brazil 215 B2
Pinhel, Portugal 63 C3
Pini, Indonesia 128 C2
Piniós →, Greece 71 B3
Pinjarra, Australia 170 B1
Pinnaroo, Australia 171 F3
Pinrang, Indonesia 129 D10
Pinsk, Belarus 81 D2
Pinyang, China 116 J5
Piombino, Italy 67 D3
Pioner, Os., Russia 91 B10
Piotrków Trybunalski, Poland 77 D4
Piqua, U.S.A. 191 E14
Piracicaba, Brazil 215 C2
Piræus = Piraiévs, Greece 71 D3
Piraiévs, Greece 71 D3
Pirajuí, Brazil 215 B1
Pirapora, Brazil 217 F7
Pirbright, U.K. 45 D2
Pirgos, Greece 71 E2
Pirin Planina, Bulgaria 73 D2
Pirineos, Spain 63 B8
Pirojpur, Bangla. 111 D2
Pirot, Serbia, Yug. 72 D9
Piru, Indonesia 129 D13
Pisa, Italy 67 C3
Pisco, Peru 213 E3
Písek, Czech. 76 B2
Pishan, China 112 D1
Pising, Indonesia 129 E11
Pistóia, Italy 67 C4
Pisuerga →, Spain 63 B4
Pitarpunga, L., Australia 171 E4
Pitcairn I., Pac. Oc. 176 H9
Piteå, Sweden 40 D5
Piteşti, Romania 75 D4
Pithara, Australia 170 A2
Piton de la Petite Rivière Noire, Mauritius 166 C1
Pitseng, Lesotho 164 A2
Pittsburg, U.S.A. 191 F10
Pittsburgh, U.S.A. 189 C1
Pittsfield, U.S.A. 189 A5
Pittston, U.S.A. 189 B4
Pittsworth, Australia 171 A8
Piura, Peru 213 B1
Pizzo, Italy 67 H7
Placentia, Canada 187 J16
Placentia B., Canada 187 H16
Placer, Phil. 130 G4
Placetas, Cuba 198 B4
Plainfield, U.S.A. 189 C5
Plainview, U.S.A. 190 G8
Plakhino, Russia 90 E9
Plant City, U.S.A. 191 J15
Plasencia, Spain 63 D3
Plata, Río de la, S. Amer. 206 F4
Platani →, Italy 67 K5
Plateau □, Nigeria 151 D5
Platí, Ákra, Greece 71 B4
Plato, Colombia 210 A1
Platte →, U.S.A. 191 E10
Plattsburgh, U.S.A. 191 C16
Plauen, Germany 58 D5
Pleasantville, U.S.A. 189 D5
Pleiku, Vietnam 125 E5
Plenty, B. of, N.Z. 175 C6
Pleven, Bulgaria 73 B3
Plevlja, Montenegro, Yug. 72 D6
Płock, Poland 77 C4
Ploieşti, Romania 75 D5
Plovdiv, Bulgaria 73 C3
Plumtree, Zimbabwe 161 D2
Plymouth, U.K. 46 M5
Plzeň, Czech. 76 B2
Po →, Italy 67 B5
Po Hai = Bo Hai, China 116 C4
Pobé, Benin 150 D3
Pobeda, Russia 91 D15
Pobedino, Russia 91 G17
Pobedy Pik, Kyrgyzstan 90 L7
Pocatello, U.S.A. 190 D5
Poços de Caldas, Brazil 215 B2
Podgorica, Montenegro, Yug. 72 E6
Podkamennaya Tunguska →, Russia 91 G10
Podolsk, Russia 81 C5
Podor, Senegal 146 A2
Pofadder, S. Africa 163 E2
Poh, Indonesia 129 C11
Pohang, S. Korea 118 G6
Point Hope, U.S.A. 193 A3
Point Pedro, Sri Lanka 110 A2
Pointe-à-Pitre, Guadeloupe 202 F5
Pointe Noire, Congo 154 D1
Poitiers, France 55 E4
Pokaran, India 106 B1
Pokataroo, Australia 171 B7
Pokrovka, Kyrgyzstan 93 B9
Pokrovsk, Russia 91 F14
Pokrovsk, Russia 81 E8
Poland ■, Europe 77
Polatsk = Polotsk, Belarus 81 C3
Polemi, Cyprus 95 B1
Polesye, Belarus 81 D2
Polewali, Indonesia 129 D10
Pŏlgyo-ri, S. Korea 118 H4
Poli, Cameroon 153 C2
Polillo Is., Phil. 130 E3
Polillo Strait, Phil. 130 E3
Polis, Cyprus 95 B1
Políyiros, Greece 71 B3
Pollensa, Spain 65 A4
Pollensa, B. de, Spain 65 A4
Polnovat, Russia 90 E7
Polotsk, Belarus 81 C3
Poltava, Ukraine 81 F4
Polunochnoye, Russia 90 F6
Polynesia, Pac. Oc. 176 G7
Pombal, Portugal 63 D1
Ponca City, U.S.A. 191 F10
Ponce, Puerto Rico 201 A1
Pond Inlet, Canada 187 C10
Pondicherry, India 107 F3
Ponferrada, Spain 63 B3
Ponta Grossa, Brazil 217 H6
Pontarlier, France 55 D8
Pontchartrain L., U.S.A. 191 J12
Ponte Nova, Brazil 215 A4
Pontedera, Italy 67 C3
Pontevedra, Spain 63 B1
Pontiac, U.S.A. 191 D14
Pontian Kecil, Malaysia 126 D3
Pontianak, Indonesia 128 C6
Pontic Mts. = Kuzey Anadolu Dağlan, Turkey 94 A4
Pontine Is. = Ponziane, Isole, Italy 67 F5
Pontine Mts. = Kuzey Anadolu Dağlan, Turkey 94 A4
Ponziane, Isole, Italy 67 F5
Poole, U.K. 46 L7
Poona = Pune, India 107 E2
Pooncarie, Australia 171 E4
Poopelloe L., Australia 171 D4
Poopó, L., Bolivia 218 C1
Popanyinning, Australia 170 B2
Popayán, Colombia 210 D1
Poperinge, Belgium 51 C1
Popigay, Russia 91 D11
Popilta, L., Australia 171 E3
Popio L., Australia 171 E3
Poplar Bluff, U.S.A. 191 F12
Popocatepetl, Mexico 194 E5
Popokabaka, Zaïre 155 E2
Poradaha, Bangla. 111 C1
Porbandar, India 107 D1
Porcupine →, U.S.A. 193 A5
Pori, Finland 43 E1
Porkkala, Finland 43 F2
Porlamar, Venezuela 211 A4
Poronaysk, Russia 91 G17
Poroshiri-Dake, Japan 121 B8
Porrentruy, Switz. 60 A2
Porreras, Spain 65 B4
Porretta, Passo di, Italy 67 C4
Port Adelaide, Australia 171 F2
Port Alberni, Canada 186 H3
Port Alfred, S. Africa 163 H6
Port Allegany, U.S.A. 189 B2
Port Antonio, Jamaica 199 B6
Port Arthur = Lüshun, China 116 C5
Port Arthur, Australia 172 C3
Port Arthur, U.S.A. 191 J11
Port-au-Prince, Haiti 200 B2
Port Augusta, Australia 171 D1
Port Bell, Uganda 156 C2
Port-Bergé, Madag. 165 B2
Port-Bouët, Ivory C. 148 E5
Port Broughton, Australia 171 E1
Port-Cartier, Canada 187 J13
Port Chalmers, N.Z. 175 J3
Port Chester, U.S.A. 189 B5
Port Darwin, Falk. Is. 224 A3
Port Davey, Australia 172 C2
Port-de-Paix, Haiti 200 A1
Port Dickson, Malaysia 126 D1
Port Elizabeth, S. Africa 163 H6
Port-en-Bessin, France 55 B4
Port Etienne = Nouâdhibou, Mauritania 140 C1
Port Fairy, Australia 171 H3
Port Fouâd = Bûr Fuad, Egypt 139 A5
Port-Gentil, Gabon 154 C1
Port Harcourt, Nigeria 151 G3
Port Harrison = Inoucdjouac, Canada 187 G11
Port Hawkesbury, Canada 187 K15
Port Hope, Canada 185 C2
Port Huron, U.S.A. 191 D14
Port Jefferson, U.S.A. 189 B5
Port Kelang = Pelabuhan Kelang, Malaysia 126 C1
Port Kembla, Australia 171 E8
Port-la-Nouvelle, France 55 H6
Port Laoise, Ireland 46 H2
Port Lavaca, U.S.A. 191 J10
Port Loko, S. Leone 147 C2
Port Louis, Mauritius 166 B2
Port Lyautey = Kenitra, Morocco 136 B4
Port MacDonnell, Australia 171 H3
Port Macquarie, Australia 171 D9
Port Maria, Jamaica 199 A4
Port Morant, Jamaica 199 C6
Port Moresby, Papua N. G. 173 C2
Port Mourant, Guyana 214 B3
Port Nelson, Canada 186 H9
Port Nolloth, S. Africa 163 E1
Port of Spain, Trin. & Tob. 204 A2
Port Pegasus, N.Z. 175 J1
Port Phillip B., Australia 171 H5
Port Pirie, Australia 171 E1
Port Radium = Echo Bay, Canada 186 D6
Port Safaga = Bûr Safâga, Egypt 139 D6
Port Said = Bûr Sa'îd, Egypt 139 A4
Port St. Johns, S. Africa 163 G8
Port San Vicente, Phil. 130 B3
Port Shepstone, S. Africa 163 F8
Port Simpson, Canada 186 F3
Port Stanley = Stanley, Falk. Is. 224 A3
Port Sudan = Bûr Sûdân, Sudan 143 B6
Port Talbot, U.K. 46 K5
Port Taufîq = Bûr Taufiq, Egypt 139 B5
Port-Vendres, France 55 H6
Port Weld, Malaysia 126 B1
Portachuelo, Bolivia 218 C2
Portage La Prairie, Canada 186 J8
Portalegre, Portugal 63 E2
Porterville, S. Africa 163 H2
Portimão, Portugal 63 G1
Portland, N.S.W., Australia 171 E7
Portland, Vic., Australia 171 H3
Portland, U.S.A. 190 B2
Portland B., Australia 171 H3
Porto, Portugal 63 C1
Pôrto Alegre, Brazil 217 K6
Porto Amboim = Gunza, Angola 160 C2
Porto Empédocle, Italy 67 K5
Pôrto Esperança, Brazil 217 G4
Porto Moniz, Madeira 223 A2
Porto Novo, Benin 150 D3
Porto Tórres, Italy 67 F2
Porto-Vecchio, France 55 H9
Pôrto Velho, Brazil 217 D3
Portobelo, Panama 197 D5
Portoferráio, Italy 67 D3
Portoscuso, Italy 67 H2
Portoviejo, Ecuador 212 C1
Portrush, U.K. 46 E3
Portsmouth, U.K. 46 L8
Portsmouth, Ohio, U.S.A. 191 E14
Portsmouth, Va., U.S.A. 191 F16
Porttipahta, Finland 43 B2
Portugal ■, Europe 63
Portuguese-Guinea = Guinea-Bissau ■, Africa 146
Porus, Jamaica 199 B3
Posadas, Argentina 220 C6
Poschiavo, Switz. 60 D6
Poshan = Boshan, China 116 D4
Poso, Indonesia 129 C11
Posoegroenoe, Surinam 214 C4
Posong, S. Korea 118 H4
Poste Maurice Cortier, Algeria 137 E3
Postmasburg, S. Africa 163 E4
Postojna, Slovenia 72 A3
Potchefstroom, S. Africa 163 D6
Potenza, Italy 67 F7
Potgietersrus, S. Africa 163 B8
Poti, Georgia 82 B3
Potiskum, Nigeria 151 B6
Potomac →, U.S.A. 191 E16
Potosí, Bolivia 218 C1
Pototan, Phil. 130 G3
Potsdam, Germany 58 C5
Potters Bar, U.K. 45 B3
Pottery Hill = Abû Ballas, Egypt 139 E2
Pottstown, U.S.A. 189 C4
Pottsville, U.S.A. 189 C3
Poughkeepsie, U.S.A. 189 B5
Pouso Alegre, Brazil 215 B3
Povenets, Russia 90 C4
Póvoa de Varzim, Portugal 63 C1
Powder →, U.S.A. 190 B7
Powell, U.S.A. 190 D6
Poyang Hu, China 116 H3
Poyarkovo, Russia 91 H15
Požarevac, Serbia, Yug. 72 C8
Pozi, Taiwan 117 B2
Poznań, Poland 77 C2
Pozoblanco, Spain 63 F4
Pra →, Ghana 149 D2
Prachin Buri, Thailand 123 G4
Prachuap Khiri Khan, Thailand 123 J4
Prague = Praha, Czech. 76 B3
Praha, Czech. 76 B3
Praid, Romania 75 B4
Praja, Indonesia 128 F9
Prang, Ghana 149 C2
Prapat, Indonesia 128 B2
Praslin, Seychelles 166 A2
Prato, Italy 67 C4
Pratt, U.S.A. 190 F9
Pravia, Spain 63 A3
Prenzlau, Germany 58 B5
Prepansko Jezero, Macedonia 72 F8
Přerov, Czech. 76 B5
Prescott, Canada 185 C4
Prescott, U.S.A. 190 G4
Presidencia Roque Saenz Peña, Argentina 220 C5
Presidente Prudente, Brazil 217 H6
Presidio, U.S.A. 190 J7
Prespa, L. = Prepansko Jezero, Macedonia 72 F8
Prestea, Ghana 149 D1
Preston, U.K. 46 G6
Preston, U.S.A. 190 D5
Prestwick, U.K. 46 E5
Prestwood, U.K. 45 B1
Pretoria, S. Africa 163 C7
Préveza, Greece 71 C1
Prey-Veng, Cambodia 125 F3
Příbram, Czech. 76 B3
Price, U.S.A. 190 E5
Prieska, S. Africa 163 F4
Prilep, Macedonia 72 F8
Priluki, Ukraine 81 E3
Prime Seal I., Australia 172 A3
Prince Albert, Canada 186 H6
Prince Albert, S. Africa 163 H4
Prince Albert Pen., Canada 186 C7
Prince Albert Sd., Canada 186 C7
Prince Charles I., Canada 187 D11
Prince Edward I. □, Canada 187 K14
Prince George, Canada 186 G4
Prince Gustav Adolf Sea, Canada 186 A8
Prince of Wales, C., U.S.A. 180 C3
Prince of Wales I., Canada 186 C8
Prince of Wales I., U.S.A. 193 B5
Prince Patrick I., Canada 186 B7
Prince Rupert, Canada 186 F3
Princes Risborough, U.K. 45 B1
Princeton, U.S.A. 189 C4
Príncipe, I. de, Atl. Oc. 132 E3
Prinzapolca, Nic. 197 B3
Pripet = Pripyat →, Europe 81 E3
Pripet Marshes = Polesye, Belarus 81 D2
Pripyat →, Europe 81 E3
Pripyat Marshes = Polesye, Belarus 81 D2
Priština, Serbia, Yug. 72 E8
Privas, France 55 F7
Privolzhskaya Vozvyshennost, Russia 81 E8
Prizren, Serbia, Yug. 72 E7
Probolinggo, Indonesia 128 F8
Proddatur, India 107 E3
Prof. Van Blommestein Meer, Surinam 214 C4
Progreso, Mexico 194 D8
Prokopyevsk, Russia 90 H9
Prome, Burma 122 E2
Prostějov, Czech. 76 B5
Provence, France 55 G8
Providence, U.S.A. 189 A6
Provideniya, Russia 91 A17
Provins, France 55 C6
Provo, U.S.A. 190 E5
Prudhoe Bay, U.S.A. 193 A5
Pruszków, Poland 77 C4
Prut →, Romania 75 C6
Pryluky = Priluki, Ukraine 81 E3
Przemysl, Poland 77 E6
Przeworsk, Poland 77 E5
Przhevalsk, Kyrgyzstan 90 L7
Pskem →, Uzbekistan 93 B3
Pskemskiy Khrebet, Uzbekistan 93 B4
Pskent, Uzbekistan 93 C3
Pskov, Russia 81 B3
Puan, S. Korea 118 G4
Pucallpa, Peru 213 C3
Pucheng, China 116 J4
Puebla, Mexico 194 E5
Pueblo, U.S.A. 190 F7
Pueblonuevo, Spain 63 F4
Puente Genil, Spain 63 G4
Puerto Armuelles, Panama 197 E3
Puerto Ayacucho, Venezuela 211 C3
Puerto Barrios, Guatemala 196 C2
Puerto Bermúdez, Peru 213 D3
Puerto Bolívar, Ecuador 212 D1
Puerto Cabello, Venezuela 211 A3
Puerto Cabezas, Nic. 197 A3
Puerto Cabo Gracias á Dios, Nic. 197 A3
Puerto Capaz = Jebba, Morocco 136 A5
Puerto Carreño, Colombia 210 C3
Puerto Castilla, Honduras 196 B3
Puerto Chicama, Peru 213 C2
Puerto Cortes, Costa Rica 197 E3
Puerto Cortés, Honduras 196 B2
Puerto Cumarebo, Venezuela 211 A2
Puerto de Santa María, Spain 63 G3
Puerto del Rosario, Canary Is. 223 D3
Puerto Deseado, Argentina 220 J4
Puerto Heath, Bolivia 218 A1
Puerto La Cruz, Venezuela 211 A4
Puerto Leguízamo, Colombia 210 E1
Puerto Madryn, Argentina 220 H4
Puerto Maldonado, Peru 213 D5
Puerto Manati, Cuba 198 B5
Puerto Montt, Chile 220 G2
Puerto Morelos, Mexico 194 D9
Puerto Padre, Cuba 198 C5
Puerto Páez, Venezuela 211 B3
Puerto Pinasco, Paraguay 219 B2
Puerto Plata, Dom. Rep. 200 A3
Puerto Princesa, Phil. 130 H1
Puerto Quepos, Costa Rica 197 D3
Puerto Rico ■, W. Indies 201
Puerto Sastre, Paraguay 219 B2
Puerto Suárez, Bolivia 218 C3
Puerto Willches, Colombia 210 B1
Puertollano, Spain 63 E5
Pugachev, Kazakstan 81 D8
Puget Sound, U.S.A. 190 A2
Púglia □, Italy 67 F8
Pugŏdong, N. Korea 118 B5
Puig Mayor, Spain 65 A4
Puigcerdá, Spain 63 B9
Pujilí, Ecuador 212 C1
Pujon-chosuji, N. Korea 118 C4
Pukaki L., N.Z. 175 G3
Pukapuka, Cook Is. 176 G7
Pukchin, N. Korea 118 C3
Pukchŏng, N. Korea 118 C5
Pukekohe, N.Z. 175 C5
Pukou, China 116 F4
Pulaski, U.S.A. 191 F15
Pullman, U.S.A. 190 B4
Pulog, Phil. 130 C2
Pülümür, Turkey 82 D2
Puná, I., Ecuador 212 D1
Punakha, Bhutan 109 B5
Punata, Bolivia 218 C1
Punch, India 107 A2
Pune, India 107 E2
Pungsan, N. Korea 118 C4
Punjab □, India 107 B2
Punjab □, Pakistan 105 D5
Puno, Peru 213 E5
Punta Arenas, Chile 220 K3
Punta Gorda, Belize 196 B2
Puntarenas, Costa Rica 197 D2
Punto Fijo, Venezuela 211 A2
Punxsatawney, U.S.A. 189 C2
Puqi, China 116 H2
Puquio, Peru 213 E3
Pur →, Russia 90 E9
Purace, Vol., Colombia 210 D1
Puralia = Puruliya, India 106 D7
Purfleet, U.K. 45 C4
Puri, India 106 F7
Purmerend, Neths. 50 C3
Purnia, India 106 C7
Pursat, Cambodia 125 F2
Purukcahu, Indonesia 128 C8
Puruliya, India 106 D7
Purus →, Brazil 217 D3
Purwakarta, Indonesia 128 E5
Puryŏng, N. Korea 118 B5
Pusan, S. Korea 118 H5
Pushchino, Russia 91 E18
Pushkino, Russia 81 E8
Putao, Burma 122 A3
Putaruru, N.Z. 175 C5
Putignano, Italy 67 F8
Puting, Tanjung, Indonesia 128 D7
Putorana, Gory, Russia 91 E10
Puttalam Lagoon, Sri Lanka 110 B1
Putten, Neths. 50 C4
Puttgarden, Germany 58 A4

Putumayo →, S. Amer. 206 C3
Putussibau, Indonesia 128 C7
Puy-de-Dôme, France 55 E6
Puy-de-Dôme □, France 55 E6
Puyallup, U.S.A. 190 B3
Puyang, China 116 E3
Puyo, Ecuador 212 C2
Pweto, Zaïre 155 F6
Pwllheli, U.K. 46 H5
Pyandzh, Tajikistan 93 G3
Pyandzh →, Afghan. 104 A5
Pyandzh →, Tajikistan 93 G2
Pyapon, Burma 122 F2
Pyärnu = Pärnu, Estonia 81 A2
Pyasina →, Russia 91 D10
Pyinmana, Burma 122 E2
Pyŏktong, N. Korea 118 C3
Pyŏnggang, N. Korea 118 E4
Pyŏngtaek, S. Korea 118 F4
P'yŏngyang, N. Korea 118 D3
Pyramid L., U.S.A. 190 D3
Pyramids, Egypt 139 B4
Pyrénées, Europe 55 H4
Pyrénées-Atlantiques □, France 55 H3
Pyrénées-Orientales □, France 55 H6
Pyu, Burma 122 E2

Q

Qaanaaq = Thule, Greenland 224 B1
Qachasnek, S. Africa 163 F7
Qahremānshahr = Bākhtarān, Iran 103 B2
Qaidam Pendi, China 112 E5
Qala, Ras il, Malta 69 A2
Qalācheh, Afghan. 104 C4
Qalāt, Afghan. 104 E4
Qal'eh-ye Best, Afghan. 104 F2
Qal'eh-ye Now, Afghan. 104 C2
Qal'eh-ye Sarkari, Afghan. 104 B4
Qal'eh-ye Valī, Afghan. 104 C2
Qalyûb, Egypt 139 B4
Qamruddin Karez, Pakistan 105 C3
Qandahār, Afghan. 104 F3
Qandahār □, Afghan. 104 F3
Qaqortoq = Julianehåb, Greenland 224 D2
Qâra, Egypt 139 B1
Qaraghandy = Karaganda, Kazakstan 90 J7
Qarāvol, Afghan. 104 A5
Qarqan, China 112 D3
Qarqan He →, China 112 D4
Qarshi = Karshi, Uzbekistan 90 L5
Qartabā, Lebanon 95 B2
Qasr 'Amra, Jordan 98 B2
Qasr Farâfra, Egypt 139 C2
Qat Lesh, Afghan. 104 C4
Qatanā, Syria 97 C2
Qatar ■, Asia 100
Qattâra, Egypt 139 B2
Qattâra, Munkhafed el, Egypt 139 B2
Qattâra Depression = Qattâra, Munkhafed el, Egypt 139 B2
Qazaqstan = Kazakstan ■, Asia 90 J6
Qazvin, Iran 103 B3
Qena, Egypt 139 D5
Qena, Wadi →, Egypt 139 D5
Qeqertarsuag = Disko, Greenland 224 C1
Qeqertarsuaq = Godhavn, Greenland 224 C1
Qeshm, Iran 103 E4
Qezi'ot, Israel 96 F1
Qianshan, China 116 G3
Qila Safed, Pakistan 105 D1
Qila Saifullāh, Pakistan 105 C3
Qilian Shan, China 112 D5
Qingdao, China 116 E5
Qinghai □, China 112 E5
Qinghai Hu, China 112 E6
Qingjiang, Jiangsu, China 116 F4
Qingjiang, Jiangxi, China 116 H3
Qingliu, China 116 J3
Qingshuihe, China 116 C2
Qinhuangdao, China 116 C4
Qinyang, China 116 E2
Qinyuan, China 116 D2
Qinzhou, China 113 J8
Qiqihar, China 113 B11
Qiryat Ata, Israel 96 B2
Qiryat Gat, Israel 96 D2
Qiryat Mal'akhi, Israel 96 D1
Qiryat Shemona, Israel 96 A3
Qiryat Yam, Israel 96 B2
Qishan, Taiwan 117 C2
Qitai, China 112 C4
Qiyang, China 116 J1
Qom, Iran 103 B3
Qomsheh, Iran 103 C3
Qondūz, Afghan. 104 B5
Qondūz □, Afghan. 104 B5
Qostanay = Kustanay, Kazakstan 90 G6
Qu Xian, China 116 H4
Quainton, U.K. 45 A1
Quairading, Australia 170 B2
Qualeup, Australia 170 C2
Quambatook, Australia 171 F4
Quambone, Australia 171 C6
Quan Long, Vietnam 125 G3
Quandialla, Australia 171 E6
Quang Ngai, Vietnam 125 D5
Quang Yen, Vietnam 125 B4
Quanzhou, Fujian, China 113 H10
Quanzhou, Guangxi Zhuangzu, China 116 J1
Quatre Bornes, Mauritius 166 B2
Quatsino, Canada 186 H3
Queanbeyan, Australia 171 F7
Québec, Canada 185 A6
Québec □, Canada 187 J12
Queen Charlotte Bay, Falk. Is. 224 A2
Queen Charlotte Is., Canada 186 F2
Queen Charlotte Sd., N.Z. 180 D7
Queen Charlotte Str., Canada 186 G3
Queen Elizabeth Is., Canada 186 B8
Queen Elizabeth Nat. Park, Uganda 156 C1
Queen Maud G., Canada 186 D8
Queenborough, U.K. 45 D6
Queenscliff, Australia 171 H5
Queensland □, Australia 168 G12
Queenstown, Australia 172 B2
Queenstown, N.Z. 175 H2
Queenstown, S. Africa 163 G6
Queguay Grande →, Uruguay 219 B1
Quela, Angola 160 B3
Quelimane, Mozam. 159 C3
Quelpart = Cheju Do, S. Korea 118 J4
Querétaro, Mexico 194 E5
Queshan, China 116 F2
Quesnel, Canada 186 G4
Quetta, Pakistan 105 D3
Quevedo, Ecuador 212 C1
Quezaltenango, Guatemala 196 C1
Quezon City, Phil. 130 E2
Qui Nhon, Vietnam 125 E5
Quibaxe, Angola 160 B2
Quibdo, Colombia 210 C1
Quiberon, France 55 D2
Quilengues, Angola 160 D2
Quillabamba, Peru 213 E4
Quilmes, Argentina 221 C5
Quilpie, Australia 168 H12
Quimper, France 55 C1
Quimperlé, France 55 C2
Quincy, Ill., U.S.A. 191 E11
Quincy, Mass., U.S.A. 189 A6
Quines, Argentina 221 A1
Quinga, Mozam. 159 B3
Quintanar, Spain 63 E5
Quinyambie, Australia 171 C3
Quirindi, Australia 171 D8
Quissanga, Mozam. 159 A3
Quito, Ecuador 212 B1
Qul'ân, Jazâ'ir, Egypt 139 E6
Qumbu, S. Africa 163 G7
Quoin Pt., S. Africa 163 H2
Quondong, Australia 171 E2
Quorn, Australia 171 D1
Quqon = Kokand, Uzbekistan 93 D4
Qurnat as Sawdā', Lebanon 95 B2
Qûs, Egypt 139 D5
Quseir, Egypt 139 D6
Qyzylorda = Kzyl-Orda, Kazakstan 90 K5

R

Raahe, Finland 43 D2
Raba, Indonesia 129 F10
Rabah, Nigeria 151 A3
Rabai, Kenya 157 F4
Rabat, Malta 69 B2
Rabat, Morocco 136 B4
Rabaul, Papua N. G. 173 B3
Rābigh, Si. Arabia 99 D3
Race, C., Canada 187 J16
Rach Gia, Vietnam 125 G3
Racine, U.S.A. 191 D12
Rădăuţi, Romania 75 A4
Radford, U.S.A. 191 F15
Radlett, U.K. 45 B3
Radom, Poland 77 D5
Radomir, Bulgaria 73 C2
Radomsko, Poland 77 D3
Rae, Canada 186 E6
Rae Bareli, India 106 C5
Rae Isthmus, Canada 186 E9
Raetihi, N.Z. 175 D5
Rafaela, Argentina 221 A4
Rafah, Egypt 139 A6
Raglan, N.Z. 175 C5
Ragusa, Italy 67 K6
Raha, Indonesia 129 E11
Rahad al Bardī, Sudan 143 D2
Rahaeng = Tak, Thailand 123 F4
Rahimyar Khan, Pakistan 105 D4
Raichur, India 107 E3
Raigarh, India 106 E6
Raijua, Indonesia 129 F11
Railton, Australia 172 B2
Rainham, U.K. 45 D5
Rainier, Mt., U.S.A. 190 B3
Raipur, India 106 E5
Ra'is, Si. Arabia 99 D2
Raj Nandgaon, India 106 E5
Raja, Ujung, Indonesia 128 A1
Raja Ampat, Kepulauan, Indonesia 129 C14
Rajahmundry, India 107 E4
Rajang →, Malaysia 126 C6
Rajasthan □, India 106 B1
Rajasthan Canal, India 106 B1
Rajbari, Bangla. 111 C1
Rajgarh, India 106 D3
Rajkot, India 107 D1
Rajpipla, India 106 E1
Rakaia →, N.Z. 175 G4
Rakan, Ra's, Qatar 100 C3
Rakaposhi, Pakistan 105 A6
Rakata, Pulau, Indonesia 128 E4
Rakhneh-ye Jamshīdī, Afghan. 104 D1
Raleigh B., U.S.A. 191 F17
Rām Allāh, Jordan 98 B1
Ram Hd., Australia 171 G7
Rama, Nic. 197 C3
Ramat Gan, Israel 96 C2
Ramatlhabama, S. Africa 163 C6
Ramechhap, Nepal 109 B4
Ramelau, Mte., Indonesia 129 F12
Ramgarh, India 106 D7
Ramla, Israel 96 D2
Rampur, India 106 A4
Rampur Hat, India 106 D8
Ramtek, India 106 E4
Ranaghat, India 106 D8
Ranau, Malaysia 126 A8
Rancagua, Chile 220 E3
Ranchi, India 106 D7
Randers, Denmark 42 B2
Randfontein, S. Africa 163 C7
Rangamati, Bangla. 111 D3
Rangia, India 106 B2
Rangitaiki →, N.Z. 175 C6
Rangitata →, N.Z. 175 H3
Rangoon, Burma 122 F2
Raniganj, India 106 D7
Raniwara, India 106 C1
Rankin Inlet, Canada 186 F9
Rankins Springs, Australia 171 E5
Ranong, Thailand 122 J3
Ransiki, Indonesia 129 C16
Rantau, Indonesia 128 D8
Rantauprapat, Indonesia 128 B2
Rapa, Pac. Oc. 176 H9
Rapid City, U.S.A. 190 D8
Rapu Rapu I., Phil. 130 F4
Rarotonga, Cook Is. 176 H7
Ra's al' Ayn, Syria 97 A5
Ra's al Khaymah, U.A.E. 101 A3
Ra's al-Unuf, Libya 138 A4
Ra's an Naqb, Jordan 98 C1
Ras Bânâs, Egypt 139 E6
Ras Dashen, Ethiopia 144 C3
Ras Mallap, Egypt 139 B5
Rasa, Punta, Argentina 220 G4
Rasca, Pta. de la, Canary Is. 223 D1
Rashad, Sudan 143 D4
Rashîd, Egypt 139 A3
Rashîd, Masabb, Egypt 139 A3
Rasht, Iran 103 B2
Rat Buri, Thailand 123 H4
Ratangarh, India 106 B2
Rath Luirc, Ireland 46 J1
Rathenow, Germany 58 B5
Ratlam, India 106 D2
Ratnapura, Sri Lanka 110 D2
Raton, U.S.A. 190 F7
Raub, Malaysia 126 C1
Raufarhöfn, Iceland 38 A5
Raukumara Ra., N.Z. 175 C6
Raurkela, India 106 E6
Ravenna, Italy 67 C4
Ravensburg, Germany 58 G3
Ravi →, Pakistan 105 D5
Rawalpindi, Pakistan 105 B5
Rawāndūz, Iraq 102 A4
Rawang, Malaysia 126 C1
Rawene, N.Z. 175 A4
Rawlins, U.S.A. 190 D6
Rawson, Argentina 220 H4
Ray, C., Canada 187 J15
Rayagada, India 106 F6
Raychikhinsk, Russia 91 H15
Rayleigh, U.K. 45 C6
Raymond, Canada 186 J5
Rayong, Thailand 123 H4
Razgrad, Bulgaria 73 B4
Ré, I. de, France 55 E3
Reading, U.K. 46 K8
Reading, U.S.A. 189 C4
Realicó, Argentina 221 C2
Ream, Cambodia 125 G2
Rebi, Indonesia 129 E16
Rebiana, Libya 138 C5
Rebun-Tō, Japan 121 A7
Recife, Brazil 217 D9
Recife, Seychelles 166 C3
Recklinghausen, Germany 59 A2
Reconquista, Argentina 220 D5
Red →, U.S.A. 191 H12
Red Bluff, U.S.A. 190 D2
Red Cliffs, Australia 171 E3
Red Deer, Canada 186 H5
Red Oak, U.S.A. 191 E10
Red Sea, Asia 132 D7
Red Tower Pass = Turnu Rosu Pasul, Romania 75 C3
Red Wing, U.S.A. 191 C11
Rédange, Lux. 52 C1
Redbridge, U.K. 45 C4
Redcliffe, Australia 171 A9
Reddersburg, S. Africa 163 E6
Redding, U.S.A. 190 D2
Redhill, U.K. 45 D3
Redlands, U.S.A. 190 G3
Redmond, Australia 170 D2
Redondela, Spain 63 B1
Redondo, Portugal 63 E2
Ree, L., Ireland 46 G2
Reefton, N.Z. 175 F3
Refahiye, Turkey 82 D1
Regensburg, Germany 58 F5
Réggio di Calábria, Italy 67 J7
Réggio nell' Emilia, Italy 67 B3
Regina, Canada 186 J7
Régina, Fr. Guiana 214 C6
Région au Vent, Réunion 166 A2
Région sous le Vent, Réunion 166 B1
Rehoboth, Namibia 162 C2
Rehovot Rām Allāh, Israel 96 D2
Rei-Bouba, Cameroon 153 C3
Reichenbach, Germany 58 D5
Reigate, U.K. 45 D3
Reims, France 55 B7
Reindeer L., Canada 186 G7
Reitz, S. Africa 163 D7
Reivilo, S. Africa 163 D5
Rekinniki, Russia 91 C17
Reliance, Canada 186 F7
Remarkable, Mt., Australia 171 D1
Rembang, Indonesia 128 E7
Remedios, Panama 197 E4
Rémire, Fr. Guiana 214 C6
Remscheid, Germany 58 D1
Rendsburg, Germany 58 A3
Rene, Russia 91 A17
Renfrew, Canada 185 B3
Rengat, Indonesia 128 C3
Renk, Sudan 143 D4
Renkum, Neths. 50 D4
Renmark, Australia 171 E3
Rennell, Solomon Is. 173 B2
Rennes, France 55 C3
Reno, U.S.A. 190 D2
Reno →, Italy 67 B5
Renovo, U.S.A. 189 B2
Republican →, U.S.A. 191 F10
Republiek, Surinam 214 C4
Repulse Bay, Canada 187 E10
Requena, Peru 213 B3
Requena, Spain 63 E7
Resht = Rasht, Iran 103 B2
Resistencia, Argentina 220 C5
Reşiţa, Romania 75 C2
Resolute, Canada 186 C9
Resolution I., Canada 187 F12
Resolution I., N.Z. 175 J1
Retalhuleu, Guatemala 196 C1
Réthimnon, Greece 71 F4
Retiche, Alpi, Switz. 60 C6
Réunion ■, Ind. Oc. 132 J9
Reutlingen, Germany 58 F3
Reval = Tallinn, Estonia 81 A2
Revelstoke, Canada 186 H4
Revilla Gigedo, Is., Pac. Oc. 180 H8
Revolyutsii, Pik, Tajikistan 93 F5
Rewa, India 106 D5
Rewa →, Guyana 214 D2
Rewari, India 106 B3
Rexburg, U.S.A. 190 C5
Rey Malabo, Eq. Guin. 153 A1
Reykjahlið, Iceland 38 B4
Reykjanes, Iceland 38 D2
Reykjavík, Iceland 38 C2
Reynosa, Mexico 194 C5
Rhayader, U.K. 46 J6
Rhein →, Europe 34 E7
Rheine, Germany 58 C2
Rheinland-Pfalz □, Germany 58 E1
Rheriss, Oued →, Morocco 136 D5
Rheydt, Germany 59 B1
Rhin = Rhein →, Europe 34 E7
Rhine = Rhein →, Europe 34 E7
Rhineland-Palatinate □ = Rheinland-Pfalz □, Germany 58 E1
Rhinelander, U.S.A. 191 C12
Rhino Camp, Uganda 156 B1
Rhir, Cap, Morocco 136 D2
Rhode Island □, U.S.A. 189 B6
Rhodes = Ródhos, Greece 71 F6
Rhodesia = Zimbabwe ■, Africa 161
Rhodope Mts. = Rhodopi Planina, Bulgaria 73 D3
Rhodopi Planina, Bulgaria 73 D3
Rhön = Hohe Rhön, Germany 58 D3
Rhondda, U.K. 46 K6
Rhône □, France 55 E7
Rhône →, France 55 H7
Rhyl, U.K. 46 H6
Ri-Aba, Eq. Guin. 153 A1
Riau □, Indonesia 128 C3
Riau, Kepulauan, Indonesia 128 C4
Riau Arch. = Riau, Kepulauan, Indonesia 128 C4
Ribadeo, Spain 63 A3
Ribatejo, Portugal 63 E1
Ribe, Denmark 42 C2
Ribeira Grande, C. Verde Is. 222 A1
Ribeirão Prêto, Brazil 215 B2
Riberalta, Bolivia 218 A1
Riccarton, N.Z. 175 G4
Rich, Morocco 136 C5
Richards Bay, S. Africa 163 E9
Riche, C., Australia 170 D3
Richfield, U.S.A. 190 E5
Richland, U.S.A. 190 B3
Richmond, N.Z. 175 F4
Richmond, Calif., U.S.A. 190 E2
Richmond, Ind., U.S.A. 191 E13
Richmond, Ky., U.S.A. 191 F14
Richmond, Va., U.S.A. 191 E16
Richmond Ra., Australia 171 B9
Richmond-upon-Thames, U.K. 45 C3
Rickmansworth, U.K. 45 B2
Ridder, Kazakstan 90 J8
Ridgway, U.S.A. 189 B2
Ried, Austria 61 A4
Riet →, S. Africa 163 E5
Rieti, Italy 67 E5
Rifstangi, Iceland 38 A5
Rift Valley □, Kenya 157 C2
Rig Rig, Chad 142 D1
Riga, Latvia 81 B2
Riga, G. of = Rīgas Jūras Līcis, Latvia 81 A1
Rīgas Jūras Līcis, Latvia 81 A1
Rīgestān □, Afghan. 104 G3
Rigolet, Canada 187 G14
Rijau, Nigeria 151 B2
Rijeka, Croatia 72 B3
Rijkevorsel, Belgium 51 A4
Rijssen, Neths. 50 C5
Rijswijk, Neths. 50 D2
Rima →, Nigeria 151 A2
Rimah, Wadi ar →, Si. Arabia 99 C2
Rimini, Italy 67 C5
Rîmnicu Sărat, Romania 75 C5
Rîmnicu Vîlcea, Romania 75 C3
Rimouski, Canada 187 J13
Rinca, Indonesia 129 F10
Ringim, Nigeria 151 B5
Ringkøbing, Denmark 42 B1
Rinía, Greece 71 E5
Rinjani, Indonesia 128 F9
Rio Branco, Brazil 217 E2
Río Branco, Uruguay 219 C3
Rio Claro, Brazil 215 B2
Rio Claro, Trin. & Tob. 204 B3
Río Cuarto, Argentina 221 B2
Rio de Janeiro, Brazil 215 C4
Rio de Janeiro □, Brazil 215 B5
Rio-del-Rey →, Nigeria 151 G4
Río Gallegos, Argentina 220 K3
Rio Grande, Brazil 217 K5
Río Grande, Nic. 197 B3
Rio Grande →, U.S.A. 180 G10
Rio Grande do Norte □, Brazil 217 D9
Rio Grande do Sul □, Brazil 217 J5
Río Hato, Panama 197 E5
Río Mulatos, Bolivia 218 C1
Río Muni = Mbini □, Eq. Guin. 153 C2
Río Segundo, Argentina 221 A2
Río Tercero, Argentina 221 A2
Riobamba, Ecuador 212 C1
Ríohacha, Colombia 210 A2
Rioni →, Georgia 34 G14
Riosucio, Caldas, Colombia 210 C1
Riosucio, Choco, Colombia 210 B1
Ripon, U.K. 46 G7
Rishiri-Tō, Japan 121 A7
Rishon le Ziyyon, Israel 96 C2
Riti, Nigeria 151 E5
Rivadavia, Argentina 221 C3
Rivas, Nic. 197 C2
River Cess, Liberia 148 D2
Rivera, Uruguay 219 A2
Riverhead, U.S.A. 189 B6
Rivers □, Nigeria 151 G3
Riversdale, S. Africa 163 H3
Riverside, U.S.A. 190 G3
Riverton, Australia 171 E2
Riverton, Canada 186 J8
Riverton, N.Z. 175 J2
Riviera di Levante, Italy 67 B2
Riviera di Ponente, Italy 67 C1
Rivière-du-Loup, Canada 187 K13
Rivière-Pilote, Martinique 203 D3
Rivne = Rovno, Ukraine 81 E2
Rivoli B., Australia 171 G2
Riyadh = Ar Riyāḑ, Si. Arabia 99 C5
Rize, Turkey 94 A6
Rizhao, China 116 E4
Rizokarpaso, Cyprus 95 A3
Rizzuto, C., Italy 67 H8
Roanne, France 55 E7
Roanoke, U.S.A. 191 F15
Roanoke →, U.S.A. 191 F16
Roatán, Honduras 196 B3
Robbins I., Australia 172 A1
Robertson, S. Africa 163 H3
Robertsport, Liberia 148 D1
Robertstown, Australia 171 E2
Roberval, Canada 187 K12
Robeson Chan., Greenland 224 A1
Robinvale, Australia 171 F4
Roboré, Bolivia 218 C3
Robson, Mt., Canada 186 H4
Roca, C. da, Portugal 34 H5
Rocha, Uruguay 219 D3
Rochefort, Belgium 51 D4
Rochefort, France 55 E3
Rochester, U.K. 45 D5
Rochester, Minn., U.S.A. 191 D11
Rochester, N.Y., U.S.A. 189 A2
Rochford, U.K. 45 C6

Rock Hill, U.S.A. 191 G15
Rock Island, U.S.A. 191 E12
Rock Springs, U.S.A. 190 D6
Rockall, Atl. Oc. 34 D4
Rockford, U.S.A. 191 D12
Rockhampton, Australia 168 H13
Rockingham, Australia 170 B1
Rockland, U.S.A. 191 B18
Rockville, U.S.A. 189 D3
Rocky Ford, U.S.A. 190 F7
Rocky Gully, Australia 170 D2
Rocky Mount, U.S.A. 191 F16
Rocky Mts., N. Amer. 180 E8
Rod, Pakistan 105 E1
Rødby Havn, Denmark 42 D3
Roden, Neths. 50 A5
Rodez, France 55 G6
Ródhos, Greece 71 F6
Roding →, U.K. 45 C4
Roermond, Neths. 50 F5
Roes Welcome Sd., Canada 186 F9
Roeselare, Belgium 51 B1
Rogagua, L., Bolivia 218 B1
Rogate, U.K. 45 E1
Roggeveldberge, S. Africa 163 G3
Rogoaguado, L., Bolivia 218 B1
Rogue →, U.S.A. 190 C1
Rohri, Pakistan 105 E4
Rohtak, India 106 A3
Roi Et, Thailand 123 F6
Rojas, Argentina 221 C4
Rojo, C., Mexico 194 D5
Rojo, Cabo, Puerto Rico 201 A1
Rokan →, Indonesia 128 B3
Rolla, U.S.A. 191 F11
Roma, Italy 67 E5
Roman, Romania 75 B5
Roman, Russia 91 G12
Romang, Indonesia 129 F13
Romāni, Egypt 139 A5
Romania ■, Europe 75
Romano, Cayo, Cuba 198 B5
Romanshorn, Switz. 60 A5
Romanzof C., U.S.A. 193 B3
Romblon, Phil. 130 F3
Rome = Roma, Italy 67 E5
Rome, Ga., U.S.A. 191 G14
Rome, N.Y., U.S.A. 189 A4
Rommani, Morocco 136 B4
Romney, U.S.A. 189 D2
Romont, Switz. 60 C1
Romorantin, France 55 D5
Roncador, Serra do, Brazil 217 E6
Ronda, Spain 63 G4
Rondônia □, Brazil 217 E3
Rong, Koh, Cambodia 125 F2
Ronge, L. la, Canada 186 H7
Ronse, Belgium 51 C2
Roodepoort, S. Africa 163 C7
Roof Butte, U.S.A. 190 F6
Roorkee, India 106 A3
Roosendaal, Neths. 50 E2
Roosevelt →, Brazil 206 C3
Roque Pérez, Argentina 221 C5
Roraima □, Brazil 217 B3
Roraima, Mt., Venezuela 211 C5
Rorschach, Switz. 60 A5
Rosa, Zambia 161 A5
Rosario, Argentina 221 B4
Rosario, Mexico 194 D3
Rosario, Paraguay 219 B2
Rosario de la Frontera, Argentina 220 C4
Rosario del Tala, Argentina 221 A5
Rosas, Spain 63 B9
Rosas, G. de, Spain 63 B9
Roscommon, Ireland 46 G2
Rose Belle, Mauritius 166 C2
Rose Hill, Mauritius 166 B2
Roseau, Domin. 203 B2
Rosebery, Australia 172 B2
Roseburg, U.S.A. 190 C2
Rosenheim, Germany 58 G5
Rosetown, Canada 186 J6
Rosetta = Rashîd, Egypt 139 A3
Roseville, U.S.A. 190 E2
Rosewood, Australia 171 A9
Rosignol, Guyana 214 B3
Roskilde, Denmark 42 C3
Roslavl, Russia 81 C4
Roslyn, Australia 171 E7
Rosmead, S. Africa 163 G5
Ross, Australia 172 B3
Rosslare, Ireland 46 J3
Rosso, Mauritania 140 D1
Rossosh, Russia 81 E6
Rostāq, Afghan. 104 A5
Rosthern, Canada 186 H6
Rostock, Germany 58 A4
Rostov, Russia 81 G6
Rostov, Russia 81 B6
Roswell, U.S.A. 190 H7
Rothaargebirge, Germany 58 D2
Rother →, U.K. 45 E6
Rotherham, U.K. 46 H7
Rothesay, U.K. 46 D4
Roti, Indonesia 129 F11
Roto, Australia 171 D5
Rotoroa, L., N.Z. 175 F4
Rotorua, N.Z. 175 C6
Rotorua, L., N.Z. 175 C6
Rotterdam, Neths. 50 D2
Rottnest I., Australia 170 B1
Rottweil, Germany 58 F2
Rotuma, Fiji 176 G5
Roubaix, France 55 A6
Rouen, France 55 B5
Round Mt., Australia 171 C9
Roura, Fr. Guiana 214 C6
Roussillon, France 55 H6
Rouxville, S. Africa 163 F6
Rouyn, Canada 187 K11
Rovaniemi, Finland 43 C2
Rovereto, Italy 67 A4
Rovigo, Italy 67 B4
Rovinj, Croatia 72 B2
Rovno, Ukraine 81 E2
Rovuma →, Tanzania 158 D3
Rowena, Australia 171 B7
Roxa, Guinea-Biss. 146 D1
Roxas, Capiz, Phil. 130 G3
Roxas, Isabela, Phil. 130 C3
Roxas, Mindoro, Phil. 130 F3
Roxburgh, N.Z. 175 J2
Royan, France 55 E3
Royston, U.K. 45 A3
Rtishchevo, Russia 81 D7
Ruahine Ra., N.Z. 175 D6
Ruapehu, N.Z. 175 D5
Ruapuke I., N.Z. 175 J2
Rub' al Khali, Si. Arabia 99 E5
Rubicone →, Italy 67 C5
Rubino, Ivory C. 148 D5
Rubio, Venezuela 211 B1
Rubtsovsk, Russia 90 J8
Ruby L., U.S.A. 190 D4
Rūdbār, Afghan. 104 G2
Rudgwick, U.K. 45 E2
Rudnogorsk, Russia 91 H11
Rudnyy, Kazakstan 90 H6
Rudolf, Ostrov, Russia 90 A9
Rufa'a, Sudan 143 C5
Rufiji →, Tanzania 158 C3
Rufino, Argentina 221 C3
Rufisque, Senegal 146 B1
Rugao, China 116 F5
Rugby, U.K. 46 J7
Rügen, Germany 58 A6
Ruhengeri, Rwanda 156 A1
Ruhr →, Germany 58 C2
Rui'an, China 116 J5
Rukwa L., Tanzania 158 C1
Rumania = Romania ■, Europe 75
Rumbêk, Sudan 143 F3
Rumford, U.S.A. 191 B18
Rumoi, Japan 121 B7
Rumonge, Burundi 156 C1
Rumuruti, Kenya 157 C2
Runan, China 116 F2
Runanga, N.Z. 175 F3
Runaway, C., N.Z. 175 C6
Runaway Bay, Jamaica 199 B3
Rungwa, Tanzania 158 C1
Runka, Nigeria 151 A4
Ruoqiang, China 112 D4
Rupat, Indonesia 128 B3
Rupert →, Canada 187 J11
Rupert House = Fort Rupert, Canada 187 J11
Rupsa, Bangla. 111 D1
Rupununi →, Guyana 214 D2
Rur →, Germany 59 B1
Rurrenabaque, Bolivia 218 B1
Rusambo, Zimbabwe 161 A5
Rusape, Zimbabwe 161 C5
Ruschuk = Ruse, Bulgaria 73 A4
Ruse, Bulgaria 73 A4
Russellkonda, India 106 F6
Russellville, U.S.A. 191 G11
Russia ■, Eurasia 91 G11
Russkaya Polyana, Kazakstan 90 H7
Rustavi, Georgia 82 B6
Rustenburg, S. Africa 163 C7
Rutana, Burundi 156 C2
Ruteng, Indonesia 129 F10
Rutshuru, Zaïre 155 C6
Ruwais, U.A.E. 101 B2
Ruwenzori, Africa 132 F6
Ruyigi, Burundi 156 B2
Ružomberok, Slovak Rep. 76 C6
Rwanda ■, Africa 156
Ryazan, Russia 81 C6
Ryazhsk, Russia 81 D6
Rybache, Kazakstan 90 K8
Rybinsk, Russia 81 B6
Rybinskoye Vdkhr., Russia 81 A5
Rylstone, Australia 171 D7
Rypin, Poland 77 B4
Ryūkyū Is. = Nansei-Shotō, Japan 121 J7
Rzeszów, Poland 77 E5
Rzhev, Russia 81 B4

S

Sa Dec, Vietnam 125 G4
Saale →, Germany 58 C4
Saarbrücken, Germany 58 E1
Saaremaa, Estonia 81 A1
Sab 'Bi'ār, Syria 97 C3
Saba, W. Indies 202 B1
Sabadell, Spain 63 C9
Sabah □, Malaysia 126 A8
Şabāḩ, Wadi →, Si. Arabia 99 D6
Sabak Bernam, Malaysia 126 C1
Sábana de la Mar, Dom. Rep. 200 A3
Sábanalarga, Colombia 210 A1
Sabang, Indonesia 128 A1
Sabarania, Indonesia 129 D17
Sabáudia, Italy 67 F5
Sabhah, Libya 138 C3
Sabie, S. Africa 163 C9
Sabinas, Mexico 194 B4
Sabinas Hidalgo, Mexico 194 C5
Sabine →, U.S.A. 191 J11
Sabirabad, Azerbaijan 82 D8
Sablayan, Phil. 130 F2
Sable, C., Canada 187 L14
Sable, C., U.S.A. 191 K16
Sable I., Canada 187 K15
Sabolev, Russia 91 E18
Sabria, Tunisia 138 C1
Sabzevār, Iran 103 B4
Sachkhere, Georgia 82 B5
Sachsen □, Germany 58 D5
Sachsen-Anhalt □, Germany 58 C4
Sacramento, U.S.A. 190 E2
Sacramento →, U.S.A. 190 E2
Sacramento Mts., U.S.A. 190 H7
Sádaba, Spain 63 B7
Sadani, Tanzania 158 C3
Sadd el Aali, Egypt 139 E5
Sade, Nigeria 151 B6
Sado, Japan 121 E6
Sadon, Russia 82 A5
Safed Koh, Afghan. 104 D6
Saffron Walden, U.K. 45 A4
Safi, Morocco 136 C2
Safīd Kūh, Afghan. 104 C2
Saga, Indonesia 129 D15
Saga, Japan 120 D1
Saga □, Japan 120 D1
Sagala, Mali 140 E3
Sagay, Phil. 130 G4
Sagil, Mongolia 112 A5
Şagir, Zāb aş →, Iraq 102 B3
Sagleipie, Liberia 148 D3
Saglouc, Canada 187 F11
Sagŏ-ri, S. Korea 118 H4
Sagres, Portugal 63 G1
Sagua la Grande, Cuba 198 B3
Saguenay →, Canada 187 J13
Sagunto, Spain 63 D8
Sahagún, Spain 63 B4
Sahara, Africa 132 D4
Saharan Atlas = Saharien, Atlas, Algeria 137 A4
Saharanpur, India 106 A3
Saharien, Atlas, Algeria 137 A4
Sahiwal, Pakistan 105 C5
Sa'id Bundas, Sudan 143 E2
Saïda, Algeria 137 A3
Sa'īdābād, Iran 103 D4
Saïdia, Morocco 136 A6
Saidu, Pakistan 105 A5
Saigon = Phanh Bho Ho Chi Minh, Vietnam 125 F4
Saijō, Japan 120 C3
Saikhoa Ghat, India 107 B6
Saiki, Japan 120 D2
Sailolof, Indonesia 129 C14
St. Albans, U.K. 45 B3
St. Albans, U.S.A. 191 B17
St.-André, Réunion 166 A3
St. Andrews, U.K. 46 D6
St. Anne, U.K. 44 A2
St. Ann's Bay, Jamaica 199 A4
St. Anthony, U.S.A. 190 C5
St. Arnaud, Australia 171 G4
St-Augustin-Saguenay, Canada 187 H14
St. Augustine, U.S.A. 191 J15
St. Austell, U.K. 46 M4
St.-Barthélemy, I., W. Indies 202 B2
St.-Benoît, Réunion 166 B3
St. Boniface, Canada 186 K8
St Brieuc, France 55 C2
St. Catharines, Canada 185 D2
St.-Cergue, Switz. 60 C1
St. Charles, U.S.A. 191 F12
St. Christopher = St. Kitts, W. Indies 202 C2
St. Cloud, U.S.A. 191 C11
St.-Denis, France 55 B6
St.-Denis, Réunion 166 A2
St. Elias, Mt., U.S.A. 193 B5
St. Elias Mts., Canada 186 D3
St.-Élie, Fr. Guiana 214 C5
St.-Étienne, France 55 F7
St.-Étienne →, Réunion 166 C1
St.-Flour, France 55 F6
St. Francis, C., S. Africa 163 H5
St. Gallen = Sankt Gallen, Switz. 60 A5
St. George, Australia 171 A7
St. George, U.S.A. 190 F4
St.-Georges, Belgium 51 C5
St.-Georges, Fr. Guiana 214 D6
St. George's, Grenada 203 L1
St. George's Channel, U.K. 46 K3
St. Georges Hd., Australia 171 F8
St. Gotthard P. = San Gottardo, Paso del, Switz. 60 C4
St. Helena ■, Atl. Oc. 223 H5
St. Helena B., S. Africa 163 G2
St. Helens, Australia 172 B3
St. Helens, U.K. 46 H6
St. Helens, U.S.A. 190 B2
St. Helier, U.K. 44 B2
St-Hyacinthe, Canada 185 B5
St-Imier, Switz. 60 B2
St-Jean, Canada 185 B5
St-Jean, L., Canada 187 K12
St-Jérôme, Canada 185 B5
St. John, Canada 187 K14
St. John's, Antigua 202 D5
St. John's, Canada 187 H16
St. Johns →, U.S.A. 191 H15
St.-Joseph, Réunion 166 C2
St. Joseph, Mich., U.S.A. 191 D13
St. Joseph, Mo., U.S.A. 191 E10
St. Joseph, L., Canada 186 J9
St. Kilda, N.Z. 175 J3
St. Kitts, W. Indies 202 C2
St.-Laurent, Fr. Guiana 214 C5
St. Lawrence →, Canada 187 J13
St. Lawrence, Gulf of, Canada 187 J14
St. Lawrence I., U.S.A. 193 A3
St.-Lô, France 55 B3
St-Louis, France 55 G7
St.-Louis, Réunion 166 C1
St-Louis, Senegal 146 A1
St. Louis, U.S.A. 191 F12
St. Lucia ■, W. Indies 203 E3
St. Lucia, L., S. Africa 163 D9
St. Lucia Channel, W. Indies 203 E3
St.-Malo, France 55 C3
St-Marc, Haiti 200 A2
St-Martin, W. Indies 202 A1
St. Mary Pk., Australia 171 D2
St. Marys, Australia 172 B3
St. Marys, U.S.A. 189 B2
St. Matthews, I. = Zadetkyi Kyun, Burma 122 J3
St. Matthias Group, Papua N. G. 173 A3
St.-Nazaire, France 55 D2
St-Niklaas, Belgium 51 B3
St.-Omer, France 55 A5
St.-Paul, Réunion 166 A1
St. Paul, U.S.A. 191 C11
St. Peter Port, Chan. Is. 44 A1
St. Petersburg = Sankt-Peterburg, Russia 81 A3
St. Petersburg, U.S.A. 191 J15
St.-Pierre, Réunion 166 C2
St.-Pierre et Miquelon □, St- P. & M. 187 J15
St.-Quentin, France 55 B6
St.-Tropez, France 55 H9
St. Vincent, W. Indies 203 H2
St. Vincent, G., Australia 171 F1
St. Vincent Passage, W. Indies 203 G3
St-Vith, Belgium 51 D6
Ste-Croix, Switz. 60 C1
Ste.-Marie, Martinique 203 C3
Ste.-Suzanne, Réunion 166 A2
Saintes, France 55 E3
Saintes, I. des, Guadeloupe 202 G5
Saintonge, France 55 F4
Saitama □, Japan 120 A8
Sajama, Bolivia 218 C1
Sak →, S. Africa 163 F3
Sakai, Japan 120 C5
Sakākah, Si. Arabia 99 B3
Sakakawea, L., U.S.A. 190 B8
Sakarya = Adapazarı, Turkey 94 A2
Sakarya →, Turkey 94 A2
Sakata, Japan 121 E7
Sakchu, N. Korea 118 C3
Sakété, Benin 150 D3
Sakha = Yakut Republic □, Russia 91 F14
Sakhalin, Russia 91 G17
Sakhalinskiy Zaliv, Russia 91 F16
Sakon Nakhon, Thailand 123 F6
Sakrivier, S. Africa 163 F3
Sal, C. Verde Is. 222 A3
Sala, Sweden 40 F3
Saladillo, Argentina 221 C4
Salado →, Argentina 221 C5
Salaga, Ghana 149 B2
Salala, Liberia 148 D2
Salālah, Oman 101 D1
Salamanca, Spain 63 C3
Salamanca, U.S.A. 189 B2
Salamis, Cyprus 95 B3
Salamis, Greece 71 D3
Salar de Uyuni, Bolivia 218 D1
Salaverry, Peru 213 C2
Salawati, Indonesia 129 C14
Salayar, Indonesia 129 E10
Salazie, Réunion 166 B2
Saldaña, Spain 63 B4
Saldanha, S. Africa 163 H1
Saldanha B., S. Africa 163 H1
Sale, Australia 171 H6
Salé, Morocco 136 B4
Salekhard, Russia 90 E8
Salem, India 107 F3
Salem, Mass., U.S.A. 189 A6
Salem, N.J., U.S.A. 189 D4
Salem, Oreg., U.S.A. 190 B2
Salerno, Italy 67 F6
Salford, U.K. 46 H7
Salida, U.S.A. 190 E7
Salima, Malawi 158 C2
Salina, Italy 67 H6
Salina, U.S.A. 190 E9
Salina Cruz, Mexico 194 F6
Salinas, Ecuador 212 D1
Salinas →, U.S.A. 190 E2
Salinas, B. de, Nic. 197 C2
Salinas Grandes, Argentina 220 D4
Salines, C. de, Spain 65 B4
Salisbury = Harare, Zimbabwe 161 B4
Salisbury, Australia 171 F2
Salisbury, U.K. 46 L7
Salisbury, Md., U.S.A. 191 E17
Salisbury, N.C., U.S.A. 191 F15
Salisbury Plain, U.K. 46 L7
Salka, Nigeria 151 C2
Salkhad, Jordan 98 A2
Salmon, U.S.A. 190 C5
Salmon →, U.S.A. 190 B4
Salmon River Mts., U.S.A. 190 C4
Salonica = Thessaloníki, Greece 71 B3
Salonta, Romania 75 B2
Salsacate, Argentina 221 A2
Salsk, Russia 81 G6
Salso →, Italy 67 K6
Salt →, U.S.A. 190 G4
Salt Creek, Australia 171 F2
Salt Fork Arkansas →, U.S.A. 191 F10
Salt Lake City, U.S.A. 190 D5
Salta, Argentina 220 C4
Saltcoats, U.K. 46 E5
Salthólmavík, Iceland 38 B2
Saltillo, Mexico 194 C4
Salto, Argentina 221 C4
Salto, Uruguay 219 B1
Salton Sea, U.S.A. 190 G3
Saltpond, Ghana 149 E2
Salûm, Egypt 139 A1
Salûm, Khâlig el, Egypt 139 A1
Salut, Is. du, Fr. Guiana 214 C6
Saluzzo, Italy 67 B1
Salvador, Brazil 217 E9
Salween →, Burma 122 F3
Salyany, Azerbaijan 82 D9
Salzburg, Austria 61 B3
Salzburg □, Austria 61 B3
Salzgitter, Germany 58 C3
Sam Neua, Laos 125 B2
Sam Ngao, Thailand 122 F3
Sama, Russia 90 F6
Samagaltai, Russia 91 J10
Samales Group, Phil. 130 L3
Samâlût, Egypt 139 C4
Samangán □, Afghan. 104 B5
Samani, Japan 121 C8
Samar, Phil. 130 G5
Samara, Russia 81 D9
Samarai, Papua N. G. 173 C3
Samarinda, Indonesia 128 C9
Samarkand, Uzbekistan 93 D1
Samarqand = Samarkand, Uzbekistan 93 D1
Sāmarrā', Iraq 102 C4
Sambalpur, India 106 E6
Sambar, Tanjung, Indonesia 128 D6
Sambas, Indonesia 128 B6
Sambava, Madag. 165 B3
Sambawizi, Zimbabwe 161 C1
Sambhal, India 106 A4
Sambhar, India 106 B2
Samburu □, Kenya 157 C2
Samchŏk, S. Korea 118 F5
Samchonpo, S. Korea 118 H5
Same, Tanzania 158 B3
Samoa Is., Pac. Oc. 168 B8
Sámos, Greece 71 D6
Samothráki, Greece 71 B5
Sampa, Ghana 149 C1
Sampacho, Argentina 221 B2
Sampang, Indonesia 128 F8
Sampit, Indonesia 128 D7
Sampit, Teluk, Indonesia 128 D7
Samsun, Turkey 94 A4
Samtredia, Georgia 82 B4
Samui, Ko, Thailand 123 K4
Samur →, Azerbaijan 82 B9
Samut Prakan, Thailand 123 H4
Samut Sakhon, Thailand 123 H4
San, Mali 140 E4
San →, Poland 77 E5
San Agustin, C., Phil. 130 L6
San Ambrosio, Pac. Oc. 206 E2
San Andres Mts., U.S.A. 190 H6
San Andrés Tuxtla, Mexico 194 E6
San Angelo, U.S.A. 190 H8
San Antonio, Belize 196 B2
San Antonio, Phil. 130 E2
San Antonio, Spain 65 C1
San Antonio, U.S.A. 190 J9
San Antonio →, U.S.A. 191 K10
San Antonio, C., Cuba 198 B1
San Antonio de los Baños, Cuba 198 B2
San Antonio Oeste, Argentina 220 G4
San Bernardino, U.S.A. 190 G3
San Bernardino Str., Phil. 130 F4
San Bernardo, I. de, Colombia 210 A1
San Blas, C., U.S.A. 191 J14
San Borja, Bolivia 218 B1
San Carlos = Butuku-Luba, Eq. Guin. 153 A1
San Carlos, Nic. 197 C2
San Carlos, Negros, Phil. 130 H4
San Carlos, Pangasinan, Phil. 130 D2
San Carlos, Uruguay 219 D2
San Carlos, Amazonas, Venezuela 211 D3
San Carlos, Cojedes, Venezuela 211 A3

San Carlos de Bariloche, *Argentina* 220 G3
San Clemente I., *U.S.A.* 190 G2
San Cristóbal, *Argentina* 220 D5
San Cristóbal, *Dom. Rep.* 200 B3
San Cristóbal, *Mexico* 194 F7
San Cristóbal, *Solomon Is.* 173 B2
San Cristóbal, *Venezuela* 211 B2
San Diego, *U.S.A.* 190 G3
San Dimitri, Ras, *Malta* 69 A1
San Felipe, *Venezuela* 211 A3
San Feliu de Guíxols, *Spain* 63 B9
San Félix, *Pac. Oc.* 206 E1
San Fernando, *La Union, Phil.* 130 C2
San Fernando, *Pampanga, Phil.* 130 E2
San Fernando, *Spain* 63 G3
San Fernando, *Trin. & Tob.* 204 C1
San Fernando de Apure, *Venezuela* 211 B3
San Fernando de Atabapo, *Venezuela* 211 C3
San Francisco, *Argentina* 221 A3
San Francisco, *Spain* 65 C2
San Francisco, *U.S.A.* 190 E2
San Francisco de Macorís, *Dom. Rep.* 200 A3
San Francisco del Monte de Oro, *Argentina* 221 B1
San Gabriel, *Ecuador* 212 A2
San Germán, *Puerto Rico* 201 A1
San Gil, *Colombia* 210 C2
San Gottardo, Paso del, *Switz.* 60 C4
San Gregorio, *Uruguay* 219 B2
San Ignacio, *Belize* 196 B2
San Ignacio, *Bolivia* 218 B2
San Ignacio, *Paraguay* 219 C2
San Ildefonso, C., *Phil.* 130 D3
San Isidro, *Argentina* 221 C5
San Javier, *Bolivia* 218 B2
San Joaquin →, *U.S.A.* 190 E2
San Jorge, *Argentina* 221 A3
San Jorge, G., *Argentina* 220 J4
San Jorge, G. de, *Spain* 63 C8
San Jorge B., *Mexico* 194 A1
San José, *Bolivia* 218 C2
San José, *Costa Rica* 197 D3
San José, *Guatemala* 196 D1
San Jose, *Luzon, Phil.* 130 D2
San Jose, *Mindoro, Phil.* 130 F2
San José, *Spain* 65 C1
San Jose, *U.S.A.* 190 E2
San José de Mayo, *Uruguay* 219 D2
San José de Ocune, *Colombia* 210 C3
San José del Guaviare, *Colombia* 210 D2
San Juan, *Argentina* 220 E3
San Juan, *Phil.* 130 J6
San Juan, *Puerto Rico* 201 A2
San Juan, *Trin. & Tob.* 204 A2
San Juan →, *Nic.* 197 C3
San Juan →, *U.S.A.* 190 F5
San Juan, C., *Eq. Guin.* 153 C1
San Juan, C., *Puerto Rico* 201 A2
San Juan Bautista, *Spain* 65 C2
San Juan de los Morros, *Venezuela* 211 A3
San Juan del Norte, *Nic.* 197 C3
San Juan del Norte, B. de, *Nic.* 197 C3
San Juan del Sur, *Nic.* 197 C2
San Juan Mts., *U.S.A.* 190 F6
San Julián, *Argentina* 220 J4
San Justo, *Argentina* 221 A4
San Lorenzo, *Argentina* 221 B4
San Lorenzo, *Ecuador* 212 A1
San Lorenzo, I., *Peru* 213 D2
San Lorenzo, Mt., *Argentina* 220 J3
San Lucas, *Bolivia* 218 D1
San Lucas, C., *Mexico* 194 D2
San Luis, *Argentina* 221 B1
San Luis, *Cuba* 198 B1
San Luis, *Guatemala* 196 B1
San Luis □, *Argentina* 221 C1
San Luis, Sierra de, *Argentina* 221 B1
San Luis Obispo, *U.S.A.* 190 F2
San Luis Potosí, *Mexico* 194 D4
San Marcos, *Guatemala* 196 C1
San Marcos, *U.S.A.* 190 J9
San Marino ■, *Europe* 67 C5
San Mateo, *Phil.* 130 C3
San Mateo, *U.S.A.* 190 E2
San Matías, *Bolivia* 218 C3
San Matías, G., *Argentina* 220 G4
San Miguel, *El Salv.* 196 D2
San Miguel, *Panama* 197 E6
San Miguel, *Spain* 65 C2
San Miguel →, *Bolivia* 218 C2
San Miguel de Tucumán, *Argentina* 220 C4
San Miguel del Monte, *Argentina* 221 C5
San Narciso, *Phil.* 130 E2
San Nicolas, *Phil.* 130 B2
San Nicolás de los Arroyas, *Argentina* 221 B4
San Pablo, *Phil.* 130 E3
San-Pédro, *Ivory C.* 148 E4
San Pedro, *Mexico* 194 C4
San Pedro de Lloc, *Peru* 213 C2
San Pedro de Macorís, *Dom. Rep.* 200 B3
San Pedro del Norte, *Nic.* 197 B2
San Pedro del Paraná, *Paraguay* 219 C3
San Pedro Sula, *Honduras* 196 C2
San Rafael, *Argentina* 220 E3
San Remo, *Italy* 67 C1
San Salvador, *Bahamas* 201 B2
San Salvador, *El Salv.* 196 D2
San Salvador de Jujuy, *Argentina* 220 B4
San Sebastián, *Spain* 63 A6
San Sebastian de la Gomera, *Canary Is.* 223 D1
San Valentin, *Chile* 206 G2
San Vicente de la Barquera, *Spain* 63 A4
Sana', *Yemen* 100 B1
Sana →, *Bos.-H.* 72 B4
Sanaga →, *Cameroon* 153 D2
Sanana, *Indonesia* 129 D13
Sanbor = Sandan, *Cambodia* 125 E4
Sánchez, *Dom. Rep.* 200 A3
Sancti-Spíritus, *Cuba* 198 B4
Sand →, *S. Africa* 163 A8
Sandakan, *Malaysia* 126 A8
Sandan, *Cambodia* 125 E4
Sandgate, *Australia* 171 A9
Sandhurst, *U.K.* 45 D1
Sandía, *Peru* 213 E5
Sandoa, *Zaïre* 155 F4
Sandomierz, *Poland* 77 E5
Sandpoint, *U.S.A.* 190 A4
Sandusky, *U.S.A.* 191 D14
Sandy C., *Queens., Australia* 168 C5
Sandy C., *Tas., Australia* 172 B1
Sandy L., *Canada* 186 J9
Sanford, *U.S.A.* 191 J15
Sanga →, *Congo* 154 B3
Sanga-Tolon, *Russia* 91 D16
Sangamner, *India* 106 F2
Sangar, *Russia* 91 E14
Sangasanga, *Indonesia* 128 C9
Sangay, *Ecuador* 212 C1
Sangeang, *Indonesia* 129 F10
Sanggan He →, *China* 116 B3
Sanggau, *Indonesia* 128 C6
Sangihe, Kepulauan, *Indonesia* 129 B12
Sangihe, P., *Indonesia* 129 B12
Sangju, *S. Korea* 118 F5
Sangkapura, *Indonesia* 128 E7
Sangmelina, *Cameroon* 153 E2
Sangonera →, *Spain* 63 F7
Sangre de Cristo Mts., *U.S.A.* 190 F7
Sanhala, *Ivory C.* 148 A4
Sanje, *Uganda* 156 D1
Sankt Gallen, *Switz.* 60 A5
Sankt Gallen □, *Switz.* 60 B5
Sankt-Peterburg, *Russia* 81 A3
Sankuru →, *Zaïre* 155 D3
Sanlúcar de Barrameda, *Spain* 63 G3
Sanmenxia, *China* 116 E1
Sannaspos, *S. Africa* 163 E6
Sannicandro, *Italy* 67 E7
Sannieshof, *S. Africa* 163 C6
Sannīn, J., *Lebanon* 95 B2
Sanniquelle, *Liberia* 148 C3
Sanok, *Poland* 77 F5
Sanshui, *China* 113 H9
Santa Ana, *Bolivia* 218 B1
Santa Ana, *Ecuador* 212 C1
Santa Ana, *El Salv.* 196 D1
Santa Ana, *U.S.A.* 190 G3
Santa Barbara, *Honduras* 196 C2
Santa Barbara, *U.S.A.* 190 F2
Santa Carlos del Zulia, *Venezuela* 211 B2
Santa Catalina I., *U.S.A.* 190 G2
Santa Catarina □, *Brazil* 217 J6
Santa Clara, *Cuba* 198 B3
Santa Clara, *U.S.A.* 190 E2
Santa Clara de Olimar, *Uruguay* 219 C3
Santa Clotilde, *Peru* 213 A3
Santa Coloma, *Spain* 63 C9
Santa Cruz, *Bolivia* 218 C2
Santa Cruz, *Costa Rica* 197 D2
Santa Cruz, *Phil.* 130 E3
Santa Cruz, *U.S.A.* 190 E2
Santa Cruz de la Palma, *Canary Is.* 223 D1
Santa Cruz de Tenerife, *Canary Is.* 223 D2
Santa Cruz del Norte, *Cuba* 198 A2
Santa Cruz del Sur, *Cuba* 198 C4
Santa Cruz do Rio Pardo, *Brazil* 215 C1
Santa Cruz I., *Solomon Is.* 176 G5
Santa Cruz Mts., *Jamaica* 199 C3
Santa Elena, *Argentina* 221 A4
Santa Elena, *Ecuador* 212 D1
Santa Elena, C., *Costa Rica* 197 C2
Santa Eugenia, Pta., *Mexico* 194 B1
Santa Eulalia, *Spain* 65 C2
Santa Fe, *Argentina* 221 A4
Santa Fe, *U.S.A.* 190 G7
Santa Inés, I., *Chile* 206 H2
Santa Isabel = Rey Malabo, *Eq. Guin.* 153 A1
Santa Isabel, *Solomon Is.* 173 A1
Santa Lucia, *Uruguay* 219 D2
Santa Lucia Range, *U.S.A.* 190 F2
Santa Luzia, *C. Verde Is.* 222 A1
Santa Maria, *Brazil* 217 J5
Santa Maria, *C. Verde Is.* 222 A3
Santa Maria, *Phil.* 130 C2
Santa Maria, *U.S.A.* 190 F2
Santa María →, *Mexico* 194 A3
Santa Marta, *Colombia* 210 A1
Santa Marta, Sierra Nevada de, *Colombia* 210 A2
Santa Maura = Levkás, *Greece* 71 D1
Santa Monica, *U.S.A.* 190 G2
Santa Rosa, *La Pampa, Argentina* 220 F4
Santa Rosa, *San Luis, Argentina* 221 B2
Santa Rosa, *Bolivia* 218 A1
Santa Rosa, *Ecuador* 212 D1
Santa Rosa, *U.S.A.* 190 E1
Santa Rosa de Copán, *Honduras* 196 C2
Santa Rosa de Río Primero, *Argentina* 221 A2
Santa Rosa I., *U.S.A.* 190 F2
Santa Tecla = Nueva San Salvador, *El Salv.* 196 D1
Santa Teresa, *Argentina* 221 B4
Santai, *China* 113 F7
Santana, *Madeira* 223 A2
Santanayi, *Spain* 65 B4
Santander, *Spain* 63 A5
Santarém, *Brazil* 217 C5
Santarém, *Portugal* 63 E1
Santiago, *Chile* 220 E3
Santiago, *Panama* 197 E5
Santiago, *Phil.* 130 C3
Santiago →, *Peru* 213 B2
Santiago, Punta de, *Eq. Guin.* 153 B1
Santiago de Compostela, *Spain* 63 A1
Santiago de Cuba, *Cuba* 198 C6
Santiago de los Cabelleros, *Dom. Rep.* 200 A3
Santiago del Estero, *Argentina* 220 D4
Santo André, *Brazil* 215 C2
Santo Antão, *C. Verde Is.* 222 A1
Santo Domingo, *Dom. Rep.* 200 B3
Santo Domingo, *Nic.* 197 C2
Santo Domingo de los Colorados, *Ecuador* 212 B1
Santo Tomás, *Peru* 213 E4
Santo Tomé de Guayana = Ciudad Guayana, *Venezuela* 211 B4
Santoña, *Spain* 63 A5
Santos, *Brazil* 215 C3
Santos Dumont, *Brazil* 215 B4
Sanza Pombo, *Angola* 160 B3
São Bernado de Campo, *Brazil* 215 C2
São Borja, *Brazil* 217 J5
São Carlos, *Brazil* 215 B2
São Filipe, *C. Verde Is.* 222 C1
São Francisco →, *Brazil* 217 E9
São Gonçalo, *Brazil* 215 C4
São João da Boa Vista, *Brazil* 215 B2
São João del Rei, *Brazil* 215 B4
São José do Rio Prêto, *Brazil* 215 A1
São José dos Campos, *Brazil* 215 C3
São Lourenço, *Brazil* 215 B3
São Luís, *Brazil* 217 C8
São Marcos, B. de, *Brazil* 217 C8
São Nicolau, *C. Verde Is.* 222 A2
São Paulo, *Brazil* 215 C2
São Paulo □, *Brazil* 217 G6
São Paulo, I., *Atl. Oc.* 223 F4
São Roque, C. de, *Brazil* 217 C9
São Sebastião, I. de, *Brazil* 215 C3
São Sebastião do Paraíso, *Brazil* 215 A2
São Tiago, *C. Verde Is.* 222 C2
São Tomé, *Atl. Oc.* 132 E3
São Tomé, C. de, *Brazil* 215 B6
São Tomé & Principe ■, *Africa* 132 E4
São Vicente, *Brazil* 215 C2
São Vicente, *C. Verde Is.* 222 A2
São Vicente, *Madeira* 223 A2
São Vicente, C. de, *Portugal* 63 G1
Saona, I., *Dom. Rep.* 200 B3
Saône →, *France* 55 D7
Saône-et-Loire □, *France* 55 D7
Saonek, *Indonesia* 129 C14
Saparua, *Indonesia* 129 D14
Sapele, *Nigeria* 151 F2
Saposoa, *Peru* 213 C2
Sapporo, *Japan* 121 B7
Sar-e Pol, *Afghan.* 104 B3
Sar Planina, *Macedonia* 72 E7
Sara, *Phil.* 130 G4
Saragossa = Zaragoza, *Spain* 63 C7
Saraguro, *Ecuador* 212 D1
Sarajevo, *Bos.-H.* 72 C6
Saramacca □, *Surinam* 214 C4
Saramacca →, *Surinam* 214 B4
Saran, *Indonesia* 128 C7
Sarandí del Yi, *Uruguay* 219 C2
Sarandí Grande, *Uruguay* 219 C2
Sarangani B., *Phil.* 130 L5
Sarangani Is., *Phil.* 130 L5
Sarangarh, *India* 106 E5
Saransk, *Russia* 81 C7
Sarasota, *U.S.A.* 191 K15
Saratoga Springs, *U.S.A.* 189 A5
Saratov, *Russia* 81 E8
Saravane, *Laos* 125 D4
Sarawak □, *Malaysia* 126 C6
Saraya, *Senegal* 146 C3
Sarda →, *India* 106 B5
Sardalas, *Libya* 138 C1
Sardarshahr, *India* 106 A2
Sardegna, *Italy* 67 G2
Sardinia = Sardegna, *Italy* 67 G2
Sarera, G. of, *Indonesia* 168 A3
Sargasso Sea, *Atl. Oc.* 222 D1
Sargodha, *Pakistan* 105 C5
Sarh, *Chad* 142 F2
Sarhro, Djebel, *Morocco* 136 D4
Sarikamiş, *Turkey* 82 C4
Sarikei, *Malaysia* 126 C6
Sariwŏn, *N. Korea* 118 E3
Sark, *Chan. Is.* 44 A2
Sarlat, *France* 55 F5
Sarmi, *Indonesia* 129 D17
Sarmiento, *Argentina* 220 H3
Sarnen, *Switz.* 60 B3
Sarnia, *Canada* 187 L11
Sarny, *Ukraine* 81 D2
Sarolangun, *Indonesia* 128 D3
Saronikós Kólpos, *Greece* 71 D3
Sarro, *Mali* 140 E4
Sarthe □, *France* 55 C4
Sarthe →, *France* 55 D4
Sartynya, *Russia* 90 E7
Sary-Tash, *Kyrgyzstan* 93 D6
Saryagach, *Kazakstan* 93 C3
Saryshagan, *Kazakstan* 90 K7
Sasabeneh, *Ethiopia* 144 E5
Sasaram, *India* 106 C6
Sasebo, *Japan* 120 D1
Saskatchewan □, *Canada* 186 H6
Saskatchewan →, *Canada* 186 H7
Saskatoon, *Canada* 186 J6
Saskylakh, *Russia* 91 D12
Sasolburg, *S. Africa* 163 D7
Sasovo, *Russia* 81 C6
Sassandra, *Ivory C.* 148 E4
Sassandra →, *Ivory C.* 148 E4
Sássari, *Italy* 67 F2
Sassnitz, *Germany* 58 A5
Sastown, *Liberia* 148 E3
Sasumua Dam, *Kenya* 157 D2
Sasykkul, *Tajikistan* 93 F6
Sata-Misaki, *Japan* 120 D2
Satadougou, *Mali* 140 F2
Satara, *India* 107 E2
Satkania, *Bangla.* 111 D3
Satkhira, *Bangla.* 111 D1
Satmala Hills, *India* 106 F2
Satna, *India* 106 D5
Sátoraljaújhely, *Hungary* 74 A5
Satpura Ra., *India* 106 E3
Satsuna-Shotō, *Japan* 121 G9
Satu Mare, *Romania* 75 A2
Satui, *Indonesia* 128 D8
Satun, *Thailand* 123 L4
Sauðarkrókur, *Iceland* 38 B3
Saudi Arabia ■, *Asia* 99
Saugerties, *U.S.A.* 189 A5
Saül, *Fr. Guiana* 214 D5
Sault Ste. Marie, *Canada* 187 L10
Sault Ste. Marie, *U.S.A.* 191 B13
Saumlaki, *Indonesia* 129 F15
Saumur, *France* 55 D4
Saunders C., *N.Z.* 175 J3
Saurbær, *Borgarfjarðarsýsla, Iceland* 38 C2
Saurbær, *Eyjafjarðarsýsla, Iceland* 38 B4
Sauri, *Nigeria* 151 B3
Saurimo, *Angola* 160 B4
Savá, *Honduras* 196 C3
Sava →, *Serbia, Yug.* 72 B7
Savage I. = Niue, *Cook Is.* 176 G7
Savalou, *Benin* 150 D2
Savanna-la-Mar, *Jamaica* 199 B1
Savannah, *U.S.A.* 191 H15
Savannah →, *U.S.A.* 191 H15
Savannakhet, *Laos* 125 D3
Savé, *Benin* 150 D2
Save →, *Mozam.* 159 D1
Savelugu, *Ghana* 149 B2
Savoie □, *France* 55 E8
Savona, *Italy* 67 C2
Sawahlunto, *Indonesia* 128 C3
Sawai, *Indonesia* 129 D14
Sawai Madhopur, *India* 106 C3
Sawara, *Japan* 120 A9
Sawatch Mts., *U.S.A.* 190 E6
Sawbridgeworth, *U.K.* 45 B4
Sawmills, *Zimbabwe* 161 C2
Sawu, *Indonesia* 129 F11
Sawu Sea, *Indonesia* 129 F11
Saxony, Lower = Niedersachsen □, *Germany* 58 B2
Say, *Niger* 141 D2
Saya, *Nigeria* 151 C1
Sayán, *Peru* 213 D2
Sayan, Zapadnyy, *Russia* 91 J10
Sayan Mts., *Russia* 84 C13
Sayasan, *Russia* 82 A7
Saydā, *Lebanon* 95 C1
Sayghān, *Afghan.* 104 C4
Sayḩut, *Yemen* 100 B3
Saynshand, *Mongolia* 113 C8
Sayre, *U.S.A.* 189 B3
Sazan, *Albania* 70 C2
Săzava →, *Czech.* 76 B3
Sazin, *Pakistan* 105 A6
Sbeïtla, *Tunisia* 138 B2
Scafell Pike, *U.K.* 46 F6
Scandinavia, *Europe* 34 C10
Scarborough, *Trin. & Tob.* 204 B1
Scarborough, *U.K.* 46 F8
Schaffhausen, *Switz.* 60 A4
Schefferville, *Canada* 187 H13
Schelde →, *Belgium* 51 A3
Schenectady, *U.S.A.* 189 A5
Scheveningen, *Neths.* 50 D2
Schiedam, *Neths.* 50 D2
Schiermonnikoog, *Neths.* 50 A5
Schio, *Italy* 67 A4
Schleswig, *Germany* 58 A3
Schleswig-Holstein □, *Germany* 58 A3
Schouten Is. = Supiori, Kepulauan, *Indonesia* 129 C16
Schouwen, *Neths.* 50 E1
Schwäbische Alb, *Germany* 58 F3
Schwaner, Pegunungan, *Indonesia* 128 C7
Schwarzwald, *Germany* 58 F2
Schweinfurt, *Germany* 58 E3
Schweizer-Reneke, *S. Africa* 163 D5
Schwerin, *Germany* 58 A4
Schwyz, *Switz.* 60 B4
Schwyz □, *Switz.* 60 B4
Sciacca, *Italy* 67 J5
Scilla, *Italy* 67 J7
Scilly Is., *U.K.* 46 M3
Scone, *Australia* 171 D8
Scoresbysund, *Greenland* 224 C3
Scotland □, *U.K.* 46 C5
Scott Inlet, *Canada* 187 C11
Scottburgh, *S. Africa* 163 F8
Scottsbluff, *U.S.A.* 190 D8
Scottsdale, *Australia* 172 B3
Scranton, *U.S.A.* 189 B4
Scunthorpe, *U.K.* 46 G8
Scutari = Üsküdar, *Turkey* 94 A2
Seal →, *Canada* 186 G8
Seaspray, *Australia* 171 H6
Seattle, *U.S.A.* 190 A3
Sebastopol = Sevastopol, *Ukraine* 81 H
Sebha = Sabhah, *Libya* 138 C
Şebinkarahisar, *Turkey* 82 C
Sebta = Ceuta, *Morocco* 136 A
Sebuku, *Indonesia* 128 D
Sebuku, Teluk, *Malaysia* 126 B
Sechura, Desierto de, *Peru* 213 C
Secretary I., *N.Z.* 175 H
Secunderabad, *India* 107 E
Sedalia, *U.S.A.* 191 F1
Sedan, *Australia* 171 F
Sedan, *France* 55 B
Sederot, *Israel* 96 D
Sedhiou, *Senegal* 146 C
Sedova, Pik, *Russia* 90 C
Seeheim, *Namibia* 162 E
Seekoei →, *S. Africa* 163 F
Sefadu, *S. Leone* 147 C
Sefrou, *Morocco* 136 B
Sefwi Bekwai, *Ghana* 149 D
Segamat, *Malaysia* 126 D
Segbwema, *S. Leone* 147 D
Seget, *Indonesia* 129 C1
Ségou, *Mali* 140 E
Segovia = Coco →, *Cent. Amer.* 180 H1
Segovia, *Spain* 63 C
Segre →, *Spain* 63 B
Séguéla, *Ivory C.* 148 C
Segundo →, *Argentina* 221 A
Segura →, *Spain* 63 F
Sehitwa, *Botswana* 162 B
Sehore, *India* 106 D
Seine →, *France* 55 B
Seine-et-Marne □, *France* 55 C
Seine-Maritime □, *France* 55 B
Seine-St.-Denis □, *France* 55 B
Seistan, Daryācheh-ye, *Iran* 103 C
Sekayu, *Indonesia* 128 D
Sekondi-Takoradi, *Ghana* 149 E
Selama, *Malaysia* 126 B
Selaru, *Indonesia* 129 F1
Selborne, *U.K.* 45 E
Sele →, *Italy* 67 F
Selemdzha →, *Russia* 91 H1
Selenga = Selenge Mörön →, *Asia* 84 C1
Selenge Mörön →, *Asia* 84 C1
Seletan, Tg., *Indonesia* 128 D
Sélibabi, *Mauritania* 140 E
Şelim, *Turkey* 82 C
Selîma, El Wâhât el, *Sudan* 143 A
Selkirk, *Canada* 186 J
Selkirk, *U.K.* 46 E
Selkirk Mts., *Canada* 186 H
Selma, *U.S.A.* 191 H1
Selowandoma Falls, *Zimbabwe* 161 E
Selpele, *Indonesia* 129 C1
Selu, *Indonesia* 129 F1
Selvas, *Brazil* 217 D
Semani →, *Albania* 70 C
Semara, *W. Sahara* 136 A
Semarang, *Indonesia* 128
Semau, *Indonesia* 129 F
Sembabule, *Uganda* 156

Sémé, *Senegal* 146 B3
Semeru, *Indonesia* 128 F7
Semey = Semipalatinsk, *Kazakstan* 90 J8
Seminole, *U.S.A.* 191 G10
Semiozernoye, *Kazakstan* 90 H6
Semipalatinsk, *Kazakstan* 90 J8
Semirara Is., *Phil.* 130 G3
Semitau, *Indonesia* 128 C7
Semiyarskoye, *Kazakstan* 90 J8
Semmering Pass, *Austria* 61 B5
Semnān, *Iran* 103 B3
Semporna, *Malaysia* 126 B8
Semuda, *Indonesia* 128 D7
Sen →, *Cambodia* 125 F3
Sena Madureira, *Brazil* 217 D2
Senaja, *Malaysia* 126 A8
Senanga, *Zambia* 161 D2
Sendai, *Japan* 121 E7
Seneca Falls, *U.S.A.* 189 A3
Seneca L., *U.S.A.* 189 A3
Senegal ■, *W. Afr.* 146
Senegal →, *W. Afr.* 132 E2
Senegambia, *Africa* 132 E2
Senekal, *S. Africa* 163 E7
Senge Khambab = Indus →, *Pakistan* 105 F3
Sengkang, *Indonesia* 129 D10
Sengua →, *Zimbabwe* 161 B2
Senhor-do-Bonfim, *Brazil* 217 E8
Senigállia, *Italy* 67 C5
Senj, *Croatia* 72 B3
Senja, *Norway* 40 B4
Senlis, *France* 55 B6
Senmonorom, *Cambodia* 125 F4
Sennâr, *Sudan* 143 D5
Sens, *France* 55 C6
Senta, *Serbia, Yug.* 72 A7
Senya Beraku, *Ghana* 149 D2
Senye, *Eq. Guin.* 153 C1
Seo de Urgel, *Spain* 63 B9
Seoul = Sŏul, *S. Korea* 118 F4
Sepik →, *Papua N. G.* 173 A1
Sepo-ri, *N. Korea* 118 E4
Sepone, *Laos* 125 D4
Sept-Îles, *Canada* 187 J13
Sequoia National Park, *U.S.A.* 190 F2
Seraing, *Belgium* 51 C5
Seram, *Indonesia* 129 D14
Seram Sea, *Indonesia* 129 D14
Serang, *Indonesia* 128 E5
Serasan, *Indonesia* 128 B6
Serbia □, *Yugoslavia* 72 D7
Serdobsk, *Russia* 81 D7
Seremban, *Malaysia* 126 C1
Serenje, *Zambia* 161 C4
Sereth = Siret →, *Romania* 75 C6
Sergino, *Russia* 90 F7
Sergipe □, *Brazil* 217 E9
Sergiyev Posad, *Russia* 81 B5
Seria, *Brunei* 127 B1
Serian, *Malaysia* 126 C5
Seribu, Kepulauan, *Indonesia* 128 E5
Sermata, *Indonesia* 129 F14
Serny Zavod, *Turkmenistan* 90 K4
Serov, *Russia* 90 F6
Serowe, *Botswana* 162 C5
Serpentine, *Australia* 170 B1
Serpukhov, *Russia* 81 C5
Sérrai, *Greece* 71 A3
Serrakhis →, *Cyprus* 95 B1
Serrat, C., *Tunisia* 138 A2
Serua, *Indonesia* 129 E14
Serui, *Indonesia* 129 D17
Serule, *Botswana* 162 C6
Sese Is., *Uganda* 156 D2
Sesepe, *Indonesia* 129 C13
Sesfontein, *Namibia* 162 A1
Setana, *Japan* 121 C7
Sète, *France* 55 G6
Sétif, *Algeria* 137 A5
Setonaikai, *Japan* 120 C4
Setouchi, *Japan* 121 H9
Settat, *Morocco* 136 C3
Setté-Cama, *Gabon* 154 C1
Setúbal, *Portugal* 63 E1
Setúbal, B. de, *Portugal* 63 F1
Seulimeum, *Indonesia* 128 A1
Sevan, *Armenia* 82 C6
Sevan, Ozero, *Armenia* 82 C6
Sevastopol, *Ukraine* 81 H4
Sevenoaks, *U.K.* 45 D4
Severn →, *Canada* 186 H9
Severn →, *U.K.* 46 K6
Severnaya Zemlya, *Russia* 91 B11
Severo-Kurilsk, *Russia* 91 F18
Severo-Yeniseyskiy, *Russia* 91 G10
Severodvinsk, *Russia* 90 D5
Sevier →, *U.S.A.* 190 E4
Sevier L., *U.S.A.* 190 E4
Sevilla, *Spain* 63 G3
Seville = Sevilla, *Spain* 63 G3
Seward, *U.S.A.* 193 B4
Seward Pen., *U.S.A.* 193 A3
Sewer, *Indonesia* 129 E16
Seychelles ■, *Ind. Oc.* 166
Seyðisfjörður, *Iceland* 38 B6
Seymchan, *Russia* 91 D16
Seymour, *Australia* 171 G5
Seymour, *S. Africa* 163 G6
Sfax, *Tunisia* 138 C3
Sfîntu Gheorghe, *Romania* 75 C4
Sha Xian, *China* 116 J4
Shaartuz, *Tajikistan* 93 G2
Shaba □, *Zaïre* 155 F5
Shaballe →, *Somali Rep.* 132 F8
Shabunda, *Zaïre* 155 D5
Shache, *China* 112 D1
Shadrinsk, *Russia* 90 G6
Shaffa, *Nigeria* 151 C7
Shagamu, *Nigeria* 151 E1
Shāh Jūy, *Afghan.* 104 E4
Shahbā, *Syria* 97 D3
Shahdadkot, *Pakistan* 105 E3
Shaḥḥāt, *Libya* 138 A5
Shahīdān, *Afghan.* 104 C4
Shahjahanpur, *India* 106 B4
Shahrig, *Pakistan* 105 D3
Shajapur, *India* 106 D3
Shakhristan, *Tajikistan* 93 D2
Shakhrisyabz, *Uzbekistan* 93 E1
Shakhty, *Russia* 81 G6
Shakhunya, *Russia* 81 B8
Shaki, *Nigeria* 151 D1
Shala, L., *Ethiopia* 144 E3
Sham, J. ash, *Oman* 101 B2
Shamâl Dârfûr □, *Sudan* 143 C2
Shamâl Kordofân □, *Sudan* 143 C3
Shamkor, *Azerbaijan* 82 C7
Shammar, Jabal, *Si. Arabia* 99 B3
Shamo = Gobi, *Asia* 84 D14
Shamo, L., *Ethiopia* 144 E3
Shamokin, *U.S.A.* 189 C3
Shamva, *Zimbabwe* 161 B4
Shan □, *Burma* 122 D3
Shandong □, *China* 116 E4
Shang Xian, *China* 116 F1
Shangani →, *Zimbabwe* 161 C3
Shangbancheng, *China* 116 B4
Shangcheng, *China* 116 G3
Shangdu, *China* 116 B2
Shanggao, *China* 116 H2
Shanghai, *China* 116 G5
Shangqiu, *China* 116 E3
Shangrao, *China* 116 H4
Shangshui, *China* 116 F2
Shani, *Nigeria* 151 C7
Shannon →, *Ireland* 46 J1
Shansi = Shanxi □, *China* 116 D2
Shantar, Ostrov Bolshoy, *Russia* 91 G16
Shantou, *China* 113 H10
Shantung = Shandong □, *China* 116 E4
Shanxi □, *China* 116 D2
Shaoguan, *China* 113 H9
Shaowu, *China* 116 J4
Shaoxing, *China* 116 H5
Shaoyang, *China* 116 J1
Shaqrā', *Yemen* 100 C1
Sharjah = Ash Shāriqah, *U.A.E.* 101 B3
Shark B., *Australia* 168 C1
Sharm el Sheikh, *Egypt* 139 C6
Sharq el Istiwa'iya □, *Sudan* 143 F5
Sharya, *Russia* 81 A7
Shashi, *Botswana* 162 B6
Shashi, *China* 116 G1
Shasta, Mt., *U.S.A.* 190 D2
Shaumyani, *Georgia* 82 C6
Shaunavon, *Canada* 186 J6
Shawan, *China* 112 C3
Shawinigan, *Canada* 187 K12
Shawnee, *U.S.A.* 191 G10
Shayib el Banat, Gebel, *Egypt* 139 C5
Shaymak, *Tajikistan* 93 F7
Shcherbakov = Rybinsk, *Russia* 81 B6
Shchuchiosk, *Kazakstan* 90 H7
She Xian, *China* 116 H4
Shea, *Guyana* 214 D2
Shebele = Shaballe →, *Somali Rep.* 132 F8
Sheboygan, *U.S.A.* 191 D12
Sheerness, *U.K.* 45 C6
Sheffield, *U.K.* 46 H7
Shefford, *U.K.* 45 A3
Shekhupura, *Pakistan* 105 C6
Sheki, *Azerbaijan* 82 C7
Shelburne, *Canada* 187 K14
Shelby, *U.S.A.* 190 B6
Shelikhova, Zaliv, *Russia* 91 D17
Shellharbour, *Australia* 171 F8
Shemakha, *Azerbaijan* 82 C9
Shenandoah, *Iowa, U.S.A.* 191 E10
Shenandoah, *Pa., U.S.A.* 189 C3
Shenchi, *China* 116 C2
Shendam, *Nigeria* 151 D5
Shendî, *Sudan* 143 C5
Shenfield, *U.K.* 45 C5
Sheng Xian, *China* 116 H5
Shenmu, *China* 116 C1
Shenqiucheng, *China* 116 F3
Shenyang, *China* 116 B6
Sheopur Kalan, *India* 106 C3
Shepparton, *Australia* 171 G5
Sheppey, I. of, *U.K.* 45 D6
Sheqi, *China* 116 F2
Sherbro I., *S. Leone* 147 D2
Sherbrooke, *Canada* 185 B6
Shere, *U.K.* 45 D2
Sheridan, *U.S.A.* 190 C7
Sherman, *U.S.A.* 191 H10
Sherpūr, *Afghan.* 104 C5
Sherpur, *Bangla.* 111 B2
Sherridon, *Canada* 186 H7
Shesheke, *Zambia* 161 D2
Shetland Is., *U.K.* 46 A9
Sheyenne →, *U.S.A.* 191 B10
Shibām, *Yemen* 100 B2
Shibata, *Japan* 121 E6
Shibetsu, *Japan* 121 A8
Shibîn el Kôm, *Egypt* 139 A4
Shidao, *China* 116 D6
Shiga □, *Japan* 120 B6
Shigaib, *Sudan* 143 C1
Shiguaigou, *China* 116 B1
Shihchiachuangi = Shijiazhuang, *China* 116 D3
Shijiazhuang, *China* 116 D3
Shikarpur, *Pakistan* 105 E4
Shikoku, *Japan* 120 D4
Shikoku □, *Japan* 120 D4
Shikoku-Sanchi, *Japan* 120 D4
Shilabo, *Ethiopia* 144 E5
Shiliguri, *India* 106 B8
Shilka, *Russia* 91 J13
Shilka →, *Russia* 91 H14
Shillong, *India* 106 C9
Shilong, *China* 113 H9
Shimabara, *Japan* 120 D1
Shimada, *Japan* 120 B8
Shimane □, *Japan* 120 B3
Shimanovsk, *Russia* 91 H15
Shimizu, *Japan* 120 B8
Shimodate, *Japan* 120 A9
Shimoga, *India* 107 F2
Shimoni, *Kenya* 157 F4
Shimonoseki, *Japan* 120 C2
Shinano →, *Japan* 121 E6
Shīndand, *Afghan.* 104 D1
Shingū, *Japan* 120 D6
Shinjō, *Japan* 121 E7
Shinkafe, *Nigeria* 151 A3
Shīnkay, *Afghan.* 104 E4
Shinshār, *Syria* 97 C3
Shinyanga, *Tanzania* 158 B1
Shiogama, *Japan* 121 E7
Shipbourne, *U.K.* 45 D4
Shippensburg, *U.S.A.* 189 C3
Shiqma, N. →, *Israel* 96 D1
Shīr Kūh, *Iran* 103 C4
Shirabad, *Uzbekistan* 93 F1
Shiraoi, *Japan* 121 B7
Shīrāz, *Iran* 103 D3
Shire →, *Africa* 158 E2
Shiriya-Zaki, *Japan* 121 C8
Shirwa, L. = Chilwa, L., *Malawi* 158 D3
Shitai, *China* 116 G4
Shivpuri, *India* 106 C3
Shiyata, *Egypt* 139 B1
Shizuoka, *Japan* 120 B8
Shizuoka □, *Japan* 120 B8
Shkoder = Shkodra, *Albania* 70 A2
Shkodra, *Albania* 70 A2
Shkumbini →, *Albania* 70 C2
Shmidta, O., *Russia* 91 B10
Shoeburyness, *U.K.* 45 C6
Sholapur = Solapur, *India* 107 E2
Shologontsy, *Russia* 91 E12
Shoshone, *U.S.A.* 190 D4
Shoshong, *Botswana* 162 C5
Shouyang, *China* 116 D2
Shreveport, *U.S.A.* 191 H11
Shrewsbury, *U.K.* 46 J6
Shrirampur, *India* 106 D8
Shuangliao, *China* 116 A6
Shuangyashan, *China* 113 B12
Shucheng, *China* 116 G3
Shule, *China* 112 D1
Shumagin Is., *U.S.A.* 193 B3
Shumikha, *Russia* 90 G6
Shunchang, *China* 116 J4
Shungnak, *U.S.A.* 193 A4
Shuo Xian, *China* 116 C2
Shurab, *Tajikistan* 93 D4
Shurchi, *Uzbekistan* 93 F1
Shurugwi, *Zimbabwe* 161 D3
Shwebo, *Burma* 122 C2
Shwegu, *Burma* 122 C3
Shymkent = Chimkent, *Kazakstan* 93 B3
Shyok →, *India* 107 A2
Shyok →, *Pakistan* 105 A6
Si Kiang = Xi Jiang →, *China* 113 J9
Si-ngan = Xi'an, *China* 113 F8
Si Racha, *Thailand* 123 H4
Siahan Range, *Pakistan* 105 E2
Siaksrindrapura, *Indonesia* 128 C3
Sialkot, *Pakistan* 105 B6
Siam = Thailand ■, *Asia* 123
Siantan, P., *Indonesia* 128 B5
Siargao, *Phil.* 130 H6
Siasi I., *Phil.* 130 L2
Siau, *Indonesia* 129 B12
Šiauliai, *Lithuania* 81 B1
Siaya □, *Kenya* 157 C1
Siazan, *Azerbaijan* 82 C9
Sibâi, Gebel el, *Egypt* 139 D6
Šibenik, *Croatia* 72 C4
Siberia, *Russia* 84 B14
Siberut, *Indonesia* 128 C2
Sibi, *Pakistan* 105 D3
Sibil, *Indonesia* 129 E18
Sibiti, *Congo* 154 D2
Sibiu, *Romania* 75 C3
Sible Hedingham, *U.K.* 45 A5
Sibolga, *Indonesia* 128 B2
Sibu, *Malaysia* 126 C6
Sibuco, *Phil.* 130 K3
Sibuguey B., *Phil.* 130 K3
Sibutu, *Phil.* 130 L1
Sibuyan, *Phil.* 130 F3
Sibuyan Sea, *Phil.* 130 F3
Sichuan □, *China* 112 G6
Sicilia, *Italy* 34 H9
Sicilia □, *Italy* 67 K6
Sicily = Sicilia, *Italy* 34 H9
Sicuani, *Peru* 213 E4
Sidéradougou, *Burkina Faso* 149 B1
Sîdi Abd el Rahmân, *Egypt* 139 A3
Sîdi Barrâni, *Egypt* 139 A1
Sidi-bel-Abbès, *Algeria* 137 A3
Sidi Bennour, *Morocco* 136 C3
Sidi Haneish, *Egypt* 139 A2
Sidi Kacem, *Morocco* 136 B4
Sidi Omar, *Egypt* 139 A1
Sidi Slimane, *Morocco* 136 B4
Sidi Smaïl, *Morocco* 136 C3
Sidney, *N.Y., U.S.A.* 189 A4
Sidney, *Nebr., U.S.A.* 190 E8
Sidon = Saydā, *Lebanon* 95 C1
Sidra, G. of = Surt, Khalīj, *Libya* 138 A4
Siedlce, *Poland* 77 C5
Sieg →, *Germany* 59 B2
Siegburg, *Germany* 59 B2
Siegen, *Germany* 58 D2
Siem Reap, *Cambodia* 125 E2
Siena, *Italy* 67 D4
Sierra Blanca Peak, *U.S.A.* 190 H7
Sierra Leone ■, *W. Afr.* 147
Sierre, *Switz.* 60 D2
Sífnos, *Greece* 71 E4
Sighetu-Marmatiei, *Romania* 75 A3
Sighişoara, *Romania* 75 C4
Sigli, *Indonesia* 128 A1
Siglufjörður, *Iceland* 38 A3
Signakhi, *Georgia* 82 B6
Sigsig, *Ecuador* 212 D1
Sigüenza, *Spain* 63 C6
Siguiri, *Guinea* 147 A5
Sihanoukville = Kompong Som, *Cambodia* 125 G2
Sijarira Ra., *Zimbabwe* 161 B2
Sikar, *India* 106 B2
Sikasso, *Mali* 140 F3
Sikhote Alin, Khrebet, *Russia* 91 H17
Sikhote Alin Ra. = Sikhote Alin, Khrebet, *Russia* 91 H17
Síkinos, *Greece* 71 E5
Sikkim □, *India* 106 B8
Sil →, *Spain* 63 B2
Silay, *Phil.* 130 G4
Silchar, *India* 107 C6
Silesia = Sląsk, *Poland* 77 D2
Silgarhi Doti, *Nepal* 109 A1
Silhouette, *Seychelles* 166 B1
Silifke, *Turkey* 94 D3
Siliguri = Shiliguri, *India* 106 B8
Siling Co, *China* 112 F3
Silistra, *Bulgaria* 73 A5
Silkeborg, *Denmark* 42 B2
Silva Porto = Kuito, *Angola* 160 C3
Silver City, *U.S.A.* 190 H6
Silver Creek, *U.S.A.* 189 A2
Silver Streams, *S. Africa* 163 E4
Silvretta, *Switz.* 60 C6
Silwa Bahari, *Egypt* 139 E5
Sim, C., *Morocco* 136 D2
Sima, *Comoros Is.* 166 B2
Simanggang, *Malaysia* 126 C6
Simbirsk, *Russia* 81 C8
Simcoe, L., *Canada* 185 C2
Simenga, *Russia* 91 F12
Simeulue, *Indonesia* 128 B1
Simferopol, *Ukraine* 81 H4
Simikot, *Nepal* 109 A2
Simla, *India* 107 B3
Simonstown, *S. Africa* 163 H2
Simplon Pass = Simplonpass, *Switz.* 60 D3
Simplon Tunnel, *Switz.* 60 D3
Simplonpass, *Switz.* 60 D3
Simpungdong, *N. Korea* 118 B5
Simunjan, *Malaysia* 126 C5
Simushir, Ostrov, *Russia* 91 G18
Sinabang, *Indonesia* 128 B1
Sinai = Es Sînâ', *Egypt* 139 B5
Sinai = Gebel Musa, *Egypt* 139 C6
Sinai, Mt. = Gebel Musa, *Egypt* 139 C6
Sinaloa, *Mexico* 194 C2
Sīnāwan, *Libya* 138 A1
Sincelejo, *Colombia* 210 B1
Sinchang, *N. Korea* 118 C5
Sinchang-ni, *N. Korea* 118 D3
Sind □, *Pakistan* 105 F4
Sind Sagar Doab, *Pakistan* 105 C5
Sindangan, *Phil.* 130 J4
Sines, *Portugal* 63 F1
Sineu, *Spain* 65 B4
Sinfra, *Ivory C.* 148 D4
Singa, *Sudan* 143 D5
Singapore ■, *Asia* 126 D3
Singaraja, *Indonesia* 128 F8
Singida, *Tanzania* 158 B2
Singitikós Kólpos, *Greece* 71 B4
Singkaling Hkamti, *Burma* 122 B2
Singkawang, *Indonesia* 128 B6
Singleton, *Australia* 171 D8
Singora = Songkhla, *Thailand* 123 L4
Singosan, *N. Korea* 118 D4
Sinhung, *N. Korea* 118 C4
Sinjai, *Indonesia* 129 E10
Sinjār, *Iraq* 102 A2
Sinkat, *Sudan* 143 B6
Sinkiang Uighur = Xinjiang Uygur Zizhiqu □, *China* 112 C3
Sinmak, *N. Korea* 118 E3
Sinni →, *Italy* 67 G8
Sinnuris, *Egypt* 139 B4
Sinop, *Turkey* 94 A4
Sinpo, *N. Korea* 118 C5
Sinskoye, *Russia* 91 F14
Sint Eustatius, I., *Neth. Ant.* 202 C1
Sint Maarten, I., *W. Indies* 202 A1
Sintang, *Indonesia* 128 C7
Sintra, *Portugal* 63 E1
Sinŭiju, *N. Korea* 118 D2
Siocon, *Phil.* 130 K3
Sioma, *Zambia* 161 D2
Sion, *Switz.* 60 D2
Sioux City, *U.S.A.* 191 D10
Sioux Falls, *U.S.A.* 191 D10
Sioux Lookout, *Canada* 186 J9
Sipalay, *Phil.* 130 H3
Siping, *China* 116 A6
Sipora, *Indonesia* 128 D2
Siquia →, *Nic.* 197 C3
Siquijor, *Phil.* 130 J4
Siquirres, *Costa Rica* 197 D3
Siracusa, *Italy* 67 K7
Şiran, *Turkey* 94 B6
Sirasso, *Ivory C.* 148 B4
Siret →, *Romania* 75 C6
Sirohi, *India* 106 C1
Sironj, *India* 106 D3
Sirsa, *India* 106 A2
Sisak, *Croatia* 72 B4
Sisaket, *Thailand* 123 G6
Sishen, *S. Africa* 163 D4
Sishui, *China* 116 E2
Sisophon, *Cambodia* 125 E2
Sitapur, *India* 106 B4
Sitges, *Spain* 63 C9
Sitka, *U.S.A.* 193 B5
Sitra, *Egypt* 139 C2
Sittang →, *Burma* 122 F3
Sittard, *Neths.* 50 G4
Sittingbourne, *U.K.* 45 D6
Siuna, *Nic.* 197 B2
Siuri, *India* 106 D7
Sivas, *Turkey* 94 B5
Sivrihisar, *Turkey* 94 B3
Sivry, *Belgium* 51 D3
Sīwa, *Egypt* 139 B1
Sīwa, El Wâhât es, *Egypt* 139 B1
Siwalik Range, *Nepal* 109 B2
Siwan, *India* 106 C6
Sjælland, *Denmark* 42 C3
Sjumen = Šumen, *Bulgaria* 73 B5
Skagafjörður, *Iceland* 38 B3
Skagerrak, *Denmark* 42 A2
Skagway, *U.S.A.* 193 B5
Skardu, *Pakistan* 105 A6
Skeena →, *Canada* 186 F3
Skegness, *U.K.* 46 H9
Skeldon, *Guyana* 214 B3
Skellefte →, *Sweden* 40 C4
Skellefteå, *Sweden* 40 D4
Skien, *Norway* 40 F2
Skierniewice, *Poland* 77 C4
Skikda, *Algeria* 137 A5
Skipton, *Australia* 171 G4
Skíros, *Greece* 71 C4
Skive, *Denmark* 42 B2
Skjálfandafljót →, *Iceland* 38 B4
Skjálfandi, *Iceland* 38 A4
Skopje, *Macedonia* 72 E8
Skovorodino, *Russia* 91 H14
Skwierzyna, *Poland* 77 C1
Skye, *U.K.* 46 B3
Skyros = Skíros, *Greece* 71 C4
Slamet, *Indonesia* 128 F6
Sląsk, *Poland* 77 D2
Slatina, *Romania* 75 D3
Slave →, *Canada* 186 F6
Slave Coast, *W. Afr.* 150 E2
Slavgorod, *Russia* 90 H8
Slavkov, *Czech.* 76 C5
Slavyansk, *Ukraine* 81 F5
Sleeper Is., *Canada* 187 G11
Sliedrecht, *Neths.* 50 E3
Sliema, *Malta* 69 B3
Sligo, *Ireland* 46 F2
Sliven, *Bulgaria* 73 C4
Slobodskoy, *Russia* 81 A8
Slochteren, *Neths.* 50 A6
Slough, *U.K.* 46 K8
Slovak Rep. ■, *Europe* 76 C6
Slovakia = Slovak Rep. ■, *Europe* 76 C6
Slovakian Ore Mts. = Slovenské Rudohorie, *Slovak Rep.* 76 C6
Slovenia ■, *Europe* 72 A3
Slovenija = Slovenia ■, *Europe* 72 A3
Slovenská Republika = Slovak Rep. ■, *Europe* 76 C6
Slovenské Rudohorie, *Slovak Rep.* 76 C6
Slovyansk = Slavyansk, *Ukraine* 81 F5
Slurry, *S. Africa* 163 C6
Slyudyanka, *Russia* 91 J11
Smartt Syndicate Dam, *S. Africa* 163 F4

Smederevo, *Serbia, Yug.* 72 C7
Smidevech, *Russia* 91 H16
Smilde, *Neths.* 50 B5
Smith Arm, *Canada* 186 D5
Smith Sund, *Greenland* 224 A1
Smithfield, *S. Africa* 163 F6
Smiths Falls, *Canada* 185 C4
Smithton, *Australia* 172 A1
Smithtown, *Australia* 171 C9
Smoky →, *Canada* 186 G5
Smoky Hill →, *U.S.A.* 191 F10
Smolensk, *Russia* 81 C4
Smolikas, *Greece* 71 B1
Smolyan, *Bulgaria* 73 D3
Smyrna = İzmir, *Turkey* 94 B1
Snæfellsjökull, *Iceland* 38 C1
Snake →, *U.S.A.* 190 B3
Snake I., *Australia* 171 H6
Sneek, *Neths.* 50 B4
Sneeuberge, *S. Africa* 163 G5
Snodland, *U.K.* 45 D5
Snøhetta, *Norway* 40 E2
Snowdon, *U.K.* 46 H5
Snowdrift, *Canada* 186 F6
Snowtown, *Australia* 171 E1
Snowy →, *Australia* 171 H7
Snowy Mts., *Australia* 171 G6
Soalala, *Madag.* 165 B2
Sobat →, *Sudan* 143 E5
Sobral, *Brazil* 217 C8
Soc Trang = Khonh Hung, *Vietnam* 125 G4
Soch'e = Shache, *China* 112 D1
Socorro, *Colombia* 210 C2
Socotra, *Ind. Oc.* 84 G9
Söderhamn, *Sweden* 40 E4
Sodiri, *Sudan* 143 C3
Sodo, *Ethiopia* 144 E3
Soekmekaar, *S. Africa* 163 B8
Soest, *Germany* 59 A3
Sofia = Sofiya, *Bulgaria* 73 C2
Sofia →, *Madag.* 165 B3
Sofiiski, *Russia* 91 G16
Sofiya, *Bulgaria* 73 C2
Sogakofe, *Ghana* 149 D3
Sogamoso, *Colombia* 210 C2
Sognefjorden, *Norway* 40 E1
Sŏgwi-po, *S. Korea* 118 J4
Sohâg, *Egypt* 139 D4
Sŏhori, *N. Korea* 118 C5
Soignies, *Belgium* 51 C3
Soissons, *France* 55 B6
Sōja, *Japan* 120 C4
Sokhumi = Sukhumi, *Georgia* 82 A3
Sokodé, *Togo* 150 C2
Sokol, *Russia* 81 A6
Sokółka, *Poland* 77 B6
Sokolo, *Mali* 140 E3
Sokoto, *Nigeria* 151 A2
Sokoto □, *Nigeria* 151 B2
Sokoto →, *Nigeria* 151 A2
Sokuluk, *Kyrgyzstan* 93 A6
Solai, *Kenya* 157 C2
Solano, *Phil.* 130 D2
Solapur, *India* 107 E2
Soledad, *Venezuela* 211 B4
Soligalich, *Russia* 81 A6
Solikamsk, *Russia* 90 F6
Solimões = Amazon →, *S. Amer.* 206 C4
Solingen, *Germany* 59 B2
Sóller, *Spain* 65 A4
Sologne, *France* 55 D5
Solok, *Indonesia* 128 C3
Sololá, *Guatemala* 196 C1
Solomon Is. ■, *Pac. Oc.* 146
Solomon Sea, *Papua N. G.* 173 B3
Solon, *China* 113 B10
Solor, *Indonesia* 129 F11
Solothurn, *Switz.* 60 B2
Solothurn □, *Switz.* 60 B2
Solunska, *Macedonia* 72 E8
Solvay, *U.S.A.* 189 A3
Solway Firth, *U.K.* 46 F5
Solwezi, *Zambia* 161 B3
Somali Rep. ■, *Africa* 145
Somalia ■ = Somali Rep. ■, *Africa* 145
Sombor, *Serbia, Yug.* 72 A6
Sombrerete, *Mexico* 194 D4
Somerset, *U.S.A.* 191 F14
Somerset East, *S. Africa* 163 H6
Somerset I., *Canada* 186 C9
Somerset West, *S. Africa* 163 H2
Someş →, *Romania* 75 A3
Somme □, *France* 55 B6
Somoto, *Nic.* 197 B1
Somport, Puerto de, *Spain* 63 B7
Son La, *Vietnam* 125 A2
Soná, *Panama* 197 E4
Sŏnchŏn, *N. Korea* 118 D2
Sondags →, *S. Africa* 163 H6
Sønderborg, *Denmark* 42 D2
Sonepur, *India* 106 F6
Song Cau, *Vietnam* 125 E5
Song Xian, *China* 116 E1
Songchŏn, *N. Korea* 118 D3
Songea, *Tanzania* 158 D2
Songhua Jiang →, *China* 113 B12
Songjiang, *China* 116 G5
Songjŏng-ni, *S. Korea* 118 H4
Songkhla, *Thailand* 123 L4
Songnim, *N. Korea* 118 E3
Songpan, *China* 113 F7
Songzi, *China* 116 G1
Sonipat, *India* 106 A3
Sonkel, Ozero, *Kyrgyzstan* 93 B7
Sonmiani, *Pakistan* 105 F3
Sonora →, *Mexico* 194 B1
Sŏnsan, *S. Korea* 118 G5
Sonsonate, *El Salv.* 196 D1
Soochow = Suzhou, *China* 116 G5
Sopi, *Indonesia* 129 B14
Sopot, *Poland* 77 A3
Sorata, *Bolivia* 218 B1
Sorel, *Canada* 185 A5
Soreq, N. →, *Israel* 96 D1
Soria, *Spain* 63 C6
Soro, *Guinea* 147 B4
Sorocaba, *Brazil* 215 C2
Sorong, *Indonesia* 129 C15
Soroti, *Uganda* 156 B3
Sørøya, *Norway* 40 A5
Sorrento, *Australia* 171 H5
Sorrento, *Italy* 67 F6
Sorsogon, *Phil.* 130 F4
Sorūbī, *Afghan.* 104 C5
Sŏsan, *S. Korea* 118 F4
Sosnovka, *Russia* 91 H12
Sosnowiec, *Poland* 77 E3
Sŏsura, *N. Korea* 118 A6
Souanké, *Congo* 154 A2
Soúdhas, Kólpos, *Greece* 71 F4
Souk el Arba du Rharb, *Morocco* 136 B4
Sŏul, *S. Korea* 118 F4
Sources, Mt. aux, *Lesotho* 164 A3
Souris, *Canada* 186 K7
Souris →, *Canada* 186 J7
Souss, O. →, *Morocco* 136 E2
Sousse, *Tunisia* 138 B2
South Africa ■, *Africa* 163
South Australia □, *Australia* 171 D2
South Bend, *U.S.A.* 191 D13
South Benfleet, *U.K.* 45 C5
South Buganda □, *Uganda* 156 D1
South C., *Australia* 168 E4
South Carolina □, *U.S.A.* 191 G15
South China Sea, *Asia* 84 G15
South Dakota □, *U.S.A.* 190 C8
South Downs, *U.K.* 46 L8
South East C., *Australia* 172 C2
South Honshu Ridge, *Pac. Oc.* 176 C3
South Horr, *Kenya* 157 B2
South I., *Kenya* 157 B2
South I., *N.Z.* 175 G2
South Nahanni →, *Canada* 186 E5
South Natuna Is. = Natuna Selatan, Kepulauan, *Indonesia* 128 B6
South Negril Pt., *Jamaica* 199 B1
South Pagai, I. = Pagai Selatan, P., *Indonesia* 128 D2
South Pass, *U.S.A.* 190 D6
South Platte →, *U.S.A.* 190 E8
South Saskatchewan →, *Canada* 186 J6
South Shields, *U.K.* 46 F7
South Taranaki Bight, *N.Z.* 175 E5
South West Africa = Namibia ■, *Africa* 162
South West C., *Australia* 172 C2
South Woodham Ferrers, *U.K.* 45 B5
Southampton, *U.K.* 46 L7
Southampton, *U.S.A.* 189 B6
Southampton I., *Canada* 187 E10
Southborough, *U.K.* 45 E4
Southend, *U.K.* 46 K9
Southern □, *Malawi* 158 D2
Southern □, *S. Leone* 147 D3
Southern Alps, *N.Z.* 175 G2
Southern Cross, *Australia* 170 A3
Southern Indian L., *Canada* 186 G8
Southminster, *U.K.* 45 B6
Southport, *Australia* 171 A9
Southwark, *U.K.* 45 C3
Southwest C., *N.Z.* 175 J1
Southwestern Pacific Basin, *Pac. Oc.* 176 K6
Soutpansberg, *S. Africa* 163 A8
Sovetsk, *Russia* 81 C1
Sovetsk, *Russia* 81 B8
Sovetskaya Gavan, *Russia* 91 H17
Soweto, *S. Africa* 163 C7
Sōya-Kaikyō = La Perouse Str., *Asia* 84 D18
Soyo, *Angola* 160 A1
Sozh →, *Belarus* 81 D3
Spa, *Belgium* 51 D5
Spain ■, *Europe* 63
Spalding, *Australia* 171 E2
Spanish Fork, *U.S.A.* 190 E5
Spanish Town, *Jamaica* 199 B4
Sparks, *U.S.A.* 190 E3
Sparta = Spárti, *Greece* 71 E2
Spartanburg, *U.S.A.* 191 G15
Spartel, C., *Morocco* 136 A4
Spárti, *Greece* 71 E2
Spartivento, C., *Calabria, Italy* 67 J7
Spartivento, C., *Sard., Italy* 67 H2
Spassk-Dalnij, *Russia* 91 J16
Spátha, Ákra, *Greece* 71 F3
Speightstown, *Barbados* 204 B1
Spence Bay, *Canada* 186 D9
Spencer, *U.S.A.* 191 D10
Spencer, C., *Australia* 171 F1
Spencer G., *Australia* 168 D3
Spenser Mts., *N.Z.* 175 F4
Spessart, *Germany* 58 E3
Spey →, *U.K.* 46 B6
Speyer, *Germany* 58 E2
Spiez, *Switz.* 60 C2
Spinazzola, *Italy* 67 F7
Spitzbergen = Svalbard, *Arctic* 34 A5
Split, *Croatia* 72 D4
Splügenpass, *Switz.* 60 C5
Spokane, *U.S.A.* 190 B4
Spoleto, *Italy* 67 D5
Sporyy Navolok, Mys, *Russia* 90 C9
Spree →, *Germany* 58 C6
Spremberg, *Germany* 58 C6
Springbok, *S. Africa* 163 F1
Springfield, *Ill., U.S.A.* 191 E12
Springfield, *Mass., U.S.A.* 189 A6
Springfield, *Mo., U.S.A.* 191 F11
Springfield, *Ohio, U.S.A.* 191 E14
Springfield, *Oreg., U.S.A.* 190 C2
Springfontein, *S. Africa* 163 F6
Springhill, *Canada* 187 K14
Springhurst, *Australia* 171 F6
Springs, *S. Africa* 163 C7
Springville, *N.Y., U.S.A.* 189 A2
Springville, *Utah, U.S.A.* 190 E5
Spurn Hd., *U.K.* 46 G8
Squamish, *Canada* 186 H3
Srbija = Serbia □, *Yugoslavia* 72 D7
Sre Umbell, *Cambodia* 125 F2
Sredinny Ra. = Sredinnyy Khrebet, *Russia* 91 D18
Sredinnyy Khrebet, *Russia* 91 D18
Sredne Tambovskoye, *Russia* 91 G16
Srednekolymsk, *Russia* 91 C15
Srednevilyuysk, *Russia* 91 F13
Sretensk, *Russia* 91 H13
Sri Lanka ■, *Asia* 110
Srinagar, *India* 107 A2
Sripur, *Bangla.* 111 B2
Stadlandet, *Norway* 40 E1
Stadskanaal, *Neths.* 50
Stafafell, *Iceland* 38 C5
Staffa, *U.K.* 46 D3
Stafford, *U.K.* 46 H7
Staines, *U.K.* 45 C2
Stakhanov = Kadiyevka, *Ukraine* 81 F5
Stalingrad = Volgograd, *Russia* 81 F7
Staliniri = Tskhinvali, *Georgia* 82 B5
Stalino = Donetsk, *Ukraine* 81 F5
Stalinogorsk = Novomoskovsk, *Russia* 81 D5
Stamford, *U.S.A.* 189 B5
Standerton, *S. Africa* 163 D8
Standon, *U.K.* 45 A4
Stanford le Hope, *U.K.* 45 C5
Stanger, *S. Africa* 163 E9
Stanislav = Ivano-Frankovsk, *Ukraine* 81 F1
Stanke Dimitrov, *Bulgaria* 73 C2
Stanley, *Australia* 172 A1
Stanley, *Canada* 186 H7
Stanley, *Falk. Is.* 224 A3
Stanovoy Khrebet, *Russia* 91 G15
Stanovoy Ra. = Stanovoy Khrebet, *Russia* 91 G15
Stansted Mountfitchet, *U.K.* 45 A4
Stanthorpe, *Australia* 171 B9
Staplehurst, *U.K.* 45 E5
Stara Planina, *Bulgaria* 73 B2
Stara Zagora, *Bulgaria* 73 C4
Staraya Russa, *Russia* 81 B4
Starbuck I., *Kiribati* 176 F8
Staritsa, *Russia* 81 B4
Starogard, *Poland* 77 A3
Start Pt., *U.K.* 46 M5
Staryy Kheydzhan, *Russia* 91 E16
Staryy Oskol, *Russia* 81 E5
State College, *U.S.A.* 189 C3
Staten, I. = Estados, I. de Los, *Argentina* 220 L4
Stavanger, *Norway* 40 F1
Stavelot, *Belgium* 51 D6
Staveren, *Neths.* 50 B4
Stavropol, *Russia* 81 H6
Stawell, *Australia* 171 G4
Steelton, *U.S.A.* 189 C3
Steenkool = Bintuni, *Indonesia* 129 D16
Steenwijk, *Neths.* 50 B5
Stefanie L. = Chew Bahir, *Ethiopia* 144 F2
Steiermark □, *Austria* 61 B5
Steinfort, *Lux.* 52 C1
Steinkjer, *Norway* 40 D2
Steinkopf, *S. Africa* 163 E1
Stellenbosch, *S. Africa* 163 H2
Stendal, *Germany* 58 B4
Stephens Creek, *Australia* 171 D3
Stepnoi = Elista, *Russia* 81 G7
Stepnyak, *Kazakstan* 90 H7
Steppe, *Asia* 84 C9
Sterkstroom, *S. Africa* 163 G6
Sterling, *U.S.A.* 190 E8
Sterlitamak, *Russia* 90 G5
Stettin = Szczecin, *Poland* 77 B1
Stettler, *Canada* 186 H5
Stevenage, *U.K.* 45 A3
Stevens Point, *U.S.A.* 191 C12
Stewart, *B.C., Canada* 186 F3
Stewart, *N.W.T., Canada* 186 D3
Stewart I., *N.Z.* 175 J1
Steynsburg, *S. Africa* 163 G6
Steyr, *Austria* 61 B4
Steytlerville, *S. Africa* 163 H5
Stikine →, *Canada* 186 F3
Stilfontein, *S. Africa* 163 D6
Stillwater, *Minn., U.S.A.* 191 C11
Stillwater, *Okla., U.S.A.* 191 G10
Štip, *Macedonia* 72 E8
Stirling, *U.K.* 46 D5
Stirling Ra., *Australia* 170 D3
Stockerau, *Austria* 61 A5
Stockholm, *Sweden* 40 F4
Stockport, *U.K.* 46 H7
Stockton, *U.K.* 46 F7
Stockton, *U.S.A.* 190 E2
Stoke, *U.K.* 45 C6
Stoke Mandeville, *U.K.* 45 B1
Stoke-on-Trent, *U.K.* 46 H7
Stokenchurch, *U.K.* 45 B1
Stokes Pt., *Australia* 172 A1
Stokkseyri, *Iceland* 38 D3
Stokksnes, *Iceland* 38 C5
Stolac, *Bos.-H.* 72 D5
Stolberg, *Germany* 59 B1
Stolbovaya, *Russia* 91 C16
Stone, *U.K.* 45 B1
Stonewall, *Canada* 186 J8
Stony Stratford, *U.K.* 45 A1
Stony Tunguska = Podkamennaya Tunguska →, *Russia* 91 G10
Stora Lulevatten, *Sweden* 40 B4
Storavan, *Sweden* 40 C4
Store Bælt, *Denmark* 42 C3
Store Creek, *Australia* 171 D7
Storlulea = Stora Lulevatten, *Sweden* 40 B4
Storm B., *Australia* 172 C3
Stormberge, *S. Africa* 163 G6
Stormsrivier, *S. Africa* 163 H5
Stornoway, *U.K.* 46 A3
Storsjön, *Sweden* 40 E3
Stort →, *U.K.* 45 B4
Storuman, *Sweden* 40 D4
Stotfold, *U.K.* 45 A3
Strahan, *Australia* 172 B1
Stralsund, *Germany* 58 A5
Strand, *S. Africa* 163 H2
Stranraer, *U.K.* 46 F4
Strasbourg, *France* 55 C9
Stratford, *Canada* 187 L10
Stratford, *N.Z.* 175 D5
Stratford-upon-Avon, *U.K.* 46 J7
Strathalbyn, *Australia* 171 F2
Straumnes, *Iceland* 38 A2
Streator, *U.S.A.* 191 E12
Strelka, *Russia* 91 G10
Strezhevoy, *Russia* 90 F8
Strickland →, *Papua N. G.* 173 B1
Strómboli, *Italy* 67 H7
Stroud Road, *Australia* 171 D8
Struer, *Denmark* 42 B2
Strumica, *Macedonia* 72 F9
Strzelecki Cr. →, *Australia* 171 A2
Stuart L., *Canada* 186 G4
Stung-Treng, *Cambodia* 125 E4
Stutterheim, *S. Africa* 163 H6
Stuttgart, *Germany* 58 F3
Stuttgart, *U.S.A.* 191 G12
Stykkishólmur, *Iceland* 38 C2
Styria = Steiermark □, *Austria* 61 B5
Su Xian, *China* 116 F3
Suakin, *Sudan* 143 A6
Suan, *N. Korea* 118 E3
Subi, *Indonesia* 128 B6
Subotica, *Serbia, Yug.* 72 A6
Suceava, *Romania* 75 A5
Suchitoto, *El Salv.* 196 D2
Suchou = Suzhou, *China* 116 G5
Süchow = Xuzhou, *China* 116 E4
Sucre, *Bolivia* 218 C1
Sudan ■, *Africa* 143
Sudbury, *Canada* 187 K11
Sudbury, *U.K.* 45 A6
Sûdd, *Sudan* 143 E3
Suddie, *Guyana* 214 B2
Sudeten Mts. = Sudetes, *Europe* 76 A4
Sudetes, *Europe* 76 A4
Sudirman, Pegunungan, *Indonesia* 129 D17
Sudr, *Egypt* 139 B5
Sueca, *Spain* 63 E8
Suez = El Suweis, *Egypt* 139 B5
Suez, G. of = Suweis, Khalîg el, *Egypt* 139 B5
Suez Canal = Suweis, Qanâ es, *Egypt* 139 A5
Sufi-Kurgan, *Kyrgyzstan* 93 D6
Sugluk = Saglouc, *Canada* 187 F11
Şuḥār, *Oman* 101 B2
Suhbaatar, *Mongolia* 113 A7
Sui Xian, *Henan, China* 116 E3
Sui Xian, *Henan, China* 116 G2
Suichang, *China* 116 H5
Suichuan, *China* 116 J2
Suide, *China* 116 D1
Suihua, *China* 113 B11
Suiping, *China* 116 F2
Suizhong, *China* 116 B5
Sukabumi, *Indonesia* 128 E5
Sukadana, *Indonesia* 128 C6
Sukaraja, *Indonesia* 128 D6
Sukarnapura = Jayapura, *Indonesia* 129 D18
Sukchŏn, *N. Korea* 118 D3
Sukhona →, *Russia* 81 A7
Sukhumi, *Georgia* 82 A3
Sukkur, *Pakistan* 105 E4
Sukkur Barrage, *Pakistan* 105 E4
Sula, Kepulauan, *Indonesia* 129 D12
Sulaco →, *Honduras* 196 C2
Sulaiman Range, *Pakistan* 105 C4
Sulak →, *Russia* 82 A8
Sulawesi □, *Indonesia* 129 C10
Sulawesi Sea, *Indonesia* 84 H16
Sulima, *S. Leone* 147 D3
Sulina, *Romania* 75 C6
Sulitjelma, *Sweden* 40 D3
Sullana, *Peru* 213 B1
Sullivan I. = Lambi Kyun, *Burma* 122 J3
Sultanpur, *India* 106 C5
Sulu Arch., *Phil.* 130 L2
Sulu Sea, *E. Indies* 84 H16
Suluq, *Libya* 138 A4
Sulyukta, *Kyrgyzstan* 93 D3
Sumalata, *Indonesia* 129 B11
Sumatera □, *Indonesia* 128 C3
Sumatra = Sumatera □, *Indonesia* 128 C3
Sumba, *Indonesia* 129 F10
Sumba, Selat, *Indonesia* 129 F10
Sumbawa, *Indonesia* 128 F9
Sumbawa Besar, *Indonesia* 128 F9
Sumbe, *Angola* 160 C2
Šumen, *Bulgaria* 73 B5
Sumgait, *Azerbaijan* 82 C9
Summer L., *U.S.A.* 190 C3
Summerside, *Canada* 187 K14
Šumperk, *Czech.* 76 B5
Sumqayit = Sumgait, *Azerbaijan* 82 C9
Sumter, *U.S.A.* 191 G15
Sumy, *Ukraine* 81 E4
Sunan, *N. Korea* 118 D3
Sunbury, *Australia* 171 G5
Sunbury, *U.S.A.* 189 C3
Sunchales, *Argentina* 221 A3
Sunchon, *S. Korea* 118 H4
Sunda, Selat, *Indonesia* 128 E5
Sunda Str. = Sunda, Selat, *Indonesia* 128 E5
Sundargarh, *India* 106 E6
Sundays = Sondags →, *S. Africa* 163 H6
Sunderland, *U.K.* 46 F7
Sundsvall, *Sweden* 40 E4
Sungai Lembing, *Malaysia* 126 C2
Sungai Patani, *Malaysia* 126 B1
Sungaigerong, *Indonesia* 128 D4
Sungailiat, *Indonesia* 128 D5
Sungaipakning, *Indonesia* 128 B3
Sungaipenuh, *Indonesia* 128 D3
Sungaitiram, *Indonesia* 128 C9
Sungari = Songhua Jiang →, *China* 113 B12
Sungguminasa, *Indonesia* 129 E10
Sunghua Chiang = Songhua Jiang →, *China* 113 B12
Sunninghill, *U.K.* 45 D1
Suntar, *Russia* 91 F13
Sunyani, *Ghana* 149 C1
Supaul, *India* 106 C7
Superior, *Nebr., U.S.A.* 190 E9
Superior, *Wis., U.S.A.* 191 C11
Superior, L., *U.S.A.* 180 E11
Suphan Buri, *Thailand* 123 G4
Supiori, Kepulauan, *Indonesia* 129 C16
Suqian, *China* 116 F4
Sūr, *Lebanon* 95 D1
Şūr, *Oman* 101 B3
Sura →, *Russia* 81 B7
Surabaja = Surabaya, *Indonesia* 128 F7
Surabaya, *Indonesia* 128 F7
Surakarta, *Indonesia* 128 F7
Surakhany, *Azerbaijan* 82 C9
Surat, *Australia* 171 A7
Surat, *India* 106 E1
Surat Thani, *Thailand* 123 K4
Suratgarh, *India* 106 A2
Surgut, *Russia* 90 F8
Surigao, *Phil.* 130 H5
Surigao Strait, *Phil.* 130 H5
Surin, *Thailand* 123 G6
Surinam ■, *S. Amer.* 214
Suriname □, *Surinam* 214 B4
Suriname ■ = Surinam ■, *S. Amer.* 214
Surkhandarya →, *Uzbekistan* 93 G1
Sürmene, *Turkey* 82 C2
Surrey □, *U.K.* 45 D2
Sursee, *Switz.* 60 B3
Surt, *Libya* 138 A3
Surt, Khalīj, *Libya* 138 A4
Surtsey, *Iceland* 38 D3
Suruga-Wan, *Japan* 120 B8
Susa, *Italy* 67 B1
Susamyr, *Kyrgyzstan* 93 B6
Susamyrtau, Khrebet, *Kyrgyzstan* 93 B6
Susanino, *Russia* 91 G16
Susquehanna →, *U.S.A.* 189 D4
Susuman, *Russia* 91 D16
Susunu, *Indonesia* 129 D16
Susuz, *Turkey* 82 C4

Sutherland, *S. Africa* 163 G3
Sutlej →, *Pakistan* 105 D5
Sutton, *U.K.* 45 D3
Suva, *Fiji* 174 A1
Suva Planina, *Serbia, Yug.* 72 D8
Suvorov Is. = Suwarrow Is., *Cook Is.* 176 G7
Suwałki, *Poland* 77 A6
Suwanose-Jima, *Japan* 121 G9
Suwarrow Is., *Cook Is.* 176 G7
Suweis, Khalîg el, *Egypt* 139 B5
Suweis, Qanâ es, *Egypt* 139 A5
Suwŏn, *S. Korea* 118 F4
Suzdal, *Russia* 81 B6
Suzhou, *China* 116 G5
Suzu-Misaki, *Japan* 121 F5
Suzuka, *Japan* 120 C6
Svalbard, *Arctic* 34 A5
Svalbarð, *Iceland* 38 A5
Svay Rieng, *Cambodia* 125 F3
Svealand □, *Sweden* 40 F3
Svendborg, *Denmark* 42 D3
Sverdlovsk = Yekaterinburg, *Russia* 90 G6
Sverdrup Chan., *Canada* 186 A9
Sverdrup Is., *Canada* 186 A8
Svir →, *Russia* 34 C13
Svishtov, *Bulgaria* 73 B3
Svobodnyy, *Russia* 91 H15
Swabian Alps = Schwäbische Alb, *Germany* 58 F3
Swakopmund, *Namibia* 162 C2
Swan Hill, *Australia* 171 F4
Swanley, *U.K.* 45 D4
Swansea, *U.K.* 46 K5
Swartberge, *S. Africa* 163 H4
Swartmodder, *S. Africa* 163 D3
Swartruggens, *S. Africa* 163 C6
Swatow = Shantou, *China* 113 H10
Swaziland ■, *Africa* 165
Sweden ■, *Europe* 40
Swedru, *Ghana* 149 D2
Sweetwater, *U.S.A.* 190 H8
Swellendam, *S. Africa* 163 H3
Świdnica, *Poland* 77 D2
Świebodzin, *Poland* 77 C1
Swift Current, *Canada* 186 J6
Swindon, *U.K.* 46 K7
Swinemünde = Świnoujście, *Poland* 77 A1
Świnoujście, *Poland* 77 A1
Switzerland ■, *Europe* 60
Sydney, *Australia* 171 E8
Sydney, *Canada* 187 J15
Sydprøven, *Greenland* 224 D2
Sydra, G. of = Surt, Khalīj, *Libya* 138 A4
Syktyvkar, *Russia* 90 E5
Sylhet, *Bangla.* 111 B3
Sym, *Russia* 90 G9
Syracuse, *U.S.A.* 189 A3
Syrdarya, *Uzbekistan* 93 C2
Syrdarya →, *Kazakstan* 90 J5
Syria ■, *Asia* 97
Syriam, *Burma* 122 F2
Syrian Desert, *Asia* 84 E7
Syul'dzhyukyor, *Russia* 91 F12
Syzran, *Russia* 81 D8
Szczecin, *Poland* 77 B1
Szczecinek, *Poland* 77 B2
Szechwan = Sichuan □, *China* 112 G6
Szeged, *Hungary* 74 C4
Székesfehérvár, *Hungary* 74 B3
Szekszárd, *Hungary* 74 C3
Szentes, *Hungary* 74 B4
Szolnok, *Hungary* 74 B4
Szombathely, *Hungary* 74 B2

T

Tabaco, *Phil.* 130 F4
Tabagné, *Ivory C.* 148 C6
Tabarka, *Tunisia* 138 A2
Ţabas, *Iran* 103 C4
Tabasará, Serranía de, *Panama* 197 E4
Tablas, *Phil.* 130 F3
Tablas Strait, *Phil.* 130 F3
Table, Pte. de la, *Réunion* 166 C3
Table B. = Tafelbaai, *S. Africa* 163 H2
Table Mt., *S. Africa* 163 H2
Tábor, *Czech.* 76 B3
Tabora, *Tanzania* 158 B1
Tabou, *Ivory C.* 148 E3
Tabrīz, *Iran* 103 A2
Tabuelan, *Phil.* 130 G4
Tabūk, *Si. Arabia* 99 B2
Tacheng, *China* 112 B3
Tach'ing Shan = Daqing Shan, *China* 116 B1
Tacloban, *Phil.* 130 G5
Tacna, *Peru* 213 F5
Tacoma, *U.S.A.* 190 B2
Tacuarembó, *Uruguay* 219 B2
Tademaït, Plateau du, *Algeria* 137 C4
Tadjoura, *Djibouti* 145 B2
Tadjoura, Golfe de, *Djibouti* 145 B2
Tadoussac, *Canada* 187 K13
Tadzhikistan = Tajikistan ■, *Asia* 93 E3
Taechŏn-ni, *S. Korea* 118 G4
Taegu, *S. Korea* 118 G5
Taegwan, *N. Korea* 118 C3
Taejŏn, *S. Korea* 118 G4
Tafalla, *Spain* 63 B6
Tafelbaai, *S. Africa* 163 H2
Tafelney, C., *Morocco* 136 D2
Tafermaar, *Indonesia* 129 E16
Taffermit, *Morocco* 136 E2
Tafiré, *Ivory C.* 148 B5
Tafnidilt, *Morocco* 136 F1
Tafraoute, *Morocco* 136 E2
Taft, *Phil.* 130 G5
Taga Dzong, *Bhutan* 109 C5
Taganrog, *Russia* 81 G5
Tagatay, *Phil.* 130 E2
Tagbilaran, *Phil.* 130 H4
Taghzout, *Morocco* 136 B5
Tagliamento →, *Italy* 67 A5
Tago, *Phil.* 130 J6
Tagomago, I. de, *Spain* 65 C2
Tagudin, *Phil.* 130 C2
Tagum, *Phil.* 130 K5
Tagus = Tejo →, *Europe* 34 H5
Tahala, *Morocco* 136 B5
Tahan, Gunong, *Malaysia* 126 B2
Tahānah-ye sūr Gol, *Afghan.* 104 F4
Tahat, *Algeria* 137 E4
Tāherī, *Iran* 103 D3
Tahoe, L., *U.S.A.* 190 E2
Tahoua, *Niger* 141 C3
Tahta, *Egypt* 139 D4
Tahulandang, *Indonesia* 129 B12
Tahuna, *Indonesia* 129 A12
Taï, *Ivory C.* 148 D3
Tai Hu, *China* 116 G5
Tai Shan, *China* 116 D4
Tai'an, *China* 116 D3
Taibei, *Taiwan* 117 A3
Taibus Qi, *China* 116 B3
T'aichung = Taizhong, *Taiwan* 117 B2
Taidong, *Taiwan* 117 C3
Taieri →, *N.Z.* 175 J3
Taigu, *China* 116 D2
Taihang Shan, *China* 116 E2
Taihape, *N.Z.* 175 D5
Taihe, *China* 116 J2
Taihu, *China* 116 G3
Taikang, *China* 116 E3
Taikkyi, *Burma* 122 F2
Tailem Bend, *Australia* 171 F2
Taimyr Peninsula = Taymyr, Poluostrov, *Russia* 91 C11
Tainan, *Taiwan* 117 C2
Taínaron, Ákra, *Greece* 71 F2
Taining, *China* 116 J3
T'aipei = Taibei, *Taiwan* 117 A3
Taiping, *Malaysia* 126 B1
Taishun, *China* 116 J5
Taita □, *Kenya* 157 F3
Taita Hills, *Kenya* 157 E3
Taitao Pen., *Chile* 206 G2
Taiwan ■, *Asia* 117
Taiwan Shan, *Taiwan* 117 B3
Taïyetos Óros, *Greece* 71 E2
Taiyiba, *Israel* 96 B3
Taiyuan, *China* 116 D2
Taizhong, *Taiwan* 117 B2
Taizhou, *China* 116 F5
Ta'izz, *Yemen* 100 C1
Tajikistan ■, *Asia* 93 E3
Tajima, *Japan* 121 F7
Tajo = Tejo →, *Europe* 34 H5
Tājūrā, *Libya* 138 A2
Tak, *Thailand* 123 F4
Takada, *Japan* 121 F6
Takaka, *N.Z.* 175 E4
Takamatsu, *Japan* 120 C4
Takaoka, *Japan* 120 A6
Takapuna, *N.Z.* 175 B5
Takasaki, *Japan* 120 A8
Takatsuki, *Japan* 120 C5
Takaungu, *Kenya* 157 F4
Takayama, *Japan* 120 A7
Takefu, *Japan* 120 B6
Takeley, *U.K.* 45 B4
Takeo, *Cambodia* 125 F3
Takhār □, *Afghan.* 104 B5
Takla Makan = Taklamakan Shamo, *China* 84 E12
Taklamakan Shamo, *China* 84 E12
Takum, *Nigeria* 151 E5
Takutu →, *Guyana* 214 D1
Tala, *Uruguay* 219 D2
Talacogan, *Phil.* 130 J5
Talaïnt, *Morocco* 136 E2
Talara, *Peru* 213 B1
Talas, *Kyrgyzstan* 93 B5
Talasskiy Alatau, Khrebet, *Kyrgyzstan* 93 B5
Talata Mafara, *Nigeria* 151 A3
Talaud, Kepulauan, *Indonesia* 129 A13
Talaud Is. = Talaud, Kepulauan, *Indonesia* 129 A13
Talavera de la Reina, *Spain* 63 D4
Talayan, *Phil.* 130 K5
Talbragar →, *Australia* 171 D7
Talca, *Chile* 220 F3
Talcahuano, *Chile* 220 F2
Talcher, *India* 106 E6
Taldy Kurgan, *Kazakstan* 90 K7
Taldyqorghan = Taldy Kurgan, *Kazakstan* 90 K7
Talgar, *Kazakstan* 93 A8
Talgar, Pik, *Kazakstan* 93 A8
Tali Post, *Sudan* 143 F4
Taliabu, *Indonesia* 129 D12
Taling Sung, *Thailand* 123 G4
Talisayan, *Phil.* 130 J5
Taliwang, *Indonesia* 128 F9
Tall 'Afar, *Iraq* 102 A3
Talla, *Egypt* 139 C4
Tallahassee, *U.S.A.* 191 H14
Tallangatta, *Australia* 171 F6
Tallarook, *Australia* 171 G5
Tallinn, *Estonia* 81 A2
Talmest, *Morocco* 136 D2
Talodi, *Sudan* 143 D4
Tālqān, *Afghan.* 104 B5
Talsinnt, *Morocco* 136 C5
Talwood, *Australia* 171 B7
Talyawalka Cr. →, *Australia* 171 D4
Tamale, *Ghana* 149 B2
Tamanar, *Morocco* 136 D2
Tamano, *Japan* 120 C4
Tamanrasset, *Algeria* 137 E4
Tamaské, *Niger* 141 C3
Tamba-Dabatou, *Guinea* 147 A4
Tambacounda, *Senegal* 146 C2
Tambelan, Kepulauan, *Indonesia* 128 B5
Tambellup, *Australia* 170 C2
Tambo de Mora, *Peru* 213 E3
Tambora, *Indonesia* 128 F9
Tambov, *Russia* 81 D6
Tamburâ, *Sudan* 143 F3
Tâmchekket, *Mauritania* 140 D2
Tamega →, *Portugal* 63 C2
Tamelelt, *Morocco* 136 D3
Tamerlanovka, *Kazakstan* 93 B3
Tamerza, *Tunisia* 138 C1
Tamgak, Mts., *Niger* 141 B4
Tamil Nadu □, *India* 107 F2
Tammerfors = Tampere, *Finland* 43 E2
Tampa, *U.S.A.* 191 J15
Tampa B., *U.S.A.* 191 J15
Tampere, *Finland* 43 E2
Tampico, *Mexico* 194 D5
Tampin, *Malaysia* 126 D2
Tamri, *Morocco* 136 D2
Tamsagbulag, *Mongolia* 113 B9
Tamworth, *Australia* 171 C8
Tamyang, *S. Korea* 118 H4
Tan-tan, *Morocco* 136 F1
Tana →, *Kenya* 157 E4
Tana →, *Norway* 40 B5
Tana, L., *Ethiopia* 144 C2
Tanahbala, *Indonesia* 128 C2
Tanahgrogot, *Indonesia* 128 D9
Tanahjampea, *Indonesia* 129 F11
Tanahmasa, *Indonesia* 128 C2
Tanahmerah, *Indonesia* 129 E18
Tanami Desert, *Australia* 168 B3
Tanana, *U.S.A.* 193 A4
Tanana →, *U.S.A.* 193 A4
Tananarive = Antananarivo, *Madag.* 165 C2
Tanannt, *Morocco* 136 D4
Tánaro →, *Italy* 67 B2
Tanchŏn, *N. Korea* 118 C5
Tanda, *Ivory C.* 148 C6
Tandag, *Phil.* 130 J6
Tandil, *Argentina* 220 F5
Tando Adam, *Pakistan* 105 F4
Tandou L., *Australia* 171 D3
Tane-ga-Shima, *Japan* 121 K2
Tanen Tong Dan, *Burma* 122 F3
Tanezrouft, *Algeria* 137 E3
Tanga, *Tanzania* 158 B3
Tangail, *Bangla.* 111 B2
Tanganyika, L., *Africa* 132 G7
Tanger, *Morocco* 136 A4
Tanggu, *China* 116 C4
Tanggula Shan, *China* 112 F3
Tanghe, *China* 116 F2
Tangier = Tanger, *Morocco* 136 A4
Tangshan, *China* 116 C4
Tanguiéta, *Benin* 150 B2
Tanimbar, Kepulauan, *Indonesia* 129 F15
Tanimbar Is. = Tanimbar, Kepulauan, *Indonesia* 129 F15
Tanjay, *Phil.* 130 H4
Tanjong Malim, *Malaysia* 126 C1
Tanjore = Thanjavur, *India* 107 F3
Tanjung, *Indonesia* 128 D8
Tanjungbalai, *Indonesia* 128 B2
Tanjungbatu, *Indonesia* 128 B9
Tanjungkarang Telukbetung, *Indonesia* 128 E4
Tanjungpandan, *Indonesia* 128 D5
Tanjungpinang, *Indonesia* 128 C4
Tanjungredeb, *Indonesia* 128 B9
Tanjungselor, *Indonesia* 128 B9
Tannu-Ola, *Russia* 91 J10
Tano →, *Ghana* 149 C1
Tanon Str., *Phil.* 130 H4
Tanout, *Niger* 141 C4
Tanta, *Egypt* 139 A4
Tantung = Dandong, *China* 116 B6
Tanunda, *Australia* 171 F2
Tanyeri, *Turkey* 82 D2
Tanzania ■, *Africa* 158
Taolanaro, *Madag.* 165 E2
Taoudenni, *Mali* 140 B4
Taounate, *Morocco* 136 B5
Taourirt, *Morocco* 136 B6
Taouz, *Morocco* 136 D5
Taoyuan, *China* 116 H1
Taoyuan, *Taiwan* 117 A3
Tapa Shan = Daba Shan, *China* 113 F8
Tapah, *Malaysia* 126 B1
Tapajós →, *Brazil* 217 C5
Tapaktuan, *Indonesia* 128 B1
Tapanahoni →, *Surinam* 214 C5
Tapeta, *Liberia* 148 D3
Tapi →, *India* 106 E1
Tapirapecó, Serra, *Venezuela* 211 D4
Tapoeripa, *Surinam* 214 C3
Tapuaenuku, Mt., *N.Z.* 175 F4
Tapul Group, *Phil.* 130 L2
Tara, *Australia* 171 A8
Tara, *Russia* 90 G8
Tara →, *Montenegro, Yug.* 72 D6
Tara →, *Russia* 90 G8
Tarabagatay, Khrebet, *Kazakstan* 90 K8
Tarābulus, *Lebanon* 95 A2
Tarābulus, *Libya* 138 A2
Tarakan, *Indonesia* 128 B9
Tarakit, Mt., *Kenya* 157 B1
Taranga Hill, *India* 106 D1
Táranto, *Italy* 67 G8
Táranto, G. di, *Italy* 67 F8
Tarapacá, *Colombia* 210 F3
Tararua Ra., *N.Z.* 175 E5
Tarbela Dam, *Pakistan* 105 B5
Tarbes, *France* 55 H4
Tarcoon, *Australia* 171 C6
Taree, *Australia* 171 D9
Tarentaise, *France* 55 E9
Tarf, Ras, *Morocco* 136 A5
Tarfa, Wadi el →, *Egypt* 139 C4
Targuist, *Morocco* 136 A5
Tarhbalt, *Morocco* 136 D4
Tarifa, *Spain* 63 H3
Tarija, *Bolivia* 218 D1
Tariku →, *Indonesia* 129 D17
Tarim Basin = Tarim Pendi, *China* 112 D2
Tarim He →, *China* 112 D3
Tarim Pendi, *China* 112 D2
Taritatu →, *Indonesia* 129 D17
Tarka →, *S. Africa* 163 G6
Tarkastad, *S. Africa* 163 G6
Tarkhankut, Mys, *Ukraine* 81 H3
Tarko Sale, *Russia* 90 E8
Tarkwa, *Ghana* 149 E1
Tarlac, *Phil.* 130 D2
Tarma, *Peru* 213 D3
Tarn □, *France* 55 G5
Tarn →, *France* 55 G5
Tarn-et-Garonne □, *France* 55 G5
Tarnów, *Poland* 77 E4
Tarnowskie Góry, *Poland* 77 E3
Taroudannt, *Morocco* 136 D2
Tarragona, *Spain* 63 C9
Tarrasa, *Spain* 63 C9
Tarshiha = Me'ona, *Israel* 96 A2
Tarso Emissi, *Chad* 142 A2
Tarsus, *Turkey* 94 C4
Tartu, *Estonia* 81 A2
Ţarţūs, *Syria* 97 B2
Tarutao, *Thailand* 123 L4
Tarutung, *Indonesia* 128 B2
Tasāwah, *Libya* 138 C2
Tash-Kumyr, *Kyrgyzstan* 93 C5
Tashauz, *Turkmenistan* 90 K4
Tashi Chho Dzong = Thimphu, *Bhutan* 109 B5
Tashkent, *Uzbekistan* 93 C3
Tashtagol, *Russia* 90 J9
Tasikmalaya, *Indonesia* 128 F6
Tasili Plat., *Algeria* 132 D4
Taskan, *Russia* 91 D16
Tasman B., *N.Z.* 175 E4
Tasman Mts., *N.Z.* 175 E4
Tasman Pen., *Australia* 172 C3
Tasman Sea, *Pac. Oc.* 176 J5
Tasmania □, *Australia* 172 B2
Tata, *Morocco* 136 E3
Tatahouine, *Tunisia* 138 D2
Tatar Republic □, *Russia* 81 C9
Tatarsk, *Russia* 90 H8
Tateyama, *Japan* 120 B9
Tathra, *Australia* 171 G7
Tatra = Tatry, *Slovak Rep.* 76 C7
Tatry, *Slovak Rep.* 76 C7
Tatta, *Pakistan* 105 F3
Tatuí, *Brazil* 215 C2
Tat'ung = Datong, *China* 116 C2
Tatvan, *Turkey* 94 C7
Taubaté, *Brazil* 215 C3
Tauern, *Austria* 61 B3
Taumarunui, *N.Z.* 175 D5
Taung, *S. Africa* 163 D5
Taungdwingyi, *Burma* 122 E2
Taunggyi, *Burma* 122 D3
Taungup, *Burma* 122 E1
Taunton, *U.K.* 46 L6
Taunton, *U.S.A.* 189 A6
Taunus, *Germany* 58 D2
Taupo, *N.Z.* 175 D6
Taupo, L., *N.Z.* 175 D6
Tauranga, *N.Z.* 175 C6
Taurianova, *Italy* 67 J7
Taurus Mts. = Toros Dağları, *Turkey* 94 C3
Tauz, *Azerbaijan* 82 C6
Tavda, *Russia* 90 G6
Tavda →, *Russia* 90 G7
Taveta, *Tanzania* 158 B3
Tavira, *Portugal* 63 G2
Tavoy, *Burma* 122 G3
Tawau, *Malaysia* 126 B8
Tawitawi, *Phil.* 130 L2
Tay →, *U.K.* 46 D6
Tay, Firth of, *U.K.* 46 D6
Tay Ninh, *Vietnam* 125 F4
Tayabamba, *Peru* 213 C2
Tayabas Bay, *Phil.* 130 E3
Taylakovy, *Russia* 90 G8
Taylor, Mt., *U.S.A.* 190 G6
Taymā, *Si. Arabia* 99 B3
Taymyr, Oz., *Russia* 91 C11
Taymyr, Poluostrov, *Russia* 91 C11
Tayshet, *Russia* 91 H11
Taytay, *Phil.* 130 G1
Taz →, *Russia* 90 E9
Taza, *Morocco* 136 B5
Tazenakht, *Morocco* 136 D3
Tazovskiy, *Russia* 90 E9
Tbilisi, *Georgia* 82 B6
Tchad = Chad ■, *Africa* 142
Tchad, L., *Chad* 142 D1
Tchaourou, *Benin* 150 C3
Tch'eng-tou = Chengdu, *China* 113 F7
Tchibanga, *Gabon* 154 C1
Tchien, *Liberia* 148 D3
Tch'ong-k'ing = Chongqing, *China* 113 G7
Te Anau, L., *N.Z.* 175 H1
Te Aroha, *N.Z.* 175 C5
Te Awamutu, *N.Z.* 175 C5
Te Kuiti, *N.Z.* 175 C5
Tebakang, *Malaysia* 126 C5
Teberda, *Russia* 82 A3
Tébessa, *Algeria* 137 A6
Tebicuary →, *Paraguay* 219 C2
Tebingtinggi, *Indonesia* 128 B2
Téboursouk, *Tunisia* 138 A2
Tébourba, *Tunisia* 138 A2
Tebulos, *Russia* 82 A6
Techiman, *Ghana* 149 C1
Tecuci, *Romania* 75 C6
Tedzhen, *Turkmenistan* 90 L3
Tegal, *Indonesia* 128 E6
Tegina, *Nigeria* 151 C3
Tegucigalpa, *Honduras* 196 C3
Téhini, *Ivory C.* 148 B6
Tehrān, *Iran* 103 B3
Tehuantepec, *Mexico* 194 F6
Tehuantepec, G. de, *Mexico* 194 F6
Tehuantepec, Istme de, *Mexico* 194 F6
Teixeira Pinto, *Guinea-Biss.* 146 D1
Tejo →, *Europe* 34 H5
Tekapo, L., *N.Z.* 175 G3
Tekeli, *Kazakstan* 90 K7
Tekirdağ, *Turkey* 94 A1
Tekman, *Turkey* 82 D3
Tel Aviv-Yafo, *Israel* 96 C2
Tel Lakhish, *Israel* 96 D2
Tel Megiddo, *Israel* 96 B2
Tela, *Honduras* 196 C3
Telanaipura = Jambi, *Indonesia* 128 C4
Telavi, *Georgia* 82 B6
Telegraph Creek, *Canada* 186 E3
Teles Pires →, *Brazil* 217 D4
Telford, *U.K.* 46 J6
Télimélé, *Guinea* 147 B2
Telpos Iz, *Russia* 34 C18
Teluk Betung = Tanjungkarang Telukbetung, *Indonesia* 128 E4
Teluk Intan, *Malaysia* 126 C1
Telukbutun, *Indonesia* 128 A6
Telukdalem, *Indonesia* 128 C1
Tema, *Ghana* 149 D3
Temax, *Mexico* 194 D8
Temba, *S. Africa* 163 C7
Temir, *Kazakstan* 90 H4
Temirtau, *Kazakstan* 90 J7
Temirtau, *Russia* 90 J9
Temma, *Australia* 172 B1
Temora, *Australia* 171 E6
Temple, *U.S.A.* 191 J10
Temuco, *Chile* 220 G2
Temuka, *N.Z.* 175 H3
Tena, *Ecuador* 212 C2
Tenasserim, *Burma* 122 H3
Tenasserim □, *Burma* 122 G3
Tendaho, *Ethiopia* 144 C4
Tendrara, *Morocco* 136 C6
Teneida, *Egypt* 139 D3
Tenerife, *Canary Is.* 223 D2
Teng →, *Burma* 122 E3
Teng Xian, *China* 116 E4
Tengah □, *Indonesia* 129 C11
Tengah Kepulauan, *Indonesia* 128 F9
Tengchong, *China* 112 H5
Tengchowfu = Penglai, *China* 116 D5
Tenggara □, *Indonesia* 129 D11
Tenggarong, *Indonesia* 128 C9
Tenggol, P., *Malaysia* 126 B3
Tengiz, Ozero, *Kazakstan* 90 H6
Tenke, *Zaïre* 155 F5
Tenkodogo, *Burkina Faso* 149 B2
Tennessee □, *U.S.A.* 191 G13
Tennessee →, *U.S.A.* 191 F13
Tennsift, Oued →, *Morocco* 136 C2
Tenom, *Malaysia* 126 B7

Tenryū-Gawa →, *Japan* 120 C7
Tenterden, *U.K.* 45 E6
Tenterfield, *Australia* 171 B9
Teófilo Otoni, *Brazil* 217 G8
Tepa, *Indonesia* 129 F14
Tepic, *Mexico* 194 D3
Teplice, *Czech.* 76 A3
Ter →, *Spain* 63 B9
Ter Apel, *Neths.* 50 B6
Téra, *Niger* 141 D1
Teraina, *Kiribati* 176 E7
Téramo, *Italy* 67 D6
Terang, *Australia* 171 H4
Tercan, *Turkey* 82 D2
Tercero →, *Argentina* 221 B3
Terek →, *Russia* 34 G16
Terek-Say, *Kyrgyzstan* 93 C4
Teresina, *Brazil* 217 C8
Terhazza, *Mali* 140 B4
Teridgerie Cr. →, *Australia* 171 C7
Termez, *Uzbekistan* 93 G1
Térmoli, *Italy* 67 E6
Ternate, *Indonesia* 129 C13
Terneuzen, *Neths.* 50 F1
Terney, *Russia* 91 J17
Terni, *Italy* 67 D5
Terowie, *Australia* 171 E2
Terracina, *Italy* 67 F5
Terralba, *Italy* 67 G2
Terranova = Ólbia, *Italy* 67 F2
Terrassa = Tarrasa, *Spain* 63 C9
Terrell, *U.S.A.* 191 H10
Terschelling, *Neths.* 50 A4
Terskey Alatau, Khrebet, *Kyrgyzstan* 93 B8
Terter →, *Azerbaijan* 82 C7
Teruel, *Spain* 63 D7
Teryaweyna L., *Australia* 171 D4
Tešanj, *Bos.-H.* 72 C5
Teshio, *Japan* 121 A7
Teshio-Gawa →, *Japan* 121 A7
Tesiyn Gol →, *Mongolia* 112 A6
Teslin, *Canada* 186 E4
Tessalit, *Mali* 140 C6
Tessaoua, *Niger* 141 D3
Tessenderlo, *Belgium* 51 B4
Tete, *Mozam.* 159 C2
Teteven, *Bulgaria* 73 B3
Teton →, *U.S.A.* 190 B6
Tétouan, *Morocco* 136 A5
Tetovo, *Macedonia* 72 E7
Tetuán = Tétouan, *Morocco* 136 A5
Teuco →, *Argentina* 220 C5
Teun, *Indonesia* 129 E14
Teutoburger Wald, *Germany* 58 C2
Tevere →, *Italy* 67 E4
Teverya, *Israel* 96 B3
Texarkana, *U.S.A.* 191 H11
Texas, *Australia* 171 B8
Texas □, *U.S.A.* 190 H8
Texel, *Neths.* 50 B3
Teynham, *U.K.* 45 D6
Teyvareh, *Afghan.* 104 D2
Tezpur, *India* 107 C6
Tha Nun, *Thailand* 122 K3
Thaba Putsoa, *Lesotho* 164 B2
Thabana Ntlenyana, *Lesotho* 70 B3
Thabazimbi, *S. Africa* 163 B7
Thai Nguyen, *Vietnam* 125 A3
Thailand ■, *Asia* 123
Thailand, G. of, *Asia* 84 G14
Thakhek, *Laos* 125 C3
Thal, *Pakistan* 105 B4
Thala, *Tunisia* 138 B1
Thallon, *Australia* 171 B7
Thalwil, *Switz.* 60 B4
Thame, *U.K.* 45 B1
Thames, *N.Z.* 175 C5
Thames →, *U.K.* 45 C6
Thane, *India* 106 F1
Thang Binh, *Vietnam* 125 D5
Thanh Hoa, *Vietnam* 125 B3
Thanh Pho Ho Chi Minh = Phanh Bho Ho Chi Minh, *Vietnam* 125 F4
Thanjavur, *India* 107 F3
Thar Desert, *India* 106 B1
Thargomindah, *Australia* 171 A4
Thásos, *Greece* 71 B4
Thaton, *Burma* 122 F3
Thaungdut, *Burma* 122 C2
Thaxted, *U.K.* 45 A5
Thayetmyo, *Burma* 122 E2
The Coorong, *Australia* 171 F2
The Dalles, *U.S.A.* 190 B3
The Frome →, *Australia* 171 C1
The Grampians, *Australia* 171 G3
The Great Divide = Great Dividing Ra., *Australia* 168 C4
The Gulf, *Asia* 84 F9
The Hague = 's-Gravenhage, *Neths.* 50 D2
The Pas, *Canada* 186 H7
The Range, *Zimbabwe* 161 C4
The Rock, *Australia* 171 F6
The Salt L., *Australia* 171 C3
The Warburton →, *Australia* 171 A2
Thebes = Thívai, *Greece* 71 D3
Thebes, *Egypt* 139 D5
Thermaïkos Kólpos, *Greece* 71 B3
Thermopílai Gióna, *Greece* 71 D2
Thermopolis, *U.S.A.* 190 D6
Thessalía □, *Greece* 71 C2
Thessaloníki, *Greece* 71 B3
Thessaloniki, Gulf of = Thermaïkos Kólpos, *Greece* 71 B3
Thessaly = Thessalía □, *Greece* 71 C2
Thetford Mines, *Canada* 187 K13
Theunissen, *S. Africa* 163 E6
Theux, *Belgium* 51 C5
Thiérache, *France* 55 B6
Thies, *Senegal* 146 B1
Thika, *Kenya* 157 D2
Thille-Boubacar, *Senegal* 146 A2
Thimphu, *Bhutan* 109 B5
þingvallavatn, *Iceland* 38 C2
Thionville, *France* 55 B8
Thíra, *Greece* 71 F5
Thisted, *Denmark* 42 B2
Thívai, *Greece* 71 D3
þjórsá →, *Iceland* 38 D3
Thlewiaza →, *Canada* 186 F8
Thomas, *U.S.A.* 189 D2
Thomasville, *U.S.A.* 191 H14
Thompson, *Canada* 186 H8
Thomson's Falls = Nyahururu, *Kenya* 157 C2
Thon Buri, *Thailand* 123 H4
Thongwa, *Burma* 122 F2
þórisvatn, *Iceland* 38 C3
þorlákshöfn, *Iceland* 38 D2
þórshöfn, *Iceland* 38 A5
Thrace = Thráki □, *Greece* 71 A5
Thráki □, *Greece* 71 A5
Three Hummock I., *Australia* 172 A1
Three Points, C., *Ghana* 149 E1
Thuin, *Belgium* 51 D3
Thule, *Greenland* 224 B1
Thun, *Switz.* 60 C2
Thunder Bay, *Canada* 186 K9
Thunersee, *Switz.* 60 C2
Thung Song, *Thailand* 123 K4
Thunkar, *Bhutan* 109 B6
Thur →, *Switz.* 60 A4
Thurgau □, *Switz.* 60 A4
Thüringen □, *Germany* 58 D4
Thüringer Wald, *Germany* 58 D4
Thurles, *Ireland* 46 J2
Thurloo Downs, *Australia* 171 B4
Thursday I., *Australia* 168 B4
Thurso, *Canada* 185 B4
Thurso, *U.K.* 46 A5
Thyolo, *Malawi* 158 E2
Thysville = Mbanza Ngungu, *Zaïre* 155 D1
Tia, *Australia* 171 C8
Tian Shan, *China* 112 C2
Tianjin, *China* 116 C4
Tianshui, *China* 113 E7
Tianzhen, *China* 116 B2
Tiaret, *Algeria* 137 A4
Tiassalé, *Ivory C.* 148 D5
Tibati, *Cameroon* 153 C2
Tiber = Tevere →, *Italy* 67 E4
Tiberias = Teverya, *Israel* 96 B3
Tiberias, L. = Yam Kinneret, *Israel* 96 B3
Tibesti, *Chad* 142 B1
Tibet = Xizang □, *China* 112 F3
Tibiao, *Phil.* 130 G3
Tibnī, *Syria* 97 B4
Tibooburra, *Australia* 171 B3
Tiburón, *Mexico* 194 B1
Ticao I., *Phil.* 130 F4
Ticehurst, *U.K.* 45 E5
Tichît, *Mauritania* 140 D2
Ticino □, *Switz.* 60 D4
Ticino →, *Italy* 67 B2
Tiddim, *Burma* 122 C1
Tidjikja, *Mauritania* 140 D2
Tidore, *Indonesia* 129 C13
Tiébissou, *Ivory C.* 148 C5
Tiel, *Neths.* 50 D4
Tiel, *Senegal* 146 B1
Tieling, *China* 116 A6
Tielt, *Belgium* 51 B1
Tien Shan, *Asia* 93 C8
Tien-tsin = Tianjin, *China* 116 C4
T'ienching = Tianjin, *China* 116 C4
Tienen, *Belgium* 51 C4
Tiénigbé, *Ivory C.* 148 C4
Tientsin = Tianjin, *China* 116 C4
Tierra de Campos, *Spain* 63 B4
Tierra del Fuego, I. Gr. de, *Argentina* 220 L3
Tiétar →, *Spain* 63 D3
Tiflèt, *Morocco* 136 B4
Tiflis = Tbilisi, *Georgia* 82 B6
Tifu, *Indonesia* 129 D13
Tigil, *Russia* 91 D17
Tignish, *Canada* 187 J14
Tigre →, *Peru* 213 B3
Tigris →, *Iraq* 84 F8
Tigyaing, *Burma* 122 C2
Tigzerte, O. →, *Morocco* 136 F2
Tîh, Gebel el, *Egypt* 139 B5
Tijuana, *Mexico* 194 A1
Tikal, *Guatemala* 196 B1
Tikamgarh, *India* 106 C4
Tikhoretsk, *Russia* 81 G6
Tikrīt, *Iraq* 102 C3
Tiksi, *Russia* 91 C13
Tilamuta, *Indonesia* 129 C11
Tilburg, *Neths.* 50 E3
Tilbury, *U.K.* 45 C5
Tilichiki, *Russia* 91 C17
Tillabéri, *Niger* 141 D1
Tílos, *Greece* 71 F6
Tilpa, *Australia* 171 C5
Tilsit = Sovetsk, *Russia* 81 C1
Timaru, *N.Z.* 175 H3
Timau, *Kenya* 157 C3
Timbedgha, *Mauritania* 140 D3
Timboon, *Australia* 171 H4
Timbuktu = Tombouctou, *Mali* 140 D4
Timhadit, *Morocco* 136 B5
Timimoun, *Algeria* 137 C3
Timiris, C., *Mauritania* 140 C1
Timişoara, *Romania* 75 C1
Timmins, *Canada* 187 K11
Timok →, *Serbia, Yug.* 72 C9
Timor, *Indonesia* 129 F12
Timor Sea, *Ind. Oc.* 168 B2
Tîna, Khalîg el, *Egypt* 139 A5
Tinaca Pt., *Phil.* 130 L5
Tindouf, *Algeria* 137 C1
Tinerhir, *Morocco* 136 D4
Tinggi, Pulau, *Malaysia* 126 D3
Tingo Maria, *Peru* 213 C3
Tinkurrin, *Australia* 170 C2
Tinogasta, *Argentina* 220 D3
Tinos, *Greece* 71 E5
Tintinara, *Australia* 171 F2
Tioman, Pulau, *Malaysia* 126 C3
Tipperary, *Ireland* 46 J2
Tiptree, *U.K.* 45 B6
Tirana, *Albania* 70 B2
Tiranë = Tirana, *Albania* 70 B2
Tiraspol, *Moldova* 81 G2
Tirat Karmel, *Israel* 96 B2
Tirebolu, *Turkey* 94 A5
Tîrgovişte, *Romania* 75 D4
Tîrgu-Jiu, *Romania* 75 C3
Tîrgu Mureş, *Romania* 75 B4
Tirich Mir, *Pakistan* 105 A5
Tirodi, *India* 106 E4
Tirol □, *Austria* 61 B2
Tirso →, *Italy* 67 G2
Tiruchchirappalli, *India* 107 F3
Tiruvannamalai, *India* 107 F3
Tisa →, *Hungary* 74 B4
Tisdale, *Canada* 186 H7
Tissint, *Morocco* 136 E3
Tisza = Tisa →, *Hungary* 74 B4
Tit-Ary, *Russia* 91 D13
Titicaca, L., *S. Amer.* 206 D3
Titiwa, *Nigeria* 151 B7
Titograd = Podgorica, *Montenegro, Yug.* 72 E6
Titov Veles, *Macedonia* 72 E8
Titovo Užice, *Serbia, Yug.* 72 C7
Titule, *Zaïre* 155 A5
Titusville, *U.S.A.* 189 B1
Tivaouane, *Senegal* 146 B1
Tívoli, *Italy* 67 E5
Tizga, *Morocco* 136 C5
Ti'zi N'Isli, *Morocco* 136 C4
Tizi-Ouzou, *Algeria* 137 A5
Tiznit, *Morocco* 136 E2
Tjirebon = Cirebon, *Indonesia* 128 E6
Tkibuli, *Georgia* 82 B4
Tkvarcheli, *Georgia* 82 A3
Tlaxcala, *Mexico* 194 E5
Tlaxiaco, *Mexico* 194 F5
Tlemcen, *Algeria* 137 A3
Tleta Sidi Bouguedra, *Morocco* 136 C2
Tmassah, *Libya* 138 C3
Tnine d'Anglou, *Morocco* 136 E2
Toamasina, *Madag.* 165 C3
Toba, *Japan* 120 C6
Toba Kakar, *Pakistan* 105 C4
Tobago, *W. Indies* 204 B1
Tobelo, *Indonesia* 129 B13
Toboali, *Indonesia* 128 D5
Tobol →, *Russia* 90 G7
Toboli, *Indonesia* 129 C10
Tobolsk, *Russia* 90 G7
Tobruk = Tubruq, *Libya* 138 A5
Tocantins →, *Brazil* 217 C6
Tochigi, *Japan* 120 A9
Tochigi □, *Japan* 120 A9
Tocumwal, *Australia* 171 F5
Tocuyo →, *Venezuela* 211 A3
Toddington, *U.K.* 45 A2
Todeli, *Indonesia* 129 C12
Todenyang, *Kenya* 157 A2
Todos os Santos, B. de, *Brazil* 217 E9
Togba, *Mauritania* 140 D2
Togian, Kepulauan, *Indonesia* 129 C11
Togliatti, *Russia* 81 D8
Togo ■, *W. Afr.* 150
Togtoh, *China* 116 B1
Toinya, *Sudan* 143 F3
Tojikiston = Tajikistan ■, *Asia* 93 E3
Tojo, *Indonesia* 129 C11
Toka, *Guyana* 214 D2
Tokachi →, *Japan* 121 B9
Tokaj, *Hungary* 74 A5
Tokala, *Indonesia* 129 C11
Tokar, *Sudan* 143 B6
Tokara Kaikyō, *Japan* 121 F9
Tŏkchŏn, *N. Korea* 118 D3
Tokelau Is., *Pac. Oc.* 176 F6
Tokmak, *Kyrgyzstan* 93 A7
Toktogul, *Kyrgyzstan* 93 B5
Tokunoshima, *Japan* 121 H8
Tokushima, *Japan* 120 C5
Tokushima □, *Japan* 120 C4
Tokuyama, *Japan* 120 C2
Tōkyō, *Japan* 120 B9
Tokzār, *Afghan.* 104 B4
Tolbukhin, *Bulgaria* 73 B5
Toledo, *Spain* 63 D5
Toledo, *U.S.A.* 191 D14
Toledo, Montes de, *Spain* 63 E4
Tolga, *Algeria* 137 A5
Toliara, *Madag.* 165 E1
Tolima, *Colombia* 210 C1
Tolitoli, *Indonesia* 129 B11
Tollesbury, *U.K.* 45 B6
Tolo, *Zaïre* 155 D2
Tolo, Teluk, *Indonesia* 129 D11
Tolosa, *Spain* 63 A6
Toluca, *Mexico* 194 E5
Tom Burke, *S. Africa* 163 A7
Tomakomai, *Japan* 121 B7
Tomar, *Portugal* 63 D1
Tomaszów Mazowiecki, *Poland* 77 D4
Tombe, *Sudan* 143 F4
Tombigbee →, *U.S.A.* 191 H13
Tombouctou, *Mali* 140 D4
Tombua, *Angola* 160 E1
Tomelloso, *Spain* 63 E5
Tomini, *Indonesia* 129 C11
Tomini, Teluk, *Indonesia* 129 C11
Tommot, *Russia* 91 F14
Tomsk, *Russia* 90 H9
Tonate, *Fr. Guiana* 214 C6
Tonawanda, *U.S.A.* 189 A2
Tonbridge, *U.K.* 45 E4
Tondano, *Indonesia* 129 B12
Tong Xian, *China* 116 C3
Tonga ■, *Pac. Oc.* 174
Tonga Trench, *Pac. Oc.* 176 G6
Tongaat, *S. Africa* 163 F9
Tongareva, *Cook Is.* 176 F7
Tongatapu Is., *Tonga* 174 B3
Tongcheng, *China* 116 G3
Tongchŏn-ni, *N. Korea* 118 D4
Tongchuan, *China* 113 E8
Tongeren, *Belgium* 51 C5
Tongguan, *China* 116 E1
Tonghua, *China* 113 C11
Tongjiang, *China* 113 B12
Tongjosŏn Man, *N. Korea* 118 D4
Tongking = Bac-Phan, *Vietnam* 125 A3
Tongking, G. of, *Asia* 84 F14
Tongliao, *China* 116 A5
Tongling, *China* 116 G4
Tonglu, *China* 116 H5
Tongnae, *S. Korea* 118 G6
Tongren, *China* 113 G8
Tongres = Tongeren, *Belgium* 51 C5
Tongsa Dzong, *Bhutan* 109 B6
Tongue →, *U.S.A.* 190 C7
Tongyang, *N. Korea* 118 D4
Tonk, *India* 106 C2
Tonkin = Bac-Phan, *Vietnam* 125 A3
Tonlé Sap, *Cambodia* 125 E3
Tonopah, *U.S.A.* 190 E3
Tonosí, *Panama* 197 E5
Tooele, *U.S.A.* 190 E5
Toompine, *Australia* 171 A5
Toora, *Australia* 171 H5
Toora-Khem, *Russia* 91 J10
Toowoomba, *Australia* 171 A9
Topeka, *U.S.A.* 191 F10
Topki, *Russia* 90 H9
Topolobampo, *Mexico* 194 C2
Torata, *Peru* 213 F5
Tordesillas, *Spain* 63 C4
Torfajökull, *Iceland* 38 D3
Torgau, *Germany* 58 C5
Torhout, *Belgium* 51 B1
Torino, *Italy* 67 B1
Torit, *Sudan* 143 F5
Tormes →, *Spain* 63 C3
Torne →, *Sweden* 40 C5
Torneå = Tornio, *Finland* 43 C2
Tornio, *Finland* 43 C2
Toronaíos Kolpos, *Greece* 71 B3
Toronto, *Australia* 171 E8
Toronto, *Canada* 185 D2
Toropets, *Russia* 81 B4
Tororo, *Uganda* 156 C3
Toros Dağlan, *Turkey* 94 C3
Torquay, *U.K.* 46 M5
Tôrre de Moncorvo, *Portugal* 63 C2
Torre del Greco, *Italy* 67 F6
Torrelavega, *Spain* 63 A5
Torremolinos, *Spain* 63 G4
Torrens, L., *Australia* 171 C1
Torreón, *Mexico* 194 C4
Torres, *Mexico* 194 B2
Torres Strait, *Australia* 168 B4
Torres Vedras, *Portugal* 63 E1
Torrevieja, *Spain* 63 F7
Torrington, *U.S.A.* 189 B5
Tortosa, *Spain* 63 C8
Tortosa, C., *Spain* 63 C8
Tortue, I. de la, *Haiti* 200 A1
Tortuga, I. La, *Venezuela* 211 A4
Tortum, *Turkey* 82 C3
Torugart, Pereval, *Kyrgyzstan* 93 D7
Torul, *Turkey* 82 C1
Toruń, *Poland* 77 B3
Tory I., *Ireland* 46 E2
Tosa-Wan, *Japan* 120 D4
Toscana, *Italy* 67 D4
Toshkent = Tashkent, *Uzbekistan* 93 C3
Toteng, *Botswana* 162 B4
Totma, *Russia* 81 A6
Totness, *Surinam* 214 B4
Totonicapán, *Guatemala* 196 C1
Tottenham, *Australia* 171 D6
Tottori, *Japan* 120 B4
Tottori □, *Japan* 120 B4
Touba, *Ivory C.* 148 B3
Toubkal, Djebel, *Morocco* 136 D3
Tougan, *Burkina Faso* 149 A2
Touggourt, *Algeria* 137 B5
Tougué, *Guinea* 147 A3
Toul, *France* 55 C8
Toulepleu, *Ivory C.* 148 D3
Toulon, *France* 55 H8
Toulouse, *France* 55 G5
Toummo, *Niger* 141 A6
Toumodi, *Ivory C.* 148 D5
Toungoo, *Burma* 122 E2
Touraine, *France* 55 D4
Tourane = Da Nang, *Vietnam* 125 D5
Tourcoing, *France* 55 A6
Tournai, *Belgium* 51 C2
Tournon, *France* 55 F7
Tours, *France* 55 D4
Touwsrivier, *S. Africa* 163 H3
Towamba, *Australia* 171 G7
Towanda, *U.S.A.* 189 B3
Townsville, *Australia* 168 G12
Towson, *U.S.A.* 189 D3
Toyama, *Japan* 120 A7
Toyama □, *Japan* 120 A7
Toyama-Wan, *Japan* 121 F5
Toyohashi, *Japan* 120 C7
Toyokawa, *Japan* 120 C7
Toyonaka, *Japan* 120 C5
Toyooka, *Japan* 120 B5
Toyota, *Japan* 120 B7
Toytepa, *Uzbekistan* 93 C3
Tozeur, *Tunisia* 138 C1
Trabzon, *Turkey* 94 A6
Trafalgar, C., *Spain* 63 H3
Trail, *Canada* 186 J4
Tralee, *Ireland* 46 J1
Tran Ninh, Cao Nguyen, *Laos* 125 B2
Trang, *Thailand* 123 K4
Trangan, *Indonesia* 129 E16
Trangie, *Australia* 171 D6
Trani, *Italy* 67 F8
Tranqueras, *Uruguay* 219 B2
Trans Nzoia □, *Kenya* 157 C1
Transilvania, *Romania* 75 C4
Transylvania = Transilvania, *Romania* 75 C4
Transylvanian Alps, *Romania* 34 F11
Trápani, *Italy* 67 J5
Traralgon, *Australia* 171 H6
Tras os Montes e Alto Douro, *Portugal* 63 C2
Trasimeno, L., *Italy* 67 D4
Trat, *Thailand* 123 H5
Traveller's L., *Australia* 171 E3
Traverse City, *U.S.A.* 191 C13
Travnik, *Bos.-H.* 72 C5
Trayning, *Australia* 170 A2
Trébbia →, *Italy* 67 B3
Trebinje, *Bos.-H.* 72 E6
Třeboň, *Czech.* 76 C3
Trece Martires, *Phil.* 130 E2
Tréguier, *France* 55 B2
Treinta y Tres, *Uruguay* 219 C3
Trelew, *Argentina* 220 H4
Tremp, *Spain* 63 B8
Trent →, *U.K.* 46 G8
Trentino-Alto Adige □, *Italy* 67 A4
Trento, *Italy* 67 A4
Trenton, *Canada* 185 C3
Trenton, *U.S.A.* 189 C4
Trepassey, *Canada* 187 J16
Tres Arroyos, *Argentina* 220 F5
Três Corações, *Brazil* 215 B3
Três Lagoas, *Brazil* 217 G6
Três Pontas, *Brazil* 215 B3
Tres Puntas, C., *Argentina* 220 J4
Três Rios, *Brazil* 215 B4
Treviso, *Italy* 67 A5
Triabunna, *Australia* 172 C3
Trichinopoly = Tiruchchirappalli, *India* 107 F3
Trida, *Australia* 171 D5
Trier, *Germany* 58 E1
Trieste, *Italy* 67 A6
Triglav, *Slovenia* 72 A2
Tríkkala, *Greece* 71 C2
Trikora, Puncak, *Indonesia* 129 D17
Trincomalee, *Sri Lanka* 110 B2
Trindade, I., *Atl. Oc.* 223 H4
Tring, *U.K.* 45 B2
Trinidad, *Bolivia* 218 B1
Trinidad, *Colombia* 210 C2
Trinidad, *Cuba* 198 B3
Trinidad, *Uruguay* 219 C1
Trinidad, *U.S.A.* 190 F7
Trinidad, I., *Argentina* 220 G5
Trinidad & Tobago ■, *W. Indies* 204
Trinity →, *U.S.A.* 191 J11
Trinity B., *Canada* 187 H16

Trinkitat, *Sudan* 143 B6
Triolet, *Mauritius* 166 A2
Tripoli = Tarābulus, *Lebanon* 95 A2
Tripoli = Tarābulus, *Libya* 138 A2
Trípolis, *Greece* 71 E2
Tristan da Cunha, *Atl. Oc.* 223 J4
Trivandrum, *India* 107 G2
Trnava, *Slovak Rep.* 76 C5
Trobriand Is., *Papua N. G.* 173 C3
Troglav, *Croatia* 72 C4
Trois-Bassins, *Réunion* 166 B1
Trois Fourches, Cap des, *Morocco* 136 A6
Trois-Rivières, *Canada* 187 K12
Troitsk, *Russia* 90 G6
Troitsko Pechorsk, *Russia* 90 E6
Trölladyngja, *Iceland* 38 C4
Trollhättan, *Sweden* 40 G2
Tromsø, *Norway* 40 A4
Trondheim, *Norway* 40 D2
Trondheimsfjorden, *Norway* 40 D2
Trout L., *Canada* 186 F5
Trouville, *France* 55 B4
Troy, *Ala., U.S.A.* 191 H14
Troy, *N.Y., U.S.A.* 189 A5
Troyes, *France* 55 C7
Trucial States = United Arab Emirates ■, *Asia* 101
Trujillo, *Honduras* 196 B3
Trujillo, *Peru* 213 C2
Trujillo, *Spain* 63 E3
Trujillo, *Venezuela* 211 A2
Truk, *Pac. Oc.* 176 E4
Trundle, *Australia* 171 D6
Trung-Phan, *Vietnam* 125 D5
Truro, *Canada* 187 K14
Truro, *U.K.* 46 M4
Trutnov, *Czech.* 76 A4
Tsageri, *Georgia* 82 A4
Tsaratanana, *Madag.* 165 B2
Tsau, *Botswana* 162 B4
Tselinograd, *Kazakstan* 90 H7
Tsetserleg, *Mongolia* 112 B6
Tshabong, *Botswana* 162 D4
Tshane, *Botswana* 162 C4
Tshela, *Zaïre* 155 D1
Tshikapa, *Zaïre* 155 E3
Tshofa, *Zaïre* 155 D4
Tshwane, *Botswana* 162 C4
Tsihombe, *Madag.* 165 E1
Tsimlyansk Res. = Tsimlyanskoye Vdkhr., *Russia* 81 F7
Tsimlyanskoye Vdkhr., *Russia* 81 F7
Tsinan = Jinan, *China* 116 D3
Tsineng, *S. Africa* 163 D4
Tsinghai = Qinghai □, *China* 112 E5
Tsingtao = Qingdao, *China* 116 E5
Tskhinvali, *Georgia* 82 B5
Tsna →, *Russia* 81 B7
Tsolo, *S. Africa* 163 G7
Tsomo, *S. Africa* 163 G7
Tsu, *Japan* 120 C6
Tsuchiura, *Japan* 120 A9
Tsugaru-Kaikyō, *Japan* 121 C7
Tsumeb, *Namibia* 162 B3
Tsumis, *Namibia* 162 C3
Tsuruga, *Japan* 120 B6
Tsuruoka, *Japan* 121 E7
Tual, *Indonesia* 129 E15
Tuamotu Ridge, *Pac. Oc.* 176 H9
Tuao, *Phil.* 130 C3
Tuatapere, *N.Z.* 175 J1
Tubarão, *Brazil* 217 J6
Tubau, *Malaysia* 126 B7
Tubbergen, *Neths.* 50 C6
Tübingen, *Germany* 58 F2
Tubruq, *Libya* 138 A5
Tucacas, *Venezuela* 211 A3
Tuchang, *Taiwan* 117 A3
Tucson, *U.S.A.* 190 H5
Tucumcari, *U.S.A.* 190 G7
Tucupita, *Venezuela* 211 B5
Tucuruí, *Brazil* 217 C6
Tudela, *Spain* 63 B6
Tudmur, *Syria* 97 C3
Tuen, *Australia* 171 B5
Tugela →, *S. Africa* 163 E9
Tuguegarao, *Phil.* 130 C3
Tugur, *Russia* 91 G16
Tukangbesi, Kepulauan, *Indonesia* 129 E12
Tukobo, *Ghana* 149 E1
Tūkrah, *Libya* 138 A4
Tuktoyaktuk, *Canada* 186 C5
Tukuyu, *Tanzania* 158 D1
Tula, *Mexico* 194 D5
Tula, *Nigeria* 151 C6
Tula, *Russia* 81 C5
Tulak, *Afghan.* 104 D2
Tulancingo, *Mexico* 194 D5
Tulare, *U.S.A.* 190 F2
Tulbagh, *S. Africa* 163 H2
Tulcán, *Ecuador* 212 A2
Tulcea, *Romania* 75 C6
Tuli, *Indonesia* 129 C11
Tuli, *Zimbabwe* 161 E3
Ṭūlkarm, *Jordan* 98 A1
Tullamore, *Australia* 171 D6
Tullamore, *Ireland* 46 H2
Tulle, *France* 55 F5
Tullibigeal, *Australia* 171 E6
Ṭulmaythah, *Libya* 138 A4
Tulsa, *U.S.A.* 191 G10
Tulua, *Colombia* 210 C1
Tulun, *Russia* 91 H11
Tulungagung, *Indonesia* 128 F7
Tum, *Indonesia* 129 D14
Tuma →, *Nic.* 197 B3
Tumaco, *Colombia* 210 D1
Tumatumari, *Guyana* 214 C2
Tumba, L., *Zaïre* 155 C2
Tumbarumba, *Australia* 171 F6
Túmbes, *Peru* 213 B1
Tumeremo, *Venezuela* 211 B5
Tumkur, *India* 107 F2
Tump, *Pakistan* 105 F1
Tumpat, *Malaysia* 126 A2
Tumu, *Ghana* 149 A1
Tumucumaque, Serra, *Brazil* 217 B5
Tumut, *Australia* 171 F6
Tunas de Zaza, *Cuba* 198 B4
Tunbridge Wells, *U.K.* 45 E4
Tuncurry, *Australia* 171 D9
Tunduru, *Tanzania* 158 D3
Tundzha →, *Bulgaria* 73 D4
Tungaru, *Sudan* 143 E4
Tungi, *Bangla.* 111 C2
Tungla, *Nic.* 197 B3
Tungurahua □, *Ecuador* 212 C1
Tunguska, Nizhnyaya →, *Russia* 91 F10
Tunis, *Tunisia* 138 A2
Tunis, Golfe de, *Tunisia* 138 A2
Tunisia ■, *Africa* 138
Tunja, *Colombia* 210 C2
Tunliu, *China* 116 D2
Tunxi, *China* 116 H4
Tuoy-Khaya, *Russia* 91 F12
Tupelo, *U.S.A.* 191 G12
Tupik, *Russia* 91 H14
Túquerres, *Colombia* 210 D1
Tura, *Russia* 91 F11
Turabah, *Si. Arabia* 99 B4
Turan, *Russia* 91 J10
Turda, *Romania* 75 B3
Turek, *Poland* 77 C3
Turfan = Turpan, *China* 112 C4
Turfan Depression = Turpan Hami, *China* 112 C4
Turgutlu, *Turkey* 94 B1
Turia →, *Spain* 63 E7
Turin = Torino, *Italy* 67 B1
Turkana □, *Kenya* 157 B1
Turkana, L., *Africa* 157 A2
Turkestan, *Kazakstan* 93 A2
Turkestanskiy, Khrebet, *Tajikistan* 93 D3
Turkey ■, *Eurasia* 94
Turkmenistan ■, *Asia* 90 K3
Turku, *Finland* 43 F1
Turkwe →, *Kenya* 157 B2
Turneffe Is., *Belize* 196 A2
Turnhout, *Belgium* 51 A4
Tŭrnovo, *Bulgaria* 73 B4
Turnu Măgurele, *Romania* 75 D4
Turnu Rosu Pasul, *Romania* 75 C3
Turpan, *China* 112 C4
Turpan Hami, *China* 112 C4
Turukhansk, *Russia* 91 F10
Tuscaloosa, *U.S.A.* 191 H13
Tuscany = Toscana, *Italy* 67 D4
Tutak, *Turkey* 82 D4
Tuticorin, *India* 107 G3
Tutrakan, *Bulgaria* 73 A4
Tuttlingen, *Germany* 58 G2
Tuva Republic □, *Russia* 91 J10
Tuvalu ■, *Pac. Oc.* 176 F6
Tuxpan, *Mexico* 194 D5
Tuxtla Gutiérrez, *Mexico* 194 F7
Tuy, *Spain* 63 B1
Tuy Hoa, *Vietnam* 125 E5
Tuyen Hoa, *Vietnam* 125 C4
Tuz Gölü, *Turkey* 94 B3
Ṭūz Khurmātū, *Iraq* 102 B4
Tuzla, *Bos.-H.* 72 C6
Tver, *Russia* 81 B5
Tweed Heads, *Australia* 171 B9
Twillingate, *Canada* 187 H15
Twin Falls, *U.S.A.* 190 D4
Two Harbors, *U.S.A.* 191 B11
Twofold B., *Australia* 171 G7
Twyford, *U.K.* 45 C1
Tychy, *Poland* 77 E3
Tyler, *U.S.A.* 191 H10
Tynda, *Russia* 91 G14
Tyne →, *U.K.* 46 F7
Tynemouth, *U.K.* 46 E7
Tyre = Sūr, *Lebanon* 95 D1
Tyrnyauz, *Russia* 82 A4
Tyrol = Tirol □, *Austria* 61 B2
Tyrrell →, *Australia* 171 F4
Tyrrell, L., *Australia* 171 F4
Tyrrhenian Sea, *Europe* 34 G9
Tyumen, *Russia* 90 G6
Tzaneen, *S. Africa* 163 B8
Tzukong = Zigong, *China* 113 G7

U

U.S.A. = United States of America ■, *N. Amer.* 190
Uasin □, *Kenya* 157 C1
Uato-Udo, *Indonesia* 129 F13
Uaxactún, *Guatemala* 196 B1
Ubá, *Brazil* 215 B4
Ubangi = Oubangi →, *Zaïre* 155 C2
Ubauro, *Pakistan* 105 E4
Ube, *Japan* 120 C2
Ubeda, *Spain* 63 F5
Uberaba, *Brazil* 215 A2
Uberlândia, *Brazil* 217 G7
Ubiaja, *Nigeria* 151 E3
Ubombo, *S. Africa* 163 D9
Ubon Ratchathani, *Thailand* 123 G6
Ubundu, *Zaïre* 155 C5
Ucayali →, *Peru* 213 B3
Uchiura-Wan, *Japan* 121 C7
Uchur →, *Russia* 91 F14
Uda →, *Russia* 91 G15
Udaipur, *India* 106 C1
Udaipur Garhi, *Nepal* 109 C4
Uden, *Neths.* 50 E4
Udi, *Nigeria* 151 F4
Údine, *Italy* 67 A5
Udon Thani, *Thailand* 123 F5
Ueda, *Japan* 120 A7
Uele →, *Zaïre* 155 A4
Uelen, *Russia* 91 A17
Uelzen, *Germany* 58 B3
Ufa, *Russia* 90 G5
Ugab →, *Namibia* 162 B2
Ugalla →, *Tanzania* 158 C1
Ugamskiy, Khrebet, *Kazakstan* 93 B4
Uganda ■, *Africa* 156
Ugep, *Nigeria* 151 F4
Ugie, *S. Africa* 163 G7
Uglegorsk, *Russia* 91 G17
Ugolyak, *Russia* 91 E13
Uige, *Angola* 160 B2
Uijŏngbu, *S. Korea* 118 E4
Ŭiju, *N. Korea* 118 C2
Uinta Mts., *U.S.A.* 190 E5
Uitenhage, *S. Africa* 163 H5
Uithuizen, *Neths.* 50 A6
Ujjain, *India* 106 D2
Újpest, *Hungary* 74 B3
Ujung Pandang, *Indonesia* 129 E10
Uka, *Russia* 91 D18
Ukerewe I., *Tanzania* 158 A1
Ukhta, *Russia* 90 E6
Ukiah, *U.S.A.* 190 D1
Ukraine ■, *Europe* 81 F3
Ulaanbaatar, *Mongolia* 113 B7
Ulaangom, *Mongolia* 112 A5
Ulan Bator = Ulaanbaatar, *Mongolia* 113 B7
Ulan Ude, *Russia* 91 J12
Ulcinj, *Montenegro, Yug.* 72 E6
Ulco, *S. Africa* 163 E5
Ulhasnagar, *India* 106 F1
Ulladulla, *Australia* 171 F8
Ullapool, *U.K.* 46 B4
Ullung-do, *S. Korea* 118 E6
Ulm, *Germany* 58 F3
Ulmarra, *Australia* 171 B9
Ulonguè, *Mozam.* 159 B2
Ulsan, *S. Korea* 118 G6
Ulungur He →, *China* 112 B4
Ulutau, *Kazakstan* 90 J6
Ulverstone, *Australia* 172 B2
Ulya, *Russia* 91 E16
Ulyanovsk = Simbirsk, *Russia* 81 C8
Ulyasutay, *Mongolia* 112 B6
Umala, *Bolivia* 218 C1
Uman, *Ukraine* 81 F3
Umaria, *India* 106 D5
Umarkot, *Pakistan* 105 F4
Umba, *Russia* 90 C5
Umboi I., *Papua N. G.* 173 B2
Umbria □, *Italy* 67 D5
Ume →, *Sweden* 40 D4
Umeå, *Sweden* 40 D4
Umera, *Indonesia* 129 C14
Umfuli →, *Zimbabwe* 161 B3
Umgusa, *Zimbabwe* 161 C2
Uminak I., *U.S.A.* 193 B3
Umkomaas, *S. Africa* 163 F8
Umm al Qaywayn, *U.A.E.* 101 A3
Umm Bāb, *Qatar* 100 D3
Umm Bel, *Sudan* 143 D3
Umm el Fahm, *Israel* 96 B2
Umm Ruwaba, *Sudan* 143 D4
Umnak I., *U.S.A.* 193 B2
Umniati →, *Zimbabwe* 161 B3
Umtata, *S. Africa* 163 G7
Umuahia, *Nigeria* 151 F4
Umvukwe Ra., *Zimbabwe* 161 B4
Umzimvubu = Port St. Johns, *S. Africa* 163 G8
Umzingwane →, *Zimbabwe* 161 E3
Umzinto, *S. Africa* 163 F8
Unac →, *Bos.-H.* 72 B4
Unalaska, *U.S.A.* 193 B2
Uncía, *Bolivia* 218 C1
Underbool, *Australia* 171 F3
Ungarie, *Australia* 171 E6
Ungava B., *Canada* 187 F12
Ungava Pen., *Canada* 180 C12
Unggi, *N. Korea* 118 A6
Union City, *U.S.A.* 189 B1
Uniondale, *S. Africa* 163 H4
Uniontown, *U.S.A.* 189 D1
United Arab Emirates ■, *Asia* 101
United Kingdom ■, *Europe* 46
United States of America ■, *N. Amer.* 190
United States Trust Terr. of the Pacific Islands, *Pac. Oc.* 176 D4
Unnao, *India* 106 B4
Uno, Ilha, *Guinea-Biss.* 146 D1
Upata, *Venezuela* 211 B5
Upemba, L., *Zaïre* 155 F5
Upernavik, *Greenland* 224 B1
Upington, *S. Africa* 163 E3
Upper Austria = Oberösterreich □, *Austria* 61 A4
Upper Hutt, *N.Z.* 175 E5
Upper Klamath L., *U.S.A.* 190 C2
Upper Volta = Burkina Faso ■, *Africa* 149
Uppsala, *Sweden* 40 F4
Ur, *Iraq* 102 E5
Ura-Tyube, *Tajikistan* 93 D3
Urakawa, *Japan* 121 C8
Ural, *Australia* 171 E5
Ural →, *Kazakstan* 34 F17
Ural Mts. = Uralskie Gory, *Russia* 90 F6
Uralla, *Australia* 171 C8
Uralsk, *Kazakstan* 81 E9
Uralskie Gory, *Russia* 90 F6
Uranium City, *Canada* 186 F6
Uranquinty, *Australia* 171 F6
Urawa, *Japan* 120 B9
Uray, *Russia* 90 F7
Urbana, *U.S.A.* 191 E12
Urbino, *Italy* 67 C5
Urbión, Picos de, *Spain* 63 B6
Urcos, *Peru* 213 E4
Urda, *Kazakstan* 81 F8
Urdinarrain, *Argentina* 221 B5
Urdzhar, *Kazakstan* 90 K8
Ures, *Mexico* 194 B2
Urfa, *Turkey* 94 C5
Urfahr, *Austria* 61 A4
Urganch = Urgench, *Uzbekistan* 90 K4
Urgench, *Uzbekistan* 90 K4
Urgut, *Uzbekistan* 93 E1
Uribia, *Colombia* 210 A2
Urk, *Neths.* 50 C4
Urmia = Orūmīyeh, *Iran* 103 A1
Urmia, L. = Orūmīyeh, Daryācheh-ye, *Iran* 103 A2
Urubamba, *Peru* 213 E4
Urubamba →, *Peru* 213 D3
Uruguaiana, *Brazil* 217 J5
Uruguay ■, *S. Amer.* 219
Uruguay →, *S. Amer.* 219 D1
Urumchi = Ürümqi, *China* 112 C4
Ürümqi, *China* 112 C4
Urup, Os., *Russia* 91 G18
Uryung-Khaya, *Russia* 91 D12
Uşak, *Turkey* 94 B2
Usakos, *Namibia* 162 C2
Usborne, Mt., *Falk. Is.* 224 A3
Usedom, *Germany* 58 A6
Ush-Tobe, *Kazakstan* 90 K7
Ushuaia, *Argentina* 220 L4
Ushumun, *Russia* 91 H15
Üsküdar, *Turkey* 94 A2
Usman, *Russia* 81 D6
Usoke, *Tanzania* 158 B1
Usolye Sibirskoye, *Russia* 91 J11
Usoro, *Nigeria* 151 F3
Uspallata, P. de, *Argentina* 220 E3
Uspenskiy, *Kazakstan* 90 J7
Ussuriysk, *Russia* 91 J16
Ust-Aldan = Batamay, *Russia* 91 E14
Ust Amginskoye = Khandyga, *Russia* 91 E14
Ust-Bolsheretsk, *Russia* 91 E18
Ust chaun, *Russia* 91 B16
Ust'-Ilga, *Russia* 91 H12
Ust Ilimpeya = Yukti, *Russia* 91 F11
Ust-Ilimsk, *Russia* 91 G11
Ust Ishim, *Russia* 90 G7
Ust-Kamchatsk, *Russia* 91 D18
Ust-Kamenogorsk, *Kazakstan* 90 J8
Ust-Karenga, *Russia* 91 H13
Ust Khayryuzova, *Russia* 91 D17
Ust-Kut, *Russia* 91 H12
Ust Kuyga, *Russia* 91 D14
Ust Maya, *Russia* 91 F15
Ust-Mil, *Russia* 91 F15
Ust-Nera, *Russia* 91 D15
Ust-Nyukzha, *Russia* 91 G14
Ust Olenek, *Russia* 91 C12
Ust-Omchug, *Russia* 91 D16
Ust Port, *Russia* 90 D9
Ust Tsilma, *Russia* 90 D6
Ust-Tungir, *Russia* 91 H14
Ust Urt = Ustyurt, Plato, *Kazakstan* 90 J3
Ust Vorkuta, *Russia* 90 D7
Ústí nad Labem, *Czech.* 76 A3
Ustica, *Italy* 67 H5
Ustinov = Izhevsk, *Russia* 82 B9
Ustye, *Russia* 91 H10
Ustyurt, Plato, *Kazakstan* 90 J3
Usu, *China* 112 C3
Usuki, *Japan* 120 D2
Usulután, *El Salv.* 196 D2
Usumacinta →, *Mexico* 194 E7
Usumbura = Bujumbura, *Burundi* 156 B1
Uta, *Indonesia* 129 E16
Utah □, *U.S.A.* 190 E5
Utah, L., *U.S.A.* 190 E5
Utete, *Tanzania* 158 C3
Uthai Thani, *Thailand* 123 G4
Utica, *U.S.A.* 189 A4
Utrecht, *Neths.* 50 D3
Utrecht, *S. Africa* 163 D8
Utrecht □, *Neths.* 50 D3
Utrera, *Spain* 63 G3
Utsunomiya, *Japan* 120 A9
Uttar Pradesh □, *India* 106 B4
Uttaradit, *Thailand* 123 F4
Uusikaupunki, *Finland* 43 F1
Uvalde, *U.S.A.* 190 J9
Uvat, *Russia* 90 F7
Uvinza, *Tanzania* 158 B1
Uvira, *Zaïre* 155 D6
Uvs Nuur, *Mongolia* 112 A5
Uwajima, *Japan* 120 D3
Uyandi, *Russia* 91 C14
Uyo, *Nigeria* 151 G4
Uyuk, *Kazakstan* 93 A4
Uyuni, *Bolivia* 218 D1
Uzbekistan ■, *Asia* 93 C1
Uzerche, *France* 55 F5
Uzgen, *Kyrgyzstan* 93 C6

V

Vaal →, *S. Africa* 163 E5
Vaal Dam, *S. Africa* 163 D7
Vaalwater, *S. Africa* 163 B7
Vaasa, *Finland* 43 E1
Vác, *Hungary* 74 A3
Vach →, *Russia* 90 F8
Vache, I.-à-, *Haiti* 200 B1
Vacoas, *Mauritius* 166 B1
Vadodara, *India* 106 E1
Vadsø, *Norway* 40 A6
Vaduz, *Liech.* 60 B5
Váh →, *Slovak Rep.* 76 D5
Vaigach, *Russia* 90 D7
Vakfikebir, *Turkey* 82 C1
Vakhsh →, *Tajikistan* 93 G2
Val-de-Marne □, *France* 55 C5
Val-d'Oise □, *France* 55 B5
Val d'Or, *Canada* 187 K11
Valahia, *Romania* 75 D4
Valais □, *Switz.* 60 D2
Valdayskaya Vozvyshennost, *Russia* 81 B4
Valdepeñas, *Spain* 63 E5
Valdés, Pen., *Argentina* 220 G4
Valdez, *Ecuador* 212 A1
Valdez, *U.S.A.* 193 B5
Valdosta, *U.S.A.* 191 H15
Vale, *Georgia* 82 B4
Valence, *France* 55 F7
Valencia, *Spain* 63 E7
Valencia, *Venezuela* 211 A3
Valencia □, *Spain* 63 E7
Valencia, Albufera de, *Spain* 63 E7
Valencia, G. de, *Spain* 63 E8
Valencia de Alcántara, *Spain* 63 E2
Valenciennes, *France* 55 A6
Valentia I., *Ireland* 34 E4
Valera, *Venezuela* 211 B2
Valjevo, *Serbia, Yug.* 72 C7
Valkenswaard, *Neths.* 50 F4
Valladolid, *Mexico* 194 D8
Valladolid, *Spain* 63 C4
Valldemosa, *Spain* 65 A3
Valle d'Aosta □, *Italy* 67 A1
Valle de la Pascua, *Venezuela* 211 B3
Vallecas, *Spain* 63 D5
Valledupar, *Colombia* 210 A2
Vallejo, *U.S.A.* 190 E2
Valletta, *Malta* 69 B3
Valley City, *U.S.A.* 190 C9
Vallorbe, *Switz.* 60 C1
Valls, *Spain* 63 C9
Valognes, *France* 55 B3
Valona = Vlóra, *Albania* 70 C2
Valparaíso, *Chile* 220 E3
Vals →, *S. Africa* 163 D6
Vals, Tanjung, *Indonesia* 129 F17
Valsad, *India* 106 E1
Valverde, *Canary Is.* 223 D1
Valverde, *Spain* 63 F3
Van, *Turkey* 94 C7
Van, L. = Van Gölü, *Turkey* 94 B7
Van Buren, *U.S.A.* 191 G11
Van Gölü, *Turkey* 94 B7
Van Rees, Pegunungan, *Indonesia* 129 D17
Vanavara, *Russia* 91 G11
Vancouver, *Canada* 186 H3
Vancouver, *U.S.A.* 190 B2
Vancouver, C., *Australia* 170 D3
Vancouver I., *Canada* 186 H3
Vandeloos B., *Sri Lanka* 110 B3
Vanderbijlpark, *S. Africa* 163 D7
Vandergrift, *U.S.A.* 189 C1
Vänern, *Sweden* 40 G3
Vang Vieng, *Laos* 125 C2
Vanga, *Kenya* 157 F4
Vangaindrano, *Madag.* 165 E2

Vankarem, *Russia* 91 A17
Vännäs, *Sweden* 40 D4
Vannes, *France* 55 C2
Vanrhynsdorp, *S. Africa* 163 G2
Vanua Levu, *Fiji* 174 A2
Vanuatu ■, *Pac. Oc.* 176 G5
Vanwyksvlei, *S. Africa* 163 F4
Vanzylsrus, *S. Africa* 163 D4
Var □, *France* 55 G8
Varanasi, *India* 106 C5
Varangerfjorden, *Norway* 40 A6
Varaždin, *Croatia* 72 A4
Varberg, *Sweden* 40 G2
Vardar →, *Macedonia* 72 F8
Vardø, *Norway* 40 A6
Varese, *Italy* 67 A2
Varginha, *Brazil* 215 B3
Varna, *Bulgaria* 73 B5
Vascongadas = País Vasco □, *Spain* 63 B6
Vāshīr, *Afghan.* 104 E2
Vasilevka = Nimneryskiy, *Russia* 91 G14
Vaslui, *Romania* 75 B6
Västerås, *Sweden* 40 F3
Västervik, *Sweden* 40 G3
Vasto, *Italy* 67 E6
Vatili, *Cyprus* 95 B2
Vatnajökull, *Iceland* 38 C4
Vatneyri, *Iceland* 38 B1
Vatomandry, *Madag.* 165 C3
Vatra-Dornei, *Romania* 75 A4
Vättern, *Sweden* 40 G3
Vaucluse □, *France* 55 G8
Vaud □, *Switz.* 60 C1
Vavau Is., *Tonga* 174 A3
Vavoua, *Ivory C.* 148 C4
Vaygach, Ostrov, *Russia* 90 D7
Vedea →, *Romania* 75 D4
Vedia, *Argentina* 221 C3
Vedra, I. del, *Spain* 65 C1
Vedrin, *Belgium* 51 C4
Veendam, *Neths.* 50 A6
Vega, *Norway* 40 C2
Vega Baja, *Puerto Rico* 201 A2
Veghel, *Neths.* 50 E4
Vegreville, *Canada* 186 H5
Vejer, *Spain* 63 H3
Vejle, *Denmark* 42 C2
Velanai I., *Sri Lanka* 110 A1
Velas, C., *Costa Rica* 197 D2
Velay, *France* 55 F7
Velddrif, *S. Africa* 163 H2
Velebit Planina, *Croatia* 72 C3
Vélez, *Colombia* 210 C1
Vélez Málaga, *Spain* 63 G5
Vélez Rubio, *Spain* 63 F6
Velika Kapela, *Croatia* 72 B3
Velikaya →, *Russia* 81 B3
Velikiye Luki, *Russia* 81 B3
Velletri, *Italy* 67 E5
Vellore, *India* 107 F3
Velsen, *Neths.* 50 C3
Venado Tuerto, *Argentina* 221 B3
Vendée □, *France* 55 D3
Véneto □, *Italy* 67 A4
Venézia, *Italy* 67 B5
Venézia, G. di, *Italy* 67 B5
Venezuela ■, *S. Amer.* 211
Venezuela, G. de, *Venezuela* 211 A2
Venice = Venézia, *Italy* 67 B5
Venlo, *Neths.* 50 F5
Venraij, *Neths.* 50 E5
Ventersburg, *S. Africa* 163 E7
Venterstad, *S. Africa* 163 F6
Ventspils, *Latvia* 81 A1
Ventuari →, *Venezuela* 211 C3
Venus B., *Australia* 171 H5
Vera, *Spain* 63 G6
Veracruz, *Mexico* 194 E6
Veraval, *India* 107 D1
Vercelli, *Italy* 67 B2
Verde Island Pass, *Phil.* 130 F2
Verden, *Germany* 58 B3
Verdun, *France* 55 B7
Vereeniging, *S. Africa* 163 D7
Verga, C., *Guinea* 147 B2
Verkhnevilyuysk, *Russia* 91 F13
Verkhneye Kalinino, *Russia* 91 G12
Verkhniy Baskunchak, *Russia* 81 F8
Verkhoyansk, *Russia* 91 D14
Verkhoyansk Ra. = Verkhoyanskiy Khrebet, *Russia* 91 E14
Verkhoyanskiy Khrebet, *Russia* 91 E14
Vermilion, *Canada* 186 H6
Verneukpan, *S. Africa* 163 F3
Vernon, *Canada* 186 H4
Vernon, *U.S.A.* 190 G9
Véroia, *Greece* 71 B2
Verona, *Italy* 67 B4
Veropol, *Russia* 91 B17
Versailles, *France* 55 C5
Vert, C., *Senegal* 146 B1
Verulam, *S. Africa* 163 F9
Verviers, *Belgium* 51 C5
Veselovskoye Vdkhr., *Russia* 81 G6
Vesoul, *France* 55 D8
Vesterålen, *Norway* 40 B3
Vestfjorden, *Norway* 40 B3
Vestmannaeyjar, *Iceland* 38 D3
Vesuvio, *Italy* 67 F6
Vesuvius, Mt. = Vesuvio, *Italy* 67 F6
Veszprém, *Hungary* 74 B2
Vevey, *Switz.* 60 C1
Vezhen, *Bulgaria* 73 B3
Viacha, *Bolivia* 218 C1
Viana, *Portugal* 63 F2
Viana do Castelo, *Portugal* 63 B1
Viborg, *Denmark* 42 B2
Vicenza, *Italy* 67 A4
Vich, *Spain* 63 B9
Vichy, *France* 55 E6
Vicksburg, *U.S.A.* 191 H12
Victor Harbor, *Australia* 171 F2
Victoria, *Argentina* 221 B4
Victoria, *Canada* 186 H3
Victoria, *Guinea* 147 B1
Victoria, *Malaysia* 126 B7
Victoria, *Malta* 69 A1
Victoria, *Phil.* 130 D2
Victoria, *Seychelles* 166 C1
Victoria, *U.S.A.* 191 J10
Victoria →, *Australia* 168 B2
Victoria, L., *Africa* 132 G7
Victoria, L., *Australia* 171 E3
Victoria, Mt. = Victoria Taungdeik, *Burma* 122 D1
Victoria Beach, *Canada* 186 J8
Victoria de las Tunas, *Cuba* 198 C5
Victoria Falls, *Zimbabwe* 161 B1
Victoria I., *Canada* 186 C7
Victoria Nile →, *Uganda* 156 B1
Victoria Point, *Burma* 122 J3
Victoria Taungdeik, *Burma* 122 D1
Victoria West, *S. Africa* 163 G4
Victorias, *Phil.* 130 G4
Vicuña Mackenna, *Argentina* 221 B2
Vidin, *Bulgaria* 73 A2
Vidisha, *India* 106 D3
Viedma, L., *Argentina* 220 J3
Vien Pou Kha, *Laos* 125 B1
Vienna = Wien, *Austria* 61 A5
Vienne, *France* 55 F7
Vienne □, *France* 55 E4
Vienne →, *France* 55 D4
Vientiane, *Laos* 125 C2
Vieques, Isla de, *Puerto Rico* 201 A3
Viersen, *Germany* 59 A1
Vierwaldstättersee, *Switz.* 60 B3
Vierzon, *France* 55 D5
Vietnam ■, *Asia* 125
Vigan, *Phil.* 130 C2
Vigo, *Spain* 63 B1
Vijayawada, *India* 107 E3
Vikna, *Norway* 40 D2
Vikulovo, *Russia* 90 G7
Vila da Maganja, *Mozam.* 159 C3
Vila de João Belo = Xai-Xai, *Mozam.* 159 F1
Vila Franca, *Portugal* 63 E1
Vila Machado, *Mozam.* 159 D2
Vila Real, *Portugal* 63 C2
Vila Real de Santo António, *Portugal* 63 G2
Vila Velha, *Brazil* 215 A6
Vilaine →, *France* 55 D2
Vilanculos, *Mozam.* 159 E2
Vilhelmina, *Sweden* 40 D3
Viliga, *Russia* 91 D17
Villa Ahumada, *Mexico* 194 A3
Villa Bella, *Bolivia* 218 A1
Villa Cañás, *Argentina* 221 B3
Villa Carlos, *Spain* 65 A6
Villa Cisneros = Dakhla, *W. Sahara* 136 B1
Villa Constitución, *Argentina* 221 B4
Villa Dolores, *Argentina* 221 A2
Villa Hayes, *Paraguay* 219 B2
Villa Maria, *Argentina* 221 B3
Villa San José, *Argentina* 221 A5
Villach, *Austria* 61 C4
Villagarcia, *Spain* 63 B1
Villaguay, *Argentina* 221 A5
Villahermosa, *Mexico* 194 E7
Villalba, *Spain* 63 A2
Villanueva de la Serena, *Spain* 63 E3
Villarreal, *Spain* 63 D8
Villarrica, *Paraguay* 219 C3
Villarrobledo, *Spain* 63 E6
Villavicencio, *Colombia* 210 C2
Villaviciosa, *Spain* 63 A4
Villena, *Spain* 63 E7
Villiers, *S. Africa* 163 D7
Vilnius, *Lithuania* 81 C2
Vilskutskogo, Proliv, *Russia* 91 B11
Vilvoorde, *Belgium* 51 B3
Vilyuy →, *Russia* 91 E13
Vilyuysk, *Russia* 91 F13
Viña del Mar, *Chile* 220 E3
Vinaroz, *Spain* 63 D8
Vincennes, *U.S.A.* 191 E13
Vinces, *Ecuador* 212 C1
Vindhya Ra., *India* 106 D3
Vineland, *U.S.A.* 189 D4
Vinh, *Vietnam* 125 C3
Vinkovci, *Croatia* 72 B6
Vinnitsa, *Ukraine* 81 F2
Vinnytsya = Vinnitsa, *Ukraine* 81 F2
Viqueque, *Indonesia* 129 F13
Vir, *Tajikistan* 93 F5
Virac, *Phil.* 130 F4
Viramgam, *India* 106 D1
Virden, *Canada* 186 J7
Vire, *France* 55 B3
Vírgenes, C., *Argentina* 220 K3
Virgin →, *U.S.A.* 190 F4
Virgin Is. ■, *W. Indies* 201 A3
Virginia, *S. Africa* 163 E6
Virginia, *U.S.A.* 191 B11
Virginia □, *U.S.A.* 191 E16
Virginia Water, *U.K.* 45 D2
Virton, *Belgium* 51 F5
Vis, *Croatia* 72 D4
Visalia, *U.S.A.* 190 F2
Visayan Sea, *Phil.* 130 G4
Visby, *Sweden* 40 G4
Viscount Melville Sd., *Canada* 186 B8
Visé, *Belgium* 51 C5
Višegrad, *Bos.-H.* 72 C6
Viseu, *Portugal* 63 C2
Vishakhapatnam, *India* 107 E4
Viso, Mte., *Italy* 67 B1
Visp, *Switz.* 60 D3
Vistula = Wisła →, *Poland* 77 A3
Vitebsk, *Belarus* 81 C3
Viterbo, *Italy* 67 E4
Viti Levu, *Fiji* 174 A1
Vitim, *Russia* 91 G12
Vitim →, *Russia* 91 G12
Vitoria, *Spain* 63 A6
Vitsyebsk = Vitebsk, *Belarus* 81 C3
Vittória, *Italy* 67 K6
Vittório Véneto, *Italy* 67 A5
Vivero, *Spain* 63 A2
Vizianagaram, *India* 107 E4
Vlaardingen, *Neths.* 50 D2
Vladikavkaz, *Russia* 82 A5
Vladimir, *Russia* 81 C6
Vladivostok, *Russia* 91 J16
Vlieland, *Neths.* 50 A3
Vlissingen, *Neths.* 50 F1
Vlóra, *Albania* 70 C2
Vltava →, *Czech.* 76 B3
Vogelkop = Doberai, Jazirah, *Indonesia* 129 C15
Vogelsberg, *Germany* 58 D3
Vohibinany, *Madag.* 165 C3
Vohimarina, *Madag.* 165 A3
Vohimena, Tanjon' i, *Madag.* 165 E1
Vohipeno, *Madag.* 165 D2
Voi, *Kenya* 157 E3
Volcano Is. = Kazan-Rettō, *Pac. Oc.* 176 C3
Volchayevka, *Russia* 91 H16
Volendam, *Neths.* 50 C3
Volga →, *Russia* 81 G8
Volga Hts. = Privolzhskaya Vozvyshennost, *Russia* 81 E8
Volgodonsk, *Russia* 81 G7
Volgograd, *Russia* 81 F7
Volgogradskoye Vdkhr., *Russia* 81 E8
Volksrust, *S. Africa* 163 D8
Vollenhove, *Neths.* 50 C5
Volochanka, *Russia* 91 D10
Vologda, *Russia* 81 A6
Vólos, *Greece* 71 C3
Volsk, *Russia* 81 D8
Volta →, *Ghana* 149 D3
Volta, L., *Ghana* 149 C3
Volta Blanche = White Volta →, *Ghana* 149 B2
Volta Redonda, *Brazil* 215 B4
Volterra, *Italy* 67 D3
Volturno →, *Italy* 67 F6
Volubilis, *Morocco* 136 B4
Volzhskiy, *Russia* 81 F7
Voorburg, *Neths.* 50 D2
Vopnafjörður, *Iceland* 38 B5
Vorarlberg □, *Austria* 61 B1
Vorderrhein →, *Switz.* 60 C5
Voríai Sporádhes, *Greece* 71 C4
Vorkuta, *Russia* 90 D7
Voronezh, *Russia* 81 E6
Voroshilovgrad = Lugansk, *Ukraine* 81 F6
Voroshilovsk = Kommunarsk, *Ukraine* 81 F5
Vorovskoye, *Russia* 91 E18
Vorukh, *Kyrgyzstan* 93 D4
Vosges, *France* 55 C9
Vosges □, *France* 55 C8
Vostok I., *Kiribati* 176 G8
Vouga →, *Portugal* 63 C1
Voznesene, *Russia* 90 D4
Voznesenka, *Russia* 91 H10
Voznesensk, *Ukraine* 81 G3
Vrangelya, Ostrov, *Russia* 91 A16
Vranje, *Serbia, Yug.* 72 E8
Vratsa, *Bulgaria* 73 B2
Vrbas →, *Bos.-H.* 72 B5
Vrede, *S. Africa* 163 D8
Vredefort, *S. Africa* 163 D7
Vredenburg, *S. Africa* 163 H1
Vredendal, *S. Africa* 163 G2
Vridi, *Ivory C.* 148 E5
Vršac, *Serbia, Yug.* 72 B7
Vryburg, *S. Africa* 163 D5
Vryheid, *S. Africa* 163 D8
Vught, *Neths.* 50 E4
Vulcano, *Italy* 67 J7
Vung Tau, *Vietnam* 125 G4
Vyatka, *Russia* 81 A8
Vyatka →, *Russia* 81 C9
Vyatskiye Polyany, *Russia* 81 B9
Vyazemskiy, *Russia* 91 H16
Vyazma, *Russia* 81 C4
Vyborg, *Russia* 90 C4
Vychegda →, *Russia* 90 E5
Vychodné Beskydy, *Europe* 76 B7
Vyshniy Volochek, *Russia* 81 B4

W

Wa, *Ghana* 149 A1
Waal →, *Neths.* 50 E5
Waalwijk, *Neths.* 50 E3
Wabash, *U.S.A.* 191 E13
Wabash →, *U.S.A.* 191 F13
Wąbrzeźno, *Poland* 77 B3
Waco, *U.S.A.* 191 H10
Wad Banda, *Sudan* 143 D3
Wad Hamid, *Sudan* 143 C4
Wâd Medanî, *Sudan* 143 C5
Waddenzee, *Neths.* 50 A3
Wadderin Hill, *Australia* 170 B3
Waddington, Mt., *Canada* 186 H3
Waddinxveen, *Neths.* 50 D3
Wädenswil, *Switz.* 60 B4
Wadhurst, *U.K.* 45 E5
Wadi Gemâl, *Egypt* 139 E6
Wadi Halfa, *Sudan* 143 A4
Waegwan, *S. Korea* 118 G5
Wageningen, *Neths.* 50 D4
Wageningen, *Surinam* 214 B3
Wagga Wagga, *Australia* 171 F6
Waghete, *Indonesia* 129 D16
Wagin, *Australia* 170 C2
Wah, *Pakistan* 105 B5
Wahai, *Indonesia* 129 D14
Wahiawa, *U.S.A.* 192 A2
Waiau →, *N.Z.* 175 G4
Waiawe →, *Sri Lanka* 110 D2
Waibeem, *Indonesia* 129 C15
Waigeo, *Indonesia* 129 C14
Waihi, *N.Z.* 175 C6
Waihou →, *N.Z.* 175 C5
Waikabubak, *Indonesia* 129 F10
Waikato →, *N.Z.* 175 C5
Waikerie, *Australia* 171 E2
Waimakariri →, *N.Z.* 175 G4
Waimate, *N.Z.* 175 H3
Wainganga →, *India* 106 F4
Waingapu, *Indonesia* 129 F10
Waini →, *Guyana* 214 A1
Wainwright, *Canada* 186 H6
Wainwright, *U.S.A.* 193 A4
Waiouru, *N.Z.* 175 D5
Waipara, *N.Z.* 175 G4
Waipawa, *N.Z.* 175 E6
Waipu, *N.Z.* 175 B5
Waipukurau, *N.Z.* 175 E6
Wairarapa, L., *N.Z.* 175 E5
Wairoa, *N.Z.* 175 D6
Waitaki →, *N.Z.* 175 H3
Waitara, *N.Z.* 175 D5
Waiuku, *N.Z.* 175 C5
Wajima, *Japan* 121 F5
Wajir, *Kenya* 157 B4
Wajir □, *Kenya* 157 B4
Wakasa-Wan, *Japan* 120 B5
Wakatipu, L., *N.Z.* 175 H2
Wakayama, *Japan* 120 C5
Wakayama □, *Japan* 120 C5
Wake I., *Pac. Oc.* 176 D5
Wakefield, *U.K.* 46 G7
Wakema, *Burma* 122 F2
Wakkanai, *Japan* 121 A7
Wakkerstroom, *S. Africa* 163 D8
Wakool, *Australia* 171 F5
Wakool →, *Australia* 171 F4
Wakre, *Indonesia* 129 C15
Wałbrzych, *Poland* 77 E1
Walcha, *Australia* 171 C8
Walcheren, *Neths.* 50 E1
Wald, *Switz.* 60 B4
Waldbröl, *Germany* 59 B3
Walembele, *Ghana* 149 A1
Walensee, *Switz.* 60 B5
Wales □, *U.K.* 46 J5
Walewale, *Ghana* 149 A2
Walgett, *Australia* 171 C7
Walhalla, *Australia* 171 H5
Walker L., *U.S.A.* 190 E3
Walla Walla, *U.S.A.* 190 B4
Wallace, *U.S.A.* 190 B4
Wallachia = Valahia, *Romania* 75 D4
Wallambin, L., *Australia* 170 A2
Wallaroo, *Australia* 171 E1
Wallerawang, *Australia* 171 E7
Wallis & Futuna, Is., *Pac. Oc.* 176 G6
Wallsend, *Australia* 171 D8
Walsall, *U.K.* 46 J7
Walsenburg, *U.S.A.* 190 F7
Waltham Abbey, *U.K.* 45 B4
Waltham Forest, *U.K.* 45 C4
Walton-on-Thames, *U.K.* 45 D2
Walvisbaai, *S. Africa* 162 C2
Wamba, *Kenya* 157 C3
Wamba, *Zaïre* 155 B5
Wamena, *Indonesia* 129 D18
Wamsasi, *Indonesia* 129 D13
Wana, *Pakistan* 105 C4
Wanaaring, *Australia* 171 B4
Wanaka, *N.Z.* 175 H2
Wanaka L., *N.Z.* 175 H2
Wan'an, *China* 116 J2
Wanapiri, *Indonesia* 129 E16
Wanbi, *Australia* 171 F2
Wandaik, *Guyana* 214 C1
Wanderer, *Zimbabwe* 161 C3
Wandsworth, *U.K.* 45 C3
Wang Saphung, *Thailand* 123 F5
Wangal, *Indonesia* 129 E16
Wanganella, *Australia* 171 F5
Wanganui, *N.Z.* 175 E5
Wangaratta, *Australia* 171 G5
Wangdu, *China* 116 C3
Wangerooge, *Germany* 58 A2
Wangi, *Kenya* 157 E4
Wangiwangi, *Indonesia* 129 E12
Wangjiang, *China* 116 G3
Wanquan, *China* 116 B3
Wanxian, *China* 113 F8
Wanzai, *China* 116 H2
Warangal, *India* 107 E3
Waratah, *Australia* 172 B2
Waratah B., *Australia* 171 H5
Warburton, *Australia* 171 G5
Warden, *S. Africa* 163 D8
Wardha, *India* 106 F4
Wardha →, *India* 106 F4
Ware, *U.K.* 45 B3
Warialda, *Australia* 171 B8
Wariap, *Indonesia* 129 C16
Warkopi, *Indonesia* 129 C16
Warlingham, *U.K.* 45 D3
Warmbad, *Namibia* 162 E3
Warmbad, *S. Africa* 163 B7
Warnemünde, *Germany* 58 A4
Waroona, *Australia* 170 C1
Warracknabeal, *Australia* 171 G4
Warragul, *Australia* 171 H5
Warrego →, *Australia* 171 C5
Warren, *Australia* 171 D6
Warren, *U.S.A.* 189 B2
Warrenton, *S. Africa* 163 E5
Warri, *Nigeria* 151 F3
Warrnambool, *Australia* 171 H4
Warsa, *Indonesia* 129 C16
Warsaw = Warszawa, *Poland* 77 C4
Warszawa, *Poland* 77 C4
Warta →, *Poland* 77 C1
Warthe = Warta →, *Poland* 77 C1
Waru, *Indonesia* 129 D14
Warwick, *Australia* 171 A9
Warwick, *U.K.* 46 J7
Warwick, *U.S.A.* 189 B6
Wasatch Ra., *U.S.A.* 190 E5
Wasbank, *S. Africa* 163 E8
Wash, The, *U.K.* 46 H9
Washim, *India* 106 F3
Washington, D.C., *U.S.A.* 191 E16
Washington, N.C., *U.S.A.* 191 F16
Washington □, *U.S.A.* 190 B3
Wasian, *Indonesia* 129 C15
Wasior, *Indonesia* 129 D16
Wassenaar, *Neths.* 50 D2
Watangpone, *Indonesia* 129 E10
Waterberge, *S. Africa* 163 B7
Waterbury, *U.S.A.* 189 B5
Waterford, *Ireland* 46 J3
Waterloo, *Belgium* 51 C3
Waterloo, *S. Leone* 147 C2
Waterloo, *U.S.A.* 191 D11
Watertown, *N.Y., U.S.A.* 191 C16
Watertown, *S. Dak., U.S.A.* 191 C10
Watertown, *Wis., U.S.A.* 191 D12
Waterval-Boven, *S. Africa* 163 C8
Watervliet, *U.S.A.* 189 A5
Watford, *U.K.* 45 B2
Watheroo, *Australia* 170 A1
Watkins Glen, *U.S.A.* 189 A3
Watling I. = San Salvador, *Bahamas* 201 B2
Watrous, *Canada* 186 J6
Watsa, *Zaïre* 155 B6
Watson Lake, *Canada* 186 E4
Wattwil, *Switz.* 60 B5
Watuata = Batuata, *Indonesia* 129 E11
Watubela, Kepulauan, *Indonesia* 129 E15
Watubela Is. = Watubela, Kepulauan, *Indonesia* 129 E15
Wauchope, *Australia* 171 D9
Waukegan, *U.S.A.* 191 D12
Wausau, *U.S.A.* 191 C12
Waverly, *U.S.A.* 189 B3
Wavre, *Belgium* 51 C3
Wâw, *Sudan* 143 E3
Wāw al Kabīr, *Libya* 138 C3
Wawa, *Nigeria* 151 C2
Waxahachie, *U.S.A.* 191 H10
Wayabula Rau, *Indonesia* 129 B13
Wayatinah, *Australia* 172 C2
Waycross, *U.S.A.* 191 H15
Waynesboro, *U.S.A.* 189 D3
Wazay, *Afghan.* 104 D5
Wazirabad, *Pakistan* 105 C6
We, *Indonesia* 128 A1
Weald, The, *U.K.* 45 E5
Weatherford, *U.S.A.* 190 H9
Webo = Nyaake, *Liberia* 148 E3
Webster City, *U.S.A.* 191 D11
Weda, *Indonesia* 129 C13
Weda, Teluk, *Indonesia* 129 C13
Weddell I., *Falk. Is.* 224 A2

Wedderburn, *Australia* ... 171 G4
Wedza, *Zimbabwe* ... 161 C4
Wee Waa, *Australia* ... 171 C7
Weemelah, *Australia* ... 171 B7
Weenen, *S. Africa* ... 163 E8
Weert, *Neths.* ... 50 F4
Weesp, *Neths.* ... 50 C3
Wei He →, *China* ... 116 E2
Weifang, *China* ... 116 D4
Weihai, *China* ... 116 D5
Weimar, *Germany* ... 58 D4
Weiser, *U.S.A.* ... 190 C4
Weishan, *China* ... 116 E4
Wejherowo, *Poland* ... 77 A3
Welkom, *S. Africa* ... 163 D6
Welland, *Canada* ... 185 D2
Wellin, *Belgium* ... 51 E4
Wellingborough, *U.K.* ... 46 J8
Wellington, *Australia* ... 171 D7
Wellington, *N.Z.* ... 175 F5
Wellington, *S. Africa* ... 163 H2
Wellington, *U.S.A.* ... 191 F10
Wellington, I., *Chile* ... 206 G2
Wellington, L., *Australia* ... 171 H6
Wellington Chan., *Canada* ... 186 B9
Wells, *U.K.* ... 46 L6
Wellsboro, *U.S.A.* ... 189 B3
Wellsville, *U.S.A.* ... 189 B2
Wels, *Austria* ... 61 B4
Welshpool, *U.K.* ... 46 J6
Welwyn Garden City, *U.K.* ... 45 B3
Wenatchee, *U.S.A.* ... 190 B3
Wenchi, *Ghana* ... 149 C1
Wenchow = Wenzhou, *China* ... 116 J5
Wendeng, *China* ... 116 D5
Wendesi, *Indonesia* ... 129 D16
Wendover, *U.K.* ... 45 B1
Wensu, *China* ... 112 C2
Wentworth, *Australia* ... 171 E3
Wenut, *Indonesia* ... 129 D15
Wenxi, *China* ... 116 E1
Wenzhou, *China* ... 116 J5
Wepener, *S. Africa* ... 163 F6
Werda, *Botswana* ... 162 D4
Werder, *Ethiopia* ... 144 E5
Werdohl, *Germany* ... 59 A3
Weri, *Indonesia* ... 129 D15
Werne, *Germany* ... 59 A3
Werribee, *Australia* ... 171 H5
Werrimull, *Australia* ... 171 E3
Werris Creek, *Australia* ... 171 C8
Wersar, *Indonesia* ... 129 C15
Wesel, *Germany* ... 59 A1
Weser →, *Germany* ... 58 B2
Wesiri, *Indonesia* ... 129 F13
West Bengal □, *India* ... 106 D8
West Beskids = Západné Beskydy, *Europe* ... 76 B6
West Cape Howe, *Australia* ... 170 D2
West Chester, *U.S.A.* ... 189 C4
West Falkland, *Falk. Is.* ... 224 A2
West Fjord = Vestfjorden, *Norway* ... 40 B3
West Frankfort, *U.S.A.* ... 191 F12
West Malling, *U.K.* ... 45 D5
West Nicholson, *Zimbabwe* ... 161 D3
West Palm Beach, *U.S.A.* ... 191 K16
West Pokot □, *Kenya* ... 157 C1
West Schelde = Westerschelde →, *Neths.* ... 50 F1
West Siberian Plain, *Russia* ... 84 B11
West Virginia □, *U.S.A.* ... 191 E15
West-Vlaanderen □, *Belgium* ... 51 B1
West Wyalong, *Australia* ... 171 E6
Westbury, *Australia* ... 172 B2
Westerham, *U.K.* ... 45 D4
Western □, *Kenya* ... 157 C1
Western □, *Uganda* ... 156 C1
Western Australia □, *Australia* ... 168 H10
Western Cape □, *S. Africa* ... 163 H3
Western Ghats, *India* ... 107 F2
Western Sahara ■, *Africa* ... 136
Western Samoa ■, *Pac. Oc.* ... 176 G6
Westernport, *U.S.A.* ... 189 D2
Westerschelde →, *Neths.* ... 50 F1
Westerwald, *Germany* ... 58 D2
Westfriesche Eilanden, *Neths.* ... 50 A3
Westland Bight, *N.Z.* ... 175 G2
Westminster, *U.S.A.* ... 189 D3
Weston, *Malaysia* ... 126 B7
Weston-super-Mare, *U.K.* ... 46 K6
Westport, *Ireland* ... 46 G1
Westport, *N.Z.* ... 175 F3
Wetar, *Indonesia* ... 129 F13
Wetaskiwin, *Canada* ... 186 H5
Wetteren, *Belgium* ... 51 B2
Wetzlar, *Germany* ... 58 D2
Wewak, *Papua N. G.* ... 173 A1
Wexford, *Ireland* ... 46 J3
Wey →, *U.K.* ... 45 D2
Weybridge, *U.K.* ... 45 D2
Weyburn, *Canada* ... 186 J7
Weymouth, *U.K.* ... 46 L6
Wezep, *Neths.* ... 50 C5
Whakatane, *N.Z.* ... 175 C6
Whale Cove, *Canada* ... 186 F9
Whangarei, *N.Z.* ... 175 B5
Wheeler Pk., *U.S.A.* ... 190 E4
Whipsnade, *U.K.* ... 45 B2
Whitby, *U.K.* ... 46 F8
White →, *Ark., U.S.A.* ... 191 G12
White →, *S. Dak., U.S.A.* ... 190 D9
White →, *Utah, U.S.A.* ... 190 E6
White Cliffs, *Australia* ... 171 C4
White Mts., *Calif., U.S.A.* ... 190 E3
White Mts., *N.H., U.S.A.* ... 191 C17
White Nile = Nîl el Abyad →, *Sudan* ... 143 E4
White River, *S. Africa* ... 163 C9
White Russia = Belarus ■, *Europe* ... 81 D2
White Sea = Beloye More, *Russia* ... 90 C5
White Volta →, *Ghana* ... 149 B2
Whitehaven, *U.K.* ... 46 F5
Whitehorse, *Canada* ... 186 D3
Whitemark, *Australia* ... 172 A3
Whiteplains, *Liberia* ... 148 D1
Whitfield, *Australia* ... 171 G5
Whitney, Mt., *U.S.A.* ... 190 F3
Whittlesea, *Australia* ... 171 G5
Wholdaia L., *Canada* ... 186 F7
Whyalla, *Australia* ... 171 E1
Whyjonta, *Australia* ... 171 B4
Wiawso, *Ghana* ... 149 D1
Wichabai, *Guyana* ... 214 D1
Wichita, *U.S.A.* ... 191 F10
Wichita Falls, *U.S.A.* ... 190 G9
Wick, *U.K.* ... 46 A6
Wickepin, *Australia* ... 170 B2
Wickford, *U.K.* ... 45 C5
Wickham, C., *Australia* ... 172 A1
Wicklow, *Ireland* ... 46 H3
Wicklow Mts., *Ireland* ... 46 H3
Wieliczka, *Poland* ... 77 E4
Wieluń, *Poland* ... 77 D3
Wien, *Austria* ... 61 A5
Wiener Neustadt, *Austria* ... 61 B5
Wiesbaden, *Germany* ... 58 E2
Wil, *Switz.* ... 60 A4
Wilcannia, *Australia* ... 171 D4
Wilge →, *S. Africa* ... 163 D7
Wilhelmina, Geb., *Surinam* ... 214 D3
Wilhelmshaven, *Germany* ... 58 A2
Wilkes-Barre, *U.S.A.* ... 189 B4
Wilkie, *Canada* ... 186 H6
Willandra Billabong Creek →, *Australia* ... 171 E5
Willebroek, *Belgium* ... 51 B3
Williams, *Australia* ... 170 C2
Williams Lake, *Canada* ... 186 H4
Williamsport, *U.S.A.* ... 189 B3
Williamstown, *Australia* ... 171 H5
Williston, *S. Africa* ... 163 G3
Williston, *U.S.A.* ... 190 B8
Willmar, *U.S.A.* ... 191 C10
Willowmore, *S. Africa* ... 163 H4
Willowvale = Gatyana, *S. Africa* ... 163 G7
Willunga, *Australia* ... 171 F2
Wilmington, *Australia* ... 171 D1
Wilmington, *Del., U.S.A.* ... 189 C4
Wilmington, *N.C., U.S.A.* ... 191 G16
Wilpena Cr. →, *Australia* ... 171 D2
Wilson, *U.S.A.* ... 191 F16
Wilsons Promontory, *Australia* ... 171 H5
Wiltz, *Lux.* ... 52 B1
Wimmera →, *Australia* ... 171 G4
Winam G., *Kenya* ... 157 D1
Winburg, *S. Africa* ... 163 E7
Winchester, *U.K.* ... 46 L7
Winchester, *Ky., U.S.A.* ... 191 F14
Winchester, *Va., U.S.A.* ... 189 D2
Wind →, *U.S.A.* ... 190 C6
Wind River Range, *U.S.A.* ... 190 D6
Windau = Ventspils, *Latvia* ... 81 A1
Windber, *U.S.A.* ... 189 C2
Windermere, *U.K.* ... 46 F6
Windhoek, *Namibia* ... 162 C2
Windsor, *Australia* ... 171 E8
Windsor, *N.S., Canada* ... 187 K14
Windsor, *Ont., Canada* ... 187 L11
Windsor, *U.K.* ... 46 K8
Windsorton, *S. Africa* ... 163 E5
Windward Is., *W. Indies* ... 203
Winfield, *U.S.A.* ... 191 F10
Wing, *U.K.* ... 45 A1
Wingen, *Australia* ... 171 D8
Wingham, *Australia* ... 171 D9
Winisk →, *Canada* ... 187 H10
Winneba, *Ghana* ... 149 E2
Winnemucca, *U.S.A.* ... 190 D3
Winnipeg, *Canada* ... 186 K8
Winnipeg, L., *Canada* ... 186 J8
Winnipegosis L., *Canada* ... 186 J7
Winona, *U.S.A.* ... 191 D11
Winschoten, *Neths.* ... 50 A6
Winslow, *U.K.* ... 45 A1
Winslow, *U.S.A.* ... 190 G5
Winston-Salem, *U.S.A.* ... 191 F15
Winterswijk, *Neths.* ... 50 D6
Winterthur, *Switz.* ... 60 A4
Winton, *N.Z.* ... 175 J2
Wisborough Green, *U.K.* ... 45 E2
Wisconsin □, *U.S.A.* ... 191 C12
Wisconsin →, *U.S.A.* ... 191 D12
Wisconsin Rapids, *U.S.A.* ... 191 C12
Wisła →, *Poland* ... 77 A3
Wismar, *Germany* ... 58 A4
Wismar, *Guyana* ... 214 B2
Witbank, *S. Africa* ... 163 C8
Witdraai, *S. Africa* ... 163 D3
Witham, *U.K.* ... 45 B6
Witley, *U.K.* ... 45 E2
Witten, *Germany* ... 59 A2
Wittenberg, *Germany* ... 58 C5
Wittenberge, *Germany* ... 58 B4
Wittersham, *U.K.* ... 45 E6
Wkra →, *Poland* ... 77 C4
Włocławek, *Poland* ... 77 C3
Woburn, *U.K.* ... 45 A2
Woburn Sands, *U.K.* ... 45 A2
Wodonga, *Australia* ... 171 F6
Woëvre, *France* ... 55 B8
Wokam, *Indonesia* ... 129 E16
Woking, *U.K.* ... 45 D2
Wokingham, *U.K.* ... 45 D1
Wolfsburg, *Germany* ... 58 C4
Wolhusen, *Switz.* ... 60 B3
Wolin, *Poland* ... 77 A1
Wollaston L., *Canada* ... 186 G7
Wollaston Pen., *Canada* ... 186 D7
Wollongong, *Australia* ... 171 E8
Wolmaransstad, *S. Africa* ... 163 D6
Wolseley, *Australia* ... 171 G3
Wolseley, *S. Africa* ... 163 H2
Wolstenholme, C., *Canada* ... 180 C12
Wolvega, *Neths.* ... 50 B5
Wolverhampton, *U.K.* ... 46 J7
Wolverton, *U.K.* ... 45 A1
Wongalarroo L., *Australia* ... 171 D4
Wongan Hills, *Australia* ... 170 A2
Wŏnju, *S. Korea* ... 118 F5
Wŏnsan, *N. Korea* ... 118 D4
Wonthaggi, *Australia* ... 171 H5
Woocalla, *Australia* ... 171 D1
Woodanilling, *Australia* ... 170 C2
Woodburn, *Australia* ... 171 B9
Woodchurch, *U.K.* ... 45 E6
Woodenbong, *Australia* ... 171 B9
Woodend, *Australia* ... 171 G5
Woodlark I., *Papua N. G.* ... 173 C3
Woodley, *U.K.* ... 45 C1
Woods, L., *Australia* ... 168 B3
Woodstock, *Canada* ... 187 K13
Woodville, *N.Z.* ... 175 E5
Woolamai, C., *Australia* ... 171 H5
Woolgoolga, *Australia* ... 171 C9
Woomera, *Australia* ... 171 C1
Woonsocket, *U.S.A.* ... 189 A6
Wooroloo, *Australia* ... 170 B2
Worcester, *S. Africa* ... 163 H2
Worcester, *U.K.* ... 46 J7
Worcester, *U.S.A.* ... 189 A6
Workum, *Neths.* ... 50 B4
Wormerveer, *Neths.* ... 50 C3
Worms, *Germany* ... 58 E2
Worplesdon, *U.K.* ... 45 D2
Worthing, *Barbados* ... 204 D2
Worthing, *U.K.* ... 46 L8
Worthington, *U.S.A.* ... 191 D10
Wosi, *Indonesia* ... 129 C13
Wou-han = Wuhan, *China* ... 116 G2
Wour, *Chad* ... 142 A1
Wousi = Wuxi, *China* ... 116 G5
Wowoni, *Indonesia* ... 129 D12
Woy Woy, *Australia* ... 171 E8
Wrangel I. = Vrangelya, Ostrov, *Russia* ... 91 A16
Wrangell, *U.S.A.* ... 193 B5
Wrangell Mts., *U.S.A.* ... 193 B5
Wrexham, *U.K.* ... 46 H6
Wright, *Phil.* ... 130 G5
Wrigley, *Canada* ... 186 E5
Writtle, *U.K.* ... 45 B5
Wrocław, *Poland* ... 77 D2
Wrotham, *U.K.* ... 45 D5
Września, *Poland* ... 77 C2
Wu Jiang →, *China* ... 113 G7
Wubin, *Australia* ... 170 A2
Wuding He →, *China* ... 116 D1
Wugang, *China* ... 116 J1
Wugong Shan, *China* ... 116 J2
Wuhan, *China* ... 116 G2
Wuhsi = Wuxi, *China* ... 116 G5
Wuhu, *China* ... 116 G4
Wukari, *Nigeria* ... 151 E5
Wulehe, *Ghana* ... 149 B3
Wuliaru, *Indonesia* ... 129 F15
Wulumuchi = Ürümqi, *China* ... 112 C4
Wum, *Cameroon* ... 153 C1
Wuning, *China* ... 116 H3
Wuntho, *Burma* ... 122 C2
Wuppertal, *Germany* ... 58 D1
Wuppertal, *S. Africa* ... 163 G2
Wuqing, *China* ... 116 C4
Würzburg, *Germany* ... 58 E3
Wuting = Huimin, *China* ... 116 D4
Wutongqiao, *China* ... 113 G7
Wuwei, *Anhui, China* ... 116 G4
Wuwei, *Gansu, China* ... 112 E6
Wuxi, *China* ... 116 G5
Wuxing, *China* ... 116 G5
Wuyi, *China* ... 116 H5
Wuyi Shan, *China* ... 116 J3
Wuyo, *Nigeria* ... 151 C7
Wuzhai, *China* ... 116 C2
Wuzhi Shan, *China* ... 113 J8
Wuzhong, *China* ... 113 E7
Wuzhou, *China* ... 113 H8
Wyalkatchem, *Australia* ... 170 A2
Wyandra, *Australia* ... 171 A5
Wyangala Res., *Australia* ... 171 E7
Wyara, L., *Australia* ... 171 B4
Wycheproof, *Australia* ... 171 F4
Wyndham, *Australia* ... 168 G10
Wynnum, *Australia* ... 171 A9
Wynyard, *Australia* ... 172 B2
Wyoming □, *U.S.A.* ... 190 D6

X

Xai-Xai, *Mozam.* ... 159 F1
Xainza, *China* ... 112 F3
Xangongo, *Angola* ... 160 E3
Xanten, *Germany* ... 59 A1
Xánthi, *Greece* ... 71 A4
Xhora, *S. Africa* ... 163 G7
Xi Jiang →, *China* ... 113 J9
Xi Xian, *China* ... 116 D1
Xiaguan, *China* ... 112 H6
Xiajiang, *China* ... 116 J3
Xiamen, *China* ... 113 H10
Xi'an, *China* ... 113 F8
Xiang Jiang →, *China* ... 116 H2
Xiangfan, *China* ... 116 F1
Xiangning, *China* ... 116 E1
Xiangtan, *China* ... 116 J2
Xiangxiang, *China* ... 116 J1
Xiangyin, *China* ... 116 H2
Xianju, *China* ... 116 H5
Xiao Hinggan Ling, *China* ... 113 A11
Xiaogan, *China* ... 116 G2
Xiapu, *China* ... 116 J5
Xichang, *China* ... 112 G6
Xichuan, *China* ... 116 F1
Xieng Khouang, *Laos* ... 125 B2
Xigazê, *China* ... 112 G3
Xiliao He →, *China* ... 116 A6
Xin Xian, *China* ... 116 C2
Xinavane, *Mozam.* ... 159 F1
Xingan, *China* ... 116 J3
Xingcheng, *China* ... 116 B5
Xingguo, *China* ... 116 J3
Xinghua, *China* ... 116 F5
Xingren, *China* ... 113 H7
Xingshan, *China* ... 116 G1
Xingtai, *China* ... 116 D2
Xingu →, *Brazil* ... 217 C6
Xingyang, *China* ... 116 E2
Xinhua, *China* ... 116 J1
Xining, *China* ... 112 E6
Xinjiang, *China* ... 116 E1
Xinjiang Uygur Zizhiqu □, *China* ... 112 C3
Xinjin, *China* ... 116 C5
Xinle, *China* ... 116 C3
Xinmin, *China* ... 116 B6
Xinning, *China* ... 116 J1
Xinxiang, *China* ... 116 E2
Xinyang, *China* ... 116 F2
Xinzheng, *China* ... 116 E2
Xinzhu, *Taiwan* ... 117 A3
Xiongyuecheng, *China* ... 116 B5
Xiping, *China* ... 116 F2
Xiuyan, *China* ... 116 B6
Xizang □, *China* ... 112 F3
Xlendi, *Malta* ... 69 A1
Xuancheng, *China* ... 116 G4
Xuanhua, *China* ... 116 B3
Xuchang, *China* ... 116 F2
Xuzhou, *China* ... 116 E4

Y

Ya'an, *China* ... 112 G6
Yaapeet, *Australia* ... 171 F3
Yabelo, *Ethiopia* ... 144 F3
Yablonovy Khrebet, *Russia* ... 91 H13
Yablonovy Ra. = Yablonovy Khrebet, *Russia* ... 91 H13
Yabrūd, *Syria* ... 97 C3
Yaeyama-Shotō, *Japan* ... 121 K5
Yagaba, *Ghana* ... 149 A2
Yagodnoye, *Russia* ... 91 D16
Yagoua, *Cameroon* ... 153 B3
Yahuma, *Zaïre* ... 155 B4
Yaiza, *Canary Is.* ... 223 C3
Yajua, *Nigeria* ... 151 B7
Yakima, *U.S.A.* ... 190 B3
Yaku-Jima, *Japan* ... 121 F9
Yakut Republic □, *Russia* ... 91 F14
Yakutat, *U.S.A.* ... 193 B5
Yakutsk, *Russia* ... 91 F14
Yala, *Thailand* ... 123 L4
Yalinga, *C.A.R.* ... 142 B4
Yalong Jiang →, *China* ... 112 H6
Yalutorovsk, *Russia* ... 90 G6
Yam Ha Melaḥ = Dead Sea, *Asia* ... 84 E7
Yam Kinneret, *Israel* ... 96 B3
Yamagata, *Japan* ... 121 E7
Yamaguchi, *Japan* ... 120 C2
Yamaguchi □, *Japan* ... 120 C2
Yamal, Poluostrov, *Russia* ... 90 D8
Yamal Pen. = Yamal, Poluostrov, *Russia* ... 90 D8
Yaman Tau, *Russia* ... 90 G5
Yamanashi □, *Japan* ... 120 B8
Yamba, *N.S.W., Australia* ... 171 B9
Yamba, *S. Austral., Australia* ... 171 E3
Yâmbiô, *Sudan* ... 143 F3
Yambol, *Bulgaria* ... 73 C4
Yamdena, *Indonesia* ... 129 F15
Yamethin, *Burma* ... 122 D2
Yamoussoukro, *Ivory C.* ... 148 C5
Yampa →, *U.S.A.* ... 190 E6
Yamrat, *Nigeria* ... 151 C5
Yamuna →, *India* ... 106 C5
Yamzho Yumco, *China* ... 112 G4
Yan, *Nigeria* ... 151 C7
Yan →, *Sri Lanka* ... 110 B2
Yana →, *Russia* ... 91 C13
Yanac, *Australia* ... 171 F3
Yanai, *Japan* ... 120 C3
Yanbu 'al Baḥr, *Si. Arabia* ... 99 C2
Yancannia, *Australia* ... 171 C4
Yanchang, *China* ... 116 D1
Yancheng, *Henan, China* ... 116 F2
Yancheng, *Jiangsu, China* ... 116 F5
Yanchuan, *China* ... 116 D1
Yanco Cr. →, *Australia* ... 171 F5
Yangambi, *Zaïre* ... 155 B4
Yangch'ü = Taiyuan, *China* ... 116 D2
Yangchun, *China* ... 113 J8
Yanggao, *China* ... 116 B2
Yangi-Yer, *Kazakstan* ... 90 K5
Yangibazar, *Kyrgyzstan* ... 93 B4
Yangikishlak, *Uzbekistan* ... 93 D1
Yangiyul, *Uzbekistan* ... 93 C3
Yangon = Rangoon, *Burma* ... 122 F2
Yangquan, *China* ... 116 D2
Yangtze Kiang = Chang Jiang →, *China* ... 116 G5
Yangxin, *China* ... 116 H3
Yangyang, *S. Korea* ... 118 E5
Yangzhou, *China* ... 116 F4
Yanhee, *Thailand* ... 122 F3
Yanji, *China* ... 113 B12
Yankton, *U.S.A.* ... 191 D10
Yanna, *Australia* ... 171 A5
Yanqi, *China* ... 112 C3
Yanqing, *China* ... 116 B3
Yanshan, *China* ... 116 H4
Yantabulla, *Australia* ... 171 B5
Yantai, *China* ... 116 D5
Yanzhou, *China* ... 116 E3
Yao, *Chad* ... 142 D1
Yaoundé, *Cameroon* ... 153 D2
Yap I., *Pac. Oc.* ... 176 E2
Yapen, *Indonesia* ... 129 C17
Yapen, Selat, *Indonesia* ... 129 C17
Yaqui →, *Mexico* ... 194 B2
Yar-Sale, *Russia* ... 90 E8
Yaransk, *Russia* ... 81 B8
Yarensk, *Russia* ... 90 E5
Yari →, *Colombia* ... 210 E2
Yarkand = Shache, *China* ... 112 D1
Yarkhun →, *Pakistan* ... 105 B4
Yarmouth, *Canada* ... 187 K14
Yaroslavl, *Russia* ... 81 B6
Yarram, *Australia* ... 171 H6
Yarraman, *Australia* ... 171 A9
Yarras, *Australia* ... 171 D9
Yartsevo, *Russia* ... 91 G10
Yashi, *Nigeria* ... 151 B4
Yasothon, *Thailand* ... 123 G6
Yass, *Australia* ... 171 F7
Yathkyed L., *Canada* ... 186 F8
Yatta Plateau, *Kenya* ... 157 E3
Yauyos, *Peru* ... 213 D3
Yavan, *Tajikistan* ... 93 F2
Yavatmal, *India* ... 106 F3
Yavne, *Israel* ... 96 D2
Yawatahama, *Japan* ... 120 D3
Yawri B., *S. Leone* ... 147 D2
Yazd, *Iran* ... 103 C4
Yazoo →, *U.S.A.* ... 191 H12
Yazoo City, *U.S.A.* ... 191 H12
Yding Skovhøj, *Denmark* ... 42 C2
Ye Xian, *China* ... 116 D5
Yealering, *Australia* ... 170 B2
Yechŏn, *S. Korea* ... 118 F5
Yecla, *Spain* ... 63 E7
Yegros, *Paraguay* ... 219 C3
Yehuda, Midbar, *Israel* ... 96 E2
Yei, *Sudan* ... 143 F4
Yekaterinburg, *Russia* ... 90 G6
Yekaterinodar = Krasnodar, *Russia* ... 81 H5
Yekhegnadzor, *Armenia* ... 82 D6
Yelanskoye, *Russia* ... 91 F14
Yelarbon, *Australia* ... 171 B8
Yelets, *Russia* ... 81 D5
Yelizavetgrad = Kirovograd, *Ukraine* ... 81 F3
Yellow Sea, *China* ... 113 E11
Yellowhead Pass, *Canada* ... 186 H4
Yellowknife, *Canada* ... 186 E6
Yellowknife →, *Canada* ... 186 E6
Yellowstone →, *U.S.A.* ... 190 B8
Yellowstone National Park, *U.S.A.* ... 190 C6
Yelwa, *Nigeria* ... 151 C2
Yemen ■, *Asia* ... 100
Yenangyaung, *Burma* ... 122 D2
Yenbo = Yanbu 'al Baḥr, *Si. Arabia* ... 99 C2
Yenda, *Australia* ... 171 E5
Yendéré, *Ivory C.* ... 148 A5
Yendi, *Ghana* ... 149 B3
Yenisey →, *Russia* ... 90 D9
Yeniseysk, *Russia* ... 91 G10
Yeniseyskiy Zaliv, *Russia* ... 90 D9
Yenyuka, *Russia* ... 91 G14
Yeola, *India* ... 106 F2
Yeovil, *U.K.* ... 46 L6
Yerbent, *Turkmenistan* ... 90 K3
Yerbogachen, *Russia* ... 91 F12
Yerevan, *Armenia* ... 82 D5
Yermak, *Kazakstan* ... 90 J8
Yermakovo, *Russia* ... 91 H15
Yerofey Pavlovich, *Russia* ... 91 H14
Yershov, *Russia* ... 81 E8
Yerushalayim = Jerusalem, *Israel* ... 96 D2
Yesan, *S. Korea* ... 118 F4

Yessey, *Russia* 91 E11
Yeu, I. d', *France* 55 D2
Yevlakh, *Azerbaijan* 82 C7
Yevpatoriya, *Ukraine* 81 H4
Yeysk, *Russia* 81 G5
Yezd = Yazd, *Iran* 103 C4
Yi →, *Uruguay* 219 C1
Yi Xian, *China* 116 B5
Yi'allaq, G., *Egypt* 139 B5
Yialousa, *Cyprus* 95 A3
Yiannitsa, *Greece* 71 B2
Yibin, *China* 113 G7
Yichang, *China* 116 G1
Yicheng, *China* 116 E1
Yichuan, *China* 116 D1
Yichun, *Heilongjiang, China* 113 B12
Yichun, *Jiangxi, China* 116 J2
Yidu, *China* 116 D4
Yihuang, *China* 116 J3
Yilan, *Taiwan* 117 A3
Yinchuan, *China* 113 D7
Ying He →, *China* 116 F3
Ying Xian, *China* 116 C2
Yingcheng, *China* 116 G2
Yingkou, *China* 116 B6
Yingshan, *China* 116 G3
Yingshang, *China* 116 F3
Yining, *China* 112 C2
Yishan, *China* 113 H8
Yishui, *China* 116 E4
Yíthion, *Greece* 71 E2
Yixing, *China* 116 G5
Yiyang, *Henan, China* 116 E2
Yiyang, *Hunan, China* 116 H1
Ynykchanskiy, *Russia* 91 F15
Yogan, *Togo* 150 E2
Yogyakarta, *Indonesia* 128 F6
Yojoa, L. de, *Honduras* 196 C2
Yŏju, *S. Korea* 118 F4
Yokadouma, *Cameroon* 153 D3
Yokkaichi, *Japan* 120 B6
Yoko, *Cameroon* 153 D2
Yokohama, *Japan* 120 B9
Yokosuka, *Japan* 120 B9
Yokote, *Japan* 121 E7
Yola, *Nigeria* 151 D7
Yolaina, Cordillera de, *Nic.* 197 C2
Yonago, *Japan* 120 B4
Yŏnan, *N. Korea* 118 E3
Yoneshiro →, *Japan* 121 D7
Yonezawa, *Japan* 121 E7
Yong Peng, *Malaysia* 126 D2
Yongampo, *N. Korea* 118 D2
Yŏngchŏn, *S. Korea* 118 G5
Yŏngdŏk, *S. Korea* 118 F6
Yŏngdŭngpo, *S. Korea* 118 F4
Yongfeng, *China* 116 J3
Yonghe, *China* 116 D1
Yŏnghŭng, *N. Korea* 118 D4
Yongji, *China* 116 E1
Yŏngju, *S. Korea* 118 F5
Yŏngwŏl, *S. Korea* 118 F5
Yongxin, *China* 116 J2
Yongxing, *China* 116 J2
Yongxiu, *China* 116 H3
Yonibana, *S. Leone* 147 C3
Yonkers, *U.S.A.* 189 B5
Yonne □, *France* 55 C6
Yonne →, *France* 55 C6
York, *Australia* 170 B2
York, *U.K.* 46 G7
York, *U.S.A.* 189 C3
York, C., *Australia* 168 B4
York, Kap, *Greenland* 224 B1
Yorke Pen., *Australia* 171 F1
Yorkton, *Canada* 186 J7
Yornup, *Australia* 170 C2
Yoro, *Honduras* 196 C3
Yos Sudarso, Pulau, *Indonesia* 129 F17
Yosemite National Park, *U.S.A.* 190 E2
Yoshkar Ola, *Russia* 81 B8
Yŏsu, *S. Korea* 118 H5
Yotvata, *Israel* 96 H2
Youghal, *Ireland* 46 K2
Youkounkoun, *Guinea* 147 A2
Young, *Australia* 171 E7
Young, *Uruguay* 219 C1
Younghusband Pen., *Australia* 171 F2
Youngstown, *U.S.A.* 191 D15
Youssoufia, *Morocco* 136 C3
Youyu, *China* 116 C2
Yozgat, *Turkey* 94 B4
Ypres = Ieper, *Belgium* 51 C1
Ysyk-Köl = Issyk-Kul, Ozero, *Kyrgyzstan* 93 B8
Ytyk-Kel, *Russia* 91 E14
Yu Shan, *Taiwan* 117 B3
Yu Xian, *Hebei, China* 116 C3
Yu Xian, *Henan, China* 116 E2
Yuanli, *Taiwan* 117 B2
Yuanlin, *Taiwan* 117 B2
Yuanling, *China* 113 G8
Yuanyang, *China* 112 H6
Yuba City, *U.S.A.* 190 E2
Yūbari, *Japan* 121 B8
Yūbetsu, *Japan* 121 A8
Yucatán □, *Mexico* 194 D8
Yucatán, Canal de, *Caribbean* 180 G11
Yucatán Pen., *Mexico* 180 G11
Yucatan Str. = Yucatán, Canal de, *Caribbean* 180 G11
Yucheng, *China* 116 D3
Yuci, *China* 116 D2
Yudino, *Russia* 90 G7
Yueqing, *China* 116 H5
Yueyang, *China* 116 H2
Yugan, *China* 116 H3
Yugoslavia ■, *Europe* 72
Yuhuan, *China* 116 H5
Yujiang, *China* 116 H3
Yukon →, *U.S.A.* 180 C3
Yukon Territory □, *Canada* 186 D4
Yukti, *Russia* 91 F11
Yuli, *Nigeria* 151 C6
Yulin, *China* 116 C1
Yuma, *U.S.A.* 190 G4
Yuma, B. de, *Dom. Rep.* 200 B3
Yumbe, *Uganda* 156 A1
Yumen, *China* 112 D6
Yun Xian, *China* 116 F1
Yungas, *Bolivia* 218 C1
Yunhe, *China* 116 H5
Yunlin, *Taiwan* 117 B2
Yunnan □, *China* 112 H6
Yunta, *Australia* 171 D2
Yupukarri, *Guyana* 214 D2
Yupyongdong, *N. Korea* 118 B5
Yur, *Russia* 91 F15
Yurgao, *Russia* 90 H9
Yuribei, *Russia* 90 D9
Yurimaguas, *Peru* 213 C3
Yuscarán, *Honduras* 196 D3
Yushu, *China* 112 F5
Yuyao, *China* 116 G5
Yuzhno-Sakhalinsk, *Russia* 91 H17
Yuzhno-Surkhanskoye Vdkhr., *Uzbekistan* 93 F1
Yvelines □, *France* 55 C5
Yverdon, *Switz.* 60 C1
Yvetot, *France* 55 B5

Z

Zaalayskiy Khrebet, *Asia* 93 E6
Zaandam, *Neths.* 50 C3
Zabaykalskiy, *Russia* 91 J14
Zabid, *Yemen* 100 B1
Zābol, *Iran* 103 C6
Zābol □, *Afghan.* 104 E4
Zabrze, *Poland* 77 E3
Zacapa, *Guatemala* 196 C1
Zacatecas, *Mexico* 194 D4
Zacatecoluca, *El Salv.* 196 D2
Zacoalco, *Mexico* 194 E3
Zadar, *Croatia* 72 C3
Zadawa, *Nigeria* 151 B6
Zadetkyi Kyun, *Burma* 122 J3
Zafra, *Spain* 63 F3
Żagań, *Poland* 77 D1
Zagazig, *Egypt* 139 A4
Zaghouan, *Tunisia* 138 B2
Zagnanado, *Benin* 150 D2
Zagora, *Morocco* 136 E4
Zagorsk = Sergiyev Posad, *Russia* 81 B5
Zagreb, *Croatia* 72 A4
Zāgros, Kuhhā-ye, *Iran* 103 C2
Zagros Mts. = Zāgros, Kuhhā-ye, *Iran* 103 C2
Zaguinaso, *Ivory C.* 148 A4
Zāhedān, *Iran* 103 D5
Zahlah, *Lebanon* 95 C2
Zailiyskiy Alatau, Khrebet, *Kazakstan* 93 A8
Zaïre ■, *Africa* 155
Zaïre →, *Africa* 132 G5
Zaječar, *Serbia, Yug.* 72 C8
Zakamensk, *Russia* 91 J11
Zakataly, *Azerbaijan* 82 B7
Zākhū, *Iraq* 102 A3
Zákinthos, *Greece* 71 E2
Zalingei, *Sudan* 143 D1
Zambeze →, *Africa* 132 H7
Zambezi = Zambeze →, *Africa* 132 H7
Zambezi, *Zambia* 161 C2
Zambia ■, *Africa* 161
Zamboanga, *Phil.* 130 K3
Zamboanguita, *Phil.* 130 J4
Zamora, *Ecuador* 212 E1
Zamora, *Mexico* 194 E4
Zamora, *Spain* 63 C3
Zamora-Chinchipe □, *Ecuador* 212 E1
Zamość, *Poland* 77 D6
Zan, *Ghana* 149 B2
Zanaga, *Congo* 154 C2
Zandvoort, *Neths.* 50 C2
Zanesville, *U.S.A.* 191 E14
Zanjan, *Iran* 103 B2
Zante = Zákinthos, *Greece* 71 E2
Zanzibar, *Tanzania* 158 C3
Zaouiet El-Kala = Bordj Omar Driss, *Algeria* 137 C5
Zaouiet Reggane, *Algeria* 137 D3
Zaozhuang, *China* 116 E4
Zapadnaya Dvina →, *Belarus* 81 B2
Západné Beskydy, *Europe* 76 B6
Zapala, *Argentina* 220 G3
Zaporizhzhya = Zaporozhye, *Ukraine* 81 G4
Zaporozhye, *Ukraine* 81 G4
Zaragoza, *Spain* 63 C7
Zaranj, *Afghan.* 104 F1
Zarate, *Argentina* 221 C5
Zaria, *Nigeria* 151 B4
Zaruma, *Ecuador* 212 E1
Żary, *Poland* 77 D1
Zarzis, *Tunisia* 138 C3
Zashiversk, *Russia* 91 D14
Zastron, *S. Africa* 163 F6
Zavitinsk, *Russia* 91 H15
Zawiercie, *Poland* 77 E3
Zāwiyat al Bayḍā, *Libya* 138 A5
Zawyet Shammâs, *Egypt* 139 A1
Zâwyet Um el Rakham, *Egypt* 139 A2
Zâwyet Ungeîla, *Egypt* 139 A1
Zayarsk, *Russia* 91 H11
Zaysan, *Kazakstan* 90 K8
Zaysan, Oz., *Kazakstan* 90 K8
Zduńska Wola, *Poland* 77 D3
Zebediela, *S. Africa* 163 B8
Zeebrugge, *Belgium* 51 A1
Zeehan, *Australia* 172 B1
Zeeland □, *Neths.* 50 F1
Zeerust, *S. Africa* 163 C6
Zefat, *Israel* 96 B3
Zeila, *Somali Rep.* 145 A1
Zeist, *Neths.* 50 D4
Zeitz, *Germany* 58 D4
Zelenograd, *Russia* 81 C5
Zelzate, *Belgium* 51 B2
Zembra, I., *Tunisia* 138 A3
Zemun, *Serbia, Yug.* 72 B7
Zendeh Jān, *Afghan.* 104 D1
Zeravshan, *Tajikistan* 93 E2
Zeravshanskiy, Khrebet, *Tajikistan* 93 E3
Zerbst, *Germany* 58 C4
Zermatt, *Switz.* 60 D3
Zernez, *Switz.* 60 C6
Zestafoni, *Georgia* 82 B4
Zeya, *Russia* 91 G15
Zeya →, *Russia* 91 H15
Zghartā, *Lebanon* 95 A2
Zhailma, *Kazakstan* 90 H5
Zhambyl = Dzhambul, *Kazakstan* 93 A4
Zhanatas, *Kazakstan* 93 A3
Zhanghua, *Taiwan* 117 B2
Zhangjiakou, *China* 116 B3
Zhangwu, *China* 116 A6
Zhangye, *China* 112 D6
Zhangzhou, *China* 113 H10
Zhanhua, *China* 116 D4
Zhanjiang, *China* 113 J8
Zhanyi, *China* 113 H7
Zhao Xian, *China* 116 D3
Zhaotong, *China* 113 G7
Zhaoyuan, *China* 116 D5
Zhayyq = Ural →, *Kazakstan* 34 F17
Zhdanov = Mariupol, *Ukraine* 81 G5
Zhecheng, *China* 116 F3
Zhejiang □, *China* 116 H5
Zheleznogorsk-Ilimskiy, *Russia* 91 H11
Zhengding, *China* 116 D3
Zhenghe, *China* 116 J4
Zhengyang, *China* 116 F2
Zhengyangguan, *China* 116 F3
Zhengzhou, *China* 116 E2
Zhenjiang, *China* 116 F4
Zhenyuan, *China* 113 G8
Zhigansk, *Russia* 91 E13
Zhijiang, *China* 113 G8
Zhitomir, *Ukraine* 81 E2
Zhlobin, *Belarus* 81 D3
Zhokhova, Ostrov, *Russia* 91 B14
Zhongdian, *China* 112 G6
Zhongxiang, *China* 116 G2
Zhuanghe, *China* 116 C6
Zhuji, *China* 116 H5
Zhumadian, *China* 116 F2
Zhuo Xian, *China* 116 C3
Zhupanovo, *Russia* 91 E18
Zhushan, *China* 116 F1
Zhuzhou, *China* 116 J2
Zhytomyr = Zhitomir, *Ukraine* 81 E2
Zibo, *China* 116 D4
Zielona Góra, *Poland* 77 C1
Zierikzee, *Neths.* 50 E1
Zigey, *Chad* 142 D1
Zigong, *China* 113 G7
Zigui, *China* 116 G1
Ziguinchor, *Senegal* 146 C1
Žilina, *Slovak Rep.* 76 C6
Zillah, *Libya* 138 B4
Zima, *Russia* 91 H11
Zimbabwe, *Zimbabwe* 161 D4
Zimbabwe ■, *Africa* 161
Zinder, *Niger* 141 D4
Zion National Park, *U.S.A.* 190 F4
Zipaquirá, *Colombia* 210 C1
Ziway, L., *Ethiopia* 144 E3
Zixi, *China* 116 J3
Zlatograd, *Bulgaria* 73 D3
Zlatoust, *Russia* 90 G6
Zlin, *Czech.* 76 C5
Zlītan, *Libya* 138 A3
Zmeinogorsk, *Kazakstan* 90 J8
Znojmo, *Czech.* 76 C4
Zomba, *Malawi* 158 D3
Zongo, *Zaïre* 155 A2
Zonguldak, *Turkey* 94 A3
Zonqor Pt., *Malta* 69 B3
Zorritos, *Peru* 213 B1
Zorzor, *Liberia* 148 C2
Zottegem, *Belgium* 51 C2
Zou Xiang, *China* 116 E3
Zouar, *Chad* 142 B1
Zouérate, *Mauritania* 140 B2
Zoutkamp, *Neths.* 50 A5
Zrenjanin, *Serbia, Yug.* 72 B7
Zuarungu, *Ghana* 149 A2
Zuba, *Nigeria* 151 D4
Zuénoula, *Ivory C.* 148 C4
Zuetina, *Libya* 138 A4
Zufar, *Oman* 101 D1
Zug, *Switz.* 60 B4
Zugdidi, *Georgia* 82 A3
Zugersee, *Switz.* 60 B4
Zuid-Holland □, *Neths.* 50 D2
Zuidhorn, *Neths.* 50 A5
Zula, *Eritrea* 144 B3
Zumbo, *Mozam.* 159 B1
Zummo, *Nigeria* 151 C7
Zungeru, *Nigeria* 151 C3
Zunhua, *China* 116 C4
Zunyi, *China* 113 G7
Zürich, *Switz.* 60 A4
Zürich □, *Switz.* 60 A4
Zürichsee, *Switz.* 60 B4
Zuru, *Nigeria* 151 B2
Zutphen, *Neths.* 50 D5
Zuwārah, *Libya* 138 A2
Zverinogolovskoye, *Russia* 90 G6
Zvishavane, *Zimbabwe* 161 D3
Zvolen, *Slovak Rep.* 76 C6
Zwedru = Tchien, *Liberia* 148 D3
Zwettl, *Austria* 61 A5
Zwickau, *Germany* 58 D5
Zwolle, *Neths.* 50 C5
Żyrardów, *Poland* 77 C4
Zyrya, *Azerbaijan* 82 C9
Zyryanka, *Russia* 91 D15
Zyryanovsk, *Kazakstan* 90 J8

DÉPARTEMENTS OF FRANCE

The following département abbreviations are featured on the map on page 55:

A.	Ain	**E8**
A.H.P.	Alpes-de-Haute-Provence	**G8**
A.M.	Alpes-Maritimes	**G9**
Ai.	Aisne	**B6**
Al.	Allier	**E6**
Ar.	Ardèche	**F7**
Ard.	Ardennes	**B7**
Ari.	Ariège	**H5**
Aub.	Aube	**C7**
Aud.	Aude	**H5**
Av.	Aveyron	**G6**
B.	Belfort	**D9**
B.R.	Bouches-du-Rhône	**B9**
B.Rh.	Bas-Rhin	**G7**
C.	Calvados	**B4**
C.A.	Côtes-d'Armor	**C2**
C.O.	Côte-d'Or	**D7**
Ca.	Cantal	**C2**
Ch.	Charente	**E4**
Ch.M.	Charente-Maritime	**E3**
Che.	Cher	**D6**
Co.	Corrèze	**F5**
Corse	Haute-Corse	**H9**
	Corse-du-Sud	**H9**
Cr.	Creuse	**E5**
D.	Dordogne	**F4**
D.S.	Deux-Sèvres	**D4**
Do.	Doubs	**D8**
Dr.	Drôme	**F7**
E.	Eure	**B5**
E.L.	Eure-et-Loire	**C5**
Es.	Essonne	**C5**
F.	Finistère	**C1**
G.	Gard	**G7**
Ge.	Gers	**G4**
Gi.	Gironde	**F3**
H.	Hérault	**G6**
H.A.	Hautes-Alpes	**F8**
H.G.	Haute-Garonne	**H5**
H.L.	Haute-Loire	**F6**
H.M.	Haute-Marne	**C7**
H.P.	Hautes-Pyrénées	**H4**
H.R.	Haut-Rhin	**C9**
H.S.	Haute-Saône	**D8**
H.Sa.	Haute-Savoie	**E8**
H.Se.	Hauts-de-Seine	**B5**
H.V.	Haute-Vienne	**E5**
I.	Indre	**D5**
I.L.	Indre-et-Loire	**D4**
I.V.	Ille-et-Vilaine	**C3**
Is.	Isère	**F8**
J.	Jura	**E8**
L.	Landes	**G3**
L.A.	Loire-Atlantique	**D3**
L.C.	Loir-et-Cher	**D5**
L.G.	Lot-et-Garonne	**F4**
Lo.	Loire	**E7**
Loi.	Loiret	**C5**
Lot	Lot	**F5**
Loz.	Lozère	**F6**
M.	Manche	**B3**
M.L.	Main-et-Loire	**D4**
M.M.	Meurthe-et-Moselle	**B8**
Ma.	Marne	**B7**
May.	Mayenne	**C3**
Me.	Meuse	**B8**
Mo.	Morbihan	**C2**
Mos.	Moselle	**B8**
N.	Nièvre	**D6**
No.	Nord	**A6**
O.	Oise	**B5**
Or.	Orne	**C4**
P.A.	Pyrénées-Atlantiques	**H3**
P.C.	Pas-de-Calais	**A5**
P.D.	Puy-de-Dôme	**E6**
P.O.	Pyrénées-Orientales	**H6**
Rh.	Rhône	**E7**
S.	Sarthe	**C4**
S.L.	Saône-et-Loire	**D7**
S.M.	Seine-et-Marne	**C5**
S.Me.	Seine-Maritime	**B5**
S.St-D.	Seine-St-Denis	**B6**
Sa.	Savoie	**E8**
So.	Somme	**B6**
T.	Tarn	**G5**
T.G.	Tarn-et-Garonne	**G5**
V.	Var	**G8**
V.M.	Val-de-Marne	**C5**
V.O.	Val-d'Oise	**B5**
Va.	Vaucluse	**G8**
Ve.	Vendée	**D3**
Vi.	Vienne	**E4**
Vo.	Vosges	**C8**
Y.	Yonne	**C6**
Yv.	Yvelines	**C5**

World: Regions in the News

Maps show the situation in June 1998

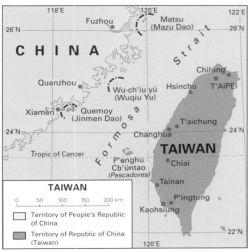

TAIWAN

0	50	100	150	200 km

☐ Territory of People's Republic of China

▨ Territory of Republic of China (Taiwan)

SOUTH CHINA SEA

0	250	500 km

▲ Philippine terr.
▼ Vietnamese terr.
■ Chinese terr.
● Taiwanese terr.
— — Philippine claim
- - - Vietnamese claim
—•— Chinese claim
······ Malaysian claim

FORMER YUGOSLAVIA

0	50	100	150	200 km

-··-··- International boundaries
-·-·- Republic boundaries
········ Province boundaries
■ Capital cities
—— Dayton Peace Agreement Boundary
▨ Muslim-Croat Federation
▨ Bosnian Serb Republic

THE BREAK-UP OF YUGOSLAVIA
The former country of Yugoslavia comprised six republics. In 1991 Slovenia and Croatia declared independence. Bosnia-Herzegovina followed in 1992 and Macedonia in 1993. Yugoslavia now comprises the remaining two republics, Serbia and Montenegro.

YUGOSLAVIA
Population: 10,881,000 (Serb 62.6%, Albanian 16.5%, Montenegrin 5%, Hungarian 3.3%, Muslim 3.2%)

Serbia Population: 6,060,000 (Serb 87.7%, excluding the former autonomous provinces of Kosovo and Vojvodina)

Kosovo Population: 1,989,050 (Albanian 81.6%, Serb 9.9%)

Vojvodina Population: 2,131,900 (Serb 56.8%, Hungarian 16.9%)

Montenegro Population: 700,050 (Montenegrin 61.9%, Muslim 14.6%, Albanian 7%)

CROATIA
Population: 4,850,000 (Croat 78.1%, Serb 12.2%)

SLOVENIA
Population: 2,000,000 (Slovene 88%)

MACEDONIA (F. Y. R. O. M.)
Population: 2,150,000 (Macedonian 64%, Albanian 21.7%, Turkish 5%)

BOSNIA-HERZEGOVINA
Population: 3,600,000 (Muslim 49%, Serb 31.2%, Croat 17.2%)

THE CAUCASUS

0	100	200 km

-··-··- International boundaries
-·-·- Republic boundaries

Georgia, Armenia and Azerbaijan achieved independence in 1991. Abkhazia, Ajaria and South Ossetia seek independence from Georgia. Chechenia has been trying to break away from Russia since 1991, but Russia has resisted with military force. Hostility also continues between Armenia and Azerbaijan over the enclave of Nagorno-Karabakh.

COUNTRIES AND REPUBLICS OF THE CAUCASUS REGION

RUSSIAN REPUBLICS IN THE NEWS

North Ossetia (Alania) Population: 695,000 (Ossetian 53%, Russian 29%, Chechen 5.2%, Armenian 1.9%)

Chechenia Population: 1,308,000 (Chechen and Ingush 70.7%, Russian 23.1%, Armenian 1.2%)

Ingushetia (Split from Chechenia in June 1993) Population: 250,000

GEORGIA
Population: 5,450,000 (Georgian 70.1%, Armenian 8.1%, Russian 6.3%, Azerbaijani 5.7%, Ossetian 3%, Greek 2%, Abkhazian 2%)

Abkhazia Population: 537,500 (Georgian 45.7%, Abkhazian 17.8%, Armenian 14.6%, Russian 14.3%)

Ajaria Population: 382,000 (Georgian 82.8%, Russian 7.7%, Armenian 4%)

ARMENIA
Population: 3,800,000 (Armenian 93%, Azerbaijani 3%)

Nagorno-Karabakh Population: 192,400 (Armenian 76.9%, Azerbaijani 21.5%)

AZERBAIJAN
Population: 7,650,000 (Azerbaijani 83%, Russian 6%, Armenian 6%, Lezgin 2%)

Naxçivan Population: 300,400

ISRAEL
Population: 5,900,000 (inc. East Jerusalem and Jewish settlers in the areas under Israeli administration. (Jewish 82%, Arab Muslim 13.8%, Arab Christian 2.5%, Druze 1.7%)

West Bank
Population: 1,122,900 (Palestinian Arabs 97% [of whom Arab Muslim 85%, Jewish 7%, Christian 8%])

Gaza Strip
Population: 748,400 (Arab Muslim 98%)

JORDAN
Population: 5,600,000 (Arab 99% [of whom about 50% are Palestinian Arab])

-··-··- 1949 Armistice Line
- - - 1974 Cease-fire Lines
Efrata Main Jewish settlements in the West Bank and Gaza Strip
■ *Halhul* Main Palestinian Arab towns in the West Bank and Gaza Strip
■ *'Amman* Capital cities

THE NEAR EAST

0	25	50 km

CENTRAL EAST AFRICA

0	50	100 km

● Towns
▲ Camps
← Refugee movements
-··-··- International boundaries
⤴ Forced repatriation

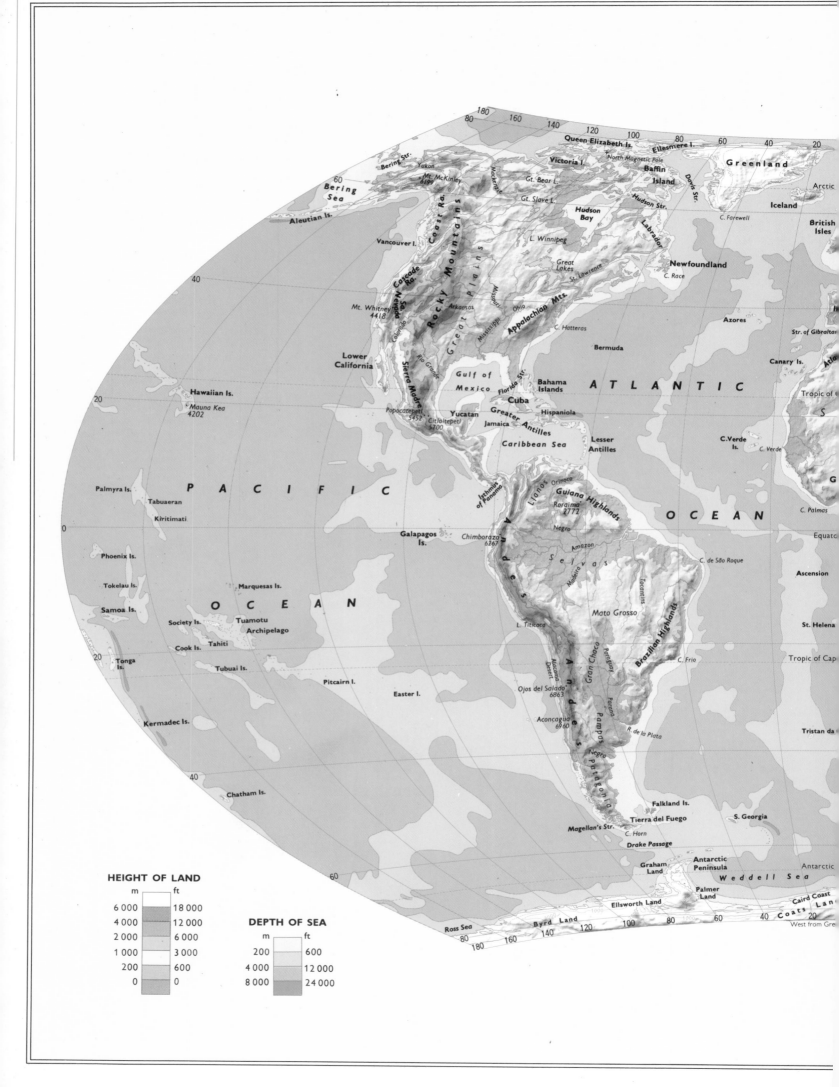

Queen Elizabeth Is. Ellesmere I.
North Magnetic Pole Greenland
Bering Str. Victoria I. Baffin
Yukon Island Davis Str.
Mt. McKinley Gt. Bear L. C. Farewell Arctic
6199 Mackenzie Iceland
Bering Gt. Slave L. Hudson Str.
Sea Hudson Labrador British
Bay Isles
Aleutian Is. L. Winnipeg
Vancouver I. Great Newfoundland
Lakes St. Lawrence C. Race

Mt. Whitney Arkansas Ohio Appalachian Mts.
4418 Missouri Azores
C. Hatteras

Lower Rio Grande Bermuda ATLANTIC
California Gulf of Bahama
Mexico Florida Str. Islands Canary Is.
Popocatepetl Cuba Str. of Gibraltar
Hawaiian Is. 5452 Yucatan Greater Antilles Hispaniola
Mauna Kea Citloitepetl Jamaica C. Verde
4202 5700 Lesser Is. C. Verde
Caribbean Sea Antilles

Palmyra Is. Isthmus Llanos Orinoco OCEAN
Tabuaeran of Panama Guiana Highlands
Kiritimati Roraima C. Palmas
2772
PACIFIC Negro Equato
Galapagos Chimborazo Andes Ascension
Is. 6267
Phoenix Is. Amazon C. de São Roque

Tokelau Is. Selvas Madeira St. Helena
Society Is. Tocantins Mato Grosso
Samoa Is. OCEAN Marquesas Is.
Cook Is. Tahiti L. Titicaca Brazilian Highlands Tropic of Cap
Tuamotu Gran Chaco C. Frio Tristan da
Archipelago Paraguay
Tonga Tubuai Is. Atacama
Is. Desert Parana
Pitcairn I. Ojos del Salado
Easter I. 6863
Aconcagua R. de la Plata
Kermadec Is. 6960 Pampas
Negro
Chatham Is. Patagonia

Falkland Is. S. Georgia
Tierra del Fuego
Magellan's Str.
C. Horn
Drake Passage
Graham Antarctic
Land Peninsula Antarctic
Palmer Weddell Sea
Land
HEIGHT OF LAND Ellsworth Land Caird Coast
m ft Ross Sea Byrd Land Coats Land
6 000 18 000 West from Gre
4 000 12 000
2 000 6 000 DEPTH OF SEA
1 000 3 000 m ft
200 600 200 600
0 0 4 000 12 000
8 000 24 000